Shropshire Wor

A glossary of archaic and provincial words, etc., used in the county

Georgina F. Jackson

Alpha Editions

This edition published in 2020

ISBN : 9789354023958

Design and Setting By
Alpha Editions
email - alphaedis@gmail.com

SHROPSHIRE WORD-BOOK,

A Glossary

OF

ARCHAIC AND PROVINCIAL WORDS, ETC.,

USED IN THE COUNTY;

BY

GEORGINA F. JACKSON.

Polonius. ——What do you read, my Lord?
Hamlet. Words, words, words.
Hamlet, II. ii. 193.

London:
TRÜBNER & CO., 57 & 59 LUDGATE HILL.
SHREWSBURY: ADNITT & NAUNTON.
CHESTER: MINSHULL & HUGHES.
1879-81.

THIS

SHROPSHIRE WORD-BOOK

Is Dedicated

TO ONE OF SHROPSHIRE KIN,

THE REV. WALTER W. SKEAT, M.A.,

A WORTHY ENGLISH SCHOLAR,

AND

THE FIRST PROFESSOR OF ANGLO-SAXON IN THE UNIVERSITY OF CAMBRIDGE.

CONTENTS.

PREFACE.

On the publication of a Glossary of the archaic and provincial words, &c., in use—or known to have been in use—in Shropshire, it seems incumbent upon me to furnish some account of the way in which the work has been carried out, in order to give assurance that it has, to the utmost of my power, been done thoroughly, and that so far it may be relied upon as trustworthy.

In the spring of 1870 I was reading the Rev. Isaac Taylor's *Words and Places*, when at p. 120 I came across two words—'*tine*' and '*tining*'—which struck a key-note in my memory, calling up recollections of the time when in early childhood I had lived in Shropshire, 'far from the busy town'—had heard the folk-speech day by day, and had shewn such aptitude for 'picking it up'—words, tones, and all—that I had not unfrequently incurred the censure of my parents for 'speaking like a little Shropshire village-child.' It was a great leap my mind took from now to then; but as clearly as if but yesterday, I heard that, in obedience to some order given, 'John Roberts wuz gwun ŏŏth 'is brummock an' mittins to the uvver leasow to *tine* a glat the ship 'ad maden.'

Then another and another phrase associated with some incident of the rural 'surroundings' of my young days rose up before me, until at last I 'made notes' of them. These I shewed to a literary man of my acquaintance whom I knew to be interested in dialects. After considering them for a few minutes, he said,

'There's the foundation here of a good Glossary; why not make one?'

That was the first idea of the work. In three days from that time it was begun 'in right good sadness.'

Word-collecting was soon in full swing. At the outset of this I was often advised to take the Glossary appended to Mr. Hartshorne's

Salopia Antiqua as the basis of mine; but I had formed for myself a plan of independent work, and to that I resolved to keep.

Ultimately, however, when my Glossarial MSS. shewed a total of more than three thousand words, I collated my work with that of Mr. Hartshorne, and from the latter made lists of words not contained in mine. These I endeavoured to verify, and in every case where I was successful in doing so I included the word in my collection, but not otherwise.

My Glossary begun, I went on steadily working in my own way till the formation of the *English Dialect Society* in 1873 led me to Cambridge to talk matters over with Mr. Skeat. From him I received much valuable help and counsel.

Two of the most important suggestions he made to me were these—to represent the sounds of the words by Glossic symbols, according to Mr. A. J. Ellis's method; and to add the localities where the words were heard or known to be used.

I saw clearly that by such an extension of my scheme a largely-increased usefulness would be given to my work in a philological point of view, and I at once made up my mind to carry it out, though it involved the cost of going over again in detail all my previous three years' work. I could grudge no pains which should tend to the more worthy accomplishing of that which I had begun with the set purpose of giving to it my best of brain and heart; for from the first it was a 'work and labour of love.' It proved a most troublesome task to localize words which in many cases had been contributed by friends who had made no notes of their whereabouts, and still more difficult was it to arrive at any trustworthy rendering of their sounds.

However, at the end of four more years of patient work my words were all fairly-well assigned to their respective districts, and their pronunciation indicated.

In order to attain this end, I had conceived the idea—based upon a general knowledge of the trend of phonetic variations in the dialect—of mapping out the county into a given number of districts, and then visiting centres of these arbitrary divisions for the purpose of collating my words, and by 'personal audition' noting their sounds.

The plan worked well, and led to many valuable results—variation of form, phonetic change, and other like noteworthy facts. It was my wont on dialecting tours, when I had been settled in head-quarters for a day or two, and had made friends with the good folk there, to begin my work by having a chat with the village blacksmith about his tools, the implements he was making or repairing, and so forth. Often on these occasions I was met with some such remark as, 'Yo' seemen to know summat about 'em, Ma'am. I could shewn yo' a noud-fashioned tool sich as I dar' say yo' never sid afore.' And then would be brought out of some dark hole or corner an obsolete agricultural implement, and all its parts and uses would be explained to me, and measurements given. And so I learnt all about *that*, and picked up many words and sounds into the bargain.

The wheelwright would then be visited, and the terms of his craft acquired in like manner. The butcher would allow me to go into his shop to see how the great joints—'slench,' 'lift,' &c.—were cut for his country customers. Some neighbouring farmer and his wife would be pleased to shew me the farm-yard, the poultry-yard, and the dairy, and thus I learnt the lore they had to teach. The school-master or mistress would tell the children 'to gather posies and bring them to school for the lady;' and then they would allow me to ask them by what names they knew the flowers they had gathered. I learnt most of my plant-names in this way, a good many bird-names also, and other things besides.

I visited the old people in their cottages, and, leading them to talk of past times, would elicit many a word now dead or dying out, and, hearing it, would note its sound.

I was often fortunate in interesting some intelligent person of the peasant-class in my work, and to such a one I would read over my MS. word-lists, which I invariably took with me. The emendations of these thus obtained were invaluable. 'That inna-d-our word—we sen so-and-so;' or, 'That'll do, nobody can mend that,' would bring out a new term to be recorded, or would confirm the accuracy of my work.

I proceeded on this plan, with more or less of interruption caused by fragile health, until the summer of 1877, when illness compelled me not only to give up a visit I was about to pay to the south-east part of the county, but also to relinquish all further investigations which would have involved fatiguing journeys. However, by methods such as I have described I had accumulated a mass of authentic information; friends had most kindly supplemented my own efforts by furnishing me with very minute answers to the crucial test-questions I had framed in order to elicit evidence upon doubtful points; and I felt, that though I would gladly have done more had strength been given to me for the work, I had yet 'done what I could,' and that I might fearlessly leave all that I was unable to do, without incurring the reproach of conscience within or of critics without.

The Introductory Grammar falls far short of my wishes, but, as far as it goes, it will, I hope, be found useful. It is, I think, the first attempt of the kind for the Shropshire dialect, and, bearing in mind what Max Müller says,—'The first grammar of a language is a work of infinitely greater difficulty than any later grammar' [*Science of Language*, p. 180],—I trust my effort may make it easier for some one coming after me to complete more worthily that which I have begun.

And now I leave my work to speak for itself: its errors are not those of carelessness, and whatever of merit it possesses may fairly be shared with those who have with the utmost kindness and cordiality given me their assistance. Of these, some have been fellow-workers with me from the beginning, others later on; but to each and all I owe a debt of gratitude for the good service they have rendered me in my arduous task. The *Shropshire Word-Book* could not have been either so copious or so complete as it is but for these helpers.

Chief amongst them are, taking them in the order of the districts:—

MR. ROBERT EDDOWES DAVIES, of Kingsland, Shrewsbury, who for upwards of eight years of my work has contributed largely to its general usefulness. His word-lists have been more especially for the SHREWSBURY, WORTHEN, and CLEE HILLS districts.

MRS. GROVES, of Great Hanwood, has done most valuable work for PULVERBATCH and WORTHEN. The *obsolete* words assigned to those districts are what she remembers her grandmother, Hannah Fletcher, using, who died in 1822, aged 86 years: the date for their decay is thus furnished.

The REV. JOHN BURD, M.A., Vicar of Chirbury, has supplied some words, &c., for the WORTHEN district.

MR. GEORGE PUGH, of Wheathill, near Wellington, has contributed a very considerable number of words for the CLEE HILLS district, also for LUDLOW, BRIDGNORTH, &c.

MR. CYRIL JOYCE, of Burford, has furnished a copious list of words from that neighbourhood—the extreme south of Salop; and MR. THOMAS MORGAN-BOUND, of Orleton, has given much valuable help in the LUDLOW district generally.

MR. HUBERT SMITH, F.R.H.S., of S. Leonard, Bridgnorth, has in various ways assisted me materially in working up the BRIDGNORTH district.

MR. W. P. BROOKES, F.R.C.S., has done very useful work in the MUCH WENLOCK district.

MR. ROBERT ANSLOW, of WELLINGTON, has sent comprehensive lists of words for that district, and many words for MUCH WENLOCK, &c.

MR. THOMAS PARTON, F.G.S., has contributed a good deal of useful information relative to *Colliery* and *Mining* terms.

MISS C. S. BURNE, of Edgmond, has done a great deal of excellent work for the NEWPORT district.

MR. A. J. MUNBY, F.S.A., of the Inner Temple, has supplied many words for the COLLIERY and NEWPORT districts.

MR. ROBERT GILL, of Hopton, Hodnet, has given a long list of words, well exemplified, for the WEM district.

The REV. JOHN EVANS, M.A., Vicar of Whixall, has been of very great assistance to the work with relation to the northern part of Salop generally, and more especially to the districts of NEWPORT, WEM, and WHITCHURCH.

The REV. WILLIAM WALSHAM HOW, M.A., Rector of Whittington, has contributed a list of words, &c., for the OSWESTRY district.

MR. ASKEW ROBERTS, of Croeswylan, both personally and by means of his '*Byegones*' columns, has given much help in the OSWESTRY district.

Three contributors to my work, who did much to enrich its pages, have passed away—the REV. J. L. SHEPPARD, M.A., Rector of Abdon; the REV. G. L. WASEY, M.A., Incumbent of Quatford and Morville; and MR. JAMES TURNER, of Wellington. The CLEE HILLS, BRIDGNORTH, WELLINGTON, and COLLIERY districts, respectively, owe a great deal to them.

MR. THOMAS HALLAM, of Manchester,—an eminently good phonetic scholar,—has from time to time given the *Glossic symbols* which indicate the pronunciation of the chief words the benefit of his revision; and more than that, for on submitting to him a 'draft' which I had framed as the basis for a synopsis of all the vowels, diphthongs and fractures, of the consonants and digraphs, I had noted as characteristics of the Shropshire folk-speech, he most kindly—in conference with me—went through it in detail; and bringing to my aid that more perfect knowledge of general phonology which he possessed, but I lacked, he enabled me to make the tabulated list of vowels, diphthongs, &c., which will be found in the opening pages of the **Grammar Outlines**—a list that cannot, as I trust, fail to be useful.

The critical revision of my proof-sheets, as it is the latest service in order of time that has been rendered to me in my arduous task, so it is the last to be placed on this record of grateful acknowledgments; but that it is very far from being the least in importance will be obvious to all those who give thought to such matters. I owe it to the good offices of my friend, the Rev. W. W. Skeat, M.A., Professor of Anglo-Saxon at the University of Cambridge, that this crowning work has been done with genuine interest, with scholarly acumen, and kindly spirit. Here I stop—the story of the book is told.

GEORGINA F. JACKSON.

White Friars, Chester,
October, 1878.

INTRODUCTION.

THE scope of this *Shropshire Word-Book* is to record—

1. **Old Words**, some more or less modified, preserved in the county
2. **Words imported**, as from Border Counties.
3. **Literary Words** used in a **peculiar** sense, marked *pec.*
4. **Literary Words** in common use, spoken with a **variation** of the received pronunciation, marked *var. pr.*
5. **Words** used in a **slangish** way, marked *sl.?*
6. **Words** which are now—or soon will be—**slang terms**, marked *sl.*
7. Some few **words** apparently **coined** in certain localities.
8. **Provincial** and **local names** of birds, plants, &c.
9. **Words** used by **Colliers** and **Miners** in the Coal-field, &c.
10. **Certain Place-names** remarkably pronounced.

Each word is assigned to the district or districts in which it is *known* to be used or, if obsolete, to have been used; but it is not meant by this that it is restricted within such boundaries. *All* that is intended to be conveyed is the *fact* that its range has so far been established.

The **Table of Districts** will shew—as has been explained in the *Preface*—that these have been arranged somewhat arbitrarily; but nevertheless great thought has been given to them, with the view of indicating by their means the trend of phonetic change, dialectic variation, and so forth.

The **topographical position** of each is determined on the *Reference Map.*

In some instances words have been recorded whose usage was apparently limited to a narrower area than that of the *District.* In such cases the more immediate neighbourhood is named where they were found to obtain; see, for example, **Besmotter**, an old word, not—so far as could be ascertained—in use in other localities than the one given.

Where a word is ascribed to several localities of which **Pulverbatch** is one, it may be safely assumed, as a general rule, that its colloquial illustration is drawn from *that* neighbourhood; the same holds good of words recorded as **common.** The exceptional cases are few, but what there are can be easily distinguished by the phonetic structure of certain words embodied in the examples, and so allotted to their respective localities—the **synopsis** of '**vowels, diphthongs,**' &c., affording the key.

The **literary citations** which illustrate the text are in the main the result of independent reading, but when they are borrowed the source from which they have been obtained is acknowledged. When several authors are quoted they are for the most part arranged in chronological order, beginning with the oldest; always excepting such as claim to be '*Salopian*,' which are usually placed *first;* and the Dictionary Quotations,—these coming almost invariably last.

By reference to the list of '**Authorities Quoted**' it will be seen which are *Salopian*, such being distinguished by †; these possess a peculiar value in connection with the *Shropshire Word-Book* of this date, for the writers of the Salopian dialect of long ago have left their impress on the Standard English of to-day.

Mr. Oliphant, in his admirable work, *Sources of Standard English*, has a good deal to say on this subject, and the gist of many of his most interesting remarks may not inaptly find a place here. To begin, then, as far back as 1220, the date of the *Ancren Riwle*, which, it is said, has, more than anything written outside the Danelagh, influenced the Standard English. It was a popular piece in the Dorsetshire dialect, and copies of it are extant in other dialects; of these the Salopian variation is the most remarkable. Following a critical comparison of the differing forms of the *Ancren Riwle*, Mr. Oliphant has a note (p. 124) here given at length:—'In Salop [1220], forms which were used in Lothian and Yorkshire seem to have clashed with forms employed in Gloucestershire and Dorset; something resembling the *Ormulum* was the upshot. In each succeeding century Salop comes to the front. *The Wohunge of ure Lauerd* seems to have been written here about 1210 (Morris's *Old English Homilies*, First Series, p. 269). In 1340, or so, the *Romance of William of Palerne* was compiled here. In 1420 John Audlay wrote his poems in the same dialect (Percy Society, No. 47). In 1580 Churchyard had not dropped all his old Salopian forms. Baxter, who came from Salop, appeared about 1650 as one of the first heralds of the change that was then passing over Standard English prose, and that was substituting Dryden's style for that of Milton. Soon after 1700, Farquhar, in his *Recruiting Officer*, gives us much of the Salopian brogue. This intermingling of Northern and Southern forms in Salop produced something not unlike Standard English.'

'Sir Ion Audlay,' the blind monk-poet of Haughmond, who wrote his verse in 1426, 'lived on the border-land between Northern and Southern varieties of English speech, as a few lines from his poems (p. 65) will shew:

'"And vij. avés to our lady,
Fore *sche* is the wel of al pité,
That *heo* wyl fore me pray."'

'Thirty years later the Southern forms seem to have lost ground in Audlay's Shire.' Ludlow Castle is more closely linked with the history and literature of the country than almost any other spot in England. 'There it was that Richard, Duke of York [he held also Sandal in Yorkshire], brought up his children.' It was from the 'Castill of Lodelowe the iij day of June' [1454] that 'a joint letter was written to their father by the future King Edward IV. and the boy Rutland, who soon after fell at Wakefield. This letter [which see in the *Paston Letters*, Vol. I. c. xi., ed. Gairdner] shews the clipped English which must have been learnt in their childhood by the York princes and their sister'—Margaret—who afterwards as Duchess of Burgundy so materially helped and influenced Caxton.

'After 1461 these clipped inflections of Ludlow (and Sandal) must have become familiar to the ears of the ladies and knights who begirt K. Edward IV. and the Kingmaker at the court of London.' In 1468 Margaret was married to Charles the Bold, and two years later she was in the Low Countries, interesting herself in that work of her countryman Caxton which was destined to fulfil such mighty ends, but of which the more immediate effects were felt on the Mother Tongue of the Duchess and the Printer. Caxton worked under the eye of Margaret. His Southern English was not approved by her; she 'found defaute' with it, and desired him 'to amend it,' and the book she bade Caxton go on with,—the first ever printed in the English Tongue,—when it came out in 1471, shewed that her own speech, fashioned on more Northern models in the far-away Shropshire home of her early years, had been brought to bear upon it: most of the Kentishman's Southern inflections were done away with, and henceforward the triumph of the Midland English as the standard for the future was assured. It had been reserved to Caxton and his Press to bring this about.

That Shropshire retains still in her folk-speech many of the *words* of the old writers will be evident to the readers of this 'Word-Book'; but the *sounds* of the words have their interest also,—their important bearings on philology,—for, to quote Dr. Murray,—*Historical Introduction to the Dialect of the Southern Counties of Scotland*, p. 90,—'Mr. Ellis's enquiry into the history of Early English pronunciation shews how much the restoration of past stages of the language is aided by what has been already done for the phonology of the existing dialects; how much greater would the aid have been if all the varieties of pronunciation in use were faithfully noted!'

In accordance with these views, the phonological part of the present work has received its due share of careful consideration. The **synopsis** of sounds contains nothing but what has been 'proven,' and may therefore be relied upon so far as it goes;—it does not pretend to represent the complete body of sounds heard in the dialect throughout Shropshire, but is given rather as a finger-post to indicate the way to that end than as the end itself attained.

The Shropshire folk-speech proper, that is, when unaffected by the impinging dialects of border counties,—notably those of Cheshire and Stafford,—is characterized in its utterance by a rhythmical cadence and quick, clipped pronunciation very difficult to attain by those 'not to the manner born.' This peculiarity is most noticeable in the ùtterance of the women, whose speaking voices, without being positively shrill, are yet pitched in an unusually high key.

It may be that these qualities of the speech come of a Welsh lineage, but it must be left for 'Scholars' to determine that. Mr. A. J. Ellis's investigations on the whole range of dialects will tend to throw light on much that makes the Salopian variety one of peculiar interest to the Student of History in Language.

TABLE OF DISTRICTS.

1. Shrewsbury.

Albrighton	N.
Condover	S.
Upton Magna	E.
Ford	W.

(a). Atcham. *Sub-district.*

Rodington	N.
Berrington	S.
Wroxeter	E.

2. Pulverbatch.

Gt. Hanwood	N.
Smethcote	S.
Condover	E.
Snailbeach	W.

3. Worthen.

The Severn	N.
Shelve	S.
Stiperstones	E.
Cherbury	W.

4. Craven Arms.

Cardington	N.
Onibury	S.
Delbury	E.
Wistanstow	W.

(b). Church Stretton. *Sub-district.*

Longnor	N.
Acton Scott	S.
Rushbury	E.
Ratlinghope	W.

5. Bishop's Castle and Clun.

Norbury	N.
R. Onny	S.
Sibdon	E.
Clun Forest	W.

6. Corve Dale and Clee Hills.

Burton	N.
Cleobury Mortimer	S.
Billingsley	E.
Stanton Lacey	W.

(c). Ludlow. *Sub-district.*

Bromfield	W.
Cleobury Mortimer	E.

7. Bridgnorth.

Sutton Maddock	N.
Chelmarsh	S.
Claverley	E.
Upton Cressett	W.

8. MUCH WENLOCK.

Little Wenlock	N.
Acton Round	S.
Linley	E.
Acton Burnell	W.

9. WELLINGTON.

Child's Ercall	N.
Leighton	S.
Kinnersley	E.
High Ercall	W.

10. COLLIERY.

Lilleshall	N.E.
Hadley	W.
Broseley	S.

11. NEWPORT.

Market Drayton	N.
Shiffnal	S.
Tibberton	W.

12. WEM.

Edstaston	N.
Hadnall	S.
Stoke-upon-Tern	E.
Middle	W.

(*d*). WHITCHURCH. *Sub-district.*

Whitchurch	N.
Prees	S.
Ightfield	E.
Whixall	W.

13. ELLESMERE.

Dudleston	N.
Shrawardine	S.
Petton	E.
West Felton	W.

14. OSWESTRY.

St. Martin	N.
Llanymynech	S.
Whittington	E.

PHONOLOGY OF THE FOLK-SPEECH.

Glossic Symbols.—These will be very easily understood by giving a little attention to the following key to the sounds which they represent, the symbols being *invariable*, viz.:—

a short as in gn*a*t.
a' fine Southern English *a* as in *a*sk, between **a** and **aa**.
aa as in b*aa*.
ae as in Provincial English n*e*t; Fr. *ê*; Germ. *ä*.
ai as in b*ai*t.
ao open Italian *o*, between *o* and *oa*.
au as in c*au*l.
e as in Southern English n*e*t.
ee as in b*ee*t.
ei as in b*i*te.
eo close Fr. *eu* in p*eu*; f*eu*.
eu as in *Eu*rope.
h' not quite *u'*, which see.
i as in kn*i*t.
i' as in *y* final in beaut*y*; happ*y*; &c.
o as in n*o*t.
oa as in c*oa*l.
oe as in open Fr. *eu* in v*eu*f; Germ. *ö*.
oo as in c*oo*l.
u as in n*u*t.
u' obscure sound as in f*a*tal; *a*bide; lunch*eo*n; &c. See **h'**.
ù between *u* and *oo*.
ue Fr. *u*; Germ. *ü*.

uo same as b*u*sh; f*u*ll; &c.

dh as *th* in *th*is.

th as in *th*in.

zh as in a*z*ure; divi*s*ion; mea*s*ure.

[·] denotes accent, as [bi'sei·d] = beside.

The foregoing is all that is necessary for the general reader to be acquainted with in order to make himself master of the simple—or compromise—Glossic, which indicates with close accuracy the pronunciation of the chief words throughout the Glossary.

The more minute analysis which in some cases is added, as for **ei** = ī [a'y; aay·; ah·; &c.], is intended for those critical students of phonology to whom Mr. A. J. Ellis's *Universal Glossic* will not be as 'the accents of an unknown tongue.'

See for extended examples of both '**Compromise**' and '**Analytic**' **Glossic** the *Specimens of the Folk-speech* following *Grammar Outlines*, &c.

GRAMMAR OUTLINES.

THE * affixed to a word denotes that it will be found more particularly explained or exemplified in the body of the **Glossary**.

ORTHOGRAPHY.

The Alphabet.—*How the letters are said together with &.*

A [aa·]	B [bai·]	C [sai·]	D [dai·]	E [ai·]
F [aef·]	G [jee·]	H [ai·ch]	I [ei·]	J [jaa·]
K [kaa·]	L [el·]	M [em·]	N [en·]	O [oa·]
P [pai·]	Q [koo·]	R [aa·r']	S [ess·]	T [tai·]
U [oo·]	V [vai·]	W [dub·l oo]	X [ek·s]	Y [wei·]
Z [zod·]	an' [u'n]	& empassy on * [em·pu'si'on·'].		

Zad an' expassy and [ek·spu'si'and] are heard about WORTHEN.

VOWELS AND DIPHTHONGS.

A.—1 = [a] in closed syllables, as, back, cat, gnat, had [ad·], that; Com. Master [mas·tu'r'], refined pronunciation; NEWPORT. See below (6) and (7).

2 = [a'], Ann [a'n·], dance [da'n·s], make [ma'k·], take [ta'k·], &c. This is the fine Shropshire **a**, still pretty general, but gradually passing away. See further, **Specimens of Folk-speech.**

3 = [aa·], mare = mar' [maa·r'], bare = bar' [baa·r'], rare = rar' [r'aa·r'], scarce [skaa·r's], &c.; Com.

4 = [:aa·], father [f:aa·dhu'r'], CLEE HILLS, *Abdon.* Cf. **A** (7). Started [st:aa·r'ti'd], warm [w:aa·r'm], Com.

5 = [aa], want [waan·t], ladder [laadh·u'r'], Com. Wash [waash·], CRAVEN ARMS; CLEE HILLS. See below (6).

6 = ĕ = [ae], wash = wesh [waesh·], catch = ketch [kaech·], Com. Thatch = thetch [thaech·], gather = gether [g(yaedh·u'r'], see **g** (2) (*consonants*); PULVERBATCH; NEWPORT. Grass = gress* [gr'aes·], NEWPORT; ELLESMERE. Master = mester [maes·tu'r'], WELLINGTON; NEWPORT; ELLESMERE. Make = mek [maek·], take = tek [taek·], before initial vowels; NEWPORT. These words are sounded [mai·], [tai·], before consonants; *ibid.* Cf. **e** (9).

7 = [ai·], father [fai·dhu'r'], master [mai·stu'r'], water [wai·tu'r'], Com.

8 = [:ai·], scarce [sk:ai·s], Com. See above (3).

9 = [ai·h'], sage = sääge [sai·h'j], CHURCH STRETTON. Ale* [ai·h'l], same [sai·h'm], LUDLOW, *Burford.*

10 = [ai], bacon [baik·n], mason [mais·n], paper, &c.; bake, name, tale, &c.; Com.

11 = [au·], call [kau·], fall [fau·], NEWPORT.

12 = [:au·], *a* before *ll*, as, all [:au·l], call, fall; Com. Talking [t:au·ki'n], Com.

13 = [a'y·], danger [da'y·nju'r'], SHREWSBURY; PULVERBATCH.

14 = [:ee·], lame [l:ee·m], NEWPORT.

15 = [ee·h'], mare = meer [mee·h'r'], share = sheer [shee·h'r'], &c.; NEWPORT.

16 = [:ee·h'], market [m:ee·h'r'ki't], BRIDGNORTH.

17 = [o], bank = bonk [bong·k], thrash = throsh [thr'osh·], can = con [kon·], &c.; Com. Apple = opple [op·l], CRAVEN ARMS; CLUN. Gather = gother [godh·u'r'], CLUN.

18 = [o'·], barrow = borrow [bo'·r'u'], CORVE DALE.

19 = [u], was (accented) [wuz·], was not [wun·u'], Com.

Ai.—1 = [aa·], fair = far [faa·r'], pair = par [paa·r'], &c.; Com.

2 = [aa], waistcoat [waas·ku't], CRAVEN ARMS.

3 = [aa·y], rain [r'aa·yn], lain [laa·yn], &c.; BISHOP'S CASTLE; CLUN.

4 = [:aa·y], rain [r':aa·yn], lain [l:aa·yn], &c.; CRAVEN ARMS; CHURCH STRETTON.

5 = [aay], rain [r'aayn], lain [laayn], &c.; SHREWSBURY; PULVERBATCH.

6 = [ae], fair [faer'·], CLUN. Cf. **ai** (1) above.

7 = [e], said [sed·], Com.

8 = [ee], rain [r'een·], drain [dr'een·], bait [beet·], &c.; NEWPORT.

9 = [ee·h'], chair [chee·h'r'], Com. Fair [fee·h'r'], &c.; NEWPORT.

10 = [i·h'], rain [r'i·h'n], drain [dr'i·h'n], NEWPORT.

Au.—1 = [a], laugh [laf·], Com.

2 = [o], laugh [lof·], COLLIERY; NEWPORT. Naughty [not·i'], NEWPORT.

3 = [:au·], daughter [d:au·tu'r'], Com.

4 = [aa·], daughter [daa·tu'r'], NEWPORT. Sauce* [saa·s], CORVE DALE.

Aw.—1 = [au·], crawl [skr'au·l], Com. Claw* [klau·], Qy. com.

2 = [:au·], gnaw [n:au·], straw [str':au·], Com.

3 = [i'·au], caw* [ki'·au], WEM.

4 = [ai·], strawberries [str'ai·br'i'z], *obsols.*; PULVERBATCH. Claws [klai·z]. See Cleys.*

5 = [ee·], claws* [kleez·].

Ay.—1 = [a'y], May [ma'y], pay [pa'y], day [da'y], &c.; SHREWSBURY; PULVERBATCH.

2 = **ai** (3) = [aa·y], day, &c.; BISHOP'S CASTLE; CLUN.

3 = **ai** (4) = [:aa·y], day, &c.; CRAVEN ARMS; CHURCH STRETTON.

4 = **ai** (8) = [ee], day, &c.; NEWPORT.

5 = [ah·y], dray* [dr'ah·y], CHURCH STRETTON.

Aye.—1 = [ay·], aye (yes) [ay·], SHREWSBURY; PULVERBATCH. Qy. com.

2 = [ahy· *or* ah·y], *idem*; NEWPORT.

E.—1 = [e] in closed syllables, as bless [bles·], peck [pek·], get [get·], wench [wen·sh], &c.; Com.

2 = [ee·], pewit [pee·wi't], PULVERBATCH. Qy. com. Cf. (6) below.

3 = [:ee·], he [:ee·], we [w:ee·]. See **Personal Pronouns.**

4 = [:ee·u'], there [dh:ee·u'r'], where [w:ee·u'r'], Com.

5 = [ai·], fever [fai·vu'r'], secret [sai·kr'i't], scheme [skai·m], &c.; Com.

6 = [:ai·], complete [ku'mpl:ai·t], &c.; Com. Pewit * [p:ai·wi't], SHREWSBURY. Me [m:ai·], NEWPORT.

7 = [aa·], serve [saa·r'v], sermon [saa·r'mu'n], certain [saa·r'ti'n], &c.; Com. Yes [yaa·s], CHURCH STRETTON. Mere [maa·r'], ELLESMERE. Cf. **mere** below (13).

8 = [aay·], yes [aay·s], CHURCH STRETTON, *Leebotwood.*

9 = [a], fetch [fach·], belly [bal·i'], Com. Cf. **a** (6).

10 = [ae], berry [baer'·i'], remlet * [r'aem·let], render * [r'aen·du'r'], ever [aev·u'r'], never [naev·u'r'], &c.; Com. Yes [yaes·], NEWPORT.

11 = [i], shelf [shilf·], clever [kliv·u'r'], seldom [sil·du'm], &c.; Com. Cf. **i** (6).

12 = [i'], in **ed**, verbal suffix pronounced as a distinct syllable, as in wanted [waan·ti'd], drowned = drown'ded [dr'uw·ndi'd], &c.; Com. Also in yes = iss [i'ss·], very general. Cf. **yes** above (7), (8), and (10).

13 = [u'], in **mere** in composition (unaccented), as Ellesmere [el·zmu'r'], Colemere [kuo·mu'r'], or more modern [koa·lmu'r'], &c.; Com. Cf. **mere** above (7); also **o** (24) (*a*).

Ea.—1 = [ai·], tea [tai·], cream [kr'ai·m], veal [vai·l], &c.; Com. Wheat [wai·t], PULVERBATCH (occasionally heard); WEM. Cf. **wheat** below (15). Leaf [lai·f], NEWPORT.

2 = [ai], beat [bait·], seat [sait·], &c.; Com. Bean [bain·], PULVERBATCH. Cf. **bean** below (14).

3 = [ai·u'], wheat [wai·u't], NEWPORT.

4 = [aa·], learn [laa·r'n], bear [baa·r'], &c.; Com. Cf. **a** (3).

5 = [:ae·], deal [j:ae·l], dead [j:ae·d], death [j:ae·th], Com. Cf. **ea** (13) below; also **d** (1).

6 = [ae], cheap [chaep·], weak [waek·], leaf [laef·], &c.; SHREWSBURY; PULVERBATCH. Qy. com.

7 = [e], team [chem·], Com. Heath [yeth·], CLUN; WEM. Cf. **heath** below (16).

8 = [:ee·h'], ear [:ee·h'r'], year, *idem.* Qy. com. Mean [m:ee·h'n], LUDLOW, *Burford.* Bear [b:ee·h'r'], wear [w:ee·h'r'], &c.; NEWPORT. Cf. **bear** above (4). Leaf [l:ee·h'f], WEM.

9 = [:ee·u'], heard [:ee·u'r'd], Com.

10 = [ee·], break [br'ee·k], great [gr'ee·t], NEWPORT.

11 = [i], feather [fidh·u'r'], Com. Measure [mizh·u'r'], Com. [miz·u'r'], ELLESMERE. Cheap [chip·], NEWPORT. Cf. **cheap** above (6).

12 = [i'aa·], beard * [bi'aa·r'd], PULVERBATCH. Qy. com.

13 = [i'ae], deal [di'ael·], dead [di'aed·], death [di'aeth·], NEWPORT. Cf. **ea** (5); also **d** (1).

14 = [i'·h'], bean [bi'·h'n], leaf [li'·h'f], Com. Stean * [sti'·h'n], PULVERBATCH. Cf. **leaf** above (6).

15 = [i'u'], beast * [bi'u'st], wheat = w'eät [wi'u't], Com.

16 = [i'·u'], beam * [bi'·u'm]. Qy. com. Heath [yi'·u'th], CHURCH STRETTON. Cf. **heath** above (7).

17 = [i'u], dead [di'ud·], LUDLOW, *Burford.*

18 = [u], heap [yup·], head [yud·], *ibid.*

19 = [ay·], clear [klay·u'r'], SHREWSBURY; PULVERBATCH; ELLESMERE.

Ee.—1 = [ee·], eighteen [a'yt·tee·n], indeed [indee·d]. See **Specimens of Folk-speech.** Indeed, *very* emphatic is [·in·dee·d], with stress on first syllable. Com. Seed [see·d] = seen, saw; NEWPORT; WEM; WHITCHURCH; ELLESMERE.

2 = [:i·], wheel [w:i·l], SHREWSBURY; PULVERBATCH. Qy. com.

3 = [i], been [bin·], seen [sin·], sheep [ship·], &c.; Com.

4 = [i'], beef [bi'f·], week [wi'k], seed [si'd·] = seen, saw; Com. Cf. **seed** above, **ee** (1).

5 = [:ai·], thee [dh:ai·], tree [tr':ai·], &c.; NEWPORT.

6 = [ee·h'], seen [see·h'n], LUDLOW, *Burford.*

Ei.—1 = [ai·], conceit [ku'nsai·t], Leighton [lai·tn], Com. Either [ai·dhu'r'], LUDLOW; NEWPORT. Qy. com.

2 = i = [aay·], neighbour [naay·bu'r']; SHREWSBURY; PULVERBATCH.

3 = i = [aay], weight [waayt·], SHREWSBURY; PULVERBATCH; NEWPORT. Height [aayt·], SHREWSBURY; PULVERBATCH.

4 = i = [a'y], eighteen [a'yt·tee·n], SHREWSBURY; PULVERBATCH.

5 = [ah·y], height [ah·yt], either [ah·ydhu'r'], NEWPORT.

6 = [ee·], neighbour [nee·bu'r'], NEWPORT.

7 = [ee·h'], reins [r'ee·h'nz], NEWPORT.

8 = [aa·], heir [aa·r'], SHREWSBURY; PULVERBATCH.

Eu = [oo], deuce (of cards) [doos·], LUDLOW.

Ew.—1 = [uw·], ewe [yuw·], dew * [dyuw·], Com.

2 = [:uu·w], mew * [my:uu·w], few [fy:uu·w], Com.

3 = [uuw], lewn * [luuwn·], *obsols.*

4 = [i':uu·w], dew [ji':uu·w], PULVERBATCH; *obsols.*?

5 = [au·], chew [chau·], LUDLOW; NEWPORT. Qy. com.

6 = [oo·], brew [br'oo·]. Qy. com. Crew * [kr'oo·], PULVERBATCH; WEM. Dew [doo·], new [noo·], Shrewsbury [soo·zbr'i'], see (11) below; NEWPORT, which in the local vernacular, = [noo·pu'r't].

7 = [oe'], sinew [sen·oe'], PULVERBATCH.

8 = [i'oe·], approximately, in few [fi'oe·], NEWPORT.

9 = [u'], sinew [sen·u'], SHREWSBURY.

10 = [u'r'], sinew [sin·u'r'], NEWPORT.

11 = [oa·], Shrewsbury [shr'oa·zbr'i'], refined; [sr'oa·zbr'i'], semi-refined; [soa·zbr'i'], Com. Shrewd [shr'oa·d], WORTHEN; CLUN; [sr'oa·d], PULVERBATCH; WEM.

Ey.—1 = [ai·], key [kai·], Com. Cleys * [klai·z].

I.—1 = [i] in closed syllables, as sit, pig, window [win·du'], frightened [fr'it·nd], &c.; Com.

2 = [i'], prill * [pr'i'l·], ivy [i'v·i'], pick [pi'k·], stick [sti'k·], &c.; Com.

3 = [a'y·], I (see **Personal Pronouns**), tidy [ta'y·di'], like [la'y·k], &c. This is the fine Shropshire diphthongal **i**; very general.

4 = [a'y], mice [ma'ys·], &c.; *idem.*

5 = [ahy· *or* ah·y] = **oi**, approximately; right = roight [r'ahy·t *or* r'ah·yt], so also night, like, &c.; NEWPORT.

6 = [ae], think [thaeng·k], till [tael·], arithmetic [u'r'aeth·mi'ti'k], &c.; Com. Cf. **e** (11).

7 = [ae·], girl [gae·r'ld], Com.

8 = [e], since [sen·s], Com.

9 = [:ee·], right [r':ee·t], bright [br':ee·t], night [n:ee·t], WEM; WHITCHURCH.

10 = [ŏŏ], with [ŏŏdh·], will (*vb.*) [ŏŏl], &c.; *S. Shr.* general. See **Verbs.**

11 = [u], with [wudh·], WEM; ELLESMERE. Muster [mus·tu'r'], NEWPORT. Bun [bun·] = bin = been; bunna [bun·u'] = binna = be not; OSWESTRY, *Whittington.*

12 = [u·], sirrah [su·r'i'], Com.

13 = [ù], will (*vb.*) [wùl·], WEM; ELLESMERE.

14 = [i'·], hiccough [i'·ku'p], Com. Cf. **gh** (3).

Ie.—1 = [i], sieve [siv·], yield [il·d], Com.

2 = [i'], field [fi'l·d], belief [bi'li'f·], &c.; Com.

(*a*) „ final in magpie [mag·pi'], SHREWSBURY; PULVERBATCH. Qy. com.

3 = [ai·], belief [bi'lai·f], NEWPORT. Field [fai·ld], sometimes heard; *ibid.*

O.—1 = [o] in many closed syllables, as nod = not, mop, top, rob, &c.; Com.

(*a*) „ rope [r'op·], yoke = yok * [yok·]. Qy. com.

2 = [u], Tom [tum·], long [lun(g], strong [str'un(g], wrong [r'un(g·], tongue [tung·g], foreign [fur'·i'n], &c.; Com. Stone [stun·], in composition and unaccented, as grind-stone = grindlestun; or of weight, 'five *stun* three,' &c.; NEWPORT. Cf. **o** = **u** in received English **onion,** and see (15), (16), (17) below.

3 = [oa·], bosom [boa·zu'm], Com. Plover [ploa·vu'r'], SHREWSBURY. Stone [stoa·n], NEWPORT. Cf. **stone** below (26).

4 = [:oa·], lose [l:oa·z], no [n:oa·], so [s:oa·], Com.

5 = [oa], fold [foad·], sold [soad·], cold [koad·], NEWPORT.

6 = [oa·h'], cold [koa·h'ld], PULVERBATCH, *Smethcote.* Cf. (21) below.

7 = [:oa·u'], afore [u'f:oa·u'r'], tore [t:oa·u'r'], porket * [p:oa·u'r'-ki't], &c.; Com.

8 = [ŏŏ], woman [ŏŏm·u'n]. Qy. com. Worsted [ŏŏs·ti'd], wool [ŏŏl·], &c.; Com. in *Mid.* and *South Shr.* Go [gŏŏ], Com. Going [gŏŏ·i'n], ELLESMERE.

9 = [oo·], gold [goo·ld], SHREWSBURY; PULVERBATCH, *obsols.* Story [stoo·r'i'], going [goo·i'n], NEWPORT.

10 = [oo·h'], more [moo·h'r'], NEWPORT.

11 = [:au·], love [l:au·v], Com.

12 = [au], morning [maur'·ni'n], &c.; Com.

13 = [a], wrong [r'an(g·], PULVERBATCH; CHURCH STRETTON. Cf. **wrong** above (2); also **ng** (2) (*consonants*).

14 = [aa], yonder [yaan·tu'r'], Com.; [yaan·du'r'], NEWPORT. See **th** (4). Foreign [faar'·i'n], CHURCH STRETTON, *Leebotwood*. Cf. **foreign** above (2).

15 = [a'y·], onion [a'y·ni'u'n], SHREWSBURY; PULVERBATCH.

16 = [aay·], „ [aay·n'u'n], CHURCH STRETTON.

17 = [ahy·], „ [ahy·ni'u'n], BRIDGNORTH.

18 = [uo], love [luov·], NEWPORT. Cf. **love** above (11). Comb [kuom], Com.

19 = [uoh'·], cord [kuoh'·r'd], SHREWSBURY, *Uffington*. Cf. **cord** below (23).

20 = [uu], for = fur [fuur'], thorn [thuur'n], Com.

21 = [ou·] = [:uu·w] when followed by **ld**, the **l** being suppressed, as fold (*sb.*) [f:uu·wd], sold [s:uu·wd], very general. Gold [g:uu·wd], WELLINGTON; NEWPORT. Qy. com. Cf. **fold** (5) and **gold** (9) above.

22 = [ou·] = [uw·], hold [uw·t], old [uw·d], fold (*vb.*) [fuw·d], cold [kuw·d], &c.; SHREWSBURY; PULVERBATCH. Qy. com.

23 = [uu], cord [kwuur'·d], CHURCH STRETTON; CLUN. Cord-wood [kwuur'd ŏŏd], PULVERBATCH; CLEE HILLS; BRIDGNORTH.

24 = [u'], so [su'], to [tu'], and sometimes go [gu'], when unemphasized; NEWPORT. Cf. **go** (8) above.

(*a*) „ in **more** in composition (unaccented), as Blakemore = Bleakmur [blee·kmu'r'], Whitmore [wit·mu'r'], &c.; NEWPORT. Cf. **e** (13).

25 = [i'·], going [gwi'·i'n], SHREWSBURY; PULVERBATCH.

26 = [oe], gone [gwoen·], bone [bwoen·], stone [stwoen·], Com.

Oa.—1 = [oa], loaf [loaf·], soap [soap·], &c.; Com. Road [r'oad·], SHREWSBURY.

2 = [oa·h'], road [r'oa·h'd], LUDLOW, *Burford*.

3 = [ù-u'], road [r'ù-u'd], load [lù-u'd], WEM. Qy. com.

4 = [uo·h'], board [buo·h'r'd], SHREWSBURY. Qy. com.

5 = [uo'·h'], board [buo'·h'r'd], WHITCHURCH.

6 = [ŏŏ-h'], oats [ŏŏ-h't·s], oäns * [ŏŏ-h'n·z], PULVERBATCH.

7 = [u], oak [wuk·], oath [wuth·], SHREWSBURY; PULVERBATCH. Qy. com. Oats [wut·s], Com. See w (3) (*consonants*).

8 = [:uu·], board = bwurd [bw:uu·r'd], PULVERBATCH. Cf. (4) and (5) above.

(*a*) „ hoar = ur [w:uu·r'], a '*wur* fros';' SHREWSBURY; PULVERBATCH.

9 = [ao·], road [r'ao·d], load [lao·d], &c.; NEWPORT.

Oa.—1 = [au·] in hoe; Com.

2 = ou = [:uu·w] in hoe; BISHOP'S CASTLE; CLUN.

3 = [oa·] in hoe; NEWPORT.

Oi.—1 = i = [ei] = [a'y], loin = line * [la'yn], join = jine * [ja'yn·], spoil [spa'yl], &c.; SHREWSBURY; PULVERBATCH; very general. Coin [kwa'yn], PULVERBATCH; *obs.?*

2 = [a'y·], oiled [a'y·ld], *ibid.* Boil [bwa'y·l], PULVERBATCH. Cf. i (3) and (4).

3 = [ahy·], spoil [spahy·l], &c.; NEWPORT.

4 = [a'·y], spoil * [spwa'·yl], BISHOP'S CASTLE; CLUN.

Oo.—1 = [ŏŏ], spoon [spŏŏn·], moon [mŏŏn·], room [r'ŏŏm·], took [tŏŏk·], &c.; Com.

2 = [oo], goose [goos·], gooseberries [gooz·br'i'z]. Cf. s (1). Shook [shook·], took [took·], *emph.* See below (7). NEWPORT.

3 = [:oo·], good [g:oo·d], coop * [k:oo·p], SHREWSBURY; PULVERBATCH. Qy. com.

4 = [oo·u'], door [doo·u'r'], floor [floo·u'r'], NEWPORT. Cf. (8) below.

5 = [oo·h'], moon [moo·h'n], LUDLOW, *Burford.*

6 = [uo], cooty * [kuot·i'], PULVERBATCH. Coother * [kuodh·u'r'], CLEE HILLS. Tooth [tuoth·], NEWPORT.

7 = [u], foot [fut·], soot [sut·], tooth [tuth·], brook [br'uk], roof [r'uf·], &c.; Com. Took [tuk·], shook [shuk·], *unemph.* Cf. (2) above. NEWPORT.

8 = [uu], floor = flur [fluur'·], door = dur [duur'·], Com. Cf. (4) above.

9 = [:oa·], choose [ch:oa·z], shook [sh:oa·k], Com. Cf. **o** (4).

10 = [oa'], coop * [koa'p·], BISHOP'S CASTLE; CLUN. Cf. **coop** above (3).

11 = [i'oo], fool [fi'ool·], pool [pi'ool·], school [ski'ool·], NEWPORT.

12 = [ue], book [buek·], nook [nuek·], WHITCHURCH, *Tilstock*.

13 = [i'ue], school [ski'uel], WHITCHURCH.

14 = [i'], Woodward (proper name) = Withart [wi'dh·u'r't], WHITCHURCH, *Whixall*. Cf. **d** (5).

Ou.—1 = [ou] = [uw], house [uwss·], mouse [muwss·], SHREWSBURY; PULVERBATCH. Qy. com.

2 = [ou·] = [uw·], housen (for houses) [uw·zn], proud [pr'uw·d], *ibid.* See further, **Specimens of Folk-speech**. Shoulder [shuw·du'r'], SHREWSBURY. This does not seem to be the normal pronunciation. Cf. **shoulder** below (14).

3 = [uwu'·], our [uwu'·r'], an hour [u' nuwu'·r']. See **Specimens of Folk-speech**. Pour (*vb.*, as of rain that has fallen) [puwu'·r']. Cf. **pour** below (10).

4 = [ou] = [uuw], bought [buuwt·], thought [thuuwt·], coarse, rough speakers; NEWPORT.

5 = [ou·] = [uuw·], shoulder [shuuw·du'r' *or* shuuw·ldu'r'], NEWPORT. Cf. **shoulder** below (9).

6 = [ou·] = [:uu·w], slough (morass) [sl:uu·w], through [thr':uu·w], PULVERBATCH.

7 = [oo·], shoulder [shoo·du'r'], CHURCH STRETTON. Sough * (*vb.*) [soo·], CLUN; WEM.

8 = [ŏŏ], pouch * [pŏŏch·]. Qy. com. Would [ŏŏd·]. See **Verbs.**

9 = [oa·], trough (for kneading) [tr'oa·], PULVERBATCH, *obsols.* Shoulder [shoa·du'r'], SHREWSBURY.

10 = [:oa·u'], your [y:oa·u'r'], Com. Pour (*vb.*, as of rain coming down) [p:oa·u'r'], SHREWSBURY. Qy. com. Cf. **pour** above (3).

11 = [au], bought [baut·], thought [thaut·], &c.; Com. See **Specimens of Folk-speech,** No. 2.

12 = [o], tough [tof·], Com. Trough [tr'of·], occasionally heard. Bought [bot·], thought [thot·], NEWPORT. Cf. (11) above.

13 = [:uo], tough [t:uof], trough [tr':uof], NEWPORT.

14 = [uo·], shoulder [shuo·dhu'r'], SHREWSBURY; PULVERBATCH. Cf. **shoulder** above (2).

15 = [uo], couch [kuoch·], coulter [kuot·u'r'], &c.; Com.

16 = [u], bound [bun·d], found [fun·d], pound [pun·d], trough [tr'uf·], &c.; Com. Should [shud·], would [wud·], NEWPORT. Cf. **would** above (8). Slough (skin of a snake) [sluf·], PULVERBATCH. Qy. com. Sough * (*sb.*) [suf·f], Com.

17 = [ů], courant * [kůr'an·t], could [kůd], PULVERBATCH. See **Verbs**.

18 = [u'], cough in composition and unaccented, as chin-cough [chin·ku'f], Com. Courant * [ku'r'an·t], CLEE HILLS.

19 = [ue] in words ending in **ous**, as curious [ki'oo·r'i'uez], &c.; WORTHEN; CLEE HILLS, *Abdon.*

Ow.—1 = [oa·], bowl (basin) [boa·l], mow (*vb.*) [moa·], &c.; Com.

2 = [ou·] = [uw·], bowl (a hoop) [buw·l], bowl (*vb.*) [*idem*], mow * (*sb.*) [muw·], bow (for arrows) [buw·], Com.

3 = [ou·] = [:uu·w], mow (*vb.*) [m:uu·w], BISHOP'S CASTLE; CLUN.

4 = [ou] = [uuw·], howl [yuuw·l], Com.

5 = [i'uuw·], cow [ki'uuw·], WHITCHURCH.

6 = [oe], cullow * [kuol·oe], killow * [ki'l·oe], &c.; PULVERBATCH, *obsols.* Burrow [bu·r'oe], *ibid.*

7 = [u'], leasow [lez·u'], meadow [maed·u'], window [wi'n·du'], &c.; Com.

8 = [u'r'], leasow [lez·u'r'], &c.; NEWPORT.

Oy.—1 = [:auy], boy [bw:auy], SHREWSBURY; PULVERBATCH; *obsols.*

U.—1 = [u] in most closed syllables, as nut, tub, but, &c.; thus, butcher = [buch·u'r'], put [put·], full [ful·], bull [bul·], &c.; Com. Pull [pul·], NEWPORT. Cf. **pull** below (8).

2 = [eu·] = [yoo·], use (*vb.*) [yoo·z], Com.

3 = [eu·] = [y:oo·], Union (work-house) [y:oo·ni'u'n], &c.; Com. Utick * [y:oo·ti'k], SHREWSBURY; NEWPORT. Qy. com. Humoursome * [y:oo·mu'r'su'm], PULVERBATCH; NEWPORT; WEM; ELLESMERE.

4 = [eu] = [yoo], use (*sb.*) [yoos·], usened * (we used) [yoos·nt], ELLESMERE; [yoos·tn], *idem*; NEWPORT.

5 = [ae], urine [aer'·i'n], Com.

6 = [eu·] = [i'oo·], music [mi'oo·zi'k], fury [fi'oo·r'i'], &c.; Com. **Musey** * [mi'oo·zi'], WHITCHURCH. Puke * [pi'oo·k], PULVERBATCH; WORTHEN. Muse * [mi'oo·ss], PULVERBATCH. Qy. com. Cornute * [kaur'·ni'oo·t], PULVERBATCH. Curious [ki'oo·r'i'uez], WORTHEN; CLEE HILLS, *Abdon*. Cf. **ou** (19).

7 = [eu·] = [i':oo·], curate [ki':oo·r'i't], fuel [fi':oo·i'l], &c.; Com. Musicianer * [mi'oo·zi'sh·'u'nu'r'], PULVERBATCH; WEM.

8 = [oo·], pull [poo·l], tune [choo·n], supple [soo·pl], dubious [joo·bu's], &c.; Com. Duke [doo·k], music [moo·zi'k], curious [koo·r'i'u's], &c.; NEWPORT. Cf. **ew** (6).

9 = [:oo·] after **r**: cruel [kr':oo·i'l], gruel [gr':oo·i'l], &c.; Com.

10 = [oo], Sukie (proper name) [shook·i'], tube [choob·], &c.; Com.

11 = [:oo·h'] before **re** in sure [sh:oo·h'r'], SHREWSBURY; PULVERBATCH. Qy. com. Cure [k:oo·h'r'], NEWPORT.

12 = [i':oo·u'] before **re** in cure [ki':oo·u'r']. Qy. com.

(*a*) = [u'] „ „ in nature [nai·tu'r'], creature [kr'ai·tu'r'], feature [fai·chu'r'], &c.; Com.

13 = [i'] in fortune [faur'·ti'n], Com.

14 = [ou·] = [uw·] in cucumber [kuw·ku'mbu'r'], Com.

15 = [ŏŏ] in cucumber [kuw·kŏŏm'·u'r'], SHREWSBURY; PULVERBATCH.

16 = [uo], duck [duok·], shut [shuot·], just [juost·], &c.; NEWPORT. Cullow * [kuol·oe], PULVERBATCH, *obsols.* Cf. **ow** (6).

17 = [ŭo], pun * [pŭon·], Com.

18 = [ů], nuchid * [nůkh·i'd], PULVERBATCH; WORTHEN; nearly *obs.* Cf. **ch** (3).

19 = [uu] before **r** in fur [fuur'·], bur * [buur'·], urchin * [uur'·chi'n], turf [tuur'·f], &c.; Com.

20 = [ae], chuck [chaek], shut * [shaet·], just [jaest·], sludge [slaej·], burying (funeral) [baer'·i'n], Com. Cf. (16) above.

21 = [ae·], bury * [bae·r'i'], LUDLOW, *Burford*; NEWPORT.

22 = [i], pulpit [pil·pi't], plumb [plim·], Com.

23 = [o], in composition with **n**, as ontidy, onlucky, &c. Qy. com. in *S. Shr.*

Ue.—1 = [oo], flue [floo], blue [bloo], due [doo], Tuesday [tooz·di' *or* chooz·di'], &c.; SHREWSBURY; PULVERBATCH; NEWPORT. Qy. com.

2 = [:oo·], true [tr':oo·], glue [gl:oo·], &c.; *ibid.*

3 = [i'], argue [aa·r'gi'], Com.

4 = [i'oo], argue * [aar'·gi'oo], WEM.

Ui.—1 = [oo], juice [joos·], SHREWSBURY; PULVERBATCH. Qy. com.

2 = [oo·], nuisance [noo·su'ns], *ibid.*

3 = [:oo·], fruit [fr':oo·t], *ibid.*

4 = [i'], build [bi'l·d], guilty [gi'l·ti'], *ibid.*

Uy.—1 = [a'y·], buy [ba'y·]; SHREWSBURY; PULVERBATCH. Qy. com.

Y.—1 = [i], hymn [im·], hyssop [iz·u'p], syllable [sin·u'bl], &c.; SHREWSBURY; PULVERBATCH. Qy. com.

2 = [ae], syrup [saer'·u'p], pyramid [paer'·u'mi'd], *ibid.*

3 = [u], sycamore [suk·u'moa·'h'r'], SHREWSBURY; PULVERBATCH; CRAVEN ARMS. Qy. com. Syringe [sul·i'nj], PULVERBATCH.

4 = [uu], myrtle [muur'·tl]. Qy. com.

5 = [a'y·], when final and accented, as by [ba'y·], my [ma'y·], why [wa'y·], &c.; SHREWSBURY; PULVERBATCH. Qy. com.

6 = [ahy· *or* ah·y] = **oi** approximately, as by [bahy· *or* bah·y], my [mahy· *or* mah·y], &c.; NEWPORT; but these words are rarely emphatic there.

7 = [i'], when final and unaccented, as in tidy [ta'y·di'], ready [r'ed·i'], &c.; pig-sty [pig·sti'], my [mi'], why [wi'], &c. Com. Cf. **ie** (2) (*a*), (*vowels, &c.*).

CONSONANTS AND DIGRAPHS, ETC.

B.—1 = **p**, as pather * = bather * = batter; ELLESMERE. Cf. **p**, below.

C.—1 = **z**: twice = twize [twa'y·z], &c.; Com. Face [fai·z], very general.

2 = **g** in carrots = garrits [gar'i'ts], carroty = garrity [gar'i'ti'], PULVERBATCH. Cf. **g** (3) below.

Ch.—1. This digraph = **sh** in bench [ben·sh], drench [dr'en·sh], wench * [wen·sh], &c.; Com.

2 = **k**, in perch (measurements of land, &c.), [paer'·k], CLEE HILLS; LUDLOW. Muchin* (a pig) [muk·i'n], WEM.

3 = [kh], a **guttural spirant**, in **muchin** [mukh·i'n], CLUN: and in nuchid* [nůkh·i'd], a nearly obsolete word, meaning ill-nourished; PULVERBATCH; WORTHEN. Cf. **gh** (5).

Cl.—1 = [kl] not [tl].

D.—1 = **j**, in deal [j:ae·l], dead [j:ae·d], death [j:ae·th], Com. Cf. **ea** (13). Darn [jaa·r'n], dew = je'ow [ji':uu·w], PULVERBATCH. See **ew** (4) (*vowels, &c.*).

2 = **t** when final after **ar**, as custard [kus·tu'r't], backward [bak·u'r't], awkward [auk·u'r't], &c.; Com. Cf. **t** (1).

3—is often omitted at the end of syllables and monosyllabic words as, landlord [lan·lu'r't], Com.; [lan·lu'r't *or* lon·lu'r't], NEWPORT; and [u'n], Com.; find [fei·n] = [fa'y·n], lend [len·], send [sen·], &c.; SHREWSBURY; PULVERBATCH. Qy. com.

4—is sometimes added to the end of words, as girl = girld [gae'·r'ld], wine = winde [wa'y·nd], gown [gou·nd] = [guw·nd], SHREWSBURY; PULVERBATCH; believed to be general with varying diphthongal sounds.

5 = **th** = [dh], Edward = Yethart [yaedh·u'r't], Woodward [wi'dh·u'r't], WHITCHURCH, *Whixall*. Cf. **th** (5) below.

Dd = **th** = [dh], ladder = lather [laadh·u'r'], edder (for *adder*) = ether [aedh·u'r'], Com.

F.—1—is usually omitted in **of**, which = **o'**.

2 = **th** in frock [thr'ok·], from [throm·] *emph.*, [thr'u'm·] *unemph.* Qy. com.

3 = **v** in feerings* = veerings [vee·h'r'i'nz], CLEE HILLS. Cf. **v** (2) below.

G.—1—as in received English generally.

2—is palatal in some words = [g(y], as get [g(yet], gether (for gather) [g(yaedh·u'r'], &c.; PULVERBATCH. Qy. com.

3 = **c** in Goldfinch = Coldfinch; WHITCHURCH. Cf. **c** (2) above.

ng is the **gutturo-nasal**.

1 = **n**: that is, nasal [n] is substituted for nasal [ng]. This usage is very extensive, more especially in words and syllables ending in **-ing**.

(*a*) *Verbal nouns*, as] hunting = huntin' [un·ti'n], running = runnin' [r'un·i'n], &c.; Com.

(*b*) *Participles* wherever occurring, as getting = gettin' [g(yet·i'n], am coming [kum·i'n], &c.; Com.

(*c*) kingdom = kin'dom [kin·du'm], Com. Nothing [nuth·i'n], anything [aen·i'thi'n], Com. Nothing [nuoth·i'n], anything [an·i'thi'n], NEWPORT. Cf. (4) below.

(*d*) *In place-names*, ending in **-ton**, as Wellington = Wellin'ton [wael·intu'n], Donnington = Donnin'ton [don·intu'n], Loppington = Loppin'ton [lop·intu'n], &c. This is a refinement upon the pronunciation of place-names as given below (6).

(*e*) In length = lenth [len·th], strength = strenth [str'en·th], Com.

2 = [n(g]. Some words, chiefly monosyllabic adjectives, ending in **ng**, have the **gutturo-nasal** sounded *weak*, as long = lung [lun(g], wrong = wrung *or* wrang [r'un(g *or* r'an(g], strong = strung [str'un(g], SHREWSBURY; PULVERBATCH. Qy. com.

3 = [ng(g, ngg]. In many words where **ng** is sounded [(g] or [g] is added, making:—

(*a*) [ng(g] where the words are final or followed by some consonants, as sing [sing(g], ring [r'ing(g], &c. Ring the bell [r'ing(g dhu' bel·], &c. Qy. com.

(*b*) [ngg], (*a*) in the middle of words between two vowels, as singer [sing·gu'r'], ringing [r'ing·gi'n], &c. Com.

(*c*) at the end of words in sentences where the following word begins with a vowel, or **h** (always mute), as bring it [br'ing·g i't], bring her [br'ing·g u'r], sing a song [sing·g u' song(g], &c.; Com.

4 = [ngk], thong = thunk [thung·k], WEM. Nothing [nuth·ingk], anything [aen·i'thingk *or* an·i'thingk], something [sum·thingk], an affected vulgar pronunciation adopted by servant girls, of town-life more especially. Cf. (1) (*c*) above.

5 = [nj] in some proper names ending in *ham*, as Bellingham = Bellinjam [bel·inju'm], &c. Qy. com.

6—is usually omitted in place-names ending in *ton*, as Wellington = Welli'ton [wael·i'tn], Donnington = Dunni'ton [dun·i'tn], Loppington = Loppi'ton [lop·i'tn], &c. Cf. (1) (*d*) above.

Gh.—1—This digraph = **k** in sigh = sike;* Com.

2 = **f** in cough, dough, enough,* slough (of a snake), sough* (*sb.*) tough, trough (for pigs); Com. See **ou** (*vowels, &c.*).

3 = **p** in hiccough [i'·ku'p], Com.

4—is silent in sough* (*vb.*), CLUN; WEM; in slough (a miry place), PULVERBATCH; in trough = [tr'oa·], a kneading vessel; PULVERBATCH.

5—is a weak **guttural spirant** = [(kh], in quaigh* [kwai(kh·], a word on the verge of obsolete, meaning as a *verb* 'to bend;' as a *noun*, a wooden vessel of 'bend ware'; CORVE DALE. The only instance in which this sound of **gh** has been noted. Cf. **ch** (3).

Gl = [gl] not [dl].

H.—1—It is recorded by Bp. Percy, in a note to an interesting MS. collection of Bridgnorth Words—now in the possession of Mr. Hubert Smith of Bridgnorth—that 'the Bridgnorth Dialect was [1774] distinguished by an almost universal misapplication of the aspirate H—applying it when it should not be, and omitting it when it should.'

The Rev. Charles Henry Hartshorne speaks [1841] to the same effect with reference to the county at large.—*Salopia Antiqua*, p. 453.

At the present time [1878] concurrent testimony goes to prove that H aspirate is *never* heard in the folk-speech of Shropshire: it is only *misapplied* by half-educated—or would be fine—speakers. People of this type always try to talk their best to '*the paas'n*,' and hence perhaps has arisen the *dicta* of the Authorities above quoted upon the use and abuse of 'poor letter H' in Salop.

2 = **y**: head = [yed· *or* yaed·], hair = yar [yaa·r], howl = yowl [yuuw·l], &c.; Com. Heath = yeth [yeth *or* yaeth], WEM; ELLESMERE; [yi'·u'th], CHURCH STRETTON. Heron = yarn [yaa·r'n], WHITCHURCH, *Tilstock.*

J.—as in received English. Cf. **d** (1) above.

K.—1—is usually pure [k], but when palatal is heard in some words = [ki'], kype* [ki'a'y·p], kibe* [ki'a'y·b], kimet* [ki'a'y·mi't], PULVERBATCH. Kerlock [ki'aeˑr'lu'k], CRAVEN ARMS; LUDLOW.

2—is dropt in **make** and **take**; COLLIERY; NEWPORT. See **a** (6), (*vowels, &c.*); also in taken = ta'en; Com.

L.—1—is silent in **-ald** and **old**, as scald = scaud [skaud·], bald [baud·], scold = scoud [skuw·d *or* sk·uu·wd], &c.; Com. See **O** (5) (21) (22), (*vowels, &c.*).

2—is silent in **-alt**, **-ault** and **-olt**, as salt = saut [saut· *or* sau·t], fault = faut [faut· *or* fau·t], bolt = bout [buw·t *or* b:uu·wt], &c.; Com. Also in **olp**: holp* [oa·p], holpen* [oa·pn].

3—is silent in **al** (1) as a prefix in *Al*mighty = A'mighty, *al*ready = a'ready, *al*most = aumust, altogether = autogether, *Al*-brighton (place-name) = Aiburton [ai·bu'r'tn *and* au·bu'r'tn], &c.; Com. (2) in false = fause [fau·ss], Com.

4—is silent when medial in some place-names, as Culmington = Cummiton [kum·i'tn], Calvington [kav·intu'n *or* kov·i'tn]. See **ng** above, (1) (*d*), also (6). Colemere = Coomer [kuom·u'r'], &c.; Com.; also in only = on'y; Com.

5 = **n**: in homily* = hominy [om·u'ni'], PULVERBATCH.

Ll.—1—is silent in all = [au·], call, and fall; call = callen (*pl.*), = caun [kau·n], fallen (*p.p.*) = faun [fau·n], NEWPORT. These instances of *call* and *fall* are somewhat exceptional and extreme, though they do obtain. 'Whatten [what dun] they *ca'* ye?' but 'Whatten they *call* 'im?' and *faun* is less usual than *fell'n*. 'E's *fell'n* down.' All = [au·], WHITCHURCH. Stalled* = staud [stau·d], NEWPORT; WEM; WHITCHURCH. Gallon = gaun* [gau·n], PULVERBATCH.

2 = **n**, in syllable* [sin·u'bl], SHREWSBURY; PULVERBATCH. Qy. com. Lilleshall (place-name) = Linsel, *obsol*. Cf. 1 (5) above.

M.—as in received English.

N.—1—falls away from *an* and is prefixed to the initial vowel of the following word:—*a narrand* = *an* arrand, *a nauf* = *an* auf,* &c. See **an** (*adjectives of numeration*).

'This letter' (N), says Sir Frederic Madden, 'by a species of prosthesis is often taken from the end of an article or pronoun and prefixed to the substantive which follows. Examples of this occur in *a noynement* for *an oynement*, *my nother*, for *myn* other. . . . The practice existed in familiar writing so late as the reign of Q. Elizabeth, and perhaps later still.'—See 'Glossarial Index' to *William of Palerne*, p. 291, ed. Skeat.

2—is generally dropt in the prepositions **in** and **on**, as '*i*' the cubbert,' '*o*' the shilf;' Com.

P.— = **b**: as pat = bat*; LUDLOW. Poke = boke*; SHREWSBURY; WEM; WHITCHURCH. Cf. **b** above.

Q = [kw], as in received English.

R.—1 = [r'] is, as a general rule, distinctly sounded, except in a very few words in which it is entirely omitted. See (4) below. It is somewhat strongly trilled in the middle of words. Its quality is similar to that of the Welsh **R**.

2—preceded by **i** is transposed in one word, thirsty = thrusty; LUDLOW.

3—preceded by **u** is transposed in a few words, as curds = cruds,* scurf = scruf; Com. Bursten = brusten; WELLINGTON. Also before **e** in pretty = perty; very general.

4—is omitted in Shrewsbury [soo·zbr'i' *or* soa·zbr'i']. See **ew** (6) and (11) (*vowels, &c.*). Parson [paas·n], scarce [skais·]. Cf. **a** (3) (*vowels, &c.*). Swarth (of grass) [swath·], worth [wuth·], curse [kus·], nurse [nus·], purse [pus·], worse [wus·], very general; but the **r** is usually sounded in nurse, purse, parson; NEWPORT. Girth [guth·], gorse [gos·], NEWPORT; ELLESMERE.

5 = **l**, in syringe = sullinge [sul·i'nzh], and in rather = lather [laa·dhu'r'], *obsols.*; PULVERBATCH. Rather = lother [lodh·u'r], *obsols.*; WHITCHURCH, *Whixall.*

S.—1 = **z** in *goose*, when this word is used either adjectively or in composition, as goose oil = gŏŏze ile [gŏŏz·a'y·l], Com. [gooz·ah·yl], NEWPORT. Gooseberries [gooz·br'i'z], *ibid.*

2 = **sh**: (1) before **u**, as suit [shoot·], suet [shoo·i't], &c.; Com. (2) before **ea** = **ĕ**, in seam [shum·], PULVERBATCH, *obs.*; [shem], CLEE HILLS.

Sh = **s** before **r**, as shrink [sr'ing·k], shrub [sr'ub·], &c.; Com. Shrewsbury [sr'oa·zbr'i]. See **ew** (11) (*vowels, &c.*).

Sp is transposed in wasp = wops;* NEWPORT. This may be rather the O.E. word retained, *wops* = *wasp*, by Metathesis.

Ss = **th** = [dh] in scissors = scithors [sidh·u'r'z], Com.

T.—1 = **d**: in not = nod, what = whad [wod·], partner = pardner [paa·r'dnu'r'], very general, but the permutation of **t** to **d** does not obtain in the district of NEWPORT. Cf. adland* and adlant,* also **d** (2) above.

2 = **ch** in team = chem [chem·], tune [choo·n], Tuesday [chooz·di'], Com. See **ue** (1) (*vowels, &c.*).

3—is dropt at the end of some past tenses, as felt = fel', kept = kep', &c.; Com. See **Strong** (and other) **verbs**. Also in other instances, as frost = fros', &c.; Com. See **Nouns** (plurals in **es** and **s**). Cf. **d** (3).

Th.—1 = O.E. þ = [th], and ð = [dh].

2 = **f** in thistle = fissle [fis·l], WORTHEN; CHURCH STRETTON; CLUN; CLEE HILLS.

3 = **d** in farther = furder [fuur'·du'r'], farthest = furdest [fuur'·du'st], LUDLOW. Cf. **d** (5) above.

4 = **t** in fifth = fift, sixth = sixt, twelfth = twelft. See **Adjectives of Numeration** (*ordinals*).

Tl = [kl] in some words ending in **ttle**, as, brittle [br'ik·l], little [lik·l], rattle [r'ak·l], very general, but not known about NEWPORT.

V.—1—is omitted in over = o'er; Com. Give (imperative) = gi'e; very general. See **Indefinite Pronouns** (*some* = *ever*, &c.).

2 = **f** in vetches = fetches* [fech·i'z], PULVERBATCH. Victual = fittle [fit·l], CORVE DALE. Cf. **f** (3) above.

W.—1—is omitted in **ward** when a last syllable, as backward = back'art, awkward = awk'art, &c., and in always = al'ays; Com.

2—is omitted when *initial* before its cognate vowel sound, as, woman = ŏŏman, wood = ŏŏd, worsted = ŏŏsted, &c.; Common throughout *Mid.* and *South Shr.*

3—is added *initially* to some words before **o** and **u** sounds, as, hot = whot [wot·], oak = wuk [wuk·], oath = wuth [wuth·], oatmeal = wutmil [wut·mi'l], &c.; SHREWSBURY; PULVERBATCH. Qy. com. in *Mid.* and *South Shr.* See **oa** (7) (*vowels, &c.*).

4—is inserted after some initial consonants, as, bone = bwun [bwoen·], stone = stwun [stwoen·], gone = gwun [gwoen·], &c.; very general. Boy = bwoy [bw:auy], SHREWSBURY; PULVERBATCH; *obsols.* Boil = bwile [bwa'y·l], PULVERBATCH. Post = pwust [pwus·t], SHREWSBURY; PULVERBATCH. Qy. com. in *S. Shr.* Coin * = quine [kwa'yn·], PULVERBATCH, *obs.?* Cord = querd [kwur'·d], CHURCH STRETTON; CLUN. See **Cordwood.***

X.—1—As in received English; Com.

2 = **ksh** in axe [ak·sh], 'a couling *aksh*;' * LUDLOW.

Y.—1—When *initial* is frequently dropt before the cognate vowel sounds **ee** and **i**, as, yield = ild, yes = iss, yesterday = isterd'y, yet = yit = it; Com.

2—is sometimes sounded *initially* before **ĕ** and **a** sounds, as, Edward * = Yedart, &c.; Com. Ale = yale [yael·]. See **Ale.***

3 = **th** = [**dh**] in yonder = thander [dhaan·du'r'], CLUN, *Hereford Border.*

Z—As in received English.

ETYMOLOGY.

NOUNS.

Plurals in en and n.—Examples of these endings are not numerous, but such as exist are for the most part of everyday use in the localities where they respectively obtain, as childeren,* childern * (a double plural), peasen,* rotten, neesen, housen, eyen, flen, shoon, &c.

All known instances of these usages will be found in the body of the Glossary.

Plurals in es and s.—Nouns of the singular number ending in **st** mostly change the **t** to **s** and add **es** to make the plural; as, crust, crusses; fist, fisses; post, posses: in the Newport district they sometimes reduplicate this plural, and say crusses-es, &c.

Instances occur where the **t** is merely dropt to form the plural; as, beast, beäs, &c.

Plural in **er**.—Only one instance known, viz. childer.*

Plurals formed by **Vowel-change**.—The known examples correspond to the literary English forms, thus—mon, men; ŏŏman, women [wi'm·i'n], tuth, tith; fut, fit; gŏŏse, or gus, gis; mouse, mice; louse, lice.

Tooth, taith; fut, fait; goose, gaise; obtain in the NEWPORT district.

Constant plurals, &c.—Many nouns have no singular form, as, aigles, afterings, cruds, drippings, fleetings, grains, &c., &c.

Some nouns are treated as plural without a plural sign, as, broth, browis; &c., &c.: of which it is said, '*they* bin good,' or 'saut,' or what not.

Nouns whose signification is that of a genuine plural, while the form is distinctly singular, are represented by *ess* = ashes.

Nouns of **time, weight, measure**, or **number**, when used collectively or with a numeral expressive of plurality, remain for the most part unchanged; as, three 'ear, six wik, ten pund, five strike, two couple, &c., &c.

Some nouns are used in the **singular form** only, as, battin, thrave, fowl, vittle, &c.

Possessive Case.—When place-names are compounded of two words, the first—being a proper noun—is generally put into the possessive case; as Wenlock's Edge, Hayton's Bent, Bieton's Heath, Exford's Green, &c., &c.

Collective nouns, expressive of large quantities, are—mort, vast, djel, dyel = deal, power, sight, &c.; the last three are of common usage.

Nouns compounded with **ful** in literary English, have in numerous instances the suffix **tle** or **le** = **ful**; as, appar*ntle** = apron-*ful*, can*tle** = can-*ful;* and so with bucke*tle*, pocke*tle*, han*tle*,* &c.: most of these will be found in the body of the Glossary. In the Newport district **ful** is **f'l**: bucket*f'l*—sometimes bucke*tle*—can*f'l*, han'*f'l;* but not can*tle*, han*tle*.

ADJECTIVES.

Adjectives of Quality.—Besides those that obtain in literary English—whether simple or derivative—with suffixes such as *ful*, *-fied*, *-ish*, *-le*, *-less*, *-some*, *-ous*, *-y*: there are many others of both classes which form an exceptional category, including old forms and remarkable words; as, bisson, brief, burrow, curst, dark, ebb, eme, gain, linnow, nesh, oval, thone, unkit, long*ful*, succour*ful*, maisteri*fied*, twisti*fied*, cad*ish*, brick*le*, aven*less*, dark*some*, light*some*, temper*some*, lunge*ous*, nuvitu*ous*, temptu*ous*, brood*y*, fume*y*, &c., &c.—these and more of like kind will be found in the body of the Glossary.

Degrees of Comparison are, as in received English, formed regularly by **er** and **est**, but double comparisons are frequent, as *more beautifuller*, *most innocentest*; examples of this are met with in the earlier writers, as—'moste *clennest* flesch of bryddes,' *Piers Pl.*, Text B., pass. xiv. l. 43; 'the *most unkindest* cut of all,' *Julius Cæsar*, III. ii. l. 187; '*more better* than Prospero,' *Tempest*, I. ii. 19; '*more corrupter* ends,' *K. Lear*, II. ii. 108; '*most straitest* sect,' Acts xxvi. 5.

The Superlative Absolute is formed by adverbial prefixes, such as mighty, right, despert, oncommon, &c., &c.

It is also expressed by similes—'as hard as brazil' *—than which nothing can be harder,—as 'sour as vargis,' 'as linnow * as a glove,' &c., &c., *ad infinitum*.

Than after the **comparative degree** is expressed by *nor* in the southern part of Shropshire, and by *till* on the N. and N.E. borders of the county: *ti'n* = till is also used in some localities.

IRREGULAR COMPARISONS.

Good	better + more[1]	better + most
Bad	worse + er	worst + est
Much	more + er	most + est
Many	"	"
Little	little + er	little + est[2]

[1] *Bettermore* [baet·ur'mur'] obtains in the NEWPORT district.

[2] 'Where love is great, the *littlest* doubts are fear.'
2 *Hamlet*, III. ii. 181.

Great is used idiomatically to express intimacy, familiarity = '**thick**'—a slang term.

Intensitives such as 'ancient owd,' 'teeny little,' are often employed.

DISTINGUISHING ADJECTIVES.

A, an [the Indefinite Article]. See **definite numerals** (*one*).

The [the Definite Article]. See **demonstrative pronouns**.

ADJECTIVES OF NUMERATION.

Definite numerals are the received Cardinal and Ordinal numbers, with certain varieties of usage.

One [wun·], Com.; [won·], N. and N.E. borders of Salop.

An [the Indefinite Article] = one = A.S. *an*, is invariably heard as **a**, the **n** falling off alike before vowels and consonants, or otherwise prefixed to the following word: *a egg; a nour* = an hour. See **n** (*consonants*).

Two = both; Com. 'I tŏŏk it i' my *two* 'onds;' 'It wuz a fŭll **wik** afore 'e could stond on 'is *two* fit.' See **both** below.

The **numerals** 21, 22, 31, 32, and other like, are counted one and twenty, two and thirty, and so on, as a common and general usage. In money this is invariably the rule for sums under forty shillings—'*six an' thirty* shillin' for a pig,' not one pound sixteen; the term *pound* being reserved till the denomination amounts to two or more, when it is 'two pund,' 'three pun' ten,' &c. In some localities—as, for instance, Shrewsbury, Worthen, Pulverbatch, and Burford—19, 29, 39, and so on, are expressed by *twenty sa' one, thirty sa' one, forty sa' one*, &c.: a method of numeration limited to the number next below the multiples of ten; *obsols.*

In counting at cards—

One is 'the odd un.'
Two „ deuce [doos·].
Three „ trey [tr'ai·].
Nine „ 'rough nine.' LUDLOW.

Score = 20 is generally employed as a reckoning of age—'four *score* isterd'y.' Cf. Ps. xc. 10.

It is also used in counting sheep, as for sale—'Them ship bin too thick o' the groun'; I'll draw a couple o' *score* [= 40] to sen' to the far nex' wik.'

Sheep are counted in the field by **couples**.

The Distributives—'**one by one**,' as of persons walking in Indian file; '**two by two**,' as of two abreast; '**two apiece**' = two to each one, '**two at once**' = two at a time.

Multiplicatives are double, two-double,* treble.

Both.—The usual form of this is **the both**—'I'll tak' *the both*.' Cf. Fr. *tous-les-deux*. See **Demonstrative Pronouns** (*the*).

Both = the two,—'I canna-d-afford *the two*;' Com.

Both = the pair on 'em, when speaking of persons or animate objects; Com. See **two** (*adjectives of numeration*).

The Ordinals exhibit few peculiarities :—

First is pronounced by children at play as firsses [fur'si'z]; 'me *firsses*;' SHREWSBURY.

Second [sek·u'nt], Com.; [si'k·u'nt], NEWPORT.

Fift * = fifth = A.S. *fífta*.

Sixt * = sixth = A.S. *sixta*.

Twelft = twelfth = A.S. *twélf*. SHREWSBURY; PULVERBATCH.

The tone = the one; NEWPORT, but rare. **The tother** = the other; Com. '*Second* has replaced the O.E. **other** = one of two; **thæt ân** = the first; **thæt other** = the second. In M.E. these became (1) **that oon** and **that other**, (2) the tone (**toon, tone**) and **the tother**.' See DR. MORRIS's *Historical English Grammar*, p. 99.

Indefinite Numerals.—**All** = whole = entire; as **all** the lot on 'em = the *entire* number. **All** the village was out = the *whole* of the inhabitants.

Many.—Large indefinite numbers are expressed by a power, a sight,* a deal [dyel *or* djel], scores, &c.; Com.

Few.*—A good *few*, a tidy good *few* = a considerable number, a concourse of people; a 'good tuthree' [tuth·r'i'] = two or three, a 'tidy tuthree,' a much smaller assemblage. These terms are also used to denote quantities, as of apples, &c.

Fractions of Quantity are 'afe [auf·, NEWPORT] = half, quarter, part; as, a *'afe* pund, *'afe* a pund, *quarter* of a pund, &c. **Part** is the fractional quantity mostly in use—'*part* of a glass' of beer; 'best *part*' = the largest portion, two *parts* = half, three *parts* = three fourths, as three *parts* of a glass of beer; but three *parts*, as of an apple cut into quarters, would be three *several* parts.

PERSONAL PRONOUNS.

[SHREWSBURY; PULVERBATCH.]

Singular.	*Plural.*
1. I	1. We
2. Thee	2. Yo'
3. A,* 'e (*masc.*); 'er (*fem.*)	3. A,* they

Singular.

1. [a'y·] *emph.*	[i'] *unemph.*
2. [dh:ee·] ,,	[dhu'] ,,
3. [aa] ,,	[u'] ,,
,, [:ee·] ,,	[i'] ,,
,, [ur'] ,,	

Plural.

1. [w:ee·] ,,	[wi'] ,,
2. [y:oa·] ,,	[yu'] ,,
3. [dh:ai·] ,,	[dhae·] ,,

[NEWPORT.]

Singular.	*Plural.*
1. I[1]	1. We
2. Thou, thee[2]	2. Yo'
3. 'E (*masc.*), 'er (*fem.*)	3. They

[1] [ah·]. [2] **Thou** and **thee** are alike pronounced as Fr. *le, me, te,* &c. [dhu'], but *emphatic* **thee** is [dhai·].

General Observations.—'Em * = them; Com. It represents an old form.

The accusative **'er** is invariably employed for the nominative **she.**

The substitution of the nominative **we** for the accusative **us** is general in the southern part of Shropshire; WORTHEN; CRAVEN ARMS; BISHOP'S CASTLE; CLUN; CORVE DALE; CLEE HILLS. 'It's mighty bad for *we;*' 'Miss Nellie's bringin' *we* some vittle.'

He and **him**[1] = **it**, which is used only in an abstract sense; BISHOP'S CASTLE; CLUN; CLEE HILLS.

'The Maister gid me this piece o' garden instead o' the other, an' I mucked *'im* well,' said John Nicholas, of Clun Hospital [1875].

'This spittle's a mighty good un',—*'e* shoots me right well.' (*Abdon.*)

Me = I, him = he, them = they, are commonly used. "*'Im* and *me* wenten—'*them* as said it,' &c.

[1] See DR. MORRIS'S *Historical English Accidence*, p. 120.

REFLEXIVE PRONOUNS.

[SHREWSBURY; PULVERBATCH.]

Singular.	*Plural.*
Myself [mi·sael·f]	Ourselves [uwu'r'sael·vz]
Theeself [dhi'sael·f]	Yoreselves [yu'r'sael·vz]
Yoreself [yu'r'sael·f]	
'Isself [izsael·f], not com.	Tharselves [dhaa·r'sael·'vz]
'Imself [imsael·f]	Themselves [dhaemsael·vz], not com.

[NEWPORT.]

Mysen [mi'saen·]	Oursens [—? saen·z]
Thysen [dhi'saen·]	Yersens [yaer'saen·z]
Yersen [yaer'sen·]	
'Issen [izsaen·]	Theirsens [dhaer'saen·z]

Sel = sen is also occasionally heard—mysel, &c.

ADJECTIVE PRONOUNS.

[SHREWSBURY; PULVERBATCH.]

Singular.	*Plural.*
My [ma'y·] *emph.*, [mi'] *unemph.*	Our [uwu'·r']
——[1]	Yore[3] [y:oa·h'r']
'Is [iz·], 'er [ur'], its[2] [it·s]	Thar [dhaa·r']

[Newport.]

Singular.	*Plural.*
My [mah·y]	Our
Thy [dhah·y]	Yer [yaer'·]
'Is [iz·], 'er [ur'], its [4]	Their [dhaer'·]

[1] **Thy** is not used.

[2] **Its**, though occasionally heard, as when addressing a very young child,—thus, 'come an' warm *its* fitties,' or 'little toeties,' is usually represented by **on it**, as well in speaking of the smaller animals as of inanimate objects; the track, hole, or marks *on it* = *its* track, hole, or marks; the legs *on it* (chair, table, &c.), not *its* legs.

[3] **Yore** = A.S. *eówer*.

[4] See note (2) above.

ABSOLUTE POSSESSIVES.

[Shrewsbury; Pulverbatch.]

Singular.	*Plural.*
Mine [ma'yn.]	Ours [uwu'r'z]
——[1]	Yores [y:oa·h'r'z]
'Is [iz·], 'ers [ur'z·]	Thars [dhaa·r'z]

[Newport.]

Mine [mah·yn]	Ourn
Thine [dhah·yn]	Yourn [yoo·h'r'n]
'Isn [iz·n], 'ersn [ur'z·n], 'ern [ur'n·]	Theirn [dhaer'n]

[1] **Thine** is not used.

DEMONSTRATIVE PRONOUNS.

The [dhu·], Com.; [dh'], Newport, before *vowels*, not before consonants.

The is used before the names of months and seasons when speaking of any particular circumstance connected with the time,—as, 'I wuz theer i' *the* June;' ''E died i' *the* Christmas.' Also before the adverb *first*, as, 'It's a pity as 'e adna done it at *the first*;' and the **Ordinals**, first, second, third, &c.: as, 'Tum come in *the second* an' Jack *the third.*' It is likewise prefixed to *both* and its equivalents. See **both** (*adjectives of numeration*).

This [dhi's·], **that** [dhat·], have the emphatic form **this 'ere** and **that there.** Cf. Fr. *ce-ci, ce-la.*

These [dhee·z], **them** = those, have the emphatic forms **these 'ere, them theer.** Cf. Fr. *ceux-ci, ceux-la.*

They = those; CORVE DALE. 'They pasen' [dhai· pai·zu'n] = those peas. *They* is occasionally found in Tudor English [1485—1600] as the plural of *the.* See DR. MORRIS's *Historical English Grammar*, p. 115.

Such [si'ch·]. Com.

Yanter [yaan·tur'] = yonder; Com.

Yander [yaan·dur'] = ,, NEWPORT.

Thander [dhaan·dur'] = ,, CLUN, *Hereford Border.*

RELATIVE PRONOUNS.

As* = who, which, that; Com.

That = who; Com. 'A girl *that* can milk.'

Whad* [wod·] = what. See **t** (1) (*consonants*).

INTERROGATIVE PRONOUNS.

Who [:oa·], Com.; [oo-u'], SHREWSBURY; PULVERBATCH. Qy. com.

Whosen = whose. '*Whosen* housen bin 'em?' CORVE DALE.

Which [wi'ch·]. **Whad.**

INDEFINITE PRONOUNS.

Each = **everyone**; '*everyone* took one' = *each* took one. Cf. SPENSER's *F. Q.*, Bk. I. c. ii. s. viii. See **Distributives** (*two apiece*).

Some; any = **e'er-a** [ae·r'u'], refined usage, **ever-a*** [aev·u'r'u']; the negative—**not any,** is **ne'er-a** [nae·r'u'], with the corresponding refined **never-a** [naev·u'r'u']; Com.

Enough [u'nuf·], *sing.* **anow*** [u'nuw·], **anew*** [u'noo·], *pl.* The distinctive use of the plural form is now [1877] dying out; and *anow,—anew* = enough, *sing.* are not unfrequently heard. See DR. MORRIS's *Historical English Accidence*, p. 147.

Either = **e'er-un** [ae·r'un], which has two degrees of refined usage, (1) **e'er-a-one** [ae·r'u'wun], and (2) **ever-a-one** * [aev·u'r'u'-wun]; Com.

Neither = **ne'er-un** [nae·r'un] has its corresponding degrees, **ne'er-a-one** and **never-a-one**; Com.

Else = or; ''Er said as 'er'd mind the child awilde I wuz out *else* [= or] I ŏŏdna-d-a lef' the 'ouse;' Com.

Summat [sum·u't] = somewhat = something; Com. *Something* has in a great measure replaced *somewhat.* This [latter] usage is as early as the thirteenth century. See Dr. Morris's *Historical English Grammar*, p. 123.

VERBS.

Verbal Inflexions.—Personal endings in the plural are formed regularly by **en** or **n**. A few examples of this usage are to be found in Spenser and Shakespeare—*F. Q.*, Bk. I. c. iv. s. xxxvii. *Mids. Night's Dream*, II. i. 56;—but it was Archaic in Spenser's time. See Dr. Morris's *Historical English Accidence*, p. 176.

En and **n** are also occasionally used in the *singular* of the *past tense*, as—I thought*en*; 'e com*en*.

Participles in numerous instances have the termination **en** or **n**. See **List of Strong** (and other) **Verbs** below.

Weak Verbs often have the **ed** and **d** of their preterite and past participle reduplicated as attack'*ded;* drown'*ded*, &c.—This is a mere vulgarism.

The present tense is frequently employed for the past, as—''e come out an' run away, an' we send after 'im.'

The negation of Verbs is made by **nad** = not. The **d** falls away from **nad** and **-na** appears as an affix to the verb—can-*na*, shan-*na*, &c.—as a general usage throughout the county; but in many places the full form **nad** is retained before **vowels**, the final **d** being sounded in a distinct kind of way, apart from the **na**. This peculiarity is represented by an intervening - (indicating pause) in the *examples* of the folk-speech, but it is omitted in the *conjugations* of the verbs in order to preserve the integrity of the negation. There are some localities—for instance Ludlow and Newport—where **-na** stands alike before vowels and consonants, and where also, but *quite exceptionally,* **not** is used for **na** before vowels, as, con*not* 'e? mun*not* I? &c.

ALPHABETICAL LIST OF STRONG VERBS, AND OTHERS OF REMARKABLE FORM.

Pres.	*Pret.*	*Part. Past.*
Arrive	Arrove [Corve Dale]	
Bear [bring forth]	bore	bore
Bear [carry]	bore	bore
Beat	beat	beat, beaten
Begin	begun	begun
Bid	bid	bid, bidden
Bind	bond,* bund *	bond,* bund *
Bite	bit	bit, bitten
Blow	blowed	blowed
Bost = burst	bost, bosted	bosten, bost, bosted
Break	broke	broken, brusten *
Chide	chid	
Choose, chose *	chose	chosen [choz·n]
Cleave [split]	clove, cleaved	cloven, cleaved
Cling	clung	clung
Climb	clomb *	clomb, clomben
Come	come, comed	comen
Creep	crope *	cropen
Crow	crowed	crowed
Delve *	delved	delved
Ding *	dinged	dinged
Do	did, done	done
Draw	drawed	drawed
Drink	drunk	drunk, drunken
Drive	druv	druv, druven
Eat	et, ete *	etten, ete
Fall	fell	fell, fellen, faun *
Feel	fel'	fel'
Fight	fought foughten *	fought, foughten *

Pres.	*Pret.*	*Part. Past.*
Find	fund *	fund *
Fling	flung	flung
Fly	fled	fled
Forget	forgot	forgot, forgotten
Forsake	forsook *	forsook,* forsooken
Freeze	froze [fr'oz·]	froze, frozen [fr'oz·n]
Get	got	got, gotten
Give	gi'ed, gid, guv, gived	gid, gi'en, gived
Go	went	gwun
Grind	grond,* grun'	grond, grun'
Grow	growed	growed
Heave * [ai·v]	hove,* heaved	hoven, heaved
Help	holp,* [oa·p] helped	holpen * [oa·pn] helped
Hew [y:uuw]	hewed	hewed
Hold [uw·t]	held	held
Keep	kep	kepen
Knead	knad,* kned	knad, kned
Know	knowed	knowed
Leap	lep *	lept
Let	let	letten
Lie	lied, lay	lain
Light *	lit	lit
Lose [l:oa·z]	lost	lost
Mistake	mistook *	mistook *
Mow	mowed	mowed
Pick	puck *	puck
Plead	plad,* pled	
Queak *	quoke *	
Reach	raught *	raught
Reap	rope *	rope
Ride	rode, rid *	rode, rid
Ring	rung	rung
Rise	riz, ruz, rose	riz, ruz, rose
Run	run	run
See	see, seed, sid	sid, sin

Pres.	*Pret.*	*Part. Past.*
Shake	shŏŏk,* shŏŏkt	shŏŏk,* shŏŏkt
Shave	shaved	shaven, shoven, shaved
Sheed [to shed or spill]	shed, sheeded	shed, shedden, sheeded
Shear	shore,* sheared	shorn, sheared
Shine	shone, [shon·] (moon) shined *	shone
Shoot	shot	shotten, shot
S'rink = shrink	s'runk	s'runken
Sing	sung	sung
Sink	sunk	sunk
Sit	sat, sot, sut	sat, sitten, sot, sutten
Sleep	slep *	slepen
Sling	slung	slung
Sow	sowed	sowed
Speak	spoke	spoke, spoken
Spin	spun	spun
Spread [spr'ai·d spr'ee·d *]	sprad,* sprod	sprad, sprod
Spring	sprung	sprung
Squeeze	squoze, squedge *	squozen, squedge
Stack	stuck *	
Stand	stood	stood, stooden
Steal	stole	stole, stolen
Stick [to kill]	stuck	stucken *
Sting	stung	stung
Stink	stunk	stunk, stunken
Stride	strode	strode
Strike	struck	struck, stricken * strucken *
Strive	strove	strove
Swear	swore	sworn
Sweep	swep	swep, swepen
Swell	swollen [swoa·n], swelled	swollen, swelled
Swim	swum	swum

Pres.	*Pret.*	*Part. Past.*
Swing	swung	swung
Take, tae	taed, took	taed, ta'en,* took, tooken
Tear [taa·r']	tore, teared [taa·r'd]	tore, teared
Teaze, toze * (wool, &c.)	toze*	toze
Think	thought, thoughten	thought, thoughten
Thrive	thruv	thruven
Throw	throwed	throwed
Tread	trod	trod, trodden
Waken	wakened	awaken
Weave	wove	woven
Weed	wed *	wed
Weep	wep *	wepen
Win	won	won
Wind	waund [w:au·nd]	waund
Wring	wrung	wrung
Write	writ,* wrote	wrote

TO BE.

[PULVERBATCH.]

AFFIRMATIVE FORM.

Part Pres. Bein'. *Part past* Bin.*

Indicative Mood.

Singular.	Present Tense. *Plural.*
1. I am	1. We bin
2. Thee bist	2. Yo' bin
3. 'E, or 'er is	3. A, or they bin

Preterite.

1. I wuz	1. We wun
2. Thee wust [wus·t̯]	2. Yo' wun.
3. A, 'e, or 'er wuz	3. A, or they wun

Perfect.

Singular.	*Plural.*
1. I've bin	1. We'n bin
2. Thee'st bin	2. Yo'n bin
3. A, 'e, or 'er's bin	3. They'n bin

Future.

1. I shall be	1. We sha'n be
2. Thee sha't be	2. Yo'n be
3. A, 'e, or 'er'll be	3. They'n be

NEGATIVE FORM.

Present Tense.

1. I amma, or amna	1. We binna
2. Thee bis'na [bis·nu']	2. Yo' binna
3. 'E, or 'er inna	3. A, or they binna

Preterite.

1. I wunna	1. We wunna
2. Thee wus'na [wus·nu']	2. Yo' wunna
3. A, 'e, or 'er wunna	3. A, or they wunna

Perfect.

1. I hanna bin	1. We hanna bin
2. Thee has'na [as·nu'] bin	2. Yo' hanna bin
3. 'E, or 'er hanna bin	3. They hanna bin.

Future.

1. I shanna or ŏŏnna be	1. We shanna or ŏŏna be
2. Thee sha'tna or ŏŏtna be	2. Yo' shanna or ŏŏna be
3. { A, 'e, or 'er shanna be 'E, or 'er ŏŏnna be	3. { A, or they shanna be They ŏŏna be

INTERROGATIVE FORM.

Present Tense.

1. Am I?	1. Bin we?
2. Bist, or bist 'ee?	2. Bin 'ee, or bin yo'?
3. Is a, 'e, or 'er?	3. Bin a, or they?

Preterite.

1. Wuz I?	1. Wun we?
2. Wust 'ee? [wus·ti']	2. Wun yo'?
3. Wuz a, 'e, or 'er?	3. Wun a, or they?

Perfect.

Singular.	*Plural.*
1. Have I bin?	1. Han we bin?
2. Hast 'ee [as·ti'] bin?	2. Han yo' bin?
3. Has a, 'e, or 'er bin?	3. Han a, or they bin?

Future.

1. Shall I be?	1. Sha'n we be?
2. Shat 'ee be?	2. { Sha'n yo' be, or shan 'ee be? / Ŏŏn yo' be, or ŏŏn 'ee be?
3. Ŏŏl a, 'e, or 'er be?	3. Ŏŏn a, or they be?

INTERROGATIVE NEGATIVE.

Present Tense.

1. { Ammad-I? / Amnad-I?	1. Binna we?
2. Bis'na thee?	2. Binna yo'?
3. { Innad-a? / Innad-'e, or 'er?	3. { Binnad-a? / Binna they?

Preterite.

1. Wunnad-I?	1. Wunna we?
2. Wus'na thee?	2. Wunna yo'?
3. { Wunnad-a? / Wunnad-'e, or 'er?	3. { Wunnad-a? / Wunna they?

Perfect.

1. Hannad-I bin?	1. Hanna we bin?
2. Has 'na thee bin?	2. Hanna yo' bin?
3. { Hannad-a bin? / Hannad-'e, or 'er bin?	3. { Hannad-a bin? / Hanna they bin?

Future.

1. { Shannad-I be? / Ŏŏnnad-I be?	1. Shanna we be?
2. Sha't na thee be?	2. { Shanna yo' be? / Ŏŏnna yo' be?
3. Ŏŏnnad-a be?	3. { Shanna they be? / Ŏŏnna they be?

TO HAVE.

[PULVERBATCH.]

AFFIRMATIVE FORM.

Infinitive Mood, To have, To A.* *Part past*, had [ad·].

Indicative Mood.

Singular.	*Plural.*
Present Tense.	
1. I've, or I han	1. We han [an·], or we'n
2. Thee'st	2. Yo' han, or yo'n
3. A,* 'e, or er's	3. They han, or a'n, or they'n
Preterite.	
1. I'd	1. We hadden [ad·n]
2. Thee had'st [ad·st]	2. Yo'hadden
3. A'd, 'e'd, or 'er'd	3. A, or they hadden
Perfect.	
1. I've had [ad·]	1. We'n had
2. Thee'st had	2. Yo'n had
3. A, 'e, or 'er's had	3. They'n had
Future.	
1. I shall a	1. We sha'n a
2. Thee sha't a	2. Yo' sha'n a
3. A, 'e, or 'er'll a	3. A sha'n a, or they sha'n a

NEGATIVE FORM.

Singular	Plural
Present Tense.	
1. I hanna [an·u']	1. We hanna
2. Thee has'na [as·nu']	2. Yo' hanna
3. A, 'e, or 'er hanna	3. They hanna
Preterite.	
1. I hadna [ad·nu']	1. We hadna
2. Thee hadsna [ad·snu']	2. Yo' hadna
3. A, 'e, or 'er hadna	3. A, or they hadna
Perfect.	
1. I hanna had	1. We hanna had
2. Thee has'na had	2. Yo' hanna had
3. A, 'e, or 'er hanna had	3. A, or they hanna had

Singular.	Future.	*Plural.*
1. I shannad-a		1. We shannad-a
2. Thee sha'tna a		2. Yo' shannad-a
3. A, 'e, or 'er shannad-a		3. A, or they shannad-a

INTERROGATIVE FORM.

Present Tense.

1. Have I? [av·i']	1. Han we?
2. Hast'ee? [as·ti']	2. Han 'ee, or han yo'?
3. Has a, 'e, or 'er?	3. Han a, or they?

Preterite.

1. Had I? [ad·i']	1. Hadden we? [ad·n]
2. Had'st 'ee? [ad·sti']	2. Hadden yo'?
3. Had a, 'e, or 'er?	3. Hadden a, or they?

Perfect.

1. Have I had?	1. Han we had?
2. Hast 'ee had?	2. Han yo' had or han 'ee had?
3. Has a, 'e, or 'er had?	3. Han a, or they had?

Future.

1. Shall I a?	1. Sha'n we a?
2. Sha't 'ee a, or ŏŏt 'ee a?	2. Sha'n yo' a, or sha'n 'ee a?
3. { Shall a, 'e, or 'er a? / Ŏŏl a, 'e, or 'er a?	3. { Sha'n a, or they a? / Ŏŏn a, or they a?

INTERROGATIVE NEGATIVE.

Present Tense.

1. Hannad-I?	1. Hanna we?
2. Has'na thee? [as·nu'dhi']	2. Hanna yo'?
3. Hannad-a, 'e, or er?	3. Hannad-a, or they?

Preterite.

1. Hadnad-I?	1. Hadna we?
2. Had'sna thee?	2. Hadna yo'?
3. Hadnad-a, 'e, or 'er?	3. Hadnad-a, or hadna they?

Perfect.

1. Hannad-I had?	1. Hanna we had?
2. Has'na thee had?	2. Hanna yo' had?
3. Hannad-a, 'e, or 'er had?	3. Hannad-a, or hanna they had?

Singular.	Future.	*Plural.*
1. Shannad-I a?		1. Shanna we a?
2. { Sha't na thee a? / Ŏŏtna thee a?		2. { Shanna yo' a, or shan 'ee a? / Ŏŏnna yo' a, or ŏŏn 'ee a?
3. { Shannad-a, 'e, or 'er a? / Ŏŏnnad-a, 'e, or 'er a?		3. { Shannad-a, or shanna they a? / Ŏŏnnad-a, or ŏŏnna they a?

TO DO.

[PULVERBATCH.]

AFFIRMATIVE FORM.

Indicative Mood.

Singular.	Present Tense.	*Plural.*
1. I do		1. We dun
2. Thee does [dus·]		2. Yo' dun
3. A, 'e, or 'er does [duz·]		3. A, or they dun
	Preterite.	
1. I did		1. We didden [did·n]
2. Thee did'st		2. Yo' didden
3. A, 'e, or 'er did		3. A, or they didden

NEGATIVE FORM.

	Present Tense.	
1. I dunna		1. We dunna
2. Thee doesna [dus·nu']		2. Yo' dunna
3. A, 'e, or 'er dunna		3. A, or they dunna
	Preterite.	
1. I didna [did·nu']		1. We didna
2. Thee didsna [did·snu']		2. Yo' didna
3. A, 'e, or 'er didna		3. A, or they didna

INTERROGATIVE FORM.

	Present Tense.	
1. Do I?		1. Dunna we?
2. Dost 'ee? [dus·ti']		2. Dun 'ee, or dunna yo'?
3. Does a, 'e, or 'er?		3. Dunnad-a, or dunna they?
	Preterite.	
1. Did I?		1. Didden we?
2. Did'st 'ee?		2. Didden 'ee, or didden yo'?
3. Did a, 'e, or 'er?		3. Didden a, or they?

INTERROGATIVE NEGATIVE.

Singular.	Present Tense. *Plural.*
1. Dunnad-I?	1. Dunna we?
2. Doesna thee? [dus·nu'dhi']	2. Dunna yo'?
3. Dunnad-a, 'e, or 'er?	3. Dunnad-a, or dunna they?
	Preterite.
1. Didnad-I?	1. Didna we?
2. Didsna thee?	2. Didna yo'?
3. Didnad-a, 'e, or 'er?	3. Didnad-a, or didna they?

CAN.

[PULVERBATCH.]

AFFIRMATIVE FORM.

Singular.	Present Tense. *Plural.*
1. I can	1. We can
2. Thee ca'st [kus·t]	2. Yo' can
3. A, 'e, or 'er can	3. A, or they can
	Preterite.
1. I could [kud]	1. We coulden [kud·n]
2. Thee cou'st [kust·]	2. Yo' coulden
3. A, 'e, or 'er could	3. A, or they coulden

NEGATIVE FORM.

	Present Tense.
1. I canna	1. We canna
2. Thee ca'sna [kas·nu']	2. Yo' canna
3. A, 'e, or 'er canna	3. A, or they canna
	Preterite.
1. I couldna [kudnu']	1. We couldna
2. Thee couldsna [kud·snu']	2. Yo' couldna
3. A, 'e, or 'er couldna	3. A, or they couldna

INTERROGATIVE FORM.

	Present Tense.
1. Can I? [kan·i']	1. Canna we?
2. Ca'st 'ee? [kus·ti']	2. Can 'ee, or can yo'?
3. Can a, 'e, or 'er?	3. Cannad-a, or canna they?

Singular.	Preterite.	*Plural.*
1. Could I?		1. Coulden I?
2. Cou'st 'ee? [kùs·ti']		2. Coulden yo'?
3. Could a, 'e, or 'er?		3. Coulden a, or they?

INTERROGATIVE NEGATIVE.

Present Tense.

1. Cannad-I?	1. Canna we?
2. Ca'sna thee? [kas·nu'dhi']	2. Canna yo'?
3. Cannad-a, 'e, or 'er?	3. Cannad-a, or canna they?

Preterite.

1. Couldnad-I?	1. Couldna we?
2. Couldsna thee?	2. Couldna yo'?
3. Couldnad-a, 'e, or 'er?	3. Couldnad-a, or couldna they?

DARE [daa·r'].

[Pulverbatch.]

AFFIRMATIVE FORM.

Part. Past. Dar'd [daa·r'd].

Indicative Mood.

Singular.	Present Tense.	*Plural.*
1. I dar *		1. We dar'n, or darden
2. Thee darst		2. Yo' dar'n, or darden
3. A, 'e, or 'er dar [1]		3. A, or they dar'n, or darden

Preterite.

1. I darst	1. We dars'en [daa·r'sn]
2. Thee darst	2. Yo' dars'en
3. A, 'e, or 'er darst	3. A, or they dars'en

NEGATIVE FORM.

Present Tense.

1. I darna *	1. We darna, or dar'dna
2. Thee dars'na	2. Yo' darna, or dar'dna
3. A, 'e, or 'er darna	3. A, or they darna, or dar'dna

Preterite.

1. I dars'na	1. We dars'na
2. Thee dars'na	2. Yo' dars'na
3. A, 'e, or 'er dars'na	3. A, or they dars'na

INTERROGATIVE FORM.

Singular.	Present Tense. *Plural.*
1. Dar I? [daa·r'i']	1. Daren, or darden we?
2. Darst 'ee?	2. Daren, or darden yo'?
3. Dar a, 'e, or 'er?	3. Daren, or darden a, or they?

Preterite.

1. Darst I?	1. Dars'en we?
2. Darst 'ee?	2. Dars'en yo'?
3. Darst a, 'e, or 'er?	3. Dars'en a, or they?

INTERROGATIVE NEGATIVE.

Present Tense.

1. Darnad-I?	1. Darna, or dar'dna we?
2. Dars'nat 'ee?	2. { Darna, or dar'dna yo? / Darnad-'ee, or dar'dnad-'ee?
3. Darnad-a, 'e, or 'er?	3. Darna, or dar'dna they?

Preterite.

1. Dars'nad-I?	1. Dars'na we?
2. Dars'nat 'ee?	2. Dars'na yo'?
3. Dars'nad-a, 'e, or 'er?	3. Dars'nad-a? dars'na they?

[1] Dr. Morris says—'The third person **dare** (O.E. *dar*) is strictly correct.' See *Historical English Accidence*, p. 184.

SHALL.

[Pulverbatch.]

AFFIRMATIVE FORM.

Singular.	Present Tense. *Plural.*
1. I shall	1. We sha'n
2. Thee sha't [shaet·]	2. Yo' sha'n
3. A, 'e, or 'er shall	3. They sha'n

Preterite.

1. I should [shud·]	1. We shoulden [shud·n]
2. Thee should'st [shud·st·]	2. Yo' shoulden
3. A, 'e, or 'er should	3. A, or they shoulden

NEGATIVE FORM.

Singular.	Present Tense.	*Plural.*
1. I shanna		1. We shanna
2. Thee sha'tna [shaet·nu']		2. Yo' shanna
3. A, 'e, or 'er shanna		3. A, or they shanna
	Preterite.	
1. I shouldna [shud·nu']		1. We shouldna
2. Thee shouldsna [shud·snu']		2. Yo' shouldna
3. A, 'e, or 'er shouldna		3. A, or they shouldna

INTERROGATIVE FORM.

Present Tense.

1. Shall I?	1. Sha'n we?
2. Sha't 'ee? [shaet·i']	2. Sha'n 'ee, or sha'n yo'?
3. Shall a, 'e, or 'er?	3. Sha'n a, or they?

Preterite.

1. Should I?	1. Shoulden we?
2. Should'st 'ee? [shud·sti']	2. Shoulden yo'?
3. Should a, 'e, or 'er?	3. Shoulden a, or they?

INTERROGATIVE NEGATIVE.

Present Tense.

1. Shannad-I?	1. Shanna we?
2. Shatna thee?	2. Shanna yo', or shan 'ee?
3. Shannad-a, 'e, or 'er?	3. Shannad-a, or shanna they?

Preterite.

1. Shouldnad-I?	1. Shouldna we?
2. Shouldsna thee?	2. Shouldna yo'?
3. Shouldnad-a, 'e, or 'er?	3. Shouldnad-a, or shouldna they?

WILL.

[PULVERBATCH.]

AFFIRMATIVE FORM.

Singular.	Present Tense. *Plural.*
1. I'll, or I ŏŏl	1. We'n, or we ŏŏn
2. Thee't	2. Yo'n, or yo' ŏŏn
3. { 'E'll, or 'er'll 'E ŏŏl, or 'er ŏŏl	3. They'n, or they ŏŏn

Preterite.

1. I ŏŏd	1. We ŏŏden [ŏŏd·n]
2. Thee ŏŏdst	2. Yo' ŏŏden
3. 'E, or 'er ŏŏd	3. They ŏŏden

NEGATIVE FORM.

Present Tense.

1. I ŏŏnna	1. We ŏŏnna
2. Thee ŏŏtna	2. Yo' ŏŏnna
3. 'E, or 'er ŏŏnna	3. They ŏŏnna

Preterite.

1. I ŏŏdna	1. We ŏŏdna
2. Thee ŏŏdsna	2. Yo' ŏŏdna
3. 'E, or 'er ŏŏdna	3. They ŏŏdna

INTERROGATIVE FORM.

Present Tense.

1. ———	1. ———
2. Ŏŏt,* or ŏŏt 'ee?	2. Ŏŏn 'ee?
3. Ŏŏt a, 'e, or 'er?	3. Ŏŏn a, or they?

Preterite.

1. Ŏŏd I?	1. Ŏŏden we?
2. Ŏŏd'st 'ee?	2. Ŏŏden yo'?
3. Ŏŏd a, 'e, or 'er?	3. Ŏŏden a, or they?

INTERROGATIVE NEGATIVE.

Present Tense.

1. ———	1. ———
2. Ŏŏtna thee?	2. Ŏŏnna yo'?
3. Ŏŏnnad-a, 'e, or 'er?	3. Ŏŏnnad-a, or ŏŏnna they?

Singular.	Preterite. *Plural.*
1. Ŏŏdnad-I?	1. Ŏŏdna we?
2. Ŏŏdsna thee, or t'ee?	2. Ŏŏdna yo'?
3. Ŏŏdnad-a, 'e, 'er?	3. Ŏŏdnad-a, or ŏŏdna they?

MAY.

[PULVERBATCH.[

AFFIRMATIVE FORM.

Singular.	Present and Past Tenses.[1] *Plural.*
1. I met	1. We met'n
2. ———	2. Yo' met'n
3. A, 'e, or 'er met	3. A, or they met'n

Past Tense.[2]

1. I may	1. We may
2. ———	2. Yo' may
3. A, 'e, or 'er may	3. A, or they may

NEGATIVE FORM.

1. I metna	1. We metna
2. ———	2. Yo' metna
3. A, 'e, or 'er metna	3. A, or they metna

INTERROGATIVE FORM.

1. Met I?	1. Met'n we?
2. ———	2. Met'n yo'?
3. Met a, 'e, or 'er?	3. Met'n a, or they?

INTERROGATIVE NEGATIVE.

1. Metnad-I?	1. Metna we?
2. ———	2. Metna yo'?
3. Metnad-a, 'e, or 'er?	3. Metnad-a, or metna they?

[1] 'Missis, *met* [= may] I gŏŏ wham to-night?' 'Well, yo' *met'n* [= may] gŏŏ after milkin', on'y yo' mus'n be sharp back to pŭt the men's supper.'

[2] *May* for *might* is of general usage—people considerably higher in rank than the peasantry employ it. 'I *may* have known what was going to happen.' 'I *may* a done it, if I'd on'y thought.'

MUST (Common Usage).

[PULVERBATCH.]

AFFIRMATIVE FORM.

Singular.	*Plural.*
1. I mun*	1. We mun
2. ———	2. Yo' mun
3. A, 'e, or 'er mun	3. A, or they mun

NEGATIVE FORM.

1. I munna	1. We munna
2. ———	2. Yo' munna
3. A, 'e, or 'er munna	3. A, or they munna

INTERROGATIVE FORM.

1. Mun I?	1. Mun we?
2. ———	2. Mun 'ee, or mun yo'?
3. Mun a, 'e, or 'er?	3. Mun a, or they?

INTERROGATIVE NEGATIVE.

1. Munnad-I?	1. Munna we?
2. ———	2. Munna yo'?
3. Munnad-a, 'e, or 'er?	3. Munnad-a, or munna they?

MUST (Refined Usage).

[PULVERBATCH.]

AFFIRMATIVE FORM.

Singular.	*Plural.*
1. I mus'	1. We mus'n
2. Thee mus'	2. Yo' mus'n
3. A, 'e, or 'er mus'	3. A, or they mus'n

NEGATIVE FORM.

1. I musna	1. We musna
2. Thee musna	2. Yo' musna
3. A, 'e, or 'er musna	3. A, or they musna

INTERROGATIVE FORM.

Singular.	*Plural.*
1. Mus' I?	1. Mus'n we?
2. Must 'ee?	2. Mus'n yo'?
3. Mus' a, 'e, or 'er?	3. Mus'n a, or they?

INTERROGATIVE NEGATIVE.

1. Musnad-I?	1. Musna we?
2. Musna thee?	2. Musna yo'?
3. Musnad-a, 'e, or 'er?	3. Musnad-a, or musna they?

TO BE.

[WORTHEN, *Cherbury.*]

AFFIRMATIVE FORM.

Part. Pres. Bein'. *Part. Past,* Bin.*

Indicative Mood.

Present Tense.

Singular.	*Plural.*
1. I bin[1]	1. We bin[1]
2. Thee bist	2. Yo' bin
3. 'E is	3. They bin

Preterite.

1. I wuz	1. We wun
2. Thee wust	2. Yo' wun
3. 'E wuz	3. They wun

Perfect.

1. I a bin	1. We'n bin
2. Thee'st bin	2. Yo'n bin
3. 'E's bin	3. They'n bin

Future.

1. I ŏŏl	1. We ŏŏl, or ŏŏn
2. Thee ŏŏt	2. Yo' ŏŏl, or ŏŏn
3. 'E ŏŏl	3. They ŏŏl, or ŏŏn

NEGATIVE FORM.

Present Tense.

1. I binna	1. We binna
2. Thee bis'na	2. Yo' binna
3. 'E inna	3. They binna

Singular.	Preterite.	*Plural.*
1. I wunna		1. We wunna
2. Thee wustna		2. Yo' wunna
3. 'E wunna		3. They wunna

Perfect.

1. I hanna bin — 1. We hanna bin
2. Thee hastna bin — 2. Yo' hanna bin
3. 'E hanna bin — 3. They hanna bin

Future.

[Shall or will.]

Singular	Plural
1. I shanna, or ŏŏnna be	1. We shanna, or ŏŏnna be
2. Thee shatna, or ŏŏtna be	2. Yo' shanna, or ŏŏnna be
3. 'E shanna, or 'e ŏŏtna be	3. They shanna, or ŏŏnna be

INTERROGATIVE FORM.

Present Tense.

Singular	Plural
1. Bin I?	1. Bin we?
2. Bist 'ee?	2. Bin yo'?
3. Is 'e?	3. Bin they?

Preterite.

Singular	Plural
1. Wuz I?	1. Wun we?
2. Wust 'ee?	2. Wun yo'?
3. Wuz 'e?	3. Wun they?

Perfect.

Singular	Plural
1. Han I bin?	1. Han we bin?
2. Hast 'ee bin?	2. Han yo' bin?
3. Has 'e bin?	3. Han they bin?

Future.

Singular	Plural
1. Shan I be, or ŏŏl I be?	1. Shan we be?
2. Shat thee be, or ŏŏl thee be?	2. Shan yo' be, or ŏŏl yo' be?
3. Ŏŏl 'e be?	3. Ŏŏl they be, or ŏŏn they be?

INTERROGATIVE NEGATIVE.

Present Tense.

Singular	Plural
1. Ammad-I?	1. Binna we?
2. Bistna thee?	2. Binna yo'?
3. Innad-'e?	3. Binna they?

Singular.	Preterite.	*Plural.*
1. Wunnad-I?		1. Wunna we?
2. Wustna thee?		2. Wunna yo'?
3. Wunnad-'e?		3. Wunna they?

Perfect.

1. Hannad-I bin	1. Hanna we bin?
2. Hast'na thee bin?	2. Hanna yó' bin?
3. Hannad-'e bin?	3. Hanna they bin?

Future.

1. Shannad-I, or ŏŏnnad-I be?	1. Shanna we, or ŏŏnna we be?
2. Shatna thee, or ootna thee be?	2. Shanna yo', or ŏŏnna yo' be?
3. Shannad-'e, or ŏŏdnad-'e be?	3. Shanna they, or ŏŏnna they be?

[1] The form **be** instead of **bin** obtains about Clun.

TO BE.

[Ludlow.]

AFFIRMATIVE FORM.

Part. Pres. Bein'. *Part. Past*, Bin.*

Indicative Mood.

Singular.	Present Tense.	*Plural.*
1. I be,[1] or I am		1. We bin, or we be
2. Yo' be, or thou bist		2. Yo' bin, or yo' be
3. 'E be, or 'e bin.		3. They bin, or they be

Preterite.

1. I wuz	1. We wun, or wuz
2. Thou wust	2. Yo' wun, or wuz
3. 'E wuz, or wun, or were	3. They wun, or wuz

Perfect.

1. I a bin	1. We a bin
2. Yo' a bin	2. Yo' a bin
3. 'E a bin	3. They a bin

Future (will).

1. Oi'll[2] be, or I ŏŏl be	1. We'll be, or we ŏŏl be
2. Yo'll be, or Thou ŏŏst be	2. Yo'll be, or yo' ŏŏl be
3. 'E'll be, or 'e ŏŏl be	3. They'll be, or they ŏŏl be

Singular.	Future (shall). *Plural.*
1. I shall be	1. We shan be
2. Thou sha't, or sha'st be	2. Yo' shan be
3. 'E shă' be	3. They shan be

NEGATIVE FORM.

Present Tense.

1. I binna, or I amna	1. We binna
2. Yo' binna, or thou bistna	2. Yo' binna
3. 'E inna	3. They inna, or binna

Preterite.

1. I wunna	1. We wunna

2nd and 3rd pers. the same.

Perfect.

1. I hanna bin	1. We hanna bin

2nd and 3rd pers. the same.

Future.

1. I ŏŏnna, or shanna be	1. We ŏŏnna or shanna be

2nd and 3rd pers. the same.

INTERROGATIVE FORM.

Present Tense.

1. Be I, or bin I?	1. Bin we, or be we?
2. Bist 'ee?	2. Bin yo', or be yo'?
3. Be 'e, or bin 'e?	3. Bin they, or be they?

Preterite.

1. Wuz I?	1. Wun we, or wuz we?
2. Wust 'ee?	2. Wun yo', or wuz yo'?
3. Wuz 'e, or wun 'e?	3. Wun they, or wuz they?

Perfect.

1. A I bin?	1. A we bin?
2. Astow,* or ast 'ee bin?	2. A yo' bin?
3. A 'e bin?	3. A they bin?

Future (will).

1. Ŏŏn, or ŏŏl I be?	1. Ŏŏn, or ŏŏl we be?
2. Ŏŏst 'ee be?	2. Ŏŏn, or ŏŏl yo' be?
3. Ŏŏn, or ŏŏl 'e be?	3. Ŏŏn, or ŏŏl they be?

Singular.	Future (shall). *Plural.*
1. Shall I be?	1. Shan we be?
2. Sha't 'ee, or sha'st 'ee be?	2. Shan yo' be?
3. Shall 'e be?	3. Shan they be?

INTERROGATIVE NEGATIVE.

Present Tense.

1. Binna I? [3]	1. Binna we?
2. Binna yo', or bistna thee?	2. Binna yo'?
3. Binna 'e?	3. Binna they?

Preterite.

1. Hanna I bin?	1. Hanna we bin?

2nd and 3rd pers. the same.

Future (will not).

1. Ŏŏna I be?	1. Ŏŏnna we be?
2. Ŏŏstna thee, or ŏŏst'n 'ee be?	2. Ŏŏnna yo' be?
3. Ŏŏnna 'e be?	3. Ŏŏnna they be?

Future (shall not).

1. Shanna I be?	1. Shanna we be?
2. Sha'tna thee be?	2. Shanna yo' be?
3. Shanna 'e be?	3. Shanna they be?

[1] The root **be** was conjugated throughout the present of the indicative as late as Milton's time—'I *be*,' 'Thou *beest*,' &c. **Bin** = O.E. *ben* = *be* + *n*, plural suffix. See Dr. Morris's *Historical English Accidence*, p. 182.

[2] *Oi* 'll [au·yl], an exceptional pronunciation of **I.**

[3] See p. li. on the **Negation of Verbs.**

TO BE.

[Bridgnorth.]

AFFIRMATIVE FORM.

Part. Pres. Bein'. *Part. Past*, Bin.

Singular.	Present Tense. *Plural.*
1. I bin	1. We bin
2. Thee bist	2. Yo' bin
3. 'E, or 'er is, or bin	3. A, or they bin

Singular.	Preterite. *Plural.*
1. I wuz	1. We wun
2. Thee wust	2. Yo' wun
3. A, 'e, or 'er wuz	3. A, or they wun

Perfect.

1. I've bin	1. We'n bin
2. Thee'st bin	2. Yo'n bin
3. 'Es, or 'er's bin	3. They'n bin

Future.

1. I shall, or wull be	1. We sha'n, or wull be
2. Thee sha't, or shan, or wull be	2. Yo'n, or yo'll be
3. E'll, or 'e wull, or 'er'll, or 'er wull be	3. They'n, or they'll, or they wull be

TO BE.

[NEWPORT.]

AFFIRMATIVE FORM.

Part. Pres. Bein'. *Part. Past*, Bin.*

Indicative Mood.

Singular.	Present Tense. *Plural.*
1. I'm	1. We'n,[1] or we bin
2. Thou art, or thou'rt[3]	2. Yo'n, or yo' bin
3. 'E's	3. They'n, or they bin

Preterite.

1. I were	1. We wun
2. Thou, or thee were	2. Yo', or ye[2] wun
3. 'E were	3. They wun

NEGATIVE FORM.

Present.

1. I amna, or ar'na	1. We arnna, or binna
2. Thou artna, or th'artna	2. Y'arnna, or yo' binna
3. 'E inna	3. They arnna, or binna

Singular.	Preterite.	*Plural.*
1. I wer'na, or wunna		1. We wer'na, or wunna
2. Thou, or thee wer'na, wunna		2. Yo', or ye wer'na, or wunna
3. 'E wer'na, or wunna		3. They wer'na, or wunna

[1] The '**n**' of 'We'*n*,' &c. in this tense = *arn* = *ar-on*—old Northern English forms, of Scandinavian origin. 'They'*n*' is less often used than they *bin*.

Ex.—'The peens [pains] 'll tek 'er . . . an' 'er'll croy [cry] out, fur the peens *a'n* loike to goo through 'er—an' that's w'en the witch 'as gotten 'is grip on 'er'—so said an Edgmond woman [1870].

[2] Ye—pronounced as French *me*, *te*, *le*, &c.—is *often* used in the affirmative; but *always* in the interrogative.

Ex.—'*Yo'* wunna gooin' to tek it off 'im, wun *ye?*' 'Ay, ah were.' 'Eh! thou'rt a bad 'un, thou art.'

[3] One authority gives in addition *Thee bist*, with its negative *Thee bistna*—stating that these forms are superseding the older 'Thou art,' &c.

Wuz obtains in the preterite throughout, as a—would be—'refined usage;' so also the negative *wuzna*. See p. li on the **Negation of Verbs**.

TO HAVE.

[NEWPORT.]

AFFIRMATIVE FORM.

Part. Pres. Havin'. *Part. Past*, Had [ad·].

Indicative Mood.

Singular.	Present Tense.	*Plural.*
1. I've, or I have [av·]		1. We'n, or we han
2. Thou, or thee hast [as·t]		2. Yo'n, or yo' han
3. 'E's		3. They'n, or they han

	Preterite.	
1. I had		1. We hadden
2. Thou, or thee hadst		2. Yo' hadden
3. 'E had		3. They hadden

NEGATIVE FORM.

Singular.	Present Tense.	*Plural.*
1. I hanna		1. We hanna
2. Thou, or thee hasna		2. Yo' hanna
3. 'E hanna		3. They hanna
	Preterite.	
1. I hadna		1. We hadna
2. Thou, or thee hadsna [?]		2. Yo' hadna
3. 'E hadna		3. They hadna

TO DO.

[Newport.]

AFFIRMATIVE FORM.

Indicative Mood.

Singular.	Present Tense.	*Plural.*
1. I do		1. We dun
2. ——?		2. Yo', or ye dun
3. 'E does		3. They dun
	Preterite.	
1. I did		1. We didden
2. ——?		2. Yo', or ye didden
3. 'E did		3. They didden

NEGATIVE FORM.

	Present Tense.	
1. I dunna		1. We dunna
2. Thou or thee, dunna or doesna		2. Yo', or ye dunna
3. 'E dunna		3. They dunna
	Preterite.	
1. I didna		1. We didna
2. Thou, or thee didna		2. Yo', or ye didna
3. 'E didna		3. They didna

CAN.

[NEWPORT.]

AFFIRMATIVE FORM.

Singular.	Present Tense.	*Plural.*
1. I con, or can		1. We con, or can
2. Thou, or thee con[1]		2. Yo', or ye con, or can
3. 'E con, or can		3. They con, or can
	Preterite.	
1. I could [ah cud]		1. We coulden
2. ——?		2. Yo', or ye coulden
3. 'E could		3. They coulden

NEGATIVE FORM.

	Present Tense.	
1. I conna, or canna		1. We conna, or canna
2. Thou, or thee conna		2. Yo', or ye conna or canna
3. 'E conna, or canna		3. They conna, or canna
	Preterite.	
1. I couldna		1. We couldna
2. ——?		2. Yo', or ye couldna
3. 'E couldna		3. They couldna

[1] *Ex.*—'Dosta think thou *con* do it?' 'Ay, to be shu-er ah *con.*' 'If Tum *conna* do it, it inna loikely as a chap loike thay [thee] *con.*'

SHALL.

[NEWPORT.]

AFFIRMATIVE FORM.

Singular.	Present Tense.	*Plural.*
1. I shall		1. We shan
2. ——?		2. Yo' shan
3. 'E shall		3. They shan

Singular.	Preterite. *Plural.*
1. I should [sh-h'd]	1. We shoulden [shud·n]
2. ——?	2. Yo', or ye shoulden
3. 'E should	3. They shoulden

NEGATIVE FORM.

Present.

1. Shanna	1. We shanna
2. Thou, or thee shanna	2. Yo', or ye shanna
3. 'E shanna	3. They shanna

Preterite.

1. I shouldna [shud·nu']	1. We shouldna
2. ——?	2. Yo', or ye shouldna
3. 'E shouldna	3. They shouldna

WILL.

[NEWPORT.]

AFFIRMATIVE FORM.

Singular.	Present Tense. *Plural.*
1. I will, or I'll	1. We win
2. Thou, or thee will [?], or thou'll, or thee'll	2. Yo' win
3. 'E will, or 'e'll	3. They win

Preterite.

1. I would [wud, or wuo·d]	1. We woulden
2. ——?	2. Yo', or ye woulden
3. He would	3. They woulden

NEGATIVE FORM.

Present Tense.

1. I winna, or wunna	1. We winna, or wunna
2. Thou or thee winna, or wunna	2. Yo', or ye winna or wunna
3. He winna, or wunna	3. They winna, or wunna

Singular.	Preterite. *Plural.*
1. I wouldna	1. We wouldna
2. Thou, or thee wouldna	2. Yo', or ye wouldna
3. 'E wouldna	3. They wouldna

Ex.—'Win ye goo to Noopert fur me, Johnny?' 'Shan ye soon a done them taters?' 'They wunna mind annythin' as I say to 'em.'

MUST.

[NEWPORT.]

AFFIRMATIVE FORM.

Singular.	*Plural.*
1. I mun	1. We mun
2. Thou, or thee mun[1]	2. Yo', or ye mun
3. 'E mun	3. They mun

NEGATIVE FORM.

1. I munna	1. We munna
2. Thou, or thee munna	2. Yo', or ye munna
3. 'E munna	3. They munna

[1] *Ex.*—'Moother, I arnna gooin' to skyule never no more.' 'Eh, my lad, but tha *mun!*' 'I shanna. The mester says we munna goo to the Mee Fear (= *May Fair*—but this is very broad), so I shanna goo anigh 'im no more.'

May is used for *might*, both among the poor and among persons of some education.

Ex.—'Well, she *may* have given the girl leave to stop over Sunday.' See p. lxiii, note (2).

FRAGMENTS OF VERBS.

TO BE.

[COLLIERY, *Oakengates.*]

Singular.	Present Tense. *Plural.*
1. I are	1. We are
2. Thoo bist	2. Yo' be
3. 'E are [or is?]	3. They be

'I saw a letter not long ago [1878] from a Shropshire carpenter (Colliery district) about the death of his wife, a young woman. He said, "The night befour she died, her said to me, Jim, I *are* very bad, my Lad, I *are* only waiting the Lord's time."'—A. J. M.

TO BE.

[ELLESMERE.]

Present Tense.

AFFIRMATIVE. *Singular.*	NEGATIVE. *Singular.*
1. I'm	1. I amma
2. Thee'st	2. Thee beestna
3. 'E's, or 'er's	3. 'E, or 'er inna

In the *Future Tense* the auxiliary **will** = wull, and **will not** = wunna. In all particulars save the foregoing this usage accords with that of PULVERBATCH.

TO BE.

[OSWESTRY.]

AFFIRMATIVE FORM.

Part. Pres. Bein'. *Part. past,* Bin.*

Indicative.

Singular.	Present Tense. *Plural.*
1. I be, or bin, or are	1. We be, or bin, or 'm = am[2]
2. Thee beest, or bin[1]	2. Yo' be, or bin, or bun[3]
3. 'E be, or bin, or are	3. They be, or bin

NEGATIVE FORM.

Singular.	*Plural.*
1. I binna, or bunna	1. We binna, or bunna
2. Thee beestna, or binna	2. Yo' binna, or bunna.[3]
3. 'E baint	3. They binna, or bunna, or baint

[1] The 2nd *pers. sing.* in use at OSWESTRY is not heard at WHITTINGTON, 2½ miles E. from that town.

[2] A little boy on being asked in school why God was called 'Our Father,' answered 'Because *we'm* His'n.'

[3] A woman said to a boy one day, '*Bun* yo' in yore senses? I think yo' *bunna.*'

'It inna' is very common, so is 'Be it?' as an interrogative. Sometimes these two go together thus:—'*It inna, be it?*' The interrogative 'Bin 'ee?' is not uncommon. Wunna = was not, and will not, is used in the *Past* and *Future Tenses* respectively.

Yo'm [yoa·m] = you am = you are, is a vulgar form; SHREWSBURY; WEM. Qy. com. '*Yo'm* a bad un!' Cf. **we'm** in the foregoing verb.

Con = can; very general.

Cannot = cosna [kus·nu'], 2nd *pers. sing.*, SHREWSBURY; [k:aus·nu'], COLLIERY; ELLESMERE.

Dare not = dorna [d:au·r'nu'], WELLINGTON.

Will = ŏŏl [ŏŏl·]; general throughout *Mid.* and *South Shr.*

Will not = ŏŏnna [ŏŏn·u'], *ibid.* (We) ŏŏn = O.E. *wolen.*

Will = wull [wùl], BRIDGNORTH; WEM; ELLESMERE; OSWESTRY?

Will not = wunna [wun·u'], *ibid.*; OSWESTRY.

Will = win [win·], = O.E. *wilen, pl.*, NEWPORT; WHITCHURCH. 'I conna keep the cows from gettin' o'er the fence, they *win* do it.'

Will not = winna * [win·u'], *pl.*, *ibid.*

Must = maun * [m:aun·], WHITCHURCH; ELLESMERE.

Must not = maunna * [m:aun·u'], *ibid.*

Must = mun, **must not** = munna; Com.

To go [gŏŏ], Com. *Pres. Part.* going [gwi'·i'n], SHREWSBURY; PULVERBATCH. [gwa'yn], CHURCH STRETTON. [gwaa·yn], BISHOP'S CASTLE; CLUN; CORVE DALE; LUDLOW. [goo·i'n], NEWPORT. [gŏŏ·i'n], ELLESMERE.

A-going—according to these various pronunciations is sometimes heard. See **A** (3) (*Glossary*).

The Past Part. is [gwun *corr.* gwoen·]; commonly.

Lukka = look you! see that! COLLIERY; used interjectionally to express surprise, or to call attention to anything being done.

Shewn * = shew, Com. 'I'll *shewn* yo'.'

Sist = seest, 2nd *pers. sing.*, COLLIERY.

Sithee = dost thee see? COLLIERY.

ADVERBS.

The subjoined classified list of **adverbs** comprises most of those in common use.

In the folk-speech **Adverbs** of **Manner** are often expressed by *adjectives*, as 'yo'n do it *easy*.' 'That thrustle does sing *sweet*,' and so forth. The usage of dropping the adverbial *-ly* obtained, according to Dr. Morris, amongst the Elizabethan writers—'*grievous* sick,' '*miserable* poor.' See *Historical English Accidence*, p. 196.

The adverb **like** is frequently employed as a redundant form—''er couldna walk *like*,' 'that's whad a toud me *like*.'

Adverbs of Negation are commonly reduplicated to express force or determination, as—'I'll *never* gŏŏ nigh that 'ouse, *never no more*.'

Adverbs of Place.—Abroad,* agate,* along,* anigh, a-one-side, aside, asiden,* athin, a-wham,* endways-on,* miles-end-ways,* pretty nigh.

Adverbs of Time.—Afore,* agen,* at-after,* arly,* awilde, by now, by-times, by-whiles, edge-o'neet, edge-o'-night,* justly,* just now,* nex'-to-nex',* now just,* now-a-days, sence,* to-morrow day, once [wun·st], Com.; [won·st], NEWPORT; ELLESMERE; twice [twei·z], Com.; [twei·st, *corr.* twahy·st], NEWPORT.

Adverbs of Manner or Quality.—Above-a-bit, aneend, anind, athatn, athatns, athisn, athisns, atwo,* backsi'fore, behappen,* belike,* caterwiff,* collywest, happen, inchmeal,* in lieu,* inturn, lather and lother = rather, lief,* lieve,* liever,* mayhappen, mebbe, most in generally, most like = very likely, on,* scatter-corner,* skewways, top-o'er-tail,* top-side-bottomest, upsi'down.*

Adverbs of Measure, Quality, Degree, &c.—Aumust, better,* despert, full,* leastways,* mighty,* ne'er-a, and never-a * = not one, nod, oncommon,* ondeniable,* onhuman,* onmerciful,* that,[1] than,[2] verra [vae·r'u'] (Newport), welly.*

[1] **That** = **so**. ''E inna *that* owd.'

[2] **Than** = **till**. See **Conjunctions**.

PREPOSITIONS.

The following is a list of the **prepositions** most commonly employed, though a few of rarer usage are included in it;—afore,* agen,* all-along-on,* along-on,* anunst,* anungst, as, at,[1] at-after,* athout, athwart, a-top,* atter, atween,* atwixt,* betwix,* by,* frommet * = fromward, i' = in,[2] o' = *of* and *on*, o'er, o'er anunst, off = from, on * = of, oërts * *and* toërts = in comparison to, right-fore-nungst, sence,* to[3] = of, tŏërt = toward.

[1] **at** = **to** and **of**. ''Ark *at* the dog!' ''Er thought nuthin *at* it.' The *former* usage is noted in the **Glossary**, the *latter* was brought under notice after that was in type. Cf. with this the Fr. *penser à*.

[2] **in** = **to** in the idiomatic phrase, **belongs in** = belongs, or pertains *to*. 'That tub *belungs i'* the brew-hus.'

[3] **to** = **of** after the verb **know**. 'I *know to* a book.'

CONJUNCTIONS.

This class of words exhibits few divergences from literary English, but the following are of frequent use—agen,* athout[2] = unless, as * = that, 'cause = because, nor * = than, onless * = except, still on = nevertheless, notwithstanding; till * and tin = than, than[1] = till.

[1] **Than** = **till**, WEM. 'I run *than* I thought I'd a dropt.' See **Adverbs of degree**.

[2] 'Yo'n never scrat a grey yed *athout* yo' tăk'n better car' o' yoreself.' Recorded as a preposition only in the body of the Glossary.

INTERJECTIONS.

Interjections and words of **interjectional** character—expletives and slight forms of oath—are constantly used, and these last often without a suspicion of 'swearing' being attached to them; of all classes of exclamation the commonest and most characteristic are—Aye, Bygum, By jings,[1] By Jove, By leddy, Chow-wow, Consarn it, Danger,* Danker, Daze my 'ounds,* Dear 'eart, Dear 'eart alive, Dear Sirs, Dear Sores,* Delp, Eh,[2] Eh gonies,* Gad, 'eart alive, Hoosack,* Lukka, My gŏŏ'niss, My 'eart alive, My ŏŏns,* Nan,* No danger,* Sarn it, Sores alive.

[1] **By jings** * = By St. Gingoulph.

[2] **Eh** is *the* indispensable interjection used by all ranks in the NEWPORT district, it = O.E. *ey*.

WEIGHTS, MEASURES, &c.

The * affixed to a word refers it to the body of the Glossary for further exemplification.

There is great diversity in the weights and measures throughout the county. The (London) *Standard*, Oct. 15th, 1878, says:—'When the Act to consolidate the law relating to weights and measures comes into operation in January next it will be found that in the county of Salop some extraordinary discrepancies still exist. It may hardly be credited, but is nevertheless a fact, that wheat alone is sold by no less than six different weights; barley by nine weights and measures different from each other; oats by four; peas, three; and beans by two. The growers of grain on one side of the county do not actually know the prices their fellow-agriculturists are receiving on the other side, and when the quotations for imperial quarters are given in the reports of Birmingham or Gloucester markets they are read [by numbers of farmers] in Shropshire as if written in an unknown tongue.'

The following **Notes**, and the **Tables** shewing the usage of *eleven* representative markets, will serve to illustrate some of the 'discrepancies' alluded to in the *Standard*.

Score * = 20 lbs. is the denomination of weight which obtains most commonly; grain, bran, gurgeons, pulse, butcher's meat in the carcase, bacon-pigs, &c., are all calculated by the *score*. Cf. **score, a definite numeral** (*Grammar Outlines*). See *N. & Q.* (5th S. x. 283).

The **Stone** is not much used, but reference to the subjoined *Tables* will show how and where.

A **pack*** (of flour) = 20 stones, each stone = 14 lbs.; MARKET DRAYTON, *Cheshire Border.*

Strike,* Bushel, Measure, are synonymous terms, but *strike* is giving place as a general usage to *bushel*, whilst *measure* is employed chiefly in the northern borders of the county. The quantities sold under these respective denominations are not, however, uniformly equal.

A [local] bushel of	grain is commonly			= 38 qts.
„	„	„	at Bishop's Castle	= 38—40 qts.
„	„	„	at Ludlow	= 40 qts.
„	„	„	at Wellington	= 39 qts.
„	„	„	at Newport	= 38 *and* 39 qts.

A **quarter** is the 16th part of a bushel; SHREWSBURY. Qy. com.

A **pot** [basket] = 5 pecks; BRIDGNORTH.
„ „ = 5 „ CORVE DALE.
„ „ = 5 pecks, sometimes 6; LUDLOW.

Two **pots** = one **bag**; *ibid.*

A **kype*** [basket] is often used as a measure for potatoes, apples, &c.; SHREWSBURY. When filled level with the top it equals a half-strike heaped.

Hoop* is a name formerly given to a peck measure, but now nearly obsolete; SHREWSBURY.

TABLE OF WEIGHTS AND MEASURES.

[*In use Nov. 1878.*]

Home Produce.—**WHEAT.**

Measure.		*Weight.*	*Market.*
Bushel or strike, 38 quarts *or* Per bag of 3 bushels or strikes	=	75 lbs. = 225 lbs. + 5 lbs. for bag	SHREWSBURY
Per sack *or* Per bag of 3 bushels of 75 lbs. each	=	11 'score' + 10 lbs. = 230 lbs. = 225 lbs. + 5 lbs. for bag = 230 lbs.	CHURCH STRETTON

WHEAT—[*continued*].

Measure.		*Weight.*	*Market.*
Per bushel	=	75 lbs.	Bishop's Castle
Per bushel or strike	=	75 lbs.	Ludlow
Per bushel *or* Per sack	=	72 lbs. / 11 'score' + 1 lb. = 221 lbs.	Bridgnorth
Per bushel of 39 quarts, or *idem*	=	75 lbs.	Wellington
Per bag of 3 bushels	=	11 'score' + 4 lbs. for bag = 224 lbs.	Newport
Per bushel, strike, or measure *or* Per bag of 3 ditto	=	75 lbs. / 11 'score' + 5 lbs. + 5 lbs. for bag = 230 lbs.	Market Drayton
Per bushel or measure	=	75 lbs.	Whitchurch
Per measure *or* Per sack of 3 measures	=	75 lbs. / 225 lbs. + 5 lbs. for bag = 230 lbs.	Ellesmere
Per bushel	=	75 lbs.	Oswestry

BARLEY.

Measure.		*Weight.*	*Market.*
Per bushel of 38 *and* of 40 quarts			Shrewsbury
Idem Per 4 bushels to a sack	=	38 quarts	Church Stretton
Per 4 bushels of 40 quarts	=	270 lbs. with bag	Bishop's Castle
Per sack	=	14 'score' = 280 lbs.	Ludlow
Per bushel of 38 *and* 32 quarts [malting] *or* Per bag [grinding]	=	10 'score' = 200 lbs. (including bag)	Bridgnorth
Per bushel of 39 quarts			Wellington
Per bag of 3 bushels of 39 quarts each Per bag [grinding]	=	10 'score' + 4 lbs. for bag = 204 lbs.	Newport
Per bushel, strike, or measure *or* Per bag of 4 bushels of 38 quarts each	=	70 lbs. / 14 'score' = 280 lbs. (including bag)	Market Drayton
Per measure	=	70 lbs., sometimes 65 lbs.	Whitchurch

BARLEY—[*continued*].

Measure.		*Weight.*	*Market.*
Per measure of 38 quarts *or* per sack of 4 measures			ELLESMERE
Per bushel of 38 quarts			OSWESTRY

OATS.

Measure.		*Weight.*	*Market.*
Per sack *or* Per sack of 9 half-strikes	=	11 'score' + 10 lbs. (including bag) = 230 lbs.	SHREWSBURY
Per sack	=	13 'score' + 10 lbs.	CHURCH STRETTON
Per sack of 4 large bushels	=	11 'score' + 10 lbs. = 230 lbs.	BISHOP'S CASTLE
Idem		*Idem*	LUDLOW
Per bag	=	8 'score' = 160 lbs. gross	BRIDGNORTH
Per sack	=	11 'score' + 10 lbs. (including sack) = 230 lbs.	WELLINGTON
Per bag of 4 bushels	=	10 'score' + 4 lbs. for bag = 204 lbs.	NEWPORT
Per bushel, strike, or measure	=	50 lbs.	MARKET DRAYTON
or Per sack of 4 ditto	=	225 lbs. (including bag)	
or Per sack	=	10 'score' = 200 lbs.	
Per measure	=	50 lbs.	WHITCHURCH
Idem		*Idem*	ELLESMERE
Idem		*Idem*	OSWESTRY

BEANS.

Measure.		*Weight.*	*Market.*
Per bag	=	12 'score' = 240 lbs. (including bag)	SHREWSBURY
Per bag of 3 bushels		*Idem*	CHURCH STRETTON
Per sack	=	12 'score' = 240 lbs. gross (seldom grown)	BISHOP'S CASTLE
Idem		*Idem*	LUDLOW
Per sack	=	10 'score' *and* 11 ditto gross	BRIDGNORTH
Per bag	=	12 'score' + 10 lbs. = 250 lbs.	WELLINGTON
Per bag of 3 bushels	=	12 'score' + 4 lbs. for bag = 244 lbs.	NEWPORT
Per bag	=	235 lbs. (including bag)	MARKET DRAYTON

BEANS—[*continued*].

Measure.	*Weight.*	*Market.*
Per sack	= 12 'score' = 240 lbs.	WHITCHURCH
Idem	*Idem*	ELLESMERE
Per bushel	= 60 lbs.	OSWESTRY

PEASE.

Measure.	*Weight.*	*Market.*
Per sack	= 11 'score' + 10 lbs. = 230 lbs. (including bag)	SHREWSBURY
Per bushel *or* Per bag of 3 bushels	= 4 'score' = 80 lbs. = 12 'score' = 240 lbs.	CHURCH STRETTON
Per bag	= 12 'score' = 240 lbs.	BISHOP'S CASTLE
Idem	*Idem*	LUDLOW
Per sack	= 10 'score' = 200 lbs. (including bag)	BRIDGNORTH
Per sack	= 200 lbs. (including bag)	WELLINGTON
Per bag of 3 bushels	= 11 'score' + 4 lbs. for bag = 224 lbs.	NEWPORT
Per bag	= 225 lbs. (including bag)	MARKET DRAYTON
Per sack	= 11 'score' + 10 lbs. = 230 lbs.	WHITCHURCH
Per bag	= 12 'score' + 5 lbs. for bag	ELLESMERE
Per —?	= 60 lbs.	OSWESTRY

MALT.

Measure.	*Weight.*	*Market.*
Per imperial bushel of 32 quarts		COMMON

FLOUR.

Measure.	*Weight.*	*Market.*
Per bushel or strike	= 56 lbs. (without bag)	SHREWSBURY
Idem	*Idem*	CHURCH STRETTON
Per sack of 5 bushels	= 280 lbs.	BISHOP'S CASTLE
Per bushel *or* Per sack of 5 bushels	= 56 lbs. = 280 lbs.	LUDLOW
Per bushel or strike	= 56 lbs.	BRIDGNORTH
Per sack of 4 bushels of 56 lbs. each	= 224 lbs.	WELLINGTON
Per sack	= 16 stones of 14 lbs. each	NEWPORT
Idem *or* Per pack *	*Idem* = 20 stones = 280 lbs.	MARKET DRAYTON

FLOUR—[*continued*].

Measure.	*Weight.*	*Market.*
Per sack of 5 bushels	= 14 'score' = 280 lbs.	WHITCHURCH
Per bushel *or* Per sack of 5 bushels	= 56 lbs. = 280 lbs.	ELLESMERE
Per sack	= 280 lbs.	OSWESTRY

BRAN, GURGEONS,* SHARPS.*

Measure.	*Weight.*	*Market.*
Per bag	1 cwt. = 112 lbs. (without bag)	SHREWSBURY
Idem	1 cwt. = 112 lbs.	CHURCH STRETTON
Per sack [*bran*] *Idem* [*gurgeons* and *sharps*]	= 112 lbs. = 168 lbs.	BISHOP'S CASTLE
Idem	*Idem*	LUDLOW
Per bushel *or* Per sack	= 56 lbs. 1½ cwt. = 168 lbs. (without bag)	BRIDGNORTH
Per sack [*bran*]	= 1 cwt. = 112 lbs.	WELLINGTON
Per bag	*Idem*	NEWPORT
Idem *or* Per Per [*gurgeons* and *sharps*]	*Idem* short cwt. = 100 lbs. 'score' = 20 lbs.	MARKET DRAYTON
Per bag [*bran*]	= 5 'score,' *or* 5 'score' + 12 lbs.	WHITCHURCH
Per sack	= 5 'score'	ELLESMERE
Per	'score' = 20 lbs.	OSWESTRY

POTATOES.

Measure.	*Weight.*	*Market.*
Per bushel or strike, which from 'getting up time' to Christmas After that time *or* Per bag of 2 bushels	= 95 lbs. = 90 lbs.	SHREWSBURY
Per heaped bushel at 'getting up time' In the spring time *or* Per bag of 2 bushels	= 96 lbs. = 90 lbs. = 180 lbs.	CHURCH STRETTON
Per bag at 'getting up time' In the spring	= 90 lbs. = 80 lbs.	BISHOP'S CASTLE

POTATOES—[*continued*].

Measure.	*Weight.*	*Market.*
Per bushel	= 80 lbs.	LUDLOW
Per bag of 9 pecks	= 180 lbs.	BRIDGNORTH
Per bag	= 10 score = 200 lbs. (including bag)	WELLINGTON.
Per pot	= 90 lbs.	NEWPORT
Per measure *or* Per bag of 2 measures	= 90 lbs.	MARKET DRAYTON
Per measure	= 80 lbs.	WHITCHURCH
Per strike which from 'getting up time' till Christmas After that time	= 95 lbs. = 90 lbs.	ELLESMERE
Per strike	= 90 or 95 lbs.	OSWESTRY

APPLES.

Measure.	*Weight.*	*Market.*
Per heaped bushel or strike, or parts thereof		SHREWSBURY
Per heaped imperial bushel, or by quarter, or peck		CHURCH STRETTON
Per pot	= 90 lbs.	BISHOP'S CASTLE
Per bushel for cider Per pot Per pot [choice fruit]	 = 80 lbs. = 20 lbs.	LUDLOW
Per pot of 5 pecks	= 63 lbs.	BRIDGNORTH
Per peck of 8 quarts, generally heaped		WELLINGTON
Per pot	= 90 lbs.	NEWPORT
Per measure	= 80 lbs.	MARKET DRAYTON
Idem	= 84 lbs.	WHITCHURCH
Idem	= 90 lbs.	ELLESMERE
Idem[1]	= 95 lbs.	OSWESTRY

PEARS.

Same as apples, excepting that 'summer fruit' is sold per 'measure' = 90 lbs., and 'winter fruit' per 'measure' = 80 lbs.; ELLESMERE.

DAMSONS.

Measure.	*Weight.*	*Market.*
Per quart[2] *or* Per heaped bushel, or strike, or parts thereof		SHREWSBURY

DAMSONS—[*continued*].

Measure.	*Weight.*	*Market.*
Per quart *or* Per pot of 2 pecks	:	CHURCH STRETTON
Per pot	= 90 lbs.	BISHOP'S CASTLE
Idem	*Idem*	LUDLOW
Idem	*Idem*	BRIDGNORTH
Idem	*Idem*	WELLINGTON
Idem	*Idem*	NEWPORT
Per measure	= 90 lbs.	MARKET DRAYTON
Per measure of 38 quarts	= 90 lbs.	WHITCHURCH
Per measure	= 90 lbs.	ELLESMERE
Idem	= 95 lbs.	OSWESTRY

[1] *Apples* are sold *retail* in Oswestry market—per hundred—the method of counting them is a simple and expeditious one. The seller takes three apples in each hand, and throws the six into the buyer's basket—repeating this process 20 times, until the 'six score the hundred' is completed.

[2] *Damsons* were sold in Shrewsbury market in 1877, for the extraordinarily high price of 1s. 2d. per quart; in 1845, a year of great scarcity, they fetched 1s. per quart.

CHEESE.

Per cwt.	= 120 lbs.	SHREWSBURY
Idem	*Idem*	NEWPORT
Per 'long' cwt.	= 121 lbs.	MARKET DRAYTON
Idem	*Idem*	WHITCHURCH

FRESH BUTTER.

Oz. to the lb.	*Market.*
16, 18	SHREWSBURY
16, 18, 20	CHURCH STRETTON
16	BISHOP'S CASTLE
16	LUDLOW
17	BRIDGNORTH
18, 22	WELLINGTON
18	NEWPORT
20, 22	MARKET DRAYTON
24 [dish]	WHITCHURCH
Idem	ELLESMERE
16, 20	OSWESTRY

SALT BUTTER.

Oz. to the lb.	*Market.*
16	COMMON

EGGS.

So many for 1s. or 6d.	COMMON

BUTCHERS' MEAT.

The weight of 'beasts' and pigs is estimated *to* the butcher by the **score**—beef so many '*score*' per side or quarter, pigs so many '*score*' the whole carcase. Calves and sheep so many lbs. per quarter. But the butcher *sells* by the lb. Weight by the **stone** is recognized, but rarely employed.

A stone of beef = 12 lbs.; LUDLOW.
,, ,, = 14 lbs.; BRIDGNORTH.
,, ,, = 8 lbs.; ELLESMERE.

LAND MEASUREMENTS, ETC.

Acre statute, usual acreage.

Acre of Hops, about half a statute acre, being as much land as is required for 1000 hop plants; LUDLOW.

Rood = *rod*, is a measure of 8 yds. *lineal*, employed for hedging, ditching, draining, &c.; Com.

The **rood** is also employed as the basis of denomination for Square Measure—a '**digging rood**,' as for cottage gardens, potatoe ground, &c., is 64 square yards, i. e. 8 × 8; Com. Cf. *N. & Q.* [5th S. x. 284].

Perch [paer'·k],	fencing or ditching,	8 yds.	*Lineal;*	CLEE HILLS.
,,	,,	,,	7 ,,	,,	LUDLOW.
,,	walling		16½ ft.		LUDLOW.

MISCELLANEOUS.

Lugg, a term in wood measurement = 149 sq. yds. of coppice wood; LUDLOW.

A Cord of Wood * measures 8 ft. long, 3 ft. 1 inch wide, and 5 ft. 1 inch high; Com.

10 **Cords of Wood** to one Charcoal-fire.

A sack of charcoal = 14 bushels.

Faggots, 120 per hundred = 6 '**score**'; CLUN; LUDLOW.

Coal, a ton = 20 cwt. of 112 lbs. each at some pits.

" " *idem* " 120 lbs. (called 'long weight') at others.

Hay, a ton = 20 cwt. of 112 lbs. each; Qy. com.

Hand-breadth * = 3 inches—sometimes used for **Hand**—a rather loose expression, signifying approximately rather than exactly; LUDLOW.

Swath * **of Hay-grass** = 39 inches; LUDLOW.

Shock of corn = 6 sheaves; WORTHEN, *Minsterley*.

Idem = 12 " LUDLOW.

Thrave * **of corn** = 24 " Com.

Boltin * **of** (thatching) **straw** = 14 lbs.; WORTHEN, *Minsterley*. Qy. com.

Battin * " " = 2 sheaves; ELLESMERE.

Thrave " " = 24 'boltin' = 336 lbs.; WORTHEN, *Minsterley*. Qy. com.

Idem *idem* = 12 'battin'; ELLESMERE.

Idem *idem* = 24 sheaves; MARKET DRAYTON.

Baker's Dozen = 13; Com.

Cider hogshead = 100 galls.; LUDLOW; BRIDGNORTH.

SPECIMENS OF THE FOLK-SPEECH.

[PULVERBATCH.]

THE following is *literatim et verbatim* what Betty Andrews—a Church Pulverbatch woman—said when relating the account of how her little boy had fallen into the brook at Cruck Meole, where she was then living [1873]. But no written characters of any kind—no 'want of stops'—*can* convey an idea of the story as poured forth by good Betty's voluble tongue—it took away one's breath to listen to it:—

"I 'eärd a scrike ma'am an' I run an theer I sid Frank ad pecked i' the bruck an' douked under an' wuz drowndin' an' I jumped after 'im an' got out on 'im an' lugged 'im on to the bonk all sludge an' I got 'im wham afore our Sam comen in—a good job it wuz for Sam as 'e wunna theer an' as Frank wunna drownded for if 'e 'ad bin I should 'a' tore our Sam all to winder-rags an' then 'e'd a bin djed an' Frank drownded an' I should a bin 'anged. I toud Sam wen 'e tŏŏk the 'ouse as I didna like it.—'Bless the wench,' 'e sed, 'whad'n'ee want? Theer's a tidy 'ouse an' a good garden an' a run for the pig.' 'Aye,' I sed, 'an' a good bruck for the childern to peck in,' so if Frank 'ad bin drownded I should a bin the djeth uv our Sam. I wuz that frittened ma'am that I didna spake for a nour after I got wham an' Sam sed as 'e adna sid me quiet so lung sence we wun married an' that wuz *eighteen* 'ear."

COMPROMISE GLOSSIC VERSION.

"Ei· ee·r'd u skr'ei·k mum un ei r'un· un dhee·r' ei sid· Frang·k ud pek·t i dhu br'uk· un dou·kt un·dur' un wuz dr'ou·ndin un ei jum·pt af·tur' im un got· ou·t on im un lug·d im on· tu dhu bong·k aul slej· un ei got· im wum· u'foa·r' our ' Sam· kum·un in· u good· job it wuz· fur' Sam· uz ee· wun·u' dhee·r' un uz Fr'ang·k wun-u' dr'ou·ndid fur' if· ee ad· bin ei shud u toa·r' our' Sam· aul· tu win·dur'-r'ag·z un dhen· ee·d u bin jed·un Frang·k dr'ou·ndid un ei· shud u bin ang·d. Ei· tou·d Sam· wen ee tŏŏk· dhu ous· ut ei· did·nu lei·k it. 'Bles· dhu wen·sh,' ee sed·, 'wod·ni waan·t?—dhee·r'z u tei·di ous· un u good· gaa·r'din un u r'un· fur' dhu pig·.' 'Ay·, ei sed, 'un u good br'uk· fur' dhu chil·dur'n tu pek· in·,' soa· if Fr'ang·k ad· bin dr'ou·ndid ei shud u bin dhu jeth·u our' Sam·—ei wuz dhat· fr'it·nd mum dhut ei did·nu spai·k fur' u nou·r' af·tur' ei got· wum· un Sam· sed· uz ee ad· nu sid· mi kwei·h't· soa· lung· sen·s wee wun mar'·id un dhat· wuz ·eit·tee·n ee·r'."

ANALYTIC GLOSSIC VERSION.

"A'y·-:ee·u'r'd-u'-skr'a'y·k-mu'm u'n-a'y-r'un· u'n-dh:ee·u'r' a'y-si'd· Fr'a'ng·k-u'd-pek·t-i'-dhu'-br'uk· u'n-duw·kt-un·du'r' u'n-wu'z-dr'uw·n di'n u'n-a'y-jum·pt a'f·tu'r'-i'm u'n got· uw·t-:on-i'm u'n-lug·d-i'm on tu'-dhu'b:ong·k :aul·-slaej·u'n-a'y-got-i'm-woem· u'f:oa·u'r'-uwu'r'-Sa'm· kum·u'n-i'n·—u' g:oo·d-job i't-wuz·-fu'r'-Sa'm· u'z-ee-wun·u'-dh:ee·u'r' u'n-u'z-Fr'a'ng·k wun·u'-dr'uw·ndi'd fu'r-i'f·-ee-a'd·-bi'n a'y-shu'd-u'-t:oa·u'r' uwu'r'-Sa'm· :aul·tu'-win·du'r'-r'a'g·z u'n-dhen·:ee·d-u'-bi'n-j:ae·d· u'n-Fr'a'ng·k-dr'uw·ndi'd u'n-a'y·-shu'd-u'-bi'n-a'ng·d. A'y-tuw·d-Sam· wen-ee-tŏŏk·-dhu'-uwss· u'z-a'y-did·nu'-la'y·k-i't. —'Bles·-dhu'-wen·sh,' ee-sed·, 'wod·ni'-waan·t?— dh:ee·u'r'z-u'-ta'y·di'-uwss· u'n-u' g:oo·d-g:aa·r'di'n u'n-u'–r'un· fu'r'-dhu'-pig·.' 'A'y·, a'y·-sed·, 'u'n-u' g:oo·d-br'uk· fu'r'-dhu'-chil-du'r'n tu'-pek·-in', s:oa-i'f-Fr'a'ng·k a'd-bin-dr'uw·n-di'd a'y-shu'd-u'-bin dhu'-j:ae·th· u'-uwu'r'-Sa'm·—a'y-wu'z-dha't·-frit·nd-mu'm dhu't-a'y-didnu'-spai·k fu'r'-u'-nuw·u'r'-a'f·tu'r' a'y-got·-woem· u'n-Sa'm-sed· u'z ee-a'd·nu' si'd·-mi'-kwa'y·h't s:oa-lung· sen·s-wee-wun-ma'r'·i'd u'n-dha't·-wu'z ·a'yt·tee·n :ee·h'r'."

The same Betty Andrews was telling how she had washed the pig's entrails at the 'prill' [stream]—and here in order to understand her story, the Glossary must be anticipated, by explaining that the pig's puddings are called respectively, the '*Roger*,' the '*Nancy*,' and the '*chitterlings*'—said Betty, 'I wuz weshin' the bally at the prill jest by the stile w'en Dick comen up—awilde I wuz talkin to 'im my *Roger* went, I run down the prill after it, an' afore I could get back the *Nancy* wuz gwun—an' I thought the very Owd Nick wuz i' the puddins.'

COMPROMISE GLOSSIC VERSION.

'Ei· wuz wesh·in dhu bal·i ut dhu pr'il jes·t bei· dhu stei·l wen Dik· kum·un up—uwei·ld ei wuz tau·kin tu im· mi Roj·ur' wen·t, ei r'un dou·n dhu pr'il· af·tur' it un ufoa·r' ei kud get bak· dhu Nan·si wuz gwun· un ei thaut· uz dhu ver'i ou·d Nik· wuz i dhu pud·inz.'

ANALYTIC GLOSSIC VERSION.

"A'y-wu'z-waesh·i'n-dhu'-bal·i'-u't-dhu'-pr'i'l·jaes·t-ba'y·-dhu'-sta'y·l wen-Dik· kum·u'n-up—u'wa'y·ld-a'y-wu'z-t:au·ki'n-tu'-im· m'i-Roj·u'r'-wen·t, a'y-r'un-duw·n-dhu'-pr'i'l· a'f·tu'r'-i't u'n-u'f:oa·u'r'-a'y-ku'd-g(yet-ba'k· dhu'-Na'n·si'-wu'z-gwoen· u'n-a'y·-thaut·-u'z-dhu'-v:ae·r'i' uw·d-Nik· wu'z-i'-dhu'-pud·i'nz."

Another anecdote of Betty Andrews—as related by herself—will conclude these 'Specimens,' which being the genuine utterances of a good representative spokeswoman of the peasant class, in a pretty central part of the County, may be taken as typical of the Shropshire folk-speech.

Betty was going in a Market-train from Hanwood to Shrewsbury, and while talking with her usual rapidity, was thus addressed by a man who was her fellow-traveller:—'W'y Missis, I should think as yo' mun a 'ad yore tongue īled [oiled] this mornin' afore yo' started.' 'No, indeed, Sir,' said Betty, 'I hanna, fur if it 'ad a bin īled it ŏŏd never a stopped. No danger!'

COMPROMISE GLOSSIC VERSION.

'Wi Mis·is, ei shud thing·k uz yoa mun u ad· yoa·r' tung·g ei·ld dhis maur'·nin ufoa·r' yoa staa·r'tid.' 'Noa indee·d Sur,' sed Bet·i, 'ei an·u fur' if it ad· u bin ei·ld it ŏŏd nev·ur' u stop·t. Noa· ·dei·njur'!'

ANALYTIC GLOSSIC VERSION.

'Wi'-Mis·i's, a'y-shu'd-thing·k u'z-y:oa mun-u'a'd· y:oa·u'r'-tung·g a'y·ld-dhis-maur'·ni'n u'f:oa·u'r'-y:oa-st:aa·r'ti'd.' 'N:oa indee·d-Su'r,' sed Be·ti', 'a'y·-a'n·u' fu'r-if-i't-a'd·-u'-bin-a'y·ld i't-ŏŏd-naev·u'r-u'-stop·t. N:oa ·da'y·nju'r'!'

DICTIONARIES CONSULTED AND QUOTED.

ASH, JOHN, *New and Complete Dictionary of the English Language.* 2 vols. London: 1775.

BAILEY, N., *Universal Etymological English Dictionary.* London: 1727; *id.* 1782.

BLOUNT, THOMAS, *Glossographia:* 'a Dictionary interpreting the Hard Words . . . now used in our refined English Tongue.' London: 1674.

BOSWORTH, REV. DR., *Compendious Anglo-Saxon Dictionary.* London: 1876.

BURGUY, G. F., *Glossaire Etymologique,* Aux xiie et xiiie siècles. Berlin: 1870.

CHAMBAUD, LOUIS M., *Dictionnaire françois-anglois,* corrigé et augmenté par lui et par M. J. B. ROBINET. Paris: 1776.

COLERIDGE, HERBERT, *Dictionary of the Oldest Words in the English Language,* A.D. 1250—1300. London: 1872.

Dictionarium Etymologicvm Latinvm. See **Querco** below.

HALLIWELL, JAMES ORCHARD, F.R.S., *Archaic and Provincial Dictionary.* 8*vo.* 3rd ed. 1855, and 8th ed. 1874.

HOTTEN, JOHN CAMDEN, *Slang Dictionary.* London: 1864.

JAMIESON, JOHN, D.D., *Etymological Dictionary of the Scottish Language.* Edinburgh: 1818.

MEADOWS, F. C., *New Italian and English Dictionary.* London: 1852.

PICK, DR. EDWARD, *French Etymological Dictionary*. London: 1869

Promptorium Parvulorum, Dictionarius Anglo-Latinus Princeps, *circa* A.D. 1440. ALBERT WAY, M.A. London: Camden Society, 1865.

QUEROO, THOMAS, DE SACRA, *Dictionarium Etymologicvm Latinvm*. *4to*. London: Imprinted by Felix Kingston for Andrew Crooke, 1648. This dictionary is useful for the old English words in its definitions.

RICHARDS, W., LL.D., *Welsh Pocket Dictionary*. London and Wrexham.

STRATMAN, DR. FRANCIS HENRY, *Old English Dictionary*, xiii., xiv., and xv. cent. Krefeld: 1867.

WAY, ALBERT, M.A. See *Promptorium Parvulorum*.

WEDGWOOD, HENSLEIGH, *English Etymology*. London: 1872.

WORCESTER, JOSEPH E., LL.D., *English Dictionary*. *4to*. London and Boston (U.S.): 1859.

WRIGHT, THOMAS, F.S.A., *Obsolete and Provincial English*. London: 1869.

CHIEF AUTHORITIES QUOTED.

The † shows that the work to which it is prefixed is either *Salopian* or near akin to the *Salopian Dialect*. See *Introduction*, pp. xvi, xvii.

† *Alexander and Dindimus*. See **Skeat**.

† *Alisaunder, K.* See *ibid.*

† Audelay, John, *The Poems of.* A specimen of the Shropshire Dialect, xv. cent. ed. J. O. Halliwell. Sm. 8*vo.* London: Percy Society, 1844.

Bible Word Book. See **Eastwood and Wright** (W. Aldis).

† Boteler, Sir Thomas, *Register of.* 'This Register embraces about eight years of the reign of Henry VIII., goes through that of Edward VI., takes in the whole of Queen Mary's, and four years of Queen Elizabeth's. . . . The Register was written in a clear, bold hand. It contained numerous entries of christenings and burials, commencing 26th November, 1538, and ending 20th September, 1562. It is believed that this valuable and interesting Register was destroyed in the calamitous fire that consumed the mansion of Sir Watkin Williams Wynn, at Wynnstay, in the year 1859.' The Rev. Charles Henry Hartshorne made extracts from the Register for private reference in 1840, but unfortunately 'in many instances modernized the spelling.' See below, **Hartshorne.**

Burns, Robert, *Works of.* Globe edition. London: 1873.

† *Byegones:* a Reprint from the columns of the *Oswestry Advertizer*, containing a good many notes on the Shropshire dialect. 1872—1878.

CHAUCER, GEOFFREY, *Canterbury Tales* (Text of Thomas Tyrwhitt). London: Routledge & Sons.

——— *Man of Lawes Tale.* See **Skeat.**

——— *Prioresses Tale.* See *ibid.*

——— *Prologue, &c.* See **Morris.**

† CHURCHYARD, THOMAS, *Poems of* (temp. Eliz., 1587). Ed. 1776, reprinted from ed. 1587 for Thos. Evans in the Strand.

EARLE, JOHN, M.A., *Philology of the English Tongue.* Oxford: 1871.

EASTWOOD, J., M.A., and WRIGHT, W. ALDIS, M.A., *Bible Word Book:* a Glossary of Old English Bible Words. London and Cambridge: 1866.

ENGLISH DIALECT SOCIETY, *Works* of the

† FARQUHAR, GEORGE, *The Recruiting Officer:* a Comedy. Second Edition. Corrected. London: Printed for Bernard Lintoth at the Cross Keys next Nando's Coffee House near Temple Bar [1705—6].

GAIRDNER, JAMES (of the Public Record Office). See *Paston Letters.*

GERARDE, JOHN, *Herball.* London, 1633, Adam Joice Norton and Richard Whitakers.

† GOUGH, RICHARD, *History of Myddle.* 1700—1701. (Facsimile reprint.) Shrewsbury: Adnitt and Naunton, 1875.

GROSE, FRANCIS, ESQ., F.A.S., *Provincial Dictionary,* with a Collection of Local Proverbs and Popular Superstitions. London: 1787. See **Pegge.**

† HARTSHORNE, REV. CHARLES HENRY, *Salopia Antiqua,* &c.; with a Glossary of Words used in the county of Salop. 8*vo.*, pp. xxii. and 640. London: J. W. Parker, 1841. The Glossary occupies pp. 299—622.

——— † Extracts from the Register of Sir Thomas Butler [Boteler], Vicar of Much Wenlock. Made for private reference, A.D. 1840. Tenby: R. Mason, printer, 1861.

Havelok the Dane. See **Skeat.**

HOLME, RANDLE, *Academy of Armory*. Folio. Printed for the Author, Chester, 1688.

HOOKER, SIR WILLIAM JACKSON, *British Flora*. 5th ed. London: 1842.

† *Inventorye*. Edm[d] Waring of Lea, Esq., deceased; taken and apprized in May 1[o] Caroli [1625]. At his howse called Ouldbury in the Parish of Bishop's Castle.—*Proceedings of the Society of Antiquaries of London*. Second Series, Vol. vi., No. iv., pp. 363—75.

Joseph of Arimathie. See **Skeat**.

Lancelot of the Laik. See **Skeat**.

† LANGLAND, WILLIAM, *Piers the Plowman* (1377 A.D.). See **Skeat**; also **Wright**.

LATIMER, BISHOP HUGH, *Seven Sermons before Edward VI.* (1549), and the *Sermon on the Ploughers* (18th Jan., 1549). London: Arber's Reprints, 1868—69.

MILTON, JOHN, *Poetical Works of*. London: W. Smith, 1840.

MORRIS, REV. DR. R., Chaucer's *The Prologue, The Knightes Tale, The Nonnes Prestes Tale*. 6th edition. Clarendon Press: 1875.

——— *Specimens of Early English* (A.D. 1298—1393) [Morris and Skeat].

——— *Historical Outlines of English Accidence*. 5th edition. London: 1876.

——— *Historical English Grammar*. 3rd edition. London: 1877.

NARES, ROBERT, M.A., F.R.S. (Ven. Archdeacon), *Glossary*. 4to. London: 1822.

Natural History. See **Wood**.

OLIPHANT, T. L. KINGTON, M.A., *Sources of Standard English*. London: 1873.

Owl and Nightingale. See **Stratmann**.

† *Palerne, William of*. See **Skeat**.

Paston Letters (A.D. 1422—1509). ed. Gairdner. 3 vols. London: Arber's Reprints, 1872—74—75.

PEGGE, SAMUEL, ESQ., F.S.A., *Supplement to the Provincial Glossary* of Francis Grose, Esq. London: 1814. See **Grose**.

Pierce the Ploughman's Crede. See **Skeat**; also **Wright**.

† *Piers the Plowman. Ibid.*

Proceedings of the Society of Antiquaries. See *Inventorye* above.

RAMSAY, ALLAN, *The Gentle Shepherd* (1725). ed. J. R. Edinburgh: 1875.

RAY, REV. JOHN, F.R.S., *Collection of English Proverbs*, and a Collection of English Words, &c. 4th edition. London: 1768.

Roister Doister. See **Udall**.

† *Salopia Antiqua.* See **Hartshorne**.

† *Salopian Shreds and Patches* (uniform with *Notes and Queries*); reprinted from *Eddowes' Shrewsbury Journal*. Contains a number of notes on the Shropshire dialect. 1874—78.

SHAKESPEARE, WILLIAM, *Works of.* Globe Edition. London: 1864.

SKEAT, REV. WALTER W., M.A., Edited by—

——— † *Alexander and Dindimus* (A.D. 1340—50, *circa*). E. E. T. S.

——— CHAUCER. *The Prioresses Tale and the Man of Lawes Tale*, &c. [Six-text ed.] Clarendon Press: 1874 and 1878.

——— *Havelok the Dane* (A.D. 1280, *circa*). E. E. T. S.

——— *Joseph of Arimathie* (A.D. 1350, *circa*). E. E. T. S.

——— † *K. Alisaunder* (A.D. 1340, *circa*). See below, *William of Palerne.*

——— *Lancelot of the Laik* (A.D. 1490—1500, *circa*). E. E. T. S.

——— *Pierce the Ploughman's Crede* (A.D. 1394, *circa*); to which is appended *God Spede the Plough* (A.D. 1500, *circa*). E. E. T. S.

——— † *Piers the Plowman*, Text A. (A.D. 1362), and *ditto*, Text B. (A.D. 1377). E. E. T. S.

——— *Specimens of Early English* (A.D. 1298—1393). See **Morris**.

——— *Specimens of English Literature* (A.D. 1394—1579). Clarendon Press: 1871.

SKEAT, REV. WALTER W., M.A., Edited by—

——— † *William of Palerne* (A.D. 1350, *circa*); to which is appended *K. Alisaunder*. See above. E. E. T. S.

SPEED, JOHN, *Theatre of the Empire of Great Britain*. London: Printed for Thomas Basset at the George in Fleet Street, and Richard Chiswel at the Rose and Crown in St. Paul's Churchyard. MDCLXXVI. The Maps of this work, pt. i., are of older date than the 'Tables of Towns,' &c.; they are of the year 1610.

SPENSER, EDMUND, *Complete Works of.* Globe Edition. London: 1877.

STRATMANN, DR. FRANCIS HENRY, *Owl and Nightingale* (xiii. cent.). Krefeld: 1868.

TRENCH, ARCHBISHOP, *The Study of Words*, 4th edition. London: 1853.

——— *English Past and Present*. London: 1855.

——— *Select Glossary* of English Words used Formerly in senses different from their Present. 2nd edition. London: 1859.

UDALL, NICHOLAS, *Roister Doister* (before A.D. 1553). London: Arber's Reprints, 1869.

WOOD, REV. J. G., M.A., F.L.S., *Illustrated Natural History*. 3 vols. London: 1863.

WRIGHT, THOMAS, M.A., F.R.S., *Early Vocabularies* (x.—xv. cent.) 2 vols. Privately printed for JOSEPH MAYER, ESQ., F.S.A., &c., 1857 and 1873.

——— † *Vision and Creed of Piers Ploughman*. 2 vols. London: 1856.

WRIGHT, W. ALDIS. See **Eastwood**.

TABLE OF ABBREVIATIONS.

adj., adjective.
adv., adverb.
A.S., Anglo-Saxon.
BUR., Burguy's *Glossaire.*
Cf., confer = compare.
CHAMB., Chambaud's *French Dictionary.*
COL., Coleridge's *Dictionary.*
conj., conjunction.
corr., correct = (Analytic Glossic).
Dan., Danish.
Dict. Etym. Lat., *Dictionarium Etymologicvm Latinvm.*
Du., Dutch.
E. D. S., English Dialect Society.
E. E. T. S., Early English Text Society.
emph., emphatic.
expl., expletive.
Fr., French.
Germ., German.
HAL., Halliwell's *Dictionary.*
Icel., Icelandic.
interj., interjection.
M. E., Middle English.
M. T., Miners' term.
N., Norse.
N. & Q., *Notes and Queries.*
obs., obsolete.
obsols., obsolescent.
O.Du., Old Dutch.
O.E., Old English.
O.Fr., Old French.
O.H., Germ., Old High German.
O.N., Old Norse.
part. adj., participial adjective.
part. past, participle past.
pec., peculiar [use].
phr., phrase.
PICK, Pick's *French Dictionary.*
Piers Pl., *Piers the Plowman.*
pl., plural.
P. Pl. Cr., *Pierce the Ploughman's Crede.*
prep., preposition.
pret., preterite.
Prompt. Parv., *Promptorium Parvulorum.*
pron., pronoun.
sb., substantive.
sl., slang.
sl.? slangish.
STRAT., Stratman's *Dictionary.*
unemph., unemphatic.
v. a., verb active.
var. pr., variety of pronunciation.
v. n., verb neuter.
W., Welsh.
WAY, Notes in *Prompt. Parv.*
WEDG., Wedgwood's *English Etymologies.*
WR., Wright's *Provincial Dict.*
WR. vocabs., Wright's *Early Vocabularies.*

SHROPSHIRE WORD-BOOK.

A GLOSSARY OF

ARCHAIC AND PROVINCIAL WORDS, ETC.

USED IN THE COUNTY.

A [u' *and* aa], (1) *pron. 3rd pers. sing. and plur.* he, they. See **Grammar Outlines**, *Pronouns.* '*A* wuz all of a dither.' 'Whad wun *a* doin' theer?' Mr. Oliphant, in his *Sources of Standard English*, p. 192, says that 'The Handlyng Synne' [Robert of Brunne, 1303] should be compared with another poem due to the same shire [Rutland], and written five hundred and sixty years later; I mean Mr. Tennyson's 'Northern Farmer.' Some of the old forms are there repeated, especially the *a*, which stands first in the following rimes:

'He ys wurþy to be shent,
For *a* doþ aȝens þys comaundment.'—p. 84.

And in a note, he adds: 'The *he* had become *ha* and then *a*; this is one of the then new forms we have rejected. Mrs. Quickly used it.' See *Hen. V.*, II. iii. The Shropshire *a* for *they* represents, according to Mr. Oliphant, the old A.S. *hi*. *They* is a Scandinavian innovation.

(2) [u'], more emphatically ['aa]. See **Grammar Outlines**, *verb* **Have**. 'We mun *a* this oven fettled afore we putten another batch in.' '. . . he sayd it was Harry Gray that thei talkyd of; and my Lord sayd, "I was besy with jn this fewe days to *a* maryd hym to a jantyllwoman jn Norfolke that schall have iiij c. marc to hyr mariage."'—*Paston Letters*, A.D. 1454, vol. i. p. 302.

(3) [u'], prepositional prefix to nouns, adjectives, and verbal nouns in *-ing*. It is equivalent to *at*, *in*, *on*, or *on the*; and represents the A.S. *æt*, at, or *on*, used in composition for *in*, *on*, *upon*.

AARON'S-ROD [ae·r'unz r'od·], *sb. Solidago Virgaúrea*, common Golden rod.—WHITCHURCH, *Tilstock*.

ABERE [u'bee·ur'], *v. a.* to bear; endure; tolerate.—ELLESMERE. 'The missis toud me I wuz to sarve them pigs an' I conna-d-*abere* it.' A.S. *aberan*, to bear, suffer.

ABIDE [u'beid·], *v. a.* to brook; to suffer; to put up with.—WEM. Qy. com. 'I canna-d-*abide* them under-'onded ways.'

'. . . would write also to my Lord of Oxford, but that he is so vexed in spirit "in thys trouble seson," that at times he cannot *abide* the signing and sealing of a letter.'—*Paston Letters*, A.D. 1450, vol. i., p. 168.

'I cannot *abide* swaggerers.'—2 *Hen. IV.*, II. iv. 118.

Icel. *bíða*, to wait; endure; suffer. Cf. A.S. *âbídan*, from *bídan*, to wait.

ABOVE-A-BIT, *adv.* to an excessive degree. Com. ''E fund as 'e'd got all the work to do 'isself, so 'e off wuth 'is smock an' went into it *above-a-bit.*'

ABROAD [u'br'aud·], *adv.*, *pec.* away; in some other direction. —PULVERBATCH. 'That peckled 'en's al'ays about the door ööth 'er chickens; I wish 'er'd tak' 'em *abroad* awilde.'

ABRON [ai·br'un], *adj.*, *obs.* auburn.—PULVERBATCH. ''Er wuz a sweet pretty babby, ööth nice *abron* ar, but too cute to live.'

'A lustie courtier, whose curled head
With *abron* locks was fairly furnished.'
Hall., *Sat.* VI. 111, S. 5, in WR.

ABUNDATION [u'bun·dai·'sh'n], *sb.*, *var. pr.* abundance. Com.

ABUSEFUL [u'beus·ful], *adj.*, *var. pr.* abusive.—PULVERBATCH; WEM.

ACHERN [ach·ur'n], *sb.* an acorn.—CLEE HILLS; WEM; ELLESMERE. 'We bin gweïn after *acherns.*' *Glans*, an acharne, Vocab. Harl. MS. 1002. *Accharne*, *okecorne*, Ort. V. In the curious inventory of the effects of Sir Simon Burley, who was beheaded 1388, are enumerated 'deux pairs des pater nosters de aumbre blanc, l'un countrefait de Atchernes, l'autre rounde.'—MS. in the possession of Sir Thomas Phillipps.—WAY, in *Prompt. Parv.*, p. 6. A.S. *æcern.*

ACHERNING [ach·ur'nin], *part.* gathering acorns.—CLEE HILLS; WEM; ELLESMERE. 'The childern bin gwun *achernin.*'

ACKER [ak·ur'], *v. n.* to tremble with passion, to chatter.—PULVERBATCH; WEM. ''Is tith far *ackered* togither' = his teeth fairly chattered. W. *achreth*, a trembling.

ACKERN [ak·ur'n], *sb.*, *var. pr.* an acorn.—SHREWSBURY; PULVERBATCH.

'. . . *hakernes* & þe hasel-notes,
& oþer frut to þe fulle: þat in forest growen.'
William of Palerne, l. 1811.

Accorne, or archarde, frute of the oke.—*Glans.* *Prompt. Parv.* Cf. **Achern.**

ACKERNING [ak·ur'nin], *part.* gathering acorns.—SHREWSBURY; PULVERBATCH. 'Bin 'ee gweïn *ackernin'?*'

ACKERSPIRE [ak·ur'speir'], *v. n.* to sprout, to germinate abnormally. Said of potatoes.—ELLESMERE; WEM. 'I doubt the tittoes 'll *ackerspire* wuth this wet.' Potatoes are *ackerspired*, when after a dry season heavy rain sets in, and the super-abundant moisture causes them to put forth new tubers, instead of increasing them in size, thus spoiling the growth. Cf. *ackerspier* in RAY's 'North Country Words,' B. 15, E. D. S.

ACQUAINTANCE [u'kwein·tuns], *sb.*, *pec.* a 'fiancé-ée.'—MUCH WENLOCK. 'Molly, do you know that Miss F—— is going to be married?' 'Well, sir, I thought I sid 'er ŏŏth an *acquaintance*.'

ADE [aid·], *sb.* a reach in the Severn. This term is 'applied by navigators of the Severn to reaches where there are eddies in the river, as Sweney [*sic*] Ade, Preen's Ade, &c.' See *The Severn Valley*, by J. Randall, 1862, pp. 69-70. *Ade* may be perhaps A.S. *ed*, which as a prefix means anew, again, as the Latin *re*, and A.S. *ea*, running water, a river.

ADLAND [ad·lund], same as **Adlant** below.—NEWPORT.

ADLANT [ad·lunt], *sb.* the border of land left at the ends of the furrows for turning the plough on. The headland. Com. To 'turn on a mighty narrow *adlant*' is a proverbial saying expressive of a very narrow escape, as from peril of death or from calamity. 'To plough the *adlants* afore the buts' is to begin a matter at the wrong end. Thus a man who asked the father's permission to propose to his daughter was said to have made a mistake, 'ploughed the *adlants* afore the buts!'

A-DONE [u'dun·], *v. a.* leave off; have done. Com. '*A-done* now w'en I spake.' Cf. **A** (2).

AFEARD [u'fee·ur'd], *adj.* afraid. Com. 'Yo needna be *afeard* o' gweïn through the leasow, they'n mogged the cow as 'iled poor owd Betty Mathus.' A.S. *áfǽran*, to terrify.

> 'For be he lewed man or elles lered.
> He not how sone that he shal ben *afered*.'
>
> CHAUCER, *C. T.*, l. 12218.

> 'And, broþer, be þou nouȝt *aferd* ·; by thenk in thyn herte,
> þouȝ þou conne nouȝt þe Crede · kare þou no more.'
>
> *P. Pl. Cr.*, l. 130.

> 'I have not scaped drowning to be *afeard* now of your four legs.'
>
> *Tempest*, II. ii. 63.

A-ferde (or trobelid, K. H. P.). *Territus, perterritus* (*turbatus, perturbatus*, K. P.). Forby, in enumerating among the provincialisms of Norfolk the word *afeard*, noticed that formerly it was not, as at present, synonymous with afraid.

> 'This wif was not afered ne affrayed.'—*Chaucer.*

The Harl. MS. indeed, renders both aferde and afrayed by *territus*, but the reading of the King's MS. agreeing with the printed editions, seems preferable. Aferde or trobelid, *turbatus perturbatus.*—*Prompt. Parv. and Notes.*

AFORE [u'foa·ur']. (1) *prep.* before; in front of. Com. 'Theer wuz the child right *afore* the 'orse an' nobody nigh, er dunna know whad fear is.' A.S. *æt-fore*, before.

'They him saluted, standing far *afore*.'
SPENSER, *Faery Q.*, B. I. canto x. 49.

(2) *adv.* before; in time past. Com. ''E's bin theer *afore* I know, so dunna tell me.'

'*Ste.* . . . He shall taste of my bottle: if he have never drunk wine *afore*, it will go near to remove his fit.'
Tempest, II. ii. 78.

AFTERCLAP [af·tur'klap·'], *sb.* an unpleasant outcome of some affair supposed to have been set at rest.—PULVERBATCH.—Qy. com. 'It's al'ays best be carful an' sen' some one as knows thar business an' then theer's no *afterclaps*.'

'For the assaults of the devil be craftie to make us put our trust in such armour, hee will feine himselfe to flie; but then we be most in jeopardie. For he can give us an *afterclap* when we least weene, that is, suddenly returne unawares to us, and then he giveth us an *afterclap* that overthroweth us, this armour deceyveth us.'—*Latimer's Sermons, in* WR.

AFTERINGS [af·tur'inz], *sb.* the last milk drawn from a cow. —PULVERBATCH. Cf. **Drippings**.

AFTER-MATH [af·tur'math·'], *sb.* a second growth of grass after the hay crop.—NEWPORT; ELLESMERE. A.S. *æfter*, after; and A.S. base, *maδ*, cognate with Lat. *metore*, to mow. Cf. **Edgrow**, also **Lattermath**.

AGATE [u'gait·], *adv.* this term expresses doing or beginning to do a thing; and is generally used with the verb 'get,' but not always. —WEM; WHITCHURCH; *Cheshire Border*. 'Whad han yo bin *agate* on?' 'Yo can get *agate* o' that job, as soon as yo'n a mind.'

'I pray you, Memory, set him *agate* again.'
O. P., v. 180, in WR.

Ash has the word, which he calls *local*. 'On the way; in a state of motion.' A gate = on gate, on the way.

AGE [aij·], *v. n.* to grow old in appearance. Com. 'The maister's beginnin' to *age* oncommon fast, an' 'e inna whad yo' met'n call so owd, about fifty, or fifty sa'one.' O.Fr. *aage;* Mod. Fr. *âge*.

AGEN [u'gen·], (1) *prep.* against. Com. ''E fat 'im a girder as sent 'im o'er, right *agen* the bonk.'

'He gripen sone a bulder ston,
And let it fleye, ful good won,
Agen þe dore, þat it to-rof.'
Havelok the Dane, l. 1792.

(2) Opposite to. Com. 'Oud it up *agen* the light an' then we shan be able to see w'eer the faut is.'

'On his rith shuldre sw[iþ]e brith,
Brithter þan gold *ageyn* þe lith.'
Havelok the Dane, l. 2141.

(3) Contiguous to. Com. 'Lave that bouk *agen* the pump w'eer I pŭt it.'

(4) Averse to; opposed to. Com. ''E wuz *agen* the weddin' altogether.'

(5) By; towards. Com. 'If I start now I shall get theer *agen* the ōnder.'

(6) *adv. conj.* by the time that; when. Com. 'Mind an' 'ăve the oven whot *agen* I come wham.'

(7) *adv.* at a future time. Com. 'I hanna got it now, but I'll gie it yo' *agen.*' A.S. *agen; commonly, ongeán;* against.

AGG, EÄG, EËG, EGG [ag·], PULVERBATCH. [ĭ'ag· *or* ĭ'eg·], CLEE HILLS. [eg·], WEM; *v. a.* to incite, to provoke. 'Joe's as quiet a fellow as ever wuz sid; 'e didna want to fight, on'y they *agged* 'im on.'

AGWINE [u'gwei·n *corr.* u'gwa'yn], *part.* a-going.—CHURCH STRETTON. 'Bin yo *agwine?*'

AID [aid·], *sb.* a gutter cut across the 'buts' of ploughed lands to carry off the water from the 'reans.'—CHURCH STRETTON; CLEE HILLS.

AIDLE [aid·l], *adj., obs.,? var. pr.* unproductive, rotten; addled; said of eggs.—PULVERBATCH; WORTHEN. 'I've 'ad despert poor luck ŏŏth my 'en's this time. I set three ŏŏth duck eggs an' two ŏŏth thar own; an' three parts on 'em wun *aidle.*'

AIDLED [ai·dld], *part. adj., var. pr.* same as 'aidle.'—CLUN. See **Nex' to nex'**. A.S. *ádl,* diseased, corrupted, putrid.

AIGLES [aig·lz], (1) *sb. pl., obs.?* spangles; tinsel ornaments of a showman's dress.—PULVERBATCH. 'Han 'ee sin Bessey Pugh sence 'er's comen back throm Lunnun; 'er's got a bonnet as shines all o'er like *aigles* on a showman.'

(2) *sb. pl., obs.* scintillations which appear on the surface of iron pots when removed from the fire. They are supposed to be Lamillæ of Salts of Iron, caused by the decomposition of the pots by the gases from the fire.—WORTHEN. 'Mind w'eer yo' put'n that marmint aw'ilde the *aigles* bin on it.'

(3) *sb. pl.* icicles.—WEM; ELLESMERE. 'It must a bin freezin 'ard i' the neet, theer's *aigles* o' ice 'angin' from the aisins.' Cf. *agglot acus, Prompt. Parv.,* and *aglet* in WEDG. Fr. *aguillette.*

AILZE [ail·z], *sb., obs.?* form of 'Alice.'—PULVERBATCH.

AINT [ain·t], *sb., var. pr.* aunt.—WORTHEN. Cf. **Naint.**

AISIN [aiz·in], *sb.* the eaves of a house. Com. 'Them Jack-squailers bin buildin' under the *aisin* agen, I see.' The singular and plural forms of this word are used indiscriminately for 'eaves;' though in some districts *aisins* has a distinct meaning as shewn below. Cf. **Easings.**

AISINS, *sb. pl.* the drops of water which fall from the eaves or 'aisin.'—SHREWSBURY, *Uffington;* NEWPORT, *Shiffnal.* 'Mother, 'ere's our Tum standin' under the *aisins* o' purpose to get wet.' 'Oud yore clack, I amma, for theer's none spottin'.'

AISIN-SPARROW [aiz·in spa'r'u'], *sb. Parus domesticus,* the common House-sparrow.—SHREWSBURY; PULVERBATCH; WEM.

AISTER [ais·tur'], (1) *sb., obsols.* the brick-work forming the back of old-fashioned fire-places, against which the polished fire-irons generally hang: sometimes it is 'spattled' or else picked out with white lines on a black ground. See **Spattled** (2).—PULVERBATCH; ELLESMERE. 'W'y look 'ow yo'n collowed yore face! as if yo'd newly comen down the chimley and kissed the *aister*.' Cf. **Backaister.** 'As black as the *aister*,' is a phrase employed to express any sooty, grimy appearance. Lambarde in his Perambulation of Kent, ed. 1596, p. 562, says that this word was in his time nearly obsolete in Kent, but that it was retained in 'Shropshyre and other parts.' See for this, *aister* in Hal., ed. 1855. O.Fr. *astre*, *aistre*, foyer; cheminée. Mot d'origine inconnue.—BUR.

(2) *sb. var. pr.* Easter.—PULVERBATCH; LUDLOW.

AITCH [aich·], *sb.* a paroxysm of suffering, as in cases of intermittent disorder; a turn of illness. Qy. com. 'They tell'n me as poor owd Matty Roberts is mighty bad.' 'Aye 'er's uset to these *aitches* every spring an' fall.' *Fainting-aitches* are attacks of faintness. *Hot and cold aitches*, alternations of heat and chill in feverish maladies.

> '"Now swete," seide alisaundrine · "seie me in what wise
> þat þat *hache* þe haldes · & how it þe takes?"
> "I-wisse," seide william · "i wol it nouȝt layne,
> sum-time it hentis me wiþ hete · as hot as ani fure,
> but quicliche so kene a cold · comes þer-after."'
>
> *William of Palerne*, l. 905.

A.S. *æce*, ache; pain; *ece*, *æce*, an unpleasant feeling; an ache.

AITHER [ai·dhur'], *pron.* either.—LUDLOW; NEWPORT. Qy. com. A.S. *ægþer*, either.

> 'Chese on *aither* hand,
> Whether the lever ware
> Sink or stille stande.'
>
> *Sir Tristrem*, p. 154, in HAL.

AITREDAN [a'y·tr'i'dan·'], PULVERBATCH; CLEE HILLS, *sb.* a mad-cap frolic; a foolish prank. 'I warrand yo' bin off now on some wild *aitredan* or other.'

ALD [:aul·d *and* :aud], *v. a.* to hold.—CORVE DALE.

> 'Curatus resident thai schul be,
> And *ald* houshold oponly.'
>
> JOHN AUDELAY'S *Poems*, p. 33.

ALE [ail·], ale. Com. [ai·h'l], LUDLOW, *Burford*. [eel·; yi'·u'l], NEWPORT. [yae·l], CORVE DALE; BRIDGNORTH. [yu'l·], CORVE DALE.

ALE-HOOF [ail·oof·'], *sb. Nepéta Glechoma*, ground ivy.—CORVE DALE; BRIDGNORTH. 'Ground Iuy,' says Gerarde, 'is commended against the humming noyse and ringing sound of the eares being put into them;' as 'a remedie against the Sciatica or ache in the huckle bone,' and for 'any griefe whatsoeuer in the eyes.' After relating these and other 'vertues' of this 'herbe,' he goes on to say: 'The women of our Northerne parts, especially about Wales and Cheshire, do tunne the herbe *ale-hoof* into their ale; but the reason thereof I know not: notwithstanding without all controuersie it is most singular against the griefes aforesaid: being tunned vp in ale and drunke, it also purgeth the head from rheumaticke humors flowing from the brain.' —*Herball*, Bk. II., p. 856.

ALE-POSSET [ail·pos·i't], *sb.* milk curdled by pouring 'old beer' into it when at boiling point. The whey strained from the curd, spiced, sweetened, and taken 'piping hot,' is considered a specific in cases of cold.—PULVERBATCH. Qy. com. 'Jack, you had better take care of that cold, I'll make you an *ale-posset* to night.' 'Thank yo', Missis, that'll tak' car o' me, nod the coud.' W. *poset*, curdled milk.

ALE-SCORE [ail·skoa·ur'], *sb.* a debt at the ale-house.—SHREWSBURY; PULVERBATCH; ELLESMERE. Qy. com. 'Tum's a cliver workman an' gets good money, but agen 'e's paid 'is *ale-score* every wik theer inna much lef' to tak' wham.'

'*Jack Cade.* There shall be no money; all shall eat and drink on my *score*.'—2 *K. Henry VI.*, IV. ii. 80.

'*Score* a pint of bastard in the half-moon.'
1 *K. Henry IV.*, II. iv. 29.

According to Wedgwood, *score* was originally a notch, then from the custom of keeping count by cutting notches on a stick, account, reckoning, number, the specific number of twenty as being the number of notches it was convenient to make on a single stick; when that number was complete the piece on which they were made was cut off [Fr. *taillée*] and called a tally.

'*Jack Cade.* And whereas, before, our forefathers had no other books but the *score* and the *tally*, thou hast caused printing to be used.'—2 *K. Henry VI.*, IV. v. 38.

A.S. *sceran*, to shear; to cut; *pp. gescoren*, shorn.

ALHALONTID [u'lal·untid], *sb.*, *obs.* the time of the 'Festival of All-Saints,' All-hallows.—WORTHIN.

'Men shulle fynde but fewe roo-bukkys whan that they be passed two ȝeer that thei ne have mewed hure heedys by *alhalwentyd*.'—*MS. Bodl.* 546, in HAL.

'Set trees at *alhallontide* and command them to prosper; set them after Candlemas and entreat them to grow.'—RAY'S *Proverbs*, p. 40.

ALL-ALONG [aul·u'lung·'], *phr.* from the first.—LUDLOW. ''E's bin comin' *all alung*.'

ALL-ALONG-ON, *prep.* owing to; in consequence of. Com. 'James France ticed the poor chap; it wuz *all alung on* 'im as 'e wuz i' the Public.'

'Bot if it is *along on* me
Of þat ȝe vnauanced be,
Or elles it be long on ȝov,
The soþe schal be proued nov.'
JOHN GOWER (A.D. 1393), *Confessio Amantis*, Bk. V.
Specim. Early Eng., xx. l. 55.

A.S. *gelang*, along of, owing to. Cf. **Along of.**

ALL AS IS IS THIS, *phr.* it comes to this.—CLUN; *Herefd. Border.* 'Now Tum, *all as is is this;* if yo' dunna stop a-wham an' be tidy I mun lave yo'! so now yo' knowen.'

ALL AS ONE, *phr.* all the same. Com. 'It's *all as one* to me.'

ALL-A-YOCK, *phr.* all awry.—WELLINGTON.

ALLELUIA [al·i'loo·'yu'], *sb. Genista tinctoria,* dyer's green-wood. —PULVERBATCH. See **Cuckoo's meat.**

ALL OF A POP, *phr.* swampy. 'That theer end o' the yord's *all of a pop* wuth las' neet's rain.'—WEM.

ALL OF A QUOB, *phr.* this expression, often used when speaking of boggy land, is sometimes also employed to denote that peculiar condition in the body of a calf or sheep which has been struck, *i.e.* died of a kind of apoplectic fit, where the extravasated blood can be felt under the skin by pressure of the hand on the parts affected. See **Quob.**

ALL ONE, *phr.* same as **All as one.** Com. The phrase 'it is all one to me' is seen in its earliest shape, *al me is an,* in the *Legend of St. Margaret* (A.D. 1200, *circa*), p. 5, E. E. T. S.: *Sources of Standard English,* p. 116.

ALL ON END, *phr.* in confusion; disorder.—LUDLOW. 'Them things bin *all on end* agen, I see.'

ALONG [u'lung·], *adv.* to send anything 'along' is to send it home, or to some place named.—CHURCH STRETTON. Qy. com. 'Shall I send the mutton *alung* now, ma'am?'

ALONG OF, same as **All along on.** Com.

> '*Her.* You, mistress, all this coil is *long of* you.'
>
> *Mid. Night's Dream,* III. ii. 339.

AMAISTER [u'mais·tur'], *v. a., obsols.* to teach.—CLUN, *Herefd. Border.* An old man near Leintwardine, speaking of his schoolmaster, said, ''E used to *amaister* me, Sir.' The term is now [1876] rarely heard.

> 'For he may mede *amaistrye* . . . .'
>
> *Piers Pl.,* Text B. 11, l. 147.

> '. . . . cesse shal we neuere
> Til mede be þi wedded wyf · þorw wittis of vs alle.
> For we haue Mede *amaistried* · with owre mery speche.'
>
> *Idem.* l. 152.

AMEN-CLERK, *sb., obs.* a parish clerk. Pegge, under 'clerk,' *Anecdotes of the English Language,* p. 318, says, 'Called *amen-clerk* in some places, and in Essex *church-clerk.*' It may be inferred that the term 'amen-clerk' was used in one place, at any rate in Shropshire, from the following entry in the Parish Register of Hopton Castle:—

> 'Anno Domi, 1636.
> 'Richardus Beb *Amenclericus* sepultus maij primo.'

AMPLE [am·pl], *adj., pec.* complete, perfect.—WEM. 'It wuz all in *ample* order agen they comen back.' Cf. **Imple.**

AMPOT [am·pu't], *sb.* a hamper.—SHREWSBURY; PULVERBATCH; WORTHEN; ELLESMERE. Qy. com. 'Poor Dick ŏŏd think it a poor Chris'mas if 'e didna 'ăve 'is *ampot;* I al'ays start it toërt New y's tit' = towards New-year's-tide.

AN' [an·], *conj.* and. Com. A.S. *and.*

'. . . . gode lawes.
He dede-maken, *an* ful wel holden.'—*Havelok the Dane*, l. 29.

ANCIENT [ain·shunt], *adj.* precocious, wise-like; said of children. Com. 'Patty wuz a mighty nice little wench, 'er went about things so stiddy an' *ancient*.' Of such children it is frequently observed that they are 'too *ancient* to live.'

ANCLER [angk·lur'], *sb.* an ancle. Com. 'The Maister's bin laid up above a wik ööth a kench in 'is *ancler*, an they sen as it 'll be a wik or nine days lunger afore 'e'll be about agen.' '*Talus* ancleow' occurs in *Archbp. Ælfric's Vocabulary*, x cent., and Mr. Wright says that 'the word *ancleow* continued in use in the English language till the fifteenth century.' See Wr. Vocabs., vol. i. p. 44. *Ancler* is probably a corruption of this old form. A.S. *ancle*, *ancleo*, an ancle.

ANDIRONS [an·di'unz], *sb.pl.*, *obsols.* ornamental iron 'uprights' placed at each end of the open hearth in old houses, serving as rests for the two iron bars, which meeting at an obtuse angle in the centre of the hearth, support the logs of the wood fire.—CLUN. *Andirons*, or, as they are quite as often called, *andogs*, may still [1875] be seen in use, though there are but few examples of them remaining.

'1447, item a pare of *andirons*.'—*Parish Accounts* of Ludlow. 'One paire of *landirons* headed with brass.'—*Inventory* . . . Owlbury Manor House, Bishop's Castle, 1625.

'. . . . her *andirons*—
I had forgot them—were two winking Cupids
Of silver, each on one foot standing, nicely
Depending on their brands.'—*Cymbeline*, II. iv. 88.

O.Fr. *landier*. *Landiron* shews the Fr. article prefixed. In the Fr. *landier*, the *l* also stands for *le*. Cf. **Cobbits**.

ANDOGS [andok·s], *sb. pl.*, *obsols.* same as **Andirons**.—CLUN. For some interesting remarks on *andirons* and *andogs*, see Hal.

ANEEND [u'neen·d], same as **Anind**.—NEWPORT.

ANEW [u'noo·], same as **Anow**.—PULVERBATCH. Qy. com.

'On kneis he faucht, felle Inglismen he slew;
Till hym thar socht may fechtaris than *anew*.'
HENRY THE MINSTREL (A.D. 1461, *circa*), *Wallace*, Bk. I.
Specim. Eng. Lit., vi. l. 324.

ANIGH [u'nei·], *adv.* near.—NEWPORT; WEM. 'The doctor never come *anigh*.'

ANIND [u'nind·], *adv.* on end; upright.—PULVERBATCH. 'The mar aived [heaved] 'er two for' fit i' the ar an' stud *anind* bout uprit,—'er wuz that frangy.'

ANOTHER GUESS SORT [u'nudh·ur'gis·sor't], *phr.* a different sort; generally taken in the sense of 'better.'—PULVERBATCH. 'Ah! the poor oud Missis wuz *another gis-sort* o' body to 'er daughter-law, 'er'd al'ays summat to 'elp out a poor family, but this 'as nuthin to spar throm 'er finery.' Wright says in his *Prov. Dict.* 'another guess' was a word in common use in the latter half of the seventeenth century.

'H'as been a student in the Temple this three years, *another ghess* fellow than this, I assure you.'—*Durfey. Madam Fickle*, 1682.

ANOW [u'nou·], *adj.* plural form of 'enough.'—SHREWSBURY; PULVERBATCH. 'Han yo' done *anow* o' tatoes? Yo' know'n as theer's the jiner an' 'is lad for dinner.'

> 'He kest the bor doun hawes *anowe*,
> And com himself doun bi a bowe.'
>
> *Sevyn Sages*, 921, in HAL.

> 'Servile letters *anow*.'
>
> MILTON, A.D. 1644. *Areopagitica*, p. 40.

A.S. *genóh*, sufficient. According to Mr. Oliphant, *genóh* gave place to *innoh* about A.D. 1120. Forty years later, about 1160, the combination 'oh' began to change to that of 'ou,' and *innoh* became *inou*. See *Sources of Standard English*, pp. 71, 80. Cf. **Anew.**

ANTY-TUMP [an·ti'tump·'], *sb.* an ant-hill.—CLEE HILLS. ''E raved an' tore like a bŭll at a *anty-tump*.'

ANUNST, ANUNGST [u'nun·st]. Com. [u'nungst], OSWESTRY. *prep.* opposite to; against. Generally used in combination with the word 'right.' 'If yo'n follow the rack alung that green leazow, yo'n see a stile right *anunst* yo', an' theer's a fŭt-road taks yo' straight to 'abberley.'

> 'And right *anenst* him a dog snarling-*er*.'
>
> BEN JONSON (A.D. 1610), *Alchymist*, Act II.

Anunst seems to be merely a variety of *anenst*, which, though recorded by Ash as 'obsolete,' still obtains in several dialects. A.S. *anemn* = anefen, which see in STRAT. Cf. **Right forenungst.**

ANVILE [anvei·l], *sb., var. pr.* an anvil.—CHURCH STRETTON. A.S. *anfilt*, an anvil.

APPARN [ap·ur'n], *sb.* an apron. Com. 'Poor owd Anna wuz a tidy ŏŏman, yo' never sid'n 'er ŏŏth a dirty cap or *apparn*.'

> '. . . . And therewith to wepe
> She made, and with her *napron* feir and white ywash
> She wyped soft her eyen for teris that she outlash.'
>
> CHAUCER, *Beryn*, *Prol.* 31, in WEDG.

O.Fr. *naperon*, grande nappe.—ROQUEFORT. O.Fr. *nape*, nappe; de *mappa*, avec changement de *m* en *n*.—BUR. *Mappula*, bearm-clað *vel* rægl. *Archbp. Ælfric's Vocabulary*, x cent. in Wr. Vocabs., vol. i. p. 26.

Barmeclothe or naprun, *Limas*. The Medulla explains *limas* to be '*vestis que protenditur ab umbilico usque ad pedes, quâ utuntur servi coci et femine. Anglice*, barm cloth.'—*Prompt. Parv. and Notes.*

APPARNTLE [ap·ur'ntl], *sb., obs.?* an apron-ful.—PULVERBATCH. 'W'eer'n'ee bin laisin', Peggy? Yo'n got a good burn.' 'I' the paas'ns piece; theer wuz pretty pickin', I've got whad yo' sin, an' a good *apparntle* o' short ears, as Jack's took wham.' Cf. **Hantle.**

APPLE-FOOT [ap·l-fut·], *sb.* an apple pasty or 'turn-over.'—PULVERBATCH; WEM. The plural form of the term is 'applefit,' but it is a stroke of rustic wit to call them 'crab-toes,' more especially when sugar has been sparingly used, and the apples in them are sour. They are often given to 'the men' for their 'bait.' 'Now, Dick, bin yo' gwein to get any bayȳe?' 'W' a'n 'ee got?' '*Apple fŭt*.' 'I think it's 'bout time to lave off them *crab-toes*, now theer's a wur [*hoar*] frost o' the groun'.'

APRICOCK [ai·pr'i'kok'], *sb.*, *obs.*? an apricot.—PULVERBATCH.

> 'Feed him with *apricocks* and dewberries.'
>
> *Mids. Night's Dream*, III. i. 169.

'Apricot,' says Mr. Wedgwood, was 'formerly *apricock*, agreeing with Lat. *præcoqua* or *præcocia*. They were considered by the Romans a kind of peach, and were supposed to take their name from their ripening earlier than the ordinary peach.'

AR [aa·r'], (1) *sb.* air. Com. ''Ow bin 'ee, ma'am?' said old A—— 'Better, thank you, since I came into this sweet Shropshire air.' 'I'm mighty glad to 'ear yo' say so, ma'am, it's right good owd fashioned *ar*, this is.' John Speed (A.D. 1676), in his *Shropshyre Described*, says, 'Wholsom is the air, delectable and good, yeilding the spring and the autumn, seed-time and harvest, in a temperate condition, and affordeth health to the inhabitants in all seasons of the year.' —*Theatre of the Empire of Great Britain*, Bk. I. ch. xxxvii. p. 71.

(2) *sb.* a hare. Com. Cf. **Yare** (1).

ARGUE [aar'·geu], *sb.* same as 'argy' (2).—WEM.

ARGUFY [aar'geufie·], *v. n.* to argue. Com. 'It's no use yo' to *argufy*, for yo'n never mak me believe to the contrairy.'

ARGY [aa·r'gi'], (1) *v. n.* to argue; to discuss persistently. Com. 'It dunna si'nify talkin'; I 'ate to 'ear folks *argy* throm mornin' till night about nuthin'.'

(2) *sb.* an argument; a contentious discussion pertinaciously carried on. Com. 'We 'ad'n a fine *argy* 'bout it, 'im an' me.'

(3) [aar'·gi'], *sb.* an embankment made to protect low-lying meadows on Severn side from the river floods.—SHREWSBURY. Mr. Hartshorne says, 'an embankment between Melverley and Llanymynech,' made to resist the overflowings of the Severn, was known as 'the *argy*.'—*Salopia Antiqua*, p. 306. A place near Kinnersley—a raised bank with a plantation of poplars and other trees—having a small brook—the 'strine' on one side, and a ditch on the other—is called by the people of that neighbourhood 'the *argy*.' W. *argae*, a stoppage; a dam.

ARLY [aa·r'li'], *adv.* early.—SHREWSBURY; WEM. Qy. com.

> 'Quhen that the brycht and fresch illumynare
> Uprisith *arly* in his fyre chare.'
>
> *Lancelot of the Laik*, Prol., l. 4.

A.S. *ǽrlíc*, early. Cf. **Yarly**.

ARN [aa·r'n], *v. a.* to earn.—SHREWSBURY; WEM. Qy. com. 'Whad bin'ee comen wham so *arly* fur? Yo' hanna *arned* yore money I'm sartin.'

> 'Fore he wyll drynke more on a dey
> Than thou cane lyghtly *arne* in twey.'
>
> *MS. Ashmole*, 61, f. 23, in HAL.

Cf. **Yarn**.

ARNESS [aa·r'ni's]; same as **Earnest,** q. v. WEM. 'Arneste or hanselle or ernest,' *Strena; Prompt. Parv.* W. *ernes.* Cf. **Hansel.**

ARNINS [aa·r'ninz], *sb. pl.* earnings. Com.

ARPIT [aa·r'pit], *adj., obsols.* quick; ready; precocious.—PULVERBATCH; CRAVEN ARMS; CHURCH STRETTON; CLEE HILLS. ''Er wuz sich a mighty *arpit* little wench, I never thought 'er'd live; it's sildom as they dun, w'en a bin so cute.' *Arpit* = M.E. *orped. Orpud, Audax; Prompt. Parv.* Cf. **Ancient.**

ARRAND [ar'·und], *sb.* a message; a commission; an errand. Com. 'W'eer's Bill?' 'Gwun a *narrand* for 'is Gran' mother.'

'One of the four and twenty qualities of a knave is to stay long at his *arrand*.'—*Howell's English Proverbs*, p. 2, ed. 1660, in HAL. A.S. *ǽrende*, a message; commission. See **N** in **Grammar Outlines** (*consonants*).

ARRANTS [ar'·unts], (1) *sb.* plural form of 'arrand' with permutation of *d* to *t.* Com. 'I like little Sally, 'er's so nimble on 'er *arrants*—dunna let the grass grow under 'er fit.'

(2) *sb. pl.* the miscellaneous contents of a market-basket after being at 'the shops.' Com. 'I've a good tuthree *arrants* to tak' wham i' that basket as I've soud the fowl out on.'

'**ARRAWIG** [aar'·u'wi'g], *sb.* an earwig.—CLUN, *Herefd. border.* 'I conna bar them nasty *arrawigs*.' Arwygyll, worme. *Aurealle.* This insect is called in Norfolk erriwiggle.—FORBY. In the Suffolk dialect arriwiggle.—MOORE. A.S. eárwigga, *vermis auricularis.*—*Prompt. Parv. and Notes.* Cf. **Erriwig.**

ARRIMAN [aar'·i'mun], *sb. Triton crestatus,* Crested Newt.—COLLIERY. The primeval drink of immortality is called 'soma' by the Hindus, and 'haoma' by the Zend branch of the Aryans. The names are identical, but the plants which produce the juices so called are different; the haoma plant grows like the vine, but its leaves are like those of the jessamine; the Indian soma is now extracted from the *Asclēpias Acida.* The Iranians, or West Aryans, describe two kinds of haoma, the white and the yellow. The latter grows on mountains, and was known to Plutarch. The Parsees of India send one of their priests from time to time to Kirmân to procure supplies of the plant for sacred uses. The white haoma is a fabulous plant which grows in heaven, in the Vouru Kasha lake, in which lake ten fish keep incessant watch upon a lizard, sent by the evil power, Agramainyus (*Ahriman*), for the destruction of the haoma. This hostile lizard is the serpent or dragon of India.—KELLY's *Indo-European Tradition and Folk-lore*, pp. 137-8.

ARRIVANCE [u'r'ei·vuns], *sb., obs.?* arrival of company.—PULVERBATCH. 'I spec' they'n be wantin' yo', Betty, to 'elp 'em a bit at the owd Maister's, I sid an *arrivance* theer as I wuz gwe'in to 'unt some barm.'

> 'For every minute is expectancy
> Of more *arrivance*.'—*Othello*, II. i. 42.

AR-SHORN-LIP [aa·r'shaur'n lip·'], *sb.* a cleft lip; a 'hare-lip.'—WEM; ELLESMERE. See **Ar** (2).

AR-SHOTTEN-LIP [aa·r'shot·n-lip·'], the same.—PULVERBATCH; CLUN. See Bk. II., *Folklore*, &c., 'Superstitions concerning Animals.'

ARTISHROW [aa·r'ti'shr'oa·'], *sb.* *Corsira vulgaris*, the shrew-mouse. —BRIDGNORTH. Cf. **Nussrow**. See Bk. II., *Folklore*, &c., 'Superstitions concerning Animals.'

AS [u'z], (1) *rel. pron.* who, which, that. Com. 'I'm sartin it wuz 'im *as* I sid comin' out o' the "George."'

(2) *prep.* on, upon. Com. ''E toud me they wun gweïn theer *as* nex' Saturday, ready for the Wakes.'

(3) *conj.* that. Com. 'They sen *as* the crannaberries bin despert scase this time.' Used also in combination with *how*. 'I 'eärd the Maister tellin' the Missis *as* '*ow* 'e wuz gweïn to Stretton far i' the mornin'.'

(4) *v. a.* has. Com. 'I sid Jack gweïn töërt the tatoe-slang; *as* a töök the sharevil ööth 'im dun 'ee think?' *As* in this case is merely an instance of the general usage in Shropshire of 'dropping the H,' but is noteworthy as being the form used by Shropshire's poet—the blind monk of Haughmond—in the fifteenth century:

> 'That holé cherche *as* bound me to,
> Grawnt me grace that fore to do.'
>
> JOHN AUDELAY'S *Poems*, p. 57.

ASGAL [az·gu'l], same as **Askal**, q. v. MUCH WENLOCK.

ASHEN-PLANT [ash·u'n plant·'], *sb.* an ash sapling cut to serve as a light walking-stick or 'cane.'—PULVERBATCH. 'Whad a despert srode lad that Tum Rowley is, 'e wants a good *ashen-plant* about 'is 'ide oftener than 'is porritch.'

> 'His *ashen* spear that quivered as it flew.'—DRYDEN.

ASIDE [u'seid·], *adv.* beside. Com. 'Mighty bad! mighty bad, poor young ööman, 'er's got the pipus [typhus] faiver—the fluency [influenza] an' 'afe a dozen plaints *aside*.' So said Sally 'Kaizwil' [*Kearswell*] of Longden, 1860 *circa*.

ASIDEN [u'sei·dn], *adv.* on one side. Com. 'Yo' hanna pŭt yore shawl on straight, the cornels bin all *asiden*.'

> 'All *asiding* as hogs fighting.'—RAY'S *Proverbs*, p. 51.

ASKAL [as·ku'l], *sb.* *Lophinus punctatus*, the smooth newt.—SHREWSBURY; PULVERBATCH. 'I carried up a barrel, ma'am, out o' the cellar into the foud, an' as I turned it the one end uvvermost theer wuz a *askal*, an' I wuz that frittened, but I 'adna squedge it, ma'am, so it 'adna 'urt me, an' that made me think as *askals* wuz more innicenter than I 'ad s'posed.' So said Betty Andrews of Cruck Meole (June, 1872). See below, **Asker**.

ASKER [as·kur'], same as **Askal**.—NEWPORT; WEM; ELLESMERE.

> 'Snakes and nederes thar he fand
> And gret blac tades gangand,
> And *arskes*, and other wormesfelle.
> That I can noht on Inglis telle.'
>
> *Homilies in Verse* (A.D. 1330, *circa*),
> *Specim. Early Eng.*, VIII. *b.* l. 177.

ASSAUT [u'saut·], (1) *sb.* attack, assault. Com. 'They 'n 'ad 'im up for *assaut.*'

'Many a cumly Knight · & oþer kid peeple
On euery side was sett · *asaute* too make.'

K. Alisaunder, l. 263.

(2) *v. a.* to attack, assault. Com. ''E *assauted* me as I was comin' throm the corn fild.'

'. . . and also bewar of spendyng of yowr stuffe of qwarellys, powdr, and stone, so that if they *assaut* yow er we come, that ye have stuffe to dyffende yow of over.'—*Paston Letters*, A.D. 1469, vol. ii. p. 381.

O.Fr. assaillir attaquer; d'où assaille, attaque, *assaut*, propr. *ad-saltus.*—Bur.

AST [as·t], *pret.* and *part. past.* asked.—Pulverbatch; Clun, *Herefd. Border.* 'Is the Màister gweïn to the far?' 'I hanna *ast* 'im.'

'He sent for me and *ast* me how I fared. . . . a toke me to him and *ast* how my suster dede, and I answeryd wyll, never better.'—*Paston Letters*, A.D. 1454, vol. i. p. 302.

Cf. **A** (1) with *a toke.*

ASTOW [as·tou], hast thou.—Ludlow.

'sadde sowes for mi sake · suffred *astow* manye.'

William of Palerne, l. 4724.

Cf. '"*Canstow* seruen," he seide . . .'

Piers Pl., Text C. pass. vi. l. 12.

AT [at·], *prep.* to. Com. 'Yo' needna be afeard, I amma gweïn to do nuthin *at* yo'.'

'Here's *at* ye, what I drink won't fat ye.'

Davy's MS. in Wr.

A.S. *æt*, at, to.

AT-AFTER [u't af·tur'], *adv.* and *prep.* after. — Pulverbatch. 'Whad time did John come in las' night?' 'A good wilde *at-after* yo'd'n gwun to bed.'

'*At after* souper goth this noble king
To seen this hors of bras, . . .'

Chaucer, *C. T.*, l. 10616.

ATHATN, ATHATNS [u'dhatn], Pulverbatch; Ludlow; Wem. Qy. com. [u'dhat-nz], Shrewsbury; Newport, *adv.* Cf. **Thatn.**

ATHIN [u'dhin·], *prep.* and *adv.* within.—Ellesmere. Qy. com.

ATHISN, ATHISNS [u'dhis·n], Pulverbatch; Ludlow. Qy. com. [u'dhis·nz], Shrewsbury; Newport, *adv.* 'Yo' bin despert oukit o'er that bit o' knittin,—canna yo' pŭt the nild [needle] through the stitch *athisn* an' nod be'ind it *athatn*? That's 'ow yo' droppen the stitches off the nilds.' Cf. **Thisn.**

ATHOUT [u'dhout·], *prep.* without.—Shrewsbury; Pulverbatch. Qy. com.

ATHWART [u'thur't], Corve Dale. [u'thwur't], Much Wenlock.

A-TOP [u'top·], *prep.* on the top; upon. Com. 'I've bin lookin' that cork-screw up an' down, an' fund it *a-top* o' the cubbert shilf after all.' Cf.—

'One heaved *a-high*, to be hurl'd down below.'
K. Richard III., IV. iv. 86.

See **A** (3).

ATTER [at·ur'], *prep.* after.—CLUN; CLEE HILLS; WELLINGTON; NEWPORT.

ATWEEN [u'tween·], *prep.* between.—PULVERBATCH; LUDLOW.

'*Attween* two theevys nayled to a tre.'
Lydgate's Minor Poems, p. 263, in HAL.

ATWIXT [u'twik·st], *prep.* betwixt, between.—LUDLOW. 'The poor chap got jammed *atwixt* the waggons; I doubt it 'll be a bad job for 'im.'

'. . . seyng that such money as is spent *a twix* yowe is but wastfully expendid and to non use vertuouse.'—*Paston Letters*, A.D. 1460? vol. i. p. 520.

Cf. **Twix.**

A-TWO [u'too·], *adv.* in two; asunder.—NEWPORT; WEM. 'The jug fell *a two* jest as I wuz 'angin' it up.'

'Do a-wei þi Maumetes · þei han trayed þe ofte;
Let breken hem *a-two* · an bren hem al to pouder.'
Joseph of Arimathie, l. 103.

A.S. *on*, in; and *twá*, two. Cf. **A** (3).

AUF [auf·], *sb.* a simpleton; a blockhead. Com. ''E took me for a *nauf*, but 'e fund 'is match.' See **N**, in **Grammar Outlines** (*consonants*). Cf. *Oaf* in WEDG.

AUKERT, AUKIT. See **Awkward.**

AULD [auld·], *adj.* old, used not in the sense of aged, but as a familiar school-boy epithet, or as a term of reproach.—LUDLOW. ''E's a reg'lar *auld* bad un.' O. Northumbrian, *ald*, old.

AUNTY [aun·ti'], (1) *adj.* quick, ready, bold, venturesome.—SHREWSBURY, *Uffington.* ''E's a *aunty* little chap is our Tum, theer inna much as 'e ŏŏnna-d-'ăve a try fur.' *Aunty* is connected with O.E. *aunters*, adventures; deeds of daring calling for high spirit and ready courage.

'Now fares Philip þe free · too fonden his myght,
And attles to þe Assyriens · *aunteres* too seeche.'
K. Alisaunder, l. 109.

Ash has *auntrith*, ventureth, an 'obsolete' word. O.Fr. *aventure* terme de chevalerie, pour désigner des combats; des périls extraordinaires.—BUR.

(2) *adj.* frisky, mettlesome; said of horses.—NEWPORT.

AUNTY-PRAUNTY [aun·ti' pr'aun·ti'], *adj.* high-spirited, proud.—ELLESMERE. ''E's a *aunty-praunty* fellow, is young John, 'E ŏŏnna bar to be pŭt upon.' This is one of those reduplicated words so often employed in the rustic speech as a more emphatic form of expression. The real signification, it will be seen, lies in the first half of the term, which seems to be a secondary meaning of 'aunty' (1).

AUSE [aus·], same as **Oss**, q. v.—CLUN; MUCH WENLOCK; NEWPORT.

AUTER. See **Halter**.

AUVE [auv·], *sb.* the handle of an axe, mattock, or pick. Com. 'Dick öön yo' len' me yore axe?' 'I canna, lad; it's at the wilrit's for a new *auve*.' This term is a corrupted form of 'helve.' A.S. *helf*, helve; handle.

AVEN [ai·vn], PULVERBATCH; CORVE DALE; CLEE HILLS; COLLIERY. [av·h'n], ELLESMERE, *sb.* prognostic; latent promise; that which contains in itself the element of some special excellence or usefulness. A thriving colt would be a good *aven* of a horse; a stick growing naturally in the form of a scythe handle a mighty good *aven* of a sned. 'Tother day as I wuz gweïn through Brown's Coppy, I sid a famous *aven* of a sned; if I'd 'ad my brummock ööth me, Mr. Jackson ööd a bin one o' 'is young ash less.' 'Yo'd'n better pray as 'e dunna ketch yo'.' Cf. **Even**.

AVENLESS [ai·vnli's], *adj.* shiftless; without any faculty for contriving.—PULVERBATCH; OSWESTRY. ''Er's a poor *avenless* wench 'er is.' Cf. **Evenless**.

AW [au·], *sb.* ear of oats.—PULVERBATCH; CLEE HILLS. 'Eels are in season when oats are in *aw*.' Proverbial saying heard about Aston Botterell. Cf. *arista*, *spica*, an *awne* of corne, an ere, or a glene, in *Prompt. Parv.*, p. 18.

AWAY TO-GO, *phr.* away with you; away he went.—WORTHEN. 'Tak' this an' *away to-go*.' A young kitchen-maid, describing the depredations of a man-servant on the pastry shelf, said, 'It wuz Lucas, ma'am, 'e comen in out o' the 'all an' took some o' the fancy pies an' *away to-go*.' In M.E. *to-go* = he went; Barbour [1375] uses *to-ga* = dispersed, as a past tense.

AWED-OUT, *phr.* in full ear.—PULVERBATCH. 'The ööäts i' the uvver fild bin *awed out*, I see.' From **Aw**, q. v.

A-WHAM [u'wu'm], *adv.* at home.—PULVERBATCH; LUDLOW. Qy. com. in S. Sh. ''E wunna-d-*a-wham* w'en the men gotten theer.' A.S. *æt*, at, and *hám*, home. See **A** (3).

AWILDE [u'weil·d], (1) *adv.* whilst.—SHREWSBURY; PULVERBATCH; ELLESMERE. 'Now then, be sharp an wesh them tuthree things *awilde* I get the batch i' the oven.'

(2) *v. n.* to have time; to wait.—SHREWSBURY; PULVERBATCH; WORTHEN; ELLESMERE. Qy. com. 'Can yo' *awilde* to draw the drink? The men bin gweïn to the fild.' This term is more often used negatively. 'I canna-d-*awilde*.' *Awile* also obtains, as a refined form. 'I can't *awile*.'—*ibid.*; CORVE DALE.

AWKWARD [au·ki't], MUCH WENLOCK. [auk·ur't], Com. [ou·ki't], PULVERBATCH; CHURCH STRETTON; CLUN, *adj.* often used in the sense of the French *difficile* as applied to persons, '*oukit* folks.'

AX, AXE [ak·s], *v. a.* to ask. Com.

'For I wol *axe* if it hir wille be
To be my wyf, and reule hir after me.'
CHAUCER, E. 326 (Six-text ed.); Skeat.

AXINS [ak·sinz], *sb. pl.* the banns of marriage. Com. 'Did'n yo' 'ear as Tum Ivans an' Patty Bowen, 'er as comes throm the tother side Sosebry, 'ad'n thar *axins* put up i' Church o' Whi'sun Sunday?' *To be axed up*, is to have the concluding banns of marriage published.

'Ye send me woord of the maryage of my Lady Jane; one maryage for an other on, Norse and Bedford were *axed* in the chyrche on Sonday last past.'—*Paston Letters*, A.D. 1472, vol. iii. p. 46.

BACHELORS' BUTTON [bach·i'lur'z but·n], *sb. Bellis perennis*, the 'Double Daisy' of the garden. Com. When flowrets cluster round the parent blossom, the name *Bachelors' button* gives place to that of *Hen-and-chickens*.

BACK-AISTER [bak·ais·'tur'], *sb.* the back of the grate immediately behind the fire.—NEWPORT, *Shiffnal*. 'Yo'n got a face as black as the *back-aister*.' Cf. **Aister**.

BACKEN [bak·n], *v. a.* to put back; to retard. Com. 'Missis, we mun *backen* dinner; the Maister's sen' word now jest as 'e ŏŏnna be in at the time.'

BACK-END [bak·end·'], *sb.* the latter end of the year. Com. 'We sha'n 'ave time to do all them little jobs to'erts the *back-end*.'

BACKERTER [bak'ur'tur'], *adv.* further back. Com. 'Shift that lung table *backerter*, nigher the wall's w'eer I want it.'

BACKERTS [bak·ur'ts], *adv.* backwards. Com.

BACKERTS ROAD ON, *phr.* wrong way before.—NEWPORT.

BACK-FRIEND [bak·fr'end], *sb.* a hang-nail. Com.

BACKSIDE [bakseid·], *sb.* the yard in the rear of a house. Com. 'The lan'lord toud me as I should 'ăve some 'en-pens pŭt at the *backside;* but I doubt 'is promises bin like pie-crusses, made to be broken.'

'Robert Hayward sett Balderton Hall and all his lands in Balderton, except his antient house and the *backside*, to one Randle Cooke a Cheshireman.'—GOUGH'S *History of Myddle*, p. 185.

BACKSI'FORE [bak·si'foa·'ur'], *adv.* wrong side before.—NEWPORT.

BAD [bad·], *adj.* ill. Com. 'Mother's *bad*, 'er canna spar me to gŏŏ to school.'

BADE [baid·], *v. a.* to bathe.—WELLINGTON; WEM. **Der.** 'bading.'

BADGE [baj·], (1) *v. a., obsols.* to cut wheat with a broad hook called a *badging-hook*.—NEWPORT. The same word as **Bag**, q. v. Cf. **Swive** and **Swivers**.

(2) *v. n., obsols.* to buy up, as of farm or garden produce, for the purpose of selling again.—PULVERBATCH; WEM.

'Ralph, the eldest son of Thomas Guest, was a sober, peaceable man; his imployment was buying corne in one markett towne and selling it in another, which is called *badgeing*.'—GOUGH'S *History of Myddle*, p. 115.

BADGER [baj·ur'], *sb.*, *obsols.* a huckster; a middle-man, between the wholesale selling farmer and the town-retailer of farm produce.—SHREWSBURY; PULVERBATCH; BRIDGNORTH; CLUN. 'A despert poor markit to-day, the *badgers* wun very shy o' buyin' an' the townsfolks 'ăd'n it all their own way; the butter went as low as a shillin', i' the ŏnder.'

'27. Item, hit hath be vsid, the Maire of Bristow anon after mighelmas, to do calle byfore hym in the yelde hall, or counseill hous, all the Bakers of Bristowe, there to vndirstand whate stuff they haue of whete. And after, whate sise they shall bake, and to assist and counseil theym in theire byeng and barganyng with the *Bagers*, such as bryngeth whete to towne, as wele in trowys, as other-wyse, by lande and by watir, in kepyng downe of the market.'—*Ordinance of the Office of Mayor of Bristol, temp. Edw. IV.*, A.D. 1479, *English Gilds.* E. E. T. S.

'Cheer up your drooping spirits,
And cease now complaining,
Although you've suffer'd hard,
Still fresh hopes there's remaining.
You see the corn is falling,
In every market town, sir,
In spite of roguish *badgers*
The price it must come down, sir.
Then thankful be to Providence,
Who heard our wretched cry,
And send us glorious crops of grain,
Our wants for to supply.'—*Old Shropshire Song.*

(2) *v. a.* to teaze; to banter.—LUDLOW. Qy. com. ''E's al'ays *badgering* some one; never 'eed im'.'

BADGING-HOOK. See **Badge** (1).

BADING [bai·din], *part. pres.* bathing.—WELLINGTON; WEM. See **Bade.**

BADLY [bad·li'], *adj.* sickly; ailing.—NEWPORT. This term is not nearly so strong as *bad*, in the sense of 'ill.'

BAG [bag·], *v. a.* to reap peas with an implement which, when applied to this purpose, is called a *baggin'-bill.*—PULVERBATCH; CORVE DALE; WELLINGTON. See **Bill.**

BAGGIN [bag·in], *sb.*, *sl.*? the farm-labourers' luncheon. An imported term which begins to supersede the old word 'bait,' q. v.—LUDLOW.

BAGGIN-BILL. See **Bag**, also **Badge.**

BAIGLE [baig·l], *sb.* an opprobrious epithet applied to a depraved woman.—PULVERBATCH; WEM. ''Er's a nasty *baigle*, that's whad 'er is.'

'*Sir To.* She's a *beagle*, true-bred, and one that adores me.'
Twelfth Night, II. iii. 195.

BAISTINS. See **Beestings.**

BAIT [bait·], SHREWSBURY; WEM; WHITCHURCH. [baayt·], PULVERBATCH; WORTHEN; LUDLOW. [boit·], OSWESTRY, *sb.* the farm-labourers' luncheon. The *baÿte time* is 10 o'clock, A.M., in ordinary seasons, but in harvest-time there is *ŏnder's baÿte*, from 4 to 5 o'clock, P.M. 'Bin yo' aumust ready for yore *ŏnder's baÿte?*' 'Aye, as soon as I've pŭt on this jag o' rākin's; it ŏŏnna 'ardly cover the ripples.'

Among the accounts of the bailiffs of Shrewsbury is a paper endorsed, 'The byll of expens don at the assyssys at Ludlow, St. Jamys Yven, a°. h. viij. xix. (24 July, 1527). Here followeth the costs don then betweyn the town and Mr. Vernan.' Among other items is:—'Paid at Lebothod (Le Botwood) for Mr. Bayleys *baytyng*, 11d.'—OWEN and BLAKEWAY'S *History of Shrewsbury*, vol. i. p. 307.

Chaucer uses the word *bayte* in the sense of to feed.

'On many a sory meel now may she *baytë*.'
CHAUCER, B. 466 (Six-text ed.), Skeat.

Icel. *beita*, to feed; to make to bite.

BAIT BAG [baayt·bag·'], *sb.* the bag in which the farm-labourers carry their luncheon to the field.—PULVERBATCH. 'Axe the waggoner w'eer 'e pŭt 'is *baÿte-bag;* if 'e pŭt it i' the cōfer for the mice to ate, like the last.' '*Bag* and bottle.'—*Robin Hood*, ii. 54, in HAL. See **Bottle** (1).

BAKE-HUS [baik·us], *sb.* a building detached from the other domestic offices, containing an oven, and used for baking purposes. The back kitchen or 'brew-'us,' as it is generally called, has an oven; and usually serves as the *bake-'us*.—PULVERBATCH. 'Put them bags o' bran an' gurgeons i' the *bake-'us*, an' lock it up; or else the one 'afe 'll find its way into the stable.' See *Prompt. Parv.*, p. 21. A.S. *bæc-hus*, a bake-house. Cf. **Hus.**

BAKESTONE [bak·stwu'n], *sb.*, *obsols.* a circular plate of iron about an inch thick, having a loop-handle for the purpose of drawing it out of the iron frame in which it is hung over the fire when wanted to bake cakes on. Com. The *bakestone*, though still occasionally to be seen in old houses, really belongs to an age that is past. 'Fatch the *bak'stwun* an' I'll mak' tuthree barley crumpits, for the Maister nor me canna ate that bread. The loaf as I've jest fatched out o' the buttery is like stir-puddin',—more fit to be ete ŏŏth a spŏŏn than a knife.' 'Barley crumpets' were extensively used in Shropshire as a substitute for bread in 1817, when, in consequence of the unprecedented bad harvest of the previous year, sound wheaten flour could not be obtained, and good bread was not to be 'gotten for gold.' In the month of October, 1816, deep snow lay on the harvest-fields, reaching to the band of the sheaves; much of the grain remained out through November, and was not 'gathered into the barn' until the frosts of December had dried it. Such is the account given by one who was herself an eye-witness of the snow-covered corn-fields. The same person saw a very different harvesting just ten years afterwards [1826], when wheat was carried on Mrs. Reynolds' farm at Longden on July the eighth, and most of the farmers in that neighbourhood had finished their harvest before the end of the same month.

'To go like a cat on a hot *bake stone*.'
RAY'S *Proverbs*, p. 222.

BALD [b:auld·], *adj.*, *pec.* unfledged.—SHREWSBURY, *Uffington.* 'Jack, I know to throstle's nist ööth five *bald* young un's in it. I fund it this mornin' on the roäd to school.' Cf. **Fliggy.**

BALD-COOT [bauld·koot·'], *sb. Fúlica atra*, the common coot.—BRIDGNORTH. Une blarye, glossed—*a balled cote*, occurs in *The Treatise of Walter de Biblesworth*, close of xiii. cent. in Wr. vocabs., vol. i. p. 165.

'As bald as a *coot*.'—RAY'S *Proverbs*, p. 220.

BALD-RIB [b:aul·r'i'b], *sb.* that part of the rib of pork which lies nearer to the neck than the spare-rib.—SHREWSBURY, *Uffington;* MUCH WENLOCK. As the *spare-rib* is *spare* of flesh, so the *bald-rib* is *bare* of flesh. Cf. **Spare-rib.**

BALE [bail·], *v. a.* to raise blisters in the flesh, as by a sting, or the bite of an insect.—SHREWSBURY; PULVERBATCH. 'The flen han bin on this poor child,—jest look 'ow they'n *baled* 'im on the back.' Cf. the following:—

'Hwone þe *bale* is alre hecst
Þonne is þe bote alre necst
For wit west a mong his sore
And for his sore hit is þe more.'
Owl and Nightingale, l. 687.

A.S. *balu; bealu.* O. Icel. *böl*, bale; misery; affliction, in STRAT.

BALEISE [bal·u's], *v. a.* to beat; to flog; to whip.—PULVERBATCH; COLLIERY.

'. . . As I a childe were
And *baleised* . . .'
Piers Pl., Text B., pass. v. l. 175.

Cf. **Bellise.**

BALK [b:auk·], (1) *sb.* a horizontal beam in the roof of a barn.—PULVERBATCH. 'I eärd a squake o'er my yed w'en I wuz throshin,' said William Evans of Castle Pulverbatch, 'an' w'en I looked up I sid a rot gweïn' alung the *balk* ööth a waizle oudin' on to the scuft on 'is neck; they fellen off the *balk*, the par on 'em, jest as they wun, on to the barn flur, an' theer I killed 'em bööäth ööth my thrashal.' This curious incident occurred as described.

The *chimley balk* is a great beam in front of an old-fashioned fire-place, where the bacon is sometimes hung to dry. *Obsols.* 'That par o' chawls mun be shifted throm the *chimley balk*, they bin gettin quite raisty.'

'To climben by the renges and the stalkes
Unto the tubbes honging in the *balkes*.'
CHAUCER, *C. T.*, l. 3626.

'*Balke* in a howse.'—*Trabs. Prompt. Parv.* Icel. *bálkr*, a beam; a partition.

(2) *sb.*, *obsols. var. pr.* a bulk or projection of masonry, as the *oven-balk*. In this case the mouth of the oven is inside the house, but the oven itself, being built outside, projects and forms a *balk*.—PULVERBATCH; ELLESMERE.

'*Iago.* Here; stand behind this *bulk.*'—*Othello*, V. i.

Cf. *Coriolanus*, II. i. 225.

(3) *sb.* an old hedge bank on which the 'quick' is planted.—NEWPORT. Icel. *bálkr*, a partition.

(4) A space left unploughed between the furrows, the result of bad ploughing. Com.

'*Balke* of a loude eryd.'—*Porca.* '*Crebro.* A *balke* bitwyne two furrowes.'—*Porca.* 'Vorat furfur, aratrum vult verteri.'—MED. HARL. MS. 2257,—*Prompt. Parv. and Notes.*

A balk in the field is a but that has been skipped in the sowing; such a *balk* is believed to portend calamity to the owner of the field. 'I see theer's a *balk* in a fild o' corn down by Steppiton, I dunna know who it belungs to, but it's no good sign anyways, theer'll be djeth i' the 'ouse afore 'arrŏŏst.' Balkyn or ouerskyppyn, *omitto.*—*Prompt. Parv.*

(5) *v. a.* to leave a space unploughed. Com. 'Sich ploughin as this ŏŏnna do for me, the one 'ăfe o' the groun's *balked.*'

'But so wel halt nô man þe plôgh, þat he ne *balkeþ* ôþer wîle.'
Gow. conf. am., l. 296, in STRAT.

'Balkyn, or to make a *balke* in a londe (in erynge of londe).'—*Porco., C. F. in porca., Prompt. Parv.*

(6) *v. a.* to hinder from using; to cause inconvenience.—ELLESMERE. Qy. com. 'I've cut the end of my finger aumust off.' 'Dear 'eart! that's a bad job; bein' at the end, it 'll *balk* you, wunna-d-it?'

BALLET [bal·u't], *sb.*, *var. pr.* a ballad. Com.

'But thee, Theocritus, wha matches?
They're no herd's *ballats*, Maro's catches.'
ROBERT BURNS, *Poems*, p. 114, l. 20.

''E toud 'er not to mak a *ballet* on it,' said of news not to be spread. A ''*ole i' the ballet*' is some part of a song or story forgotten.

BALL-STONE, (1) *sb.* iron-stone lying in balls, found above the 'top coal.'—COLLIERY; M. T. See **Coal-Field.**

(2) *sb.* a kind of limestone.—MUCH WENLOCK.

BALLY [bal·i'], (1) *sb.* the belly; the old pronunciation. Com.

'A great bolle-full of benen · were betere in his wombe,
And wiþ þe randes of bakun · his *baly* for to fillen.'
P. Pl. Cr., l. 763.

A.S. *bælig*, idem, properly a bag.

(2) *sb.* a litter of pigs. Com. 'I shall keep that sow on, 'er brought ten pigs the first *bally* an' twelve the next, an' reared 'em all.' Cf. **Farrow.**

(3) *v. n.* to grow abdominous.—PULVERBATCH; ELLESMERE. Qy. com. ''E use' to be as thin as a red yerrin; but faith, 'e *ballies* well sence 'e went to the paas'ns.'

BALLY-PROUD [bal·i'pr'oud], *adj.* dainty; fastidious in respect of food. ''E wuz welly clemmed wen 'e come to me, an' now 'e's got *bally-proud.*' See above.

BALLYS [bal·i's], *sb. pl.* blacksmith's bellows. Qy. if restricted to this sense.—WEM; ELLESMERE. The form *balyws* occurs in Tundale, p. 34, Hal. Cf. **Blow-bellys.** See **Bellys.**

BANDS [baandz], *sb. pl.*, *var. pr.* banns of marriage.—COLLIERY. 'A pit-girl who presented herself with her "chap" to "put up the *bands*," confounded both parson and clerk by giving her name as *Loice-Showd.* They could make nothing of it, and had to defer publishing the banns until the girl's proper appellation could be ascertained. It proved to be—upon making inquiries in an adjoining parish—*Alice Harwood!*' This is by no means a solitary instance of the ignorance of their rightful names which obtains amongst the pit-folk and others of the peasant class. See Bk. II., *Folklore,* &c., 'Nicknames' and 'Sirnames.'

BANGER [bang·ur'], (1) *sb.* a hard blow. Com. 'I gid 'im sich a *banger* as 'e ŏŏnna forget in a 'urry.'

(2) *sb.* a three 'grained' pikel used for 'gathering scutch.'—WHITCHURCH.

BANG-SWANG [bang·swang·'], *adv.* without thought; headlong.—CLEE HILLS.

BANK [bangk·], refined pronunciation of 'bonk,' q. v. A.S. *banc,* a bank; a hillock.

BANKY-PIECES. See **Bonky-pieces.**

BANNERING [ban·ur'in], *sb.* and *part. adj.* perambulating the parish boundaries.—SHREWSBURY. See Bk. II., *Folklore,* &c., 'Customs connected with Days and Seasons' (*Holy-Thursday*).

BANNUT [bann·ut], *sb. Nux juglaus regica,* a large kind of walnut. Com. *Banne-note-tre* occurs in a *Metrical Vocabulary* (perhaps), xiv. cent., and Mr. Wright remarks on it 'This is by much the earliest example of the word I have met with.' See Wr. vocabs., vol. i. p. 181.

BANTER [ban·tur'], *v. a., pec.* to beat down, as in price.—SHREWSBURY; WEM; ELLESMERE. Qy. com. 'Peggy,' said Richard Price of Welshampton, 'I've bin to the Baumur after that pig, but they wanten too much money for 'im. I sed to 'Liza Downes, I dunna want to *banter* yo down in price, if yo thinken yo can get more for 'im by tăkin' 'im to Ellesmur far'; tăk 'im, I've toud yo whad I mane to give.' Cf. **Bate.**

BAR [baa·r], (1) *sb.* a bear. Com. 'I dunna like that Australian bif, yo never knowen w'ether it's lion or *bar* yo bin ātin.' So said John Cotton of Hanwood [1873]. A.S. *bera,* a bear.

(2) *v. a.* to bear; to tolerate. Com. 'I canna *bar* that, an' whad's more, I ŏŏnna ăve it.'

(3) *v. a.* to deprive of.—SHREWSBURY; PULVERBATCH. 'Oh! 'er's sich a fav'rit, 'e canna *bar* 'er anythin' 'er axes fur.'

'Heaven and fortune *bar* me happy hours!
Day, yield me not thy light; nor night thy rest!'
King Richard, IV. iv. 400.

(4) *v. a.* to prevent. 'I'll *bar* 'im gwī'in theer.'—CLUN.

(5) [baar·], *v. a.* to claim possession or privilege; to make choice

of. The term is used by children at play.—ELLESMERE. 'I say, Bill, I *bar* that bat.' Cf. **Barley**, *infra*.

(6) *v. a.* to ignore, as of a bad hit. A playground term.—CLUN. Qy. com. 'Oh! we'll *bar* that.'

(7) *adj.* bare; naked. Com.

BARBINE [baa·r'bein], *sb. Convolvulus Arvensis*, small bind-weed.—SHREWSBURY, *Hanwood*. Cf. **Devil's guts** and **Billy-Clipper**.

BAR-FUT [baa·r'fut], *adj.*, *var. pr.* having the feet uncovered; barefoot. Com.

'Frauncеys bad his brethern
Bar-fot to wenden.'—*P. Pl. Cr.*, l. 594, ed. WR.

BAR-FUT CUSTARD [baa·r'fut kus·tur't], *sb.*, *obsols.*? a 'bystin' custard not enclosed in a crust.—PULVERBATCH. 'We'n mak a dish o' *bar-fut custart* ŏŏth that bystin for the men's supper; it'll be a trate for 'em.' Cf. **Bystin Custard**.

BARGE [baa·r'j], (1) *v. n.* to curve outwards; to bulge, as of the sides of a tub, a wall, &c.—WHITCHURCH, *Whixall*. Cf. 'Bulk' in WEDG.

(2) *sb.* a term applied to anything large. 'A great *barge* of a thing.' —WHITCHURCH, *Whixall*.

(3) *adj.*, *obsols.* large; protuberant. 'A great *barge-bellied* thing.'—PULVERBATCH.

BARGS [baa·r'ggz], *interj.* a schoolboy's term. Crying *bargs* entitles him to a short withdrawal from a game, and exemption from penalties that would otherwise have been incurred.—SHREWSBURY.

BARIN' [baa·r'i'n], *part.* laying bare the stone; a quarrying term. —MUCH WENLOCK. Cf. **Onbear**.

BARK [baa·r'k], *v. a.* to kick the skin off a person's shins. Com. ''E rawled 'im about shameful, an' *barked* 'is shins beside.'

BARLEY [baa·r'li'], *v. a.* same as **Bar** (5), q. v. Com.

BARLEY-CHILD [baa·r'li'-cheild·], *sb.* a child born in wedlock, but which makes its advent within six months of marriage. The metaphor lies in the allusion to the time which elapses between *barley sowing* and *barley harvest*.—MUCH WENLOCK, *Acton Burnell*.

BARLIS [baa·r'liss], *v. a.* same as **Bar** (5), q. v. Com. CLEE HILLS.

BARM [baa·r'm], *sb.* yeast. Com.

'And sometimes make the drink to bear no *barm*.'
Mids. Night's Dream, II. ii. 8.

A.S. *beorma*, barm; yeast.

BARNACLES [baa·r'nu'klz], (1) *sb. pl.* spectacles. —NEWPORT. *Barniques*, spectacles.—*Vocab. de Berri* in WEDG.

(2) *sb. pl.*, *obsols.* an instrument applied to the nose of a savage bull to subdue his violence. Com. The *barnacles* are somewhat like the figure of 8 in form, consisting of two rings connected midway by short bars, through which a screw passes. The upper ring is jointed in the centre, while the lower one is correspondingly divided. *This*

is put into the bull's nostrils, and held there by the screw which serves to tighten the *barnacles* at pleasure. The upper ring is attached to the point of each horn by means of a chain, thus keeping the lower one from dropping and impeding the animal while grazing.' 'It gies the bŭll plenty to do to think on 'is nose w'en the *barnacles* bin on,' said Thomas Cliffe, the 'village blacksmith' of Tilstock, when describing the instrument and its uses [Sept. 1874]. Cf. 'Barnacles' in WEDG.

BARN-DOOR-SAVAGE, *sb.*, *sl.*? a clodhopper.—SHREWSBURY.

BARNISH [baa·r'nish], *v. n.* to grow stout and well-favoured; to 'fill out,' as youths do who have ceased to grow in height.—PULVERBATCH; MUCH WENLOCK; WELLINGTON; NEWPORT. 'I spect the young squire's lef' college: 'e's as tall as a young poplar, an' as thin as a pikel-stail; but 'e'll *barnish* now for a couple o' 'ears, an' mak a fine fellow. I 'ope 'e'll be as good a maister an' lan'lord as the owd un.'

BARROW [baar'·u'], *sb.* a child's pinafore.—SHREWSBURY, *Uffington.* 'Oud your *barrow*, Polly, for some apples.' Cf. **Brat.**

BARS-ARS [baa·r'z aa·r'z], *sb. pl.* bear's hairs; threads of filmy white, fringing greater masses of cloud, said to betoken some sort of weather; but the popular mind is not at one, whether it be fair or foul.—CHURCH STRETTON; MUCH WENLOCK.

BASE-CHILD [bais·cheild], *sb.* an illegitimate child.—WORTHEN; CLUN; BRIDGNORTH; MUCH WENLOCK.

'1689 Expences at ye sealing a bond to saue the Jifh [Justice] Rarmely from a *bace child*—00-01-00.'—*Parish Accounts*, CLUN.

Cf. **Love-child.**

BASK [bask·], *v. n.* to cough asthmatically.—WEM. 'That theer poor oud mon's very bad, 'e'll sit afore the fire *baskin'* an' spittin' all day lung.'

BASS [bass·], *sb.* a slaty substance found in coal which will not cinerate. Com. Called 'dundick' in Derbyshire. See **Coal-field.**

BASSET-END [bas·i't end·], *sb.* the end of the workings on the rise of the mine.—COLLIERY, M. T.

BASTE [baist·], (1) *v. a.* to sew slightly; to tack together the several pieces of a garment with long stitches preparatory to more permanent work. Com. ''Er's pŭt mighty slim work i' this gownd, it inna much better than *basted.*'

'*Bene.* . . . The body of your discourse is sometime guarded with fragments, and the guards are but slightly *basted* on neither.'—*Much Ado about Nothing*, I. i. 288.

Cf. *Rom. of the Rose*, 104.

'*Baste* couture grossière, faufilure; vb. *bastir*, aujourd'hui *bâtir*, attacher de pièces les unes aux autres en les cousant à grands points; de l'ahal. *bestan*, raccomoder, rapiécer, du subst. *bast.*'—BUR. '*Bastyn* clothys *subsuo; sutulo.*'—*Prompt. Parv.* O.H. Germ. *besten*, baste; sew, in STRAT.

(2) *v. a.* to flog; to beat. Com. 'Tum, I'll *baste* yore back fur yo

in another 'afe minute if yo dunna be quiet. Whad bin 'ee prokin the ess out o' the grate athatn fur? I've on'y now jest claned up the fire-place.'

'*Dro. S.* . . . I think the meat wants that I have.
Ant. S. In good time, sir; what's that?
Dro. S. Basting.'—*Comedy of Errors*, II. ii. 59.

Strutt mentions *Baste the bear* as an incident in games; a form of punishment by which 'a boy couching down is laden with the clothes of his companions, and then buffeted by them.'—*Sports and Pastimes*, p. 387, ed. 1833.

O.N. *beysta*, to beat; to thrash. Dan. *böste*, to drub; to belabour, in WEDG.

BAT [bat·], (1) *sb.*, *obs.?* a kind of light club-like implement used by washerwomen for the purpose of beating the clothes.—MUCH WENLOCK. Shakespeare has *batlet* for the same thing.

'*Touch* . . . I remember, when I was in love . . .
The kissing of her *batlet* and the cow's dugs
That her pretty chapt hands had milked.'
As You Like It, II. iv. 49.

A.S. *bat*, a bat; club;—of Celtic origin. Cf. **Bat-staff.**

(2) *sb.* a heavy blow.—WHITCHURCH. Qy. com. in N. Shr. ''E gied 'im sich a *bat*.'

'That xal be asayd be this *batte!*
What, thou Jhesus? ho ȝaff the that?'
Coventry Mysteries, p. 296, in HAL.

(3) *sb.*, *sl.?* speed.—SHREWSBURY; WHITCHURCH. Qy. com. Of a person running or riding as hard as he can they say, ''E's gŏŏin at a pretty *bat*.'

(4) *v. a.* to beat with force.—SHREWSBURY; PULVERBATCH; WHITCHURCH. Qy. com. 'Polly, afore yo make that door, gŏŏ an' fatch a box o' slack to rake the fire; an' bring the shovel alung ŏŏth yo to *bat* it down well as it shanna burn through.'

(5) *v. a.* to strike lightly; to tap.—LUDLOW. Mothers *bat* their children in playful reproof. The expression is a common one.

'*Battede* hem on þe bakkes · to bolden heore hertes.'
Piers Pl., Text A, pass. iii. l. 192.

Cf. Pope's 'Gay *pats* my shoulder, and you vanish quite.'

(6) *v. a.* to wink, or rather to move the eyelids up and down quickly. Com. ''E *bats* 'is eyes like a louse i' the ess.' Cf. **Bate,** a term in falconry, which describes the similar motion of a hawk's wings when trying to get away from 'fist' or 'perch.' Fr. *battre les ailes.*

BATCH [bach·], (1) *sb.* a quantity baked at one time, as of bread or pies. Com.

'*Achil.* How now, thou core of envy!
Thou crusty *batch* of nature, what's the news?'
Troilus and Cressida, V. i. 6.

'Bahche; batche, or bakynge.'—*Pistura*, *Prompt. Parv.* A.S. *bacan*, to bake.

(2) *sb.* the quantity of corn sent to the mill for one grinding, and the quantity of flour returned from it. Com.

'Shrewsbury, April 18, 1796.
'The Inhabitants of the United Parishes of this Town
May have their Corn Ground at
Kingsland Windmill
For Sixpence a Bushel.

N.B.—No Toll or Gratuity will be taken. A Cart will go regularly through the Town two or three Times a Week to fetch and deliver the *Batches.*'—*Old Handbill.*

Cf. **Grist.**

(3) *sb.* a lot or quantity of anything; 'a *batch* of papers,' letters, &c. Com.

BATCH-CAKE [bach·kaik], *sb.* a small 'oven-bottom' loaf made for immediate use. Com. In farm-houses the large loaves are made in two parts, a lesser on a greater, like what bakers call a 'cottage loaf.' The *batch-cake,* on the contrary, is of one undivided portion. 'We mun mak' a couple o' *batch-cakes* to save cuttin' the new bread, for theer is but a cantel o' the owd left.'

BATCH-FLOUR [bach·flour'], *sb.* an inferior quality of flour for common household bread; produced chiefly from wheat, though barley, rye, and even rice are sometimes admitted into its composition. Com.

BATE [bait], *v. a.* to remit; to lessen in price. Com. 'Mate's desport dear, tenpence a pound, tak' it or lave it; 'e ŏŏdna *bate* a half-penny.' Cf. **Banter.**

'*Laf.* Yes, good faith, every dram of it, and I will not *bate* thee a scruple.'—*All's Well,* II. iii. 234.

'*Sic.* Sir, the people
Must have their voices; neither will they *bate*
One jot of ceremony.'—*Coriolanus,* II. ii. 144.

BATHED [baidh·d], *part. adj., obsols.* sodden; underdone: said of meat.—PULVERBATCH; WORTHEN; CORVE DALE. 'Betty, your fire's bin too slow, the meat isn't enough, it's *bathed* like somethin' between roasted an' boiled.'

BATHER [baadh·ur'], *v. a.* to tread down.—CLEE HILLS. 'The young turkies *bather* the mowin' grass sadly.' Cf. **Pather.**

BATHY [baidh·i'], *adj.* same as **Bathed.**—SHREWSBURY. Cf. **Beethey.**

BAT-STAFF [bat·stu'f], *sb., obs.?* same as **Bat** (1).—PULVERBATCH; BISHOP'S CASTLE; CLUN. '*In the Great Chamber . . .* twelve bedstaves with a *battstafe.*'—*Inventory . . .* Owlbury Manor-House, Bishop's Castle, 1625. Cf. 'Batte-staffe,' *Perticulus fustis batillus* in *Prompt. Parv.* with WAY's Note, p. 26. See **Buck.**

BATTER-DOCK [bat·ur'dok], *sb. Rumex obtusifolius,* broad-leaved Dock.—ELLESMERE. 'Beware of a breed if it be but a *batter-dock*' is a proverbial saying heard about Welshampton. It implies the need of caution in dealing with persons who come of a family characterized by 'failings.' RAY, p. 82, has—'Beware of breed; *Cheshire*, i. e. an ill breed.'

BATTIN [bat·in], *sb.* a truss of straw, consisting of two sheaves secured by bands of straw round the middle.—ELLESMERE. The term is used in the singular form only. Twelve *battin* make a thrave, q. v. Cf. **Boutin.**

BAUSON [baus·n], *sb.* an over-corpulent person. Com. 'Whad a great *bauson* 'e's givun.'

BAUTERED [bau·tur'd], *adj.* tangled; 'unkempt:' said of hair.—ELLESMERE. Cf. Shakespeare's 'boltered,' signifying 'clotted.'

> 'For the *blood-boltered* Banquo smiles upon me.'
> *Macbeth*, IV. i. 123.

BAUTERY [baut·h'r'i'], *idem.*—WELLINGTON.

BAUTIN [baut·i'n], same as **Battin**, q. v.—LUDLOW. Cf. **Boutin.**

BAWME [baum·], *sb. Melissa officinalis*, the herb-balm.—PULVERBATCH. 'I doubt that family's mighty bad off, the poor ŏŏman said 'er'd 'ad nuthin but a drop o' *bawme* tay all the wik.' '*Bawme*, herbe or tre, *Balsamus Melissa.*'—*Prompt. Parv.*

BAY [bai·], *sb.* a compartment of a barn used as a storehouse for threshed straw, or grain in the straw before it is threshed. Com.

> 'Earth
> By Nature made to till, that by the yearly birth
> The *large-bayed* barn doth fill.'—*Drayton* in WEDG.

Cf. **Dunce-hole.**

BAYLY [bai·li'], SHREWSBURY; WHITCHURCH. [baayl·i'], PULVERBATCH; LUDLOW, *sb.* the head of the working staff on a farm; a bailiff. His duties are very multifarious: he gives directions to the men under him; where there is not a shepherd he manages the flocks, he shears the sheep, measures hedges, sows broadcast, leads the field in harvest, &c. &c. 'Aye, *Bayly* 'ere, an' *Bayly* theer, as if I could be i' twenty places at once. I dunna know who'd be *Bay̆ly*.'

> 'Seth sekelar men schul have non soulys in kepyng;
> And pytton here personache to ferme to a *baylé*.'
> JOHN AUDELAY'S *Poems*, p. 33.

'. . . Abraham Puller, of Edgboulton . . . was a long time *Bayly* to my lady Corbett, of Acton Reyner, alias Acton Reynold.'—GOUGH'S *History of Myddle*, p. 73.

> 'Ther nas *baillif*, ne herde, ne other hyne,
> That he knew his sleighte and his covyne.'
> CHAUCER, *The Prologue*, l. 603, ed. Morris.

Hic ballivus, a baylé. *Nominale*, xv. cent. in Wr. vocabs., vol. i. p. 211.

BAZ [baz·], *v. a.* to beat; to thrash.—WEM. 'Young chap, I'll *baz* yore back if yo binna sharp.' Cf. **Baste** (2), also **Beat.**

BE [bi'·], an intensitive prefix, as *be*-fangle, *be*-spattle, &c. Com.

BEÄM [bi'·u'm], *sb.*, *var. pr.* a beam of wood.—PULVERBATCH;

CORVE DALE; WEM.—Qy. com. 'The 'ouse is despert low, an' a great *beäm* across the kitchen as yo' met'n knock yore yed agen.'

BEAN-HAULM [bi'·h'n aum·']. See **Haulm**. The general pronunciation of *bean* is that of the fractured diphthong as noted above, though it may be heard occasionally as *bane*.

BEAR [baer'·], *sb.* the large block of sandstone forming the hearth or base of the furnace on which the molten iron rests. 'After being subjected to the great heat of the iron it becomes metamorphosed, and represents a hard, solid block of stone mixed with iron in one heterogeneous mass, when it is pulled out and called the furnace-*bear*.'—COLLIERY, *Iron-works*.

BEÄRD [bi'aa·r'd], (1) *sb., var. pr.* the beard.—PULVERBATCH. Qy. com. 'The beärd won't pay for the shaving' is a proverbial saying analogous to the French—'*Le jeu ne vaut pas la chandelle.*' 'Peggy, the Maister's gid me that owd 'edgerow atween the barley bonks for tatoes, if I'll rid it; but I 'ardly think *the beärd 'll pay for the shavin'*.' 'Well, John, pŭttin' one thing anunst another, I think it ŏŏl; theer's some good owd stouls in it as ŏŏd mak' us firein' for 'afe the winter.'

(2) *v. a.* to thicken the lower part of a hedge by putting thorns into it.—PULVERBATCH. Qy. com. As the top of a hedge is 'brushed,' so the lower part is *beärded*, by putting the 'brushings' into the thin places. 'I've tined the glat, an' *beärded* the bottom, so as the pigs canna proke through.'

BEÄS [bi'u'ss], *sb. pl.* beasts, meaning cattle. Com. Cf. **Bests**.

BEÄST [bi'u'st], *sb., var. pr.* an animal of the bovine species. Com.

BEÄST-LEECH [bi'u'st-leech·], *sb.* a cow-doctor, a hedge-farrier.—PULVERBATCH; CHURCH STRETTON; BRIDGNORTH. Qy. com. in S. Shr.

'One Peter Braine, an excellent *Beast-Leech*.'—GOUGH'S *History of Myddle*, p. 120.

'Also that it lyek yow that John Mylsent may be spoken to, to kep well my grey horse, and he be alyve, and that he spare no met on hym, and that he have konnyng *lechys* to look to hym.'—*Paston Letters*, A.D. 1470, vol. ii. p. 413.

Cf. **Cow-leech**.

BED-HILLIN' [bed·il·in], *sb.* the covering of a bed; usually a 'home-made' quilt.—WEM.

'I remember the soldiers fetched bedding from Newton, for the use of the soldiers there. [Abright Hussey.] They tooke onely one coarse *bed hilling* from my father.'—GOUGH'S *History of Myddle*, p. 8.

BED-OF-BEEF, *sb.* the flank; in the living animal the intestines lie on it as on a bed—hence its name.—NEWPORT. Qy. com.

BEEF [beef·], *sb., pec.* an ox or cow intended for slaughter.—CLUN. They *kill a beef* at Clun only once in three months. A butcher explained as a reason for this [1875] that the inhabitants of Clun were 'a very *oukit* sort of folk,' who would probably not buy the meat if provided for them at their own doors, though they would willingly 'send for it all the way from Bishop's Castle!' Cf. Fr. *un bœuf*. See **Bif**.

BEESTIN'-CUSTARD, *sb.* 'beestings' flavoured with spice, sweetened, and baked in a dish lined with paste. Com. Cf. **Barfut-custard.**

BEESTINGS [bees·tinz], NEWPORT; ELLESMERE. [bais·tinz], SHREWSBURY. [bwa'ysti'n], CLUN. [bi'·sti'nz], PULVERBATCH; BRIDGNORTH, *sb.* the milk taken from the cow immediately after calving. It is of a peculiar richness, and has the property of thickening when cooked, as ordinary milk does with the addition of eggs. Ash has *beestings*, which he calls a corrupted spelling of *biestings*. A.S. *beost, bystings*. Ger. *biest-milch*. See 'beestings' in WEDG. der. 'beestin'-custard,' &c.

BEESTIN'-PUDDING, *sb.* 'beestings' made into a batter with flour, to which are added sugar and carraway seeds; then tied in a cloth and boiled.—ELLESMERE. Qy. com.

BEETH [beedh·], *v. n.* to decay; to wither.—CORVEDALE.

BEETHED [beedh·d], (1) *part. past.* decayed; withered.—*ibid.*

(2) same as **Bathed**, q. v.—*ibid.*

BEETHY [beedh·i'], (1) *adj.* dank; sodden: said of fallen leaves. —CRAVEN ARMS; CLUN.

(2) *adj.* sodden; underdone: said of meat.—*ibid.* Cf. **Bathy.**

BEETLE [beet·l], *sb.* a heavy, iron-bound wooden mallet, used for driving iron wedges into wood for the purpose of splitting it.—CRAVEN ARMS; CLUN.

'There goes the wedge where the *beetle* drives it.'
RAY'S *Proverbs*, p. 167.

'Betylle, *malleus*.'—*Prompt. Parv.* A.S. *býtl*, a mallet. Cf. **Mall.**

BEFANGLED [bi'fang·ld], same as **Fangled**, q. v.—WEM. See **Be.**

BEGGARED [beg·ur'd], *part. adj.* impoverished: said of land that has been 'let down' from want of manure and tillage. Com.

BEGGARLY [beg·ur'li'], *adj.* poor, as applied to land. '*Beggarly* land' is land that will not yield well. Com.

BEGGAR'S-NEEDLE, *sb. Scandix Pecten*, Venus comb.—WELLINGTON.

BEHAPPEN [bi'apn], *adv.* perhaps; like enough. Com. '*Be'-appen*,' says Jack Dallow, 'is a saying current about Bridgnorth.' See Bk. II., *Folklore*, &c., 'Popular and Proverbial Sayings.' Cf. **Mayhappen.**

BELIKE [bi'leik·], same as **Behappen.**—SHREWSBURY; MUCH WENLOCK; WEM.

'Thys sedicious man [Isaiah] goeth also forthe, sayinge, . . . Thy wyne is myngeled wyth water. Here he medeleth with vinteners, *be like* ther were bruers in those dayes, as ther be nowe.'—LATIMER, *Sermon* iii. p. 86.

BELL [bel·], *v. n.* a shortened form of bellow, applied to cattle. Not common.—MUCH WENLOCK. A.S. *bellan*, to roar; to bellow. Cf. **Bellock** (1).

BELL-HORSE, *sb.*, *obs.* the leader of a string of pack-horses.—CORVE DALE. The *bell-horse* was so named from its carrying a bell attached to its neck, the sound of which served as a guide to the others along the dark, winding roads which they traversed, while laden with charcoal or other produce. As late as 1840 or thereabouts—perhaps later still—strings of pack-horses might have been seen, presenting a striking and picturesque appearance as they threaded their way through rough, stony tracks, their bridles gaily decorated, and conducted by men of gipsy-like mien. See '*Bell-horses, bell-horses*, what time of day?'—Bk. II., *Folklore*, &c., 'Games.'

BELLISE [bel·i'ss], *v. a.* a corrupted form of *baleise*, q. v.—LUDLOW. The term is not common.

BELLOCK [bel·u'k], (1) *v. n.* to bellow; to roar. Com. ''Ark the cow *bellockin'*; 'er wants 'er cauve, see 'ow 'er elder's pounded, poor thing.' See **Bell.**

(2) *v. n.* to cry vociferously. Com. 'We maden 'im gŏŏ to school, 'is faither an' me, an' 'e *bellocked* all the röäd as 'e went.'

BELLYS [bel·i'ss], *sb.* bellows.—SHREWSBURY; PULVERBATCH; CLUN.

'Jeremiah, blow the fire;
Puff, puff, puff;
Beat, Jack; strike, Tum;
Blow the *bellys*, old man.'
Children's Doggerel Verse.

'j par de *belwes*' is mentioned in a deed relating to the Pastons before A.D. 1444.—*Paston Letters*, vol. iii. p. 419.

Cf. **Ballys.** See **Blow-bellys.**

BELLY-VENGEANCE [bel·i' ven·junss], *sb.* weak beer. Com. 'Pretty 'arrŏŏst drink, indeed! w'y it inna-d-a bit better nor *belly-vengeance.*'

BELOWNDER [bi'lound·ur'], *sb.* a noise as of something heavy falling.—PULVERBATCH. 'Jest after we wenten to bed las' night I 'eärd sich a *belownder*; an' whad should it be but one o' the cheeses 'ad tumbled off the shilf.'

BELT [bel·t], *v. a.* to beat; to castigate.—SHREWSBURY; WEM. Qy. com.

BELTER [bel·tur'], *sb.* anything of an extraordinary size.—*ibid.* 'My ŏŏns, whad a *belter!*' said a gardener, on digging up an immense potato. See **Belt**, so also **Banger** (1), q. v. from **Bang.**

BENNET [ben·i't], *sb.* *Pimpinella Saxifraga*, common Burnet-saxifrage.—CRAVEN ARMS, *Stokesay.* Cf. **Old man's plaything.**

BENT [bent·], (1) *sb.* a strong spiked grass-stalk. Com. In various parts of Shropshire several species of grass are distinguished as *bents*, not one of which is the 'Bent-grass' of botanical authors; as, for instance, *Alopecúrus pratensis*, Meadow Fox-tail-grass; and *Phleum pratense*, Cat's-tail-grass. The peasant children pluck *bents*, and fashion them into coronets and other pretty quaint devices. They employ them also as threads upon which to string wild strawberries. The term is generally used in the plural form.

'June is drawn in a mantle of dark grass green; upon his head a garland of *bents*, king-cups, and maiden-hair.'—*Peacham*, p. 419, in WR.

'*Hoc gramen*, *A*ᵉ bent.'—*English Vocabulary*, xv. cent., in Wr. vocabs., vol. i. p. 191. Mr. Wright observes of this, 'The word *bent* was applied usually to the long, coarse grass growing on the moors, but often in a more general sense to grass of all kinds.' O.H. Germ. *binuz*, a bent, in STRAT. Germ. *binse*, rush; bent-grass.

(2) *sb.* the declivity of a hill; a hollow in a hill.—CORVE DALE; MUCH WENLOCK. *Hayton's Bent* is an example of this application of the term.

> 'And downward on an hil under a *bente*,
> Ther stood the temple of Marz, armypotente.'
> CHAUCER, *The Knightes Tale*, l. 1123, ed. Morris.

BERE [bee·ur'], (1) *sb. Hordeum vulgare*, white square winter barley, four or six rowed.—CORVE DALE. '*Hoc essaticum An*ᵉ bere.' —*Pictorial Vocabulary*, xv. cent. in Wr. vocabs., vol. i. p. 264.

'In 1124 the new form *bærlic*, our *barley*, replaces the old *bere*, which still lingers in Scotland.'—*Sources of Standard English*, p. 64.

A.S. *bere*, barley.

(2) *sb.*, *obsols.* a pillow-case.—BISHOP'S CASTLE; CLUN. This term is now [1876] very rarely heard. Ash has it, ed. 1775.

'*The Brushing Chamber.* One fayre Presse. *In the Seid Presse.* eight paire of flaxen pillow *beares*, one course Pillow *beare*. *Inventory* . . . Owlbury Manor-House, Bishop's Castle, 1625.'

> 'For in his male he hadde a *pilwebeer*,
> Which that, he seide, was oure lady veyl.'
> CHAUCER, *The Prologue*, l. 694, ed. Morris.

'iij fyne pelow *beres*' are named in Dame Elizabeth Browne's Will, A.D. 1487.—*Paston Letters*, vol. iii. p. 464.

BERRIN [baer'i'n], *sb.* a burying; a funeral. Com. 'Theer wurz a power o' folk at the owd Squire's *berrin*.' A.S. *beorgan*, to cover over.

BESMATTER [bi'smat·ur'], *v. a.* to daub; to dirty.—WEM; LUDLOW. A corruption of the old form *besmotter*.

BESMOTTER [bi'smot·ur'], *v. a.*, *obsols.* to smear or daub with mud or other sticky dirt.—WHITCHURCH, *Tilstock*. The word is now [1877] only heard occasionally amongst old people.

> 'Of fustyan he werede a gepoun
> Al *bysmotered* with his habergeoun.'
> CHAUCER, *The Prologue*, l. 76, ed. Morris.

Ash gives as 'obsolete' *besmottrid*, besmutted; bedawbed. Jamieson has *besmottrid*, bespattered; fouled. A.S. *besmitan*, to besmut; defile. Du. *smodderen*, to dirty; daub.

BESMUDGE [bi'smuj·], *v. a.* to smear; to soil; to daub.—SHREWSBURY. 'W'y, Tummy, w'eerever han yo bin to *besmudge* yoreself all o'er athatns?' Shakespeare has *besmirch* in a similar sense.

> 'Our gayness and our gilt are all *besmirch'd*
> With rainy marching in the painful field.'
> *K. Henry V.*, IV. iii. 110.

BESOM [bee·zum]. Com. [bez·um], LUDLOW, *Burford.* [biz·um], CLUN, *sb.* a broom made of birch twigs.

> 'They have need of a *beesom* that sweep the house with a turf.'
> RAY'S *Proverbs*, p. 78.

A.S. *besem, besm,* a besom; a broom.

BESPATTLE, BESPOTTLE [bi'spat·l], WEM. [bi'spot·l], LUDLOW, *v. a.* to bespatter. Cf. **Spattle** (1). See **Be.**

BESSY-BRIN-TAIL [bes·i' br'i'n tail·], *sb.* same as **Brand-tail,** q. v. CLUN, *Twitchen.*

BESTED [bes·ti'd], (1) *part. adj., sl.?* cheated; overreached—what is understood by the slang term 'done.' A word often heard in markets and fairs. Com. 'I changed sid [seed] ŏŏth owd Medlicott, but 'e's *bested* me; mine wuz good six-rowed corn as 'e 'ad, an' this poor, lathy, lean-eared stuff ŏŏl 'ardly gie the sid back.'

(2) *ib.* beaten at any game; defeated. Com. 'Charlie Grice an' me wun 'ăvin a game at "Jack-stones," but I *bested* 'im quick: 'e inna much of a 'and at it.' Jamieson has '*best,*' struck; beaten; which he refers to 'baist,' to overcome. Icel. *beysta,* ferire. Cf. **Baste** (2).

BEST-HUS [best·us], *sb.* a cow-house.—CLUN, *Herefd. Border.* Cf. pronunciation of **Beast** above. See **Hus.**

BESTS, *sb. pl.* beasts.—*ibid.* Cf. **Bĕăs.**

> 'In which that poure folk of that village
> Hadden her *bestes* and her herbergage.'
> CHAUCER, E. 201 (Six-text ed.), Skeat.

O.Fr. *beste.* Lat. *bestia.*

BET AND BURN, *v. a., obsols.,* this phrase designates an agricultural process adapted to the improvement of rough grass land. It consists of paring off the surface soil with an implement called a 'betting-iron,' collecting it into heaps, burning it, and when in a charred state digging it a spade's depth into the ground.—PULVERBATCH; WORTHEN. 'It's a rough plack, but I'm gweïn to *bet an' burn* it; the turf ess is capital for tatoes.' A field on the 'Huglith Farm' is called the *Bettin' Leasow,* from having been treated in the manner above described about the year 1804. *Betting and burning* is still [1871] practised in the neighbourhood of Minsterley.

A.S. *bétan,* to improve; to make better. Cf. 'Beat,' E. D. S., B. vi., also 'Denchering,' in HAL. See **Betting-iron** below.

BETTER [bet·ur'], *adv., pec.* more. Com. '*Better* than a mile.'

BETTERLY [bet·ur'li'], *adj.* superior. Com. 'Tum Roberts is a tidy young chap, 'e's got the garden in a *betterly* condition than 'is faither 'ad.'

BETTERMOST [bet·ur'must], (1) *adj.* best. Com. '*Bettermost* sort of folk.'

(2) *adj.* used to express in excess of; more than. Com. 'Well, Mary, 'ow fare did'n 'ee sen' yore naint?' 'W'y the *bettermost* 'afe o' the way.'

BETTING-IRON [bet·i'n ei·ur'n], *sb.*, *obsols.* the implement used to pare off the turf in the process of 'betting and burning,' as related above. A description of the 'flaying spade,' further on, taken from eye testimony and actual measurement, will—on the authority of one who knew the *betting-iron*—apply equally well to it.

BETTY-GO-TO-BED-AT-NOON, *sb.* *Ornithógalum umbellatum*, common Star of Bethlehem.—ELLESMERE. This plant owes its local name to the circumstance of its flowers closing about mid-day. Sir William Hooker, in his 'British Flora,' says, "Linnæus imagines that the roots of *Ornithógulum umbellatum* are the 'Doves' Dung' which was sold so dear at the siege of Samaria, as mentioned in 2 Kings vi. 25. They are still much used for food in the Levant." Cf. **Peep-o'-day.**

BET-WELL [bet·wi'l], *sb.* the wicker, bottle-shaped strainer placed over the spigot-hole within the mash-tub, to prevent the grains passing through into the wort.—WELLINGTON; WHITCHURCH, *Whixall.* Cf. **Pooch** (1).

BETWIX [bi'twik·s], *prep.* betwixt; between.—SHREWSBURY; PULVERBATCH. ''Er's a mighty pretty 'eifer; yo ŏŏnna see a better *betwix* this an 'ereford.' Cf. **Atwixt.**

> 'He seith he can no difference fynde
> *Bitwix* a man that is out of his mynde
> And a man which that is dronkelewe.'
>
> CHAUCER, C. 494 (Six-text ed.), Skeat.

'And he wold fayne have a resonable end *betwyx* us, wher to he wyll helpe, as he seythe.'—*Paston Letters*, A.D. 1479, vol. iii. p. 266.

'Mr. Oliphant says that the O.E. *betwox* appears for the first time as *betwix* in the Peterborough Chronicle, drawn up in the Midland speech of 1120. That about the year 1250 Layamon's poem was turned into the English of the day, and *betwyx* became *betwixte.*'—*Sources of Standard English*, pp. 58—153.

BEZZLE [bez·l], *v. n.* to drink hard; to sot.—PULVERBATCH; WELLINGTON.—Qy. com.

'They that spend their youth in loitering, *bezzling*, and harlotting.' —MILTON (A.D. 1641), *Animad. upon Remons. Def.*

See **Bezzle** in HAL.

BEZZLER [bez·lur'], *sb.* a toper; a sot.—*ibid.* ''E's a reg'lar *bezzler.*'

> 'Oh me! what odds there seemeth 'twixt their cheer
> And the swoln *bezzle* at an alehouse fire.'
>
> *Hall's Satires*, v. 2 (A.D. 1597), in HAL.

BIBSTERS, *sb. pl.*, *obs.* ale-sellers.—SHREWSBURY.

'That the Bailiffs should make Serjeants for whom they could answer, the Serjeants to account for issues and estreats of courts, and

Bibsters' fines every quarter.' (Orders issued by the Corporation and selected from Exchequer books.)—PHILLIPS' *History of Shrewsbury*, p. 161.
Cf. **Tensors.**

BIF [bi'ff·], *sb.*, *var. pr.* beef. Com. ''E made a great mistake—liked vail [*veal*] better nor *bif*,' was said of one who married the niece instead of the aunt.

BIG-SORTED [big·sau·r'tid], *adj.* proud; stuck-up. Com. They say of such a person, ''E's as *big-sorted* as ess.'

BILBERRY [bil·br'i'], *sb. Vaccinium Myrtillus*, whortleberry.—WELLINGTON; WEM.

'There pinch the maids as blue as *bilberry*.'
Merry Wives of Windsor, V. v. 49.

'*Billberries* . . . are termed whortleberries or windberries.'—*Academy of Armory*, Bk. ii. ch. v. p. 81.
See 'Bilberry' in WEDG. Cf. **Wimberry.**

BILE [bei·l], *sb.* a boil. Com. Mr. Halliwell says *bile* is 'the genuine word. It is found in the early editions of Shakespeare, and in most early writers.'
'Laid to as a cerot with pitch, it resolueth pushes and *biles*.'—HOLLAND'S *Pliny*, xx. 13 (A.D. 1634).
Cf. **Bwile** (2).

BILL [bil·], *sb.* a bill-hook; a sickle-shaped implement, having a handle about five feet in length, which admits of its being used with both hands. It is employed for various agricultural purposes—reaping peas, 'brushing' hedges, &c., &c. Com.
'. . . although it bee but a pickavill, a *trouse bill*, or a clubbe staff.'—GOUGH'S *History of Myddle*, p. 35.
'Scythes and sneads, *hedge-bills*, and broad hooks.'—*Auctioneer's Catalogue* (Stoddesden), 1870.
'*Falcis*, wudu-bil, siþe, rifter.'—*Latin and Anglo-Saxon Glosses*, xi. cent., in Wr. vocabs., vol. ii. p. 35. *Hoc falcastrum*, a bylle. *Nominale*, xv. cent., in Wr. vocabs., vol. i. p. 235.
Cf. 'Much Ado,' III. iii. 44. See **Bag.**

BILLY-BAT, *sb. Pleiótus communis*, Long-eared Bat.—PULVERBATCH; CHURCH STRETTON. '*Billy-bat* come under my 'at.' Cf. **Hat-bat.**

BILLY-BITER, *sb. Parus cæruleus*, the Blue Titmouse.—BRIDGNORTH. From the furious way in which the female bird 'bites' the fingers of bird-nesting boys comes the appellation *Billy-biter*.

BILLY BLACKCAP, *sb. Pyrrhula rubicella*, the Bullfinch.—BRIDGNORTH. Cf. **Bud-nope.**

BILLY-BUTTON, same as **Bachelor's button**, q. v.—ELLESMERE.

BILLY-CLIPPER, same as **Barbine**, q. v.—PULVERBATCH.

BILLY-HOOTER, *sb. Súrnium Alúco*, common Brown Owl.—CLUN. Cf. **Oolert.**

BILLY WHITETHROAT, same as **Peggy Whitethroat**, q. v.—BRIDGNORTH.

BIN [bin·], (1) been; are. See **Grammar Outlines** *verb* 'To Be.'

> 'And winking Mary-buds begin
> To ope their golden eyes;
> With every thing that pretty *bin*
> My lady sweet, arise.'
> *Song in Cymbeline*, II. iii.

> 'Blushes that *bin*
> The burnish of no sin,
> Nor flames of ought too hot within.'
> CRASHAW (first half 17th cent.), in NARES.

(2) *sb.* a corn-coffer.—NEWPORT; LUDLOW.

'The word *binna* occurs in a deed of the year 1263, in Chron. W. Thorn, 1912, where it signifies a receptacle for grain.'—WAY.

> 'Wel cowde he kepe a gerner and a *bynne*.'
> CHAUCER, *The Prologue*, l. 593, ed. Morris.

A.S. *bin*, a manger. Cf. **Cofer**, also **Cub** (1).

BINDS [beindz·], *sb. pl.* strata lying upon the coal; a sure indication of coal beneath.—COLLIERY; M. T. *Binds* are locally distinguished as 'blue,' 'grey,' &c. See **Coal-field**.

BING [bingg·], (1) *sb.* a kind of store-room or small granary within a larger one, or within a 'bay;' which can be locked up, and into which grain can be put in bulk after it is threshed and before it is 'bagged up.'—SHREWSBURY; WELLINGTON.

> 'You might have seen them throng out of the town,
> Like ants when they do spoil the *bing* of corn.'
> SURREY'S *Poems*, p. 191, ed. Bell.

Bynge, *Theca, cumera.*—*Prompt. Parv.* Sw. *binge*, a heap. See 'Bing' in WEDG. Cf. **Bin** (2).

(2) *sb.* a receptacle for flour.—SHREWSBURY; PULVERBATCH. Qy. com. '*In the great Buttery* one *binge*.'—*Inventory* . . . Manor-House, Owlbury, Bishop's Castle, 1625.

In the Indenture of delivery of Berwick Castle, in 1539, occurs, 'in the pantre, a large *bynge* of okyn tymbar with 3 partitions.'—*Archæol.* xi. 440, WAY.

(3) *sb.* a place railed off from the cow-house in which fodder is kept in readiness for feeding the beasts.—NEWPORT; WHITCHURCH; OSWESTRY.

BIRDS'-EGGS [bur'd·z eg·z], *sb. Siléne inflata*, Bladder Campion.—CRAVEN ARMS, *Stokesay*.

BIRD'S-EYE [bur'd·z ei], *sb. Veronica Chamædrys*, Germander Speedwell.—SHREWSBURY.

BISCAKE [bis·kaik], *sb., var. pr.* a biscuit. Com.

BISHOPPED [bish·u'pt], (1) *part. adj.* confirmed.—PULVERBATCH; WELLINGTON; ELLESMERE.—''Er wuz *bishopped* i' Sosebry a wik las' Tuesday.'

> 'And *metropolitanus*
> And baptisede and *busshoppede*.'
> *Piers. Pl.* [C. xviii. 267], p. 559, ed. Wr. (Notes).

A.S. *biscoped*, confirmed.

(2) *part. adj.* said of milk that has been burnt to the pan in boiling. —BISHOP'S CASTLE. This use of the term may occasionally, but very rarely, be heard in an isolated kind of way throughout the county; it seems to be nearly obsolete. A corrupted form, ''ishopped,' has been noted, but probably it was an individual instance. In the neighbourhood of Craven Arms and about Welshampton some of the old people say when the milk is burnt, 'The bishop's pŭt 'is fŭt in it.'

'When a thinge speadeth not well, we borowe speach and saye, The *bysshope* hath blessed it, because that nothinge speadeth well that they medyll withall. Yf the podeche be burned to, or the meate over rosted, we saye, The *bysshope* hath put his fote in the potte, or The *bysshope* playd the coke, because the byshopes burn who thei lust and whosoever displeaseth them.'—*Tyndale, Obedience of a Christen Man*, 1535, in WR.

Jamieson has the following: 'Bishop's Foot; it is said, *The Bishop's foot has been in the broth*, when they are singed.' And observes, 'This phrase seems to have had its origin in times of Popery, when the clergy had such extensive influence that hardly anything could be done without their interference.'

(3) *part. adj., sl.* a horse is said to be *bishopped* when his teeth are artificially marked for purposes of deception with regard to his age. Com.

BISOM. See **Besom**. 'Scopæ, *verriculam*, a bissom.'—DUNCAN'S *Appendix Etymologiæ*, A.D. 1595, E. D. S., B. xiii. A.S. *bism*, a besom.

BISSON [bis·u'n], *adj., obs.?* blind.—BRIDGNORTH. 'The poor owd mon's aumust *bisson*.' 'Aye, 'is eyes han bin bad a good bit.'

'. . . your *bisson* conspectuities.'—*Coriolanus*, II. i. 70.

In the Lindisfarne or Durham MS. of the Latin Gospels we have the word 'caeci' (S. Mat. ix. 28), with the Old Northumbrian Gloss. above, 'bisena *vel* blinde,' i. e. *bissen* or *blind* men, the *a* being the nom. pl. ending. A.S. *bisen*, blind.

BIT [bit·], *sb.* the wide part or blade of an agricultural shovel.—MUCH WENLOCK.

BIT-BAT [bit·bat·'], same as **Billy-bat**, q. v.—SHREWSBURY; WEM.

BLACK-BESS [blak bes·], *sb.* any small black beetle is so called. Com. Two *black-besses* that were sent for entomological examination proved to be respectively, *Amara familiaris* and *Leistis fulvibarbis*. 'I ketched two *black-besses*, ma'am, an' pŭt 'em in a box to sen' to yo, but w'en I went to start the box, I opened it to see wun they all right, an' theer I fund as they 'ad etten one another; an' I couldna get two more nod then, an' I wuz that vexed,' said Betty Andrews of Cruck Meole (1872).

BLACKBIRD, *sb. Turdus torquatus*, the Ring Ouzel.—BRIDGNORTH.

BLACKCAP, *sb. Parus ater*, the Cole Titmouse.—BRIDGNORTH.

BLACK-HEADED TOMTIT, *sb. Parus major*, the Great Titmouse. —BRIDGNORTH. Cf. **Tom-noup**.

BLACK-JACKS, *sb. pl.* the heads of the Ribwort Plantain, *Plantago lanceolata*.—COLLIERY, *Lilleshall*. Cf. **Fighting-cocks**.

BLACK-MULLOCK [blak mul·uk], *sb.* peat-turf.—WHITCHURCH, *Whixall Moss;* ELLESMERE. *Turf-mullock* is the refuse of the peat which has been cut for burning. Cf. **Mullock.**

BLACK-QUARTER [blak·kwau·r'tur'], *sb., obs.* In the domestic economy of a cottage it is called *black-quarter* when there is no milk, the cow being 'dry for calving,' or when the store bacon is finished before the new flitch is ready for eating.—PULVERBATCH.

BLACKSMITH, *sb. Emberiza citrinella,* Yellow Bunting, or Yellow Ammer.—BRIDGNORTH. *Blacksmith* is evidently a play upon the name *Yellow Hammer,* as it is often spelt.

Speaking of this bird, Mr. Yarrell says, 'I have ventured to restore to it what I believe to have been its first English name, Yellow Ammer, although it appears to have been printed Yellow Ham and Yellow Hammer from the days of Drs. William Turner and Merrett to the present time. The word *ammer* is a well-known German term for Bunting, in very common use. Thus Bechstein employs the names Schnee-ammer, Grau-ammer, Rohr-ammer, Garten-ammer, and Gold-ammer for our Snow Bunting, Corn Bunting, Reed Bunting, Ortolan or Garden Bunting, and Yellow Bunting. Prefixing the letter *h* to the word appears to be unnecessary, and even erroneous, as suggesting a notion which has no reference to any known habit or quality in the bird.'—*History of British Birds,* vol. i. p. 518, 3rd ed. 1856.

BLACKSMITH'S DAUGHTER, *sb.* a hanging lock.—PULVERBATCH. 'I mus' pŭt the *blacksmith's daughter* on the garden wicket, fur I see the straibries bin gweïn too fast.'

BLACK STONE, *sb.* a vein of iron-stone lying on both sides of 'Lightmoor Fault.'—COLLIERY; M. T.

'The Black Stone and Blue Flats are rich and valuable iron-stones. These stones occur in nodules, and produce from 1000 to 1600 tons per acre. The famous cold blast iron of the Lilleshall Company is made from equal mixtures of Black Stone, Blue Flats, and Penny Stone, with a little proportion of others.'—*Notes on the Shropshire Coal-Field,* by T. PARTON, F. G. S., 1868.

Cf. **Penny Stone.** See **Blue Flats.**

BLADE [blaid·], (1) *v. a.* to trim a hedge by 'feathering' it to the. top —CLEE HILLS.

'Bladyn' herbys or take away the bladys.'—*Detirso, Prompt. Parv.*

A.S. *blǽd,* a leaf; branch; twig.

(2) *sb.* that timber in a roof which goes at an angle from the top of the 'king post' to the beam of the 'principal.'—CLUN. The *blade* is known in Cheshire as the *back.*

BLAEBERRY [blai·br'i'], *sb.* same as **Bilberry,** q. v.—COLLIERY.

'Nae birns, or briers, or whins e'er troubled me,
Gif I cou'd find *blae-berries* ripe for thee.'
ALLAN RAMSAY, *The Gentle Shepherd,* II. iv. p. 34.

BLANKS AND PRIZES, *sb. pl.* a dish of beans and bacon. Com. The *blanks* are the beans, the *prizes* the morsels of bacon which are somewhat sparsely distributed amongst them. To prepare this popular dish, the bacon must be cut into 'dice,' fried, and then poured with its 'liquor' into the ready-boiled beans: all must then be stirred together with a seasoning of pepper, and—as the old cookery books say—'messed forthe.'

BLATHER [blaadh·ur'], (1) *sb.* noisy, senseless prate; empty flattery; humbug.—WEM. 'Sich *blather!* I hanna-d-a bit of patience wuth it.' Cf. **Bledder** (2).

> 'But I shall scribble down some *blether*
> Just clean aff-loof.'—ROBERT BURNS, *Poems*, p. 77, l. 33, c. 2.

(2) *v. n.* to prate senselessly, &c.—*ibid.* 'Theer's never no 'eed to be tŏŏk on 'im, 'e *blathers* an gosters all day lung.' '*Balbutio*, to bladder.'—DUNCAN'S *Appendix Etymologiæ*, A.D. 1595, E. D. S., B. xiii.

BLEDDER [bled·ur'], (1) *sb.* a bladder.—PULVERBATCH; LUDLOW.

> 'Wiþ a face as fat · as a full *bledder*
> Blowen bretfull of breþ. . . .'—*P. Pl. Cr.*, l. 222.

'Bleddyr, *vesica.*'—*Prompt. Parv.* A.S. *blædre*, a bladder.

(2) *sb.*, *sl.*? chatter; prate.—LUDLOW. 'Shet yore *bledder*' is equivalent to 'Hold your tongue.' Cf. **Blather** (1).

BLESSING [bles·in], *sb.* a small quantity given over the measure in selling milk, &c.—SHREWSBURY; PULVERBATCH; COLLIERY. 'They'n begun to sell milk at both housen at Churton; I shall gŏŏ to the poor owd Missis, 'er gies capital mizzer an' a good *blessin'* into the bargain.'

BLETHER [bledh·ur'], *sb.* a bladder.—SHREWSBURY; PULVERBATCH. 'Look at them lads makin' a fŭt-ball o' that *blether*; they'n bost it jest now.'

> 'An' bid him burn this cursed tether,
> An', for thy pains, thou'se get my *blether*.'
> ROBERT BURNS, *Poems*, p. 33, l. 18, c. 2.

BLIND [bleind·], *adj.* abortive: said of blossoms.—SHREWSBURY; PULVERBATCH. 'I shanna-d-ăve above 'afe a pint o' straibries this 'ear, the blows bin all *blind.*' See **Blow**.

BLIND-BALL [bleind·baul], *sb.* the fungus *Lycoperdon Bovista.*—SHREWSBURY; PULVERBATCH. See **Fuzz-ball**.

BLIND-BUFF [bleind buff·], same as **Blind-ball**.—CLUN.

BLIND-BUZZARD [bleind buz·ur't], (1) *sb. Melolontha vulgáris*, the common Cockchafer. Com.

(2) *sb. Lucánus cervus*, the Stag Beetle.—COLLIERY.

BLIND-MAN'S-HOLIDAY [blein monz ol·i'di'], twilight. Com. Florio has, '*Feriáto*, vacancy from labour; rest from worke; *blind-man's-holyday*,' in HAL.

BLIND SIEVE [bleind·siv], *sb.*, *obsols.* a sieve—in appearance like a tambourine—made of sheepskin, and not perforated. Com. The *blind sieve* was formerly much used in granaries for dressing corn, and is still so employed by cottage-folk for their 'laisins.' By a peculiar eddying motion given to it—which it requires an 'expert' to do—the chaff and lighter parts of the grain are brought to the surface, in the middle of the sieve, and can be easily removed. The grain is cleansed very effectually by this simple process. Cf. **Rieing sieve.**

BLIND-WORM [bleind·wur'm], *sb. Anguis fragilis*, the Slow-worm. Com. Cf. **Ether.**

'Newts, and *blind-worms*, do no wrong.'
Mids. Night's Dream, II. ii. 11.

'*Hec scutula*, a blynde-worme.'—*Nominale*, xv. cent., in Wr. vocabs., vol. i. p. 223.

BLINK [blingk·], (1) *v. n.* to glimmer; to burn in a faint, fitful manner.—PULVERBATCH. 'The fire wuz mighty doggit this mornin', it kep' *blink, blink, blinkin'*, I thought I should never a got the men's breakfast.'

'For me, I swear by sun an' moon,
An' every star that *blinks* aboon,
Ye've cost me twenty pair o' shoon
Just gaun to see you.'
ROBERT BURNS, *Poems*, p. 34, l. 8.

O.Dutch, *blinken (micare, splendere)*, to blink; gleam. Dan. *blinke*, to blink; shine.—STRAT.

(2) *sb.* a glimmer; a spark of fire.—PULVERBATCH; CLUN; LUDLOW. 'I raked the fire las' night, thinkin' to be up yarly, an' it burnt out; theer wunna-d-a *blink* left.'

BLINKED [blingkt·], *part. adj., obsols.* said of butter-milk that from exposure to the sun's rays has acquired a peculiar, bitter, ill flavour. —PULVERBATCH. 'W'y this butter-milk 'is as bitter as sût—I toud yo' as it ŏŏd be *blinked* if it wunna covered o'er, the sun wuz shinin' right into the steen.' Jamieson has 'to blink,' to become a little sour; a term used with respect to milk and beer. He suggests a 'gloss' on this by way of query—giving the derivation, Germ. *blinken*, coruscare—'as struck with lightning, which, we know, has the effect of making liquids sour; or as denoting that of *sunshine*, or of the heat of the weather.'

BLOB [blob·], (1) *sb.* a blister; a watery pustule. Com. 'Dick's got a bad leg; it come jest a little *blob*, an' sprad all o'er 'is leg like S. Anthony's fire.'

(2) *sb.* a bubble. Com. 'That fresh drink dunna-d-'afe work, on'y jest a *blob* 'ere an' theer.' 'By-gum, Missis, be'appen it inna-d-able!'

(3) *sb.* a drop.—PULVERBATCH. Qy. com. 'The swat stood on 'is foryed i' *blobs* as big as pase.'

'Though both his eyes should drop out like *blobbes* or droppes of water.'—Z. Boyd, in WEDG.

(4) *v. a.* to let out a secret. Com. 'I'll tell yo' a saicrit, Mary, if yo'n mind nod to *blob*.' Cf. 'Blabbe, wreyare of cownselle,' in *Prompt. Parv.*, p. 37.

BLOBBER [blob·ur'], (1) *sb.* saucy, idle chatter. Com. 'Oud yore *blobber*.' Cf. 'Blaberyn, or speke wythe-owte resone,' in *Prompt. Parv.*, p. 37.

(2) *v. n.* to cry without tears in a broken, noisy way, as children do

who have not much cause of complaint. Com. 'Whad bin 'ee *blobberin'* fur, Tum? nobody's 'urtin' yo'.' See 'Blobure' (blobyr), with Way's notes, in *Prompt. Parv.*, p. 40.

BLOCKING-AXE [blok·inak·s], *sb.*, *obs.* an axe employed for squaring timber, having a handle so curved horizontally, right and left, as to save the knuckles of the workman.—MUCH WENLOCK.

BLOCKY, BROCKY [blok·i'], WEM. [br'ok·i'], PULVERBATCH, short and stout. 'Yore new waggoner's despert *brocky*, 'e'll want a lungish pitchin' pikel.'

BLOOD-STICK [blud·stik·'], *sb.* a kind of club used by farriers to drive in the 'flues' when bleeding an animal. Qy. com. See **Flues.**

BLOOD-WORT [blud·wur't], *sb.* *Erythræa Centaúrium*, common Centaury.—PULVERBATCH, *Hanwood.* Cf. **Sanctuary.**

BLOODY-BUTCHERS [blud·i' buch·ur'z], *sb.* *Orchis Mascula*, early purple Orchis. Com. This is the 'dead men's fingers' of Shakespeare. See *Hamlet*, IV. vii. 172.

BLOODY-WARRIOR [blud·i' waa.r'·i'u'r'], *Cheiranthus Cheiri Sanguineus*, the very dark double Wall-flower.—ELLESMERE.

BLOOM [bloo·m], *sb.* a mass of iron as it comes out of the puddling furnace before it is hammered and sent through the rolls.—COLLIERY, *Iron-works.* Kennett, MS. Lansd. 1033, mentions a rent for ovens and furnaces called bloom-smithy-rent, in HAL.

BLOW [blou·], (1) *sb.* bloom; blossom.—SHREWSBURY; PULVERBATCH. Qy. com. 'Theer's a good *blow* o' the plum-trees this 'ear.' 'The bread ŏŏna keep w'ile the corn's i' the *blow*' is an expression frequently heard in the hot weather of blossoming time, when bread is apt to become 'ropy.'

(2) *v. n.* to come into leaf.—SHREWSBURY, *Uffington.* 'The 'edges bin beginnin' to *blow*; they'n soon be i' full lef if this weather lasses.'

> '& buskede him out of þe buschys · þat were *blowed* grene,
> & leued ful louely · þat lent grete schade.'
>
> *William of Palerne*, l. 21.

BLOW-BELLOWS [bloa·bel·'u'ss], *sb. pl.* a pair of bellows.—NEWPORT.

'. . . After that cometh suggestion of the divel, this is to say, the divel's *belous*, with which he bloweth in man the fire of concupiscence.'—CHAUCER, The Persones Tale (*secunda pars, penitentiæ*).

BLOW-BELLYS [bloa·bel·'i'ss], *idem.*—PULVERBATCH; WEM; ELLESMERE. ''As any one sid the *blow-bellys*? I canna get this fire to tind.' Cf. **Ballys.** See **Bellys.**

BLOWS [bloa·z], *sb. pl.* affairs; things to be done.—PULVERBATCH; WORTHEN. To be 'full of blows' is a phrase equivalent to having 'many irons in the fire.' 'I canna-d-aw'ile to fettle that this mornin', I'm *fŭll o' blows.*'

BLUE-BACK [bloo·bak·'], *sb.* *Turdus piláris*, the Fieldfare.—MUCH WENLOCK.

BLUE-BELL, *sb. Hyacinthus, non-scriptus,* Wild Hyacinth.—SHREWSBURY. Generally used in the plural form *Blue-bells.*

BLUE-BONNET, *sb.* same as **Billy-biter,** q. v.—BRIDGNORTH.

BLUE-BOTTLE, *sb. Centauréa Cýanus,* Corn Blue-bottle. Com.

BLUE-CAP, the same as **Blue-bonnet.**—BRIDGNORTH.

BLUE FLATS, *sb.* a valuable iron-stone.—COLLIERY; M. T.
'This iron-stone, which occurs in nodules of all imaginable shapes, is full of the fossil *Unio* or *Anthracosia,* and impressions of the vegetable Lycopodiaceæ.'—*Notes on the Shropshire Coal-field,* by T. PARTON, F.G.S., 1868.
See **Black Stone,** also **Coal-field.**

BLUE FOX-GLOVE, *sb. Campanula Trachélium,* Nettle-leaved Bell-flower.—WHITCHURCH, *Tilstock.*

BLUE-HEADS [bloo·edz], *sb. pl.* the flowers of *Scabiosa succisa.*—CORVE DALE. Cf. **Devil's-bit.**

BLUNGE [blunzh·], *v. a.* to knead or mix up hastily, as of dough or dumpling.—ELLESMERE; WEM. 'Now, Jenny, be sharp an' *blunge* up a bit o' dumplin' for the lads, or they wunna think it's 'Amp'n [*Hampton*] Wakes.'

BOAR-SEG [boa·ur' seg·], *sb.* a boar that has been gelt.—CLEE HILLS. Qy. com.

BOAR-THISTLE [boa·ur' thiss·l], *sb. Carduus lancelolatus,* Spear Plume-thistle.—CLEE HILLS. Qy. com.

BOASOM [boa·zum], *sb., var. pr.* bosom. Com.

BOBBERSOME [bob·ur'sum], *adj., sl.?* free; lavish.—NEWPORT. 'Dunna yo be too *bobbersome* wi' yore money.'

BOBBISH [bob·ish], *adj., sl.?* pretty well and bright in health and spirits. Com.

BODGE [boj·], (1) *v. a.* to patch clumsily; to mend roughly. Com. 'Theer, I've tore my gownd! I canna-d-awilde to mend it properly, nod now, so I mun *bodge* it up.' Cf. **Botch.**

(2) *sb.* a rough patch; a clumsy, bungling job of any kind. Com. Cf. Shakespeare's *bodged* for 'bungled.'—3 *K. Henry VI.* I. iv. 19.

BOES [boaz·], *sb. pl. Pediculi humani; insecta parva comâ infantum.*—SHREWSBURY; PULVERBATCH; LUDLOW. Cf. **Bugs.** See Bk. II., *Folklore,* &c., 'Superstitions concerning Insects.'

BOFFLE [bof·l], *v. a., var. pr.* to confuse; to baffle. Com. 'I knowed right well 'e wuz tellin' me a lie, so I cross-waund 'im a bit an' soon *boffled* 'is story.'

BOIT. See **Bait.**

BOKE [boak·], (1) *v. n.* to thrust at, as with a rail or stake.—SHREWSBURY; WEM; WHITCHURCH. ''E pooled a stake out o' the 'edge an' *boked* at 'im.' *Boke* is another form of *poke;* but a curious distinction is made between the *b* of the one word and the *p* of the other; they are used 'with a difference.' As B is a heavier letter than P, so to *boke* is a heavier action than to *poke*. A man *bokes* with a rail or other thick piece of wood, and *pokes* with a light stick. See B and P in **Grammar Outlines** (*consonants*).

(2) *v. n.* to stare about in a stupid, half-blind way; to shy, when used with reference to a horse.—WEM, *Hopton*. ''E went alung the rŏoäd *bokin* an' startin' at everythink, till I thought I c'u'd niver a druv 'im 'ere.'

BOLTIN [boal·ti'n], same as **Battin**; refined pronunciation.—SHREWSBURY; PULVERBATCH; CLUN. Der. 'boutin.'

BOND [bond·], (1) *pret.* and *part. past*, bound.—NEWPORT; WEM; ELLESMERE.

'Three hundred foxes took Sampson for Ire,
And alle her tayles he togider *bond*.'
CHAUCER, B. 3222 (Six-text ed.), Skeat.

Cf. **Bund** (1).

(2) *sb.* a straw band for binding sheaves.—*ibid.*

'"Canstow seruen," he seide · "other syngen in a churche,
Other coke for my cokers · other to the cart picche,
Mowe other mowen · other make *bond* to sheues."'
Piers Pl., Text C. pass. vi. l. 14.

'The *Bond* is that as ties the Corn into Bundles.'—*Academy of Armory*, Bk. III. ch. iii. p. 73.

Cf. **Bund** (2).

(3) *sb.* the load of coal or iron-stone to be drawn up. Com. M. T.

(4) [bon· *or* bond·], *sb.* a band or gang of pit-men working together.—COLLIERY; M. T. ''E works i' the *bon*'.'

BONDSMEN [bonz·men], *sb. pl.* men working in a *band*, whose duty it is to remove the coal after it has been 'holed' by the 'holers;' first knocking away the 'sprags,' q. v. Com. M. T.

BONK [bongk·], *sb.* a sloping height; a steep pitch or incline in a road. Com. 'Mr. Gittins o' Churton 'ad a prime mar' spiled the tother day gweïn down Welbi'ch [*Welbatch*] *bonk*; the waggoner must a bin a nauf to gŏŏ down a place like that athout scotchin'.'

'Quhil the reflex of the diurnal bemys
The beyn *bonkis* kest ful of variant glemys.'
GAWIN DOUGLAS (A.D. 1513), *Prol. of the XII Buk of Eneados. Specim. Eng. Lit.*, xiii. l. 62.

Cf. **Bonky-pieces**.

BONKIE [bongk·i'], *sb.* a girl employed on the 'bank' as a 'bonksman' is.—COLLIERY; M. T.

BONKSMAN [bongks·mun], *sb.* a man on the 'bank' who disposes of the coal as it comes to the surface.—COLLIERY; M. T.

BONKY-PIECES [bongk·i' pee·si'z], *sb. pl.* steep, sloping fields.—PULVERBATCH. Qy. com. 'I tell yo' a double plough's no chonce i' them *bonky-pieces*, they'n chuck it out spite o' yore tith.' Cf. **Sidelant leasow**.

BONNY [bon·i'], *adj.* comely; stout—what the French understand by *embonpoint*; quite a distinct sense from the Scottish 'bonnie.' The term is not of very frequent use.—PULVERBATCH; CORVE DALE; CLEE HILLS. 'Betty Jenkins praises 'er pastur's; whad a bonny ŏŏman 'er's gwun! 'er wuz a poor torrel the las' time I sid 'er.'

BOOK [buek·], WHITCHURCH, *Tilstock*;—school book. [ski'uel buek·]. Cf. Scotch 'Buik.'

BOOGIE [bŏŏg·i'], *sb.* a supernatural being; a spectre; a household sprite.—SHREWSBURY; PULVERBATCH; WORTHEN.

'*K. Edw.* . . . For Warwick was a *bug* that fear'd us all.'
3 *K. Henry VI.* V. ii. 2.

W. *bwgan*, a bugbear. Cf. **Bugabo.** See Bk. II., *Folklore*, 'The Bŏŏgies an' the Saut-box.'

BOOSEY [boo·zi'], *sb.* the upper end of the cow-stall where the fodder lies. Com. 'Booc or boos, netystalle.'—*Prompt. Parv.* A.S. *bós, bósig*, a stall; manger; crib.

BOOSEY-PASTURE, *sb.* ground claimed by the off-going tenant at Lady Day for the use of his cattle up to the first of May, on which to consume hay, turnips, and such produce as is not allowed to be taken off the farm.—PULVERBATCH. Qy. com.

BOOSEY-STAKE, *sb.* the stake to which the cow is fastened in the *boosey* by a 'cow-chain.'—WEM. Qy. com. Cf. **Stelch** (2).

BORE-PASSER [boa·ur' pas·ur'], *sb.* a gimlet.—WORTHEN. 'Persowre (or wymbyl), *Terbellum.*'—*Prompt. Parv.* Cf. **Nail-passer.**

BORROW [bo'·r'u'], *sb., var. pr.* a barrow.—CORVE DALE.

BOSH [bosh·], (1) *sb.* the rough, bristly part of a boar's head between the ears.—PULVERBATCH. Qy. com.

(2) *sb.* the curly front of a bull's head between the horns.—*ibid.*

'*Leon* . . . The steer, the heifer, and the calf
Are all call'd neat.
. . . How now, you wanton calf?
Art thou my calf?
Mam. Yes, if you will, my lord.
Leon. Thou want'st a rough *pash* and the shoots that I have
To be full like me.'—*Winter's Tale*, I. ii. 128.

BOSS [boss·], (1) *sb.* a protuberance of iron in the top part of the spindle in which the brandarts were placed. Com. See **Brandarts.**

(2) *sb.* a hassock. Com.
'1778. for a *Boss* for the Communion 0. 8. 0.'—*Churchwardens' Accounts*, Hopton Castle, Salop.

BOST [bost·], (1) *v. a., var. pr.* to burst. Com. 'I doubt we sha'n 'ăve to *bost* that door open, for the kay canna be fund 'igh, low, nor level.'

(2) a slight imprecation. Com. '*Bost* that chap, w'y couldna-d-'e a lef' that lather w'eer I pŭt it? an' then I should a 'ad it.'

BOSTEN [bos·n], *part. adj.* full to repletion; burst.—SHREWSBURY; ELLESMERE. Qy. com. 'I conna tak' no more, Missis, I'm welly *bos'n.*'

BOTCH [boch·], *v. a.* to patch old clothes, but not necessarily in a rough and clumsy way.—NEWPORT. Cf. **Bodge** (1). See 'Botch' in WEDG.

BOTTLE [bot·l], (1) *sb.* a small wooden barrel or keg for carrying drink to the field. Com. *Bottles* vary in size: those used by the ploughman or labourer hold about three pints, while the harvest-men's *bottles* contain from two to six quarts. 'Tell Bill to tak' the 'ackney mar' an' start off ŏŏth them two *bottles* an' bay̆te-bags to the turmit fallow—it's aumust the middle o' the day.' 'Bag and bottle.' —*Robin Hood*, ii. 54, in HAL. Cf. **Costrel.**

(2) *sb.* a bundle of hay.—PULVERBATCH; CORVE DALE; ELLESMERE. 'I axed the Maister to let me 'ăve a bit of 'ay; 'e said 'e darna sell, but 'e'd gie me a *bottle*, as the cow wuz nigh cauvin.'

> 'Al-though it be nat worth a *botel* hey.'
> CHAUCER, H. 14 (Six-text ed.), Skeat.

> 'I have a great desire to a *bottle* of hay.'
> *Mids. Night's Dream*, IV. i. 37.

'To look for a needle in a *bottle* of hay' is a common proverb which occurs in *Clarke's Phraseologia Puerilis*, 1655. See HAL.

> 'A thousand pounds, and a *bottle* of hay,
> Is all one thing at Doom's-day.'
> HOWELL'S *Proverbs*, ed. 1660, in HAL.

'*Botelle* of hey.'—*Fenifascis.* '*Botelle* of haye, *botteau de foyn.* Aske you for the hosteller, he is aboue in the haye lofte makynge *botelles* (or *botels*) of hay, *boteller.*'—PALSG. 'In Norfolk it denotes the quantity of hay that may serve for one feed.'—FORBY.—*Prompt. Parv. and Notes.*

BOTTLE-TIT, *sb. Parus caudatus*, the Long-tailed Tit-mouse.—LUDLOW. Cf. **Can-bottle.**

BOTTOMLEY BAY, *sb.*, *var. pr.* Botany Bay.—NEWPORT; WHITCHURCH. See 'Sosebry' in *Place Names.*

BOUGHS [bou·z], to be 'up in the *boughs*' is a phrase signifying to be put quickly out of temper; to be easily offended.—SHREWSBURY; PULVERBATCH; CORVE DALE; CLEE HILLS. ''Er wuz all *up i' the boughs* in a minute.' Cf.—

> 'Now in the croppe, now doun in the breres.'
> CHAUCER, *The Knightes Tale*, l. 674, ed. Morris.

BOUGHT OFF THE PEGS, *phr. sl.*? said contemptuously of second-hand or 'slop-made' clothing.—SHREWSBURY; PULVERBATCH; WEM. ''E *bought it off the pegs*, it ŏŏnna do 'im much joy.'

BOUK [bou·k], (1) *sb.*, *obsols.* a bucket of what is technically known as 'bend ware.'—PULVERBATCH. Cf. **Quaigh.**

(2) *sb.* a pail with an upright handle, used for various purposes of brewing, dairy-work, &c.—WEM; WHITCHURCH; ELLESMERE.

'He beareth Azure, a Milk-Pail, Argent. This is the Badge and Cognizance of the Milk-Maids, whom I have heard give this sort of vessel several denominations; of some it is called a Pail, a Cruck, an

Eshon; of others a *Bouk.'—Academy of Armory*, Bk. III., ch. viii. p. 335.

A.S. *buc*, a bucket. See Bk. II., *The Bouk*, 'A Descriptive Poem.'

(3) *sb.* a large barrel used for drawing water in sinking purposes. Com. M. T.

(4) *sb.* the box of a wheel.—PULVERBATCH.

BOUKIN [bou·ki'n], *sb., obsols.* same as **Bush** (2).—PULVERBATCH; CLEE HILLS.

BOUSTER [bou·stur'], *sb., var. pr.* a bolster. Com.

BOUT [bou·t], *sb.* a course in knitting round a stocking.—PULVERBATCH; WELLINGTON. ''Ou bin 'ee gettin' on ŏŏth that stockin?' 'I'm at the quirk ŏŏthin a *bout* or two.'

(2) *sb.* a turn once up and down a ploughed field. Com. The number of *bouts* to a 'but' varies according to the nature of the soil, on stiff land fewer than on dry, light ground. To *bout up* is to ridge ground for turnips.—CLEE HILLS.

(3) *sb.* a turn of illness. Com. 'I'm glad to 'ear poor John's better, 'e's 'ad a bad *bout* on it; 'e's bin o' the box three months.' *On the box* means dependent on the sick club.

(4) *sb.* a party.—PULVERBATCH. 'They'd'n a big *bout* at the uvver 'ouse las' wik.'

BOUTHERS [bou·dhur'z], *sb.pl.* boulders; paving-stones.—NEWPORT.

BOUTIN [bou·ti'n], usual pronunciation of 'boltin,' q. v. James France of Pulverbatch said of an uncomely woman-servant that, ''Er wuz jest like a *boutin* o' straw ŏŏth one bun' round it.' See **Bund**. Cf. **Bautin**.

BOW [boa·], *sb.* a steel fire-guard encompassing the kitchen fire-place. Rings usually encircle the top rod of the *bow* for the children to play with.—SHREWSBURY; PULVERBATCH. Qy. com.

BOWERY [bou·h'r'i'], *sb.* a bower; a shady recess.—SHREWSBURY; MUCH WENLOCK.

BOW-HAULER, BOW-HAULIER [buo'au·lur', buo'au·lyur'], *sb., obsols.* a man who by means of a rope drags a barge along the Severn. —MUCH WENLOCK. The *first* form of the word obtains between Coalport and Buildwas; the *second* about Cressage.

'With regard to the mode of hauling barges, an obvious improvement would be the opening of a good towing-path along the river, and the substitution of horses for men in this slavish labour. That this project is perfectly feasible, even on the most difficult banks, has been shown by the laudable and successful experiment of Mr. Reynolds, of Ketley, who formed a path for horses near his manufactories at Coalport, and carried it on through rugged banks, and over some of the worst fords, for a distance of two miles, to the Iron Bridge.'—REV. J. NIGHTINGALE'S *Description of Shropshire*, p. 41, ed. 1810.

BOWL [bou·l], (1) *sb.* a child's hoop.—SHREWSBURY; PULVERBATCH; ELLESMERE. 'Now, Tummy, dunna bring yore *bowl* o' the causey; gŏŏ i' the lane, yo'n 'ăve a better run theer.'

(2) *v. a.* to trundle; to wheel, as of a perambulator, &c.—SHREWSBURY; PULVERBATCH; MUCH WENLOCK. An inquiry after an invalid girl was answered by the assurance that she was better, as she had been *bowled out* in her chair.

BOX-BARROW [bok·sbaar'·u'], *sb.* a hand-barrow for carrying cut grass.—ELLESMERE.

BOX-HARRY, *v. n.*, *sl.*? to take things as they are; to 'rough it.'—SHREWSBURY; CLEE HILLS. Qy. com.

BRADE [br'aid·], (1) *sb.* breadth; width.—PULVERBATCH. 'The *brade* o' my 'and.'

'& deliuer þe londes a-ȝen · in lengþe & in *brede.*'
William of Palerne, l. 3055.

A.S. *brǽde*, breadth; width.

(2) *sb.* a breadth or width of any kind of stuff from selvage to selvage.—SHREWSBURY; PULVERBATCH; WEM; ELLESMERE. ''Ow many *brades* han 'ee got'n·in yore gownd? it looks mighty skimity.'

BRADLING [br'ad·li'n], *part. adj.* brooding: as a hen over her chickens.—WEM; WHITCHURCH. A.S. *brǽdan*, to spread; to stretch out. Cf. **Broodle.**

BRAG [br'ag·], *sb.* praise; boast. Com. 'Han 'ee tasted Clar's drink lately?' They praisen it oncommon.' 'Ugh! good beer needs no *brag.*'

Cf. 'Good wine needs no *bush.*'—See *P. Pl. Cr.*, l. 706.

BRAGGABLE [br'ag·u'bl], *adj.* very good; commendable.—PULVERBATCH. ''Ow's Dick likin' 'is plack?' 'Oh! 'e ses it's nuthin' *braggable*, they bin cummudgin sort o' folks.'

BRAGGLIN' [br'ag·lin], *part. adj.* swaggering; boasting.—WELLINGTON. 'Oud Barber wuz *bragglin'* o'er them byests o' 'isn at the far.'

BRANDARTS [br'and·ur'ts], *sb. pl.*, *obs.* four iron arms fixed into the 'boss' of a spindle, in a flour-mill, for the purpose of carrying the upper mill-stone. Com. What are called 'balance-irons' have now superseded the old *brandarts.* See **Boss** (1).

BRAND-IRON [br'and·ei·'ur'n], (1) *sb. obs.*? a branding-iron; an instrument employed to brand horses or cattle with their owners' names, when animals belonging to different persons were turned out on the same hill-common. The *brand-iron* was made hot to sear the animal with the stamp. Com. See **Burn-mark.**

(2) *sb.* a similar instrument to the foregoing, still used for branding agricultural implements, such as spades, forks, &c., with the owner's name. Com.

(3) *sb.*, *obs.* a frame to keep up the logs on the fire.—BISHOP'S CASTLE.

'*The kytchynge* . . . six broches, two *brandirons*, one fire forke.'—*Inventory* . . . Owlbury Manor-House, Bishop's Castle, 1625.

A.S. *brand-isen*, a tripod or andiron; an 'iron' to support 'brands' of wood.

BRAND-TAIL [br'an·tail], *sb.* *Ruticilla phœnicura*, the Redstart. —CLUN. The name *Brand-tail* has like allusion with *Redstart* to the flame-coloured feathers in the bird's tail. Cf. **Fire Brand-tail.**

BRASH [br'ash·], (1) *sb.* the loppings off trees used for heating brick ovens, &c. Com. 'I've got a famous 'ŏŏd-pil; the Maister soud me the *brash* off two ash trees for ten shillin', an' it'll las' me a twel'-month.' See **Cordwood.** Cf. **Trouse.**

(2) *sb.* a watery rash or eruption on the skin.—PULVERBATCH. 'The child's got a *brash* on 'im like as if 'e wuz nettled; but I spect it's on'y throm 'is tith.'

BRASS [br'ass·], (1) *sb.* copper coin. Com. 'I tell John 'e should ax the Maister to pay 'is wages in silver, for agen I've lugged two five-shillin' papers o' *brass* all the way to Sosebry; it swags me down.' The *brass* thus spoken of was the heavy copper money of the reign of George III.; 'two five shillin' papers' of which would weigh seven and a half pounds avoirdupois. The term *brass* is now (1877) occasionally heard as slang for money of any kind; but it is really a respectable old word in the restricted sense of copper—or its equivalent, bronze—coin.

'Wiþ-out pite, piloure · pore men þow robbedest,
And bere here *bras* at þi bakke · to caleys to selle.'
Piers Pl., Text B., pass. iii. l. 195.

See also St. Matt. x. 9.

(2) *sb.* shamelessness; impudence. Com. ''Er's got a face as big as a warmin'-pon, an' as much *brass* in it.'

'Can any *face of brass* hold longer out.'
Love's Labour Lost, V. ii. 395.

BRASSY [br'ass·i'], *adj.* bold; shameless. Com. 'That's a *brassy*, impudent young scoundrel; 'e'll stick at nuthin short o the gallus.'

BRAT [br'at·], (1) *sb.* a coarse 'over-all' made with sleeves, worn by dairy-maids when milking.—PULVERBATCH. Qy. com.

'And a *bratt* to walken in by daylight.'
CHAUCER, *C. T.*, l. 16349.

A.S. *bratt*, a cloak. W. *brat*, a clout; a rag. Gael. *brat*, a mantle; apron; cloth, in WEDG.

(2) *sb.* a child's pinafore. Com. Cf. **Barrow.**

(3) *sb.* a contemptuous term for a child. Com.

'Thy *brat* hath been cast out, like to itself,
No father owning it.'—*Winter's Tale*, III. ii. 88.

BRAWN [br'aun·], *sb.* a boar pig. Com.

'A brinded pig will make a good *brawn* to breed on.'—RAY'S *Proverbs*, p. 52.

Cf. **Boar-seg.** See 'Brawne of a bore' in *Prompt. Parv.*, p. 48.

BRAZIL [br'az·il], *sb.* iron pyrites; *sulphuret of iron*, of which the component parts average—sulphur, 52·15; iron, 47·85.—Com. M. T. *Brazil* is found chiefly in the 'yard coal.' William Humphreys of Arscott, a collier, described it as 'growing' in large round masses of a hundred-weight or more, very hard, but when cut through resembling broken brass in appearance. He said he had once met with some in the 'thin coal' at Le Botwood, but it was 'very rar to find it out o' the yard coal.' *Brazil* is so extremely hard as to have given rise to a common proverbial saying, 'As hard as *brazil*.' It, however, decomposes rapidly when laid in heaps and moistened with water. Vitriol is made from it. This mineral—though not known in the locality as *brazil*—occurs in large masses in the Flintshire coal measure. One seam is called the 'brassy coal,' from the quantity of it mingled with the coal. Cf. 'Brasyle' in *Prompt. Parv.*, p. 47.

BREAD AND CHEESE [br'ed·un chee·z], (1) *sb.* the Yellow Ammer. So called from the peculiar intonation—almost articulation—of its song.—BRIDGNORTH. See **Blacksmith.**

(2) *sb.* the first young leaves of the hawthorn: children eat these, and call them *bread and cheese*.—SHREWSBURY; ELLESMERE.

(3) *sb.* the seed-vessels of *Malva sylvestris*, common Mallow: eaten by children as *bread and cheese*.—SHREWSBURY; WEM. Cf. **Cheeses.**

BREAK [br'aik·], *v. n.* the explanation of this *may* be given by citing Mr. G. Christopher Davies in the following:—

'There is a peculiarity of the Ellesmere water which I can scarcely account for, but which, I am informed, some other sheets of water in England also present. To use the local name, it *breaks*. Every summer, for a longer or shorter time, the water becomes full of some matter held in suspension. In appearance it is like small bran, rendering it impossible sometimes to see more than a foot through the water. The mere becomes of a greenish hue, and to leeward, where it is the worst, it gives rise to a very disagreeable smell. It is always worse in hot weather. To the eye the matter held in suspension seems to consist of husk-like pieces of fibre, such as might be stripped off a plant. From this I was inclined to think that the Anacharis is chiefly to blame for this appearance, and that in some way the outer coating of the plant sloughs off and floats during its decay in the water. This is, however, but a supposition. The other meres do not *break* to such an extent, but they are not so full of the Anacharis, and the water is probably purer. While the water is *broken* the fish refuse to bite.

'A correspondent of the *Field* said the organism causing the *break* was *Ectrinella articulata*, a doubtful genus, some authors considering it a vegetable, and some an animal organism. It is depicted in Sowerby's English Botany, vol. xxii. p. 208, tab. 2555.'—*Mountain, Meadow, and Mere*, pp. 16, 17, ed. 1873.

BREAKSTUFF [br'ee·kstuf], *sb.*, *var. pr.* breakfast.—COLLIERY.

BREAK THE YEAR, *phr.* this is a term of servant-life. In the rural districts it is customary to 'hire' for the year, and servants leaving before the expiration of the twelve-months are said to *break the year*, which it is considered a discreditable thing to do, and loss of 'a character' may be the penalty. Com. In the N. and N.E. borders of Shropshire, Christmas is the 'hiring-time,' but throughout the county generally, it is on or about the first of May. 'Bessy mak's a many Mays i' the 'ear, an' 'er's send 'er yarnest back twize this 'irin'; 'er *broke 'er 'ear* from Longd·n, an' agen from the Moat: 'er's a rollin' stwun an' that never gethers no moss.'

BREAK-UP [br'aik·up], *v. n.* to clear up: said of the weather. Com. 'What do you think, James, will it be fine to-day?' 'I dunna know whad to say, ma'am, the weather's caselty; but be'-appen it 'll *break-up*.' They say, too, the clouds will *break-up;* that is, open and disperse. Compare with this Shakespeare's use of the term, in the sense of to break open.

'*Leon. Break up* the seals and read.'
Winter's Tale, III. ii. 132.

'*Glou. Break up* the gates, I'll be your warrantize.'
1 *K. Henry VI.*, I. iii. 13.

BREAST [br'est·], *v. a. To breast* a hedge is to lay thorn-boughs on the top of the hedge-bank, to prevent sheep or other animals browsing the hedge, or breaking down the top of the bank.—ELLESMERE. Cf. **Beärd** (2).

BREBIT. See **Brevit** (1). An old woman said of a cat that was continually hunting about for food, ''Er's al'ays ibbidgin' an' snibbidgin', an' *brebitin'* about.'

BREE [br'ee·], *sb. Túbanus bovínus;* the Gad-fly.—PULVERBATCH; CLEE HILLS; WEM. Cf. **Breese.**

BREECH [br'i'ch·], *v. a.*, *obsols.*? to cut the wool from about the roots of the sheep's tails before shearing-time.—PULVERBATCH. ''E's gwun to *brich* them ship.' Cf. **Burl.**

BREECHING-WOOL [br'i'ch·in ŏŏl], *sb.*, *obsols.*? the wool cut off as described above.—*Ibid.* It is used for padding harness. 'That *brichin-ŏŏl* mun be weshed an' sprad i' the sun; the sadler 'll want it nex' wik.' Cf. **Burlings.**

BREESE [br'eez·], *sb.* same as **Bree**, q. v.—WEM.

'The *breese* upon her, like a cow in June.'
Antony and Cleopatra, III. x. 14.

'*Hic brucus*, a breas.'—*Nominale*, xv. cent., in Wr. vocabs., vol. i. p. 223. 'Brese.'—*Locusta, asilus.* 'A brese, *atelabus, brucus, vel locusta.*'—CATH. ANGL. '*Atelabus*, a waspe or a brese.'—ORT. VOC. 'Brese or long flye, *prester.*'—PALSG. A.S. *brimsa*, tabanus.—*Prompt. Parv. and Notes.* Cf. **Briz.**

BREVIT, BREBIT, BRIVIT [br'ev·i't], PULVERBATCH; CLEE HILLS; LUDLOW. [br'eb·i't], WHITCHURCH. [br'iv·i't], SHREWSBURY; CLUN; WEM; ELLESMERE.

(1) *v. n.* to search; to pry; to examine inquisitively. 'Who's bin *brevitin'* i' my drawer? ever see sich a rumpus it's in.'

(2) [br'ev·i't], PULVERBATCH. [br'iv·i't], SHREWSBURY; CLUN, *sb.* a minute search. 'I've lost the kay o' the owd beer, an' canna find it up nur down; but I'll 'ăve another *brevit* for it.' Cf. **Hunt.**

BRIAR-BOSS [brei·ur' boss·], *sb.* the gall of the Wild Rose, formed by the insect known as *Cynips rosâe.* See Bk. II., *Folklore*, &c., 'Superstitious Cures' (*toothache*). Cf. **Buzzy ball.**

BRIBIT [br'ib·i't], *sb.* a short visit.—WHITCHURCH, *Whixall.*

'Where's Margaret—isn't she at home?' 'No, sir, but 'er's on'y gwun on a *bribit* to owd Molly Price's.'

BRICKLE [br'ik·l], *adj.* brittle.—PULVERBATCH. Qy. com. 'Chaps, yo' mun mind 'ow yo' 'ondlen that corn; the straw's despert *brickle*—yo'n lose all the yeds.' Cf. **Britchy**.

'Fraile, *brickle*, soone broken. Fragilis. *Brickle* glass was quickly dashed a sunder. Futilis glacies ictu dissiluit. Virg.'—BARET, *Alvearie*, A.D. 1580.

BRIDE-WEED, *sb. Linária vulgaris*, yellow Toad-flax.—SHREWSBURY.

BRIEF [br'i'f·], (1) *adj.* prevalent; general. Com. 'Han yore childern 'ad the maizles? I 'ear as a bin mighty *brif* about.' Bailey has *brief*, common or rife, ed. 1782.

(2) *adj.* busy; bustling.—WEM; ELLESMERE. ''Er wuz that *brif* about clānin' the 'ouse down w'en I seed 'er, 'er couldna-d-aw'ile to spake to me.'

(3) *adv.* quick.—CLUN. 'Now then, be *brif* an' finish that job.' Compare with this Shakespeare's use of the term in the following citation:—

'——Follow me with speed; I'll to the king:
A thousand businesses are *brief* in hand.'
K. John, IV. iii. 158.

(4) *sb.* a writing setting forth the circumstances by which a poor person has incurred loss, as by fire—the death of a horse, cow, &c. Such a one takes the *brif* about to collect money for his indemnification.—WORTHEN.

BRIMBLES [br'im·blz], *sb.pl.*, *var. pr.*, *obs.*? brambles.—PULVERBATCH. 'I mun push tuthree *brimbles* i' the glat till it can be tined.'

BRITCHY [br'ich·i'], *adj.* brittle.—WEM. 'The straw's that *britchy* yo canna 'ardly tie it up into boutins.' A.S. *breotan*, to break. Cf. **Brickle**.

BRIVIT. See **Brevit** above.

BRIZ [br'iz·], corrupted form of **Breese**, q. v.—WEM.

BROACH [br'oa·ch], (1) *sb.*, *obs.* the woollen yarn wound on the spindle as it was spun from the wheel. It was shaped somewhat like the 'float' of a fishing-line, high in the middle, and tapering at each end, and was about five inches in length. A piece of paper twisted round the spindle made the foundation upon which the *broach* was constructed, and held it firm when taken off. To give it additional support when removed from the spindle for the further process of winding for twisting, a stick was passed through it. It is probable that it owed its name to this stick, which was—*in se*—the *broach* proper.—PULVERBATCH. 'If yo' bin gwĕĭn to wind that yorn, mind an' nod scrobble the nose o' the *broach*, or yo'n 'ăve it in a soor mess.' O.F. *broche*, *brocque*.—BUR. *Brocque* meant a great variety of pointed things of wood or iron.—PICK.

(2) *v. a.*, *obsols.* to transfix as with a spit.—PULVERBATCH. ''Er *broached* the spit right through the breast o' the turkey.'

'*Broach'd* with the steely point of Clifford's lance.'
3 *Henry VI.*, II. iii. 16.

O.F. *brocer*, *brocher*, piquer.—BUR.

BROACHER [br'oa·chur'], *sb.* a very large sharp-pointed knife.—PULVERBATCH; WHITCHURCH. 'This is a good *broacher* for a flitchen.' About Whixall (Whitchurch) the term *broacher* is applied to anything very large. This has probably arisen from the association of ideas between the big knife and the great pieces it is required to cut.

BROCKY. See **Blocky.**

BROGGIL [br'og·i'l], *sb.* brawl; angry squabble.—WEM. A person on Stanton-on-Hine Heath said, 'Them theer neighbours of ours bin aukert folks to live anunst, but we never consarn 'em, an' so we never 'ăve no *broggil* wuth 'em.' W. *broch*, din; wrath: *brochus*, a fuming; blustering. Cf. Ital. *imbroglio*, perplexity; trouble: *imbroglione*, a fomenter of quarrels. E. *broil*, a contraction of *broggil*.

BROODLE [br'oo·dl], *v. a.* to brood, as a hen over her chickens.—PULVERBATCH; NEWPORT; WEM; ELLESMERE. Cf. **Bradling.**

BROODY [br'oo·di'], *adj.* A hen when wanting to sit is said to be *broody*. Com.

BROOIT [br'oo·i't], *sb.* a good bite of herbage.—CLEE HILLS. ''E's a ploughin' up that meado', an' theer's a good *brooit* on it for the yeows.' Fr. *brouter*, to browse; to nibble. It is proverbially said by the French of an industrious man. 'L'herbe sera bien courte s'il ne trouve de quoi *brouter*.'—CHAMB.

BROOZLE [br'oo·zl], same as **Broodle.**—WORTHEN; WEM.

BROSELEY [br'oa·zli'], *sb.* a clay pipe: so called from the place of its manufacture—*Broseley* (Salop). Com.

BROSTERING [br'os·tur'in], *adj.* domineering; overbearing.—WHITCHURCH, *Whixall.* 'Sich a *brosterin'* fellow 'e is.' *Broster*, greatness; majesty.—*Lexicon Cornu-Britannicum.*

BROTH [br'oth·], *sb.* broth, always in the plural. Com. 'They bin good; let's han tuthree more.'

BROTHE [br'oa·dh], *v. a.* to thicken broth with oatmeal or flour.—SHREWSBURY; PULVERBATCH; WORTHEN; CLUN. 'The Missis come i' the kitchen to get the chaps breakfasts, an 'er took waiter an' bacon liquor an' *brŏthed* it ŏŏth' flour; but the chaps they couldna bar it, an' my brother 'e comen wham,' said a young servant-girl.

BROTHIN [br'oa·dhin], *sb.* oatmeal or flour put into broth to give it consistency.—*ibid.*

BROUSE [br'ous·], *sb.*, *obsols.* the finer trimmings of hedges, such as brambles, &c.—MUCH WENLOCK.

'Amang the *brouys* of the olyve twestis
Seir smaill fowlys wirkand crafty nestis.'
GAWIN DOUGLAS (A.D. 1513), *Prol. of the XII. Buk of Eneados. Specim. Eng. Lit.*, xiii. l. 165.

O.Fr. *broce*, menu bois, *broussailles* (derive de *broce*).—BUR. Cf. **Brushings.** See **Trouse.**

BROWIS [br'ou·is], *sb.* a pottage made by pouring boiling water upon slices of bread seasoned with pepper and salt, and adding to it a lump of butter and a shred of onion. Com.

'They thank'd him all with one consent,
But especially maister Powes,
Desiring him to bestow no cost,
But onely beefe and *browes.*'
King's Halfe-Pennyworth of Wit, 1613, in Wr.

'*Hoc pulmentum*, browys.'—*Nominale*, xv. cent., in Wr. vocabs., vol. i. p. 241. A.S. *briw*, pottage.

BROWN SHEELERS [br'oun shee·lur'z], *sb.pl.* hazel nuts fully ripe and ready to drop out of their husks. Com. 'I got a pocketle o' nuts o' Sunday, an' they wun aumust all *brown sheelers;* it looks as if Pousbry Wakes wunna fare off.'

BROW SQUARE [br'ou· squaa·r'], *sb.*, *obs.* a three-cornered linen kerchief bound about the head of a new-born baby.—Worthen. Cf. **Cross-cloth.**

BRUCK [br'uk·], *sb.*, *var. pr.* a brook. Com. A.S. *brôc*, a spring; brook; rivulet.

BRUM [br'um·], (1) *sb. Cýtisus Scoparius*, common Broom. Com. The young shoots of broom yield a fine bitter, and a decoction of them is frequently taken as a tonic under the generic term of 'yarb tay.' They are also from the same property occasionally used instead of hops for 'fresh drink.' 'Yo should'n get some *brum* tay this spring-time, John; it's a mighty good thing for the stomach.' 'Aye, it is; but it's a power better ŏŏth some barley in it.'

(2) 'It inna wuth w'ile sendin' for 'ops for this drop o' fresh drink; get a 'antle o' nice young *brum.*'

'In the Corporation Accounts of Shrewsbury, 1519, it is ordered that brewers are not to use hops in their brewings under a penalty of vis. viijd. Hops were in use some time before this, for in 1428 the Parliament were petitioned to prevent the use of them, as being a wicked weed.'—Phillip's *History of Shrewsbury*, p. 168.

Perhaps *broom* was used at that time for bittering ale. See Bk. II., *Folklore*, &c., 'Superstitions concerning Plants.'

(4) *sb. Galium verum*, yellow Bed-straw.—Craven Arms.

BRUMMOCK [br'um·u'k], *sb.* a short, strong hook for wood-cutting purposes. Com. 'W'eer's John Roberts gwun?' 'I spect 'e's gwun up to the uvver groun' to tine; I sid 'im tak' 'is *brummock* an' mittens an' 'is bay̆te-bag.'

'. . . Hee was sent to Shrewsbury goale for fellony, where hee hired a silly boy to procure him instruments to breake prison. The boy brought to him a bar of iron and a broaken *broome hooke*, and with these he pulled out severall stones, and made a hole through the stone wall of the dungeon, and soe escaped, but left the tooles behinde him.'—Gough's *History of Middle*, p. 80.

BRUND [br'und·], Pulverbatch. [brun·], Wem, *sb.* a log of wood.

'Pŭt a good *brund* o' the fire an' back it ŏŏth slack, an' then it 'll las' all the ŏnder.'

'So þat child wiþ-draweþ is hond.
From þe fur & þe *brond*,
þat haþ byfore bue brend
Brend child fur dredeþ!
Quoþ Hendyng.'
Proverbs of Hendyng (A.D. 1272—1307).
Specim. Early Eng., iii. l. 185.

'Bronde of fyre. *Facula, fax. ticio torris.*'—*Prompt. Parv.* 'Hic fax —cis, a bronde.'—*Nominale*, xv. cent., in Wr. vocabs., vol. i. p. 229. Cf. **Christmas brund.**

BRUSH [br'ush·], (1) *sb.* stubble: of leguminous crops only.—CLEE HILLS.

(2) *v. a.* to take a crop of peas, beans, or vetches off a field.—*Ibid.*

(3) *v. a.* to trim hedges. Com.

'Cf. Fr. *brosser*, courir à travers des bois & des brousailles: to run through woods or bushes; to *brush* along.'—CHAMB. Also, 'Brusche, *Bruscus.*'—*Prompt. Parv.*

BRUSHING-HOOK, *sb.* a sickle-shaped hook with a long handle, used for *brushing* hedges. Com. Cf. **Bill.**

BRUSHINGS, *sb.pl.* the trimmings off hedges. Com.

'*Brossailles, broussailles*, epines, ronces, &c., croissant dans les forêts & en d'autres endroits: briars; thorns; brambles; bushes.' —CHAMB. 'Bruschalle, *Sarmentum; earnentum; arbustum.*'—*Prompt. Parv.* Cf. **Brouse.**

BRUSTEN [br'us·tu'n], *part. past*, broken.—WELLINGTON. Cf.—

'& wolden *brusten* þe best · nad he be the liȝttere.'
William of Palerne, l. 154.

where *brusten* has the meaning of hurt severely; damaged.

Brusten = A.S. *borsten*, p.p. of *berstan*, to burst *Berstan* became *bresten* in Chaucer. Cf. Icel. *bres;* Swed. *brista*, to break violently.

BUCK [buk·], (1) *sb.* a **T** shaped end to the plough-beam, having notches in it for the purpose of regulating the draught of the plough. The 'shackle' goes into it to which the horses are yoked. Cf. **Copsil** (3).

'The *Buck* is the iron which the Horses are tyed unto.'—*Academy of Armory*, Bk. III. ch. viii. p. 333.

(2) *v. a., obs.* to wash heavy, coarse linen, or the home-spun yarn of which it was commonly made, by the process described under **Buck-wesh** below.—PULVERBATCH. 'We sha'n 'ăve a bumpin' weshin' nex' wik; theer's six an' twenty slippin's o' yorn to *buck*, beside 'afe as many sheets an' smocks.'

'Do-wel shal wasshen and wryngen it.
. . . .
Do-bet shal beten it and *bouken* it.'
Piers Pl., pass. xiv., l. 8939, ed. WR.

Wedgwood says of *buck*, as applied to washing, that 'the true derivation of the word is seen in Gael. *bog*, moist, soft, tender, and as a verb, to steep or soak.'

Der. **Bucking** (2). Cf. **Bucking** (1).

BUCK-BASKET [buk·bas·'ki't], *sb.*, *obs.* a large basket used for carrying the linen at the 'buck-wesh,' q. v.—PULVERBATCH. Qy. com.

'*Fal.* . . . . They conveyed me into a *buck-basket*.
Ford. A *buck-basket!*
Fal. By the Lord, a *buck-basket!* rammed me in with foul shirts, and smocks, socks, foul stockings, greasy napkins; that, Master Brook, there was the rankest compound of villanous smell that ever offended nostril.'—*Merry Wives of Windsor*, III. v. 88—92.

BUCKING [buk·in], (1) *sb.* a state of profuse perspiration; a 'sweating,' caused by violent exertion, said of man or horse.—PULVERBATCH; CLUN; WEM. 'I carried the batch an' the bran throm Habberley Mill, but it gid me a *buckin'*.' *Bucking*, soaking in perspiration, may perhaps be referred to the same root as **Buck** (2). Cf. **Swelter** (2).

(2) *sb.*, *obs.* synonym for 'buck-weshing,' q. v. A shortened form. —PULVERBATCH. 'A *buckin'* an' a soapin'.'

'*Mrs. Page.* . . . Look, here is a basket: if he be of any reasonable stature he may creep in here: and throw foul linen upon him, as if it were going to *bucking*: or—it is whiting-time—send him by your two men to Datchet-mead.'—*Merry Wives of Windsor*, III. iii. 140.

BUCKING-STONE. See **Buck-wesh.** At Grub's Gutter, near Hopton Castle, Salop, there is a large stone which still (1875) bears the name of the *bucking-stone*.

BUCK-LEE [buk·lee·'], *sb.*, *obs.* a lye of wood-ashes obtained from burning green 'brash' or fern, the latter being esteemed the best.—PULVERBATCH. Qy. com. Cf. **Ess-balls.** See Bk. II., *Folklore*, &c., 'Superstitions concerning Days and Seasons' (*Christmas*).

BUCKLES [buk·lz], *sb.pl.* small pointed rods twisted and doubled in the centre, used by thatchers.—ELLESMERE. *Buckles* are employed for the top and eaves of a roof; the intermediate thatching pegs, which are not twisted, are called *lugs*. Shakespeare has *buckle*, to bend.

'And as the wretch, whose fever-weaken'd joints,
Like strengthless hinges, *buckle* under life.'
2 *K. Henry IV.*, I. i. 141.

BUCK-WESH *or* **WESHIN'** [buk·wesh·' *or* wesh·'i'n], *sb.*, *obs.* a large wash of heavy, coarse linen which took place about every three months.—PULVERBATCH; CLUN. Qy. com. In the *buck-wesh* no soap was used, but the linen was boiled in the *buck-lee* described above. It was then carried to a neighbouring stream or spring, and laid upon a smooth stone or a block,—the 'stoul' of a tree standing permanently by the margin of the water often served for the purpose,—there the linen was beaten with a 'batstaff,' after which operation it was well 'swilled' in the pure water. This mode of washing obtained till 1832—40, if not later. A wash of finer linen was called a 'soaping.'

'They bin 'ăvin' a busy wik at Wilderley, a big *buck-weshin'*, *soapin'* an' ship-shearin'.'

'*Mrs. Ford.* . . . You were best meddle with *buck-washing.*'—*Merry Wives of Windsor*, III. iii. 166.

Cf. **Buck** (2).

BUDGET [buj·i't], *sb.* a satchel of bass-matting in which workmen carry their tools.—SHREWSBURY; MUCH WENLOCK.

'O.Fr. *boge*, *bouge*, sac (de cuir), *bogette*, *bougette*, valise; d'où l'ancien anglais *bogett*, aujourd'hui *budget*, que nous avons emprunté . . . . La racine de ce mot se retrouve dans le celtique et l'allemand: ancien irlandais *bolc*; gallois *bolg*, *builg*, ahal; *bulga*, de *belgan*, *pelkan*.'—BUR. Cf. **Frail**.

BUD-NOPE. See **Nope**.

BUFFER [buf·ur'], *sb.*, *sl.?* the master of a household.—SHREWSBURY, *Uffington*; WHITCHURCH, *Prees*. 'I reckon the *buffer* 'll 'ăve to pay for it.' Cf. **Gaffer** (1).

BUFFET-STOOL, *sb.*, *obs.* a stool. Halliwell says, 'variously described.' '*The Low Parlor*, six *buffett-stooles*. *Inventory* . . . Owlbury Manor-house, Bishop's Castle, 1625. Bofet, thre fotyd stole.'—*Tripes.* See Way's note. *Prompt. Parv.*, p. 41. Cf. **Joint-stool**.

BUFT [buf·t], (1) *v. a.*, *var. pr.* to knock about with any soft substance; to buffet.—WHITCHURCH; ELLESMERE. 'I took my 'at an' *bufted* 'im reet well about the yed; I wouldna thrash 'im.'

(2) *v. n.* to stammer.—SHREWSBURY; PULVERBATCH; CLUN. ''Ow that lad *bufts* to-day.' 'Aye, 'e al'ays does 'gen rain.'

BUFTER [buf·tur'], *sb.* a stammerer.—SHREWSBURY; PULVERBATCH; CLUN; NEWPORT. Cf. O.E. *buffere*, stutterer, in STRAT. In Isaiah, xxxii. 4, where our version has 'the tongue of the stammerers,' the Vulgate version has 'lingua balbonum.' Wyclif translates *balbonum* by '*of bufferes*.'

BUFTY [buf·ti'], same as **Buft** (2).—NEWPORT. ''Er *bufties* a bit in 'er talk.' This term is not commonly used.

BUGABO [bŏŏg·u'boa], *sb.* an imaginary object of terror; a hobgoblin.—PULVERBATCH; LUDLOW. '*Bugabo's* comin', Tummy, if yo' binna still.' Cf. **Boogie**.

BUGAN [bŏŏg·h'n], *sb.* the evil spirit; the devil.—LUDLOW, *Herefd. Border*. 'If yo' dunna be qweet I'll let *bugan* tak' yo.'

Mr. Oliphant, speaking of a collection of poems which he believes to have been compiled between 1220 and 1250, and now printed in 'An Old English Miscellany' (Early English Text Society), says, 'We see in page 76 a Celtic word brought into English, a word which Shakespeare was to make immortal. It is said that greedy monks shall be "bitauht þe puke;" that is, given over to the Fiend. The Welsh *pwcca* and *bwg* mean "an hobgoblin;" hence come our *bugbears* and *bogies*.'—*Sources of Standard English*, p. 154.

See **Bŏŏgie**.

BUGGIES [buog·i'z], same as **Bugs**, q. v.—PULVERBATCH; ELLESMERE.

BUGLES [beu·glz], *sb.pl.* beads of any kind.—SHREWSBURY.

BUGS [bug·z], WEM. [buog·z], LUDLOW, *sb.pl. Pediculi humani*, same as **Boes**, q. v. 'I've bin drămin' about *bugs* i' my yed; theer's sure to be sickniss for some on us i' the 'ouse,' said Jane Philips of Lee Brocklehurst. On being asked by what name *bugs*—as usually understood by that appellation—would be distinguished from these *pediculi*, she answered, 'Bed-bugs.'

'Bug,' says Mr. Cyril A. Greaves, 'is the old English equivalent to the Latin *insectum*, and in Kent all insects are popularly called *bugs* . . . Various kinds of insects are specified by the suffix *bug* to their own name, as 'beetle-bug,' &c. The sleep-staying pests which only we call *bugs*, are with them 'bed-bugs.'—*Science Gossip*, June, 1874, p. 140.

BULGE [bul·zh], *v. a., pec.* to dint.—LUDLOW. 'Somebody's gid that new milk-tin a fine knock an' *bulged* the side in.' Cf. **Dinge.**

BULL [bul· *or* buol·], *sb.* the 'coupling' which fastens harrows together so as to give full play to both, in accommodating each harrow to the inequalities of the land.—CLEE HILLS.

BULLED [buol·d], *part. adj., obsols.* swollen: said of cheese that from some cause generate fermentation after being pressed, and consequently rise and bulge.—PULVERBATCH. *Bulled* is a corrupted form of O.E. *bolled*, swelled.

> 'His Bodi was *Bolled* · for wraþþe he bot his lippes.'
> *Piers Pl.*, Text A, pass. v. l. 67.

See also Exodus ix. 31. Dan. *bolne.* Sw. *bulna*, to swell; to bulge.

BULL-HEAD [bul· *or* buol·yed·'], (1) *sb. Cottus góbio*, Miller's Thumb.—CLEE HILLS. Qy. com. Cf. '*Hic mullus* A^{ω}, a bulhyd.'—*Pictorial Vocabulary*, xv. cent., in Wr. vocabs., vol. i. p. 253.

(2) *sb.* the tadpole.—PULVERBATCH.

'A Frog [is] first a *Bull-head*, then a Frog-tail, then a Frog.—*Academy of Armory*, Bk. ii. ch. xiv. p. 325.

BULLIRAG [bul·i'r'ag], (1) *v. a.* to banter; to teaze.—LUDLOW.

(2) *sb.* a banterer; a person who teazes.—*Ibid.* ''E's a reg'lar *bullirag*—never lets one be.'

BULLS' EYES [buol·z eiz], *sb.pl.* holes in cheese caused by the whey not having been properly pressed out, or from having had too much rennet put into the milk.—PULVERBATCH. 'I dunna like this cheese, it's got too many *bulls' eyes* in for me.' Cf. **Eyes.**

BULL-STUB [bul· *or* buol·stub], *sb.* a bull that has been gelt.—CLEE HILLS. Qy. com.

BUM [bum·], *sb.* a contracted form of 'bum-bailiff; a sheriff's officer. Com. 'I 'ear theer's gweïn to be a sale at Betchcot, they'n 'ad the *bums* i' the 'ouse for a fortnit.'

BUMBLE [bum·bl], *sb.* the Humble bee; one of the species *Bombus.* —CLEE HILLS. 'Eh! theer's a big *bumble.*'

BUMMIL [bum·i'l], *v. a.* to beat; to pound. —LUDLOW. Cf. **Pommel.** See B and P in **Grammar Outlines** (*consonants*).

BUND [bund·], (1) *pret.* and *part. past,* bound.—SHREWSBURY; PULVERBATCH. 'Mother, whad'n 'ee think! I've jest sid 'em takin' my nuncle off to Sosebry 'firmary, ŏŏth 'is yed *bund* up; 'e's fell off the ruff at the Squire's, an's aumust killed.' A.S. *bindan,* to bind; *p. t., þu bunde.* Cf. **Bond** (1).

(2) [bun· *or* bund·], *sb.* same as **Bond** (2).—*ibid.* See **Boutin.**

BUNDATION [·bundai·shu'n], *sb.* an abundance. Com. 'Theer'll be a *bundation* o' fruit o' them ras'b'ry-canes I spect.' Cf. **Abundation.**

BUNNIL [bun·il], *sb.* a beverage made from the crushed apples after nearly all the juice has been expressed for the cider. The chief ingredient is *water!*—CLEE HILLS.

BUNT [bunt·], (1) *v. a.* to push with the head as calves do. Com. Cf. **Pote.**

(2) [bùnt], *sb., obsols.* a third swarm of bees from one hive.—NEWPORT. The first is the 'swarm,' *par excellence;* the second, the 'cast;' the third, the *bunt;* the fourth—of rare occurrence—the 'couch.' Old Dinah Shuker of Edgmond, a good authority, said [1874] of the last two terms, 'Very owd words them bin, theer's fe'ŏo [Gl. fi'eo·] as knows o' them nĕems now-a-days. Folks getten noo nĕems for things.' Cf. **Ob** and **Play.**

BUR [bur'·], (1) *sb.* the sweetbread of a calf. Com.

(2) *sb.* a whetstone for scythes. Com.

(3) *sb.* a rough excrescence on trees.—CHURCH STRETTON. Gael. *borr,* a knot; lump; swelling, in WEDG. Cf. **Canker** (3).

(4) *sb.* the hooked scaly head of *Arctium Lappa,* common Burdock. Com.

'. . . Hateful docks, rough thistles, kecksies, *burs.*'
K. Henry V., V. ii. 52.

Fris. *borre, burre.* Dan. *borre.*—Idem in WEDG.

BURL [bur'l], *v. a.* to cut the wool from about the roots of sheep's tails before shearing time.—PULVERBATCH; NEWPORT; ELLESMERE. In the manufacturing of cloths the process of clearing it of the knots, ends of thread, and the like, with little iron nippers called *burling-irons,* is termed *burling.* Todd, in WEDG.

'Burle of clothe, *Tumentum.*'—*Prompt. Parv.* Cf. **Breech.**

BURLINGS [bur'l·i'nz], *sb.* the wool cut off as described above.—*ibid.*—Cf. **Breeching-wool.**

BURN [bur'n], *sb.* a burden; a bundle.—SHREWSBURY; PULVERBATCH; MUCH WENLOCK; WEM. 'Well, I think I've done my shar' for to-day. I got a gŏŏd *burn* o' laisin afore my breakfast, an' two sence; an' fat a *burn* o' sticks throm the coppy to yeät the oven.'

'Then Isaake speaketh to his father, and taketh a *burne* of stickes, and beareth after his father, and saieth . . .'—*Chester Plays*, l. 65.

BURN-MARK, (1) *sb., obs.* the mark on an animal's hide made by the **Brand-iron** (1), q. v.—PULVERBATCH. Qy. com.

(2) *sb.* the stamp of the **Brand-iron** (2) on tools and implements.—*Ibid.*

BURROW [buˑr'oe], (1) *v. a.* to bore.—PULVERBATCH. 'Them ship han *burrowed* thar backs i' the dyche bonk i' the sandy leasow till the roots o' the trees bin bar'.' Cf. A.S. *borian*, to bore.

(2) *adj.* sheltered; shady—'the *burrow*-side of the hedge.'—MUCH WENLOCK.

'þis cowherd comes on a time · to kepen his bestes
Fast by-side þe *boruȝ* · þere þe barn was inne.'
William of Palerne, l. 9.

A.S. *beorgan*, to shelter: *beorh*, a defence; refuge. Cf. **Succourful.**

BURY [baeˑr'i'], (1) *sb.* a rabbit-burrow.—LUDLOW, *Burford.* A.S. *beorh.* Cf. **Burrow** (2).

(2) *sb.* a hole in the ground in which potatoes are kept for winter use, covered with straw and soil.—LUDLOW; NEWPORT. A.S. *beorgan*, to protect; keep; preserve. Cf. **Hod, Hog,** and **Tump.**

BUSH [buoshˑ], (1) *sb.* an iron socket fastened into the centre or 'eye' of the lower mill-stone, in which the spindle that carries the upper mill-stone rotates. Com. See **Cockhead.**

(2) *sb.* that part of a wheel which fits into the nave, and in which the axle works: it is made of iron, and fastened inside the nave or centre of the wheel by means of longitudinal ribs. Com. Cf. **Boukin.**

'One paire of *bushes* . . . one paire of *bushes* soles.'—*Inventory* . . . Owlbury Manor-House, Bishop's Castle, 1625.

'The *Busshes* are Irons within the hole of the Nave to keep it from wearing.'—*Academy of Armory*, Bk. III. ch. viii. p. 332.

BUSK [buskˑ], *sb.* a piece of wood or 'sheet-iron' worn down the front of women's stays to keep them straight. Com. Nares—who is wrong in supposing the term obsolete—gives the following, amongst other quotations, illustrating the use of the *busk* in the Elizabethan period:—

'Her long slit sleeves, stiffe *buske*, puffe verdingall,
Is all that makes her thus angelical.'
JOHN MARSTON (A.D. 1599), *Scourge of Villanie*, II. vii.

'Fr. *busc;* petit bâton dont se servent les Dames pour tenir leur corps de jupe en état.'—CHAMB.

BUSSOCK [busˑukˑ], *sb., sl.*? a donkey.—ATCHAM; WEM.

BUT [butˑ], (1) *sb.* a space of ploughed land, comprising a certain number of furrows, determined by the character of the soil. Com. See **Feerings.**

'*Hec amsages An*ᵉ, a *but* of lond.'—*Pictorial Vocabulary*, xv. cent., in Wr. vocabs., vol. i. p. 270.

(2) *sb.* the stump of a tree; the thick end of anything. Com.

O.N. *butr*, the trunk, stump of a tree. Fr. *bout*, the end. W. *pwt*, any short, thick thing; stump, in WEDG. Cf. **Stoul** (1).

(3) *sb.* an esculent root, such as a turnip, carrot, &c.—PULVERBATCH.

(4) *v. n.* to form such-like esculent roots.—*Ibid.* 'Yore garrits an' inions looken well, John.' 'Aye, but I doubt they bin on'y toppy; I dunna think as they bin *buttin'* well.'

BUTTERED ALE [but·ur'd ail], *sb.* ale boiled with butter, lump sugar, spice, and eggs—said to be an excellent specific for cold. Com. It is made thus: boil a pint of ale with a lump of butter in it, beat up two eggs with sugar and spices, pour the boiling ale upon the eggs, stirring briskly.

BUTTER-LEAVES, *sb. pl.* leaves used in packing the butter for market. Com. Various kinds of leaves are employed for this purpose—the sycamore, the nut, &c. Sometimes the Sicilian beet (*Beta cicla*) is cultivated expressly for the sake of its long, cool, green *butter-leaves.*

BUTTER-MIT, *sb.* a shallow tub for washing the butter in. Com. Cf. **Kemlin.**

BUTTER-MONEY, *sb.* the money which is the farmer's wife's perquisite from the sale of her butter, eggs, &c.—SHREWSBURY; WEM. 'Things wenten very low i' the market to-day, Missis; I hanna brought yo' much *butter-money.*'

'And when the father on the earth did live,
To his sonnes fancie he such way did give;
For at no season he the plow must hold,
The summer was too hot, the winter cold;
He robs his mother of her *butter-pence*,
Within the alehouse serves him for expence.'
Taylor's Workes, 1630, in WR.

'She's thrimlin' for her *bŭtter-brass*, her *bŭtter-brass*, her *bŭtter-brass*,
She's thrimlin' for her *bŭtter-brass*, but willn't thrimle lang.'
'Bobby Bank's Boddernent,' in the *Folk-Speech of Cumberland*, by A. J. GIBSON, p. 25.

Cf. **Spattling-money.**

BUTTERY [but·h'r'i'], *sb.* the pantry of a cottage or farm-house.—PULVERBATCH; WEM. 'Cuddlin' i' the buttery' is a phrase equivalent to 'cupboard-love.' 'Theer's a power too much *cuddlin' i' the buttery* gwein on.' '*Hec botolaria, An*[m], a botry.'—*Pictorial Vocabulary*, xv. cent., in Wr. vocabs., vol. i. p. 274.

BUTTING-IRON, *sb.* an implement for peeling the bark off trees.—MUCH WENLOCK. Qy. com. Cf. O.Dutch *botten*, butt; *pellere*, in STRAT.

BUTTY [but·i'], (1) *sb.* a fellow-workman; a partner in any business. Com.

(2) *sb.* a contractor who agrees to raise the minerals to bank at so much per ton, or per dozen; the latter applying to the iron-stones,

representing about two tons.—COLLIERY; M. T. Cf. **Charter-master.**

(3) *sb.* a fellow, as of a shoe, a glove, &c.—SHREWSBURY; CLEE HILLS. 'I've fund one shoe, but canna see the *butty* no-w'eer.' Cf. **Marrow.**

(4) *v. n.* to cohabit, as man and wife.—COLLIERY. 'Did'n'ee 'ear as Jim Tunkiss wuz come up throm the "Black country" an' brought three childern to the parish?' 'Eh! I didna know 'e wuz married.' 'Well, I reckon 'e inna married, but 'e's bin *buttyin'* alung o' one o' them Monsells.'

BUZZY-BALL [buz·i' baul·'], *sb.* same as **Briar-boss**, q. v.—CHURCH STRETTON. See also Bk. II., *Folklore*, &c., 'Superstitious Cures (*chin-cough*).

BWILE [bwei·l], (1) *v. a.* to boil.—PULVERBATCH; LUDLOW. 'Theer wuz four couple axed up o' Sunday ready for May weddins.' 'Aye, behappen they'n find it easier to get married than to keep the pot *bwilin*.'

'Sche sette a caldron on þe fyr;
In which was al þe hole atir,
Wheron þe medicine stod,
Of ius of water and of blod
And let it *buile* in such a plit,
Til þat sche sawh þe spume whyt.'

JOHN GOWER (A.D. 1393), *Confessio Amantis*, Book V. *Specim. Early Eng.* xx. l. 295.

(2) *sb.* same as **Bile**, q. v.—LUDLOW, *Burford.*

BWOISTIN. See **Beestings.**

BWOY [bwoi·, *corr.* bw:auy], *sb.*, *obsols.*, *var. pr.* a boy.—SHREWSBURY; PULVERBATCH. 'Jack's gwun a big strung *bwoy;* it's time 'e wuz gettin' 'is own crust.'

BWUNS [bwun·z, *corr.* bwoen·z], *sb. pl.*, *var. pr.* bones. Com. 'Pŭt some yarbs to them *bwuns;* they'n mak' tuthree broth.'

BY [bei·], (1) *prep.*, *pec.* against. — WORTHEN; WHITCHURCH; ELLESMERE. Qy. com. 'I never knowed no 'arm *by* 'im' (Ellesmere). 'E's a tidy mon, sir, leastways I know nuthin' *by* 'im' (Whixall). In this sense of 'against' our translators have used the word *by*—1 Cor. iv. 4: 'I know nothing *by* myself; yet am I not hereby justified'—where the Greek words fully bear out the meaning of 'I am not conscious of anything *against* myself.'

'Ac it is noght *by* the bisshope
That the boy preacheth.'

Piers Pl. Prol., l. 160, ed. WR.

The same sense would seem to be implied in *by-name*, a term of reproach.

(2) *prep.*, *pec.* with.—WORTHEN; BISHOP'S CASTLE. 'I dunna know whad to do *by* 'im.'

BY-BLOW [bei· bloa·], *sb.* an illegitimate child.—COLLIERY. Qy. com. This word is found in BAILEY, ed. 1782.

'*Sal.* Thou speak'st not like a subject; what's thy name?
Fil. My name is Draco.
Sal. Of the Athenian Dracos?
Fil. No, of the English Drakes. Great Captain Drake
[That sail'd the world round] left in Spain a *by-blow*,
Of whom I come.'—*The Slighted Maid*, p. 27, in WR.

BY-GUM [bi'gaem· *or* bi'gum·], a slight oath; an expletive. Com.

BY JINGS [bei· jing·z], *interj.* used chiefly by children to express approbation of what is thought to be clever or witty.—SHREWSBURY; ELLESMERE. '*By jings!* Surrey, lad, yo'n copped that.'

'While Willie lap, an' swoor *by jing*,
'Twas just the way he wanted
To be that night.'
ROBERT BURNS, *Poems*, p. 45, l. 7, c. 2.

Cf. *By jingo* in HAL.

BY-LEDDY [bei· ledi'], *expl.* an adjuration or oath corrupted from 'by our Lady,' the Blessed Virgin.—NEWPORT, *Market Drayton.*

BYLET [bei·let, *corr.* ba'y·let], *sb.* a river island; land lying between the divergent branches of a stream, as, for instance, between the natural course of a brook and the mill-stream, or 'flem,' q. v.—SHREWSBURY*; PULVERBATCH; CLEE HILLS; BRIDGNORTH; MUCH WENLOCK.

'William Benbow is rated to the poor on St. Mary's books for *bylet* [the island at Coton-hill] and tan-house, in every year from 1652 to 1664 inclusive, with the exception of 1663, when it is *Martha Benbow* for *the bilett*.'—Note on the Benbow family in OWEN and BLAKEWAY'S *History of Shrewsbury*, vol. ii. p. 390.

'BRIDGNORTH HORTICULTURAL SOCIETY.

'The second annual Exhibition was held on the *Bylet*, Low Town, yesterday. . . .'—*Eddowes's Shrewsbury Journal*, Sep. 9, 1874.

BYNOW [bi'nou·], *adv.* by this time. Com. 'They'n a got theer *bynow*, I spect.'

BYSTIN-CUSTARD, same as **Beestin'-custard**, q. v.—PULVERBATCH. Cf. **Barfut-custard**.

BYSTINS. See **Beestings**.

BYTACK [bei·tak], *sb.* a farm taken by the tenant of a larger farm, to which it is, as it were, *tacked* on. The land only being wanted, the house and 'building' are let separately.—PULVERBATCH; WELLINGTON. Qy. com. 'Theer 'll be a bundation o' housen to be 'ad, for one 'afe o' the farms bin let *bytack*.' '*Tack*, a lease; possession for a time.'—JAMIESON.

BY-TAIL [bei·tail], *sb.* the right handle of a plough: it is fastened to the 'shell-board.' The left handle is called the 'master-tail,' and is fastened to the foot of the plough.—CLUN; BRIDGNORTH.

BY-WHILES [bi'weil·z], *adv.* at times.—CORVE DALE. See **Owlert**.

CADDAS [kad·u's], *sb.*, *obsols.* a fine worsted galloon or ferret, now chiefly employed in decorating horses, but at one time used for 'recruiting colours.'—SHREWSBURY. 'Theer's lots o' young chaps listed this May; the *caddas* wuz flyin' about Sosebry streets above a bit.'

'*Serv.* He hath ribbons of all the colours i' the rainbow . . . inkles, *caddisses*, cambrics, lawns.'—*Winter's Tale*, IV. iv. 208.

Caddis, in the Gloss. to the 'Globe Edition' of Shakespeare, is said to have its name from its resemblance to the 'caddis-worm.'

Cadas *Bombicinium*. *Cadas* appears to have signified flocks of silk, cotton, wool, or tow, used for stuffing gamboised garments. In the curious poem by Hue de Tabarie, at Middle Hill, entitled '*Coment le fiz Deu fu armé en la croyz*', is this passage—

'*Pur aketown ly bayle blaunche char e pure*
Pur cadaz e cotoun de saunk fu le encusture.'

MS. Heber, No. 8336.

In the petition against excess of apparel, 1463, it is thus mentioned; 'No yoman &c to were in the aray for his body eny bolsters, nor stuffe of woole, coton, or *cadas*, nor other stuffer in his doubtlet, save lynyng accordyng to the same.'—ROT. PARL. '*Cadas* or crull, *saijette*.'—PALSG. '*Cardarce, pour faire capiton;* the tow or coursest part of silke, wherof sleaur is made.'—COTGR. Nares explains *caddis* to be a sort of worsted lace.—*Prompt. Parv. and Notes.*

CADDISSED [kad·i'st], *part. adj.* dusted with red powder: said of sheep.—CLEE HILLS. 'Maister, I ŏŏnder yo' liken yore lomb's *caddissed* athatn.'

CADE [kai·d], (1) *sb.* a pet. Com. ''E's a reg'lar *cade:*' said of a spoiled child. A *cade-lamb* is a lamb brought up by hand. Cf. *Kod-lomb* in Wr. vocabs., vol. i. p. 245.

(2) *v. a.* to pet; to bring up tenderly. Com.

CADISH [kai·dish], (1) *adj.* spoiled by over-indulgence.—PULVERBATCH. Qy. com. 'Jenny Preece 'as pŭt 'er lad to a wilrit; but 'e'll never stop throm 'is mammy, 'e's so *cadish.*'

(2) *adj.* docile; gentle: said of animals.—SHREWSBURY; NEWPORT.

CADY [kai·di'], same as **Cadish** (1).—CHURCH STRETTON.

CAFF [kaf·], (1) *sb.* an implement for hoeing and earthing up potatoes.—CLUN; LUDLOW. '. . . . *caffs* and hoes.'—*Auctioneer's Catalogue* (Stoddesden), 1870. Cf. **Kibe.**

(2) *v. a.* to clean and earth up potatoes.—LUDLOW.

CAKEY [kai·ki'], *adj.*, *sl.?* weak of intellect; silly.—SHREWSBURY; WELLINGTON; WEM; ELLESMERE. 'Now then, whad's wrang wuth yo'? Bin 'ee cryin' fur a biled aip'ny, yo' *cakey* piece?'

CAKING [kai·kin]. See Bk. II., *Folklore*, &c., 'Customs.'

CALAMINCA, *sb.* a sort of red shale—a mixture of red and yellow clay, marl, and sand.—COLLIERY, *Madeley;* M. T.

CALL [kaul·], (1) *sb.* occasion; necessity. Com. ''E'd no *call* to say that on 'er.'

(2) *v. a.* to abuse; to vilify. Com. ''Er *called* 'im fur everythin'; the worst name as 'er could lay 'er tongue to wuz too good for 'im.'

CALL-WORDS TO ANIMALS. *Cows* :—Cow-up, cow-up, coop, coop [kuuw·oop, kuuw·oop, kù·p, kù·p]. The last two words are used as they near home. Com. Hoap, hoap, hoap [·ùŏŏp, ùŏŏp, ùŏŏp], CLUN. Hie-up [·ei·up], or how-up [uuw·oop], is to drive them. Com.

Calves :—Mog, mog, mog [·mog, mog, mog]. Com.

Pigs :—Dack, dack, dack [·dak, dak, dak], SHREWSBURY; CHURCH STRETTON; LUDLOW. Guey, guey, guey [·gueaiy, gueaiy, gueai·y], CORVE DALE. Guep, guep, guey [·guep, guep, gue·i'], CLUN. Nack, nack, nack [·nak, nak, nak], SHREWSBURY; PULVERBATCH; CHURCH STRETTON; ELLESMERE. Pig, pig, pig [·pi'k, pi'k, pi'k], PULVERBATCH; ELLESMERE. Poo-ik, poo- -ik [puo·i'k, puo··i'k], to pigs at a distance.—WORTHEN. Ric, ric, ric [·r'i'k, r'i'k, r'i'k], SHREWSBURY; MUCH WENLOCK; WELLINGTON; WHITCHURCH. Yup, yup, yu-up [·yù·p, yù··p, yù··ùp], with an increase of pitch on *up*.—CRAVEN ARMS. Stoo, stoo, rree [·stoo, stoo, ..r'ee··] is to drive pigs. Com.

'They say in my contrye, when they cal theyr hogges to the swyne troughe, Come to thy myngle mangle, come pyr, come pyr.'—LATIMER, *Sermon* iii. p. 98.

Horses. See **Waggoners' Words.**

CALL-WORDS TO POULTRY. *Fowls* :—Chuck, chuck, chuck [·chaek, chaek, chaek], SHREWSBURY; PULVERBATCH. [·chuk, chuk, chuk]. Com. [·chùk, chùk, chùk], ELLESMERE; WHITCHURCH. Shoo [shù··] is to drive them. Com.

Chickens :—Chick, chick, chick [·chik, chik, chik], SHREWSBURY. Qy. com. Tweet, tweet, tweet [·twi'·t, twi'·t, twi'·t], ELLESMERE.

Ducks :—Weet, weet, weet [·wi'·t, wi'·t, wi'·t], ELLESMERE. Wid, wid, wid [·wi'd, wi'd, wi'd], SHREWSBURY; PULVERBATCH; CHURCH STRETTON; CLUN; LUDLOW. Widdy, widdy, widdy [·wid·i', wid·i', wid·i'], CLEE HILLS.

Geese :—Gus, gus, gus [·gus, gus, gus], CRAVEN ARMS; CHURCH STRETTON; CLUN; LUDLOW. Lag, lag, lag [·lag, lag, lag], SHREWSBURY; PULVERBATCH; ELLESMERE. Hoo-lag [·oo lag] drives them on. *Ibid.* as for **Lag.**

Turkeys :—Pen, pen, pen [·pen, pen, pen], SHREWSBURY; PULVERBATCH. Pur, pur, pur [·pur', pur', pur'], PULVERBATCH; WORTHEN; CRAVEN ARMS; CLUN.

CAMOMINE [kam·u'mein], *sb., var. pr. Anthemis nóbilis*, Chamomile. Com.

CAMPERING [kam·pu'r'in], *adj., obsols.* mettlesome; high-spirited. —PULVERBATCH. 'Young Dicken rides a fine *camperin'* 'orse to markit.' 'Aye, an' 'e's a fine *camperin'* fellow 'isself.'

Dan. *kämpe*, to fight.

CANARY [ku'nae·ri']. 'Give a cat a canary' is a phrase analogous to 'Tell that to the marines,' implying disbelief in an improbable story.—SHREWSBURY. 'Chow-wow, "Give a cat a *canary*," dunna tell me none o' yore rōmance.'

CANBOTTLE [kan·bot·l], *sb. Parus caudatus*, the long-tailed Titmouse.—SHREWSBURY; BRIDGNORTH; NEWPORT. Cf. **Bottle-tit.**

CANDLE OF THE EYE, *phr.* the pupil of the eye.—SHREWSBURY; PULVERBATCH; WORTHEN; WEM. Ray gives, 'The Bird of the Eye, the Sight or Pupil. *Suffolk.*' See p. 70, ed. 1768. Cf. **Pea of the eye.**

CAN-DOUGHS [kan doa·z], *sb. pl., obs.* small, oblong cakes made for the breakfast-table.—LUDLOW. Perhaps *can-doughs* = portions of *dough* baked in *cans;* just as bakers call loaves baked in tins 'tin-loaves.'

CANK [kang·k], (1) *v. n.* to cackle as geese.—PULVERBATCH; WORTHEN; CLEE HILLS; ELLESMERE.

(2) *v. n.* to talk rapidly; to gabble.—WELLINGTON.

(3) *sb.* a fit of ill-humour.—SHREWSBURY; PULVERBATCH. 'I toud 'er a bit o' my mind, an' 'er 'uff'd an' ding'd an' went off in a fine *cank.*'

CANKER [kang·kur'], (1) *sb.* rust in wheat. Com.

> '*Poins.* O, that this good blossom could be kept from *cankers.*'
> 2 *K. Henry IV.*, II. ii. 102.

(2) *sb.* a species of dry-rot in turnips. Com.

(3) *sb.* an unhealthy excrescence on trees or plants, preventing kindly developments, and causing a withered, dead appearance. Com. Cf. **Bur** (3).

> 'Full soon the *canker* death eats up that plant.'
> *Romeo and Juliet*, II. iii. 30.

(4) *sb.* verdigris.—SHREWSBURY. Qy. com.

'Nay, I tell you it is old truth, long rusted with your *canker*, and now new made bright and scoured.'—LATIMER, *Serm.* p. 30 (Parker Society).

'What is this but a new learning; a new *canker* to rust and corrupt the old truth?'—*Id.* p. 31.

(5) *v. a.* to envenom by verdigris, brass, or copper, so as to cause ulceration.—SHREWSBURY. Qy. com. 'Yo' shouldna let the child play ŏŏth brass; if 'e pŭts it in 'is mouth it 'll *canker* it.'

(6) *sb.* a sore in the mouth popularly believed to be caused by the venom of verdigris, brass, or copper. Com. Lat. *cancer*, a canker. This 'mouth disease' is known in medicine as *Cancrum oris*, a foul ulcer inside the lips and cheeks of children—rarely of adults—often arising from bad food or bad constitution. The following curious entry in the *Register of Sir Thomas Boteler*, Vicar of Much Wenlock, may justify the introduction here of the term *canker* in a usage adopted by the medical profession.

'1544. 5th July . . . The said Joan child, single woman, of the age of 22 years, deceased, and died upon the disease of a *Canker* within her mouth, under the root of her tongue, which as her father said she chanced to have through the smelling of Rose-flowers.'

CANKERED [kang·kur'd], (1) *part. adj.* affected with canker. Com. 'Them cabbidge ŏŏn mak' nuthin this 'ear—they bin poor *cankered* tack.' See **Canker** (3).

(2) *adj.* cross; ill-tempered.—WEM, *Shawbury.*

'We had neuer such a *cankered* carle,
Were neuer in our companie.'—*Percy Folio*, i. 48.

'——if *canker'd* Madge, our aunt,
Come up the burn, she'll gie's a wicked rant.'
ALLAN RAMSEY, *The Gentle Shepherd*, I. ii. p. 21.

Ray has 'A *cankred* Fellow, Cross, Ill-condition'd.' A North-country word.

CANKEROUS [kang·kr'us], *adj.* venomous.—PULVERBATCH. 'The poor child's got a despert leg throm that car'less wench pŭttin' the warmin' pan i' the bed—it's sich a nasty *cank'rous* thing to be burnt ŏŏth.' See **Canker** (4), also (5).

CANNA. See **Grammar Outlines**, *verb* **Can.**

'An' forward, tho' I *canna* see,
I guess an' fear!'
ROBERT BURNS, *Poems*, p. 54, l. 17.

CANT [kant·], (1) *v. n.* to gossip; to carry tales. Com. 'That keeper's al'ays *cantin'* to the Squire about somebody; but if 'e dunna mind 'is owd rabbit grins, an' let other folks alone, I'll put a scotch on 'is w'ĕĕl afore lung.' Cf. **Clat** (1).

(2) *sb.* a tattler; a tale-bearer. Com. ''Er's a reg'lar owd *cant*, that's whad 'er is.' Cf. **Clat** (2).

(3) *sb.* gossip; tattle. Com. ''Er's never athout some *cant* to tell yo' on, gŏŏ w'en yo' will.'

CANTEL [kan·tel], *sb., obsols.* a corner; a small piece left, as of bread.—PULVERBATCH. 'We mun bake to-morrow, I see, as theer's on'y one loaf an' a bit of a *cantel* as 'll 'ardly see breakfast o'er.'

'For nature hath nat take his bygynnyng
Of no partye ne *cantel* of a thing,
But of a thing that parfyt is and stable.'
CHAUCER, *The Knightes Tale*, l. 2150, ed. Morris.

'*Hec quadra*, a cantel of brede.'—*Pictorial Vocabulary*, xv. cent., in Wr. vocabs., vol. i. p. 258. O.Fr. *chantel, cantel*, coin, morceau. —BUR.

CANTING-QUARTER [kan·tin kwaur'tur'], *sb.* from Candlemas Day to May-Day is called *canting-quarter.*—PULVERBATCH. Candlemas is the beginning of the 'laying season' in the poultry-yard; and about the same time farm-house servants are 'hired for May.' These events give rise to much chit-chat, or, as it is called, *cant*, amongst the house-wives.

'Does your goose lay?
Does your maid stay?'

is a familiar couplet, which aptly illustrates the kind of thing that has given rise to the term *canting-quarter.*

CANTLE [kan·tl], *sb., obsols.* a can-ful.—SHREWSBURY; PULVERBATCH. 'Han' 'ee 'ad a good "Tummasin" this time?' 'Well, as the owd sayin' is, "Them as 'ad'n most mouths 'ad'n most mate." Mrs. Ward an' Mrs. Ambler an' most o' the good owd 'ouse-keepers gid'n us a *cantle* for every one. We'd'n pretty nigh a 'oop a piece.' 'Oh! a tidy Christmas batch.' Cf. **Thinkle.** See Bk. II., *Folklore*, &c., 'Customs connected with Days and Seasons' (*S. Thomas's Day*).

CAPLIN [kap·li'n], *sb., obsols.* a piece of strong leather made of horse-hide, laced by thongs or strips of eel-skin to the two parts of a flail respectively; viz., to the 'swipple' and the 'hand-staff.' The *caplins* are in their turn similarly united, thus giving to the flail the requisite swing when in use.—PULVERBATCH. Qy. com.

'The *Caplings*, the strong double Leathers made fast to the top of the Hand-staff and the top of the Swiple.'—*Academy of Armory*, Bk. III., ch. viii. p. 333.

'Cappe of a fleyle.'—*Prompt. Parv.*, p. 61. Cf. **Nile.**

CAREYN [kaar'·i'n], (1) *sb., obsols.* a foul carcase, as of an animal that has died from disease.—ELLESMERE.

'He crouke3 for comfort · when *carayne* he fynde3
Kast vp on a clyffe · þer costese lay drye;
. . . .
Falle3 on þe foule flesch · & fylle3 his wombe.'
Alliterative Poems, The Deluge (A.D. 1360, *circa*).
Specim. Early Eng., xiii. l. 459.

O.Fr. *charoigne* de *caro* (nominatif *carnis*).—BUR.

(2) *sb.* an opprobrious epithet applied to a woman or girl of dirty habits.—SHREWSBURY; ELLESMERE. 'Yo' bin a nasty, dirty *careyn*, that's whad yo' bin.'

'Out, you green-sickness *carrion!* out, you baggage!
You tallow face!'—*Romeo and Juliet*, III. v. 157.

CARFUL [kaa·r'ful], *adj.* careful. Com. An old form.

'3e schul 3ild a *carful* counte on dredful domys-day.'
JOHN AUDELAY'S *Poems*, p. 21.

CARNEY [kaa·r'ni'], *adj.* giddy; thoughtless. — SHREWSBURY. 'Mary, w'eer's them matches as I sen' yo' to fatch?' 'I forgot 'em, mother.' 'Forgot! yo' bin al'ays forgettin'; I never see sich a *carney* piece i' my days.' Cf. *Carny*, B. vii., E. D. S.

CARPENTER [kaa·r'pentur'], *sb. Porcellio scaber*, the Wood-louse. Generally used in the plural form, *carpenters*.—NEWPORT.

CARRIAGE [kaar'·i'j], *sb.* a sling attached to the leathern girdle worn by a mower, in which he carries the whetstone at his back.—PULVERBATCH; CHURCH STRETTON. Cf. **Sling.**

CASE [kais·], *v. a.* to skin. Com. 'I never sid a nimbler girld i' my life; 'er'd *case* them rabbits awilde yo' bin lookin' which way to begin.' This term, though used chiefly with respect to small animals, as rabbits, hares, squirrels, &c., is not restricted to them; rooks are *cased* in preparing them for pies.

'*First Lord.* We'll make you some sport with the fox ere we *case* him.'—*All's Well That Ends Well*, III. vi. 111.

CASE-HARDENED [kais·aa·'r'dnd], *part. adj.* impenetrable to all sense of shame or moral rectitude.—PULVERBATCH; ELLESMERE. Qy. com. ''E's a *case-hardened* scoundrel; if 'e dunna come to the gallus it 'll su'prize everybody as knows 'im.' 'Aye, 'e wuz al'ays a despert srode lad.'

'*Case-hardened*, obdurate; hardened in impiety.'—BAILEY, ed. 1727.

CASE-KNIFE [kais·neif], *sb.* a carving-knife of the common type, without sheath or *case* of any kind.—PULVERBATCH. 'Why dunna yo' get the *case-knife* to cut the bacon? Yo'n 'urt yoreself worse than the flitchen ŏŏth that little thing.'

CASELTY, CASERTLY [kas·u'lti'], SHREWSBURY; ATCHAM; WEM. [kaz·ur'tli'], PULVERBATCH; WEM. (1) *adj.* uncertain; doubtful: said of the weather. Com. See **Break-up.**

(2) *adj.* insecure; hazardous: as of a wall or stack out of the perpendicular.—PULVERBATCH. 'Now, John, ŏŏn 'ee think o' yore stack by daylight? It looks mighty *casertly*.'

(3) *adj.* dangerous; critical: as of the state of a person in illness. —PULVERBATCH. 'Poor owd Betty Jones lies in a very *casertly* condition; they sen 'er leg an' thigh bin broke, an' it's a bad job at 'er age; but 'er met as well a bin killed on the spot.'

CASEYS [kai·zi'z], *sb. pl.*, *var. pr.* 'causeys,' paths or roads between the beds from which the peat, or 'turf,' as it is called, is cut on Whixall Moss.—WHITCHURCH.

'Haremeare Mosse was incompassed round with the water of this Meare; howbeit, the neighbours did gett some *turves* upon it; which they carryed over the water in boats; butt Sir Andrew Corbet caused a large *causey*, or banke, to bee raised throw the water, soe that teames and carts might easily passe from Haremeare Heath to the Mosse, and the turves (which beefore were had freely) were sold at 8d a yard, that is, 80 square yards, to cutt and lay upon, which yeilded a loade for the best teame thatt was.'—GOUGH'S *History of Myddle*, p. 30.

See *Causey*, B. xiv., E. D. S. Cf. **Causey**, below.

CASP [kasp·], *sb.* the cross-bar at the top of a spade-handle. Com. 'The *casp* o' that spade's cracked, I see; it mun 'ăve a cramp pŭt through it.'

'The head, or handle, or *kaspe* (of a spade).'—*Academy of Armory*, Bk. III., ch. viii., p. 337. Cf. **Critch.**

CAST [kast·], (1) *v. a.* to throw over; to fling: as of animals for purposes of farriery. Com. 'We'n 'ad a despert job to *cast* that cowt; 'e gid Jim a pote as 'e ŏŏnna forget in a 'urry.' Icel. *kasta;* Swed. *kasta;* Dan. *kaste*, to throw.

(2) *part. past.* thrown over; flung: said of sheep that have accidentally got on their backs, and cannot regain their footing. Com. 'Dick, yo' mun run for life to the fare end o' Wuken [*Oaken*, a field at Pulverbatch]; theer's a yeow *cast* i' the briers, an' 'er'll be djed direc'ly; tak the brummock ŏŏth yo' to cut the briers.'

(3) *v. a.* to bring forth prematurely: said of cows.—SHREWSBURY; PULVERBATCH; CLEE HILLS. 'Daisy's *cast* 'er cauve.'

'Thy ewes and thy she-goats have not *cast* their young.'—Genesis xxxi. 38.

See also Malachi iv. 11. Cf. **Pick** (1).

(4) *part. past., obsols.?* defeated; thrown over; condemned: as in a law-suit.—SHREWSBURY; PULVERBATCH. 'Theer's bin a lung law-shoot about a right o' rŏŏäd; but the newcomer's got *cast:* it's bin a rŏŏäd for marr'in' an' berrin' this forty 'ear. I thought if they coulden stop it, it wuz mighty odd to me.'

'1541. Memorandum that the 10th day of this instant month of Feb[ry], in the year of our Lord 1541, here was buried W[m] Lowe, a Cheshire man born, which William was a lad of 18 years of age or thereabouts, *cast* by the verdict of 12 men at the s[d] Sessions holden here. . . .'—*Register of Sir Thomas Boteler*, Vicar of Much Wenlock.

'. . . It is not a strang thing for Mr. Lloyd to impose upon his neighbours, as appeares by his stopping of a footway over his back side, for which he was sued and *cast.*'—GOUGH'S *History of Myddle*, p. 109.

'Well, my dear Ladies, said he . . . Is sentence given?

'It is, Sir Charles—He took my hand, . . .—I have hopes, my dear Miss Byron, that you are *cast.*'—*Sir Charles Grandison*, vol. vi. p. 194, ed. 1766.

(5) *v. n.* to yield; to produce.—CLEE HILLS. 'Well, Tummas, 'ow did that w'eät *cast* as yo' wun throshin'?' 'Middlin' like, considerin' the saison; but it dunna *cast* like it did last 'ear.' Cf. **Out-cast.**

(6) *v. a.* a hunting term. Com. A huntsman is said to *cast* his hounds when, the scent being lost, he takes them on the line of the hunted animal, or to the right or left, in order to recover it. The old hunting rule is to *cast forwards* for a fox; and to *cast backwards* for a hare, as this animal almost always tries to 'double' back again.

(7) *sb.* a second swarm of bees in the season from one hive. Com. See **Bunt** (2).

CASTLING [kass·dlin], *sb.* an abortive calf.—SHREWSBURY. See **Cast** (1).

CASTREL [kas·tr'el], *sb.* a worthless person.—CLEE HILLS. Cf. **Wastrel** (1).

CAT [kat·], *sb., obs.?* a stand formed of three pieces of wood, ornamentally turned or carved, crossing each other in the middle; it could be set up at either end, and would still have three feet on the ground at the vertices of a triangle. Com. The *cat* was intended to hold a plate of hot cakes or buttered toast before the wood-hearth, so general in farm-house and cottage throughout Shropshire up to the beginning of the present century, and still [1874] occasionally to be seen. 'I'll butter the flaps straight off the backstwun, if yo'n fatch me a plate an' the *cat* to put it on—they'n keep whot till tay.'

CAT-BRAIN [kat·br'ain], *sb.* a rough clayey kind of soil full of stone. —WELLINGTON. Cf. **Rotch.**

CATCHING-TIME [kach·in tei·m], *sb.* It is called *catchin' time* when in a wet season they *catch* every minute of favourable weather for field work.—SHREWSBURY; CLEE HILLS.

CATER-CORNELLED [kai·tur' kaur'neld], *adj.* irregular of form; out of proportion: said of any material that won't cut to a required shape.—PULVERBATCH. 'I never sid sich a *cater-cornelled* thing as this; for turn it which way yo' ŏŏn, yo' canna get it squar' nor round.' Cf. **Wanty.**

CATER-CORNERED, *adj.* diagonal.—WELLINGTON. A house standing diagonally to the street would be *cater-cornered.* Cf. **Endways-on.**

CATER-WIFF, *adv.* across; from one side to the other in an oblique direction, as a tipsy person would go.—WEM, *Burlton.* 'I seed as 'e wunna sober by the way 'e went *cater-wiff* alung the rŏŏăd.'

CATS' EYES [kat·s eiz], *sb. Epilobium angustifolium,* Rose-bay, Willow Herb.—CRAVEN ARMS, *Stokesay.*

CATS' GALLOWS [kat·s gal·u'ss], *sb.* a kind of leaping-pole made by children, consisting of a stick laid horizontally upon two forked sticks placed upright in the ground.—SHREWSBURY; PULVERBATCH. Called also *cat gallows.*—LUDLOW; NEWPORT. *Jumpin' cats' gallusses* is a favourite game with children.

CAT'S HEAD, *sb., obs.* a 'pit-head' standing on three legs. Com. M. T. See **Pit-head.** Cf. **Cat.**

CAT'S TAIL, *sb. Aconitum Napěllus,* Wolf's-bane.—LUDLOW.

CAUF [kauf·], (1) *sb., var. pr.* a calf. Com.

> 'A cow and a *cauf,* a yowe and a hauf,
> And thretty gude shillin's and three;
> A vera gude tocher, a cotter-man's dochter,
> The lass with the bonie black ee.'
>
> ROBERT BURNS, *Poems,* p. 255, l. 21, c. 2.

(2) *sb.* a silly, stupid person. Com. 'Yo' great *cauf,* could na yo' do that bit'n a job athout me 'ăvin' to tell yo' the same thing twize o'er?'

'*C. Custance.* You great *calfe* ye should haue more witte, so ye should . . .'—*Roister Doister,* Act ij. Sc. iiij. p. 37. Cf. **Auf.**

CAUSEY [kaus·i'], (1) *sb.* a paved foot-path, often raised above the general level. Com. 'The waiter's out all alung the flat aumust level ŏŏth the *causey.*'

'This plain aforesaid named Laboriæ, is confined on both sides with the great *causeis* or high waies raised by the consuls.'—HOLLAND'S *Pliny,* xviii. 11 (A.D. 1634).

> 'Ye dainty Deacons, an' ye douce Conveeners,
> To whom our moderns are but *causey*-cleaners!'
>
> ROBERT BURNS, *Poems,* p. 27, l. 23.

Our received word 'causeway' is a corruption of *causey;* an old spelling of which, according to Mr. Skeat, was *calcie,* from Lat. *calceata via,* a way made with lime; whence Span. *calzada,* a paved way; and Fr. *chaussée,* the same thing: from which last comes directly Eng. *causey.* Cf. **Caseys.**

(2) *sb.* a narrow paved yard at the back of a house; also a pavement surrounding, or partly surrounding, a house. Com. 'Sally, han' yo' aumust done sloppin' out theer?' 'I've on'y got the *causey* to swill; I shanna be lung.'

CAUVE [kau·v], same as **Cauf** (1). Com.

CAUVE KIT [kau·v kit], *sb.* a kind of 'loose box' in the cow-house where the sucking calves are kept. Com. Cf. **Cote**, from which *Kit* is probably corrupted.

CAVALDRY, CAVALTRY [kav·u'ldr'i', kav·u'ltr'i'], *sb.*, *var. pr.* cavalry, having special reference to the 'Yeomanry Cavalry.' Com. The interchange of *d* and *t* is determined rather by individual usage than by any other law; but *cavaltry* is the more general form. In an old diary kept by an 'Oswestrian,' early in this century, there is the following:—'The *cavaldry* called up in Oswestry to quell the colars at Chirk, Jany. 1, 1831.' See *Byegones*, 25 Oct. 1876.

CAVE [kaiv·], (1) *v. n.* to give way, or fall in, as earth that is undermined.—PULVERBATCH. 'Two men wun buried alive in sinkin' a well at Le Bot'ood las' wik; it *caved* in on 'em six yards dip.'

(2) [keiv·], SHREWSBURY. [keev·], NEWPORT. [kaiv·], WEM; ELLESMERE; OSWESTRY, *v. a.* to turn over; to tilt up, so as to empty. 'Now then, look afore yo', or yo'n *cave* that bouk o'er an' sheed all the milk.' Cf. **Kale** (2).

CAW [ki'·au], WEM. See **Croup.**

CHAG [chag·], *sb.* a branch of broom or gorse.—PULVERBATCH; ELLESMERE. 'Theer's a djel o' bread, beside apple-fit, so mind an' ăve the oven whot; pŭt tuthree more *chags* o' brum in, an' cliër it well.' Cf. **Jag** (3).

CHAMBER [chaim·bur'], *sb.* a sleeping apartment on the ground-floor. — SHREWSBURY; PULVERBATCH; WEM. Bed-rooms on an upper story are called 'upstars' [upstairs]. 'It's a despert poor little 'ouse; no loft o'er it, but *chambers* ŏŏth lime flurs, an' I canna bar a place athout *upstars*.'

CHAMBLE, CHOMBLE [cham·bl], PULVERBATCH. [chom·bl], SHREWSBURY; WEM. (1) *v. a.* to gnaw; to nibble: as rats and mice do. 'Yo'n got a nice lot o' cheese; I 'ope the mice ŏŏnna tak' a fancy to *chamble* 'em, for they bin pretty good judges in a cheese.' Cf. **Chassel.**

(2) *v. a.* to peck; to break into small fragments: as birds do seed. —*Ibid.* 'Dunna pŭt the canary so much sid to *chamble* an' flirt about; 'e covers the window-sill ŏŏth 'is chimblin's.'

CHANCE-CHILD [chans· chei·ld], *sb.* an illegitimate child.—SHREWSBURY. Cf. **Love-child.** See **Base-child.**

CHANCE-PENNY-STONE, *sb.* the highest bed of iron-stone in the coal-field.—COLLIERY; M. T.

'After the preponderance of vegetable remains in all the lower measures, a change is discovered here in the shape of a great abundance of *Leptæna Scabicula.* This fossil, it is believed, has only been found in the Penny iron-stones; in many instances it forms the nucleus for the nodules of iron-stone. Another characteristic of this Penny-stone is the presence of *Megalichthys Hibberti, Gyracanthus, Formosus,* and *Conuleniæ.*'—*Notes on the Shropshire Coal-Field,* by T. PARTON, F.G.S., 1868.

CHANEY [chai·ni'], *sb., var. pr.* china. Com.

CHAP [chap·], (1) *sb.* a farm servant: of such, all below the 'bayly' are *chaps.* Com. Abbreviated from **Chapman.**

(2) *sb.* a familiar appellation for man or boy, as 'fellow' is in 'polite circles.' Com.

> 'An' ane, a *chap* that's damn'd auldfarran,
> Dundas his name.'
> ROBERT BURNS, *Poems*, p. 11, l. 21.

(3) *sb.* an admirer; a sweetheart. Com. The country girl speaks of her *chap*, as the town-bred damsel does of her 'young man.' A lady was expostulating with her maid-servant upon some unwise love affairs which had come under her notice—'I know it's all right whad yo' sen, Ma'am,' said the girl, 'but indeed, Missis, I canna 'elp it; I've bin in trouble alung o' the *chaps* ever sence I knowed anythin'.' The lady looked into Fanny's blue eyes and—believed her!

CHAPMAN [chap·mu'n], *sb., obsols.* a buyer. — PULVERBATCH. 'Whad sort on a far han'ee 'ad to-day?' 'A mighty 'onest un—every mon kep' 'is own; I took a right useful cow an' cauve an got never a *chapman*—nod a biddin'.' This old word *chapman* formerly meant *seller* as well as *buyer;* a trader; a merchant. A.S. *ceápmann*, a merchant; a market-man.

> 'þanne micthe *chapmen* fare
> þuruth englond wit here ware,
> And baldelike beye and sellen,
> Oueral þer he wilen dwellen.'
> *Havelok the Dane*, l. 51.

> 'In Surrye whylom dwelte a companye
> Of *chapmen* riche, and therto sadde and trewe,
> That wyde-wher senten her spicerye,
> Clothes of gold, and satins riche of hewe.'
> CHAUCER, B. 135 (Six-text ed.), Skeat.

> Beauty is bought by judgment of the eye,
> Not utter'd by base sale of *chapmen's* tongues.'
> *Love's Labour Lost*, II. i. 16.

> '*Par.* Fair Diomed, you do as *chapmen* do,
> Dispraise the thing that you desire to buy.'
> *Troilus and Cressida*, IV. i. 75.

> 'When *chapman* billies leave the street,
> And drouthy neebors, neebors meet,
> As market-days are wearing late,
> An' folk begin to tak the gate.'
> ROBERT BURNS, *Poems*, p. 91, l. 1.

'In the days of Edward I.,' says Mr. Oliphant, 'we find scores of French words, bearing on ladies' way of life, employed by our writers. . . . The English *chapman* and *monger* now withdrew into low life, making way for the more gentlemanly foreigner, the *marchand.*' Mr. Oliphant makes further mention of *chapman*, as—together with other words which he enumerates—'still struggling for life,' at the close of the sixteenth century.—*Sources of Standard English*, pp. 236—302.

CHAPMONEY [chap·muni'], *sb.*, *obsols.* money which the seller gives back to the buyer for 'luck.'—PULVERBATCH; WEM. Qy. com. 'I gid seven pun ten for 'er at the far, an' got five shillin' for *chap-money.*'

CHARLES'S WAIN [chaa·r'lzi'z wain], *sb.* the constellation *Ursa Major.*—BISHOP'S CASTLE; CLUN; MUCH WENLOCK.

'*First Carrier.* Heigh ho! an it be not four by the day, I'll be hanged: *Charles' wain* is over the new chimney, and yet our horse not packed. What, ostler!'—1 *K. Henry IV.*, II. i. 2.

In the Staunton edition is the following note:—'*Charles' wain.* The vulgar appellation for the constellation called the Bear, and a corruption of the *Chorles* or *Churls* (i.e. rustic's) wain.' Cf. **Jack and his waggon.**

CHARM [chaa·r'm], SHREWSBURY; PULVERBATCH; NEWPORT; WEM; ELLESMERE. [chaam·], CORVE DALE. (1) *sb.* the intermingled and confused song of all the morning birds. ''Ow the birds bin singin' this mornin'; the coppy's all on a *charm.*'

'Sweet is the breath of morn, her rising sweet,
With *charm* of earliest birds . . .'

Paradise Lost, Bk. iv. l. 641.

'I *cherme* as byrdes do whan they make a noyse a great nomber togyther.'—*Palsgrave*, in Hal.

Hence, perhaps, 'a *charm* of goldfinches,' meaning a company of them,' given by Strutt in 'Terms used in Hawking.'—*Sports and Pastimes*, p. 38, ed. Hone, 1833.

(2) *sb.* a murmuring noise; a hum, as of many voices. 'Whad a *charm* them childern bin mākin i' school.' A.S. *cyrm*, a noise; shout.

CHARTER-MASTER, *sb.* same as **Butty** (2).—COLLIERY; M. T.

CHASSEL [chas·h'l], *v. a.* to nibble, as rats do corn.—CORVE DALE. 'The rots han *chasselled* awaȳ one 'afe o' the w'ĕăt i' the rick.' Cf. **Chamble.**

CHASSELLINGS [chas·h'linz], *sb. pl.* cut or nibbled grains of corn which fall out in the 'tail-ends,' q. v.—CORVE DALE. Cf. **Chimb-lings.**

CHASTISE [chastei·z], *v. a.*, *pec.* to suspect; to accuse.—SHREWSBURY; PULVERBATCH. 'It's 'ard to say w'en a thing's gwun who 'as it. I *chastised* Joe on it; but 'e flatly denied, an' toud me so straīght for'at w'eer an' w'en 'e lef' it, as I believe 'e's innicent.'

CHATOES. See **Potatoes.**

CHATS [chat·s], *sb. pl.* small branches and twigs used for firing.—SHREWSBURY; PULVERBATCH; ELLESMERE; OSWESTRY. 'Dick, run an' fatch tuthree dry *chats* to pŭt i' the oven, I canna get this big 'ŏŏd to burn.'

'Love of lads and fire of *chats* is soon in and soon out.'—*Darbish. Ray's Proverbs*, p. 42.

Ash has '*chat-wood*, small brushwood for fire.'

CHATTER-PIE, *sb. Pica caudáta*, the Magpie.—BRIDGNORTH.

'And *chattering pies* in dismal discords sung.'
3 *Henry VI.*, V. vi. 48.

CHATTY IRONSTONE, *sb.* crumbling, tender iron-stone.—COLLIERY; M. T.

CHAW [chau·], (1) *v. a.* to masticate; to chew.—PULVERBATCH; NEWPORT. Qy. com.

'. . . But still as you are fishing *chaw* a little white or brown bread in your mouth, and Cast it into the Pond about the place where your flote swims.'—*The Compleat Angler*, ch. viii. p. 172.

A.S. *ceówan*, to eat; chew.

(2) *v. a., pec.* to mumble in speaking.—LUDLOW. 'Dunna *chaw* your words; spake 'em.'

CHAWL [chau·l], (1) *sb.* a pig's cheek; a cheek of bacon.—SHREWSBURY; PULVERBATCH; CLUN; NEWPORT; WEM. 'Bacon wuz a bit chepper at the far; I bought a prime par o' *chawls* for 7*d.* a lb., an' yo' could'n 'ăve a good flitchen at 8*d.*'

'Hee was byglich ybownde · on bothe twoo halues,
Bothe his *chaul* & his chynne · with chaynes of yren.'
K. Alisaunder, l. 1119.

Chavylbone or chawlbone, *Mandibula.* 'A chafte, a chawylle, a chekebone; *maxilla*, . . *mandubila* . . .'—CATH. ANGL. In the Latin-English Vocabulary, Harl. MS., 1002, f. 140, occurs the word '*brancus*, a gole, or a chawle.'—*Prompt. Parv. and Notes.* A.S. *ceaflas*, *nom. pl.* jaws; cheeks. Cf. **Choul** (1).

(2) *v. a.* to chew; to munch.—SHREWSBURY; LUDLOW. 'Whad 'nee got i' yore mouth, *chawlin'* athatn?' Cf. **Chaw** (1).

CHEAPEN [chep·n], *v. a.* to ask the price of anything.—SHREWSBURY; PULVERBATCH; CLUN; WEM. ''Ow's butter gweïn this mornin'?' 'I dunna know, I hanna *chep'ned* it.'

'*Kite.* . . . . Ay, about an hour hence walk carelessly into the market-place [Shrewsbury], and you'll see a tall slender Gentleman *cheapning* a Pennyworth of Apples, with a Cane hanging upon his Button . . . . . .

'*Smith.* A tall slender Gentleman, you say, with a Cane! Pray what sort of Head has the Cane?

'*Kite.* An Amber Head with a Black Ribband.'—FARQUHAR'S *Recruiting Officer*, Act III. Scene.—A Chamber.

Chepyn, *Licitor.* 'To chepe, *taxare;* Chepe, *precium.*'—CATH. ANGL. In Caxton's *Boke for Travellers*, a servant who is sent to market is thus directed: 'So chepe for us of the venyson, *si nous bargaigne.*' Palsgrave gives the verb. 'To bargen, chepe, bye and sell, *marchander.* Go cheape a cappe for me, and I wyll come anone and bye it.' A.S. ceápian, *negotiari.*—*Prompt. Parv. and Notes.*

CHEER [chee·h'r'], *sb., var. pr.* a chair. Com.

CHEESES [chee·ziz], *sb. pl.* the seed-vessels of *Malva sylvestris*, common Mallow. Com. John Clare, the Northamptonshire poet, has a reminiscence of childish games with these *cheeses*, when he says—

'The sitting down when school was o'er
Upon the threshold of the door,
Picking from mallows, sport to please,
The crumpled seed we call a *cheese*.'

'*Les petits fromageons*' is the name given by French children to the 'crumpled seed' of the Mallow.

CHEM [chem·], *sb.* a team of horses.—PULVERBATCH; WEM; ELLESMERE. 'Theer wuz a grand stand-off at the love-carriage las' Saturday—thirteen waggins. Mr. Bromley's *chem* come in first, an' Ben looked pretty proud on 'is for' 'orse; 'e gid two shillin' for a star for 'im.' See **Love-carriage.**

CHESPIT [ches·pit], *sb.* a cheese-vat.—WEM; ELLESMERE.

CHESWIT [chez·wi't], same as **Chespit.**—SHREWSBURY; PULVERBATCH; CLUN. 'I never sid sich a noggen fellow as that cowper is. I axed 'im to mak' me a squar' frame for crame cheese, an' 'e's gwun an' made a *cheswit* big anuf to shoot a Cheshire mon.'

'Casiarium,' glossed '*chese-wate*,' occurs in a *Metrical Vocabulary*, perhaps xiv. cent., in Wr. vocabs., vol. i. p. 178.

CHILDER [chil·dur'], *sb. pl.* children.—NEWPORT.

'Of mouth of *childer* and soukand,
Made þou lof in ilka land.'

Metrical English Psalter (before A.D. 1300).
Specim. Early Eng., II. viii. 5.

Mr. Oliphant, speaking of the changes at work in the English of about A.D. 1120, says, '*Cildru* turns into *cyldren*, for the South of England, unlike the North, always loved the plural in *en*, of which the Germans are so fond.' And he observes of Ormin, who wrote about A.D. 1200, 'He uses *childre* for the plural of *child*, and the former still lingers in Lancashire as *childer*;' adding, 'Our corrupt plural *children* came from the South, as also did *brethren* and *kine*.'—*Sources of Standard English*, pp. 70—102.

Mr. Earle says, '*Brethren* and *children* are cumulate plurals. They have added the *-en* plural form on to an elder plural; for *brether* and *childer* were plurals of "brother" and "child".'—*Philology of the English Tongue*, pp. 316, 317. A.S. *cild*, a child; pl. *cildra*, *cildru*. Cf. **Childermas-Day.**

CHILDERIN [chil·du'r'in], *sb. pl.* children.—NEWPORT. A form of rare occurrence.

'God that made se and sond,
With blody woundis he sall stond,
Come ye alle on ryȝt hond,
ȝe *chylderin* that han servyd me.'

Songs and Carols of the Reign of Henry VI., xvii. p. 2.
Warton Club Publications, 1856.

CHILDERN [chil·dur'n], *sb. pl.* children. Com.

'And play as *chylderne* done in strete.'

Early Eng. Miscel., iii. p. 10.
Warton Club Publications, 1855.

CHILL [chil·], *v. a., pec.* to warm; to take the chill off any liquid. Com. 'Bring that 'orn, wench, to *chill* this drink for the Maister's baÿte; 'e öönna like to 'ave it cowd, sich a djurn day as this.'

CHIMBLINGS [chim·blinz], *sb. pl.* bits gnawed or pecked off.—SHREWSBURY; PULVERBATCH; WEM. 'The rots or mice han cut the bags i' the granary, an' I know theer's my 'at full o' *chimblin's* on the flur.' See **Chamble.** Cf. **Chassellings.**

CHIMBLINS [chim·blinz], *sb. pl., var. pr.* chilblains. Com. 'Mother, I canna bar ööth these *chimblins* no lunger, they itchen so.' 'Well, dunna scrat 'em no more than yo' can 'elp, an' I'll axe yore faither to fatch a good 'olly bough to squitch 'em ööth; it's the best remëddy as I know to—but it gies yo' whad fur at the time.'

CHIMLEY. See **Chimney** below.

'1808. April 13th, sweeping workhouse *Chimley* / 6d.'—*Parish Accounts*, Much Wenlock.

'The auld guidwife's weel-hoordet nits,
Are round an' round divided,
An monie lads' an' lasses' fates
Are there that night decided:
Some kindle, couthie, side by side,
An' burn thegither trimly;
Some start awa, wi' saucy pride,
An' jump out-owre the *chimlie*
Fu' high that night.'

ROBERT BURNS, *Poems*, p. 45, l. 26.

CHIMLEY-JAWM [chim·li jau·m], *sb., obsols.* the solid masonry forming the sides of the fire-place as seen in old houses.—PULVERBATCH. 'Theer's nuthin' lef' but the *chimley-jawm*,' said old Hannah Fletcher, describing the utter wreck of her house, which was swept away by the flood occasioned by the bursting of a water-spout on the Stiperstones, May 27th, 1811. The cottage thus alluded to skirted the side of the little brook which flows through the Pulverbatch Outrack; and there was literally nothing left of it 'but the *chimley-jawm*,' on which hung a ham, and on a nail over it the good old dame's bonnet; these escaped being carried away. The furniture was all swept off by the flood, with the exception of the tall oak-cased clock, which stood against the western wall of the cottage; this wall was borne in by the violence of the flood, and seems to have impelled the clock across the kitchen, as it was found leaning against the before-mentioned *chimley-jawm*, as a person faint and weary might lean against a prop. It was absolutely uninjured; the very glass was saved without a crack. This clock yet [1878] 'survives' with the same glass face it had 'at the time of the flood,' in the possession of the grand-daughter of H. F.——. A 'batch' of bread, just taken out of the oven when the storm burst, was carried by the stream to Stapleton, a distance of three miles; the loaves, swollen to an immense size, were taken out at Stapleton church-yard. A pot of gold pieces, twenty-seven 'spade ace guineas,' was never recovered; it was believed to have been buried in the silt left by the flood, and in future ages may be brought to light as 'treasure trove.' It must have been a shedding-off of the water-spout which thus devastated the little homestead in the Pulverbatch Outrack; the main body of water striking off through Habberley and Minsterley, as will be seen from the subjoined account of the 'Minsterley Flood' condensed from the *Shrewsbury Chronicle* of the period.

'In the afternoon of Monday, 27th May, 1811, there was a violent storm of thunder, lightning, and hail. Near the White Grit, hailstones, two inches in circumference, lay almost a foot deep. About five o'clock a cloud burst upon the Stiperstones, and a torrent of water rushed down the hill-side, sweeping away several cottages of the White Grit miners. The body of water, however, divided: one portion took a direction through Habberley, but the greatest quantity pursued its course along the valley through which Minsterley brook runs, and overwhelmed everything which lay in its way; trees were torn up by the roots, and one containing about 80 feet of timber floated over meadows for more than a mile. Between five and six o'clock the water reached Minsterley, and flooded almost every house in the village. Mr. Vaughan, a farmer, was swept from his fold and carried several hundred yards through the bridge, where the current threw him upon a pigsty, whence he climbed to the roof of a house and was saved. His sister was swept into the branches of a tree. Thirteen persons in the 'Angel' public-house saved themselves by clinging to the rafters when the water reached the second story. The stables, with all other contiguous buildings, were swept away, but 17 horses swam out. Three persons were drowned here. At Pontesford the flood burst into Mr. Heighway's house through the windows; the walls gave way and four people perished. Two ladies climbed on the roof and were saved. At this place the water was at least 20 feet deep. The house and mill at Plox Green were "swilled" away. Great damage also was done at Hanwood. The torrent, following the course of Meole brook, reached Shrewsbury about half-past ten at night with a tremendous roaring noise. All the houses near Coleham Bridge were flooded, and the street in front of the factory was inundated to the depth of nearly three feet by an instantaneous gush. The force of the stream turned the current of the Severn, which rose near the English Bridge four feet in less than ten minutes. The consternation caused in Shrewsbury was intense, as the event happened in the night and in a time of drought, and people rushed from their rooms half dressed and not knowing where to go.'

Owen and Blakeway, in their *History of Shrewsbury*, vol. i. p. 585, referring to the foregeing event, say, 'A subscription was immediately begun in Shrewsbury to supply the loss sustained by nearly 200 families of cottagers, and the sum of £1862 10*s*. 8*d*. was collected in a few weeks; of which £1322 15*s*. 6*d*. was disbursed to the sufferers, and 25 per cent returned to the subscribers. The liberality of the contribution was enhanced by the consideration that two other charitable subscriptions were going on at the same time: one for the British detained as prisoners by Bonaparte, and the other for the distress occasioned in Portugal by the invasion of the French.'

CHIMNEY [chim·bli'], Pulverbatch; Clun. [chim·di'], Clun; Clee Hills. [chim·li'], Shrewsbury; Pulverbatch; Much Wenlock.

CHIN-COUGH [chin·ku'f], *sb.* the whooping-cough. Com. See Bk. II., *Folklore*, &c., 'Superstitious Cures' (*chin-cough*).

CHINE OF PORK, *sb.*, *obsols.* a longitudinal cut on each side of the backbone gives the *chine*, which is afterwards subdivided into small 'hunks.' The *chine* may be cut broad or narrow to suit the circumstances of the household. The ordinary breadth in a large pig is about three inches. Com. 'Cut a good *chine*, Landy, as the offil lasses us most the 'ear; the flitchens an' the 'ams bin wantin' for rent an' other things.' See **Offil.**

A Chine of Pork is one of the dishes in a 'Bill of Fare for Grand Feasts' given by Randle Holme.—*Academy of Armory*, Bk. III. ch. iii. p. 78.

CHINK-CHINK, *sb. Fringilla cœlebs*, the Chaffinch.—BRIDGNORTH. So called from its ringing, musical 'call-note.'

CHISEL [chiz·l], same as **Chassel**, q. v.—CRAVEN ARMS.

CHITTERLING PUFFS [chit·h'lin puf·s], *sb. pl.* puffs made of pastry, filled with a kind of mince-meat made of 'chitterlings' (q. v. below) and other ingredients.—SHREWSBURY; ELLESMERE. Qy. com. A Welshampton woman gave the following receipt for making *chitte'lin' puffs:* 'Yo maun wesh the chitte'lin's in a many waiters, then soak 'em four days in saut an' waiter, an' then two days in fresh waiter, an' after that yo maun bile 'em till they bin thin and clier thin, an' then 'ack 'em as small as small, an' get some corrans an' rais'ns an' some candied pĕĕl an' spice, an' 'ack some apples, an' blend 'em all together, an' mak' puffs on it, or—if yo liken better—standin' pies.'

CHITTERLINGS [chit·h'linz], *sb. pl.* the 'puddings,' or intestines, of a pig. Com. *Chitterlings*, after being thoroughly cleansed by a process such as that described in the preceding 'gloss,' are prepared for table by boiling them—the smaller ones being plaited together—and cutting them into short lengths. Served up thus, or else fried, they are eaten with mustard and vinegar, and are considered quite a delicacy of farm-house or cottage fare. 'Get some o' them *chitte'lins* an' fry 'em for the men's supper, they bin mighty fond on 'em.'

Chytyrlynge, *Scrutellum.* 'Chiterlynge, *hilla.*'—CATH. ANG. 'Chyterling, *endoile.*'—PALSG. Horman says, 'Let us have trypis, chetterlyngis, and tryllybubbys ynough, *suppedita aulicoctia ad satietatem.*' Skinner derives the word from Teut. kutteln, *intestina.*—*Prompt. Parv. and Notes.* Cf. **Roger.**

CHITUP [chit·u'p], *sb.* a saucy, pert, forward girl.—PULVERBATCH; CLUN. 'Dun yo think as I wuz gwein to be 'ectored o'er by a little *chitup* like that? I soon let 'er know as 'er'd got the wrang pig by the ear.'

CHOICE [chois·s], *adj.*, *pec.* careful of, as valuing highly.—SHREWSBURY; PULVERBATCH. Qy. com. 'They han but that one little lad, an' they bin mighty *choice* an' tid on 'im—'e's sadly spiled.'

CHOKE-PEAR [choa·k paa·r'], *sb.* a very hard kind of winter pear.—ELLESMERE, *Montford.*

CHOMBLE. See **Chamble.**

CHOSE [choa·z], *v. a.*, *var. pr.* choose. Com. ''Er didna *chose* to start alung ŏŏth we, so we lef'n 'er a-wham.'

An indenture written at SHREWSBURY, 'ye v day of October the vth yere of the Reigne of Kynge Edward the iiijth,' contains the following: 'Also it shall be lawfull for the said John C & his eyrys to electt & *chose* any other honest or lawfull prest,' &c.—OWEN and BLAKEWAY'S *History of Shrewsbury*, vol. ii. p. 469.

'Therfore let oure kynge, what tyme hys grace shalbe so mynded to take a wyfe to *chose* hym one whych is of god, that is, whyche is of the housholde of fayth.'—LATIMER, *Sermon* i. p. 34.

CHOUL [chou·l], (1) *sb.* same as **Chawl** (1).—ELLESMERE.

'So hard Rofyn rogud his roll,
That he smot with his *choule*,
Aȝayns the marbystone.'
JOHN AUDELAY'S *Poems*, p. 77.

(2) *sb.* the stump of a tree.—WEM. Cf. **Stoul** (1).

CHRISTIAN [kr'is·chu'n], *sb.* this appellation is given to an animal as expressive of superior intelligence. Com. 'W'y 'e'd get on that wall,' said a woman, of a favourite dog, 'an' bark like a *Christian* 'e ŏŏd, 'e knowed so well who wuz a-comin'.'

CHRISTMAS BRON' [kr'is·mus br'on], *sb.*, *obsols.*? a yule log.—WORTHEN.

CHRISTMAS-BRUND, *idem.*—PULVERBATCH. Cf. **Brund.**

CHUCK [chaek· *and* chuk·], (1) *sb.* a cut of beef extending from the horns to the ribs, including the shoulder-piece. — SHREWSBURY. Country butchers have 'cuts' such as the *chuck*, 'slench,' &c., to meet the requirements of their farm-house customers. See **Slench.**

(2) *v. a.* [*id.*] to throw; to toss. Com. '*Chuck* them orts to the pigs, Surrey.'

(3) *v. n.* a call to fowls. See **Call-words.**

'And with that word he fleigh down fro the beem,
For it was day, and eek his hennes alle;
And with a *chuk* he gan hem for to calle,
For he hadde founde a corn, lay in the yerd.'
CHAUCER, *Nonne Prestes Tale*, l. 353, ed. Morris.

(4) [chuk·], *sb.* a term of endearment to a child. Com. 'Now, *chuck*, come an' a yore new coat on, we bin gweïn to see the 'ousekeeper at the Squire's.'

'*Macb.* Be innocent of the knowledge, dearest *chuck*,
Till thou applaud the deed.'—*Macbeth*, III. ii. 45.

CHUCKIE, diminutive of **Chuck** (4).

'I wat she is a daintie *chuckie*,
As e'er tread clay!'
ROBERT BURNS, *Poems*, p. 108, c. 2, l. 27.

CHUMP [chump·], *sb.* a log of wood for the fire.—SHREWSBURY; WORTHEN. 'Fatch a *chump* to put o' the fire, an' then it'll las' us till we bin ready for bed.' Cf. **Brund.**

CHUNDER [chun·dur'], *v. n.* to mutter; to grumble.—NEWPORT. See **Junder.** Cf. **Munger.**

CHURCHING MICE, *phr.* murmuring in an under-tone.—PULVERBATCH; WHITCHURCH. 'I al'ays tell 'em whad I think right out; I dunna like *churchin' mice*, they bin never the wiser then.'

CHURL [chur'l·], *sb. Cheiranthus Cheiri;* the common Wall-flower. —COLLIERY. Cf. **Bloody Warrior.** See **Wall-flower.**

CHURN-DRILL [chur'n·dr'il], *sb.* a flat, edged tool, used in drilling holes for blasting; it is worked with the hands alone, not, as is the ordinary 'drill,' with the hammer. Com. **M. T.**

CHURNING [chur'·nin], *part. adj.* working the 'churn-drill.' *Ibid.*

CHURN-OWL, *sb., obsols. Caprimulgus Europæus;* the European Goat-sucker.—BRIDGNORTH. Called *Churn-owl* from the peculiar cry the bird utters—'chur-r-r! chur-r-r!' Cf. **Night-hawk.**

CLACK [klak·], (1) *sb.* a contemptuous term for a woman's tongue.—SHREWSBURY; PULVERBATCH; WELLINGTON. Qy. com. 'Whad a *clack* that ŏŏman 'as! 'Er puts me in mind o' Betty Andras o' Cruck Meole, w'en the chap i' the market-train gweïn to Sosebry said to 'er, "W'y, Missis, I should think yo' ïled yore tongue this mornin' afore yo' started." But Betty wunna short fur a nanser to 'im; no danger! "No, indeed, sir," 'er said, "I didna; it runs fast anuf athout ïlin'!"'

> 'Þar mid þu *clackest* oft and longe
> And þat is on of þine songe.'
>
> *Owl and Nightingale*, l. 81.

O. Dutch, *klacken;* O. Icel. *klaka*, clack.—STRAT. Cf. **Clat** (3).

(2) *sb.* noisy, unmeaning talk. *Ibid.* 'I tak' no more 'eed on 'er *clack* than a nowd 'en cacklin'.'

(3) *sb.* the valve of a pump.—PULVERBATCH; WELLINGTON. Qy. com. 'I canna get a drop o' waiter out o' the pump; I dunna know w'ether it's the *clack* or the bucket, but summat's wrang.' Cf. **Clicket** (3).

(4) *sb.* the valve of bellows.—SHREWSBURY; PULVERBATCH. Qy. com. ''Ow can yo' espect them *bellys* to blow w'en yo'n got yore knee agen the *clack?*'

(5) *sb.* a smart slap.—SHREWSBURY. 'Mother, Mary's gid our little Sam a *clack* o' the side on 'is yed.' 'Well, jest let me ketch 'er, an' I'll gie 'er Jack-up-the-orchut.'

Claque; coup du plat de la main.—CHAMB.

CLACKER, *sb.* a wooden rattle used to frighten birds. Com. 'It's a pity to see a nice bwoy like Jim stuck i' the leasow to frighten crows; 'e inna lazy, fur 'e works the *clacker* right well.

Cf. Fr. *claquet*, the clapper of a mill.—CHAMB.

CLAM [klam·], (1) same as **Clem,** q. v.—CLUN, *Hereford Border.*

> 'My intrails
> Were *clamm'd* with keeping a perpetual fast.'
>
> *Roman Actor*, II. ii., MASSINGER (first half 17th cent.) in Nares.

Bailey has '*Clammed*, starved with hunger;' ed. 1782.

(2) *vb.* to pull all the bells at once in ringing a peal. Com. 'I spec the weddin's come off; I 'ear Wes'bry bells ringin' an' *clammin'* like fury.'

CLAMPER [klam·pur'], *sb.* anything big, cumbrous, troublesome, or obstructive, would come under the signification of this term.—WORTHEN, *Cherbury.*

CLANE [klain·], (1) *v. a.* and *adj., var. pr.* clean. Com. A.S. *clǽnan*, to clean; *clǽn*, clean. See *Sources of Standard English*, p. 116.

(2) *v. a.* to change the morning dress; to arrange the afternoon toilette; not necessarily to perform the ablutions also. Com. 'Han'ee sid Mary about?' 'Iss, I met 'er now jest at the top o' the stars, gwein to *clane* 'er fur tay.'

(3) *adv.* entirely; quite. Com. 'Sally, the Maister's jest bin an' toud the Missis as the fox 'as bin i' the night an' tŏŏk all them gullies —they bin *clane* gwun, 'e hanna lef' one. The Missis is in a fine fanteeg, an' pŭts the faut on yo' fur nod seein' as they wun safe i' the crew; so yo'd'n better bewar'.'

'Medleth namore with that art, I mene,
For, if ye doon, your thrift is goon ful *clene.*'
CHAUCER, G. 1425 (Six-text ed.), Skeat.

Cf. *Ps.* lxxvii. 8; *Is.* xxiv. 19. A.S. *adv. clǽne*, entirely.

(4) *adj.* clear; pure; with regard to complexion; wholesome looking. Com. ''Er wuz a mighty pretty girld; sich a *clane* skin an' clier red an' w'ite.'

CLANLY [klan·li'], *adj.* clean and neat of habits.—PULVERBATCH; ELLESMERE. Qy. com. ''Er's a *clanly*, tidy ŏŏman, an' the best 'uz'ife i' the parish.' A *clanly dab* is a slattern. Cf. **Dab** (4).

'þe stede stod ful stille · þouȝh he sterne were,
While þe kniȝt him sadeled · & *clanli* him greiþed.'
William of Palerne, l. 3288.

A.S. *clǽnlic*, pure; cleanly.

CLANSE [klanz·], (1) *v. a., var. pr.* to clear; to free from impurities or superfluous matter; to cleanse.—PULVERBATCH. This word is not used in the sense that *clean* is, with regard to domestic economies. 'A dose o' camomine tay ŏŏd do that cowd good; it ŏŏd *clanse* the stomach—theer's nuthin like yarb tay.'

'And *clanse* here consyans clene and kepe charite.'
JOHN AUDELAY'S *Poems*, p. 14.

'On vche braunche was a word · of þhreo maner enkes;
Gold and Seluer he seis · and Asur forsoþe.
'þis makeþ', quod þe wiht · þe marke of gold;
And 'þis saues', quaþ þat wiht · þe seyne of seluer;
And 'þis *clanses*' · as þe Asur kennes.'
Joseph of Arimathie, l. 198.

A.S. *clǽnsian*, to cleanse; to purify; to clear.

(2) *sb.* the after-birth of a cow.—PULVERBATCH. Qy. com. A.S. *clǽnsung*, a cleansing; purification. Cf. **Cleaning.**

CLANSING-SIEVE [klan·zi'n siv], *sb.* a large sieve used in brewing to strain the hops from the wort.—SHREWSBURY; PULVERBATCH; WEM.

Hoc colatorium, a clenyng-sefe, under the head of '*Panducsator cum suis Instrumentis*,' occurs in *Pictorial Vocabulary*, xv. cent., in Wr. vocabs. vol. i. p. 276.

CLAP [klap·], (1) *v. a.* to lay down hastily. Com. 'I *clapt* the kay o' the drink down somew'eer, an' now I canna find it.'

(2) *v. a.* to set down in writing. Com. 'I mus' *clap* down a few arrants, or else I shall forget the one 'afe.'

(3) *v. a.* to sit down hastily. Com. ''Er *clapt* 'erself down on the first cheer 'er come to.'

(4) *v. a.* to close, as of the double doors or gates of a farm-yard. Com. 'Tum, *clap* them gates together, ŏŏt 'ee?' 'W'en I've got the ship out o' the foud.'

(5) *v. a.* to apply, as of a poultice or plaister, &c. Com. 'It's on'y a bit of a scrat; I'll *clap* a slip o' plaister on it jest now.'

> 'He'll *clap* a shangan on her tail,
> An' set the bairns to daud her
> Wi' dirt this day.'
>
> ROBERT BURNS, *Poems*, p. 29, l. 18.

(6) *v. a.* to smack; to slap, as a sign of approbation. Com. Cf.—

> 'And he *clapte* him with þe tre
> Rith in þe fule necke so.'
>
> *Havelok the Dane*, l. 1821.

(7) *sb.* a smack; a slap of encouragement. Com. 'Well said, Jack! Yo' desarve a *clap* o' the back for that.' 'But yo' *clappen* too 'ard.'

CLAPPERCLAW [klap·u'r'klau·], *v. a.* to scold and abuse with the tongue.—PULVERBATCH. Qy. com. 'I believe 'er *clapperclawed* 'im shameful.'

CLAPPERCLAWING, a round of abuse. *Ibid.* ''Er gid 'im sich a *clapperclawin'* as 'e never 'ad.'

CLARY [klaa.r'·i'], *sb. obs.*? a shrill noise; a ringing cry.—PULVERBATCH; WORTHEN. (1) 'It shewns the time o' 'ear; the rooks bin makin' a pretty *clary*.' (2) 'Bin the 'ounds out to-day? I thought I 'eärd thar *clary*.'

Cf. 'Clari'sonous [*clarisonus*, Lat.], sounding loud or shrill.'—BAILEY, ed. 1727.

CLAT [klat·], (1) *v. n.* to tattle; to propagate idle tales.—PULVERBATCH. ''Er's al'ays *clattin'* about somebody.' Cf. **Cant** (1).

(2) *sb.* a tattler; a tale-bearer.—*Ibid.* Cf. **Cant** (3).

> 'Clit, *clat*, clit,
> Yore tongue shall be slit;
> An' every little dog in the town
> Shall 'ăve a bit.'
>
> *Shropshire 'Nursery Rhyme.'*

Cf. *Tell tale tit* in Halliwell's *Nursery Rhymes of England*, p. 76.

'*Glaud*. That *clatteran* Madge, my titty, tells sic flaws
Whene'er our Meg her canker'd humour gaws.'
ALLAN RAMSAY, *The Gentle Shepherd*, III. ii. p. 42.

(3) *sb.* a contemptuous term for a woman's tongue.—ELLESMERE. 'Whad a *clat* that woman 'as! Did'n'ee ever 'ear sich a nize 'er mak's?' Cf. **Clack** (1). A.S. *clatrung*, anything that makes a clattering.

CLAW [klau·], *v. a.* to seize hold of; to snatch at.—SHREWSBURY. Qy. com. 'Now, childern, yo' needna *claw* out o' the basket as soon as it's pŭt down, yo'n get whad's in it none the sooner.'

'He *claws* it as Clayton *claw'd* the pudding, when he eat bag and all.'—RAY'S *Proverbs*, p. 220.

A.S. *clawian;* O.H. Germ. *klawen*, to claw; clutch.—STRAT.

CLAWS, CLEES, CLEYS [klau·z], ELLESMERE; WEM. [klee·z], SHREWSBURY; CLUN. [klai·z], PULVERBATCH; WORTHEN; BISHOP'S CASTLE, *sb. pl.* the respective parts of a cloven-foot. 'Tak' car' as yo' scauden the pig's fit well, so as the *cleys* ŏŏn come off aisy athout tarrin 'em.'

Randle Holme, in his *Academy of Armory*, enumerates amongst the parts of 'The Legs and Feet of a Bull, Oxe, or Cow,' the *clees* or hoofs, which is termed double-*clawed*, or cloven-footed.—Bk. II. ch. xi. p. 171. Of a sheep, hoofs or *claws*.—*Ibid.* p. 177. Swine's feet, *claws* or hoofs.—*Ibid.* p. 181.

'*Claw*, or *cle* of a beste. *Ungula*.'—*Prompt. Parv.*

Minsheu (ed. 1617, p. 97) has the following:—'2051. The *Cleyes* of Crabbes, Scorpions, &c., à Lat. Chelae ārum; idem Gr. χηλαὶ, q. σχηλαὶ, à σχίζω, i.[e.] findo, to cleave asunder, quia fissae videntur in duas partes, *because they are divided and cloven asunder*.'

A.S. *clawu*, a claw; *clea*, *cleo;* id. pl. *cleawan*, *cleawn*.

CLAY-COLD [klai· koa·ld], *adj.* quite cold; lifeless. Com. (1) 'W'eerever han'ee 'ad this child? it's fit an' 'an's bin *clay-cold*—it's welly starved to djeth.' (2) 'The body wuz *clay-cold* w'en it wuz fund.'

CLEACH [klee·ch], (1) *v. a.* to clutch.—CLEE HILLS.

'þenne Sir Gauan bi þe coler *cleches* þe kniȝt.'
The Anturs of Arther, &c., 48, 7, in STRAT.

(2) *v. a.*, *obsols.* to lade out in a skimming kind of way, so as not to disturb the bottom.—PULVERBATCH. 'Tak' a spŏŏn an' fatch a spot o' crame; *cleach* it under carfully, nod to disturb the milk much, or we shan 'ăve it sour.'

CLEACH-HOLE [klee·ch oal], *sb.*, *obsols.* a place scooped out in the bed of a brook, to collect water for domestic purposes.—PULVERBATCH. 'Mind as yo' dunna muddy the *cleach-'ole;* I shall want it clier for weshin' the butter.'

CLEACH-NET [klee·ch net], *sb.* a hand-net, similar in form to a 'shrimping-net,' used in shallow, muddy waters to catch 'pinks' or other small fish. — SHREWSBURY. A good '*cleachin'-waiter*,' as described by John Cotton of Hanwood, is water disturbed by rain, in which the *cleach-net* may be used unperceived by the fish.

CLEANING, (1) *sb.* same as **Clanse** (2).—ATCHAM. Qy. com.

(2) *sb.* a cleansing drink given to the cow at the time of calving.—*Ibid.* Cf. **Clanse** (1).

CLEAT, CLET, CLUT [klee·t], WHITCHURCH. [klet·], WELLINGTON. [klut], PULVERBATCH; WORTHEN, *sb.* a small wedge. 'The cogs o' this sned binna-d-as tight as they oughten to be; I mun get some *cluts* for 'em afore I can begin to mow.'

Randle Holme has '*Plow-Clates*, a kind of Wedge to raise the Beam higher or lower.'—*Academy of Armory*, Bk. III. ch. viii. p. 333.

'Clête, cleat (clate), wedge; *cuneus*.'—STRAT.

'Clyte, or clote, or vegge (clete or wegge). *Cuneus*.'—*Prompt. Parv.*

CLEES. See **Claws.**

CLEM [klem·], *v. a.* to pinch with hunger; to famish. Com. *Starve* is never used in this sense; it is applied to cold only. 'They sen Jack Pugh's tŏŏk to gaol fur poachin', an' the poor ŏŏman an' childern bin *clemmed* an' *starvin'*; they hanna-d-a bit o' bread nor a lump o' coal i' the 'ouse.'

'I cannot eat stones and turfs, say. What, will he *clem* me and my followers? Ask him an he will *clem* me; do, go.'—BEN JONSON, *Poetaster*, I. ii. (first half 17th cent.), in WR.

'You been like Smithwick, either *clem'd* or borsten. *Chesh.*'—RAY'S *Proverbs*, p. 227.

Du. *klemmen*, to pinch; O.L. Germ. (bi)*klemman*; O.H. Germ. (bi)*chlemmen*, to clam. See STRAT. Cf. **Clam** (1).

CLEM-GUT [klem· gut], (1) *sb.* poor food.—PULVERBATCH. 'I canna ate that, it's reg'lar *clem-gut*.'

(2) *adj.* poor; unsatisfying: said of food.—*Ibid.* 'I dunna like them *clem-gut* apple-fit for bayte; theer's nuthin like a good lommack o' bread an' cheese.'

A field at Northwood, Ellesmere, is called *Clem gutts.*

CLEM-GUTTED [klem· guti'd], *part. adj.* said of one who eats ravenously, as if hunger-pinched.—NEWPORT, *Shiffnal.*

CLENT [klent·], *v. n., obsols.* to dry, as grass, &c.; a hay-field term. —BRIDGNORTH. 'Them nettles mun be cut an' lef' to *clent*, ready for the bottom o' the rick.'

CLET. See **Cleat.**

CLEYS. See **Claws.**

CLICK [klik·], (1) *sb.* a sharp, unexpected blow. Com. 'I gid 'im sich a *click* i' the ear-'ole.'

(2) *v. a.* to close; to snap.—PULVERBATCH. 'Did'n a *click* the wicket after 'em?'

CLICKET [klik·i't], *sb., obsols.* the fastening of a gate.—CRAVEN ARMS, *Stokesay.* An iron link is attached to the gate by means of a staple; this link is terminated by a short hasp-like bolt. On the gate-post is an iron plate, having in it a kind of key-hole, into which the before-mentioned bolt fits, much after the manner of the fastening of a trunk, thus securing the gate.

'*Hec sericula, A*[a] clykyt' occurs in an *English Vocabulary.*, xv. cent. in Wr. vocabs. vol. i. p. 203. Cf. Lat. *sera*, a moveable bolt or bar for fastening doors, and the *sericula* is represented by the *clicket* still to be seen in some parts of Shropshire; there is one such now (1873) on the wicket which leads from Stokesay Castle into the adjoining churchyard. 'Clykett, *clitorium, clavicula.*' 'A clekett, *clavis.*'—CATH. ANG. 'Clyket of a dore, *clicquette.*'—PALSG. The French term *cliquet*, in Low Latin *cliquetus*, seems properly to have signified a latch.

'*Pessulus versatilis, Gall. loquet.*'—DUC.

Thus the gloss (*temp.* Ed. II.) Gautier de Bibelesworth (*close of* xiii. *cent.*) renders it—

'Par *cliket* et cerure (lacche and hok).
Ert la mesoun le plus sure.'
Arund. MS. 220 *f.* 302 *b.*

Chaucer, however, uses the word in the sense that is here given to it, '*clavicula*, a lytel keye.'—ORTUS. Thus in the *Merchant's Tale*—

'. . . . he wold suffre no wight bere the key,
Sauf he himself · for of the smal wiket,
He bare alway of silver a *cliket.*'
Prompt. Parv. and Notes.

'Statuentes quod in ostio domus librariæ sit una serura *clikat* vulgariter nuncupata, de qua quilibet socius dicti nostri Regalis Collegii habeat clavem unam: quod quidem ostium singulis noctibus serari volumus.'—From chap. lx. of the *Statutes given to King's College, Cambridge*, by the Founder, King Henry VI., in the year 1446.

(2) *v. a.*, *obsols.* to fasten the wooden latch of a door by inserting a peg above it, thus preventing it from being raised.—CHURCH STRETTON. Wooden latches of the kind referred to, at one time common throughout Shropshire, are now [1873] fast disappearing. They are raised on the outer side of the door by the simple expedient of pulling a string which is fastened to the latch within, and passed through a hole in the door.

(3) *sb.* the valve of a pump.—CRAVEN ARMS, *Stokesay*. Cf. **Clack** (3).

(4) Same as **Cleat**, q. v.—LUDLOW, *Deepwood, Bromfield.*

(5) *sb.* a thin board, having four or five small arched apertures, placed before the mouth of a hive in the winter months to protect the bees from mice or other vermin.—PULVERBATCH; CRAVEN ARMS.

(6) *v. a.* to protect the hives by means of a *clicket*. 'Han 'ee *clicketed* the bees?'—PULVERBATCH; CRAVEN ARMS.

CLIER [klei·ur'], *v. a.* and *adj.*, *var. pr.* clear. Com. 'Hanna yo' *cliered* them things away yet?'

CLIERINGS [klei·ur'inz], *sb.*, *obs.* the middle quality of dressed hemp or flax, between the fine tow and the 'noggs' or 'hurds.'—PULVERBATCH. 'The waiver's made rar' cloth o' the *clierins;* I'll mak' the lads some shirts—they ŏŏnna want a scrattin' pwust.'

CLINKER [kling·kur'], (1) *sb.* a cinder of iron dross, composed of a small proportion of iron mixed with earthy impurities.—COLLIERY; M. T.

'The colliers are coming here,
Is still the talk and tattle;
For they have left their cinder-hills,
Where *clinkers* sore did rattle.'

The Battle of Chirk Bank, a ballad published by R. Minshull, Oswestry, Jan. 4th, 1831.
Byegones, August 16, 1876. See **Cavaldry**.

(2) *sb.* a hard, incombustible cinder of coal. Com. 'I dunna like Short Hill coal, it's so full o' *clinkers*. Now the Arscott coal burns away to ess, an' yo'n done ŏŏth it.'

(3) *v. n.* Coals are said to *clinker* when they cake firmly together in burning.—COLLIERY; M. T.

(4) *sb.* a smart blow. Com. 'Fatch 'im a *clinker* i' the mouth.'

(5) *sb.*, *obsols.* a nail used by shoemakers for protecting the toes of heavy boots. Com. A *clinker* has a rectangular head, curved at the extremity, so as to lie close to the toe leather. Half a dozen of these nails are required for a boot, but steel 'tips' are generally superseding them. 'Tell the cobbler to pŭt some *clinkers* at the nose o' them boots, or they'n soon be spurred out playin' at marvils.'

CLINKER HILLS, *sb. pl.* high heaps of iron dross cinders.—COLLIERY; M. T. See **Clinker** (1). The 'Clinker hill riots,' which took place near Wellington, in Feb. 1821, are still remembered as a matter of local history. The colliers rose in opposition to the iron-masters on a reduction of their wages, assembling between Dawley and Malin's Lee to the number of about 3000, with the intention of injuring and stopping various works. The Yeomanry were called out under the command of Lieutenant-Col. Cludde—a fray ensued; the colliers occupied the *clinker hills*, and hurled stones and *clinkers* on the cavalry, seriously hurting some. The cavalry fired upon the colliers, killed two, and severely wounded others. Ultimately several were made prisoners and committed to take their trial at the Salop spring assizes, March 25th, 1821. Sentence of death was passed upon two; one, however, was reprieved, the other was hanged on the 7th of April following. The rest, nine in number, were imprisoned for a term of nine months, with hard labour. A detailed account of the 'riots,' given in the *Salopian Journal* of Feb. 7th, 1821, was reprinted in *Shreds and Patches*, August 2nd, 1876.

CLIP [klip·], (1) *v. a.* to embrace; to fondle. Com.

'& whan þe sunne gan here schewe · & to schine briȝt,
þe hende & hinde · bi-gunne to a-wake,
& maden in-fere þe mest murþe · þat man miȝt diuise,
wiþ *clipping* & kessing · and contenaunce fele,
& talkeden bi-twene · mani tidy wordes.'

William of Palerne, l. 3076.

'He kisseth hire, and *clippeth* hire ful oft.'

CHAUCER, *C. T.*, l. 10,287.

Mar. 'O, let me *clip* ye
In arms as sound as when I woo'd.'

Coriolanus, I. vi. 29.

A.S. *clyppan*, to embrace; clasp; clip.

(2) *v. a.* to cut wool, as of a sheep; or hair, as of horses, &c. Com.

'And sleping in hir barme vp-on a day
She made to *clippe* or shere his heer awey.'
CHAUCER, B. 3257 (Six-text ed.), Skeat.

'Clyppyn, *Tondeo.* Clyppynge, *Tonsura.* A clippynge howse, *tonsorium.*'—CATH. ANG. In Norfolk to *clip* signifies now to shear sheep, and the great annual meeting at Holkham was commonly termed the Holkham *clip* or clipping. FORBY.—*Prompt. Parv. and Notes.*

Icel. *klippa*, to clip, cut; *klippa hár*, to cut hair.

(3) *sb.* the quantity of wool from the shearing of a flock.—CLEE HILLS. Qy. com. 'Whad sort on a *clip* han 'ee 'ad this *'ear?*' 'Oh, mighty middlin', thank yo'.'

(4) *sb.* a 'clamp' of iron perforated at each end. It is applied as a bandage to a weak or fractured part of an implement; wire is passed through the holes at the ends to draw it up to the requisite degree of tightness.—PULVERBATCH. Qy. com. 'Tak' them twins down to the blacksmith's shop, an' 'ăve a bit of a *clip* put on, or else yo'n be losin' the tines.'

'1594. It thom̃s adderton for three *clypes* of iron for settynge to the newe pylpitt vj[d].'—*Churchwarden's Accounts of the Abbey*, Shrewsbury.

CLIP-ME-TIGHT, *sb.* the scapula of a fowl, with the coracoid bone attached.—CLEE HILLS. Cf **Lucky-bone.**

CLIPPING THE CHURCH. See Bk. II., *Folklore*, &c., 'Customs connected with Days and Seasons' (*Shrove Tuesday*).

CLOD [klod·], *sb.* shale found in the coal-measures.—COLLIERY; M. T. See **Coal-Field.** Cf. **Clunch.**

CLOD-COAL, *sb.* one of the lowest coal-seams; a good smelting coal. —COLLIERY; M. T. See **Coal-Field.**

CLOD-MALL [klod·maul], (1) *sb., obs.?* a large wooden hammer employed for breaking clods.—PULVERBATCH.

'Then every man had a *mall*,
Syche as thei betyn *clottys* withall.'
Huntyng of the Hare, ll. 91, 92.

'A clottynge malle, *occatorium.*'—CATH. ANG., in WAY.

(2) *v. a.* chiefly used in the participial form; metaphorically, to imply retributive justice.—*Ibid.* ''E'll a 'is day o' *clod-malling*,' said a poor dying woman of one who had done her grievous wrong.

CLOG [klog·], (1) *v. a.* to steep seed-grain in lye or a solution of 'blue vitriol,' in order to destroy the parasitic fungus (*Puccinia*) which produces smut.—CLEE HILLS. Cf. **Pickle.**

(2) *sb.* a strong leather shoe with a wooden sole. Com. When the leather soles of such shoes are worn out, it is a general practice to have them replaced with wooden ones. The man who does this is called a *clogger*.

'*Cloggs* are shooes with thick wooden soles.'—*Academy of Armory*, Bk. III. ch. i. p. 14.

(3) *sb.* a kind of under-shoe worn by women to protect their feet from wet. Com. This *clog* consists simply of a thick wooden sole, the heel of which is usually 'iron-clad.' Two leather straps are attached to the sides, which, being tied by a string over the instep of the wearer, keep the *clog* in position. Germ. *klotz*, a block, log; *klotzschuh*, a clog or wooden shoe.—WEDG.

(4) *sb.* a billet of wood fastened to the foot of an animal to prevent it straying far from a certain limit. Com. 'Clogge, *Truncus.*'—*Prompt. Parv.* '*Trunculatus*, Plaut. Clogged, or that weareth a *clog.*'—*Dict. Etym. Lat.*

CLOG-FAIR-DAY [klog· faer' daa·y], *sb.* S. Thomas's Day.—BISHOP'S CASTLE; CLUN. See Bk. II., *Folklore*, &c., 'Customs connected with Days and Seasons.'

CLOGGER. See **Clog** (2).

CLOGGING. See Bk. II., *Folklore*, &c., 'Customs connected with Days and Seasons' (*S. Thomas's Day*).

CLOMB [klom·], *pret.* and *part. past*, climbed. — SHREWSBURY; PULVERBATCH; CORVE DALE; NEWPORT. ''E *clomb* up the wuk-tree after the ackerns.'

'That Phebus, which that shoon so clere and bryghte,
Degrees was fyue and fourty *clombe* on hyghte.'
B. 12 (Six-text ed.), Skeat.

'So *clomb* this first grand thief into God's fold.'
Paradise Lost, iv. l. 192.

Dr. Morris notes the preterite *clomb* as 'obsolete' in his *Historical English Accidence*, p. 159. See **Grammar Outlines** (*strong verbs*).

CLONTERING [klon·tur'in], *part. adj.* walking with heavy, clattering steps, as if caused by clumsy, ill-fitting shoes.—SHREWSBURY; WHITCHURCH. 'Theer 'e göös *clonterin'* ööth 'is clogs alung the street.'

CLOS' [klos·], *sb.* a small field near the house.—PULVERBATCH; CLUN; CLEE HILLS. 'Whad sha'n we play at?' 'We'n run 'ar' an' 'oun's three times round Gittins's *clos'* afore the bell rings' (Churton School). A field at Aston Botterell is called *Dove-'us-clos'*.

'. . . also that John Qwale shall not have Gyns *close* nor the Chyrche *close*, as he has taken them to farm.'—*Paston Letters*, A.D. 1474, vol. iii. p. 112.

CLOSEM [kluz·u'm], *v. a.* to grasp in a close embrace.—WEM. 'They *closem'd* out o' one another, an' wros'led together a good bit afore we could part 'em.'

CLOTH [kloth·], *sb.* linen, in contradistinction to calico. Com. 'Yo' think be'appen as I dunna know the difference twix *cloth* an' calica, but yo' bin mista'en; theer's too many thrids gwun through my fingers in linen an' öölen fur that: an' as to yore fine "Union," it's neither one nor tother.'

CLOUT [klou·t], (1) *sb.* a rough patch.—SHREWSBURY; PULVERBATCH. Qy. com. This term is more especially applied to cobblers' patches; but a rough board nailed on to a wooden paling would also be called a *clout*. 'Them owd boots binna wuth tappin'; but tak' 'em to Bradley an' axe 'im to pût a *clout* under the 'eel, an' then they'll las' a bit lunger.'

'Better see a *clout* than a hole out. They that can cobble and *clout* shall have work when others go without.'—RAY's *Proverbs*, p. 89.

'Spare none but such as go in *clouted* shoon.'
2 *K. Henry VI.*, IV. ii. 195.

See also *Cymbeline*, IV. ii. 214; also Joshua ix. 5.

Clowte of a schoo, *Pictasium*. Palsgrave gives the verb 'to cloute, *carreler, rateceller*. I had nede go *cloute* my shoes, they be broken at the heles.'—*Prompt. Parv. and Notes.*

Sir Frederic Madden says, 'The verb is preserved in Belgic, *klutsen, kluteren*, to cobble or repair.' See Glossarial Index to *William of Palerne*, ed. Skeat, p. 262. As a verb, *clout*, to mend, to patch, is of frequent occurrence in the early writers, and some of the later ones; as, for instance, Burns.

(2) *sb.* a plate of iron going half way round that part of an axle-tree which works within the stock of a wheel. It protects the wood and keeps the wheel steady when rotating.—PULVERBATCH. Qy. com.

'The *Clouts*, or *Axell-tree Clouts*, the Iron plates nailed on the end of the Axell-tree to save it weareing.'—*Academy of Armory*, Bk. III. ch. viii. p. 339.

'A clowte of yrne, *crusta, crusta ferrea, et cetera ubi*, plate.'—CATH. ANG., in WAY. Cf. **Hurter**.

(3) *sb.* a cloth or rag applied to mean purposes: as a 'babby-*clout*,' a 'dish-*clout*,' an 'oven-*clout*.' Com.

'Ycrammed ful of *cloutes* and of bones.'
CHAUCER, C. 348 (Six-text ed.), Skeat.

'And hing our fiddles up to sleep,
Like baby-*clouts* a-dryin.'
ROBERT BURNS, *Poems*, p. 29, l. 22, c. 2.

'*Clowte* of clothe (cloute or ragge). *Scrutum, panniculus, pannucia.*'
—*Prompt. Parv.*

A.S. *clút*, a little cloth; clout.

(4) *sb.* a blow. Com. 'I'll gie yo' sich a *clout* yo' never 'ad'n, if yo' dun that agen.'

'The kinges sone, kene and proud
Gaf kyng Richard swylke a ner *clout*,
That the fyr of his heyen sprong.'
R. Coer de Lion, l. 768.

'And radly raght him a *clowte*.'
Huntyng of the Hare, l. 174.

(5) *v. a.* to beat; to deal blows. Com. 'Nancy Smith *clouted* that chap right well for 'is imperence; 'er didna spar' 'im, an' sarved 'im right an' all.'

'*C. Custance*. . . . Come hither if thou dare,
I shall *cloute* thee tyll thou stinke . . .'
Roister Doister, Act iiij. sc. iij. p. 65.

Jamieson has, 'To *clout*, to beat; to strike—properly with the hands.' Cf. Du. *klotsen*, to strike on.

CLOUTING-NAILS [klou·tin nailz], *sb. pl.* large square-headed nails used for strengthening the heels of heavy boots.—SHREWSBURY; PULVERBATCH. Qy. com. Cf. **Clinker** (5).

'Wiþ his knopped schon · clouted full þykke.'
P. Pl. Cr., l. 424.

Cf. **Clout** (1).

CLUNCH [klun·sh], *sb.* a species of shale found in the coal-measures. —COLLIERY; M. T. See **Coal-Field.** Cf. **Clod.**

Bailey has, 'Clunch, *blue*-clunch, a substance which is found next the coal, upon sinking the coal-pits at *Wednesbury*, in *Staffordshire*.' ed. 1782.

CLUT. See **Cleat.**

CLUTTERED [klut·ur'd], *part. adj.* clotted; coagulated, as of milk or blood.—ATCHAM; WEM. 'That milk's gettin' *cluttered*.'

'The *clothred* blood, for eny leche-craft,
Corrumpeth, and is in his bouk i-laft.'
CHAUCER, *The Knightes Tale*, l. 1887, ed. Morris.

'*Grumeau de sang*, a clot or *clutter* of coagulated blood.'—COTGRAVE, in Wr. O.Du. *klotteren*, clotter. *Coagulare.*—STRAT.

COAL-CAKES [koal kai·ks], *sb. pl.* cakes of dough taken from the 'batch' and baked in the mouth of the oven before the fuel is cleared out. Eaten with the addition of a lump of butter, these cakes are excellent.—CLUN; CLEE HILLS.

COAL-FIELD, *sb.* The 'Shropshire Coal-field' possesses many features of peculiar interest, alike to the Geologist and the Mining Engineer: for the former there are formations of different 'strata,' beautiful sections, faults and dykes, and effects of denudation,—while for the latter there are the varied characteristics of the coal-seams and bands of iron-stones. The names of the 'strata' of the *Shropshire Coal-field* may not inaptly find a place in a *Shropshire Word-Book*. They are comprised for the most part in the following 'section taken from a cutting in the Old Park Colliery, near Oakengates, which contains all the coals and iron-stones that peculiarly characterize the field, with the exception of what is found in the Madeley section,' added below.

SECTION OF PUDLEY HILL PITS.

	Thickness of Strata.			Thickness to Coal.		
	yds.	ft.	in.	yds.	ft.	in.
Soil	0	0	8			
Clay	1	1	0			
Loose Rock	1	2	0			
COAL	0	1	0	3	1	8
Blue Clod	4	0	0			
Red Clunch	3	0	0			
Top Rock	8	0	0			
White Clod	3	0	0			
Brown Clunch	5	0	0			
Red and Blue Clod	3	1	0			
Carried forward ...	29	2	8			

	Thickness of Strata.			Thickness to Coal.		
	yds.	ft.	in.	yds.	ft.	in.
Brought forward ...	29	2	8			
White Binds	4	2	0			
Blue Clod	7	0	0			
Brown Clunch	4	1	0			
Red and Blue Clod	4	0	0			
Blue Clod	7	0	0			
Thick Rock	17	0	0			
Strong Blue Clod	16	0	0			
Stinking Rock	16	1	0			
COAL	0	1	9			
Rock	0	1	6			
COAL	0	0	9			
Fire Clay	0	2	0			
COAL	0	1	0	109	0	8
Strong Binds	6	0	0			
White Rock	18	0	0			
Red Clod	1	2	0			
Brickman's Measure	3	2	0			
Rough Rock	17	0	0			
Rough Binds	6	0	6			
Dark Clod	3	2	6			
Dark Rock	8	2	0			
Rock Binds	5	0	0			
Strong Clod	4	1	6			
Blind Bass	1	0	0			
Ballstone Clod	5	0	0			
TOP COAL	1	1	6	191	0	8
Bass	0	1	0			
Slaty Measure	4	1	6			
Half-yard Coal	0	1	6			
Double Coal Rock	2	0	0			
DOUBLE COAL	2	0	0	201	1	8
Yellow Stone Clod	1	2	6			
YARD COAL	0	2	9			
Parting	0	1	6			
Blue Flat Clod	1	2	6			
Pitch of Casses	1	2	0			
White Flat Clod	3	1	9			
BIG FLINT COAL	1	0	0	211	2	8
Flint Rock	7	2	0			
Penny Stone Clod	6	2	0			
STINKING COAL	1	1	0			
Upper Clunches	9	0	0			
SILK OR CLUNCH COAL ...	0	2	0			
Clunches	0	2	6			
TWO FOOT AND BEST COALS ...	1	1	4			
RANDLE AND CLOD COALS ...	1	1	8	240	1	2
Little Flint Rock	4	0	0			
LITTLE FLINT COAL	0	1	6			
Total	244	2	8	244	2	8

MADELEY SECTIONS.

			yds.	ft.	in.	
Little Flint Rock	...	...	3	1	0	
Crawstone Measure	...	...	1	0	0	
COAL ...	...	...	0	1	0	
Crawstone Crust	...	...	1	2	7	
Lancashire Ladies COAL		...	0	0	9	Not worked.
Rock, hard ...	...	...	0	2	0	
Ditto ...	...	...	1	0	0	

Wenlock Limestone underlies this at Lincoln Hill.
Notes on the Shropshire Coal-Field, by T. PARTON, F.G.S., 1868.

COAL-HOD [koa·l od], *sb.* a wooden coal-scuttle.—PULVERBATCH; NEWPORT. 'Bucket, saucepan, and *coal-hod*.'—*Auctioneer's Catalogue* (Forton Hall), 1875.

COAL-NAMES. The nomenclature of coal-seams is, as a rule, purely arbitrary; but the *same seam*, after being once named, will maintain its title right through a coal-field, if properly identified according to relative position or mineral characteristics. The following list comprises most of the names given to seams in the N.E. Shropshire Fields. Such as have the * prefixed will be found more especially mentioned under their respective letters in the body of the Glossary.

SEAMS.			PLACES WHERE WORKED.
Best	Coal	...	Common.
Blackstone	,,	...	Donnington, E. of Lightmoor Fault.
Bottom	,,	...	Madeley.
Chance	,,	...	Wombridge.
* Clod	,,	...	Donnington, Oakengates, Dawley.
Clunch	,,	...	Donnington, Wombridge, Oakengates.
Cover	,,	...	Dawley.
* Curly	,,	...	Common.
* Double	,,	...	Donnington, Oakengates, Dawley.
Flint	,,	...	Donnington, Wombridge, Malin's Lee, Dawley.
* Flint, Little	,,	...	Donnington, Wombridge, Oakengates, Dawley, Madeley, Amies (near Broseley).
Flint, Big	,,	...	Oakengates.
Foot	,,	...	Donnington, Wombridge.
* Fungus	,,	...	Donnington, Wombridge.
Gainey, Upper	,,	...	Madeley.
Gainey, Little	,,	...	Madeley.
Gainey, Main	,,	...	Madeley.
Gur	,,	...	Donnington, Wombridge.
Half-yard	,,	...	Oakengates.
Kennel	,,	...	Donnington, E. of Lightmoor Fault.
Lancashire Ladies	,,	...	Donnington, E. of Lightmoor Fault. *Madeley* (not worked).
Laver	,,	...	Dawley.
Lower	,,	...	Dawley, Madeley.
Randle	,,	...	Donnington, Wombridge, Dawley.
Rider	,,	...	Madeley.
Sill	,,	...	Dawley, Malin's Lee.

SEAMS.			PLACES WHERE WORKED.
Sill, Lower	,,	...	Dawley.
Silk or Clunch	,,	...	Oakengates.
* Stinking	,,	...	Dawley, Oakengates.
Stinking, Small	,,	...	Donnington.
Stone	,,	...	Donnington.
Sulphur	,,	...	Common.
* Top	,,	...	Donnington, Wombridge, Oakengates, Dawley.
Tow	,,	...	Donnington, E. of Lightmoor Fault.
Two-foot	,,	...	Donnington, Wombridge, Oakengates, Dawley, Malin's Lee.
Three-quarter	,,	...	Donnington, Wombridge.
* Yard	,,	...	Common.

COB [kob·], (1) *sb.* the chief; the leader.—SHREWSBURY; PULVERBATCH. Qy. com. 'Tum's gettin' too big for that job; 'e's bin *cob o'* the walk this lung wilde.' A.S. *copp*, the head; top.

(2) *v. a.* to surpass; to exceed.—*Ibid.* The relation of any surprising or improbable feat will often call forth, 'Well, that *cobs* Dolly, an' Dolly *cobbed* the devil.' A.S. *idem.* Cf. **Cop** (2).

COBBITS [kob·its], *sb. pl.*, *obsols.* two iron bars having knobs at the upper end to rest upon the andirons; meeting at the opposite extremity on the centre of the hearth, they form a kind of cradle for the firewood.—CLEE HILLS.

'1 Paire of *Cobbits*' is an item of an inventory—of about 1758—found in an old chest at Aston Botterell, in the neighbourhood of which place the term still (1873) lingers amongst the old people, though the things which it expresses are rarely to be seen. Ray gives 'a *Cob-iron*, an Andiron,' as an Essex and Leicestershire word (ed. 1768). Cf. **Andirons.**

COBBLE-NOBBLE, *v. a.* to rap on the head with the knuckles.—PULVERBATCH. Qy. com. 'I'll *cobble-nobble* yore yed, if yo' dunna be quiet.'

COBBLES [kob·lz], (1) *sb. pl.* stones broken for laying on roads.—SHREWSBURY. Qy. com.

'*Hic rudus*, *A*[e] a cobyl-stone.'—*Pictorial Vocabulary*, xv. cent., in Wr. vocabs., vol. i. p. 256.

A *cobbledy road* is a rough road.

(2) *sb. pl.* small lumps of coal. Com. 'Pŭt tuthree *cobbles* o' the fire as'll burn up quick.' *Cobbledy coal* is coal in small lumps, free from slack, and having no large pieces in it.

COBBLETICUT. See Bk. II., *Folklore*, &c., 'Games.'

COB-NUT [kob· nut], *sb.* the conquering nut in the game of **Cobbleticut**, q. v. Com. 'I'll shewn yo' a *cob-nut* as 'as cobbed twenty; it's as 'ard as brazil, an' ŏŏl cob twenty more yet.' See **Cob** (2).

COCKAMEG [kok·u'meg], *sb.* a short prop at an oblique angle from the roof of the mine to the top of the 'sprag,' used whilst 'holing' where coals are tender.—COLLIERY; M. T. See **Sprag** (4).

COCKER [kok·ur'], *sb.*, *obsols.* a sock; a short stocking.—SHREWSBURY; PULVERBATCH. 'How old is the child?' 'Oh, 'er's on'y a little un; 'er inna-d-out o' *cockers* yet.'

> 'And cast on me my clothes · yclouted and hole,
> My *cokeres* and my coffes · for colde of my nailles.'
>
> *Piers Pl.*, Text B., pass. vi. l. 62.

'*Cokeres*, short woollen socks or stockings, without feet, perhaps worn as gaiters. A.S. *cocer*, a sheath; Du. *koker*, a sheath; a case; a quiver.'—*Glossarial Index* to Text B., small ed., Skeat.

COCKET [kok·i't], *adj.* saucy; pert; petulant.—SHREWSBURY; PULVERBATCH. Qy. com. 'Yo' nee'na be so *cockit* about it. I toud yo' fur yore own good—but yo'n fine it out.'

COCKHEAD [kok·ed], *sb.* the top part of the spindle which carries the upper mill-stone in a flour-mill; this stone rests on a pivot on the top of the *cockhead*. Com. The lower mill-stone is stationary on a frame of iron or wood; the spindle goes through the centre of it. See **Bush** (1).

COCKSCOMB [kok·s kŭm], *sb. Rhinanthus Crista-Galli*, common Yellow-rattle.—CLUN; MUCH WENLOCK. The country folk consider that when the seeds of this plant rattle in their capsules it is time to mow the hay-grass. Cf. **Rattle-box**.

COCK'S EGG [kok·s eg], *sb.* an abortive egg.—PULVERBATCH; WORTHEN. See Bk. II., *Folklore*, &c., 'Superstitions concerning Birds and Eggs.'

COCKSHUT [kok·shaet], *sb.* a long, rough, steep field.—LUDLOW. In the same neighbourhood a wood is often called *cockshut*. As a place-name the term occurs repeatedly in the nomenclature of Shropshire.

CODLOCKS [kod·luks], *sb. pl.* small pieces of coal or stone.—COLLIERY; M. T. See **Craws of Iron-stone**. Cf. **Cobbles**.

COFER [koa·fur'], *sb.* a chest; more especially one used in stables to hold corn for the horses.—SHREWSBURY; PULVERBATCH; WORTHEN; ELLESMERE. 'I fund out w'eer the eggs göën; theer wuz sixteen 'id under the corn i' the *cofer*. Tum may well a the Maister's 'ackney fat!'

'Cofur, *cista*.'—*Prompt. Parv.* *Capsa*, glossed *cofer*, occurs in a *Metrical Vocabulary* (perhaps), xiv. cent., in Wr. vocabs., vol. i. p. 176.

O.Fr. *cofre*, cofin; panier; corbeille; de *cophinus*.—BUR. Cf. **Bin** (2); also **Cub** (1).

COGGLE [kog·l], *v. n.* to be shaky, as of a rickety piece of furniture.—SHREWSBURY. Qy. com. 'Dear 'eart! 'ow this table *coggles*; it's swilkered my tay all o'er the cloth.'

COGS [kog·z], (1) *sb. pl.* the short handles on the pole of a scythe. Com.

'The *koggs* are the handles of the sythe.'—*Academy of Armory*, Bk. III. ch. viii. p. 322.

(2) *sb. pl.* pieces of iron on a horse's shoe, to raise the heel from the ground.—SHREWSBURY. Cf. **Corking**.

COIN [kwoin·, *corr.* kwa'yn·], *v. a.*, *var. pr.*, *obs.*? to coin.—PULVERBATCH. 'I ŏŏdna 'ăve 'im,—nod if 'e'd *quine* 'is skin into goold—no I ŏŏdna.'

COLDFINCH, *sb.* the Yellow Ammer.—WHITCHURCH. See **Blacksmith.**

COLLAR-PROUD [kol·ur' pr'oud], *adj.* restive: said of a horse that won't go steady in harness.—NEWPORT.

COLLOGUE [ku'loa·g], *v. n.* to unite and plot together to the disadvantage of others.—PULVERBATCH; WEM. Qy. com. 'No danger o' e'er-a-one o' them tellin', they bin all *collogued* together.' 'Aye, I dout they bin a bad lot.'

'Why, look ye, we must *collogue* sometimes, forswear sometimes.'
Malcont., O. Pl. iv. 94, in Nares.

'. . . . .
A blackguard smuggler, right behint her,
An' cheek-for-chow, a chuffie vintner,
Colleaguing join;
Picking her pouch as bare as winter
Of a' kind coin.'
ROBERT BURNS, *Poems*, p. 10, l. 34.

COLLOW [kol·u'], (1) *sb.* soot, such as is commonly seen on a fire-grate, pots, or kettles. Com. See **Colly**, below.

(2) *v. a.* to blacken with soot.—*Ibid.* 'W'y, Bessy, 'ow yo'n *collowed* yore face!' 'Oh, no 'arm in a bit o' clane *collow.*' People *black* themselves with coal, but *collow* themselves with soot.

Colwyd (colowde, P.), *carbonatus.* 'To colowe, make blacke with a cole, *charbonner.*'—PALSG. *Prompt. Parv. and Notes.*

N. *kola*, to black or smut with coal; *kolut*, smutted. Aasen. in WEDG.

COLLY [kol·i'], *sb.* and *v. a.* same as **Collow.**—NEWPORT.

'Nor hast thou *collied* thy face enough, stinkard!'
BEN JONSON, *Poetaster*, IV. v. in Nares.

'To see her stroaking with her ivory hand his [Vulcan's] *collied* cheekes, and with her snowy fingers combing his sooty beard.'—*Cœlum Britan.*, B. 4, 1634. *Ibid.*

Cf. Shakespeare's '*collied night,*' *Mids. Night's Dream*, I. i. 145; also *Othello*, II. iii. 206.

COLLY-WEST [kol·i' west], *adj.* and *adv.* awry; out of the direct line. Com. 'Yore bonnet's stuck on *colly-west*, like a mawkin in a corn-leasow.'

COME-ON, *v. n.* to grow; to improve. Com. 'Them yerlins *comen-on* right well.'

COME-THY-WAYS, *phr.* come here; an encouraging form of address. Com. Noticed by Halliwell as occurring in Shakespeare.

COMICAL [kom·i'kul], (1) *adj.*, *pec.* disagreeable; queer in temper. —SHREWSBURY; PULVERBATCH. Qy. com. ''Er's a good-sorted ŏŏman; but 'er's got some *comical* cornels in 'er temper.'

(2) *adj., pec.* bad; dangerous; said of roads.—PULVERBATCH. Qy. com. 'Our Tum's talkin' o' gweïn across the Longmynt to Sen Tandras [S. Andrew's] far. I tell 'im 'e mus' mind, or 'e'll get into 'djed mon's 'ollow,' for it's a *comical* rŏăd, 'specially if theer comes on a mug.' See **Dead Man's Fair.**

COMIC-STRUCK [kom·ik str'uk], *adj.* struck with amazement.—SHREWSBURY; PULVERBATCH. Qy. com. 'Dunna stand starrin'-like summat *comic-struck;* pŭt yore shuther to it, an' 'elp 'im.'

COMING-FLOOR [kum·i'n flur'], *sb.* the floor of a malt-house on which the barley is spread to germinate. Com.

'*A Couching Floore*, a Floor made of Plaister of Paris, smooth and even, which no water will hurt, where the wet Barley is laid to come.

'*The Comeing of Barley or Malt* is the spritting of it as if it cast out a Root.

'*Wither it* is to cast it abroad on the Kill Floor when it is come, that the comeings may wither away, and for the Barley to dry. It must be turned every twelve hours.'—*Academy of Armory*, Bk. III., ch. iii. p. 105.

See **Couch** (1), also **Witherins.**

CONE-UPON-CONE, *sb.* 'peldor,'—see further, **Curlystone,**—called *cone-upon-cone* on account of its crystallization assuming that form. COLLIERY; M. T. Cf. **Dog-roof.**

CONQUER [kong·kur'], *sb.* a snail-shell. In the children's game of pitting snail-shells one against the other, that which breaks its opponent is called the *conquer.*—SHREWSBURY; ELLESMERE; OSWESTRY. Qy. com. Cf. **Cob-nut.**

CONSAIT [kunsai·t], (1) *sb., var. pr.* conceit. Com.

(2) *sb.* opinion. Com. 'I hanna much *consait* of 'er.'

(3) *v. a.* to fancy. Com. 'I couldna *consait* to ate after that ŏŏman, 'er looks so grimy.'

(4) *v. a.* to conceive; to imagine; to apprehend. Com. 'Mother, Bessy Leach wuz at school this mornin', an' 'er face is all red from the maisles; think I shall 'ăve 'em?' 'Dunna yo' go to *consait* 'em; think nuthin' about it.'

'If any man *conceit* that this is the lot and portion of the meaner sort onely, and that Princes are priuiledged by their high estate, he is deceiued.'—*The Translators to the Reader*, in *Bible Word-Book*, p. 122.

CONSARN [ku'nsaa·r'n], *vb.* and *sb., var. pr.* concern. Com.

CONSARNMENT [ku'nsaa·r'nmu'nt], *sb.* concern; business.—PULVERBATCH. Qy. com 'Richu't wanted me to tell the Maister as the turmits wun gweïn less faster than they shoulden; but I toud 'im it wuz no *consarnment* o' mine.'

CONSARN YO', an expletive; a slight imprecation. Com. Cf. **Sarn** (1).

CONTRAPTIONS [ku'ntr'ap·shu'nz], *sb. pl., sl.?* odds and ends; small matters.—SHREWSBURY. 'Whad'n'ee lef' all them *contraptions* theer fur, messin' about?'

COODLE [kŏŏd·l], *v. n.* to get close together, as a flock of chickens does.—SHREWSBURY; PULVERBATCH. Cf. **Coother.**

COOLER [koo·lur'], *sb.* a large and somewhat shallow oval tub used in brewing. Com. See **Turnel.**

COOM [kuom·], *sb., var. pr.* a comb. Com. A person flushed as from anger or drink is said to have 'raddled 'is *cŏom.*' 'I should think yo'n bin 'avin' a spot o' rum i' yore tay, yo'n *raddled yore cŏom.*' The metaphor is borrowed from the reddening of the wattles and comb of a cock when excited. Ray has, 'He's raddled,' in his *Proverbial Periphrases of one drunk*, p. 69.

COOP [k:oo·p], SHREWSBURY; PULVERBATCH. [koa'p·], CLUN, *v. a.* to tighten; to draw in: a term of needlework. 'Anne, yo'n got one side o' this sem lunger than the other, yo' mun *coop* it in a bit or else unpick it.'

COOTER [kuo·tur'], *sb., var. pr.* coulter; that part of a plough which cuts and forms the furrows. Com. See **Plough.**

COOTH [kooth·], *sb.* a cold.—WEM; WHITCHURCH; ELLESMERE; OSWESTRY. 'That child's ketcht a *cooth* somew'eer.' A.S. *coð*, a disease; a malady.

COOTHER [kuodh·ur'], same as **Coodle,** q. v.—CLEE HILLS.

COOTY [kuot·i'], *adj., obsols.* snug; comfortable; cosy.—PULVERBATCH. 'Whad a nice *cŏoty* bonnet yo'n got!' 'Aye, it's odds to whad a war'n now-a-days ŏŏth thar ears all bar.' Cf. **Tutty.**

COP [kop·], (1) *sb.* the highest part of a 'but' in ploughed land.—PULVERBATCH; CORVE DALE. A.S. *copp*, the head; top; apex.

(2) *v. a.* to surpass; to exceed.—CLEE HILLS; ELLESMERE. 'Well, that's *copped* all as ever I sid afore.' A.S. *idem.* Cf. **Cob** (2).

COPPY [kop·i'], *sb.* a wood; a plantation. Com.

'This Castle [Myddle] stood at, or in, the north-east corner of a pretty large parke . . . On the south side there is a place called the Lane, which lyes betweene the *Coppy* (which was part of the parke) and Webscott grounds . . . The timber of part of this parke was long since falne; but the timber of those partts which are called the higher parke and the *coppy* were fallne about fifty yeares agoe, and sold to Mr. Thomas Atcherley of Marton, and Thomas Wright, of the same.'—GOUGH'S *History of Myddle*, p. 29.

COPSIL [kop·si'l], (1) *sb., obs.* a wedge for keeping the coulter of an old-fashioned wooden plough in its place and at a proper angle to the beam.—WEM, *Hopton.* The *copsil*, or, as it was some times called, the *cop-wedge*, was generally attached to the beam of the plough by a short chain to prevent its being lost. When it was taken out of the hole in the beam, through which the coulter passed, the latter would be quite loose and could be removed at pleasure for repairs. The *copsil* in fastening the coulter was vertical, or nearly so, to the beam. In modern iron-ploughs a horizontal cramp secured by a screw and nut on the opposite side of the beam fulfils the office of the old *copsil.* The substance of the foregoing description was given by two old farm-labourers, who made their statements quite independently of each other, Decem. 1874. *Copsils* of this kind fell out of use when iron ploughs became general, about 1835—1840.

Mr. Wright's edition of *Piers Ploughman* has a frontispiece copied from a coloured drawing on the fly-leaf of a MS. of *Piers. Pl.* in Trinity College Library, Cambridge, marked there R. 3, 14, the date of which, according to Mr. Skeat, is quite the end of the 14th cent. The plough depicted in the drawing has the coulter passing through the beam and secured by a wedge—an arrangement corresponding exactly with that of the coulter and *copsil* as it obtained in the first half of the 19th cent.

The sense of the term *copsil* as given above is probably the primary one, from A.S. *cop*, top, apex, and *sul* or *syl*, a plough. A secondary meaning may afterwards have attached to it, and the word been used for any wedge or peg. 'Two pair of Cotterells or *Copsoles*' are mentioned in an *Inventory* . . . Owlbury Manor-House, Bishop's Castle, 1625. Cf. **Cottril.** Randle Holme, after describing the parts of a yoke, says, 'He beareth Gules, a *Cop-sole* and Pin, with the chain Pendant, Argent, By the name of *Copsole*.'—*Academy of Armory*, Bk. III., ch. viii. p. 335.

(2) *sb.* The term *copsil* is given to the cramps on the plough-beam which, by means of screws and nuts, secure and adjust the wheels of the plough.—ELLESMERE. An application of the old word to a modern usage; perhaps an isolated instance.

(3) *sb.* a piece of iron describing an arc, welded to the end of the plough-beam, perforated and furnished with pins, for adjusting the width and regulating the draught of the plough. Cf. **Buck** (1). In this third sense of the term *copsil* reverts to the etymology before suggested. It terminates the head of the beam, and is the 'cop' or highest part of the plough when working. In Piers Ploughman's plough the apex of the curved beam where the wedge enters appears to be the 'cop' of the plough.

COP-WEDGE [kop· wej], *sb.*, *obs.* See **Copsil** (1).

'*Intersimcnium*, glossed *wegge*,' occurs in the description of a plough and its parts in *Metrical Vocabulary* (perhaps), xiv. cent. in Wr. vocabs., vol. i. p. 180. Cf. **Kay** (2).

CORD [kwur'·d], *sb.*, *var. pr.* cord.—CHURCH STRETTON; CLUN.

CORDWOOD [kwur'd ŏŏd], *sb.* the medium-sized portions of fallen trees cut into lengths, and ranked in 'cords' measuring 8 ft. long, 3 ft. 1 inch wide, and 5 ft. 1 inch high.—PULVERBATCH; CLEE HILLS; BRIDGNORTH. *Cordwood* is chiefly intended for charcoal, so when a fall of timber takes place the trunks of the trees are sold to a timber-merchant, the 'brash' or small fuel is carted away, the *cordwood* is prepared. Then comes the charcoal-burner, makes for himself a hut of poles and turf, and remains on the spot till he has manufactured the *cordwood* into charcoal,—a 'ticklish' process, which requires constant attention day and night.

'. . . Hee became a timber-man, and purchased all the timber in Kenwick's Parke [about 1600] . . . hee bought all the Oakes at 12*d.* a tree, and had the Ash and Underwood into the bargaine, but hee wanted sale for it. It is said that hee would sell wood for fewell at

4*d*. per waine loade, and because hee wanted vent for *Cordwood* hee erected a Glasse-house to consume some of his Charcoale, which house is called the Glasse-house to this day.'—GOUGH'S *History of Myddle*, p. 140.

Blount says, 'A *Cord of wood* ought to be eight foot long, four foot broad, and four foot high, by Statute.'—*Glossographia*, p. 161.

CORKING [kaur'·ki'n], *sb.* a piece of iron on a horse's shoe, to raise the heel from the ground.—PULVERBATCH; BISHOP'S CASTLE. Cf. **Cogs** (2).

CORMLET [kaur'·mlet], *sb.*, *var. pr.* a great eater.—CHURCH STRETTON, *Le Botwood. Cormorant* is evidently meant.

CORN [kau·r'n], *sb.* wheat, in contradistinction to other grain. Com.

CORNCRAKE [kau·r'n kr'aik], *sb. Ortygometra crex*, the Landrail.—SHREWSBURY; PULVERBATCH. Cf. **Landrake.**

'The blysfull byrdis bownis to the treis,
And ceissis of thare heuinlye armoneis;
The *Corncraik* in the croft, I heir hir cry;
The bak, the Howlat, febyll of thare eis
For thare pastyme, now in the ewinnyng fleis.'
SIR DAVID LYNDESAY, *Poems*, ed. Fitzedward Hall, D.C.L., E. E. T. S.

See Bk. II., *Folklore*, &c., 'Superstitions concerning Birds and Eggs.'

CORNED, *part. adj.* full of drink; intoxicated.—WELLINGTON.

'Or elles a draught of moyste and *corny* ale.'
CHAUCER, C. 315 (Six-text ed.), Skeat.

'*Corny*, strong of the corn or malt.'—*Glossarial Index*, p. 221.—*Ibid.*

CORNEL [kau·r'nel], *sb.*, *obsols.*? a corner.—SHREWSBURY; PULVERBATCH. 'Poor owd mon, 'e's so bad ŏŏth the rheumatic, 'e inna-d-able fur a day's work; 'e's more fit fur the chimley *cornel*.' Bailey calls this an 'old word,' ed. 1782. W. *cornel*, a corner; an angle.

CORNEL-CUBBERT, *sb.*, *obsols.*? a corner cupboard.—*Ibid.*

CORNISH [kau·r'nish], *sb.* a cornice.—PULVERBATCH. 'As theer's two windows, I think it ŏŏd be best to carry the *cornish* all alung.'

'Cornice or *Cornish* is the top and over-seeling moulding on the top of a piece of Wainscot.'—*Academy of Armory*, Bk. III., ch. iii. p. 100.

CORNUTE [kaur'neu·t], *v. a.*, *pec. obs.* to correct; to chastise.—PULVERBATCH; WORTHEN. ''E's gettin' a despert srode lad; 'is faither mun *cornute* 'im, 'e tak's no 'eed o' me.'

CORVE [kau·r'v], *sb.* a large round basket, bulging in the middle, and having twisted handles. It holds a bushel or more, and is used for general purposes, such as carrying turnips to cattle, chaff, &c., &c. —CORVE DALE. Cf. **Kype.**

COSTLY [kos·tli'], *sb.*, *obsols.* a game at cards very similar to 'cribbage.'—SHREWSBURY; ELLESMERE. Qy. com. This game, according to Strutt, is mentioned as *Costly Colours* in the *Complete Gamester*, 1674. See Bk. II., *Folklore*, &c., 'Games.'

COSTREL [kos·tr'il], *sb.* a small keg or barrel for carrying drink to the field.—BISHOP'S CASTLE; CLUN. 'The men bin gwine to the fild; fill the two-quert *costrel* for 'em.' '*Hic colateralis*, a costrille.'—*Nominale*, xv. cent., in Wr. vocabs., vol. i. p. 232.

'Costred or costrelle, grete botelle. *Onopherum*. . . . *Costerellum* or *costeretum*, in old French *costeret*, signified a certain measure of wine or other liquids; and a *costrell* seems properly to have been a small wooden barrel, so called because it might be carried at the side, such as is carried by a labourer as his provision for the day, still termed a *costril* in the Craven dialects.'—*Prompt. Parv. and Notes.*

Cf. **Bottle** (1).

COTE [koat·], *sb.* a hovel, frequently made of gorse or ling—erected for the shelter of animals out at grass. Com. 'Put them yerlins i' the *cote* leasow, an' some dry litter i' the foud; theer'll be a snow afore mornin'.'

'1588. One Richard Reynolds of Bagley, near Cockshut in this county [Salop], was on the 19th day of July, being the second day of the assize, put into the Pillory at Shrewsbury, by order of the Privy Council, and had both his ears cut off by Richard Stubbs, then appointed by the Bailiffs to be executioner. His crime was setting fire to a *sheep-cote* of one Gammer, his brother-in-law, wherein was a great number of sheep, and all burned.'—PHILLIP'S *History of Shrewsbury*, p. 200.

'þer sat is ship up-on þe sond,
But grim it drou up to þe lond;
And þere he made a litel *cote*,
To him and to hise flote.'
Havelok the Dane, l. 737.

'God hath swich fauour sent hir of his grace,
That it ne semed nat by lyklinesse
That she was born and fed in rudenesse,
As in a *cote* or in an oxe-stalle,
But norished in an emperoures halle.'
CHAUCER, B. 398 (Six-text ed.), Skeat.

'And learn'd of lighter timber, *cotes* to frame,
Such as might save my sheepe and me fro shame.'
The Shepheard's Calender, December, st. xiii., ed. 1617.

'*Sec. Brother.* . . . Might we but hear
The folded flocks penn'd in their wattled *cotes*.'
MILTON, *Comus*.

A.S. *cot*; O.Dutch, *kote*; '*casa*,' cote.—STRAT.

COTHER [kudh·ur'], *v. n.* to bustle; to fuss.—WEM. 'Whad's 'er come 'ere fur, *cotherin*' an' messin' about?'

COTTER [kot·ur'], (1) *v. a.* to mend up old garments.—CLUN;

ELLESMERE. 'I maun git that owd gownd an' *cotter* it up; it'll do for me to war w'en the weather gets warmer, wunna-d-it?'

(2) *sb.* same as **Cottril**, below.—WEM.

COTTRIL [kot·r'il], (1) *sb.* an iron pin passing through a shutter, and fastened on the inside by a peg fitting into a hole at the end.—PULVERBATCH.

'. . . tow paire of *Cotterells* or Copsoles.'—*Inventory* . . . Owlbury Manor-house, Bishop's Castle, 1625.

Cf. **Copsil** (1).

(2) *v. a.* to fasten by means of a *cottril.*—*Ibid.* 'Han yo' made the door an' *cottrilled* the shutter?'

COUCH [kuoch·], (1) *sb.* a bed of barley when germinating for malt. Com.

'If the grain be of a dark colour, and many corns have brown ends, we judge them to have been heated in the mow, and they seldom come well in the *couch.*'—*Aubrey's Wilts, MS. Royal Soc.*, p. 304, in HAL.

'*Couch the Barley* is to take it out off the wet and lay it on the Flooer a foot thick, for as large a compass as the Weeting will contain.' —*Academy of Armory*, Bk. III., ch. iii. p. 105.

(2) *sb.* a bed of any kind of grain.—CHURCH STRETTON; CLEE HILLS. Fr. *couche*, layer; stratum.—CHAMB.

(3) *sb.*, *obsols.* a fourth swarm of bees from one hive.—NEWPORT. See **Bunt** (2).

(4) *v. n.* to stoop low down; to cower; to crouch. Com. 'I know that lad's after the eggs; 'e wuz *cöochin'* under the 'ay-stack isterday.'

'& þat witty werwolf · went ay bi-side,
& *kouchid* him vnder a kragge · to kepe þis two beris.'
William of Palerne, l. 2240.

'*Sec. Lord.* He can come no other way but by this hedge-corner.

. . . But *couch*, ho! here he comes.'—*All's Well that Ends Well*, IV. i. 24.

O.Fr. *colche; couche*, [Lat.] de *collocare*, mettre, placer, poser.—BUR.

COULING-AXE [kau·li'n ak·'sh], *sb.*, *obsols.* a farm-labourer's implement for stocking up earth.—LUDLOW.

COURANT [kŭr'an·t], (1) *sb.* a hasty journey; a quick walk.—PULVERBATCH. 'A pretty *courant* I've 'ad for nuthin.'

O.Fr. corre, courre; courir, se mouvoir, poursuivre de *currere*. Corant, part. prés. empl. subst. courant.—BUR.

Der. 'couranting.'

(2) *sb.* an assembly; a social gathering; a merry-making.—PULVERBATCH. 'They'n 'ad a pretty *courant* at the christening—above twenty folks, beside the Gossips.'

(3) [ku'r'an·t], *sb.* a great fuss or talk about anything.—CLEE HILLS. 'A perty *courant* 'er's made about it.'

COURANTING [kŭr'an·ti'n], (1) *part. adj.* going about from place to place gossipping and carrying news.—PULVERBATCH. ''Er met fine summat else to do than gweïn *courantin'* round the parish.'

(2) [ku'ran·ti'n]. See Bk. II., *Folklore,* &c., 'Customs connected with Days and Seasons' (*S. Thomas's Day*).

COURTED CARDS [koa·ur'ti'd kaa·'r'dz], *sb. pl., obsols.* the court cards of a pack taken collectively: *a* 'court card,' but *so many* 'courted cards.'—SHREWSBURY; PULVERBATCH. Cf. **Faced Cards.**

COVERSLUT [kuv·ur'slut], *sb.* a clean apron over a dirty dress. Com.

COW-CAP [kou·kap], *sb.* a metal knob put on the tip of a cow's horn.—CLUN; ELLESMERE.

COW-CHAINS, *sb. pl.* chains for tying cattle by the neck when in the stall.—CRAVEN ARMS. Qy. com. 'Three dozen *cow-chains* in lots.'—*Auctioneer's Catalogue* (Longville), 1877. See **Cow-ties.** Cf. **Sole.**

COWCOOMER, COWCUMBER [kou·kŏŏmur'], SHREWSBURY; PULVERBATCH. [kou·kumbur'], Com.; *sb., var. pr.* a cucumber.

COWD [koud·], *adj.* cold. Com.

COWERSLOP, COWSLOP [kou·h'r'slop], SHREWSBURY; PULVERBATCH. [kou·slop], WORTHEN, *sb., var. pr. Primula veris,* common Cowslip. '*Primeveyre*' glossed '*cousloppe,*' occurs in *The Treatise of Walter de Biblesworth,* xiii. cent., in Wr. vocabs., vol. i. p. 162.

COW-FOOT [ki'ou·fut, *corr.* ki'uuw·fut], *sb. Senécio Jacobæa,* common Rag-wort.—WHITCHURCH, *Tilstock.*

COW-LEECH, same as **Beast-leech,** q. v.—WEM.

COWP [kou·p], *sb.* a pen or coop for rabbits.—CRAVEN ARMS. Cf. **Cub** (4), also O.Dutch, *kuipe,* in STRAT.

COWPER [kou·pur'], *sb., obsols.* a cooper.—PULVERBATCH; CLUN; WEM. 'Missis, the *cowper's* comen to 'oop the tub.'

'Item, to indyte a *cowper* at Geyton wheche slow a tenaunt of Danyell at Geyton.'—*Paston Letters,* A.D. 1451, vol. i. p. 190.

'*Hic cuperius,* a cowper.'—*Nominale,* xv. cent., in Wr. vocabs., vol. i. p. 212.

Couper, O.Dutch, *kuiper,* cooper.—STRAT.

COW-QUAKERS [kou· kwaikur'z], *sb. Briza media,* common Quaking-grass.—ELLESMERE.

'*Phalaris pratensis* is called also *Gramen tremulum;* in Cheshire, about Nantwich, *Quakers* and Shakers; in some places *Cow-quakes.*' —GERARDE's *Herball,* Bk. I. p. 87. Cf. **Quakers.**

COWS-AN'-CAUVES, *sb.* the flower-spikes of *Arum maculatum,* Cuckow-pint.—SHREWSBURY; PULVERBATCH; WORTHEN. Cf. **Ladies and Gentlemen.**

COW-SHARN [kou shaa·r'n], *sb.* cow-dung.—SHREWSBURY; PULVERBATCH. 'The best thing as ever I met ŏŏth fur bad legs is a *cow-sharn* pŭltis.' 'Aye; 'ow dun 'ee mak' it?' 'Tak a 'antle o' wutmil an' as much *cow-sharn* as 'll mix well together, an' pŭt it on the leg, it'll swage the swellin' an' mak' it as cool as a cowcŏŏmer.'

'They say that bull's *sherne* is an excellent complexion, forsooth, to set a fresh rosat or vermilion colour on in the ball of the cheeke. —HOLLAND'S *Pliny*, vol. ii. p. 327.

'*Shorn* is the Dung of Oxen and Cows.'—*Academy of Armory*, Bk. II., ch. ix. p. 173.

A.S. *scearn;* O.Icel. *skarn;* L.Germ. *scharn*, dung.—STRAT.

COWSLOP. See **Cowerslop.**

COWT [kout·], *sb.* a colt. Com. 'Pŭt the cowt i' the chains an' let 'im gŏŏ a bout or two, an' yo'n see 'ow 'e osses.'

'Yet aft a ragged *cowte's* been known
To mak' a noble aiver.'
ROBERT BURNS, *Poems*, p. 37, l. 37.

COWTHER [kou·dhur'], *v. a.* to chase; to drive.—CHURCH STRETTON. 'Hie after 'em, Rover! *cowther* 'em out, theer's a good dog.' Cf. **Scowther.**

COW-TIES, same as **Cow-chains.**—CLEE HILLS; LUDLOW. Qy. com. '25 chain *cow-ties.*'—*Auctioneer's Catalogue* (Stoddesden), 1870.

CRABBIT [kr'ab·i't], *adj., var. pr.* peevish; sour-tempered. Com. 'Our Maister's mighty *crabbit* to-day, 'e's bin on sence daylight.' Cf. **Crousty.**

'Or lee-lang nights, wi' *crabbit* leuks,
Pore ower the devil's pictur'd beuks.'
ROBERT BURNS, *Poems*, p. 6, l. 3.

CRAB-VARJIS [krab vaa·r'ji's], *sb.* the juice of crab-apples: said to be good for sprains. Com. ''Ow's Tummas?' 'Well, 'e's laid by ŏŏth a kench in 'is ancler.' 'Whad'n'ee pŭt on it?' 'I pŭt a pultis made ŏŏth *crab-varjis*—theer's nuthin better to swage away the swellin'.'

CRACKNUTS [kr'ak·nuts], *sb. pl.* nut-crackers. Com. 'Han 'ee sid Jack's new *cracknuts*?' 'Whad, 'is tith?' 'No; 'e's made a par o' *cracknuts* ŏŏth a 'azel twig.'

'Then for that pretty trifle, that sweet fool,
Just wean'd from's bread and butter and the school;
Cracknuts and hobbihorse, and the quaint jackdaw,
To wear a thing with a plush scabberd-law.'
FLETCHER'S *Poems*, p. 244, in WR.

CRAFT [kr'aft], *sb., var. pr.* same as **Croft** (1), q. v.—SHREWSBURY; ELLESMERE.

'For me, thank God, my life's a lease,
Nae bargain wearing faster,
Or, faith! I fear that with the geese
I shortly boost to pasture
I' the *craft* some day.'
ROBERT BURNS, *Poems*, p. 36, l. 36.

CRAITCHY [kr'aich·i'], (1) *adj.* dilapidated; tumble-down. Com. 'It's a bit o' good groun'; but a terrable *craitchy* owd 'ouse.'

(2) *adj.* infirm of health; poorly; ailing. Com. 'Tum's wife's a poor *craitchy* piece—al'ays complainin'.'

CRAKE [kr'aik·], (1) *v. n.*, *var. pr.* to creak. Com.

(2) *v. a.* to divulge; to confess.—WELLINGTON.

(3) *v. n.* to murmur; to grumble.—SHREWSBURY. 'Now, Polly, yo'n a to göö, so it's no use to *crake*.'

> 'And *Craken* aȝeyn þe Clergie · Crabbede wordes.'
> *Piers Pl.*, Text A., pass. xi. l. 65.

(4) *v. n.* to ail; to complain of illness.—SHREWSBURY; PULVERBATCH. 'I've got a despert sick 'ouse—three childern down o' the maisles, an' another beginnin' to *crake*.' This seems to be a variety of *croak*, in the same sense.

CRAME [kr'ai·m], *sb.* cream. Com. *Quactum*, with the gloss. *crayme*, occurs in a *Metrical Vocabulary*, (perhaps) xiv. cent., in Wr. vocabs., vol. i. p. 178. See *Piers Pl.* under *Cruds*.

CRANE, CRAWN [kr'ain·], OSWESTRY. [kr'au·n], BRIDGNORTH, *sb.* *Ardea cinerea*, the Heron. Cf. **Yarn**.

CRANNABERRIES [kr'an·u'bae·'r'i'z], *sb. pl.*, *var. pr.* the fruit of *Vaccinium Oxycóccos*, Cranb. rries. Com.

CRAP, CROP [kr'ap·], PULVERBATCH; WEM. [kr'op·], SHREWSBURY; CRAVEN ARMS, *sb.* the settlings of ale or beer at the bottom of a barrel, sometimes used instead of barm. 'Han'ee ever a spot o' barm as yo' can gie me, Missis?' 'No; but yo' can 'a some *crap*.' O.Dutch, *krappe*, crap; refuse.—STRAT.

CRAP, *sb.* a crop, as of grain.—ELLESMERE.

> ''Twas when the stacks get on their winter hap,
> And thack and rape secure the toil-won *crap*.'
> ROBERT BURNS, *Poems*, p. 24, l. 26.

CRAPPINS, *sb.* places where the coal 'crops out' on the surface soil.—COLLIERY; M. T.

CRATCH [kr'ach·], (1) *sb.* a hay-rack. Com.

> '. . . . . þe sturnest stede · in hire stabul teiȝed,
> . . . .
> . . . . durst no man him neiȝhe,
> ne be so bold of his bodi · on his bak to come,
> but euer stod teied in þe stabul · wiþ stef irn cheynes;
> & queyntliche to his *cracche* · was corue swiche a weie,
> þat men miȝt ligge him mete · & wateren atte wille.'
> *William of Palerne*, l. 3233.

'*Cratches* and mangers.'—*Auctioneer's Catalogue* (Stoddesden), 1870.
'Two sheep-*cratches*.'—*Idem* (Longville), 1877.

'In stabulo sit presepe,' with the gloss. *creeche*, over *presepe*, occurs in *The Treatise of Alexander Neckham*, xii. cent., in Wr. vocabs., vol. i. p. 106.

In the Wickliffite version, the manger in which our Saviour was laid is called a *cratche* (Luke ii. 7). 'Cratche for horse or oxen, *crèche*.' —PALSG. '*Creiche*, a cratch, rack, oxe-stall, or crib.'—COTG. WAY, in *Prompt. Parv.*, p. 103.

Cf. **Crib** (1).

(2) *sb.* the rack-like tail-board of a cart or waggon. Com. 'John, turn down the *cratch* o' the cart, an' fatch that bit o' trouse down out o' the W'ite leasow; an' tine that glat w'eer the ship getten i' the meadow.'

(3) *sb.* a rack suspended from the ceiling of a cottage or farm-house kitchen, where the 'flitchens' are kept or fire-arms placed. Com. 'Yo' shoulden al'ays pŭt the gun on the *cratch* w'en it's loaded—s'pose the childern wun to get out on it; it's best to pŭt it out o' thar raich.'

(4) *v. a.* to eat heartily. Com. 'Well, Tummas, 'ow bin'ee gettin' on?' 'I'm despert wek, Maister, but I'm beginnin' to *cratch* a bit.'

CRATCHER, *sb.* a hearty eater. Com. ''Ow does yore new mon oss, Yedurt?' 'Well, 'e's a right good *cratcher;* I dunna know much else about 'im yet.'

CRATER [kr'ai·tur'], *sb.*, *var. pr.* a creature. Com.

CRAW [kr'au·], *sb.* the first stomach of a bird into which the food enters. — SHREWSBURY; PULVERBATCH; NEWPORT; ELLESMERE. '*Crawe* or crowpe of a byrde or oþer fowlys. *Gabus, vesicula*.'—*Prompt. Parv.* Cf. **Crop** (3).

CRAWN. See **Crane.**

CRAWS OF IRON-STONE, *sb. pl.* lumps of iron-stone.—COLLIERY; M. T. 'Clod mixed with large *craws of iron-stone* and codlocks found 24th May, 1867, on the west side of Lightmoor Fault, between the Tow coal and the Gur coal.' See **Codlocks.**

CRAW-STONE, *sb.* the lowest vein of iron-stone in the Shropshire coal-field.—COLLIERY; M. T. *Craw-stone* was described by a miner as 'a hard, uncouth stone, much disliked by furnace men.'

'In the "*Craw-stone* iron-stone" has been found the fossil *Unio* or *Anthracosia*.'—*Notes on the Shropshire Coal-Field*, by T. PARTON, F.G.S., 1868. See **Coal-field.**

CREEPING SAILOR, (1) *sb. Saxifraga sarmentosa.* Com. Cf. **Pedlar's Basket.**

(2) *sb. Sedum acre*, Wall-pepper.—SHREWSBURY, *Uffington.*

CREW [kr'oo·], *sb.* a pen for ducks and geese.—PULVERBATCH; WEM. 'Dunna loose them ducks out o' the *crew* afore they'n laid, else they'n dab thar eggs somew'eer as we sha'n never find 'em.'

Bailey has '*Swine-crue*, a swine-sty or hog-sty. An old word.' ed. 1782.

CRIB [kr'ib·], (1) *sb.* a receptacle for fodder used in fields and in farm-yards for animals lying out during the winter months. Com. 'I've put clane litter on the fowd, an' filled all the *cribs*.'

'Six cattle fodder *cribs*, in lots.'—*Auctioneer's Catalogue* (Longville), 1877.

'Let a beast be lord of beasts, and his *crib* shall stand at the king's mess.'—*Hamlet*, V. ii. 88.

Cf. Is. i. 3. '*Crybbe*, or cracche, or manger, *Presepium*.'—*Prompt. Parv.*

A.S. *cribb;* O.Dutch, *kribbe;* O.H. Germ. *crippa*, crib.—STRAT. Cf. **Cratch** (1).

(2) *sb.* a lock-up; a bridewell.—WELLINGTON.

CRICKER [kr'ik·ur'], (1) *sb.* an itinerant dealer in coarse, common earthenware.—CORVE DALE. Cf. **Crick-man.**

(2) *sb.* a sorry old horse, such as itinerant vendors of earthenware often employ to convey their merchandise.—PULVERBATCH. 'W'y owd Jarvis ŏŏdna own sich a brute as that for a *cricker*.' Cf. **Keffel.**

CRICKET [kr'ik·i't], *sb.* a low wooden stool. Com. The *cricket* is rectangular in form, but longer than wide; it is closed in at the ends and sides, and so stands as upon a frame, instead of legs. A curvilinear aperture at the top admits the hand for carrying it. Pl. D. *krukstool*, a three-legged stool.—WEDG.

CRICK-HORSE, same as **Cricker** (2).

CRICK-MAN, CRICK-WOMAN [kr'ik·mu'n, kr'ik·ŏŏmu'n], same as **Cricker.**—SHREWSBURY. Cf. **Tickney-man,** &c.

CRICKNEY-WARE, *sb.* coarse, common earthenware.—CORVE DALE. Cf. **Tickney-ware.**

CRICKS, *idem.*—SHREWSBURY; CLUN. Cf. **Crocks.**

CRIDDOW [kr'id·oe], *sb., obs.?* a person shrunk or bowed down from age, poverty, or sickness.—PULVERBATCH. 'Molly's gwun a poor *criddow* sence Tummas died,—'e wuz a mighty tidy mon.'

CRIDDOWED, *adj., obs.?* shrunk; bowed down.—*Ibid.* 'Poor owd Ben is *criddowed* sence I sid 'im. I can remember 'im a fine camperin' young chap, an' the best daincer i' the parish.'

CRIFTER [kr'if·tur'], *sb.* a small croft, q. v.—WORTHEN.

CRIM'LY [kr'im·li'], *adj.* crumbling.—SHREWSBURY; WEM. 'That theer cheese is all *crim'ly;* it'll never 'oud together ti'n yo' getten wham.' Cf. **Crudly.**

CRIN [kr'in], *sb.* a small ravine in a hill.—WEM. 'I toud 'im if 'e went alung one o' them *crins* as 'e'd be sure to come to it.' There is a spot between Lee Brockhurst and Hawkstone—a little ravine in the hills close to 'Hollow-way-mouth'—the site of a cottage called the *Crin*—'Morrises o' the *Crin*.' Fr. *cren*, a notch.—COTGRAVE. Lat. *crena.*

CRINK [kr'ing·k], *sb.* a very small, sweet summer apple.—SHREWSBURY; CLEE HILLS. Hence a term of endearment to children. Mothers say, 'Come 'ere my little *crink* or *crinkie*.'

CRINKS, *sb. pl.* small apples left on the tree after the general gathering.—SHREWSBURY; PULVERBATCH; WEM; ELLESMERE. Always in the plural, except that children sometimes say they've 'fund a *crink*, or a *crink-apple*.'

CRIP [kr'ip·], *v. a.* to cut the ends of the hair.—PULVERBATCH.

CRIT [kr'it·], *sb.* a cabin or hut on the 'bank.'—COLLIERY; M. T.

CRITCH [kr'ich·], same as **Casp**, q. v.—CHURCH STRETTON.

CROCK [kr'ok·], *sb.* a coarse earthenware vessel wider at the top than the bottom, having a loop-handle at the side. Com.

'And lerned men a ladel bugge · with a long stele,
þat cast for to kepe a *crokke* · to saue þe fatte abouen.'
Piers Pl., Text B., pass. xix. l. 275.

A.S. *croc; crocca*, a crock; pot; pitcher. Cf. **Stean.**

CROCK-BUTTER, *sb.* butter salted and put down in a *crock* for winter use. Com.

CROCK-NEEST-EGG, *sb.* an imitation egg of earthenware.—NEWPORT.

CROCKS, *sb. pl.* coarse, common earthenware. Com. At Newport the finer kinds of earthenware come under this designation. A set of chamber-ware would be called 'a set of *crocks*.'

'þar ys also whyt cley & reed for to make of *crokkes* & steenes & oþer vessel.'—JOHN OF TREVISA (A.D. 1387), *Description of Britain*, *Specim. Early Eng.*, xviii. l. 46. Cf. **Cricks.**

CROCK-SHOP, *sb.* a china shop.—NEWPORT.

CROFT [kr'oft·], (1) *sb.* a small grass field. Com.

'þenne schul ȝe come bi a *Croft* · but cum ȝe not þer-Inne;
þe *Croft* hette coueyte-not.'
Piers Pl., Text A., pass. vi. l. 62.

A.S. *croft*, idem. See **Craft.**

(2) *sb.* a water-bottle for the table.—SHREWSBURY; ELLESMERE.

'Water-*croft* and tumbler.'—*Auctioneer's Catalogue* (Shrewsbury), 1876.

Croft is probably a corrupted form of Fr. *carafe*, the same thing. See *Shreds and Patches*, 3rd May, 1876.

CROODLE [kr'oo·dl], *v. a.* to crouch; to shrug; to draw together, as from cold. Com. 'Them cauves wanten thar suppin—it's a djurn mornin'; see 'ow they bin *croodlin'* thar four fit together, poor things.'

(2) *v. a.* to cuddle; to cherish.—PULVERBATCH. Qy. com. 'Theer dunna winnock, darlin'; come to mother an' 'er'll *croodle* yo' a bit.'

CROP [kr'op·], (1) *v. n.* to yield a crop or a harvest.—PULVERBATCH. Qy. com. 'Them tatoes *croppen* well.'

(2) See **Crap** (1).

(3) Same as **Craw**, q. v.—PULVERBATCH; LUDLOW. A.S. *crop*, idem.

CROPE [kr'oa·p], *pret.* crept.—PULVERBATCH; CORVE DALE; CLEE HILLS.

'Ac þow þi-self sothely · shamedest hym ofte,
Crope in-to a kaban · for colde of þi nailles.'
Piers Pl., Text B., pass. iii. l. 190.

CROPIN' [kr'oa·pi'n], *part. adj.* rumbling in the bowels.—CORVE DALE; WEM. 'Jack, what were you cracking nuts for in church on Sunday?' 'Please, ma'am, theer wuz a lady as sat afore me as wuz *cropin'* so,—I cracked the nuts as 'er shouldna be 'eärd.'

CROSS-CLOTH [kr'os· kloth], *sb., obs.* a square of linen folded crosswise, and laid on a child's head to protect the 'opening.'—WORTHEN. The *cross-cloth*, together with the 'skull-cap' and 'plucker-down,' formed the head-gear of an infant a century ago—1770—or thereabout. The *skull-cap* was a tight-fitting cap of linen which went over the *cross-cloth;* to this was attached the *plucker-down*—an invention designed to keep the child from throwing its head back. It consisted of two linen bands, which, being secured to the cap at one end, were at the other fastened to the shoulders of the child's dress, thus keeping the head in position. Cf. **Brow-square.**

CROSS DAY, the Festival of the Holy Innocents.—PULVERBATCH. See Bk. II., *Folklore*, &c., 'Superstitions concerning Days and Seasons.'

CROSS-WAUND [kr'os wau·nd], (1) *part. adj.* cross-examined.—PULVERBATCH; WEM. ''E thought to get the saicrit out; 'e questioned an' *cross-waund* me all manner o' ways, but 'e missed it.'

(2) *adj.* ill-tempered.—*Ibid.* 'Yo'n never stop yore 'ear out ŏŏth 'er; 'er's sich a *cross-waund* piece.'

CROUP [kr'ou·p], *v. n.* to caw.—PULVERBATCH. 'I shouldna 'eed 'im or whad 'e said no more than a crow *croupin'*.'

'*Crocio*, to *crowp* like a rauine.'—DUNCAN'S *Appendix Etymologiæ*, A.D. 1595, B. xiii. E. D. S.

CROUSTY [kr'ou·sti'], *adj.* cross; peevish; irritable. Com. 'Yo' canna look at the Maister this mornin', 'e's that *crousty*.'

CROUT [kr'ou·t], *v. n.* to beg with importunity; to crave.—SHREWSBURY; PULVERBATCH; WEM; ELLESMERE. 'That ŏŏman's never satisfied, whadever 'er 'as; 'er keeps *croutin'* all the wilde.'

CROW-FIG [kr'oa· fig], *sb. Strychnos Nix-vomica*, the Vomit-nut of Bengal.—NEWPORT; WHITCHURCH. 'Somebody's gied the poor dog some *crow-fig*, an' pisoned 'im.'

CROWNER [kr'ou·nur'], *sb.* a coroner. Com.

'Sir Myles Stapylton, knyght, with other yll dysposed persones, defame and falsly noyse me in morderyng of Thomas Denys, the *Crowner*.'—*Paston Letters*, A.D. 1461, vol. ii. p. 27.

'*First Clown*. Is she to be buried in Christian burial, that wilfully seeks her own salvation?

'*Sec. Clown*. I tell thee she is; and therefore make her grave straight: the *crowner* hath sat on her, and finds it Christian burial.' —*Hamlet*, V. i. 4.

CROWNER'S QUEST, *sb.* a coroner's inquest. Com.

'*Sec. Clown*. But is this law?

'*First Clown*. Ay, marry, is't; *crowner's quest* law.'—*Hamlet*, V. i. 23.

CRUDDLED [kr'ud·ld], *part. adj.* curdled. Com.

'*Crudle* (Job x. 10), to curdle, the form in which the word appears in modern editions of the Bible.'—*Bible Word-Book*, p. 137.

CRUDLY [kr'ud·li'], *adj.* crumbling: said of cheese.—PULVERBATCH; WEM. Qy. com. 'How came this cheese to be broken so?' 'Please, ma'am, it wuz *crudly*, an' it tumbled all to pieces.' Cf. **Crim'ly.**

CRUDS [kr'ud·z], *sb. pl.* curds produced by scalding the whey after cheese-making, and adding to it a small quantity of butter-milk. Com.

'. . . . bote twey grene cheeses,
And a fewe *Cruddes* and Craym · and a þerf Cake.'
Piers Pl., Text A., pass. vii. l. 269.

Curde (crudde), *Coagulum.* 'Cruddes of mylke, *mattes*.'—PALSG.—*Prompt. Parv. and Notes.*

Cf. **Fleetings.** See **Jowters** (2).

CRUK [kr'uk·], *v. n.*, *obs.*? to sprout.—PULVERBATCH. 'Bad 'arroost weather, John; the corn's *crukin'* sadly.'

CRUKS O' MAUT, *sb.*, *obs.*? malt-dust.—*Ibid.* See **Coming-floor.**

CRUPTURED [kr'up·tyur'd], *part. adj.*, *var. pr.* ruptured.—CHURCH STRETTON.

CRYING THE MARE. See Bk. II., *Folklore*, &c., 'Customs' (*harvest*).

CUB [kub·], (1) *sb.* a chest used in stables to hold corn for the horses. —CLEE HILLS. Cf. **Cofer.**

(2) *sb.* a boarded partition in a granary to store corn.—CLUN; CLEE HILLS. Cf. **Bing** (1).

(3) *sb.* a boarded partition in a malt-house where the sacks of barley are kept.—CLUN.

(4) *sb.* a pen for poultry or rabbits. It is a low wooden 'lean-to,' divided into compartments about two feet wide, each having a door and fastening.—SHREWSBURY; PULVERBATCH; CLUN. 'Han'ee pŭt the chickens i' the *cub*, an' made the doors?'

'A hen-house; a place where poultrie is kept; a *cub*.'—*Nomencl.* in WR.

Nares has '*To cub*, to confine in a narrow space.' He takes it to be 'a familiar corruption of to *coop*.'

'To be *cubbed* upon a sudden, how shall he be perplexed.'
Burt. Anat. Mel., p. 153.

CUBBERT [kub·ur't], *sb.*, *var. pr.* a cupboard. Com.

'*In the greate Parlor*, two *Cubberts*, one Duble virginall upon a *Cubert*.'—*Inventory* . . . . Owlbury Manor-House, Bishop's Castle, 1625.

CUCKOO'S BEADS [kuok·ooz beedz], *sb. pl.* Hawthorn berries.—ELLESMERE. 'We'n mak' a necklis o' *cuckoo's beads* if yo'n come alung wuth me to them 'awthuns.' Cf. **Haws.**

CUCKOO'S BREAD AND CHEESE, *sb. Oxalis acetosella*, common Wood Sorrel.—PULVERBATCH; CLUN; WEM. See **Cuckoo's Meat.**

CUCKOO'S CAPS, *sb.* *Aconitum napellus*, Wolf's bane.—WEM; ELLESMERE. Cf. **Monk's Cowl**.

CUCKOO'S FOOT ALE, *sb.*, *obs.* ale drunk by the colliers on first hearing the cuckoo's note. See Bk. II., *Folklore*, &c., 'Customs.'

CUCKOO'S MATE, *sb.* *Yunx torquilla*, the Wryneck.—BRIDGNORTH. This bird appears about the same time as the cuckoo, hence its name of *Cuckoo's Mate*.

CUCKOO'S MEAT, *sb.* *Oxalis acetosella*.—SHREWSBURY.

'Wood Sorrell, or Cuckow Sorrell, is called in Latine *Trifolium acetosum;* the Apothecaries and Herbalists call it *Alleluya* and *Panis Cuculi*, or *Cuckowes meate*, because either the Cuckow feedeth thereon, or by reason when it springeth forth and floureth the Cuckow singeth most, at which time also *Alleluya* was wont to be sung in Churches.'—GERARDE'S *Herball*, Bk. ii. p. 1202.

Cf. **Alleluia**.

CUCKOO'S SHOE, *sb.* *Viola canina*, Dog-violet.—WORTHEN.

CUCKOO'S SOUR, *sb.* *Oxalis acetosella*.—PULVERBATCH.

'*Trifolium*, geaces-sure, *vel* þri-lefe, occurs in *Archbp. Ælfric's Vocabulary*, x. cent.; and Mr. Wright says in a footnote, '*Geaces-sure* or *gæces-sure*, literally *cuckoo's-sour*, was the plant we now know by the name of wood sorrel, which is still called in some parts of the country *cuckoo sorrel*.'—See *Vocabs.*, vol. i. p. 30.

CUCKOO'S SPIT, *sb.* the frothy substance found upon hawthorn twigs, &c., which contains the small green larva of *Cicado spumaria*. It is popularly believed to be the expectoration of the cuckoo. Com.

CUCKOO'S STOCKINGS, *sb.* *Lotus corniculatus*, common Bird's-foot-trefoil.—CRAVEN ARMS, *Stokesay*.

CULLOW [kuol·oe], *adj.*, *obs.?* pale; wan; dejected.—PULVERBATCH. 'Poor Betty, the dairy-maid, looks despert *cullow* sence 'er's married, dunna-d-'er?' 'Aye, aye, 'er dunna lick the crame-mundle now.'

CULLINGS [kul·inz], *sb. pl.* the residue, as of a flock of fatted sheep, of which the best have been picked out.—CLEE HILLS. 'Maister, them's *cullin's*, they ŏŏnna do for me.'

> 'Those that are big'st of bone I still reserve for breed;
> My *cullings* I put off, or for the chapman feed.'
> DRAYT., *Nymph.*, vi. p. 1496, in WR.

'*Cullynge*, or owte schesynge. *Seperacio, Segregacio*.'—*Prompt. Parv.*

CUMMUDGEON [ku'muj·i'n], *adj.*, *var. pr.* niggardly; parsimonious; close.—PULVERBATCH. 'Whad sort o' folk bin them comen to the New Farm?' 'Well, they bin queer *cummudgeon* sort o' folk; they bin gweïn to get 'arroost in ŏŏth butter-milk, so yo' met'n know w'eer they comen from.'

CUNGIT [kunj·it], *sb.*, *obs.* a road in a mine driven out of the main road for the convenience of drawing the coals.—COLLIERY; M. T. Now called a 'drawing-road.' See **Spout-road**.

CUNNING-MAN, *sb.* a diviner; a magician; a charmer.—SHREWSBURY; ELLESMERE.

'*Smith.* Well, Master, are you the *Cunning Man?*
'*Kite.* I am the Learned *Copernicus.*
'*Smith.* Well, Master, I'm but a poor Man, and I can't afford above a Shilling for my Fortune.'—FARQUHAR'S *Recruiting Officer,* Act III. Scene.—A Chamber [Shrewsbury].

Cf. **Wise-man.** See Bk. II., *Folklore,* &c., 'Charming and Charms.'

CURCHEY [kur'·chi'], *sb.* and *vb., var. pr.* a curtsey. Com. As a verb *curchey* is not much used; women and girls *make* or *drop* a *curchey.*

'These meeke folke that meetes you in the streete
Will *curchie* make, or shewes an humble spreete,
This argues sure they have in Wales been bred
Or well brought up and taught where now they dwell.'
CHURCHYARD'S *Poems,* p. 387. ('Of Shrewsbury.')

CURLY-COAL, *sb.* coal which assumes a curly or conchoidal fracture. It has no particular position; a portion of ordinary seams of coal will often present this peculiarity. Com.—M. T.

CURLY-STONE, *sb.* 'peldor' or 'cement-stone,' assuming a curly fracture. It is composed of lime, silica, and alumina in various proportions, and is found generally in the strata containing the ironstones.—COLLIERY; M. T. Cf. **Cone-upon-cone,** also **Dog-roof.**

CURST [kur'st·], *adj.* wicked; bad; mischievous.—WORTHEN; CLUN. ''E's a little *curst* chap.'

'Be she as foul as was Florentius' love,
As old as Sibyl and as *curst* and shrewd
As Socrates' Xanthippe . . . .'
Taming of the Shrew, I. ii. 70.

'A *curs'd* cur must be tied short.'
RAY'S *Proverbs,* p. 94.

See *Curst,* B. xii., E. D. S. Cf. **Shrewd.**

CUSH-COW [kuosh· *and* kush· kou], *sb.* a cow without horns.—NEWPORT; WEM. Such a cow is often elliptically called a *cush.* In the Swaledale dialect *cush* is a call-word to cows. See C. i., E. D. S. Icel. *kussa,* a cow; *kus,* a call to cows. Cf. **Moillet.**

CUSTARD-CUPS, *sb. Epilobium hirsútum,* great hairy Willow-herb.—WELLINGTON.

CUSTURT [kus·tur't], *sb., var. pr.* custard. Com.

CUT [kut·], SHREWSBURY; ELLESMERE. [kuot·], NEWPORT, *sb.* a canal. See *Cut,* C. vi., E. D. S.

CUTE [keu·t], *adj.* quick; intelligent; knowing. Com.

CUTS [kut·s], *sb. pl.* lots; slips of unequal length, which, being placed within the hand, the upper ends only visible, are drawn to determine any matter at issue: either the longest or the shortest of them is decisive, according to agreement previously made.—PULVERBATCH; WORTHEN. Qy. com.

'Now draweth *cut*, er that we ferrer twynne;
He which that hath the schorteste schal bygynne.
. . . .
Anon to drawen every wight bigan,
And schortly for to tellen as it was,
Were it by aventure, or sort, or cas,
The soth is this, the *cut* fil to the knight.'

CHAUCER, *The Prologue*, ll. 835—845, ed. Morris.

'*Cut*, or lote. *Sors*.'—*Prompt. Parv.* W. *cwtws*, a lot. See Glossarial Index to *Man of Lawe*, &c., ed. Skeat.

CUTTIN' THE GONDER'S NECK OFF. See Bk. II., *Folklore*, &c., 'Customs' (*harvest*).

DAB [dab·], (1) *sb.* a slight blow, generally with the back of the hand. Com. 'If I'd a bin as nigh 'im as yo' wun, I'd a gid 'im a *dab* i' the mouth.'

(2) *sb.* a small quantity. Com. 'We'n a poor *dab* o' butter this wik; the cauves ta'en jest all the milk, an' the Maister says 'e ŏŏnna 'ave thar yeds broke ŏŏth the churn-staff—so we canna 'ăve it both ways.'

(3) *v. a.* to set things down anywhere but in their right place. Com. 'Now dunna *dab* that down 'afe way; pŭt it in its place at wunst.'

(4) *sb.* an untidy, thriftless woman. 'Aye, aye! a mon mun ax 'is wife 'ow they bin to live, an' 'e's got a poor *dab* to 'elp 'im alung.' See **Clanly.**

(5) *sb.* any turn of work done out of regular course. Com. 'Our reg'lar wesh is every three wik; but we bin often 'bliged to 'ăve a bit of a *dab* between.'

(6) *adj.* slight; irregular; out of course. Com. 'A *dab* cleaning;' a *dab* wash.

(7) *v. a.* to do things, such as washing or dusting, in a slight, superficial manner. Com. 'Mary, jest *dab* me tuthree cloths through as'll las' till Monday; it dunna matter bīlin' 'em fur wunst.'

DAB-CHICK, *sb. Gallinula chlóropus*, the Water Hen.—WELLINGTON. Qy. com. Cf. **Douker.**

DAB-HAND, *sb.* a skilled hand; an adept. Com. 'I dout as I canna manage that job; yo'd'n better ax Tum to do it—'e's a *dab-hand* at them sort o' things.' Cf. **Don-hand.**

DACKY [dak·i'], *sb.* a sucking pig.—SHREWSBURY; CHURCH STRETTON; LUDLOW. See **Call-words,** *Pigs.*

DADE [daid·], *v. a.* to lead children when learning to walk.—SHREWSBURY; ATCHAM; PULVERBATCH; MUCH WENLOCK; WEM. 'I'd rather *dade* a child six month than it should larn to creep.'

'Which nourish'd and bred up at her most plenteous pap,
No sooner taught to *dade*, but from their mother trip.'
DRAYT., *Polyolb.*, song i., in WR.

DADING-STRINGS, *sb. pl.* the leading-strings by which a child is held up when learning to walk.—*Ibid.* ''Im a mon! W'y 'a's 'ardly out o' the *dadin'-strings* yit!'

DAFFISH [daf·ish], *adj.* shy; bashful. — PULVERBATCH; CLEE HILLS; WEM. ''Er's a mighty nice young ŏŏman; a little bit *daffish*, but that's a djel better than bein' too boud.' Compare with this, the following:—

'The word *daffte* still [about 1200] keeps its old sense, *humilis*; it has been degraded, like *silly* (beatus).'—*Sources of Standard English*, p. 103.

Cf. also O.Swed. *döf*, stupid.

DAFFODOWNDILLY [daf·u'dou·'ndili'], *sb. Pseudo Narcissus*, common Daffodil. Com.

'Strowe me the ground with *Daffadowndillies*,
And Cowslips, and Kingcups, and loved Lillies.'
SPENSER, *The Shepheard's Calender*, April, l. 140.

DAG [dag·], (1) *v. a.* to sprinkle clothes with water preparatory to mangling or ironing.—PULVERBATCH. 'Send the ōnder's baÿte to the leasow, an' *dag* them clo'es afore yo' go'n to milk.' 'Daggen, O.Icel. *döggva*, dag; moisten; sprinkle.'—STRAT.

(2) *v. a.* to trail in the wet or dirt. Com. 'Molly, w'y dunna yo 'oud yore petticoats up out o' the sludge; yo' bin *daggin* 'em 'afe way up yore legs.'

DAGGLE LOCKS [dag·l loks], *sb. pl.* same as **Burlings**, q. v.—ELLESMERE, *Welshampton.*

DAGGLY [dag·li'], (1) *adj.* wet; showery—a *daggly* day.—SHREWSBURY; CHURCH STRETTON; WEM; ELLESMERE. Cf. **Dag** (1).

(2) *adj.* scattered.—CLUN. Francis Rawlings, the old clerk of Clun Church, said that whereas the old men from the Hospital used to sit in a gallery by themselves, they 'wun now [1873] *daggly* all about.'

DAIRYMAID [dae·r'i'maid], *sb.* a post formed of a bough, usually off an oak tree, with the smaller branches lopped to serve as pegs, upon which the dairy vessels are hung in the open air after being scoured.—PULVERBATCH. Cf. **Vessel-maid.**

DALLOP [dol·up], *sb.* a quantity not measured—as of fruit or potatoes; a mass or lump of anything. Com. W. *talp*, a mass; a lump.

DAN [dan·], *sb.* a small tub used for drawing coals from the workings to the main road where the skips are loaded.—COLLIERY; M. T. *Danning* is drawing the coals in the *dans*, which is done by boys. See **Slipes.**

DANGER, DANKER [dang·ur'], ATCHAM; ELLESMERE. [dang·kur'], CLUN, an imprecatory expression of a mild type. '*Danger* my neck!' '*Danker* it wunst!' Cf. **No danger!**

DANG-SWANG [dang·swang], *adv.* vigorously; with might and main.—PULVERBATCH; WEM; WHITCHURCH. 'Now, chaps, gö̆ö̆ at it *dang-swang*, an' get the barley cocked afore the je'ow falls.'

A farmer, comparing the military prowess of Blucher and General Lord Hill, said to the Rev. E. Nevile, Vicar of Prees, 'Lord Hill's so cool an' so cute, w'ile Blucher goes *dang-swang* at 'em.'

DANKING [dang·kin], *adj.* loose; dangling; 'a *dankin'* coat.'—SHREWSBURY.

DANKS [dang·ks], *adj.* dwarfish: said of people.—NEWPORT. Cf. **Durgy.**

DANNING. See **Dan.**

DAR, DARNA. See **Grammar Outlines** *verb* **Dare.** ''It me if yo' *dar*; but yo' *darna*.'

'For y *dar* nouȝt for schame · schewe him mi wille.'
William of Palerne, l. 938.

'For which thou art i-bounden as a knyght
To helpe me, if it lay in thi might,
Or elles art thou fals, I *dar* wel sayn.'
CHAUCER, *The Knightes Tale*, l. 294, ed. Morris.

'What's this!—I canna bear't! 'tis waur than hell
To be sae burnt with love, yet *darna* tell!'
ALLAN RAMSAY, *The Gentle Shepherd*, II. ii. p. 27.

DARK [daa·r'k], *adj.*, *obsols.*? blind.—PULVERBATCH; WELLINGTON; NEWPORT.

'This Richard Gough lived to a great age, and was *darke* twenty yeares beefore hee dyed, and yett was very healthful.'—GOUGH'S *History of Myddle*, p. 96.

Dryden has 'a *dark* old man.' A.S. *dearc*, dark. Cf. **Bisson.**

DARKSOME, (1) *adj.* dark; obscure; ill-lighted.—SHREWSBURY; PULVERBATCH. 'I thought the place mighty *darksome* after ours; the windows wun little an' the sailin' [ceiling] low, the beäms aumust touchin' yore yed.'

'. . . . thence united fell
Down the steep glade, and met the nether flood,
Which from his *darksome* passage now appears.'
Paradise Lost, Book IV. l. 232.

(2) *adj.* gloomy; melancholy; sad.—PULVERBATCH. 'Aye, them wun *darksome* days—sorrow 'pon sorrow; we wun 'bliged to lave the 'ouse, an' the two poor little childern died'n,—all athin a fortnit.'

DARN [jaa·r'n], *v. a.*, *var. pr.* to darn.—PULVERBATCH. Qy. com. 'I think yo'd'n better *djarn* yore stockin's than mess at that crochetin' all day.'

DASHBOARDS [dash·bwur'dz], *sb. pl.* upright boards put on the sides of a waggon for the purpose of enlarging the interior body when required for a large load, as of lime, &c.—LUDLOW.

'Broad wheel waggon, with iron arms, thripples, and *dashboards*.'—*Auctioneer's Catalogue* (Stoddesden), 1870.

DAUBER [dau·bur'], *sb., obsols.* a plasterer.—BISHOP'S CASTLE, *Walcot. Cementarius*, glossed *dawber*, occurs in a *Metrical Vocabulary*, (perhaps) xiv. cent., in Wr. vocabs., vol. i. p. 181. See Way's note on *dawber* in *Prompt. Parv.*, p. 114.

DAUNTED [daun·ti'd], *adj., pec.* shy; timid.—NEWPORT.

DAW [dau·], *sb.* fire-clay found on coal, giving it a soft, sticky surface, and preventing its ready ignition. It has the appearance of mould when dry.—WHITCHURCH, *Tilstock.* 'I conna kind that fire this mornin', the coal's all over *daw* an' mess; I never seed sich a thing.' *Daw* is perhaps merely a variation of *daub.*

DAWNY [dau·ni'], *adj.* mouldy; mildewed: said of hay.—CRAVEN ARMS. 'The 'ay's gettin' mighty *dawny;* it's lain out so lung, an' theer's bin a power o' rain on it.'

DAZE MY 'OUNDS [daaz· mi' ŏonz], an expletive; a slight oath.—BRIDGNORTH.

'In the Third period [1250—1350] we find *daþeit, dahet* (O.Fr. *deshait, dehait, dehet*) = ill betide. In subsequent writers it became *daþet*, which has given rise to *dase you! dise you! dash you!*'—DR. MORRIS'S *Historical English Accidence* [interjections], p. 336.

DEAD MAN'S FAIR [jed· monz faa·r'], *sb., obs.?* the fair held at Church Stretton on S. Andrew's Day. It acquired this ominous name from the circumstance, it is said, of the number of men who in attempting to cross the hills on their return home after attending the fair, lost their way and perished.

DEAF-EARS [jef· eer'z], *sb. pl.* the valves of an animal's heart. Com.

DEAF-NUT [jef· nut], *sb.* a nut with an abortive kernel. Com. ''E dunna crack many *djef-nuts*' is said of one who has a well-fed appearance.

'Jamieson observes that deaf signifies properly stupid, and the term is transferred in a more limited sense to the ear. It is also applied to that which has lost its germinating power; thus in the North, as in Devonshire, a *rotten nut* is called *deaf*, and barren corn is called deaf corn, an expression literally Ang. Sax. An unproductive soil is likewise termed deaf.'—WAY, in *Prompt. Parv.*, p. 116.

DEA-NETTLE [dee· net·'l], *sb. Lamium album*, white Dead-nettle.—PULVERBATCH.

'*Archan* . . . . de-netle.'—*Semi-Saxon Vocabulary*, xii. cent., in Wr. vocabs., vol. i. p. 91.

DEÄRN, DEÜRN [jaa·r'n], PULVERBATCH. [di'aa·r'n], CORVE DALE. [di'ur'·n], CLUN, *adj., obsols.* eager; bent. 'I knowed I mun be sharp, for 'e wuz *djarn* on it,'—*i. e.* bent upon having it. A fair or market term. See **Deurn** below.

DEAR SORES [dee·-ur' soa'h'r'z], PULVERBATCH. [dee·h'r' sur'z], ELLESMERE, *interj.* perhaps connected with the Sacred Wounds in some form of adjuration.

DEATH [jeth·], the common pronunciation.

'’Ere's a toast as the w'eel rolls on;
Djeth is a thing we bin all sure on;
If life wuz a thing as money could buy,
The rich ŏŏd live an' the poor ŏŏd die.'

DEATH-PINCH [jeth·pinsh], *sb.*, *obsols.*? a black mark in the flesh which looks as if caused by a pinch, but as a matter of fact arises from a diseased state of the blood.—PULVERBATCH. Marks of this kind are believed to foreshadow approaching death. 'Betty, jest look at my arm, 'ow black it is! I hanna 'urt it as I know on; is it whad they callen a *djeth-pinch*?—gid me to prepar'.'

DECK [dek·], (1) *sb.*, *obsols.* a pack of cards.—SHREWSBURY; PULVERBATCH; ELLESMERE.

(2) *sb.* the cards played out; the 'board' at a round game.—SHREWSBURY; PULVERBATCH.

'Whiles he thought to steal the single ten,
The king was slily finger'd from the *deck*!'
3 *K. Henry VI.*, V. i. 44.

DELF [delf·], *sb.*, *obsols.* a stone quarry.—PULVERBATCH. 'Theer wuz a skimperin o' snow, an' the poor owd man missed the rack an' tumbled into the *delf*, an' 'urt 'is-self badly.'

In the Wickliffite version, 2 Chron. xxxiv. 10, the expression occurs, 'stonys hewid out of þe *delues* (eþer quarreris).'—Cott. MS. Claud. E. ii. '*Aurife-della*, a gold *delfe*.'—Vocab. Harl. MS. 1002.—WAY, in *Prompt. Parv.*, p. 118.

A.S. *delf*, a delving; a digging. Cf. **Delve**, also **Standelf**.

'DELP [del·p], *interj.* a contraction of 'God help,' used to express pity.—PULVERBATCH.

DELVE [del·v], (1) *v. a.* to dig two spade's depth.—NEWPORT. Cf. **Graff**.

'Conscience comaunded þo · al crystene to *delue*,
And make a muche mote . . . . . .'
Piers Pl., Text B., pass. xix. l. 361.

'Where is more love, who hath more happie daies,
Than those poore hynds, that digges and *delves* the ground?'
CHURCHYARD's *Poems*, p. 113, l. 8.

(2) *v. n.* to dig and turn over the soil in a purposeless way, as children do.—PULVERBATCH; WEM. 'Let the childern alone, they bin on'y *delvin'* i' the on-dug groun', doin' no 'arm.' A.S. *delfan*; O.Fris. *delva*; O.H. Germ. *telban*, delve; grave; dig.—STRAT.

(3) *v. n.*, *pec.* to slave; to drudge.—PULVERBATCH. 'I'm tired till I can 'ardly lug a leg; I han to *delve* at them tatoes w'ile yo' bin runagatin' about after nuts an' slons, tarrin' yore rags off yore back.'

DENIAL [di'nei·h'l], *sb.* detriment; hindrance; drawback. Com. 'Poor Dick's lost 'is arm i' the throshin' machine; it'll be a great *denial* to 'im, but 'e met as well a bin killed.'

DEURN [jur'n], (1) *adj.*, *obsols.*? hard; stern; severe.—PULVERBATCH. 'Yo' mun mind 'ow yo' dailen ŏŏth 'im, for 'e's a *djurn* hond;

I 2

to get a bargain out'n 'im is summat like gettin' blood out on a cab-bitch stalk.'

Compare *deärn* above; the terms appear to be cognate and to be allied to M.E. *derf*, A.S. *dearf*, O.Icel. *diarfr*, firmus, durus, gravis, in STRAT.

(2) *adj.*, *obsols.*? cold; biting.—PULVERBATCH. 'Good mornin', Mr. Bromley; it's a mighty *djurn* winde.' 'Aw! yo'd'n think so if yo'd'n bin w'eer I han—a-top o' Big Huglith'; it'll shave a mon clane athout lather or razzor.'

DEVER [dev·ur'], (1) *sb.* duty.—CORVE DALE; LUDLOW. 'I'll do my *dever*, Sir.'

'To prey Grenefeld to send me feythfully word, by wrytyn, who Clement Paston hath do his *dever* in lernyng. And if he hathe nought do well, nor wyll nought amend, prey hym that he wyll trewly belassch hym, tyl he wyll amend; and so ded the last maystr, and the best that ever he had, att Caumbrege. And sey Grenefeld that if he wyll take up on hym to brynge hym in to good rewyll and lernyng, that I may verily know he doth hys *dever*, I wyll geve hym x marcs for hys labor, for I had lever he wer fayr beryed than lost for defaute.'—*Paston Letters*, A.D. 1458, vol. i. p. 422.

Fr. *devoir*, duty.

(2) *v. n.*, *var. pr.* to try; to attempt; to endeavour.—SHREWSBURY. Qy. com. 'I'm afeard as I shanna be able to do 'em this wik; but I'll *dever* to let yo' han 'em.'

DEVIL [div·l], *sb.* so pronounced when speaking of the devil *per se*, but in composition the word follows ordinary usage. See below.

DEVIL'S BEDSTEAD [dev·lz bed·sti'd], *sb.*, *sl.* the four of clubs, a card which is considered 'unlucky.'—CLEE HILLS. Qy. com.

The *Slang Dictionary*, p. 119, has 'Devil's bed-post, the four of clubs.' See CAPT. CHAMIER's novel of *The Arethusa*.

DEVIL'S BIT, *sb.* *Scabiosa succisa*, the Devil's bit Scabious.—SHREWSBURY. The root of this plant has the appearance of being cut off abruptly, or bitten [radix præmorsa].

Gerarde calls it *Morsus Diaboli*, *Diuels bit*, and says: '. . . . Old fantasticke charmers report that the diuell did bite it for enuie, bicause it is an herbe that hath so many good vertues, and is so bineficiall to mankinde.'—See GERARDE's *Herbal*, Bk. II. p. 587, ed. A.D. 1597.

Cf. **Blueheads** and **Gentlemen's Buttons**.

DEVIL'S CHURN-STAFF, *sb.* *Euphorbia helioscopia*, Sun Spurge.—ELLESMERE, *Welshampton*. This plant probably owes its name of *Devil's Churn-staff* to the acrid milky juice contained in its stems.

DEVIL'S COACH-HORSE, *sb.* *Ocypus olens*, the Rove Beetle or Common Black Cocktail.—SHREWSBURY. Qy. com.

DEVIL'S CORN, *sb.* *Stellaria holóstea*, Greater Stitchwort.—SHREWSBURY, *Uffington*. Called *Devil's Eyes* about Wrexham.

DEVIL'S CURRY-COMB [dev·lz kur'i' kuom], *sb.* *Ranunculus arvensis*, Corn Crowfoot.—WELLINGTON. This plant is said to be extremely injurious to cattle. Some farmers discussing the merits of certain 'stiff' soil, one of them exclaimed, 'It's full o' the *Devil's Curry-comb.*' 'Yes,' said another, 'and the fallows al'ays throw up the "Beggar's Needle."'

Ranunculus arvensis is a very common weed on all strong soils in Shropshire. Its extremely acrid properties have doubtless led to its association with the Evil One; his *curry-comb* being suggested, probably, by its comb-like achenium.—*Science Gossip*, p. 228, Oct. 1870.
See **Beggar's Needle.**

DEVIL'S GUTS, *sb. Convolvulus arvénsis*, Small Bindweed.—SHREWSBURY. The name of *Devil's Guts* is given to this plant from the circumstance of its roots running very deep into the ground, and being difficult of extirpation. Cf. **Barbine.**

DEVIL'S LONTUN, *sb., obs.* Devil's lantern; the *Ignis fatuus.* Cf. **Jack-o'-the-lanthorn.**

DEVIL'S MEN AND WOMEN, *sb.* the fruit spike of *Arum maculatum.*—SHREWSBURY. The red berries are *men*, the green ones *women*. Cf. **Ladies and Gentlemen.**

DEVIL'S POSY, *sb. Allium ursínum*, Broad-leaved Garlic.—PULVERBATCH, *Hanwood.* It would seem that the horrible fœtid odour of this plant is thought by the rustic mind to be a fitting 'bouquet' for the Prince of Darkness.

DEVIL'S SNUFF-BOX, *sb.* same as **Blind-ball**, q. v.—WELLINGTON. This appellation may, no doubt, be ascribed to the snuff-like powder with which the fungus is charged in its mature state, and to which very baneful properties are popularly attributed. See **Fuzz-ball.**

DEW [dyou·], SHREWSBURY; WORTHEN. [ji'ou·], PULVERBATCH. [doo·], NEWPORT, *sb.* 'We'n 'ad a big *je'ow* i' the night, Yedart.' 'Aye, a mighty big un; we sha'n a a whot day.'

> 'And all the day it standeth full of *deow*,
> Which is the teares, that from her eyes did flow.'
>
> SPENSER, *Astrophel*, l. 192, p. 561.

DHU-STONE [deu·stone *and* joo·stwun], *sb.* basalt, of a black or very dark colour, quarried at TITTERSTONE CLEE. *Dhu*—the local spelling—is a mistake. *Dhu* = W. *du*, black; sable.

DIBBIN-STICK [dib·in stik], *sb.* a setting-stick.—SHREWSBURY; CRAVEN ARMS; ELLESMERE.

> '*Perdita.* I'll not put
> The *dibble* in earth to set one slip of them.'
>
> *Winter's Tale*, IV. iv. 100.

DICHE [dei·ch], *sb.* a ditch by a hedge-side. Com. 'It'll be no sich a job to clane that *diche* out, it's so o'er-growed wuth brombles.'

'The Roll of the Court Leet of the Manor of Bromfield, Shropshire, for the 2nd October in the 4th year of King James I. (1607). . . . . At this court for avoyding of controversies betwext Wm. Lane and Rich. Bevan: It is now with the Lord's consent, and assent of Wm Lane, ordered, that Richard Bevan, who hath broken the lord's former order betwext them, shall hensforth have and repossede two Ridges hitherto in controuersye, and so save the sayd Lane from harmes with sufficient hedge and *diche* of his lande adionyning. And this vnder peine of x*s*, a curia in curiam.'—*English Gilds, their Statutes and Customs*, E. E. T. S.

'To þare *diche* . . . . .'—*Owl and Nightingale*, l. 1239.

A.S. *dīc;* O.Fris. *dīk;* O.Icel. *dīk; dīki;* ditch; dike.—STRAT. Cf. Drain.

DICHE-BONK, *sb.* the embankment on the hedge-side of a ditch. Com. 'Yo' can see the mark o' the wil [wheel] 'afe way up the *diche-bonk;* it's a ŏŏnder they wunna boăth killed.'

DICHER [dei·chur'], *sb.* a ditcher: generally used in conjunction with hedger—a hedger and ditcher. Com. 'The fellow's a perty good 'edger an' *dicher;* but as to stack-makin' an' thatchin', w'y 'e's no better than an owd ŏŏman.' A.S. *dīcere*, a ditcher.

DIDSTAFF [did·stu'f], *sb., obs., var. pr.* a distaff.—PULVERBATCH.

DIMMERY [dim·ur'i'], (1) *sb.* a dark, ill-lighted room or passage.—SHREWSBURY; PULVERBATCH. 'Whad a *dimmery* this place is; w'y yo' canna see from one end to the other, an' it inna that big.' A.S. *dym*, dim; dark.

(2) *sb.* a building or shed in a builder's yard where tools, mortar, and odd things are kept.—SHREWSBURY.

(3) *sb., obs.* a place attached to old churches where the grave-digger's tools were (perhaps) kept.—*Ibid.*

'Underneath this church [S. Chad's], on the north side, is a vaulted room, called the *dimery;* which place probably has been used as a repository for the bones and skulls of the dead, and might receive its name from the Saxon word *dwimora*, ghosts, which in times of ignorance and superstition were supposed to haunt such places; or more likely from the common word dim, dark; a *dimery*, or dark room or place.'—PHILLIPS's *History of Shrewsbury*, p. 89.

DIMMY-SIMMY [dim·i' sim·i'], *adj.* conceited; languishing.—WORTHEN.

DINDERS [din·dur'z], *sb. pl.* Roman coins found at WROXETER [Uriconium]. Spelt *dynders* by Kennett, in HAL.

'The Roman coins found here (Wroxeter) are a proof of the antiquity of the place; the inhabitants call them *dinders*, a corruption of the Roman *denarius*.'—PHILLIPS's *History of Shrewsbury*, pp. 199, 200.

DING [ding·], (1) *v. a.* to dash down with violence.—WHITCHURCH.

'But Do-wel shal *dyngen* hym adoun,
And destruye his myghte.'
Piers Pl., pass. xx. l. 6273, ed. WR.

O.N. *dengia*, to hammer; *dengia einum niðr*, to ding one down, in WEDG.

(2) *v. n., obsols.* to impress forcibly: chiefly used in the way of taunting.—PULVERBATCH; CLUN. 'The Missis 'as bin *dingin'* at me,' said Mary Davies, 'about Bessey knittin' the Maister a stockin' in a

day; so I toud 'er if I couldna knit a stockin' in a day, I could mak' 'im a shirt, an' I went at it dang-swang an' did it.' Mary Davies and Bessey Coxall, two servants of the 'old school,' lived with Mrs. Bromley, of Castle Pulverbatch, about the year 1817. Workers such as they, may be considered like many of the words of their time, to have become 'obsolete.'

(3) [ding·g], *sb.* a buzzing noise in the ears.—SHREWSBURY. 'Dear 'eart! I've sich a *ding* i' my ears, jest like a swarm o' bees.'

DINGE [din·zh], (1) *v. a.* to dint; to knock in.—SHREWSBURY. Qy. com. 'Dun 'ee know who's *dinged* the tay-pot athisn? It looks as if it 'ad bin fell o' the flur.' O.N. *dengia*, to hammer. Cf. **Bulge.**

(2) *sb.* a dint.—*Ibid.*

DINNER-WHILE, *sb.* dinner-time.—COLLIERY. 'I've bin workin' i' my *dinner-w'ile*, Sir.'

DIP [dip·], (1) *adj., var. pr.* deep; cunning; crafty. Com. '*Dip* as the North' is a proverbial phrase current in Shropshire, signifying very crafty.

(2) *sb.* the part of a mine below the level; the part above the level is called the *basset*.—COLLIERY; M. T.

DIPNESS [dip·ni's], *sb., var. pr.* deepness; slyness.—PULVERBATCH. Qy. com. ''Ow yo' cropen off to the wakes athout sayin' ever-a word; I'll remember yo' fur yore *dipness*.'

DIPPER, *sb. Alcédo I'spida*, the Kingfisher.—BRIDGNORTH.

DISANNUL [dis·u'nul], *v. a., pec.* to inconvenience; to disturb; to turn out.—PULVERBATCH; CORVE DALE; WEM. (1) 'Yo' can come in, yo' ŏŏnna *disannul* the ladies.' (2) ''E thought to end 'is days theer, but this new lan'lord's *disannulled* 'im altogether.'

DISCORDEDEN [diskaur'·di'du'n], *pret.* disagreed.—CLEE HILLS. 'Well, I met a bin ŏŏth 'im now, on'y we *discordeden* a bit.' O.Fr. *discorder*, disputer; quereller.—BUR.

DISGEST [dizgest·], *v. a.* to digest. Com. 'I'm a sight better than I wuz; yarb-tay did me most good of anythin'. I could aumust *disgest* a pimple-stwun.'

> 'Sowre whey and curds can yeeld a sugred tast
> Where sweete martchpane, as yet was never knowne:
> When emptie gorge, hath bole of milke embrast;
> And cheese and bread, hath dayly of his owne,
> He craves no feast, nor seekes no banquets fine,
> He can *disgest* his dinner without wine.'
>
> CHURCHYARD's *Poems*, p. 113, l. 18.

'*Disgestive Faculty* assimilates the nourishment, into the substance of that part where it is.'—*Academy of Armory*, Bk. II. chap. xvii. p. 414.

DISH-WASHER, *sb. Motacilla yarrellii*, the Pied Wagtail.—BRIDGNORTH.

DISTRESS [distres·s], *sb., pec.* strain; stress; application of force. —WEM. 'Theer wunna be no *distress* on that theer 'edge tin after 'arvest,'—*i. e.* till after the corn is cut, and animals are turned into the field, who will strain, or try, the strength of the fence.

DITHER [didh·ur'], *v. n.* to tremble with cold; to shiver. Com. 'I'm starved till I *dither*, an' my tith chatter.' 'That's a pity, for yore tongue can chatter fast enough.' Cf. **Acker.**

DIVINING-ROD, *sb., obsols.* a rod made of Hazel or twigs of Wych Elm, used for purposes of divination.—CORVE DALE; LUDLOW. See Bk. II., *Folklore*, &c., 'Charming and Charms.'

DIZENIN' [diz·h'nin], *sb.* a 'dressing;' a scolding.—WEM. ''Er give 'im a fine *dizenin'* w'en 'e did come wham.' Cf. *Dizen* = to dress.

DO [doo·], *sb.* a festivity; an entertainment. Com. 'I s'pose as theer's to be a fine *do* at the Squire's w'en the weddin' comes off.'

DOCK [dok·], (1) *v. a., obsols.* to cut off the tails of horses to the stump; also to cut close the ears of dogs. Com. The latter practice is made criminal under the Cruelty to Animals Act. 'That dog ŏŏd look better if 'is ears wun *dockt*, but we darna now.'

'He [Sir Charles Grandison] seldom travels without a set, and suitable attendants; and, what I think seems a little to savour of singularity, his horses are not *docked*. Their tails are only tied up when they are on the road. . . . .

'But if he be of opinion that the tails of these noble animals are not only a natural ornament, but are of real use to defend them from the vexatious insects that in summer are so apt to annoy them (as Jenny just now told me was thought to be his reason for not depriving his cattle of a defence which nature gave them), how far from a dispraise is this humane consideration! And how in the more minute as well as we may suppose in the greater instances, does he deserve the character of the man of mercy, who will be merciful to his beast.' —*Sir Charles Grandison*, vol. i. p. 257, ed. 1766.

'*Dokkyn̄*, or smytyn̄' a-wey the tayle. *Decaudo.*'—*Prompt. Parv.* O.N. *dokr*, a short, stumpy tail.—WEDG.

(2) *v. a.* to cut off, in any general sense, so as to shorten.—PULVERBATCH. Qy. com. 'I dunna know whad folks wanten ŏŏth a yard o' stuff 'angin' at thar 'eels; I should like to tak' 'em to the choppin'-block an' *dock* 'em.'

'His heer was by his eres ful round i-shorn,
His top was *docked* lyk a preest biforn.'
CHAUCER, *The Prologue*, l. 590, ed. Morris.

'*Dokkyn̄*' or shortyn̄. *Decurto, abbrevio.*'—*Prompt. Parv.*

(3) *v. a.* to shorten: as of a baby's clothes.—WEM; ELLESMERE. 'We maun *dock* the child's clothes nex' wik, the weather's gettin' warmer.'

(4) *v. a., pec.* to put off: as of apparel.—SHREWSBURY. 'It's no use, I mun *dock* this gownd off, it's swelterin' me to djeth.' Cf. **Doff.**

DOCTOR'S MON, *sb.* a medical man's assistant. Com. 'I should think theer's somebody very bad at the shop; I sid the Doctor theer this mornin', an' the *Doctor's mon* this onder.'

DOCTOR'S STUFF, *sb.* medicine. Com.

DODDERING [dod·h'r'i'n], *part. adj.* trembling; shaking: as from age or sickness, like palsied people do.—CORVE DALE. Cf. **Dither.**

DODGER [doj·ur'], *sb. Sherardia arvensis*, creeping Plume-thistle. CORVE DALE.

DOFF [dof·], *v. a.* to put off; to do off.—SHREWSBURY; PULVERBATCH; NEWPORT; WEM. 'If yo' mainen work, *doff* that jacket; yo' bin like owd Jack Jones—ate till yo' swat, an' work till yo' starve.'

> '. . . . . . do as ich þe rede,
> *dof* bliue þis bere-skyn · & be stille in þi cloþes.'
>
> *William of Palerne*, l. 2343.

> 'Shee also *dofte* her heavy haberjeon,
> Which the faire feature of her limbs did hyde.'
>
> SPENSER, F. Q., Bk. III. c. ix. st. xxi.

DOG [dog·], *sb.* the link at the end of the chain fastening it round the cow's neck.—CLEE HILLS. Qy. com. See **Cow-chains.**

DOG-DAISY [dog·dai·'zi'], *sb. Anthémis cotula*, stinking Chamomile. —WHITCHURCH, *Tilstock*. Cf. **Maise.**

DOGGIE [dog·i'], *sb., sl.* the overlooker at the pit's mouth.—COLLIERY; M. T. Cf. **Reeve** (1).

DOG-HANGIN', *sb.* a large social gathering.—CORVE DALE. Mr. Halliwell says a *dog-hanging* was a wedding feast where money was collected for the bride.

DOG-MEN [dog·men], *sb. pl., obs.* church beadles.—BISHOP'S CASTLE; CLUN. Countrymen coming into church were often followed by their dogs, which were driven out by the beadles, who thus acquired the name of *dog-men*. This office ceased to exist about 1830.

'July 17th, 1741. Then agreed with Henry Howells to give him Ten shillings untill Lady Day next for *Whiping the doggs* out of the Church servise Time, and keeping people from Sleeping in Church During Divine service, and to be paid him by the Churchwardens that are in Office for the time Being.'—*Churchwarden's Accounts*, Clun.

DÓG-ROOF, *sb.* same as **Curly-stone**, q. v. The miners give it this name from its fancied resemblance to the roof of a dog's mouth.— COLLIERY; M. T.

DOG'S LEAVE, *phr., sl.?* without permission.—SHREWSBURY.

DOLLIES [dol·i'z], *sb. pl.* bolsters of straw put under the eaves of a stack to make them project, and so throw the wet off better.—PULVERBATCH.

DOLLY [dol·i'], (1) *sb.* a washing implement.—SHREWSBURY; ELLESMERE. Qy. com. The lower part of the *dolly* is made of a solid block of wood, 8 inches deep and 6½ inches wide; it is of circular shape, and so cut through at the two opposite diameters as to form four wedge-shaped feet 4½ inches in depth. Into the centre of this block is fitted an upright handle 2 ft. long, having a cross-bar at the top 15 inches long; held by this, the *dolly* is worked with an up and down motion, which pounds the dirt out of the clothes.

(2) *v. a.* to cleanse the clothes with the *dolly* or the 'dolly-peg.'—*Ibid.*

DOLLY-PEG, *sb.* an implement similar in intention to the dolly, but differing from it in form and mode of action. A circular piece of wood 1½ inch thick and 8 inches in diameter has inserted into it six stout pegs about 7 inches in length; on the upper side of it is an upright handle 2 ft. 2 inches long, having a cross-bar 7 inches long, about 4 inches below the top; the operator holds the *dolly-peg* by this, and with a strong twisting motion shakes and rubs the clothes in the water, so as to cleanse them very effectually.—*Ibid.* Cf. **Peggy.**

DOLLY-TUB, *sb.* the deep tub adapted to the purpose, in which the clothes are 'dollied.'—*Ibid.* Cf. **Washing stock.**

DON [don·], *v. a., obsols.* to put on: as of clothes—more especially gay attire; to dress up.—PULVERBATCH. 'Did'n'ee see Bessy Leach at the club? wunna-d-'er *donned* off?' See **Donnings.**

'And costly vesture was in hand to *don.*'
Turbvile's Ovid, 1567, f. 145, in HAL.

'What, should I *don* this robe, and trouble you?'
Titus Andronicus, I. i. 189.

'*Do oñ* clothys, or clothyn'. *Induo, vestio.*'—*Prompt. Parv.* Cf. **Doff.**

DONCASS [dong·ku's], *v. n.* to saunter.—CLEE HILLS. 'W'eer bin yo' off *doncassin'* to now?'

DONEY-WAGGON [doa·ni' wag·u'n], *sb.* a waggon with skeleton sides.—ATCHAM.

DON-HAND, *sb.* an expert; an adept.—PULVERBATCH; CLEE HILLS. 'Tummas, they tellen me as yo' bin a *don-'and* at stack-makin' an' thetchin'; can 'ee spar' us a wik?' Cf. **Dab-hand.**

DONNINGS [don·i'nz], *sb. pl., obsols.*? fine clothes.—PULVERBATCH. 'Sally Price 'as got on all 'er *donnin's* I should think; w'y 'er's 'anged ŏŏth ribbints like a pedlar's basket.' See **Don.**

DOOR-CHEEKS, *sb. pl.* door-posts.—WEM. See Exod. xii. 22, ed. 1640.—HAL.

DOOR-JAWMS, *sb. pl., var. pr.* door-posts or jambs.—PULVERBATCH.

DOSOME [doa·sum], *adj.* hearty; thriving: said of animals.—WEM.

'Loik dangling of a babby, then the Huntsman hove him up,
The dugs a bayin' roind him, while the gemmen croid, "Whoo-hup!"
As *doesome* cauves lick fleetings out o' th' piggin in the shed,
They worried every inch of him, aw but his tail an' yed.'
Farmer Dobbin: 'A Day wi' the Cheshire Fox Dugs.'
R. E. EGERTON WARBURTON'S *Hunting Songs*, v. xviii. p. 94.

A.S. *dugan*, to thrive (= Germ. *taugen*).

DOSSIL [dos·i'l], *sb.* a satisfying quantity.—WEM. ''Er give 'im a good *dossil* o' dumplin'.'

DOUBLE-COAL [dub·l koal], *sb.* a good coal for manufacturing purposes, much used.—COLLIERY; M. T. See **Coal-field.**

DOUBLE COUPLE [dub·l kup·l], *sb.* twin lambs. Com. Reduplication of this kind is very general in Shropshire—*two twins*, for twins. Betty Roberts of Castle Pulverbatch, speaking of her daughter, said, 'Yo' remember Saa·ra, Ma'am; well, 'er got married, an' in a twelvemonth er wuz pŭt to bed of a *double birth o' two twins*.' Betty's auditor computed these to be eight children! On a gravestone in Edgmond churchyard (Salop) is the following epitaph (date A.D. 1800):—

'They were *Two Twins* in Birth both join'd;
Great is their gain in Hopes to find.'

Cf. **Two-double.**

DOUGH. See **Duff.**

DOUK [dou·k], *v. a.* to stoop or lower the head. Com. ''E *douks* 'is yed like a gonder gwein under a barn-door' is a current Shropshire saying.

'*M. Mery.* Curtsie . . . *douke* you and crouche at euery worde.'—*Roister Doister*, Act. j. Sc. iiij. p. 26.

DOUKER [dou·kur'], *sb. Podiceps minor*, the Little Grebe.—WELLINGTON. Qy. com. Bewick calls this 'The small *Doucker*.' See *British Birds*, vol. ii. p. 171, ed. 1832. '*Hic mergulus*, *A*", a dokare.' —Wr. vocabs., vol. i. p. 253. Cf. **Dab-chick.** See **Jack-douker.**

DOUST [dou·st], (1) *sb.* dust.—SHREWSBURY; PULVERBATCH; CHURCH STRETTON. 'Them up-stars rooms bin in a fine mess o' dowl an' *doust*, they wanten a right good frotin'.'

'LI. Also, that no Sadeler, Boche', Baker, ne Glover, ne none other persone, caste non Intrelle ne fylth of Bestes donge, ne *doust*, over Severne brugge, ne beyond the seid Brugge in the streme.' See 'Ordinances of Worcester,' temp. Ed. IV. (1467), in *English Gilds, their Statutes and Customs*, E. E. T. S.

(2) *v. a.* to beat.—PULVERBATCH; WEM. '*Doust* 'is jacket for 'im, Surrey.'

DOUSTER, (1) *sb.*, *var. pr.* a duster.—SHREWSBURY.

(2) *sb.* a heavy blow.—PULVERBATCH; WEM. 'It fell sich a *douster*.'

DOUT [dou·t], *v. a.* to extinguish; to do out. Com. '*Dout* them candles, Sally; theer 'll be light enough to talk by then, if that's all yo'n got to do.'

'*Doon' owte*, or qwenchyñ' (liȝth, K; lyth, H.). *Extinguo.*'—*Prompt. Parv.*

DOUTER, *sb.* a candle extinguisher. Com.

DOWL [dou·l], (1) *sb.* the downy fibres of a feather; down. Com.

'*Ariel.* You fools! . . . . . the elements,
Of whom your swords are temper'd, may as well
Wound the loud winds, or with bemock'd-at stabs
Kill the still-closing waters, as diminish
One *dowle* that's in my plume.'—*Tempest*, III. iii. 65.

'Young *dowl* of the beard.'—*Howell*, sect. i., in HAL.

(2) *sb.* the light downy substance which collects under beds and about bedroom floors, &c. Com.

(3) *v. a.*, *sl.*? to abuse: as big boys do little ones, too often.—SHREWSBURY. 'George Davies *dowled* poor little Joe Cartri't shameful gweïn to school; a great lungeous lout 'e is!'

(4) *v. a.*, *obsols.* to mix or knead up in a hurry: as of bread or dumpling.—PULVERBATCH. 'We bin gettin' short o' bread, I see; I mun *dowl* up a pot-cake for tay, an' the men can 'a cake an' drink fur thar supper.' Cf. **Blunge.**

DOWLER, *sb.*, *obsols.* a cake or dumpling made in a hurry.—*Ibid.* 'Look sharp an' mak' a bit of a *dowler* to 'elp out the men's dinners.'

DOWN-FALL [dou·nfaul], *sb.* a fall of rain, hail, or snow. Com. 'It's despert coud; we sha'n a a *down-fall* afore lung.'

DOWNY [dou·ni'], *adj.*, *sl.* crafty. Com. 'A *downy* trick.'

DRAG [dr'ag·], *sb.* a timber bar used for drawing timber out of 'workings.'—COLLIERY; M. T.

DRAGGER [dr'ag·ur'], *sb.* advantage; start.—OSWESTRY. *Dragger* is a term used by boys when running a race: the known good runners give the inferior ones a 'start,' varying in distance according to their powers; this they call giving *dragger*, a simple mode of what racing men would term 'handicapping.'

A writer, Edeirnion, in *Byegones*, March 4th, 1874, p. 29, says, 'I fancy the word *dragger* is confined to the Welsh border, and I take it to be a corruption of the Welsh word *rhagor*. Rhag = before; difference; precedence, with the termination "or." Suppose one Welsh boy challenging another to a race, and the following dialogue to ensue: "A redi di râs hefo fi?" "Gwnaf, faint o *ragor* a gaf fi?" "Wel cymer haner can llath." This would be exactly synonymous with the term *dragger* as used by Oswestry boys.'

DRAGON'S-BLOOD, *sb.* *Geranium Robertianum*, Herb Robert.—PULVERBATCH.

DRAIN [dr'een· *and* dr'i·h'n], *sb.* a large, deep, wide, open ditch for draining the Wealdmoors.—NEWPORT. A *gutter* is a small, narrow ditch for the same purpose. Cf. **Diche**, also **Sough** (1).

DRAW [drau·], (1) *v. a.* to take bread out of the oven. Com. 'Han 'ee *drawed* the bread?'

'*Draw the Bread* when it is well Baken; then it is taken out of the Oven.'—*Academy of Armory*, Bk. III. ch. iii. p. 86.

'*Drawe* forthe owte of þe ovyne. *Effurno.*'—*Prompt. Parv.*

(2) *v. a.* to take cattle out of meadow-land that the grass may grow for hay.—PULVERBATCH. 'Yo' mun see to the 'edges round them meadows, they mun be *drawed* an' dressed nex' wik.' See **Dress.**

(3) *v. a.* to let off water from wet fields by means of aids.—CLEE HILLS. 'Han 'ee *drawed* them aids?' See **Aid.**

DRAW-BONE [dr'au·boan *or* bwun], *sb.* the 'merry-thought' (*clavicles*) of a fowl.—PULVERBATCH; WORTHEN. This bone gets its local name of *draw-bone* from the custom practised by young people of *drawing* or pulling it in order to determine which of them will be soonest married. The bone, held at each extremity by two persons, is pulled between them till it breaks; the one in whose hand the shorter piece remains will be the first to enter the marriage state, but the other will have '*the lungest cubbert!*'

DRAWING-ROAD, *sb.* same as **Cungit**, q. v.—COLLIERY; M. T. Cf. **Spout-road.**

DRAWT [dr'aut·], *sb.* the full balancing range of steelyards; that which is weighed at one balance.—PULVERBATCH. Qy. com. 'My stilyards ŏŏna weigh more than 56 [lbs.] at a *drawt.*'

DRAWT-HORSE [dr'aut· aur's], *sb.* a draught-horse, *i. e.* a waggon-horse.—PULVERBATCH; BRIDGNORTH.

DRAWTS [dr'auts·], *sb.* a pair of dentist's forceps.—PULVERBATCH. Qy. com. 'The las' tuth I 'ad out I suffered a martidom; the *drawts* slipt twize, an' it 'ad to be punched out.' '*Drawte* or pulle. *Tractus,*' in *Prompt. Parv.* See *Draht* in STRAT.

DRAY [dr'ah·y], *sb.* a squirrel's nest.—CHURCH STRETTON.

'The nimble squirrel noting here,
Her mossy *dray* that makes.'
DRAYTON'S *Quest of Cynthia*, p. 626, in Nares.

DRAYTON DIRTY FAIR, *sb.* The fair known in the north of Shropshire by this name is a long-established cattle fair, held at Market Drayton in the end of October. The bad weather usually prevailing at the time has given it its name. Formerly the old-fashioned farmers of the district were much exercised in their minds if their winter wheat was not sown by the *Dirty fair.*

DREEP [dr'eep·], *v. n., var. pr.* to drip.—SHREWSBURY.

DRENCH [dr'en·sh], (1) *sb.* a draught or potion for horses or cattle. Com.

'*Drenches;* Drinks or Mashes given to Horses to cleanse them.'—*Academy of Armory*, Bk. III. ch. iii. p. 89.

'. . . . . . if the sleepy *drench*
Of that forgetful lake benumb not still.'
Paradise Lost, Bk. II. l. 73.

A.S. *drenc*, a drink; drench.

(2) *v. a.* to administer the potion. Com. A.S. *drencan*, to make to drink.

DRENCHING-HORN, *sb.* a horn into which the *drench* is put, as a convenient means of pouring it down the animal's throat. Com. 'Look sharp an' fatch the *drenchin'-'orn* out o' the shad, an' 'elp me to *drench* the cow, or else 'er'll be djed.' A.S. *drenc-horn.*

DRESS [dr'es·], *v. a.* Applied to meadows, this term signifies to break and scatter the dung upon them; to pick off stones, sticks, &c. See **Draw** (2).

DRESSEL, DRESSER [dr'es·el], SHREWSBURY, *Uffington.* [dr'es·ur'], Com. (1) *sb., obsols.* an old-fashioned piece of kitchen furniture, consisting of a long, narrow table, having a row of drawers to the front, and surmounted by a high range of shelves for dishes: the sides of this, reaching about half way to the top, are enclosed and made into a cupboard for smaller pieces of crockery. A *dresser* of this kind and a tall clock were formerly considered quite indispensable to 'tidy' young people about to begin housekeeping. 'Aye, it begins to look like marr'in' w'en the clock an' *dresser's* bought; I s'pose the nex' thing ŏŏl be the axin's.' *Fr. dressoir*, a side-board.

DRESSER, (2) *sb.* an implement which combines hammer and 'pick;' being a hammer at one end, and very sharp, like a 'pick' at the other: strong iron clamps secure it to the handle. It is used for setting props and general heavy work.—COLLIERY; M. T.

DREVEN [dr'ev·n], *sb.* a person or thing in a state or condition of dirt.—WEM. 'Look at that child, whad a *dreven* 'er is! 'er mus' a bin i' the slurry.'

DRIBBLE [dr'ib·l], (1) *v. n.* to rain slowly; to fall in drops.—SHREWSBURY; PULVERBATCH. Qy. com.

(2) *v. n.* to do anything in a feeble kind of way.—SHREWSBURY; ATCHAM; ELLESMERE. Qy. com. 'Now, Sarah, if yo' bin gweïn to milk the cow, milk 'er, an' dunna *dribble* at 'er.'

(3) *v. a.* to let fall drop by drop; to leak.—SHREWSBURY; PULVERBATCH. Qy. com. 'The rayn-tub's lost a 'oop, an's *dribblin'* all the waiter out.'

'. . . . . . ten thousand casks,
For ever *dribbling* out their base contents.'
COWPER, *The Task*, Bk. IV. l. 505.

(4) *v. a.* to deal out in very small quantities.—ATCHAM; WEM; ELLESMERE. 'Dunna *dribble* the barley out athatns—gie me a good feed for the fowl at wunst.'

DRIBLETS [dr'ib·li'ts], *sb. pl.* very small quantities.—ATCHAM; WEM.

DRIBLINGS [dr'ib·linz], *idem.*—ELLESMERE.

DRIDBENCH [dr'id·bensh], *sb.*, *obs.* a wrinkle; a crease.—WORTHEN. (1) 'Poor Jazey Humphries! 'er's gettin' a nowd ŏŏman; the *dridbenches* is beginnin' to shew in 'er for'yed.' (2) 'It wuz a *dridbench* i' the child's shirt as wuz 'urtin' 'im made 'im so fretchit.'

DRIFT-HOUSE [dr'if·t u's], *sb.* the lofty covered way out of a farm-yard under which a loaded waggon can be drawn.—WEM. Qy. com.

DRIFT-WAY. The same.

DRINK, *sb.* ale. Com. 'Whad sort o' *drink* dun they keep at that public?' 'Well, nuthin' to brag on; it wunna much better than *fresh-drink* the las' time as I wuz theer.' Very strong old 'October' ale is called *beer;* 'old *beer*,' 'harvest *beer*.' See **Fresh-drink.**

DRINK-MEAT [dr'ing·k mait], *sb.* ale boiled, thickened with oat-meal, and spiced.—PULVERBATCH. Qy. com. 'The cowman's got a despert bad coud; I'll mak' 'im a stodger o' *drink-mate* fur 'is supper, an' gie 'im a good swat.'

DRIP [dr'ip·], *v. a.* to take the last milk from a cow.—NEWPORT; WEM; WHITCHURCH. Cf. **Strip.**

DRIPPING-BOWL, *sb.* a wooden bowl used to *drip* the cows into. —*Ibid.*

DRIPPINGS, *sb.* the last milk drawn from a cow.—*Ibid.* Cf. **Afterings,** also **Strippings.**

DRIVE A HEAD, *phr.* to effect an entrance into the solid stratum of coal, mineral, &c.—COLLIERY; M. T.

DRODSOME [dr'od·su'm], *adj.* dreadful; alarming.—BRIDGNORTH.

DROP OUT, *v. n.* to quarrel; to fall out.—PULVERBATCH; CLUN; WEM. 'If that shoot o' clo'es inna done agen the club, yo' an' me sha'n *drop out.*'

DROPPING-TIME, *sb.* a showery time.—PULVERBATCH; WELLINGTON; WEM.

DROUPEN [dr'oup·h'n], *part. adj., obsols.* drooping.—PULVERBATCH; ELLESMERE. 'Yore cabbidge plants looken rather *droupen,* John.' 'Aye, they want'n a drop o' rayn; but they'n prink up to'rt night.'

> 'But true it is that, when the oyle is spent,
> The light goes out, and weeke is throwne away:
> So, when he had resignd his regiment,
> His daughter gan despise his *drouping* day,
> And wearie wax of his continuall stay.'
>
> SPENSER, *F. Q.,* Bk. II. c. x. st. xxx.

O.Icel. *drûpa,* droup (droop).—STRAT.

DROVIER [dr'oav·yur'], *sb., var. pr.* a drover.—PULVERBATCH; WEM. 'Who'd a thought on a fine camperin' young fellow like that comin' to be a *drovier?*'

'Robert Mather was a stranger in this country; hee came hither to serve Sir Humphrey Lea as his Bayly. Hee was a person very expert in buying and selling of Catle, and had a commission, to be one of the King's purveyors, which was an office to buy fatt beasts for the King's houshould. . . . . . . These purveyors were likewise *drovyers,* who bought catle in this country, and brought them into Kent to sell again.'—GOUGH'S *History of Myddle,* p. 74.

DRUDGER [dr'uj·ur'], *sb., var. pr.* a cook's flour-dredger.—SHREWSBURY; PULVERBATCH; CRAVEN ARMS; CLUN; WEM.

DRUMBLE [dr'um·bl], (1) *v. n., obsols.* to be sluggish; to dawdle. —PULVERBATCH. 'Come, pluck up yore fit, an' dunna gŏŏ *drumblin'* alung, as if yo' wun 'afe asleep.'

'*Mrs. Ford.* What, John! Robert! John! Go take up these clothes here quickly. Where's the cowl-staff? look, how you *drumble!*'—*Merry Wives of Windsor,* III. iii. 156.

(2) *sb., obsols.* a dull, inactive person.—*Ibid.* 'The poor owd mon's aumust done now; an' 'e wuz al'ays a poor *drumble.*'

(3) *sb., obsols.* a rough wooded dip in the ground; a dingle.—NEWPORT.

DRUMBY-HOLE [dr'um·bi' oal], *sb.* same as **Drumble** (3).—ELLESMERE. 'I got to gŏŏ to Linëa' to-neet, an' I dunna know 'ow to pass the *drumby-'ole* near the Cut bridge, fur they sen theer's frittenin theer.' Cf. **Dumble-hole.**

DRUMMIL [dr'um·i'l], (1) *sb.* a worn-out horse.—PULVERBATCH; WELLINGTON.

(2) *sb.* a dull, sluggish person.—PULVERBATCH. 'I dunna know w'ich is best, mon or 'orse, fur they bin bŏăth poor *drummils*.' Cf. **Drumble** (2), also **Keffel**.

DRUMMING [dr'um·in], *sb.* a sound beating. Com.

DRUV [dr'uv·], *pret.* and *part. past*, drove; driven. Com. 'I 'ear Medlicott's lost the cow 'e bought at the far, an' I dunna ŏŏnder at it; 'er milk 'ad bin pounded so lung, an' 'er wuz o'er-*druv*, an' it brought on the milk faiver.' See **Rid** (1).

DRY [dr'ei·], (1) *adj.* thirsty. Com. 'Weer'n'ee got the bottle, lads? fur I'm as *dry* as a ragman's 'prentice.' 'Be'appen yo'n 'ad a red yurrin fur yore dinner.'

> 'And now my conclusion I'll tell,
> For, faith, I'm confoundedly *dry*.'
> ROBERT BURNS, *Poems*, p. 50, l. 26.

(2) *adj.* having no milk: said of cows. Com.

(3) *v. a.* to cause a cow to lose her milk; to disperse it medicinally. Com. 'I've done gweïn to market now; the Maister's drenched six o' the cows to *dry* 'em fur feedin'.'

> 'Leaue milking and *drie* vp old mulley thy cow,
> The crooked and aged, to fatting put now.'
> TUSSER'S *Fiue Hundred Pointes of Good Husbandrie* [August].

DUBBIN [dub·in], *sb.* soft grease, such as is produced from the boiling of tripe: it is used for the purpose of softening and preserving strong leather.—SHREWSBURY; PULVERBATCH; WEM. Qy. com. 'Maister, we'n got no *dubbin* for the gears; mun I do 'em ŏŏth gŏŏze-ile?'

DUBBIN' SHEARS, *sb.* shears used to trim closely-cropped hedges. —WHITCHURCH.

DUBBIT [dub·i't], *adj.* blunt; dull; 'a *dubbit* axe.'—WEM.

DUBOUS [joo·bus], (1) *adj., var. pr.* dubious; doubtful; not very sure.—SHREWSBURY; PULVERBATCH; WEM. Qy. com. 'Aye, I 'ear they bin gweïn into business, but I'm rather *jubous* w'ether it 'll answer.' An undecided person is said to be '*jubous*-minded.'

(2) *adj., pec.* suspicious.—PULVERBATCH. 'I dunna like to 'ăve anythin' to do ŏŏth that ŏŏman, 'er's of sich a *jubous* turn; 'er thinks everybody's robbin' 'er.'

DUCK'S-FROST, *sb.* a slight frost.—CLEE HILLS. Cf. **Ketch o' Frost**.

DUFF [duff·], (1) *sb., var. pr.* dough. Com. 'As busy as a dog in *duff*' is a proverbial saying heard in some parts of Shropshire.

(2) *sb.* the stomach.—LUDLOW. ''E tŏŏk me *duff*,' said a man in evidence at a police court. On being asked to explain, he said, ''E 'it me i' the stomach.' Cf. **Nanny**.

DUMBLE-HOLE [dum·bl oal], *sb.* a pit-fall; a dangerous hollow.—

PULVERBATCH. 'Thee'st better mind them *dumble-'oles*; it's a comical rŏăd, Surrey.' Cf. **Drumby-hole.**

DUNCE-HOLE [dun·s oal], *sb.* same as **Bing** (1).—WELLINGTON; WEM. 'Yo'd'n better get the *dunce-'ole* cliered out; we sha'n want it w'en we throshen to-morrow.'

DUNCHED [dun·sht], *part. adj., obs.* knocked; bruised.—WORTHEN. 'Look, 'ow that drawer's *dunched*; that wunna done by no far manes.'

'*Dunchyn*' or bunchyn'. *Tundo.*'—*Prompt. Parv.*

Dan. *dunke*; Swed. *dunka*, dunch; 'tundere.'—STRAT.

DUN EARTH, *sb.* a stratum of earth, said to be so called from its colour.—COLLIERY, *Donnington*; M. T.

DUNGEVIL [dung·h'vi'l], *sb.* a garden-fork.—CRAVEN ARMS; CORVE DALE. Cf. **Sharevil.**

DUN-NETTLE [dun·net·'l], *sb. Labium purpúreum*, red Dead-nettle. —CRAVEN ARMS, *Stokesay.* Cf. **French-nettle.** See **Tormentil.**

DUNNUK [dun·u'k], *sb.* a dung-fork.—SHREWSBURY. A corruption of *dung-hook.* Cf. **Tummy-awk.**

DUNNY [dun·i'], *adj.* hard of hearing, and stupid, as a consequence. —PULVERBATCH; CLUN; CLEE HILLS. 'W'y, Dick, thee bist as *dunny* as a pwust! I've 'ooted till they coulden 'a 'eärd me at Churton.'

DURGY [dur'·gi'], *adj.* dwarfish.—PULVERBATCH. Generally used in a contemptuous way. 'Dun yo' think as I'm gweïn to be bate by a *durgy* chap like that?' A.S. *dweorg*, a dwarf. Cf. **Danks.**

DUTCH [duch·], *adj.* fine, affected, in language.—SHREWSBURY; PULVERBATCH; WEM; WHITCHURCH. 'Sally's got so mighty *Dutch* sence 'er's gwun to the paas'n's, 'er dunna know 'ow to talk to poor folk.' ''E talks as *Dutch* as Darnford's dog:' proverbial saying heard in the neighbourhood of Whitchurch.

'*Dutch*' = *Deutsch* = *German.* Compare the following:—

'The word *Dutch* is an adjective signifying national, and was the name by which the old Teutons called themselves, in contradistinction to other people whose language they were unable to understand.'—DR. MORRIS's *Historical English Grammar*, p. 4.

DUZZY [duz·i'], *adj.* deafish; stupid; confused.—WHITCHURCH. (1) ''E's lother *duzzy*; 'e doesna 'ear very well.' (2) 'I'm mighty *duzzy* this mornin'.' *Duzzy* = dizzy. A.S. *dysig.* Cf. **Dunny.**

DWINDERED [dwin·dur'd], *part. adj.* wasted in appearance.— WEM. 'Dear 'eart alive! 'ow bad an' *dwindered* 'er looks sence I seed 'er.' See below.

DWINE [dwei·n, *corr.* dwah·yn], *v. n.* to waste away: chiefly used in the participial form, *dwining*, but not common.—NEWPORT.

'but duelfulli sche *dwined* a-waie · boþe dayes & niȝtes,
& al hire clere colour · comsed for to fade.'

William of Palerne, l. 578.

A.S. *dwinan*; O.Dutch *dwínen*; O.Icel. *dvína*, dwine; waste.— STRAT. Der. 'dwindered.'

EÄG. See **Agg**. 'W'y 'ow can I blame the lad w'en yo' bin al'ays eäggin 'im on?'

EAR-APPARN [ee·h'r' ap·ur'n], *sb.* an apron turned up at about half its length and stitched at the sides, thus forming a pocket, into which the gleaner puts the short ears of corn as she gathers them.—ELLESMERE.

EAR-BAG, same as **Ear-apparn**.—PULVERBATCH. 'Theer wuz pretty pickin' i' the Mars'-fild, I got five 'antle an' my *ear-bag* swag füll; theer's a sight o' short ears—the straw's so despert brickle.'

EAR-BRAT, *sb.* a child's pinafore sewed up in the same way and for the same purpose as the **Ear-apparn**, above.—ELLESMERE.

EARNEST [yaa·r'nist], *sb., obsols.* deposit money given to bind a bargain, as on hiring a servant.—PULVERBATCH. Qy. com. 'Jack, I thought yo' wun 'ired at the Bonk.' 'Aye, so I wuz, but I send my *yarnest* back; they bin too yarly for me, they wanten the night as well as the day.'

'. . . and from his coffers
Received the golden *earnest* of our death.'
K. Henry V., II. ii. 168.

'This simple token or poore *earnest* peanie.'—*Bibl. Eliotæ*, 1559 ded., in HAL.

W. *ernes*. Cf. **Arness**.

EASEMENT [ai·zmunt], *sb.* ease; relief.—SHREWSBURY; PULVERBATCH; LUDLOW. Qy. com. 'It's a great *aisement* to my mind as the Maister's got that corn lugged at last.'

'. . . & so for *esement* of a man himsilf, & for *esement* of his neiȝbour, it is not expressid in holi scripture þat a man schulde singe. & ȝit goddis forbode, but þat, into *esement* of him-silf & also of his neiȝbour, a man mai singe, pleie, & lauȝe vertuoseli, & þerfore merytorili.'—REGINALD PECOCK, *The Repressor* (A.D. 1449, *circa*). *Specim. Eng. Lit.*, v. *a.* ll. 76—78.

EASINGS [ee·zinz], same as **Aisin**, q. v.—WEM.

'The out sides of an House . . . The Eaves or *Easeings*.'—*Academy of Armory*, Bk. III. ch. xii. p. 451.

Eaves = O.E. *yfes*, *efese* = margin, edge.

'We sometimes find *esen*-droppers = eaves-droppers; *esen* = O.E. *efesen*, eaves.'—DR. MORRIS's *Historical English Accidence*, p. 100.

EASINGS-SPARROW, same as **Aisin-sparrow**, q. v., of which it is a more refined pronunciation.

EASY MELCHED [aizi' mel·sht], *part. adj., obsols.*? said of a cow that yields her milk easily.—PULVERBATCH. 'I like to milk Daisy, 'er's so *aisy melched*, an' gi'es aumust a cantle o' milk.' Cf. **Soft melched**.

EBB [eb·], *adj.* shallow; near the surface. Com. 'Will this dish do to make the fitchock pie in?' 'No, it's too *ebb*; we sha'n be 'ăvin' the jessup runnin' all under the bread i' the oven.'

'1794, Novr. 1—Sowed what they have plowed these 2 dayes. I

am convinced that it is too *ebb* plow'd. Will tells me it's deep enough for any plowing.'—*Bailiff's Diary*, Aston, Oswestry. *Byegones*, 1877, p. 342.

'Nothing "ebbs," unless it be figuratively, except water now; but "ebb," oftener an adjective than anything else, was continually used in our earlier English with a general meaning of shallow. There is still a Lancashire proverb, "Cross the stream where it is *ebbest*."

'"This you may observe ordinarily in stones, that those parts and sides which lie covered deeper within the ground be more firm and tender, as being preserved by heat, than those outward faces which lie *ebb*, or above the earth."'—Holland, *Plutarch's Morals*, p. 747.

'"It is all one whether I be drowned in the *ebber* shore, or in the midst of the deep sea." Bishop Hall, *Meditations and Vows*, cent. ii.'—ARCHBP. TRENCH, *Select Glossary*, p. 67.

ECALL [ek·ul], *sb. Gécinus víridis;* the Green Woodpecker.—CLEE HILLS. Drayton calls this bird 'the laughing *hecco*.' *Polyolbion*, xiii. p. 915. Cf. **Laughing bird**, also **Yockel**.

EDDISH [ed·ish], *sb.* the after-growth of clover.—PULVERBATCH. Qy. com. Cattle are liable to injurious distension from eating *eddish*. 'The young beäs han broke into the clover *eddish*—run for yore life; we sha'n 'ăve 'em swelled as big as 'ogshits' [hogsheads]. See Way's note (1) in *Prompt. Parv.*, p. 135; also E. D. S., B. xv. A.S. *edisc*, aftermath. Cf. **Edgrow**.

EDGE [ej·], *sb.* the ridge of a hill. As a compound form this term is often met with throughout the county; as Wenlock-*Edge*, Benthall-*Edge*, Yeo [View] -*Edge*, &c.

EDGE-O'-NEET, *sb.* twilight; night-fall.—WEM. See below.

EDGE-O'-NIGHT, same as above.—SHREWSBURY; PULVERBATCH; CHURCH STRETTON. Qy. com. "Now, if yo' bin gweïn to Churton, start, an' nod lave it till *edge-o'-night* as yo' al'ays dun—prowlin' the lanes i' the dark.'

EDGROW [ed·gr'oa], *sb.* a second crop of grass after the hay-crop.—PULVERBATCH; WEM; ELLESMERE; OSWESTRY.

'*Recidiva*, ed-growung.'—*Archbp. Ælfric's Vocabulary*, x. cent., in Wr. vocabs., vol. i. p. 39.

Edgrow, greese (edgraw, herbe, K. ete growe, greese, H. P.). *Bigermen, regermen.*

'The Medulla explains *bigermen* to be the mixed grain called in the *Promptorium* MESTLYONE, but it seems here to signify after-grass, or after-math, still called *edgrow* in some parts of England.'—*Prompt. Parv. and Notes.*

Cf. **Eddish**, also **After-math**.

EDWARD [yed·ur't], Com. [yed·ud], BRIDGNORTH. [yed·ut], CLUN. [yedh·ur't], WHITCHURCH.

'*E* before a vowel at the beginning of words, as *Eadweard*, *Eoforwic*, was clearly sounded like *y* or the High-Dutch *j*. Thus we still write *York;* and *Yedward* is found in Shakespeare [1 *K. Henry IV.*, I. ii. 149]; and *Earl* is in Scotland sounded *Yerl*, like the Danish *Jarl*.'—FREEMAN'S *Old English History*, p. xviii.

EECLE [ee·k·l], *sb.* an icicle. — SHREWSBURY; PULVERBATCH; WORTHEN; CLUN. 'It's bin a snirpin' fros' sence it lef' off rainin'; theer's *eecles* at the aisins a yard lung.' '*Ikyl* (iekyll, W.), *Stiria.*'—*Prompt. Parv.* 'A.S. ises-ȝicel, *glacialis stiria*,' in WAY. Cf. **Aigles** (3).

EEG. See **Agg.**

EEL. See **Ale.**

EGG, *v. a.* to incite; to provoke.—WEM.

> '. . . . . . burnes he sent
> enuiously to þemperour · & *egged* him swiþe
> bi a certayne day · bataile to a-bide.'
>
> *William of Palerne*, l. 1130

> 'Adam and Eue · he *egged* to ille,
> Conseilled caym · to kullen his brother.'
>
> *Piers Pl.*, Text B., pass. i. l. 65.

'Ill *egging* makes ill begging.'—RAY'S *Proverbs*, p. 101.

A.S. *eggian*, to egg; to excite. Cf. **Agg.**

EGGS-AND-BACON, *sb. Narcissus incomparibilis bicoloratæ.* — ELLESMERE.

EH, GONIES! [ai·gon·iz], *interj.* a corrupted form of Romish oath = '*agonies*.'—COLLIERY; NEWPORT.

ELDED [el·di'd], *part. past.*, *var. pr.* ailed.—PULVERBATCH; CLUN. 'I 'ad the Club Doctor to 'im, but 'e didna seem to know whad *elded* 'im, so I 'suaded 'im to göö to the Firmary, an' they maden a cure on 'im direc'ly.' See **Elding**, below.

ELDER [el·dur'], *sb.* the udder of a cow, mare, or other large animal. Com. 'The mar' ninted alung töërt wham at a pretty rate; 'er wuz glad to see the cowt, for 'er *elder* wuz as 'ard as a stwun.'

ELDER-WINE [el·dur' wein·d], *sb.* wine made from *elder-berries.* Com. 'I made a spigot-stean o' *elder-winde* las' 'ear, an' fund it very useful—the Maister's so subject to ketch cowds; an' I mull a good joram fur 'im, an' püt 'is fit in warm waiter, an' 'e's as right as a trivit i' the mornin'.'

ELDING, *part. pres.*, *var. pr.* ailing.—PULVERBATCH. 'So poor owd Molly's ended up at last, as one met say, fur 'er's bin *eldin'* a lung wilde.'

ELDRAKE [el·dr'aik], same as **Ell-rake**, q. v.—NEWPORT.

ELLERN [el·ur'n], *sb. Sambucus nigra*, the Elder.—CLUN; CORVE DALE.

> 'Iudas he Iapede · with þe Iewes seluer,
> And on an *Ellerne* tree · hongede him after.'
>
> *Piers Pl.*, Text A., pass. i. l. 66.

Hyldyr, or eldyr (hillerntre, K. ellernetre, HARL. MS. 2274; ellorne tre, P.), *Sambucus.*

'It was supposed that Judas hanged himself upon an Elder tree, and Sir John Maundeville, who wrote in 1356, speaks of the tree as being still shewn at Jerusalem. *Voiage*, p. 112.'—*Prompt. Parv. and Notes.*

Sambucus, suev, *ellarne;* occurs in a *Vocabulary of the Names of Plants*, of the middle of xiii. cent., in Wr. vocabs., vol. i. p. 140.

ELLFIT [el·fit], *sb., obsols.* the crested foam on ale when fermenting in open vessels.—PULVERBATCH. 'I think we sha'n be lucky in 'ăvin' plenty o' barm this time—theer's a beautiful *ellfit*.' It seems probable that the *ale-vat* or *fat*, from having held the drink while fermenting, has given its name in a corrupted form to the result of the fermentation itself.

ELL-RAKE [el·r'aik], *sb.* a large rake with long iron teeth used in clearing the field.—PULVERBATCH. Qy. com. 'Theer'll be mighty little lef' fur the laisers; they'n bin draggin' that *ell-rake* ever sence daylight, very different to the poor owd Maister—'e never 'ad it raked but jest after the waggin.' The *ell-rake* follows at the heel of the person using it, and may therefore be a corrupted form of *heel-rake*, the *h* being an absent element of the word. Cf. **Eldrake**, above.

EM [em·], *pers. pron.* them. Com. *Em* is not a contraction of *them*, though usually printed as if it were—'*em*—but it represents the old *heom*, *hem*.

> 'But criste kingene kynge · kniȝted ten,
> Cherubyn and seraphin · such seuene and an-othre,
> And ȝaf *hem* myȝte in his maieste · þe muryer *hem* þouȝte;
> And ouer his mene meyne · made *hem* archangeles,
> Tauȝte *hem* bi þe Trinitee · treuthe to knowe,
> To be buxome at his biddyng · he bad *hem* nouȝte elles.'
>
> *Piers Pl.*, Text B., pass. i. ll. 107—110.

> '*Pros.* Being once perfected how to grant suits,
> How to deny them, who to advance, and who
> To trash for overtopping, new created
> The creatures that were mine, I say, or changed '*em*,
> Or else new form'd '*em* . . . . . .'
>
> *Tempest*, I. ii. 82, 83.

Mr. Oliphant says that, 'in the Rushworth Gospels, the English version of which is dated by Wanley at A.D. 900 or thereabouts, we find in S. Matt. ii. 4 *heom* employed for *hig*, just as we say in talking, "*I asked 'em*."' And again, speaking of the changes which were taking place in the English language about A.D. 1120, he says, 'The Old English *heora* and *him* now change into *here* and *hem*. This last we still use in phrases like, "*give it 'em well;*" and this Dative Plural drove out the old Accusative *hi*.'—*Sources of Standard English*, pp. 42, 44, 58.

EME [ee·m], *adj.* near; direct. Com. 'Yo' bin gŏŏin a mighty lung way round; cross them filds, it's the *emest* rŏăd a power.' *Eme*, regularly declined in every degree, obtains throughout the county, but is in most general use in the northern parts, where it is constantly heard. A.S. *anemn* = *anefen* = *onefen* = *on-eme*. Cf. **Anunst** = *anemn* = *anefen* = *on-eme-s* + *t* (excrescent). Cf. **Gain** (1).

EMPASSY ON, *sb.* the symbol & = and. Com. *Empassy on* is a corruption of *and per se*. The symbol & expresses *and* by itself (*i. e.*

in a single sign), and was read as '*and per se;*' it originally meant *et*, and is merely &, written with one stroke of the pen. Compare &c. = *et* cætera = *and* the rest.

'The letters A, O sometimes meant *words*, viz. the words "a" or "oh!" They were then called *A-per-se-A* and *O-per-se-O*, or simply *A-per-se*, &c. "*A-per-se*" also meant "excellent."'—*Romance of Partenay*, 1148.

See **Grammar Outlines** (*alphabet*).

END [en·d], *v. a.* to kill; to put an end to. Com. 'Why dunna yo' *end* the poor thing out on its misery?'

'For ho so woneþ in þis word · & wol nouh[t] y-knowe
þat him is demed to deie · & doom schal abide,
Hit is riht þat þe rink · be reufully *ended*.'
Alexander and Dindimus, l. 1062.

'*Doug.* The Lord of Stafford dear to-day hath bought
Thy likeness, for instead of thee, King Harry,
This sword hath *ended* him.'—1 *K. Henry IV.*, V. iii. 9.

A.S. *endian*, to end.

ENDWAYS-ON, *adv.* endways, *i. e.* with the end abutting upon, as, 'the house standing *endways-on* to the street.'—NEWPORT.

ENEMY [en·u'mi'], *sb.*, *obsols.* an insect.—PULVERBATCH. 'Theer's a *enemy* o' the child's night-gownd!' 'Whad a good job yo' sid'n it afore 'e went to bed!'

ENMES [en·mi'z], *sb. pl.*, *obsols.* enemies.—SHREWSBURY, *Uffington.* It is interesting to find this old form, which is found in the writings of the blind monk of Haughmond, still [1878] lingering amongst the aged folk who live under the shelter of Haughmond Hill.

'O Jhesu, so I the beseche,
Ryȝt with her fulli speche
Thou graunt myn *enmes* grace.
Here mysdedis here to mende
Out of this word or thai wynde
Fader, thou ȝif ham space.'
JOHN AUDELAY'S *Poems*, p. 62.

ERCLE [ur'·kl], *sb.* a watery blister.—PULVERBATCH. 'Our John's got a despert bad leg; theer come a little *ercle* on it, an' 'e scrat it, an' it turned to the 'sipelas, an' it's swelled as big as my middle' [waist].

ERRIN [aer'·i'n], *sb.*, *var. pr.* urine. Com. An old man at Buildwas, working in a garden under the superintendence of a young mistress, observed of a certain plant that 'it ŏŏd be better fur some *errin.*' 'Red-herring or fresh?' naïvely asked the lady. 'W'y *ne'erun*, Miss,' replied the man with some emphasis; '*errin* sich as yo' an' me maken.'

ERRIWIG [aer'·i'wig], *sb.* an earwig.—SHREWSBURY; PULVERBATCH. Qy. com. 'Looks like a throttled *erriwig*' is proverbially said of one who has a startled appearance. Cf. **Arrawig.**

ES-HOOK [es·uk], *sb.* a hook at the extremity of a waggon-horse's traces, in the form of the letter S. A hook of this kind is also used to unite the two ends of a broken chain. Com.

ESS [ess·], *sb.* ashes. Com. 'Yore garden seems to be a very stiff sile, John; if I wuz yo' I'd sprade some *ess* an' sut on, it ŏŏd do a sight o' good, an' mak' it a power more mīldy; I pŭt a 'oop o' lime on my īnion bed.'

'ESSE, Ashes. *Chesh.* *Sheer the* ESSE, *i. e.* separate the dead Ashes from the Embers. *Chesh.*'—BAILEY, ed. 1782. A.S. *æsce*, ashes.

ESS-BALLS, *sb. pl.*, *obs.* balls made of the ashes of wood or fern damped with water; they were afterwards sun-dried.—PULVERBATCH. Qy. com. These balls were used for making '*buck-lee*,' q. v. 'Molly, pŭt a couple o' them *ess-balls* i' the furnace an' fill it up ŏŏth waiter fur the lee, an' mak' 'aste to yore w'ĕĕl, or that slippin' ŏŏnna be done to-day.' *Ess-balls* wére sold in Shrewsbury market in 1811, and probably much later on, as *buck-washing* was practised for many years after that date. See **Buck-wesh.**

ESS-HOLE, *sb.* the ash-pit in front of a kitchen grate. Com.

ESS-ROOK, *sb.* a dog or cat that likes to lie in the ashes.—PULVERBATCH. 'This kitlin' inna wuth keepin'—it's too great a *ess-rook*.' Cf. **Rook** (1).

ETE [ee·t], *pret.* and *part. past.* ate; eaten.—PULVERBATCH. Qy. com. 'Is there any o' that rearin' o' pork left?' 'No, Missis; the baÿly *ete* it fur 'is supper las' night.'

'Þar þai offerd, praid, and suank,
Thre dais noþer *ete* ne dranc."

Cursor Mundi (A.D. 1320, *circa*).
Specim. Early Eng., vii. l. 42.

ETHER [aedh·ur'], Com. [aeth·ur'], OSWESTRY; *sb.* *Pelias berus*, the Adder, or common Viper. Shropshire rustics say—

'If the *ether* 'ad the blindworm's ear,
An' the blindworm 'ad the *ether's* eye,
Neither mon nor beäst could safe pass by.'

They also say of a person out of breath that ''e blows like a *ether*.' It is popularly believed that the *ether* can only die at sunset; even if apparently killed in the morning, it will retain life till the going down of the sun. See **Ether's-nild**, below.

ETHERINGS [aedh·ur'inz], *sb. pl.* pliant boughs, as of hazel, intertwined through the upright stakes of a hedge to bind the top and keep it even. Com. 'I see they'n bin tarrin' the 'edge above-a-bit; the *etherins* bin gwun, they'n a the stakes next.' A.S. *edor*, what bounds, or defends; *eðer*, a hedge.

ETHER'S-MON, *sb.* *Cordulegaster annulatus*, a large, long-bodied Dragon-fly.—WEM; ELLESMERE. See below.

ETHER'S-NILD, the same as above.—PULVERBATCH. It is believed that this Dragon-fly indicates by its presence the vicinity of the Adder, whence its local names—*Ether's-mon* and *Ether's-nild* [needle]. In some parts of Scotland it is called the *Flying Adder*, and in America it is said to be known as the *Devil's Darning-Needle.*

EVEN [ee·vn], *sb.* a dull, slow, stupid person.—CLUN. ''Ow does yore girld ause?' 'Oh! 'er's no good, 'er's as big a *even* as ever wuz in a 'ouse.' Cf. **Aven** and **Avenless.**

EVENING [ee·vni'n], *sb., pec.* the afternoon of the day. The day is divided into morning, middle of the day, and *evening.* Night begins about six o'clock.—SHREWSBURY; MUCH WENLOCK. Qy. com.

'10th. August 1788. The meeting held on Monday *evening* last was adjourned to be holden to-morrow *Evening* at three of the Clock.

27th. March 1808. Divine Service will begin here this *evening* at half past two of the Clock.'—*Churchwardens' Accounts*, Much Wenlock. Cf. **Onder.**

EVER-A. 'Is there *ever-a* wisket as I could 'ăve?'

'Now tell me wha was your father,' she says;
'Now tell me wha was your mother.
And had ye ony sister?' she says,
'And had ye *ever a* brother?'
Fair Annie, a Scotch Ballad, first printed in
HERD's *Collection of Scotch Songs*, 1769.

See **Grammar Outlines** (*indefinite pronouns*).

EVER-A-ONE, either of them. Com. A good many years ago, Mr. Thos. Morris of Burley—who was a 'wag,' and deaf to boot—laid a wager that he would get 'summat to drink' at a certain house which 'proved the rule' of Shropshire hospitality by being its 'exception.' He went there accordingly, and was met with the usual greeting—''Ow bin 'ee this mornin'?' not, however, followed by the equally usual, 'Whad'll yo' tak'?' 'Drink or cider,' he replied, '*ever-a-one*, I dunna car' w'ich.' ''Ow's the Missis?' he was asked. Again affecting not to understand the question, he repeated, 'Drink or cider, *ever-a-one*, I dunna car' w'ich.' He gained his wager. '*Ever-a-one*' tapped his neighbour's barrels! See **Grammar Outlines** (*indefinite pronouns*).

EVER-SO, *adv.* however much; in any case. Com. This term is constantly heard in such expressions as 'I'd as lief walk as ride if I'd a 'orse *ever-so*.' 'I couldna ate that if it wuz *ever-so*.'

EVE'S SCORK, *sb. Pomum Adami*, the larynx.—PULVERBATCH. 'Daddy, whad's this lump i' yore neck?' 'W'y it's *Eve's scork*, child—owd Mother Eve ete the apple 'erself, but 'er gid the *scork* to Faither Adam, an' all men's 'ad'n this lump ever sence.' See **Scork.**

EVIL [ee·vl], *v. a.* to turn the ground lightly over with a *sharevil* [fork]—CHURCH STRETTON, *Leebotwood.* 'Get a sharevil an' *evil* them beds o'er.' See **Sharevil.**

EVIL-EYE, *sb.* an eye that charms. Com. ''E's a nasty down-lookin' fellow—looks as if 'e could cast a *nĕv'l-eye* upon yo'.' See Bk. II., *Folklore*, &c., 'Charming and Charms.'

EXCISE [ekseiz], *v. a., pec.* to extort; to exact.—ELLESMERE.

EXPASSY AND = *et*-per-se-and. See **Empassy on.**

EXPECT, *v. a., pec.* to think; to imagine, without reference, necessarily, to the future. Com. 'I *expect* they'd'n rar' raps at owd Peggy's Cākin', an' kep'n it up till daylight; Jack never come to fother till seven o'clock.'

EYE [ei·], *sb.* the germ bud of a potato-tuber. Com. See **Eyen**, below.

EYEABLE [ei·u'bl], *adj.* pleasing to the eye.—PULVERBATCH. Qy. com. 'This gownd's pŭt together despert slim; jest made *eyeable*, an' nod to las' too lung.'

EYEBRIGHT [ei·br'eit], *sb.* *Veronica Chamædrys*, Germander Speedwell.—PULVERBATCH.

'Blue *eyebright!* loveliest flower of all that grow
In flower-loved England! Flower whose hedge-side gaze
Is like an infant's! What heart does not know
Thee, cluster'd smiler of the bank where plays
The sunbeam on the emerald snake, and strays
The dazzling rill, companion of the road.'—EBENEZER ELLIOTT.

Cf. **Bird's Eye.**

EYELET-HOLES, *sb. pl.* small holes worked in the material of a garment, &c., to admit hooks or cord for fastening purposes; a term of sewing craft. Com. 'I dunna like 'ooks an' eyes, they comen ondone; *eyelet-'oles* bin best for fastenment.'

'*Oeillet*, petit trou qu'on fait à une étoffe pour passer un cordon. *Eyelet*.'—CHAMB.

EYEN [ei·n *or* ei·h'n], *sb. pl.* eyes.—CORVE DALE. 'They'n the frummest tatoes as be, an' more'n that, they'n the ebbest *eyen*.'

'Thanne ran repentance · and reherced his teme,
And gert wille to wepe · water with his *eyen*.'
Piers Pl., Text B., pass. v. l. 62.

'With that adowne out of her christall *eyne*
Few trickling teares she softly forth let fall,
That like to orient perles did purely shyne
Upon her snowy cheeke. . . . . .
SPENSER, *F. Q.*, Bk. III. c. vii. st. ix.

EYES [ei·z], *sb. pl.* holes in bread and in cheese, caused in the former case by the fermentation set up by the yeast; in the latter by defective management in the process of cheese-making.—WEM; WHITCHURCH. 'I like,' said a young farmer, 'bread full of *eyes*, cheese without any, an' ale as 'll make yore *eyes* star' out o' yore 'ead.'

'*Bad Cheese*, That is . . . White and dry, the Butter of it being in the Market when it is making; too Salt, full of *Eyes*, not well prest, but hoven and swelling.'—*Academy of Armory*, Bk. III. ch. v. p. 244.

Cf. **Bull's eyes.**

FA' [fau], *v. n., var. pr.* to fall. — NEWPORT. 'Tek keer ye dunna *fa'*.'

'Nae mair then, we'll care then,
Nae farther can we *fa'*.'
ROBERT BURNS, *Poems*, p. 57, l. 23, c. 2.

See Ll in **Grammar Outlines** (*consonants*).

FACED-CARDS [fai·zd kaa·'r'dz], *sb. pl.* the court-cards of a pack.—PULVERBATCH. Qy. com. Cf. **Courted-cards.**

FAD [fad·], (1) *sb.* a whim; a fancy; a speciality. 'Full o' *fads.*' Com.

(2) *sb.* one who is difficult to please in **trifles**; a tiresomely particular person. Com. 'Everybody toud me as I should never stop ŏŏth sich a noud *fad*, but I stayed ŏŏth 'er seven 'ear, an' a good Missis 'er wus to me.'

FAD-ABOUT, *v. n.* to look after affairs in a quiet way. Com. 'The poor owd Maister canna do much now—on'y *fad-about* a bit; but, as the sayin' is, "one par o' eyes is wuth two par o' 'ands."'

FADDLE-AFTER, *v. a.* to pay minute attention to a person; to be solicitous about—and complying with—*fads.* Com. 'Bessy's a rar' plack up at the owd 'all; nuthin 'ardly to do but *faddle-after* the Missis, draw the drink, an' sich like.' Cf. **Taddle.**

FADDY, *adj.* particular; fanciful; fussy. Com. 'I ŏŏdna mind doin' twize the work, but the Missis is so dreadful *faddy* yo' never knowen w'en a thing's right.'

FAGGIT [fag·i't], (1) *sb., var. pr.* a bundle of sticks, or of heath, for fuel.—SHREWSBURY; CLUN. Qy. com. 'Dun 'ee want any yeth this evenin', Missis?' 'Yes; how much have you?' 'On'y about 'afe a dozen *faggits;* yo'd better tak' 'em all.'

'*Fagott*, Fassis, strues. CATH.'—*Prompt. Parv.* W. *ffagod*, a faggot; a bundle. Cf. **Kid** (1).

(2) *sb.* a term of opprobrium for a false, hypocritical woman. Com. 'That ŏŏman's a reg'lar owd *faggit*—'er imposes on the paas'n shameful.'

FAGGITS, *sb. pl.* a kind of sausages made of the liver and lights of a pig, boiled with sweet herbs, and finely chopped; then covered with the 'veil' of the pig, and baked on an oven-tin. The *faggits* are oblong in form, and about an inch and a half thick.—SHREWSBURY; PULVERBATCH; WORTHEN. Cf. **Spice-balls.** See **Veil.**

FAIBERRY [fai·br'i'], *sb. Ribes Grossulária*, common Gooseberry.—PULVERBATCH; CORVE DALE; COLLIERY. Generally used in the plural form *Faiberries.* Cotgrave has this word in v. *Groiselles.*—HAL. Ray, in *South and East Country Words*, gives '*Feabes* or *Feaberries*, Gooseberries, *Suff. Leicestersh. Thebes* in Norf. Ash has '*Feaberries*, a local word,' and Grose has it as N. = North.

FAIBERRY-BUSH, *sb.* a gooseberry-bush.—PULVERBATCH; CORVE DALE; COLLIERY. 'Hie away to the *faib'ry-bush* an' fatch my 'ankercher as I pŭt theer to w'ĭt'n.'

'In English Goose-berry bush, and *Fea-berry bush* in Cheshire, my native country.'—GERARDE'S *Herball*, Bk. II. p. 1324.

FAIGH [fai·], *sb.* iron-stone measure with iron-stone ore in it.—COLLIERY, *Madeley;* M. T.

FAIN [fein· *corr.* faayn·], *adv., obsols.*? gladly. —PULVERBATCH. 'I'd *fayn* gŏŏ to the far o' Thursday on'y fur gettin' them turmits in afore theer comes rayn.'

'& *fayn* sche wold þan in feiþ · haue fold him in hire armes
to haue him clipped & kest . . . . .'
William of Palerne, l. 858.

'*Lear*. Dost thou know me, fellow?
'*Kent*. No, sir; but you have that in your countenance which I would *fain* call master.
'*Lear*. What's that?
'*Kent*. Authority.'—*K. Lear*, I. iv. 30.

'For I am sixteen and my time is a-wastin';
I *fain* would get married if I knew the way.'
Old Ballad.

A.S. *fægen*, *fægn*, fain; glad. Icel. *feginn*.

FAIRISHES, *sb. pl.*, *var. pr.*, *obs.* fairies.—BRIDGNORTH.

FALL [faul·], (1) *v. a.* to let fall. Com. 'I should never trust that child ŏŏth a lookin'-glass, 'er'll be sure to *fall* it.'

'*Seb*. . . . Draw thy sword: one stroke
Shall free thee from the tribute which thou payest;
And I the king shall love thee.
Ant. Draw together;
And when I rear my hand, do you the like,
To *fall* it on Gonzalo.'—*Tempest*, II. i. 295.

(2) *v. a.* to fell trees. Com.

(3) *sb.* the act of felling trees. Com. 'The young Squire says w'en 'e comes of age 'e'll *fall* a sight o' timber; an' a grand *fall* theer'll be, fur 'is poor owd nuncle ŏŏdna 'ăve a sprig touched in 'is time.'

(4) *sb.* the autumn.—NEWPORT.

'What crowds of patients the town-doctor kills,
Or how, last *fall*, he raised the weekly bills.'—DRYDEN.

Cf. **Fall o' the leaf**, below.

FALLAL [fallal·], *sb.* nonsense; jocoseness; exaggerated civility; 'humbug.'—SHREWSBURY; PULVERBATCH. Qy. com. 'I canna believe a word 'e says, 'e's so much *fallal* about 'im.'

FALLER, *sb.* a feller of timber. Com. 'The *fallers* bin on Esridge [Eastridge] coppy agen; I thought they fellen a pretty good shar' last 'ear.'

FALL O' THE LEAF, *phr.* the season of autumn.—SHREWSBURY; PULVERBATCH; WEM. Qy. com. 'Ah! poor fellow, 'e's desport wek; 'e'll 'ardly see o'er the *fall o' the lef*.'

FANCICAL [fan·si'kul], *adj.*, *obsols.*? fanciful. — PULVERBATCH; WEM; ELLESMERE. 'I want a plaȳn dacent bonnit—none o' yore *fancical* finery fur me.'

FANG [fangg·], (1) *v. a.* and *v. n.* to lay hold of.—PULVERBATCH. 'W'y didna yo' *fang* out o' the 'ĭnd-bwurd' [hind-board] 'o' the tumbril w'en yo' sid'n the turmits tum'lin' all alung the lane?'

'Wheither sholde *fonge* the fruyt,
The fend or hymselve.'
Piers Pl., pass. xvi. l. 10992, ed. Wr.

'Destruction *fang* mankind! Earth, yield me roots!'
Timon of Athens, IV. iii. 23.

'*Fangyñ* or latchyñ (lachyn or hentyn, K. H.). *Apprehendo.* To *fang* or seize, A.S. fang, *captura*, fangen, *captus*, is a verb used by R. Brunne and various writers as late as Shakespeare.'—*Prompt. Parv. and Notes.*

(2) *sb.* the prong of a fork, of any kind.—Shrewsbury; Pulverbatch. 'Look 'ere, Sally, this sort o' clānin' ŏŏnna do fur me; jest see 'twixt them *fangs*—theer's dirt enough to set garrits in.'

FANGED, *part. adj.* furnished with fangs.—*Ibid.* 'Axe Tummas to len' me 'is five-*fanged* sharevil; the groun's so fine it runs throu' this.'

FANGLED, *part. adj.*, *obsols.* showily trimmed, as with ribands or 'bugles;' bedizened.—Shrewsbury; Pulverbatch. ''Er bonnit wuz *fangled* all o'er ŏŏth ribbints like a pedlar's basket.'

'. . . . . . A book? O rare one!
Be not, as is our *fangled* world, a garment
Nobler than that it covers.'—*Cymbeline*, V. iv. 134.

Cf. **New-fangled.**

FAN-PECKLES [fan·pek·'lz], *sb. pl.* freckles.—Wem; Whitchurch. Perhaps a corruption of *fawn-speckles*, to which freckles may not inaptly be likened. Grose has, '*Farn-tickled*, freckled. N.' Cf. **Sun-speckles.**

FANTEAG [fantai·gg *and* fantee·gg], *sb.* a fit of ill-temper; a pet. Com. 'The Missis is in a pretty *fantaig;* the Maister's gwun to the far an' tŏŏk the kay o' the flour-rŏŏm ŏŏth 'im—an' the fire i' the oven fur bakin'.'

FANTOM [fan·tu'm], (1) *adj.* flimsy.—Newport. 'It's poor *fantom* stuff.'

(2) soft; flabby.—Newport; Wem. ''Er's bin that poorly 'er arms han gotten quite *fantom.*'

'*Fantome* Flesh, when it hangs loose on the Bone.'—Ray [*North Country Words*], p. 29. 'C'est un vrai *fantôme* se dit d'un homme maigre . . .'—Chamb. Cf. O.Fr. *fantosme* de *fantasma.*—Bur.

FAR [faa·r'], *sb.*, *var. pr.* a fair. Com. '*Far* indeed! theer's too many *fars*—they wun used to be ev'ry month, then a comen ev'ry fortnit, an' now they'n got 'em ev'ry wik; I'm *farred* to djeth!'

FARE [faer'·], (1) *sb.* a track, as of a rabbit.—Oswestry. A.S. *faru*, a journey. Cf. **Muse.**

(2) *adv.* far; distant.—Shrewsbury; Pulverbatch; Wem; Ellesmere. 'How far is it to Longden?' 'Well, it's a mile alung the lane, but it inna-d-'afe as *fare* across the filds.'

'Fingered ladies whose womanlike behaviour and motherlike housewifry ought to be a lighte to al women that dwell aboute you, but is so *fare* otherwise, that, unless ye leave them landes to marye them wythall, no man wyll set a pinne by them when you be gone.' —ROBERT CROWLEY'S *Select Works* (A.D. 1549), ed. J. M. Cowper, E. E. T. S.

FARRIN' [faa·r'i'n], *sb.*, *var. pr.* a fairing; a present from a fair.—PULVERBATCH. Qy. com. 'See whad a perty 'ankercher Jim bought me for a May *farrin'*, an' these papers o' Dorri't'n gingerbread.'

FARROW [faar'·u'], (1) *v. a.* to bring forth a litter of pigs.—PULVERBATCH; ELLESMERE. Not a term of frequent use in the first-named locality, and is perhaps an imported word.

'A Swine or Sow, *Farroweth*: the young ones are called a *Farow* of Pigs.'—*Academy of Armory*, Bk. II. ch. vii. p. 134.

(2) *sb.* a litter of pigs.—*Ibid.*

'*First Witch.* Pour in sow's blood, that hath eaten
Her nine *farrow* . . .'—*Macbeth*, IV. i. 65.

A.S. *fearh*; O.H. Germ. *farh*; Lat. *porcus*; farrow.—STRAT.

FARTHING-BAG, *sb.* the second stomach of a cow.—PULVERBATCH; CLUN. ''Er's bund i' the *farthin'-bag*.'

FASTENMENT [fas·nmu'nt], *sb.* a fastening of any kind. Com. 'If yo' go'n as fare as Stepit'n [Stapleton], tell Jones to come up an' put a *fas'nment* o' the brew-'us door.'

'Door-*fastenments*.'—*Auctioneer's Catalogue* (Church Stretton), 1877. See below.

FASTNESS, *sb.* a fastening, as of bolt, bar, &c., to door, gate, or window.—WEM. 'That theer bull's bin 'ilin the dur o' 'is place, an' bruk the *fas'ness*.' See **Hile.**

FAT, *pret.* and *part. past.* fetched. Com. ''E *fat* up the 'ackney mar' out o' the leasow to tak' the owd Maister wham.'

Among the borough accounts of Shrewsbury for the year 1506 is the item—'For ale that was *fat* in the chambyr and that servaunts dranke bytwixt melys ijs viijd.'—OWEN and BLAKEWAY'S *History of Shrewsbury*, vol. i. p. 280. Cf. **Fot.**

FATCH, *v. a.* to fetch. Com. 'Run an' *fatch* me the sharevil, ŏŏt 'ee?'

'Many wedous with wepyng tears cam to *fache* ther makys A-way.'
Chevy Chase. Specim. Eng. Lit., vii. l. 118.

FATHER-LAW [fai·dhur' lau], *sb.*, *obsols.* a father-in-law.—PULVERBATCH; WEM. 'Dunna yo' think as I'm gweïn to be married to live ŏŏth my *faither-law*—if 'e ŏŏnna tak' a 'ouse, I stop awham.'

FAUN, *part. past.* fallen.—NEWPORT.

'O Woman lovely, Woman fair!
An Angel form's *faun* to thy share,
'Twad been o'er meikle to gien thee mair,
I mean an Angel mind.'
ROBERT BURNS, *Poems*, p. 205, l. 4, c. 2.

See Ll in **Grammar Outlines** (*consonants*).

FAUSE [fau·ss], *adj.* artful; deceitful. Com. 'They'n got a new 'ousekeeper at the 'all, I 'ear; dun'ee know anythin' on 'er?' 'Well, nod much—'er manages the Squire's lady; but from whad folks sen on 'er, I should think 'er's as *fause* as *fause*.'

'Wi' lightsome heart I pu'd a rose,
Fu' sweet upon its thorny tree;
And my *fause* luver stole my rose,
But ah! he left the thorn wi' me.'

ROBERT BURNS, *Poems*, p. 206, l. 19.

(2) *v. a.* to coax; to wheedle. Com. 'I want a new gownd agen the Wakes; I mus' try an' *fause* my Maister o'er to get me one.'

FAUT [fau·t], (1) *sb.* fault; error. Com. 'Oh no! yo' bin never i' no *faut;* yo' bin the lily-w'ite 'en as never lays astray, yo' bin.'

'Bot þat oþer wrake þat wex · on wyȝeȝ hit lyȝt
Þurȝ þe *faut* of a freke · þat fayled in trawþe.'

Alliterative Poems, The Deluge (A.D. 1360, *circa*).
Specim. Early Eng., xiii. l. 236.

'Then never range, nor learn to change,
Like those in high degree;
And if ye prove faithful in love,
You'll find nae *faut* in me.'

ALLAN RAMSAY, *Song XIV.*, p. 51.

O.Fr. *faute.*

(2) *sb.* the imputation of a fault; blame. Com. 'They laiden the *faut* o' Joe, but I dunna think as the poor bwoy wuz to blame.'

'I haue yherde hiegh men · etyng atte table,
Carpen as þei clerkes were · of cryste and of his miȝtes,
And leyden *fautes* vppon þe fader · þat fourmed us alle.'

Piers Pl., Text B., pass. x. l. 103.

(3) *sb.* a defect. Com. 'Theer's a *faut* i' that beäm; I doubt as it'll never bar Jack-tiles.'

'Þenne he seiȝ a newe chaumbre-wouh · wrouȝt al of bordes,
a dore honginge þer-on · haspet ful faste,
A child cominge þorw · his come was nout seene,
Siþen lenges a-while · and a-ȝein lendes,
wiþ-outen *faute* oþer faus · as þei fore seiden.'

Joseph of Arimathie, l. 268.

'*Fawte*, or defawte. *Defectus.*'—*Prompt. Parv.*

(4) *sb.* a dislocation in the seam of coal or ore in a mine.—M. T. 'Comin' to a *faut*' is a metaphorical phrase frequently employed to express 'let or hindrance' in any of the ordinary affairs of life.

FAUTY, (1) *adj.* guilty; blameworthy. Com. 'I knowed 'e wuz *fauty* as soon as I sid 'is face, for all 'e denied it, but I plankt it on 'im,' *i. e.* convicted him of the offence.

'And if they [the byshoppes] be founde necligente or *fauty* in theyr duties oute with them.'—LATIMER, *Sermon* ii. p. 66.

'ONE diligent seruiture, skilfull to waight
more comelieth thy table than other some eight,
That stand forto listen, or gasing about,
not minding their dutie, within nor without.

Such waiter is *fautie* that standeth so by,
 vnmindful of seruice, forgetting his ey.
If maister to such giue a bone for to gnaw,
 he doth but his office, to teach such a daw.'
TUSSER, *Fiue Hundred Pointes of Good Husbandrie*, ed. E. D. S., p. 189.

(2) *adj.* defective; imperfect; in bad condition. Com. 'My shoes bin gettin' *fauty*, an' this snow ŏŏl find 'em out.'
'*Fawty*, or defawty. *Defectivus*.'—*Prompt. Parv.*

FAVOUR [fai·vur'], *v. a.* to bear a family likeness.—SHREWSBURY; PULVERBATCH; WEM. Qy. com. 'That's a pretty babby o' Matty Wigley's.' 'Aye, 'er's a good-lookin' ŏŏman, an' it *favours* 'er family strungly.'

'Good faith, methinks that this young Lord Chamont
Favours my mother, sister, doth he not?'
BEN JONSON, *Case is alter'd*, iii. 1, in NARES.

Mr. Nares' note on the foregoing is, 'The *Mother* had been dead some time.' Cf. **Feature.**

FEÄK [fi'·u'k *or* fi'aek·], (1) *sb.* a sharp twitch or pull.—SHREWSBURY; PULVERBATCH; WORTHEN. Qy. com.

(2) *v. a.* to give a sharp twitch or pull.—*Ibid.* 'I know w'en our Maister's in a bad 'umour, fur 'e al'ays *feäks* 'is wescut down.'

FEÄRN [fi'aa·r'n], *sb.*, *var. pr.* fern. Com. 'Theer wuz a power o' feärn cut on Huglith, an' burnt to make ess-balls on.' This was said in reference to a circumstance dating about 1805. A.S. *fearn*, fern. See **Ess-balls.**

FEATURE [fai·chur'], *v. a.* to resemble in feature.—SHREWSBURY; PULVERBATCH; WEM. Qy. com. 'Ben *faichurs* 'is faither, but all the rest favour the mother's side.' Cf. **Favour.**

FEBRIWERRY-FILL-DICHE, *sb.* the month of February, which is usually a wet one.—PULVERBATCH. Qy. com. 'Now Chris'mas is turned we sha'n be glad to see the end of owd Janniwerry-freeze-the-pot-by-the-fire an' *Febriwerry-fill-diche*—that's like a tuthless owd ŏŏman as 'ad three nuts to crack, an' 'er said, "If I could crack this an' another I should on'y a one lef' to crack."'

'Feb, *fill the dike*
With what thou dost like.'
TUSSER, *Februaries husbandrie.*

'*February fill dike*, Be it black or be it white;
But if it be white, It's the better to like.'
RAY'S *Proverbs*, p. 33.

FEED [fee·d], *sb.* food; pasture. Com. 'I hanna sid more *feed* o' the groun' fur many a 'ear than is this time, an' now jest 'allantide.' Shakespeare has *feeding* in the sense of pasturage, tract of land.

'*Shep.* They call him Doricles; and boasts himself
To have a worthy *feeding*. . . . .'
Winter's Tale, IV. iv. 169.

Cf. **Keep** (3).

FEEDING-TIME, *sb.* warm, showery weather. — SHREWSBURY; PULVERBATCH. Qy. com. 'It's a fine *feedin'-time* fur the corn an' turmits, but it maks the 'aȳ lag.'

FEERINGS [fee·h'r'inz], *sb. pl.* spaces of ploughed land from eight to more yards in width.—SHREWSBURY; PULVERBATCH. Qy. com. *Feerings* differ from 'buts' in being made as level as possible; 'buts' are high on the ridge, and correspondingly low in the 'reän:' 'buts' are on wet lands—*feerings* on dry lands. Cf. **But** (1). See **Veerings.**

FEG [feg·], *sb.* long, rank grass, which cattle refuse to eat unless they have no other. Com.

FEL' [fel·], *pret.* and *part. past* felt. Com. 'I *fel'* so bad all o'er as if I wuz gweïn to 'ăve a faiver, but I tŏŏk a good jorum o' drink-mate an' it throwed it off.' See T (3) in **Grammar Outlines** (*consonants*).

FELL, (1) *pret.* and *part. past.* fallen. Com. 'They sen as poor Jack's *fell* off the stack an' broke 'is leg.'

'Ten masts at each make not the altitude
Which thou hast perpendicularly *fell.*'
K. Lear, IV. vi. 54.

Cf. **Faun.**

(2) *v. a.* to hem down the inside of a seam: a sewing term. Com. 'Run that sem up an' *fell* it down.'

FELLEN, *v. n., pret. pl.* fell. Com. 'We *fellen*, the par on us, as we wun runnin' down the bonk.'

'Firste þorw þe we *fellen* · fro heuene so heighe;
For we leued þi lesynges. . . . . .'
Piers Pl., Text B., pass. xviii. l. 309.

FELLIES [fel·iz], *sb. pl.* the curved pieces of wood which form the circumference of a wheel. Com. The number of *fellies* in a wheel vary according to its size, but there are two spokes in each.

'The *Fellees* or *Felloes* are the pieces which compass the Wheel, the Wheel Rim, which are . . . . . in number.'—*Academy of Armory*, Bk. III. ch. viii. p. 332.

'*Felwe* of a qwele (whele, P.). *Circumferencia*—*Prompt. Parv.* A.S. *felge.*—*Idem.*

FENDING AND PROVING, *phr.*, *obsols.*? disputing; arguing for and against.—PULVERBATCH. 'Han they settled about the fŭt-way yet? theer's bin a sight o' *fen'in' an' provin'*; it wuz to be settled at the Court Leet.' Grose gives this phrase as 'common' in his *Provincial Glossary.*

'To *fend and prove*, i. e. to wrangle; vitilitigo, altercor.'—ADAM LITTLETON'S *Lat. Dict.* 1735, *sub voc.* in E. D. S., C. vi.

FESCUE [fes·keu], *sb.*, *obs.* a pointer used in teaching children to read.—PULVERBATCH; WORTHEN. 'I see yo' binna-d-in a 'umour to larn this mornin'; lave the *fescue* an' the Psalter an' run to Churt'n fur me, yo'n do it better w'en yo' comen back.'

'Lewed men may likne ȝow þus · þat þe beem lithe in ȝoure eyghen,
And þe *festu* is fallen · for ȝowre defaute.'
Piers Pl., Text B., pass. x. l. 277.

Mr. Skeat's note on the foregoing is—Cf. 'Quid consideras *festucam*,' at l. 262, above [Matt. vii. 3].

Mr. Way refers to this same passage in *Piers. Pl.*, and adds, 'The Medulla likewise renders "*festuca*, festu, or a lytel mote." The name was applied to the straw or stick used for pointing, in the early instruction of children: thus Palsgrave gives "festue, to spell with, *festev*." Occasionally the word is written with *c* or *k*, instead of *t*, but it is apparently a corruption. "*Festu*, a feskue, a straw, rush, little stalk, or stick, used for a fescue. *Touche*, a fescue; also, a pen or a pin for a pair of writing-tables." COTGR.' —*Note in Prompt. Parv.*, p. 158.

FETCHES [fech·iz], *sb. pl.* vetches. — PULVERBATCH; OSWESTRY. 'Everall's got some famous winter *fetches* i' the Fut-way fild—they'n 'elp 'is fother out.'

> 'This is said by hem that be not worth two *fetches*.'
> CHAUCER, *Troil. and Cres.*, iii. 887, in *Bible Word-Book.*

'*Fetche*, corne, or tare (fehche, K.). *Vicia*, UG. *in vincio, crobus*, C. F.'—*Prompt. Parv.* See **Fitches**.

FETTERIN' [fet·h'r'in], *part. adj.* pottering about.—CLUN; WEM. 'The warden wuz al'ays *fetterin'* i' the church,' said Francis Rawlings, of Clun [1873].

FETTLE [fet·l] (1), *v. a.* to put in order; to repair; to make ready. Com. A parish clerk of Cound [Salop] gave notice—during the time of Divine Service—of a vestry meeting, in the following terms: 'This is to give you all notice that theer'll be a meetin' in the vestry nex' Toosd'y wik—'ould, I'm wrung—nex' Toosd'y as ever comes I mane—to *fettle* the pews and so forth.'

> 'Wen hit watȝ *fettled* & forged · & to þe fulle grayþed,
> Þenn con dryȝttyn hym dele · dryȝly þyse wordeȝ;
> "Now Noe," quod oure lorde · art þou al redy?
> Hatȝ þou closed þy kyst · with clay alle aboute?"'
> *Alliterative Poems, The Deluge* (A.D. 1360, *circa*).
> *Specim. Early Eng.*, xiii. l. 343.

> 'John bent vp a good veiwe bow,
> & *ffetteled** him to shoote:
> the bow was made of a tender boughe,
> & fell downe to his footee.'
> *Guye of Gisborne*, l. 60. *Percy Folio MS.*, vol. ii. p. 230, ed Hales and Furnivall.

* '*ffetteled*, prepared; addressed him.'—*Verbum Salopiense.* Note by BP. PERCY.—*Ibid.*

The only instance of Shakespeare's use of the word *fettle* occurs in the following passage:—

> '*Capulet.* How now, how now . . . . .
> Thank me no thankings, nor proud me no prouds,
> But *fettle* your fine joints 'gainst Thursday next,
> To go with Paris to Saint Peter's Church,
> Or I will drag thee on a hurdle thither.'
> *Romeo and Juliet*, III. v. 154.

L

'Prov. Eng. *fettle*, to set in order; Mœso-Goth. *fetjan*, to adorn, make *fit*; allied to A.S. *fetel*, a fetter, and E. *fit*. See Diefenbach, i. 373.'—*Glossarial Index to Specim. Early Eng.*

(2) *sb.* state; order; condition. Com. 'Yo'n fine the lanes in a despert *fettle* now, ŏŏth the snow gweïn away.'

FEW [fyou·], *adj., var. pr.* few. Com. 'Theer wunna but a *fyeow* pars on that tree—they met'n a lef' 'em alone.'

> 'If hops look browne,
> go gather them downe.
> But not in a deaw,
> for piddling with *feaw*' [*feawe*, ed. 1577].
> TUSSER'S *Fiue Hundred Pointes of Good Husbandrie*, ed. E. D. S., p. 427.

A.S. *feáwe*, few. See **Grammar Outlines** (*indefinite numerals*).

FID [fi'd·], *v. a.* to chew fodder and eject it from the mouth, when, from being imperfectly masticated, it cannot be swallowed.—CLEE HILLS. 'Maister, that owd mar' *fids* 'er fother—'er's got no tith at all.'

FIDDLE-FADDLE [fid·l fad·l], *v. n.* to trifle; to dawdle.—PULVERBATCH. Qy. com. 'I canna think whad yo'n bin *fiddle-faddlin'* about all mornin'—'ere it's jest baȳte time an' the milk things never done up.'

FIDGE [fi'j·], (1) *sb.* a fidget; a restless person. 'A reg'lar owd *fidge*.'—SHREWSBURY. Qy. com. Cf. **Fad** (2).

(2) *v. a.* and *v. n.* to be fidgety or restless.—*Ibid.* ''Er's al'ays *fidgin'* about—'er canna be still 'erself nor let other folk be.'

> 'In gath'rin votes you were na slack;
> Now stand as tightly by your tack;
> Ne'er claw your lug, an' *fidge* your back,
> An' hum an' haw;
> But raise your arm, an' tell your crack
> Before them a'.'
> ROBERT BURNS, *Poems*, p. 10, l. 21.

FIERY-BRAN'-TAIL, *sb.* the Redstart.—PULVERBATCH, *Hanwood*. See **Brand-tail**.

FIFT [fi'f·t], fifth. Qy. com. An old form.

> '& swiche duel drow to hert · for his dedus ille,
> þat he deide on þe *fifte* day · to talke þe soþe.'
> *William of Palerne*, l. 1322.

> 'King Henry the *Fift*, too famous to live long.'
> 1 *K. Henry VI.* i. 1 [ed. 1623], in *Bible Word-Book.*

Adnepos, fifte sune; *Adneptis*, fifte dohter, occur in *Supplement to Archbp. Ælfric's Vocabulary*, x. or xi. cent., in Wr. vocabs., vol. i. p. 51. See **Grammar Outlines** (*adjectives of numeration*).

FIGARIES [fi'gae·r'i'z], *sb. pl.* fanciful attire; fantastic ornaments, as of ribands, bows, flowers, &c.—SHREWSBURY; ATCHAM; PULVERBATCH; CLUN; WEM. Qy. com. ''Er's got all manner o' *figaries* about 'er.' Perhaps *vagaries* = whimseys is meant.

FIGÁRIMENTS [fi'gae·r'i'mu'nts], *sb. pl.* same as **Figaries.** Qy. com. 'I should like it made nate an' plain—no *figárimenta* about it.'

FIGGETTY-DUMPLING [fig·i'ti' dum·pli'n], *sb.* a pudding made by lining a basin with paste and then filling it with figs cut in pieces, currants, a little candied peel, treacle, and water, covering it with paste, and boiling it for some hours. It is said to be 'nod 'afe bad.'—ELLESMERE.

FIGHTING-COCKS, *sb. pl. Plantago lanceolata.*—Qy. com. It is a favourite amusement with children to try to strike off the head of one plantain-stalk by hitting it with another, whence the name *Fighting-cocks.* See **Black Jacks.**

FILBEARD [fil·bi'u'r'd], *sb.* a filbert.—SHREWSBURY; PULVERBATCH. Qy. com. *Filbeard* is found in Tusser, p. 75, ed. E. D. S.

'*Fylberde,* notte. *Fillum.* DICC.'—*Prompt. Parv.* See below.

FILBEARD-TREE, *sb.* the cultivated *Corylus Avellana,* filbert-tree. —*Ibid.* 'I never sid the *filbyard-trees* covered ŏŏth lamb-tails [catkins] as they bin this 'ear' [1879]. '*Hic fullus,* a fylberd-tre,' occurs in a *Nominale,* xiv. cent., in Wr. vocabs., vol. i. p. 229, and Mr. Wright has the following note upon it: 'The Latin should be *fillis.* Filberde-tree, *Phillis.*'—*Prompt. Parv.* Gower, *Confes. Amant.,* vol. ii. p. 30 (ed. Pauli), has misrepresented the story of Phillis and Demophoon, in Ovid, in order to give a derivation of this word.

'"And Demephon was so reproved,
That of the Goddes providence
Was shape suche an evidence
Ever afterward ayein the slowe,
That Phillis in the same throwe
Was shape into a nutte-tre,
That alle men it mighte se,
And after Phillis *philliberde*
This tre was cleped in the yerde."'

FILD [fi'l·d], *sb.* a field. Com. The curious expression, 'a *fild* of land,' is often heard.

'By occasion of thys texte [Rom. xv. 4] (most honorable audience) I haue walked thys Lente in the brode *filde* of scripture and vsed my libertie, and intreated of such matters as I thought mete for this auditory.'—LATIMER, *Sermon* vii. p. 182.

Tusser has *fildes* for fields, ed. 1557. A.S. *feld; fild,* a field; pasture; plain.

FILDEFARE [fi'l·di'faa·'r'], *sb. Turdus piláris,* the Fieldfare.—SHREWSBURY; PULVERBATCH.

FILDFARE, *sb.* same as above.—LUDLOW.

'he com him-self y-charged · wiþ conyng & hares,
wiþ fesauns & *feldfares* · and oþer foules grete.'
William of Palerne, l. 183.

A.S. *feala-for,*—*Idem.* See **Blue-back,** also **Shredcock.**

FIND [fei·nd], *v. a.* to provide for; to supply—more especially with food. Com. 'I call three shillin' a day big wages, an' *find* 'em in mate an' drink.'

'Then havest thow londes to lyve by,
Quath Reson, "other lynage ryche
That *fynden* the thy fode?"'

Piers Pl., p. 514, ed. WR.

'By housbondrye of such as God hire sente,
Sche *fond* hireself, and eek hire doughtren tuo.'

CHAUCER, *The Nonne Prestes Tale*, l. 9, ed. Morris.

By an 'Assessment of the Corporation of Canterbury,' made in 1504, the following were the rates of wages declared payable:—'Every labourer from Easter to Michaelmas, with meat and drink, 4*d*. per day, *finding* himself, 10*d*.; and from Michaelmas to Easter, with meat and drink, 4*d*.; without, 8*d*. Mowers per day, with meat and drink, 8*d*.; *finding* themselves, 14*d*. By the acre, with meat and drink, 4*d*.; without, 8*d*. Reapers per day, with meat and drink, 6*d*.; *finding* themselves, 10*d*.; by the acre, with meat and drink, 14*d*.; without, 28*d*.'—HASTED'S *Antiquities of Canterbury*, 1801, vol. ii., Appendix.

A.S. *findan*, to find.

FINGERS-AND-TOES, *sb.* a diseased form of turnip—caused by the attacks of an insect—where the root has departed from the natural growth and become branched and clubbed. Com. See *Fingers and toes*, E. D. S., C. vi.

FINGER-STALL, *sb.* a covering—usually the finger of a glove—for a sore finger or thumb. Com. 'We 'ad'n a busy day o' Friday, whad ööth churnin', bakin' pork-pies, an' renderin' lard; an' to mak' amends I cut my finger, but I clapt a *finger-stall* on an' went at it as if nuthin' wuz the matter.' Mr. Halliwell says, '*Finger-stall* does not appear to be in the dictionaries. It is in common use, and occurs in *Florio*, p. 139.'

FINISHED, *part. adj.* weak of intellect is expressed by 'not quite *finished*.'—WORTHEN, *Cherbury*. Cf. **Half-soaked.**

FINNIKIN [fin·i'kin], *adj.* over-nice; mincing; finical. Com. 'I dunna know whad the fellow wanted ööth sich a *finnikin* piece as 'er—ööth fingers too fine to ketch out o' the pig-trough.'

FIR-BALLS, *sb. pl.* fir cones.—SHREWSBURY; CLUN; WEM.

FIR-BOBS, *idem.*—PULVERBATCH.

FIR-BRUSHES [fur'·br'aesh·'i'z], *sb.* the needle-foliage of fir trees.—CLUN. Cf. Way's note on *Fyyre* in *Prompt. Parv.*, p. 162.

FIRE-BRAN'-TAIL, same as **Fiery-bran'-tail**, q. v.—CLUN, *Twitchen*; OSWESTRY.

FIRE-FORK, *sb.* a long-handled, two-pronged fork for stirring up the fuel in a brick-oven.—PULVERBATCH. 'Sally, yo' should'n a brought the *fire-fork* an' the slut afore yo' putten yore 'ands i' the flour.'

'*The Kytchynge* . . . one *fireforke* two wodden peeles.'—*Inventory* . . . Owlbury Manor-House, Bishop's Castle, 1625. Cf. **Oven-pikel.**

FIRMARY [fur'·mu'r'i'], *sb.* an infirmary. Com. 'Well, I hanna much consate o' them Club Doctors; if yo'd send 'im to the *Firmary* 'e'd get the best 'elp as could be 'ad.'

'Chambers wiþ chymneyes · & Chapells gaie;
And kychens for an hyȝe kinge · in castells to holden,
And her dortour y-diȝte · wiþ dores ful stronge;
Fermery and fraitur · with fele mo houses.'
P. Pl. Cr., l. 212.

'Fermerye. *Infirmaria.*'—*Prompt. Parv.*

FIRST-BEGINNING, *sb.*, *pec.* the beginning. Qy. com. 'The *first-beginnin'* on it wuz a little pimple no bigger than a pin's yed, an' it fumed an' turned to Tantony's-fire, an' the poor owd chap's gotten a despert leg.'

FIRST-POLE, *sb.* the ridge piece of the roof-timbers.—CLUN.

FISGIG [fiz·gig], (1) *sb.* this term implies a kind of loose 'shagginess,' as of fuzzy hair, or of the ill-connected garnish of a dress.—PULVERBATCH. 'Whad ŏŏth frills an' furbelows, 'er wuz all of a *fisgig*.'

(2) *sb.*, *sl.*? sharp, small beer.—SHREWSBURY; PULVERBATCH. Qy. com. 'A drop o' *fisgig* to cut yore throät.'

FISK [fi's·k], *v. n.* to wander; to roam about idly.—SHREWSBURY, *Uffington*. 'Mother, owd Kitty James wuz at the 'arves'-wham at Upton Magna.' 'Bless me! I never sid sich a ŏŏman as 'er fur *fiskin'* about; no matter whad's gweïn on, 'er's sure to be at it.'

'And what frek of þys folde · *fisketh* þus a-boute.'
Piers Pl., Text C., pass. x. l. 153.

Mr. Skeat's note on this passage is:—'*Fisketh*, wanders; roams. As this word is scarce, I give all the instances of it that I can find. In *Sir Gawayne and the Grene Knight*, ed. Morris, l. 1704, there is a description of a fox-hunt, where the fox and the hounds are thus mentioned:—

"& he *fyskes* hem by-fore · þay founden hym sone"—*i. e.* and he (the fox) runs on before them (the hounds); but they soon found him. "Fyscare abowte ydylly; Discursor, discursatrix, vagulus vel vagator,vagatrix."—*Prompt. Parv.*, p. 162. "Fiskin abowte yn ydilnesse; Vago, giro, girovago."—*Ibid.*

"Such serviture also deserveth a check,
That runneth out *fisking*, with meat in his beck" [mouth].
TUSSER, *Five Hundred Points*, &c., ed. Mavor, p. 286.

"Then had every flock his shepherd, or else shepherds; now they do not only run *fisking* about from place to place, . . but covetously join living to living."—WHITGIFT'S *Works*, i. 528.

"I *fyske*, i. e. fretille. I praye you se howe she *fysketh* about."—PALSG. "*Trotière*, a raumpe, fisgig, *fisking* huswife, raunging damsell."—COTG.

"Then in a cave, then in a field of corn,
Creeps to and fro, and *fisketh* in and out."
Dubartas (in Nares).

"His roving eyes rolde to and fro,
He *fiskyng* fine, did myncing go."
KENDALL'S *Flower of Epigrammes*, 1577 (Nares).

"Tom Tankard's cow . . . .
Flinging about his halfe aker, *fisking* with her tail."
Gammer Gurton's Needle, i. 2.

"*Fieska*, to *fisk* the tail about; to *fisk* up and down."—*Swed. Dict.*, by J. Serenius. "*Fjeska*, v. n. to fidge; to fidget; to *fisk*."—*Swed. Dict.* (Tauchnitz).'

To the examples of the word *fisk* cited in the foregoing note may be added the following:—'But whan a stronger than he commeth vpon hym, whan the light of goddes word is ones reueled, than he is busi, then he rores, then he *fyskes* a brode, and styrreth vp erronius opinions, to sclaunder godds word.'—LATIMER, *Sermon*, iv. p. 104.

FISKY, *adj.* frisky, as of a kitten, &c.—SHREWSBURY, *Uffington*. Cf. **Fisk**, above.

FITCHES [fich·i'z], *sb. pl.* vetches. Com.

'Some countries are pinched of medow for hay,
yet ease it with *fitchis* as well as they may.
Which inned and threshed and husbandlie dight,
keepes laboring cattle in verie good plight.

In threshing out *fitchis* one point I will shew,
first thresh out for seede of the *fitchis* a few:
Thresh few fro thy plowhorse, thresh cleane for the cow,
this order in Norfolke good husbands alow.'
TUSSER, *Fiue Hundred Pointes of Good Husbandrie* [December].

FITCHET [fich·i't], *sb. Putorius fœtidus*, the Polecat.—SHREWSBURY; WEM; ELLESMERE. In the last two of these districts *fitch* is sometimes heard instead of *fitchet*. The form *fitchew* occurs in *P. Pl. Cr.*, l. 295, and in *K. Lear*, IV. vi. 124.

FITCHET-PIE, *sb.* a pie made of apples, onions, and bacon: sometimes cheese is substituted for the bacon, but it is a departure from 'old usage.' This pie gets its name—*fitchet*—from the strong, unsavoury odour it emits in baking.

FITCHOCK [fich·u'k], same as **Fitchet**, above. — SHREWSBURY; PULVERBATCH; CLUN; CORVE DALE; LUDLOW. It is worthy of remark, as showing the decay of provincialisms, that some words linger on with a wrong meaning; thus in Corve Dale some there begin [1874] to call a *hedgehog* a *fitchock*.

FITCHOCK-PIE, same as **Fitchet-pie**, 'made after the original receipt.' The form *fitchock-pie* follows *fitchock* in localities.

FITHERFEW [fidh·ur'feu], *sb. Pyréthrum Parthénium*, common Feverfew. Com.

'. . . In English, *Fedderfew* and *Feuerfew* . . . . . It is vsed both in drinks, and bound to the wrists with bay salt, and the pouder of glasse stamped together, as a most singular experiment against the ague.'—GERARDE's *Herball*, Bk. ii. p. 653.

'*Fedyrfu* or fedyrfoy, herbe. *Febriffuga*.'—*Prompt. Parv.*

A.S. *feferfuge*, Feverfew, a herb. See *Featherfew*, E. D. S., C. ix.

FITHERS [fidh·ur'z], *sb. pl.*, *var. pr.* feathers. Com. 'Look sharp an' strip them *fithers*, I want 'em to put in a bouster.'

FITS AND GIRDS, *phr.* fits and starts.—PULVERBATCH; WELLINGTON; WEM; ELLESMERE. 'Theer's no 'eed to be tŏŏk o' that chap, 'e's all by *fits an' girds.*'

'By *fits and girds*, as an ague takes a goose.'
RAY'S *Proverbs*, p. 272.

Cf. **Hobs and Girds.**

FITTIES [fit·i'z], *sb. pl.* little feet: children's term. Com.

FITTLE, *sb.* victual.—CORVE DALE. See V (2) in **Grammar Outlines** (*consonants*).

FLABBOUS [flab·us], *adj.* a term applied to a slovenly, loose, ill-fitting garment.—MUCH WENLOCK. A coined word probably.

FLAG [flag·], *v. n.* to fade.—SHREWSBURY; PULVERBATCH. 'If yo' lăven them flowers i' the sun they'n *flag.*'

FLAG-BASKET, *sb.* a soft, flexible basket, made of *flags*—a generic term for *reeds*—chiefly used by workmen for carrying their tools in.—SHREWSBURY; PULVERBATCH. 'I've bought satchels an' made bags fur school till I'm tired, an' now I'll get a *flag-basket*, an' see if that'll las' 'em.' Cf. **Frail**, also **Budget.**

FLAKE [flai·k], *v. n.* to bask in the sun.—CLUN; ELLESMERE.—'I seed a ruck o' lads an' dogs *flakin'* o' that sunny bonk o'er-anunst the pentice' (Welshampton).

FLAKY-SPAR [flai·ki' spaa·r'], *sb. Calcic carbonate*, Calc-spar.—PULVERBATCH, *Snailbeach*; M. T. The local name given to this spar is very likely due to the manner in which its beautiful rhomboidal prisms sever or *flake.*

FLANNEN [flan·i'n], *sb.*, *var. pr.* flannel. Com.

'I wad na been surpris'd to spy
You on an auld wife's *flainen* toy.'
ROBERT BURNS, *Poems*, p. 74, l. 19, c. 2.

W. *gwlanen*, flannel; from *gwlan*, wool.

FLANS, *sb. pl.* stony pieces of coal that won't burn.—CLEE HILLS. 'No ŏŏnder theer's no fire, that coal's nuthin' i' the world but *flans.*' Cf. **Bass.**

FLAP, *sb.* a tea-crumpet. — SHREWSBURY; PULVERBATCH; WEM. 'I went to see the poor owd Missis las' wik, an' fund 'er busy makin' *flaps*, so I buttered 'em off the bak'stwun, an' we'd'n a rar' joram, an' a good bit o' cant into the bargain.' Molly Preece of Church Pulverbatch, who followed the calling of a crumpet-maker [1838], was generally known in her neighbourhood as *Pally Flap.* See **Flap-jack**, below. Cf. **Pikelets.**

FLAP-JACK, same as **Flap**, above.—COLLIERY.

'*First Fisherman.* . . . . . . Come, thou shalt go home, and we'll have flesh for holidays, fish for fasting days, and moreo'er puddings and *flap-jacks*; and thou shalt be welcome.'—*Pericles*, II. i. 87.

Flap-jack appears to be generally glossed *pancake.* See NARES and HALLIWELL.

FLASH [flash·], *sb.* a shallow pool of water left after heavy rains or floods.—CLUN; ELLESMERE; OSWESTRY.

'*Flasshe*, watyr. *Lacuna*, CATH. Plasche, or *flasche*, where reyne watyr stondythe (or pyt).' '. . . . The following distinction is here made: Plasche, flasche, or broke: *Torrens, lacuna.* Plasche, or flasch after a rayne: *Colluvio, colluvium*.'—*Prompt. Parv. and Notes.*

FLATS, *sb. pl.* same as **Feerings**, q. v.—WHITCHURCH.

FLAT-STONE, a measure of iron-stone.—COLLIERY; M. T.

FLAX, *sb. Curruca cinerea*, common Whitethroat.—NEWPORT. Cf. **Jack-straw**. See **Hay-tick**.

FLAY [flai·], (1) *v. a.* to pare the turf off grass land. Com. See **Flaying-spade**, below.

(2) *sb.* part of a plough: it goes before the coulter, and pares off the surface of the ground, turning it under the furrow which the plough makes, and so burying grass or weeds more effectually than could otherwise be done. Com. 'Be sure an' pŭt the *flay* dip enough to cover it under.'

'Iron wheel plough with *flay*.'—*Auctioneer's Catalogue* (Stoddesden), 1870. Cf. **Skelp**.

FLAYING-SPADE, *sb., obs.*? an implement for paring off the surface of rough grass land for burning.—WHITCHURCH, *Tilstock*. The *flaying-spade* is about nine inches broad and three inches deep; it is slightly curved and 'dishing' in shape. The handle, which is about four feet in length, is made of a rude stick naturally formed for adaptation to the purpose of working the implement, that is, after the manner of a 'breast plough.' See **Betting-iron**.

FLEAK [flek·], *sb.* a hurdle. — OSWESTRY. '*Hec cratis*, a flek.' *Nominale*, xv. cent., in Wr. vocabs., vol. i. p. 234.

'*Fleyke*, or hyrdylle, *Plecta, flecta, cratis*.'—*Prompt. Parv.* See Way's note. 'O.Icel. *fleki*; O.Du. *vlaek*, fleak (flaik), hurdle,' in STRAT.

FLECKED [flek·t], *part. adj., obsols.* spotted; streaked.—PULVERBATCH. 'Ah! it wuz pretty down i' the Glibe [*Glebe*]; I could a stopt theer all day to watch the little prill, an' look at the grass *flecked* ŏŏth sunshine through the trees, an' think 'ow we wun used to swingle theer.' The *Glebe* here spoken of is the beautiful wooded dell—through which a brook 'flows on, for ever, ever'—situated between Churton and Castle Place.

'. . . . . and wonderful foules,
With *flekked* fetheres · and of fele coloures.'
Piers Pl., Text B., pass. xi. l. 321.

'The grey-eyed morn smiles on the frowning night,
Chequering the eastern clouds with streaks of light,
And *flecked* darkness like a drunkard reels
From forth day's path, and Titan's fiery wheels.'
Romeo and Juliet, II. iii. 3.

Cf. Du. *vlek*, a spot; whence *vlekken*, to spot.

FLED [fled·], (1) *pret.* and *part. past.* flew; flown. Com. 'The 'en *fled* across the path.' 'The cork's *fled* out o' the bottle.'

'And than anone one of the byrdes *fledde* fro the tree to saynt Brandon.'—*The Golden Legend*, ed. Wynkyn de Worde. Publications of Percy Society, 1844.

(2) *part. past.* taken; gone: as of crops—roots or cereals—that from fly, worm, or other causes have failed either wholly or in part. Com. 'They'n be a poor crop o' turmits; they bin most on em *fled*, an' the rest looken despert simple.'

(3) *part. past.* gone; faded: as of colour.—SHREWSBURY; PULVERBATCH. Qy. com. 'I doubt it ŏŏnna be sarviceable; I'd a gownd summat like it wunst, an' the colour all *fled* afore ever it wuz wesht.'

FLEETINGS [flee·tinz], *sb. pl.* same as **Cruds**, q. v.—WHITCHURCH, *Cheshire Border.* In the process of preparation, the *fleetings* rise to the surface of the whey, and are then skimmed off, whence the term.

'To *fleet*, or skim the cream, is a verb still commonly used in East Anglia, and the utensil which serves for the purpose is termed a *fleeting*-dish. "I *flete* mylke, take away the creame that lyeth above it whan it hath rested."—PALSG. "*Esburrer*, to fleet the creame potte; *laict esburré*, fleeted milke; *maigne*, fleeted milke, or wheye." —Hollyband's Treasurie. "*Escremé*, fleeted, as milke, uncreamed." —COTG. A.S. flet, *flos lactis*.'—WAY, in *Prompt. Parv.*, p. 166.

FLEM [flem·], *sb.* a mill-stream, *i. e.* the channel of water from the main stream to the mill, below which the streams reunite.—SHREWSBURY; PULVERBATCH. 'We wenten smack into another "trap" [vehicle] jest on the *flem* bridge at the Hook-a-gate; it's a great ŏŏnder them or us didna gŏŏ o'er into it.' *Flem* is a corrupt form of *flum*, an old word found in the early writers. The expression 'the *flum* Jordan' occurs in the *Story of Genesis and Exodus* [A.D. 1230, *circa*], ed. Morris, l. 806, E. E. T. S. *Flum* also occurs in *Layamon*, l. 542, and *Ormulum*, l. 10342 (both about A.D. 1200). It is probably O.Fr. *flum*, from Lat. *flumen*, a river. Cf. *Flam* in E. D. S., B. xiv. See **Bylet.**

FLEN [flen·], *sb. pl.* fleas.—SHREWSBURY; PULVERBATCH; BISHOP'S CASTLE; CLUN; CORVE DALE; CLEE HILLS. Qy. com. in S. Shr. 'I couldna sleep for the *flen*; I wuz scroutin at 'em all night.'

> 'Awake, thou cook,' quod he, 'god yeue the sorwe,
> What eyleth the to slepe by the morwe?
> Hastow had *fleen* al nyght, or artow dronke?'
>
> CHAUCER, H. 17 (Six-text ed.), Skeat.

Old Munslow of the Thresholds, Salop, a well-known local 'character' in his day—about 1820—was wont to say 'as God made the ŏŏnts, but the devil made the rots an' *flen*.' He held a singular persuasion that the Supreme Being created only what was good and useful; and that to the Prince of Darkness might be ascribed the existence of all that was the reverse of these. Hence his dictum upon the '*rots an' flen*.' A.S. *fleá*, pl. *fleán*. Cf. **Fluff.** See **Ŏŏnt.**

FLESH-FORK, *sb.* a long, two-pronged, iron fork for getting up meat out of a pot or caldron—the prongs are curved at the end.—PULVERBATCH. Qy. com. 'Dick s'ore 'e could ate more poncake than we could'n stick the *flesh-fork* throu'.' Compare 1 *Sam.* ii. 13, 14, where the *flesh-hook* is said to have 'three teeth.' *Flesh-hook* occurs in Chaucer:—

'Ful hard it is, with *fleischhok* or with eules
To ben yclawed, or brend, or i-bake.'
Sompnour's Tale, 7312, in *Bible Word-Book*.

FLESH-MEAT, *sb.* butcher's meat. Com. 'Pŭddin' an' pancake's all very well wunst an' a way, but theer's nuthin' like a good dinner o' *flesh-mate* fur satisfyin' the stomach, as I 'eärd a lickle girld say w'en 'er wuz stuck ŏŏth 'er pancake—"Oh dear! throat full an' belly empty!"'

FLIGGY [flig·i'], (1) *adj.* birds whose down is changing to feathers are said to be *fliggy*.—CLEE HILLS.

'. . . . it is reported, the seid sone hath geve gret sylver to the Lords in the north to bryng the matier a bowte, and now he and alle his olde felaweship put owt their fynnes, and arn ryght *flygge* and mery, hopyng alle thyngis and shalbe as they wole have it.'—*Paston Letters*, A.D. 1461, vol. i. p. 544.

'*Flygge* as bryddis. *Maturus, volatilis.* "Flyggenesse of byrdes, *plumevseté*."—PALSG. A.S. *fliógan*, volare; *flyge*, fuga.'—*Prompt. Parv. and Notes.* Cf. **Flush** (1).

(2) *adj.* birds when imperfectly plucked are said to be *fliggy*.—CLEE HILLS.

(3) *adj.* very light in the crop and small in the ear; said of grain.—PULVERBATCH; CLEE HILLS; WEM; ELLESMERE. 'W'y it ŏŏnna stond to the scythe, it's so nation *fliggy*.' Cf. **Lathy** (2).

(4) *adj.* soft, as from saturation.—WEM. 'Trăpsin' about i' the wet's made my boots as *fliggy* as con be.'

FLIGHT [flei·t], (1) *sb.* a crop.—CLEE HILLS; CLUN; LUDLOW. 'Theer'll be another *flight* o' mushrooms after a bit.' Cf. **Hit**.

(2) a family.—PULVERBATCH; CLEE HILLS; WEM. ''E married agen, an' now theer's a second *flight*.'

FLINT-COAL, *sb.* It will be seen by reference to **Coal-field** and **Coal-names**, pp. 90, 91, that there are two seams of *Flint-coal*, which are distinguished as *Big* and *Little*: the former is a 'good burning coal,' the latter a 'good smelting coal.'

'"The Big Flint" has no characteristic fossil, but the "Little Flint" has imbedded in it the stems of *Stigmaria*, composed of sandstone. The rock overlying it also contains similar specimens.'—From *Notes on the Shropshire Coal-Field*, by T. PARTON, F.G.S., 1868.

FLISKEY [flis·ki'], *sb.* a slovenly, ill-dressed woman.—WHITCHURCH. ''Er's an owd *fliskey* as ever wuz seed.'

FLIT [flit·], *v. n.* to remove from one house to another; to change the abode.—SHREWSBURY; NEWPORT; WHITCHURCH; ELLESMERE. Qy. com.

'Thow sall haiff leiff to fysche, and tak the ma;
All this forsuth sall in our *flyttyng* ga.
We serff a lord; thir fysche sall till him gang.'
HENRY THE MINSTREL (A.D. 1461, *circa*), *Wallace*, Bk. I.
Specim. Eng. Lit., l. 396.

'To *flitte* from place to place is no poyncte of lightenesse of man;

but an euident signe of the charitee, that suche as folowe the steppes of the Apostles ought to haue.'—UDAL's *Erasmus* [1548], *Luke*, fol. 51 *b*, in *Bible Word-Book*.

'Wi' tentie care I'll *flit* thy tether
To some hain'd rig,
Whare ye may nobly rax your leather,
Wi' sma' fatigue.'
ROBERT BURNS, *Poems*, p. 54, l. 15, c. 2.

'*Flyttiñ* or remevyñ (away).' —*Prompt. Parv.* Dan. *flytte*,—*Idem.* Cf. **Shift** (4).

FLITCHEN [flich·i'n], (1) *sb.* a flitch of bacon. Com. 'I shall tak' a *flitchen* an' a couple o' 'ams to the nex' far; they'n sell well now that the green pase bin comen in.'

'Fower *flitchins* of bacon and Martlemas beef.'—*Inventory*, Stratford on Avon MSS., in WR.

(2) *sb.* a fat child, or over-fed person. Com. 'Inna-d-e gotten a great *flitchen*?'

FLITTER-MOUSE, *sb. Pleiótus communis*, the Long-eared Bat.—WEM.

'And giddy *flitter-mice* with leather wings.'
BEN JONSON, *Sad Shepherd*, ii. 8, in Nares.

Cf. **Bit-bat**, also **Leather-bat**.

FLOAT, *v. a.* to irrigate meadow-land by means of sluices and flood-gates. Com. 'Owd Mrs. Byuman [Beamond] wuz a reg'lar mănikin; I've sid 'er ŏŏth a noud red cloak on, *floatin'* the Barn meadow w'en it wunna fit fur no ŏŏman to be out.'

FLOATING-SHOVEL, *sb.*, *obsols.*? a long, narrow spade used for draining purposes: it is about three inches longer, and two and a half inches narrower, in the blade than an ordinary spade is.—PULVERBATCH. Cf. **Grafting-tool** (2).

FLOMMUCKY [flum·u'ki'], *adj.* slovenly; ill-dressed.—SHREWSBURY; WORTHEN. 'A *flommucky* sort o' ŏŏman.'

FLUES [floo·z], *sb. pl.* farriers' lancets. Qy. com. This term is always used in the plural form. The *flues* consist of several lancets, varying in size, which close into a 'haft' like the blades of a pocket-knife.—See **Blood-stick**.

FLUFF [fluf·], (1) *sb.* a flea.—CHURCH STRETTON; WEM; ELLESMERE. Generally heard in the plural form *fluffs*. A.S. *fleá*, a flea. Cf. **Flen.**

(2) *v. a.* to clean from fleas, as dogs and cats do.—*Ibid.* 'The dog's *fluffin'* 'imself.'

FLUMBRY [flum·br'i'], *sb.*, *var. pr.* flummery made from oats—thus: the oats, having been kiln-dried, are ground, husks and all; they are then soaked in water for three or four days till they become sour, after which the water is strained from them and boiled to a jelly. This is eaten with milk or beer, and even with wine 'amongst the betterly people.'—SHREWSBURY; CLUN. *Flumbry* seems to have been introduced by the Welsh, with whom, in many places, it is a staple article of food. W. *Llymru*, flummery.

FLUR, *sb.* a floor. See Oo (8) in **Grammar Outlines** (*vowels*, &c.).

FLUSH [flush·], (1) *adj.* fledged. Com. 'Tum knows to a thrustle's nist ŏŏth five young uns, but they binna *flush* yet.' Cf. **Fliggy** (1).

(2) *sb.* a show, as of early grass.—PULVERBATCH; WEM. 'I call it a lat spring, now close upon Maȳ-Daȳ, an' no grass—on'y a bit of a *flush*.'

(3) a sudden rise in a stream, such as would be caused by a thunder-storm a few miles up: it rapidly subsides, and thus differs from a flood.—SHREWSBURY; PULVERBATCH; WORTHEN; CLUN; WEM. 'Theer's a fine *flush* i' the Sivern; they'n ketcht it among the Welsh 'ills someweer.' Compare SPENSER's '*flushing* blood,' that is, flowing rapidly.—*F. Q.*, Bk. IV. c. vi. st. xxix. Cf. **Shut** (4).

(4) *adj.* liberal; lavish. Com. ''E's more *flush* ŏŏth 'is money than sense.'

(5) *sb.* a hand of cards all of one suit. Com. See for this, HAL.

FLUSKER [flus·kur'], (1) *v. n.* to hurry. Qy. com. 'I *fluskered* to get all done an' be ready for church.' *Flusker* would seem to be a corrupted form of *fluster*. O.Norse, *flaustr*, precipitancy; over-haste, in WEDG.

(2) *sb.* a state of confusion. Qy. com. 'I warrant if we bin in a *flusker* somebody's sure to come.'

FLUTTER [flut·ur'], *v. a.* to agitate; to confuse; to make nervous. Qy. com. 'I tell yo' whad—it inna a good thing to live athin crow o' the lan'lord's cock, fur on a busy day the Squire's aumust sure to come in, an' it *flutters* me till I dunna know whad I'm sayin' to 'im.'

(2) *sb.* a state of agitation, &c. Qy. com. 'It pŭt me all of a *flutter*.'

FLY-FLAP, *sb.* the 'clapper' used by butchers to hit flies with.—PULVERBATCH. Qy. com. 'I toud 'im whad wuz the matter; I come dab on 'im jest like a butcher's *fly-flap*.'

FLY-GANG, *sb.* a band of labourers who engage to do harvesting or other work for the farmers, and take it by the piece. The *fly-gang* is headed by a *gaffer*.—NEWPORT. See **Gaffer** (3). Cf. **Taskers**.

FOLLOW, *sb.*, *var. pr.* a fallow.—LUDLOW, *Burford*.

FOLLOWER, *sb.* a dairy utensil: it is used for pressing the curd in the cheese-vat.—CLEE HILLS.

'Cheese-vats, *followers*, and suitors.'—*Auctioneer's Catalogue* (Stoddesden), 1870.

FOOT [fut·], (1) *sb.* feet (of measure). Com. 'I want a bwurd about four *fut* lung pŭt by the back-dur fur the men's bottles.'

> 'Made hem to huppe · half an hundret *foote*,
> forte seche boþem · þer þei non seiȝen.'
>
> *Joseph of Aramathie*, l. 14.

(2) *sb.* the body of a plough.—WHITCHURCH. Qy. com.

> 'My *plow-fote* shal be my pyk-staf · and picche atwo þe rotes,
> And helpe my culter to kerue · and clense þe forwes.'
>
> *Piers Pl.*, Text B., pass. vi. l. 105.

The *plow-fote* of Piers the Plowman was not, however, the *body* of the plough, but was an appendage to the beam for regulating the depth to which the plough should enter the earth—'a staye to order of what depenes the ploughe should go.' See Mr. Skeat's *Notes* on *P. Pl.*, E. E. T. S., p. 161.

In the description of a plough in *The Treatise of Walter de Biblesworth*, close of xiii. cent., '*Le chef e le penoun*' is glossed 'the plouheved and the *foot*.'—WR. vocabs., vol. i. p. 168.

Amongst the seventeen 'Parts of a Plow' enumerated by Randle Holme is 'The *Foot*,' which, he says, 'is the piece of Hooked or Bended Wood, at the end of the Plow, under the Suck; which is to keep it from going too deep in the earth.'—*Academy of Armory*, Bk. III. ch. viii. p. 333.

FOOT-ALE, *sb.* ale given to the older workmen by an apprentice or 'new hand' as an entrance fee on taking his place amongst them. —PULVERBATCH; NEWPORT. Qy. com. 'Jack, yo' munna be away o' Monday, theer's two *fut-ales* to be paid.'

FOOTING, (1) *sb.* same as **Foot-ale**, above.—*Ibid.*

(2) *sb.* a fine demanded by craftsmen from gentlefolk who make experimental use of their implements of trade. Qy. com.

FOOTSOME [fut·sum], *sb.* neat's-foot oil.—PULVERBATCH; WORTHEN.

FORECAST [for'·kast], (1) *sb.* forethought. Com. '*For'cast* 's the best afe o' the work; if yo' dunna know whad yo' bin gweïn about, 'ow shan'ee know 'ow lung it'll tak'.'

'*Forecast* is better than work-hard.'
RAY'S *Proverbs*, p. 109.

(2) [for'kas·t], *v. a.* to plan beforehand; to contrive. Com. ''E hanna *for'casted* well, or 'e ŏŏdna a comen to a faut athisns.'

'Richard Eavans was never marryed, and I think hee had noe inclination that way, but lived as if hee designed to bee his owne heire, but did not *forecast* to keepe any thing to maintaine him if hee happened to live unto old age.'—GOUGH'S *History of Myddle*, p. 189.

'To *forecast*. Prospicere, prouidere, præcognoscere.' — BARET, *Alvearie* [1580], in *Bible Word-Book*.

'Dere broþer,' quaþ Peres · 'þe devell is ful queynte;
To encombren holy Churche · he casteþ ful harde,
And fluricheþ his falsnes · opon fele wise,
And for he *casteþ to-forn* · þe folke to destroye.'
P. Pl. Cr., l. 485.

'Of. *Caste* for to goōn, or purpose for to dōn' any othyr thynge.' —*Tendo, intendo*, in *Prompt. Parv.*

FORE-END [for'·end·'], (1) *sb.* the beginning of a week, month, or year.—ELLESMERE. Qy. com.

'. . . . . . . and, this twenty years,
This rock and these demesnes have been my world:
Where I have lived at honest freedom, paid

More pious debts to heaven than in all
The *fore-end* of my time.'—*Cymbeline*, III. iii. 73.

Cf. **Forrat-part.**

(2) *sb.* the fore-part of a thing—'the *for'-end* o' the waggin'.'—PULVERBATCH. Qy. com.

FOREIGNER [fur'·i'nur'], *sb.*, *pec.* a stranger; one who belongs to another neighbourhood or county.—CHURCH STRETTON. Qy. com. 'Dun'ee know who that mon is? I've sid 'im about this good wilde.' 'No, 'e's a *furriner* i' these parts; 'e's from 'ereford way they tellen me.'

'Upon this common [Haremeare] there is a great store of free stone very usefull for building. The inhabitants within the Mannor pay to the Lord one shilling for every hundred (that is six score) foot of stone, but *Forainers* paye one shilling and sixpence.'—GOUGH'S *History of Myddle*, p. 32.

FORE-TOKEN [for'·toa·'kn], *sb.*, *obsols.* a warning.—PULVERBATCH. 'Jack come wham star'in like a throttled ar, an' said 'e'd sid summat i' the Boggy-leasow glimmerin' like a pot o' brimston', an' it wuz sure to be a *for'-token*. The chaps persuaden 'im it wuz the Devil's lontun, an' frittened 'im out on 'is wits.' 'Well, it'll be a mighty good job if 'e tak's warnin', fur 'e's a despert gallus chap.'

'To loke yf he him wolde amende,
To him a *fore-token* he sende.'
GOWER, *MS. Soc. Antiq.* 134, f. 56, in HAL.

FORGOTTEN, *adj.* neglected; out of the way.—CORVE DALE. A very secluded little hamlet in 'the Dale' was described as a '*forgotten* kind of place.' Cf. **Forsaken**, below.

FORNICATE, *v. a.*, *pec.* to tell lies; to invent falsehoods = to forge. —SHREWSBURY; PULVERBATCH. Qy. com. 'It wus a downright lie, an' 'e can *fornicate* 'em as fast as a 'orse can trot.'

FORRAT [for'·u't], *adj.*, *var. pr.* forward; early. Com. 'John Griffi's 'as got a capital crop o' *forrat* 'tatoes—'e says they bin the best an' yarliest i' this country; 'e al'ays reckons to a new 'tatoes fur King Charlie' [May 29th].

'Yes! there is ane; a Scottish callan—
There's ane; come *forrit*, honest Allan!
Thou need na jouk behint the hallan,
A chiel sae clever.'
ROBERT BURNS, *Poems*, p. 114, l. 5, c. 2.

Cf. **Frum** (1).

FORRAT-PART, *phr.* same as **Fore-end** (1).—SHREWSBURY.

FORSAKEN, *adj.* a term chiefly applied to a very evil person, or a very remote place.—CORVE DALE. Cf. **Forgotten**, above.

FORSOOK, *pret.* for *part. past*, forsaken. Com.

'*Emil.* Hath she *forsook* so many noble matches,
Her father, and her country, and her friends?'
Othello, IV. ii. 125.

'. . . . . . what vast regions hold
The immortal mind that hath *forsook*
Her mansion in this fleshly nook.'
MILTON, *Il Penseroso*, l. 91.

FORTY-LEGS, *sb. Julus terrestris*, the common Millipede.—PULVERBATCH.

FORTY-SA'-ONE LIKE OBITCH'S COWT, *phr.* a common expression—heard with variations in different localities, as Roden or Rowson for *Obitch*—applied to persons of a 'certain age' who affect youthful manners. See **Grammar Outlines** (*adjectives of numeration*), p. xlv.

FOR'YED [for'·yed·'], *sb.*, *var. pr.* the forehead.—PULVERBATCH. Qy. com. 'Aye, I dar'say yore sorrow is summat like owd Tunkiss's, w'en 'e cried fur 'is wife tell the tears runnen up is *for'yed*.'

FOSSET [fos·i't], *sb.* a faucet.—SHREWSBURY; PULVERBATCH. Qy. com. 'I brewed a drop o' fresh drink i' the spigot-stean; ðŏn yo' be so good as len' me yore *fosset*, fur mine's split.'

'. . . you wear out a good wholesome forenoon in hearing a cause between an orange-wife and a *fosset*-seller.'—*Coriolanus*, II. i. 79.

'*Fausset*, petite brochette de bois, servant à boucher le trou que l'on fait à un tonneau. *Faucet* or peg.'—CHAMB. Cf. Lat. *fauces*.

FOT [fot·], *pret.* fetched.—NEWPORT. ''E *fot* a jug o' eel fur 'em.' 'Also he that tolde me this seid that it were better for yow to come up than to be *fotte* out of your house with streingth.'—*Paston Letters*, A.D. 1461, vol. ii. p. 54. Cf. **Fat.**

FOTHER [fodh·ur'], (1) *sb.* fodder, more especially *dry* food, such as hay, cut straw, &c. Com.

'For men, I've three mischievous boys,
Run de'ils for rantin' an' for noise;
A gaudsman ane, a thrasher t'other,
Wee Davock hauds the nowte in *fother*.'
ROBERT BURNS, *Poems*, p. 104, l. 37.

'*Alitudo*, fothur,' occurs in an A.S. *Vocabulary*, viii. cent., in Wr. vocabs., vol. ii. p. 100. 'A.S. *fóder*, *fódder*; O.Icel. *fóðr*; O.H. Germ. *fuotar*, fodder; *pabulum*.'—STRAT.

(2) *v. a.* to give horses and cattle their fodder. Com. 'W'y, Tum, whadever han 'ee bin doin'? yo' hanna gid them beäs' thar *fother*; an' yo' hanna littered anythin' as I can see. By gum! yo' bin bwun-lazy; our Maister ðŏl a to come an' *fother* 'em 'isself jest now.' The rule is to *fother* horses and cattle, *feed* sheep, and *serve* pigs. Cf. the following:—

'With her mantle tucked vp
Shee *fothered* her flocke.'
Percy Folio MS., *Loose Songs*, p. 58.

FOUD, *sb.* a farm-yard: the term is not restricted to any one part of a farm-yard; as, for instance, to a space bedded up for stock; but it comprehends the whole enclosure. Sometimes, but rarely, it is called 'the *fould*.' Com. 'They bin yarly folks; the cows bin milked an' out o' the *foud* every mornin' afore six.'

'The Garden [of the Parsonage House] containeing about the eighth parte of an acre; the Fowl yard containeing about the eighth parte of an acre; the yard containeing about a quarter of an acre; the *Fould* yarde containeing about the sixteenth parte of an acre.'—GOUGH'S *History of Myddle*, p. 21.

A.S. *fald*, a fold.

FOUGHTEN, *pret.* and *part. past*, fought.—NEWPORT. Qy. com. 'They stooden up an' *foughten* an' 'itten out like men; but they 'adna *foughten* manny minutes afore the Sergeant coom oop, an' they wun soon parted then.'

'William & his wiȝes · so wonderli *fouȝten*,
þat þei felden here fon · ful fast to grounde.'
William of Palerne, l. 3414.

'At mortal batailles hadde he ben fiftene,
And *foughten* for oure feith at Tramassene
In lystes thries, and ay slayn his foo.'
CHAUCER, *The Prologue*, l. 62, ed. Morris.

Cf. Shakespeare's 'well-*foughten* field.'—*K. Henry V.*, IV. vi. 18.

FOUL, *adj.* plain; homely of feature; ugly. Com. An old man who was towing a barge on the canal near Ellesmere, was met by a bevy of nice-looking girls; he courteously lowered the tow-line and stood on one side to make way for them, regarding them attentively, but with a most respectful air, as one by one they filed past him; then, as the last went by, he said, as if to himself, 'Well, w'ich way bin all the *foul* ones gwun this evenin', I wonder!'

'If thou be fair, ther folk ben in presence
Shew thou thy visage and thyn apparaille;
If thou be *foul*, be fre of thy dispence,
To gete thee frendes ay do thy trauaille;
Be ay of chere as lyght as leef on lynde,
And lat him care, and wepe, and wringe, and waille!'
CHAUCER, E. 1209 (Six-text ed.), Skeat.

'*Aud.* I am not a slut, though I thank the gods I am *foul.*'
As You Like It, III. iii. 39.

A.S. *fúl*, foul.

FOULS, *sb.* a sort of gathering in the cleft of the foot to which horned cattle are subject. Com. A.S. *fúl*, foul; corrupt. See Bk. II., *Folklore*, &c., 'Superstitious Cures.'

FOUR-CROSSES, *sb.* the point at which two roads intersect.—SHREWSBURY; ELLESMERE. Qy. com. At Bicton and at Baschurch respectively a public-house with the sign of the '*Four-Crosses*' marks the crossing of two roads [1878].

FOUR-O'-CLOCK [foo·h'r' u' klok], *sb.* the farm-labourers' meal between dinner and supper.—NEWPORT. An Edgmond plough-boy at a night-school—about 1867—spelt t, e, a—sounding the letters in the broad 'vernacular' of his class—and paused for the word. 'What do you have between dinner and supper?' said his teacher. '*Foor-o'-clock*,' was the very decided answer. 'But what does your mother have?' '*Tay*,' said the boy. Cf. **Onder's-bayte.**

FOUR-SQUARE [foa·ur' skwaa·r'], *adj.* quadrangular; square; cubical. Com. 'What box are you going to take with you, Price?' said a lady to her maid-servant. 'Only a bit on a wooden un, Ma'am—a *four-squar'* un,' said Price, at the same time showing her Mistress the box in question, which was literally 'square' on every side.

'Upon the same riuer [Thames] is placed a stone bridge, a worke verie rare and maruellous, which bridge hath (reckoning the draw bridge) twentie arches made of *foursquare* stone, of height threescore foote, and of breadth thirty foote, distant one from another twentie foote.'—STOW, *Annals*, p. 2 [A.D. 1601], in *Bible Word-Book.*

'O fall'n at length that tower of strength,
Which stood *four-square* to all the winds that blow!'
TENNYSON'S *Ode on the Death of the Duke of Wellington.*

See Exodus xxxviii. 1; Rev. xxi. 16. 'Fowre Square. *Quaarus.* —*Prompt. Parv.* Cf. **Three square.**

FOUSTY [fou·sti'], *adj., var. pr.* fusty; ill-smelling; unclean.— BRIDGNORTH. ''E smells *fousty*, as if 'e never weshed 'isself.'

'. . . . where the dull tribunes,
That, with the *fusty* plebeians, hate thine honours,
Shall say, against their hearts, "We thank the gods,
Our Rome hath such a soldier."'—*Coriolanus*, I. ix. 7.

Cf. **Frousty.**

FOX [fok·s], *sb. Vulpes vulgáris*, the Fox. Reynard is almost invariably spoken of by the rustic folk as '*The Fox;*' just as people generally say '*the* butcher,' '*the* tax-collector,' and so forth—they thus make a kind of personage of him. *A* stoat, *a* weasel, has committed depredations in the poultry-yard, but '*the* fox 'as bin i' the night an' töök all the young turkies.' Perhaps it is because Shropshire is so thoroughly a fox-hunting county that Reynard is honoured with this 'distinguishing adjective' as a mark of respect! See *Reynolds* in REV. W. D. PARISH'S *Dictionary of Sussex Dialect* [E. D. S.].

FOXES OR THE FI' FINGERS, *phr.* when a thing is believed to have been stolen, it is figuratively said that 'the *foxes or the fi' fingers* han got it.'—CORVE DALE.

FRAIL [fr'ei·l *corr.* fr'aay·l], *sb.* a workman's satchel made of 'rush' or some similar thing.—CLUN, *Hereford Border.*

'. . . . and take his felawe to witnesse,
What he fonde in a *freyel* · after a freres lyuynge.'
Piers Pl., Text B., pass. xiii. l. 94.

Mr. Skeat remarks on this: '*Freyel* is the Low Lat. *frælum*, a rush-basket or mat-basket, especially for containing figs and raisins. See "Frayle of frute, *Palata, carica*," in *Prompt. Parv.*, and Mr. Way's note. To the examples there given I can add the following:—"Bere out the duste in this figge-*frayle*, Asporta cinerem in hoc syrisco."— *Hormanni Vulgaria*, leaf 149. *Frail* is still used in Essex to mean a rush-basket, as noted by Mr. Jephson. Also in Kennett's *Parochial Antiquities* the glossary has "*Frayle*, a basket in which figs are brought from Spain and other parts." He cites the phrase "in uno *frayle* ficuum" from an account dated 1424-6. Palsgrave has "*Frayle* for fygges, *cabas, cabache*." See *cabas, cabasser*, in Cotgrave. Also *Babees Book*, ed. Furnivall, p. 200, note to l. 74.' Cf. **Flag-basket.**

FRAISE [fr'ai·z], *sb., obs.* a kind of pancake eaten with sweet sauce: it was thicker than the ordinary pancake, and made with a 'stiffer' batter.—CLEE HILLS, *Stoddesden.*

> 'For fritters, pancakes, and for *frayses*,
> For venison pasties, and minst pies.'
>
> *How to Choose a Good Wife*, 1634, in HAL.

'*Hoc frixum*, a froys,' occurs in a *Nominale*, xv. cent., in Wr. vocabs., vol. i. p. 242. Mr. Wright has the following note upon it:—'A *froise* was a sort of pancake. The word is still used in the dialect of the eastern counties. It appears to have been a favourite dish with the monks; for Gower (*Conf. Amant.*, vol. ii. p. 92), describing the troubled sleep of Sompnolence, says—

> "Whan he is falle in suche a dreme,
> Right as a ship ayein the streme
> He routeth with a slepy noise,
> And brustleth as a monkes *froise*,
> Whan it is throwe into the panne."'

See Bk. II., *Folklore*, &c., 'Customs connected with Days and Seasons' (*Mid-lent Sunday*).

FRANG [fr'ang·], *sb.* a very broad iron fork used for getting in coal, loading potatoes, &c.—CLEE HILLS. Cf. **Frank** (1), below.

FRANGY [fr'anj·i'], *adj.* restive; impatient of restraint; said of horses chiefly.—SHREWSBURY; PULVERBATCH. Qy. com. 'The mar' seems *frangy* this mornin'.' 'Aye, 'er dunna like lävin' the cowt; 'er ŏŏnna let the grass grow under 'er fit in comin' back.'

FRANK [fr'ang·k], (1) *sb.* same as **Frang**, above.—LUDLOW (not common); WEM.

(2) *v. a.* to throw or scatter about, as of manure, hay, &c.—LUDLOW. 'E's *frankin'* it all about.'

FRANT [fr'an·t], (1) *sb.* a fit of violent passion in a child; a state of extreme irritability in an older person.—PULVERBATCH; WORTHEN; CORVE DALE. 'What's the matter with baby?' ''E's on'y in a *frant*, Ma'am, 'cause the cat ŏŏnna be mauled.'

(2) *v. n.* to kick and scream with passion.—*Ibid.* ''Ow the child *frants*.'

FRATCHETY [fr'ach·i'ti'], *adj.* peevish; irritable.—MUCH WENLOCK; NEWPORT. See *Fracchyñ*, and Way's note on it, in *Prompt. Parv.*, p. 175. Cf. **Fretchet.**

FREE, *adj.* frank; generous; affable. Com. 'A more *freeer*, 'onourabler, comfortabler young fellow than Edward Breeze wus never in company.' So said a man travelling in a 'Market-train' from Shrewsbury to Hanwood [1871].

> 'þe feiȝtful & *fre* · & euer of faire speche,
> & seruisabul to þe simple · so as to þe riche.'
>
> *William of Palerne*, l. 337.

'Also I prey yow to recomand me in my most humbyll wyse unto the good Lordshepe of the most corteys, gentylest, wysest, kyndest, most compenabyll, *freest*, largeest, most bowntesous Knyght, my Lord the Erle of Arran, whych hathe maryed the Kyngs sustyr of Scotland.' —*Paston Letters*, A.D. 1472, vol. iii. p. 47.

A.S. *freó*; Germ. *frei*, free. Cf. **Free-spoken**, below.

FREE-HOLLY, *sb.* the smooth, upper foliage of *Ilex Aquifólium*, common Holly.—LUDLOW, *Burford*. None but *Free-holly* is used by the Burford folk for decorating their houses at Christmas-tide [1874].

FREE-OUDER, *sb.*, *var. pr.*, *pec.*, *obs.*? a free-holder, *i. e.* a land-owner, in contradistinction to a tenant. — PULVERBATCH. 'Who 'ad'n'ee at the *free-ouders*' meetin' 'isterd'y?' 'Well, we'd'n Mr. Jackson, Mr. Freme, an' the two Jondrells—nod furgettin' owd John Hughes, the thatcher.'

FREE-SPOKEN, *adj.* frank; candid; unreserved, in address. Com. Milton employs this term—'*Free-spoken* and plain-hearted men.'

FRENCH BROOM [fr'en·sh br'um], *sb.* *Cytisus Laburnum.* — PULVERBATCH. Cf. **Golden showers**. See **Brum** (1).

FRENCH NETTLE, *sb.* *Lamium purpúreum*, red Dead-nettle.—WHITCHURCH, *Tilstock*. Cf. **Dun-nettle**.

FRESH, (1) *adj.* intoxicated; exhilarated with drink—'not drunken, nor sober, but neighbour to both.' Com. ''Ow did the Maister come wham las' night?' 'Oh, on'y jest *fresh*—a bit markit-peärt, nuthin' more.' Cf. Eng. *frisk*, *frisky*, from A.S. *fersc*; O.N. *friskr*.

(2) *adj.* in good condition, as of a beast when half fatted.—PULVERBATCH; WEM. Qy. com. 'Wun them bŭllocks fat?' 'Well, nod very, considerin' they wun perty *fresh* w'en they wun pŭt'n up.'

FRESH-DRINK, *sb.* table-beer. Com. 'I never pŭt above a strike an' 'afe o' maut to them two barrels, an' it mak's nice peärt *fresh-drink*.' See **Drink**.

FRETCHET [fr'ech·it], *adj.* peevish; irritable. Com. 'I wish as the weather ŏŏd clier up to lug that corn, fur it's makin' the Maister deepert *fretchit*.' A.S. *fretan*, to fret.

FRILL [fr'i'l·], *sb.* a piece of fleshy fat surrounding the entrails of a pig: it has the appearance of being puckered like a frill, whence its name. Com. Margaret Penlington of Welshampton described the *frill* as 'a piece of rumfled fat rōw'ded wuth red.' See *frill* in WEDG.

FRITTEN [fr'it·n], *v. a.*, *var. pr.* to frighten. Com. A.S. *áfyrhtan*. —*Idem*.

FRITTENIN [fr'it·ni'n], *sb.* a ghost; an apparition.—ELLESMERE; WEM. 'I darna gŏŏ past Coomur [Colemere] lane ends—folks sen as theer's *frittenin* to be seed theer after dark.'

FROD, *sb.* ice-rubbish; as *ground-ice*, which rises to the surface of the Severn; or *drift-ice*, which comes down the stream.—BRIDGNORTH. O.Fr. froit; froid, *frigidus*.—BUR.

FROG-STOOLS, *sb. pl.* 'toad-stools'—some of the species *Agaricus.*—SHREWSBURY; PULVERBATCH. Qy. com. 'Aye, theer'll be no mushrooms this 'ear, now the *frog-stools* bin comin'.'

FROMMET [fr'om·u't], (1) *prep., var. pr., obsols.* in a direction going straight *from* a place; *fromward* as opposed to *toward.*—PULVERBATCH. 'W'eer wun yo' w'en yo' sid'n me?' 'W'y I wuz gweïn *frommet* the stack-yurd *töërt* the cow-'us.'

'Give ear to my suit, Lord; *fromward* hide not Thy face.'—*Paraphrase of Psalm lv.*, by Earl of Surrey.

'Varying up and down, *towards* or *fromwards* the zenith.'—Cheyne, in TODD'S *Johnson.*

See 'The Suffix "*-ward*,"' N. & Q. [5th S. x. 521]. A.S. *fromweardes*, from without; beyond.

(2) *adj.* right hand (off-side)—a harvest-field term.—PULVERBATCH; CLEE HILLS. *Töërt* is left hand, thus, suppose the waggon loaded and ready to be bound, the man on the top calls 'ropes,'—the ropes are thrown up to him. 'W'eer ŏŏn'ee 'ave it?' he asks of the men on the ground; the reply is, 'Put it down the *frommet* way.' He throws it from his *left* hand instead of *right.* 'Theer, now yo'n chucked it down the *töërt* way.'

FRONT [fr'un·t], *v. n.* to plump; to swell, as young tender meat does in cooking.—PULVERBATCH; CLEE HILLS; WEM. 'I knowed well enough it wuz owd mutton w'en I sid it i' the pot—it didna *front* a bit.' Jamieson has 'To *front*' in this sense.

FROST-KETCHEN, *part. adj.* frost-bitten. Com.

FROST-NAILS, *sb. pl.* spike-headed nails put into horses' shoes to prevent them slipping on frozen, icy roads. Com.

'*Frost-Nails*, with sharp pointed heads.'—*Academy of Armory*, Bk. III. ch. iii. p. 89. See **Roughed.**

FROTHY [fr'oth·i'], *adj.* light in the ear: said of wheat that has suffered from blight.—LUDLOW, *Cleobury Mortimer.* Cf. **Fliggy** (3).

FROTING [fr'oat·in], *part. adj., obs.?* a thorough house-cleaning—'rubbing up' and 'scrubbing down.'—PULVERBATCH. 'We mun pŭt the spinnin'-w'ĕel by now till after Maÿ-Daÿ; nex' wik theer'll be the buckin' an' the pewter clānin', an' then a reg'lar *frotin'* from the top to the bottom.'

'Hee unclosed þe caue · unclainte þe barres,
And straihte into þe stede · stroked hym fayre.
Hee raught forthe his right hand · & his rigge *frotus*,
And coies hym as he kan. . . . .'

K. Alisaunder, l. 1174.

'Al þe longage of þe Norþhumbres, & specialych at ȝork, ys so scharp, slyttyng & *frotyng*, & vnschape, þat we Souþeron men may þat longage vnneþe vnderstonde.'—JOHN OF TREVISA (A.D. 1387), *Description of Britain. Specim. Early Eng.*, xviii. *a*, l. 209.

O.Fr. frotter de [Lat.], *fricare.*—BUR.

FROUSTY [fr'ou·sti'], *adj.* dull; heavy-looking, as from lack of sleep; half awake; not half washed.—PULVERBATCH. Qy. com. 'W'y yo' looken as sleepy an' *frousty* this mornin' as if yo' 'adna bin i' bed las' night; gŏŏ an' swill yore face ŏŏth some cowd waiter, it'll mak' yo' 'afe as sharp an' sweet agen.' Cf. **Frousty.**

FRUM [fr'um·], (1) *adj.* forward; early ripe. — PULVERBATCH; WORTHEN; CORVE DALE; WEM. 'Them bin a capital sort o' 'tatoes, the *frum* kidneys.' A.S. *frum-ripe*, early ripe.

(2) *adj.* strong; heavy, as of a crop, or of corn in the ear.—ELLESMERE, *Welshampton.* 'That crop i' the Breäry Craft's a rar' *frum* un, it'll ild a mizzer an' 'afe to the thrave.' A.S. *fram*, *from*, strong; vigorous. Cf. Germ. *fromm*, excellent.

FRUMP, *sb.* a contemptuous term for an old woman who affects youthful airs and dress.—PULVERBATCH.

FRUMPED, *part. adj.* tricked out in youthful fashion, as of an old woman.—*Ibid.* 'The owd girld wuz *frumped* up like a yeow dressed lomb fashion.'

FRY [fr'ei·], (1) *sb.* a swarm of kinsfolk.—PULVERBATCH. 'Well, I'm right glad them folks bin gwe'in out of our parish, we sha'n be rid o' the ool [whole] *fry*; I should think Ponsert 'ill ŏŏd be best fur them.'

'And them before the *fry* of children yong
Their wanton sportes and childish mirth did play.'
SPENSER, *F. Q.*, Bk. I. c. xii. st. vii.

'What a *fry* of fools is here!'—*Beaumont and Fletcher.*

Bailey—ed. 1782—has '*Fry*, a multitude; a company.'

(2) *sb.* the liver and lights of a pig dressed by *frying.* Com. 'The men bin mighty fond o' *fry;* w'en yo'n cut whad'll do fur dinner sen' the rest to poor owd Molly.' Ash has '*Fry*, from the verb, a dish of anything fried.' Cf. **Harslet.**

FUKE [feu·k], *sb.*, *obsols.?* a stray lock of hair.—PULVERBATCH. 'I wish yo'd'n put that *fuke* o' yar out o' yore eyes; yo' looken jest like a muntin [mountain] cowt.' '*Fukes*, the Locks of the Head. O[ld].'—BAILEY, ed. 1727. A.S. *feax*, hair of the head.

FULL [ful·], *adv.*, *pec.* quite. Com. 'This'll do *fŭll* as well.'

'. . . The first suit is hot and hasty, like a Scotch jig, and *full* as fantastical.'—*Much Ado about Nothing*, II. i. 79.

(2) *sb.*, *var. pr.* fill; sufficiency; generally applied to drink. ''E's 'ad 'is *full*,' i.e. he has had as much as he can take without becoming intoxicated.—SHREWSBURY. Qy. com.

'With the grace of God, or hyt were nyghte,
The yeant had his *fulle* of fyghte.'
MS. *Cantab.*, Ff. ii. 38, f. 66, in HAL.

FULLAR [ful·ur'], *sb.* the tool employed to make a *fullaring* with. See below.

FULLARING, *sb.* the groove in a horse-shoe into which the nails are inserted.—PULVERBATCH. Qy. com.

FULLOCK [ful·uk], *v. n.* to shoot a marble in an irregular way by jerking the fist forward instead of hitting it off by the force of the thumb only. Qy. com. 'Oh, that inna far; 'e's *fullockin'*.' When shooting marbles at 'ring-taw' the closed hand is rested on the ground, and the marble projected by the thumb acting upon it like a spring: to *fullock* is then considered dishonourable, but it is allowed in 'long-taw' when aiming at a single marble. Cf. *Fullock*, E. D. S., C. ii.

FUME [feu·m], *v. n., pec.* to inflame.—PULVERBATCH; WEM; ELLESMERE. 'It was on'y a bit on a briar-scrat, an' it tŏŏk to *fume* an' swelled all up 'is arm.'

FUMEY, *adj.* hasty; passionate.—*Ibid.* 'The Maister's as *fumey* as the mouth o' the oven this mornin'; yo' mun mind 'ow yo' dailen ŏŏth 'im.'

'*Fumer de colère*, to fume; to be in a rage.'—CHAMB.

FUND [fun·d], *pret.* and *part. past*, found. Com. 'I've bin after the mushroms sence afore five o'clock this mornin'.' 'Han 'ee *fund* any?' 'Aye, a right good tuthree; but the best part on 'em I *fund* i' the uvver leasow.'

'Til þat he haueden godard *funde*,
And brouth biforn him faste bunde.'
Havelok the Dane, l. 2376.

See DR. MORRIS'S *Historical English Accidence*, p. 161 (5).

FUNDLESS, *sb., obsols.*? a thing accidentally found.—PULVERBATCH. 'I 'ad sich a *fundless* this mornin'.' ''Ad'n'ee; whad did'n'ee find?' 'W'y I fund our paas'n's pus, an' 'e gid me 'afe-a-crownd fur the findin'.' Cf.—

'& þouȝh he as *fundeling* where founde · in þe forest wilde.'
William of Palerne, l. 502.

FUNGUS COAL, *sb.* the coal which bears this name is chiefly confined to the north of the field, and is good for nearly every purpose. —COLLIERY; M. T. See **Coal-names**.

FUNNY, *adj.* bad; capricious: said of the temper. Com. ''Er's a nice sort of girld enough, but 'er's got a *funny* temper.'

FUR, *sb.* (1) the indurated sediment found in the bottom of tea-kettles. Com. 'The kettle's got a *fur* inside a ninch thick.'

(2) *adv., var. pr.* far: the 'degrees' are *furder*, *furdest*.—LUDLOW. See Th (3) in **Grammar Outlines** (*consonants*). Cf. **Fare** (2).

FURNACE [fur'·nis], *sb.* the large boiler used in brewing. Com. 'Sixty gallon brewing *furnace*, grate and fittings.'—*Auctioneer's Catalogue* (Church Stretton), 1877.

'*Hec fornax-eis An*[m] a fornys,' occurs under the head of '*Panducsator cum suis Instrumentis*,' in a *Pictorial Vocabulary*, xv. cent., in Wr. vocabs., vol. i. p. 276.

FURNAIG [fur'nai·g], *v. n., obsols.*? to revoke at cards.—PULVERBATCH.

FUSSOCK [fus·uk], *sb.* a big, dirty, greasy woman.—PULVERBATCH; WEM. '’Er's a reg'lar owd *fussock*.'

FUSTIAN BLANKETS, *sb. pl.*, *obs.* 'One payre of gersy blanketts, one payre of *fustian blanketts*,' are items of an *Inventory* taken at Owlbury Manor-House, Bishop's Castle, 1625. *Fustian blankets* are said to be identical with the homespun blankets made as late as the beginning of the present century, which were a mixture of wool and 'herdes' [rough hemp]. One of these blankets—the yarn for which was spun by Alice Fletcher, of Castle Pulverbatch, in 1804—shows that the warp was of 'herdes,' the woof of wool. It is of thick and warm, but somewhat coarse, texture, and of a 'whitey-brown' colour, the wool being unbleached.

Fustian blankets are of frequent mention in old inventories, as, for instance, that of '*Sir John Fastolf's Wardrobe*,' A.D. 1459. 'Item, ij *fustian blanketts*, every of hem vj webbys.'—*Paston Letters*, vol. i. p. 482. See **Jarsey Hillin'**.

FUTHER [fudh·ur'], *v. n.* to fuss or fidget about.—SHREWSBURY.

FUZZ-BALL, *sb. Lycoperdon Bovista.*—WELLINGTON; NEWPORT.

'*Tubera terra.* Fusse-balls or Puckfists. *Fusse-balls* are no way eaten: the pouder of them doth dry without biting: it is fitly applied to merigalls, kibed heeles, and such like.

'The dust or pouder hereof is very dangerous for the eyes, for it hath been often seen, that diuers haue been pore-blinde euer after, when some small quantitie thereof hath been blowne into their eyes.

'The countrey people do vse to kill or smother Bees with these *Fusse-balls* being set on fire, for the which purpose it fitly serueth.'—GERARDE's *Herball*, Bk. III. p. 1584.

Cf. **Blind-ball**, also **Devil's Snuff-box**.

GABY [gai·bi'], *sb.* a simpleton; one who gapes and stares about in ignorant wonder.—LUDLOW; WEM.

'Dan. *gabe*, to gape; *gabe paa*, to stare at. N. *gape*, to stare, to gape; *gap*, a simpleton.'—WEDG. Cf. **Gauby**.

GAFFER [gaf·ur'], (1) *sb.*, *obsols.* a title given to an aged father or grandfather—and of address, equivalent to 'Master,' the head of a house. The term as thus applied is one of perfect respect.—CLUN, *Hereford Border*. Cf. **Buffer**.

(2) *sb.*, *obsols.* a synonym for 'Mr.' or 'Sir' in the same locality. *Gaffer*, according to Mr. Halliwell, 'was formerly a common mode of address,' meaning '*friend, neighbour*.'

'"O, why do you shiver and shake, *Gaffer* Grey?
And why does your nose look so blue?"
"'Tis the weather that's cold,
And I'm grown very old,
And my doublet is not very new;
Well-a-day!"'—*Old Song*.

Bailey—ed. 1727—gives, '*Gaffer*, a Country Appellation for a Man.'

(3) *sb.* a head workman; the foreman of a band of labourers—as of harvest-men—who makes the agreement as to the terms of their work. Com. See **Fly-gang.**

GAFFIN [gaf·in], *part. adj.* jesting; bantering.—PULVERBATCH, *Hanwood.* 'Never yo' 'eed 'im, 'e's on'y *gaffin* a bit.'

GAFTY [gaf·ti'], *adj.* sly; tricky.—WEM; ELLESMERE. ''E's sich a *gafty* chap, yo' never knowen whad's the nex' thing 'e'll be after.'

GAIN [gai·n *and* gaay·n], (1) *adj.* near; short; direct.—SHREWSBURY; PULVERBATCH. 'My man, can you tell me the best way to the Hills from here [Stapleton]? I understand there's a coursing match there to-day.' 'Well, sir, the *gainest* waÿ ŏŏd be the Squire's bridle-roäd, it'll tak' yo' up to Wilderley as straïght as the crow flies; but yo' mun mind, sir, to keep to the wickets; nod throu' gates, or be'appen yo'n be landed in a ŏŏd.'

> 'At a posterne forth they gan to ryde
> By a *geyn* path, that ley oute a side.'
> JOHN LYDGATE (A.D. 1420, *circa*), *The Storie of Thebes. Specim. Eng. Lit.*, iii. *b*, l. 1002.

'*Geyne*, redy, or rythge forth. *Directus.* In the Eastern counties *gain* signifies handy, convenient, or desirable; and in the North, near, as "the *gainest* road," which seems most nearly to resemble the sense here given to the word.'—*Prompt. Parv. and Notes.*

Mr. Skeat ascribes *gain* to 'O.Swed. *gen*, direct; Icel. *gegn*, direct, ready, from Icel. prep. *gegn*, over against.'—See *Joseph of Arimathie*, p. 81. Cf. **Eme.**

(2) *adj.* handy; convenient.—SHREWSBURY; PULVERBATCH; LUDLOW; WELLINGTON; NEWPORT. 'Tak' the side-basket, it'll be *gainer* fur the gig than the market-basket, 'cause o' the 'andle.'

> 'Þe aþel auncetereȝ suneȝ · þat adam watȝ called,
> To wham god hade geuen · alle þat *gayn* were.'
> *Alliterative Poems, The Deluge* (A.D. 1360, *circa*). *Specim. Early Eng.*, xiii. l. 259.

Icel. *gegn*, serviceable; *gegna*, to meet; suit.

(3) *adj.* tractable; easy to manage.—PULVERBATCH; CLEE HILLS. 'The 'eifer's as *gain* as if 'er'd been milked seven 'ear; 'er walks up to the stelch as knowin' as can be.'

GALENY [gulai·ni'], *sb.* *Númida meleágris*, the Guinea-fowl, or Pintado.—SHREWSBURY; PULVERBATCH. Qy. com.

'*Galeny*, old cant term for a fowl of any kind; now a respectable word in the West of England, signifying a Guinea-fowl. Lat. *gallina.*' —*Slang Dictionary*, p. 140.

GALL [gau·l], (1) *sb.* a sore place; an abrasion of the skin.—PULVERBATCH; CLEE HILLS. 'The child's never 'ad a *gall* on it sence it wuz born till now; they tellen me as it's from 'is eye-tith.'

'But London can not abyde to be rebuked, suche is the nature of man. If they be prycked, they wyll kycke. If they be rubbed on the *gale:* they wil wynce.'—LATIMER, *Sermon on the Ploughers*, p. 23.

'*Galle*, soore yn mann' or beeste. *Strumus*, marista.'—*Prompt. Parv.*

'Fr. *gale*, scurf; itch; callum, callus; hardened skin.'—PICK.

(2) *v. a.* and *v. n.* to fret; to chafe. Com. 'Young cowts bin apt to *gall* i' the shuther,' is a saying metaphorically applied to young folk who are impatient of the restraints of work.

'"þe hors was . . . *galled* upon þe bak(e)."—*Gower's Confess. Amant.*, ii. 46,' in STRAT.

'*Ham.* . . . . Let the *galled* jade wince, our withers are unwrung.' —*Hamlet*, III. ii. 53.

'Touch a *gall'd* horse on the back, and he'll kick [or wince].'—RAY'S *Proverbs*, p. 112.

Fr. '*Se galer*, to scratch or rub.'—CHAMB.

(3) *sb.* a stiff, wet, 'unkind' place in plough-land.—PULVERBATCH; CLEE HILLS. The term is usually employed in the plural form. 'Theer couldna be spected much off that fild o' land, theer's sich a power o' wet *galls* in it.' Grose has '*Galls.* Sand-galls, spots of sand through which the water oozes. Norf. and Suf.' See *Gall* in WEDG. W. *gwall*, a defect. Cf. **Slade** (1).

(4) *sb.* the oak-apple, by which name this excrescence is usually distinguished.—ELLESMERE. '*Galle*, oke appyll.'—*Prompt. Parv.* See **Oak-ball.**

GALLOWAY [gal·u'wai], *sb.* a horse fourteen hands high; between a pony and a horse of larger growth.—BRIDGNORTH. Qy. com.

ADVERTISEMENT.

WHITCHURCH RACES.

'To be Run for upon Preese Heath near White Church in Shropshire, the 23rd of May next, being Tuesday in Whitson Week, a Purse of Ten Guineas, by *Galloways* not exceeding 14 Hands high, to carry Nine Stone, all under to be allowed Weight for Inches, paying half a Guinea entrance. . . . . .'—ADAMS'S *Weekly* [Chester] *Courant*, April 5—12, 1738.

'Breakfast being finished, the chivalry of the Hall prepared to take the field. The fair Julia was of the party, in a hunting-dress, with a light plume of feathers in her riding-hat. As she mounted her favourite *Galloway*, I remarked with pleasure that old Christie forgot his usual crustiness, and hastened to adjust her saddle and bridle.'—WASHINGTON IRVING (A.D. 1822), *Bracebridge Hall* (Hawking).

GALLOWS [gal·us], *adj.* mischievous; naughty; applied to boys chiefly. Com. ''E's a *gallus* bird, that is,—'e's bin i' the orchut agen after them apples.'

'*Ros.* . . . .
For he hath been five thousand years a boy.
Kath. Ay, and a shrewd unhappy *gallows* too.'
Love's Labour Lost, V. ii. 12.

Cf. **Ontidy.**

GALT [gau·t], *sb.* a spayed female pig.—PULVERBATCH; CLEE HILLS. Qy. com.

'*Hic frendis A'* galt,' occurs in an *English Vocabulary*, XV. cent., in

Wr. vocabs., vol. i. p. 204. Mr. Wright explains *galt* as 'a boar-pig.' '*Galte* (or gylte) swyne. *Nefrendus.*'—*Prompt. Parv.* '*Galte*, O.Icel. *galti* (aper), young boar.'—STRAT. Grose has '*Gawts and Gilts*, hog-pigs and sow-pigs. N.' Cf. **Gilt.**

GAMBREL [gam·br'il], *sb.* a crooked piece of wood used by butchers to expand and hang carcases upon.—SHREWSBURY; PULVERBATCH; ELLESMERE. Qy. com.

GAME, *sb.* fun, often derisive fun. Com. 'I'll 'elp yo' to mak' yore *game* o' me, yo' imperent young puppy; if yo' comen athin my raich, I'll turn yo' double an' bost yo'.'

> 'Ne of hir doughter nought a word spak she
> Noon accident for noon aduersitee
> Was seyn in hir, ne neuer hir doughter name
> Ne nempned she, in ernest nor in *game*.'
> CHAUCER, E. 609 (Six-text ed.), Skeat.

A.S. *gamen*, a sport; a play; a taunt; a scoff.

GAMMOCKS [gam·uks], *sb.* rough play. Qy. com. 'Them chaps bin al'ays up to some *gammocks*—now that poor fellow's got 'is shuther pŭt out.' A.S. *gamen*, sport; play.

GAMMY [gam·i'], *adj.*, *sl.*? lame. Com. 'A *gammy* fŭt.'

GANGREL [gang·r'il], *sb.*, *obsols.*? a gaunt, lean, long-limbed person or animal. (1) 'Whad a *gangrel* that Tum Perks is gwun—'e's as lung as a lather, an' as thin as a thetchin' peg.'

(2) 'It'll tak a good djel to feed that owd sow, 'er's sich a *gangrel*.'

GARLANDS. See **Virgins' Garlands.**

GARRITS, *sb. pl.*, *var. pr.* carrots.—PULVERBATCH.

GARRITY, *adj.*, *var. pr.* carroty.—*Ibid.* 'I knowed well enough it wuz one o' the Burguins by 'is *garrity* yar; they'd'n better keep 'im out o' the stack-yurd, else it'll ketch fire.'

GATED [gait·i'd], *part. past*, set a-going, as in the phrase *gated and geared*, below.—WHITCHURCH; ELLESMERE.

GATED AND GEARED, *phr.* made to work 'true' together: said of the several parts of an agricultural implement.—*Ibid.* See **Geared.**

GATE-ROAD, *sb.* the main-road, or level, in a mine.—COLLIERY; M. T. See **Gob-gate-road.**

GAUBY [gau·bi'], same as **Gaby**, q. v. Com. 'Now then, yo' great *gauby*, get out o' the way.' See below.

GAUBY-FAR, *sb.* The first Saturday in the year and the first Saturday after May-Day are respectively distinguished as *Gauby-far*. On these days country servants—'chaps' and 'wenches,'—'*gaubies*,' as they are called for the nonce—come into the town to spend their wages and see the sights.—SHREWSBURY. 'Nex' Saturday 'll be *Gauby-far*—theer'll be a grand show in ribbints an' rags.' See **Break the Year.**

GAUBY-MARKET, the market-day which follows next after

Christmas Day, observed as above.—WELLINGTON; NEWPORT. See Bk. II., *Folklore*, &c., 'Wakes, Fairs,' &c.

GAUKY [gau·ki'], *sb.* an awkward, stupid, badly-mannered person. —SHREWSBURY; PULVERBATCH; WELLINGTON. Qy. com. 'Han 'ee sid the new dairy-maid?' 'Aye, as great a *gauky* as anybody ŏŏd wish to see—ŏŏth a garrity yed, an' as foul as if 'er wuz made fur spite.' ''Ark at Jack! an' they sen as yo' bin o'er yed an' ears in love ŏŏth 'er.'

'Þe gome þat gloseth so chartres · for a *goky* is holden.
So is it a *goky*, by god · þat in his gospel failleth,
Or in masse or in matynes · maketh any defaute.'
Piers Pl., Text B., pass. xi. ll. 299, 300.

'Now *gawkies*, tawpies, gowks, and fools,
Frae colleges and boarding-schools,
May sprout like simmer puddock-stools
In glen or shaw;
He wha could brush them down to mools,
Willie's awa!'
ROBERT BURNS, *Poems*, p. 122, l. 19.

A.S. *geác*; O.Icel. *gaukr*, a cuckoo; whence, a fool; a simpleton. See STRAT.

GAUN [gau·n], (1) *sb.* a gallon.—PULVERBATCH. 'Tell the cowper to mak' a good strung four-*gaun* payl.'

'1584. 32 galanes of the best ale at vjd ob. a *gaune* xiij s viij d.'—*Accounts of the Shearmen's Company*, Shrewsbury.

(2) *sb.* a pail, one of the staves of which, being left much longer than the rest, forms an upright handle. It holds about a gallon, and is used for lading the drink, in the process of brewing.—NEWPORT; ELLESMERE. Qy. com. Cf. **Lade-gaun.**

GAUP [gau·p *and* gi'au·p], (1) *v. n.* to gape; to open the mouth. Qy. com. 'One o' the chickens belungin' to the brown 'en got squedge i' the wicket, an' I thought it wuz djed, but I 'eld it o'er the smoke, an' warmed it ever so lung, an' at last it begun to *gaup*; I wuz pretty glad, fur Missis is despert choiçe on 'em.'

'And with a *galping* mouth hem alle he keste.'
CHAUCER, F. 350 (Six-text ed.), Skeat.

O.Du. *galpen*, gaup, in STRAT.

(2) *v. n.* to stare about vacantly, with the mouth open as well as the eyes. Qy. com. 'I dunna know whad yo' wanten i' town—nuthin to do but *gi'-aup* at the shop-windows.' See **Gauby-Far.**

GAWM [gau·m], (1) *v. a., obsols.*? to grasp.—PULVERBATCH; CLUN; WEM. 'We'd'n a rar' batch o' laisin' this mornin'—I'd thirteen 'antle, as much as ever I could *gawm*.'

(2) *v. a., obsols.*? to bite through.—PULVERBATCH. 'Yo'n cut the bread i' sich clouters [rough thick pieces], nobody can *gawm* it.' See *Goam* in E. D. S., B. xiv.

GAWT. See **Galt.**

GAY-POLE [gai· poal], *sb., obsols.* a pole placed across the interior of a chimney, from which are suspended the hangers for the pots and kettles.—BRIDGNORTH. Cf. **Sway-pole.**

GEARED [gee·h'r'd], *part. past*, fitted up with its several parts; said of an agricultural implement.—WHITCHURCH; ELLESMERE. A.S. *gearwian*; to make ready; to prepare. Cf. **Gated.** See **Gated and Geared.**

GEARING, (1) *sb.* the projecting rail on the fore-part of a cart or waggon.—NEWPORT; WHITCHURCH.

(2) *sb.* the harness and trappings of a cart-horse.—CRAVEN ARMS. Qy. com.

'Waggon Horses with their *Gearing.*' 'Suit of chain *gearing.*' 'Suit of shaft *gearing.*'—*Auctioneer's Catalogue* (Longville), 1877.

A.S. *gearwa*, clothing.

GEARS [gee·h'r'z], *sb. pl.* same as **Gearing** (2), above. Com.

'Suit of long *gears.*' 'Suit of thillers *gears.*'—*Auctioneer's Catalogue* (Stoddesden), 1870.

GEARUM [jee·h'r'um], *sb.* order; good condition; serviceable fitness for a purpose.—PULVERBATCH. ''Ow is it yo' binna at the turmits to-day, Molly?' 'Indeed, Maister, I couldna gŏŏ; my back's bad an' my limbs achen, an' I'm altogether out o' *gearum.*' A.S. *gearo*, ready; prepared.

GEE, GEE-HO. See **Waggoner's Words to Horses.**

GEE-HO-PLOUGH [jee oa· plou], *sb.* a plough drawn by two horses abreast. Qy. com.

'Two sets of *G. O.* back bands and traces, in lots.'—*Auctioneer's Catalogue* (Longville), 1877. Called *Gee-woa-plough.*—NEWPORT.

GENTLE-LOIN, *sb.* the lean part of the loin of a bacon-pig, between the ham and the flitch.—BISHOP'S CASTLE; CLUN. Cf. **Griskin.**

GENTLEMAN'S-BUTTONS, *sb. pl.* the flowers of *Scabiosa succisa.*—WHITCHURCH, *Tilstock.* Cf. **Blue-heads.**

GEOLTITUDES [ji'ol·titeudz], *sb. pl.* bursts of passionate temper.—PULVERBATCH, *Condover.* Cf. **Tantrums.**

GEOMMOCKS [ji'om·uks], *sb. pl.* shreds; tatters.—WORTHEN; WEM. ''Er gownd's all in *geommocks.*'

GETHER [gedh·ur'], *v. n.* to ramify, as of young corn.—PULVERBATCH. 'That crop looks thin, Bayly.' 'Never mind, it'll look better after awilde, w'en it begins to *gether.*' Cf. **Stoul** (2).

GETHERIN', *sb.* the 'Offertory' collection in church.—PULVERBATCH; CLUN. Qy. com. 'Whad sort on a *getherin'* 'ad'n a on Sunday?'

GIB [gib·], (1) *sb.* a wooden prop used to support the coal when being 'holed.'—COLLIERY; M. T. Cf. **Sprag** (4).

(2) *sb.* a piece of iron of a peculiar shape—not unlike the half of a hollow square—used in connecting machinery together.—COLLIERY; M. T.

(3) *sb.*, *obsols.*? the handle of a walking-stick. — BRIDGNORTH; ELLESMERE.

GIBBED-STICK, *sb.*, *obsols.*? a hooked stick.—*Ibid.* '*Gib-staff*, a quarter-staff,' is given by both Ray and Grose as a North-county word. Cf. **Kibba.**

GID [gid·], *sb.* a dizziness to which sheep are liable—caused by *hydatids*.—CLEE HILLS. Cf. E. *giddy*, also **Kimet** (1).

GIE [gi'·], *v. a.* give: used in the imperative mood and in some tenses of the other moods. Com. '*Gie* the child that apple as 'e wants.' 'It'll *gie* 'em summat to do.'

'Fortune! if thou'll but *gie* me still
Hale breeks, a scone, an' Whisky gill,
An' rowth o' rhyme to rave at will,
Tak' a' the rest,
An' deal't about as thy blind skill
Directs thee best.'

ROBERT BURNS, *Poems*, p. 9, l. 19.

GI'ED [gi'·d], *pret.* gave.—*N.* and *N. E. Shr. Border.*

'Oh I had wooers aught or nine,
They *gied* me rings and ribbons fine;
And I was fear'd my heart would tine,
And I *gied* it to the weaver.'

ROBERT BURNS, *Poems*, p. 227, ll. 2—4, c. 2.

GI'EN [gi'·n], *part. past*, given.—*Ibid.*

'He ne'er was *gi'en* to great misguidin',
Yet coin his pouches·wad na bide in;
Wi' him it ne'er was under hidin',
He dealt it free:
The Muse was a' that he took pride in,
That's owre the sea.'

ROBERT BURNS, *Poems*, p. 71, l. 25, c. 2.

GIES [gi'·z], *v. a.* gives. Com.

'My Peggy smiles sae kindly,
It makes me blithe and bauld,
And naething *gies* me sic delight,
As wauking of the fauld.'

ALLAN RAMSAY, *The Gentle Shepherd*, I. i. p. 6.

GIFTS [gif·ts], *sb. pl.* white spots on the finger-nails; said to foretoken gifts. Com.

'A *gift* on the thumb
Is sure to come;
A *gift* on the finger
Is sure to linger.'

Children sometimes read the spots on their nails thus—beginning with the thumb and ending with the little finger:—'*Gift*, theft, friend, foe, journey to come.'

GIGGING SIEVE [gig·i'n siv], *sb.* a sieve, worked by a crank, used in a flour-mill for the first process of taking out the rough husks or other hard substances. Com.

GILLOFER [jil·u'fur'], *sb. Cheiranthus Cheiri*, common Wall-flower, and *Mathiola*, Stock, are included in this term, which is usually employed in the plural form. — ELLESMERE. Qy. com. 'Them *gillofers* smellen sweet, they'n be beautiful fur the posy.'

'*Gillofer*, or *Gelofer*. The old name for the whole class of carnations, pinks, and sweet-williams; from the French *girofle*, which is itself corrupted from the Latin *cariophyllum* . . . . .'

'Here spring the goodly *gelofers*,
Some white, some red, in showe,
Here prettie pinkes with jagged leaves,
On rugged rootes do growe.
The John so sweete in showe and smell,
Distincte by colours twaine,
About the borders of their beds,
In seemlie sight remaine.'

Plat's Flowers, &c., in *Cens. Lit.*, viii. 3, in NARES.

Shakespeare has *Gillyvors*, which Mr. Nares says is 'a step of the progress to our modern *Gilliflower*.'

'*Perdita*. . . . The fairest flowers of the season
Are our carnations and streak'd *gillyvors*.'

Winter's Tale, IV. iv. 82.

'*Gyllofre*, herbe. *Gariophilus*.'—*Prompt. Parv.*

'*Giroflée*, fleur odoriférante; la plante qui la porte. Stock-gilly-flower. De la giroflée jaune, Wall-flower.'—CHAMB.

GILLY-HOOTER [jil·i' oo·tur'], *sb. Súrnium Alúco*, Brown Owl.—ELLESMERE.

GILLY-OWLET, *sb. Strix flammea*, White Owl—the young birds.—CLUN, *Hereford Border*. Cf. **Owlert.**

GILT [gil·t], *sb.* a young sow that has not had a litter.—PULVERBATCH; CLEE HILLS. Qy. com.

'Capital sow in pig.' 'Do. *gilt* in pig.'—*Auctioneer's Catalogue* (Stoddesden), 1870.

'*Suilla*, vel *sucula*, gilte,' occurs in *Archbp. Ælfric's Vocabulary*, x. cent., in Wr. vocabs., vol. i. p. 22.

'*Gylte*, swyne. A *gilt*, or gaut, signifies in the North a female pig that has been spayed. . . . . Any female swine is called a *gilt* in Staffordshire.'—*Prompt. Parv. and Notes.*

A.S. *gilte*; O.Icel. *gilta*, young sow.—STRAT. Cf. **Galt.**

GIN [jin·], *sb.*, *obsols.* a contrivance for hoisting minerals out of the shaft—chiefly used in sinking. It is a 'drum' fixed on an upright shaft, supported by a rude frame-work of timber: this 'drum'—made to revolve by horse-power—winds up the ropes employed in raising the 'barrels' to the surface.—M. T. Com.

Gin is found in the early writers in the twofold sense of an ingeniously-constructed machine and of an artful or crafty device. Chaucer has it in both these. An instance of the former occurs in *The Squieres Tale*, where it is related that the magic 'stede of bras' would bear its rider at his pleasure—

'And turne ayeyn, with wrything of a pin.
He that it wroughte coude ful many a *gin*.'
F. 128 (Six-text ed.), Skeat.

'*Troclea*, the *gyn* whyche is called a crane.'—ELYOT.

'*Exostra*, a vice or *gin* of wood, wherewith such things as are done within, out of sight, are showed to the beholders by the turning about of wheeles.'—*Junius's Nomenclator*, by Fleming, in WAY.

'O.Fr. *engien*, *engin*; machine de guerre; ruse, finesse; machinerie, tromperie; de *ingenium*.'—BUR.

GIN-BARRELS, *sb. pl.*, *obsols.* the barrels used to bring up minerals out of the shaft.—M. T. Com. 'Al'ays comin' an' gööin' like *gin-barrels*.'

GIN-HORSE, *sb.*, *obsols.* the horse which works the *gin*.—*Ibid.*

GIN-RING, *sb. obsols.* the circle which the *gin-horse* traverses in working the *gin*.—*Ibid.*

GIRD [gur'd·], *v. a.* to pull violently.—WEM. 'Dunna yo' *gird* the rop' athatn.' As a verb, *gird*, to strike, to cut, is found in the early writers.

'& whan þe duk was war · þat he wold come
boute feyntice of feuer · he festned his spere,
& grimly wiþ gret cours · eiȝþer *gerdeþ* oþer.'
William of Palerne, l. 1240.

'And to thise cherles two he gan to preye
To slen him, and to *girden* of his hed.'
CHAUCER, *C. T.*, l. 14,464.

At a later period *gird* was used in a metaphorical sense—to cut or lash with wit or sarcasm. Shakespeare has this use of the word both verbally and substantively.

'*Sic.* Nay, but his taunts.
Bru. Being moved, he will not spare to *gird* the gods.'
Coriolanus, I. i. 260.

'*Luc.* I thank thee for that *gird*, good Tranio.'
Taming of the Shrew, V. ii. 58.

GIRDER [gur'·dur'], *sb.* a heavy blow.—PULVERBATCH. Qy. com. 'I gid 'im a pretty *girder*.' A.S. *gyrd*, a staff; rod.

GIRL, GIRLD [gae·r'l, gae·r'ld], *sb.*, *pec.* a single woman of any age. Com. The alternative pronunciations are dependent upon the education or refinement of the speaker.

'. . . My uncle John Gough dyed, butt my aunt Katherine survived him. Shee was soe extreeme fatt that shee could not goe straite foreward through some of the inward doores in the house, butt did turne her body sidewayes; and yett shee would go up staires and downe againe, and too and fro in the house and yard as nimbly, and tread as light as a *girl* of 20 or 30 years of age.'—GOUGH'S *History of Myddle*, p. 101.

Cf. Lone-girl.

GIS-AN-GULLIES, *sb. pl.* the blossoms of *Salix capréa*, great round-leaved Sallow.—SHREWSBURY; PULVERBATCH; WEM. Qy. com.

Gis-an'-Gullies = Geese and Goslings. See Bk. II., *Folklore*, &c., 'Superstitions concerning Plants.'

GIZZAN, GIZZANT [giz·u'n], CLEE HILLS. [giz·u'nt], PULVERBATCH; WEM, *sb.* 'Shall I 'elp yo' to a wing, Miss G——? Dun yo' perfer the liver or the *gizzant*?'

Pegge gives, '*Gizzen*, the stomach of a fowl, &c., Lanc.'

'We have *gyssarne* in an early MS. collection of medical receipts at Lincoln, apparently in the same sense' [of gizzard].—HAL.

GLAB [glab·], *sb.* a talkative, tattling person.—PULVERBATCH. 'Yo' met'n as well gie the bell-man a groat to cry it as tell Nancy Price anythin'—'er is sich a *glab*.' 'No, I think yo'd'n better tell 'er an' save yore fourpence.' Cf. **Clat** (2).

GLADSOME [glad·sum], *adj.* joyous; cheery; pleasant.—PULVERBATCH. 'Well, Richut, 'ow bin'ee? I 'spected to see yo' as *gladsome* as a butterfly, an' 'ere yo' bin lookin' as dismal as a mug in November.'

'As when a man hath ben in poure estaat,
And clymbeth vp, and wexeth fortunat,
And ther abydeth in prosperitee,
Swich thing is *gladsom*, as it thinketh me.'
CHAUCER, B. 3968 (Six-text ed.), Skeat.

A.S. *glæd*, glad; cheerful; pleasant.

GLANTH [glan·th], *sb.* a shade or tone of colour.—CORVE DALE. 'The barley innad 'urt—it's on'y jest a nice *glanth* on it.' This was said of barley that had stood much wet weather.

GLASTER [glas·tur'], *sb.* milk and water.—PULVERBATCH; WEM; OSWESTRY. 'Aye, this is milk like milk, nod sich *glaster* as yo' getten i' the towns.' W. *glasdwr*.—*Idem*.

GLAT [glat·], (1) *sb.* a broken down opening in a hedge.—PULVERBATCH; BISHOP'S CASTLE; CORVE DALE; LUDLOW; WEM. 'Them ship bin all i' the lane, Maister, I doubt theer's a *glat* somew'eer i' the leasow fence.'

(2) *sb.* a gap in the mouth caused by loss of teeth.—PULVERBATCH. 'Dick, yo' bin a flirt; I thought yo' wun gweïn to marry the cook at the paas'n's.' 'Aye, but 'er'd gotten too many *glats* i' the mouth fur me.' See *Gat-toothed*, in WEDG.

(3) *sb.* the 'vacant place' made by death.—PULVERBATCH. 'So the poor owd Squire's gwun! It'll be a lungful wilde afore that *glat's* maden up—theer ŏŏnna be another like 'im.'

GLAVER [glai·vur'], *v. a.* to flatter with a view to self interest; to cajole.—WEM. ''E *glavered* 'im o'er till at last 'e stud 'im a quart.'

'And þat wicked folke · wymmen bi-traieþ,
And bigileþ hem of her good · wiþ *glauerynge* wordes.'
P. Pl. Cr., l. 52.

W. *glafru*, to flatter.

GLEDE [glee·d], *sb.* a red spark of fire.—SHREWSBURY; PULVERBATCH. Qy. com. 'Theer wuz a nice *glede* o' fire i' the grate w'en I got up this mornin'.'

'Of knith ne hauede he neuere drede,
þat he ne sprong forth so sparke of *glede*.'
Havelok the Dane, l. 91.

'Her house sae bien, her curch sae clean,
I wat she is a dainty chucky;
And cheerlie blinks the ingle-*gleed*
Of Lady Onlie, honest Lucky!'
ROBERT BURNS, *Poems*, p. 252, l. 19, c. 2.

A.S. *glêd*, a burning; fire.

GLEDES, *sb. pl.* clear, glowing red cinders; glowing wood embers out of a bread-oven.—SHREWSBURY; PULVERBATCH. Qy. com. The *gledes* from oven-fuel are often collected into a tin pail for the purpose of making, or keeping, a dish of food hot, which they do very effectually. 'Sally, pŭt the men's 'tatoe-pie o'er them *gledes* as come out o' the oven, to keep warm for supper.'

'And as glowande *gledes* · gladieth nouȝte þis werkmen,
þat worchen & waken · in wyntres niȝtes,
As doth a kex or a candel · þat cauȝte hath fyre & blaseth.'
Piers Pl., Text B., pass. xvii. l. 217.

'Loke how that fire of smal *gledes*, that ben almost ded under ashen, wol quicken ayen, whan they ben touched with brimstone, right so ire wol evermore quicken ayen, whan it is touched with pride that is covered in mannes herte.'—CHAUCER, *The Persones Tale* (*De Ira*).

'For there no noisy railway speeds,
Its torch-race scattering smoke and *gleeds*.'
LONGFELLOW, *Prelude to Tales of a Wayside Inn*.

A.S. *glêd*; O.Fris. *glêd*; O.Du. *gloed*, glowing coal.—STRAT.

GLEDY [glee·di'], *adj.* red; glowing; clear; said of a fire.—SHREWSBURY; PULVERBATCH. Qy. com. 'Mind to 'ăve a nice *gledy* fire fur makin' the suppin', else yo'n get it groud.'

'The cruel ire, as reed as eny *gleede*.'
CHAUCER, *The Knightes Tale*, l. 1139, ed. Morris.

GLEM [glem·], *sb.* a gleam; a ray of sunshine.—PULVERBATCH. Qy. com. 'Han 'ee 'ad e'er a swarm o' bees it? Theer's bin some nice *glems* to-day.'

'Als þe knithes were comen alle,
þer hauelok lay, ut of þe halle,
So stod ut of his mouth a *glem*,
Rith al swilk so þe sunne-bem;
þat al so lith wa[s] þare; bi heuene!'
Havelok the Dane, l. 2123.

A.S. *glæm*, a gleam; brightness.

GLEMMY, *adj.* said of the weather when there are gleams of sultry heat, or alternating sunshine and showers.—*Ibid.* 'This *glemmy* weather's grand for feedin' the corn, now its dropped the blow.' ''Ow lung dun 'ee reckon from blow-drop till 'arroost?' 'About five wik.'

GLIBE [glei·b], *sb.*, *var. pr.*, *obsols.* the glebe.—PULVERBATCH. See **Flecked**.

GLID [glid·], *sb.*, *obsols. Milvus regális*, the Kite. Com. 'Bessey, run i' the orchut an' look after them young ducks—I see a *glid* about, an' the 'en's under the pen, an' canna defend 'em.'

'*Milvus*, glida,' occurs in *Archbp. Ælfric's Vocabulary*, x. cent., in Wr. vocabs., vol. i. p. 29. Mr. Wright remarks upon it—'*Glede* continued to be the usual English name for the kite till a comparatively late period.' He refers, for example, to an *English Vocabulary*, xv. cent., p. 188 of the same volume, where '*Hec Milvus A*ᵉ, glede,' is found. A.S. *glida*, a kite. Cf. **Kite.**

GLINT [glin·t], (1) *v. a.* to dry; to wither: the sun *glints* grass and corn.—CLEE HILLS.

(2) *adj.* dull, as of the edge of a knife—'the knife's *glint*.'—WELLINGTON.

GLOR [glau·r'], *sb.* fat. — PULVERBATCH; WEM. The following humorous dialogue—heard in the neighbourhood of Pulverbatch—is supposed to be *cawed* by two crows, one of which has found a carrion that the other desires to share:—

First Crow. 'All *glor*, all *glor!*'
Sec. Crow. 'W'eer is it? w'eer is it?'
First Crow. 'Down i' the moor, down i' the moor.'
Sec. Crow. 'Shall I come alung? shall I come alung?'
First Crow. 'Bar bwuns, bar bwuns!'

Pegge gives '*Glore*, fat. North.,' and '*Glur*, soft fat. Lanc.' Cf. *Glor* in E. D. S., C. v.

GLOR-FAT, *adj.* excessively fat; an over-fed beast would be said to be *glor-fat*.—PULVERBATCH; WEM. See *Gloar-fat* in HAL.

GLUE, *sb.*, *pec.* the gum which exudes from the bark of hardy stone-fruit trees.—SHREWSBURY; PULVERBATCH. See **Lammas-plum.**

GLUE-WARM, *adj.* lukewarm.—SHREWSBURY. 'Mix the waiter fur naidin' [kneading] nod more than *glue-warm*.' Cf. **Lew-warm.**

GLUT [glut·], *sb.* a long continuance of wet weather.—PULVERBATCH. 'We hanna 'ad sich a *glut* o' rain this lung wilde.'

GLYDE [glei·d], (1) *v. n.* to squint.—WEM. Qy. com.

Ash gives '*Gly*, to look asquint (a local word).' Jamieson has 'To Gley, *Glye*, to squint.'

'*Hec stroba*, a woman glyande,' and '*Hic strabo-nis*, a glyere,' occur in a *Nominale*, xv. cent., in Wr. vocabs., vol. i. p. 225. Mr. Wright explains 'Glyande' as '*Glyante*, squinting.'

See '*Glyare* or goguleye,' in *Prompt. Parv.*, with WAY's note. Cf. **Squine.**

(2) *sb.* a squint.—*Ibid.*

GOB [gob·], (1) *sb.* a lump of dough or bread; also of cheese.—SHREWSBURY, *Uffington.* 'Mother, canna yo' spar me that *gob* o' duff to mak' pot-balls on?' 'No, fur I'm gwein to mak' a pie fur yore faither's supper.'

'*Hec massa An*ᵉ, a gobet of dow,' occurs—under the head of *Pistor cum suis Instrumentis*—in *Pictorial Vocabulary*, xv. cent., in Wr. vocabs., vol. i. p. 277.

'Gobet, lumpe. *Frustrum, massa.* Gobet, parte, Para. The word gobbet formerly implied not only a lump, but generally a piece or portion of anything. . . . . . "Gobbet, a lumpe, or a pece, *monceau, lopin, chanteau.*" — PALSG. The derivation appears to be from "*Gobeau*, a bit, gobbet, or morsell." COTG.'—*Prompt. Parv. and Notes.*

(2) *sb.* the crumb or middle part of a loaf, from which the crust has been broken off.—LUDLOW, *Worcestershire Border.* 'Some chaps 'ad'n some bayte at a public, an' pěělenen the loaf. W'en the owd ŏŏman come in, 'er says—liftin' up 'er 'onds—"Whad's to become o' the *gob?*"'

'Gobet of a broke thynge (of hole thinge, P.). *Fragmen, fragmentum.*'—*Prompt. Parv.*

(3) *sb.* a rough sod, or clump of coarse grass in a pasture-field.—SHREWSBURY, *Uffington.*

'*Gleba*, a gobet of erthe,' in WAY. Cf. **Hobs and Gobs.**

(4) *sb.* a mass of refuse matter.—COLLIERY; WEM; ELLESMERE. 'They'n turned a fine *gob* o' sludge out o' that diche—hanna they?'

(5) *sb.* the 'worked out' part of a coal-mine.—COLLIERY; M. T. To *build the gob* is to prop the walls of the excavations with timber, as each miner proceeds with his work, in order to prevent them falling in upon him. See **Gob-gate-road**, below.

GOBBLE [gob·l], (1) *v. a.* to sew or mend in a rough kind of way. —SHREWSBURY. Qy. com. ''Ere Sally, tak' this owd petticut an' *gobble* it up—it inna wuth wastin' time o'er, but it'll do to wesh in.'

GOBBY [gob·i'], *adj.* rough; uneven.—PULVERBATCH. Qy. com. 'This knittin's despert onshooty, but I canna 'elp it—the yorn's so *gobby.*'

GOB-GATE-ROAD, *sb.* a main road carried into the *gob.*—COLLIERY; M. T. See **Gob** (5), above; also **Gate-road.**

GOD A'MIGHTY'S LADY-COW, *sb. Coccinella septem punctata*, the Lady-bird.—PULVERBATCH. 'This well-known insect is dedicated to Our Lady, as appears by the German name *Marien-käfer* or *Gottes-kühlein*, in Carinthia *Frauenküele.* In Brittany it is called *la petite vache du bon Dieu*, and Bohem. *Bozj krawicka*, God's little cow, has the same meaning.'—WEDG.

The Welsh name for the 'Lady-bird' is '*Y fuwch coch fach*' = the little red cow. See **Lady-cow.**

GOIN' A-TUMMASIN'. See Bk. II., *Folklore*, &c., 'Customs connected with Days and Seasons' (*St. Thomas' Day*).

GOLDEN AMBER, *sb.* the Yellow Ammer.—CLUN. See **Blacksmith.**

GOLDEN-CHAINS, *sb. pl.* the flowers of *Cytisus Laburnum.* Qy. com.

GOLDEN-SHOWERS, *idem.*—PULVERBATCH.

GOLDFINCH, *sb. pec.* same as **Coldfinch**, q. v.—PULVERBATCH.

GOLORE [gu'loa·h'r'], *adv.* in abundance; always concluding the phrase or sentence in which it is used—'We'n apples *golore.*'—CORVE DALE. 'Gaelic, *gu léor*, enough, from *leór*, an adj. signifying sufficient, with the prefix *gu*, which is used for converting an adj. into an adverb.'—Note in E. D. S., C. iii. p. 30.

GONDER [gon·dur'], (1) *sb.*, *var. pr.* a gander. Com. 'I'm gweïn to kill my owd *gonder*, Maister; I've 'ad 'im five an' twenty 'ear, an' I know as I should never get my owd tith throu' 'im, so I'll dress 'im fur the markit, an' tak' 'im to Soseb'ry o' Saturd'y.' Thus spake Betty Matthews of Castle Pulverbatch [1833], and—she sold her '*gonder!*'

(2) *v. n.* to mope about.—PULVERBATCH. 'That fellow's good fur nuthin' but *gonder* about like a kimet ship.'

GONE COLD, *part. past*, become cold. Com.

GOOD FEW. See **Indefinite Numerals**, p. xlvi.

GOODIES-TUESDAY, *sb.*, *obsols.* Shrove-Tuesday.—PULVERBATCH; CLUN; CLEE HILLS. 'Mother, did'n'ee 'ear whad our lickle Sam said?—as 'e knowed why it wuz called *Goodes'-Choozd'y* wuz 'cause Mam al'ays made poncakes. Inna-d-'e mighty arpit?' Called *Gütis-Tuesday.*—WEM. Grose has '*Gooddit*, Shrove-tide. North.'

GOOD OLD HAS BEEN, *phr.* said of persons or things that have past their prime.—PULVERBATCH. ''Er's a *good owd 'as bin*' was remarked of a sometime beauty who had lost all pretension to be considered such.

GOOLD [goo·ld], *sb.*, *var. pr.*, *obsols.* gold.—SHREWSBURY; PULVERBATCH; OSWESTRY. *Goold* is a lingering form, which dates from the time of George IV., when it was a 'shibboleth' of good breeding.

GOOM [goo·m], (1) *sb.* a swelling, as from a sprain.—CLEE HILLS. ''Ow did'n yo' come by that *goom* o' yore 'ond?' 'I gid it a kench, but I'll get some ïles [oils] to it to linnow it a bit.'

(2) *sb.*, *var. pr.* the gum. Qy. com. 'I think 'e'll ăve a tuth through afore lung—they bin very 'ard i' the *gooms.*'

GOOM-TITH, *sb. pl.* molar teeth. Qy. com. 'It wuz one o' my *goom-tith* as ached so, it warched an' nagged, an' gid me no pace, so I went to 'ave it drawed; an' the mon, 'e pŭt the pinsons on it an' gid one pool, an' out it comen—but it gid me whad fur.'

Cf. '*Les dents maschelieres*, The cheeke-teeth, *Jaw-teeth*, grinders.' —COTGRAVE, in *Bible Word-Book*, p. 278.

GOOSE-APPLE, *sb.*, *obsols.*? a green, juicy cooking-apple, excellent for sauce.—PULVERBATCH; WELLINGTON, *Upton Waters.*

GOOSE-GOGS, *sb. pl.* gooseberries.—OSWESTRY.

GORSE-BIRD, *sb. Fringilla cannábina*, the Brown Linnet.—CLUN. See below.

GORSE-HATCHER, same as above.—BRIDGNORTH. This name points to the bird's habit of making its nest under gorse-bushes.

GORSE-THATCHER, same as above.—CHURCH STRETTON.

GORST [gor'·st], *sb. Ulex Europæus*, common Furze.—Com. *S. Shr.* 'I'll 'ăve a foud 'urdled out by that shad an' waund ŏŏth *gorst*—it'll be warm fur the beäs to ate thar turmits.'

'1643. Payd for 5 loads of *Gorste* to stop the breaches in the church & placing the same with chardges 17 s.

'1649. Rec^{d}. for old *gorste* that was taken out of the breaches in the north side of the church 3 s.'—*Churchwardens' Accounts of the Abbey*, Shrewsbury.

> 'Þe fox & þe folmarde · to þe fryth wyndeȝ,
> Hertes to hyȝe heþe · hareȝ to *gorsteȝ*,
> & lyouneȝ & lebardeȝ · to þe lake-ryftes.'
>
> *Alliterative Poems, The Deluge* (A.D. 1360, *circa*).
> *Specim. Early Eng.*, xiii. l. 535.

'*Herba iras*, gorst.'—*Anglo-Saxon Vocabulary*, xi. cent., in Wr. vocabs., vol. i. p. 68. A.S. *gorst*. Cf. **Goss**.

GORSTY, *adj.* abounding with 'gorst'—'a *gorsty* bonk.'—Com. *S. Shr.*

GOSS [gos·], same as **Gorst**.—NEWPORT; WEM; ELLESMERE.

> 'Tooth'd briers, sharp furzes, pricking *goss* and thorns.'
>
> *Tempest*, IV. i. 180.

'*Goss*, Furze. Kent. Called in the North gorse.'—GROSE.

GOSSIPS [gos·sips], *sb. pl.* sponsors in Holy Baptism.—PULVERBATCH; WEM; OSWESTRY. 'Yo'd'n a pretty gran' Chris'nin' I 'ear—who wun the *gossips*?' '*Gossips* enough, fayth! if they'd'n pickt the parish they couldna-d-a fund two better talkers.'

'1540. 12 March thro lycens was christened at Wylley, Agnes the dought^{er} of Ric^{d} Charlton of this towne of Wenlok and of Jone his wife, *Gossibbes* wer Sr Thos Boteler of Wenlok aforesaid Vicar, and Maistres Agnes wif Maist^{r} Ric^{d} Lacon Lord of Wylley aforesaid, and the wife of Wm Davys of Apley Lode.'—*Register of Sir Thomas Boteler*, Vicar of Much Wenlock.

'They had mothers as we had; and those mothers had *gossips* (if their children were christened) as we are.'—BEN JONSON, *The Staple of News, The Induction.*

'*Gossip* is still used by our peasantry in its first and etymological sense, namely, as a sponsor in baptism—one *sib* or akin in *God*, according to the doctrine of the mediæval Church, that sponsors contracted a spiritual affinity with one another, with the parents, and with the child itself.

'"*Gossips*," in this primary sense, would ordinarily be intimate and familiar with one another—would have been so already, or through this affinity would have become so; and thus the word was next applied to all familiars and intimates. At a later day it obtained the meaning which is now predominant in it, namely, the idle profitless talk, the "commérage" (which word has exactly the same history), that too often finds place in the intercourse of such.'—ARCHBP. TRENCH, *Select Glossary*, pp. 95, 96.

See WAY's note in *Prompt. Parv.*, p. 204. A.S. *god-sibb*, a gossip; sponsor.

GOSTER [gos·tur'], (1) *sb.* swagger; vapouring talk; empty compliment.—WEM; ELLESMERE. 'Gie us none o' yore *goster*—dun'ee think as folks han no better sense till believe it?'

(2) *v. n.* to swagger, &c.—*Ibid.* Pegge gives '*Goyster*, to brag and swagger;' but does not add locality where used.

GO THY WAYS, *phr.* chiefly addressed to children when bidding them begone in a good-humoured kind of way.—SHREWSBURY. Qy. com. This phrase, according to Mr. Oliphant, is found for the first time in the *Handlyng Synne* [1303], p. 346.

'Þou mayst þan sykerly *go þy weye*.'
See *Sources of Standard English*, pp. 191—194.

Shakespeare uses it:—

'*King.* *Go thy ways*, Kate:
That man i' the world who shall report he has
A better wife, let him in nought be trusted,
For speaking false in that. . . . . .'
K. Henry VIII., II. iv. 133.

See **Come thy ways.**

GOWD [gou·d], *sb.*, *var. pr.* gold.—WELLINGTON; NEWPORT. Qy. com.

'The rank is but the guinea stamp;
The man's the *gowd* for a' that.'
ROBERT BURNS, *Poems*, p. 227, l. 28, c. 2.

See **Grammar Outlines** (*vowels*, &c.), **O** (9), (21).

GOWDEN [gou·dn], *adj.*, *var. pr.* golden.—*Ibid.*

'Thou paints auld Nature to the nines,
In thy sweet Caledonian lines;
Nae *gowden* stream thro' myrtles twines,
Where Philomel,
While nightly breezes sweep the vines,
Her griefs will tell!'
ROBERT BURNS, *Poems*, p. 114, l. 12, c. 2.

GOWND [gou·nd], *sb.*, *var. pr.* a gown. Com.
'1756. Pd. for a *Gownd* for An Bridwaters ,, 8 - 9.'—*Churchwardens' Accounts*, Hopton Castle.

GRACE [gr'ai·s], *sb.*, *var. pr.* grease. Com. 'Whad! han they 'ad a sale up at the 'ill?' 'Oh, aye! they bin gwun all to raddle an' rags, an' urchins' [hedgehogs'] *grace*—I never 'spected they'd'n do any good.'

GRAFF [gr'af·], *sb.* a spade's depth in digging.—PULVERBATCH; WEM; WHITCHURCH; OSWESTRY. Qy. com.
'The measure of this leape [Humphry Kinaston's] was afterwards marked out upon Knockin Heath, upon a greene plott by the wayside that leads from Knockin towards Nescliffe, with an H and a K cut in the ground at the ends of the leape. The letters were about an elne long, and were a spade *graff* broad and a spade *graff* deep. These letters were usually repaired yearely by Mr. Kinaston of

Ruyton. I confesse I have seen the letters, but did not take the measure of the distance.'—GOUGH'S *History of Myddle*, p. 29.

'A.S. *grafan;* O.Icel. *grafa;* O.H. Germ. *graban*, to grave; dig.' —STRAT.

GRAFTING-SHOVEL [gr'af·tin shuv·l], *sb.* a digging-spade.—WHITCHURCH, *Tilstock*.

GRAFTING-TOOL, (1) *sb.* a crescent-shaped implement for cutting the turf, preparatory to making the drains in grass-land—PULVERBATCH. Not much used now [1879].

(2) *sb.* a long spade used for draining purposes.—LUDLOW. See **Floating-shovel.**

(3) *sb.* a curved spade shorter in the iron part than the draining-tool: it is much used in 'rabbiting,' as it digs down to the hole at two semi-circular cuts, whereas a common spade would require three or four to the same end—it thus expedites matters.—CLEE HILLS.

GRAINING IN THE HORN, *phr.* A ring appears on a cow's horn with every calf she has after the first one, this is called *graȳnin' i' the 'orn.* Hence, by metaphor, a woman waxing in years is said to be *graȳnin' i' the 'orn.* Also, as it is the practice of dishonest cattle-dealers to file out the *grains* or rings in a cow's horn, in order to make her appear younger than she is; so, a woman, who by artificial means tries to give herself a more youthful appearance, is said to 'tak' the *graȳns out'n 'er 'orns.*'—PULVERBATCH. See below.

GRAINS [gr'ei·nz, *corr.* gr'aayn·z], (1) *sb. pl.* the rings in a cow's horn.—PULVERBATCH. 'That cow's ten 'ear owd—fur I counted seven or eight *graȳns* in 'er 'orn.'

(2) [gr'aayn·z], PULVERBATCH. [gr'ain·z], NEWPORT; WEM, *sb. pl.* the prongs of a hay-fork. 'Did'n'ee 'ear that mon's djed at the 'Firmary?' 'Ŏo-a?' ''Im as 'ad the pikel *graȳns* potched throu' 'is 'ond—the Doctor said it brought on tiddinus [tetanus] or summat.'

'*Grain* in *pl.* the prongs of a fork.'—JAMIESON.

'Dan. *green*, branch; bough; prong of a fork.'—WEDG.

GRANCH [gr'an·sh], (1) *v. a.* and *v. n.* to craunch; to crush forcibly with the teeth; to grind.—SHREWSBURY; PULVERBATCH. Qy. com. 'Them curran'-cakes as yo' buyen bin nasty things—they *granch* under yore tith like ātin' cinders.' 'Yo' shud'n gŏŏ to Plimmer's, an' then yo'd'n 'ăve 'em good.'

(2) *sb.* a hard bite.—*Ibid.* 'Jest see 'ow I broke my tuth; theer wuz a bit of a stwun i' that curran'-cake, an' I gid it a *granch*, an' split a piece off my tuth—I'll gŏŏ w'eer yo' tellen me fur 'em agen.'

(3) *v. a.* to bite greedily; to snatch at, in eating.—PULVERBATCH. 'All them ship ŏŏn *granch* that bit o' grass up in no time.' Cf. **Raunch.**

GRANNOWED [gr'an·oed], *part. adj.* ingrained with dirt.—WEM; ELLESMERE. Compare *granyt* = dyed in grain, in the following lines:—

'In crammysyn cled and *granyt* violat,
With sangwyne cape, the selvage purpurat.'
GAWIN DOUGLAS (A.D. 1513), *Prol. of the XII. Buk of Eneados. Specim. Eng. Lit.* xiii. l. 15.

Cf. **Grinnowed.**

GRANNOWS [gr'an·oez], *sb. pl.* streaks of dirt left in clothes from bad washing; the term is chiefly applied to body-linen.—*Ibid.* Cf. **Grinnows.**

GRANNY-REARED, *part. adj.* over-indulged; coddled—as if brought up by a more fond than wise grandmother. Com. 'Whad a spiled, pinnikin lickle thing that child is!' 'Aye, 'er looks like a *granny-reared* un—duna-d-'er?'

GRANSIR [gr'an·sur'], *sb., obs.* a grandsire.—WORTHEN. 'I've lef' the two little uns alung ŏŏth thar *gransir.*'

'Both perles prince and kyng veray;
His gracious *granseres* and his grawndame,
His fader and moderis of kyngis thay came,
Was never a worthier prynce of name.'
JOHN AUDELAY, *Lines on K. Henry VI.*, p. viii.

'*Grawnsyre*, faderys fadyr (grawncyr, S. grauncer, P.). *Avus.*'—*Prompt. Parv.*

GRASS-HOOK [gr'as· uk], *sb.* a small hook attached to the head of a scythe-pole which fastens into the scythe and keeps it steady.—PULVERBATCH. Qy. com.

GREEN [gr'ee·n], *adj.* inexperienced; raw.—SHREWSBURY; PULVERBATCH. Qy. com. 'Whad can yo' expect from a *green* young wench like that?—fur my part I'd as lif' be athout as none the better.'

'*Riv.* Why with some little train, my Lord of Buckingham?
'*Buck.* Marry, my lord, lest, by a multitude,
The new-heal'd wound of malice should break out;
Which would be so much the more dangerous
By how much the estate is *green* and yet ungoverned.'
K. Richard III., II. ii. 127.

GREEN-HOND, *sb.* one who is unskilled, as an apprentice or new beginner at any kind of work.—*Ibid.* 'Aye, it's done pretty well fur a *green-'ond*—yo'n get saisoned to it afore seven 'ear.'

GRESS [gr'es·], *sb.* grass. — NEWPORT; ELLESMERE; OSWESTRY. 'Nancy Robuts married agen, dun'ee say? W'y 'er's 'ardly let the *gress* grow green on 'er poor 'usban's grave.'

'Was neuere non þat mouhte þaue
Hise dintes, noyþer knith ne knaue,
Þat he felden so dos þe *gres*
Bi-forn þe syþe þat ful sharp is.'
Havelok the Dane, l. 2698.

A.S. *græs*, grass.

GREWED [gr'oo·d], (1) *part. adj.* stuck to the saucepan in boiling; said of milk, porridge, &c.—WEM; ELLESMERE. See **Growed.**

(2) *part. adj.* fastened in, as of smut or dirt attaching to the skin. —*Ibid.* See **Growed** (2).

GREY-HUN [gr'ai· un], *sb.* a greyhound.—PULVERBATCH. 'We'n three dogs, but the *grey-'un* an' the pŷnter bin the Squire's.'

'O.N. *grey, grey-hundr*, a bitch.'—WEDG.

GREY-MARE, *sb.* a managing, rather than a ruling, wife.—PULVERBATCH. Qy. com. 'The *grey-mar's* the best 'orse—'e ŏŏdna do much good athout 'is wife.'

GRID [gr'id·], *sb.* a grating over a drain. Com. ''Ow did'n yo' come off i' the starm? We'd'n a reg'lar flood; the waiter run through the 'ouse like a bruck—the *grid* wuz stopt up at the back.'

GRIDDLE [gr'id·l], (1) *sb., obsols.?* a gridiron. — SHREWSBURY; PULVERBATCH.

'A strong fur he let make and gret,
And a *gredel* theropon sette.'
MS. Coll. Trin. Oxon. 57, in HAL.

'Craticulam,' glossed '*gridil*,' occurs in the *Treatise of Alexander Neckam*, xii. cent., in Wr. vocabs., vol. i. p. 102. W. *greiddyll*, a gridiron.

(2) *v. a.* to broil; to grill.—*Ibid.* 'Sally, we'n get on ŏŏth our work, an' never mind any reg'lar dinner to-day—we can *griddle* a slice o' 'am fur our tay, an' get it yarly.' 'Aye, I think as that'll be best.' W. *greidio*, to scorch; to singe.

(3) *sb.* a grill of some sort.—*Ibid.* 'We mun get the Maister a bit of a *griddle* fur 'is tay—'e's bin a lung journey.'

GRIG [gr'ig], (1) *sb.* a bantam fowl.—PULVERBATCH; CLEE HILLS. 'They'n gid me a couple o' *grigs*—a cock an' a 'en.'

(2) *sb. Calluna vulgaris*, common Ling. Qy. com. 'What advantages then might bee made of some great mosses in Lancashire and elsewhere, that lye near to coal and limestone, and therefore might well be spared without making fuell dear, and improved at a very small charge, and for the present yield little or no profit, save some *grigg* or heath for sheep.'—*Aubrey's Wilts, MS. Royal Soc.*, p. 304, in HAL.

Ray has '*Grig*, Salopiensibus Heath,' in his '*Catalogue of Local Words* Paralleled with Welch.' W. *grug*, heath; ling.

GRIG-BESOM, *sb.* a broom made of 'grig.' Qy. com. 'I like a *grig-besom* fur sweepin' the imbers out o' the oven, an' then a clane maukin' to finish up ŏŏth.' *Grig-besoms* are in much request for barn-floors.

GRIME [gr'ei·m], *sb.* smut grained in—differing from 'collow,' which is mere surface soot.—CLEE HILLS. Qy. com. 'That ŏŏman's face hanna sid waiter lately—look at the *grime*.'

'*Ant. S.* What complexion is she of?

'*Dro. S.* Swart, like my shoe, but her face nothing like so clean kept: for why, she sweats; a man may go over shoes in the *grime* of it.

'*Ant. S.* That's a fault that water will mend.

'*Dro. S.* No, sir, 'tis in grain; Noah's flood could not do it.'—*Comedy of Errors*, II. ii. 106.

Dan. *grim*, soot; smut; dirt.

GRIN [gr'in·], *sb.* a snare, as for a hare or rabbit, &c. Qy. com. 'Whad's the matter ŏŏth the cat's fut?' 'I 'spect it's bin ketcht in a *grin*, an' 'e's got a poacher's reward.'

'Þe loverd þat sone underȝat
Lim and *grine* and wel ihwat
Sette and leide þe for to lacche
Þu come sone to þan hacche
Þu were inume in one *grine*
Al hit abohte þine schine.'
Owl and Nightingale, ll. 1055—1059.

'Even as a bird
out of the foulers *grin*,
Escaped away,
right so it fareth with us.'
STERNHOLD and HOPKINS (A.D. 1599), *Ps.* cxxiv. 7, in *Bible Word-Book*.

A.S. *grin*, a snare. **Der.** 'grinned.'

GRINDLE-STONE, *sb.* a grind-stone. Qy. com. 'Jack, I shall want yo' to turn the *grindle-stwun* fur me to sharpen the axe.' See *grindelston*, in STRAT.

GRINNED, *part. past*, trapped in a 'grin.' Qy. com. See above.

GRINNERED, GRINNERS, same as **Grinnowed**, &c., below.—NEWPORT.

GRINNOWED [gr'in·oed], *part. adj.* ingrained with dirt.—SHREWSBURY; PULVERBATCH. 'I ŏŏdna gie anythin' to sich a nasty slanny; 'er clo'es bin all *grinnowed* ŏŏth dirt, an' 'er face is as black as the aister.' Cf. **Grannowed**.

GRINNOWS [gr'in·oez], *sb. pl.* same as **Grannows**, q. v.—SHREWSBURY; PULVERBATCH. 'I canna get the *grinnows* out if I rub the piece out, they'n bin biled in so many times.'

GRIP [gr'ip·], *sb.* a very small water-channel cut in the ground for the purpose of letting the rain run off.—CHURCH STRETTON, *Longnor*.

'Þan birþe men casten hem in poles,
Or in a *grip*, or in þe fen.'
Havelok the Dane, l. 2102.

'*Gryppe*, or a gryppel, where watur rennythe a-way in a londe, or watur forowe. *Aratiuncula, aquagium, aquarium.* "*Aratiuncula, fossa parva que instar sulci aratur.*"—CATH. The term *grype* occurs in an award, dated 1424, relating to the bounds of lands of the Prior of Bodmin, as follows: "the bounde that comyth thurgh the doune—goyng don to another stone stondynge of olde tyme in the bank of a *grype*,—and so the diche (called Kenediche) and the *gripe*, &c."—Mon. Ang., new ed. from Harl. Cart., 57 A. 35.

'In Norfolk, Forby states that a trench, not amounting to a ditch, is called a grup; if narrower still, a *grip;* and if extremely narrow, a gripple.'—*Prompt. Parv. and Notes.*

'O.Du. *grippe* (*sulcus*), grip; trench; ditch.'—STRAT.

GRISKIN [gr'is·kin], *sb.* a lean piece out of the loin of a bacon-pig, lying between the ham and the flitch.—BISHOP'S CASTLE; CLUN.

'In Salop the old Scandinavian *gris* (the Sanscrit *grishti*) is used [1220] instead of *pig;* hence our *griskin:* some curious English rimes in the *Lanercost Chronicle* turn on the former word.'—*Sources of Standard English*, p. 123.

The following are the rimes referred to by Mr. Oliphant in the passage quoted above:—

'Willy *Gris*, Willy *Gris*,
Think quhat thou was, and quhat thou is.'

Mr. Wright alludes to the same rimes in his Glossary to *Piers Pl.* when explaining the word '*grys*,' which occurs about three times throughout that work.

'*Gryce*, swyne or pygge. *Porcellus, nefrendis.*'—*Prompt. Parv.*

See *Gris* in JAMIESON.

GRIST [gr'ei·st], *sb.* the quantity of corn ground at once, usually a bag, *i. e.* three bushels.—CLUN. 'Tell the milner to fetch the *grist* to-daay̆, an' saay̆ I shall want the batch i' the mornin'.'

'And moreouer, that all Dowers of the Cite and suburbis of the same, grynd att the Cite is myllis, and noo where els, as long as they may have sufficiaunt *grist*, vppon such paynis as of old be ordned and provided yn that be-halfe.'—'Ordinance of the "Gild of the Bakers." Exeter, temp. 22 Edw. IV. to 1 Richard III.,' in *English Gilds, their Statutes and Customs*, E. E. T. S.

'All bring *grist* to your mill.'—RAY'S *Proverbs*, p. 194.

Jamieson gives, '*Grist*, fee paid at a mill for grinding.'

A.S. *grist*, a grinding. Cf. **Batch** (2).

GROATS [gr'au·ts], *sb. pl.* dregs or grounds of oatmeal.—NEWPORT. A.S. *grút*, coarse meal.

GROND [gr'ond·], *pret.* and *part. past*, ground. — SHREWSBURY; PULVERBATCH. 'The waggoner said 'e couldna sleep fur that lad—'e *grond* 'is tith all night as if 'e'd bin gnawin' a w'et-stwun.'

'A few verbs have *ou*, which has arisen out of an *o* or *oo*, as ground = *grond* (*groond*) = [O.E. *pret.*] *grand.*' — DR. MORRIS'S *Historical English Accidence*, p. 161.

GROPE [gr'oap·], *v. n.* to catch trout with the hands, by feeling for them in the holes and sheltered places of a stream.—PULVERBATCH. Qy. com. 'I can do no good ŏŏth a net ketchin' trout—I like to *grope* fur 'em best under the stouls an' bonks.'

'Look what ther is, put in thyn hand and *grope*,
Thow fynde shalt ther siluer, as I hope.'
CHAUCER, G. 1236 (Six-text ed.), Skeat.

'*Gropyñ* or felyñ wythe hande. *Palpo.*'—*Prompt. Parv.*

A.S. *grápian*, to lay hold of.

GROUND [gr'ou·nd *and* gr'ou·n], *sb.* farm-land, or some portion of it: 'gwun round the ground' = gone round the farm; 'the uvver groun' = the upper or higher part of a farm.—PULVERBATCH. Qy. com. 'It's a rar' farm that's no bad *ground*' is a proverbial saying analogous to 'It's a fair flock that has no black sheep,' and is similarly applied.

GROUTS, GROUTINS [gr'ou·ts], PULVERBATCH. [gr'ou·tinz], WEM, *sb. pl.* settlings of beer; the thick sediment deposited by the 'drink' at the bottom of the cooler, or otherwise in the barrels. 'Sally, han yo' bin stoupin' the barrel? Look at this drink, all full o' *grouts*—on'y fit fur the wesh-tub.'

'N. *grut*, dregs; *gruten*, grouty; muddy.'—WEDG. Cf. **Crap.**

GROWED [gr'ou·d], (1) *part. adj.* stuck to the pan in boiling: said of milk, &c.—SHREWSBURY; PULVERBATCH; CLUN. 'W'y, Bessy, this suppin's bwiled till it's all *growed* to the pot—whad says owd Nancy Andrus o' Churton Green?—

"It's saut, sour, an' sutty,
Thick, *growed*, an' lumpy,
Like the Devil's porritch."'

Lancelot, in the *Merchant of Venice* (II. ii. 18), uses the expression *grow to*, and the following note upon it is found in the edition of the Clarendon Press Series (*Select Plays*). '*Grow-to*, a household phrase applied to milk when burnt to the bottom of the saucepan, and thence acquiring an unpleasant taste. "Grown" in this sense is still used in Lincolnshire (BROGDEN'S *Dict. of Prov. Words*, &c.).' Cf. **Bishopped** (2), also **Grewed** (1).

(2) *part. adj.* ingrained with dirt—a term chiefly applied to the skin.—SHREWSBURY; PULVERBATCH. 'That poor child's never 'afe weshed—the dirt's reg'lar *growed* in tell yo' met'n sow sids i' the ridges on 'er neck.' Cf. **Grewed** (2). See **Grime.**

GROZIER [gr'oazh·yur'], *sb., var. pr., obsols.*? a grocer.—SHREWSBURY; PULVERBATCH. 'Whad *grozier* dun yo' dale ŏŏth?' 'Well, I al'ays gŏŏ to Bromley's—yo' sin one knows the family.' See **-ier.**

GRUBBY [gr'ub·i'], *adj.* small; poor; stunted.—SHREWSBURY; PULVERBATCH. Qy. com. 'The cabbitch bin poor *grubby*-lookin' things this time.'

GRUMPY [gr'um·pi'], *adj.* peevish; testy; ill-tempered.—SHREWSBURY; PULVERBATCH. Qy. com. '"Grumpy," whad els yo' to-day? Yo' bin as *grumpy* as yo' knowen 'ow to be—if I canna plase yo' I shall jest gie yo' lave to plase yoreself.'

GUDGEONS [guj·unz], (1) *sb. pl.* the iron pivots in the wooden axle of a wheel-barrow.—PULVERBATCH; LUDLOW. 'Tell the smith to mak' a par o' *gudgeons* fur the wilbarrow.'

'The *gudgions* of the spindle of a wheele.'—*Nomenclator*, in WR.

(2) *sb. pl.* the pinions on which a windlass turns. Com. M. T.

GULCH [gul·sh], *v. a.* to swallow greedily with a sucking noise.—

PULVERBATCH. Qy. com. 'Jim Tunkiss is no better than a wench at 'arroost-work, but 'e can *gulch* the drink out o' the bottle as well as e'er a chap i' the fild.'

'Du. *gullen*, to swallow greedily; suck down,' in WEDG.

Cf. **Guttle**, also **Loach** (1).

GULL [gul·], *sb.* an unfledged gosling.—CLUN; CLEE HILLS.

'And verily 't would vex one to see them, who design to draw disciples after them, to lead a crew of *gulls* into no small puddles by having obtained the repute of being no meanly understanding *ganders*.' —TRENCHFIELD (A.D. 1671), *Cap of Grey Hairs*, p. 8.

Mr. Wedgwood says *gull* simply means an 'unfledged bird.' So Shakespeare has it:—

> 'And being fed by us you used us so
> As that ungentle *gull*, the cuckoo's bird,
> Useth the sparrow. . . . .'
>
> 1 *King Henry IV.*, V. i. 60.

See also the 'naked *gull*' in *Timon of Athens*, II. i. 31. Cf. the Celtic:—W. *gwylan*; Cornish, *gullan*; Bret. *gwelan*, a sea-gull. Hence, perhaps, *gull*, an appellation given to other birds. Cf. **Gully**, below.

GULLET [gul·it], (1) *sb.* a parcel or portion, as of a field.—LUDLOW. ''E's a good *gullet* o' that side the fild.'

'And the residewe beinge xx. li. lyeth in sundrye *gullettes* in severall townes and shers.'—*Ludlow Muniments, temp. Edw. VI.*, in WR.

(2) *sb.* a long, narrow piece of land.—WELLINGTON. 'I've bin down the *gullet* gettin' rawnies.' Cf. **Slang**.

(3) *sb.* a passage opening out of a street—a 'cul-de-sac,' not a thoroughfare.—SHREWSBURY. 'I say, w'eer does that ŏŏman live as maden yore gownd?' 'W'y, 'er lives up that *gullet* by Hughes the painter's shop, o' yore left-hand side as yo' gwun up the Cop.'

'Fr. *goulet*, a narrow entrance to a harbour; O.Fr. *goule* for *gueule*.' —PICK. Cf. **Shut** (2).

GULLY, same as **Gull**, above. Com.

GUMPY [gum·pi], *adj.* lumpy; uneven.—PULVERBATCH. 'This ŏŏllen yorn's mighty *gumpy*—it'll mak' a rough stockin'.' Cf. **Gobby**.

GUN [gun·], *sb.*, *obsols.* a broad-cast turnip-sower of a peculiar description. It is a hollow tin cylinder about ten feet long, divided into compartments, each of which has apertures furnished with slides to open or close at pleasure—the upper one is for admitting the seed, the lower one for letting it out. The slide by which the seed is distributed is perforated with holes of various sizes for the purpose of regulating the quantity of seed to be sown. The *gun* is held by two handles, and the man who uses it carries it before him in a horizontal position, shaking it as he goes along.—CLEE HILLS.

GURGEONS [gur·junz], *sb. pl.* coarse refuse from flour. Com. *Gurgeons* are produced from the inner skin of the grain. They are lighter in substance than '*sharps*,' with which they are often confounded, owing to the respective terms being applied without discrimination to the different kinds of refuse meal obtained from the processes of 'dressing' the flour.

Cf. 'Fr. *escourgeon*, a kind of base and degenerate wheat, which being ground yields very white, but very light, and little nourishing meal.'—HOWELL'S *Dictionary*, ed. 1673.

'O.Fr. *escourchier*, *escorce*; de *cortex*.'—BUR.

'*Cortex*, a rinde or bark; a shell or pill.'—*Dict. Etym. Lat.*

See **Sharps**.

GUTH [guth·], *sb.*, *var. pr.* a girth.—NEWPORT; ELLESMERE.

GUTTER [gut·ur'], (1) *sb.* a narrow (natural) water-course, generally flowing into a brook—Grub's *Gutter*; Hope *Gutter*, &c.—CLUN.

(2) *sb.* The fissures or rifts in the Longmynd (Stretton Valley side) are locally known as *gutters*.—CHURCH STRETTON. Whatever their producing cause may have been—geologists differ as to that—these *gutters* now serve as channels for the mountain streamlets, which, issuing from spring or bog, flow down them—almost invariably from their summits—to the valley below.

O.F. *gutiere*. 'Fr. *gouttière*, a channel or gutter.'—WEDG.

(3) [guot·ur']. See **Drain**.

GUTTLE [gut·l], *v. a.* to drink greedily.—WEM. Qy. com. 'Them chaps binna fur work, all they wanten's to *guttle* the drink down thar throttles.' See *Guttle*, in WEDG. Cf. **Gulch**.

GYLAND [gei·land], *sb.* a sloping piece of land; a high bank.—OSWESTRY, *Welsh Border*. W. *ceulan*, a hollow bank; *Y-geulan*, a sloping bank.

H. The remarks on the omission of this letter as an aspirate, in **Grammar Outlines**, p. xxxviii., may be aptly illustrated by the word *house* as spelt in an inscription in the entrance hall of the old half-timbered dwelling-place in Bridgnorth, which was built by Richard Forster, A.D. 1580, and in which Bp. Percy was born, A.D. 1729. The inscription runs thus:—

EXCEPT · THE · LORD · BVILD · THE
OWSE THE · LABOVRERS · THERE · OF ·
EVAIL · NOT · ERECTED BY R · FOR ·
* 1580

The quaint use of the symbol * to represent the last syllable of For*ster* is very curious, and probably exemplifies the local pronunciation of *star* at that period. Something very like it obtains in many parts of Shropshire at this day.

HACK [ak·], (1) *v. a.* to chop; to mince. Com. 'Now, *'ack* them garrits, an' get the bif an' bacon up fur the men's dinner.'

'And leet comaunde anon to *hakke* and hewe
The okes olde, and leye hem on a rewe
In culpous wel arrayed for to brenne.'
CHAUCER, *The Knightes Tale*, l. 2007, ed. Morris.

O.Du. *hacken*, to chop; to cut.

(2) *sb., obsols.* the heart, liver, and lights of a pig, undivided.—ELLESMERE, *Welshampton.*

''*Hack*, the Lights, Liver, and Heart altogether.'—*Academy of Armory*, Bk. II. ch. ix. p. 181.

Cf. **Haslet.**

(3) *sb.* a small pick used in getting coal.—COLLIERY; M. T. Ash has this, which he calls 'a local word;' and Bailey—ed. 1782—says it is 'North Country.' Cf. **Maundrel.**

HACK-AVE, *sb.* the handle of a 'hack.'—*Ibid.* See **Auve.**

HACKER, *sb.* a short, strong, slightly curved implement of a peculiar kind, for chopping off the branches of fallen trees, &c.—CLEE HILLS; LUDLOW, *Cleobury Mortimer* (Forest of Wyre). Cf. **Brummock.**

'Axe, *hacker*, mittins, and other small tools.'—*Auctioneer's Catalogue* (Stoddesden), 1870.

HACKLE [ak·l], (1) *sb.* a cone-shaped covering of straw placed over bee-hives to protect them from wet and cold.—PULVERBATCH; CLUN; NEWPORT.

Compare '*Heyke*, garment. *Lacerna*,' with Way's note in *Prompt. Parv.*, p. 232. Also, 'A.S. *hacele;* Goth. *hakuls;* O.Icel. *hökull;* O.H.Germ. *hachul, hackle*, garments,' in STRAT.

(2) *v. a.* to cover the hives with 'hackles.'—*Ibid.* 'It's gettin' time to '*ackle* an' clicket the bees—theer'll be a snow afore lung.'

(3) *v. a.* to cover out-standing corn, by placing inverted sheaves over the 'mow' in such a manner that the straw spreads out, and forms a weather-thatch to throw off wet.—*Ibid.* 'I 'spect the glass is gweïn down, fur they'n begun to '*ackle* the corn i' the lung leasow, an' I see the Maister busy among 'em.' Cf. **Hattock.**

HACKLING-SHEAVES, *sb. pl.* the sheaves turned down over the 'mow.'—*Ibid.* Cf. **Hattocks.**

HACKNEY [ak·ni'], *sb.* a saddle-horse—an easy-paced, ambling nag. —PULVERBATCH. Qy. com. 'Whad! han'ee got two '*ackneys?*' 'Aye, that's a spon new un fur the Missis—the jockey's comin' to break it nex' wik.'

> 'Er we had riden fully fyue myle,
> At Boughton vnder Blee vs gan atake
> A man, that clothed was in clothes blake,
>
> . . . .
>
> His *hakeney*, that was al pomely grys,
> So swatte, that it wonder was to see;
> It semed he had priked myles three.'
>
> CHAUCER, G. 559 (Six-text ed.), Skeat.

> 'Syne to thi tennandis & to thi wawafouris
> If effy *haknays*, palfrais, and curfouris.'
>
> *Lancelot of the Laik*, l. 1730.

'*Hakeney* horse. *Bajulus, equiferus.*'—*Prompt. Parv.*

O.Fr. *hacquenée.*

HADDEN. See **Grammar Outlines**, *verb* **Have.**

'& tit þanne told eche til oþer · here tenes & here sorwe,
þat sadly for eiþers sake · *hadden* suffred long.'
William of Palerne, l. 1014.

HADNA. See **Grammar Outlines,** *verb* **Have.**

'*Sym.* I wad na baulk my friend his blithe design,
Gif that it *hadna* first of a' been mine.'
ALLAN RAMSAY, *The Gentle Shepherd*, II. i. p. 25.

HAG [ag·], (1) *sb.* a plantation; a coppice; or part of a wood enclosed for any special purpose.—WELLINGTON.

'This said he led me over holts and *hags*,
Through thorns and bushes scant my legs I drew.'
FAIRFAX' (A.D. 1600) *Tasso*, viii. 41, in Nares.

There is a farm called the *Hag* a few miles south of Bridgnorth, in the parish of Highley, and not far from the Forest of Wyre.

Mr. Halliwell says, 'The park at Auckland Castle was formerly called the *Hag*.'

'A.S. *haga;* O.Du. *hage* (*haghe*); O.Icel. *hagi*, locus sepe circumdatus.'—STRAT. Cf. **Hay.**

(2) *sb.* an allotment of timber for felling.—CLEE HILLS; LUDLOW; BRIDGNORTH.

When a wood is to be cut down and a number of men are engaged to do it, they conduct the operation on this wise:—they range themselves at the edge of the wood at about forty yards apart, then they start, proceeding in straight lines through the wood, hewing down the underwood, and hacking the outer bark of the trees with their 'hackers' as they go along; shouting to each other in the mean while, in order to keep their respective distances, till they reach the farther limit. The lines thus cleared form the boundaries of the *hag* apportioned to each man to fell.

A line of demarcation of this kind is called by the wood-cutters in the neighbourhood of Cleobury Mortimer a '*bliss*,'—they make a *bliss*, and in doing it '*brase*'—as their term is—the outer bark of the trees, *i. e.* cut and slash it: in using this expression *brase* they preserve an old word, meaning—according to Mr. Halliwell—'to make ready; to prepare,' in its early sense, applying it as they do, to their work of preparation for the *hag*. See *Hagways*, N. and Q. [5th S. xi. 257.]

(3) *sb.* work taken by contract; a job of work.—PULVERBATCH; WORTHEN; ELLESMERE. 'Whad! bin'ee roäd-makin', James?' 'No, I'm on'y doin' a bit of a '*ag* fur owd Tummas—'e's gwun to 'is club to-day.'

HAGGIS [ag·is], *sb.* Not the 'Great chieftain o' the puddin'-race,' the Scotch '*Haggis*,' immortalized by Burns, but the smaller entrails of a calf; what the 'chitterlings' are in a pig.—CLUN.

'*Omasus, i. tripa vel ventriculus qui continet alia viscera*, a trype, or a podynge, or a wesaunt, or *hagges*,' in WAY.

HAGGIT [ag·i't], *part. adj.*, *var. pr.* harassed; careworn; emaciated; 'hagged.'—PULVERBATCH. 'Poor Nancy Poppet looks despert '*aggit*, as if 'er worked 'ard an' far'd 'ard.'

Ash has '*Hagged*, tormented; harassed.' See *Hag*, in WEDG.

HAGGLE [ag·l], (1) *v. a.* to cut and carve in notches.—SHREWSBURY; WEM; ELLESMERE. Qy. com. 'Dunna yo' '*aggle* the mate i' that way—I conna bar to see it.'

> 'Suffolk first died: and York, all *haggled* over,
> Comes to him, ...'
>
> *K. Henry V.*, IV. vi. 11.

'The manner of carving is not only a very necessary branch of information, to enable a lady to do the honours of her table, but makes a considerable difference in the consumption of a family. . . . . . Some people *haggle* meat so much as not to be able to help half a dozen persons decently from a large tongue, or a sirloin of beef; and the dish goes away with the appearance of having been gnawed by dogs.'—*Domestic Cookery*, p. vi. ed. 1812—1815 (?).

'Sw. dialect, *hagga*, to hew.'—WEDG. Cf. **Kag** (3).

(2) *v. n.* to dispute; to bicker.—SHREWSBURY; PULVERBATCH; WEM. Qy. com. 'Who said it ŏŏnna?—yo' wanten to '*aggle*, dun'ee—yo' bin al'ays ready for cross-plādin'.'

'Fris. *hagghen*, rixari.—Kilian,' in WEDG.

'*Rixor*, to braule, to scould, to strive and quarrel.'—*Dict. Etym. Lat.* Cf. **Argy** (1).

(3) *v. n.* to drive a hard bargain; to be tedious in coming to an agreement about price. Qy. com. ''E's a rar' chap to drive a bargain, 'e'd '*aggle* a nour fur sixpence.' Cf. **Higgle**.

HAIFER [ai·fur'], *sb.*, *var. pr.* a heifer.—CORVE DALE; CLEE HILLS. '*Hayfare*' is given as the gloss of '*juvenca*' in a *Metrical Vocabulary*, perhaps xiv. cent., in Wr. vocabs., vol. i. p. 177.

See '*Hekfere, Juvenea*,' with Way's note in *Prompt. Parv.*, p. 234. A.S. *heáhfore*, a heifer.

HAIHOW [ai·ou], *sb. Gecinus viridis*, the Green Woodpecker.—BRIDGNORTH, *Chelmarsh*. '*Pimard*, a heighaw, or woodpecker.'—COTGRAVE's *French Dictionary*. See **Ecall.**

HAIRY-TAILOR, *sb.* the caterpillar of *Arctia caja*, the Tiger-moth. CLUN, *Twitchen*. Cf. **Tommy-Tailor.**

HALF-SOAKED, *part. adj.* said of persons of feeble mind or of silly expression.—SHREWSBURY; WHITCHURCH. 'That chap looks as if 'e wuz on'y '*afe-soaked*.' Cf. **Finished.**

HALF-STRAINED, *part. adj.* simple; silly; half-witted. Qy. com. 'Well, I think the Maister wuz to blame to trust a '*afe-strained* auf like 'im, ŏŏth a sperited 'orse—'e met a bin sure 'e'd spile it.'

HALLANTID [al·untid], *sb.*, *obsols.* the time of the 'Festival of All-Saints.'—PULVERBATCH. Cf. **Alhalontid.**

HALTER [aut·ur'], Com. [ou·tur'], LUDLOW, *sb.* It is commonly said of a person in impotent rage that he is 'as mad as a tup in a '*auter*.'

HAMES [ai·mz], *sb. pl.* the two crooked pieces of wood which encompass a horse-collar, and to which the traces are attached.—PULVERBATCH; NEWPORT. Qy. com.

'Les cous de chivaus portunt esteles,' with '*hames*' as the gloss of '*esteles*,' occurs in *The Treatise of Walter de Biblesworth*, xiii. cent., in Wr. vocabs., vol. i. p. 168.

'*Attelle*, terme de Bourrelier, espece de planche chantournée qu'on attache au devant des colliers des chevaux de charrettes. The *haum*.' —CHAMB.

'Du. *haam*; hame; horse-collar.'—STRAT. Cf. **Homes.**

HAN. See **Grammar Outlines,** *verb* **Have.**

> '& gode sire, for godes loue · also greteþ wel oft
> alle my freyliche felawes · þat to þis forest longes,
> *han* pertilyche in many places · pleide wiþ ofte.'
> *William of Palerne*, l. 361.

> 'For al ys good that hath good ende,
> When ȝe *han* mended ȝe *han* do mys,
> This ys no nay.'
> JOHN AUDELAY'S *Poems*, p. 54.

'"They *han*," which you may read in Chaucer, and hear in Yorkshire and Derbyshire, is a contraction, *hav-en*.'—PEGGE'S *Anecdotes of the English Language*, p. 202, ed. 1814.

A.S. *habban*, to have.

HAND-BREADTH. See **Weights and Measures,** p. xciii.

'*Hand-breadth* (Ex. xxv. 25), a measure of length now rarely used; a palm. Horses are still measured by *hands*. Compare Ezek. xl. 43.' —*Bible Word-Book*.

'Others have thought, that it [the grape of Amomum] commeth from a shrubbe like Myrtle, & carieth not aboue a *hand-bredth*, or 4 inches in height.'—HOLLAND'S *Pliny*, xii. 13, in *ibid.*

> 'She's bow-hough'd, she's hein shinn'd,
> Ae limpin' leg a *hand-breed* shorter;
> She's twisted right, she's twisted left,
> To balance fair in ilka quarter.
> . . . .
> Sic a wife as Willie had,
> I wad na gie a button for her.'
> ROBERT BURNS, *Poems*, p. 207, l. 14, c. 2.

'Hande Brede. *Palmus*.'—*Prompt. Parv.*

A.S. *hand-brǽd*, a hand's breadth.

HANDKERCHER [ang·kur'chur'], *sb.* a handkerchief. Qy. com.

> '*Oliver*. . . . . . if you will know of me
> What man I am, and how, and why, and where
> This *handkercher* was stained.'
> *As You Like It*, IV. iii. 97.

'Handcloth (Sax. *hondclath*) was the old and more proper word for that which we now call a *Handkercher*.'—BLOUNT, *Glossographia*, p. 298.

See '*Kerche*,' with Way's note, in *Prompt. Parv.*, p. 272.

Cf. **Hanshaker.**

HANDLASS, *sb.* a windlass. Com.—M. T.

HANDY-PANDY. See Bk. II., *Folklore*, &c., 'Games.'

HANGMAN'S-WAGES, *sb. pl.*, *sl.*? money paid before-hand for work. SHREWSBURY. See HAL.

HANSEL [an·sl], (1) *sb.* the first money received in the day on the sale of goods.—SHREWSBURY; PULVERBATCH. Qy. com. 'Bless yo', Missis, tak' summat off me jest fur *'ansel;* I've carried my basket all mornin' an' never soud a crock. Thank yo', Missis, I'll spit on this, an' 'ope it'll be lucky.'

> 'And, fiercely drawing forth his blade, doth sweare
> That who so hardie hand on her doth lay,
> It dearely shall aby, and death for *handsell* pay.'
>
> SPENSER, *F. Q.*, Bk. VI. c. xi. st. xv.

'It is a common practice among the lower class of hucksters, pedlars, or dealers in fruit or fish, on receiving the price of the first goods sold that day, which they call *hansel*, to spit on the money, as they term it, for good luck.'—GROSE, *Popular Superstitions.*

'*Hansel* (from the Brittish *honsel*); he that bestows the first money with a Tradesman, in the morning of a Fair or Market, is said to give him *Handsel*, quasi *Handsale.*'—BLOUNT'S *Glossographia*, p. 298.

'"Hansale, *Strena.*"—CATH. "Strena est bona sors, *Anglice* hansell."—ORTUS. "Hansell, *estrayne.* I hansell one, I gyue him money in a mornyng for suche wares as he selleth, *ie estrene.*"—PALSG.' *Prompt. Parv. and Notes.*

'O.Icel. *handsal*, handsel (hansel).'—STRAT.

A.S. *hand-sylen*, a giving into the hands. Cf. **Arness.**

(2) *v. a.* to try, or use, a thing for the first time.—PULVERBATCH. Qy. com. 'I never sid sich a time fur wet; I thought to *'ansel* my new bonnet o' Wissun-Sunday, but it rayned all day lung—it'll get owd a-lyin' by.'

> '. . . . . and Rose þe dissheres,
> Godfrey of garlekehithe · and gryfin þe walshe,
> And vpholderes an hepe · erly bi þe morwe
> Geuen glotoun with glad chere · good ale to *hansel.*'
>
> *Piers Pl.*, Text B., pass. v. l. 326.

'". . . To hanselle, *strenare, arrare.*"—CATH. ANG. "*Estreiné*, handselled, that hath the handsell or first use of."—COTG.' See WAY.

HANSHAKER [an·shukur'], *sb.*, *var. pr.* a handkerchief.—WELLINGTON. Cf. **Handkercher.**

HANTLE [an·tl], *sb.* a handful. Qy. com. 'I'll scaud a *'antle* o' 'ops an' bind it to the mar's leg—it'll bring the swellin' down.'

Hantle, in Southern Scotch, means a good many, a considerable number or quantity; and Dr. Murray says, 'the word seems to be *hand-tal*, a hand-tale or number.'—*Dialect of the Southern Counties of Scotland*, p. 178.

See **Grammar Outlines** (*nouns compounded with 'ful'*), p. xliii.

HAPPEN [ap·n], *adv.* perhaps; probably.—COLLIERY. '*'Appen* I shall be theer.'

'"Now faire words makes fooles faine;
& that may be seene by thy Master & thee;
ffor you may *happen* think itt soone enoughe
when-euer you that shooting see."'
Northumberland betrayed by Dowglas, l. 181. *Percy, Folio MS.*, vol. ii. p. 224, ed. Hales and Furnivall.

Pegge gives, '*Happen* and *Haply*, perhaps. Happen I may go. Derb.' Cf. **Mayhappen**. See **Behappen**.

HARDEN [aa·r'dn], *v. a., pec.* to air clothes—damp from the washing.—CLUN, *Herefd. Border.* 'Mind as yo' *'ard'n* them things afore yo' putten 'em away.' A.S. *heardian*, to harden.

HARD-YEDS [aa·r'd yedz], *sb. pl.* the hard, globose heads of *Centauréa-nigra*, black Knapweed.—WELLINGTON.

HARIFFE [ae·r'if], *sb. Galium Aparíne*, Goose-grass or Cleavers. Com.

'*Hec uticella*, haryffe,' occurs in a *Nominale*, xv. cent., in Wr. vocabs., vol. i. p. 226. Mr. Wright has the following note upon it:—'In Gloucestershire the name *hairiff* is given to the plant called more usually goose-grass or cleavers; . . . in the north it is applied to catchweed.' See '*Hayryf*,' in *Prompt. Parv.*, with Way's note.

HARNISH [aa·r'nish], (1) *sb.* horse-trappings; harness.—PULVERBATCH; LUDLOW; WEM. 'The *'arnish* mus' be brought i' the kitchen, it's gettin' quite mouldy.' See below.

(2) *v. a.* to put the harness on horses.—*Ibid.* 'Tell Jack to *'arnish* the mar'; I' want to gŏŏ as fare as the Beäs-leech, fur that cow's despert bad.'

John Audelay uses this form in the sense of to garnish or decorate:—

'. . . . . he is a gentylmon and jolylé arayd,
His gurdlis *harneschit* with silver, his baslard hongus bye.'
Poems, p. 16.

'O.Fr. *harnascher, harnacher*, garnir, équiper . . . . . Ce mot ne dérive pas de l'allemand *harnisch*; . . . c'est le contraire qu'il eût fallu admettre . . . [c'est] du celtique: kymri *haiarn*, anc. breton *hoiarn*, irlandais *iaran*, fer.' See further, in BUR.

HARROOST [aar'·ŭost], *sb., var. pr.* harvest. — SHREWSBURY; PULVERBATCH. '*Back o' harrŏost*' is after the harvest. 'W'en's yore wakes, Tum?' 'Oh, *back o' 'arrŏost*.' **Der.** 'harroosting.'

HARROOST-DRINK, *sb.* strong, twelvemonth-old ale. — *Ibid.* They'n got some o' the best owd beer at Goff's o' Wes'ley as ever I tasted.' 'Aye, they wun al'ays noted fur good *'arrŏost-drink*.' See **Drink**.

HARROOSTING, *sb.* the act of getting in the harvest.—*Ibid.* 'Our Dick's gwun ŏŏth Jack Sankey an' a lot on 'em down tŏërt Atcham an' Emstrey a-*'arrŏostin'*—yo' sin they bin yarlier down theer; they'n get three wiks *'arrŏost* wages, an' be back time enough fur ours.'

HARRY-LONG-LEGS, *sb. Tipula gigantéa*, Great Crane-fly. Com.

"'*Arry, 'Arry-lung-legs,*
Couldna say 'is prars;
Ketcht 'im by the lef' leg,
An throwed 'im down stars.'
Children's Doggerel Verse.

HARSLET [aar'·sli't], *obsols.?* same as **Haslet**, q. v.—CLEE HILLS. Mr. Halliwell glosses this word, 'A pig's chitterlings,' and quotes, 'A haggise, a chitterling, a hog's *harslet*.'—*Nomenclator*, p. 87.

In the *Domestic Cookery*, p. 64, ed. 1812—1815 (?), there are directions for dressing a *Pig's Harslet*:—'. . . chop the liver, sweetbreads, &c., . . . when mixed, put all into a cawl, and fasten it up tight with a needle and thread. Roast it on a hanging jack, or by a string.' This would be a *haggis*. Alternative instructions are—'Or serve in slices with parsley for a *fry*.' Cf. **Fry** (2).

HARVEST-BEER, same as **Harroost-drink**. Qy. com.

HARVEST-GOOSE. See Bk. II., *Folklore*, &c., 'Customs' (*harvest*).

HASAM-JASAM [ai·zum jai·zum], *adj.* equal, as in weight, size, or value.—PULVERBATCH. 'Theer wuz fifteen faggits i' one lot, an' sixteen i' the tother, an' I püt 'em little an' big together, to mak' 'em as '*äsam-jäsam* as I could.'

HASK [as·k], *sb.* a hoarse, hard cough.—NEWPORT; WEM; WHITCHURCH. ''E's gotten sich a '*ask* on 'im.'

'He hath a great *haskness*, gravi asthmate implicatur.'—*Horman*, in WEDG. See below. Cf. **Hoost**, also **Wisk**.

HASKY [as·ki'], *adj.* harsh; dry; arid.—WEM; WHITCHURCH. 'A '*asky* cough;' ''*asky* winde;' ''ard an' '*asky* land.' See *harske* or *haske*, with Way's note, in *Prompt. Parv.*, p. 228. Icel. *heskr*, *hastr*, harsh.

HASLET [as·li't], *sb.*, *obsols.?* the heart, liver, and lights of a pig, taken out entire—with the wind-pipe attached.—PULVERBATCH; CLUN. 'We shanna a to bwile the pot o' Friday, theer'll be the '*aslet* fur the men's dinners.'

'There was not a hog killed within three parishes of him, whereof he had not some part of the *haslet* and puddings.'—OZELL (first half 18th cent.), *Rabelais*, Bk. iii. ch. 41, in Nares.

'*Haslet* [probably of *Haste*, F. a Spit, because being usually roasted], the Entrails of a Hog.'—BAILEY, ed. 1727.

'Fr. *hastille, hasterel, hastemenue*, the pluck or gather of an animal.' —WEDG. Cf. **Harslet**, also **Hack**.

HASP [as·p], *sb.* a fastening for the lid of a box—a folding clasp with staple attached which falls over the lock: the staple fits into an aperture on one side of the key-hole, and is there secured by the bolt of the lock. Com. 'I lost the kay, an' didna like to break the '*asp*, so I knocked a bwurd out o' the bottom.'

'And underneþe is an *hasp*, shet wiþ a stapil and a clasp.'
R. Coer de Lion, l. 4083, in STRAT.

'*Clavis vel sera*, hespe,' occurs in *Semi-Saxon Vocabulary*, xii. cent., in Wr. vocabs., vol. i. p. 92.

'"Haspe of a dore, *clichette*."—PALSG. "*Agraphe*, a claspe, hook, brace, grapple, haspe."—COTG. In this last sense the word *haspa* occurs in the Sherborn Cartulary, MS. . . . . where, among the gifts of William the sacrist (xii. cent. ?), is mentioned, "*Missale cum haspâ argenteâ*."'—WAY.

Bailey—ed. 1782—has, 'An *Hasp*, a Sort of fastening for a Door, Window, &c.'

A.S. *hæps*, *hæsp*, a hapse, hasp, the hook of a hinge. Cf. **Clicket** (1).

HASTENER [ai·snur'], *sb.* a long funnel-shaped tin vessel for warming 'drink' quickly: when used for this purpose it is put *into* the fire, not *upon* it, as a saucepan would be.—CRAVEN ARMS. See *Hastener*, in WEDG. Cf. **Horn.**

HAT [at·], *pret.*, *obsols.* heated.—PULVERBATCH. 'Whad'n'ee bin doin' all mornin' ?—I '*at* the oven an' knad the bread afore the men comen in fur thar bayte, an' yo'n bin pītherin' o'er them tuthree milk-things all this wilde.'

HAT-BAT, *sb.* the Long-eared Bat.—PULVERBATCH; WORTHEN. Cf. **Billy-bat**, also **Flitter-mouse.**

HATCHEL, same as **Hetchel**, q. v.—CLEE HILLS.

'An *Hatchel*, of which there are several sorts, one finer than another, these are long Iron Pinns set orderly in a Board with which Hemp and Flax is combed into fine haires.'—*Academy of Armory*, Bk. III. ch. iii. p. 106.

HAT-FULL-OF-FEATHERS, (1) *sb.* the nest of the Long-tailed Titmouse.—OSWESTRY.

'Meanwhile Rupert, wandering listlessly about the pool, and keeping his eye on the bushes, discovered the most beautifully-constructed nest of any of our English birds—that of the long-tailed tit. This nest was about as large as a small cocoa-nut, and just the shape of one, with a small hole in the side, near the top, to admit the birds. It was made of mosses, feathers, and hair, and was encrusted on the outside with lichens, until it looked as if it were spangled with frosted silver. Inside, it was so full of fine soft feathers, that it quite justified the name it bears among the country lads of a "*hat full of feathers*."' —G. CHRISTOPHER DAVIES, *Rambles and Adventures of Our School Field-Club*, p. 136, ed. 1875.

(2) *sb.* the nest of the Willow Wren.—OSWESTRY.

This nest 'is a rounded structure with a hole in the side, through which the bird obtains admission into the interior. . . . The materials of which it is composed are generally leaves, grasses, and moss, and the interior is lined with a warmer bed of soft feathers.'—WOOD'S *Natural History* (Birds), vol. ii. p. 281.

HATHORN [aath·ur'n], *sb.*, *var. pr.* the hawthorn.—PULVERBATCH. 'I went to Cunder [Condover] church o' Wissun-Sunday to see the poor owd Maister's grave, an' come the fut roäd across the Park back—it wuz grand, the '*athurn* trees wun blowed as w'ite as a sheet.'

HATTOCK [at·uk], *v. a.* to cover reaped corn in the field with *hattocks.* See below. Cf. **Hackle** (3), also **Hood.**

HATTOCKS, *sb. pl.* sheaves of corn inverted over the 'mow' to protect it from wet. The two end sheaves of the 'mow,' which consists of eight sheaves, are taken as *hattocks* for the remaining six.—ELLESMERE, *Welshampton*. Compare O.N. *höttr* (later *huttr*), which had, according to Cleasby, the primary meaning of the cowl of a cloak, and seems to be allied to *hetta*, a hood, with A.S. *hæter*, clothing; apparel. Whence *hatt* + *ock*, a covering.

'An *Hattock* is three Sheafs laid together.'—*Academy of Armory*, Bk. III. ch. iii. p. 73.

Grose gives '*Hattock*, a shock of corn containing twelve sheaves, N.

Cf. **Hackling-sheaves**, also **Hooders**.

HAUL [aul·], *v. a.* to carry coal.—SHREWSBURY; LUDLOW.

'1805. Decr. 7th, *Hawling* Load Coals to the workhouse. 1 - 0 - 0.' —*Parish Accounts*, Much Wenlock.

Cf. **Lug** (1).

HAULIER [aul·yur'], *sb.* a man who carts coal, &c. for hire.—SHREWSBURY; ELLESMERE. 'I've bin to Philips the *'aulier* to axe 'im w'en 'e can fatch me a lŏoäd o' cŏäl from the Cut-w'arf' [Ellesmere]. See **-ier**. Cf. **Jagger**.

HAULM [aum·], *sb.* pease-straw; bean-stalks, &c.—PULVERBATCH. Qy. com.

'*Culmus*, healm,' occurs in *Archbp. Ælfric's Vocabulary*, x. cent., in Wr. vocabs., vol. i. p. 38, and Mr. Wright remarks upon it:—'The straw of corn, as well as the stalks of many other plants, are [*sic*] still called *haulm* in many of our provincial dialects.'

'A.S. *healm*; O.Sax., O.H. Germ. *halm*; O.Icel. *halmr*, halm (haum), *culmus*.'—STRAT.

HAW. See **Waggoners' Words to Horses**.

HAWS [au·z], *sb. pl.* the fruit of *Cratægus Oxyacántha*, Hawthorn. Com.

'*Hawes*, hepus, & hakernes · & þe hasel-notes,
& oþer frut to þe fulle. . . . . . .'
William of Palerne, l. 1811.

Cf. **Hippety-haws**. See **Hips**, also **Cuckoo's-beads**.

HAY, *sb.*, *obsols.* a plantation; a wood; a coppice: formerly a portion of a forest, or wood, enclosed for special purposes, as of deer-keeping, feeding swine, &c., but in this sense the term is become *obsolete*.—WELLINGTON. A gamekeeper of Lord Forester's said [1868], 'We'n seventeen *'ays* about 'ere, an' we cut'n [thin] one every 'ear, so it'll be seventeen 'ears afore the Arcall [Ercall] is cut agen.' A group of small coppices in the neighbourhood of Wellington is known as the 'Black Hays.' The entrance to the king's *Hay* in the forest of Mount Gilbert, otherwise known as the Wrekin forest, is still called *Hay*-gate. *Hay* enters into the names of several places about Wellington, as Horse-*hay*, Hinks-*hay*, &c. It occurs in like manner in other parts of Salop. 'The *Hay*' near Coalport was formerly a portion of Shirlot Forest. 'The *Hays*' and '*Hay* House' are the names of farms which lie a few miles south of Bridgnorth; and two others which border on the Clee Hills are called respectively '*Hay*-more' and '*Hay*-farm.' On the west side of the county, northward of Worthen, there is a farm on what is called the Forest of *Hayes*—south of this is *Hay*-wood. About half a mile from Westbury there is a mill at *Hay*-ford. Then, near the southern limits of the county, not far from Ludlow, is *Hay* Park. Other instances might be adduced, but those here given will be sufficient to show how the old word *hay* = enclosure, once obtained in Shropshire.

'In the edition of the Ortus in Mr. Wilbraham's library, *clausura*, is rendered "a closse, or a heye." *Haye* occurs elsewhere in the sense of an enclosure; thus in the gloss on the "*liber vocatus equus*," called in the Promptorium "*Distigius*," written by John de Garlandiâ, occurs "*Cimiterium*, chyrche-haye."—Harl. MS. 1002. In the Golden Legend it is said, "he had—foule way thorugh *hayes* and hedges, woodes, stones, hylles and valeys."—f. 68, b.' WAY, p. 221.

'O.Fr. *haie*, clôture en général; du bas-allemand *haeghe*, enclos.' —BUR.

Compare 'A.S. *haga*; O.Du. *hage* (*haghe*); O.Icel. *hagi*, locus sepe circumdatus.'—STRAT. See below. Cf. **Hag** (1).

HAYMENT, HEYMENT, *sb.*, *obs.* a fence; a boundary. This word, mentioned by Mr. Hartshorne as having come under his notice in a parish book pertaining to Smethcot, and which he subsequently found to mean, 'the hedge which encircles part of the churchyard,' seems to have had a wide range throughout Shropshire. Though for the most part restricted in its application to the boundary—of whatever kind it were—which enclosed the churchyard, yet it was not necessarily so.

Gough, in his *History of Myddle*, pp. 10, 11, at the date of 1770, says, that a certain bridge over a brook 'some years past was out of repaire, and the parishioners of Baschurch parish did require the parish of Myddle to repaire one half of this bridge. . . . Rowland Hunt of Boreatton, Esq. . . . living in Baschurch parish, was very sharp upon the inhabitants of Myddle parish beecause they refused to repair half the bridge. But the parishioners of Myddle answeared that the brooke was whoaly in the parish of Baschurch, and was the *Hayment* or fence of the men of Baschurch parish, betweene their lands, and the lands in Myddle parish. . . .' At p. 33 of the same work, Gough says, speaking of Billmarsh Green, 'This is a small common, much controverted, whether it lyes in the Lordship of Myddle, or in the parish of Broughton, and libertyes of Salop. . . . But all Billmarsh was formerly a common, and it should seem that this Greene was left out of it when it was incloased, for all other places make *Heyment* from Bilmarsh except this Greene.'

In p. 65 of *A Lecture on Quatford, Morville and Aston Eyre 800 Years Ago*, by the Rev. George Leigh Wasey, M.A. (Bridgnorth, 1859), the following old custom at Quatford is recorded:—'The wall round the churchyard, extending two hundred and seventy yards, is apportioned between the following nine properties in the parish, which are bound by immemorial usage to keep certain lengths of it in fixed repair, on the application of the churchwardens: the Careswell Charity estate; Daniel's mill; Mr. Pitman's estate at Eardington, late Mr. Duppa's; Mrs. Oldbury's; Mr. Rutter's; the Hay farm, now Mr. Walker's property; Lord Sudeley's farm at the Knowle; Mr. Hudson's at the Deanery; and Mr. Norton's at Eardington.'

The portions of the churchyard wall for these 'Properties' to repair so many yards each are marked out on the vestry map, which is called 'the Map of the *Hayments*.'

The following extract is from the *Churchwardens' Accounts*, Clun:—'Agreed at a Vestry Meeting held for the parish of Clun, the 24th Day of May 1755, for the Repairs of the Church and the Churchyard Wall or *Hayments*, as follows. . . .'

In the *Churchwardens' Accounts*, Hopton Castle, are the following entries:—'1747, Pd. Willm Bottwood for mend-g *Hayment* 0 - 17 - 0.

'Pd. Mr. Beale for Timbr. 1 - 1 - 0.

1766. for Railing the Church *hayment* at two pence f. 0 - 12 - 0.'

The churchyard at Hopton Castle is still [1875] enclosed by a wooden paling on its south side, though it is no longer called the *hayment*.

Gough glosses the proper name *Hayward*, 'a keeper or overseer of *Hayment*.' See *History of Myddle*, p. 197. *Hayment* is made up of Fr. *haie*, and Fr. suffix, '*ment*.' See **Hay**, above.

HAYTICK, *sb.* common Whitethroat.—OSWESTRY. This bird, when alarmed, flies about the tall grass uttering a '*tick*-ing' sound, from which it gets its name, *Haytick*. See **Flax**. Cf. **Utick**.

HE, used for **It**. See **Grammar Outlines** (*personal pronouns*), p. xlviii.

> 'A! nay! lat be; the philosophres stoon,
> Elixir clept, ...
> For al our craft, whan we han al ydo,
> And al our sleighte, *he* wol nat come vs to.
> *He* hath ymaad vs spenden mochel good.'
>
> CHAUCER, G. 867, 868 (Six-text ed.), Skeat.

Cf. **Him**, below.

HEAD [yed·], Com. [yad·], BISHOP'S CASTLE; CLUN. [yud·], LUDLOW, *Burford*.

HEAD-OUT [yed· out], *v. a.* to 'drive a head' in advance of the general workings.—COLLIERY. See **Drive a head**.

HEAD-COLLAR [yed· kol·'ur'], *sb.* a kind of bridle put on to a horse for the purpose of fastening him to the manger,—an arrangement of leather straps, passing over the nose, under the throat, and round the neck of the animal. A rope—which is sometimes called the *shank*—is attached to the *head-collar*, and by it the horse is tied up in his stall.—ELLESMERE. Qy. com.

HEAD-STALL [ed·stul *and* yed·stul], *sb.*, *obsols.*? same as **Head-collar**, above.—ATCHAM; ELLESMERE.

> '. . . . . one did take
> The horse in hand within his mouth to looke:
> . . . .
> Another, that would seeme to have more wit,
> Him by the bright embrodered *hed-stall* tooke.'
>
> SPENSER, *F. Q.*, Bk. V. c. iii. st. xxxiii.

'. . . . his horse hipped with an old mothy saddle and stirrups of no kindred; . . . . . and with a half-checked bit and a *head-stall* of sheep's leather.'—*Taming of the Shrew*, III. ii. 58.

HEAP [yep·], Com. [yup·]. CLUN; LUDLOW, *Burford*, *v. a.* and *sb.* to heap; a heap. See **Scutch-yup.**

HEARKEN-OUT, *v. n.* to be on the watch for information.—SHREWSBURY; NEWPORT. Qy. com. 'We'n *'eark'n-out*, an' mebbe we shan 'ear o' summat'—having reference to the subject of inquiry.

HEART [aa·r't], *sb., pec.* state; condition; said of ground.—PULVERBATCH. Qy. com. 'It'll do mighty well this time athout muck, the groun' 's in good *'eart*, an' well claned.'

HEARTEN, *v. a.* to cheer; to encourage; to invigorate.—PULVERBATCH; NEWPORT; WEM. Qy. com. This term is usually employed with one or other of the prepositions, *up* or *on*. 'Come in an' 'ăve a dish o' tay—it'll *'earten* yo' *on*—yo'n find it a good way to Powtherbitch [Pulverbatch], an' all up 'ill.'

'*Prince.* My royal father, cheer these noble lords
And *hearten* those that fight in your defence:
Unsheathe your sword, good father; cry "Saint George!"'
3 *K. Henry VI.*, II. ii. 79.

'*Roger.* Kind Patie, now fair fa' your honest heart,
Ye're aye sae cadgy, and have sic an art
To *hearten* ane. . . . .'
ALLAN RAMSAY, *The Gentle Shepherd*, I. i. p. 11.

A.S. *hyrtan*, to encourage; comfort.

HEART-WELL [aa·r't wel·], *adj.* in good general health.—SHREWSBURY; PULVERBATCH. Qy. com. 'I'm pretty *'eart-well*, God be thankit, on'y infirm'd.'

HEAVE [ai·v], (1) *v. a., var. pr.* to lift. Com. '*'Aive* that pot off the fire, them tatoes bin done.'

'& comande þe couherde · curteysli and fayre,
to *heue* vp þat hende child · bi-hinde him on his stede.'
William of Palerne, l. 348.

'He was schort schuldred, brood, a thikke knarre,
Ther nas no dore that he nolde *heve* of barre,
Or breke it at a rennyng with his heed.'
CHAUCER, *The Prologue*, l. 550, ed. Morris.

See **Hove**, also **Heler.**

(2) *v. n.* to rise; said of bread when 'laid in sponge;' or of cheeses that rise up in the middle in consequence of the whey not having been thoroughly pressed out. Com. (1) 'I doubt this bread'll be sad, it dunna *'aive* well—the barm's bin fros'-ketcht, I spect.' (2) 'Theer's won o' them cheese *'aivin'* I see—we maun keep that fur ourselves—it wunna do fur the markit.' Cf. **Bulled.**

(3) See Bk. II., *Folklore, &c.*, 'Customs connected with Days and Seasons' (*Easter Monday*).

HEAVER [ai·vur'], (1) *sb., obsols.* a kind of vertical, sliding shutter across the doorway of a barn, made to fit into grooves in such a way that it can be lifted, or *'aived*, out at pleasure—whence its name. Qy. com. When grain was thrashed on the barn-floor with a 'thrashal' [flail], the *heaver* was employed to close up the lower part of the barn door-way, and so prevent the grain escaping by the—otherwise—open door of the barn.

(2) *sb.*, *obsols.* a kind of 'blower,' or winnowing machine without sieves. A handle is turned that works a fan—from a box at the top of the machine the grain falls over the thin edge of a board, and being met by a blast of wind from the fan, the light grain and dust are *'aived* out. Qy. com.

HEAVING. See as for **Heave** (3).

HEAVING-DAYS, *sb. pl.*, *obsols.* Easter Monday and Easter Tuesday: so called from the custom of *heaving* on those days. Qy. com. See above.

HEAVY [ev·i'], *adj.* stern.—WHITCHURCH; ELLESMERE. 'Yo' look'n very *'eavy* at me.'

HEDGE-BILL. See **Bill.**

HEEL [ee·l], *sb.* the top crust of a loaf cut off, or the bottom crust remaining.—PULVERBATCH. 'Cut a loaf through to sen' to the leasow, that *'eel* ŏŏnna be enough.' A remaining *corner* is called the *heel* of the loaf at CLUN. Burns has 'kebbuck-*heel*,' i. e. the remaining part of a cheese:—

'O Wives, be mindfu', ance yoursel
  How bonie lads ye wanted,
An' dinna, for a *kebbuck-heel*,
  Let lasses be affronted
    On sic a day!'—*Poems*, p. 19, l. 7.

Cf. **Cantel.**

HEEL-RAKE. See **Ell-rake.**

HEEL-TAPS, *sb. pl.* small quantities of ale, &c. left in the glasses. Com. 'Now, drink up yore *'eel-taps*, an' ăve another jug — the evenin' 's young yet.'

HEET, HEIT. See **Waggoners' Words to Horses.**

HEFT [ef·t], PULVERBATCH; CLEE HILLS; LUDLOW. [if·t], WEM.

(1) *sb.* a heavy weight. *A dead heft* is a weight that cannot be moved; as, for instance, the huge trunk of a fallen tree, would be *a dead heft* to a horse that was made to pull at it.

(2) *v. a.* to lift; to try the weight of a thing by lifting.—*Ibid.* 'W'y, Betty, han yo' carried that basket all the way?' 'Iss, an' yo' jest *heft* it.' 'My 'eart! it is a good *'eft.*' Shakespeare has *heft* in the sense of heaving:—

'. . . he cracks his gorge, his sides,
With violent *hefts.* . . . .'
    Winter's Tale, II. i. 45.

'A.S. *hebban;* O.Sax. *hebbien;* O.H.Germ. *heffan;* O.Icel. *hefja;* Goth. *hafjan*, to heave.'—STRAT.

HELER [ee·lur'], *sb. obs.?* one who covers or conceals a thing. This old word is preserved in a proverbial saying heard in the neighbourhood of Stoddesden:—'The *heler* 's as bad as the heaver;' which is analogous to, 'The receiver's as bad as the thief'—he who *heles*, or hides, is equally guilty with him who *heaves*, i. e. 'lifts,' which latter word has an old meaning of to steal, still retained in the modern term 'shop-*lifting*.'

> '"I-wisse," þan seyde william · "i wol no lenger *hele*,
> My liif, my langor, & my deþ · lenges in þi warde."'
>
> *William of Palerne*, l. 960.

A.S. *helan*, to cover; to conceal. Cf. **Hill**. See **Heave** (1).

HELL-HUN [el·un], *sb.*, *var. pr.* a hell-hound.—NEWPORT; WHITCHURCH. A poor old man whom a pack of ruffianly lads had hooted at and pelted, said of them, to a magistrate at Whitchurch, that 'they wun a paasle o' '*ell-'uns*.'

> 'ȝe ben to þe *helle-hond* · holliche i-like.'
>
> *Alexander and Dindimus*, l. 792.

> 'A cry of *hell-hounds* never ceasing bark'd
> With wide Cerberean mouths full loud, and rung
> A hideous peal. . . . .'
>
> *Paradise Lost*, Bk. II. l. 654.

A.S. *helle-húnd*, *idem*. See **Grey-hun** for *hound*.

HEMP-BUT, *sb.*, *obs.* a plot of garden ground, or a piece of a field on which hemp was grown.—WEM; ELLESMERE.

'It is observed that if the chiefe person of the family that inhabits in this farme [Cayhowell] doe fall sick, if his sicknesse bee to death, there comes a paire of pidgeons to the house about a fortnight or a weeke before the person's death, and continue there untill the person's death, and then goe away. This I have knowne them doe three severall times. 1st Old Mr. Bradocke, fell sicke about a quarter of a yeare after my Sister was maryed, and the paire of pidgeons came thither, which I saw. They did every night roust under the shelter of the roofe of the kitchen att the end, and did sit upon the ends of the side raisers. In the day time they fled about the gardines and yards. I have seene them pecking on the *hemp-butt* as if they did feed, and for ought I know they did feed.'—GOUGH'S *History of Myddle*, p. 47.

HEMPERT [em·pur't], *sb.*, *obs.* ground specially appropriated to hemp, whether of the garden or of a 'close.'—PULVERBATCH. 'So I see Mr. Goff 'as let the '*empert* into the stack-yurd—well, well, I s'pose as theer's more barley than 'emp wanted now-a-days.' *Hempert* is doubtless a corruption of *hemp-yard*.

HEN-AND-CHICKENS. See **Bachelors'-button.**

HEN-SCRATS, *sb. pl. cirri*,—filaments of white cloud crossing the sky like net-work.—PULVERBATCH; WHITCHURCH. Qy. com.

HERDEN [ur'd·h'n], *adj.* made of 'herdes,' q. v., below.—PULVERBATCH; CLUN; CLEE HILLS. 'The waiver's maden a nice piece o' 'uckaback of the '*erden* yorn—it'll do mighty well for the men's tablecloths.'

'The Inventory of the effects of Sir John Conyers, of Sockburne, Durham, 1567, comprises "vij harden table clothes, iv s.—xv. pair of harden sheats, xx s." Wills and Inv. Surtees Soc. i. 268,' in WAY.

See **Hurden**. Cf. **Noggen**.

HERDES [ur'd·z], *sb.*, *obsols.?* coarse, or refuse, flax or hemp.—PULVERBATCH; CLEE HILLS.

'*Hyrdys* or *herdys* of flax or hempe. *Stuppa.* "*Stupa*, hyrdes of hempe, or of flax. *Stupo*, to stop with hurdes."—MED. MS. CANT. "*Extupo, Anglice*, to do awaye hardes or tawe. *Stupa*, stub, chaf, or towe."—ORTUS. The word occurs in the Wicliffite version, Judges xvi. 9; "And sche criede to him, Sampson! Felisteis ben on þee, which brak þe boondis as if a man brekith a þrede of herdis (*filum de stupâ*, Vulg.) wriþun wiþ spotle." "Heerdes of hempe, *tillage de chamure* (? *chainvre*) *estovpes.*"—PALSG. "Hirdes, or towe, of flaxe, or hempe, *stupa.*"—BARET.' *Prompt. Parv. and Notes.*

'*Stúpa, vel stuppa, quòd cortici lini proximum*, ... The course part of flaxe.'—*Dict. Etym. Lat.*

Mr. Halliwell observes of *Herdes*, that it is 'still in use in Shropshire.' A.S. *heordas*, the refuse of tow. See **Hurds.** Cf. **Nogs.**

HESPEL [es·pil], *v. a.* to worry; to harass; to tease; to 'bother.'—SHREWSBURY; PULVERBATCH; WORTHEN; CLEE HILLS. 'They dun '*espel* that poor wench shameful—er's on throm mornin' till night, an' 'afe the night as well, fur now the childern han got the chin-cuff 'er 'as to be up an' down ŏŏth them.' Cf. **Huspel.**

HETCH, *sb.*, *var. pr.* a hatch, as of chickens, &c.—PULVERBATCH.

HETCHEL [ech·il], *sb.*, *obs.* a carding implement for dressing hemp or flax—a board with rows of iron teeth set in it—the fibre was thrown across the *hetchel* and pulled through it.—PULVERBATCH; WORTHEN.

'*Hechele*' (noun) and '*hechelet*' (verb) are the respective glosses of '*serence*' and '*serencet*' in the following lines:—

'La serence dout pernet,
E vostre lyn serencet.'
The Treatise of Walter de Biblesworth, xiii. cent., in Wr. vocabs., vol. i. p. 156.

Blount has, '*Hitchel* (Tut. *hechel*), a certain instrument with iron teeth to dress flax or hemp.'—*Glossographia*, p. 308.

'O.Du. *hekel*; O.H.Germ. *hachele*, hatchel (heckle).'—STRAT.

Cf. **Hatchel.** See **Swingle** (1), also **Tewter.**

HEYMENT. See **Hayment.**

HIE [ei·], *v. n.* to hasten—used in the imperative mood with the adverb *away*, has the meaning of 'be quick and go,' but is not often heard.—SHREWSBURY; PULVERBATCH. 'Now then, '*ie away* an' fatch me yore throck to pŭt on, else yo'n be late fur school agen.'

'Elles go by vs som, and that as swythe,
Now, gode sir, go forth thy wey and *hy* the.'
CHAUCER, G. 1295 (Six-text ed.), Skeat.

Hie, in combination with *up*, is employed in urging cows forward. See **Call-words** (*cows*). A.S. *higan, higian*; to make haste.

HIFT. See **Heft.**

HIGGLE [ig·l], *v. n.* to chaffer; to drive a hard bargain.—ELLESMERE.

'*Plume*. . . . Pretty Mrs. Rose—you have—let me see—how many?

'*Rose*. A Dozen, Sir, and they are richly worth a Crown.

'*Bul*. Come, Ruose; I sold fifty Strake [strike] of barley to-day in half this time; but you will *higgle* and *higgle* for a penny more than the Commodity is worth.

'*Rose*. What's that to you, Oaf? I can make as much out of a Groat as you can out of fourpence I'm sure. The Gentleman bids fair, and when I meet with a Chapman, I know how to make the best of him, and so, Sir, I say for a Crown-piece the Bargain's yours.'—FARQUHAR'S *Recruiting Officer*. Scene—The Market-place, Shrewsbury.

Cf. **Haggle** (3).

HIGGLER [ig·lur'], *sb.* same as **Badger**, q. v.—NEWPORT; ELLESMERE. Qy. com.

HIGHFUL [ei·ful], *adj.* haughty—'a *'ighful* dame.'—MUCH WENLOCK.

HIGHFULLY, *adv.* haughtily; with a distant manner.—*Ibid.* 'I didna gŏŏ, 'cause 'er on'y axed me *'ighfully*.'

HIGHRANGER [eir'ai·nzhur'], *sb.*, *var. pr.*, *obsole. Hydrangea hortense*.—SHREWSBURY; PULVERBATCH. 'I pŭt the *'ighranger* out i' the garden to get the sun, an' the winde's wouted the pot o'er an' broke it all to pieces.'

HIKE [ei·k], *v. a.* to throw; to toss; to injure with the horns; said of cattle.—NEWPORT; WEM; WHITCHURCH; ELLESMERE. About the middle of the present century there lived in the neighbourhood of Whixall a covetous old farmer, who, to prevent boys from trespassing on his land in nutting season, turned a 'running' bull into his fields. In about a week's time he himself was killed by this same bull—whereupon 'they māden a ballet on 'im.' The last verse ran thus:—

'E got 'is wealth,
By fraud an' stealth,
As fast as 'e could scraup it;
Theer com'd a bull,
An' cracked 'is skull,
An' *'iked* 'im in a saw-pit.'

The gravestone placed over this victim of his own greed, in the old churchyard—Whixall—still [1874] retains the traces of a chiselled gallows—showing the estimation in which he was held while living. Cf. **Hile**, below; also **Hite** (1).

HILE [ei·l], *v. a.* to strike with the horns as cattle do, so as to cause injury; to gore.—PULVERBATCH; NEWPORT; WEM; WHITCHURCH. (1) 'Our John's in a pretty way—them bŭllocks han *'iled* 'is new plaiched 'edge an' tore it all to winders.' (2) 'Them cows 'll *'ile* one another if they binna parted.'

'The terms *hile* and *hike* (see above), though often used indiscriminately for "horning," are clearly not, *in se*, synonymous—the attack of a savage bull consists of two processes; he first *hiles*, or gores, and then *hikes*, or tosses.' *Hile* = *hik-le*, the frequentative form.

See **I** (5), p. xxviii., for the Newport pronunciation of these two words.

HILL [il·], *v. a.* to cover.—SHREWSBURY; PULVERBATCH. Qy. com. (1) 'Please, Ma'am, shall I *'ill* you up afore I göö?' said a little maid to her invalid mistress, the covering of whose bed she was preparing to arrange for the night [1874]. (2) 'Mind an' *'ill* them tatoes well ööth feärn w'en yo' tumpen 'em.'

'. . . . . . . and pertiliche bi-holdes
hov hertily þe herdes wif · *hules* þat child,
& hov fayre it fedde · & fetisliche it baþede,
& wrouȝt wiþ it as wel · as ȝif it were hire owne.'
William of Palerne, l. 97.

'And alle þe houses ben *hiled* · halles and chambres,
Wit[h] no lede, but with loue · and lowe-speche-as-bretheren.'
Piers Pl., Text B., pass. v. l. 599.

'A rof shal *hile* us boþe o-nith,
Þat none of mine, clerk ne knith,
Ne sholen þi wif no shame bede,
No more þan min, so god me rede!'
Havelok the Dane, l. 2082.

'1544. For covering off W. Smyths grave v[d].
'1545. For covering off Thomas Warmynchames grave iij[d].
'1553. For leynge my lords grave and others ij[s] iiij[d].
'1558. For iiij bushells off lyme for pavyng ye Churche & *hyllyng* graves ther xx[d].'—*Treasurer's MS. Accounts of the Cathedral*, Chester.

'*Hyllyñ*' (coueren), *Operio, tego, velo.* "*Tego*, to hille; *tegmen*, an helynge."—MED. MS. CANT. "I hyll, I wrappe or lappe, *ie couvre; you must hyll you wel nowe a nyghtes, the wether is colde*."—PALSG. "*Palier*, to hill ouer, &c."—COTG.' *Prompt. Parv. and Notes.*

'A.S. *helan; O.H.Germ. hullen; Goth. huljan; O.Icel. hylja*, to hill; to cover.'—STRAT.

Der. 'hilling.' Cf. **Heler.**

HILLERS [il·ur'z], *sb. pl., obsols.* dwellers on hill-common; people who go to the 'hills' for the purpose of gathering wimberries.—PULVERBATCH. See **Wimberries.**

HILLING [il·in], *sb., obsols.* the binding or covering of a book.—PULVERBATCH; WELLINGTON. 'Tummy, yo'd'n better pŭt some brown paper on them school-books, or else the *'illin's* öön be spiled afore the wik's out.'

'*Hyllynge*, or coverynge of what thynge hyt be. *Coopertura, coopertorium, operimentum.* "*Tegmentum*, a hyllynge, a couerynge."—ORTUS. "*Hyllyng*, a coueryng, *couverture*."—PALSG. The accounts of the churchwardens of Walden comprise the item, "*A le Klerk de Thakstede pur* byndynge, *hyllynge et* bosynge *de tous les liveres en le vestiarye*."—Hist. of Audley End, p. 220.' *Prompt. Parv. and Notes.*

Cf. **Hulling.**

HIM, used for **It.** See **Grammar Outlines** (*personal pronouns*), p. xlviii.

'A! nay! lat be; the philosophres stoon,
Elixir clept, we sechen faste echoon;
For, hadde we *him*, than were we siker ynow.'
CHAUCER, G. 864 (Six-text ed.), Skeat.

Cf. **He**, above.

HIP-BOSS [ip· boss], *sb.* same as **Briar-boss**, q. v.—CLEE HILLS. See **Hips**, below.

HIPPETY-HAWS [ip·i'ti' au·z], *sb. pl.* same as **Haws**, q. v., children's term.—SHREWSBURY. See **Hips**, below.

HIPPETY-HAW TREE, *sb.* the hawthorn.—*Idem; ibid.*

HIPS [ip·s], *sb. pl.* the berries of *Rosa canina*, common Dog-rose. Com. *Hips* are generally associated with 'haws'—*hips and haws.*

'*hawes, hepus* & hakernes. . . .'
William of Palerne, l. 1811.

'Fie upon *heps* (quoth the fox) because he could not reach them.'—RAY'S *Proverbs*, p. 110.

A.S. *heópe*, the fruit of the dog-rose. See **Haws**.

HIT [it·], *sb.* a good crop.—PULVERBATCH; CLUN; CLEE HILLS. 'Theer's a perty good *hit* o' turmits this time.' 'Aye, the weather 'appens to shute 'em.'

HITE [eit· *corr.* a'y·t *and* ahy·t], PULVERBATCH; CHURCH STRETTON. [ahy·t *and* ait·], CLEE HILLS, *Abdon*. (1) *v. a.* to toss; to throw: the term is of general application.

(1) 'Poor owd Sally Wildblood's 'ad a mighty narrow 'scape up at Shep'n filds, 'er wuz gwei'n alung the leasow, an' the bŭll tŏŏk after 'er an' ketcht 'er jest as 'er raught the stile; 'e 'iled 'er legs an' then '*ited* 'er clane o'er into the Drench Lane.' 'Dear Sores! 'er met as well a bin killed.'

(2) 'We'd'n rar raps o' Sruv-Toosday ŏŏth the bwoys tossin' thar poncakes; Dick '*ited* 'is right o'er 'is yed, an' Bob send 'is up the chimley—Sam fell 'is i' the ess, an' then Tum 'ad 'is face collowed ŏŏth the pon.'

Farm-house kitchens are sometimes the scenes of great mirth on Shrove-Tuesday, when the farm-labourers celebrate the Feast of Pancakes—not only does each one toss a pancake, but if he fail to eat it before another is fried, he has to submit to having his face blacked with the frying-pan.

Hite = hike (see *ante*) by the common weakening of *k* to *t*.

(2) [a'yt·], *v. a.* to raise the hand as a signal.—PULVERBATCH; WEM. 'I've bin to the top o' the bonk to call Jack; the winde wuz so 'igh I couldna mak' im 'ear, but I '*ited* my 'ond at 'im, an' 'e'll come.'

HIVER-HOVER [iv·ur' ov·ur'], *adj.* wavering; undecided. Qy. com. 'Did'n yo' gŏŏ?' 'No, I wuz '*iver-'over* about it fur a bit, but as I said I ŏŏdna, I didna.'

HOB AND CATCH, *phr.* bit by bit; just as one can—as of getting in harvest in a bad season.—CRAVEN ARMS. Cf. **Catching-time**.

HOBBETY-HOY [ob·iti' oi·'], *sb.* a youth between boyhood and manhood. ''Twixt man an' boy.'—PULVERBATCH. Qy. com. 'Yo' dunna think I'd tak' up ŏŏth a *'obbety-'oy* like that fur a sweet'eart!—it'll be a better sort o' mon than 'im as'll get me i' the 'umour.' Tusser has the third season of man's age:—

'21 . . kepe vnder sir *hobbard de hoy*.'—See p. 138, ed. E. D. S.

> 'A *Hober-de-hoy*, half a man and half a boy.'
>
> RAY'S *Proverbs*, p. 57.

Cf. **Lobber-te-loy.**

HOB-JOB, *adv.* off-hand; without deliberation.—CLEE HILLS. ''E did *'ob-job* at a ventur'.'

HOBS AND GIRDS, *phr.* fits and starts.—PULVERBATCH. 'Theer's no 'eed to be took o' that fellow, 'e's all by *'obs an' girds*—yo' never knowen w'en yo' han 'im.' Cf. **Fits and Girds.**

HOBS-AND-GOBS, *sb. pl.* inequalities of surface.—PULVERBATCH; CLEE HILLS. 'Theer's some difference betwix them two turmit-fallows—the one's all *'obs-an'-gobs* like 'orses' yeds, an' the tother's as fine as a īnion-bed.' Cf. **Gob** (3).

HOBS-AND-JOBS, *sb. pl.* snatches; odd times.—WEM. 'We mun get that done by *'obs-an'-jobs*.' Cf. **Hob and Catch.**

HOD [od·], (1) *sb.* a store-heap of potatoes, or turnips, covered with straw and soil to protect them from frost.—ELLESMERE.

(2) *v. a.* to cover potatoes, &c. as above.—*Ibid.* Cf. **Hog** (3).

HODGE [oj·], *sb.* the large paunch in a pig.—CLUN. Cf. **Roger.**

HODGEN [oj·in], *sb. Erináceus Europæus*, the Hedgehog.—MUCH WENLOCK, *Cressage.* Cf. **Urchin.**

HOE [au·], SHREWSBURY; PULVERBATCH; ELLESMERE. Qy. com. [ou·], BISHOP'S CASTLE; CLUN, *sb.* and *v. a.* a hoe; to hoe.

> 'Some like sowin', some like mōwin';
> But of all the games that I do like,
> Is the game of turmit-'ōwin'.'
>
> *Local Doggerel Verse.*

O.H.Germ. *houwan*; Fr. *houe*, to hoe. Du. *houwer*, cognate with the O.H.G. *houwa*, a pick, or hoe. See WEDG.

HOG [og·], (1) *sb.* a male sheep of the first year.—BISHOP'S CASTLE; CLUN; CLEE HILLS.

'*The Sheep and beastes. Imprimis*, six wethers, nyne tupp or *hoggs*, thirteene *hoggs* & barren ewes, eleven heefers, foure steares, one bull, two geldings, two fylles, one Coult, one nagg, and six stales of Bees, lxij[li] xv[s] viij[d].'—*Inventory* . . . Owlbury Manor-house, Bishop's Castle, 1625.

> 'The lee-lang night we watch'd the fauld,
> Me and my faithfu' doggie;
> We heard nought but the roaring linn,
> Amang the braes sae scroggie;

But the howlet cry'd frae the castle wa',
The blitter frae the boggie,
The tod reply'd upon the hill,
I trembled for my *Hoggie.*'

ROBERT BURNS, *Poems*, p. 269, l. 36.

'*Hog*, a young sheep of the second year . . . Du. *hokkeling*, a heifer, beast of one year old. From being fed in the *hok* or pen.'—WEDG. Cf. **Hogget**, below.

(2) *v. a.* to trim a hedge by sloping it to the top, like the roof of a house.—SHREWSBURY; ATCHAM; ELLESMERE. *Hog* = hag = hack. Cf. **Blade.**

(3) *sb.* and *v. a.* same as **Hod**, q. v.—NEWPORT; WEM. Cf. **Bury**, also **Tump.**

HOGGET [og·i't], *sb.* same as **Hog** (1), above.—PULVERBATCH. Cf. **Thave.**

HOG-MANE, *sb.* a horse's mane cut quite short, so as to stand erect. —ELLESMERE. Cf. *Hog* (5), in HAL.

HOGSHET [og·shi't], *sb., var. pr.* a hogshead. 'Yo'n get a right good traicle *'ogshet* fur the valley o' 'afe-a-crownd—I 'ad one off Bromley the grozier, an' it lasted, fur a wesh-tub, 'ears.'

HOLD [ou·t], *sb.* place of safety, as a hole under a bank where fish lie; the retreat of any wild animal. Qy. com.

Mr. Oliphant, speaking of the French Romance of Sir Tristrem, which was Englished about 1270, says, 'Some new substantives are found. In page 25 a castle is called a *hold.*'—See *Sources of Standard English*, p. 160.

Cf. *Ps.* lxxi. 2.

HOLD YO' [ou·d yu'], *phr.* 'hold fast'—an expression of the harvest-field—addressed to the man on the load when the waggon is about to move on. Com.

HOLD YOUR HOLD [ou·d yur' ou·'t], *phr.* meaning primarily 'hold fast,' but with a secondary sense of 'Stop,' or 'Gently there,' when a person is either walking or talking too fast.—WEM.

HOLE [oa·l], *v. a.* to excavate; to cut round a block of coal in such a way as to detach it for removal. Com.—M. T.

'Holyñ', or boryn'. *Cavo, perforo, terebro.* "To hole, *cavare, perforare, &c., ubi*, to thyrle."—CATH. ANG. "*Palare, cavare, forare, Anglice*, to hole, or to bore." Equiv. John de Garlandiâ.'—*Prompt. Parv. and Notes.*

A.S. *holian*, to hollow; to make a hole. See **Sprag** (3).

HOLERS [oa·lur'z], *sb. pl.* men employed to *hole.*—*Ibid.* See **Bondsmen.**

HOLP [oa·p], *pret., sing., obsols.* helped.—SHREWSBURY; PULVERBATCH. 'I *'ŏ'p* 'im ŏŏth that bag on 'is shŭther.'

'Heo hath *holpe* a thousand out
Of the develes punfolde.'

Piers Pl., pass. v. l. 3756, ed. WR.

'*Ant. E.* A man is well *holp* up that trusts to you.'
Comedy of Errors, IV. i. 22.

A.S. *healp*, p. t. of *helpan*, helped; assisted.

HOLPEN [oa·pn], (1) *pret., pl., obsols.* helped.—*Ibid.* 'Poor owd Tummas an' me wun al'ays good frien's, an' *'ō'p'n* one another as neighbours shoulden.' A.S. (we) *hulpon*, p. t. of *helpan*, helped; assisted.

(2) *part. past, obsols.* helped.—*Ibid.* 'I doubt they bin a avenless set—they dunna ought to be bad off, they'n bin *'ō'p'n* more than anybody i' the parish.'

'For I haue . . . seith cryst . . . .
. . . . blynde men *holpen*,
And fedde ȝow with fisshes · and with fyue loues,
And left baskettes ful of broke mete · bere awey who so wolde.'
Piers Pl., Text B., pass. xvi. l. 124.

'Yo have no need to be *holpen* with any part of my labour in this thing.'—LATIMER, *Sermons*, p. 34, in *Bible Word-Book*.
See *Ps.* lxxxiii. 8. A.S. *holpen*, p.p. of *helpan*, to help.

HOLUS-BOLUS [oa·lus boa·lus], *adv.* impulsively; without deliberation.—SHREWSBURY; PULVERBATCH; CLEE HILLS. Qy. com. ''E never thinks 'ow it's gweïn to end, but gwuz at it *'ōlus-bōlus*.'

HOMBER [om·bur'], *sb.* a hammer. Com. To go ''omber an' pinsons' at a thing is to set about it with determination and force. 'So yo' couldna finish the Wakes athout a fight I 'ear.' 'I'd nuthin' to do ōōth it, Maister, it wuz Jack Pugh an' Dick Morris—the constable parted 'em wunst, but they watchen 'im away, an' then wenten *'omber an' pinsons* at it again—but they'n 'ăve 'em in fur it yit.'
The form '*hambyr*' for *malleus* occurs in *Prompt. Parv.*, p. 225.

HOMES [oa·mz], same as **Hames**, q. v.—WEM.
'The *Trill Homes*, are the peeces of wood made fast to the collar about the horse neck, to which hooks and the chains are fixed. The *Homes* are the wooden peeces themselves.'—*Academy of Armory*, Bk. III. ch. viii. p. 339.

HOMMACK [om·uk], *v. a.* to dash; to destroy by want of careful using: said chiefly of dress.—SHREWSBURY; WEM. Qy. com. 'Look at that wench, 'ow 'er's *'ommacked* 'er new bonnet.'

HOMMACKIN', *adj.* awkward; clumsy. Qy. com. ''Er's a great *'ommakin'*, on-gain lookin' wench—'er mus' spruce up an' look sharp about 'er, else 'er ōōnna be theer lung.'

HOMMAGED [om·ijd], *part. adj.* severely censured.—WEM. ''E wuz badly *'ommaged* about it, an' 'e wunna do it agen in a 'urry.'

HOMPERED [om·pur'd], *part. adj.* harassed; worried; troubled. Qy. com. 'God 'elp the poor ōōman—'er'll be despertly *'ompered* ōōth them two twins.'

'"whan al þe cuntre was umbe-cast · with clene men of armes,
to haue þe take þer tit · & to dethe *hampred;*
I tok here souerayne sone · so saued i þe þere."'
William of Palerne, l. 4694.

HOND [on·d], *sb.* a hand. Com.

'And oche eday thi masse thou here,
And take halé bred and halé watere
Out of the prestis *hond;*
Soche grace God hath ȝif the,
ȝif that thou dey sodenly
Fore thi housil hit schal the stond.'
JOHN AUDELAY'S *Poems*, p. 81.

'And at this same tyme were hurt Lordes of name—. . . . . the Lord of Stafford in the *hond,* with an arowe.'—*Paston Letters*, A.D. 1455, vol. i. p. 331.
A.S. *hond.*

HONDLE [on·dl], *v. a.* to handle.—SHREWSBURY; PULVERBATCH. Qy. com. 'Yo' *'ondlen* that pikel as if it wuz a gate-pwust; slout it under the swath athisn, an' shift yore fit a bit faster, or we shanna finish 'arrŏost by Chris'mas.'

'He was fayr man, and wicth,
Of bodi he was þe beste knicth
þat euere micte leden with here,
Or stede onne ride, or *handlen* spere.'
Havelok the Dane, l. 347.

HONE [oa·n], *v. n.* to yearn; to long.—PULVERBATCH; NEWPORT. (1) 'That poor cow's *'ōnin'* after 'er cauve an' lowin' pitiful.' (2) ''E canna do no good at school, 'e does so *'one* fur 'ome.'
'She brought a servant up with her, said he, who *hones* after the country, and is actually gone, or soon will.'—*Sir Charles Grandison*, vol. i. p. 241, ed. 1766.

HOOD [uod·], *v. a.* same as **Hattock,** q. v.—WHITCHURCH. A.S. *hód*, a hood.

HOODERS [uod·ur'z], *sb. pl.* same as **Hattocks,** q. v.—*Ibid.* Cf. **Hoodwinks,** below.

HOODWINKS [ud·wingks], *sb. pl.* same as **Hooders,** above.—WEM. Compare this use of the term *hoodwink*, in the sense of a *covering*, with the—apparently—kindred meaning it bears in the following passage:—

'*Caliban.* Good my lord, give me thy favour still.
Be patient, for the prize I'll bring thee to
Shall *hoodwink* this mischance; . . . .'
Tempest, IV. i. 206.

HOOFLOCK [uf·luk], PULVERBATCH. [of·luk], CLEE HILLS, *sb.* the fetlock of a horse. The term is metaphorically applied to clumsy ancles. 'Whad *'uflocks* 'er 'as!—bif to the anclers like a Lancashire bŭllock.'

HOOKER [ook·ur'], *sb.* a large quantity: a term generally employed in combination with 'pretty.' Com. 'My eye! we'n got a *pretty 'ooker* o' tail-ends fur the fowl—the Maister hanna furgot us this time.'

HOOKINGS [ook·inz], *sb. pl.* two long spells of work, with an interval of rest between.—NEWPORT, *Cheswardine.* A man who works by *hookings*, i. e. early and late, with an intervening 'siesta,' is said to do two days' work in the twenty-four hours. An arrangement corresponding to this is known to miners as 'double-shift.'

HOOP [oop· *and* wop·], *sb., obsols.* a peck measure.—SHREWSBURY; PULVERBATCH. 'The pars bin so chep, they binna wuth twopence a *'oop.'*

In the *Accounts of the Ludlow Churchwardens* for the year 1548 is the following:—'item to Coke for whitlymynge the churche ij dayes worke, and for a bushelle and a *whop* of lyme xxd. ob.'

Price, in his *History of Oswestry*, quotes an old 'accompt' of the third year of the reign of Elizabeth, which contains a charge for 'saullt,' viz., 'Allso, payde for a *hoope* of saullt for the byff xd.,' and another for 'a *hoope* of whette for brede.'

An *Inventory*, taken at Owlbury Manor-House, 1625, comprises—'*In the Corne Chamber over the Stables*—one strike, one *hopp*, one halfe Bushell.'

'According to Kennett, MS. Lansd. 1033, the *hoop* contained two pecks; but in his Glossary, p. 147, he says only one peck.'—HAL.

HOOSACK [oos·ak], *interj.* an exclamation, equivalent to '*Eureka*,' uttered upon finding a thing, or recovering that which has been lost. —PULVERBATCH. 'Dick fund 'is knife w'en we wun gettin' the barley-stack in—I 'eärd 'im cry "*'oosack!*" an' I said, "W'ast'ee fund, Dick?" an' 'e says, "My knife, lad—I'm perty glad."'

HOOST [oos·t], *sb.* a cough; said of cattle.—NEWPORT. 'The cows han gotten a bit'n a *'oost.*'

'Now colic-grips, an' barkin' *hoast*,
May kill us a'.'
ROBERT BURNS, *Poems*, p. 9, l. 9.

Mr. Oliphant, speaking of the Northumbrian Psalter—A.D. 1250—says, 'We now find *hâs* (*raucus*) becomes *haast;* hence the Scotch substantive *hoast*. We of the South have put an *r* into the old adjective, and call it *hoarse*.'—*Sources of Standard English*, p. 150.

'Hoose, or cowghe (host, or cowhe, K. host, or cowgth, S. hoost, HARL. MS. 2274). *Tussis*. "An host, *tussis;* to host, *tussire*."—CATH. ANG.' *Prompt. Parv. and Notes.*

'A.S. *hwósta;* O.Icel. *hósti;* O.H.Germ. *huosto;* O.Du. *hoest*, host (hust), *tussis*.'—STRAT. Cf. **Hask.**

HOOTCHING [uo·chin], *part. adj.* crouching; huddling.—SHREWSBURY; ATCHAM; PULVERBATCH; WEM; ELLESMERE. Qy. com. 'Come out—*'ootchin'* i' the cornel theer.' *Hootching* is generally used with reference to a *corner*, and so differs from **Couch** (4), q. v.

HOPPER [op·ur'], (1) *sb., obsols.* a kind of open box of—what is technically called—'bend-ware,' for carrying seed; it is slung across the shoulder of the sower, and usually rests on his left hip, being hollowed on one side to fit the person, whilst on its outer side there is a short, upright handle, by which he holds it.—PULVERBATCH; CLEE HILLS.

> 'And hange myn *hoper* at myn hals · in stede of a scrippe;
> A busshel of bredcorne · brynge me þer-inne;
> For I wil sowe it my-self. . . . .
>
> *Piers Pl.*, Text B., pass. vi. l. 63.

'Seed *hopper* and strap.'—*Auctioneer's Catalogue* (Stoddesden), 1870.

'*Hopur* of a seed lepe (or a seed-lepe, HARL. MS. 2274). *Satorium, saticulum.* "*Seminarium vas quo ponitur semen*, an hopre."—MED.' *Prompt. Parv. and Notes.*

(2) *sb.* a funnel for supplying grain to the mill-stones. Com.

> '. . right by the *hopper* wol I stand,
> (Quod John) and seen how that the corn gas in.
> Yet saw I never by my fader kin,
> How that the *hopper* wagges til and fra.'
>
> CHAUCER, *C. T.*, ll. 4034—4037.

'*Hopur* of a mylle, or a tramale. *Taratantara.*—CATH. *Farricapsium.*—DICC. "An hopyr, *ferricapsa, est molendini; saticulum, satum, seminarium.*"—CATH. ANG. The proper distinction is here made between the *hopper*, . . . so termed from the hopping movement given to it, and the seed-leep, which was also called a *hopper.* "*Hopper* of a myll, *tremye.*"—PALSG.' *Prompt. Parv. and Notes.*

'A.S. *hoppere (saltator)*, hopper; (hoper) *infundibulum.*'—STRAT.

'*Infundibulum*, a tunnell whereinto liquor is powred when vessels are filled, an *hopper* of a mill, &c.'—*Dict. Etym. Lat.*

HOPPER-TROUGH [op·ur' tr'uf], *sb.* a kind of box into which the grain is put to be conveyed between the mill-stones. The grain runs out of the *trough*, through the *hopper*, into the 'eye' of the upper mill-stone. Com. Mr. Way would seem to confound the *hopper* with the *hopper-trough*, when he says, 'the *hopper*, or the *trough* wherein the grain is put in order to be ground, mentioned by Chaucer, *C. T.*, ll. 4034—4037, &c.' See Note in *Prompt. Parv.*, p. 246.

HOPS AND GIRDS, same as **Hobs and Girds**, q. v.—WORTHEN.

HORN [aur'·n], *sb.* same as **Hastener**, q. v.—PULVERBATCH.

HOT [ot·], *v. a.* to make hot; to heat. Com. 'Draw some drink an' '*ot* it fur the men's suppers.'

HOUD, *v. a., var. pr.* hold. Cf. **Hout.**

HOUD YO'. See **Hold yo'.**

HOUD YORE 'OUT. See **Hold your hold.**

HOUSEL [ous·il], *sb.* household goods.—SHREWSBURY; PULVERBATCH. 'I 'ear as theer's to be two days' sale at the "George"—one fur live stock, an' another fur '*ousel.*'

HOUSEN [ou·zn], *sb. pl.* houses. Com. "'*Ousen* bin despert scase about theer, folks dunna shift about like they dun i' the town, they keepen on, one generation after another.'

HOUSE-PLACE, *sb.* the large kitchen, or general living room of a farm-house.—WHITCHURCH.

HOUSING [ou·sin], *sb., obsols.* the large leather cape attached to the collar of a waggon-horse's gears, which can be raised or lowered at will; when laid down, it serves to protect the horse's neck from wet. Com.

'*Housse de cheval de harnois*, a sheep or goat's skin laid upon the collar of a team horse.'—CHAMB.

HOUT. See **Hold**.

HOVE [oav·], *pret.* heaved; lifted.—CLEE HILLS. ''E come an '*ove* me out o' the gig afore 'e '*ove* 'is wife out.'

'For his swerd he *hof* up heye,
And þe hand he dide of fleye,
Þat he smot him with so sore.'
Havelok the Dane, l. 2750.

A.S. *hóf*, p. t. of *hebban*, lifted.

HOVEL [ov·il], (1) *sb.* same as **Cote**.—SHREWSBURY; PULVERBATCH; ELLESMERE. Qy. com. 'Dun'ee call that a 'ouse to live in?—w'y it's no better than a '*ŏvil* fur cattle to 'erd in.'

'*Hovyl* for swyne, or oþer beestys. *Cartabulum, catabulum*.'—*Prompt. Parv.*

'O.Lat. *Catabolum*, a stable; a beast house.'—*Dict. Etym. Lat.*

(2) *sb.* a shed adjoining a cottage, where coal, wood, &c. are kept; also a mean dwelling-place.—PULVERBATCH. Qy. com.

'*Hovyl*, lytylle howse. *Teges*.'—*Prompt. Parv.*

'O.Lat. *Tegestas*, a cover or cottage.'—*Dict. Etym. Lat.*

HOWGY [ou·ji'], (1) *adj.* huge.—CLUN; CLEE HILLS. ''E fat a great '*owgy* stwun an' pŭt agen the gate, so as it shouldna be opened.'

The form *howgy* occurs, according to Mr. Halliwell, in Skelton, ii. 24. 'Huge, *hougy*,' is found in STRAT.

(2) *adj.* large.—*Ibid.* An old man at Clun said that the living of that place was not very ''*owgy*,' i. e. not 'good' or 'rich.'

(3) *adj.* 'great,' meaning very intimate.—*Ibid.* 'They bin gotten mighty '*owgy*.' Cf. **Great** in **Grammar Outlines** (*adjectives*).

HUD [ud·], *v. a.* to collect, or gather together.—LUDLOW. 'Oh! 'e'll be sure to '*ud* it all up.'

HUDDIMUK [ud·i'muk], *v. n.* to do things on the sly.—PULVERBATCH; WEM. 'I dunna know about 'em bein' so poor—they carri'n a good cheek, an' it strikes me they'n '*uddimuk* an' junket by tharselves, an' al'ays looken poor to get all they can.'

HUDDIMUKERY, *adj.* close; sly: as in hiding away money or valuables of any kind.—WELLINGTON; COLLIERY; ELLESMERE. 'I fund a bran'-new shillin' in a noud canister, w'en I wuz clānin' down that top shilf; I 'spect Jim 'ad pŭt it theer—I dunna like sich '*uddermukery* ways.' Compare the two foregoing terms, expressive of secresy or concealment, with O.E. *hude*, to hide:—

'& he ful listli hem ledes · to þat loueli schippe,
& tauȝt bi-hinde tunnes · hem to *hude* þere.'
William of Palerne, l. 2743.

Compare them also with 'hugger-mugger' in the following citations:—

'. . . . . the people muddied,
Thick and unwholesome in their thoughts and whispers,
For good Polonius' death; and we have done but greenly,
In *hugger-mugger* to inter him.'—*Hamlet*, IV. v. 84.

'But one thing I have to request, proceeded my Uncle—It is, that we may have a joyful Day of it; and that all our neighbours and tenants may rejoice with us. . . . . No *hugger-mugger* doings—Let private weddings be for doubtful happiness.'—*Sir Charles Grandison*, vol. vi. p. 280, ed. 1766.

Mr. Oliphant says that, Tyndale was the first 'to give us the term "*huker-muker*," which has been but little changed.'—*Sources of Standard English*, p. 294.

It would seem as if *huddimuk* and *huddimukery* were words 'made up' of O.E. *hude* and the last half of that term of Tyndale's, which he brought into the Mother Tongue in the sixteenth century.

HUF [uf·], *sb.*, *var. pr.* a hoof. Com.

HUFF [uf·], *sb.* a pet; a slight fit of hasty temper.—LUDLOW. Qy. com. Cf. **Miff.**

HUFFED [uf·t], *adj.* offended; put out of temper. Qy. com.

'But then to see how ye're negleckit,
How *huff'd*, an' cuff'd, an' disrespeckit!'
ROBERT BURNS, *Poems*, p. 3, l. 6.

HUFFLE-FOOTED [uf·l fut·id], same as **Huffle-heeled**, below.—WEM.

HUFFLE-HEELED, *adj.* clumsy-footed; shuffling in gait.—PULVERBATCH. ''E'll mak' a prime militia-mon—w'y 'e's 'umpbacked an' *'uffle-'eeled!* I call it a waste o' the king's cloth.' See **Hooflock.**

HUFLOCK. See **Hooflock.**

HUG-A-MA-TUG, same as **Clip-me-tight**, q. v.—CLEE HILLS.

HUK [uk·], *sb.*, *var. pr.* a hook. Com.

HULKY [ul·ki'], *adj.* heavy; stupid.—WEM.

'Imagin her with thousand virgins guided
Unto her fearefull toombe, her monster-grave:
Imagin how the *hulky* divell slyded
Along the seas smooth breast, parting the wave:
Alasse poore naked damsell ill provided,
Whom millions without heavens help cannot save.'
HEYWOOD, *Troia Britanica*, 1609, in WR.

HULL (1) *sb.* an outer covering or husk, as of nuts, pease, beans, &c. SHREWSBURY; PULVERBATCH; CLUN; NEWPORT. Qy. com. 'Chuck them beän-*'ulls* o'er to the pigs afore yo' gin 'em the wesh.'

'*Hoole*, or huske. *Siliqua*. *Hoole* of pesyn', or benys, or oþer coddyd frute. *Techa*.—CATH. *in fresus*. In the recipe for "blaunche perreye" it is directed to "sethe the pesyn in fyne leye," and then rub them with woollen cloth, and "þe holys wyl a-way."—HARL. MS. 279, f. 25. "Hull of a beane or pese, *escosse*. Hull or barcke of a tree, *escorce*."—PALSG. "*Gousse*, the huske, swad, cod, hull of beanes, pease, &c."—COTG.' *Prompt. Parv. and Notes*.

'*Hull*, the Cod of Pulse, Chaff, &c.'—BAILEY, ed. 1727.

A.S. *hule*; O.Du. *hulle*; husk, as of corn, &c. Cf. **Hulling**.

(2) *v. a.* to take off the husks, as of nuts; to shell, as of beans, pease, &c.—*Ibid.* (1) 'I've bin *'ullin* walnuts all day, so I shanna want a par o' gloves fur Sunday.' (2) 'Gie Jim the side-basket o' pase, an' 'e'll *'ull* 'em afore 'e gwuz to church, an' throw the pessum to the pigs.'

'Bestes to hulde' occurs in *William of Palerne*, l. 1708. *Hulde* is explained in the *Glossarial Index*, p. 280, 'to flay, to take off the covering or hide;' and Sir Frederick Madden's note on the word is quoted as follows:—' "From the same root proceeds the modern verb *to hull*, to take off the *hull* or husk. It corresponds to the Goth. *and-huljan*, Lu. x. 22. Hence also A.S. *hyldere*, a butcher." '

(3) *v. a.* to take off, as of the crust of a pie, or to lift up the meat in it, to get to that which lies beneath.—PULVERBATCH. 'Yo' bin *'ullin'* an' ortin' that pie as if it wunna fit to ate.'

HULLING [ul·in], *sb.* the binding of a book.—WELLINGTON.

'O.H.Germ. *hullen*; Goth. *huljan*; O.Icel. *hylja*, to hill; to cover.' —STRAT. See **Hilling**.

HULLOCK [ul·uk], *sb.* a lazy, worthless fellow.—CLEE HILLS. Cf. *Hulk* (1), in HAL.

HUMBER [um·bur'], *sb.* the common Cockchafer.—CLEE HILLS.

Compare '*Humber* [of *Hummen*, Teut. to make a humming Noise, because it flows with a murmuring Noise], the Name of a River,' in BAILEY, ed. 1727.

'O.Du. *hommelen* (*bombilare*).'—STRAT. Cf. **Blind-buzzard** (1), also **Huz-buz**.

HUMOURSOME [yoo·mur'sum], *adj.* peevish; out of temper; in a state of mind when nothing pleases.—PULVERBATCH; NEWPORT; WEM; ELLESMERE. 'The child's well enough, but 'e's spiled till 'e's that *'umoursome* 'e dunna know whad to do ŏŏth 'isself.'

Compare Shakespeare's 'humorous' in a similar sense:—

'Yet such is now the duke's condition,
That he misconstrues all that you have done.
The duke is *humorous*; . . . .'

As You Like It, I. ii. 277.

Humoursome is employed at Burford (Salop) with the signification of good, or pleasant, in regard of temper.

HUNT [unt·], *v. a.*, *pec.* to search for. Com. 'Han yo' sin the kay o' the one-w'y-drink? I've bin *'untin'* it up an' down—likely an' onlikely—an' canna find it now'eer.' 'It wuz o' the shilf i' the cornel-cubbert the las' time I sid it, but if it inna theer now, yo' mun *'unt* till yo' find'n it, an' then yore labour ŏŏnna be lost.'

'Seek till you find, and you'll not lose your labour.'
RAY'S *Proverbs*, p. 155.

HURDEN, same as **Herden**, q. v.
'What from the *hurden* smock, with lockram upper bodies, and hempen sheets, to wear and sleep in holland.'—R. BROME (first half 17th cent.), *New Acad.*, iii. p. 47, in Nares.

HURDS, same as **Herdes**, q. v.
'Now that part [of the flax] which is utmost, and next to the pill or rind, is called tow or *hurds*.'—HOLLAND'S *Pliny*, vol. ii. p. 4, in Nares.

HURRIFUL [u·r'i'ful], *adj.* quick; hasty; precipitant.—PULVERBATCH; CLEE HILLS. 'It inna the *'urriful* sort o' folk as bringen the most to pass, fur they runnen about athout thar yed ŏŏth 'em.'

HURST [ur's·t], (1) *sb.* a wooded eminence or knoll.—CLUN.

'. . . . . From each rising *hurst*,
Where many a goodly oak had carefully been nursed.'
DRAYTON.

Hurst, in combination, is of not infrequent occurrence as a place-name throughout Salop:—Black*hurst*, Brock*hurst*, Holly*hurst*, Under*hurst*, Lily*hurst*, Mud*hurst*, &c.
Bailey says—ed. 1727—'*Hurst*, joined with the Names of Places, denotes that they took their Name from a Wood or Forest.'

(2) *sb.* a bed of shingle in the Severn is called a *hurst*.—MUCH WENLOCK.
'Du. *horst*, a brake, bushy place; Germ. *horst*, a tuft or cluster, as of grass, corn, reeds, a clump of trees, heap of sand, crowd of people.'—WEDG.

HURTER [ur'·tur'], *sb.* an iron plate edged with steel, fastened—by 'langets' or stays—on to the axle of a 'tumbrel' to keep the wheel from wearing into the axle-tree: the steel edge works against the 'boukin,' q. v.—PULVERBATCH. Qy. com.

HUS [us·], *sb.* house, in composition:—wain-*'us*, cow-*'us*, bake-*'us*, brew-*'us*, maut-*'us*, &c. Com.
Compare 'sceapa-*hus*,' 'corn-*hus*,' 'mealt-*hus*,' &c., in the *Supplement to Ælfric's Vocabulary*, x. or xi. cent., in Wr. vocabs., vol. i. p. 58.
A.S. *hús*, a house.

HUSPEL [us·pil], *v. a.* to drive away; to put to rout.—CORVE DALE; WELLINGTON; WEM; ELLESMERE. 'I'll *'uspel* yo' childern off that causey, yo' bin jest like a kerry o' 'ounds up an' down:' so said a Welshampton woman [1873].
'*Huspylyn̄*', or spoylyn̄'. *Spolio, dispolio.* In old French *housepouillier*, or *harpailleur*, implies a thievish marauder, "*homme qui vole les geus de la campagne, vagabond.*"—ROQUEF. "*S'houspiller l'un l'autre*, to tug, lug, hurry, tear one another, &c."—COTG.' *Prompt. Parv. and Notes.*
Cf. **Hespel**.

HUSSY, HUSWIFE [uz·i'], CLEE HILLS. [uz·if], PULVERBATCH; ELLESMERE, *sb.*, *pec.*, *obsols.* a case for holding sewing materials, such as thread, needles, and buttons. It is made of a strip of some suitable material, and is fitted up with longitudinal 'casings' for the thread, and with pockets for the buttons, &c. It rolls up when not in use, and fastens with a loop and button.

HUZ-BUZ, *sb.* same as **Blind-buzzard,** q. v. — COLLIERY. Cf. **Humber.**

-IER, a noun suffix = **er,** as in drov*ier*, groz*ier*, haul*ier*, q. v. Til*ier* for till*er* is found in the Wycliffite version [A.D. 1388], Luke xiii. 7: 'And he seide to the *tilier* of the vynȝerd.' The plural *tilieris* occurs in Luke xx. 9: 'A man plauntide a vynȝerd, and hiride it to *tilieris*.'

IFTIN'-AN'-ANDIN', *sb.* hesitation.—SHREWSBURY. 'I axed that ŏŏman about the weshin', an' after a good bit o' *iftin'-an'-andin'* 'er said 'er'd come—but 'er didna seem to car' about it.'

ILD [il·d], *v. n.*, *var. pr.* to yield.—PULVERBATCH; WEM; ELLESMERE. ''Ow does the corn *ild*, William?' 'Well, but mighty middlin', the ears bin lathy—theer wuz a djel o' strung winde w'en it wuz in blow, an' knocked it about.'

Compare Shakespeare's '*ild*—'God '*ild* you:'—*As You Like It*, III. iii. 76.

ILL-BLENDED, *adj.* morose; bad-tempered.—PULVERBATCH; CLEE HILLS; WEM. ''E's a *ill-blended*, down-looking, hang-dog fellow as ever yo' sid'n.'

ILL-CONTRIVED, *adj.* bad-tempered; cross-grained.—PULVERBATCH. 'Yo' bin as contrairy an' *ill-contrived* as yo' knowen 'ow to be, but it ŏŏnna be lung till Maȳ-Daȳ, then yo' sha'n gŏŏ somew'eer else to shewn yore tempers.'

IMBERS [im·bur'z], *sb. pl.*, *var. pr.* embers.—PULVERBATCH; WEM. 'The fire'll tak' no 'arm, theer's nuthin' but a few *imbers* i' the grate.'

IMITATE, *v. n.*, *pec.* to attempt.—WEM; ELLESMERE. ''E's bin *imitatin'* at drivin' the 'orses the las' wik or two, but 'e inna-d-up to much.' [Common in Norfolk.—W. W. S.]. Cf. **Make a mock.**

IMP, *sb.* a scion; a slip; a shoot.—CORVE DALE; CLEE HILLS.

> '. . . . . "I was sum tyme a frere,
> And þe couentes Gardyner · for to graffe *ympes*."'
> *Piers Pl.*, Text B., pass. v. l. 137.

'"*Impe*, or graffe. *Surculus, novella*."—CATH.' *Prompt. Parv.* 'Dan. *ympe*; Swed. *ymp*, imp, *surculus*.'—STRAT.

IMPLE [im·pl], *adj.* same as **Ample,** q. v.—CLEE HILLS.

INCH-MEAL, *adv.* inch by inch; little by little; minutely, as in seeking for a thing.—CLEE HILLS. 'Well, it conna be theer, I've looked it *inch-meal*.'

'*Caliban.* All the infections that the sun sucks up
From bogs, fens, flats, on Prosper fall and make him
By *inch-meal* a disease!'—*Tempest*, II. ii. 3.

INCH-SMALL, same as **Inch-meal**.—WEM. See **Ins-small**.

IN GOOD BEHOPES, *phr.* hopeful.—WEM; ELLESMERE. 'I wuz *in good be'opes* as I should a got theer afore the poor fellow died, but I didna.'

IN GOOD SADNESS, *phr.* in good earnest; in all seriousness.—PULVERBATCH; WEM. (1) 'Now set about that job *in good sadness*, as if yo' mănen to do it.' (2) 'It's sure to be the truth, for 'e toud me *in right good sadness*.'

'*M. Mery.* . . And will ye needes go from vs thus in very deede?
R. Royster. Yea, *in good ſadneſſe*.'
Roister Doister, Act iij. Sc. iij. p. 46.

'Therfor ȝe, britheren, bifor witynge kepe ȝou silf, lest ȝe be disseyued bi errour of vnwise men, and falle awei fro ȝoure owne *sadnes* [a propriâ *firmitate*, Vulg.].'—2 *Pet.* iii. 17, Wicliffite Version, ed. A.D. 1388.

'"*Sad. Sadly, Sadness*," says Archbp. Trench, "had once the meaning of earnest, serious, sedate, "set," this last being only another form of the same word. The passage from Shakespeare quoted below marks "sadly" and "sadness" in their transitional state from the old meaning to the new; Benvolio using "sadness" in the old sense, Romeo pretending to understand him in the new.

"*Ben.* Tell me in *sadness* who she is you love?
Rom. What, shall I groan, and tell you?
Ben. Groan? why, no;
But *sadly* tell me who."
Romeo and Juliet, I. i. 205.'
Select Glossary, pp. 192, 193.

Cf. '*Sadnesse. Soliditas, maturitas. Sadnesse*, yn porte and chere *idem est*.'—*Prompt. Parv.*

IN GOOD SOOTH, *phr.*, *obs.* of a truth; indeed.—PULVERBATCH; WORTHEN. 'Theer's bin parlour-laisers theer all wik—*in good sooth*, I amma gweïn to scrape thar orts after 'em.'

'*Kent.* Sir, *in good sooth*, in sincere verity,
Under the allowance of your great aspect,
Whose influence . . . .'
K. Lear, II. ii. 111.

A.S. *sóð*, truly; verily; of a truth.

INION [ei·ni'un], *sb.*, *var. pr.* an onion.—SHREWSBURY; PULVERBATCH. See **O** (15) (16) (17) in **Grammar Outlines** (*vowels*, &c.).

INKLE [ingk·l], *sb.*, *obs.* coarse tape.—PULVERBATCH. 'If yo' bin gweïn to markit, be so good as bring me a pen'orth o' *inkle* fur my linsey appern—nod w'ite—if yo' canna get it striped, bring blue caddas.'

'*Serv.* He hath ribbons of all the colours i' the rainbow . . . *inkles*, caddisses, cambrics, lawns.'—*Winter's Tale*, IV. iv. 8.

'As thick as *inkle* weavers.'—*Proverbial Saying.*

Cf. **Caddas**.

IN LIEU [in loo·], *adv.* instead; in exchange for.—PULVERBATCH. 'The Maister said 'e'd gie me the top adlant i' the "Red-buts" fur tatoe ground, an' 'e mun 'a a couple o' days work i' the 'arrŏost *in lieu.*'

'But, poor old man, thou prunest a rotten tree,
That cannot so much as a blossom yield
In lieu of all thy pains and husbandry.'
As You Like It, II. iii. 65.

Cf. Fr. *au lieu de.* See **Inturn.**

INSENSE [insen·s], *v. a.* to instruct; to make clear to the understanding. Com. 'If 'e dunna bring the things right I canna 'elp it—I *insensed* 'im well into it.'

'The olde bokes of Glastenbury shall you *ensence,*
More plainly to vnderstande this forsayd matere.'
The Lyfe of Ioseph of Armathia, l. 363.

'. . . Don John your brother *incensed* me to slander the Lady Hero. —*Much Ado about Nothing*, V. i. 242.

Ray has, 'To *Insense*, to inform: a pretty word used about *Sheffield*, in *Yorkshire.*'

INSIGHT [in·sit], *sb.* the entrance into the 'workings' from the bottom of the shaft. Com.—M. T.

INS-SMALL. See **Inch-small,** of which it is a corrupted form.—PULVERBATCH. 'I've sarched the 'ouse *ins-small*, an' canna find it 'igh, low, nor level.'

IN-TAK [in·tak], *sb.* an *in-take*, i. e. a piece—say an acre or thereabouts—of reclaimed waste land, enclosed and taken into a farm.—WEM; ELLESMERE. 'I 'ad for'casted to a laid the new *in-tak* down [sown it with permanent grass seed] this time, but I doubt I canna manage it now.' Cf. **Bytack.**

IN THE FACE O' FLESH, *phr.*, *obsols.* equivalent to 'in the body.' —WEM. 'Eh, dear! but I'm reet glad to see yo' *in the face o' flesh* agen after all this lung time.'

INTURN [intur'n·], *adv.* instead.—SHREWSBURY; LUDLOW. 'I'll do it *inturn* o' yo'.' Cf. **In lieu.**

INWARDS [in·ur'dz], *sb.* the heart, liver, &c. of a pig or lamb.—WEM.

'*Intestina*, smæl þearmas, *vel* inneweard,' occurs in *Archbp. Ælfric's Vocabulary*, in Wr. vocabs., vol. i. p. 44.

ISS. See **Yes.**

ISTERD'Y [is·tur'di'], *adv.*, *var. pr.* yesterday. Qy. com. '*Isterd'y* wuz a wik' = yesterday week.

IT, *conj.*, *var. pr.* yet. Com.

ITEM [ei·tum], *sb.*, *pec.* a hint.—SHREWSBURY. Qy. com. 'I sid the Maister comin', so I gid 'im the *item.*'

'My Uncle took notice, that Sir Charles had said, he guessed at the writer of the note. He wished he would give him an *item*, as he called it, whom he thought of.'—*Sir Charles Grandison*, vol. vi. p. 266, ed. 1766.

IVVY [iv·i'], *sb.*, *var. pr. Hedera Hélix*, common Ivy. Com.

> ''Olly an' *ivvy* wun runnin' a race,
> 'Olly gid *ivvy* a smack i' the face;
> *Ivvy* run wham to tell 'is Mother,
> 'Olly run after 'im an' gid 'im another.'
>
> *Children's Doggerel Verse.*

JACK [jak·], (1) *sb. Corvus monédula*, the Jackdaw.—BRIDGNORTH.

(2) *sb. Esox lúcius*, a (young) Pike.—ELLESMERE.

(3) *sb.*, *obs.* a drinking vessel of leather. A *Jack* of this kind was preserved until quite a recent period at Corra—the Calverhall of the Ordnance map—not far from Whitchurch (Salop). It was shown in the Art Treasures' Exhibition at Wrexham, 1876, and was catalogued, '1075. Leather *Jack* (pint) mounted with silver rims, inscribed—

> "Jack of Carrow is my name,
> Don't abuse me then for shame."

—Mr. Whitehall Dod.' A local tradition was formerly current at Corra that a certain traveller, half dead with fatigue, being helped on his way by a refreshing draught of nut-brown ale at that place, by way of thank-offering, charged his estate with a sum of money yearly, to provide a *Jack* of ale at a cost of 1d. for future wayfarers in Corra. The village inn at the present day [1879] is called '*The Old Jack.*'

There is an account of the *Jack of Corra*, substantially the same as that given above, in BAGSHAW'S *History*, *Gazetteer*, *&c. of Shropshire*, 1851, p. 305.

Minsheu (ed. 1617) has, '6013. A *Jacke* of Leather to drink in, because it somewhat resembles a *Jacke* or coat of maile; Vi. Jugge, Pot.'

Phillips—*New World of Words*, 7th ed., 1720—gives, amongst other meanings of the word *Jack*, that of 'a sort of great Leathern Pitcher to put Drink in.'

Ash has, '*Jack*, a kind of leather cup, a large jug for liquor.'

Mr. Halliwell says that *Jack* 'has the same meaning as *Black-jack*,' which he glosses, 'a large leather can formerly in great use for small beer.' Both Grose and Pegge give the term *Jack* as signifying a measure; the former says, 'half a pint,' the latter, 'a quarter of a pint.'

JACK-A-DANDY, *sb.* the dancing light sometimes seen on wall or ceiling, reflected from the sunshine on water, glass, or other bright surface.—NEWPORT. The same term is applied to a *lady* in the following verse, and apparently with a kindred—metaphorical—sense:—

'My love is blithe and bucksome,
And sweet and fine as can be;
Fresh and gay as the flowers in May,
And lookes like *Jack-a-Dandy*.'
Song, '*Harry and Mary*,' in *Wit and Drollery*, 1682.

JACK-AN'-'IS-CHEM [team], *sb.*, *obs.*? *Ursa Major.*—PULVERBATCH.

JACK-AND-HIS-WAGGON, *idem.*—PULVERBATCH; ELLESMERE.

JACK-AND-HIS-WAIN, *idem.*—OSWESTRY. Cf. **Charles's Wain**.

JACK-DOUKER, same as **Douker**, q. v.—WEM.

JACK-NICOL [jak nik·u'l], *sb. Fringilla carduëlis*, the Goldfinch. —WEM; ELLESMERE.

JACK-O'-THE-LANTHORN, *sb.*, *obs.* the *Ignis fatuus.*—CLEE HILLS. Cf. **Devil's-lontun**.

JACK-O'-TWO-SIDES, *sb. Ranunculus arvensis.*—WELLINGTON, *High Ercall*. See **Devil's Curry-comb**, also **Worry-wheat**.

JACK-PLAYNE [jak plaa·yn], *sb.*, *var. pr.* the first plane used for taking off rough surfaces.—CLUN. *Jack-plane*, as usually pronounced, is a common enough term.

JACK-SQUEALER [jak squai·lur'], *sb. Cýpselus apus*, the Swift.—CHURCH STRETTON; BRIDGNORTH. Qy. com. This bird's loud piercing cry has obtained for it the name of *squealer*.

JACK-STONES, (1) *sb. pl.* pebbles—usually white ones—used in playing the game known by the same name. Qy. com. See below.

(2) *sb.* a children's game played with stones.—*Ibid.* Considerable dexterity is required in throwing up and catching the *Jack-stones*—five in number—and the game throughout is a pretty and interesting one.

JACK-STRAW, *sb. Curruca cinerea*, common Whitethroat.—SHREWSBURY. The name of *Jack-straw* is given to this bird from the straw-like material with which it builds its nest. Cf. **Flax**.

JACK-TILES, *sb. pl.* roofing-tiles, so called from the place where they are made—*Jack-field*, Broseley (Salop).

JACK-UP-THE-ORCHARD, *sb.* a threat—*ignitum pro terribile.* Com. 'If yo' dunna tak' car' I'll shewn yo' *Jack-up-the-orchut*.'

JAG [jag·], (1) *v. a.* to carry hay, &c. in a cart.—COLLIERY. Qy. com. Der. 'jagger.' Cf. **Haul**.

(2) *sb.* a small cart-load. Qy. com. 'Tak' the light waggin an' fatch them tuthree rākin's, they'n on'y be a bit of a jag.'

'A *Jagg of Hay* is a small load of hay.'—*Academy of Armory*, Bk. III. ch. iii. p. 73.

(3) same as **Chag**, q. v.—WEM.

JAGGER, *sb.* one who carts for hire. Qy. com. 'So John Ivans is turned *jagger*, I 'ear!' 'Aye, an' it's a poor *jag* 'e'll mak' on it, fur I dunna know w'ich is the biggest drummil, 'im or the owd 'orse.' Cf. **Haulier**.

JAGGLE [jag·l], *v. a.* to cut badly and unevenly.—PULVERBATCH. 'Them scithors mun gŏŏ to Soseb'ry to be grond—jest look 'ow they *jagglen* the stuff—somebody's bin nōsin' an' taȳlin' faib'ries ŏŏth 'em.' Cf. **Haggle** (1).

JANGLING [jang·lin], *part. adj.* the idle talking which is fruitful of 'evil speaking, lying, and slandering.' Com. 'Them women bin al'ays *janglin'*—it ŏŏd look better on 'em to mind thar own business, an' let other folks mind thars.'

'*Jangling*, is whan man speketh to moche before folk, and clappeth as a mille, and taketh no kepe what he sayth.'—CHAUCER, *The Persones Tale* (*De Superbia*).

'*Iangelyn̄*', or iaveryn̄'. *Gar(v)ulo, blatero.* "*Iangler*, to jangle, prattle, tattle saucily, or scurvily."—COTG.' *Prompt. Parv. and Notes.*

'Du. *jangelen;* O.Fr. *jangler*, to jangle, *garrire, blaterare.*'—STRAT.

'Il faut chercher une (autre) origine à *jangler*, et elle se trouve sans doute dans le hollandais *jangelen.*'—BUR.

JANNIWERRY-FREEZE-THE-POT-BY-THE-FIRE, *sb.* the month of January.—PULVERBATCH. Qy. com.

'A kindly good Janiuéere,
Fréeseth pot by the féere.'
TUSSER, *Januaries husbandrie.*

'*Janiveer freeze the pot by the fire.*
If the grass grow in Janiveer,
It grows the worse for't all the year.'
RAY'S *Proverbs*, p. 33.

See **Febriwerry-fill-diche.**

JARN. See (1) **Darn**, (2) **Deärn.**

JARSEY [jaa·r'zi'], (1) *sb., obs.* the fine combings of wool.—PULVERBATCH.

'*Jersey* is the finest Wool taken out of other sorts of Wool by combing it with a Jersey-Comb.'—*Academy of Armory*, Bk. III. ch. vi. p. 286.

Ash has, '*Jersey.* Combed wool prepared for spinning, yarn spun from combed wool.' And he gives, as the adjective from this, '*Jersey*, made of *Jersey.*' See below.

(2) *sb., obs.* a coarse fabric of loose texture, made of '*jarsey*' spun into worsted.—*Ibid.* 'As coä'se as *jarsey*' is a proverbial saying still extant, and applied to any material of inferior quality. Der. 'jarsey-hillin'.'

(3) *sb., obsols., sl.?* the hair.—*Ibid.* 'Yo' wanten yore *jarsey* cropt.' Compare the slang term '*Jazey*,' a wig—'the cove with the *jazey*, i. e. the Judge.' See *Slang Dictionary*, p. 161.

JARSEY-HILLIN', *sb., obs.* a bed-covering of '*jarsey*' (2) quilted with refuse wool-combings between the double-fold material.—*Ibid.* 'I think yo' bin prepar'd fur the winter ŏŏth two par' o' blankets an' a *jarsey-'illin'.*'

'One payre of *gersy* blanketts' is comprised in an *Inventory* . . . . Owlbury Manor-House, Bishop's Castle, 1625.

See WAY in *Prompt. Parv.*, p. 240. Cf. **Bed-hillin'**, also **Fustian blankets**.

JARSEY-WOOLSEY, *sb.*, *obs.* a dress material cunningly woven of fine worsted yarn and linen thread—warp and woof often of diverse colours, as of dark blue and orange, or brown,—a pretty fabric of changing hue and serviceable quality, entirely 'home-made.'—*Ibid.* 'Aye, theer's nuthin' wars like the owd-fashioned *jarsey-ŏŏlsey*, it beäts yore merinoes out o' sight.'

JAUNDERS [jon·dur'z], *sb.*, *var. pr.* the jaundice. Com. 'Poor owd mon! 'e's bin bad a lungful time, an' now they sen it's turned to the black *jaunders*.' Cf. **Yallow-wort**.

JAWM. See **Chimley-jawm** and **Door-jawms**.
'The *Jaumes* or Peers, the window Sides.'—*Academy of Armory*, Bk. III. ch. xiii. p. 473.

JAZEY [jai·zi'], *sb.*, *obs.*? a form of the (woman's) name Joyce—there was a *Jazey* Humphreys at Castle Pulverbatch [1838].

JEALOUSY [jel·u'si'], *sb. Sedum rupestre*, St. Vincent's Rock Stone-crop (garden plant).—PULVERBATCH, *Arscott*. See **Link-moss**.

JED, *adj.*, *var. pr.* dead. Com. See **Grammar Outlines** (*consonants*), **D** (1) for similar examples.

JEF-EARS. See **Deaf-ears**.

JEF-NUTS. See **Deaf-nuts**.

JENNY-RAILS, *sb.* the tramway.—COLLIERY; M. T.

JENNY-WAGGON, *sb.* the truck—loosely hooped with iron round the load—on which coal or iron-stone comes up the pit, and is pushed from the pit's mouth by the 'bonkies.'—COLLIERY; M. T.

JEÖW. See **Dew**.

JERKS [jur'·ks], *sb.* the heart, liver, and lights of a lamb.—WEM. Cf. **Pummice**.

JERUSALEM STAR, *sb. Hypericum calycinum*, large-flowered St. John's Wort (garden plant).—PULVERBATCH, *Hanwood*.

JESSUP [jes·up *and* jez·up], *sb.* juice; syrup out of fruit pies and puddings.—PULVERBATCH; NEWPORT; WEM. 'W'en the rŭbub's so young it gwuz all to *jezzup*, an' w'en the pŭddin' 's cut it's nuthin' but duff.'

JETH, JETH-PINCH. See **Death** and **Death-pinch**.

JETTY [jet·i'], (1) *v. n.* to agree; to be in concord.—WEM. 'The new cow *jetties* reet well alung wuth the others.'

(2) *sb.* a state of evenness or uniformity.—*Ibid.* 'The new buildin' an' the 'ouse bin all of a *jetty*,' i. e. not detached—all under one roof.
Shakespeare has *jutty* with exactly the opposite meaning—that of projection :—

'. . . . . . . No *jutty*, frieze,
Buttress, nor coign of vantage.'
Macbeth, I. vi. 6.

JIGGIN. See **Waggoners' Words to horses.**

JIMMY [jim·i'], *adv.* airily; jauntily.—PULVERBATCH; WORTHEN; WEM. 'The owd mon an' ŏŏman wun comin' alung together as *jimmy* as yo' pläsen.'

JINE, *v. a.* and *v. n.*, *var. pr.* to join. Com. It is related of a certain parish clerk of Upton Magna, that upon one occasion, when there was a 'strike' amongst the village choir, he found himself compelled to sing 'solo'—he managed to go through one verse, then he stopped, turned with an appealing look to the congregation, and said, 'Them as can *jine*, come *jine*, come *jine*, fur it's a misery to be athisn!'

JOB [job·], *v. a.* to pierce or stab suddenly with any sharp-pointed instrument.—SHREWSBURY; PULVERBATCH; WEM. 'Whad maks yo' lame, Tummas?' 'W'y I *jobbed* one o' the tines o' the sharevil i' my big toe.' 'Han'ee 'ad it dressed?' 'I 'ad it charmed, an' the sharevil, so I 'spect it'll tak' no 'arm.' Ash has to *job* in the same sense.

'To *job* signifies in the East Anglian dialect to peck with the beak, or with a mattock.'—WAY, in *Prompt. Parv.*, p. 263.

JOBLOCKS [job·luks], *sb. pl.* fleshy, hanging cheeks.—PULVERBATCH. ''E's a fine par o' *joblocks*, 'e looks as if 'e didna crack many djef nuts.'

JOCKEY [jok·i'], *sb.* a horse-breaker.—SHREWSBURY; PULVERBATCH. Qy. com. 'We sha'n a pretty well o' folks o' Monday—theer'll be the ship-shearers, an' the wilrits, an' owd Billy Davies the *jockey*, an' 'is lad bin comin' to break two cowts.'

'From *Jack* (or, with the Northern pronunciation, *Jock*), in the sense of a person in an inferior position. *Jocky* was specially applied to the servant who looked after horses, now almost confined to the rider of a race-horse.'—WEDG.

JOHN-GO-TO-BED-AT-NOON, same as **Betty-go-to-bed-at-noon,** q. v. —NEWPORT.

JOHNNY-KNOCK-SOFTLY, *sb.*, *sl.?* a slow, dawdling, awkward workman. Qy. com. 'I dunna know whad the Maister wanted ŏŏth sich a *Johnny-knock-softly* as that.'

JOHNNY-WOP-STRAW, *sb.*, *sl.?* a farm-labourer. Qy. com. Cobden applied the term '*chop-stick*' to the same class of people.

JOINT-STOOL, *sb.*, *obs.* Mr. Halliwell says, 'A stool framed by joinery work, at first so called in distinction to stools rudely formed from a single block;' he quotes from the *Unton Inventories*, p. 1, '*Ioyned stole*.'

'*In the greate Parlor* . . . fowre low stooles, Thirteene *joyned stooles*.' —*Inventory* . . . Owlbury Manor-House, Bishop's Castle, 1625.

Cf. **Buffet-stool.**

JOMPERT [jom·pur't *and* jom·pu't], *sb.*, *obsole.* a large, coarse, earthenware cup with two close-fitting handles—a kind of 'porringer.'

—PULVERBATCH; WEM; ELLESMERE. 'Have you brought the things out of the gig, Jack? Take care of that cup.' 'Dun yo' mane that *jompe't*, Missis?—it's a rar' un for a joram o' drink-mate!'

JONNACK [jon·uk], *adj.* true-hearted; fair-dealing; honourable. Qy. com. 'Bill said 'e ŏŏdna, an' 'e didna, 'e's al'ays *jonnack*—whad says owd Ben—I'd sooner tak' 'is word than many a man's wuth.'

JORAM [joa·r'um], *sb.* a large quantity of good eatables or drinkables—'a rar' *joram*.' Qy. com.

JOSEY [joa·zi'], *sb.* form of 'Joseph.'—COLLIERY.

JOUR [jou·h'r' *and* ji'ou·r'], *v. n.*, *obsols.* to mutter, or grumble in an undertone; generally used in the participial form—*jouring*.—PULVERBATCH. 'Whad's the matter ŏŏth yo', Dick?—yo' bin al'ays *jourin'* an' mungerin' at the table—han'ee got summat as is too good fur yo'?'

'I pray that Lord that did you hither send,
You may your cursings, swearings *jourings* end.'
ROBERT HAYMAN'S *Quodlibets*, 1628, in Nares.

Mr. Nares explains *jouring* as 'swearing,' and adds, 'Perhaps a coined word, from *juro*, Latin.' Cf. **Munger**.

JOWL [jou·l], PULVERBATCH. Qy. com. [joa·l], ATCHAM; WEM, (1) *v. a.* to knock, as of the head. 'Whad bin yo' lads cross-plădin' about?—I'll *jowl* yore yeds together direc'ly, an' that'll end the matter.' *Jowl* is a corruption of *Choul*. See **Choul** (1).

(2) *sb.* a washing mug.—NEWPORT. A *Staffordshire-Border* term, apparently. Cf. **Stean**.

JOWTERS [jou·tur'z], (1) *sb. pl.* cabbage-plants that boll instead of forming hearts.—PULVERBATCH. 'My cabbidge bin most turned *jowters*.'

(2) *sb. pl.* large flakes of curd.—PULVERBATCH. In the process of curd-making, if the whey breaks into large flakes, they are *jowters*—if into very small ones, 'the cruds bin moithered.' See **Cruds**.

JOY, *sb.*, *pec.* service.—SHREWSBURY; PULVERBATCH; WELLINGTON. 'Well, a good thing is a good thing after all, an' a bad un does yo' no *joy*.'

JUFFET [juf·it], *v. n.* to jump or fidget about.—WEM. 'Whad bin yo' childern *juffetin'* about athatn fur?'

JUMBLEMENT, *sb.* a state of confusion. Qy. com. 'Dear 'eart alive! whad a *jumblement* yo'n got them plums in—afore ever I get to Soseb'ry they'n be in sich a mingicummumbus, I shall never part 'em.'

JUNDER, (1) *v. n.* to mutter; to grumble in an undertone.—PULVERBATCH. 'I'd ten times sooner folks ŏŏd'n spake out whad they han to say than gŏŏ *junderin'* to tharselves—if they wun my childern I'd 'elp 'em to *junder*.' Cf. **Chunder**.

(2) *sb.* frogs' spawn.—CRAVEN ARMS; CHURCH STRETTON. Cf. **Tather** (1).

JUNKET [jungk·it], *sb.*, *obsols.* a feast; a furtive entertainment.—'The Missis an' some on 'er owd cronies wun 'ăvin' a rar' *junket* o' buttered flaps, an' the Maister come wham onexpected an' ketcht 'em.'

JUNKETING, *part. adj.*, *obsols.* wastefully feasting and entertaining.—*Ibid.* ''Er'll ruin 'er 'usband ŏŏth 'er *junketin'* ways—it's an owd sayin', but a very true un, "The ŏŏman can throw out ŏŏth a spŏŏn whad the mon'll throw in ŏŏth a spade."'

JURGY [jur'gi'], *adj.* contentious; inclined to pick a quarrel.—CLEE HILLS. 'The agent wuz mighty *jurgy*, I 'ad to mind whad I said to 'im.' Cf. Lat. *jurgiōsus*, quarrelsome.

JURN. See **Deurn.**

JUSTLY, *adv.*, *pec.* exactly—with regard to time.—NEWPORT. 'I conna come not now—not *justly* now.'

JUST NOW [jaest nou·], *adv.* this term comprises a twofold meaning with regard to time—past and future—at a considerable interval from the moment of speaking. Com. (1) 'Call Jack to 'is bayte.' 'I did *jest now.*' 'W'en?' 'This 'our agŏŏ.' (2) 'The bŭtcher-boy's brought the mate, an' wanted to know about the shooit—I toud 'im as that 'ŏŏd do *jest now*, at-after 'e'd bin 'is roun's—'e needna gŏŏ back fur it.'

'*Just now*,' says Dean Alford, 'in its strict meaning, imports nearly at the present moment, whether before or after. Yet general usage has limited its application to a point slightly preceding the present, and will not allow us to apply it to time to come. . . . We have the double use of the term (that is, for past and future time) preserved in provincial usage in the Midland and Northern counties.'—*The Queen's English*, p. 210, 2nd ed. 1864.

Ray gives '*Near now*, Just now, not long since, *Norf.*,' in '*South and East Country Words.*' Cf. **Now just.**

KAG [kag·], ATCHAM; PULVERBATCH; WEM. [ki'ag·], CHURCH STRETTON, *Leebotwood*, (1) *sb.* a projecting piece left on a tree or shrub when a branch has been severed from it.

(2) *sb.* a tooth standing alone.—PULVERBATCH. 'I hanna but this one *kag* lef', an' I should be better athout that, fur it's as sore as a bile.'

Compare '*Dentes exerti*, *gag* teeth, or teeth standing out.'—*Nomenclator*, 1585, p. 29, in HAL.

(3) *v. a.* to cut badly and unevenly, so as to leave projections.—CHURCH STRETTON, *Leebotwood.* 'See 'ow yo'n *kyagged* the bacon.' Cf. **Snag** (1).

KAGGLE [kag·l], *v. n.* to struggle to keep up and make the best of circumstances.—PULVERBATCH; WEM. ''Ow dun'ee manage, Betty, ŏŏth the ruff raïnin' in so bad?' 'Well, we bin obleeged to *kaggle* on some'ow—we 'ad'n to pool the bed out, an' pŭt the cooler to ketch it.'

KALE [kai·l], (1) *sb.* a turn.—WELLINGTON. '*Kale* for *kale*,' to drink alternately;—'It's my *kale* now,' *i. e.* my turn to drink—are harvest-field expressions in passing the bottle.

Compare '*Sors*, a lot, or *keauill*, a chance, a deale,' in DUNCAN'S *Appendix Etymologiæ*, A.D. 1595, E. D. S., B. xiii., and O.Du. *cavel*, 'sors,' in STRAT.

(2) [kai·l], SHREWSBURY. [kei·l *corr.* kaayl·], PULVERBATCH, *v. a.* to tilt up, as of a cart, so as to empty; to turn over. 'W'en Dick brings the nex' tumbril load o' turmits, tell 'im to *kaÿle* 'em up i' the orchut fur them yeows.' Cf. **Cave** (2).

KAMING [kai·min], (1) *part. adj.* issuing forth in a stream, as bees when leaving the hive to swarm.—NEWPORT. Cf. **Towthering.**

(2) *part. adj.* making rude mocking noises to annoy a person. —*Ibid.*

KATIE-BRAN'-TAIL, *sb.* the Redstart.—LUDLOW. Cf. **Bessy-brin-tail.**

KAY [kai·], (1) a key—an old pronunciation. Com.

'And cal the clargé to ȝour counsel, that beryn Cristis *kay*,
And holdist up holé cherche the prynce of Heven to pay.'
JOHN AUDELAY'S *Poems*, p. 20.

'The[y] locked the dore / and than went theyr way.
Cayphas and Anna / of that kept the *kay*.'
Lyfe of Joseph of Armathia, l. 53.

'Either through gifts, or guile, or such like waies,
Crept in by stouping low, or stealing of the *kaies*.'
SPENSER, *F. Q.*, Bk. IV. c. x. st. xviii.

'A.S. *cǽg*; O.Fris. *kei*, *kai*, key; *clavis*.'—STRAT.

(2) *sb.*, *obs.* same as **Cop-wedge**, q. v.—PULVERBATCH.

(3) *v. a.* to make, or to bind, round, as of the top of a well, with timber or masonry—'*kayin*' the top o' the well.'—CORVE DALE.

'"*Key*, or knyttynge of ij. wallys, or trees yn an vnstabylle grownde. *Loramentum*."—CATH. The Catholicon explains *loramentum* to mean boarding or frame-work compacted together, as in the construction of a ceiling. . . . . "*Key* to knytte walles toguyder, *clef*."—PALSG.' *Prompt. Parv. and Notes.*

KAYS. See **Keys.**

KEACH [kee·ch], same as **Cleach**, q. v.—PULVERBATCH; WEM.

KEACH-HOLE, same as **Cleach-hole**, q. v.—PULVERBATCH; WEM.

KECK-HONDED, *adj.* left-handed, and awkward in consequence, or by metaphor.—PULVERBATCH. 'Ketch out, yo' *keck-'onded*, avenless thing.'

KECKLE-STOMACHED, *adj.* squeamish; queasy.—PULVERBATCH. 'I'm so despert *keckle-stomached* lately, I should 'aive my 'eart out if I wuz to see a yar in anythin'.'

Ash has, '*Keckle*, to keck, to heave the stomach.' He derives '*keck*' from Du. *kecken*, to cough. Cf. **Kickle-stomach.**

KEDLOCK, *sb. Sinapis arvensis,* wild Mustard, Charlock. Qy. com. Cf. **Kerlock.**

KEECH [kee·ch], (1) *sb.* a cake of consolidated fat, wax, or tallow.—PULVERBATCH; WEM. (1) 'Theer's a good *keech* o' fat on them broth, tak' it off carfully.' (2) 'I've got a good *keech* o' bees-wax this time; I shall tak' it to the Soseb'ry 'Firmary, they'n gie the wuth on it theer.' Compare 'tallow-*catch*' in 1 *K. Henry IV.*, II. iv. 252.

Nares says, 'It is highly probable that tallow-*keech* is here the right reading,' and in support of his opinion quotes 'Dr. [Bp.] Percy' as follows:—'A *keech* of tallow is the fat of an ox or cow, rolled up by the butcher in a round lump, in order to be carried to the chandler. It is the proper word in use now.'

Shakespeare applies the term *keech* to a butcher's wife—2 *K. Henry IV.*, II. i. 101; and to a butcher's son—Wolsey—*K. Henry VIII.*, I. i. 55.

(2) *v. n.* to consolidate, as warm fat, wax, &c. does in cooling.—PULVERBATCH; WEM; OSWESTRY. 'Dunna mess yore fingers ŏŏth it awilde it's warm, let it *keech*, an' then it'll break off aisy—them mole candles dunna do to carry about.'

KEEP [kee·p], (1) *v. a., pec.* to maintain. Com. ''E's a right tidy fellow, but hanna-d-a chance to get on; 'e 'as 'is poor owd mother to *keep*, an' a crippled sister—'e says if it wunna fur them 'e ŏŏdna stop naigerin' [working like a negro] 'ere.'

(2) *sb., pec.* maintenance. Com. 'A chap like that inna wuth 'is *keep*, an' say nuthin' about wages.'

(3) *sb., pec.* pasture. Com. 'Theer's bin a good Miămas spring—plenty o' *keep* to las' till Chris'mas if the groun' should keep bar' [free from snow].' See **Out at keep.** Cf. **Feed.**

(4) *v. a., pec.* to attend, as of the market.—SHREWSBURY; PULVERBATCH. Qy. com. 'I 'ear our owd neighbour's gwun to live twix Wenlock and Bridgenorth, so they can *keep* which market they'n a mind.'

'*Rose.* . . . . My Father is a Farmer within three short Miles o' the Town: we *keep* this Market—I sell Chickens, Eggs, and Butter, and my Brother Bullock there sells Corn.'—FARQUHAR's *Recruiting Officer*, Act III. Scene—The Market-Place [Shrewsbury].

Ash gives *keep* in the same sense.

KEEVE. See **Cave** (2). Ash has '*keeve*,'—which he calls 'a local word,'—'to overturn; to empty a cart.' Bailey—ed. 1782—gives, 'To *keeve*,' in the same sense as '*Cheshire*.'

KEFFEL [kef·i'l], (1) *sb.* a sorry, worthless horse.—PULVERBATCH; WELLINGTON; NEWPORT; WEM. Richardson—a Derbyshire man—uses this word:—'Old Robin at a distance on his Roan *keffel*.'—*Clarissa Harlowe*, vol. ii. p. 130, ed. 1774.

W. *ceffyl*, a horse. Cf. **Kirby.**

(2) *sb.* a lazy, good-for-nothing fellow.—*Idem.* 'Couldna Tum 'Ŏŏd bring yo' a bit'n a jag o' coal?' 'Well, I dunna know—they bin poor *keffils*, bŏăth mon an' 'orse.' Cf. **Drummil.**

KELL [kel·], (1) *sb.* the omentum, or caul, of a slaughtered pig.—WELLINGTON.

'Rim or *kell* wherein the bowels are lapt.'—*Florio*, p. 340, in HAL.
Mr. Halliwell says *kell* means 'any covering like network.'
'Kelle, *Reticulum, retiaculum.*'—*Prompt. Parv.*, p. 270.
See Mr. Way's Note, *idem*. Cf. **Veil.**

(2) *sb.* a film, or scale, on the eye; a cataract.—NEWPORT. An old man at Edgmond said of his wife, ''Er's got a *kell* o' won oi, an' 'er's dark o' the tother.'

KELTER [kel·tur'], (1) *sb.*, *obsols.*? wealth; accumulated money.—PULVERBATCH. 'The daughter'll be a ketch fur somebody, the owd chap 'as yeps o' *kelter*.' Jamieson has '*kelter*, money.'

(2) *v. a.* to amass; to collect.—*Ibid.* 'I've bin out *kelterin'* all day, but got mighty little pelf.'

KENCH [ken·sh], (1) *sb.* a twist or wrench,—a sprain. Com. 'I thought it wuz on'y a bit of a *kench*, but agen mornin' it wuz swelled as big as two, an' Dr. Wildin' said as theer wuz a splinter broke, an' I mun gŏŏ o' my club, fur I shouldna be uprit fur a month.'

(2) *sb.* a big piece or lump.—WEM. 'The Missis give 'im a reet good *kench* o' bread an' chees', an' send 'im off.' *Kenchin'* is an alternative term used in precisely the same way. Cf. **Slench** and **Slenchin'.**

KENSPECKLE, *adj.* conspicuous—a term applied chiefly to dress.—CORVE DALE. Probably an imported word. See *Kenspeckle*, in WEDG.

KEOUP [ki'ou·p *or* kyou·p], (1) *v. n.* to bark, or yelp, incessantly, as a cur does.—PULVERBATCH. 'I couldna get a bit o' sleep fur that dog *kyoupin'* all night.'

(2) *sb.* a yelping cur.—*Ibid.* 'I 'ate them lickle *kyoups*, they binna wuth thar keep, let alone payin' fur.' Cf. **Keout.**

(3) *v. n.* by metaphor—to scold.—*Ibid.* 'I ŏŏdna live ŏŏth that ŏŏman whadever 'er'd gie me—'er *kyoups* from mornin' till night.'

(4) *sb.* a scold.—*Ibid.* 'The Missis wuz sich a *kyoup.*'

KEOUSE [ki'ou·s *or* kyou·s], *v. a.* to chase; to drive away.—PULVERBATCH; WORTHEN; CLEE HILLS. 'The pigs bin i' the garden—w'eer's the dog, to *keouse* 'em out?' Cf. **Scout.**

KEOUT, KEOUT-DOG [ki'ou·t *or* kyou·t], *sb.* a little, sharp, vigilant, barking dog.—PULVERBATCH; WEM. 'Snap's a rar' *kyout*, 'e ŏŏnna let nobody gŏŏ nigh the 'ouse athout lettin' 'em know.'

Cf. 'Make bandog thy *scoutwatch*, to barke at a theefe.'—TUSSER, *Good husbandlie lessons*, l. 19, p. 20, ed. E. D. S.
'O.Fr. *escout, estre en escout*, écouter attentivement, épier.'—BUR.
Cf. **Keoup** (2).

KERLOCK [ki'er'·luk *or* kyer'·luk], same as **Kedlock**, q. v.—CRAVEN ARMS; CLEE HILLS; LUDLOW.

KERRY, (1) *sb.* a clamorous inquiry about anything.—WHITCHURCH. 'Theer wuz sich a *kerry* after it.'

'O.Fr. *querre;* quérir, faire une enquête, demander, requérir.'—BUR.

(2) *sb.* a noisy troop or pack, as of children or dogs.—NEWPORT; ELLESMERE. (1) 'Oh! 'ere's a *kerry* o' lads; let's run.' (2) 'Them childern bin like a *kerry* o' 'oun's up an' down the place.'

KESTER, *sb.* a form of the proper name Christopher.—NEWPORT.

'he said, "come hither *Kester* Norton,
a ffine ffellow thou seemes to bee;
some good councell, *Kester* Norton,
this day does thou giue to mee."'
Risinge in the North, ll. 61—63. *Percy Folio MS.,* vol. ii. p. 212, ed. Hales and Furnivall.

Mr. Halliwell gives '*Kester*' as a '*North*' form.

KETCH, (1) *v. a., var. pr.* to catch. Com.

(2) *sb.* a part of a song.—PULVERBATCH. 'Whad sort of a finishin' night 'ad'n'ee—pretty good singin'?' 'Aye, several right good songs, beside a *ketch* or two; but Mr. John Oakley's "Pedlar Jew" wuz the best thing I ever 'eärd, an' the best sung.'

'Come, Hostis, give us more Ale, and our Supper with what haste you may, and when we have sup'd, let's have your Song, Piscator, and the *Ketch* that your Scholer promised us, or else Coridon will be doged.'—*The Compleat Angler,* ch. xi. p. 208, ed. 1653.

KETCH-O'-FROST, *sb.* a slight hoar frost. Com. 'Theer wuz a bit of a *ketch-o'-fros'* last night, an' these w'ite frosses al'ays brings rain.' Cf. **Duck's-frost.**

KEX [kek·s], *sb.* the dry stalk of the hemlock, and of some other species of umbelliferous plants.—PULVERBATCH; WELLINGTON; WEM. Qy. com. 'Ben, I toud yo' to bring some *kex* in fur spills; yo' gwun at them matches as if they comen fur nuthin', but yo'n fine it out some dark mornin' w'en theer is none.'

'And as glowande gledes · gladieth nouȝte þis werkmen,
þat worchen & waken · in wyntres niȝtes,
As doth a *kex* or a candel · þat cauȝte hath fyre & blaseth.'
Piers Pl., Text B., pass. xvii. l. 219.

'As hollow as a gun; as a *kex.*'
RAY'S *Proverbs,* p. 222.

See WAY in *Prompt. Parv.,* p. 278. W. *cecys,* hollow stalks; hemlock.

KEYS [kai·z *and* kee·z], (1) *sb. pl.* the clustering fruit of *Fráxinus excélsior,* common Ash. Qy. com.

'*Hoc fraccinum,* a *kay* of a nesche.'—*Nominale,* xv. cent., in Wr. vocabs., vol. i. p. 228. See **Kay** (1).

(2) *sb.* the fruit of *Acer Pseúdo-plátanus,* greater Maple, or Sycamore.—PULVERBATCH. Qy. com.

(3) *sb. pl., obs.?* iron tips used for shoeing bullocks.—CORVE DALE.

KIBBA [kib·u'], *sb., obsols.* a long walking-staff, held—not at the top, as an ordinary walking-stick is, but—in the middle, like an 'alpenstock.'—WEM. Such a stick was once quite common in Shropshire, and may still [1874] occasionally be seen. Cf. **Gibbed-stick.** See *Kibble* (3), in HAL.

KIBBLE [kib·l], *v. a.* to crush, or grind, coarsely, as of barley, pease, &c. Qy. com. 'Pŭt that bag o' barley across the owd mar' an' tak' it to 'Abberley mill, an' get 'em to *kibble* it aw'ile yo' stoppen, or we sha'n be short o' feed afore Sunday's o'er.'

KIBBLETY [kib·lti'], *adj.* stony, and, as a consequence, rough and jolting: said of roads.—WHITCHURCH. See **Cobbles** (1).

KIBE, KIVE [ki'ei·b], PULVERBATCH. [kei·b], CLUN. [kei·v], SHREWSBURY, *sb.* an implement used by cottage gardeners for 'stocking' up the ground between the potato rows prior to the operation of earthing the potatoes. It is about a foot long, and four inches broad at the cutting end: the handle is three feet and a half in length. The form of the implement is similar to that of an adze, and it is used in the same way. Cf. **Caff** (1).

KICKLE-STOMACH, *sb.* a squeamish stomach.—WEM. See **Keckle-stomached.**

KID [kid·], (1) *sb.* a bundle of small sticks for firewood.—WELLINGTON; NEWPORT; WEM.

'*Kyd*, fagot. *Fassis* (*fasciculus*, P.). "A kidde *ubi* fagott."—CATH. ANG. "Kydde, a fagotte, *falourde*."—PALSG.' *Prompt. Parv. and Notes.* Cf. **Faggit** (1).

(2) *v. a.* and *v. n.* to make up bundles, or *kids*, of small brushwood for fuel.—*Ibid.* 'Yo' can cut that brash an' get it *kidded*.'

KIDDLE [kid·l], *v. n.* to emit a flow of saliva from the mouth; to slaver. Qy. com. 'The child *kiddles* badly cuttin' its tith, but I al'ays think it's best—they binna so likely fur fits.'

KIDLING-BIB [kid·li'n bib], *sb.* a baby's slavering-bib.—*Ibid.*

'*Hoc salmarium, A*' slaveryng-clout,' occurs in an *English Vocabulary*, XV. cent., in Wr. vocabs., vol. i. p. 203.

KIDMAW [kid·mau], *sb.* the stomach of a calf prepared for rennet. —WORTHEN, *The Gravels*; CRAVEN ARMS; CLUN. Cf. **Mawskin.**

KIGGLING [kig·li'n], *adj.* unsteady; tottering. Qy. com. 'Dunna pŭt the crame-stane on that *kiggling* bench—it'll tipe o'er an' tak' the butter to markit down the gutter.'

KILL, *sb.*, *var. pr.* a kiln. Com. 'They tellen me as them furrin 'tatoes bin *kill*-dried afore they comen 'ere, so they bin no good fur settin'.'

'The *kil* house' is named in an *Inventory* . . . Owlbury Manor-House, Bishop's Castle, 1625.

'The dog of the *kill*,
He went to the mill
To lick mill-dust:

The miller he came
With a stick on his back,—
Home, dog, home!
. . . .'

J. O. HALLIWELL'S *Nursery Rhymes of England*, CCCLIX.

'Kylne (f)or malt dryynge (*Kyll*, P.). *U(s)trina*, C. F.'—*Prompt. Parv.*

KILLODDY [kil·odi'], *v. a.*, *obs.* to dry hemp-stalks over a fire made in a hole in the ground. (See below.) It was the first process in hemp dressing.—PULVERBATCH. See **Tewter.**

KILLODDY-PIT, *sb.*, *obs.* the hole in the ground in which the fire was made for *killoddying* the hemp-stalks. —*Ibid.* There was a *killoddy-pit* on the 'Green' at Castle Pulverbatch: it was in use about the year 1800. 'I 'ear Medlicott's lost another yeow i' the *killoddy-pit;* it's a great ŏŏnder to me they dunna fill it up, it hanna bin used this ten 'ear, an' this is the second—if nod the third—ship they'n fund djed in it.' The 'Green,' and the 'Oaken'—an adjacent hill—were formerly a sheep-walk.

KILLOW [ki'l·oe], *v. n.*, *obsols.* to dry by the heat of the sun, as grass or herbs.—PULVERBATCH. (1) 'The 'ay̆ ŏŏnna *killow* as lung as this weather lasses—it wants more sun.' (2) 'Dunna shift them yarbs out o' the sun, they binna *killowed* anow.' Cf. **Glint** (1).

KIMET [ki'ei·mit *and* kei·mit], (1) *adj.* dizzy: said of sheep that are suffering from hydatids on the brain.—PULVERBATCH; CLUN; CORVE DALE. 'The Maister's killed the owd ship—we sha'n a *kyimet* mutton fur dinner an' *kyimet* pie fur supper—agen the end o' the wik we sha'n all be as *kyimet* as the ship.' See below. Cf. **Gid.**

(2) *adj.* silly; half-witted.—SHREWSBURY; PULVERBATCH; CLUN; WEM. 'Thee bist as *kyimet* as a noud ship—turnin' round an' starrin' about fur things w'en they bin under yore nose.'

(3) *adj.* perverse of temper; intractable.—OSWESTRY. A waggoner, speaking of a cart-horse, said, 'I dunna like them churn-yedded uns, they bin al'ays so *kimit;* I like a good nag's-yedded un.'

'When I com nār to Skeàl-hill, I fūnd oald Aberram Atchisson sittin on a steul breckan steàns to mend rwoads wid, an' I ax't him if I med full my ledder pwokes frae his heap. Aberram was varra *kaim't*, an' tell't ma to tak' them 'at wasn't brocken if I wantit steàns, sooa I tell't him hoo it was an' oa' aboot it.'—'Joe and the Geologist,' in *The Folk-Speech of Cumberland*, by A. C. Gibson, F. S. A., p. 4.

Mr. Gibson adds the Glossarial Note, '*Kaim't*, literally crooked, but used to signify cross or peevish.'

The Cumberland *kaim't* and the Shropshire *kimet* point to an origin common to both. W. *cam*, crooked. Cf. **Kim-kam**, below.

KIM-KAM, (1) *adj.* all awry.—WELLINGTON.

'*Sic.* This is clean *kam.*
Bru. Merely awry. . . . .'

Coriolanus, III. i. 305.

(2) *adj.* perverse.—WEM. 'Let's a none o' yore *kim-kam* ways.' W. *cam.* Cf. **Kimet** (3), above.

KIMNEL, (1) *sb.* the shallow tub in which butter is washed and salted when fresh from the churn.—NEWPORT.

'Churn and *kimnel.*'—*Auctioneer's Catalogue* (Forton Hall), 1875. Cf. **Butter-mit**.

(2) *sb., obs.* a brewing vessel; a cooler (?).

'*The Seller* one *kymnell* . . . one small *kymnell* . . . one tundish.' —*Inventory* . . . Owlbury Manor-House, Bishop's Castle, 1625.

'He goth, and geteth him a kneding trough,
And after a tubbe, and a *kemelin.*'
CHAUCER, *C. T.*, l. 3622.

'She's somewhat simple indeed, she knew not what a *kimnel* was, she wants good nurture mightily.'—BEAUMONT and FLETCHER, *The Coxcomb*, iv. 7, in Nares.

Ray, amongst his '*North Country Words,*' gives '*A Kimnel*, or *Kemlin*, a Powdering Tub.'

'*Kymlyne*, or kelare, vesselle (kynlyn, S. P.), *Cunula.* In a roll of 2—5 Edw. I., among the miscellaneous records of the Queen's Remembrancer, a payment occurs, "*Stephano le Ioignur, pro j. Kembelinâ subtus cisternam Regis*, vijd." The Latin-Engl. Vocabulary, Roy. MS. 17, C. xvii., gives, under the head "*ad brasorium pertinencia*, Kymnelle, *cuna;* Kunlione, *cunella.*" Thos. Harpham of York bequeaths, in 1341, "*unum plumbum, unam cunam, quæ vocatur* maskefat, *et duas parvas cunas quæ vocantur* gylefatts, *duas* kymelyns, *et duos parvos barellos.*"—Testam. Ebor. i. 3. "Kynmell, *quevue, quevuette.*"—PALSG.' *Prompt. Parv. and Notes.*

KIND [kin·d], (1) *v. a.* and *v. n.* to ignite.—WHITCHURCH; ELLESMERE. (1) 'I conna *kind* the fire wuth these chats, they binna dry.' (2) 'The fire wunna *kind* this mornin', do whad I wull.'

O.N. *kynda*, to set fire to. Cf. **Tind**.

(2) [kei·nd], *adj.* genial; flourishing; thriving:—'the groun's nice and *kind;*' 'the plants dunna grow so *kind* under them trees;' 'the pig looks mighty *kind.*' Com. Cf. **Kindly** (2).

(3) [koi·nd *corr.* kayh·nd], *adj.* healthy; wholesome: said of the skin.—NEWPORT. ''Er's got a noice *koind* skin on 'er own.' Cf. **Clane** (4).

KINDLE [kin·dl], (1) *sb.*—in *kindle*—is to be with young. (1) Of rabbits. Com. (2) *obsols.* of kittens.—PULVERBATCH.

'Kynled, or *kyndelyd* in forthe bryngynge of yonge beestys. *Fetatus.*' —*Prompt. Parv.* Cf. **Kittle** (1).

(2) *v. n.* to bring forth young. (1) Rabbits. Com. (2) *obsols.* kittens. —PULVERBATCH. 'Wha'n'ee think?—the cat's *kindled* in Betty's ban'-box an' spiled 'er best bonnit.'

'*Orlando.* Are you native of this place?

'*Rosalind.* As the cony that you see dwell where she is *kindled.*'— *As You Like It*, III. ii. 358.

'*Kyndlyñ*, or brynge forthe yonge kyndelyngys. *Feto.* The expression "*genimina viperarum,*" Vulg., Luke iii. 7, is in the Wicliffite version rendered "Kyndlyngis of eddris. . . ." In the St. Alban's Book mention is made of "a kyndyll of yonge cattes." Palsgrave gives the verb to "kyndyll as a she hare or cony dothe, whan they bring forthe yonge." . . . Compare Germ. kindlein, *proles*.'—*Prompt. Parv. and Notes.*

Cf. **Kittle** (2).

KINDLY [kei·ndli'], (1) *adv.* heartily.—SHREWSBURY; PULVERBATCH. Qy. com. 'Well, I wish yo' good-night, Missis, an' thank yo' *kindly* for me.'

'The ground of al goodnes curatis schuld be the cause,
And knyt hem *kyndly* togedur al the clergé.
. . . .
With mercé and with mekenes the treuth for to teche,
The comawndmentis of Crist to kepe *kyndly*
. . . .
ffore ȝe ben scheperdys al one.'

JOHN AUDELAY'S *Poems*, p. 36.

'. . . . .
In walks the little dog,
Says, "Pussy! are you there?
. . . .
Mistress Pussy, how d'ye do?"
"I thank you *kindly*, little dog,
I fare as well as you."'

J. O. HALLIWELL'S *Nursery Rhymes of England*, DLXVII.

(2) *adv.* well; thriving.—PULVERBATCH. Qy. com. 'The yerlins [yearlings] looken *kindly*, Mr. Jones, they'n got a good slike [sleek] coät on 'em.' 'Aye, I fettled 'em well all winter, but w'ether they'n paȳ's a question.' Cf. 'Kuyndeliche' = well, in the following:—

'"Peter!" quod a Plouȝ-Mon · and putte forþ his hed,
"I knowe him as *kuyndeliche* · as Clerk doþ his bokes."'

Piers Pl., Text A., pass. vi. l. 29.

KINGDOM-COME, *sb.* a state of pleasure in some newly-acquired happiness.—SHREWSBURY; PULVERBATCH; WEM. 'Poor owd Betty's in 'er *kin'dom-come* now 'er's gotten Jack wham agen.'

KINGFISHER, *sb.*, *pec. Calépteryx virgo*, Demoiselle Dragonfly.—WEM. Cf. **Sting-fisher.**

KING-O'-THE-WIK, *sb.* Friday, on which day it is popularly believed the weather will attain its climax, be it of shine or shower. —PULVERBATCH. Qy. com. 'Fair or foul, Friday's bound to be *king-o'-the-wik*.'

'Friday's a day as'll ăve its trick,
The fairest or foulest day i' the wik.'

Proverbial Weather-Rime.

'Right as the Friday, sothly for to telle,
Now it schyneth, now it reyneth faste,
Right so gan gery Venus overcaste

The hertes of hire folk, right as hire day
Is gerful, right so chaungeth sche array.
Selde is the Fryday al the wyke i-like.'
CHAUCER, *The Knightes Tale*, ll. 676—681, ed. Morris.

KINTER [kin·tur'], (1) *sb.* a cover.—WELLINGTON. "Er's done me a bad turn under *kinter* on a good un.'

(2) *v. a.* to cover. '*Kinter* it o'er.'—*Ibid.* Cf. **Kiver.**

KIPE [kei·p *and* ki'ei·p], *sb.* a strong osier basket with a twisted handle on each side, of circular form, but wider at the top than the bottom: it is computed to hold about half a bushel, and is used for general gardening purposes.—SHREWSBURY; PULVERBATCH; CORVE DALE; COLLIERY; WEM; ELLESMERE. 'I'll get owd Price in Coleham to mak' me a couple o' *kipes* the right mizzer, fur whad we buy'n at the country shops ŏŏnna-d-oud 'afe a strike yept, let alone level full.'

Ash gives '*Kipe* (a *local* word), a basket in the form of the lower frustrum of a cone, containing about a bushel; a coarse kind of wicker basket, wider at top than bottom.'

See **Kype** in *Weights and Measures*, p. lxxxv. Cf. **Corve**, also **Wisket** (1).

KIRBY, *sb.* a poor old horse.—OSWESTRY, *Welsh Border.* Cf. **Keffel** (1).

KISSING-BUSH, *sb.* a bunch of evergreens or mistletoe garnished with ribands and fruit, which is hung in the kitchen, or hall, at Christmas-tide. Qy. com. 'It dunna look much like Chris'mas, nod a bit o' 'olly an' ivvy, let alone a *kissin'-bush*—scrat an' clane an' cook is all our folks thinken on.'

KISSING-CRUST, *sb.* rough, protuberant crust on a loaf. Com. 'I like a *kissin'-crust* ŏŏth plenty o' good fresh butter on it.' 'Aye, the *crus'* is sweeter than the *kissin'*, I tak' it.'

KITCHEN, *sb., pec., obsols.* a large caldron or kettle furnished with a tap—designed to keep a supply of hot water by the kitchen fire—technically called a 'fountain.'—PULVERBATCH. Qy. com. 'Tak' car' to keep plenty o' waiter i' the *kitchen*, else yo'n 'ave it to-bost.'

KITE, *sb. Tinnúnculus Alaudarius*, the Kestrel.—OSWESTRY. Cf. **Glid.**

KITLING, *sb.* a kitten. Qy. com. 'The owd mar' 's as playful as a *kitlin'*.'

'A wanton widow Leezie was,
As cantie as a *kittlin;*
But Och! that night, amang the shaws,
She gat a fearfu' settlin!
She thro' the whins, an' by the cairn,
An owre the hill gaed scrievin,
Whare three lairds' lands met at a burn,
To dip her left sark-sleeve in,
Was bent that night.'
ROBERT BURNS, *Poems*, p. 47, l. 20.

Ash gives '*Kitling* (not so common a word), A kitten, a young cat.

'*Kytlynge*. *Catillus, catunculus*. "*Catulus*, a whelpe or a kytlynge."—ORTUS.' *Prompt. Parv. and Notes*.

'*Catulus*, . . a whelp, a *kitling*, the little yong of any beast.'—*Dict. Etym. Lat.*

'*Chaton*, petit chat; kitten, a *kittling*.'—CHAMB.

KITTLE [kit·l], (1) *sb.*—in *kittle*—is the state of being with young: said of cats. Qy. com. Cf. **Kindle** (1).

(2) *v. a.* to bring forth 'kitlings.' Qy. com.

'A Cat *kittleth*; a Litter of kittleings.'—*Academy of Armory*, Bk. II. ch. vii. p. 134.

'"Kyttell as a catte dothe, *chatonner*. Gossyppe, whan your catte kytelleth, I praye you let me haue a kytlynge (*chatton*)."—PALSG. "*Chatonner*, to kittle, or bring forth young cats. *Caller*, to kittle as a cat. *Faire ses petits*, to whelp, *kittle*, kindle, farrow," &c.—COTG.' WAY, in *Prompt. Parv.*, p. 277.

Cf. **Kindle** (2).

KIVE. See **Kibe**.

KIVER [kiv·ur'], (1) *v. a.* to cover.—CLUN. 'I've jest *kivered* the basket o'er.'

In *Rev.* xix. 8, the Wicliffite version—ed. A.D. 1388—has, 'And it is ȝouun to hir, that sche *kyuere* hir with white bissyn schynynge.'

(2) *sb.* a cover—'put the *kiver* on.'—CLUN; CORVE DALE; BRIDGNORTH; MUCH WENLOCK.

(3) *sb.*, *obsols.* a shallow meat-dish of coarse, brown earthenware.—PULVERBATCH; ELLESMERE. 'Put the men's dinner i' the oven to keep whot, an' wauve the *kiver* o'er it.' The term is fast dying out. A redundant form, *kiver-dish*, is occasionally employed about Pulverbatch.

KNAB [nab·], *v. a.* to bite gently and playfully. Horses *knab* each other when in good temper. Qy. com. Du. *knabbelen*, to gnaw.

KNABBIN', *sb.* a bite of herbage; short pasture.—PULVERBATCH. 'Yo' can turn the cows i' the little fild—theer's tidy *knabbin'* on it—awilde the edgrow gets a bit strunger.' Cf. **Brooit.**

KNACKER [nak·ur'], *sb.* a worn-out horse quite unfit for work. Qy. com. 'If 'e tak's that poor owd *knacker* to markit agen, 'e'll a the p'lice on 'im fur cruelty.'

Ray gives 'A *knacker*, One that makes Collars and other Furniture for Cart-horses,' amongst '*South and East Country Words*.'

Mr. Wedgwood says, 'It would seem that the office of slaughtering old worn-out horses fell to the *knacker* or coarse harness-maker, as the person who would have the best opportunity of making the skins available.'

Hence, then, the application of the term *knacker* to a horse fit only for the *knacker's* slaughter-house—the *knacker's-yard*, as it is called. Cf. O.N. *knackr*, a saddle.

KNAD [nad·], *pret.* and *part. past*, *obsols.* kneaded.—PULVERBATCH. 'This bread's *knad* too stiff, it'll be as 'ard as a cobbler's w'et-stwun afore the wik's out.' Cf. **Kned.**

KNAGGY [nag·i'], *adj.* cross; ill-tempered. Com. 'I should think the owd fellow's pŭt 'is clogs on the wrang fit this mornin'—'e's as *knaggy* as 'e knows 'ow to be.'

Dan. *knag*, a knot. Cf. **Nag** (1).

KNAP [nap·], (1) *sb.* a low hill; a mound.—PULVERBATCH. There is a little round hill at Castle Pulverbatch called the *knap;* it is one of two mounds which appear to have been thrown up and entrenched; the other—lower than the *knap*, and square in form—is called the 'Castle Ring.' They are contiguous, and surmount a natural steep.

'1543. 5 March. Agnes, daughter of John Chistoke departed, somtyme deacon or Clerk of this Churche, who departed of the pestilens the first day of September in the er of our Lord God MDxxxij, who was a full honest server of the Churche and taught scolers playne song & prick song full well, so that the Churche was well served in his tyme; buryed he was in the churche yard on the *knapp* uppon the right hand as ye entre into the Porche, abowte vij cloth yards frō the porch whose sowle God Almighty take to m̄cy. Amen.'—*Register of Sir Thomas Boteler*, Vicar of Much Wenlock.

Knap is applied to a hill-top in the following:—'And both these riuers running in one, carying a swift streame, doe make the *knappe* of the said hill very strong of situation to lodge a campe vpon.'—NORTH'S *Plutarch*, *Sylla*, p. 507, in *Bible Word-Book*, p. 285.

Cf. *Nab* Scar = *Knap* Scar (opposite Grasmere).

Ash gives '*Knap*, a little hill rising on all sides.'

'W. *cnap*, a knob, hill.'—STRAT.

(2) *sb.* a slight blow.—BISHOP'S CASTLE; CLUN. ''E gid 'im a *knap* o' the yad ŏŏth a stick.'

Jamieson has this word in the same sense. Tusser employs it as a verb: '*Knap* boy on the thums.'

Du. *knappen*, to crack. See **Knoup.**

KNAP-KNEED, *adj.* knock-kneed.—PULVERBATCH. 'I've 'eard as "a friend in need is a friend indeed," so one met say as poor owd Ben's a friend *in-kneed*, or whad they callen *knap-kneed*.'

KNATTER [nat·ur'], *v. n.* to find fault incessantly about trifles.—PULVERBATCH. 'I wish yo' ŏŏdna *knatter* all the wilde about nuthin', the poor wench dunna know whad to do to be right—'er's farly cowed down.'

KNATTERED, *part. adj.* peevish; irritable.—NEWPORT; WEM.

KNEADING-MIT, *sb.* a four-sided wooden vessel used for kneading purposes: it is longer than broad, and narrower at the bottom than the top, and is furnished at each end with a close-fitting handle by which to carry it.—SHREWSBURY; PULVERBATCH.. Qy. com. Sometimes it is called by one or other of the older terms, *kneading-trow*, or *kneading-turnel*. See below.

KNEADING-TROW [tr'oa·], *sb.*, *obsols.* a thing similar in shape to the *kneading-mit* above, but much bigger, in fact, it is a rude piece of furniture, standing on four legs, having a (detached) flat lid which fits closely on to it, so that when covered it serves as a table, and is about the height of one.—SHREWSBURY; PULVERBATCH.

An Inventory dated at Aston Botterell, about 1758, comprises '1 *Neading Troafe.*'

> 'Anon go get us fast into this in
> A *kneding trough* or elles a kemelyn,
> For eche of us; but loke that they ben large,
> In which we mowen swimme as in a barge.'
>
> CHAUCER, *C. T.*, l. 3548.

See **Gh** (2) (4) in **Grammar Outlines** (*consonants*).

KNEADING-TURNEL, *sb.*, *obsols.* same as **Kneading-trow**, above.—NEWPORT; WEM; ELLESMERE. Cf. **Turnel.**

KNED, same as **Knad**, q. v.—WORTHEN. A.S. *cnedan*, to knead; p.p. *cneden.*

KNIT [nit·], (1) *v. n.* to unite, as of a broken bone.—SHREWSBURY; PULVERBATCH; NEWPORT. 'Tum Jones is gweïn to the 'Firmary ŏŏth 'is arm; it wuz badly set, an' it's *knit* crukit; they sen as it'll 'ăve to be broke agen, to be pŭt straïght.'

'The verb to *knit* is used by old writers in the sense of to unite. Thus in Sloane MS. 3548, f. 99, *b.* is given an extraordinary nostrum "for to knyt synous þat are brokyne. Take greyte wormes þat are called angeltwycthys, and lat hem dry in þe sunne, and þen beyte hem to powder, and strew þat powder in þe wounde, and yt shall knytte to-geder. *Probatum est sepissime.*"'—WAY, in *Prompt. Parv.*, p. 279.

A.S. *cnyttan*, to tie; to make a knot. See below.

(2) *v. a.* to join, or close, firmly together.—PULVERBATCH. 'W'en a mon *knits* his lips athatn, it shewns the temper's none o' the best.'

'*Knyttynge*, or ioynynge, or rabetynge to-gedyr of ij bordys, or oþer lyke. *Gumfus.*'—*Prompt. Parv.*

(3) *v. n.* to set, or form, for fruit, as blossoms do.—PULVERBATCH; NEWPORT. 'I think theer'll be a good 'it o' apples this time—they seemen to be *knit* like traces o' īnions.'

> 'It is better to *knit* than blossom.'
>
> RAY'S *Proverbs*, p. 127.

'*Knyttynge* to-gedyr, *Nodacio, connodacio, connexus.*'—*Prompt. Parv.*

'*Nōdo*, to knit or tie knots, to button.'—*Dict. Etym. Lat.*

(4) *v. n.* to cluster, or hang, together, as bees do in swarming.—PULVERBATCH; NEWPORT. 'I never like to see the bees *knit* on the ground—it's a sure sign of a berrin.'

Compare *Judges* xx. 11: 'They were all *knit* together as one man.'

KNIVES AND FORKS, *sb. Lycopodium clavatum*, common Club-moss.—CLUN, *Hopton Castle.* Cf. **Lamb's-tails.**

KNOBBLE [nob·l], *v. a.* to hammer; to knock, but not forcibly.—PULVERBATCH. 'My Gran'mother's *knobbled* me many a time ŏŏth the wil-pin [wheel-pin] w'en I hanna carded the rolls well,' said Hannah Bevan [1879].

KNOCKING ABOUT, *phr.* a common every-day expression, which takes in a wide range of meaning—a number of people moving about, going hither and thither, are said to be '*knocking about;*' things incapable of motion are '*knocking about* the place;' current rumours, &c., are equally '*knocking about;*' as, for example, when an old ballad-tune was sought to be recovered, an inquiry about it was met by the assurance that 'it was *knockin' about* the country, an' somebody wuz safe to get it.'

KNOGS. See **Nogs.**

KNOPPLE [nop·l], (1) *v. n.* to rule; to be the head over.—PULVERBATCH. ''E shanna *knopple* o'er me.' Cf. A.S. *cnaepp*, top, in STRAT.

(2) *sb.* a small lump.—WORTHEN. 'Cut me a tidy piece o' bread an' a nice *knopple* o' cheese.'

'O.Du. *knoppe* (*nodus, bulla, gemma*), knop, button, bud.'—STRAT.

KNOT. See **Posy-knot.**

KNOUP [nou·p], *v. a.* to toll the church-bell.—CLEE HILLS. ''E's on'y *knouped* the bell seven times, so 'e'll on'y be 'ere seven year.' This observation bore reference to a current belief that when—according to the rites of induction—a clergyman tolls the bell on being put into possession of his church, the number of years he will hold the living are fore-*told* by the same number of strokes on the bell. *Knoup* is evidently a corrupted form of M.E. *knap*, to strike, used in the sense of to *toll* in the following:—

'*M. Mery*. . . . farewell Roger olde knaue,
Good night Roger olde knaue, knaue *knap*.
Pray for the late maister Roister Doisters soule,
And come forth parish Clarke, let the passing bell toll.
Pray for your mayster sirs, and for hym ring a peale.'
Roister Doister, Act. iij. Sc. iij. p. 46.

Cf. **Knap** (2).

KNOW TO, *phr.* to know the whereabouts of a thing—a more definite expression than *know of*, which is understood to mean rather the knowledge that a certain thing is somewhere, than that it is in any particular spot. Com. 'Dost 'ee *know to* the brummock, Dick?' 'Aye, I sid the wench 'ăve it jest now—cuttin' sticks fur the oven.'

KNURL [nur'l·], (1) *sb.* a knot in timber.—PULVERBATCH; WEM. 'Tak' it a bit lower, yo' canna saw through that *knurl*, it's "as 'ard as brazil."'

'*Nodus*, a knot, a *knurl*. . .'—*Dict. Etym. Lat.*

Sw. *knorla*, to twist.

(2) *sb.* a short, stiff, thick-set person.—ATCHAM; PULVERBATCH; WEM. 'Whad a stumpy *knurl* Dick keeps!—'e dunna grow a bit.' ''E may well be a *knurl*, 'is nasty owd Faither's punned 'im into the yerth aumust.' Chaucer has '*knarre*' in the same sense:—

'The MELLERE was a stout carl for the nones,
Ful big he was of braun, and eek of boones;
. . . .
He was schort schuldred, brood, a thikke *knarre*.'
The Prologue, l. 549, ed. Morris.

R

'In Homer's craft Jock Milton thrives;
Eschylus' pen Will Shakespeare drives;
Wee Pope, the *knurlin*, 'till him rives
Horatian fame;
In thy sweet sang, Barbauld, survives
Even Sappho's flame.'
ROBERT BURNS, *Poems*, p. 114, l. 15.

KNURLED, *adj.* stunted; dwarfed.—PULVERBATCH. 'The cabbitch dunna come on kindly, they bin all knotted an' *knurled*—theer's no growth in 'em.'

KOLING [koa·lin], *sb.* a rough-tasting apple, like the crab, found in cider-orchards.—LUDLOW.

KYERLOCK. See **Kerlock.**

KYOUP. See **Keoup.**

KYOUSE. See **Keouse.**

KYOUT. See **Keout.**

KYPE. See **Kipe.**

KYVE. See **Kive.**

LACE, *v. a.* to beat; to thrash.—PULVERBATCH; CRAVEN ARMS. Qy. com. 'If that lad wuz mine I'd *lace* 'im as lung as I could stand o'er 'im.'

Pegge gives '*Lace*, to thresh a person. "I *laced* his jacket for him." North.' Cf. **Leather.**

LADE-GAUN, same as **Gaun** (2), q. v.—NEWPORT. See *Ladyn̄*, with Way's note, in *Prompt. Parv.*, p. 283.

'A.S. *hladan;* O.H.Germ. (*h*)*ladan;* O.Icel. *hlaða*, to lade [= to load].'—STRAT.

LADIES AND GENTLEMEN, *sb.* the flower-spikes of *Arum maculatum.*—SHREWSBURY. Cf. **Devil's Men and Women.** See **Cows and Cauves.**

LADIES'-PURSES, *sb. pl.* the flowers of the *Calceolaria.* Qy. com.

LAD-LICKED, *part. adj.* beaten, vanquished by a youth.—PULVERBATCH. 'So some o' the owd warriors [village pugilists] got beaten, I 'ear.' 'Aye, the owd uns bin 'ard-fisted, but the young uns bin nimble, yo' sin, an' so owd Jim got *lad-licked.*' See **Lick** (1).

LAD'S-LOVE, *sb. Artemisia abrotanum*, Southern-wood.—PULVERBATCH. Qy. com. Cf. **Old-Man.**

LADY-COW, *sb. Coccinella septem punctata*, the Lady-bird. —SHREWSBURY; WEM. Qy. com.

'*Lady-cow, lady-cow*, fly thy way home,
Thy house is on fire, thy children all gone,
All but one that ligs under a stone,
Fly thee home, *lady-cow*, ere it be gone.'
J. O. HALLIWELL'S *Nursery Rhymes of England*, DXXXIII.

Mr. Halliwell says the foregoing stanza 'is of very considerable antiquity, and is common in Yorkshire.'

Mr. Wedgwood remarks that 'the comparison of a beetle to a cow seems strange, but in other cases the names of certain animals are given to insects of different kinds,' and he instances the large black beetle—'The Devil's Coach-horse' [q. v. *ante*], called in O.N. *Jötun-oxi*, the Giant's ox. He says, 'The name *Lady-bird*—rapidly supplanting that of *Lady-Cow*—was probably given to the pretty little beetle which bears it as being more appropriate to a flying creature;' but adds that '*bird* here may be a corruption of *bode*, or *bud*, a name given to insects of different kinds—*sharn-bode*, dung-beetle, *wool-bode*, hairy caterpillar.' He gives as his authority for this, 'E. Adams on names of insects in Philolog. Trans.'

See **God-A'mighty's Lady-Cow.**

LADY-GLOVE, *sb. Digitalis purpúrea*, purple Foxglove.—ELLESMERE. One of the French names for the *Digitalis* is '*gants de notre Dame.*' See **Lady's-fingers,** below.

LADY-GRASS, *sb. Dactylis elegantissima*, variegated Cocksfoot-grass; the striped 'riband-grass' of the garden. Qy. com. Cf. **Lady's-ribands.**

LADY'S-FINGERS, *sb.* same as **Lady-glove.**—CLUN. So likewise in French it is '*doigts de la Vierge.*'

LADY-SMOCK, *Cardamine pratensis*, common Bitter-cress. Com.

'When daisies pied and violets blue
And *lady-smocks* all silver white
And cuckoo-buds of yellow hue
Do paint the meadows with delight.'
Love's Labour Lost, V. ii. (*the Song*).

'This plant (*Cardamine*) is called in English Cuckowe-flower, at the Namptwich in Cheshire, where I had my beginning, *Ladie Smocks*, which hath giuen me cause to Christen it after my Countrey fashion.'—GERARDE'S *Herball*, Bk. II. p. 261.

'Looking down the Meadows, [I] could see here a Boy gathering Lillies and *Lady-smocks*, and there a Girle cropping Culverkeys and Cowslips all to make Garlands suitable to this pleasant Month of May.'—*The Compleat Angler*, ch. xi. p. 214, ed. 1653.

'*Ladies Smock*, an Herb, otherwise called *Cuckoo Flower.*'—BAILEY, ed. 1727.

LADY'S-RIBANDS, same as **Lady-grass,** q. v.—PULVERBATCH. Cf. **Love's-laces.**

LADY-WITH-THE-TEN-FLOUNCES, the Goldfinch. — CLUN. Children's term. Cf. **Sheriff's-Man.** See **Jack-Nicol.**

LAG [lag·], *v. n.* to fall behind; to come slowly on; to retard. Com. 'Now then, come alung; 'ou yo' done *lag* behind.'

'Then farre behind they come I troe, that strive to run before,
We must goe *lagging* on, as legges and limmes were lame.'
CHURCHYARD'S *Poems*, p. 68, l. 27.

The slow movements of geese coming up from pasture are accelerated by the call '*lag, lag, lag.*' See **Call-words.**

'W. *llag*, loose; slack; sluggish. Gael. *lag*, feeble; faint,' in WEDG. See **Lag-last**, below.

LAG-END, (1) *sb.* the heaviest portion, either of work or of weight.—PULVERBATCH. 'Yo' al'ays gin me the *lag-end* o' the sack.'

(2) the remainder; the latter end.—PULVERBATCH. 'Poor oud fellow! it's very 'ard to know want at the *lag-end* on 'is days.'

> '*Wor.* . . I could be well content
> To entertain the *lag-end* of my life
> With quiet hours. . . . .'
>
> 1 *K. Henry IV.*, V. i. 24.

LAGGENS, *sb. pl.*, *obsols.* refuse pieces and strips of wood, used to 'line out'—*i. e.* make level—a roof, under the tiles.—BRIDGNORTH.

LAGGERMENTS, *sb. pl.*, *obsols.* fragments; odds and ends of pieces left from work.—PULVERBATCH. 'Pick up yore *laggerments*, they bin all o'er the 'ouse.' Cf. **Libbets.**

LAG-LAST, *sb.* a loiterer. Com. 'Now then, shift yore fit; I warrant yo' bin al'ays *lag-last*.' Compare *K. Richard III.*, II. i. 90.

LAMBS'-TAILS, *sb.* same as **Knives and Forks**, q. v.—CLUN, *Hopton Castle.*

LAMB-TAILS, *sb.* the catkins of *Corylus Avellana*—Hazel and Filbert trees.—SHREWSBURY; PULVERBATCH.

LAMMAS-PLUM, *sb.* a dark, purple plum, which has its 'due season' for becoming ripe at Lammas-tide—the first week in August. —PULVERBATCH; WEM. 'Whad bin yo' ātin', Jack?' 'On'y a bit o' glue off the *Lammas-plum* tree.' See **Glue.**

LAMMEL [lam·il], *v. a.* to beat—a school-boy's term.—WELLINGTON. Qy. com.

Bailey—ed. 1782—gives 'To *Lamm*, to baste one's Shoulders, to drub one.'

'O.N. *lemja*, to give a sound drubbing; N. *læmja*, to beat,' in WEDG.

LANDRAKE [lan·dr'aik], *sb.*, *var. pr.* the Landrail.—CLUN; BRIDGNORTH. See **Corncrake.**

LANGET [lang·it], (1) *sb.* the iron socket into which the 'tree' of a spade fits.—PULVERBATCH; BISHOP'S CASTLE; CLUN.

(2) *sb.* a somewhat long and narrow iron stay, such as is used in securing a 'hurter' to the axle-tree of a tumbrel.—PULVERBATCH.

'*Langate* or *Languet* (from the Fr. *langue*, a tongue), a long and narrow piece of land or other thing.'—BLOUNT'S *Glossographia*, p. 363.

Grose has '*Langot* (of the shoe), the strap of the shoe. N.'

LANTUN [lan·tun], *sb.*, *var. pr.* a lantern. Qy. com. Cf. **Lantun.**

LANTUN-PUFF, same as **Lontun-puff**, q. v.—WEM.

LAP [lap·], *v. a.* to fold; to wrap; to envelop. Com. (1) ''Ere, *lap* that 'ankercher up afore yo' pütten it away.' (2) 'Fatch my ŏŏllen shawl to *lap* round the child—it'll be starved gweïn o'er the 'ill, fur it's a mighty cowd night.'

'þan wist william wel · bi þe bestes wille,
þat he þe hert & þe hinde · hade þere slayne,
him & his loueliche lemman · to *lappe* in þe skinnes.'
William of Palerne, l. 2576.

The Wicliffite version—ed. A.D. 1388—has, 'And whanne the bodi was takun, Joseph *lappide* it in a clene sendel.'—*Matt.* xxvii. 29.

'*Lappyn̄*', or whappyn̄' yn cloþys (happyn to-gedyr, S. wrap togeder in clothes, P.). *Involvo.* "*Plica*, to folde, or lappe. *Volvo*, to turne, or lappe."—MED. Palsgrave gives the following phrases: "Lappe this chylde well, for the weather is colde, *enuelopez* bien, &c. Lappe this hoode aboute your head, *affubley vous de ce chaperon.*" '—*Prompt. Parv. and Notes.*

See **Lapt**, below.

LAPE [lai·p], *v. a.* to lap with the tongue, as dogs, &c.—WHITCHURCH; ELLESMERE.

'And if hym lyst for to *lape* · þe lawe of kynde wolde
That he dronke at eche diche · ar he for thurste deyde.'
Piers Pl., Text B., pass. xx. l. 18.

O.Du. *lapen*, *Idem.*

LAPESING [lai·pu'sin], *part. pres.* dabbling, as in water or 'slop' of any kind.—ELLESMERE. 'Them childern bin al'ays *lapesin'* i' the waiter; I never seed the like on 'em.'

LAPPED O'ER TONGUE, *phr.*, *sl.*? tasted; drunk.—ATCHAM; ELLESMERE. Qy. com. 'It's as good drink as iver wus *lapped o'er tongue.*'

LAPT, *part. adj.* folded; inwrapped; enclosed; enveloped. Com. (1) 'Han'ee *lapt* them tuthree things in a good strung paper as ŏŏnna be likely to-bost?' (2) 'The poor child's scauded 'er fŭt despertly.' 'Wha'n'ee pŭt to it?' 'Well, we'n *lapt* it round ŏŏth traicle an' flour, it's the best remeddy theer is fur fatchin' the fire out.'

'The towne is built, as in a pit it were,
By water side, all *lapt* about with hill.'
CHURCHYARD's *Poems*, p. 70, l. 2. (Towne of Breakenoke.)

'Here doth two Corpse lie sleeping here,
The Husband & the Wife most dear,
Lapt up in Clay they must remain
Till Christ doth call them out again.'
Epitaph in Clungunford Churchyard.

'"*Obvolvo*, to lappe about. *Involutus*, *i. circumdatus*, lapped or wrapped. *Involutio*, a lappynge in."—ORTUS. "To lappe, *volvere*, *convolvere*. To lapp in, *intricare*, *involvere*," &c.—CATH. ANG. This verb is used most commonly in the sense of wrapping as a garment.' —WAY, in *Prompt. Parv.*

See **Lap**, above.

LARK-HEELED, *adj.* having a long projecting heel.—PULVERBATCH. Qy. com. 'Bin yo' sure yo'n got the instep o' that stockin' wide enough?—'cause Charlie's rather *lark-'eel'd*, yo' knowen.'

LARN. See **Learn**.

LARRANCE [laar'·uns], *sb.*, *var. pr.* the 'Genius' of idle people.

They are said to have *Larrance* on their back. Com. 'That chap's got *Larrance on 'is back*, 'e dunna do 'afe a nour's work in a day.'

LARRUM [laar'·um], *sb.*, *var. pr.* the alarum of a clock. Qy. com. 'Dick, yo' mind an' get up w'en yo' 'ear the *larrum*.' 'Iss, Missis'—but Dick muttered to himself—'I get too much *larrum* [scolding], so be'appen I shanna 'ear it!'

LARRUP [laar'·up], *v. a.* to beat.—OSWESTRY.

'Du. *larp*, a lash; *larpen*, to thresh in a peculiar manner, bringing all the flails to the ground at once.—Bomhoff,' in WEDG.

LARRY [laar'·i'], *sb.* a confused noise, as of a number of people all talking together.—PULVERBATCH. 'I 'eärd a fine *larry* las' night—folks gweïn down the Moat lane.'

LAT [lat·], (1) *sb.* a lath. Com. Usually heard in the plural form—'one o' them *lats*.'

'*Latas*,' explained by Mr. Wright as '*laths*,' occurs in *The Dictionarius of John de Garlande*, first half xiii. cent., in Wr. vocabs., vol. i. p. 137.

'A.S. *latta*; O.Du. *latte*; O.H.Germ. *latta*, lat (lath), *asser*,' in STRAT.

(2) *adj.* slow; tedious. Com. 'Yo'n find it a *lat* job to shift all them 'urdles by yoreself.'

> 'þenne com þe kyng Eualac · and fullouht askes;
> In þe nome of þe fader · Ioseph him folwede,
> Called him Mordreyns · "a *lat* mon" in trouþe.'
>
> *Joseph of Arimathie*, l. 695.

Mr. Skeat gives the following Glossarial Note, p. 65:—'Mordreyns is explained to mean "tardieus en creanche," slow of belief. A *lat mon* = a slow or sluggish man; lit. a *late* man.'

'A.S. *læt*; O.Sax. *lat*; O.Icel. *latr*; Goth. *lats*, lat; *tardus*,' in STRAT.

(3) *adj.* backward; late.—SHREWSBURY; PULVERBATCH. Qy. com. 'Mr. Clarke's ŏŏäts bin *lat*, but they wunna sowed tell after May-Daȳ, an' the Mŏät-'all groun' 's never very yarly—an' as the owd sayin' is—"*lat* sowin' mak's *lat* mowin'."' See **Lat-time**.

LATCH, *v. a.* to survey the underground workings of a mine. Qy. com.—M. T. Called *dialling* in Derbyshire.

LATHER [laadh·ur'], (1) *sb.*, *var. pr.* a ladder. Com.

'*The Carte howse*, two tumbrels with bare wheeles, fowre *lathers*, twelve Gutter powles for the Water Course.'—*Inventory* . . . Owlbury Manor-House, Bishop's Castle, 1625. A.S. *lædder*, *Idem*.

(2) [laa·dhur'], *adv.*, *obsols.* rather.—PULVERBATCH. Cf. **Lother**.

LATHY [lath·i'], (1) *adj.* thin; spare of frame.—PULVERBATCH. 'I think o' pŭttin' Jim to a trade, 'e's a poor *lathy* lad—nod fit fur 'ard work.'

'*Lethy* or weyke, Flexibilis.'—*Prompt. Parv.*

(2) *adj.* light and poor in the ear: said of grain.—*Ibid.* 'It'll be a poor ild this time, the ears bin despert *lathy* an' green.' Cf. **Fliggy** (3).

LATITAT [lat·i'tat], *sb., obsols.* senseless talk.—PULVERBATCH. 'None o' yore *latitat;* yo' bin about as wise as a suckin' gully.'

LATNESS, same as **Lattance**, below.—ELLESMERE.

LATTANCE, *sb.* an impediment in the speech.—PULVERBATCH; WEM. 'It's a sad denial to the poor lad 'ăvin' sich a *lattance* in 'is speech.' 'Ah! 'e can swar fast enough.' *Lat*, with a kindred meaning of hindrance, occurs in the following:—

> '"And as that I am feithful knycht and trew,
> At nycht to yow I enter ſhall againe,
> But if that deth or other *lat* certañ,
> Throw wich I [may] have ſuch Impediment,
> That I be hold, magre myne entent."'
>
> *Lancelot of the Laik*, l. 958.

A.S. *lǽtan*, to hinder.

LATTENING [lat·nin], *part. adj.* retarding.—PULVERBATCH; WEM. 'This cowd weather's mighty *latt'nin'* to the tillin'.'
A.S. *lǽtan*. See **Lattin'**, below.

LATTERMATH [lat·ur'muth], *sb.* same as **Aftermath**, q. v.—LUDLOW. 'Whad sort'n a *lattermuth* han yo'?'
'Lateward hay, *latermath*.'—*Hollyband's Dictionarie*, 1593, in HAL.
A.S. *lator*, later; and A.S. base, *mað*.

LAT-TIME, *sb.* a backward season.—SHREWSBURY; PULVERBATCH. Qy. com. 'It's a many 'ears sence we 'ad'n sich a *lat-time* as this [1879]—I remember one 'ear w'en the damsons wun as green as grass at Churton Wakes [1st Sunday after Sep. 27th], but that mus' be forty 'ear ago, or close upon it' [1839?]. Cf. **Lat** (3).

LATTIN', *part. adj.* hindering—'the rain is very *lattin'*.'—CLEE HILLS. Cf. **Lattening**.

LAUGHING-BIRD, *sb.* the Green Woodpecker.—WEM. See **Ecall**.

LAWN [lau·n], *sb., obsols.* a term still employed by some of the older gentry to designate the park-like area which is adjacent to their houses, and through which runs an approach, formerly called the 'coach-road'—now, the 'carriage-drive' (at Berwick this has an extent of half a mile or thereabout).—SHREWSBURY; NEWPORT; OSWESTRY. Qy. com. The *lawn* is distinguished from the park proper by having no deer in it; the home stock graze its pasture, but when its acreage is very extensive it is occasionally let as a 'ley'—as at Berwick. 'I canna tell who rents Berwick *lawn* sence Mr. Gough o' Gravel 'Ill 'eld it, but I sid a lot o' ship an' cattle i' the park as I went by, an mighty good sorted things they wun.'

> '"And þus I went wide-where · walkyng myne one,
> By a wilde wildernesse · and bi a wode-syde.
> Blisse of þo briddes · [abyde me made,]
> And vnder a lynde vppon a *launde* · lened I a stounde,
> To lythe þe layes · þo louely foules made."'
>
> *Piers Pl.*, Text B., pass. viii. l. 65.

'. . . . . . clothed al in greene,
On honting be thay riden ryally.
And to the grove, that stood ful faste by,
In which ther was an hert as men him tolde,
Duk Theseus the streyte wey hath holde.
And to the *launde* he rydeth him ful righte,
For thider was the hert wont have his flighte.'
CHAUCER, *The Knightes Tale*, l. 833, ed. Morris.

'*First Keeper*. Under this thick-grown brake we'll shroud ourselves;
For through this *laund* anon the deer will come;
And in this covert will we make our stand,
Culling the principal of all the deer.'—3 *K. Henry VI.*, III. i. 2.

'then went they downe into the *Lawnde*
these Noblemen all 3
eche of them slew a hart of greece
they best that they cold see.'
Adam Bell, Clime of the Cloughe, and William of Cloudeslee, l. 419. *Percy Folio MS.*, vol. iii. p. 92, ed. Hales and Furnivall.

Mr. Furnivall gives a footnote:—'*Lawnde*, a clear space in a forest.' A Glossarial Note—p. 558—by Mr. Viles, says—'"*Lawne*, a plain, untilled ground."—*Bullokar's Dict.*, 1656,' and adds, [other] 'old dictionaries define *laund*, "a piece of ground that never was tilled,"' and instances 'Oaken *Lawn*,' a rugged common bordering Salop on the Staffordshire side.

Granted the foregoing, it seems probable that a farm called the *Lawn*, situated midway between Castle Pulverbatch and Habberley (Salop), has retained the appellation it bore when yet 'untilled ground.' A rabbit-warren which skirts it on one side is known as the '*Lawn* Hill.'

Ash gives '*Lawn*, an open space between woods.'

Bailey—ed. 1782—has '*Lawn*, a great Plain in a Park, or between two Woods.'

'*Lawnde* of a wode. *Saltus*. Camden, in his Remains, explains *laund* as signifying a plain among trees. Thus in the account of the hunting expedition, Ipomydon, 383, the Queen's pavilion was pitched at a "laund on hight," whence she might command a view of all the game of the forest. . . . . . "*Indago*, a parke, a huntyng place, or a lawnde."—ORTUS. "A lawnde, *saltus*."—CATH. ANG. "Launde a playne, *launde*."—PALSG. "*Lande*, a land or launde, a wild untilled shrubbie or bushy plaine."—COTG.' *Prompt. Parv. and Notes.*

W. *llan*, a clear space.

LAWTER [lau·tur'], *sb.* the complement of eggs for a 'sitting' laid by the mother-bird before she broods: a term of the poultry-yard.—SHREWSBURY; PULVERBATCH; WORTHEN; WELLINGTON; WEM. ''Er's a capital goose, 'er brought twelve gullies the first hetch, an' 'er's laid seven eggs o' the secont *lawter*.'

Grose gives 'Laster, or *Lawter*, thirteen eggs to set a hen. N.'

LAY, *v. a.* This term, when applied to a thorn-hedge, means, to renew it by cutting it down on both sides, hewing out the old wood and stumps, leaving—or placing—standards at given distances, and then—

having first carefully split them lengthwise—*laying* down the young shoots, intertwining them basket-fashion between the uprights.—NEWPORT; ELLESMERE. Cf. **Pleach.**

LAYERS, *sb. pl.* the quick-thorn shoots which are laid down to form the hedge.—*Ibid.*

'Pl. D. *lage*, a row of things laid in order . . . *afleger*, a layer or offset of a plant laid in the ground to strike root.'—WEDG.

Cf. **Pleachers.**

LAYLOC [lai·luk], (1) *sb.*, *var. pr. Syringa vulgaris*, common Lilac. Qy. com.

'Then all comes crowdin' in; afore you think
The oak-buds mist the side-hill woods with pink,
The cat-bird in the *laylock* bush is loud,
The orchards turn to heaps o' rosy cloud.'

J. R. LOWELL.

(2) *adj.* the colour 'lilac.' Qy. com.

Layloc for *lilac* was the pronunciation of fashionable, 'high life' folk in the days of George IV. See *Philology of the English Tongue*, p. 149.

LAY ME IN, *phr.* cost me. Com. 'That melch cow *lay me in* £20, but 'er's a rar' good un.'

LAY-O'ERS-FOR-MEDDLERS, *sb.* an undefinable term, used to ward off a child's troublesome inquisitiveness.—SHREWSBURY; PULVERBATCH. 'Whad'n'ee got i' the basket, Mother?' '*Lay-o'ers-fur-meddlers*, an' yo' sha'n be sarved first.' Perhaps the idea of a switch, to *lay over* the shoulders, is meant to be conveyed in this figure of speech.

LAZE, LAZING. See **Lease, Leasing.**

LAZY-BACK, *sb.*, *obsols.* the frame for holding the bakestone over the fire.—BRIDGNORTH. Cf. **Maid** (3).

LEAF, (1) *sb.* a layer of fat spreading over certain portions of the interior carcase, as of pigs and poultry; the *leaf* of a pig is melted down for lard—the *leaf* of a goose for goose-oil—the *leaf* of a fowl for chicken-oil, and so on. Com. The sense of *leaf* here given is in unison with Mr. Wedgwood's assertion that 'the radical meaning [of *leaf*] seems something flat.' Gr. λεπας (lep-as), a scale.

(2) See **Lef.**

LEARN [laa·r'n *and* lur'n·], *v. a.* to teach. Com. 'I should like to *larn* the bwoy my own trade, but 'is Mother's tŏŏk a fancy to mak' 'im a counter-skipper.'

'But woldest þou for godes loue · *lerne* me my Crede.'

P. Pl. Cr., l. 402.

'And, modyr, I pray yow thys byll may recomend me to my sustyrs bothe, and to . . . . . Syr John Stylle, and to pray hym to be good mastyr to lytyll Jak, and to *lerne* hym well.'—*Paston Letters*, A.D. 1467, vol. ii. p. 319.

'*Cal.* You taught me language; and my profit on't
Is, I know how to curse. The red plague rid you
For *learning* me your language!'—*Tempest*, I. ii. 364.

See *Pss.* xxv. 4—8; cxix. 66.

A.S. *lǽran;* Germ. *lehren,* to teach. Du. *leeren* has the twofold meaning of to teach and to learn, just as Prov. E. *learn* has.

LEASE [lai·z], SHREWSBURY; PULVERBATCH; WORTHEN; ELLESMERE. Qy. com. [lee·z], NEWPORT; WHITCHURCH; OSWESTRY, *v. a.* and *v. n.* to pick up and gather together the scattered ears of corn in a harvest-field; to glean. 'It wunna use't to be so i' the poor owd Maister's time, he al'ays loost the neighbours in among the mows, to *laise* afore the mob comen—but now yo' mun stop till every shof's out, an' the ell-rake dragged o'er till theer inna-d-a ear lef'.'

'"Ac who so helpeth me to crie · or sowen here ar I wende,
Shal haue leue, bi owre lorde · to *lese* here in heruest,
And make hem mery þere-mydde · maugre whoso bigruccheth it."'
Piers Pl., Text B., pass. vi. l. 68.

'Gleaning or *Leesing* or Songoing, is gathering of the loose **Ears** of Corn, after Binding and Loading.'—*Academy of Armory,* **Bk. III.** ch. iii. p. 73.

'Goth. *lisan,* to lease, gather, collect; Matt. vi. 26; vii. 16. Germ. and Du. *lesen;*' E. *lease,* to glean.'—SKEAT'S *Mœso-Gothic Dictionary.*

LEASING [lai·zin *or* lee·zin], according to localities above, *sb.* the corn that has been *leased,* whether tied up in bundles or—in the case of short ears—collected in the 'ear-bag' [q. v.] of the gleaner. 'Weer's yore Faither workin' to-day, Tum?' ''E inna workin' no-weer—'e's throshin' the *laisin'* i' Kite's barn [Cothercot].'

'As the waggoner of Mr. Menlove, of Wackley, near Ellesmere, was walking backwards and whipping one of the horses in the harvest-field, a few days since, his feet got entangled in some *leasing* which threw him down, and the wheels passing over him, he was killed on the spot.'—*Salopian Journal,* Sept. 19th, 1804, in *Byegones,* July 23rd, 1879.

LEASOW [lez·u'], *sb.* a pasture-field. Com. The term is also applied to a corn-field, but this is a degenerate use of it: the old folk in Corve Dale at this date [1874] reprove the younger ones for employing the word '*corn-leasow.*' 'I' the lane w'en a ought to be i' the *leasow*' is proverbially said of one who is not in the right place at the right time.

'*Pascua,* læswe,' occurs in an *Anglo-Saxon Vocabulary,* xi. cent., in Wr. vocabs., vol. i. p. 80.

Mr. Wright gives the following note:—'This is the modern *leasow*—a word still in use, in some parts of England, in the significa-tion of a pasture-field.' In John x. 9, where the A. V. has 'pasture,' the Wicliffite version—ed. A.D. 1388—has 'lesewis:'—'And he schal go ynne, and schal go out, and he schal fynde *lesewis.*'

A.S. *lœsu,* a pasture; common. Cf. **Lezzer.**

LEASTWAYS, *adv.* at least. Com. 'I 'ope Jack'll gŏŏ ŏŏth 'is Faither to work soon—*leastways,* the Maister promised me 'e'd tak' 'im.'

Leastways is a corruption of *least-wise,* a form which Mr. Pegge notes as being a substitution, by the 'Natives of LONDON,' for 'at least.' He vindicates the word from vulgarity by quoting its literary use,—'"At least-wise."—*Life of Lord Herbert of Cherbury,* p. 9,'—and says, '*Weise* is a German word, signifying *manner;* and will as fairly combine with *least* as with those words which are its usual associates, viz., *like*-wise, *other*-wise, &c.'—*Anecdotes of the English Language*, p. 56, ed. 1814.

LEATHER [ledh·ur'], *v. a.* to beat; to thrash. Com. 'Yo' tell 'im, if 'e dunna let yo' alone comin' throm school, yore Faither 'll *leather* 'im athin a ninch on 'is life.'

Grose has '*Leather*, to beat. N.' **Der.** 'leathering.'

LEATHER-BAT, *sb.* Long-eared Bat.—BRIDGNORTH. See **Billy-bat,** also **Flitter-mouse.** Cf. **Leathering-bat,** below.

LEATHERING, *sb.* a beating; a sound drubbing. Com. 'I gid 'im sich a *leatherin'* as 'e never wuz maister on afore.'

LEATHERING-BAT, same as **Leather-bat,** above.—CLUN.

LEAVE [leev·], *v. a.* to let; to allow; to permit.—SHREWSBURY; ELLESMERE. A term chiefly used in asking for a favour to be granted. (1) 'Missis 'as sen' to know if yo'll *leave* 'er 'ăve a can o' waiter out o' the pump, an' 'er'll thank yo' kindly.' (2) 'Mary, axe yore Mother if 'er'll *leave* yo' gŏŏ alung ŏŏth me to the Club.'

'"Now god *leue* neure," quod repentance · "but þow repent þe rather,
þe grace on þis grounde · þi good wel to bisette,
Ne þine ysue after þe ·" . . . .'

Piers Pl., Text B., pass. v. l. 263.

'And *leue* sho mo him y-se
Heye hangen on galwe tre,
þat hire haued in sorwe brouth.'

Havelok the Dane, l. 334.

See Mr. Skeat's 'Glossarial Note' on *leue*, in *Havelok*, p. 131.
A.S. *lýfan;* Germ. *er lauben*, to allow; permit.

LEDGEN [lej·h'n, *sometimes* lej·h'nd], *v. a.* to close the seams of wooden vessels which have opened, either from having been left too long dry, or in consequence of the 'grouping' being broken; in the former case simple immersion in water will *ledgen* the tub or pail, in the latter it is cooper's work.—WEM; ELLESMERE.

Compare '*Legge*, ouer twarte byndynge (ouer wart, S. ledge, P.). *Ligatorium*,' in *Prompt. Parv.*

LEECH. See **Beăst-leech.**

'*Leche*, mann or woman. *Medicus, medica.* "A leche, *aliptes, empiricus, medicus, cirurgicus.*"—CATH. ANG. "Leche, a surgion, *servrgion.*"—PALSG. The appellation was used to denote those who professed any branch of the healing art, as well as the ladies, who frequently supplied the place of the regular practitioners.'—*Prompt. Parv. and Notes.*

A.S. *lǽce;* Dan. *læge*, a physician; surgeon.

LEF, (1) *sb., var. pr.* a leaf.—SHREWSBURY; PULVERBATCH. Qy. com. 'I dunna know exac'ly whad time it wuz w'en the Squire come 'ere, I know the trees wun i' the *lef*—but they al'ays gwun to Lunnon the best part o' the 'ear.'

'"Ac þow art like a lady · þat redde a lessoun ones,
Was, *omnia probate* · and þat plesed here herte,
For þat lyne was no lenger · atte leues ende.
Had [she] loked þat other half · and þe *lef* torned,
[She] shulde haue founden fele wordis." . . .'

Piers Pl., Text B., pass. iii. l. 337.

'A.S. *leáf;* O.Du. *loof;* O.Fris. *lâf;* O.Icel. *lauf;* O.H.Germ. *laub;* Goth. *laubs*, leaf.'—STRAT.

(2) *sb.* a large leaf—usually a cabbage leaf—upon which raspberries are disposed, as upon a platter, and so carried to market, and sold. —*Ibid.* 'They wun sellin' razb'ries at 4d. a *lef* i' Sosebry o' Saturday; they binna tied to mizzer by the *lef*, but they bin genarlly about a pint, an' I should think these one nigh a quart.'

LENNOW. See **Linnow.**

LENT-CORN, *sb.*, *obsols.* spring wheat.—NEWPORT. A.S. *lencten*, the spring. See below.

LENT-GRAIN, *sb.* barley, oats, and pease (but not wheat)—which are sown in the early spring-tide—are included in this term.—SHREWSBURY; PULVERBATCH. Qy. com.

'As lynne-seed & lik-seed · & *lente-seedes* alle;
Aren nouht so worþhi as whete · . . . .'

Piers Pl., Text C., pass. xiii. l. 190.

See **Lent-tilling.**

LENTH [len·th], *sb.* length. Com. A form of frequent occurrence in the early writers.

'& þus of *lenþe* & of large · þat lome þou make;
Þre hundred of cupydeȝ · þou holde to þe *lenþe*,
Of fyfty fayre ouer-þwert · forme þe brede.'

Alliterative Poems, The Deluge (A.D. 1360, *circa*).
Specim. Early Eng., xiii. ll. 314, 315.

'Item, j. pece of fyne lynen clothe, yerd brode, of lvj. yerdys of *lenthe*.'—*Inventory*. . . . A.D. 1459, in *Paston Letters*, vol. i. p. 480.

'A.S., O.Icel. *lengð*; O.Du. *lengde*, length.'—STRAT.

LENT-SIDNESS, *sb.* the spring seed-time.—SHREWSBURY; PULVERBATCH. Qy. com. A.S. *leuctentid*, the spring-time.

LENT-TILLIN', *sb.* the crops of *Lent-grain*. See above.—*Ibid.*

LEP, (1) *v. a.* and *v. n.* to leap.—SHREWSBURY; PULVERBATCH. 'That mar' 's a right good un to *lep;* 'er took the quick-'edge into the Broad-meadow, an' *lep* it like a buck.'

'þanne *lep* he vp liȝteli · & loked al a-boute.'

William of Palerne, l. 702.

'He was so wimble and so wight,
From bough to bough he *lepped* light.'

SPENSER, *The Shepheards Calender*, March, l. 453.

(2) *sb.* a leap.—MUCH WENLOCK.

(3) *v. n.* to boil soft and tender: said of pease.—CLEE HILLS. 'Them pase *leppen* well.' See below.

LEPPERS, *sb. pl.* grey pease that soften well in boiling.—PULVERBATCH. 'I can get a couple o' shillin' a bag more fur them pase—they bin sich good *leppers*.'

LEPPIN'-PASE, same as above.—CHURCH STRETTON.

LESTIAL. See **Restial.**

LEWN [lou·n], *sb., obsols.* a church-rate.—SHREWSBURY; PULVERBATCH; WORTHEN; CLUN; WELLINGTON; WEM; ELLESMERE. 'It inna lung sence the *lewn*-getherer wuz 'ere, an' theer's another *lewn* cast las' vestry-meetin'.'

'November, 1582, a cessemente or *lewne*,' was laid upon the parishioners for repairs. — *Churchwardens' Accounts*, St. Mary's, Shrewsbury.

'1690. Hugh Greenly being poore his *leaune* not paid, 00 - 00 - 08.' —*Churchwardens' Accounts*, Clun.

'1776. Collected by *Lewn*, 5 - 12 - 3.'—*Churchwardens' Accounts*, Hopton Castle.

'October 15th, 1840. At a vestry meeting held in the Parish Church . . . . for the purpose of granting a *lewn* for the use of the Church,' &c.—*Churchwardens' Accounts*, Ellesmere.

A.S. *læ̂n*, a loan.

LEWN-PAPER, *sb., obsols.* a rate-paper.—*Ibid.*

LEW-WARM [loo·], *adj.* tepid; lukewarm. Qy. com. 'Sally, fill the three quart can o' waiter fur naidin' [kneading], nod more than *lew-warm*—the weather's 'ot enough to pŭt it out o' the pump.' *Lew-warm* is a redundant form. O.E. *lew* means warm, as shown in the following citations:—

> 'Hwan þe deuel he[r]de that,
> Sum-del bigan him forto rewe;
> With-drow þe knif, þat was *lewe*
> Of þe seli children blod.'
>
> *Havelok the Dane*, l. 498.

'Y wolde that thou were could, ethir hoot; but for thou art *lew*, and nether cold, nether hoot, Y schal bigynne to caste thee out of my mouth.'—*Apocalypse*, iii. 16. Wicliffite Version, ed. A.D. 1388.

Jamieson gives '*Lew*, *Lew-warm*, tepid.' Cf. **Glue-warm.**

LEZZER [lez·ur'], same as **Leasow,** q. v.—NEWPORT.

'*Hæc pascua pascuæ est locus herbosus pascendis animalibus aptus*, Anglice a lesur.'—*MS. Bibl. Reg.* 12 B. i. f. 13, in HAL.

LIABLE, *adj., pec.* eligible.—NEWPORT. An Edgmond woman asked if she were *liable* to a blanket from the Provident Society.

LIBBETS [lib·its], *sb. pl.* rags in strips.—PULVERBATCH. 'Pike up yore *libbets* an' laggerments, an' nod 'ăve 'em all o'er the 'ouse-flur a-this a-way.' Compare '*lippe*,' which has the sense of a slip, a shred, in the following:—

> 'And sith þat þis sarasenes · scribes, & Iuwes
> Han a *lippe* of owre byleue · . . . . .'
>
> *Piers Pl.*, Text B., pass. xv. l. 493.

Cf. **Laggerments.**

LICH-FOWL [lei·ch foul], *sb.* the European Goat-sucker.—WEM, *Hopton.*

'*Lich-fowle,* the reputed unlucky Night-Raven, so called from the Saxon *Lic* or *Lich,* i. e. a dead corps; Country people by corruption call these *Scritch-Owles,* or *Lich-Owles.*'—BLOUNT'S *Glossographia,* p. 374.

See *Lich-owl,* in NARES. Cf. **Night-hawk,** also **Churn-owl.**

LICK, (1) *v. a.* to beat; to thrash. Com.

> 'But, Davie, lad, I'm red ye're glaikit;
> I'm tauld the Muse ye hae negleckit;
> An' gif it's sae, ye sud be *licket*
> Until ye fyke;
> Sic hauns as you sud ne'er be faikit,
> Be hain't wha like.'
>
> ROBERT BURNS, *Poems,* p. 103, l. 27.

See **Lad-licked.**

(2) *v. a.* to surpass; to excel—'that *licks* all as ever I sid.' Com.

LICKING, *sb.* a beating. Com.

LICKLE [lik·l], *adj., var. pr.* little. Qy. com. See **Tl** in **Grammar Outlines** (*consonants*).

LICK THE CRAME-MUNDLE, *phr.* a figure of speech borrowed from the dairy—and applied to the dairy-maid—to express 'lives well.'—PULVERBATCH. For example see **Cullow.** Cf. **Mundle** (1).

LIDS, *sb. pl.* pieces of wood from twelve to eighteen inches in length, laid horizontally on the props that support the roof of a mine, for the purpose of giving them additional firmness. Com.—M. T. Pieces of wood of like kind are called *caps* in Derbyshire.

LIE, *v. n., pec.* to sleep—'the child *lies* with its mother'—'*lies* by itself.' Com.

'Wherfor I have purveyd that ye shall have the same drawte chamer that ye had befor ther, as ye shall *ly* to your self.'—*Paston Letters,* A.D. 1453, vol. i. p. 251.

LIEF [lif·], *adv.* soon; readily; willingly.—SHREWSBURY; PULVERBATCH. Qy. com. 'I'd as *lif* sit i' Powtherbitch stocks fur a nour, as I'd gŏŏ to Church i' that fine bonnit to be starred at.'

'And as for your tenants of Drayton, as I canne understond by hem, they be ryght gode and trew hertyd to you to ther powers, and full fayn wold that ye had it a yen in peasse, for they had as *leffe* al most be tenants to the Devell as to the Duke.'—*Paston Letters,* A.D. 1465, vol. ii. p. 194.

'*Jaques.* I thank you for your company; but, good faith, I had as *lief* have been myself alone.'—*As You Like It,* III. ii. 269.

Mr. Oliphant remarks with reference to Caxton's *Renard the Fox,* A.D. 1481, that 'it contains many old Teutonic words, now obsolete, which we could ill afford to lose:' he enumerates some of these, and amongst them is '*lief.*'—*Sources of Standard English,* p. 286.

See **Lieve,** below.

LIE I' THE LUNG FITHERS, *phr.* to sleep in the straw in a barn or out-house. Qy. com. 'Yo' bin up yarly this mornin', Jack; but I 'spect yo' *lied i' the lung fithers* las' night.' See **Lie.**

LIE UP, *v. n.* to be housed at night: said of horses, cattle, &c.—NEWPORT.

LIEVE [lee·v], *adv.* same as **Lief,** above. ''E'd as *lieve* goo as not.' —NEWPORT.

'I once saw it laid down in an old-fashioned book of good manners,' says Mr. Oliphant, 'that it was vulgar to say, "I would as *lieve* do it." For all that, let each of our English writers who has a well-grounded hope that he will be read a hundred years hence, set himself heart and soul to revive at least one long-neglected English word.'—*Sources of Standard English*, p. 318.

LIEVER, *adv., cmp.* sooner; rather; more willingly. ''E'd *liever* goo till stop.'—*Ibid.*

'So gret liking & loue i haue · þat lud to bi-hold,
þat i haue *leuer* þat loue · þan lac al my harmes.'
William of Palerne, l. 453.

'Barow swor to me be his trowth that he had *lever* than xls., and xl. that his lord had not comawndyd hym to com to Gressam.'—*Paston Letters*, A.D. 1450, vol. i. p. 111.

'For *lever* had I die then see his deadly face.'
SPENSER, *F. Q.*, Bk. I. c. ix. st. xxxii.

LIFTER, *sb.* a smart blow—'jest gie 'im a good *lifter.*'—SHREWSBURY; WEM. Cf. **Rifter.**

LIFT-OF-BEEF, *sb.* the upper part of a leg of beef cut lengthwise. —CLUN; CLEE HILLS. Cf. **Slench.**

LIFT-OF-PORK, *sb.* the 'fore-quarter' of a porkling pig, *i. e.* the 'hand,' 'breast,' and 'belly-piece.'—SHREWSBURY.

LIG, *sb.* a lie. Qy. com.

LIGGER, *sb.* a liar.—*Ibid.* 'If Jack toud yo' that, it's a *lig*, an' 'e's a *ligger*—yo' can tell 'im as I say so.'

'Folk whilk I ne knewe serued to me;
In hering of ere me boghed to he,
Outen sones to me *lighed* þai.'
Metrical English Psalter, xvii. (A.D. 1300, *ante*), [*Ps.* xviii. 45]. *Specim. Early Eng.*, II. l. 113.

'A.S. *leógan;* Du. and Germ. *leugen;* O.E. *lig*, to tell lies.'

LIGHT, (1) *v. n.* to dismount; to alight. Com. 'Maister, the Squire called this mornin', but 'e ŏŏdna *light* as yo' wunna-d-in,—'e took a glass o' ale at the 'orse-block, an' said 'e should want the grey-'un o' Monday.'

'Þar þai þam thoght to rest and slepe;
Þar did þai Mari for to *light*,
Bot son þai sagh an vgli sight.
. . . .
Quan Iesus sagh þam glopnid be,
He *lighted* of his moder kne.'
Cursor Mundi (A.D. 1320, *circa*).
Specim. Early Eng., vii. ll. 231—238.

'I woulde haue *lyghted* from my horsse, and taken my swerde by the poynt, and yelded it into hys graces handes.'—LATIMER, *Sermons*, iiii. p. 119.

'"but *light* now downe, my lady gay,
light downe & hold my horsse,
whilest I & your father & your brether
doe play vs at this crosse."'
The Child of Ell, ll. 33, 34. *Percy Folio MS.*, vol. i. p. 134, ed. Hales and Furnivall.

See *Genesis* xxiv. 64. A.S. *lihtan*, to alight from a horse.

(2) *v. n.* to descend and settle, as a bird after flight. Com. 'Is a gweïn to *light*?' 'W'y, 'er 'as *lit*—canna yo' see?'

'whon god sende an Angel · in-to Galile,
. . . .
to A Maiden ful meke · þat Marie was hoten,
And seide, "Blessed beo þou flour · feirest of alle!
þe holigost with-Inne þe · schal lenden and *lihte*."'
Joseph of Arimathie, l. 81.

See *Matt.* iii. 16. Compare 'Let thy mercy *lighten* upon us,' in the *Te Deum Laudamus* (Prayer-Book version). A.S. *lihtan*, to descend.

(3) *v. n.* to fall in with by chance; to come upon unexpectedly. Com. 'Very often w'en yo' bin lookin' fur one thing yo' *light* on another—I wuz brevetin' fur the nail-passer, an' *lit* on Freddy's silver pencil as wuz gid up fur lost.'

'And in such sort that his offering might be acceptable to Iupiter, and pleasant to his citizens to behold: did cut downe a goodly straight growen young oke, which he *lighted* on by good fortune.'—NORTH'S *Plutarch*, 'Romulus,' p. 30, in *Bible Word-Book*.

(4) *adj.* thin; poor: said of crops. Com. 'Them crops looken despert *light*.' A.S. *leóht*, light (of weight). Cf. **Shire**.

LIGHT-BOWT, *sb.* a thunder-bolt.—PULVERBATCH; NEWPORT. Qy. com. 'Theer's bin a power o' damage done by the storm las' Monday, no less than three *light-bowts* fell, an' a mar' an' cowt wun killed at 'Abberley—I sid one gweïn ziggle-zaggle down the sky, an' ööndered w'eer it ööd fall.' Compare 'levin [= lightning] bolt' in the following:—

'The morning dawned full darkly,
The rain came flashing down,
And the jagged streak of the *levin-bolt*
Lit up the gloomy town:
The thunder crashed across the heaven,
. . . .'
AYTOUN, *The Execution of Montrose*.

Spenser has '*levin-brond*' for thunder-bolt. See *F. Q.*, Bk. VII. c. vi. st. xxx.

LIGHT-CAKE, *sb.* same as **Flap**, q. v.—CHURCH STRETTON; CLUN. Cf. **Pikelet**.

LIGHTED, *part. past*, *obs.* confined; delivered of a child.—PULVERBATCH; MUCH WENLOCK. 'Gran, Mammy's sen' me to tell yo' as we'n got another babby—'er wuz *lighted* afore Dad come wham las' night.' 'Ah, well-a-day wratch! theer wuz anow on yo' afore, 'er nee'na a sen' yo' throu' the snow to tell me that.'

'1802. March 5. a poor Straing woman *Lighted* on the road. 0 - 2 - 6.'—*Parish Accounts*, Much Wenlock.

'And miracles of mydwyves · & maken wymmen to wenen,
þat þe lace of oure ladie smok · *liȝteþ* hem of children.'
P. Pl. Cr., l. 79.

'And I shalle say thou was *lyght*
Of a knave-childe this nyght.'
Towneley Mysteries, p. 107, in HAL.

'*Lighted*, a woman when brought to bed is said to be *lighted*, i. e. lightened. North,' in PEGGE.

A.S. *gelihtan*, lighten (make lighter).

LIGHTSOME, (1) *adj.* cheerful; gay.—PULVERBATCH. ''Er wuz a good-tempered, *lightsome* girld, but 'er soon droupt off.'

'& a *lightsome* bugle then heard he blow
ouer the bents soe broune.'
Sir Cawline, l. 80. *Percy Folio MS.*, vol. iii. p. 7, ed. Hales and Furnivall.

(2) *adj.* brisk: said of beer.—*Ibid.* 'It wunna strung, but nice *lightsome* drink.'

LIGHT-TIMBERED, *adj.* light of bone: said of horses chiefly. Com.

LIKE. See **Grammar Outlines** (*adverbs*), p. lxxxi.

LIKELY, *adj.*, *pec.* hopeful; promising.—PULVERBATCH. Qy. com. 'Them bin *likely* avens fur makin' two good pigs, John.' 'Aye, the 'og's a good strung pig, but the gawt's a piddlin' āter,—minces an' mommocks the mate about—I'm afeard 'er ŏŏnna mak' much.'

LIMBER [lim·bur'], (1) *adj.* lithe; supple; pliant. Qy. com. 'W'y, John, yo' getten younger instid o' owder—yo' gwun alung as *limber* an' as lissom as a lad o' nineteen.' 'Aye, I could daince the Sailor's-'ornpipe yit, ŏŏth a pretty good fiddler.'

'*Her.* Verily!
You put me off with *limber* vows.'
Winter's Tale, I. ii. 47.

'"*Mol*, soft, supple, tender, lithe, *limber*."—COTGR.,' in WAY.

Cf. **Lissom.**

(2) *v. a.* to soften; to supple.—WEM. ''E *limbered* 'is jīnts wuth iles.'

LIME-ASH, *sb.*, *obsols.*? a compost of sifted ashes and mortar beaten together; a rough kind of flooring for kitchens or out-houses is made of it.—PULVERBATCH.

LIMER [lei·mur'], *sb.* to 'come *limer*' over a person is to take an unfair advantage of him, thus:—'Three lime-burners gŏŏ to a public fur some yale, two young uns an' a owd un; the owd un tak's car' to sit i' the middle, so as the jug passes backerts an' forrats—'e gets as much agen drink as the young uns.' Hence the saying—''E's a-comin' *limer* o'er him.'—CLEE HILLS, *Cleobury Mortimer.*

LIMMOCKS, *sb. pl.* rags; bits.—ATCHAM; WEM. ''Er's tard 'er pinner all to *limmocks*.'

LING, *sb. Erica Tetralix*, Cross-leaved Heath. Qy. com. Dan. *lyng*, heath. Cf. **Grig** (2).

LINK, *v. a.* to fasten the doors.—BISHOP'S CASTLE, *Lydbury North*. Cf. **Make** (1).

LINKERING, *part. adj.* lingering; loitering; 'loafing about'—generally used with a reduplicated form—'lonkering.'—PULVERBATCH; WEM. 'Jack, yo' lock that 'tato-'ouse, an' look roun' the buildin' to-night, theer's a lot o' tramps *linkerin'* an' *lonkerin'* about the lanes—I'll shift 'em if a bin theer to-morrow.'

LINK-MOSS, same as **Jealousy**, q. v.—PULVERBATCH.

LINNOW, LENNOW [lin·u'], Qy. com. [len·u'], WORTHEN; CLEE HILLS; LUDLOW; ELLESMERE, (1) *adj.* limp; flexible; pliant. 'These starched things bin as *linnow* as the dish-clout, the Maister 'll never pŭt 'is collars on like this.' 'As *linnow* as a glove' is a current proverbial saying.

Pegge has '*Lennock*, slender, pliable. Lanc.' Cf. Germ. *linde*, soft.

(2) *v. a.* to make pliant—but the term is not very often used in this way.—*Ibid.*

LIN-PIN, *sb.* the iron pin which goes through the axle of a wheel; a linch-pin.—PULVERBATCH. Qy. com.

Amongst the several parts of a wheel enumerated under the head of '*Nomina pertinencia ad Carectarium*,' in an *English Vocabulary*, xv. cent., in Wr. vocabs., vol. i. p. 202, are, '*Hic axis, A' axyl-tre*,' and next in order, '*Hoc humullum, A'* lyn-pyne.'

'*Lin-pin*, Lint-pin, *s.* The linch-pin.'—JAMIESON.

LINT, *sb.*, *pec.* the flocculent dust which collects in rooms, more especially in bed-rooms.—NEWPORT. Cf. **Dowl** (2).

LINTY, *adj.* idle; lazy.—PULVERBATCH; WORTHEN; WELLINGTON; NEWPORT. Qy. com. 'Yo' bin as *linty* as yo' knowen 'ow to be, but I'll brush yore jacket fur yo' direc'ly, if yo' dunna stir a bit faster.'

'"*Lentus*, slowe and febulle, or lethy, moyste."—MED. MS. CANT. "*Lentesco*, to waxe slowe or lethy, *i. tardum esse*."—ORTUS,' in WAY. *Prompt. Parv.*, p. 302.

LIP, *sb.* the turned-up bit on the toe of a horse's shoe, which keeps the animal's hoof from pressing forward when travelling.—PULVERBATCH. Qy. com. Cf. **Corking.**

LISSOM [lis·um], (1) *adj.* agile; supple; lithe; free of movement in every joint and limb. Com. 'The owd school-maister gets o'er the stiles as *lissom* as a lad.' 'Aye, aye, 'e hanna stŏŏd in as many wet diches as I han, or 'e ŏŏdna be so limber.'

Pegge gives '*Lissom*, limber, relaxed. North.'

A.S. *lið*; N. *lide*, to bend the limbs, whence lithe, lithesome, and Prov. E. *lissom*. Cf. **Limber** (1).

(2) *sb.* a layer; a stratum.—CORVE DALE; CLEE HILLS. 'Yo'

sin, Sir, in burnin' lime we pŭtten first a *lissom* o' coal, an' then a *lissom* o' lime-stwun.' Cf. **List**, below.

(3) [liz·um], same as **List**, below.—PULVERBATCH.

LIST, *sb.* the close, dense streak sometimes seen in a loaf which has not risen properly.—PULVERBATCH. 'I canna tell w'ether it's the faut o' the flour or the barm, but the bread hanna ruz well—jest look whad a *list* is all alung the bottom o' the loaf.'

'O.Fr. *liste*, bande . . . de l'ahal. *lista*, bande; allmod. *leiste*, bordure.'—BUR. Compare A.S. *list* (edge of cloth).

LITCH [lich·], (1) *sb.* a bunch of hay or grass.—CORVE DALE.

(2) *sb.* a lock of tangled, matted hair.—CLEE HILLS. 'Yore yar's all i' *litches*, I conna get the cōom through it.'

LITHERMON'S-LOÄD [lidh·ur' munz], *sb.*, *obsols.*? a greater load than can well be carried at one time, but is nevertheless undertaken to save the trouble of another journey — a 'lazy-man's-load.'—PULVERBATCH. 'Now, yo' bin al'ays fur carryin' *lithermon's-loäd*—the one 'afe's tumblin' off, an' yo'n a to fatch it, an' that's 'ow lazy folks al'ays han the most trouble.' O.E. *lither*, bad, wicked, has a secondary meaning of 'lazy' in some of the early writers.

'& thou lett them of their leake · with thy *lidder* turnes!'
Death and Life, l. 249. *Percy Folio MS.*, vol. iii. p. 67, ed. Hales and Furnivall.

'Some *litherly* lubber more eateth than twoo,
yet leaueth vndone that another will doo.'
TUSSER, *Fiue Hundred Pointes of Good Husbandrie*, ed. E. D. S., p. 174.

Ray [1691] gives '*Lither*, idle, lazy, slothful' in 'North Country Words,' also in 'South.'

Jamieson has '*Lidder*, sluggish,' and '*Lythyrnes*, sloth.'

A.S. *lyðer*, bad.

LOACH, *v. a.* (1) to drink greedily.—PULVERBATCH. 'I 'ate to see Colliers come i' the fild, they bin good fur nuthin' but *loach* the bottle,' *i. e.* to drink out of the 'bottle.'

Compare 'To *lurch*, devour, or eate greadily, *ingurgito*,' in BARET'S *Alvearie*, A.D. 1580. Low Latin *lurcare*, to swallow food greedily. Cf. **Gulch**.

(2) *v. n.* to suck hard.—*Ibid.* 'The babby seems strung, 'e *loaches* away at 'is titty.'

LOAF-O'-BREAD, *sb.*, *pec.* a loaf. Com. '"Them as gwun a borrowin' gwun a-sorrowin'"—but I shall be 'bliged to borrow a *loaf-o'-bread*, fur the milner never brought the batch till after dinner, an' I canna bar ōnder's bakin'.'

'*Hic panis*, *A*ͤ lof of bred,' occurs in an *English Vocabulary*, xv. cent., in Wr. vocabs., vol. i. p. 198.

LOBBER-TE-LOY, same as **Hobbety-hoy**, q. v.—WORTHEN.

Cf. 'Du. *loboor*, a raw, silly youth,' in WEDG.

LOCKERS, *sb. pl.* pieces of wood or iron placed within the circumference of the wheel of a waggon, or 'skip,' to 'scotch' it when going down an incline. Com.—M. T.

'O.N. *lok*, anything that serves for a fastening,' in WEDG.

LODGED, *part. adj.* laid flat, as by rain or wind: said of grain or grass. Qy. com. 'That corn ŏŏl be despert bad to cut—it inna-d-on'y *lodged*, but tathered.'

'We'll make foul weather with despised tears;
Our sighs and they shall *lodge* the summer corn,
And make a dearth in this revolting land.'
K. Richard II., III. iii. 162.

See **Tather** (2).

LOF, *v. n.* and *sb.* to laugh; a laugh.—COLLIERY; NEWPORT.

'. . . . . and falls into a cough;
And then the whole quire hold their hips and *loffe*.'
Midsummer Night's Dream, II. i. 55.

Mr. Halliwell says, *lof* 'occurs in Mother Hubbard, and is a genuine old form.' A.S. *hlihhan*, to laugh; pt. t. *ic hlóh*.

LOGGY [log·i'], *adj.*, *obsols.?* thick-set; weighty: said of animals.—PULVERBATCH; ELLESMERE; WEM. 'John's pig weighed more than 'e 'spected—it looked short, but it wuz *loggy*.' Cf. **Blocky**.

LOLLOCK [lol·uk], *v. n.* to lounge, or loll, or idle about.—ELLESMERE. Compare Icel. *lulla*, to loll about. See **Lollup**, below. Cf. **Lozzock**.

LOLLOCKIN'-CHEER, *sb.* an easy-chair; a lounging chair.—*Ibid.* Compare 'Du. *lollebancke*, a couch, lounging bench,' in WEDG.

LOLLUP, same as **Lollock**, above.—SHREWSBURY; PULVERBATCH. 'Yo'd'n better be i' the fallow, Tum, than *lolloppin'* about the foud.'

LOMB [lom·], *sb.* a lamb. Com. An old form.

'And as a *lomb* and ennosent,
To be lad to sacrefyce to fore present,
Of Ann and Kayface;
Of Pilate, Erod, and moné mo.'
JOHN AUDELAY'S *Poems*, p. 60.

'For as the *lomb* toward his deth is brought,
So stant this Innocent bifore the king.'
CHAUCER, B. 617 (Six-text ed.), Skeat.

'*Lombe*, yonge schepe. *Agnus*, *agnellus*.'—*Prompt. Parv.*

'A.S., O.Sax., O.Icel., Goth., O.H.Germ. *lamb*, lamb.'—STRAT.

LOMMOCK [lom·uk], *sb.* a big lump; a thick piece—'a *lommock* o' cheese.' Qy. com. Cf. **Lownder** (1).

LONDON-LACE, same as **Lady-grass**, q.v.—CLUN. Cf. **Love's-laces**.

LONE-GIRL, *sb.* a single, solitary woman, for whom there is no kinsman's shielding care. Com.

'. . . A hundred mark is a long one for a poor *lone woman* to bear: and I have borne, and borne, and borne, and have been fubbed off, and fubbed off, and fubbed off, from this day to that day, that it is a shame to be thought on.'—2 *K. Henry IV.*, II. i. 35.

See **Girl**.

LONG [lung·], *adj.*, *pec.* tall. Com. 'Jack says 'e canna bar this new Scotch bayly, 'e's as *lung* as a lather, an' as thin as a rail; 'e should like to mak' 'is coffin out on a spout, an' bury 'im in a suff!'

'"My name is *longe* Wille."'

Piers Pl., Text B., pass. xv. l. 148.

'Hw he was fayr, hw he was *long*,
Hw he was with, hw he was strong.'

Havelok the Dane, l. 1063.

'If he were as *long* as he is lither, he might thatch a house without a ladder. *Chesh.*'—RAY's *Proverbs*, p. 200.

LONGFUL, *adj.* excessively long, as applied to time.—PULVERBATCH. Qy. com. 'Yo'n bin a *lungful* wilde gweïn to the blacksmith's shop.' 'Theer wuz four 'orses to be shoe'd afore I could be sarved.'

LONG-KNEELING, *sb.*, *obsols.* the English Litany.—PULVERBATCH; WORTHEN; ELLESMERE. 'It wuz despert warm an' clos' i' church o' Sunday—theer wuz three wenten out poorly, afore the *lung-kneelin'*.'

LONGSOME, *adj.* long; tiresome; dreary.—PULVERBATCH; WEM. 'It's a despert *lungsome* rŏäd 'twix the Mŏät an' Steppiton, but I've gwun it many a dark night, an' never sid anythin' worse than myself.' 'Humph, yo' 'ad'n but one other to see!'

Prior uses the expression a '*longsome* plain.'

Mr. Earle says, 'This formative [some] is one that is in present activity. In Sir J. T. Coleridge's *Memoir of Keble*, p. 364, we find a new [?] adjective on this model, namely, *long-some*:—"It is thought to labour under the fault of being *long-some*." But perhaps we see here only an imitation of the German *langsam*.'—*Philology of the English Tongue*, p. 332.

LONK [long·k], *sb.* the groin. — PULVERBATCH; CRAVEN ARMS. 'Whad mak's Bob limp athatn?' ''E's gotten a bwile in 'is *lonk*, poor bwoy.' 'Whad's 'e pŭt to it?' 'Some cobbler's wax.' ''E'd better a some groun'sel pultis to it to-night.'

Lanke, glossed the hip-joint, occurs in Stratmann, 'and leiþ is (*his*) leg o *lonke*.'—Wr. *Pol. Songs*, 156. O.Du. *lanke*, O.H.Germ. *lancha*, lank.'

LONKERING. See **Linkering**.

LONTUN, *sb.*, *var. pr.* a lantern.—PULVERBATCH. 'Dick, ŏŏt 'ee len' me yore *lontun* to gŏŏ i' the tallit?—mine's got a 'ole in it.' Cf. **Lantun**.

LONTUN-PUFF, *sb.*, *obsols.* hurry; petulant haste.—PULVERBATCH. 'I gid 'er a bit o' my mind, an' 'er tŏŏk off in a perty *lontun-puff*.' Cf. **Lantun-puff**.

LOOED [loo·d], *part. adj.*, *obsols.* thwarted; 'check-mated.' — PULVERBATCH. 'I thought to a bought that cow, but 'fund I was *looed*—the Maister sen' 'er to the las' far.' From the game of *Loo* (of French origin).

LOOK, (1) *v. a.* and *v. n.* to seek; to search for. Qy. com. (1) 'Whad bin'ee brevitin' i' that box fur, Mary?' 'W'y, I'm *lookin'* my thimble—I canna think w'eer it's gwun.' (2) ''E says 'is brother's got a place fur 'im, an' that'll be a sight better than 'ăvin' one to *look*.'

(2) *v. n.* to expect. Qy. com. 'Now I've pŭt them cubberts an' drawers straight, I shall *look* fur 'em to be [or, *look* to find 'em] kep' so.'

'Certaine of my frendes came to me wyth teares in theyr eyes, and tolde me, they *loked* I should haue bene in the tower the same nyghte.'—LATIMER, *Sermon* iii., p. 83.

Cf. *Acts* xxviii. 6. Mr. Halliwell gives *look*, in the several foregoing senses, as 'North.'

LOOSE [loo·s], (1) *v. a.* to discharge, as of firearms, &c.—SHREWSBURY; PULVERBATCH. Qy. com. 'Look at the child!—'e's playin' ŏŏth the gun.' 'It ŏŏnna 'urt 'im, I al'ays *loose* it off afore I come in.'

'*Titus*. . . . You are a good archer, Marcus;
[*Gives the arrows.*]
. . . .
To it, boy! . . *loose* when I bid.'
Titus Andronicus, IV. iii. 58.

'I spyed hym behynde a tree redy to *lowse* at me with a crosbowe.'
—*Palsgrave*, in HAL.

(2) *v. a.* to let go; to set free. Qy. com. 'Bessy, remember to *loose* the goose off 'er nist soon i' the mornin', else 'er'll break all 'er eggs.'

'*Pol.* You know, sometimes he walks four hours together,
Here in the lobby.
Queen. So he does, indeed.
Pol. At such a time I'll *loose* my daughter to him:
Be you and I behind an arras then;
Mark the encounter: . . . . . .'—*Hamlet*, II. ii. 162.

Compare *Acts* xxvii. 40.

(3) *v. a.* to let out. Qy. com. 'Gŏŏ yo' forrat an' *loose* the cauves out o' the cauve-kit, an' I'll come after an' drip the cows.'

(4) *v. a.* to let in. Qy. com. 'Whad time wuz it w'en yo' *loosen* the cowman in las' night?' 'It wuz aumust mornin', but I toud 'im as I shouldna *loose* 'im in agen.'

LOP-LOLLARD, *sb.*, *obsols.* a lazy fellow.—PULVERBATCH. ''E's sich a o'er-grown *lop-lollard*, 'e's too lung or too lazy to oud 'imself uprit.' Compare Icel. *lullari*, a sluggard. See *Lollard* in WEDG.

LORRY, LURRY, *v. a.* to drag along with violence.—WHITCHURCH.

LOSELLING [loz·u'lin], *adj.* idling.—WHITCHURCH. A formative of O.E. *losel*, a worthless fellow. Cf.:—

'Somme leyde here legges aliri · as suche *loseles* conneth,
And made her mone to pieres · and preyde hym of grace:
"For we haue no lymes to laboure with · lorde, y-graced be ȝe!"'
Piers Pl., Text B., pass. vi. l. 124.

Compare also '*loselyche*' in pass. xii. l. 213, which appears in Wright's edition as '*losselly*,' with the gloss given to it,—'in a disgraceful, good-for-nothing manner.' Cf. **Lozzock**.

LOT, *v. a., var. pr.* to allot.—PULVERBATCH; WEM; ELLESMERE. 'Theer's to be a Vestry-meetin' o' Monday to *lot* the pews.' 'Be'appen they'n do the same as they did'n at our Church—*lot* 'em, an' then clap "Free" on 'em at-after.' A.S. *hleótan*, to appoint or ordain by lot.

LOTH [loth·], *adj., var. pr.* unwilling; loath.—PULVERBATCH. Qy. com. 'I wuz mighty *loth* to gŏŏ, but they o'er-persuaden me, an' I went.'

> 'eiþer þonked oþer · many þousand siþes,
> & lauȝt seþe here leue · þouȝh hem *loþ* were.'
> *William of Palerne*, l. 5201.

LOTHER [lodh·ur'], *adv., obsols.* rather. — WHITCHURCH. Cf. **Lather** (2).

LOUK [lou·k], *sb.* a severe blow; a hard hit. Qy. com. 'W'en I wuz choppin' sticks at the block, a piece bounded up an' gid me sich a *louk* i' the face—it met as well a blinded me.'

LOUSE'S-LATHER, *sb.* the ladder-like breach made in knitting by dropping a stitch.—PULVERBATCH. 'W'y, 'ere's a pretty *louse's-lather*—one, two, three, four—five bouts back, 'ow's that to be gotten up?'

LOUT [lou·t], *sb.* a clownish, under-bred fellow. Com. 'Nod all the fine clo'es i' Sosebry ŏŏl ever mak' a gentleman on 'im, 'e's sich a *lout*.'

> '*R. Royster*. Thou iuftleft nowe to nigh.
> *M. Mery*. Back al rude *loutes*.'
> *Roister Doister*, Act iij. Sc. iij. p. 48.

> 'And you will rather show our general *louts*
> How you can frown than spend a fawn upon 'em,
> For the inheritance of their loves and safeguard
> Of what that want might ruin.'—*Coriolanus*, III. ii. 66.

LOVE-CARRIAGE. See Bk. II., *Folklore*, &c., 'Customs.'

LOVE-CHILD, *sb.* an illegitimate child.—PULVERBATCH.
For some admirable remarks on the use of this term '*love-child*,' see ARCHBP. TRENCH'S *Study of Words*, pp. 49, 50.
Cf. **Base-child**. See **Chance-child**.

LOVE'S-LACES, *sb.* riband-grass.—PULVERBATCH.
'. . . vsually of our English women it is called *Lady laces* or painted Grass: in French *Aiguillettes d'Armes*.'—GERARDE'S *Herball*, Bk. I. p. 26.
Cf. **Lady's-ribands**.

LOVE-SPINNING, *sb., obs.* a spinning 'Bee.' — PULVERBATCH. 'Bin 'ee gweïn to Betty Mathus's *love-spinnin'*, Matty?' 'No, I've broke the barrel o' my wil.' 'Well, tak' yore lung-wil, they wanten as many 'ŏŏl spinners as thrid—it's men's linseys as a bin măkin'.'
Betty Mathews lived at the turnpike-gate house at Castle Pulverbatch, about the year 1800, where and when the *love-spinning* referred to above took place. See, further, Bk. II., *Folklore*, &c., 'Customs.'

LOW [lou·], *adj., obsols.* flavourless; insipid.—PULVERBATCH. 'Yo' bin mighty spar'in' o' yore saut i' this suppin'—it's despert *low*.'

LOWN [lou·n], (1) *sb.* a vertical course of straw in thatching.—CORVE DALE.

(2) *v. n.* to grow stout and comely in person: said of youths,—'that young fellow *lowns.*'—CLEE HILLS. Cf. **Barnish.**

LOWNDER, (1) *sb.* a thick slice.—PULVERBATCH. 'I gid the poor chap a good *lownder* o' bread an' cheese, an' a spot o' fresh drink, an' mighty glad 'e wuz on it.' Cf. **Lowner,** also **Lommock.**

(2) a blow.—*Ibid.* 'I gid 'im sich a *lownder* as 'e ŏŏnna furget soon.' Cf. **Belownder.**

LOWNER, same as **Lownder** (1), above.—WEM; ELLESMERE.

LOZZOCK [loz·uk], *v. n.* to lie down idly, instead of being at work. —WEM. ''E went an' *lozzocked* i' the 'ay i' the tallant instid o' awin' them turmits, as I toud 'im.' The participle *lozzockin'* has a wide meaning, and is often used as an intensitive to 'idle'—'a *lozzockin'* idle fellow.' Cf. **Lollock,** also **Loselling.**

LUCKY-BONE, *sb.* the coracoid bone of a fowl.—SHREWSBURY. Qy. com. This bone carried in purse or pocket is believed to bring money-fortune, whence the name—*lucky-bone.* See **Clip-me-tight.**

LUG, (1) *v. a.* to cart; to carry; to drag. Com. *Haul* is sometimes employed when speaking of carrying coal: about Newport they *carry* hay, and *draw* coal; but *lug* is the term of wide acceptance and general usage as glossed above; anything or everything that can be carried, is '*lugged,*'—from a baby to a waggon-load of corn. (1) 'They wun gwein to *lug* barley this mornin', but afore they could get the waggins out it begun to rain.' (2) 'That poor wench seems as if 'er could scace *lug* 'er legs after 'er, let alone *lug* the child—I doubt 'er inna lung fur this world.'

'1794, Feby 5—Getting on some lime rubbish on Long Meadow, the stuff from Tinsley's old house. *Luggd* the bricks from it to build a pit in garden.'—*Bailiff's Diary,* Aston, Oswestry. *Byegones,* 1877, p. 316.

'Make seruant at night *lug* in wood or a log,
let none come in emptie but slut and thy dog.'
TUSSER'S *Fiue Hundred Pointes of Good Husbandrie,* ed. E. D. S., p. 177.

(2) *v. a.* to pull, as of the ears. Qy. com. 'If 'e dunna mind, I'll *lug* 'is ears as lung as a donkey's.'

'Swed. *lugga,* to lug, pull.'—STRAT.

(3) *sb.* a rod used in roof-thatching.—ELLESMERE.

'Þu seist þat ich am manne loþ
And ever euch man is wiþ me wroþ
And me mid stone and *lugge* þreteþ
And me tobursteþ and tobeteþ.'
Owl and Nightingale, l. 1609.

See **Buckles.** Cf. **Springle** (2).

LUKE'S-TID, *sb.* St. Luke's Day—the time of the Festival of St. Luke.—CLEE HILLS.

LUKKA, *interj.* Look you! = See that! an expression evincing surprise at — or calling attention to — something being done.— COLLIERY.

LUMBER, *sb.* mischief; trouble. Com. 'That lad's al'ays i' some *lumber.*' 'Whad's 'e bin doin' now?' 'Breakin' windows—'is poor Mother's got two-an'-ninepence to pay, an' dunna know 'ow to get a bit o' bread fur the rest on 'em.'

LUMP, *sb.* a good-sized child.—WORTHEN, *Cherbury.* 'How big are your children?' 'Oh, they bin *lumps.*'

LUNGE [lunj·], (1) *v. a.* to use unfairly, as of eating food by stealth, &c.—PULVERBATCH. Qy. com. 'Ate as much mate as yo' wanten, but dunna *lunge* it.' Cf. **Munge** (1).

(2) *v. a.* to abuse; to ill-treat with violence.—WEM. ''E knocked 'im down and *lunged* 'im shameful.'

LUNGEOUS [lun·jus], *adj.* malicious; spiteful; cruel. Com. 'I ŏŏdna 'ăve that fellow among my cattle on no account, 'e's the most *lungeous* brute to poor dumb beäs as ever wuz about a place.'

LUNGFUL, LUNGSOME. See **Longful** and **Longsome**.

LURRY. See **Lorry**.

LUTE [loo·t], *sb.* a worthless person.—CLEE HILLS. 'Yo' binna thinkin' o' marryin' that mon, Sal—w'y 'e's a reg'lar *lute.*' Compare *luther* in the following:—

> 'I deme men þat don ille · and ȝit I do wel worse,
>
> . . . .
>
> Þus I liue loueles · lyk A *luþer* dogge,
> Þat al my breste Bolleþ · for bitter of my galle.'
>
> *Piers Pl.*, Text A., pass. v. l. 98.

A.S. *lyðer*, bad; wicked.

L-WOOD, *sb.* a plantation running in two lines, one down the slope of a hill, the other, meeting it at its base in such a way as to give the wood — when seen at some distance off — a likeness to the letter L; whence the name given to it.—WHITCHURCH.

MAESTUR [maes·tur'], *sb., var. pr.* same as **Maister**, q. v.— WELLINGTON; NEWPORT; WHITCHURCH; ELLESMERE.

MAG [mag], (1) *v. a.* to teaze incessantly.—LUDLOW. 'Canna yo' be queet, an' nod *mag* me so?'

(2) *sb.* a chatterer.—*Ibid.* The term is sometimes reduplicated, as, 'I never 'eärd sich a *mag-mag* as yo' in all my days.'

Pegge gives '*Magging*, prating, chattering. Chesh.'

MAGPY [mag·pi'], *sb., var. pr.* the Magpie.—SHREWSBURY; PULVERBATCH; CLUN. Qy. com.

> 'Devil, devil, I defy thee,
> *Magpy, magpy*, I go by thee.'

The form *Magpy* occurs in a list of bird-names given by Randle Holme, *Academy of Armory*, Bk. II. ch. xiii. p. 308.
Cf. **Chatter-pie**, and **Mag** (2), above.
See Bk. II., *Folklore*, &c., 'Superstitions concerning Birds and Eggs.'

MAID, (1) *sb.* a light portable frame used for hanging clothes upon; a clothes-horse. Com.
Called 'Tamsin [Thomasine] in Kent.'—PEGGE.
See **Maiden** (1), below.

(2) *sb., obs.* a round straw mat—having a bow-handle—used as a kind of breastplate to protect the person when lifting a large iron pot off the fire: the pot rested against it, and was carried by the 'ears' on each side.—BISHOP'S CASTLE; CLUN.

(3) *sb., obs.* same as **Lazy-back**, q. v.—BRIDGNORTH.

MAIDEN, (1) same as **Maid** (1), above. Com.

(2) same as **Dolly** (1), q. v.—BRIDGNORTH.

MAISE [mai·z], *sb.* stinking Chamomile.—WELLINGTON. See **Maythig**, also **Dog-daisy**.

MAISTER [mai·stur'], (1) *sb.* an employer.—SHREWSBURY; PULVERBATCH. Qy. com.

> 'þe segges were a-slepe þan · þat it schuld ȝeme,
> al but þe mest *maister* · to munge þe soþe.'
> *William of Palerne*, l. 2735.

(2) *sb.* a husband.—*Ibid.*

(3) *sb.* a title of address to a superior or elder.—*Ibid.* Cf. **Gaffer** (1).
'O.Fr. *maïstre*, qui, par suite du fréquent emploi, devint de bonne heure *maistre*, d'où les orthographes *meistre*, *mestre*, maître, . . . chef . . . . . du latin *magister*.'—BUR.
Cf. **Maester**.

MAISTERIN', (1) *adj.* imperious; authoritative; assuming the airs of a master; overbearing.—PULVERBATCH; WHITCHURCH; ELLESMERE. ''E seems a *maisterin'* sort o' mon, that.' 'Oh, aye! 'e can do the *maisterin'* part right well, but a bit o' 'ard work ŏŏd shoot 'im a sight better.' Spenser has this word in the sense of controlling:—

> '. . . with *maystring* discipline doth tame.'
> *F. Q.*, Bk. IV. c. ix. st. ii.

MAK [mak·], *v. a.* to make. Qy. com. 'Whad bin 'ee gweïn to *mak* o' that?—it inna-d-enough fur a gownd, is it?'

> 'Amang squilk was broght a writte,
> O Seth þe name was laid on it;
> O suilk a stern þe writt it spak,
> And of þir offerands to *mak*.'
> *Cursor Mundi* (A.D. 1320, *circa*).
> *Specim. Early Eng.*, vii. l. 28.

'An' whyles twalpennie worth o' nappy
Can *mak* the bodies unco happy.'
ROBERT BURNS, *Poems*, p. 3, l. 34.

A.S. *macian;* O.Fris. *makia*, to make.

MAKE [mai·k *and* mak·], (1) *v. a.* to bar; to bolt; to fasten, as of doors or shutters. Qy. com. 'Turn out these dogs an' cats, an' *make* the doors an' shutters, it's gettin' on fur bed-time.'

'. . . . . . she will well excuse
Why at this time the doors are *made* against you.'
Comedy of Errors, III. i. 93.

'*Rosalind*. . . . . *make* the doors upon a woman's wit, and it will out at the casement.'—*As You Like It*, IV. i. 162.

Pegge gives '*Make the door*, or *windows*, i. e. fasten them. North. Salop., Leic.'

Low Dutch, *mak to*, to shut, or fasten; '*mak to het door*,' shut the door. Cf. **Link**.

(2) *v. a.* to secure by shutting up, as of a dog, a stray animal, &c. Qy. com. 'Yo'd'n better *mak* that dog up i' one o' the bings, fur if yo' tie'n 'im up be'appen 'e'll hong 'imself afore mornin'.'

MAKE A MOCK, *phr.* to half do a thing—to do it neither wholly nor perfectly.—WEM. 'It's no use 'im *mäkin' a mock* on it, if 'e conna do it, 'e'd better let it alone, an' let somebody else try thar 'ond.' Cf. **Imitate**.

MAKE-SHIFT, *v. n.* to manage; to contrive; to do with or without a thing, as the case may be. Com. 'I'd sooner *mak'-shift* any how than be al'ays borrowin' like they bin.'

'Good husband and huswife, will sometime alone,
make shift with a morsell and picke of a bone.'
TUSSER, *Huswiferie*, ed. E. D. S., p. 175.

'Sad will I be, so bereft,
Nancy, Nancy!
Yet I'll try to *make a shift*,
My spouse, Nancy.'
ROBERT BURNS, *Poems*, p. 186, l. 15.

MALKIN [mau·kin], (1) *sb.* an oven-mop made of rags. Qy. com. 'Now then, wet the *maukin*, an' fatch the tin to püt the gledes in.'

'The *Maukin* is a foul and dirty Cloth hung at the end of a long Pole, which being wet, the Baker sweeps all the Ashes together therewith, which the Fire or Fuel, in the heating of the Oven, hath scattered all about within it.'—*Academy of Armory*, Bk. III. ch. vi. p. 293.

'*Hoc tersorium, An*ᵐ, a malkyn,' under the head of '*Pistor cum suis Instrumentis*,' occurs in a *Pictorial Vocabulary*, xv. cent., in Wr. vocabs., vol. i. p. 276.

'*Malkyne*, mappyl, or oven swepare. *Dossorium, tersorium.* "Malkyn for an ouyn, *frovgon*." — PALSG. Holliband renders "*Wavdrée*, the clout wherewith they clense or sweepe the ouen, called a maukin."'—*Prompt. Parv. and Notes*.

See *Malkin*, in WEDG. Cf. **Slut** (1).

(2) *sb.* a scarecrow, made up of old ragged garments into a rude representation of a human figure. Qy. com. 'The Bayly's pŭt sich a rar' good *maukin* i' the corn-leasow—anybody ŏŏd think it wuz a livin' mon.'

Nares gives '*Malkin*, a diminutive of Mary; of *mal* and *kin*. Used generally in contempt. Hence, as Hanmer says, a stuffed figure of rags was, and in some places still is, called a *malkin*.'

'Forby gives *maukin* as signifying either a dirty wench, or a scarecrow of shreds and patches.'—WAY.

See below. Cf. **Mommet** (1).

(3) *sb.* a slovenly, showily-dressed — would-be-fine-and-fashionable—girl or woman. Qy. com. 'Sally, if yo' gŏ'n to town i' that owd cloak an' them fithers an' flowers stuck i' yore 'at, yo'n a to carry the flag for the biggest *maukin* i' the far.'

'*Bru.* All tongues speak of him, ...
. . . .
. . . . the kitchen *malkin* pins
Her richest lockram 'bout her reechy neck,
Clambering the walls to eye him.'

Coriolanus, II. i. 224.

MALL [mau·l], same as **Beetle**, q. v.—WEM; OSWESTRY.

'. . . . . and with mighty *mall*
The monster mercilesse him made to fall.'

SPENSER, *F. Q.*, Bk. I. c. vii. st. 51.

'Malyet, betyl (*malle* or malyet, H. P.). *Malleolus*.'—*Prompt. Parv.*
O.Fr. *mail;* Lat. *malleus*, a hammer, mallet.

MALL-BEETLE, same as above.—CLUN; CLEE HILLS.

MAMMOCK, MOMMOCK [mam·uk *and* mom·uk]—both pronunciations obtain, but the latter is the more usual one—*v. a.* to cut into fragments; to mangle, break up, or crumble away, so as to cause waste: said of food. — SHREWSBURY; ATCHAM; PULVERBATCH; WORTHEN; WEM; WHITCHURCH; ELLESMERE. 'Dunna *mommock* that good mate, yo'n be glad o' worse than that some day.'

'. . . he did so set his teeth and tear it; O, I warrant, how he *mammocked* it.'—*Coriolanus*, I. iii. 71.

Bailey—ed. 1727—has '*To Mammock* [prob. of *Man*, Brit. little or small, and *Ock* a Diminutive], to break into Bits or Scraps.'

Ash gives '*Mammock*, to tear; to break into shapeless pieces.'

Cf. **Ort**, also **Mommock** (2).

MAMMOCKS, MOMMOCKS, *sb. pl.* fragments; viands 'mammocked,' or broken up into scraps. — *Ibid.* 'Look at all these *mommocks* throwed about — "wilful waste brings woful want," remember.'

'Where you were wonte to haue
cawdels for your hede,
Nowe must you mouche
Mammocks and lumps of bred.'

Magnyfycence, l. 2034, SKELTON'S *Works*, i. 291.

Minsheu—ed. 1617—has '*Mammockes*, peeces; Vi. fragments—peeces.'

Bailey—ed. 1782—gives '*Mammock* [probably of *Man*, C. Br. little, and *Ock*, Dim.] a Fragment, Piece, or Scrap.'
Ash has '*Mammock*, a shapeless piece.'

MANIKIN [man·i'kin], *sb.*, *obsols.* a masculine woman.—PULVERBATCH. 'It inna to be 'spected as poor Mary can top-an'-ta̅yle turmits like that great *mănikin* as lives nei̅ghbour to her—but 'er's a tidy little ŏŏman i' the 'ouse.' Compare Shakespeare's '*mankind*,' used in the similar sense of having a masculine nature:—

> '*Leon.* Out!
> A *mankind* witch! Hence with her, out o' door.'
> *Winter's Tale*, II. iii. 67.

MANK [mang·k], *sb.* a roguish trick; a prank.—CLUN; WEM. 'Yo' bin up to yore *manks* theer agen—bin 'ee?'

MANSH [man·sh], *v. a.*, *var. pr.* to mash.—PULVERBATCH; ELLESMERE. 'The Missis said I wuz to *mansh* the 'tatoes, an' 'er'd pŭt the butter an' crame—an' to mak' 'em good.'

M'APPEN [map·n], contraction of **Mayhappen**, q. v. '*M'appen* 'er met, an' *m'appen* 'er metna' = perhaps she will—perhaps she won't.—ELLESMERE, *Welshampton.*

> 'Lal Dinah Grayson's fresh, fewsome, an' free,
> Wid a lilt iv her step an' a glent iv her e'e;
> She glowers ebbem at mé whativer I say,
> An' meàstly mak's answer wid "*M'appen* I may!"
> "*M'appen* I may," she says, "*m'appen* I may;
> Thou thinks I believe the', an' *m'appen* I may!"'
> Lal Dinah Grayson, v. i., in *The Folk-speech of Cumberland*, by A. C. Gibson, F.S.A.

MAR [maa·r'], (1) *sb.*, *var. pr.* a mare. Com. ''Er's a rar' good trottin' *mar*—'er is.' A.S. *mære*, a mare; O.N. *mar*, a horse. Cf. **Mere** (1). See **A** (3) (15) in **Grammar Outlines** (*vowels*, &c.).

(2) *sb.*, *var. pr.* a mere.—ELLESMERE; OSWESTRY. A circuit of a few miles in the neighbourhood of Ellesmere embraces several beautiful 'meres.' Not the least remarkable for their loveliness are 'Blackmere' and 'Kettle-mere, which lie contiguous to each other. A gentleman riding down the lane which skirts them, said to a boy whom he met, 'My lad, can you tell me the name of this water?'—pointing towards 'Kettle-mere.' 'Oh, aye, sir; it's *Kettle-mar'*.' 'How deep is it?' 'Oh, it's no bottom to it, and the tother's deeper till that, Sir.' See **E** (13) in **Grammar Outlines** (*vowels*, &c.).

MARCH-MALLOWS [maa·r'ch mal·uss], *sb. Malva sylvéstris*, common Mallow.—SHREWSBURY; PULVERBATCH; CLUN. Qy. com. '*March-mallus* stewed into a tay is a mighty good thing fur swellin' as comes from rheumatiz,' said Isabella Pearce, of the Twitchen.

'The mallow—is very much used by the Arabs medicinally; they make poultices of the leaves to allay irritation and inflammation.'—*Domestic Life in Palestine*, p. 323, in WEDG.

'*Malva*, æ, es malache, μαλάχα, παρὰ τὸ μαλάσσειν, quod est mollire. *The herb mallows.*'—*Dict. Etym. Lat.*

MARKET-PEÄRT, *adj.* exhilarated, rather than positively intoxicated, by drink—a return-from-market-condition. Com. See **Fresh** (1).

MARLIN, *sb., var. pr. Hypotriorchis æsalon,* the Merlin.—BRIDGNORTH.

MARMINT, MARMOT [maa·r'mint], PULVERBATCH. [maa·r'mut], CLEE HILLS, *sb., obsols.* a three-legged iron pot—holding about four quarts—to be hung over the fire. 'Bring me the *marmint,* to bile some linsid fur the cow's drench.'

'2 Potts—1 *Marmitt,*' are comprised in an *Inventory,* dated at Aston Botterell, about 1758.

'*Marmite;* sorte de pot de fer, de cuivre, &c. où l'on fait bouillir les viandes dont on fait du potage. A porridge pot; a seething pot. "La *marmite* est bonne chez lui. He keeps a good table."'—CHAMB.

MARRED [maa·r'd], *part. adj.* petted; foolishly indulged; spoilt.—WHITCHURCH; ELLESMERE. ''Er's *marred* that lad tell 'e'll never be no good to 'isself nor nobody else.'

> 'Be wise who first doth teach thy childe that Art,
> Least homelie breaker *mar* fine ambling ball.
> Not rod in mad braines hand is that can helpe,
> But gentle skill doth make the proper whelpe.'
>
> TUSSER, ed. E. D. S., p. 185.

Cf. **Cadish.**

MARRIED ALL O'ER, *phr.* said of women who after their marriage fall off in appearance, and become poor and miserable-looking.—PULVERBATCH; WEM; ELLESMERE. 'Han'ee sid Mary Gittins lately?' 'Iss, dunna-d-'er look bad? Aye, 'er's *married all o'er!*'

MARROW [maar'·oe], (1) *sb.* a friend; a companion; a mate—'a play-*marrow.*'—WEM; WHITCHURCH; ELLESMERE.

> '"O stay at hame, my noble lord,
> O stay at hame, my *marrow.*
> My cruel brother will you betray
> On the dowie houms o' Yarrow."'
>
> *The Dowie Dens o' Yarrow* (first *printed,* A.D. 1803), in *Border Minstrelsy,* ii. p. 373.

'With theefe and his *marrow*' occurs in Tusser, ed. E. D. S., p. 134.

'Marwe, or felawe yn trauayle (or mate, *marowe,* P.). *Socius, compar.* The term marrow used in this sense is . . . retained in the Northern, Shropshire, and Exmoor dialects. . . . It occurs in the Townl. Myst., p. 110.'—*Prompt. Parv. and Notes.*

See below. Cf. **Butty** (1).

(2) *sb.* a fellow; one of a pair, as of shoes, &c.—*Ibid.* (1) 'They wun off the same ship, Sir; this leg's the *marrow* o' the one yo' seed.' (2) 'That inna the *marrow* o' the boot the child's got on, it belungs to another.'

Bailey—ed. 1782—has '*Marrows,* Fellows; as, *my Gloves are not Marrows,*' a 'North Country' Word.

Jamieson gives '*Marrow,*' with the several meanings of 'a companion,' 'a married partner,' 'one of a pair.'

See above. Cf. **Butty** (3).

MARVELS [maa·r'vh'lz], *sb. pl., var. pr.* marbles.—SHREWSBURY; PULVERBATCH. Qy. com. ''Ow many *marvels* 'ast 'ee got, Dick?' 'Forty, lad—I won fifteen stoneys an' six alleys off Jack Ivans, 'side whad I 'ad afore.' Mr. Halliwell gives '*marvels*' for marbles as a Suffolk word.

MASED [mai·zd], *part. adj.* stupefied; confused; made giddy.—PULVERBATCH; COLLIERY. 'Poor Jack Robe'ts fell off the lather isterd'y, a-sarvin' the thetcher—'e wunna much 'urt, on'y a bit *mased*, but 'e met as well a bin killed.'

> 'þat witerly he couþe no word · long þer-after spek,
> but stared on here stifly · a-stoneyd for ioye,
> þat he cast al his colour · and bi-com pale,
> and eft red as rose · in a litel while.
> so witerly was þat word · wounde to hert,
> þat he ferd as a *mased* man · . . . .'
>
> *William of Palerne*, l. 884.

> 'She seyde, she was so *mased* in the see
> That she forgat hir mynde, by hir trewthe.'
>
> CHAUCER, B. 526 (Six-text ed.), Skeat.

Mr. Oliphant, speaking of the *Ancren Riwle* [A.D. 1222, *circa*], says, 'Many Norse words are found for the first time in this work,' and he gives a list of these,—amongst them is 'Mased, *delirus*. O.N. *masa*, to chatter confusedly.'—*Sources of Standard English*, p. 122.

Cf. **Maskered.**

MASEY [mai·zi'], *adj.* confused.—WEM.

MASH, (1) *sb.* a preparation, as of bran mixed with water, given to horses and cattle. Com. 'The mar's got a nasty wisk, 'er'd better 'ăve a warm *mash* to-night.'

'Drenches; Drinks or *Mashes* given to Horses to cleanse them.'—*Academy of Armory*, Bk. III. ch. iii. p. 89.

'A commixture, a *mash*.'—*Florio*, p. 111, in HAL.

(2) *v. a.* and *v. n.* to pour boiling water upon the malt intended for brewing, mixing it well together with the mashing-staff. Com.

(3) *v. a.* and *v. n.* to infuse, as of tea.—SHREWSBURY; ELLESMERE. Qy. com. 'I'll pŭt the tay to *mash* aw'ile I clane me.'

Jamieson has *mask* in the same sense, and gives '*Masking-pat*, a tea-pot.'

MASHING-BASKET, same as **Bet-well,** q. v.—ELLESMERE.

MASHING-MUNDLE, *sb., obsols.* a brewing utensil used for stirring the malt in the 'mashing-tub,' and the 'drink' in the 'furnace.'—ELLESMERE, *Welshampton*. See below. Cf. **Mundle** (1).

MASHING-STAFF, same as above.—PULVERBATCH; CRAVEN ARMS; CHURCH STRETTON; WEM. Qy. com.

'*Mashing-staff*, pouch and taps.'—*Auctioneer's Catalogue* (Longville), 1877.

MASHING-TUB, *sb.* a tub—either round or oval in form—in which the malt is *mashed* in the process of brewing. Com.

'Three oak *mashing-tubs.*'—*Auctioneer's Catalogue* (Church Stretton), 1877. See **Mash** (2), above.

MASH-RULE, same as **Mashing-mundle**, above.—NEWPORT.

'*Mash-rule*, ladder, and sieve.'—*Auctioneer's Catalogue* (Forton Hall), 1875.

'Maschel, or rothyr, or *maschscherel. Remulus, palmula, mixtorium.* This term evidently implies the implement used for mashing or mixing the malt, to which, from resemblance in form, the name 'rudder' is also given. In Withal's little Dictionary, enlarged by W. Clerk, among the instruments of the Brew-house is given "a rudder, or instrument to stir the meash-fatte with, *motaculum.*"'—*Prompt. Parv. and Notes.*

MASK, same as **Mass**, below.—OSWESTRY.

MASKERED [mas·kur'd], (1) *part. adj.* confused; bewildered, as by losing the way in fog, or snow, or darkness.—PULVERBATCH; MUCH WENLOCK; WELLINGTON; COLLIERY; WEM. 'It wuz a great mercy the poor fellow wunna lost—'e got *maskered* i' the snow-storm o' the 'ill, an' w'en it cliered off 'e wuz miles out on 'is road.'

Maskered is the *malskrid* of *William of Palerne*, with the *l* left out:—

'& told here þanne as tit · treweli al þe soþe,
how he had missed is mayne · & *malskrid* a-boute.'—l. 416.

Compare 'Mask, *v. a.* = bewilder; *part.* "maskede."—*Legend of St. Brandan*, 115,' in COL.

(2) *part. adj.* confused; 'bothered'—'*maskered* wuth the mon's talk.' —WEM.

Pegge has '*Masker'd*, stunned; also nearly choaked. North.'
Cf. **Mased.**

MASLIN-KETTLE, *sb.* a brass, or a tinned-copper, preserving-pan.—CLEE HILLS; ELLESMERE, *Welshampton.*

'*Maslin kettle.*'—*Auctioneer's Catalogue* (Stoddesden), 1870.

'Take a quarte of good wyne, and do it in a clene *mastelyn panne*, and do therto an ownce of salgemme.—*MS. Med. Rec.*, xv. cent.' in HAL.

A.S. *mæslen, mæstlen*, brass; *mæstling*, a brass vessel. Cf. **Meslin-kettle.**

MASS, *sb.*, *var. pr.* acorns; mast. — PULVERBATCH; ELLESMERE. 'Theer's a good 'it o' *mass* this 'ear—rar' raps fur the pigs an' gis.'

Grose gives '*Mass*, acorns (mast), Exmoor.'

A.S. *mæst*, food, such as acorns, berries, and nuts. Germ. *mast*, Perhaps related to Goth. *mats*, food. See **Mask**, above.

MASTER-TAIL, *sb.* the left handle of a plough.—CLUN; BRIDGNORTH.

'The *Master handle* is that on the left hand, which he [the man] holdeth while he cleareth the Plow from clogging earth.'—*Academy of Armory*, Bk. III. ch. viii. p. 333.

See **By-tail.**

MATE, *sb.*, *var. pr.* meat. Com. 'We'n 'ad a bit o' *mate* out o' the owd dish,' said a peasant-man, when telling how the old Rector had been able to take his Sunday duty again.

'. . . it coste me of my noune propr godes at that tyme more than vj. merkes in *mate* and drynke.'—*Paston Letters*, A.D. 1450, vol. i. p. 133.
See **Meat.**

MAUL [mau·l], *v. a.* to pull about; to handle roughly. Qy. com. 'Shepherd's a mighty good-tempered dog—'e lets the childern *maul* 'im as much as they'n a mind, an' never snaps 'em.'

MAUN, MAUNNA, must; must not. See **Grammar Outlines**, p. lxxx.

'He begged, for Gudesake! I wad be his wife,
Or else I wad kill him wi' sorrow:
So e'en to preserve the poor body in life,
I think I *maun* wed him to-morrow, to-morrow,
I think I *maun* wed him to-morrow.'
ROBERT BURNS, *Poems*, p. 195, ll. 10, 11.

'With glooman brow the laird seeks in his rent:
'Tis no to gie; your merchant's to the bent:
His honour *maunna* want, he poinds your gear;
Syne driven frae house and hald, where will ye steer?'
ALLAN RAMSAY, *The Gentle Shepherd*, I. ii. p. 19.

Mr. Oliphant says that the Scandinavian *munnde* of the 'Ormulum' is found as *mone* in 'Havelok the Dane,' written 80 years later:—

'I wene that we deye *mone*
For hunger . . . . .'—l. 840.

He remarks that 'this *mone* is almost the Scotch *maun*.'—*Sources of Standard English*, p. 165.
Cf. **Mun.**

MAUNCHER [mau·nshur'], *sb.* a stone crusher. Com. M. T. Cf. **Mansh.**

MAUNDER [mau·ndur'], *v. n.* to wander about, as if without settled purpose.—CLEE HILLS. 'Ow's Jack gwe'in on?' 'Oh, 'e's no good, 'e gwuz *maunderin'* about like some owd cow.'
See *Maunder* in HAL. Cf. **Gonder** (2).

MAUNDREL [maun·dr'il], *sb.* a pick, sharp-pointed at each end, used in 'getting' coal. Com. M. T.
Pegge gives this word for 'North.' Mr. Halliwell says that it occurs in 'Howell, 1660, sect. 51.'

MAUT [mau·t], *sb., var. pr.* malt. Com.

'O, Willie brew'd a peck o' *maut*,
And Rob and Allan cam to see;
Three blyther hearts, that lee-lang night,
Ye wad na find in Christendie.'
ROBERT BURNS, *Poems*, p. 200, l. 17, c. 2.

MAWKIN. See **Malkin.**

MAWKSED [mauk·st], *part.* roughly fingered; rumpled; made untidy.—ELLESMERE. 'Dear 'eart alive! 'ow yo'n *mawksed* that apparn, w'y it wuz on'y clane on at tay-time.'

MAWKSING, *part. adj.* sauntering; loitering.—SHREWSBURY;

ATCHAM; PULVERBATCH; WEM; ELLESMERE. 'I've knit a stockin awilde we'n bin *mawksin'* the lanes after a bit o' laisin'—a sign we hanna 'ad much to do.'

MAWMSEY [mau·mzi'], *adj.* sleepy; stupid, as from want of rest, or from over-drinking.—PULVERBATCH; WEM. 'Merry nights măk'n sorrowful mornin's—I'm despert *mawmsey* to-day, an' shanna be right tell I'm pool'd through the sheets agen.'

MAWN [mau·n], *sb., var. pr.* a mane.—WEM.

MAWSKIN [maus·kin *and* mau·skin], *sb.* the stomach of a calf prepared for rennet—WORTHEN; NEWPORT. A.S. *maga*, the stomach. Cf. **Kidmaw,** also **Rindless.**

MAY, (1) *v. a., var. pr.* make.—COLLIERY; NEWPORT. 'Oi'll *may* that warm fur ye.' See **A** (6) in **Grammar Outlines** (*vowels*, &c.). See also **Mek.** Cf. **Mak.**

(2) *pron., var. pr., emph.* me.—*Ibid.*

'there he tooke a ring of his ffingar right,
& to that squier raught itt hee,
& said, "beare this to my Lady bright,
for shee may thinke itt longe or shee *may* see."'
Bosworth Feilde, l. 524. *Percy Folio MS.*, vol. iii. p. 254, ed. Hales and Furnivall.

'In and near Newcastle, Staffordshire, *me* is to-day pronounced *may*.'—Glossarial Note by Mr. Viles, p. 560, *ibid.*

See **Grammar Outlines** (*personal pronouns*), Note (1), and compare *emph.* **thee.**

MAY-BE, *adv.* perhaps.—NEWPORT.

'Or *maybe* in a frolic daft,
To Hague or Calais taks a waft,
To make a tour, an' tak a whirl,
To learn *bon ton*, an' see the worl'.'
ROBERT BURNS, *Poems*, p. 4, l. 27.

Cf. **May-happen,** below. See **Mebbe.**

MAY-FLOWERS, *sb. pl.* the flowers of *Caltha Palústris*, common Marsh Marigold.—PULVERBATCH; NEWPORT. See Bk. II., *Folk-lore*, &c., 'Customs connected with Days and Seasons' (*May-Day*).

MAY-GRASS, *sb.* Greater Stitchwort.—PULVERBATCH. See **Devil's Corn.**

MAY-HAPPEN, *adv.* perhaps.—ELLESMERE, *Welshampton.*

'And able for to helpen al a schire
In any caas that mighte falle or *happe*.'
CHAUCER, *The Prologue*, l. 585, ed. Morris.

Dr. Morris glosses *happe*, to happen, befall; 'whence,' he says, '*happy*, mis-*hap*, per-*haps*, may-*hap*. O.E. *happen*, happy; O.N. *happ*, fortune; W. *hap*, luck.'

Cf. **Happen,** also **Behappen.** See **Mappen.**

MAYTHERN [mai·dhur'n], *sb.* stinking Chamomile.—CORVE DALE; CLEE HILLS.

'*Ameroke*,' glossed '*mathen* (*maythe*),' occurs in *The Treatise of Walter de Biblesworth*, xiii. cent., in Wr. vocabs., vol. i. p. 162.

See below. Cf. **Moithern.**

MAYTHIG [mai·dhig], same as above.—CORVE DALE.

'*Herba putida*, mægða,' occurs in *Archbp. Ælfric's Vocabulary*, x. cent., and '*Hec embroca*, *A^e* maythe,' in an *English Vocabulary*, xv. cent., both in Wr. vocabs., vol. i. pp. 31—190.

Mr. Wright has a footnote on the latter, referring to '*maythe;*' it is as follows:—'Camomile (the *anthemis cotula* of botanists), still called in some districts *may-weed;* the A.S. *mageða*.'

'Mayde wede, herbe, or maythys. *Melissa, amarusca*.'—*Prompt. Parv.* Cf. **Maise.**

MEÄKING [mi'·u'kin], *adj.* sickly; ailing; lacking energy.—PULVERBATCH; WEM. 'Kitty wuz al'ays a poor *meäkin'* thing, nod likely to get 'er livin' like the rest.'

MEAL [mee·l], *sb.* the quantity of milk given by a cow, or by cows, at one time. Com. 'The cows sinken i' thar milk fast, I can see it less every *meal*—it shewns the time o' 'ear.'

'Each shepherd's daughter with her cleanly peale,
Was come a field to milk the morning's *meale*.'
BROWN'S *Pastorals*, B. I., Song iv. p. 99, in Nares.

A.S. *mǽl*, that which is marked out; a portion,—time, meal.

MEAL-MOUTHED, *adj.* the very opposite of 'plain-spoken'—reluctant to speak the honest truth, when to do so might be 'inconvenient.'—PULVERBATCH. 'Yo' bin so despert *meal-mouthed*—afeard o' späkin' w'en yo' should'n, an' w'en yo' binna wanted yo' can rackle too fast, a power.'

Mr. Nares says that 'this term, which survives in the form of *mealy-mouthed*, appears to have been the original word.' He explains it as meaning 'Delicate-mouthed, unable to bring out harsh or strong expressions,' and quotes the following as an illustrative example of this usage:—

'Who would imagine yonder sober man,
That same devout *meale-mouthed* precisian,
That cries good brother, kind sister, &c.
. . . . who thinks that this good man,
Is a vile, sober, damn'd polititian?'
MARSTON, *Sat.* ii. A.D. 1598.

Minsheu—ed. 1617—gives, '8523. *Meale mouthed*, or faire spoken. Hujusmodi *etiam apud Lat:* sunt loquendi formulæ qui de homine perblando dicunt, mel, et rosas loquitur, *ita et nos* meal-mouthed, quasi qui farinam loqueretur, cujus verba blanda sunt, et mollia instar farinæ.'

MEAL'S-MEAT, *sb.* food enough for a meal.—SHREWSBURY; PULVERBATCH. Qy. com. 'I gid the mon a shillin' an' a *meal's-mate* fur 'is job.'

'You ne'er yet had
A *meal's-meat* from my table, as I remember,
Nor from my wardrobe any cast suit.'
BEAUMONT and FLETCHER, *Honest Man's Fortune*, ii. 403, in WR.

Mr. Wright says of *meal's-meat* that it is 'still used in Norfolk.' 'Forby has *Meal's-victuals*. See ii. 212.'—HAL. See **Meat**, below.

MEAR, (1) *sb.*, *obs.* a boundary.—CLUN; CLEE HILLS.

'The forest, as well as the Honor of Clun, adjoined Kerry upon the boundary; and in a suit, in the time of Queen Elizabeth, between the Crown and several freeholders and copyholders of Clun, the boundary of the forest was minutely set out, and is thus deposed to:—At Reilth, in the County of Salop, the 8th day of May, in the 18th year of the reign of Queen Elizabeth (1576), Moris ap Owen, of Reilth, Yeoman, of the age of 4 score years or thereabouts, being sworn to the *meares* of the forest, and having described them so as to exclude Kerry, on being examined how he knoweth the *meares* to be as aforesaid, saith that "about sixty years last past, at which time the Lords of Clun had and held Jura Regalia within the Lordship of Clun. And the Lords of Kery held also Jura Regalia within the Lordship of Kery; he saw two men hanged, whose names he doth not now remember, for certain offences by them before committed and done; the one of the said two men was hanged within the Lordship of Clun, at the side of the Brook called the Rithor, by the Steward and Officers of the Lordship of Clun; and the other man was hanged within the Lordship of Kery, on the other side of the said Brook, within less than a bow-shot to the other, by the Steward and Officers of the Lordship of Kery; and saith that the said two men were hanged on one day."'—From a Paper on '*Ancient Documents relating to the Honor, Forests, & Borough of Clun*,' read before the 'Archæological Institute' at Shrewsbury, in August, 1855, by Thos. Salt, Esq., and 'privately printed.'

'The minutes of the proceedings of a Court Swainmote of Humphrey Briggs, Esq., for his Forest of Clee, . . . held at Emstrey, in the 15th year of James 1st, ... describe the boundary line of the "Clives," or open downs, all round the hill [Brown Clee], the several townships being divided from each other, at the point where they touch the Forest by a landmark, most frequently by an oak called a *mear-oak*, the boundaries being called *mears*.'—From a Paper on '*The Clee Forest and the Clee Hills*,' by William Purton, Esq., published in the '*Transactions of the Severn Valley Naturalists' Field Club*' for 1865—1870, pp. 7—9.

'*Mere* set þou whilk ouerga þai ne sal,
Ne turne to hile þe land with-al.'
Metrical English Psalter, ciii. (A.D. 1300, *ante*).
[*Ps.* civ. 9]. *Specim. Early Eng.*, ii. l. 19.

'The Trojan Brute did first that citie fownd,
And Hygate made the *meare* thereof by West,
And Overt gate by North . . . . . .'
SPENSER, *F. Q.*, Bk. III. c. ix. st. xlvi.

'The furious Team, that on the Cambrian side,
Doth Shropshire as a *mere* from Hereford divide.'
DRAYTON, *Polyolbion* [A.D. 1613—1622], i. p. 807, in Nares.

'*Meer*, marke be-twene ij. londys. *Meta*, *meris*, C. F. (divia, interfinium, K.).'—*Prompt. Parv.*

Ash has '*Meer*, a boundary.' A.S. *mǽre*, *gemǽre*; Du. *meere*; O.N. *mœri*, a boundary.

(2) [mee·u'r'], *sb.* a line of stones down a field, which have been

picked out of the plough's course, and so left by idle farmers long ago. Such is the explanation current at Ditton Priors (Clee Hills) of the *mears* existing there at this date [1875].

Mr. Purton, in his Paper on '*The Clee Forest*' before quoted, says of the old word *mear* that, though obsolete as meaning a boundary, 'it is a singular fact that it was, not many years ago, and probably is now, in familiar use about Ditton Priors, with which neighbourhood this report [minutes of the Brigg's Court] especially identifies itself. It is applied to heaps of stones collected off the fields and left in rows down the middle of them. The old *mears* between the parishes were probably fixed in the same way, the oaks being the more enduring landmarks. Sometimes it is a *mear oak*, sometimes an oak in a *mear*, in one place "where a birtch did lately stand."'

Ash has '*Meer*, a strip of green between ploughed lands.'

Grose gives '*Meer*, a ridge of land between different properties in a common field. Glouc.'

'In Norfolk, according to Forby, a Mara-balk, or mere, is a narrow slip of unploughed land, which separates properties in a common field. "*Limes est callis et finis dividens agros*, a meere."—MED. M.S. CANT. . . . . . Elyot gives "*Cardo*, mere, or boundes which passeth through the field." The following occurs in Gouldman: "To cast a meer with a plough, *urbo*. A meer, or mark, *terminus, meta, limes*."' —WAY.

See **Mear-oak**, below.

MEARED, *part. adj., obs.* marked out; bounded.—OSWESTRY.

In a copy, dated 1714, of the Terrier of the Oswestry Schools' lands, taken in 1635, is the following:—'Item, One parcel of meadowing in a meadow there called Gweirglodd Jenn Gouth, lying betwixt ye lands of Edward Evans gent on ye one side, and *meared* by two oakes one att each end thereof, and ye lands of Robert Powell, Esq. *meared* on that side by three *mear stones*.'—See *Byegones*, Sept. 8th, 1875, p. 299.

Ash gives '*Meered*, having a boundary, bounded by a meer.'

The verb to *mere*, to have a common boundary, occurs in a document *temp.* Henry VIII., 1543, in *State Papers*, v. 309. See WAY.

See **Mear-stone**, below.

MEAR-OAK, *sb., obs.* a landmark,—'by a landmark, most frequently by an oak called a *mear-oak*.'—CLEE HILLS.

'Mos antiquorum in divisione agrorum, *ramum* ex arbore palma *decerptum cum fructibus* pro termino figere solebunt.'—MINSHEU, —ed. 1617—p. 299.

See below, also **Mear**, above.

MEAR-STONE, *sb., obs.* a boundary-stone,—'ye lands . . . . meared on that side by three *mear stones*.'—OSWESTRY.

'"A meyre stane, *bifinium, limes*."—CATH. ANG. "*Terminalis lapis*, a mere stone, laide or pyghte at the ende of sundry mens landes."—ELYOT.' See Way's Note in *Prompt. Parv.*, p. 333.

Minsheu has 'Mearstones, *rectius* mearck-stones, *sunt lapides terminales, qui unius cujusque* terras limitant, et discurrunt. Marck *enim est limes ut prolixe disputat*.'

Ash gives '*Meerstone*, a merestone, a stone set up as a boundary between lands.'

A.S. *gemǽre*, a termination; limit. See **Meared**, above.

MEAT, *sb.* food; the generic term—so much a day and his *meat.* Com.

> 'This knyght is to his chambre lad anon,
> And is vnarmed and to *mete* yset.'
>
> CHAUCER, F. 173 (Six-text ed.), Skeat.

'A.S. *mete;* O.Icel. *matr;* Goth. *mats;* O.H.Germ. *maz*, meat (*cibus; esca*).'—STRAT.

Cf. **Flesh-meat.** See **Mate.**

MEATY [mai·ti], *adj.* fleshy: said of cattle.—PULVERBATCH. Qy. com. 'Them bŭllocks binna to say fat, but they bin *mātey*—thick o' the rib.' See **Flesh-meat.**

MEBBE [meb·i'], contraction of **Maybe**, q. v., and the more usual form.—NEWPORT. Cf. **M'appen.**

MEGRIMS [mai·gr'imz], *sb. pl., pec.* antics; gesticulations.—PULVERBATCH; ELLESMERE. Qy. com. 'Them childern wun naughty i' church, they wun măkin' *maigrims* an' witherin' one to another all the wilde.' See *Megrims* in WEDG.

MEK, *v. a., var. pr.* make—'*mek* 'er a coop o' tay.'—COLLIERY; NEWPORT. See **A** (6) in **Grammar Outlines** (*vowels*, &c.), also **May** (1).

MELCH [mel·sh], (1) *adj.* soft; mild, as of wind or weather.—PULVERBATCH. 'Theer's a nice *melch* winde this mornin'—mild as Maȳ.'

(2) *adj.* milk-giving.—SHREWSBURY; PULVERBATCH; WORTHEN. Qy. com. 'Bin them barren or *melch*, Maister?' 'They bin dried fur feedin'.'

'Sche was *melche. Lai le freine,*' in STRAT.

MELCH-COW, *sb.* a cow giving milk; a dairy-cow—'a new *melch-cow.*'—*Ibid.*

> '. . . . . then at the farm
> I have a hundred *milch-kine* to the pail.'
>
> *Taming of the Shrew*, II. i. 359.

'*Smolgiuto*, sucked or *milched* dry.'—FLORIO, A.D. 1680.

'O.H.Germ. *melcher*, milch (melch).'—STRAT. See **Easy Melched.**

MENAGERIE [mu'najur'i'], *sb., pec.* a confused state of things; a litter; a collection of odds and ends. Com. ''Eart alive, childern, whad a *menagerie* yo'n got 'ere!'

MENGE. See **Minge.**

MENT, *pret.* mended.—CORVE DALE.

MEOW [mi'ou· *or* myou·], *v. a.* and *v. n.* to make a wry mouth; to make distorting grimaces.—SHREWSBURY; PULVERBATCH. ''E bats 'is eyes an' *myows* 'is mouth like summat kyimet.'

> 'Sometime like apes that *mow* and chatter at me.'
>
> *Tempest*, II. ii. 9.

'*Mowyn̄*, or make a mow, *Valgio, cachinno.*'—*Prompt. Parv.*

'*Faire la moue à quelqu'un;* to make mouths at one.'—CHAMB.

'O.Fr. *moe;* Du. *mouwe;* mouth (mow).'—PICK. Cf. **Morums.**

MERE [mee·h'r'], (1) *sb.* a mare.—NEWPORT.

'Forthledand hai to *meres* ma,
And gresse to hinehede of men swa,
Þat þou outelede fra erthe brede.'
Metrical English Psalter, ciii. (A.D. 1300, *ante*).
[*Ps.* civ. 14]. *Specim. Early Eng.*, ii. l. 29.

'In a tabard he rood upon a *mere*.'
CHAUCER, *The Prologue*, l. 541, ed. Morris.

'*Meere*, horse. *Equa*.'—*Prompt. Parv.*
A.S. *mære;* O.H.Germ. merhe, a mare. Cf. **Mar** (1).

(2) *sb.* a large natural sheet of water—a lake. The *meres*, as a lake system, obtain in *N. Shr.*

'. . . . . Our weaver here doth will
The muse his source to sing, as how his course he steers;
Who from his natural spring, as from his neighb'ring *meres*
Sufficiently supply'd, shoots forth his silver breast.'
DRAYTON'S *Polyolbion* [A.D. 1613—1622], xi. p. 861, in Nares.

Mr. Nares remarks that *mere* is 'still used in Cheshire and elsewhere for the lakes of the country.'

Mr. Halliwell also notes the term as 'still in use.' He quotes the following:—'A *mere*, or water whereunto an arme of the sea floweth.' —Baret, 1580.

'*Mere*, watur (mer, or see, water, W.). *Mare*.'—*Prompt. Parv.*
A.S. *mere*, a lake; pool. See **Mar** (2). Cf. **Pool**. See Bk. II., *Folklore*, &c., 'Legends.'

MERE-BALLS. See **Moss-balls.**

MERE-SIDE, *sb.* the margin of the mere.—*Ibid.* The *mere-side* at Ellesmere affords a most charming walk, the *Mere-gardens* adding to its natural attractions.

MERRY-TREE, *sb.*, *obsols.* a tree bearing a small, wild cherry.—WEM; ELLESMERE.

'*Merise tree*' occurs in Phillips' *New World of Words*, 7th ed. 1720.

'*Merise*, espèce de fruit rouge à noyau plus petit que la cerise. A kind of small, bitter cherry.'—CHAMB.

MESLIN-KETTLE, same as **Maslin-kettle**, q. v.—NEWPORT.
'Brass *meslin kettle*.'—*Auctioneer's Catalogue* (Forton Hall), 1875.

MESS, (1) *v. n.* to trifle; to expend time upon frivolous employment. Com. ''Ow lung bin 'ee gweïn to *mess* o'er that crochet?—yo'd'n better by 'afe be knittin' a stockin'.'

(2) *v. a.* to squander; to waste. Com. ''Er's *messed* all 'er wages away, an' got nuthin', as yo' met say, to shewn fur 'em.'

METHEGLIN [mi'theg·lin], *sb.* a fermented liquor made of honeyed water, obtained by thoroughly washing the 'comb,' when drained of the honey: in a high class brew the 'comb' is sometimes washed in a little 'fresh beer' to hasten the fermentation; but the strength of the liquor is dependent upon the quantity of honey it contains. *Metheglin*, when well made, and refined and matured by age, is a 'cordial' of no mean order—a homely 'liqueur' of potent quality.—

PULVERBATCH; NEWPORT. Qy. com. ''Ow'n yore bees turned out this time, Molly?' 'Mighty middlin'—plenty o' dry cŏom, but despert lickle 'oney; I dunna think I shall 'ăve a spiggit-stane o' *metheglin*.'

'*Evans*. And given to . . . taverns and sack and wine and *metheglins*.'—*Merry Wives of Windsor*, V. v. 166.

'*Metheglin* (Br. *Meddiglin*), a kind of drink in *Wales* made of Wort, Herbs, Spice, and Honey sodden together.'—BLOUNT's *Glossographia*, p. 408.

Mr. Halliwell says, '*Metheglin* was anciently made of a great variety of materials. See a receipt for it in *MS. Sloane*, 1672, f. 127.'

See Mr. Way's Note on 'must' in *Prompt. Parv.*, p. 349.

W. *meddyglyn*, hydromel, mead.

MEX. See **Mix.**

MEZZLED [mez·ld], *adj.* affected with a disease to which swine are subject—a kind of measles which appear in the tissues of the flesh, in the form of white, semi-opaque spots, and render it quite unfit for use. It is popularly supposed that food given to pigs when it is too warm, will induce a *mezzled* condition of flesh. Com. 'Tak' car' as yo' dunna gie them lickle pigs thar mate too warm, or we sha'n 'ăve 'em all *mezzled*.'

> 'Hog *measeled* kill,
> for flemming that will.'
>
> TUSSER, *Fiue Hundred Pointes of Good Husbandrie* [Octobers abstract].

'The *Measils* or *Meazle*, they are like Hail-stones spread in the Flesh, and especially in the leaner part of the Hog; this is a Disease proper to this Beast, for no other in the World (as *Aristotle* saith) is troubled therewith. . . . . . .'—*Academy of Armory*, Bk. II. ch. ix. p. 181.

'Masyl, or mazil, sekenesse, *Serpedo, variola*, Maselyd. *Serpiginosus, vel serpigionatus*.'—*Prompt. Parv.*

'*Variolæ*: postulæ quibus cutis sit varia: *Measills*.'—*Dict. Etym. Lat.*

'Du. *maese*, spot, stain, mark; *maeselen*, measles.'—WEDG.

MIÄMAS [mei·h'mus], *sb.* Michaelmas; the 'Festival of St. Michael and all Angels.'—PULVERBATCH; WEM; ELLESMERE. 'We mun be thinkin' about the rent, *Miämas* is drawin' nigh.' *Miämas* is a variation of *Mihelmas*, a form that sprang, according to Mr. Nares, from a current and familiar usage, which for a long time obtained, of pronouncing the proper name *Michael* as *Mihel*. Both words occur in Tusser:—

> 'Then spare it for rowen, till *Mihel* be past.'
>
> 'Be mindfull abrode of *Mihelmas* spring.'
>
> *Fiue Hundred Pointes of Good Husbandrie* [August].

An earlier instance of the form, '*Myhelmas* Day,' is found in the *Paston Letters*, A.D. 1465, vol. ii. p. 244.

MICH [mich·], *v. n.*, *obs.*? to crouch; to huddle, as in a corner.—PULVERBATCH; WORTHEN. 'The poor owd ŏŏman's gettin' mighty simple, 'er canna do much but *mich* i' the cornel.'

'"To *mich* in a corner, *deliteo.*"—Gouldman,' in WAY.
Cf. **Hootching.**

MIDDLE, *sb.* the waist. Qy. com. 'I dunna like pŭttin' a strap round a child's *middle* to dade ŏŏth—it mak's 'em inclined to peck forrat.'

'On heu hire her is fayr ynoh,
Hire browe broune, hire eȝe blake,
Wiþ lossum chere he on me loh;
Wiþ *middel* smal & wel ymake.'
Specim. of Lyric Poetry (A.D. 1300, *circa*). 'Alysoun.'
Specim. Early Eng., iv. *a*, l. 16.

'Full many Ladies often had assayd
About their *middles* that faire belt to knit.'
SPENSER, *F. Q.*, Bk. V. c. iii. st. xxviii.

'*Myddyl*, of þe waste of mannys body. *Vastitas.*'—*Prompt. Parv.*

MIDDLING, *adj.* indifferent; not well, nor yet ill—a poor kind of state: said of the health. Com.

MIDDLING-SHARP, *adj.* tolerably well. Com.

MIDGEN [mij·in], *sb.* the omentum of a slaughtered pig.—ELLESMERE.
'*Midgin*, the mesentery of a hog, commonly called the Crow. North.'—PEGGE.
See **Kell** (1).

MIDGEN-LARD, *sb.* an inferior kind of lard made from the fat of the intestines.—PULVERBATCH; NEWPORT; ELLESMERE.

MIFF, (1) *sb.* a pet; a slight ill-humour.—WHITCHURCH.
'She is in a little sort of *miff* about a ballad.'—ARBUTHNOT.
Pegge has '*Miff*, displeasure, ill-humour: He left me in a *miff*. North.'
See *Miff* in WEDG. Cf. **Huff.**

(2) *v. n.* to take offence hastily.—WHITCHURCH. ''E *miffed* at it direc'ly.'

MIFFY, *adj.* apt to take offence; touchy.—*Ibid.*

MIGHTY, *adj.*, *pec.* very. Com. 'Rogers the tailor bought a pig at the far, but 'e's a *mighty* poor aven.' ''E'll feed well on cabbitch, yo'n see!—'e'll mak' a tidy lump by Chris'mas.'
'Itē y[e] 19 of Marche, 1614, for stoppage of the water of Seaverne out of the Churche beinge then a *mighty* great flood, xviij d.'—*Churchwardens' Accounts of the Abbey*, Shrewsbury.

MIGHTY-BAD, *adj.* very ill,—in regard of health. Com.

MILDY [mil·di'], *adj.* loose; fine; crumbling, as of soil.—PULVERBATCH. 'The fros' 'as done a power o' good, the ground breaks up as *mīldy* an' as fine as a īnion-bed.'

MILE, (1) *sb.*, *sing.* for *pl.* miles—'about two *mile* across the filds.' Com.

'At þe Castel of Carboye · þer he beden hade,
was fiftene *myle* · fro sarras I-holden,
And oþer fiftene *myle* · fro þenne as þei leiȝen.'
Joseph of Arimathie, ll. 417, 418.

A.S. *míl*, a mile. Cf. **Foot** (1).

(2) *v. n.*, *var. pr.* to work and labour hard; same as **Moil**, q. v. ''E's *milin'* at it.'—COLLIERY.

(3) *v. n.*, *var. pr.* to drudge; to 'moil,' in the restricted sense of working in filth and mire, of such kind as would cleave to the labourer.—WORTHEN. ''Ow them chaps bin *mīlin'* i' the mixen, they bin all o'er muck.' Cf. **Moil.**

MILES END-WAYS, *adv.* an undetermined distance; a long way—miles vaguely computed without reference to point or direction, whence or whither. Com. 'Everybody wants the thetcher at the same time—the Maister rid *miles end-ways* the tother day after a mon.' ''E'd better a mounted the lather instid o' the 'orse; the owd Maister use't to thetch w'en 'e wuz above seventy.' Compare 'mile wei' used in an analogous manner, though with a diverse meaning, in the following:—

'alle þe surgens of salerne · so sone ne coþen,
haue lesed his langour · and his liif saued,
as þe maide meliors · in a *mile wei* dede.'
William of Palerne, l. 1578.

MILING [mei·lin], *part. adj.* dirty and laborious—'a *mīlin'* job.'—COLLIERY. See **Mile** (2), above.

MILK-FORK, same as **Dairy-maid**, q. v.—ELLESMERE.

MILK-LEAD, *sb.* a shallow, leaden cistern for laying milk in; it is furnished with a plug beneath, upon the withdrawal of which the milk flows through, leaving the cream resting on the '*lead*,' from whence it is afterwards removed in a quite pure state. Qy. com. 'Now, dunna star' about yo' an' let the crame run through, as well as the milk.'

'Two *milk leads* and frame.'—*Auctioneer's Catalogue* (Longville), **1877.**

MILLER, *sb. Muscicapa grisola*, Spotted Fly-catcher—the *young* bird.—BRIDGNORTH.

MILNER, *sb.* a miller. Com. '**If yo'** sin the *milner*, tell 'im we sha'n want a batch **groud nex'** wik.'

'*Hic molendinarius*, a milner,' occurs in a *Nominale*, xv. cent., in Wr. vocabs., vol. i. p. 212.

'O.Icel. *mylnari*; O.H.Germ. *mulnari*, milner,' in STRAT.

MINCING, *part. adj.* tripping; walking with short steps, in an affected manner. 'Jest see our Mary! 'er gwuz *mincin'* alung as if 'er wuz daincin' on eggs an' afraid o' breakin' 'em—'er's gotten despert big-sorted sence 'er went to live at the 'All.'

'*Portia.* I'll hold thee any wager,
When we are both accoutred like young men,
I'll prove the prettier fellow of the two,

. . . .
. . . . . and turn two *mincing* steps
Into a manly stride . . . . . .'
Merchant of Venice, III. iv. 67.

MINGE, MENGE [min·zh], PULVERBATCH; CLEE HILLS. [men·zh], ELLESMERE, *v. a.* to mix; to mingle. 'Tell the cowman to gie the 'eifer a good bran mash, an' to *minge* it up well—nod lave any dry lumps in.'

'*Mynge*' occurs in the Wicliffite version—ed. A.D. 1388—'. . in the drynke that she meddlid to ȝou, *mynge* ȝe double to hir.'—*Rev.* xviii. 6. '. . . whos blood Pilat *myngide* with the sacrifices of hem.'—*Luke* xiii. 1.

'Medle, or *mengyn̄ge* to-gedur of dyuerse thynges. *Mixtura.*'—*Prompt. Parv.*

A.S. *mengan*; O.Fris. *menga*, to mix, mingle. Cf. **Munge** (2).

MINGICUMMUMBUS [minj·i'ku'mum·'bus], *sb.* an agglomeration; an inseparable mass, as of pounds of butter stuck together, or of things of diverse kinds shaken together into a state of hopeless confusion.—PULVERBATCH. 'Ööl the owd mar' be fit fur markit o' Saturday, Maister?—the young un jogs so, we sha'n a the butter all in a *mingicummumbus.*' The term is clearly a 'coined' one. Cf. **Minge**, above.

MINIKIN [min·i'kin], (1) *adj.* small; delicate.—PULVERBATCH; WEM. 'It's a *minikin* lickle thing fur six months owd, but a pretty child.'

Tusser has '*minnekin* Nan,' p. 20, ed. E. D. S.

'A *minikin* wench, a smirking lasse.'—Florio, p. 315, in HAL.

(2) *sb.* a slight, delicate, affected girl—'sich a *minikin* as 'er is.'—*Ibid.* 'A *minikin*, a fine mincing lass,' Kennett MS., is quoted by Mr. Halliwell, who remarks that the word is 'still in use in Devon.'

MINTY [min·ti'], *adj.*, *obsols.* mitey, as of cheese, &c.—SHREWSBURY; CRAVEN ARMS.

'*Vermes*, Anglice myntys,' occurs in a *Metrical Vocabulary*, perhaps xiv. cent., in Wr. vocabs., vol. i. p. 176. Mr. Wright has the following note upon it:—'The word *mint*, in the signification of a mite, is still preserved in the dialects of the west of England.'

MISDEEDED, *adj.* miserly; covetous—'a *misdeeded* owd mon.'—CLUN, *Clungunford.*

MISDEEMFUL, *adj.* suspicious.—PULVERBATCH; CHURCH STRETTON; CLEE HILLS. 'Mrs. Morris is so *misdeemful*, 'er thinks everybody's chaitin' 'er—be'app'n 'er mizzers other folk's cloth by 'er own yard.'

'*C. Custance.* Surely this fellowe *misdeemeth* some yll in me.'—*Roister Doister*, Act iiij. Sc. iij. p. 62.

A.S. *déman*, to judge, and Lat. prefix, *mis* = less.

MISDEENFUL, MISDAINFUL, same as above—corrupted forms. —WEM.

MISELTOE-THRUSH, *sb.* *Turdus viscivorus*, Missel-thrush. —WORTHEN; CLUN.

'This bird . . . is not migratory, excepting in so far as it moves off in considerable flocks into Herefordshire and Monmouthshire for the sake of the mistletoe, which abounds in the orchards there, on the viscous berries of which it delights to feed; whence it has obtained its familiar name of missel, or *mistletoe-thrush*.'—*Science Gossip*, p. 166, A. D. 1873.

Cf. **Missel-bird**, below. See **Thrice-cock**.

MISERD [mei·zur'd], *sb.*, *var. pr.* a miser; an avaricious man. Qy. com. 'Aye, 'e's jest like all the lot on 'em—'is Faither wuz as great a *miserd* as ever lived, an' 'is owd Nuncle too.'

MISFORTUNE, *sb.*, *pec.* an illegitimate child-birth. Com. See **Love-child**.

MISSEL-BIRD, same as **Miseltoe-thrush**, above, q. v.—BRIDGNORTH.

Called '*Missell Bird*, or Shrit,' in the *Academy of Armory*, Bk. II. ch. xii. p. 279.

MITHER. See **Moither**.

MITTENS [mit·inz], *sb. pl.* gloves worn by hedgers and woodmen, to protect their hands and arms from injury whilst about their work; they are made of stout hide, and reach halfway to the elbow; they have no fingers like an ordinary glove—the hand-part is undivided—but there is a pouch for the thumb. Com. 'I lost a capital par o' *mittins* the tother day; I 'anged 'em o' the 'edge ŏŏth my baÿte-bag, aw'ile I wuz clānin' the diche, an' somebody stole 'em.'

'Brushing-hooks, axes, broomhooks and *mittens*.'—*Auctioneer's Catalogue* (Longville), 1877.

'Twey *myteynes*, . . maad all of cloutes,' are named, as forming part of the apparel of 'The poor Ploughman,' in *P. Pl. Cr.*, l. 428.

'To handle without *mittins*.'—RAY'S *Proverbs*, p. 60.

'O.Fr. *Mitan*, moitié, milieu . . . . . M. Grandgagnage, derive mitan de l'ahal. *mittamo* (medius). . . . . . Notre *mitaine* appartiendrait-il à cette famille? *Mitaine* est un gant où il n'y a qu'une séparation, pour ainsi dire gant séparé en deux moitiés.'—BUR.

MIX, MEX [mik·s], Qy. com. [mek·s], PULVERBATCH, *v. a.* to clean out, as of stable or cow-house litter. 'Theer use't to be a lad kep' to *mex* the cows, sarve the pigs, an' do all the rough work.'

Randle Holme has, under 'Terms used by Cow-herds:'—'*To Mexon*, is to make clean their Houses from Dung.'—*Academy of Armory*, Bk. II. ch. ix. p. 173.

'A.S. *mix*, *meox*; Fris. miox, miux; mix (mux), *stercus*.'—STRAT.

MIXEN, *sb.* a dunghill. Com.

'Better wed over the *Mixon* than over the Moor,' is given by Ray as a '*Cheshire Proverb*,' and he adds a note:—'That is, hard by or at home, the *Mixon* being that heap of compost which lies in the yards of good husbands, than far off, or from *London*. The road from *Chester* leading to *London* over some part of the Moor-lands in *Staffordshire*, the meaning is,' &c. See *Proverbs*, pp. 235, 236.

Pegge has '*Mixon*, a dunghill. Kent.'

A.S. *mixen*, a dunghill.

MIZZLE [miz·l], *v. n.* to rain softly, in small, fine, imperceptible drops.—SHREWSBURY; PULVERBATCH; WELLINGTON; NEWPORT; WEM.

> 'Up, Colin up! ynough thou morned hast;
> Now gynnes to *mizzle*, hye we homeward fast.'
> SPENSER, *The Shepheards Calender*, November, l. 208.

MIZZLING, *part. adj.* descending thickly, in soft, fine drops, like mist,—'a *mizzling* rain.'—*Ibid.*

'O.N. *mistr*, G. *mist*, Du. *miest*, thickness of the air, mist; *missen*, *miesten*, *mieselen*, nebulam exhalare, rorare tenuem pluviam; *mieselinge*, nebula.—Kilian,' in WEDG.

MOACH [moa·ch], *v. n.* to lounge, or 'hang about,' idly.—WEM. ''E's no good, 'e does nuthin' but *moach* about from mornin' tell neet.' Cf. '*Mich*, to skulk,' in HAL.

MOBLE [mob·l], (1) *v. a.* to muffle the head and shoulders in warm wraps.—SHREWSBURY. 'I never sid sich a ŏŏman, 'er *mobles* 'erself up in that owd 'ŏŏd an' shawl, an' sits by the fire, tell 'er's as nesh as nesh—'er'd be a power better if 'er 'ad to knock about like me.'

> "*First Player.* 'But who, O who, had seen the *mobled* queen——'
> *Ham.* 'The *mobled* queen?'
> *Pol.* That's good: '*mobled* queen' is good.
> *First Player.* 'Run barefoot up and down, threatening the flame
> With bisson rheum; a clout upon that head,
> Where late the diadem stood; and for a robe
> About her . . . . . a blanket.'"—*Hamlet*, II. ii. 524—526.

(2) *v. a.* to put on an abundance of warm wraps for general comfort, as when setting out for a cold journey, or such like.—PULVERBATCH; NEWPORT; WEM. 'Yo' mun *moble* yourself well up, it's a despert, raw, cowd night.' The past participle, followed by the adverb *up*, is perhaps more frequently used—'*mobled up*.' 'Mind as yo' bin *mobled up* right well afore yo' start.'

MOG [mog·], (1) *v. a.* and *v. n.*, *obsols.* to move from one place to another, as of cows changing pasture; to move off or away.—PULVERBATCH. (1) 'Tell John to *mog* the cows i' the mornin'—it's time as they wenten i' the Cote Leasow.' (2) 'Now then, *mog* off fur the cows, or they ŏŏnna be out o' the foud by six' (A.M.). Cf. **Shift** (3) (4).

(2) *v. n.*, *obsols.* to exchange; a term of cards employed in the game of 'Costly.'—SHREWSBURY; ELLESMERE. Qy. com. See **Costly.**

MOGGY, *sb.* a young calf. Com.

MOIL [mwoi·l *and* moi·l], *v. n.* to labour; to slave; to drudge in dirty work: generally, but not necessarily, used in combination with 'toil'—'*moil and toil.*'—PULVERBATCH; WEM. Qy. com. 'Yo' met'n *mwoil an' toil* a couple o' 'ours, an' 'ardly get a wisket full—it's a despert bad crop, but yo' canna look fur anythin' else off that wet groun', the 'tatoes rot afore they comen to anythin'.'

'. . mounchynge in their maungers, and *moylynge* in their gaye manoures and mansions, and so troubeled wyth loyterynge in theyr Lordeshyppes.'—LATIMER, *Sermon on the Ploughers*, p. 26.

'GOod husbandmen must *moile & toile*,
to laie to liue by laboured feeld.'
TUSSER, *Introduction to the Booke of Husbandrie*, p. 13, ed. E. D. S.

Bailey—ed. 1782—gives 'To Moil [*moil*, old Word for *mule*, q. d. to labour like a Mule], to work with might and main, to drudge.'
Cf. **Mile** (2) (3).

MOILLED, MOILLET [mwoi·ld], PULVERBATCH. [moi·lh't *and* mwoi·lh't], CHURCH STRETTON, *Leebotwood*, (1) *adj.* hornless. 'I ŏŏdna-d-a car'd if the Maister 'ad soud that Bishop's Castle cow ŏŏth 'er wide 'orns, but to sell my pretty little *mwoilled* 'eifer—it did vex me.'
W. *moel*, bare, bald. Cf. **Oush-cow**.

(2) [mwoi·ld], *adj.* borderless, as of a cap.—PULVERBATCH. 'I like the childern to war nightcaps, it keeps the bousters clane, an' they done as well *mwoilled* as bordered.'

MOITHER, MITHER [moi·dhur' *and* mei·dhur'], both pronunciations obtain, and appear to be used indifferently, (1) *v. a.* and *v. n.* to distract; to perplex; to 'bother.' Com. (1) 'Them women's clack *mitherd* the poor chap tell 'e didna know whad 'e wuz sayin'.' (2) 'The Missis 'as gid me sich a power o' jobs all wantin' doin' at wunst, that I'm far *mithered*, an' canna tell which to start on first.' (3) 'Do it which way yo'n a mind, an' dunna *moither* me ŏŏth it.'
Perhaps connected with Du. *moedden*; Germ. *ermüden*, to tire.

(2) *v. n.* to talk incoherently—to ramble, as in feverish sleep, or delirium. Com. 'I thought the poor child wuz gweïn to 'ăve a faiver, fur 'er burnt like a coal, an' *moithered* all night.'
Bailey—ed. 1782—gives '*Welly Moidered*, almost crazed. *Chesh.*'

MOITHERED, *part. adj.* broken into very small flakes: said of curds. See **Jowters** (2).

MOITHERN, same as **Maythern**, q. v.—CORVE DALE, *Stanton Lacey*.

MOLE [moa·l], *sb.* a mould; a form. Com. 'Pŭt the pŭddin' i' the round *mole*, it looses best out o' that.'
'O.Fr. *Mole*, moule; ital. modano, esp., port., avec renversement du *l*, molde; de *modulus*.'—BUR.

MOLLYCOT, *sb.* a man who busies himself in such household matters as are peculiarly the woman's province: a derisive term. Com. ''E's whad I call a useful man in a 'ouse athout bein' a *mollycot*.' Compare Shakespeare's 'cot-quean' as applied to Capulet.—*Romeo and Juliet*, IV. iv. 7.

MOMBLE [mom·bl], (1) *sb.* a bungling job—''e'll mek a *momble* on it.'—NEWPORT.

(2) *v. a.* and *v. n.* to bungle; to do things in a clumsy way.—*Ibid.*

MOMBLED-UP, *part. adj.* dressed up awkwardly and ridiculously. —*Ibid.* Cf. **Moble** (2), also **Mommocked-up**.

MOMBLEMENT, *sb.* confusion; disorder.—PULVERBATCH. 'Mary, yo' al'ays get these drawers into a *momblement* an' mess w'enever yo' gŏ'n to 'em.'

MOMMET [mom·i't], (1) *sb.* a scarecrow.—CORVE DALE, *Stanton Lacey.*

> '——that ever any man should look
> Upon this *maumet*, and not laugh at him.'
> *Old Play*, in NARES.

Compare O.E. *mawmet*, an idol:—

> 'Do a-wei þi *Maumetes* · þei han trayed þe ofte;
> Let breken hem a-two . . . .'
> *Joseph of Arimathie*, l. 102.

Cf. **Malkin** (2).

(2) *sb.* a ghost; a spectre.—PULVERBATCH; ELLESMERE. 'I'd as lif gŏŏ i' the night as the day, I amma afeard o' *mommets*.'

MOMMOCK, (1). See **Mammock.**

(2) *v. a.* to dissipate; to squander.—WEM. ''E *mommocked* all 'is money away i' no time.'

(3) *v. a.* to tumble; to disarrange; to throw into confusion.—NEWPORT. 'See 'ow yo'n *mommocked* a' the clane things as Oi'd jŏost fo'ded.'

(4) *sb.* a litter.—*Ibid.* 'Eh! ye notty childern—mekkin sich a *mommock* all o'er the pleace.'

(5) *v. n.* to romp about, putting things into confusion. — *Ibid.* 'Dunna *mommock* about athatns,' is a common form of reproof.

MOMMOCKED-UP, *part. adj.* dressed up fantastically and absurdly. *Ibid.* Cf. **Mombled-up.**

MOMMOCKS. See **Mammocks.**

MON, *sb.* a man. Com. A form of frequent occurrence in the early writers.

> 'A *mon* to have iiij. benefyse, anoder no lyvynge,
> This is not Godys wyl.'
> JOHN AUDELAY'S *Poems*, p. 40.

MOON-DAISY, *sb.* *Chrysánthemum Leucánthemum*, great white Ox-eye.—CRAVEN ARMS.

MOOR [moa·ur' *and* moo·ur'], (1) *sb.* a tract of low-lying marsh land, as the 'Wealdmoors,' 'Bagley Moors,' &c.—*N. Shr.*

> 'And so forleost þe hund his fore
> And turnþ aȝen eft to þan *more*
> Þe fox can creope bi þe heie
> And turne ut from his forme weie
> And eft sone cume þar to
> Þonne is þes hundes smel fordo.'
> *Owl and Nightingale*, l. 818.

> 'Therto the frogs, bred in the slimie scowring
> Of the moist *moores* . . . . . .'
> SPENSER, *Virgils Gnat*, l. 230.

Mr. Halliwell says that 'in Suffolk any uninclosed land is called a *moor*.'

'A.S. *mór*; O.Icel. *mór*; O.Du. *moor, moer*; M.H.Germ. *muor*, moor.'—STRAT. Cf. **Moss.**

(2) *sb.* a low, marshy meadow by the water side.—WELLINGTON; NEWPORT. The term is used generically—'So and So has a good crop of hay off his *moors*,' the hay itself being, nevertheless, called 'meadow-hay.' But such-like meadows are often distinguished by *Moor* as a proper name—the 'Far *Moor*,' the 'Gossy *Moor*,' the 'Pigeon *Moors*,' &c. Compare Mr. Halliwell's note above.

MOOR-HEN, *sb.* the Water-Hen.—BRIDGNORTH.

'*Môrhen*, moor-hen. Wr. *Pol. Songs*, 158,' in STRAT.

Cf. **Morant**, below. See **Dab-chick.**

MOP, (1) *sb.*, *obs.*? a hiring fair.—LUDLOW; BRIDGNORTH. See Bk. II., *Folklore*, &c., 'Wakes, Fairs,' &c.

(2) *sb.* the gall of the Wild Rose.—SHREWSBURY, *Uffington*. The village school children give the name of *mop* to the pretty rose-gall, because they use it as such, for the purpose of cleaning their slates. 'Mary, we'n tak' dog's leave an' gŏŏ through the coppy this mornin' to 'unt *mops* to clane our slates w'en we bin loost out o' school—ŏŏn'ee come alung?' 'Aye, I'll come, but we mun tak' car' as the keeper dunna see us; 'e'll gie us *mops* else, an' be'appen stails as well.' See **Briar-Boss.**

MORAL [mu·r'ul], *sb.*, *pec.* the exact likeness; the express image; the model.—SHREWSBURY; CHURCH STRETTON. Qy. com. 'Dear 'eart alive! that little wench is the very *murral* on 'er Gran'mother, 'er'll be the owd ŏŏman o'er agen if 'er lives to see sixty sa' one.'

Mr. Nares says '*Moral* was sometimes confounded with *model*, and used for it; and I believe still is, by the ignorant.' He quotes the following:—

'Fooles be they that inveigh 'gainst Mahomet,
Who's but a *morral* of Love's monarchie.'

H. Const. Decad., 4 *Sonn.* 4.

MORANT, same as **Moor-Hen**, above.—BRIDGNORTH.

MORBAN [maur'·ban], *sb.* a silly person.—WHITCHURCH, *Whixall*. 'Whad a crazy owd *morban* it is:' said of an old man who was playing off some foolish antics.

MORF [maur'·f], *sb.* a thick, tangled crop, as of hair, weeds, &c.—PULVERBATCH; WEM. 'Whad a *morf* o' yar that fellow's got! it looks as if 'e'd cŏŏmed it ŏŏth a three-futted stool.' Cf. **Tellif.**

MORT [mau·r't], *sb.* a great deal; an abundance.—COLLIERY; NEWPORT.

'The next thing to being a man of property, was to have possessed worldly goods which had been "made away wi'," it scarcely mattered how. Indeed, even to have "made away wi' a *mort* o' money" one's self, was to be regarded as a man of parts and of no inconsiderable spirit.

'"Yo're in a *mort* o' trouble, Sammy, I mak' no doubt," remarked one oracle, puffing at his long clay.

'"Trouble enow," returned Sammy, shortly, "if yo' ca' it trouble to be on th' road to th' poor-house."'—FRANCES H. BURNETT, *That Lass o' Lowrie's*, A Lancashire Story, p. 90, ed. 1877.

Ash has '*Mort* (from the Islandick *margt, but judged inelegant*), a great quantity.'

Bailey—ed. 1782—gives '*Mort*, a great Abundance,' as '*Lincolnshire*.'

'O.N. *margt*, neuter of *margr*, much; *mart* (adv.), much.'—WEDG.

MORTIFY [mau·r'ti'fei], *v. a.* and *v. n.*, *pec.* to vex; to provoke; to disappoint; to abase. Com. ''E thinks 'imself a mighty fine fellow i' the Parish, but stop till the vestry-meetin', w'en 'e gets afore Mr. Jackson an' Dickin, they'n *mortify* 'is ambition fur 'im, yo'n see.' Compare *K. Henry V.*, I. i. 26.

MORUMS [moa·r'umz], *sb. pl.* mocking grimaces.—CRAVEN ARMS. 'Please, Sir, 'e's makin' *morums* at me.' Probably connected with the old word 'mow' or 'moe,' a wry face. Compare the following:—

> 'And other-whiles with bitter mockes and *mowes*
> He would him scorne . . . .'
>
> SPENSER, *F. Q.*, B. VI. c. vii. st. xlix.

'*Hamlet*. It is not very strange; for mine uncle is king of Denmark, and those that would make *mows* at him while my father lived, give twenty, forty, fifty, an hundred ducats a-piece for his picture in little.' —*Hamlet*, II. ii. 381.

'*Mowe*, or skorne. *Vangia, vel valgia*, CATH. *et* C. F. (*cachinna*, P.).' —*Prompt. Parv.*

'To make a *moe* like an ape. Distorquere os.'—BARET, *Alvearie*, A.D. 1580.

Cf. **Meow.**

MOSEY [moa·zi'], *adj.* dry; flavourless; 'woolly,' as apples, pears, &c. become when over-kept. Com. 'Them Goose-apples bin the sort to keep till Chris'mas, these yallow uns gwun as *mosey* an' pithy—like an owd turmit.'

Grose gives '*Mosey*, Mealy, a mosey apple. Glouc.'

MOSS, *sb.* a tract of wild marsh land; a morass; a peat-bog, as 'Whixall Moss,' 'Brown Moss,' &c.—*N. Shr.*

'*Mosses*, so moorish and boggy places are called in *Lancashire*.'—BLOUNT'S *Glossographia*, p. 421.

'O.N. *mosi*; Germ. *moos* . . . . . moss-grown, swampy, or moory places. *Donau-moos*, *Erdinger-moos*, tracts of such land in Bavaria.' —WEDG. Cf. **Moor** (1).

MOSS-BALLS, *sb. pl.* balls—sometimes called *Mere-balls*—found in Colemere, a long, narrow lake, rather more than two miles from Ellesmere; they are described by Mr. G. Christopher Davies as follows:—

'Peculiar to this mere [Colemere] . . . . . are the green *moss-balls* (*Conferva Ægagropila*), and brown balls composed of fir leaves. It is supposed that the bottom of the mere is troubled with conflicting eddies and currents, caused no doubt by springs, and that these currents catch up the fir leaves that fall from the trees on the south side of the mere, and roll them up, together with particles of *confervæ*, into balls of different sizes, even up to two feet in diameter. The *moss-balls* are composed entirely of *confervæ*. The currents convey these balls to the opposite side of the mere, and there they may be found in thousands at a depth of three or four feet. The cohesion of each ball is perfect.'—*Mountain, Meadow, and Mere*, p. 21, ed. 1873.

MOTE [moa·t], *sb. Tinea tapetzella*, the Clothes-moth. Com. 'The Missis says the *motes* han ete the Maister's top-coät all in 'oles—sarve it right an' all; 'er met a gid it to some poor owd fellow, to a kep' 'im warm, an' then it ŏŏdna a 'ad a *mote* in it.'

'And make to ȝou sachels that wexen not oolde, tresoure that failith not in heuenes, whidir a theef neiȝith not, nether *mouȝt* destruyeth.'—*Luke* xii. 33, Wicliffite version, ed. A.D. 1388.

'*Mouȝte*, clothe wyrme. *Tinea.* "*Mought*, that eateth clothes, *uers de drap.*"—PALSG.' *Prompt. Parv. and Notes.*

A.S. *moðþe;* O.Du. *motte*, a moth.

MOTHER, *sb.* a slimy, turbid substance concreted in stale beer or vinegar.—PULVERBATCH. Qy. com. Both Ash and Jamieson have the word in this sense. See *Mother*, in WEDG.

MOTHERING-SUNDAY. See Bk. II., *Folklore*, &c., 'Customs connected with Days and Seasons' (*Mid-Lent Sunday*).

MOTHER-LAW, *sb.*, *obsols.* a mother-in-law.—PULVERBATCH. 'I toud 'im if 'e couldna afford to tak' a 'ouse to lave me w'eer I wuz, fur I wunna gweïn to no *mother-law*.' See **Father-law**.

MOTTO, *sb.* the mark at which quoits are thrown.—BRIDGNORTH. Pegge gives *Motty*, for the same thing, as 'Derbyshire.'

MOULD [moa·ld], *v. a.* and *v. n.* to make the dough into loaves, &c. —SHREWSBURY; PULVERBATCH. Qy. com. 'Yo' met'n begin to *mould* up, the oven ŏŏl be ready agen yo' bin; an' get the proper skiver, I dunna like a fork:—

"Them as pricken ŏŏth fork or knife,
Ŏŏn never be 'appy, maïd nur wife."'

Amongst the 'Terms used by Bakers,' given by Randle Holme, are the following:—'*Mould* it [the bread], make it into Loaves or Roulls.' '*Prick the Loafe*, is to make little holes on the top of the Loafe with a Bodkin.'—*Academy of Armory*, Bk. III. ch. iii. pp. 85, 86.

'*Moolde* breed. *Pinso, pisto.*'—*Prompt. Parv.*

'One muldinge planke, one mouldinge trough with a cover,' are mentioned amongst other things belonging to '*The Back howse*,' in an *Inventory*, dated at Owlbury Manor-House, Bishop's Castle, 1625.

The '*muldinge planke*' would probably be the board upon which the loaves were made up, and the '*mouldinge trough*' like the '*kneading-trow*' described on p. 239, *ante*.

'*Hic panificator, Anᵐ*, a mouldere,' occurs under the head of '*Pistor cum suis Instrumentis*,' in a *Pictorial Vocabulary*, xv. cent., in Wr. vocabs., vol. i. p. 276; and Mr. Wright gives a note, to explain '*mouldere*' as 'The person who makes the dough into loaves.'

MOULD-BOARD [mou·ld buo·h'r'd], *sb.* that part of a plough which turns the furrows—the 'breast.'—ELLESMERE.

Randle Holme enumerates 'The *Mould Board*' amongst 'The parts of a Plow.' *Academy of Armory*, Bk. III. ch. viii. p. 333.

See **Shell-board.**

MOULDIWARP [moa·ldi'waa·r'p], PULVERBATCH. [mou·di'waar'·p], NEWPORT; OSWESTRY, *sb.* *Talpa Europœa*, the Mole. 'Yo' keepen yore dog well, Tummas, 'e's as alike as a *mouldiwarp*.' 'Aye, 'e keeps 'isself—'e's turned poacher! I 'spect to 'ăve 'im grinned or shot afore lung.'

> 'In which like *Moldwarps* nousling still they lurke.'
>
> SPENSER, *Colin Clouts come Home Again*, l. 763.

> '"Master, Master, see you yonder faire ancyent,
> yonder is the serpent & the serpents head,
> the *mould-warpe* * in the middest ffitt,
> & itt all shines with gold soe redde."'
>
> *Earle of Westmorlande*, l. 77. *Percy Folio MS.*, vol. i. p. 303, ed. Hales and Furnivall.

'* "Taulpe: f. The little beast called a Mole or *Moldewarp*."—Cotgrave. In Yorkshire *Mowldywarp* still.' Note by Mr. FURNIVALL.—*Ibid.*

Grose gives '*Mould-warp*, a mole. N.'

Mould(i)warp is, literally, *earth-caster*, from 'A.S. *molde;* O.Icel. *mold;* Goth. *mulda*, earth; and A.S. *weorpan;* O.Icel. *verpa;* Goth. *vairpa*, to throw, cast.'—See STRAT.

MOULDIWORT [moa·ldi'wur't *and* mou·li'wur't], same as above.—SHREWSBURY; WELLINGTON; WEM.

'He beareth Argent, a Mole (or *Mouldwart*), Sable. It is as black as a Coal, and soft as Velvet; having only his Feet, and a little tip at the Nose, of flesh colour. It is termed a *Want*, and a *Mouldwarp*.'—*Academy of Armory*, Bk. II. ch. x. p. 204.

> 'Whyles mice and *moudieworts* they howkit.'
>
> ROBERT BURN'S *Poems*, p. 2, l. 4.

Cf. **Ŏŏnt.**

MOUNT [mou·nt], *sb.* an embankment; a mound, artificially raised, as for ornamental grounds.—PULVERBATCH. 'I remember seein' the poor owd Squire in 'is green coăt, potchin' Snowdrops i' the *mount* up the drive, ŏŏth 'is walkin'-stick; an' they blowen as fresh now as they did'n twenty 'ear agŏŏ.'

MOUNTING [mou·ntin], *part. adj.*, *var. pr.* moulting, as birds.—SHREWSBURY; PULVERBATCH. Qy. com. 'Whad a pelrollock that peckled 'en looks now 'er's *mountin'!*' 'Aye, 'er'll be like yo', Bessie—look better w'en 'er gets new clo'es on.'

'*Mowtynge.* *Deplumacio.* "Mowter, *vide* moulter—*quando avium pennæ decidunt*."—GOULDM.' *Prompt. Parv. and Notes.*

Lat. *mutare*, to change (the feathers).

MOUSE-EAR, *sb.* *Stachys Germanica*, downy Woundwort (garden plant).—PULVERBATCH.

'*Mowseer*, herbe. *Muricula* (*auricalis muris*, K. P.).'—*Prompt. Parv.*

'*Auricula muris.* The hearbe *Mouse-eare*.'—*Dict. Etym. Lat.*

MOUTER [mou·tur'], *v. n.*, *var. pr.* to rot; to crumble with decay; to moulder—generally used in the past participial form. Qy. com. 'I dunna think the stillige safe fur a big barrel, the sides bin *moutered* as well as the legs.'

MOUTH-MAULING, (1) *sb.* a volley of abusive language.—PULVERBATCH. 'If I could get at 'im I'd gie 'im sich a *mouth-maulin'* as 'e never 'ad afore.' See **Maul**.

(2) *sb.* indistinct, drawling utterance; untunable singing.—*Ibid.* 'Yo' may call it chantin' or whad yo'n a mind, but I call it *mouth-maulin'*, fur nobody can tell whad they sen.'

MOW [mou·], (1) *sb.* a cluster of standing sheaves—generally six or eight.—SHREWSBURY; PULVERBATCH; ELLESMERE. Qy. com.

Tusser has *mow* in the sense of a stack:—

'Sharpe cutting spade, for the deuiding of *mow*.'
Husbandlie furniture, p. 38, ed. E. D. S.

'Look to the Cow, and the Sow, and the *Wheat-mow*, and all will be well enow. *Somerset*.'—RAY'S *Proverbs*, p. 271.

A.S. *múga*; O.N. *múgr*, a stack; a heap. Cf. **Stuck**.

(2) [mou·], *v. a.*, *var. pr.* to mow.—BISHOP'S CASTLE; CLUN. 'Dun yo' see that mon *mōwin'* them wuts?' A.S. *máwan*, to mow. See **Hoe**.

(3) See **Meow**.

MOW-BURNT, *adj.* heated in the stack, as of hay, oats, &c., which have not been seasoned properly before stacking. Qy. com. 'Bill says 'e thinks the 'ay's toasted a bit too much, but the cattle āten it, an' dun well—it's none the worse fur bein' a bit *mow-burnt*.'

'Corne being had downe (any way ye alow),
should wither as needeth, for *burning in mow*:
Such skill appertaineth to haruest mans art,
and taken in time is a husbandly part.'
TUSSER, *Fiue Hundred Pointes of Good Husbandrie* [August].

'*Mow-burn* is occasioned by the Hay being stack'd too soon, before its own juice is thoroughly dried, and by Norfolk people is called the *Red Raw*; not such as is occasioned by stacking it when wet with Rain, which is a nasty musty and stinks.'—*Tusser Redivivus* (A.D. 1710), in E. D. S. ed., p. 290.

Pegge gives '*Mow-burnt-hay*, hay that has fermented in the stack. York.' See **Mow** (1), above.

MUCHIN, MUCKIN [mukh·i'n], CLUN. [muk·in], WEM, *sb.* a pig. 'I've bought a fresh *muckin*, wun'ee come an' see 'im?'

W. *mochyn*; Gael. *muk*, a pig.

MUCK, *sb.* and *v. a.* manure; to manure (land). Com.

Mr. Oliphant, speaking of *The Bestiary*—a poem in the East Midland Dialect, written about A.D. 1230—remarks:—'There are many Scandinavian words found here;' and he enumerates, amongst others, '*Muck.* Icel. *mykr*.'—*Sources of Standard English*, p. 131.

MUCKER, *sb.* a state of dirt and confusion.—COLLIERY.

MUCKERED, *adj.* said of milk that has acquired a bad flavour—but not become sour—by being kept in a close place.—PULVERBATCH. 'Bessie, this milk ŏŏnna do fur the child, it's *muckered*—I doubt yo'n 'ad it i' the cubbert, else it ŏŏdna a gwun like this.' See **Muckery**, below.

MUCKERING, *adj.* living, or working, in a dirty, slovenly manner. —PULVERBATCH. Qy. com. 'I like plenty o' clier waiter throwed down the dairy; none o' yore *muckerin'* work, moppin' about the milk-pons—the butter's sure to tell yo' on it.'

MUCKERY, *adj.* damp; close, as of the weather.—PULVERBATCH. 'This *muckery* weather's despert bad fur the corn, it'll mak' it spurt.' Jamieson has '*Moch*, *Mochy*, close; misty.' Cf. **Muggy**, below.

MUCKETER, *sb.* a child's pinafore.—CLEE HILLS.

Mr. Nares supposes *mucketer* to be a corruption of '*Muckender*,' a pocket-kerchief—a *mouchoir;* but adds that Baret, in his *Alvearie*, refers '*mucketter* to *bib*.' See *Mucketer*, *Muckender*, in WEDG.

MUG, *sb.* a mist; a fog.—PULVERBATCH.

MUGGY, *adj.* foggy; damp; close. Qy. com. 'Theer wuz sich a *mug* this mornin' yo' couldna see 'afe-a-dozen yards afore yo'—we'n 'ad a power o' *muggy* weather lately.'

'O.N. *mugga*, dark, thick weather,' in WEDG.

Compare W. *mwg*, smoke.

MUGWOOD, *sb.*, *var. pr. Artemísia vulgáris*, Mugwort.—WORTHEN. *Mugwood* seems to be a hybrid form, due probably to some confusion between the respective names, *Mugwort* and *Wormwood* (*Artemisia Absinthium*); but compare the following, on the matter of pronunciation:—

'Mogwort, al on as seyn some, modirwort: lewed folk þat in manye wordes conne no ryȝt sownynge, but ofte shortyn wordys, and changyn lettrys and silablys, þey coruptyn þe o. in to u. and d. in to g. and syncopyn i-smytyn a-wey i. and r. and seyn mugwort.'—*Arundel MS.* 42, f. 35 vo., in WAY.

MULLIGRUBS, *sb.* the colic. Qy. com. 'Sick of the *mulligrubs* with eating chopp'd hay.'—RAY's *Proverbs*, p. 60.

MULLOCK, *sb.* dirt; rubbish, as of the refuse of masons' work, gardeners' sweepings, &c.—SHREWSBURY; PULVERBATCH; CORVE DALE; WEM. 'Whad bin'ee gweïn to do ŏŏth all this *mullock?* yo' mun clier it all away afore Sunday.'

'The *mullok* on an hepe ysweped was,
And on the floor ycast a canevas,
And al this *mullok* in a syve ythrowe,
And sifted, and ypiked many a throwe.'

CHAUCER, G. 938—940 (Six-text ed.), Skeat.

Grose gives '*Mullock*, Dirt or rubbish. N.'

Mullock is a diminutive = O.E. *mull* + *ock*.

'Muk, or duste (mul, K. S. *mull*, P.) *Pulvis*. The term *mull* is still retained in the Eastern counties, and in the North, and signifies, according to Forby, soft, breaking soil. "Molle, *pulver*, *et cetera ubi* powder."—CATH. ANG. Compare Low Germ. and Dutch, *mul;* Ang.-Sax. *myl, pulvis.* "Mullock, or mollock, *vide* dust, or dung."—GOULDM.' *Prompt. Parv. and Notes.*

See **Black-mullock.**

MULLOCKY, *adj.* untidy; all in a litter.—CHURCH STRETTON.

MUMCHANCE [mum·chans], *adv.* stupidly silent.—PULVERBATCH. 'W'y dunna yo' spake, lad?—an' nod stand *mumchance* theer like a dummy in a draper's shop.'

Mr. Halliwell says that 'in Devon a silent, stupid person is called a *mumchance,* Milles' MS. Gloss.' He refers the term to an 'old game, mentioned by Cotgrave and others, in which, according to some, silence was an indispensable requisite.' See *Mum-chance,* in WEDG.

MUMRUFFIN [mum·r'uf·'in], *sb.* the long-tailed Titmouse.—CLUN, *Clungunford;* BRIDGNORTH. See **Canbottle.**

MUN, *aux. vb.* must. Com.

'I *Mun* be maried a Sunday,
I *mun* be maried a Sunday,
Who foeuer ſhall come that way,
I *mun* be maried a Sunday.'
Roister Doister, The fourth Song, p. 87.

Mr. Oliphant says that in the 'Ormulum' [A.D. 1200, *circa*] Ormin uses 'a new Scandinavian auxiliary verb, which is employed even now from Caithness to Derbyshire. Such a phrase as *I mun do this* is first found in his work; the *mun* is the Scandinavian *muna,* but *mune* in the "Ormulum" implies futurity more than necessity.'—*Sources of Standard English,* p. 104.

Cf. **Maun.**

MUNCORN [mungk·ur'n], *sb., obsols.* mixed corn—wheat and rye ground together for bread-meal.—PULVERBATCH. '*Muncorn* bread's very sweet an' good, but theer's nuthin' like a bit o' good w'eäten flour.'

'And mene *mong-corn bred* · to her mete fongen,
And wortes flechles wroughte · & water to drinken.'
P. Pl. Cr., l. 786.

'Some *mixeth to miller the rie with the wheat,*
Temmes *lofe* on his table to haue for to eate:
But sowe it not mixed, to growe so on land,
least rie tarie wheat, till it shed as it stand.'
TUSSER, *Fiue Hundred Pointes of Good Husbandrie* [September].

Tusser called this mixed corn '*mestlen.*'

'Mestlyone, or *monge corne* (or . . . mongerne, S.). *Mixtilio,* bigermen.'—*Prompt. Parv.*

See WAY'S Note. A.S. *mengan,* to mix. Cf. **Munker.**

MUNDLE [mund·l], (1) *sb.* a utensil variously employed for purposes of stirring, as a mashing-*mundle* (q. v. *ante*), a cream-*mundle,* &c.; but the term is most often heard in the dairy, where the *mundle* is in constant requisition for stirring the cream in the deep 'steans' in which it is gathered for the churn. A *cream-mundle* is a flattish piece of wood, sometimes divided at the lower and broader end in such a way as to admit of the cream passing through it, thereby making the necessary operation of stirring the cream about, much more effectual. Com.

'*Mundle*, a pudding-slice. Derb.'—PEGGE.

See **Lick the crame-mundle.**

(2) *v. n.* to bungle; to do a thing awkwardly.—PULVERBATCH; CHURCH STRETTON. 'Dear 'eart alive! 'ow yo' bin *mundlin'* o'er that bit on a job; 'ere, gie it me if yo' canna do it no better—I hanna one bit o' patience to see yo' messin' at it athatn.'

MUNGE [munj·], (1) *v. n.* to eat greedily and by stealth.—PULVERBATCH. 'That girld's al'ays *mungin'*, 'er never gwuz i' the buttery athout 'elpin' 'erself—'er met never get a meal's-mate, an' look at 'er *munge, munge, mungin'*.'

'"I monche, I eate meate gredyly in a corner, *ie loppine.*"—PALSG. Bp. Kennett gives "to *munge*, to eat greedily; Wilts."—Lansd. MS. 1033.'—WAY'S Note in *Prompt. Parv.*, p. 342.

(2) same as **Minge**, q. v.—PULVERBATCH. A corrupted form apparently.

MUNGER [munj'ur'], *v. n.* to mutter; to grumble in an undertone. —PULVERBATCH; WEM. 'W'y dunna yo' say whad yo' han to say?—an' nod *munger* about the 'ouse athatn, like a 'umbly-bee in a churn.' Connected with O.E. *munge*, to tell, speak:—

'þan gan Meliors *munge* · þe meschef þat hir eyled;
þat oþer comsede to carp · of cumfort & ioie,
& eþer *munged* of þe mater · þat þai most louede.'
William of Palerne, ll. 831—833.

'A.S. *myngian*; O.H.Germ. *munigon*, to admonish.'—STRAT.

Cf. **Junder** (1).

MUNKER, *sb.*, *obsols.* mixed corn,—wheat and rye grown together as a crop, for grinding into bread-meal.—BRIDGNORTH, *Worfield.* It is said that the old practice of sowing wheat and rye together in this part of Shropshire arose, primarily, from a doubt whether the land would produce a good crop of wheat, therefore the rye—which was not so likely to fail—was sown also.

'If soile doe desire to haue rie with the wheat,
by growing togither, for safetie more great,
Let white wheat be ton, be it deere, be it cheape,
the sooner to ripe, for the sickle to reape.'
TUSSER, *Fiue Hundred Pointes of Good Husbandrie* [September].

The term *Munker* is evidently corrupted from **Muncorn**, q. v.

MURGY [mur'gi'], *sb.* a contemptuous term for a miner or collier.—WELLINGTON. Compare '*Murche*, lytyll man,' in *Prompt. Parv.*, upon which Mr. Way remarks:—'This name for a dwarf does not appear to be retained in any of the local dialects, although preserved, as it would appear, in the sirname *Murchison.*'

MURRAL. See **Moral.**

MUSE, SMUSE [meu·s], PULVERBATCH; WELLINGTON. Qy. com.

[smeu·s], WEM, *sb.* a small hole or 'run' through a hedge, made by a hare or rabbit in its track.

'Take a hare without a *muse*,
And a knave without excuse,
And hang them up.'
HOWELL'S *English Proverbs*, p. 12, *a*, in Nares.

'——I know your *musees*, your inlets and outlets, and wherever the rabbets pass, the ferret or weezel may venture.'—RAVENSCROFT, *Careless Lovers*, 1673, in Wr.

Cf. **Fare** (1).

MUSEY [meu·zi'], *adj.* inquisitive.—WHITCHURCH; ELLESMERE. 'Tak' car' whad yo' bin about, 'er's very *musey*.'

MUSICIANER, *sb.*, *obsols.* a performer on a musical instrument,—a musician.—PULVERBATCH; WEM. Qy. com. 'Who 'ad'n'ee fur a *musicianer* at the daincin'?' 'One o' the blind Tithers [Tudors] o' the Gattin played the fiddle [1815]—that wuz all the music we 'ad'n.'

'He beareth Argent, a *Musicioner* playing on a Treble Vial, cloathed all in blew with a Scarlet Cloak hanging on his back, Hat Sable, Feather Gules. This is the Crest of *Fidler* in *Countryton*.'—*Academy of Armory*, Bk. III. ch. iii. p. 156.

MUST, *sb.* ground apples (for cider).—CLEE HILLS. Cf. **Pomice**.

MUST-TUB, *sb.* the tub into which the apple-pulp is put, in the process of cider making.—*Ibid.*

'*Must tub*.'—*Auctioneer's Catalogue* (Stoddesden), 1870.

MUZZLE, *v. n.* to root with the snout, as pigs do.—PULVERBATCH. 'Tell Humphrey Robe'ts to send a dozen rings fur the little pigs, they bin beginnin' to *muzzle*, I see.' Mr. Halliwell has this for 'Devon.'

MY OONS, *interj.* perhaps a corruption of some Romish adjuration having reference to the 'Sacred *Wounds*.' Com. The term in its present form seems to be pretty old, and Farquhar *may* have heard it by 'Severn Side:'—

'*Braz.* Will you fight for the Lady, Sir?
Plume. No, Sir, but I'll have her notwithstanding.
Thou Peerless Princess of Salopian Plains,
Envy'd by Nymphs and worship'd by the Swains—
Braz. Oons, sir! not fight for her!
Plume. Prithee be quiet—I shall be out—'
. . . .
Recruiting Officer, Act III. Scene.—The walk by the Severn Side [Shrewsbury].

NAB [nab·], (1) *v. a.*, *sl.?* to dupe; to trick. Com. The Rev. Wm. Gilpin of Church Pulverbatch, preaching to his rural congregation in Churton Church—about 1836—said, 'Some of you, some of you, calling yourselves honest men go to the fair to buy and to sell, and when you come back, you boast that you "*nabbed* the chap!"'

'*Nab* me, I'll *nab* thee.'—RAY'S *Proverbs*, p. 274.

(2) *v. a.*, *sl.?* to seize hold of unexpectedly. Com. 'The "Bobbies" 'an bin lookin' out for them poachin' chaps a good wilde, but they *nabbed* 'em at the far.'

'Dan. *nappe*, to snatch; snatch at; pluck.'—WEDG.

NAG [nag·], (1) *v. a.* and *v. n.* to irritate the temper by constant fault-finding; to carp. Com. 'I'm despert sorry fur poor Samwel; 'e wuz a right tidy mon afore 'e got married, but 'is wife's *nagged* 'im, tell 'e's bin far druv to drink—as yo' met'n say—by a ŏŏman's tongue.'

'N. *nagga*, to gnaw; to irritate, plague, disturb.'—WEDG.

(2) *v. n.* to keep up a slight but constant pain; to gnaw, as of an aching tooth. Com. 'I couldna sleep las' night fur the tuth-ache, it wunna to say violent, but kep' *nag*, *nag*, *naggin'* all the wilde till about four o'clock.'

NAGER [nai·gur'], *sb.*, *var. pr.* an auger.—CLUN. 'Fowre *nagers*' are enumerated amongst sundry miscellaneous items in an *Inventory*, dated at Owlbury Manor-House, Bishop's Castle, 1625.

'*Terebrum*, navegar,' occurs in *Archbp. Ælfric's Vocabulary*, x. cent. See Wr. vocabs., vol. i. p. 16. *Nauger* is the correct form, not *auger*.

NAIL-PASSER, *sb.* a gimlet. Com. Called a 'Nail-piercer' by Randle Holme. Cf. **Bore-passer**.

NAINT, *sb.* an aunt.—SHREWSBURY; PULVERBATCH; ELLESMERE. Qy. com. 'As yo' comen throm school, Mary, gŏŏ by the Bonk an' axe 'ow yore Nuncle's ancler is, an' tell yore *Naint* I'm gweïn to Soseb'ry o' Saturd'y if 'er wants a narrand.' Cf. **Aint**, also **Nuncle**.

NAKED AS A ROBIN, *phr.* quite naked: said chiefly of an un-dressed child,—'W'y yo' bin as *naked as a robin*.' Com.

NAKED-LADY, *sb.* *Colchicum autumnale*, the Autumnal Crocus.—SHREWSBURY.

NAN, *interj.* and *interrog.*, *obsols.* this term is equivalent to the 'I beg your pardon' of modern 'polite society,' when an observation has been either not heard or not understood; it scarcely amounts to 'What do you say?' *Nan* is very seldom used now; only a few of the aged folk seem to retain it [1875].—PULVERBATCH; CHURCH STRETTON; CLUN.

Pegge has '*Nan*, used as an interrogation; as—Nan? *i. e.* What did you say? Kent.' See *Anan* in HAL.

NANCY, *sb.* the pudding in a pig which is next in size to the paunch.—PULVERBATCH. See **Roger**.

NANNY, (1) *sb.* same as **Nancy**, above. CLUN. See **Hodge**.

(2) *sb.* the stomach.—WELLINGTON. Cf. **Duff** (2).

NANNY-NINE-HOLES, *sb.* *Lampetra fluviátilis*, the Lampern.—SHREWSBURY; PULVERBATCH. Qy. com.

NAP-AT-NOON, same as **Betty-go-to-bed-at-noon**, q. v.—ELLESMERE.

NATION, *adv.*, *sl.?* very,—'*nation* cowd.' Com. Pegge gives this for 'Kent, Norf., and Suff.'

NATIVE [nai·tiv], *adj.*, *pec.* used elliptically for 'native place,'—'Worthen's my *native.*' Com.

NATURE, *sb.*, *pec.* natural goodness; nutrition: said of food.—NEWPORT. A shopkeeper observed to one of his customers [1872] that, having tried the Australian meat, he found he could not recommend it, for it was 'so overdone, there seemed to be no *nature* left in it.'

NAVE [nai·v], *sb.* a prop to support the shaft of a loaded cart when the horse is out; it is made of a strong oak-branch having three forks, which serve for feet—the branch being inverted.—PULVERBATCH.

Grose has '*Nape*, or Nepe. A piece of wood that hath three feet, used to support the fore part of a loaded waggon. N.' Cf. **Vamp.**

NAY-WORD, *sb.* a by-word.—PULVERBATCH; CLEE HILLS. 'I ŏŏnna be the first to be married at the new church; I amma gweïn to be a *nay-word* to all the parish.'

'. . . if I do not gull him into a *nay-word*, and make him a common recreation, do not think I have wit enough to lie straight in my bed.'—*Twelfth Night*, II. iii. 146.

NEAR, NEAR-FISTED, *adj.*, *pec.* penurious; stingy; grasping. Com. 'It's nuthin' like the same place sence the poor owd Missis died, they bin so *near* an' grindin'—nobody likes to gŏŏ nigh the 'ouse.'

'*Near*, covetous. North. As, He is a *near* man.'—PEGGE.

NECK, *v. a.* to kill fowls by pulling their necks out, or rabbits by giving them a blow on the back of the neck.—SHREWSBURY; WHITCHURCH. Qy. com.

NECK-HOLE, *sb.* the nape of the neck. Com.

NEEDLESS [need·lis], (1) *adj.*, *pec.* shiftless; helpless.—PULVERBATCH. 'I'm despert sorry fur that mon, 'e's got sich a *needless* piece fur a wife—'is wages bin gwun afore 'e 'as 'em—an' 'e's right tidy 'isself.'

(2) *adj.*, *pec.*, *obsols.* nameless: said of an unbaptized infant.—ELLESMERE, *Welshampton.* 'Whad'n'ee call that child?' 'Oh, it's *needless* yet, poor thing, it hanna bin chris'ned.'

NEEDNA, *v. a.* need not; have no occasion to be, &c. Com.

'*Roger.* I *needna* mak' sic speed my blood to spill,
I'll warrant death come soon enough a-will.'
ALLAN RAMSAY, *The Gentle Shepherd*, I. i. p. 9.

NEELD. See **Nild.**

NE'ER-A, contraction of **Never-a**, q. v.

NEESENIN', *part. adj.* nesting—seeking for birds' nests.—NEWPORT. See **Nests.**

NEEST, *sb.*, *var. pr.* a nest.—NEWPORT; ELLESMERE. See **Nests.**

NESH [nesh·], (1) *adj.* delicate; tender: said of the health or physical constitution. Com. (1) 'It wunna likely as a poor little *nesh* child like 'er could do; it ŏŏd tak' a strung girld i' that place.'

(2) 'Yo' lads be off out o' doors, an' nod rook round the fire—yo'n be as *nesh* as a noud ŏŏman.'

'Wummon is of *nesche* flesche.'
Owl and Nightingale, l. 1387.

'"God saue the Queene of England," he said,
"for her blood is verry *neshe*,
as neere vnto her I am
as a colloppe shorne from the flesh."'
King James and Browne, l. 119. *Percy Folio MS.*, vol. i. p. 141, ed. Hales and Furnivall.

(2) *adj.* poor-spirited; lacking energy.—WEM. ''Er's a *nesh* piece, 'er dunna do above 'afe a day's work, an' 'er's no use at all under a cow [milking a cow].'

'A.S. *hnesc;* O.Du. *nesch;* Goth. *hnasqus;* nesh, *mollis, tener.*'—STRAT.

NEST, *adv.* next.—COLLIERY.

'And sum sais bot þe *nest* yeire
Foluand . . . .'
Cursor Mundi (A.D. 1320, *circa*). *Specim. Early Eng.*, vii. l. 5.

A.S. *neahst;* Dan. *næst*, nighest; next. Cf. **Nigh.**

NESTS, *sb. pl.* [nee·zn], SHREWSBURY; NEWPORT; WEM; OSWESTRY. [nes·i'z], SHREWSBURY; CLUN; CORVE DALE; LUDLOW. [nis·i'z], PULVERBATCH; WORTHEN; CLUN. [nis·ts], SHREWSBURY; PULVERBATCH; WORTHEN; CLUN. [nee·sts], ELLESMERE. Of the different plurals of *nest* obtaining in the Shrewsbury district, it may be observed that *neesen* is one chiefly employed by the aged folk; a fact which seems to point to the conclusion that it is *in se* the oldest form of all that are here given.

NEVER-A, *adv.* not a, or one. Com. 'Theer's *never-a* spot o' milk i' the 'ouse.'

'he had *neuer a* penny left in his pursse,
neuer a penny but 3,
& one was brasse, & another was lead,
& another was white mony.'
The Heir of Lin, ll. 33, 34. *Percy Folio MS.*, vol. i. p. 176, ed. Hales and Furnivall.

See *Matt.* xxvii. 14.

NEVER-A-ONE, none; neither. Com. '*Never-a-one* on 'em ossed to 'elp.' See **Grammar Outlines** (*indefinite pronouns*).

NEW-FANGLED, *adj.* new; new-fashioned; novel, as of some pursuit or 'hobby.'—SHREWSBURY; PULVERBATCH; ELLESMERE. Qy. com. (1) 'I'll a none o' them *new-fangled* ways; I like things done as they bin use't to be, an' I know yo' canna mend 'em.' (2) 'W'y, dear 'eart alive! Jenny, whad *new-fangled* fashions han yo' got i' yore yed now?' said a Welshampton woman to her daughter, who was just come home from her 'place' with newly-acquired tastes, which she was busily disclosing.

'So *newefangel* ben they of hir mete,
And louen nouelries of propre kynde.'
CHAUCER, F. 618 (Six-text ed.), Skeat.

'At Christmas I no more desire a rose
Than wish a snow in May's *new-fangled* mirth.'
Love's Labour Lost, I. i. 106.

Mr. Oliphant says that Chaucer was the first to use '*Newfangel*.' Mr. Nares and the editors of '*The Bible Word-Book*' alike remark of *New-fangled* that it is 'not yet quite obsolete.' See *Fangle*, in WEDG. Cf. **Fangled** (*ante*).

NEW-YIS-TIDE, *sb.*, *obsols.* the New-year's-tide; the beginning of the year.—PULVERBATCH. A couplet which sets forth that the days attain a slightly increased length at this season runs as follows:—

'*New-yis-tide*
A cock-stride.'

NEX'-TO-NEX', *adv.* in order of succession; consecutively,—'three nights *nex'-to-nex'*.'—SHREWSBURY; CLUN. Qy. com.

NICE, *adj.* over-particular; fastidious—in regard of food. Com. ''E shall shift 'is fit from under my table, 'e's got'n so despert *nice*, theer's nuthin' good enough fur 'im.'

'*Portia.* In terms of choice I am not solely led
By *nice* direction of a maiden's eyes.'
Merchant of Venice, II. i. 14.

'More *nice* than wise.'—RAY'S *Proverbs*, p. 203.

NIGH, *adv.* and *prep.* near—regularly compared, as, ''E never come *nigh*, fur all 'e promised.' 'Draw up *nigher* the fire.' ''E stŏŏd at the top *nighest* the Maister.' Com.

'—was *neiȝe* atte deþe.'—*William of Palerne*, l. 1511.

'And *neigh* the castel swiche ther dwelten three.'
CHAUCER, B. 550 (Six-text ed.), Skeat.

'*Prospero.* Why, that's my spirit!
But was not this *nigh* shore?
Ariel. Close by, my master.'
Tempest, I. ii. 15.

A note in the *Bible Word-Book* says that *nigh* is 'a common provincialism in Suffolk.' See DR. MORRIS'S *Historical English Accidence*, p. 108.

A.S. *neáh, néh;* sp. *nýhst*, nigh, nighest, of which the comp. is *nearr'a*. Cf. **Nest**, also **Anigh**.

NIGHT-HAWK, *sb.* the European Goat-sucker.—CLUN, *Clungunford Hill* and *Shelderton Rocks;* OSWESTRY. See *Nyghte Crowe* in *Prompt. Parv.* with WAY'S Note. Cf. **Churn-owl**, also **Lich-fowl**.

NIGHT-JAR, same as above.—BRIDGNORTH.

NILD [nil·d], (1) *sb.*, *var. pr.* a neeld—old form for needle. Com. 'Come an' look my knittin'-*nild*—theer's a good child.' 'W'y yo'n stuck it i' yore cap, Gran!' Slight stitching that won't hold is said to have been 'sewed ŏŏth a wut [hot] *nild* an' a burnin' thrid.'

'We, Hermia, like two artificial gods,
Have with our *neelds* created both one flower,
Both on one sampler, ...'
Midsummer Night's Dream, III. ii. 204.

'*Acus*, nelde,' occurs in a *Semi-Saxon Vocabulary*, in Wr. vocabs., vol. i. p. 94. A.S. *nǽdl*, a needle.

(2) *sb.* a needle used in stemming holes for blasting.—PULVERBATCH, *Arscott.* Qy. com. M. T. Cf. **Pricker.**

NILE, same as **Caplin,** q. v.—CORVE DALE; LUDLOW.

NIMBLE-TAILOR, *sb.* the Long-tailed Titmouse.—BRIDGNORTH. See **Bottle-tit.**

NINE-CORNS, *sb., sl.* the last after-supper pipe.—CLEE HILLS. Qy. com. 'I'll gŏŏ an' a my *nine-corns*, an' then I'll be off to bed.'

NINETED, *adj.* addicted to evil ways. Com. ''E's a *nineted* pippin': said of a vicious youth.

NINTE [nei·nt], (1) *v. a.* to beat. Qy. com. 'Billy, if yo' dunna come back an' get on wuth that leasin' I'll *ninte* yore 'ide fur yo'': so said 'Jack-the-Rot's' daughter to her boy.

(2) *v. n.* to go along.—CLEE HILLS; LUDLOW; BRIDGNORTH. 'They wun comin' alung as fast as the pony could *ninte.*'

NIPPIT [nip·it], *v. n.* to go quickly; to hurry.—CRAVEN ARMS. 'W'en I 'eärd the w'istle, didnad I *nippit?*'

NISGAL [niz·gul], (1) *sb.* the smallest and weakliest of a brood of any kind of domestic fowls.—PULVERBATCH. 'I've nussed this poor lickle *nisgal* in ŏŏl this two days an' nights, an' see 'ow peärt 'e's gotten.'

(2) *sb.* the smallest of a litter of pigs.—CLUN; LUDLOW.

NITTY [nit·i'], *adj.* bright; sparkling: said of ale. Com. 'I wuz frittened w'en I tapped the ale, it looked jest like barm i' the jug; but w'en I poured it i' the glass it wuz *nitty*, an' as clier as sack.'

'Nitid (*nitidus*), clean, . . . fair, bright.'—BLOUNT'S *Glossographia*, p. 435.

'Lat. *nitido*, to make bright or clear.'—*Dict. Etym. Lat.*

NO, *adv., pec.* not. Com. 'Well, I carna w'ether yo' dun it or *no*, it's all the same to me.'

NOBBLETY, same as **Noggety,** below.—WEM.

NOBBY, *sb.* a sucking foal.—SHREWSBURY; PULVERBATCH; CRAVEN ARMS.

NOD, *adv.* not. Com. See **T** (1) in **Grammar Outlines** (*consonants*).

NOD 'AFE BAD, *phr.* very good. Com. 'Well, Joe, did they give you what you liked?' asked a clergyman of an old man who had just had a capital dinner in the rectory kitchen. 'W'y, iss, Sir,' said Joe, doggedly, 'they pŭt me a bit o' bif, an' it *wunnad 'afe bad.*' To express approval or opinion in this negative, doubtful fashion is a characteristic of Shropshire folk, and, until it is understood, is often a source of vexation to strangers who dwell in their midst, as when a clergyman recently come to his benefice heard himself thus appraised 'Our paas'n *inna so bad* as some, that's all I 'ave to say fur 'im;'—he was much disturbed, till a friend assured him that the remark was meant to convey the speaker's decided approbation of his rector.

NO DANGER, *interj.* Not at all likely! Nothing of the kind!—a deprecatory exclamation constantly in use, *àpropos*, or *malàpros*, to the occasion. Com. 'So I 'ear yo' bin gweïn to be married, Tum. '*No daïnger*, Missis—axin' i' church inna marryin', an' I amma come to that yit.' See **A** (13) in **Grammar Outlines** (*vowels*, &c.). Cf. **Danger**.

NOGGEN [nog·n], (1) *adj.*, *obsols.* made of *nogs*,—coarse refuse of flax or hemp.—PULVERBATCH; CLEE HILLS.

'*In the trunk at the end of the Presse. Imprimis* eyghtenne payre of hempten sheets and six paire of *noggen* sheets vij^{s}.'—*Inventory* . . . Owlbury Manor-House, Bishop's Castle, 1625.

Cf. **Herden**.

(2) *adj.*, *obsols.* dull; stupid; rough.—PULVERBATCH; CLEE HILLS; MUCH WENLOCK; WELLINGTON. 'A *noggen* mother's better than a gowden faither:' so said old Molly Johnson of Wrockwardine, then [1857] in her ninety-fourth year; she was speaking of a young family left motherless, and she gave it as the 'experience of life' that the homely old proverb was a true saying.

NOGGEN-YEDDED, same as **Noggle-yedded**, below.—WEM.

NOGGETY [nog·uti'], *adj.* big; clumsy, as of the head of a walking-stick.—PULVERBATCH, *Arscott*. 'Han yo' sid my stick?' 'No; whad sort wuz it—a 'ooked un?' 'No; a *noggety-yedded* un.' Cf. **Nobblety**.

NOGGLER, *sb.*, *obsols.* a stupid person; a blockhead.—PULVERBATCH. See **Noggling**, below.

NOGGLE-YEDDED, *adj.*, *obsols.* thick-headed; stupid.—PULVERBATCH. ''E's a *noggle-yedded* auf—nuthin' better.' Cf. **Noggen-yedded**, above.

NOGGLING, *adj.*, *obsols.* bungling; blundering. — PULVERBATCH. 'Well, yo' han maden a *nogglin'* job o' that, any ways.' 'Whad did'n'ee spect different, w'en yo' knowed as I wuz nuthin' but a *noggler* afore I started on it.' See **Noggler**, above.

NOG-MAN [nog·mun], *sb.*, *obs.* a country weaver.—PULVERBATCH. 'Poor owd Spake [Speake] the *nog-man* called to beg a spot o' drink; it's 'ard times ŏŏth 'im now nobody spins—'e tells me 'e gets a bit o' yorn from the factory, an' waives it 'imself, an' it shoots them folks as bin too lazy to spin fur tharselves.' Sometimes a rope-maker was called a *nog-man*.

NO GREAT SHAKES, *phr.* not good for much; 'below par.' Com. ''Ow bin'ee, Matty?—I hanna sid yo' this lung wilde.' 'Well, indeed, I'm *no great shakes*: I've bin tossicated ŏŏth one thing or other, the bwoy breakin' is leg an' that—'e met as well a bin killed.'

NOGS, *obsols.* same as **Herdes**, q. v.—PULVERBATCH; CLEE HILLS. Der. 'noggen' (1).

NONE, *adv.*, *pec.* a very short time; next to no time, as of going or coming. Com. 'Now, Ted, I want yo' to run a narrand for me, an' yo' mun be *none* away, else the Maister ŏŏl be 'ere afore yo.'

NON-PLUSH, *sb.*, *var. pr.*, *pec.* a position of difficulty or disadvantage.—PULVERBATCH. Qy. com. 'Poor owd Mr. Ambler! 'e wuz the best mon i' the parish ŏŏth 'is chem—'e ŏŏdna see a poor neĭghbour at a *non-plush* fur a bit o' coal, or anythin' else as men or 'orses coulden do.'

NONSICAL, *adj.*, *var. pr.* nonsensical—in a disagreeable way.—PULVERBATCH; WEM. 'Never 'eed whad that fellow says, 'e's al'ays on ŏŏth 'is *nonsical* talk.'

NOOK-SHOTTEN, (1) *adj.* having many sharp turns and angles.—WHITCHURCH, *Whixall.* An old farmer cautioned a certain person against taking a short cut across some fields because the way was very '*neuk-shotten.*'

'—that *nook-shotten* isle of Albion.'
K. Henry V., IV. v. 14.

'Layamon [A.D. 1205, *circa*] has the word *nook* (angulus). . . . . The poet, speaking of a mere, says, "Feower *noked* he is." . . . There are some other common words, which he is the first English writer to use.'—*Sources of Standard English*, pp. 114, 115.

(2) *part. adj.* stationed—as a matter of idle habit—in the chimney-corner:—'Sich a *neuk-shotten* thing inna wuth 'er saut.'—WHITCHURCH, *Tilstock.*

'Kate sits i' the *neuk*,
Suppin' hen broo;
Deil tak' Kate,
An' she be a noddin' too.'
ROBERT BURNS, *Poems*, p. 276, l. 1, c. 2.

See **Oo** (12) in **Grammar Outlines** (*vowels*, &c.).

NOON-SPELL, *sb.* the labouring-man's luncheon-time.—WELLINGTON. Pegge has '*Noon-scape*, the time when labourers rest after dinner. Lanc.' Cf. **Bait.**

NOPE, BUD-NOPE [noa·p], *sb. Pyrrhúla rubicilla*, the Bullfinch.—BRIDGNORTH. *Nope* = *ope* = *aupe*, and *avpe* = *alpe*, the word used for bullfinch in the following:—

'——nightingales,
And *alpes*, and finches, and wode-wales.'
Rom. of the Rose, l. 658.

'To philomell the next, the linet we prefer;
And by that warbling bird, the wood-larke place we then,
The red-sparrow, the *nope*, the red-breast, and the wren.'
DRAYTON'S *Polyolbion*, Song xiii., in Wr.

Randle Holme gives '*Nope*' in a category of birds, '*Canorous*, or of a Singing kind;' but as he includes '*Bulfinch*' also in the same list, he probably did not identify them as being one and the same bird.—*Academy of Armory*, Bk. II. ch. xiii. p. 309.

'*Nope*, a bullfinch. Suff.'—PEGGE. See *Alpe* in HAL. Cf. **Plum-budder.**

NOPES, *sb. pl.*, *obs.*? children,—a term employed amongst the mining population.—COLLIERY.

Compare E.E. 'knape; A.S. *cnapa*; O.Fris. *knapa*; O.Sax. *cnapo*; O.Icel. *knapi*, a boy,' in STRAT.

NOR, *conj.*, *pec.* than,—'better *nor* that.'—CLEE HILLS; LUDLOW; NEWPORT.

'"& more *nor* this, he dyes for your Loue,
Therfore, Lady, show some pittye."'
Will Stewart and Iohn, l. 83. *Percy Folio MS.*, vol. iii. p. 219, ed. Hales and Furnivall.

'For some few bags of cash, that, I wat weel,
I nae mair need *nor* carts do a third wheel.'
ALLAN RAMSAY, *The Gentle Shepherd*, IV. ii. p. 66.

Grose gives '*nor*' for than as 'North.'

NORATION [noar·ai·shun], *sb.* a fussy, discussional talk about a matter,—'much ado about nothing.' Clearly an *oration* is meant. Com. 'Poor owd Nelly! 'er went off verra sŏodden Mŏond'y wuz-a-wik. Ah went in theer o' the Sŏond'y evenin', an' as soon as iver Ah looked at 'er Ah seed as 'er were tuk for dyeath, an' Ah sez to 'er daater, "Merier," Ah sez, "yer Mŏother looks verra baad." "Eh!" 'er sez, "Ah dunna think as 'er's no wus till wot 'er 'as bin." "Merier," Ah sez, "tae moi woord fur it, 'er's strŏok fur dyeath, an' yo' 'ad ought to sen' fur the doctor—oither the doctor *or* the paarson," Ah sez, "fur theer'll be sich a *noration* all o'er the pleace if we letten 'er doi wi'out annyun;" an' Ah went across baack agen to our 'ouse an' axed moi Maester, wud 'e goo fur the paarson to owd Nelly?—an' 'e'd taen 'is boots off, an' were jŏost gooin' ŏop the steers, an' 'e sed, "No, they med goo thersens,"—an' Ah sez to 'im, "My laad," Ah sez, "Ah'll do moi dooty by owd Nelly as Ah expec' to 'ăve someun to do it by may," an' wi' thaat Ah set off fur the Rector mysen, jŏost as Ah were, an' dark at noight, an' twelve o'clock afore 'e raught baack to owd Nelly's, an' the fus' thing as 'e did—soon's iver 'e got in—'e brot out a spot o' braandy out'n 'is pockit, an' 'e axed me, "'Ad Ah iver-a fresh egg i' the 'ouse?" an' Ah sed, "Eh dear! yes, Sir," Ah sez, "plenty o' eggs;" an' 'e toud me to breek won an' part the yolk fro' the woite, an' blend it ŏop wi' the braandy; so Ah blent it ŏop as 'e toud me, an' 'e gi'ed it owd Nelly 'issen, an' it sim'd to nŏorish 'er loike, an' 'er continnied on till mornin', an' went off verra quoite jŏost after we'd 'adden our brekfasses—Ah knowed 'er were strŏok fur dyeath soon as iver Ah seed 'er o' the Sŏond'y noight' [Edgmond, 1872].

NOSE [noa·z], *v. a.*, *pec.* to take the blossoms off black currants and gooseberries preparatory to preserving them. Qy. com. 'We *nosed* about eight quarts o' black curran's after milkin' time, an' then theer wuz a great side-basket o' gooseb'ries to *nose*.'

NOTTAMY [not·u'mi'], *sb.*, *var. pr.* a thin, meagre person,—one worn to 'skin and bone' by illness or worry; an anatomy. It was remarked of a certain 'faddy' mistress, concerning her maid-servant, that ''er'd werrited the poor girld till 'er wuz a rāel *nottamy!*'

NOW JUST, *adv.* a point of time immediately preceding the present.

Com. 'W'y, Maister, w'eer'n'ee bin? The Squire wuz 'ere *now jest*, an' wanted to see you.' Cf. **Just now.**

NOWT [nou·t], *sb.* nothing; naught: a term employed by the rougher class of speakers.—WELLINGTON; COLLIERY; NEWPORT.

> 'þan was þe godwif glad · and gan it faire kepe,
> þat it wanted *nouȝt* · þat it wold haue.'
>
> *William of Palerne*, l. 72.

A.S. *náwiht*, naught.

NUCHID, *part. adj.*, *obs.*? stunted in growth in consequence of having been ill-fed and neglected: said of animals.—PULVERBATCH; WORTHEN. 'That pig o' Molly Robe'ts's is *nuchid;* it'll never come to nuthin'.'

Ray gives '*Nush'd*, Starved in the bringing up,' in *South and East Country Words*.

See **Ch** (3) in **Grammar Outlines** (*consonants*, &c.). Cf. **Stoken.**

NUNCLE [nungk·l], *sb.* an uncle. 'Dun yo' call yore *Nuncle* a noud mon? W'y my *Nuncle* Ben lived to be a 'undred an' two, an' yore's inna-d-above four-score!'

Mr. Nares says that *Nuncle* was 'originally a familiar contraction of *mine uncle*, and was the customary appellation of the licensed fool to his superiors.' So Shakespeare has it in *K. Lear*, I. iv., v., where the Fool repeatedly addresses Lear as *Nuncle.*

Mr. Nares also says that in Beaumont and Fletcher's *Pilgrim*, IV. i., 'when Alinda assumes the character of a fool, she meets Alphonso and calls him *nuncle;* to which he replies by calling her *naunt*, by a similar change of *aunt*.' Cf. **Naint.** See **N** (1) in **Grammar Outlines** (*consonants*, &c.).

NUNTY [nun·ti'], *adj.* handy; convenient.—CLEE HILLS. 'Ah! they 'adna sich *nunty* things to get on ŏŏth the work forty 'ear ago.'

NURKER [nur'·kur'], *sb.* something that is more than good—of superlative worth or excellence.—LUDLOW. 'Whad sort'n a milker's that cow, Maister?' 'Whad sort'n a milker? W'y 'er's a reg'lar *nurker*.'

NURSERY [nur's·r'i'], *sb.*, *pec.* a nursling.—WEM.

NUSS-ROW, *sb.* the Shrewmouse. Qy. com. See **Artishrow.**

NUTCRACKER, *sb. Sitta Europœa*, the Nuthatch.—BRIDGNORTH.

NUVITUOUS [nuv·i'chus], (1) *sb.*, *obs.*? a rarity; a dainty; a 'bonne-bouche.'—PULVERBATCH; WORTHEN, *Minsterley*. 'I went to see poor owd Mrs. Farley o' Wren'all [Wrentnall], an' 'er gid me a piece o' Marigold-cheese—it wuz a *nuvituous;* I hanna sid one fur 'ears.'

(2) *adj.*, *obsols.*? nourishing.—CHURCH STRETTON.

OAF. See **Auf.**

OAK-BALL, *sb.* an oak-apple.—SHREWSBURY. Cf. **Gall** (4). See Bk. II., *Folklore*, &c., 'Customs connected with Days and Seasons' (*Twenty-ninth of May*).

OANED, *part. adj.* made hard by congestion of the milk-ducts: said of a cow's udder.—WELLINGTON; WEM. 'That brind'ed cow's elder's badly *oaned.*' See **Oäns**, below. Cf. **Pounded (2).**

OÄNS, OONS [öö-h'n·z], PULVERBATCH. [oo·nz], CHURCH STRETTON, *sb. pl.* lumps in the udder of a cow, consequent upon the milk-ducts having been overcharged. 'Betty, yo' mun rub that cow's elder, theer's *oäns* in it as 'ard as a stwun.'

OASINS [oa·zinz], *sb.* chaff mixed with light grain.—PULVERBATCH. 'Jack, yo' hanna 'afe winnud that corn; I got a blind-sieve fûll o' *oasins* out on a strike.' See below.

OAZEZ, *sb. pl.* light grains that are winnowed out, covered with the husk or chaff.—CLEE HILLS. Cf. **Tail-ends.**

OB [ob·], *sb.* a third swarm of bees in one season from the same hive.—CLEE HILLS. Cf. **Bunt (2).** See **Play (2),** also **Cast** (7).

OBITCH'S COWT. See **Forty sa' one,** &c.

ODDLINGS, *sb. pl.* things of diverse sorts or sizes.—PULVERBATCH. 'Them 'tatoes i' that wisket's *oddlin's.*'

'A thread-bare shark; one that never was a soldier yet lives upon lendings. His profession is skeldering and *odling;* his bank Paul's, and his warehouse Pict-hatch.'—BEN JONSON, *Every Man out of his Humour,* in Nares. See Mr. Nares' Note upon it.

ODD-MARK, *sb., obsols.* that portion of the arable land of a farm set apart for a particular crop as it comes in order of rotation under the customary cultivation of the farm. Thus, a farm on the 'four-course' system, having 200 acres arable land, apportioned into equal parts for grain and green crops—as wheat followed by turnips, barley or oats by clover or vetches—would have 50 acres *odd-mark.*—CLEE HILLS.

ODDMENTS, *sb. pl.* odds and ends. Com. 'The Maister bought a lot o' *oddments* at the sale at Betchcot; some on 'em wun useful enough, but the most part wun rubbitch.'

ODDS, (1) *v. a.* to alter; to set to rights.—PULVERBATCH; CRAVEN ARMS. 'We mun *odds* this, it öönna do to lave it athatn.'

(2) *sb.* difference. Com. 'Yo'n find the *odds* w'en yo' gwun to another plack.'

(3) *adj.* different. Com. 'Yo' bin *odds* to me if yo' can drink sich belly-vengeance as this.'

O'ER-ANUNST, *prep.* over-against. — WEM; ELLESMERE. See **Anunst.**

O'ER-GET, (1) *v. a.* to escape, as by trick or strategy.—PULVERBATCH; CLEE HILLS; NEWPORT. 'They wun jaggin 'im off to jail, but 'e managed to *o'er-get* 'em.' Cf. **O'er-run (1),** below.

(2) *v. a.* to recover from; to get over.—PULVERBATCH. 'That child's never farly *o'er-got* the maisles; theer's bin summat lankerin' about it ever sence.'

O'ER-LOOKED, *part. adj.* bewitched; spell-bound; fascinated, as by an 'evil eye.'—PULVERBATCH. 'I should think we wun *o'er-looked* to lave the Green an' come 'ere—we'n 'ad nuthin' but ill-luck ever sence.'

> '. . . . . . . Beshrew your eyes,
> They have *o'er-look'd* me and divided me.'
> *Merchant of Venice*, III. ii. 15.

Cf. *Merry Wives of Windsor*, V. v. 87. See Bk. II., *Folklore*, &c., 'Witchcraft.'

O'ER-RUN, (1) *v. a.* to escape by flight. Com. ''E *o'er-run* me, else 'e'd a 'ad a good strappin'.' Cf. **O'er-get** (1), above.

(2) *v. a.* to leave, as of work, or some unfinished task. Qy. com. 'I'v' bin despert onlucky ööth my pou'try this 'ear; theer's three 'ens *o'er-run* thar nists after the eggs wun chipped.'

O'ER-SEEN, *part. adj.* blinded; deluded; deceived.—PULVERBATCH; CLUN; ELLESMERE. 'Fur my part, I never thought 'er any great shakes, but the Missis wuz despertly *o'er-seen* in 'er.'

> 'Thou, Collatinè, shalt oversee this will;
> How was I *overseen* that thou shalt see it!'
> SHAKESPEARE, *Lucrece*, l. 1206.

OËRTS [oaur'ts], *prep.* in comparison to.—PULVERBATCH. 'The corn's frummer i' the yed *oërts* as last 'ear.' Cf. **Toërts**.

OFF, *prep., pec.* from,—'took it *off* 'im.' Com.

OFFIL [of·il], *sb., var. pr., pec.* every part of a carcase that does not come under the recognized category of the larger pieces and joints,—as of a pig, all but the flitches and hams.—PULVERBATCH; ELLESMERE. Qy. com. 'I dunna like to see the flitchen cut afore May̆-Day̆, an' it nee'na be, if the *offil* is used carful.' See **Chine of Pork**.

OILS [ei·lz], *sb. pl., pec.* lotions and liniments of all kinds. Com.

OLD-GIRL, *sb.* an 'old maid.' Com. See **Girl**.

OLD-MAN, *sb.* Southern-wood. Com. See **Lad's-love**. Cf. **Old-Woman**.

OLD-MAN'S-PLAYTHING, same as **Bennet**, q. v.—*Ibid.*

OLD-RUFFLER, *sb., sl.* the ace of spades.—CLEE HILLS. Cf. **Devil's Bedstead**.

OLD-WOMAN, *sb. Artemísia argentéa*, Silvery Wormwood.—CLUN; WHITCHURCH, *Tilstock*. Cf. **Old-man**.

OLLERN, *sb. Alnus glutinosus*, the Alder.—CORVE DALE.

'*Alnus*,' glossed '*alr*,' occurs in an *A.S. Vocabulary*, xi. cent., in Wr. vocabs., vol. i. p. 79. Cf. **Orl**, also **Owler**.

OMBER. See **Homber**.

ON [on·], (1) a prefix = *un*. See **On-merciful**, **On-tidy**, &c., below. Qy. com. in *Mid.* and *S. Shr.* It is an old form.

'Þe wordes scholle be ised
Wiþe-oute wane and eche;
And *onderstand*, hi moȝe bi sed
In alle manere speche
Ine lede;
Þat euerich man hi sigge moȝe
And cristny for nede.'

WILLIAM OF SHOREHAM (A.D. 1307—1327).
De Baptismo, Specim. Early Eng., vi. l. 66.

(2) *prep.* of. Com. 'They tooken out *on* 'im, or else 'e'd a o'er-got 'em.'

'Were such things here as we do speak about?
Or have we eaten *on* the insane root
That takes the reason prisoner?'

Macbeth, I. iii. 82.

(*a*) *prep.* in combination with *lay*:—*To lay on*, to beat. 'They *laiden on* the poor chap.'

'. . . *Lay on*, Macduff.'—*Macbeth*, V. viii. 33.

(3) *adv.* in combination with a verb. Com.

(*a*) *To be on*, (1) to work or bustle about. 'They *wun on* all day lung.' 'Now yo' *bin on*, bin 'ee?'

(2) to talk about, usually in the way of complaint. ''E's *bin on* ŏŏth me agen about that cowt gettin' i' the fild.'

(*b*) *To come on*, to thrive; to grow. 'Yore lombs hanna *comen on* much.'

(*c*) *To go on*, to scold. 'Dunna *gŏŏ on* to the child, 'er couldna 'elp it.' 'They *wenten on* to the young ŏŏman shameful.'

(*d*) *To hold on*, to pause. ''*Oud on*, Surrey, till I come up.'

(*e*) *To keep on*, to continue; persist. 'They *keppen on*, an' ŏŏdna let it drop.'

(*f*) *To take on*, (1) to feign. ''Er *took on* as 'er wuz mighty bad.' ''E *took on* 'im soft.' *To take on soft* is to assume an air of hopeless stupidity, as country people often do in a witness-box when called upon to give evidence upon some point which they wish to ignore.

(2) to grieve; to lament. ''Er *took on* sadly w'en a toud'n 'er as Yedut wuz djed.'

(*g*) *To think on*, to remember. 'I'll buy some more yarn o' Saturd'y, if I can *think on*.' Cf. **Remember**.

ONBEAR [onbaer'·], *v. a.* to remove the stratum of earth lying over the stone: a quarrying term.—CLUN; BRIDGNORTH. Cf. **Barin'**.

ONBEARING [onbaer'·in], *sb.* a superincumbent weight.—PULVERBATCH; CLUN; BRIDGNORTH. 'That beäm's despert wek for sich a *onbearin'*.'

ONCOMMON, *adv.*, *pec.* very. — SHREWSBURY; PULVERBATCH; WORTHEN. Qy. com. 'I'll tak' a bit more, if yo' plaisen,—yore pŭddin's *oncommon* good.'

'Wi' that I pulled my vittles out, and zat a horse-barck, atin of 'em, and *oncommon* good they was.'—R. D. BLACKMORE, *Lorna Doone*, A Romance of Exmoor, p. 243, ed. 1878.

ONDENIABLE, *adv.* very; extremely,—''er's *ondeniable* spicy.'—SHREWSBURY; PULVERBATCH; WORTHEN. Qy. com.

ONDER [oa·ndur'], (1) *sb., obsols.* the afternoon. In places where this term obtains the day is divided into morning, middle of the day, *ōnder*, and night. 'I thought to a finished the fūt o' my stockin' this *ōnder*, an' now it's aumust six o'clock at night, an' it inna done. I've been despert linty.' The word *ōnder* [*sb.*] is used more or less throughout the *eastern* half of Shropshire. A line drawn from ELLESMERE to MIDDLE, thence to PULVERBATCH, and on to LUDLOW would roughly determine its range on that side.

Mr. Garnett says, 'This word [*onder*] appears in our glossaries in nine or ten different shapes, all equally corrupt. The true form is *undorn*, or *undern*; Goth. *undaurn*, A.S. *undern*, G. *untern*. The word is sagaciously referred by Schmeller to the prep. *unter*, anciently denoting *between* [cf. Sansk. *antar*, Lat. *inter*, the true cognates of our *under*], q. d. the *intervening* period; which accounts for its sometimes denoting a part of the forenoon, or a meal taken at that time, and sometimes a period between noon and sunset. It occurs in the former sense in Ulphilas, *undaurni-mat* [lit. undernmeat], Luc. xiv. 12; in the latter in the Edda [Voluspa], where the gods are said to have divided the day into four parts—*myrgin*, morning; *mitheandag*, noon; *undern*, afternoon; *aftan*, evening.'—GARNETT'S *Philological Essays*, p. 59. Cf. **Evening**.

(2) *v. n., obsols.* to continue to work well in the after part of the day.—CRAVEN ARMS, *Norton*; CORVE DALE, *Stanton Lacey*. ''E's a rar chap for work i' the mornin', but 'e dunna *ōnder* well.'

(3) *v. n., obsols.* to go down: said of the sun.—PULVERBATCH. 'The sun's beginnin' to *onder*.'

ONDER'S-BAȲTE. See **Onder**, above, and **Bait**. Cf. **Four-o'clock**.

ONE DOG, ONE BULL, *phr.* signifies 'fair play.' — COLLIERY. This saying had its rise in the practice of bull-baiting—a brutal custom which lingered on in Shropshire till about the year 1841. The *Bullring* is still the name of a small space in Ludlow, at the top of Corve Street.

See Bk. II., *Folklore*, &c., 'Wakes, Fairs,' &c.

ONE-WAY-DRINK, *sb.* beer of medium quality which contains the full strength of the malt and hops apportioned to it—no ale having been first drawn, nor weaker beer afterwards made, from the brew.—PULVERBATCH; WORTHEN. Qy. com. 'Tak' a jug an' draw some *one-way-drink* for the wilrit.'

ONGAIN, (1) *adj.* awkward; inconvenient.—PULVERBATCH; CLEE HILLS. 'Yo'n find that ampot mighty *ongain* I doubt; for whad yo' wanten it's too big a power.' See **Gain** (2). Cf. **Ungain**.

(2) *adj.* intractable.—*Ibid.* 'This pony's so *ongain* I canna get it nigh the 'orse-block.' See **Gain** (3).

ONHUMAN, UNHUMAN [oneu·mun], PULVERBATCH. [uneu·mun], ELLESMERE, *adv.* extraordinarily. 'Poor fellow! 'e's *onhuman* thin; 'e's gwun to nuthin' but skin an' bwun.'

ONLESS, *conj.* unless.—PULVERBATCH; WORTHEN. Qy. com. in *S. Shr.* 'I wuz fŏŏăst to gŏŏ alung ŏŏth 'er; 'er said *onless* I went 'er naint ŏŏdna loose 'er out.'

'At this court, for avoyding a controuersye betwext John wigley and John Chepp concerning the right vse of a way at a place called the water-byde, Richard Genins and George ffaulkoner, produced in court as witnesses for and on the behalf of John Wigley, being sworn before the stuard and homage, depose and say as followeth. I. Richard Genins sayth that Margory Davies, sometime dwelling on Chep Street, wold not remove her habitacion *onles* she might haue away conveniently and quietly to passe from the kings high way to and from a pasture called Hadwell,' &c.—'The Roll of the Court Leet of the Manor of Bromfield, Shropshire, for the 2nd October in the 4th year of James I. (1607).' *English Gilds, Their Statutes and Customs*, E. E. T. S.

ONLUCKY, UNLUCKY [onluk·i'], PULVERBATCH; WORTHEN. [un-luk·i'], LUDLOW; ELLESMERE, *adj.* In one or other of these forms the term is general, meaning mischievous, as applied to bad boys, or to cows, &c. breaking fence.

(1) 'Theer's that *onlucky* bwoy bin chuckin' stwuns agen at them gis, an's broke one o' thar wings.' Cf. **Ontidy**.

(2) 'The cow's so *onlucky* 'er's fŏŏăst to 'ăve a yok on.' Sometimes they say, ''Er's got 'er *onlucky* baids on'—referring to the yoke.

ONMERCIFULLY, *adv., pec.* excessively; extraordinarily.—PULVERBATCH. 'I should think yo' han got a rig out this Maȳ—yo' bin *onmercifully* fine.'

ONRIG, *v. a.* and *v. n.*, *obsols.*? to undress.—PULVERBATCH; WEM. 'Now, Missis, dinner's waȳtin'.' 'Well, gie me time to *onrig*; yo' bin in a despert 'urry; yo'd'n better 'ăve the dinner to meet one 'afe way to church.'

ONSHOOTY, *adj.* uneven; irregular.—PULVERBATCH. Qy. com. in *S. Shr.* 'Ow bin yore turmits this time?' 'Well, they bin mighty *onshooty*; they'n missed five or six buts together.'

ONSHUT [onshaet· *and* onshut·], *v. a.* to unyoke the horses from the implements.—PULVERBATCH. Qy. com. 'Yo'd'n better *onshet* an' gŏŏ wham; it inna fit for mon or 'orse to stond out i' this rain.'

Compare '*onschet*'—explained as 'un-shut, *i. e.* opened'—in the following:—

> 'Gymp gerraflouris thar royn levys *onschet*,
> Fresch prymross, and the purpour violet.'
>
> GAWIN DOUGLAS (A.D. 1513), *Prol. of the XII. Buk of Eneados.* *Specim. Eng. Lit.*, xiii. l. 121.

See **Shut** (1) and (5).

ONTIDY, UNTIDY [ontei·di'], PULVERBATCH; WORTHEN. [un-tei·di'], LUDLOW; ELLESMERE; *adj.* loose or depraved in habits. As with 'Onlucky,' so with this term—whether the prefix take the form of 'on' or 'un'—it is current throughout the county. '*Gallus*,' '*Onlucky*,' '*Ontidy*' are the three degrees of comparison as regards ill conduct, *ontidy* being the superlatively bad. 'Them three young youths bin bad uns—Jack's as *gallus* a dog as ever lived, Sam's that *onlucky* 'e's al'ays in some lumber, but Tum's right *ontidy*; I doubt 'e'll stretch a auter some day.'

'On-tydy *Intemptatus* (*intemptus*, *durisipus*, *intemperatus*.).'—*Prompt. Parv.*

ONWEEDY, *adj.* soon done or got through.—CHURCH STRETTON. 'Missis, that flour's bin mighty *onweedy*; it's done a'ready.' Cf. **Weedy**.

ŎŎL, *sb.*, *var. pr.* wool. Com. in *Mid.* and *S. Shr.* 'Al'ays strokes 'er the right way o' the *ŏŏl*, Miss,' said an old farmer, who wished to point out to a young lady how it was he got on so well with his wife. See **W** (2) in **Grammar Outlines** (*consonants*, &c.).

ŎŎLERT, *sb.* an owl,—the term is applied generically. Qy. com.

One night in the early part of the present century a certain Alick Young lost his way in the Eastridge Coppy. He cried out, 'Lost, lost!' in the hope of being heard, and of gaining help. A voice replied, 'Who-o-o.' 'Alick Young, the saddler, Sir, of Minsterley,' said he. 'Who-o-o,' repeated the voice. Again the man answered as before, and again came the 'Who-o-o.' Alick Young in some way recovered the lost path, and himself told the story of how he had answered an '*ŏŏlert's who?*' in Eastridge Coppy.

There is a Shropshire saying—'I live too nigh the ŏŏd to be afeard of a *ŏŏlert*.'

A.S. *úle*; Icel. *ugla*; Germ. *eule*; Lat. *ulula*; an owl.

'*Uulula*. An owle or *howlet*.'—*Dict. Etym. Lat.*

See **Billy-hooter**. Cf. **Owlerd**.

ŎŎLERT-MOTH, *sb.* one of the order *Lepidoptera Noctuidæ*, believed to be *Plusia gamma*, Gamma Moth.—PULVERBATCH. The local name of '*ŏŏlert*' is probably given to this moth from its nocturnal habits. Flying about in the dusk of autumn evenings, it often at such times finds its way into dwelling-houses.

ŎŎLLENLY, *adj.*, *obsols.* simple-minded; credulous.—PULVERBATCH. 'I al'ays liked Tummas as a neighbour; 'e wuz a good-nātured, *ŏŏllenly* mon—if 'e couldna do no good, 'e'do no 'arm.'

ŎŎNNA BE SAID, *phr.* won't be advised. Qy. com. 'I've toud 'er an' toud 'er whad that fellow wuz, but 'er *ŏŏnna be said*, an' now 'er's got to sup sorrow by spŏŏntles.'

ŎŎNS, (1) See **My ŏŏns**.

(2) See **Oāns**.

ŎŎNT, *sb.* a mole.—PULVERBATCH; WORTHEN; MUCH WENLOCK; CORVE DALE. Qy. com. in *S. Shr.* 'If yo' wanten a *ŏŏnty*-skin pus, yo' shoulden gŏŏ to owd Wilkes, the rot-ketcher; 'e ketches *ŏŏnts* an' stoats an' po'-cats an' all sorts o' varmint.'

'*Talpa*,' glossed '*wont*,' occurs in a *Metrical Vocabulary*, perhaps xiv. cent., in Wr. vocabs., vol. i. p. 177.

'A.S. *wand*; want (wont), *talpa*.'—STRAT.

Cf. **Mouldiwort**. See *sub voce* **Flen**. See Bk. II., *Folklore*, &c., 'Superstitions concerning Animals' (*moles*).

ŎŎNTY-TUMP, *sb.* a wanty-tump,—a mole-hill.—*Ibid.* See **Tump** (1).

ŎŎSTED, *sb.* a term used to denote quickness.—PULVERBATCH; CHURCH STRETTON; CLEE HILLS. 'They wenten like the *ŏŏsted.*' 'They growen like the *ŏŏsted.*' The notion of a ball of worsted (pronounced *ŏŏsted*) set free in rapid motion as it falls and rolls away from a knitter is said to be implied in this curious expression.

ŎŎT, wilt: used elliptically for 'wilt thou.' See **Grammar Outlines,** *verb* **Will,** p. lxv.

'Ketch out, *ŏŏt?*' The speaker was one of two boys, who, toiling up the Wyle Cop (Shrewsbury) under the weight of a heavy basket of clothes, had set down their load, and, after resting for a few seconds, were about to resume it. Just as the boy spoke, two clergymen passed. 'Did you hear that, Sir?' said the younger one to his companion, the Rev. William Gorsuch Rowland. 'No; what was it?' 'The boy said, Sir, "*Ketch out, ŏŏt?*"—take hold, wilt thou?' This incident occurred in 1846.

Ŏŏt = M.E. *wolt.* See DR. MORRIS'S *Historical English Accidence,* p. 187.

OOTER [oo·tur'], same as **Hastener,** q. v.—CLEE HILLS; WEM. *Hotter* = *heater* is meant. See **Hot.** A.S. *hát.*

OOZY [oo·zi'], *adj., pec.* dull; sluggish.—WEM; WHITCHURCH; ELLESMERE. 'That wench dunna seem to oss very well, 'er's that *oozy* 'er hanna won bit o' stir in 'er—'er's as lazy as Ludlam's dog that laid 'im down to bark.'

Ray gives this quoted proverb 'with a difference'—'that lean'd his head against a wall to bark.'—p. 219.

OPPLE, *sb., var. pr.* an apple. Qy. com.

OPPLE-GOB, *sb.* a dumpling made by enclosing an apple in a lump of dough, and boiling it.—SHREWSBURY; CRAVEN ARMS; CLUN; WEM. Cf. **Gob** (1).

OPPLE-SCOPPLE, *v. n.* to scramble for sweetmeats, as children do. —CLUN.

ORL, same as **Ollern,** q. v.—LUDLOW, *Herefd. Border.* There is a village called *Orleton* a few miles to the S.W. of Ludlow, but in Herefordshire.

ORNARY, (1) *adj., var. pr.* inferior; ordinary. Com. 'Whad! Jack's a-wham agen—I thought 'e went to the Bonk.' 'Aye, but the livin' theer wuz so *ornary,* the bwoy couldna stop.'

(2) *sb., var. pr.* a public dinner for farmers attending the markets; an 'ordinary'—a '*table-d'hôte.*' Com. 'A poor far, I doubt—theer wus a despert fi'eow at the Unicorn *ornary.*'

'LADIES' ORDINARY.—At the *Talbot* on *Tuesday,* the *Raven* on *Wednesday,* the *Talbot* on *Thursday,* and the *Raven* on *Friday.*'

'GENTLEMEN'S ORDINARY.—At the *Raven* on *Tuesday,* the *Talbot* on *Wednesday,* the *Raven* on *Thursday,* and the *Talbot* on *Friday.*'—From a 'Correct List' of Shrewsbury Races in 1774, reprinted in *Salopian Shreds and Patches,* vol. i. p. 68.

'*Ordinaire,* maison où l'on donne à manger. An *ordinary;* an eating-house. Jusqu'à quand mangerai-je à l'*ordinaire?* How long shall I eat at the *ordinary?*'—CHAMB.

ORT [aur't·], *v. a.* to pick out the best part of a mess of food and leave the rest—'the pig *orts* 'is mate.'—CLEE HILLS.

Jamieson gives '*To Ort, v. a.* To throw aside provender.' Cf. **Mammock** (1). See below.

ORTS, *sb. pl.* broken meat; scraps; fragments that are left—not, like 'mammocks,' in a worthless state—but fit to be eaten. Com. 'Yo' bin too nice, a power; if yo' canna ate good *orts* from the Maister's table, yo' mun clem tell yo' binna so bally-proud.'

> 'Let him have time a beggar's *orts* to crave,
> And time to see one that by alms doth live
> Disdain to him disdained scraps to give.'
>
> SHAKESPEARE, *Lucrece*, l. 985.

See *Troilus and Cressida*, V. ii. 158.

'Evening *orts* are good morning fodder.' 'To make *orts* of good hay.'—RAY'S *Proverbs*, pp. 103, 205.

'*Ortus*, releef of beestys mete. *Ramentum*.'—*Prompt. Parv.*

See *Orts* in WEDG.

OSS [os·], (1) *v. a.* to offer; to attempt. Com. ''Er'll never *oss* to pŭt anythin' in its place as lung as 'er can get through 'em.'

Ray gives '*Ossing* comes to bossing' as a 'Cheshire' proverb: he explains '*ossing*' as 'offering or aiming to do.'—p. 48.

(2) *v. n.* to show promise; to 'shape.' Com. 'I think the chap knows his work, 'e *osses* pretty well.' Cf. **Ause**. See below.

OSSMENT, *sb.* attempt, as indicative of skill.—SHREWSBURY; PULVERBATCH; OSWESTRY. 'I doubt 'e'll never do no good—I dunna like 'is *ossment*.'

OUKIT. See **Awkward**.

OUT, *adv., pec.* away from home, as upon an excursion or a visit. 'I shall be *out* for three weeks.' Com.

OUT AT TACK. See **Tack** (3).

OUTCAST, *sb.* the surplus weight or measure gained by millers and maltsters in converting wheat and barley into flour and malt. Qy. com. See **Weights and Measures**, pp. lxxxvi, lxxxviii.

OUTRACK, *sb., obsols.* a tract of land, formerly waste.—PULVERBATCH. The name still lingers on, but the *outrack*, as such, is a thing of the past. There were three *outracks* in the parish of Church Pulverbatch, viz., Pulverbatch, Wilderley, and Wrentnall. They were uninclosed lands leading from the cultivated ground to open common. The Pulverbatch *outrack* abutted at one end on 'Waken' [Oaken]—a sheep-walk—and at the other upon Cothercot Hill; the Wilderley one led up to the hills which stretch towards the Longmynd; and the Wrentnall one opened out on Longden Common. The farmers held the privilege of turning their animals—sheep, cattle, or ponies—into these *outracks*, and from thence to the hills or common. When the flocks and herds were taken off the common, they were driven into the *outracks*, which were then closed at the opposite end by a gate or barrier of some kind, in order to keep the animals within bounds, while the work of separating them was carried on by their respective owners.

The *outracks* are now enclosed: the Pulverbatch one has more than one small freehold within its boundaries. Comfortable homesteads at this date (1874) occupy the place of the 'wattle and dab' tenements erected by the early settlers on the waste: one of these primitive dwelling-places was standing in the year 1858 or thereabouts. It had been occupied by the same family of Roberts from father to son through many generations.

The first acknowledgment of 'manorial rights' made by the dwellers on the *outrack* was late in the eighteenth century, when John Fletcher was required to pay to the Manor of Condover eighteen pence per annum for his house and the ground then attached to it.

Jamieson has '*Out-rake.* An extensive walk for sheep or cattle.' See *Outrake* in E. D. S., B. vii. Cf. **Rack.** See **Chimley-jawm.**

OUTRIDER, *sb., pec.* a commercial traveller. Com. 'W'eer's young Blakeway now?' ''E's gwun to be *outrider* to some Lunnon 'ouse.'

OVAL, OVIL [oa·vul], WHITCHURCH. [oa·vil], PULVERBATCH; WORTHEN; WEM, *adj.* conceited; self-complacent; supercilious. 'Did'n'ee see Bill Jones, 'ow *ovil* 'e wuz in 'is new shoot?—'e thinks 'isself somebody now 'e's a bwun-polisher.'

OVEN-PEEL, same as **Peel,** q. v. Com.

'Strong fire-shovel and poker, and *oven-peel.*'—*Auctioneer's Catalogue* (Church Stretton), 1877.

OVEN-PIKEL, *sb.* same as **Fire-fork,** q. v. Com. See **Pikel.**

OVEN-SWEEP, OVEN-SWOOP, *sb.* same as **Malkin** (1).—PULVERBATCH. 'If yo' putten the *oven-sweep* o' the dairy-pegs, yo'n a the Missis after yo'.' A.S. *ofen,* oven; and *swápan,* to sweep, brush.

OVEROVE [ov·u'r'oav], *part. past.* over-hove = over-risen: said of bread which has fermented too much when in the dough, and, as a consequence, runs flat in the oven instead of rising.—ELLESMERE.

OVER-RIND [ov·ur'eind], PULVERBATCH. [ov·ur'ind], ELLESMERE, *part. adj.* a loaf which has so risen in the oven as to leave a hollow space between the top crust and the body of the loaf is said to be *over-rind;* and is caused by an excess of yeast, or by unsound flour.

OVERWEEST [oa·vur'weest], *part. adj.* completely covered with liquid.—WEM; ELLESMERE. 'I say, Mary, dunna yo' furget to see as that pork's *overweest* i' the brine.' A.S. *ofer,* over; and *wesan,* to macerate, soak.

OVIL. See **Oval,** above.

OWD LAD, OWD NICK, OWD SCRAT, *sb.* respective soubriquets for the Devil, of which the first two are most in requisition. Com. 'Jack, ŏŏn yo' gŏŏ a narrand fur me to-night?—yo' ŏŏnna be afeard o' the *Owd Lad* ketchin' yo'.' 'Oh no! Missis, I amma-d-afeard o' 'im, 'e's lookin' after somebody as 'e inna so sure on.'

> 'O THOU! whatever title suit thee,
> Auld Hornie, Satan, *Nick,* or Clootie.'
> ROBERT BURNS, *Poems,* p. 31, l. 2.

OWD LAD'S CORN, same as **Devil's corn,** q. v.—SHREWSBURY, *Uffington.*

OWLER, *sb.* the Alder.—WELLINGTON; WEM. There is a place near Wem called 'The *Owlers*,' and a road called the '*Owlery* Lane.' See **Orl.** Cf. **Woller.**

OWLERD, *sb.*, *var. pr.* an owl not quite fully grown; an owlet.—CORVE DALE. 'Them owls an' *owlerds*, they liven in a barn, an' theer they sitten on a beäm: by-w'iles they sin a mouze an' they droppen on 'im, an' ketchen 'im, an' getten 'im i' their baik, an' chawen 'im, an' squaigen 'im, an' crushen 'im, an' sŏoken 'im till theer inna nuthin' left on 'im, an' then they droppen the quid.' Cf. **Ŏŏlert.**

OWNER [oa·nur'], *sb.*, *obsols.*? a proprietor of barges.—SHREWSBURY; BRIDGNORTH. This term is often used as a prefix of title, much as one would say, 'Captain So and So.' 'I see them three barges of *Owner* Lowe's bin lyin' alung side Frankwell w'arf yet, I s'pose a bin waitin fur a rise i' the river.'

'*Ow(n)ere* of a schyp, or schyp-lord. *Navarchus.*'—*Prompt. Parv.* See **Trowman.**

OX-EYE, *sb.* the Great Titmouse.—BRIDGNORTH. See **Black-headed Tomtit.**

OXSLOP [ok·slop], *sb.*, *var. pr.* *Primula elátior*, Oxlip Primrose.—SHREWSBURY; ELLESMERE.

'I know a bank where the wild thyme blows,
Where *oxlips* and the nodding violet grows.'
Midsummer Night's Dream, II. i. 250.

See SKEAT'S *Etym. Dict.* Cf. **Cowslop.**

PACK, (1) *sb.*, *obsols.* twenty stones of flour,—a survival probably of the old custom of conveyance by pack-horses.—MARKET DRAYTON, *Cheshire Border.* See **Weights and Measures**, p. lxxxv.

(2) *sb.* a pedler's bundle, as of dress-pieces, tea, &c.—SHREWSBURY; PULVERBATCH; ELLESMERE. Qy. com.

'A small *pack* becomes a small pedler.'
RAY'S *Proverbs*, p. 157.

Du. Germ. *pack*, a bundle.

PACK-GOODS, *sb.* the dress-pieces or such like, carried in the pack.—*Ibid.* 'I dunna think it's wuth w'ile makin' up sich poor slaizy stuff, yo' met'n potch straws through it—it's al'ays the case ŏŏth *pack-goods.*'

PACKMAN, *sb.* a pedler who carries a pack.—*Ibid.* 'Some folks thinken they get great bargains off the *packmen*, but I dunna like thar flaunty trash, so I never 'arbour 'em nor taymen—gŏŏ to a good shop, I say, an' then yo'n be used well.'

PACK-STAFF, *sb.* a pedler's staff, serving the two-fold purpose of supporting his *pack*, and of a cloth-yard for measuring his *pack-goods.*—ELLESMERE. 'As plain as a *pack-staff*' is an old proverbial simile almost superseded at the present day by the equally appropriate, 'as plain as a pike-staff.'

'Not riddle-like, obscuring their intent,
But *pack-staffe* plaine, uttering what thing they mean.'
HALL's *Satires*, Prol. to Bk. iii., in Nares.

PADDLE [pad·l], (1) *sb.*, *obs.* a small spade-like implement which was attached to the plough for the purpose of clearing the soil from the 'breast' when it became clogged. Com. Called *plough-paddle* more frequently.

'The Plow Staff and *Paddle*, by which the Man cleaneth the Plow from clogged Earth or Mould.'—*Academy of Armory*, Bk. III. ch. viii. p. 333.

(2) *sb.* a small crescent-shaped spade used by mole-catchers.—WELLINGTON.

PANAKIN [pan·u'kin], *sb.*, *obsols.*? a very small pan, beforetime called a 'pimpert,' q. v.—PULVERBATCH.

PANNEL, *sb.*, *obs.* a pillion.—BISHOP'S CASTLE. Some old people in this locality at the present day [1875] remember the *pannel* being in use.

'*The tow Stables* one *pannel* . . .'—*Inventory* . . . Owlbury Manor-House, Bishop's Castle, 1625.

'"& on our Mill horsses full swift wee wyl ryd,
with pillowes & *pannells* as wee shall provyde."'
Kinge and Miller, l. 174. *Percy Folio MS.*, vol. ii. p. 155, ed. Hales and Furnivall.

'*Pannell* to ryde on, *batz*, *panneau*.'—Palsgrave, in HAL.

PARLOUR-LEASER [lai·zur'], *sb.*, *obsols.* a person who—'having a friend at court'—has permission to glean before the field is cleared.—PULVERBATCH. 'By-gum! I shanna trouble to gŏŏ after that leasow—the *parlour-laisers* han bin o'er it.' Cf. **Taskers'-leasers.** See **Lease.**

PATCH, *sb.* a small grass-field, generally lying contiguous to the house.—SHREWSBURY; PULVERBATCH; CLUN; CLEE HILLS; WELLINGTON. 'Tell Yedart to fatch the mar' up out o' the *patch*—the Maister wants 'er to gŏŏ to the far.' Cf. **Piece** (2), also **Clos'.**

PATHER [padh·ur'], (1) *v. a.* to tread down = patter,—'*pathered* the snow down i' the foud.'—ELLESMERE. Cf. **Bather.**

(2) *v. n.* to move lightly over a surface, scarcely touching it, as an insect does,—'a fly *patherin'* about the child's face.'—PULVERBATCH. Cf. **Pither-pather.**

(3) *v. n.* to fidget; to shuffle about on the feet uneasily.—WEM.

PAUME [pau·m], *sb.* the palm of the hand.—SHREWSBURY; PULVERBATCH. 'Tummas is one as ŏŏnna do much athout summat i' the *paume*.'

'And as þe hande halt harde · and al þynge faste
Þorw foure fyngres and a thombe · forth with þe *paume*.'
Piers Pl., Text B. pass. xvii. l. 157.

'O.Fr. *paume*, plat de la main.'—BUR.

PAUME-SUNDAY, *sb.* Palm-Sunday.—*Ibid.* 'We bin drawin' mighty nigh Aister, nex' Sund'y's *Paume-Sunday.*'
'O.Fr. *paume;* palme, branche en feuille de palmier.'—BUR.

PAYL [pai·l *and* paayl·], *v. a.* to beat; to thrash; to punish as with fists.—PULVERBATCH; WELLINGTON; WEM. 'If I could raich 'im I'd *paÿl* 'im black an' blue.' This is perhaps a varied form of Shakespeare's *pay*:—
'*Falstaff* . . . . . but I followed me close, came in foot and hand; and with a thought seven of the eleven I *pay'd*.'—1 *K. Henry IV.*, II. iv. 242.
Pegge has '*Peyl*, to strike, or beat. Lanc.'

PEAKING [pee·h'kin], PULVERBATCH. [pee·kin], WEM, *adj.* sickly; drooping: said of young poultry for the most part. 'A wet May 's bad for turkies; I've lost several, an' theer's more looks very *peäkin'*.'

'And as poore sillie hen . . . .
Soone droopes and shortly then beginnes to *peake*.'
TUSSER, p. 158, ed. E. D. S.

PEAKY, same as above.—ATCHAM; WELLINGTON.

PEA OF THE EYE, same as **Candle of the Eye**, q. v.—ELLESMERE.

PEA-RISERS, PEA-RISES [r'ei·zur'z], NEWPORT. [rei·siz], ELLESMERE, *sb. pl.* pea-rods, or sticks.
'A pese *rys*' occurs in *The Treatise of Walter de Biblesworth*, xiii. cent., in Wr. vocabs., vol. i. p. 154. See **Rise** (1) and (2).

PEÄRT [pee·ur't *and* pi'ur'·t], *adj.* brisk; lively,—well in health and bright in spirits. Com. 'I'm glad to see yo' so *peärt* agen, John.' 'Thank yo', Maister, I'm a djel better, but Mr. Glover says I shall never be my own mon agen.'

'There was a tricksie girle, I wot, albeit clad in grey,
As *peart* as bird, as straite as boult, as freshe as flowers in May.'
WARNER'S *Albions England*, 1592, in Wr.

'Quick she had always been, and "*peart*" (as we say on Exmoor), and gifted with a leap of thought too swift for me to follow.'—R. D. BLACKMORE, *Lorna Doone*, A Romance of Exmoor, p. 283, ed. 1878.
Cf. **Market-peart.**

PEÄRTEN, PEÄRTLE [pi'ur'·tn], SHREWSBURY; PULVERBATCH. Qy. com. [pyur't·l], WEM, *Hopton*, *v. a.* and *v. n.* to revive; to enliven; to cheer. (1) 'Oh! yo'n soon *pearten* up, yo' beginnen to look better a'ready.' (2) ''Er quoite *pyurtled* 'im ŏop w'en 'er come wŏam.'

PEÄRTISH, *adj.* diminutive of **Peärt.**—LUDLOW. Qy. com. ''Ow bin yo'?' 'Oh, *peartish*-like.'

PEASEN [pai-zun], *sb. pl.* peas; pease (collective).—CORVE DALE.

'Al þe pore peple · pese-coddes fetten,
Bake Benes in Bred · þei brouhten in heor lappes.
. . . .

Honger eet þis in haste · and asked aftur more
Þen ne þis folk for fere · fetten him monye
Poretes, and *Peosen* · for þei him plese wolden.'
Piers Pl., Text A. pass. vii. l. 285.

Grose gives '*Peasen*. Pease. Berks.'

O.E. *pese* (sing. sb.), pl. *pesen*. The modern *pea* is a false form. See DR. MORRIS's *Historical English Accidence*, p. 97.

A.S. *pise*, pl. *pisan*; Lat. *pisum*.

PECK, PICK [pek·], SHREWSBURY; PULVERBATCH; WORTHEN. [pik·], WEM; ELLESMERE, *v. n.* to pitch forward; to go head first; to over-balance. 'Mind the child dunna *peck* out on 'is cheer.'

'*Porter*. You i' the camlet, get up o' the rail;
I'll *peck* you o'er the pales else.'
K. Henry VIII., V. iv. 95.

PECKLED, *adj.* speckled,—'a *peckled* 'en.' Com.

'*Peckled*' occurs in Burton's *Anatomy of Melancholy* [A.D. 1621], p. 94, in NARES.

PECKLED-DICK, *sb.* the Goldfinch.—BRIDGNORTH. Cf. **Seven-coloured-Linnet**. See **Jack-Nicol**.

PECKLEDY-PIED, *adj.* speckled with black and white. Com.

PEDLAR'S-BASKET, *sb.* *Saxifraga sarmentosa*. — PULVERBATCH. To the gay appearance of this plant—its leaves lined with red, its flower-stalks streaming like ribands—the appellation of *Pedlar's-basket* is doubtless due. Cf. **Creeping-sailor** (1).

PEEL, *sb.* a kind of flat shovel of wood or iron, fastened to a long handle, used for putting bread, &c. into the oven, and also for taking the same out again. Com. 'Bring the oven-swoop an' the *peel*, we sha'n be ready for 'em in a minute.'

'Two wodden *peeles*' are enumerated amongst other effects in 'The Kytchynge,' in an *Inventory*, dated at Owlbury Manor-House, Bishop's Castle, 1625.

'He beareth Sable, a Baker, with a *Peel* in his both hands Bend-ways, with a Loaf of Bread upon it, Or. Others who give a fuller description of it, Blazon it thus, a Baker with his *Peel* in his hands bendwise, with a Loaf thereon, Or, a Cap on his head, his Waistcoat stripped above his Elbows, Argent, Breeches and Hose, Grey, Shooes, Sable; having an Oven fixed to the dexter side, Gules. This was the ancient Crest of the Bread Bakers of *Chester*, which now they have relinquished.'—*Academy of Armory*, Bk. III. ch. iii. p. 85.

'*Pele* of owen, K. *peel* for þe ovyn. *Palmula*, *pellica* (*pala*, P.).'—*Prompt. Parv.*

O.Fr. *pele*; It. *pala*, a shovel, spade. See BUR.

PEEP-O'-DAY, same as **Betty-go-to-bed-at-noon**, q. v.—WEM.

PEFFEL [pef·i'l *and* pef·l], (1) *v. a.* to peck at in a worrying manner. — ATCHAM; PULVERBATCH; CLUN; WEM; ELLESMERE. 'Them birds bin *peffelin'* out that turmit sid sadly.'

(2) *v. a.* to beat; to knock about; to abuse with violence.—WEM. ''E *peffeled* 'im reet well about the yed wuth 'is fisses.'

PEGGY, (1) same as **Dolly-peg**, q. v.—SHREWSBURY; ELLESMERE.

(2) same as **Dolly** (2).—*Ibid.*

PEGGY-NINE-HOLES, same as **Nanny-nine-holes**, q. v. — WHITCHURCH.

PEGGY, PEGGY-WHITETHROAT, *sb.* *Sylvia trochilus*, the Willow Warbler; *Sylvia rufa*, the Chiff-chaff; and *Sylvia sibilátrix*, the Wood Warbler, are respectively and alike called *Peggy* and *Peggy-Whitethroat.* Qy. com. See **Billy-Whitethroat.** Cf. **Jack-straw.**

PELCH, *sb.* a fat, corpulent person.—ELLESMERE. ''E's gettin' a deepert *pelch.*'

PELL [pel·], (1) *v. a.* to make bare, as of sheep or cattle eating down a pasture, &c.—PULVERBATCH; WELLINGTON; NEWPORT; WEM; ELLESMERE. 'Them ship han *pelled* that fild as bar' as yore 'ond.' Fr. *peler*, to make bare; to peel. Cf. **Pill.**

(2) *v. a.* and *v. n.* to pick; to take in small bits: said of food chiefly, as when children help themselves surreptitiously.—WORTHEN; CHURCH STRETTON. 'The lad *pelled* an' *pelled* at the dumplin' till 'e *pelled* it all away.'

PELL-NECKED, *adj.* having the neck bare of wool: said of sheep,—'a *pell-necked* yeow.'—PULVERBATCH; WORTHEN; ELLESMERE.

'*Hec adasia, A*ᵉ pylled hew,' occurs in a *Pictorial Vocabulary*, xv. cent., in Wr. vocabs., vol. i. p. 250.

'Pylled as one that wanteth heare, "*pellu.*"' Palsgrave, in HAL. See Cotgrave, *sub voce* **Pill.**

PELROLLOCK, *sb.* a faded, ill-dressed, worn-down looking woman. —PULVERBATCH; MUCH WENLOCK. 'Jim France 'as jined the 'totallers.' 'A good thing an' all fur 'is family—'is wife looks a poor *pelrollock*, an' 'is childern 'afe clemmed.'

PELT, *sb.* a sheep-skin of which the wool has fallen away from the living animal, in consequence of 'skin disease' of some kind.—SHREWSBURY; WELLINGTON.

PEN, (1) *v. a.* and *v. n.* to shut up; to confine. Com. 'I think it's a shame to *pen* the poor childern i' the 'ouse all day; a bit o' fresh ar ŏŏd do 'em a sight more good.'

> 'To be a mirrour to all mighty men,
> In whose right hands great power is contayned,
> That none of them the feeble over-ren,
> But alwaies do their powre within just compasse *pen*.'
> SPENSER, *F. Q.*, Bk. V. c. ii. st. xix.

A.S. *pyndan*, to shut in; restrain.

(2) *sb.* a shoot for grafting.—ATCHAM; PULVERBATCH; WELLINGTON. 'The owd gardener's pŭt five different *pens* i' the big par tree, so we sha'n 'ăve a sortment if they growen.'

(3) *v. a.* to pick the soft quills out of poultry when preparing them for the table.—SHREWSBURY; PULVERBATCH; NEWPORT; WEM. See below.

PEN-FEATHERED [fidh·ur'd], *part. adj.* having an under-growth of young feathers. Qy. com. 'I want to send some o' them ducks to markit, but I see they bin desport *pen-fithered*—it'll tak' more time to *pen* 'em than a bin wuth.' See below.

PEN-FEATHERS [fidh·ur'z], *sb. pl.* the young, newly-developed quill-feathers as they appear at moulting time. Qy. com. Cf. **Pens.**

PENNY, *adj.* very full of 'pens:' said of fowls, &c. Qy. com. See **Pens**, below.

PENNY-RYAL, *sb., var. pr. Mentha palégium,* Penny-royal.—PULVERBATCH. Qy. com. 'Robin-run-i'-the-'edge, an' Dragon's-blood, an' *Penny-ryal,* bin mighty good yarbs to tak' i' the Spring-o'-the 'ear fur clansin' the blood.'

Tusser enumerates '*Peneriall*' amongst 'Seedes and Herbes for the Kitchen.' See E. D. S. ed., p. 94.

PENNY STONE, *sb.* an iron-stone measure.—COLLIERY; M. T.

'The *Penny Stone* is the most remarkable and productive iron-stone in Shropshire. It is composed of a series of nodules, producing from 2,000 to 2,600 tons to the acre, and—as proved by smelting—contains about 35 per cent. of iron. The cavities of these nodules are filled up with sulphate of baryta, silicate of alumina, carbonate of lime, and crystals of zinc-blende. A curious feature in connexion with this seam is the presence of petroleum. In certain parts the work appears as though it had undergone a washing of tar. It is said that at one time petroleum abounded in the coal measures, producing as much as 1,000 gallons per week.

'The *Penny Stone* is interesting with its appearance and evidence of the piercing by burrowing worms, which have left, as a writer says, "heaps of excretions at the doors of their dwellings." This iron-stone contains numerous marine organic remains, the characteristic marine fossil being the *Leptœna Scabicula,* occurring also in the mountain limestone. Several species of Nautilus, Bellerophon, Orbicula, Unio, Terebratula, Lingula, &c., associated with the bones and scales of the *Megalichthys Hibberti,* and the *Gyracanthus Formosus.*

'Another characteristic fossil is the *Orbicula Reflexa.*'—*Notes on the Shropshire Coal-field,* by T. PARTON, F.G.S. 1868.

See **Black Stone,** also **Chance Penny Stone.**

PENS, *sb. pl.* the rudimentary quills of feathers, as of fowls, ducks, &c.—SHREWSBURY; PULVERBATCH; NEWPORT. Qy. com.

'His flaggy winges, when forth he did display,
Were like two sayles, in which the hollow wynd
Is gathered full, and worketh speedy way:
And eke the *pennes,* that did his pineons bynd,
Were like mayne-yardes with flying canvas lynd;
. . . .

SPENSER, *F. Q.*, Bk. I. c. xi, st. x.

'*Pennes,* quills.'—Maundeville, p. 269, in HAL.

'*Hec pluma,* a fedyre; *Hec penna,* a *penne; Hoc ilum,* the pyf of the *penne,*' occur *seriatim* under the head of '*Partes Animalium,*' in a *Nominale,* xv. cent., in Wr. vocabs., vol. i. p. 221.

'O.Fr. *penne*, plume; de [Lat.] *penna*.'—BUR.
Cf. **Pen-feathers**. See **Pugs** (2).

PENTICE [pen·tis], *sb.* the shed attached to a smithy, in which horses are shod.—PULVERBATCH; WORTHEN; ELLESMERE.

An ancient building called the *Pentice*, attached to S. Peter's Church, Chester, was taken down, A.D. 1801-6. Hanshall—the county historian—gives the following copy of a record having relation to it:—

'1616. Aug. 23. King James came here. He went to the Cathedral, and passed from thence along Shoemaker's-row to the *Pentice*, where he was banqueted, and had presented to him a gilt bowl, with 100gs. in it.'

Pentice is a shortened form of *appentice*, that which is *appended;* and further, the last syllable of this French word was before Shakespeare's time—according to Mr. Earle—anglicized into 'house,' making a sort of compound, *pent-house*. See *Philology of the English Tongue*, p. 292.

Bailey—ed. 1782—gives '*Pentice*, a Penthouse; also a Shed.'

'*Pentyce*, of an howse ende. *Appendicium*. "A pentis, *appendix, appendicium, apheduo*, (sic) *ut dicit Brito; et dicitur profectum, si de ligno, menianum, si de lapidebus*."—CATH. ANG.' *Prompt. Parv. and Notes.*

'*Appentis*, bâtiment bas & petit, qui est appuyé contre un plus haut. A shed, an out-house.'—CHAMB.

PERK. See **Land Measurements** (*Perch*), p. xcii.

PERK-UP, *v. n.* to look up in a bright, cheerful way after a state of depression from whatever cause proceeding. Com. 'Well, John. I'm mighty glad to see as yo' bin beginnin' to *perk-up* a bit, yo'n 'ad a bad bout, but now yo'n made a start, I 'ope yo'n soon be yore own mon agen.'

'. . when suddenly *up* the face
Of the Piper *perked* in the market place.'
ROBERT BROWNING, *The Pied Piper of Hamelin*, st. viii.

PESSUM [pes·um], *sb.* pease-haulm—a contracted form. Com. 'Theer wuz a noud rot-ketcher as wuz called "Dicky *Pessum;* w'en a wuz a young mon, a wuz sen' to stop a glat the pigs maden i' the stack-yord, 'e rommed some *pessum* i' the 'ole, an' wuz called "Dicky *Pessum*" ever atter.'

The term *pessum* is sometimes, oddly enough, applied to bean-straw, as in the neighbourhood of Wem, where they speak of *bean-pessum*. Cf. **Bean-haulm.**

PESTLE, *sb.* the fore-leg of a slaughtered pig, between the knee and the flitch.—PULVERBATCH; ELLESMERE. 'We'n 'ăve a pair of *pestles* an' a fowl boiled on Friday, then theer'll be broth for the men's breakfasts.'

Grose gives '*Pestle-of-pork*, a leg of pork. Exmoor.'

'"*Pestels* of venison."—WARNER'S *Antiq. Culin*, p. 98. "*Pestell* of flesshe, *jambon*."—Palsgrave,' in HAL.

Cf. **Shackle-bone.**

PEWIT [pee·wi't *and* pai·wi't], *sb. Vernellus cristátus*, the Lapwing.—SHREWSBURY; PULVERBATCH. Qy. com.

Randle Holme says, 'The Lapwing cries *Teewit*.'—*Academy of Armory*, Bk. II. ch. xiii. p. 310.

PIANET [peian·it], (1) *sb.* *Pæonia officinalis*, common Peony.—PULVERBATCH. Qy. com. 'Er'd got a posy as big as a besom, ŏŏth three *pianets*, an' a armful o' gilliflowers.'

(2) *sb.*, *obsols.* the Magpie.—WORTHEN; OSWESTRY. See **Chatter-pie**, also **Magpy.**

PICK [pik·], (1) *v. a.* to bring forth a calf prematurely.—ATCHAM; WORTHEN; ELLESMERE. Cf. **Cast** (3).

(2) *v. a.* to bring forth a foal prematurely.—PULVERBATCH; WEM.

(3) See **Peck.**

PICKLE, *v. a.* to steep seed-corn in lye, &c., preparatory to sowing. —PULVERBATCH. Qy. com. See **Clog** (1).

PIDDLING, *part. adj.* picking; dainty: used with reference to taking food.—PULVERBATCH. 'I doubt it'll tak' a despert w'ile to feed this pig, 'e's sich a *piddlin'* āter.'

'We took up our knives and forks, laid them down, and took them up again; . . . . *piddled*, sipped; but were more busy with our elbows than with our teeth.'—*Sir Charles Grandison*, vol. ii. p. 165, ed. 1766.

PIE-BALD. See **Skew-bald.**

PIECE [pee·s], (1) *sb.* an intermediate meal given to children, usually consisting of a piece of bread and butter. Com. 'Yo' shan' a no more *pieces* afore dinner, yo'n bin *piece, piece, piecin'*, all mornin', an' then when the garden stuff's done [cooked], yo'n ate nuthin'.' The 'garden stuff' is the cottage dinner of vegetables.

'I find the word [*piece*] in a little book of children's verses, '*Stories for Alice*' (Philadelphia, 1857), by a lady of English descent living in Chester, county Pennsylvania.

"And on the dresser you will find
At twelve o'clock your *piece*.

The *piece* was two nice corn-meal cakes."'—*N. and Q.*, 4th Series, vol. vi. p. 249.

(2) *sb.* a field.—CHURCH STRETTON; CORVE DALE; CLEE HILLS.

'I removed the house to another *peice*, called the Old Feild . . . The *peice* from whence the house was removed is to this day called Ored's *peice*.'—GOUGH'S *History of Myddle*, p. 83.

Cf. **Patch.**

(3) *sb.* a somewhat contemptuous term for a woman. Com. ''Er's a poor *piece;* w'y 'er dunna know 'ow to wesh 'er 'usban's shirt fur all 'er brags 'erself for everythin'.'

PIED-FINCH, *sb.* *Fringilla cœlebs*, the Chaffinch. Qy. com. So called from its parti-coloured plumage. Cf. **Pine-finch.**

PIE-FINCH, same as above. — SHREWSBURY; CHURCH STRETTON; BRIDGNORTH; NEWPORT.

PIG-COTE, *sb.*, *obsols.*? a pig-sty.—PULVERBATCH.

'*Hec porcaria, A*[e] swyn-cote,' occurs in an *English Vocabulary*, xv. cent., in Wr. vocabs., vol. i. p. 204.

PIGGIN [pig·in], (1) *sb.*, *obsols.* a wooden bowl. Com. The *piggin* was formerly used for eating porridge or other 'supping' out of; it gave place to the 'pollinger,' which in its turn was supplanted by the ordinary earthenware basin, or tin can. *Piggins* were in common use during the era of pewter platters. As the wooden *piggin* gave place to other eating vessels, so there was a progressive refinement in food and language, as the following Shropshire doggerel sets forth :—

'Dame an' porridge,
Missis an' broth,
Madam an' tay.'

'2 *Piggins*' are comprised in an *Inventory*, dated at Aston Botterell about 1758.

'Heigh, diddle, diddle,
The cat an' the fiddle;
The cow jumped o'er the moon,
The little dog laughed to see sich sport;
And the *piggin* ran after the spoon.'
Shropshire version of the 'Old Nursery Rhyme.'

Cf. **Quaigh** (1). See **Treen**.

(2) *sb.* a wooden pail, one of the staves of which being left much longer than the rest, forms an upright handle.—WEM. A *piggin-calf* is a calf reared by hand, and is so called from the *piggin* being used to hold its 'supping.'

Ray has 'A *Piggin*, a little Pail or Tub, with an erect Handle,' amongst 'North Country Words.' Cf. **Gaun** (2).

PIG-GRASS, PIG-RUSH, *sb. Polygonum aviculare*, common Knot-grass.—WELLINGTON. The pest of light soils in some parts of Salop.

PIG-NUT, *sb. Bunium flexuosum*, common Earth-nut.—PULVERBATCH.

'And I with my long nails will dig thee *pig-nuts*.'
Tempest, II. ii. 172.

PIGS-PARSNIP, *sb. Heracleum sphondylium*, common Cow-Parsnip.—WELLINGTON.

PIKE, (1) *sb.* a toll-bar; a turnpike-gate. Com.

(2) *v. a.* to pick.—PULVERBATCH. Qy. com. 'We met'n as well *pike* a bit i' the owd stubble as sit under the 'edge waitin' fur the tother—they hanna finished luggin' the barley yet.'

'"he calles them knaues your hignes keepe,
with-all hee calls them somewhatt worsse,
he dare not come in without a longe staffe,
hees ffeard lest some bankrout shold *pike* his pursse."'
The pore man & the Kinge, l. 108. *Percy Folio MS.*, vol. iii. p. 201, ed. Hales and Furnivall.

'O.Du. *pecken* (*manticulari*); pike (pick).'—STRAT.

(3) *sb.* a pick.—NEWPORT. O.Du. *picke.*—*Idem.*

(4) *sb.* a hay-fork; a pitch-fork.—CLEE HILLS; LUDLOW. '*Pikes* and rakes.'—*Auctioneer's Catalogue* (Stoddesden), 1870.

'A rake for to hale vp the fitchis that lie,
a *pike* for to pike them vp handsom to drie.'
TUSSER, *Husbandlie furniture*, p. 37, ed. E. D. S.

'A.S. *pic*, a pike; *aculeus, cuspis.*'—STRAT.

PIKEL [pei·ki'l], *sb.* a hay-fork; a pitch-fork. Com.

'One dozen *pikels* in lots.'—*Auctioneer's Catalogue* (Longville), 1877.

'For the Pitchfork (or *Pikel*, which we vulgarly call it) it is an Instrument much used in Husbandry for their Loading and Stacking of Hay and Corn.'—*Academy of Armory*, Bk. III. ch. viii. p. 331.

Gough, in his *History of Myddle*, makes repeated mention of a '*pike-evill*,' apparently the same thing as a *pikel*—'*pikeavell* grains'—'a long *pikeevill*,' &c. At this day *evil* is similarly used in composition by Shropshire folk for the names of other kinds of fork. See **Dung-evil**, also **Sharevil**. Cf. **Evil**.

PIKELET [pei·klet], *sb.* a tea-crumpet.—SHREWSBURY; LUDLOW; BRIDGNORTH; NEWPORT.

'However, Mrs Jerome herself could not deny that Janet was a very pretty-spoken woman: "She al'ys says she niver gets sich *pikelets* as mine nowhere; I know that very well—other folks buy 'em at shops—thick, unwholesome things, you might as well eat a sponge."'—GEORGE ELIOT, *Scenes from Clerical Life* (Janet's Repentance).

Bailey—ed. 1782—gives '*Bara-picklet* [*Welsh*] Cakes made of fine Flower kneaded with Yeast.'

Cotgrave has French '*popelins*, soft cakes of fine flour, &c., fashioned like our Welsh *barrapyclids*.' W. *bara*, bread. See **Flap**, also **Light-cake**.

PIKES, *sb. pl.* short 'buts' ploughed in pointed furrows of graduated lengths; filling up spaces—left by the long 'buts' lying at right angles—in fields of irregular form.—PULVERBATCH. Qy. com. A.S. *pic*, a point.

PILES [pei·lz], *sb. pl.* the awns of barley.—PULVERBATCH; CRAVEN ARMS; CLEE HILLS; WEM. Qy. com.

PILING-IRONS, *sb.* an implement for removing the awns.—*Ibid.*

'. . riddles, sieves, and barley *piling-irons* in lots.'—*Auctioneer's Catalogue* (Longville), 1877.

PILINGS, *sb. pl.* trusses of threshed-out straw.—NEWPORT. 'Rots bin nippers for *pilin's*.'

PILL, *v. a.* to strip; to deprive of the outer skin or covering; to peel.—SHREWSBURY; PULVERBATCH; CHURCH STRETTON. Qy. com.

'Lads mak'n poor laisers gener'lly—they'n al'ays got a stick to *pill*, or anythin' but bend thar backs to the stubble.'

> 'The skilful shepherd *pilled* me certain wands.'
>
> *Merchant of Venice*, I. iii. 85.

'Pyllyn̄, or *pylle* bark, or oþer lyke. *Decortico*.'—*Prompt. Parv.*

'Fr. *peler*, to bauld or pull the haire off; also to *pill*, pare, barke, unrinde, unskin.'—COTG. Cf. **Pell** (1).

PILLOW-COAT, *sb.* a pillow-case, or cover.—SHREWSBURY; PULVERBATCH. Qy. com. See **Bere** (2).

PILPIT, *sb.* a pulpit.—SHREWSBURY; PULVERBATCH. Qy. com. The form is an old one.

> 'Thus ȝe prechyn the pepul and in the *pylpit* opynlé
> The vij workys of mercé mekelé to fulfyl.'
>
> JOHN AUDELAY'S *Poems*, p. 41.

PIMKIN [pim·kin], *sb., var. pr.* a small earthen pan used for boiling infant's food in, &c.,—a pipkin.—PULVERBATCH; CRAVEN ARMS. 'Mind as that *pimkin* 's clane afore yo' pŭt the child's pap in.'

PIMMIROSE, *sb., var. pr. Primula vulgaris*, common Primrose,—'*pimmiroses* an' cowerslops.'—SHREWSBURY; PULVERBATCH.

PIMPERT, *sb., obs.?* a very small pan—an 'egg-saucepan.'—PULVERBATCH. See **Panakin.**

PIMPING, *sb.* a small, delicate creature.—PULVERBATCH. 'The baby's but a little *pimpin'* fur a twel'month owd.'

PIMPLE, *sb., pec.* a pebble.—SHREWSBURY; PULVERBATCH. 'Whad bin 'ee trimplin' at?' 'Theer's a *pimple* i' my boot, an' it's blistered my fŭt.' Cf. **Pumple-stones.**

PIN, *sb.* the middle place for a horse,—between the shafter and the leader in a team of three.—WELLINGTON; WEM. 'Yo'd'n better pŭt that cowt i' the *pin* a bit.' A.S. *pyndan*, to shut up; to restrain. See **Pin-horse.**

PIN-BONE, *sb., obsols.?* the great protuberance at the top of the thigh bone or *femur*—the *Trochanter major*.—PULVERBATCH. 'The rheumatic 's bad enough anyw'eer, but it's wust i' the *pin-bwun* o' the 'ip, fur yo' can carry a bad arm, but a bad leg ŏŏnna carry yo'.'

PINK-FINCH, same as **Pied-finch**, q. v.—WEM; ELLESMERE. So called from its querulous note. Cf. **Chink-chink.**

PINFOLD, *sb.* an enclosure for stray animals; a pound.—PULVERBATCH; NEWPORT; WEM. 'Han'ee pŭt them strafes i' the *pinfoud*?'

'And if thy horse breake his tedure, and go at large in euery man's corne and grasse, then commeth the pynder, and taketh hym, and puttoth hym in the *pynfolde*, and there shall he stande in prison, without any meate, vnto the tyms thou hast payde his raunsome to the pynder, and also make amendes to thy neyghbours for distroyenge of theyr corne.'—FITZHERBERT'S *Husbandrie* [A.D. 1523], ed. 1767, p. 95.

See *Two Gentlemen of Verona*, I. i. 114.

'*Hoc inclusorium*, a *pyn-fold*,' occurs in a *Nominale*, XV. cent., in Wr. vocabs., vol. i. p. 239.

A.S. *pyndan*, to shut in; and *fald*, a fold.

PIN-HORSE, *sb.* the middle horse in a team.—WELLINGTON; WEM; ELLESMERE. See **Pin.** Cf. **Pinner** (1).

PINK [ping·k], *sb. Leúciscus phoxínus*, the Minnow.—SHREWSBURY; PULVERBATCH; WORTHEN; CORVE DALE; LUDLOW. Qy. com.

'Pinchbrooke is now cald Peynesbrooke, and perhaps might take his name from those small and litle fishes called *Pinks*, which are common in great multitudes in such brookes.'—GOUGH'S *History of Myddle*, p. 39.

'For the *Minnow* or *Penke*, he is easily found and caught in April, for then he appears in the Rivers.'—*The Compleat Angler*, ch. iv. p. 96, ed. 1653.

Pegge has '*Pink*, the fish called the minnow. North.'

PINKERN [ping·kur'n *and* ping·knur'n], *sb.*, *var. pr.*, *obsols.* a very narrow boat used on the Severn—a *pinkstern.* This is a river term, which still lingers on amongst the Severn bargemen, though rarely used. It was heard in December, 1875, at Shrewsbury, and about the same time in the S.E. of Salop—at Cleobury Mortimer, or Neen Sollers. 'Whad a *pinkern* that is o' yore's!' 'Aye, but it's an oncommon 'andy boat.'

Compare Fr. '*Pinque*, petit bâtiment de charge qui est rond à l'arrière,' in CHAMB. Icel. *espingr;* a long boat. See *Pink* (4) in SKEAT's *Etym. Dict.*

PINNER, (1) *sb.* same as **Pin-horse**, q. v.—PULVERBATCH; NEWPORT.

(2) *sb.* a pinafore. Com.

PIN-ROWED [pin·r'oad], *adj.* a term applied to butter which, having been imperfectly worked after the salt has been added to it, is, as a consequence, full of white streaks.—PULVERBATCH; WELLINGTON. Qy. com. 'Butter wuz chepper o' Saturd'y, I 'ear.' 'Aye, some *pin-rowed* stuff as wunna fit to ate; but good butter kep' its price.'

PINS-AND-NEEDLES, *sb. Hypnum serpens*, Creeping Feather-moss. —SHREWSBURY. The little stalks or '*seta*,' of this pretty moss, bear upon their summits the spore-cases or capsules—these are the *pin's heads.*

PINSONS [pin·su'nz], (1) *sb.* pincers. Com. 'Gie me the omber an' *pinsons* 'ere, an' I'll soon fatch the nail out.'

'*Pynsone. Tenella.*'—*Prompt. Parv.*

(2) *sb.* a dentist's forceps,—'the tuth broke i' the *pinsons.*'—SHREWSBURY.

'*Pynsone*, to drawe owt tethe. *Dentaria.*'—*Prompt. Parv.*

Mr. Way says, 'The term seems to be a diminutive of the *Fr. pince.*' See his Note.

'*Pince*, petites tenailles, qui servent a differens usages.' Pincers, nippers.—CHAMB. Cf. **Drawts.**

PIP, (1) *sb.* a single blossom terminating a pedicel, as the cowslip, or a peduncle, as the primrose, &c.—SHREWSBURY; PULVERBATCH. Qy. com.

(2) *v. a.* to pick off the blossoms or 'pips' of cowslips, &c.—*Ibid.* 'I promised the Missis as the childern shoulden get 'er a basket o' cowerslops, an' now 'er wants 'em *pipped;* an' it's a despert lat job picking the *pips* fur winde.'

(3) *sb.* a pippin, as of an apple, orange, &c. Com.

(4) *sb.* a spot of any of the suits on playing cards,—generally used in the plural form, as 'counting the *pips*,' when computing a hand. Com.

PIPE-DRINK, *sb.*, *sl.?* light ale esteemed by smokers,—'nice little *pipe-drink.*'—WEM. Qy. com.

PISSANNAT, *Idem.*—WEM.

PISSANT, *sb.* an insect of the genus *Formica*,—the common Ant. —SHREWSBURY; PULVERBATCH; ELLESMERE.

PITCH [pich·], (1) *v. a.* to throw the hay, sheaves, &c., on to the waggon in the harvest-field. Com. 'Yore new waggoner 's despert short an' stiff, I dunna know 'ow e's to *pitch* at 'arrŏost—'e'll want a good lung *pitchin'-pikel.*'

'"Canstow seruen," he seide · . . . .
. . . . "other to the cart *picche.*
Mowe other mowen · other make bond to sheues."'
Piers Pl., Text C, pass. vi. l. 13.

(2) *sb.* the quantity taken at one time for 'pitching.' Com. 'Jack ŏŏnna 'urt 'imself—'e dunna tak' more at a *pitch* than yo' coulden pŭt on ŏŏth a toastin'-fork.'

PITCHER, (1) *sb.* the man who 'pitches' the hay, &c., when loading the harvest-waggon. Com.

(2) *adj.* ill-tempered; cross-grained.—ATCHAM; WEM. 'The Maister 's mighty *pitcher*, yo'd'n better mind whad yo' bin doin'.'

PITCHERS, PITCHETS, PICHOCKS [pich·ur'z], SHREWSBURY; ELLESMERE. [pich·uts], PULVERBATCH. [pich·uks], CORVE DALE, *sb. pl.* bits of broken crockery used as playthings by children. A little girl admiring her mother's new tea-china, exclaimed, 'Eh! ŏŏdna they maken pretty *pitchets*?'

PITCHERS, *sb. pl.* earthenware vessels of the finer kinds, common china included.—SHREWSBURY. See **Crocks.**

PITCHER-SHOP, same as **Crock-shop.**—SHREWSBURY.

PITCHING-PIKEL, *sb.* a pitch-fork. Com. See **Pitch** (1), also **Pikel.**

PIT-GRATE, *sb.* the grating-covered ash-pit in front of a kitchen fire-place.—SHREWSBURY; WORTHEN; WELLINGTON; ELLESMERE. Cf. **Purgy-hole.**

PITHERING [pei·dhur'in], *part. adj.* trifling; dawdling.—ATCHAM; PULVERBATCH; WEM. 'I canna think whad yo'n bin *pitherin'* at all mornin'—I could a done twize as much in 'afe the time.'

PITHER-PATHER [pidh-ur' padh·ur'], same as **Pather** (2), PULVERBATCH; WELLINGTON. 'I felt summat *pither-patherin'* about my neck an' flirted it off, an' it wuz a great yerriwig.' Cf. E. *pit-a-pat.*

PIT-ROT, *sb.* a contemptuous term for a miner or collier.—WELLINGTON.

PIT-WOOD, *sb.* timber-wood for the common purposes of mining operations. For these Larch is the best adapted, from its greater pliancy. Com.—M. T.

PIZE [pei·z], *expl.* a strong form of expression; a mild kind of anathema.—WHITCHURCH. (1) 'What the *pize* han yo' got to do wi' it?' (2) '*Pize* on them naughty lads, conna they let that poor cat alone?'

'My Uncle was petulant. . . . He ran into all those peculiarities of words, for which you have so often raillied him—His *adsheart*, . . . his *What a pize*, his hatred of *shilly-shally*.'—*Sir Charles Grandison*, vol. vi. p. 63, ed. 1776.

See J. O. HALLIWELL's *Nursery Rhymes of England*, DLXI.

PIZY [pei·zi], *adj.* peevish; irritable,—'a *pizy* owd maid.'—WELLINGTON; NEWPORT.

PLACK [plak], (1) *sb.* a plot of ground.—PULVERBATCH; CORVE DALE; ELLESMERE. 'Yo'n got a good *plack* for tatoes i' the fallow, Tummas.' 'Perty well, o'ny theer's sich a morf o' chicken-weed.' See **Placket** (1), below.

(2) *sb.* an allotment of work; a job.—WEM; ELLESMERE; OSWESTRY. 'Yedut wunna want for work this good bit, the Squire's gid 'im a *plack* as'll las' 'im o'er Miämas.'

(3) *sb.* a situation; a berth.—PULVERBATCH; CORVE DALE. Qy. com. 'John's a rar *plack* at the paas'n's, 'e looks as if 'e didna crack many djef nuts.'

PLACKET [plak·it], (1) *sb.* the diminutive of '*plack*,' a plot of ground.—CORVE DALE. A little hamlet built on some old common allotment is called, 'The Golden *Plackets*.' See **Plack** (1), above.

(2) *sb.*, *obsols.* the slit in the skirt of a woman's dress which admits of its being passed over the head.—PULVERBATCH. Qy. com. 'Mind as yo' maken the *placket* lung enough i' my gownd, or else it'll tar every time it gwuz on.'

Pegge has '*Placket-hole*, a pocket-hole. York. From the Scots.'

PLACKET-BOARD [buo·h'r'd], *sb.* the back-board of a waggon. It slips inside the 'cratch,' and is used when the load being of a loose nature, such as lime, is liable to shed through the open 'cratch.'—WHITCHURCH; ELLESMERE.

PLAD, *pret.* pleaded.—PULVERBATCH. 'The Missis ŏŏd a turned 'er off, but the Maister, '*e plad* for 'er.'

'And long for hir forsothe he *pladde*.'—*Chron. Vilodun.*, p. 108, in HAL. See **Pled.**

PLADE [plai·d], *v. n.* to argue.—PULVERBATCH. To *cross-plade* is to contradict. 'Tummas an' me han bin *plădin'* an' *cross-plădin'* about them apples; 'e says as they wun got afore Miämas, an' I say as they wunna.'

PLADE PARDON. See **Plead-pardon.**

PLANK, *v. a.*, *pec.* to charge 'point-blank' so as to inculpate; to convict.—PULVERBATCH. 'It's no use yo' sayin' yo' didna, fur 'ere the eggs bin to spake fur tharselves, so yo'n *plankt* the lie on yoreself.'

PLAY, (1) *v. n.* to swarm: said of bees.—PULVERBATCH; BRIDGNORTH. 'Two 'ives *played* in one day, Sir.' The bees are said to *play* high, or *play* low, as the case may be.

(2) *sb.* the first swarm of bees in the season from one hive.—CLEE HILLS.

'A *play* of bees in May's wuth a noble the same day;
A *play* in June's perty soon;
A *play* in July 's nod wuth a butterfly.'

Local Doggerel Rime.

See **Bunt** (2).

(3) *v. n.* to fly high and sweep through the air, as rooks do.—PULVERBATCH. ''Ow the rooks *playen* about to-day!—it's a sign we sha'n ăve a starm afore lung.'

(4) *v. n., pec.* to do no work; to spend the time in idleness.—SHREWSBURY; PULVERBATCH; NEWPORT. 'Theer's mighty little doin' at the mines now; the men wun *playin'* one 'afe thar time las' wik, an' theer wuz a lot sacked [discharged] las' reck'nin'.'
A.S. *plegian*, to amuse one's self.

PLAZEN [plai·zn], *sb. pl.* places, *i. e.* situations, as for domestic servants.—NEWPORT. '*Plazen* 's none so plentiful as what they wuz:' said the mother of an aspiring maid-of-all-work [1880].

PLEACH [plai·ch], *v. a.* to remake a hedge by intertwining, &c.—same as **Lay**, q. v.—SHREWSBURY; PULVERBATCH; WORTHEN; CLEE HILLS; OSWESTRY. Qy. com. 'I'll back John to *plaich* a 'edge ŏŏth any mon, 'e does it like basket-work.'

'And all her husbandry doth lie in heaps.
. . . .
. . . . . her hedges even-*pleach'd*,
Like prisoners wildly overgrown with hair,
Put forth disorder'd twigs. . . . . .'
K. Henry V, V. ii. 42.

PLEACHERS, same as **Layers**, q. v.—PULVERBATCH; CLEE HILLS; WELLINGTON.

PLEAD PARDON [plai·d], *phr.* to ask pardon. Qy. com. 'Well, I tell yo' whad, if yo' dunna *plade pardon*, yo'n lose yore plack, fur I 'eärd the Maister say so.'

PLED, *pret.* pleaded.—WORTHEN. ''E *pled* ŏŏth me to gie the poor chap another chance.'
'The well-known story of the presbyter deposed from his office for forging the Acts of Paul and Thecla, although he *pled* that he had done so from the love of Paul.'—*Contemporary Review*, p. 602. April, 1869.
Pled is an established Scotticism. Cf. **Plad**.

PLIM, (1) *adj., var. pr.* perpendicular; plumb. Com. 'The oven inna set *plim* to the grate.'
(2) *v. a.* to adjust by plumb-line. Com.

PLIM-BOB, *sb.* the line and plummet.—WHITCHURCH.

PLOUGH [plou·]. The parts of a plough here presented in a tabulated form, will be found explained as they occur in the order of their respective initial letters in the body of the Glossary:—

Buck (1), ELLESMERE. (The *locality* was omitted in its proper place.)
By-tail.
Cooter.
Copsil (1) (2) (3).
Cop-wedge.
Foot (2).
Flay (2).
Kay (2).
Master-tail.
Mould-board.
Paddle.
Shell-board.
Skelp (2).
Suck.
Tails.

PLOUGH-MONDAY, *sb., obs.* the Monday next after Twelfth-Day. —PULVERBATCH; ELLESMERE. See Bk. II., *Folklore, &c.*, 'Customs.'

PLUCK, *sb.* the heart, liver, and lights of a sheep,—'ship's yed an' *pluck.*' Com. See *Pluck* in WEDG. Cf. **Pummice.**

PLUCKER-DOWN. See **Cross-cloth.**

PLUCKING [pluk·in], (1) *part. adj.* twitching.—PULVERBATCH.

(2) *sb.* a nervous twitching; S. Vitus's Dance.—PULVERBATCH; WORTHEN; WEM. 'Mother, theer's summat the matter ŏŏth my eye—it's *pluckin'.*' 'I wish yo'd'n a *pluckin'* i' yore 'eels to get out o' my roäd.'

PLUG, *v. a.* to pull; to pluck,—''Er's *pluggin'* my yar.'—SHREWSBURY; PULVERBATCH; CLEE HILLS. Cf. **Pug.**

PLUM-BIRD, *sb.* the Bullfinch.—PULVERBATCH.

PLUM-BUDDER, same as above.—WORTHEN. To the Bullfinch's well-known habit of feeding on the buds of fruit-trees is this local name doubtless due. See **Nope.**

PLUTS, *sb. pl.* temporary pools of water.—BRIDGNORTH. Connected with E. *plod* = to walk through puddles. See SKEAT'S *Etym Dict.* Cf. **Flash.**

PODGEL [poj·il], *v. n.* to do anything in a clumsy way.—WHITCHURCH.

PODGELLING, *part. adj.* clumsy; awkward.—*Ibid.* 'Whad bin 'ee *podgellin'* at?—I never seed sich a *podgellin'* fellow.'

POKE-PUDDING, *sb.* the Long-tailed Titmouse.—BRIDGNORTH. See **Bottle-Tit.**

POLLINGER, *sb., var. pr., obs.?* a one-handed cup of coarse pottery, used for broth, milk, &c., for farm-servants,—a porringer. Sometimes called a *pollinger-cup.*—PULVERBATCH; WORTHEN. 'Al'ays bread the men's *pollingers*, an' pŭt the bread an' cheese o' the table o'er night.' See **Piggin** (1).

POMICE [pum·i's], *sb.* the apple-pulp after the juice has been expressed through the 'cider-hairs.'—CLEE HILLS.

'*Pomace* (from *poma*), the dross of Cyder pressings; Pugs, some call it Muste.'—BLOUNT'S *Glossographia*, p. 501.

Cf. **Must,** also **Pouse** (3).

POMMELLER, *sb.* a pavior's mallet.—NEWPORT. Cf. **Punner.**

POMPERS, POMPETS [pom·pur'z], WORTHEN. [pom·pets], PULVERBATCH, *sb. pl., obsols.* shallow vessels of coarse earthenware for setting milk in for skimming.

PONSHOVEL, *sb.* a shovel slightly turned up at the sides, used for spreading lime.—WHITCHURCH.

PŎŎCH [pŏŏch·], (1) *sb., var. pr.* a wicker strainer placed over the spigot-hole within the mash-tub to prevent the grains passing through into the wort.—PULVERBATCH; WORTHEN; CRAVEN ARMS; CLUN.

'*Pouches* and racking taps.'—*Auctioneer's Catalogue* (Church Stretton), 1877. A.S. *pocca*, a pouch. Cf. **Mashing-basket.**

(2) *v. n., var. pr.* to thrust out the lips in a sullen, discontented manner; to pouch, or pout.—WEM.

PŎŎCHIN [pŏŏch·in], *sb.* a wicker eel-trap.—MUCH WENLOCK; WELLINGTON. Cf. **Pŏŏch** (1), above.

POOL [pool·], (1) *sb.* a large natural sheet of water,—a lake, as 'Marton-Pool,' with which several streams are connected. 'Llyn-clys Pool,' &c. The *Pools* lie for the most part in *N. Shr.* It may be noted here that the term *Lake* is never employed in Shropshire folk-speech to denote a large sheet of water; when used, it means a small, temporary puddle,—'the roäd's all in *lakes* after the rain.'

Compare '*Pool*, or ponde of watyr. *Stagnum*,' in *Prompt. Parv.*

'A.S. *pôl*; O.Du. *poel*; M.H.Ger. *pfuol*, a pool.'—STRAT.

Cf. **Mere** (2). See Bk. II., *Folklore*, &c., 'Legends.'

(2) [poo·l], *v. a.* and *v. n.*, *var. pr.* to pull. Com. 'Well, Jane, yo'n got married, I 'ear.' 'Aye, an' I amma afeard but whad we sha'n do well, an' one *pool* each way.' Both pull together is what Jane Binsley meant to express.

'1565 It. for Wm Roe the yongers table and his mans about *pooling* downe the window ij wykes ix[s] iiij[d].'—*Churchwardens' Accounts of the Abbey*, Shrewsbury.

POOLING-BONE, same as **Draw-bone,** q. v.—SHREWSBURY; ELLESMERE.

PORE [poa·ar'], (1) *v. a.* and *v. n.* to intrude.—PULVERBATCH; CLEE HILLS. ''Er hanna invited me, so I shanna *pore* myself.'

> 'In every hous he gan to *pore* and prie,
> And begged mele and chese, or elles corn.'
>
> CHAUCER, *C. T.*, l. 7320.

(2) *v. a.* to thrust.—WORTHEN. 'I *pored* a sight o' thurns i' the 'edge, but a lot o' greet jowts [big, rough lads] comen an' maden another glat.'

PORKET, *sb.* a young pig fatted for killing—a porkling.—SHREWSBURY; PULVERBATCH; WEM. Qy. com. 'I shall feed up a couple o' them little pigs fur *porkets*, they'n do fur present use an' save the big bacon.'

PORKY, *adj.* stout; corpulent.—PULVERBATCH; WEM. ''Ow the young Maister 's barnished!—'e's gettin' quite *porky*.'

POSH [posh·], (1) *sb.* a sudden gush, as of water, &c. Com. 'Whad'n'ee think that child's done?—pool'd the spigot out o' the mashin'-tub, an' the drink come out sich a *posh*, 'e met as well a bin scauded to djeth.'

(2) *sb.* a heavy rain-fall, as of a thunder shower. Com. 'Yo'd'n better fatch them tuthree räkin's, fur be'appen we sha'n 'ăve a *posh* o' wet toërt middle day w'en the sun an' winde get'n together.' Compare M.E. *pash* = dash. See *Piers Pl.*, Text A. pass. v. l. 16.

POSS, *v. a.* to plash up and down in the water, as washerwomen do when rinsing their clothes. Com. 'These things bin ready fur swillin', get plenty o' waiter an' *poss* 'em well to clier 'em.'

'And therin thay keste hir, and *possede* hir up and downe, and sayd, take the this bathe for thi slewthe and thi glotonye.'—*MS. Lincoln*, A. 1. 17, f. 253, in HAL.

Jamieson gives 'To *Pouss*, to drive clothes hastily backwards and forwards in the water in the act of washing.' See *Piers Pl.*, Prol., l. 151. E. *push* = M.E. *posse* = O. Fr. *pousser* = Lat. *pulsare*.

POSSEL, *sb.* a state of soft, wet, swampy saturation.—WHITCHURCH. 'Yo' conna gŏŏ o' the leasow now, the ground's all of a *possel*.'

POSTS [poas·i'z], SHREWSBURY; ELLESMERE. [pŭo·u's], PULVERBATCH. [puos·n], CHURCH STRETTON. [puos·ts], CLUN, *sb. pl.* posts.

POSY [poa·zi'], *sb.* a bunch of flowers; a nosegay. Com.

'A pretie *Posie* gathered is of Flowers, Hearbes, and Weedes

. . . .

This *Posie* is so pickt, and choysely sorted throw
There is no Flower, Herbe, nor Weede, but serves some purpose now.'
GEORGE GASCOIGNE'S *Posies* (A.D. 1573), ed. Hazlitt, vol. i. p. 20.

'O Luve will venture in, where it daur na weel be seen,
O luve will venture in, where wisdom ance has been;
But I will down yon river rove, amang the wood sae green,
And a' to pu' a *Posie* to my ain dear May.

The primrose I will pu', the firstling o' the year,
And I will pu' the pink, the emblem o' my dear,
For she's the pink o' womankind, and blooms without a peer:
And a' to be a *Posie* to my ain dear May.'
ROBERT BURNS, *Poems*, p. 205.

The plural form *posies* is used for growing flowers. See below.

POSY-KNOT, *sb.* a flower-bed. Com. 'Mother, they bin măkin' the paas'n's garden so nice—sich pretty *posy-knots*, diaments, an' rounds, an' some like a fir-bob; Dick the gardener says theer'll be sich pretty *posies*, pollyantuses, an' riccaluses, qulips, an' all sorts,—the blue segs bin to go by the pool, an' the pianets into the s'rubbery.'

'When our . . garden . . . .
Is full of weeds, her fairest flowers chok'd up,
Her fruit trees all unprun'd, her hedges ruin'd,
Her *knots* disorder'd, and her wholesome herbs
Swarming with caterpillars.'
K. Richard II., III. iv. 46.

POT. See **Weights and Measures**, p. lxxxv.

POTATOES [tai·tu'z], SHREWSBURY; PULVERBATCH. Qy. com. [ti'ae·tu'z], CLUN. [chaat·u'z], BRIDGNORTH. [tit·uz], ELLESMERE, *sb. pl.* potatoes.

POT-BALL, *sb.* a dumpling made of dough; a piece of dough about the size of an egg is thrown into a pot of boiling water, and boiled till it rises to the surface, when it is taken out and served with hot treacle,—it is 'nod 'afe bad.' Com.

Randle Holme enumerates 'A *Pot Ball* or Dumpling . . of Bread,' amongst the dishes for the 'First Course' in a 'Bill of Fare.'—*Academy of Armory*, Bk. III. ch. iii. p. 79.

POT-CAKE, *sb.* a cake of dough baked in an iron pot over the fire. —PULVERBATCH. Qy. com. 'That Jäzey Owen's a poor needless piece, 'er's messed all the bit o' laisin' away i' *pot-cakes*, instid o' yeätin' the oven.' Cf. **Coal-cakes.**

POTCH, *v. a.* and *v. n.* to poke; to thrust. A weak form of *poke*. Qy. com. A little school-child was complained of to his teacher for '*potching* pins' into his neighbour.

'True sword to sword, I'll *potch* at him some way.'—*Coriolanus*, I. x. 15.

POTE [poa·t], *v. a.* to push or kick with the feet. Com. 'Them lads han *poted* these sheets through a'ready.'

Ash gives '*Pote* (*a local word*), to push.'

Mr. Skeat says that '*pote* is nothing but our common verb, to put, in the original sense of, to push. To put out, when used of a snail putting out its horns, means, to push out; another variety is "pout," which means, to push out the lips . . . .'

'*Pote* is closely allied to "but," to push with the horns.'—'*Local Notes and Queries*' in *Manchester Guardian*, Jan. 26th, 1874.

See **Put** (1).

POTECARY [pot·i'kaer'i], *sb.*, *obsols.* an apothecary.—SHREWSBURY; PULVERBATCH. ''Er's bin tăkin' stuff from Pugh the *potecary*, an' 'e's as good as a doctor, on'y 'e hanna walked the 'ospitals.'

'He is agreid to pay the *potycarye* aftyr that he have the inventory fro yow.'—*Paston Letters*, A.D. 1472, vol. iii. p. 48.

Mr. Pegge says, 'I incline to believe that it [*Potecary*] is radically the Spanish word *boticario*, as *botica* in that language more emphatically signifies the shop of an apothecary, as opposed to the itinerant empirick: and the permutation of *b* and *p* is very common. . . . . .'

'In the Comedy of the Four P's by J. Heywood, published 1569, one of them is the *Poticary* . . . . They are the *Poticary*, the *Pedlar*, the *Palmer*, and the *Pardoner*. Heywood, who was a man of learning, would hardly have made a *Poticary* one of his characters, had he not been conscious that he was right, when there were so many others with the same initial that would have answered the purpose. . . . .' —*Anecdotes of the English Language*, p. 72.

In M.E. no other form was used,—Chaucer has '*potecarie*,' *C. T.*, l. 12786.

POTHERY [pudh·ur'i'], *adj.* hot; close.—SHREWSBURY; PULVERBATCH; WEM. Qy. com. 'It wuz mighty *pothery* about three o'clock this ŏnder—I thought we shoulden a 'ad thunder, but it cliered off.'

POUNDED [pou·ndid], (1) *part. adj.* pent up, as of a stream which has been dammed.—PULVERBATCH; WEM. 'They'n bin gropin' fur trout I spect, I see the bruck's *pounded*.' A *mill-pound* is the back-water which is held in reserve for the supply of the mill.

'þat *pound* ys byclypped aboute wiþ six score rooches . . . . . and þre score ryuers eorneþ in-to þat *pound*, and non of ham alle eorneþ in-to þe se bot on.'—JOHN OF TREVISA [A.D. 1387], *Description of Britain*. *Specim. Early Eng.*, xviii. *a.* ll. 94—97.

'*Punden*, A.S. *pyndan*, to shut up, *includere*.'—STRAT.

(2) *part. adj.* pent up and overcharged: said of milk and the mammæ.—*Ibid.* (1) 'That child may well look bad, gettin' nuthin' but *pounded* milk every night; its mother 's bin i' the filds this wik or nine days, toppin' an' buttin' turmits, an' 'er couldna mind it same as if 'er wuz a-wham.' (2) 'Tak' car' an' drip them cows clane, or we sha'n be 'ăvin oäns i' thar elders—see 'ow a bin *pounded.*' Cf. **Oaned.**

POUNDS-OF-SUGAR, *sb. pl.* the seed-vessels of the Foxglove.—PULVERBATCH.

POUNDSTONE [pou·nsi'n], *sb.* dirt lying next under the coal,—the coal-floor. Com.—M. T.

POUK [pou·k], (1) *sb.* a sty on the eye.—PULVERBATCH; LUDLOW; NEWPORT.

(2) *sb.* a small spot or pustule of any kind.—SHREWSBURY; ELLESMERE. *Pouk* = *pock.*

'Scab is a dry sore, proceeding from a *Pouk*, or waterish Blister.' —*Academy of Armory*, Bk. II. ch. xvii. p. 428.

'*Hec porigo*, a poke,' occurs in a *Nominale*, xv. cent., in Wr. vocabs., vol. i. p. 224.

O.Du. *poeke*, idem. Cf. **Puckle.**

POUSE [pou·s], (1) *sb.* a mixed and varied crop of grain and pulse, as oats, pease, and vetches; oats and vetches; oats, barley, and pease—frequently used as green fodder for horses.—CRAVEN ARMS; CLEE HILLS; BRIDGNORTH.

'*Pousse*'—explained in the 'Glosse' as *pęase* [= pulse] —occurs in *The Shepheards Calender* [August]:—

> '*Per.* That shall yonder heardgrome, and none other,
> Which over the *pousse* hetheward doth post.'—l. 46.

(2) *sb.* refuse, as of the fragments of pods after threshing pulse, or of clover when the seed has been milled out, &c.—WORTHEN; CLEE HILLS; WELLINGTON. *Pouse*, in a similar sense of refuse, is used in Lancashire. Many years ago a very old lady, a native of that county, on being asked by Mr. Jackson, 'Whether during her long life she had not witnessed great changes?'—*àpropos* to society—replied: 'Well, the chief changes I have seen are, that the "*pouse*" is become quality, and the quality "*pouse*"!'

(3) *sb.* the refuse of the apple pulp when all the cider has been expressed—the 'caput mortuum.'—WORTHEN; CLEE HILLS. Cf. **Pomice.**

POWER, *sb.* a great deal; a great quantity or number. Com. 'By-gum, Master, if I'd a knowed as I'd a bin so thirsty to-day, I'd a drank a *power* more isterd'y.' So said a butcher—who had been 'in his cups' the preceding day—to a country gentleman, as riding together across the Hills to a fair at Church Stretton, they stopped at a brook-side to water their horses, and the speaker dismounting, made a cup of his palm, and drank copiously from the stream.

'*Bull.* But if the conjuror be but well paid, he'll take pains upon the ghost and lay him, look ye, in the Red Sea—and then he's laid for ever.

'*Gardn.* Why, John, there must be a *power* of spirits in that same Red Sea, I warrant ye they are as plenty as fish.'—ADDISON'S *Drummer*, in Wr. Cf. **Sight.**

POWERATION, *sb.* a great quantity,—'a *poweration* o' rain.' Com. Cf. **Mort.**

PRAISEN [pr'ai·zn], *v. a., p. t., pl.* praise. Com. 'Han'ee tried this newfangled coffee as they sen's made thrum dandelions?—I wuz thinkin' o' gettin' some, fur they *praisen* it oncommon.'

> '. . william þat bold barn · þat alle burnes *praisen.*'
> *William of Palerne*, l. 617.

PRAR [praa·r'], *sb., var. pr. pec.* an implied imprecation, a prayer,—'I gid 'im a *prar.*'—SHREWSBURY; PULVERBATCH. Qy. com.

PRARS, *sb. pl., var. pr.* prayers. Com. 'Good night, Missis, an' God bless yo':' said William Chidley to a friendly neighbour,—'Good-night, young Missis'—to her daughter. 'Good-night, Chidley,' responded the old 'Missis,' 'an' God bless yo'; I 'ope yo' thinken on God, an' dunna furget to say yore *prars.*' 'Say my *prars!*' replied Chidley, 'no, I dunna furget 'em, I say 'em every night—the Lord's *prar*, an' the Belif, an' the Ten Commandments, an' a power on it.'

PRAUNCE [pr'au·ns], *v. n.* to deport one's self in a high and mighty kind of way.—SHREWSBURY; PULVERBATCH. 'Yo' shoulden jest see him *praunce* about as if 'e wuz Lord o' the Manor; 'e'll do it a bit too much, an' then be'appen 'e'll gŏŏ down faster than 'e got up.'

> 'So growen great, through arrogant delight
> Of th' high descent whereof he was yborne,
>
> . . . .
>
> That, when the knight he spyde, he gan advaunce
> With huge force and insupportable mayne,
> And towardes him with dreadfull fury *praunce.*'
> SPENSER, *F. Q.*, Bk. I. c. vii. sts. x. xi.

PRAUNTING [pr'au·ntin], *part. adj.* prancing; curvetting: said of a mettlesome horse.—SHREWSBURY; PULVERBATCH. Qy. com. Cf. **Aunty-praunty.**

PRIAL [pr'ei·ul], *sb.* three cards of one kind,—a term employed in the games of Costly, Commerce, &c., and which is known to be corrupted from *pair-royal.* Qy. com.

'A pair is a pair of any two, as two kings, two queens, &c. A *pair-royal* is of three, as three kings, three queens, &c.'—*The Complete Gamester*, p. 106, in NARES. See **Costly.**

PRICKER, same as **Nild** (2).—OSWESTRY, *St. Martins*; M. T.

'*Punctorium*, a prykker.'—*Nominale MS.*, in HAL.

A.S. *prica*, a prick; a point.

PRILL, *sb.* a streamlet of clear water, a rill; a runnel from a spring.—PULVERBATCH; CHURCH STRETTON; CLUN; MUCH WENLOCK; WELLINGTON; WEM. 'I wuz mighty glad to see the poor owd place agen after so many 'ears—I could aumust a cried w'en I sid the little *prill* runnin' an' ripplin' alung the very same as w'en gran'mother wuz alive, an' I fatched waiter from the well fur her tay,—it seemed the on'y thing lef' as wunna changed.' Cf. **Rindel.**

PRINK-UP, *v. n.* to revive, as plants do when recovering from transplantation.—PULVERBATCH; WEM; ELLESMERE. 'The sun's laid them cabbidge-plants flat o' the groun', but they'n *prink-up* w'en the je'ow comes on 'em.'

> 'Do you not see howe these newe fangled pratling elfes,
> *Prinke up* so pretty late in every place?'
>
> *Old Play*, in NARES.

Cf. **Perk-up.**

PRITCH [pr'ich·], (1) *sb.* a staff of wood about three feet in length, steel-pointed at one end, and attached at the other, by two iron 'eyes' to the axle-tree of a cart. Its purpose is to 'scotch' the cart, when going up-hill, which it does by means of the steel-pointed end sticking into the ground, at a given distance from the axle-tree. On level ground, the *pritch* either drags after the cart, or otherwise is held up beneath it, by a short chain and a hook. Com. *Pritch* is a weak form of *prick*. A.S. *prica*, a prick; a point.

(2) *sb.* a long pole furnished with an iron fork at one end, used by Severn boatmen for propelling their boats,—a river term.

PRIVY [pr'iv·i'], *sb. Ligustrum vulgare*, common Privet,—'the *Privy*-'edge is in blow.'—WEM; ELLESMERE.

> 'Set *priuie* or prim
> Set boxe like him.'
>
> TUSSER [Septembers abstract], p. 33, ed. E. D. S.

PRIZE [pr'ei·z], *v. a.* to force up, or open; to compel to let go, as by wrestling with, or by any other means. Com.

Compare Shakespeare's 'bony *priser*'—the strong wrestler who could *lift* and *throw over* his antagonist—in, *As You Like It*, II. iii. 8. See **Proz.**

PRODIGAL, *adj.*, *pec.* proud; upstart.—PULVERBATCH; WORTHEN; WEM. ''E's a poor *prodigal* auf—dunna know whose legs 'e stands on, but be'appen 'e'll find it out w'en 'e buys 'is own shoes.'

PROFFER [pr'of·ur'], *v. a.* to offer; to tender a service. Com. 'One o' yo' chaps mun gŏŏ an' 'elp Jones to-day, they *profferedem* us a mon w'en we wun throshin', an'

> "Giff-gaff's a good fellow,
> One good turn desarves another."'

'And the knyȝtis neiȝeden, and scorneden hym, and *profreden* vynegre to hym.'—*Luke* xxiii. 36, Wicliffite version [A.D. 1388].

PROFLIGATE, *adj.*, *pec.* prolific. Qy. com. 'I like them w'ite 'tatoes as they callen "Farmers' Glories"—they bin the most *profligate*.'

PROKE [pr'oa·k], (1) *v. a.* to poke, as of the fire, &c.,—'dunna *proke* the fire.' Qy. com. W. *procio*, to thrust; to stab.

(2) *v. a.* and *v. n.* to poke into or about; to obtrude—'*prokin'* in every 'ole an' cornel.' 'Al'ays *prokes* 'er nose into other folks's business.' Qy. com.

PROKER, *sb.* a poker. Qy. com.

'Basnett stept out at the back doore and Hinton with him, and comeing to the oven on the backside, Basnett tooke a peele with which they put bread into the oven, and Hinton tooke a pole which they call an oven *proaker*.'—GOUGH'S *History of Myddle*, p. 189.

PRONG, *sb.*, *pec.* a silver or plated fork; in contradistinction to the common steel fork of two or three 'fangs.' Com.

'Six superior quality electro-plated dinner *prongs*.'—*Auctioneer's Catalogue*, 1877.

Pegge has '*Prong*, a fork; as a hay-prong, a muck-prong. North.' See **Fang** (2).

PROSPERATION, *sb.*, *var. pr.* prosperity.—MUCH WENLOCK.

'*Prosperation*
to the
Corporation.'

See Bk. II., *Folklore*, &c., 'Customs' (*Bailiff's Feast, Wenlock*).

PROUD-TAILOR, *sb.* the Goldfinch.—MUCH WENLOCK. See Mr. Nares on this name—which he says is a Warwickshire one—for the Goldfinch. Cf. **Sheriff's-Man**. See **Jack-Nicol**.

PROVOKE, *v. a.*, *pec.* to revoke,—'to *provoke* a bargain,' is an expression often heard.—WEM.

PROZ [pr'oz·], *pret.* prized; forced by any means, not necessarily by leverage,—'We *proz* 'im off:' said of making a dog let go his hold.—WHITCHURCH. See **Prize**.

PUCK [puk·], *pret.* picked,—'bin them pars shuk or 'and *puck*?'—CLUN; CORVE DALE; CLEE HILLS; MUCH WENLOCK; WELLINGTON.

PUCKLE, *sb.* a pimple; a pustule: diminutive of *pock*.—PULVERBATCH; WEM.

Du. *puckle*—*idem*. Cf. **Pouk** (2).

PUFF-BALL, *sb.* same as **Fuzzy-ball**, q. v.—SHREWSBURY; LUDLOW.

PUG, *v. a.* to pull, as of entangled hair.—CLEE HILLS.

Jamieson has '*To Pug*, to pull. Perths.' Cf. **Plug**.

PUGS, (1) *sb. pl.* tangled locks or ends of hair.—CLEE HILLS. Cf. **Litch** (2).

(2) same as **Pens**, q. v.—SHREWSBURY.

PUKE, *sb.* an emetic.—PULVERBATCH; WORTHEN. 'That child inna well, 'er'd better 'ăve a *puke* i' the mornin'.'

PUMMICE [pum·is], *sb.* the heart, liver, and lights of a lamb. —CLUN.

'*Sheep Pummices* is the Head, Heart, Lights, Liver, and Wind-pipe of a Sheep all hanging together. *Lambs Pum[m]ices*, is the same of a Lamb.'—*Academy of Armory*, Bk. III. ch. iii. p. 88.

See **Jerks**, also **Race** (2).

PUMPLE-STONES, *sb. pl.* pebble-stones.—ATCHAM.

Pegge has '*Pumple*, a pimple. Pumple nose. North.' Cf. **Pimple**.

PUN [pŭon·], *v. a.* to knock; to beat; to pound. Com.

(1) 'Please, Ma'am, it wuz only Betsey *punning* Sally down to lay the cloth.' Such was the explanation given to a lady who enquired of her maid-servant the meaning of a repeated knocking she had heard at a backstairs door. Sally was not knocked down, but was reminded of her duty by Betsey '*punning* at the door!'

(2) 'The Maister says I mun *pun* the bif-steak, but nuthin' ŏŏl ever mak' it tender.' 'Tell 'im to sen' it to our 'ouse, I can pŭt seven set o' tith about it, as ŏŏn soon mak' it tender.'

'*Thersites.* He would *pun* thee into shivers with his fist, as a sailor breaks a biscuit.'—*Troilus and Cressida*, II. i. 42.

'To stampe or *punne* in a morter.'—*Florio*, p. 6, in HAL.

PUND, *sb. pl.* pounds,—''e gid six *pund* odd fur it.' Com.

'A gold ring drow he forth anon
An hundred *pund* was worth þe ston.'
Havelok the Dane, l. 1633.

A.S. *pund*, sing. and pl. alike.

PUNGLED, *part. adj.* embarrassed in money matters. 'If Mr. —— had a large income he would not be so *pungled* as he is.'—WHITCHURCH. Compare '*Pung*, a purse,' in HAL.

PUNISHMENT, *sb.*, *pec.* pain.—ELLESMERE, *Welshampton*. 'I maun get this tuth drawed, fur I conna bar the *punishment* no lunger.'

PUNK, *sb. Polyporous squamosus*, the Scaly Polyporous. A white fungus growing on decayed ash-trees, which in its dry state is possessed of great elasticity, and will rebound like an Indian-rubber ball.—BISHOP'S CASTLE; CLUN.

PUNNER, *sb.* a pavior's mallet.—NEWPORT. See **Pun**. Cf. **Pommeller**.

PUNSE, *v. a.* to kick.—NEWPORT. 'The red moggy *punsed* Daddy i' the face:' said a little Edgmond child.

PURGY [pur'·gi'], *adj.* conceited; consequential. — SHREWSBURY; ATCHAM; PULVERBATCH; WEM. 'Well, yo' nee'na be so *purgy*, yo' bin none so 'onsome, an' if yo' han a bit o' money, I dar'say a little 'orse can carry it.'

PURGY-HOLE, *sb.* the grated ash-pit in front of a kitchen fire-place.—NEWPORT. Cf. **Pit-grate**.

PURLED, *part. adj.* become lean, by reason of injury or overwork: said of beasts,—'that beäst looks *purled*.'—WELLINGTON.

PURPLE DEA-NETTLE, *sb.* the red Dead-nettle.—PULVERBATCH. See **French-nettle**. Cf. **Dea-nettle**.

PUT [put·], (1) *sb.* an attack, as by a cow.—CLEE HILLS. ''Er made a pŭt at me, but I got out on 'er roäd.'

Jamieson gives 'To *Put*, to push with the head or horns.'

'*Puttyn̄* or schowyn̄. *Impello, trudo.* To put, or push, as with the head or horns, a verb still in use in Yorkshire, has been derived from

bouter, to butt. Robert Brunne uses it in this sense, App. to Pref. cxciv. "To putte, pellere."—CATH. ANG.' *Prompt. Parv. and Notes.*
Mr. Skeat says that *put* is of Celtic origin—Gael. *put*; Corn. *poot*; W. *pwtio*, to push; hence the Danish *putte*. And if Fr. *bouter* be related, which is doubtful, it is from a Celtic source. See **Pote**. Cf. **Bunt** (1).

(2) *v. n.* to attack; to fly upon, as a dog would,—'Now *püt* at 'im, lad.'—*Ibid.*

(3) *sb.* an attempt; an endeavour. — WORTHEN; CLEE HILLS. 'Yo'n do it some time, fur yo' hanna maden a bad püt at it.'

PUT-ABOUT, *part. adj.* distressed; annoyed. A woman would be *put-about* by the loss of her husband, or by the breaking of her best tea-cups—though perhaps not equally so. Com.

PYEL, *sb.* an outcry; a clamour.—SHREWSBURY; CHURCH STRETTON; WEM. 'Owd Sammy Griffi's wunna so sharp as a should be: they wun oncommon good to 'im at Onslow 'all, an' one day a wuz 'ăvin' some toast an' swig theer, w'en a mon comen in an' says, "Sammy, yore wife 's djed." "No danger!" says Sammy. "'Er is, though, indeed," says the mon. "Well," answered Sammy, "jest yo' wait'n till I've done this drink, an' then yo'n 'ear me mak' a pretty *pyel*."' [*Peal* is meant.]

QUACK [kwak·], *adj.* silent; close.—PULVERBATCH; WORTHEN. 'Yo' met'n trust Jem, 'e's al'ays *quack* w'en it's wanted—if anybody gi'es 'im sixpince 'e'll never tell; but it's a pris'ner.'

QUAIGH, (1) *sb., obsols.* a cup, of—what is known to coopers, as—'bend-ware;' a turned round cup with a short, upright handle.—CORVE DALE. *Quaighs*, though now (1875) scarcely to be met with, were, fifty years ago, almost as common on kitchen and farm-house tables as earthenware drinking-vessels. *Quaighs* of a large size were used as pails.
Jamieson has '*Quaich, Quegh*, a small and shallow drinking cup with two ears. Ir. Gael. *cuach*, a cup or bowl.'
Cf. **Piggin** (1) and (2), also **Bouk** (1). See **Treen.**

(2) *v. a., obsols.* to bend; to turn,—'*quaigh* the branch round the end o' the wall:' said of training a fruit-tree.—CORVE DALE, *Stanton Lacey*. See **Gh** (5) in **Grammar Outlines** (*consonants*, &c.).

QUAIL, *v. n., obsols.* to languish; to fail; to fall sick.—BRIDGNORTH. Spenser employs this word in the sense of to wither or perish:—
'The braunch once dead, the budde eke needes must *quaile*.'—*Shepheards Calendar*, November, l. 91.
Pegge has '*Quail*, to fail; to fall sick; to faint. North.'
Compare Du. *kwelen*, to languish.

QUAKERS, *sb.* common Quaking-grass.—SHREWSBURY; PULVERBATCH; WORTHEN; WEM. See **Cow-quakers.**

QUANK, *adj.* still; quiet,—'as *quank* as a mouze.'—CORVE DALE; CLEE HILLS. Pegge gives this word for 'Cheshire.'

QUARRIES [kwor'·iz], *sb. pl.* square flooring-tiles.—SHREWSBURY; PULVERBATCH. Qy. com. 'The kitchen flur wuz sich nice *quarries*—as red as a cherry.'

O.Fr. *quareaus*, i. e. *quadrellus*, de Lat. *quadrum*; Fr. *carreau*, a square. See BUR.

QUARTER [kwaar'·tur'], *v. n.* to drive a cart in a lane with deep ruts, in such a way as to keep each wheel clear of them.—LUDLOW; BRIDGNORTH.

QUARTERS, *sb. pl.* to 'make *quarters* good,' means to keep in with the publicans by dividing custom. Thus, if a farmer going to market were to 'put up' at one house, and go to another 'for a glass,' in order to maintain just relations with both—he would 'make his *quarters* good.'—BRIDGNORTH. 'Now, then, Bob, come wham.' 'I conna yet, I got to gŏŏ to the Swan to *mak' my quarters good*.' Compare the 'keep fair *quarter*,' of Shakespeare, *Comedy of Errors*, II. i. 108.

QUAT, *adv.* close; still, as a hare on her form: used metaphorically also,—'to keep *quat*,' so as not to attract notice.—CORVE DALE.

Mr. Nares says '*Quat* is used for the sitting of a hare.' Cf. **Squat** (2).

QUAWK [kwau·k], *v. n.* to caw, as crows.—SHREWSBURY; PULVERBATCH; WEM.

'E'en roused by *quawking* of the flopping crows,' Clare, in WEDG. Cf. **Croup.**

QUEAK [kwee·k], *v. a.* to press, or squeeze.—CLUN. 'I shall be fŏoäst to get another box, I conna *queak* all these things i' this.' See **Quoke.** Cf. **Tweak** (2).

QUEASY [kwaiz·i], *adv.* affected with nausea; squeamish; sick at the stomach.—SHREWSBURY; PULVERBATCH. 'I dunna know how folks can ate fat bacon fur thar breakfast, it makes me feel *quaizy* to look at it.'

'. . letyng yow weet that the worlde semyth *qweysye* heer.'—*Paston Letters*, A.D. 1473, vol. iii. p. 98.

'I, with your two helps, will so practise on Benedick that, in despite of his quick wit and his *queasy* stomach, he shall fall in love with Beatrice.'—*Much Ado About Nothing*, II. i. 399.

QUEECE [kwee·s], *sb. Columba palumbus*, the Ring-Dove, or Wood-Pigeon.—CHURCH STRETTON; NEWPORT. Called '*Queese*' by Randle Holme. Cf. **Quice**, below.

QUEENING [kwin·in], *sb.* a fine-flavoured sweet apple, common in the cider-orchards.—LUDLOW.

'The *Queening*, is a fair and striped Apple, and beautiful in its Season being a kind of Winter Fruit.'—*Academy of Armory*, Bk. II. ch. iii. p. 48.

QUEET [kwee·t], *adv., var. pr.* quite.—CLUN, *Herefd. Border.* Cf. **Quite.**

QUERD, QUERDŎŎD. See **Cord, Cordwood.**

QUERRY [kwae·r'i'], *sb., var. pr.* a stone-quarry.—CHURCH STRETTON.

QUERT [kwur't·], *sb.*, *var. pr.* a quart,—'a two-*quert* costrel.'—BISHOP'S CASTLE; CLUN.

QUICE, QUISTE [kwei·s], SHREWSBURY; PULVERBATCH; WORTHEN; CLUN; LUDLOW; WEM; ELLESMERE; OSWESTRY. [kwei·st], CRAVEN ARMS, *sb.* the Ring-Dove, or Wood-Pigeon.

Grose gives '*Quice*, a wood-pidgeon. Glouc.' See **Queece**, above.

QUICK, *sb.* young hawthorn for planting hedges. Com. 'Theer's bin too much tinin', an' now it's all djed stuff an' staggers a 'undred 'ear owd—the 'edge wants riddin', an' some good *quick* set, like Mr. Jackson's done the Quaker's meadow.'

Compare '*Vivus*, Quicke, or lively greene.'—*Dict. Etym. Lat.* A.S. *cwic*, alive. Cf. **Sate** (1).

QUID, *sb.* a cud = that which is chewed.—CORVE DALE. See example *sub voce* **Owlerd**.

QUILE, QUOIL, *sb.* a heap of hay from which the cart is loaded for carrying.—WELLINGTON; NEWPORT.

QUININ. See **Queening**.

QUIRK [kwur'·k], *sb.*, *obsols.* the clock of a stocking,—an ornamental device knitted at the ancle.—PULVERBATCH. 'I al'ays think w'en I'm knittin' a stockin' as the waidiest part 's o'er w'en I get to the *quirk*, an' w'en the 'eel's bond down, it's aumust as good as done.'

'Then have they neyther stockes to these gay hosen, not of cloth (though never so fine) for that is thought too base, but of jarsey, worsted, crewell, silke, thred, and such like, or els, at the least of the finest yawn that can be got, and so curiously knit with open seame down the legge, with *quirkes* and clockes about the anckles, and sometime (haplie) interlaced with golde or silver threds, as is wonderfull to beholde.'—STUBBES' *Anatomy of Abuses* [A.D. 1595], p. 31.

QUITE, *adv.* quiet.—NEWPORT.

> 'That every cristen wight shal han penance
> But if that he his Cristendome withseye,
> And gon al *quite*, if he wol it reneye?'
>
> CHAUCER, *C. T.*, l. 15916.

See **I** (5) in **Grammar Outlines** (*vowels*, &c.).

QUIVVY [kwiv·i'], *sb.* a knack,—'theer's a bit of a *quivvy* in plantin' these s'rubs.'—WELLINGTON.

QULIPS [keu·lips], *sb. pl.*, *var. pr.* tulips.—PULVERBATCH.

QUOB [kwob·], *sb.* a marshy spot in a field; a quagmire.—PULVERBATCH; CHURCH STRETTON; WELLINGTON; WEM. See **All of a Quob**.

QUOBBY, *adj.* flabby; wanting solidity.—PULVERBATCH; WEM. 'I dunna think it's solid fat, 'e's *quobby*—more inclined to be dropsical.'

QUOKE [kwoa·k], *pret.* squeezed; pressed.—CLUN. ''E *quoke* me so 'ard:' said a girl of her lover. See **Queak**.

RABBITS'-MEAT, *sb.* the red Dead-nettle.—WHITCHURCH, *Tilstock.* See **Dun-nettle.**

RACE, (1) *sb.* the heart, liver, and lights of a pig.—SHREWSBURY; WELLINGTON; COLLIERY. See **Haslet.**

(2) *sb.* the same of a lamb. — WELLINGTON; COLLIERY. See **Pummice.**

(3) *sb.* the same of a calf.—SHREWSBURY; PULVERBATCH; WELLINGTON; COLLIERY.

RACK, (1) *sb.* a rude, narrow pathway, such as sheep would make in their walk; a path or track through a wood.—PULVERBATCH; WORTHEN; WELLINGTON. 'I wuz ketcht i' the snow-storm gweïn o'er the 'ill, an' missed the *rack* an' got maskered, but wuz pretty glad w'en I sid Cothercot.'

Mr. Walter White, when speaking of his walk from Cherbury towards the Stiperstones, says: 'Starting anew I came presently to the "*rack*"—that is—a dim track leading up the wild hill which then rose in my way . . . . . The "*rack*" ascends to a lonesome table-land patched with gorse, bracken, and rushes.'—*All Round the Wrekin*, p. 65, ed. 1860.

See **Outrack.**

(2) *v. a.* to refine ale by drawing it off, clearing the cask of the dregs, and then putting it back, sometimes with the addition of a little isinglass and loaf sugar, if not deemed sufficiently clear, after which process it is closely bunged up. Qy. com. 'The Maister likes to *rack* the ale, but fur my part, I think it feeds better on the crap, an' it'll be clier enough an' gie it time.' See *Rack* in WEDG.

RACKLE [r'ak·l], (1) *v. n.* to make a clattering noise,—to rattle.—PULVERBATCH. Qy. com. 'I think a bin luggin' barley at the Bonk, I 'ear the waggins *rackle*.' See **Tl** in **Grammar Outlines** (*consonants*, &c.).

(2) *sb.* noisy, chattering talk.—*Ibid.* 'Owd yore *rackle*, wench, theer's no sich a thing as püttin' a word in edgeways.'

(3) *sb.* a very talkative person.—*Ibid.* ''Er's a despert *rackle*—'er is.'

RACK OF EYE, *phr.* to work by *rack of eye*, is to be guided by the eye without line or rule.—PULVERBATCH; WEM. 'John, yo' binna gweïn mighty straïght ŏŏth yore job theer.' 'Well, Maister, I canna do it no better by *rack of eye*, an' theer's sich a tellif o' scutch to root up.'

RADDLING, *sb.* bribery; the act of bribing.—SHREWSBURY. This term is said to have originated in a rough custom of marking with *raddle* [= ruddle] the houses of persons suspected of taking bribes for political purposes at election times. 'I spect the Rads han bin doin' a lot o' *raddlin'* this time, I sid two or three 'ousen raddled above a bit.' 'Aye, an' theer'd be a sight more if they wun all raddled as took bribes.' Said *apropos* to the usages which obtained at the General Election, 1880.

RAKE, (1) *v. a.* to cover: said of fires, which, when required to be kept alive throughout the night, are smothered with inferior coal that will merely smoulder if left undisturbed. Com. 'I dunna think it tak's a bit more coal to *rake* the fire than light it, fur w'en it's coked it tinds direc'ly.' Compare the following citations:—

'And whan he sey noon other remedye,
In hote coles he hath him-seluen *raked;*
For with no venim deyned him to dye.'
CHAUCER, B. 3323 (Six-text ed.), Skeat.

'. . . Here in the sands
Thee I'll *rake* up.'—*King Lear*, IV. vi. 281.

Palsgrave—A.D. 1530—explains *rake* thus, 'to cover anything in the fire with ashes.' See HAL.

(2) *v. a.* to clear the grate of ashes. Com. 'Bessy, yo' hanna *raked* out this grate—it's 'afe fŭll o' ess—I canna do ŏŏth sich muckerin' work, an' it inna likely as the fire ŏŏl tind.'

'*Pistol.* Elves, ...
Where fires thou find'st *unraked* and hearths unswept,
There pinch the maids as blue as bilberry;
Our radiant queen hates sluts and sluttery.'
Merry Wives of Windsor, V. v. 48.

RAKINGS, *sb.* scattered grain raked off the stubble after the main crop has been carried. Com. 'We hanna much to do now, on'y a bit o' spring w'ëat an' a jag or two o' *rakin's* to carry.' A.S. *racian*, to rake together.

RAGGED-ROBIN, (1) *sb. Lychnis Flos-Cuculi*, Meadow Lychnis.—PULVERBATCH.

(2) *sb.* a rolled jam-dumpling of which the paste is flaky, or ragged, in appearance.—PULVERBATCH. ''Ere's a rar' *raggit-robin*, lads, to blow out all the crivices' [in the stomach].

RAGGED-ROBINS, *sb.* a vein of iron-stone lying on the west side of Lightmoor Fault, so called from its ragged appearance.—COLLIERY, *Lilleshall;* M. T.

RAGGLING, *adj.* said of anything working roughly or unevenly,—'*ragglin'* 'arrows.'—ATCHAM.

RAISTY. See **Reasty.**

RALLY [r'al·i'], (1) *sb., pec.* a violent, clamorous ringing of a bell.—WORTHEN. 'They gidden the bell a pretty *rally*, as if they wun gweïn to 'ăve the 'ouse down.' Cf. Fr. *rallier*, to call together.

(2) *sb., pec.* an angry scolding; a sound rating.—PULVERBATCH. 'If I could see 'er, I'd gie 'er a *rally* as ŏŏd pay 'er fur the new an' the owd.'

RAMMEL [r'am·il], *sb.* reddish earth, neither clay nor sand—not fertile, a foe to vegetation.—WELLINGTON. 'I wunna tak' that garden, it's all *rammel.*'

RAMMELLY, *adj.* of the nature of 'rammel.'—SHREWSBURY. 'It ŏŏnna do in 'ere, Maister, the groun's too *rammelly.*'

RAMSONS, *sb. Allium Ursinum*, broad-leaved Garlic.—CLEE HILLS.

'The leaues of *Ramsons* be stamped and eaten of diuers in the Low-countries, with fish for a sauce, euen as we do eate green-sauce made with sorrell.'—GERARDE'S *Herball*, Bk. I. p. 180.

See **Devil's Posy**.

RANDAN [ran·dan·'], (1) *sb.* a string of words conveying no particular information,—'a pack of nonsense;' foolish talk.—PULVERBATCH; WORTHEN. Qy. com. 'I never 'eärd sich a fellow, 'e's al'ays talking some *randan* as yo' bin none the wiser fur.' To talk *randan* is to talk at *random*,—the words are cognate.

'*Randone*, or longe renge of wurdys, or other thynges. *Haringga*. . . *Haringga* seems here to be given for *harenga*, or *arenga*, a public declamation. See Ducange.'—*Prompt. Parv. and Notes.*

Connected with O.Fr. *randon*, force; violence; impétuosité.—BUR. See **Random-shot**, below.

(2) *adj.* continuous, purposeless, senseless, as applied to talk.—PULVERBATCH; WHITCHURCH; ELLESMERE. Qy. com. 'Sich *randan* talk, I conna mak' ne'ther tops nur tails on it—it far mithers me.'

RANDOM-SHOT, *sb.* a wild young fellow.—PULVERBATCH; WEM. ''Ow's Tum ossin'—'ow's 'e gweïn on?' 'I dunna know, I doubt 'e's but a *random-shot*.' Compare *random* = in a lavish way, in the following:—

'When my son grew to man's estate, hee had leave to live more at *random* (*liberius vivendi fuit potestas*).'—*Terence in English*, 1641, in WR. Connected with O. Fr. *randon*, same as above.

RANDY [r'an·di'], (1) *sb., sl.?* a frolic; a 'spree.'—SHREWSBURY; WELLINGTON. Qy. com. 'Inna that chap come to 'is work this mornin'?—I'll be bound 'e's on the *randy* agen.'

Cf. 'O.Fr. *randir*, s'avancer avec impétuosité, presser vivement.'—BUR.

(2) *adj.* self-willed; hard to manage.—ATCHAM. 'A despert *randy* chap.'

RANDY-ROW [rou·], *sb., sl.?* a noisy merry-making.—WELLINGTON; WEM. 'They bin 'ăvin' a perty *randy-row*.'

RANTIPOLE [r'an·ti'poal], *sb.* a rude, romping, boisterous child, of either sex.—PULVERBATCH. 'Whad a great rompin', rip-stitch *rantipole* that girld is!'

'. . No! they have had their whimsey out . . . and quiet good souls as they are by that time become, they go on without *Rantipoling*, in the ordinary course of reasonable creatures.'—*Sir Charles Grandison*, vol. vii. p. 214, ed. 1776.

There is [1877] a cottage near Longden (Salop) which bears the name of *Rantipole Hall*, but why or wherefore is not known.

RAP [r'ap·], *v. a.* to exchange; to swap.—PULVERBATCH; CLEE HILLS. Qy. com. 'Ben Jones wanted to *rap* his owd mar' fur Preece's pony, but Tummy wunna to be done athatn; 'e said—"Aye, ketch a noud 'orse ŏŏth chaff!"'

RAPS, (1) *sb. pl.* merry-makings; sports; fun of any kind. Com. 'Well, Bill, 'ow bin 'ee?—I hanna sid yo' sence Stretton far; whad sort o' *raps* 'ad'n'ee?' 'Oh! we'd'n rar' *raps*—never got'n wham till break-o'-day.' Perhaps connected with Du. *rap*; Sw. *rapp*, brisk.

(2) *sb. pl.* news. Com. 'Come in 'ere, Ben, into this cornel an' warm yore fit—now, whad bin the best *raps* töërt 'Abberley?' 'Nod much, Missis, on'y Everall's stacks bin burnt.' ''Eart alive! yo' dunna say so.'

RAT AND SCAT, *phr.*, *obsols.* a contemptuous expression applied to a company or set,—'they bin a bad lot, *rat an' scat*.'—PULVERBATCH.

RATHES, RAVES [r'ai·dhz], WHITCHURCH, *Tilstock.* [r'ai·vz], CORVE DALE; CLEE HILLS, *sb. pl.* the movable side-rails of a cart or waggon, put on for carrying a greater load, as of hay or corn at harvest-time. Palsgrave has '*Raves* of a carte,' but gives no French equivalent. In *The Treatise of Walter de Biblesworth*, xiii. cent., it is said that—

> 'Checune charette ke meyne blés,
> Deyt aver *redeles* au coustés;'—

'*redeles*' being glossed '*rayes*' (*ronges*). See Wr. vocabs., vol. i. p. 168. Cf. **Ripples.**

RATLING, *sb.* the smallest pig of a litter.—SHREWSBURY; PULVERBATCH; WORTHEN; OSWESTRY. 'William aumust al'ays buys the *ratlin'*, 'cause 'is wife is sich a good 'and at tiddlin' 'em on—'er never fails to make a good bacon on 'em.' Cf. **Reckling.**

RATON, *sb.* a young rat.—NEWPORT.

> 'Wiþ þat ran þere a route · of *ratones* at ones,
> And smale mys with hem · mo þan a þousande,
> And comen to a conseille · for here comune profit.
> . . . .
> A *raton* of renom · most renable of tonge
> Seide . . . .'
>
> *Piers Pl.*, Text B., *Prol.*, ll. 146-58.

> 'An' heard the restless *rattons* squeak
> About the riggin.'
>
> ROBERT BURNS, *Poems*, p. 38, l. 17.

'*Ratun*, or ratōn. *Rato*, *sorex*.'—*Prompt. Parv.*

RATTLE-BOX, *sb.* same as **Cockscomb**, q. v.—ELLESMERE.

RATTOCKS, *sb. pl.* the very small potatoes, used for feeding pigs.—ELLESMERE. 'Now, Jenny, yo' gŏŏ an' pick up them *rattocks* o' tittoes, an' wesh 'em to bile fur the pig, an' then w'en we killen 'im yo' sha'n a the brains.' The brains of a pig thoroughly cleansed, and then boiled, and seasoned with butter, pepper, and salt, are esteemed as a delicacy of cottage fare.

RAUGHT [r'au·t], (1) *pret.* and *part. past*, reached.—PULVERBATCH. 'I went to church athout my book, but Mr. Smith *raught* me one out o' thar pew.'

> 'þere þe pres was perelouste · he priked in formest,
> & blessed so wiþ his briȝt bront · a-boute in eche side,
> þat what rink so he *rauȝt* · he ros neuer after.'
>
> *William of Palerne*, l. 1193.

'He smiled me in the face, *raught* me his hand,
And, with a feeble gripe, says . . . . . .'
K. Henry V., IV. vi. 21.

'The auld guidman *raught* down the pock,
An' out a handfu' gied him.'
ROBERT BURNS, *Poems*, p. 46, l. 1, c. 2.

(2) *pret.* and *part. past*, arrived, and, as one would say, 'got to,' a destination,—''E started afore 'is Faither an' may, but 'e hanna *raught* yet;' 'The poor lad were welly gone afore the Doctor *raught* to 'im.'—WELLINGTON; COLLIERY; NEWPORT; WEM; WHITCHURCH. *Raught* as a transitive form does not obtain in these districts.

'& went forþ on here way · wiȝtly and fast,
til þei redli hade *rauȝt* · to grete rome euene.'
William of Palerne, l. 4823.

A.S. *rǽcan tó*, to reach to; pt. t. *rǽhte tó*. See *sub voce* **Noration.**

RAUNCH [r'au·nsh *and* r'aun·s], *v. a.* to tear up; to bite at eagerly, as of grass: said of cattle,—'They'n be glad to *raunch* that feg up w'en they can get nuthin' else.'—PULVERBATCH. *Raunch an' scraunch* is to snatch greedily; to grasp at,—'Look at that ŏŏman *raunchin' an' scraunchin'*; 'er'll be all o'er the fild afore the others bin in at the gate:' said *apropos* of a gleaner. Compare Spenser's—

'Hasting to *raunch* the arrow out.'
The Shepheards Calender, August, l. 100.

RAVES. See **Rathes.**

RAWL [r'au·l], *v. a.* to pull roughly about. Com. 'They *rawlened* the poor chap about an' abused 'im shameful.' Cf. **Yawl.**

RAWM [r'au·m], *v. a.* to eat greedily.—PULVERBATCH. 'The young beäs ŏŏn *rawm* up all that feg w'en theer's a snow o' the ground.' Cf. **Raunch.**

RAWNERS, RAWNIES [r'aun·ur'z], WEM. [r'au·niz], WELLINGTON, *sb. pl.* rotten, worthless branches of trees. See **Rawny-boughs,** below.

RAWNING, *adj.* a term applied to the movements of a big, awkward man.—WHITCHURCH, *Whixall.* See **Rawny,** below.

RAWN-PEGS, same as **Rawners,** above.—WELLINGTON.

RAWNY [r'au·ni'], *adj.* a term applied to the appearance of a large-built and awkward man,—'a great *rawny* fellow.'—WHITCHURCH, *Whixall.* Perhaps *brawny* is meant, but see **Rawning,** above.

RAWNY-BOUGHS, same as **Rawners,** above.

RAW-YEDS, a corrupted form, apparently, of **Roits,** q. v.

RAYE, *sb.*, *obs.* a rail.—SHREWSBURY.

'1634. Itm̃ for nayles & setting up the dore of the *raye* that compasseth the Communion table 1d.'—*Churchwardens' Accounts of the Abbey*, Shrewsbury.

'*Redeles*,' the side-*rails* of a cart, is explained by '*rayes*' in *Walter de Biblesworth.* See *sub voce* **Rathes.**

REAN [r'i'·h'n], PULVERBATCH; CORVE DALE. [r'ee·n], CRAVEN ARMS. [r'ai·n], WEM; WHITCHURCH, *sb.* the furrow between the 'buts' of ploughed lands for carrying off the water.

> 'Cayme, husbantes crafte thou must goe towe,
> And Abell a sheapharde be.
> Therefore of cornes fayer and cleane
> That growes one rigges out of the *reian*,
> Cayme, thou shalt offer, as I meane,
> To God in magistie.'
>
> *The Death of Abel, Chester Plays*, vol. i. p. 36.

'A *Ree-an* is the distance between two buts.'—*Academy of Armory*, Bk. III. ch. iii. p. 73.

REAP [r'ee·p *and* r'ai·p], *v. a., pec.* in combination with *up,*—to revive the memory of painful bygones, in a sense antagonistic to that of letting 'the dead past bury its dead.' Com. 'Yo' nee'na *reap up* about the poor owd mon bein' i' jail—that's forty 'ear agŏŏ.'

REAR [r'ae·r'], (1) *v. a.* to raise: especially applied to making pork-pies. Com. 'We'n 'ad a busy mornin'; the bŭtcher wuz 'ere the first thing cuttin' up the pig, an' sence then I've rendered the best lard an' the midgen-lard, an' *reared* four an' twenty pies, beside a batch of apple-fit—an' got i' the oven.' 'My 'eart! but yo' han bin busy.'

(2) *adj.* under-done: said of cooked meat. Com. 'I can do with beef or mutton a bit *rear*, but veal an' pork should be done well.'

> 'There we complaine of one *reare*-roasted chick
> Here meat worse cookt nere makes us sick.'
>
> HARRINTON'S *Epigrams*, iv. 6 [A.D. 1615], in Wr.

Mr. Nares remarks of *rear* in this sense that it is 'not yet quite disused.' A.S. *hreáw*, raw.

REARING OF PORK [r'ae·r'in], *sb.* the loin of a porkling pig.—SHREWSBURY; PULVERBATCH. Qy. com. 'We'n ăve some curly greens ŏŏth the *rearin' o' pork*, an' score it fine to mak' the cracklin' crisp.'

REASTY [r'ai·sti' *and* r'ee·sti'], *adj.* rancid: said of bacon. Com. 'It's a bad kitchen fur keepin' bacon—it al'ays gwuz *raisty*—the sailin's [ceiling] low, an' nod much ar in it.'

> 'lay flitches a salting
> Through follie too beastlie
> Much bacon is *reasty*.'
>
> TUSSER, *Fiue Hundred Pointes of Good Husbandrie* [Novembers Abstract].

'*Resty* flees' is given as the gloss of '*chars restez*' in *The Treatise of Walter de Biblesworth*, xiii. cent., in Wr. vocabs., vol. i. p. 155.

'Reest, as flesche (*resty*, P.). *Rancidus*.'—*Prompt. Parv.*

'*Restie*, or rustie bacon.'—Nomenclator, 1585, p. 86, in HAL.

See *Reasty*, in WEDG. Cf. **Reechy** (2).

REBBLING [r'eb·lin], *part. pres., var. pr.* revelling,—'drinkin' an' *rebblin'*.'—PULVERBATCH; CRAVEN ARMS.

RECKLING [r'ek·lin], *sb.* the smallest and usually the last born of a litter, as of pigs, puppies, &c.—WELLINGTON. The term is not a very common one. Cf. **Rickling.**

RECKON [r'ek·n], *v. n., pec.* to imagine; to suppose; to apprehend. Com.

> '. . . . . which to shake off
> Becomes a warlike people, whom we *reckon*
> Ourselves to be.'—*Cymbeline*, III. i. 53.

RED, *v. a.* to comb out the hair.—PULVERBATCH.
Jamieson gives 'To *Red.* To disentangle . . . *To red the head*, or *hair*, to comb out the hair.' See **Redding-comb,** below. Cf. **Rid** (5), also **Reeve** (2).

RED-CAP, *sb.* the Goldfinch. — NEWPORT. Cf. **Seven-coloured-Linnet.** See **Jack-Nicol.**

REDDING-COMB [kuom·], *sb.* a dressing-comb. —PULVERBATCH. 'W'y dunna yo' *red* yore yar, Bessy?—it looks as if it 'adna 'ad a *reddin'-cŏom* through it fur a month.' See **Red,** above. Cf. **Ridding-comb,** also **Reeving-tooth-comb.**

REDDINS [r'ed·inz], *sb., var. pr.* the sirname Meredith.—CLEE HILLS, *Aston Botterell.* 'Who bin them two?' 'W'y, owd *Reddins* o' Didlick an' Bidey [Bytheway] o' Stotherton.'

RED-ROW [r'oa·], *sb.* the stage of reddish tinge which barley assumes just before ripening.—PULVERBATCH; CLEE HILLS. Qy. com. 'Allen o' Steppiton 's cut barley afore ours is i' the *red-row.*'

REECHY [r'ee·chi'], (1) *adj.* dirty; smoky; unwashed,—in appearance.—PULVERBATCH. ''Er's a grimy, *reechy* lookin' thing, I shouldna like to ate after 'er.'

> '. . . . . the kitchen malkin pins
> Her richest lockram 'bout her *reechy* neck.'
> *Coriolanus*, II. i. 225.

A.S. *réc*, smoke.

(2) *adj.* rancid, as of butter, or bacon.—WEM; ELLESMERE. 'That butter 's nasty *reechy* stuff—I conna ate it.' Cf. **Reasty.**

REED-SPARROW, (1) *sb. Sylvia phragmítis*, the Sedge-Warbler. Com.

(2) *sb. Sylvia arundinacea*, Reed Warbler. Common in the vicinity of large sheets of water, where the Reed, *Arundo Phragmites*, abounds. '*Hic palustrus*,' glossed '*a rede-sparowe*,' occurs in a *Nominale*, xv. cent., in Wr. vocabs., vol. i. p. 221. Cf. **Water-Sparrow.**

REEPLE [r'ee·pl], *sb.* a beam placed horizontally against the 'face' of the coal to prop it, being itself supported by 'sprags.'—COLLIERY, *Old Park;* M. T.

REEVE [r'ee·v], (1) *sb.* the underground overlooker of the pits.—COLLIERY; M. T.

'*Reve*, lordys serwawnte. *Prepositus.*'—*Prompt. Parv.*
A.S. *gerēfa*, a steward, bailiff, agent. Cf. **Doggie.**

(2) *v. a.* to comb out the hair.—CLUN. 'Mind, Ruth, as yo' *reeve* yore yar well.' See **Reeving-tooth-comb.** Cf. **Red.**

(3) *v. a.* to contract into wrinkles, as of the nose or forehead,—'Dunna *reeve* yore nose,' *i. e.* don't *pull up* your nose, as at anything displeasing. Com. Du. *ruyffelen,* to wrinkle. Cf. **Rivelled.**

(4) *v. a.* to draw, or gather up—a term of sempstressy. Qy. com. 'We sha'n get the throck done afore night—if yo'n *reeve* the skirt, I'll sew it on.' See **Reeving-string**, below.

REEVINGS, *sb. pl.* gathers.—PULVERBATCH. Qy. com. 'Mary, see 'ow yore gownd's tore out o' the *reevin's*.'

REEVING-STRING, *sb.* a string put in for the purpose of drawing or gathering up. Qy. com. 'The *reevin'-string* 's comen out o' the neck o' the child's pinner—jest len' me yore bodkin 'afe a minute to run it in agen.'

Bailey—ed. 1782—has 'To *Reeve* . . . a Term used by Sailors, for to put in or pull through.'

REHEARSE, *v. n., pec.* to rise on the stomach, as of food which disagrees.—SHREWSBURY. 'That pie wuz too good fur me, it *re'earsed* all day after.' Compare Fr. *rehercer,* to go over again, like a harrow (Fr. *herce*) over a ploughed field. Cf. **Repeat.**

REITS [r'ei·ts], *sb. Ranunculus fluitans* (Lam.), Water Crowfoot.—SHREWSBURY. The water-weed to which old Severn fishermen give the name of *Reits*, and which abounds in the shallows of the Severn, is the 'tresses fair' of Sabrina, in Milton's *Comus.*

'Seaweeds were formerly called Reets. Bishop Kennett has the following note,—"Reits, seeweed of some called reits, of others wrack, and of the Thanet men wore," &c. "*Leppe,* sea-grasse, sea-weed, reets."—COTG.' See Mr. Way's Note in *Prompt. Parv.*, p. 431. See **Roits.**

REJOICE [r'i'jei·s], *v. n., pec.* same as **Rehearse**, above.—PULVERBATCH.

REMEMBER, *v. a., pec.* to remind. Com. '*Remember* me to sen' down to Littlehales's fur some vinegar, w'en Dick calls fur 'is baskit—'e gwuz by the shop, an' 'e'll do a narrand fur me, I know.'

'I'll speak of her no more, nor of your children;
I'll not *remember* you of my own lord,
Who is lost too.'—*Winter's Tale,* III. ii. 231.

'*Remember,* to put in mind of: If you will *remember* me of it. North.'—PEGGE.

REMLET [r'em·lu't], *sb., obsols.*—PULVERBATCH. 'I bought it chep, it wuz jest a bit on a *remlet.*'

'Remelawnt (remenaunt, *residuum,* F.). *Residuus, reliquus.* The use of the obsolete form of the word remnant appears in the Craven Glossary, v. *Remlin,* and in Palmer's Devonshire Words, v. *Remlet.* It occurs in the inventory of effects of a merchant at Newcastle, in 1571, in whose shop were certain "yeardes of worssett in Remlauntes." Durham Wills and Inv., Surtees Soc., vol. i. 362.'—*Prompt. Parv. and Notes.*

RENDER, *v. a., pec.* to melt down out of the natural state: said chiefly of lard and suet. Com. 'Be sure be carful w'en yo' *render* the lard, the pot's got thin i' the middle, an' it'll ketch direc'ly.'
Grose gives '*Render* . . . to melt down. To *render* suet. N.'

REP [r'ep·], *sb., obs.* a reaping by gift-work.—PULVERBATCH. A.S. *rip*, a reaping. See Bk. II., *Folklore*, &c., 'Customs' (*harvest*).

REPEAT, same as **Rehearse**, q. v.—SHREWSBURY; LUDLOW.

RESTIAL, *sb., obs.* a fee for burial within the Church, including the charge for tolling the bell.—SHREWSBURY.
'1634. Itm̄ paid to the Lord Bishop's secretary and other officers to pc̄ure a mitigation of *Restalls* within our Church, and two letters from the Lord Bishop, 10ˢ/.'—*Churchwardens' Accounts of the Abbey*.
Called '*Lestial*' in the *Churchwardens' Accounts of S. Julian's*.

RICKLING, same as **Ratling**, q. v.—NEWPORT.

RID [r'id·], (1) *pret.* rode.—PULVERBATCH. 'We wenten to the far to buy ship—the Maister druv, an' I *rid* the grey mar':' so said John Griffith of Exford Green [1871].
'*Brazen*. . . . I have Reason to remember the time, for I had two-and-twenty Horses killed under me that day.
'*Wor*. Then, Sir, you must have *rid* mighty hard.
'*Bal*. Or perhaps, Sir, . . . you *rid* upon half a dozen Horses at once.'—FARQUHAR'S *Recruiting Officer*, Act III. Scene—The Market-Place [Shrewsbury].
'I remember two young fellows who *rid* in the same squadron of a troop of horse, who were ever together.'—*Spectator*, Aug. 24, 1711.

(2) *v. a.* to dispatch; to get work out of hand.—PULVERBATCH. 'Tummas is a good workman, 'e'll *rid* as much i' one day as some folks dun i' two.'

'We, having now the best at Barnet field,
Will thither straight, for willingness *rids* way.'
3 *King Henry VI.*, V. iii. 21.

(3) *v. a.* to clear, as of land by stubbing up the furze, &c. Com.
'1621. Laid out in stocking up of the gorst in Kingsland, making the same into faggottes, and *ridding* and making cleane the growndes, vˡˡ iiijˢ vjᵈ.'—*Bailiffs' Accounts*, in OWEN and BLAKEWAY'S *History of Shrewsbury*, vol. i. p. 574.
Dan. '*rydde*, to grub up, to clear.'—WEDG. **Der.** 'ridding.'

(4) *v. n.* to expectorate.—WORTHEN; CHURCH STRETTON; WELLINGTON. 'I wuz coughin' an' *riddin'* all night.'

(5) same as **Red**, q. v.—ELLESMERE.

RIDDING, *sb.* the act of clearing, as of land from furze, &c. Com. 'The Maister gid me a plack o' 'tato ground fur the *riddin'*, an' a famous crop it brought.'

RIDDING-COMB [kuom·], same as **Redding-comb**, q. v.—ELLESMERE. 'Fatch the *riddin'-cōom*, an' let me *rid* the child's yar.'

RIDGE, RUDGE, *sb.* a space of ploughed land,—same as **But** (1), q. v.—CRAVEN ARMS; BRIDGNORTH. At Chelmarsh when a man sows a '*ridge*' wholly at once it is called a '*ridge at a wiff;*' but when he goes once up and once down it is a '*ridge at a bout.*'

'. . . of cornes fayer and cleane
That growes one *rigges* out of the reian.'
Chester Plays, vol. i. p. 36.

'*Rygge*, of a lond. *Porca.*'—*Prompt. Parv.* See **Rean.**

RIDGE-BAND [r'izh· *and* r'ich· band], *sb.* the strong leathern band which goes over the saddle of cart-harness, and holds up the shafts.—LUDLOW. In *The Treatise of Walter de Biblesworth*, close of xiii. cent., it is said that—

'. . . . . . ly limounere,
Ke porte à dos une dossere.'

'*Limounere*' is glossed 'thillo-hors,' *i. e.* shaft-horse; and '*dossere* has '*rige-leyther*' given as its synonym. See Wr. vocabs., vol. i. p. 168. A.S. *hrycg*, the back, and *bend*, a band.

RIDLESS [r'id·lis], (1) *sb.* a riddle; a conundrum. Qy. com. 'Well, whad did'n 'ee do, if theer wuz no daincin'?' 'W'y we played'n at turn the trancher an' blind-man's-buff till we wun tired, an' then begun to tell *ridlesses*, an' whad twix puzzlin' to fine 'em out, and then cryin' the weds, we gotten to three o'clock i' the mornin'.' A riddle given in *The Treatise of Walter de Biblesworth* is supplemented by—

'Red that *redeles*, red qwat it may beo.'
See Wr. vocabs., vol. i. p. 161.

A.S. *rǽdels*, a riddle, from *rǽdan*, to interpret, *read.*

(2) *sb.* a doggerel rime; an improbable story,—any 'rigmarole.' Qy. com. A servant-girl, who was a Dissenter, objected to going to Church on the plea that, whereas in Chapel they had new prayers every Sunday, in Church they had 'on'y the same owd *ridless* o'er an' o'er agen!'

'And there was Christe, but fygured and described in cerimonies / in *redles* / in parables and in darke prophesies.'—WILLIAM TYNDALE (A.D. 1528), *Obedience of a Christian Man. Specim. Eng. Lit.*, xvi. l. 12.

RIE [r'ei·], *v. a.*, *obs.* to sift grain by shaking it round a sieve in such a manner as to bring the chaff and light grains to the surface, from whence they can be removed.—PULVERBATCH; WORTHEN.

'I can riddle an' I can *rie*,
Toss a pancake an' rear a pie.'

The 'branches of useful knowledge' set forth in the above couplet, represented generically all those arts of housewifery which, in the 'good old times,' young country-women esteemed it honourable to practise.

RIEING-SIEVE, same as **Blind-sieve**, q. v.—*Ibid.*

RIFF, (1) *sb.* the itch.—PULVERBATCH; WEM. Qy. com.

(2) *sb.* the mange.—*Ibid.*

RIFLE [r'ei·fl], *v. a.* to ruffle, as of the temper. Com. 'If 'e'd gwun on much lunger 'e'd a *rifled* my temper, an' I should a toud 'im what I thought.'

RIFTER, same as **Lifter**, q. v.—CLEE HILLS.

RIG, (1) *sb.* a sprain, as of the back.—CLEE HILLS.

(2) *v. a.* to sprain.—*Ibid.* 'The mar' 's *rigged* 'er back, an' I've gid my arm a kench a-tryin' to oud 'er.' See **Kench** (1).

(3) *sb.* to 'run a *rig*' on a person is to banter him unsparingly. Qy. com.

RIGGIL [r'ig·il], *sb.* a male animal partially gelt. Com.

RIGHT-FORENUNGST, *prep.* over-against. — OSWESTRY. See **Anunst**, also **O'er-anunst**.

RIGOL [r'ig·h'l], (1) *sb.* a small gutter or channel in land, made to lead water off.—PULVERBATCH. 'I've made a bit of a *rigol* to carry the waiter off the posy-knot.' Compare Shakespeare's 'Watery *rigol*' —*Lucrece*, l. 1745.

'O.Fr. *rigole*, canal, conduit pour l'écoulement des caux . . . . du celtique: kymri *rhig*, entaille, coupure; *rhigol*, sillon, fossé.'—BUR. Cf. **Grip**.

(2) *sb.* a groove.—PULVERBATCH; OSWESTRY. 'Yo'n pertended to dust this room, an' jest look at the dirt i' the *rigol* round the table.'

RIGOT, same as **Rigol**, above.—WEM.

Amongst the 'Terms used in the Gentle Craft' [shoe-making], Randle Holme has, '*Channelling the Sole;* is making a *riggett* in the outer Sole for the Wax Thread to lie in.'—*Academy of Armory*, Bk. III. ch. iii. p. 99.

Pegge gives '*Riggot*. A gutter. Lanc.'

RILE, *v. n.* to move about uneasily; to fidget,—generally used in combination with 'wriggle.'—PULVERBATCH. 'I couldna 'ear the one 'afe Mr. Gilpin said—them childern wun *rilin'* an' wrigglin' about i' the Chancel all the wilde.' See **Roil**.

RIMING [r'ei·min], *adj.* falling, as of mist; same as **Mizzling**, q. v.—'*rimin'* weather.'—WORTHEN.

RINDEL [r'in·dl], *sb.* a small stream.—WHITCHURCH, *Prees*. A.S. *rynele*, a stream, runnel. Cf. **Prill**.

RINDLESS [r'in·dlis *and* r'in·dles], *sb.* the stomach of a calf prepared for rennet.—PULVERBATCH. 'This *rindlis* dunna come well; I mus' remember to tell Rowson to send us the maw from our own cauf, then we sha'n be sure on it comin'.' It is believed that the *rindless* obtained from a calf whose 'nursing mother' grazes the pasture common to the dairy-stock will have a special effect on the milk of the dairy, causing it to coagulate—or '*come*,' as it is termed—with almost absolute certainty.

'Renlys, or *rendlys*, for mylke. *Coagulum*.'—*Prompt. Parv.* Cf. **Mawskin**.

RIPPER, *sb.* a crescent-shaped implement used for trimming the edges of gutters.—WHITCHURCH.

RIPPLES [r'ip·lz], *sb. pl.* the movable rails put on the sides of a cart or waggon when it is required to carry a more than ordinary load, as, for instance, at harvest-time.—PULVERBATCH; WORTHEN; CORVE DALE; WEM. They say about Cherbury that a man has 'got the *ripples* on' when, though not absolutely drunk, he has yet taken a greater quantity of drink than he can well carry. Thus a wife extenuated her husband's insobriety: 'Well, 'e 'ad the *ripples* on,'—drunk he was not, though he had exceeded his rightful allowance. Cf. **Thripples.** See **Rathes.**

RISE [r'ei·s], (1) *sb.* a long, slender stick; a branch.—PULVERBATCH; CHURCH STRETTON; CLEE HILLS. 'Yo' mun get a good lung *rise* as'll raich them swallows' nists, an' proke 'em down, else we sha'n a dirty windows.'

'þanne [buskede] a bold kniht · & to a bow stirte,
þe sote-sauerede frut · sone to pulle.
But al so raþe as þe rink · gan þe *ris* touche,
Doun fel he wiþ dul · ded in þe place.'
Alexander and Dindimus, l. 129.

'Then vnto London I dyd me hye,
Of all the land it beareth the pryse:
"Hot pescodes," one began to crye,
"Strabery rype," and "cherries in the *ryse*."'
JOHN LYDGATE (A.D. 1420, *circa*), *London Lyckpeny*. *Specim. Eng. Lit.*, III. *a*. 9.

Du. *rijs*; Germ. *reis*, a twig.

(2) *v. a.* to rod peas.—PULVERBATCH; NEWPORT; ELLESMERE. 'I wanted to *rise* the tother row o' pase, but I fell short o' sticks.' See **Pea-risers.**

(3) *v. a.* to beat,—'*rise* 'is back.'—WEM.

RISING [r'ei·sin], *sb.* a beating with a light stick,—''E gid the lad a good *risin'*.'—PULVERBATCH.

RIVELLED [r'iv·ld], *part. adj.* wrinkled.—SHREWSBURY; PULVERBATCH. Qy. com. 'Martha begins to shewn age—'er neck an' 'ands bin all *rivelled* an' s'runk.'

'A *riueld* skynne, a stinkyng breath; what than?
A tothelesse mouth shall do thy lippes no harme.'
SIR THOMAS WIAT (A.D. 1540, *circa*), *Satire*, III. l. 61.

In Ephes. v. 27 the Wicliffite version—A.D. 1388—has '*ryueling*,' where the A. V. has '*wrinkle*.' Cf. **Reeve** (3).

RIVEL-RAVEL [r'iv·l r'av·l], (1) *sb.* nonsense,—'sich *rivel-ravel*.'—CLUN, *Herefd. Border*.

'And a great deal more of such *rivel-ravel*, of which they knew no more than the man in the moon.'—*The High German Looking-Glass*, 1709, in WR.

(2) *adj.* nonsensical,—'sich *rivel-ravel* stuff.'—*Ibid.*

ROAD, *sb.*, *pec.* way, manner,—of doing a thing. Com. 'Yo' come by [stand aside], an' I'll shewn yo' the *rodd* [way to do it].'

ROB [r'ob·], (1) *sb.* a very stiff preserve,—the term seems to be restricted to black-currant jam.—PULVERBATCH. 'I think Missis biles 'er jam too lung, it's as 'ard as black-currant *rob*.'

Pegge has '*Robb*, a stiff jelly made from fruit, and denominated accordingly, as *Elder-Robb*; called in the South *Jam*.'

Fr. *rob*; It. *robbo*; Sp. *rob*; Arab. *robb*; the thickened juice of fruits.

(2) *sb.* a tangle, as of thread, twine, &c.—'all on a *rob*.' Com.

ROBBLE, *sb.* an entanglement,—same as **Scrobble** (1), q. v.—WEM; OSWESTRY.

ROBIN-RUN-I'-THE-'EDGE, *sb.* *Glechóma hederácea*, Ground-Ivy. Com.

ROBIN'S-PINCUSHION, *sb.* the gall of the Wild Rose.—CLUN. See **Briar-boss.** Cf. **Mop** (2).

ROBS, *sb. pl.* quantities.—ATCHAM; WEM. 'Han yo' fund any?' 'Aye, *robs* on it.'

ROCHE [r'och·], *sb.* loose, crumbling rock; earth much mixed with stone; a sub-soil of earth and gravel.—PULVERBATCH; WELLINGTON. 'It ŏŏnna bring much aside o' the 'ill, theer inna much sile, an' whad is is *roche*.'

'*Roche*, ston. *Rupa, rupes*.'—*Prompt. Parv.*

'O.Fr. *roche*; rocher, écueil.'—BUR.

Fr. '*Roche*, rock. Il y a quelque anguille sous *roche* (il y a quelque chose de caché dans l'affaire). There's a snake in the grass.'—CHAMB.

Cf. **Rammel.**

ROCHY [r'och·i'], *adj.* of the nature of *roche*,—hard: said of soil that turns up in lumps.—PULVERBATCH; WEM. Cf. **Rammelly.**

RODEN'S-COWT. See **Forty-sa'-one**, &c.—PULVERBATCH; CLEE HILLS.

RODNEY, same as **Rattling**, q. v.—ELLESMERE, *Welshampton*.

ROGER, *sb.* the paunch of a pig,—same as **Hodge**, q. v. Com. See **Nancy.**

ROIL [r'oi·l *corr.* r'ahy·l], same as **Rile**, q. v.—ATCHAM; WEM.

ROITS [r'oi·ts], same as **Reits**, q. v.,—a broader pronunciation of the term. See **Raw-yeds.**

ROMANCE [r'oa·mans], (1) *sb.* that 'silly jesting which is not convenient'—having a show of truth. Com. 'I should never 'eed whad that fellow says, 'e's so full on 'is *rómance*.'

'O.Fr. *romans*; histoire fabuleuse.'—BUR.

(2) *v. n.* to exaggerate in narration; to relate a circumstance in such a jesting kind of way as to throw doubt upon its verity. Com. 'Now, Ben, dunna *románce*, but tell me straight forrat 'ow it 'appened,—yo' bin too fond o' *románcin'*, theer's no knowin' w'en yo' spake the truth.' O.Fr. *romancier*. See BUR.

ROMBLING, *adj.*, *pec.* restless. Com. 'The child's bin *romblin'* all night—I couldna sleep for it.'

ROMMELLY, *adj.* fat; greasy.—PULVERBATCH; CHURCH STRETTON. ''Ow's yore pig gettin' on, Tummas?' 'Oh! right well—'e'll mak'

30 score by Chris'mas.' 'Well, I dunna like 'em so big, the bacon ates so *rommelly*.'

ROMPSTAL [r'omp·stul], *sb.* a romping girl.—PULVERBATCH. ''Er's a great *rompstal*—more fur play than work.'

RONGE [r'onj·], *v. n.* to reach; to try to attain, as by stretching or effort.—PULVERBATCH. 'Jones's cattle bin al'ays *rongin'* o'er the 'edge after nettles—it's a sign the pastur' 's bar.' 'Well, let 'em *ronge*, it's thar own fence.'

RONGING-HOOK, *sb.* a hooked stick, or a stick furnished with a hook, for pulling dead branches out of trees.—*Ibid.* 'Jim made me a capital *rongin'-'ŏŏk* ŏŏth a stail of a pitchin'-pikel, an' pŭt a iron 'ŏŏk at it—it's a sight better than a 'ŏŏkit-stick.'

RONK [r'ong'k], (1) *adj.* strong; vigorous; luxuriant—in growth, as of wheat or potatoes. Qy. com. 'Them 'tatoes bin *ronk* i' the top, I dunna know 'ow the bottoms bin.' Cf. *Gen.* xli. 5.

(2) *adj.* cunning; bad; mischievous,—'a *ronk* owd file;'—'a *ronkish* lad.' Qy. com.

> 'Þat watȝ þe rauen so *ronk* · þat rebel watz euer.'
> *Alliterative Poems, The Deluge* (A.D. 1360, *circa*), *Specim. Early Eng.*, xiii. l. 455.

A.S. *ranc*, proud; haughty; rebellious.

ROOK, (1) *v. n.* to huddle; to lie close, as fowls do.—SHREWSBURY; PULVERBATCH. (1) 'They wun thick enough o' the groun' afore, an' now Jack's comen an' brought 'is wife an' two childern, so they bin farly *rooked* up.' (2) 'The fowls bin inclined to *rook* under the stack-frames an' wain-'us—it's a sure sign of a snow.'

> 'What is mankynde more unto yow holde
> Than is the scheep, that *rouketh* in the folde?'
> CHAUCER, *The Knightes Tale*, l. 450, ed. Morris.

> 'The raven *rook'd* her on the chimney's top.'
> 3 *K. Henry VI.*, V. vi. 47.

Low Germ. *hurken*, to squat down.

(2) *sb.* the iron key used for winding up a kitchen-grate when it is too wide.—WEM.

ROOT-WOUTED [wou·tid], PULVERBATCH. [wau·tid], WEM, *part. past*, up-rooted. 'The wïnde 's broke a lot o' trees i' the park, an' *root-wouted* some o' them big elms.' See **Wout**, also **Wawt**.

ROP [rop·], *sb.*, *var. pr.* a rope. Com. See *sub voce* **Frommet** (2).

ROPE [r'oa·p], (1) *pret.* and *part. past*, reaped.—PULVERBATCH; CLEE HILLS. 'Yo' remember'n John Pugh.' 'I should think I do, I've *rope* ŏŏth 'im many a day—we use't to tak' 'arrŏost all round Cantlop an' Cunder an' theer w'en I wuz a young fellow.'

(2) *sb.* the 'trail' of a woodcock.—PULVERBATCH. See below.

ROPES, *sb. pl.* the entrails of a sheep,—'the ship's *ropes*.'—PULVERBATCH. Grose gives '*Ropes.* Guts. N.'
A.S. *roppas*, bowels; entrails.

ROPY [r'oa·pi'], *adj.* viscous; stringy: said of bread, also of beer. Com. 'Look at this bread, Dick, it'll pool into nex' wik, it's that *ropy.*' Hot, damp weather will cause both bread and beer to become *ropy*, and it is curious that the former, when in this state, will infect sound bread,—a loaf laid upon a shelf where *ropy* bread had stood would speedily become unsound in like manner. 'Yo' munna pŭt the new bread o' that shilf w'eer the las' batch wuz, or we sha'n be 'ăvin' it *ropy* afore it's cowd.' Beer will become *ropy* when insufficiently boiled or bittered. 'Now see, an' bwile that drink well, or we sha'n 'ăve it *ropy* this muckery weather.'

'Ropynge, ale or oþer lycowre (*ropy* as ale, K. H.). *Viscosus.*'—*Prompt. Parv.*

ROUGH [r'uf·], *sb.* a wooded slope,—steeply inclined. Com. 'Ah, Joe, I fund out w'y yo' couldna tell w'eer the text wuz o' Sunday—yo' wun nuttin' i' Wildin's *rough* (Sheptonfields), an' 'e's gweïn to get a summons for yo'.'

ROUGHED [r'uf·t], *part. past*, made rough, as with frost-nails: said of horses' shoes. Com. Randle Holme has '*Frosted*' in the same sense. See **Frost-nails**.

ROUNCING [r'ou·nsin], *adj., obsols.* roaring; boisterous,—'a *rouncin'* fire;'—'a *rouncin'* winde.'—PULVERBATCH; WORTHEN.

ROUNDS, *sb.* a turn once up and down a ploughed field.—WHITCHURCH. See **Bout** (2).

ROUND-SHAVING, *sb., sl.?* a sharp reprimand.—PULVERBATCH. 'If yo' dun that agen, yo'n get sich a *roun'-shavin'* yo' never 'ad'n afore.'

ROUSE [r'ous·], *sb.* rubbish, as of garden refuse—bean-tops, immature fruit, &c.,—'rucks o' *rouse.*'—PULVERBATCH; CORVE DALE; WEM; OSWESTRY.

ROUSTY, *adj.* rusty. Com.

'*Scaber*, rough, *rowstie.*'—DUNCAN'S *Appendix Etymologiæ*, A.D. 1595, E. D. S., B. xiii.

ROUTE [r'ou·t], (1) *sb.* a party; an assembled company.—PULVERBATCH. 'They bin 'ăvin' a big *route* at the Squire's.'

'but for [to] telle þe a-tiryng · of þat child þat time,
þat al þat real *route* · were araied fore.'
William of Palerne, l. 1942.

'O.Fr. *route;* compagnie, bande.'—BUR. Cf. **Bout** (4).

(2) *sb.* a disturbance; a commotion.—*Ibid.* 'They'd'n a pretty *route* at Powtherbitch Wakes.' ''Adna? whad wun a doin'?' 'W'y fightin' like mad.'

'To make *rowtte* into Rome with ryotous knyghtes,
Within a sevenyghte daye with sex score helmes.'
Morte Arthure, MS. Lincoln, f. 57, in HAL.

'O.Fr. *route* . . . confusion, désordre; de *ruplus, rupta.*'—BUR.

(3) *v. n.* to low; to cry, or make a noise, as animals do when restless.—PULVERBATCH. 'Did'n yo' fother them beäs well las'

night? they wun *routin'* till I couldna get a wink o' sleep,—no, I couldna.'

'. . . . . and made hem *rowte*
Als he weren kradelbarnes:
So dog þe child þat moder þarnes.'
Havelok the Dane, l. 1911.

'*Mugio*, to *rowt* like a nowt,' occurs in Duncan's *Appendix Etymologiæ*, A.D. 1595, E. D. S., B. xiii.

Grose gives 'Rowt. To rowt or rawt, to lowe like an ox or cow. N.'

'A.S. *hrutan*; O.Fris. *hruta*; O.Icel. *hriota*, route, *mugire*.'—STRAT.

(4) *sb.* the cry, or noise, made by restless animals.—*Ibid.* 'The ship bin makin' a pretty *route*.'

(5) *v. a.* to turn up out of the earth, as pigs do with the snout,—'*routed* the 'tatoes up.' Com.

ROUTY, *adj.* rutty; full of wheel tracks,—'a *routy* road.' Com.

ROW'DED [r'oa·did], *adj.* having alternate rows of fat and lean: said of bacon chiefly. Com. 'Axe Molly Dovas'on to cut me a nice *row'ded* bit o' bacon, I canna do ŏŏth it so very fat.'

ROWDY, same as above. Com.

ROWSON'S COWT. See **Forty-sa'-one**, &c.—WORTHEN.

ROZZEN-IN, *v. n.* to set to work in a determined, vigorous manner. —WEM. ''E ketcht out o' the pikel an' *rozzened-in* than I thought 'e'd a dropt.'

RUBBER, *sb.* a mower's whet-stone.—LUDLOW, *Burford*.

'The *rub* or buckle stone which husbandmen doe occupie in the whetting of their sithes.'—HARRISON'S *Description of England*, Pt. ii. p. 64.

Cf. **Bur** (2).

RUCK, (1) *v. a.* to crease; to rumple. Com. 'Jest see 'ow yo'n *rucked* yore apparn—whadever han 'ee bin doin'?'

'O.N. *hrucka*, to wrinkle.'—WEDG.

(2) *sb.* a rough crease; an aggregation of creases. Com. 'The poor child's clo'es bin all in a *ruck* from maulin' it about—no ŏŏnder at it cryin'.'

'N. *hrukka*, a wrinkle.'—WEDG.

(3) *sb.* a heap,—'a *ruck* o' stwuns.' Com.

'O.Swed *ruka*, ruck; heap.'—STRAT.

(4) *v. a.* to gather into heaps. Com. 'Jack, I want yo' i' the fallow to *ruck* scutch ready for burnin'.'

RUCKS AN' YEPS, *phr.* analogous to '*ducks and drakes*,' as applied to squandering property.—PULVERBATCH. Qy. com. 'Yo'n got a pretty place 'ere, Maister.' 'Aye, lad, it's took me many a 'ear's 'ard work to get it together, but I doubt it'll soon be made *rucks an' yeps* on w'en I'm gwun.' *Yep* = heap.

RUDGE. See **Ridge**.

RUFF, *sb.* a roof. Com. 'Dunna shift that lather, we wanten it 'ere—the men bin gweïn o' the *ruff* to fettle it, it looses the wet in.'

'1581. September. Pd. for trussynge up the *ruffe* of the churche end, vjd.'—*Churchwardens' Accounts*, S. Mary's, Shrewsbury.

'*Ruffe* of an hows.'—*Prompt. Parv.*

RUNDEL [r'un·dl], (1) *sb.*, *obsols.* a pollard oak.—PULVERBATCH. These pollards are usually spoken of as 'old *rundels*,' because for many years oaks have not been polled, consequently what there are must be of old growth, but it does not of necessity follow that a *rundel* must be 'hollow,' as sometimes explained. Farmers were formerly allowed to top trees for the wood they required, as for repairs of implements, &c.; the privilege, however, became abused, and a stop was put to it. 'We darna cut a bough now-a-days, else theer's a capital three-fanged bough 'angs o'er the beän leasow ŏŏd mak' a rar' nave; but the Squire ŏŏnna 'äve a wuk cut fur the world—'e canna bar the sight of a *rundel*.' Cf. **Runnel**.

(2) *sb.* by metaphor,—an aged person who has outlived the friends and companions of early years.—*Ibid.* 'All the owd neighbours bin gwun, an' lef' a poor *rundel* like me.' 'Oh! yo'n las' a good wilde yet, Molly—*rundels* bin mostly 'ard.'

(3) *sb.* a dwarfed, stunted person or animal.—*Ibid.* 'Yore new waggoner's a despert *rundel*, it'll be more than 'e can do to raich the 'orse's yed.' Cf. **Runt**, below.

RUNLET, *sb.*, *obs.*? a shallow, round tub, used for brewing purposes. —PULVERBATCH; BISHOP'S CASTLE. 'I'm a bit doubtful o' the barm, pŭt some wort i' the *runlet*, an' try if it'll come [work].'

'Tow small *Runletts*' are enumerated amongst other things in 'The Seller,' in an *Inventory*, dated at Owlbury Manor-House, Bishop's Castle, 1625.

RUNNABLE, *adv.* by rote; fluently, as of a repetition lesson well prepared or well said.—PULVERBATCH. 'Billy, han yo' gotten yore spellin' *runnable*, an' yore catechis' an' yore collic'?' 'Iss, Mother.' 'That's a good child—yo'n soon be a scholard.' See Mr. Skeat on '*renable*' in *Notes on Piers Pl.*, C. i. 176, p. 23.

RUNNEL, *sb.* an old stunted tree, usually a pollard, and hollow.—ATCHAM; WELLINGTON; WEM. Cf. **Rundel** (1).

RUNT, same as **Rundel** (3). — PULVERBATCH; WELLINGTON; OSWESTRY. Qy. com.

RUNTED, *adj.* stunted in growth.—*Ibid.* 'The 'eifer dunna change 'er cŏŏat kindly—I think 'er's *runted* throm bad winterin'.'

RUTTLING [r'ut·lin], *sb.* and *part. pres.* rattling; gurgling—that peculiar noise in the throat often observed in dying persons. Qy. com. 'It's nigh all o'er ŏŏth 'im, poor owd mon, 'e's *ruttlin'* i' the throät.'

'O.Du. *rotelen*, to rottle, rattle.'—STRAT.

RYAL [r'ei·ul], (1) *adj.* royal,—'the *ryal* family.' Qy. com.

'And cround our quene in *ryal* aray.'
JOHN AUDELAY'S *Poems*, p. ix.

(2) *adj.* 'high and mighty;' independent,—in a bad sense.—WEM. ''E wuz mighty *ryal*, I can tell yo', w'en I toud 'im whad the Maister said.'

SAD, *adj.* close; heavy: said of bread which, owing to bad yeast or from being ill made, has not risen properly, or, being well made and baked, has been shaken before becoming 'set' or cold. Com. 'O, Missis, yo'n mak' the loaf *sad* if yo' bin so rough ŏŏth it,' said a servant-girl to a lady who had taken up a loaf hot out of the oven, and hastily dropped it.

'*Sad*, heavy, close Bread.'—*Academy of Armory*, Bk. III. ch. vii. p. 317.

Sad, in the sense of firm, heavy, clayey, occurs in *Alexander and Dindimus*:—

'For to sowe & to sette · in þe *sad* erthe.'—l. 912.

'*Sad*, or hard. *Solidus.*'—*Prompt. Parv.*

Cf. **Sammy**.

SADE [sai·d], to cloy; to satiate.—PULVERBATCH; WEM. Qy. com. 'Dick says 'e can ate as much poncake as 'e could stick a pikel through, but 'e'll find as they'n soon *sade* 'im.'

'To *sade*, cloy, *satio*.'—Coles' Lat. Dict. in HAL.

'"Of worldes winne *sad*."—Walter Mapes [A.D. 1162, *circa*], 341. A.S. *sæd*; O.Sax. *sad*; O.Icel. *saðr*; Goth. *saþs*; O.H.Germ. *sater* (*satur*), satiate,' in STRAT.

SADING, *part. adj.* cloying; satisfying.—*Ibid.* 'This shooity dumplin' 's despert *sadin'*, I canna ate no more on it.'

SAGE-CHEESE, *sb.* an ordinary cheese with a sprinkling of sage in the curd. Qy. com. When *sage-cheese* is made it is usually at the end of the dairy season; the cheese then being difficult to dry, sage is rubbed into the curd to act as a 'drier.' 'We'n rub a bit o' *sage* i' this crud, it'll 'elp to dry it, an' we bin all fond on a bit o' *sage-cheese*.' In some dairies an imitation of Cheddar cheese is sometimes made, by pounding sage leaves and adding the juice expressed from them to the customary curd.

Randle Holme has, '*Sage*, or Mint, or Marigold Cheese.'—*Academy of Armory*, Bk. III. ch. viii. p. 335.

SAKE [sai·k], *sb.* a land-spring; a place where the water oozes out on the surface soil.—WEM; WHITCHURCH; ELLESMERE. Cf. **Seek** (2).

SAKY, *adj.* having wet patches: said of fields.—WELLINGTON; WEM; ELLESMERE.

SALLET, *sb.* a salad.—SHREWSBURY; PULVERBATCH; CLEE HILLS; ELLESMERE. Qy. com.

'. . . . Wherefore, on a brick wall have I climbed into this garden, to see if I can eat grass, or pick a *sallet*, ... which is not amiss to cool a man's stomach this hot weather.'—2 *K. Henry VI.*, IV. x. 9.

'*Sallet*, is either Sweet Herbs, or Pickled Fruit, as Cucumbers, Samphire, Elder Buds, Broom Buds, &c., eaten with Roasted Meats.' —*Academy of Armory*, Bk. III. ch. iii. p. 84.

O.Lat. '*Salata.* Sallets.'—*Dict. Etym. Lat.* '*Insaláta*, salad (food of raw herbs).'—MEADOWS' *Ital. Dict.*

SALLY, *sb.* the name applied generically to every species of Osier, and to other Salices of semi-arboreal habit. Com.

'Near to the shady bank where slender *sallies* grow.'
DRAYTON, *The Muses' Elysium, Nymphal* VI.

'. . . . the cherries on the wall must be turning red, the yellow *Sally* must be on the brook, wheat must be callow with quivering bloom, and the early meadows swathed with hay.'—R. D. BLACKMORE, *Lorna Doone*, A Romance of Exmoor, p. 515, ed. 1878.

'*Amera* seal' occurs in *Latin and Anglo-Saxon Glosses*, xi. cent., in Wr. vocabs., vol. ii. p. 8, and Mr. Wright gives the explanation:—'The willow, still called the *sally* on the border of Wales and in the West of England.'

Dr. Stratmann gives the plural form of the word, '*salyhes*,' as occurring in an 'Anglo-Saxon and Early English Psalter.'

Wyclif has *salewis*, Ps. cxxxvi. (*or* cxxxvii.) 2.

A.S. *sealh;* O.H.Germ. *sal(a)ha;* Lat. *salix.* Cf. **Withy.**

SALLY-BED, *sb.* a plantation of *Sallies*,—an Osier-holt.—WEM. Cf. **Withy-bed.**

SAMCLOTH [sam·klu'th], *sb., obsols.* a sampler.—PULVERBATCH; WEM.

Randle Holme enumerates amongst 'The School Mistris Terms of Art,' 'A *Samcloth*, vulgarly a Sampler.'—*Academy of Armory*, Bk. III. ch. iii. p. 98.

SAMMY, *adj.* close; clammy; heavy: said of bread.—WEM. Cf. **Sad.**

SANCTUARY [sang·kteuh'r'i'], *sb., var. pr.* common Centaury.—PULVERBATCH; CLUN; COLLIERY. See **Bloodwort.**

SAPY [sai·pi'], *adj.* moist; slimy,—the first stage of putrescence: said of meat. Qy. com. 'This close, muggy weather the mate gets *sapy* direc'ly.' Cf. Low Du. *sapp*, juice; wet.

SARCH, SEARCH, (1) *sb.* a sieve—about two feet in diameter—made of sheep-skin drilled with holes, used in granaries for sifting the dust from grain.—BISHOP'S CASTLE; CLUN; BRIDGNORTH. Cf. **Blind-sieve.**

(2) *sb., obs.* a sieve similar to the above, formerly in general use in small flour-mills throughout Shropshire, for sifting flour of very fine quality. It obtained as late as 1835, if not later.

'The *Searce* or *Searcer*, it is a fine Sieve with a Leather cover on the top and bottom of the Sieve Rim, to keep the Dant or Flower of any Pulverized Substance, that nothing be lost of it in the Searceing.'—*Academy of Armory*, Bk. III. ch. viii. p. 337.

Ash has '*Searce.* A fine kind of sieve or bolter.'

Bailey—ed. 1782—gives 'A *Sarse*, a Sort of Sieve.'

'O.Fr. *saas; sas;* tamis, sas. Bas Lat. *sedatium* . . . . de *seta* (= *setaceum*) crin. . . . . parce qu'ils [les tamis] sont faits de crins, signification qu' a *seta*.'—BUR.

'Fr. *Sas*, tissu de crin attaché à un cercle de bois, & qui sert à passer de la farine, du plâtre, &c. Sieve, *searce*.'—CHAMB.

(3) *sb., obs.* a strainer (?).—CLEE HILLS.

'1 Brass Kettell & *Sarch*—0-1-6,'—'1 brass Kettle & *Search*—0-1-6,' are items of an *Inventory* dated at Aston Botterell about A.D. 1758.

There are [1873] aged persons in the neighbourhood of Abdon who remember brass kettles fitted up with strainers after the manner of a fish-kettle, but the term *sarch*, or *search*, appears to be obsolete.

'j. *sars* of brasse,'—'j. *sarche* of tre,' are enumerated amongst things pertaining to the '*Coquena*,' in the 'Inventory of Sir John Fastolf's Goods,' A.D. 1459.—*Paston Letters*, vol. i. p. 490.

Pegge has '*Serce*, a strainer for gravy, &c. York.'

SAR-CLOTH, *sb., obs.* a plaister.—PULVERBATCH; WORTHEN. ''Is back keeps despert bad, an' 'e's wore a *sar-cloth* all winter.'

'*Ligatura*,' glossed '*sar-clað*,' occurs in *Archbp. Ælfric's Vocabulary*, x. cent., in Wr. vocabs., vol. i. p. 20.

Ash gives '*Searcloth*. A kind of plaister; a large plaister.'

'*Cerat*. A Plaister made of Waxe, Gommes, &c., and certain Oyles; Wee also call it, a cerot or *seare-cloth*.'—COTGRAVE'S *French Dictionary*.

A.S. *sár-clað*, a sore-cloth. Cf. **Shar-cloth.**

SARN [saa·r'n], (1) *expl.* '*Sarn it*' is a forcible form of expression not amounting to an oath. Com. '*Sarn it* wunst! I've talked to 'im solid an' sairious, an' I've plagued 'im, but it's no use—'e wull 'ave 'er; an' this is whad I look at, 'er conna work, an' whad good'll 'er be to 'im!' So reasoned a girl (from the neighbourhood of Ellesmere) upon her brother's choice of a wife. Cf. **Consarn-yo'.**

(2) *sb.* a culvert.—CLUN; CORVE DALE. W. *sarn*, a causeway; a paving. Cf. **Sough** (1).

SARVE [saa·r'v], (1) *v. a.* to serve. Com.

'Mans wisdome scatereth / divideth, and maketh sectes / while the wisdome of one is that a white Cote is best to *sarve* God in / and a-nother saith, a blacke / a-nother, a grey / [a]nother, a blew.'—WILLIAM TYNDALE [A.D. 1528], *Obedience of a Christian Man*. *Specim. Eng. Lit.*, xvi. l. 353.

(2) *v. a.* to give pigs their food. Com. 'Jack, yo' can *sarve* the pigs awilde I pŭt the gis an' ducks up.' See **Fother** (2).

SARVER, *sb.* a round, shallow basket holding a single 'feed' of corn.—PULVERBATCH. Qy. com. ''As the mar' 'ad 'er 'ay? Then yo' can gie 'er a *sarver* fŭll o' ŏŏats.' Cf. **Server.**

SARVING, *sb.* the quantity of food given at one time: said of pigs chiefly. Com. 'Gie the fat pigs a good *sarvin'* the las' thing—the nights bin lung.'

SATE [sai·t], (1) *sb.* young thorn set for hedges; usually protected by posts and rails.—PULVERBATCH; WORTHEN. 'The cowts han broke down the pwus an' rails—gwun through the *sate*-'edge, an' trod it down fur two or three yards.' Cf. **Seat.**

(2) *sb.* a kind of wedge-shaped chisel, used by blacksmiths for cutting bars of iron in lengths,—a 'set.' Com.

SATE-ROD, *sb.* a tough hazel rod twisted round the neck of the 'set,' and forming a handle, which is preferred to an iron one, as it causes less jar to the hand when the 'set' is struck for the purpose of cutting off a length of iron. Com. '*Sate-rods* binna so much used now' [1874]—said a Hanwood blacksmith—'sence they'n made it a trespass to gŏŏ i' the coppies to get the 'āzel twigs.'

Randle Holme has the following amongst 'Terms used by Smiths:'—'*Seat Rod* or Punch Rod; is With or Wreathen stick turned about the Head of a fire punch to hold it on the hot Iron, while it is striking through or making a hole in it.'—*Academy of Armory*, Bk. III. ch. iii. p. 89.

SAUCE [saa·s], *sb.* vegetables, or any other additions to the dinner-table, which are eaten with meat.—CORVE DALE, *Stanton Lacey.*

SAVATION [saivai·shun], (1) *sb.* saving, as of a person or thing.—PULVERBATCH. Qy. com. 'I like a good wide apparn to come round yo'—it's a great *savation* to yore gownd.'

'And for the *savacion* of my maisters horse, I made my fellowe to ryde a wey with the ij. horses; and I was brought forth with befor the capteyn of Kent.'—*Paston Letters*, A.D. 1465, vol. i. p. 132.

(2) *sb.* saving,—in the sense of economy.—*Ibid.* 'I dunna think theer's much *savation* in burnin' ŏŏd; if yo' mun pay a mon to cleave it, yo' met'n as well buy coal.'

SAVE-ALL, *sb.* a money-box with an aperture in the top for dropping 'pennies saved' into.—NEWPORT.

SAVERN-TREE [sav·ur'n], *sb. Juniperus sabina.*—PULVERBATCH, *Hanwood.*

'*Hec samina*, *An*^ce a saveryn,' occurs in a *Pictorial Vocabulary*, xv. cent., in Wr. vocabs., vol. i. p. 265. Mr. Wright supposes it to be *Juniperus sabina.* '*Savern-tea*' is supposed to procure abortion. See **Savin-tree**, below.

SAVIN-TREE, same as **Savern-tree**, above.—PULVERBATCH; WEM. The properties imputed to a 'tea' made from this shrub (see above) are alluded to in the following lines:—

'. . . And when I look
To gather fruit, find nothing but the *savin-tree*,
Too frequent in nunnes' orchards, and there planted,
By all conjecture, to destroy fruit rather.'

MIDDLETON, *Game of Chess*, C. I. 6, in Wr.

'*Saveyne*, tree. *Savina.*'—*Prompt. Parv.*

SAVVER [sav·ur'], *sb.* a small quantity; a morsel; a taste: said of food,—'theer inna-d-a *savver* on it lef'.'—PULVERBATCH; ELLESMERE; WEM. Pegge has this word for Derbyshire.

Compare '*Savowre* or tast. *Sapor.*'—*Prompt. Parv.*

'O.Fr. *Savor*, *Savour*; goût, saveur; de *sapor.*'—BUR.

SAWTH [sau·th], *sb.* saw-dust.—CORVE DALE.

SAYLY [sai·li'], *adj.*, *obsols.* thin; flimsy.—WORTHEN. 'This new flannin's sad *sayly* stuff, they dunna make nuthin' as good as it used to be.' Cf. **Slazy** (1).

SCALDED-APPLE, *sb. Lychnis diurna*, Red Campion.—PULVERBATCH.

SCALLION, *sb. Allium Ascalonicum*, a kind of small onion,—the Ascalonian garlic.—LUDLOW.

'*Hec hinnula*, a scalyone,' occurs in a *Nominale*, xv. cent., in Wr. vocabs., vol. i. p. 225.

'*Hinnula*, cepula [a small onion].'—DUCANGE. Cf. **Sheelot.**

SCAR-CROW [skaa·r' kr'oa], *sb.* a figure made of straw and dressed in man's clothes, set up in fields and gardens to affright birds. Com. 'It wuz rar' raps to 'ear the 'unters shoutin' to the *scar-crow* to know which way the fox went.' This form of the common word *scare-crow* is an old one apparently:—

> 'Lik'st a strawne *scar-crow* in the new sowne field,
> Rear'd on some sticke, the tender corne to shield.'
>
> HALL'S *Satires*, iii. 7, in Nares.

Minshew—ed. 1617—has, 'a *Scar-crow*, any device to fright birds, compositum *à* Scar, i. terrere & Crow i. Cornix . . .'

Mr. Nares says that 'other old dictionary-writers have it in this form.' See **Malkin** (2).

SCATTER-CORNER, *adv.* diagonally.—CORVE DALE. Some members of 'The Severn Valley Field-Club' were directed by an old man at Wilderhope to go '*scatter-corner*' through a field. Cf. **Cater-cornered.**

SCAUD [skau·d], *v. a.* and *v. n.* to scald. Com. 'The poor child wuz *scauded* dreadful—the skin wuz all rivelled up.'

> 'I'm sure sma' pleasure it can gie,
> Ev'n to a deil,
> To skelp an' *scaud* poor dogs like me,
> An' hear us squeel!'
>
> ROBERT BURNS, *Poems*, p. 31, l. 11.

'O.Du. *schauden*, to scald.'—STRAT.

SCHOLARD [skol·ur'd], *sb.*, *var. pr.* a scholar. Com. ''As Jack lef' school yet?' 'No, I want 'im to gŏŏ another quarter, 'e's but a poor *scholard*.'

'*Kite.* O! Carolus! Why Carolus is Latin for Queen Ann; that's all.

'2d. *Mob.* 'Tis a fine thing to be a *scollard*—Sergeant, will you part with this?'—FARQUHAR'S *Recruiting Officer*, Act II. Scene—The Street [Shrewsbury].

SCLENCH [sklen·sh], *v. a.* to check water at boiling point, by dashing cold water into it.—PULVERBATCH. 'Yo'd'n better *sclench* that waiter afore it all bwiles away.'

SCONCE [skon·s], (1) *sb.* a tin candlestick with a reflector at the back, made to hang flat against a wall. Qy. com.

'*Hic absconsus*, *A*ͤ sconse'—under the head of *Nomina Pertinencia Ecclesie*—occurs in an *English Vocabulary*, xv. cent., in Wr. vocabs., vol. i. p. 193. Mr. Wright has the following note upon it:—'A sort of candlestick made to be attached to the wall. The word is still in use for such candlesticks in the North of England.' See *Sconce* (2), in WEDG.

(2) *sb.*, *sl.*? a contemptuous term for a person's head.—LUDLOW. Qy. com. 'That fellow's *sconce* inna wuth the carryin'.'

'*Ant. S.* . . . .
If you will jest with me, know my aspect,
And fashion your demeanour to my looks,
Or I will beat this method in your *sconce*.

'*Dro. S. Sconce*, call you it? so you would leave battering, I had rather have it a head: an you use these blows long, I must get a *sconce* for my head, and *insconce* it too; or else I shall seek my wit in my shoulders.'—*Comedy of Errors*, II. ii. 32—38.

See *Sconce* (1), in WEDG.

SCOOT [skoo·t], *sb.* a small irregular plot of ground; an odd piece, as of cloth, &c. Com. (1) 'I'll pŭt a fyeow cabbitch o' that *scoot* down by the bruck.' (2) 'The Missis gid me a good *scoot* o' linsey as'll mak' Joe a good wascut.'

'A.S. *sceat;* O.Fris. *skat;* O.Du. *schot;* O.Icel. *skaut;* Goth. *skauts;* O.H.Germ. *scoz*, a corner. . . .'—STRAT.

SCORCH [skaur'·ch], *v. a.* to rub with stones, as a hearth or door-step.—SHREWSBURY; WORTHEN; WEM. 'Whad's the good o' me *scorchin'* the 'earth if yo' keep'n prokin' the ess o'er it all the wilde?'

SCORCHING-STONES [stwunz], *sb. pl.* rubbing-stones.—*Ibid.*

SCORE [skoa·ur'], (1) *v. a.* to make circles, zigzags, or other devices, with the rubbing-stones on doorsteps, &c. Com.

'N. *skura;* to rub, scrape, scour.'—WEDG.

(2) *v. a.* to scratch; to cut superficially. Com. (1) 'The spŏons bin *scored* all o'er.' (2) 'Yo'n gwun too dip i' *scorin'* this leg o' pork, yo'n cut i' the flesh—the Maister 'll say swar w'en it's sarved.' A.S. *scýrian;* O.N. *skera*, to cut.

(3) *sb.* 20 lbs. in weight: used generally in the singular form,—'the pig 'll mak' 30 *score* by Chris'mas.' Com. See **Weights and Measures**, p. lxxxiv.

SCORING-STONES, same as **Scorching-stones**, above. Com. See **Score** (1), above.

SCORK [skau·r'k], *sb.* the core of an apple,—'the *scork* stuck in Adam's throät.' Com. In the *Treatise of Walter de Biblesworth*, xiii. cent., amongst the parts of an apple and what to do with them, the following occurs:—

'La pipinette engettez,
Les pepynes dehors plauntez.'

La pipinette is glossed 'the *scoree*.'—Wr. vocabs., vol. i. p. 150.

The core of an apple is called the *score* in Gloucestershire. See **Eve's-scork**.

SCOT, *sb.* an ale-house reckoning.—CORVE DALE. Qy. com.

'O.Fr. *escot* . . . de l'allemand: ancien frison *skot*, suédois *skott*, anglais *scot*, all. mod. *schoss*, impôt.'—BUR.

Cf. **Shot.**

SCOTCH, (1) *v. a.* and *v. n.* to stop, or retard, a wheel, as of a waggon, &c.,—in going up-hill this is done by placing a stone on the road, and backing the 'shafter' till the wheel rests upon it, by which means it is kept from going back, and the horses are relieved from the strain of the load while they are breathed; in going down-hill a drag is put on the wheel. Com. 'Yo' mind to *scotch* gweïn down the Baich bonk, else it'll tak' the shafter off 'is fit.'

'*Scotch a wheel*, to stop it from going backward. Lanc.'—PEGGE.

(2) *v. a.* to make a barrel steady by placing a wedge on each side of it.—PULVERBATCH. Qy. com. 'Dunna yo' pŭt them wedges out o' the way, I shall want 'em w'en I tun the drink to *scotch* the barrels ŏŏth.'

'Fr. *accoter;* to underprop, shore, bear up, stay from shaking or slipping. Cotgr.,' in WEDG.

SCOTCH-GOTHERUM [godh·ur'um], *sb.* a term applied to any material of coarse, loose texture.—PULVERBATCH; WORTHEN. 'W'y didna yo' get summat as ŏŏd war, an' nod sich *scotch-gotherum* as this?'

Compare '*caurimauri*'—explained as the name of some coarse, rough material—in *Piers Pl.*, Text A., pass. v. l. 62.

SCOUT, *v. a., pec.* to chase; to drive away,—same as **Keouse,** q. v. —WEM. A.S. *sceótan,* to send forth. See *sub voce* **Keout.**

SCOWTHER [skou·dhur'], same as above.—PULVERBATCH. 'Well done, little Spot!—it's a famous dog to *scowther* the 'ens out o' the garden.' Cf. **Cowther.**

SCRAMMEL, STRAMMEL [skr'am·el], WEM. [str'am·il], PULVERBATCH, *sb.* a lean, gaunt, ill-favoured person or animal. (1) 'That theer piece as Jones 'as married, 'er's a reg'lar poor *scrammel* to look at.' (2) 'Whad a great *strammel* of a pig that is as John bought at the far.' Cf. **Gangrel.**

SCRAT, (1) *v. a.* and *v. n.* to scratch; scratched,—'dunna *scrat* athatn,'—'the cat *scrat* the child.' Com.

'On the sege then sate y,
And he *scrattud* me fulle vylensly.'
MS. Cantab. Ff. ii. 38, f. 152, in HAL.

'And ylkane *skratte* othyr in the face,
And thaire awen flesche of ryve and race.'
Hampole, MS. Bowes, p. 215, in HAL.

Mr. Oliphant says that the word '*scratch* arose in Salop.' See *Sources of Standard English,* p. 124.

(2) *sb.* the itch. Com.

(3) *v. n.* to work hard for a poor living. Com. 'Aye, poor ŏŏman, 'er knows whad it is to *scrat* afore 'er pecks.'

(4) *v. n.* to hurry; to make haste. Com. 'I mun *scrat* alung ŏŏth my work, else I shanna get to the raps afore dark.'

(5) *sb.* an avaricious person. Com. 'Jest yo' look at Molly Andras—an owd *scrat* 'er is—'er wants the laisin' all to 'erself.'

(6) See *sub voce* **Owd Lad.**

SCRATCHIN', *sb.* a term applied to meat that is dried up and shrivelled from being over-roasted,—'done to a *scratchin'*.' Qy. com.

SCRATCHIN'-CAKE, *sb.* a cake made with the *scratchin's* of lard (see below) mixed with flour, rolled out about an inch thick, and baked. Qy. com.

SCRATCHIN'S, *sb. pl.* the small crisp bits left from the 'leaf' after the lard has been all melted out. Com. *Scratchin's* are considered a *bonne-bouche*, either made into cakes (as above) or simply eaten with bread. The refuse of them pressed down and caked together is used for dog-meat.

SCRAUP [skr'au·p], (1) *v. a., var. pr.* to scrape; to make a scraping noise. Com. 'Jack, yo' should'n mak' better 'aste o'er yore dinner, an' nod be *scraupin'* yore plate for more w'en I've shut my knife.' In farm-houses where the old customs are still observed, the men, employed on the farm, dine at a long table set apart for them, while the master and his family take their dinner at the same time from a square table in the middle of the kitchen. The master carves for all. At 'the men's table' neither knives nor forks are provided, but each man uses his own clasp-knife, which serves the twofold purpose of cutting his food and conveying it to his mouth. If he wants a second helping, he *scrapes* his plate with his knife to call the master's attention to the fact. The head waggoner is 'master of the ceremonies' at 'the men's table,' and when he has finished his dinner, he closes his knife with a snap, as a signal for all to rise and leave the table. This custom has given rise to a saying current among farm-servants—'It's time for me to a *shut my knife*,' that is, to have finished any matter in hand.

'O.Du. *schrapen*, to scrape.'—STRAT.

(2) *sb.* a greedy, avaricious person. Com. 'Poor owd fellow!—'e's bin a reg'lar *scraup* all 'is life, an' now 'e's gwun an' left all.' Cf. **Scrat** (5).

SCRAWL [skr'au·l], (1) *v. n.* to crawl; to creep, as a child does about a floor. Com. 'I shouldna lay 'im down so much now, 'e ought to be takin' 'is fit, fur if 'e begins to *scrawl* 'e'll mak' some work.'

(2) *v. n.* to move slowly and laboriously about, as a very weak or tired person does. Com. 'I got out i' the sun a bit isterd'y, but fel' so wek I could 'ardly *scrawl*.'

'To *scrall*, stir; *motito*.'—COLES' *Lat. Dict.*

(3) *sb.* a tangle, as of thread, &c. Com. 'W'en yo' turn them slippin's [skeins] o' the 'edge, see as yo' dunna get 'em in a *scrawl*—it mak's 'em so taidious to wind.' Cf. **Scrawly**, below.

(4) *sb.* a hobble; a difficulty. Com. 'I never sid sich a ŏŏman as that Betsy Davies—'er's al'ays gettin' i' some *scrawl*.' 'Well, an' sarve 'er right, 'er's al'ays prokin' 'er nose w'eer 'er inna wanted.'

(5) *v. n.* to wrangle; to quarrel.—WEM. Qy. com. 'Them folks bin al'ays *scrawlin'* among theirselves.'

SCRAWLING, *adj.* mean; worthless,—'a *scrawlin'* fellow.' Com.

SCRAWLY, *adj.* twisted; entangled: said of growing corn, of which the ears have been turned in different directions by the wind.—CLEE HILLS. Cf. **Tather** (2).

SCRIKE, *v. n.* and *sb.* to shriek; a shriek,—'*scriked* till yo' met'n a 'eärd 'er a mile off,'—'gid sich a *scrike*.' Com.

> 'The little babe did loudly *scrike* and squall,
> And all the woods with piteous plaints did fill.'
> SPENSER, *F. Q.*, Bk. VI. c. v. st. xviii.

> 'with that a greiuous *scrike*
> among them there was made,
> & euery one did seeke
> on something to be stayd.'
> *The Drowning of Henery the I. His children*, l. 81. *Percy Folio MS.*, vol. iii. p. 159, ed. Hales and Furnivall.

N. *skrika*, to shriek, scream.

SCRIMMER, *sb.* a niggardly person.—PULVERBATCH. 'It's little use axin' 'er fur anythin'—the poor *scrimmer*, 'er grudges 'er own needs, let alone anybody else's.'

SCRIMMITY, *adj.* mean; stingy.—PULVERBATCH. ''Er's as jubous as 'er's *scrimmity*—weighs the flour out, an' then the bread after it's baked; be'appen 'er thinks as I should ate the duff.'

SCRINCH [skr'in·sh], *sb.* a morsel; a 'wee bittie,'—'gie me jest a *scrinch*.' Com.

SCRIP, *v. a.* and *v. n.* to snatch; to snatch at—hastily or greedily. Com.

SCROBBLE [scr'ob·l], (1) *sb.* a state of difficulty or trouble—generally brought about by folly or ill conduct; a scrape.—PULVERBATCH. 'E's got 'isself into a pretty *scrobble* ŏŏth 'is gammocks.' See **Robble.** Cf. **Scrawl** (4).

(2) *sb.* a tangle,—'a *scrobble* o' thrid.'—*Ibid.* Cf. **Scrawl** (3).

(3) *v. a.* to entangle; to ravel.—*Ibid.* 'Yo'n *scrobble* that yorn if yo' binna more carful o'er windin' it.'

(4) *v. n.* to scramble.—SHREWSBURY; PULVERBATCH. Qy. com. 'I remember the poor owd free-owder Jondrell, 'e use't to chuck apples o'er the 'edge fur us childern to *scrobble* for [1817].'

SCROODGE, SCRUDGE [skr'oo·j, skr'uj·], *v. n.* to squeeze; to press or thrust in, as between two persons. Com. 'Plaze, Sir, Tum Jones is *scrudgin'* on to our form.' Compare Spenser's '*scruze*' = squeeze:—

> 'Tho up he caught him twixt his puissant hands,
> And having *scruzd* out of his carrion corse
> The lothfull life . . . .'
> *F. Q.*, Bk. II. c. xi. st. xlvi.

SCROUT [skr'ou·t], *v. n.* to scratch vigorously,—'*scroutin'* at the flen all night.'—CLEE HILLS.

SCRUF [skr'uf·], *sb.* scurf. Qy. com. 'That pig dunna grow a bit, 'e's reg'lar 'ide-bond, an' a *scruf* on 'is back as thick as a twopenny piece.' See **R** (3) in **Grammar Outlines** (*consonants*, &c.).

SCRUF-O'-THE-NECK, *sb.* the nape of the neck.—NEWPORT.

SCUFF, SCUFT, &c., same as above. Com. See *Scuff*, in WEDG.

SCUFFLE [skuf·l], (1) *sb.* a garden implement used for cutting off weeds at the roots,—generally known as a Dutch hoe. Com. Du. *schoffel*:—*idem.*

(2) *v. a.* to cut up weeds with the *scuffle.* Com. Du. *schoffelen*:—*idem.* See WEDG.

SCUPPERED [skup·ur'd], *part. adj., obsols.* crumpled; turned black, as by blight or frost: said of leaves.—PULVERBATCH. 'Theer must a bin a ketch o' fros' las' night, see 'ow the tatoe-tops bin *scuppered.*'

Mr. Halliwell says that *scuppered* is 'A Herefordshire word, according to Urry's MS. additions to Ray.'

SCUT [skut·], *sb.* the tail of a hare or a rabbit.—PULVERBATCH; CLEE HILLS.

Randle Holme gives amongst 'Terms for the Tails of several sorts of Beast,'—'An Hare & Cony, the *Skutt*, or *Scutte*.'—*Academy of Armory*, Bk. II. ch. vii. p. 133.

The *Prompt. Parv.* gives '*Scut*, hare.'

SCUTCH [skuch·], *sb. Triticum répens*, Couch-grass. Com. Cf. **Squitch** (1).

SCUTCH-YUP, *sb.* a heap of *scutch*; a rubbish heap.—LUDLOW, *Burford.* See **Heap**.

SEARCH. See **Sarch.**

SEAT [see·t], *sb.* a 'quick' thorn, or other growing hedgerow shrub,—'a thorn *seat*,'—'a crab *seat*.'—WEM. Cf. **Sate** (1). See **Quick.**

SEEDNESS, *sb.* seed-time.—WEM. Qy. com. in *N. Shr.*

> '. . . . . as blossoming time
> That from the *seedness* the bare fallow brings
> To teeming foison. . . . . . .'
>
> *Measure for Measure*, I. iv. 42.

Cf. **Sidness.**

SEEK, (1) *v. n.* to percolate: said of water finding its way, it *seeks* out of a hill, *seeks* into a pit.—NEWPORT.

(2) *sb.* a place which water *seeks* into, or out of. A pit that is supplied by surface-drainage—that has no spring—and becomes dry in dry weather, is a *seek*;—there is a *seek* in the draining-pipe if the drain lets out the water.—*Ibid.* Cf. **Sake.**

SEG, *sb.* a term applied generically to *all Irises*, whether wild or cultivated, and to other plants also having 'flag'-like leaves,—the large aquatic species of *Carex*, &c. Com. About Wem it is proverbially said of a person giving way to noisy expressions of impotent rage, that 'he roars like a bittern at a *seg*-root.' The bittern has long been an extinct bird in that neighbourhood, but years ago his cry—the 'hollow, booming noise,' as Bewick designates it—may have been heard across the swampy flats of the district.

> 'Imeind mid spire and grene *segge*.'
>
> *Owl and Nightingale*, l. 18.

'*Carex*, segg.' '*Gladiolum*, secgg,' occur in *Anglo-Saxon Vocabulary*, xi. cent., in Wr. vocabs., vol. i. p. 67.

'*Segge*, of fenne, or wyld gladōn. *Accorus*.' '*Segge*, star of the fenne, *Carix*.'—*Prompt. Parv.*

A.S. *secg*, a sedge.

SEG-BOTTOM, *sb.* a rush-bottom for a chair.—SHREWSBURY; PULVERBATCH. Qy. com. 'Fur my own part I like ŏŏden cheers best fur the kitchen—the *seg-bottoms* las' none.'

SEG-BOTTOMED, *adj.* rush-bottomed,—'a *seg-bottomed* cheer.'—*Ibid.*

SEGGER. See **Sogger** (1).

SEN, *v. a., pr. t., pl.* a contracted form of *sayen*,—'folks *sen* so.' Com.

'Sum men *sayn* these selé frerys thai han no consyans.'
JOHN AUDELAY'S *Poems*, p. 29.

'. . . . . þis matter is asked,
Boþe to lered and to lewed · þat *seyn* þat þey leueden
Hollich on þe grete god.'—*P. Pl. Cr.*, l. 25.

SENCE [sen·s], *adv.* and *prep.* a contracted form of O.E. *sithens*,—'it's a lungful wilde *sence* 'er wuz 'ere.' Com.

'I hearde once a tale of a thinge yat was done at Oxforde xx yeres a go, and the lyke hath bene *sence* in thys realme as I was enformed of credible persons.'—LATIMER, *Sermon* iv. p. 119.

SEND, *v. a., pec.* to accompany on the road. Com. 'Yo' nee'na gŏŏ yet—stop an' 'ăve a bit o' supper, an' we'n *send* yo' [go with you] a tidy bit o' the way at-after.'

SENNOW [sen·oe], *sb.* a sinew.—PULVERBATCH.

'Yf his clothe be xviii. yerdes longe, he wyl set hym on a racke, and streach hym out wyth ropes, and racke hym tyll the *senewes* shrinke a gayne, whyles he hath brought hym to xxvii yardes.'—LATIMER, *Sermon* iii. p. 87.

Dr. Stratmann gives '*senuwen*' as occurring in Layamon's Brut, and also several other early examples of the form. See **Sinnow**.

SENNOW-GROWED, *part. adj.* contracted: said of the ligaments of a joint.—*Ibid.* 'I think it's a bad thing fur Dick to carry 'is arm in a sling so lung; it'll be gettin' *sennow-growed*, an' 'e'll 'ăve a stiff jīnt as lung as 'e lives.'

SEROP [saer'·up], *sb.* syrup.—SHREWSBURY; PULVERBATCH. Qy. com. 'We mun a some Elder *serop* made, it's sich a useful thing i' the 'ouse fur cowds an' that, but I doubt the berries ŏŏnna ild well this 'ear.'

'Tryakill, droggis, or electuary,
Seroppys, sewane, sugur, & Synnamome.'
GAWIN DOUGLAS (A.D. 1513), *Prol. of the XII. Buk of Eneados*. *Specim. Eng. Lit.*, xiii. l. 145.

'Ital. *siroppo*; Sp. *xarope*, *xarabe*, *axarabe*, from Arab. *charāb*, a frequent word among the Arab doctors.'—WEDG.

SERPCLOTH, SIRPCLOTH, *sb.*, *obs.* This word occurs in the *Churchwardens' Accounts*, Hopton Castle (Salop), as follows:—

'1753. For a quarter of Cloth for yᵉ *Serpcloth* 0 - 0 - 8½
For washing the *Serp Cloth* t[w]yes 0 - 3 - 0
For washing the *Serpcloth* 0 - 1 - 6

'1766. for a *Sirp Cloth* 14 yards 2 - 11 - 4
for making the *Sirpcloth* 0 - 10 - 6.'

'Surplice—*sirpcloth* in the North of England, xvii cent.,' occurs in Mr. Mackenzie Walcott's *Popular Dict. of Sacred Archæology*, p. 567, ed. 1868. See **Cloth.**

SERVE, same as **Sarve** (2), q. v.

SERVE, SERVER, *sb.* a sieve like a **Blind-sieve,** q. v., used for a horse's feed.—BRIDGNORTH. See **Sarver.**

SERVING, same as **Sarving,** q. v.

SET, *v. a.*, *pec.* to let. Com. 'I 'ear they'n *set* the 'ill Farm at last.' 'Aye, but they'n tolled it o' tuthree filds o' land fur the nex' neīghbour.'

'. . . therefore, when my father and Richard Jukes had lost one halfe yeare's rent, they *sett* it [Haremeare Warren] at six pounds per ann. to Mr. Hall of Balderton.'—GOUGH'S *History of Myddle*, p. 32.

SETLESS, (1) *sb.* a bench built into a recess by the fireplace, forming a permanent seat in the 'ingle-neuk.'—PULVERBATCH. 'The owd ŏŏman wuz sittin' o' the *setless* anunst the chimley-jawm the las' time I sid 'er, an' 'er toud me then 'er fel' mighty bad.'

'On þe *setle* of unhele,' *i. e.* in the seat of ill-health, occurs in *Old English Homilies*, ii. 59, ed. Morris.

'Opon the *setil* of his magesté,' *i. e.* on the throne of his majesty. —HAMPOLE'S *Pricke of Conscience*, l. 6122.

'A common *settle* drew for either guest.'
DRYDEN, *Baucis and Philemon*, l. 44.

A.S. *setl;* Goth. *sitls;* Germ. *sessel;* Lat. *sella* [= *sed-la*], a seat.

(2) *sb.* a raised platform, or shelf, of bricks or tiles, built round a dairy for the milk-pans to stand upon.—NEWPORT; ELLESMERE.

Compare the *settle* mentioned in Ezek. xliii. 14, 17, which Mr. Nares conjectures to have been 'a kind of ledge or flat portion of the altar,' and of which he says, 'the clearest account seems to be in the Assembly's annotations' [Assembly of Divines, 1643?]:—

'. . . . From thence two cubits to the round ledge, or bench, or *settle*, of a cubit broad, that went round about it [the altar].—This ledge or bench seems to be for them that served at the altar to stand upon, and to go upon, round about the altar.' See further in NARES.

SETTINGS, *sb.* two props and a horizontal beam used to support the sides and roof of the waggon-road of a mine. Com.—M. T.

SEVEN-COLOURED-LINNET, *sb.* the Goldfinch.—CHURCH STRETTON; CLUN; BRIDGNORTH; WELLINGTON; NEWPORT. Cf. **Peckled-Dick.** See **Jack-Nicol.**

SEVERN [siv·ur'n *and* siv·h'n]. An idiomatic usage commonly obtains in speaking of the Severn; it is simply designated *Severn*, without a preceding *the* as is usual for river-names. 'Theer must a bin 'eavy rain upperts—*Sivern* wuz risin' fast, it ruz above two fŭt awilde I wuz in town.'

'1583-4. This yeare and the xxj*th* day of Septembe' being S[t] Mathews daye and also the fayre daye in Shreusberie the horsse fayre was kept in the backesyde of Edward Myntoons in Franckvill in a teynter crofte there becawse *Syvern* wat' coverid over all the usuall place of the horsefayre there at that tyme.'—*Early Chronicles of Shrewsbury* (*Taylor MS.*), in *Transactions of the Shropshire Archæological and Natural History Society.*

William Langland speaks of the Thames in the same way:—

'Take two stronge men · and *in themese* cast hem.'
Piers Pl., Text B., pass. xii. l. 161.

Referring to this, Mr. Skeat remarks that 'this use of the name of a river (without the definite article preceding it) is still common in many parts of England, and sounds well; it seems to add to the dignity of the river. I take the opportunity of recording here that I heard a good instance of it at Cleobury Mortimer. One boy said to another—"If yo' dunna take care, yo'll fall into *Severn*." I did not overhear the rest of the conversation, which must have referred to some adventure at a distance, since the Severn does not come at all near to Cleobury. The interesting point was the use of William's idiom at the supposed place of his birth.'—*Notes*, p. 290.

See example *sub voce* **Mighty.**

SEYNY-TREE [sain·i'], *sb.* the Laburnum,—the leaves are thought to resemble *senna*-leaves, whence the name, *seyny-tree.*—WEM; ELLESMERE. See **French Broom.**

SHAB-RAG, *sb.* a term of contempt applied to persons of dirty, depraved appearance.—LUDLOW. 'Yo' great idle *shab-rag*, get out o' my sight, or I'll shift yo'.'

SHACKET [shak·it], *sb.* a child's night-gown.—WEM; ELLESMERE. 'See as yo' ar'n the child's *shacket*, fur if 'e gets a cooth it'll be the djeth on 'im.'

SHACKLE-BONE [shak·l bwun], *sb.* the hind leg of a pig's carcase, between the foot and the joint at which the ham is cut off.—PULVERBATCH. Cf. **Pestle.**

SHACKLING, (1) *adj.* unstable,—not to be relied upon.—PULVERBATCH. Qy. com. 'I can never bargain ŏŏth 'im, 'e's sich a *shacklin'* fellow.'

(2) *adj.* idling; dawdling; shiftless: chiefly applied to men,—'a *shacklin'* fellow.'—NEWPORT; WEM; WHITCHURCH. Qy. com.

SHAD [shad·], *sb.*, *var. pr.* a shed,—'pŭt them turmits i' the *shad.*'—PULVERBATCH; CLEE HILLS.

'the other Lyes att home like summers cattle *shadding.*' *
Hollowe me Fancye, l. 39. *Percy Folio MS.*, vol. ii. p. 31, ed. Hales and Furnivall.

* 'Getting into a shed or the *shade.*' Note by Mr. FURNIVALL.

SHAD-BIRD, *sb.*, *obsols.*? *Tringöides hypoleuca*, the Common Sandpiper.—SHREWSBURY. Before the erection of weirs at Worcester and other places on the Severn, *shad* used to ascend the river; they came up about the middle of April, the time of the arrival of the Common Sandpiper, and it is probable that the Severn fishermen, connecting the appearance of the bird with the advent of the shad-fishing season, gave to it the local appellation of *Shad-bird*.

SHAD-SALMON, *sb.*, *obs.* small salmon of from five pounds' to eight pounds' weight—so called by the old Severn fishermen because they arrived with the *Shad.*—*Ibid.*

SHAKE [shai·k *and* shae·k], *v. n.*, *pec.* to be about—a term of conjecture,—'*shekin* a mile' = about a mile:—'the pig 'll *shake* twenty score.'—CLUN; LUDLOW. *Shake* is a metaphorical expression, evidently borrowed from the act of weighing in scales or on a balance, in which movement is necessarily implied.

SHAKED [shak·t], *part. adj.* split or cleft, as by sun or wind: said of green wood.—CLUN. Cf. **Spauled.**

SHALLIGONAKED [shal·i'gŏŏnaikit], *sb.* and *adj.* a term applied to a jacket, or such like, for out-door wear; made of light, thin, flimsy material.—SHREWSBURY; PULVERBATCH; BISHOP'S CASTLE. 'Whad good ŏŏl that fine *shalligonakit* thing be?—it'll cut a poor figger on a wet day.'

SHANK [shang·k], *sb.*, *obsols.* a rope by which a horse is tied up in the stall.—ELLESMERE. See **Head-collar.**

SHANNA. See **Grammar Outlines,** *verb* **Shall.**

'Go on, my lord! I lang to meet you,
An' in my house at hame to greet you;
Wi' common lords ye *shanna* mingle,
The benmost neuk beside the ingle
At my right han' assigned your seat.'
ROBERT BURNS, *Poems*, p. 151, l. 20, c. 2.

SHAR-CLOTH, same as **Sar-cloth,** q. v.—SHREWSBURY; OSWESTRY.

SHAREVIL [shaar'·u'vl], *sb.* a garden-fork.—SHREWSBURY; ATCHAM; PULVERBATCH; ELLESMERE; OSWESTRY. Qy. com. 'Tak' the *sharevil* an' the kipe, an' gŏŏ an' get up some o' them frum tatoes out o' the slang.' See **Sherevil,** also **Evil.** Cf. **Dungevil.**

SHARN. See **Cow-sharn.**

SHARP [shaa·r'p], (1) *adj.* quick; active. Com. 'Now then, be *sharp* o'er that job—theer's a power to do afore milkin' time.'

'Hast thow be *scharpe* and bysy
To serve thy mayster trewely?'
MS. Cott. Claud., A. ii. f. 141.

'*Scharpnesse*, or swyftenesse. *Velocitas.*'—*Prompt. Parv.*

(2) *adj.* well; in health. Com. ''Ow bin 'ee this mornin'?' 'Oh, right *sharp*; 'ow bin yo'?'

(3) *adj.* cold; frosty; nipping. Com. 'It's a *sharp* mornin', Tummas.' 'Aye, theer's bin a ketch o' fros' las' night.'

SHARPS, *sb. pl.* coarse siftings of flour. Com. *Sharps*, as explained by a miller, are the small kernel which has not been ground fine enough to pass with the flour through the 'dressing' machinery. *Sharps* are of various degrees of goodness: some are ground over again into a coarse quality of flour, others are sold off for purposes of pig-feeding, &c., without undergoing any further process. These differences are due to the diverse methods of grinding and 'dressing' adopted in different mills. See **Gurgeons**.

SHAVES [shai·vz], (1) *sb. pl.* fragments of hemp-stalk adhering to the tow.—PULVERBATCH. Called '*Shoves*' by Randle Holme.

'Low Du. *scheve*, the shives or broken fragments of stalk that fall off in dressing flax or hemp.'—WEDG.

(2) *sb. pl.* shafts.—PULVERBATCH. 'The 'orse run away, knocked the gate pwust down, an' broke the *shaves* o' the cart right short off.'

SHAVING-BRUSH, (1) *Centauréa nígra*, black Knapweed.—CRAVEN ARMS, *Stokesay*. Cf. **Hard-yeds**.

SHEAR [shee·h'r'], *v. a.*, *obs.* to reap.—CLEE HILLS.

'*Scheryn̄*', or repe corne.'—*Prompt. Parv.*

A.S. *sceran*, to shear, shave, cut off. Cf. **Swive**.

SHEARERS, *sb. pl.*, *obs.* reapers who used a sickle—called a 'saw-sickle'—having a serrated edge.—*Ibid.* The *shearers* grasped a handful of corn and cut it off, placing it on a band—for the after convenience of binding—and so on, handful by handful, until the sheaf was completed. They left a high stubble, but as level as if it had been shaved off. The *shearers* were Irishmen or nailers from the 'Black Country,' who, before the introduction of reaping machines, presented themselves in gangs at the different farm-houses at harvest time for the purpose of cutting the wheat. The sickle they used is a thing of the past, the scythe now taking its place when the corn is too much 'laid' for the machines to cut it.

'1793 August 12—I let the wheat to reap to Roger Furbow, &c., for six shillings per acre, with an allowance of beer, which they accomplished in a very neat manner, being done with *sickles*, which does it much better than in the common way with *hooks*.'—*Bailiff's Diary*, Aston, Oswestry. *Byegones*, 1877, p. 297.

'*Hic messor An*ͤ a scherer.—*Hec fals An*ͤ a sekylle,' occur in a *Pictorial Vocabulary*, xv. cent., in Wr. vocabs., vol. i. p. 277.

Cf. **Swivers**. See **Swiving-hook**.

SHEED, (1) *v. n.* to let fall; to scatter,—grain when over-ripe *sheeds*. Com. A.S. *sceádan*, to separate.

(2) *v. a.* to spill; to slop,—'see, as yo' dunna *sheed* that milk.' Com.

'O Molly read these letters,
Which I have written here,
And if you will but read them,
You will *sheed* many a tear.

. . . .

The Gallant Hero, A Ballad, printed by J. WAIDSON, Doglane, Shrewsbury, A.D. 1812, *circa*.

'the litle boy had a horne
of red golde that ronge;
he said, "there was noe Cuckolde
shall drinke of my horne,
but he shold itt *sheede*
Either behind or beforne."'

Boy and Mantle, l. 181. *Percy Folio MS.*, vol. ii. p. 311, ed. Hales and Furnivall.

SHEEL [shee·l], *v. a.* and *v. n.*, *var. pr.* to shell, as of nuts, peas, &c.—PULVERBATCH. 'The lads bin al'ays rongin' after the nuts; by the time they'n *sheel*, theer'll be none left.' Cf. **Shull**, also **Brown-sheelers**.

SHEELOT [shee·lot], *sb.*, *var. pr.* the shallot,—same as **Scallion**, q. v.—LUDLOW. Fr. *échalote*,—idem.

SHELL-BOARD, *sb.* the 'breast' of a plough—the part which turns the furrows. Qy. com.

Shell-board is a variation of *shield-board*,—'*Teschuchoun*,' glossed 'the *cheld-brede*,' occurs in the description of a plough and its several parts, in *The Treatise of Walter de Biblesworth*, xiii. cent., in Wr. vocabs., vol. i. p. 169.

Randle Holme has, the '*Shell-Board*,' amongst the 'Terms of all the parts of a Plow.' Cf. **Mould-board**.

SHEM-RIPPED, *adj.* opened at the seam: said of boots or shoes of which the upper leather has separated from the sole. Qy. com. 'These bought boots dunna stand war like wham made uns, they bin *shem-ripped* afore yo'n wore 'em a month.'

SHEPHERD'S-NEEDLE, same as **Beggar's-needle**, q. v.—WELLINGTON.

SHERES. See **Shires**.

SHEREVIL [shae·r'u'vl], same as **Sharevil**, q. v.—WELLINGTON.

SHERIFF'S-MAN, *sb.* the Goldfinch.—PULVERBATCH; CLUN; CLEE HILLS; MUCH WENLOCK. Cf. **Proud-tailor**. See **Jack-nicol**.

SHERRY [shae·r'i'], *sb.* a short piece of wood used to shore up a gate-post when the lower part is worn away.—CORVE DALE; LUDLOW; BRIDGNORTH.

'Hit had *shoriers* to shoue hit vp · þre shides of o lengþe.'
Piers Pl., Text C. pass. xix. l. 20.

SHET [shaet·], *v. a.* to shut,—an old form.—SHREWSBURY; PULVERBATCH. Qy. com.

'& ȝepli ȝomen þan dede · þe ȝates *schette*.'
William of Palerne, l. 3649.

'He knokked faste, and ay, the more he cryed,
The faster *shette* they the dores alle.'
CHAUCER, B. 3722 (Six-text ed.), Skeat.

A.S. *scyttan*, to lock up; pt. t. *ic scytte*. See **Shut**, also **Onshut**.

SHETH [shaeth·], *sb., var. pr.* a sheath, as for scissors, &c.—WEM ; ELLESMERE. Cf. **Shuth.**

SHEWN [shoa·n], *v. a.* to shew [= old infinitive *shewen*],—'let me *shewn* you 'ow to do that.' Com.

'"For that belongeth to thoffice
Of prest, whose ordre that I bere,
So that I wol nothing forbere
That I the vices one by one
Ne shall the *shewen* everichone."'
JOHN GOWER (A.D. 1393), *Confessio Amantis*, vol. i. p. 50, ed. Pauli.

SHIFT, (1) *v. a.* to change, as of clothes. Com. 'I al'ays *shift* my gownd as soon as I come in throm Church,—it's best be carful.' 'I run off jest as I wuz,—never stopt to *shift* myself nor nuthin',' is a frequent apology for presenting an untidy appearance.

'*First Lord.* Sir, I would advise you to *shift* a shirt; the violence of action hath made you reek as a sacrifice.'—*Cymbeline*, I. ii. 1.

'*Schyftynge* or chaũngynge. *Mutacio.*'—*Prompt. Parv.*

'A.S. *sciftan;* O.Du. *schiften;* O.Icel. *skipta*, to shift; *mutare.*'—STRAT.

(2) *sb.* a substitute; a change. Com. 'Be'appen yo' could pick a throck out o' this owd gownd, it ŏŏd do fur a *shift* a time or two.'

(3) *v. a.* to remove; to move away. Com. 'Now, look sharp, an' *shift* them milk-things, or I'll *shift* yo'.'

'And elde hent good hope · and hastilich he *shifte* hym,
And wayued awey wanhope. . . . .'
Piers Pl., Text B., pass. xx. l. 166.

'*First Serv.* Where's Potpan, that he helps not to take away? He *shift* a trencher? He scrape a trencher!'—*Romeo and Juliet*, I. v. 2.

'*Schyftynge* or removynge. *Amocio.*'—*Prompt. Parv.*

(4) *v. n.* to move from one house to another. Com. 'Oŏn'ee be so good to gie us a 'elpin' 'ond?—we bin gweïn to *shift* to-morrow; the Maister, 'e's promised to sen' the chem fur the tuthree goods:—I 'ope yo'n do better, John, than we han; they sen three *shifts* bin as bad as a fire, an' I know a bin.' Cf. **Flit.**

(5) *sb., obsols.* a woman's or girl's undermost garment. Com. 'Our 'Liza's a mighty nice little sewer, 'er's made a pinner an' a *shimmy* 'er own self.' 'My good woman, say a pinafore and a *shift*, then I shall understand you.' The term *shift*, which in the march of refinement ousted the old word *smock*, has in its turn been almost superseded; that modern affectation, *shimmy*—a corrupt form of chemise—being now considered more polite. See **Smock** (1).

(6) *v. n.* to manage. Com. 'Yo' mun *shift* fur yoreself now, I canna 'elp yo' no lunger.'

'*Steph.* Every man *shift* for all the rest, and let no man take care for himself.'—*Tempest*, V. i. 256.

Cf. **Make-shift.**

SHIMMY. See **Shift** (5), above.

SHIM-WHITE, *adj.* a clear, bright white.—ELLESMERE. A.S. *scíma*, brightness.

SHINED, *pret.* did shine: said of bright, glittering objects,—'the spar *shined* like diamants.' Qy. com.

'. . and the earth *shined* with his glory.'—*Ezek.* xliii. 2.

Dr. Morris says '*shinde* occurs in the fourteenth century.' See *Historical English Accidence*, p. 166. A.S. *scínan*, to shine, glitter.

SHIP, *sb.* a sheep; sheep. Com.

SHIP-BURROWS, *sb. pl.* excavations on hill-sides or ditch-banks made by sheep boring into them in rubbing their backs.—PULVERBATCH. See **Burrow** (1).

SHIPPEN [ship·un], *sb.* a cow-house.—WHITCHURCH; ELLESMERE, *North Border*. An imported *Cheshire* word apparently.

'Whi is not thi table sett in thi cow-stalle,
And whi etist thou not in thi *shipun* as wele as in thin halle.'
MS. Digby 41, f. 8, in HAL.

'*Bostar, vel boviale*, scipen,' occurs in *Supplement to Ælfric's Vocabulary*, x. or xi. cent., in Wr. vocabs., vol. i. p. 58.

A.S. *scypen*, a stall, stable. Cf. **Best-hus**.

SHIP-SHEARING, *sb.* the rent-day,—'the Clives' *ship-shearin'*.'—CORVE DALE. Figurative expressions of this kind are common in Shropshire.

SHIRE [shei·ur'], *adj.* thin; scanty: said of crops.—PULVERBATCH. 'Theer's a despert *shire* crop o' barley this time—on the bonks the straw inna-d-as lung as a wik's beärd.'

'Shyrenesse, thynnesse, *delievre*.' 'Shyre, nat thycke, *delie*.'—Palsgrave, in HAL.

SHIRES [shee·r'z]. 'Down i' the *Sheres*' is a phrase noted by Mr. Skeat as obtaining at Ludlow, where it is used with reference to other counties, more especially the manufacturing ones, in a depreciatory kind of way. The expression is quite a common one in Kent, Surrey, or Sussex, but it is singular to find it employed in a County which is itself a *Shire*. The form *Shere* occurs in Beaumont and Fletcher's *The Burning of the Pestle*, IV. v.—

'Rejoice, oh English hearts, rejoice, rejoice, oh lovers dear,
Rejoice, oh city, town, and country, rejoice eke, every *shere*.'

SHIVE [shei·v], (1) *sb.* a thin slice, as of bread, bacon, &c.: said of bread chiefly. Com. 'The poor owd Missis is very bad off, they sen.' 'Whad a pity!—'er wuz too good-natured; 'er gid the loaf an' as to beg the *shive*.' 'Well, as the owd sayin' is—"yo' shouldna ondress yo' afore yo' gwun to bed."'

'. . . and easy it is
Of a cut loaf to steal a *shive*, we know.'
Titus Andronicus, II. i. 87.

'Give a loaf and beg a *shive*.' 'To cut large *shives* of another man's loaf.'—RAY'S *Proverbs*, pp. 192, 175.

'*Hec lesca*, a schyfe,' occurs, under the head of '*De Panibus et*

Partibus Eorum,' in a *Nominale*, xv. cent., in Wr. vocabs., vol. i. p. 241. Mr. Wright explains *schyfe* as a *shive* or slice.

'Schyvere, of brede or oþer lyke (*schyve*, K. S. P.). *Lesca*, scinda.' —*Prompt. Parv.*

'O.Du. *schive*; M.H.Germ. *shibe*, shive, round, slice.'—STRAT.

(2) *sb.*, *var. pr. Schœnoprasum tenuifolium*, Chives.—PULVERBATCH. Qy. com. 'These broth ŏŏd be all the better fur tuthree *shives* in 'em.'

'Fr. *cive*, *civette*, a chive, scallion or unset leek. Cotgr.,' in WEDG.

'*Civette*, petite herbe potagère, qu'on mange aussi en salade. Chives or cives, a species of small onion.'—CHAMB.

Cf. **Scallion.**

SHIVER [shei·vur'], same as **Shive** (1), above.—WEM. Cf. **Sliver.**

SHOF [shof·], *sb.* a sheaf.—PULVERBATCH; CRAVEN ARMS; WEM. Qy. com.

'Scheffe, or scheef (schefe or schofe, S. *schof*, K.). *Garba*, *gelima*.' —*Prompt. Parv.*

A.S. *sceáf*; Du. *shoof*; a sheaf. See **Shoves.**

SHOO, *interj.* a word used to drive poultry. Com.

'*Shough*, *shough!* up to your coop, peahen!'
BEAUMONT and FLETCHER, *Maid in the Mill*, V. i.

'He cannot say *shooh* to a goose.'—RAY'S *Proverbs*, p. 193.

'To cry *shooe*, *shooe*, as women do to their hens.'—*Florio*, p. 477, in HAL.

Cf. Germ. *scheuchen*, to scare, frighten, drive away. See **Call-words to Poultry** (*Fowls*).

SHOODS [shood·z], *sb. pl.* husks of oats,—'this wutmil's fŭll o' *shoods*.'—PULVERBATCH.

'*Shoods*. Oat-hulls. N.'—GROSE.

SHOOK, *pret.* for *part. past*, shaken. Com.

'*K. John.* Hadst thou but *shook* thy head or made a pause
When I spake darkly what I purposed.'—*K. John*, IV. ii. 231.

'. . . . all heaven
Resounded, and had earth been then, all earth
Had to her centre *shook*.'—*Paradise Lost*, Book VI. l. 219.

SHOOK, SHOOKY, familiar forms of Susan. Com.

SHOON [shoo·n], *sb. pl.* shoes.—NEWPORT. An old woman at Edgmond, relating how her son-in-law wanted to get all her goods 'off' her, and how she would not let him, said,—'I amna gooĭn to doff my *shoon* afore I gooes to bed—no! 'e mun work same as we didden' [1874].

'clouȝtand kyndely his *schon* · as to here craft falles.'
William of Palerne, l. 14.

'His *shoon* of Cordewane.'
CHAUCER, B. 1922 (Six-text ed.), Skeat.

'Ye've cost me twenty pair o' *shoon*
Just gaun to see you;
And ev'ry ither pair that's done,
Mair taen I'm wi' you.'
ROBERT BURNS, *Poems*, p. 34, l. 9.

A.S. *scó, sceó*, a shoe; pl. *sceós, sceón*.

SHOOT [shoo·t], *v. a.* and *sb.*, *var. pr.* to suit; a suit,—'this cap wunna *shoot* 'er;'—''e's got a new *shoot* on.' Com.

SHOOTER, SHOOTER-BOARD, *sb.* a board placed between cheeses under the press. Com. 'Yo' munna clane them *shooter-bwurds* ŏŏth the milk things, else we sha'n a sour milk.'

'eleven chefats [cheese-vats], five *shooters*,' are enumerated amongst other dairy vessels in an *Inventory* dated at Owlbury Manor-House, Bishop's Castle, 1625.

SHOOTY, *adj.* even; regular.—PULVERBATCH. Qy. com. (1) 'This yorn inna nigh so *shooty* as the tother—I doubt it'll mak' gobbety sort o' knittin'.' (2) 'The tatoes bin peepin' 'ere an' theer, but nod at all *shooty*.' Cf. **Suity**.

SHORE [shoa·ur'], *pret.* sheared,—'who *shore* the ship?'—CLEE HILLS.

'His scarlet mantell than *shore* he.'—*Syr Isenbras*, 127, in HAL. See *Canterbury Tales*, l. 13958.

SHOT, *sb.* an ale-house reckoning. Qy. com. 'Now, chaps, whad'n'ee a to drink—ale or short [spirits]?—an' I'll stand *shot*.'

'*Launce*. . . . I reckon this always, that a man is . . . . never welcome to a place till some certain *shot* be paid, and the hostess say "Welcome!"'

'*Speed*. Come on, . . . I'll to the ale-house with you presently; where for one *shot* of five pence, thou shalt have five thousand welcomes.'—*Two Gentlemen of Verona*, II. v. 7—10.

'. . . when good-fellows meet at the Tavern or Alehouse, they at parting call for a *Shot*, *Scot*, or Reckoning: and he is said to go *Scot free* that pays not his part or share towards it.'—BLOUNT'S *Glossographia*, p. 575.

Cf. **Scot**, also **Ale-score**.

SHOUL [shou·l], (1) *v. a.* to shed the first teeth.—PULVERBATCH. 'The poor lickle wench looks despert foul now er's *shoulin'* 'er tith.'

(2) *v. n.* to shuffle in gait.—WORTHEN; OSWESTRY.

SHOULDNA. See **Grammar Outlines**, *verb* **Shall**.

'You *shouldna* paint at angels mair.'
ROBERT BURNS, *Poems*, p. 117, l. 11.

SHOUTHER, (1) *sb.* a shoulder.—SHREWSBURY; PULVERBATCH.

'Their gun's a burden on their *shouther*;
They downa bide the stink o' powther.'
ROBERT BURNS, *Poems*, p. 13, l. 13.

See **Ou** (14) in **Grammar Outlines** (*vowels*, &c.).

(2) *v. a.* to shoulder; to carry on the shoulder.—*Ibid.* 'Look sharp an' *shŏother* that off.'

SHOUTHER HIGH, *phr.* a metaphorical expression = on a bier.—*Ibid.* 'Yo'n be right w'en yo' sin me *shŏother 'igh'* was the not infrequent remark of a certain man to his wife when quarrelling with her.

SHOVES [shoa·vz], *sb. pl.* sheaves.—PULVERBATCH; CRAVEN ARMS; WEM. Qy. com. 'I see 'em throwin' down the mows an' feelin' the *shoves*, I spect they bin thinkin' o' luggin'.'

'Schokkyn' *schovys*, or oþer lyke. *Tasso, congelimo.*'—*Prompt. Parv.* See **Shof.**

SHRAG, *v. a.* to snap; to bite.—CLEE HILLS. 'Hie, *shrag* 'im, Towzer, lad!'

SHREDCOCK, *sb.* the Fieldfare.—ELLESMERE. See **Fildefare,** also **Stormcock.**

SHREWD [sr'oa·d], PULVERBATCH; WEM. [shr'oa·d], WORTHEN, *Cherbury,* adj. badly-disposed; wicked; vicious. ''E's gwun a despert *srōde* lad, an' no ŏŏnder, fur 'e's never chid, do whad 'e ŏŏl.'

'& sone as a schrewe schuld · þe *schrewedest* he þou3t.'
William of Palerne, l. 4643.

'. . . she is intolerable curst
And *shrewd* and froward.'
Taming of the Shrew, I. ii. 90.

See *Shrewd* in ARCHBP. TRENCH'S Select Glossary, pp. 198, 199. '*Schrewyd, Pravatus, depravatus.*'—*Prompt. Parv.* Cf. **Curst.**

SHROPSHIRE [sr'op·sheir'], *sb.* a dish of fried eggs and bacon.—WHITCHURCH. Waggoners and such-like folk, stopping for refreshment at a public-house, will say, 'Can yo' gie us any *S'ropshīre?*'

SHROPSHIRE-FAR' [sr'op·shur'], same as above. Qy. com. 'We'n nuthin' but eggs an' bacon—owd *S'ropshire-far'*—to offer yo'.'

SHULL, *v. a., var. pr.* to shell, as of pease,—'*shull* them paze.'—SHREWSBURY; NEWPORT; WHITCHURCH. *Pea-shulls* are pea-shells. Cf. **Hull** (1) and (2), also **Sheel.**

SHUT [shaet· *and* shut·], (1). See **Shet.**

(2) *sb., obsols.* a narrow alley,—sometimes a 'cul-de-sac,' but usually—in Shrewsbury it is always—a thoroughfare.—SHREWSBURY; WELLINGTON; ELLESMERE; OSWESTRY. The term *Shut,* in this sense, is fast dying out in Shrewsbury; the 'Gullet *Shut*' is now [1874] called the 'Gullet Passage,' and so with other sometime *Shuts,* they are 'Passages' at the present day.

'From the Stalls or Mardol-head the street itself of Mardol branches off to the right, but the straight-forward course which we are now pursuing brings us into the narrow street called Shoplatch: at the entrance to which is the passage of *Gullet-Shut.* A *shut* in Shrewsbury language denotes, not, as might be imagined, a *cul-de-sac,* or alley shut at one end, but, on the contrary, one open at both extremities, enabling the pedestrian, for it is pervious only to such, to *shoot* or move rapidly from one street into another.'—*Blakeway Salop MSS.* (A.D. 1817, *circa*), in Bodleian Library.

'Don't you know the muffin-man,
Don't you know his name—
Don't you know the muffin-man
That lives in our lane?
All round the Butter-Cross,
Up by Saint Giles's,
Up and down the *Gullet Shut*,
And call at Molly Miles's.'

Old Shrewsbury Ditty.

Molly Miles is believed to have kept a noted Tavern called '*The Gullet*,' of which some account is given in the *Blakeway Salop MSS.* Cf. **Gullet** (3).

(3) *v. a.* to throw off—to shoot, as of water from a roof. Qy. com. 'Tak' car' as yo' maken that ruff steep enough, else it ŏŏnna *shut* the waiter off.' See **Water-shutten.**

(4) *sb.* the increase of a river from rain.—CLUN, *Herefd. Border.* 'Theer's a tremenjus *shut* o' waiter i' the river:' said of the rising of the Teme. Cf. **Flush** (3).

(5) *v. a.* to yoke horses to the implements. Qy. com. 'Tell Jack to *shet* a couple o' 'orses to that par o' twins, an' gŏŏ o'er Roger's-Brum ŏŏth 'em—theer's a power o' scutch i' that fild as mun be fat up afore the 'arrows gwun on.' See **Onshut**, also **Shutting**, below.

(6) *v. a.* to empty, as of a sack, &c.: used in the past participial form chiefly. Qy. com. 'Them bags hanna bin *shut* yit, Maister, so we sha'n be fŏŏast to get some more afore we can send in the rest o' the barley.'

(7) *adj.* quit; free,—'I wuz mighty glad to get *shet* on 'er.' Com.

(8) *sb.* the act of getting quit of; deliverance,—'good *shut* o' bad rubbitch.'—WORTHEN. See **Shuttance**, below.

(9) *v. a.* and *sb.* to join two pieces of iron by over-lapping them, and then hammering them together at red-heat till they become firmly compacted. Com. When two pieces of iron have been badly united they call it a 'cold *shut*;'—'it ŏŏnna las' lung, 'e's made a *cold shut* on it.' Blacksmiths understand a difference between *shutting* and welding iron,—to *shut* is to unite two separate pieces—to *weld* is to turn part of a piece back upon itself, and hammer it until the whole becomes a solid body again, and assumes the required form.

SHUTH [shuth·], *sb., var. pr.* a sheath,—'han'ee sid the *shuth* o' my scithors?'—PULVERBATCH. A *knittin'-shuth* is a cylindrical sheath attached to the waist of the knitter for holding the end of the needle off which she is knitting. Cf. **Sheth.**

SHUTTANCE, *sb.* riddance,—'good *shuttance* on 'er.' Com. See **Shut,** (8) above.

SHUTTING, *sb.* a yoking—the length of time the horses are yoked for field work; this varies with the season: early in November, after the corn seed-time, the farmers make 'one *shutting*,' i. e. the horses go to the field about 8 A.M., and are not brought back until three or four o'clock in the afternoon; but in the spring-time, at the 'Lent-sidness,' they make a 'double *shutting*,' the horses being at work from 6 A.M. to 12, and from 2 to 6 P.M.—PULVERBATCH. Qy. com. See **Shut** (5).

SICH [sich·], *pron.* such. Com. Spenser employs the form :—

'But rather joyd to bee then seemen *sich*.'
F. Q., Bk. III. c. vii. st. xxix.

It is found in other early writers also.

SICK, *adj.*, *pec.* eager; desirous.—WORTHEN; WEM. ''E wuz oncommon *sick* to gŏŏ, but I ŏŏdna let 'im.'

SIDE-BASKET, *sb.*, *obsols.* a shallow basket without a handle, straight on one side and curved on the other,—adapted for carrying butter, eggs, &c. to market on horseback. It was formerly a general custom for farmers' wives and daughters to ride to market, carrying their dairy and poultry-yard produce with them in *side-baskets* on this wise,—a wallet stuffed with hay or straw was thrown across the saddle, to form a support or pad for the baskets—the curved sides of which fitted upon it—they were then secured by means of a strap passing over the saddle, one on each side of the horse, the market-woman sitting between them, often with a third basket on her knee. At Church Stretton, at the present date [1880], there may be seen on most market-days a few women on horseback, with their *side-baskets*, coming down the Burway road from the villages on the other side of the Longmynd, into the town; but crossing the hills in this fashion is dying out, an ordinary market-cart can now be used, thanks to the great improvements that have been made in the mountain-road.

SIDELANT-LEASOW [sei·dlunt], *sb.* a steep, sloping field.—PULVERBATCH. Farms having many such fields are said to be 'despert 'ard to work, they'n so much *sidelant* ground in 'em.' *Sidelant* = side-land, *i. e.* land lying on the *side* of a declivity. Cf. **Bonky-pieces.** See **Leasow.**

SIDE-RAZOR [r'az·ur'], *sb.* a beam in the roof to which the rafters are fastened,—the 'purlin.'—CLUN.

SIDNESS, same as **Seedness**, q. v. Qy. com. in *Mid.* and *S. Shr.*

SIDTH [sidth·], *sb.* the measurement of the side of an object,—'lenth, width, and *sidth*.'—CORVE DALE.

SIE [sei·], (1) *v. a.* to strain milk. Qy. com. 'Now, look sharp, an' *sie* the milk, an' pŭt the men's suppers, an' then yo' can gŏŏ an' see whad's gweïn on at the Wakes.'

'*Cyyd* (cyued, P.), or cythyd and clensyd, as mylke, or oþer lyke (licoure, P.). *Colatus.*' '*Syynge* or clensynge (syftynge, S.). *Colacio, colatura.*'—*Prompt. Parv.*

'A.S. *sihan;* O.H.Germ. *sihan;* O.Du. *sigen;* O.Icel. *sia*, to sigh (*sie*), *colare*.'—STRAT.

(2) *sb.* a milk-sieve. Qy. com. 'I like a tin *sie* best, they bin a power sweeter than the ŏŏden uns.'

'. . . a kind of Wooden Dish with a large round hole in the bottom of it with a Rim about it, which is by Milk Women called a *Seigh;* and having a Cloth tied about the hole, Milk runs through it, which takes away all hairs from the Milk; this in our Country is termed *Seighing* of Milk.'—*Academy of Armory*, Bk. III. ch. viii. p. 335.

'My cloake itt was a verry good cloake,
. . . .
I have had itt this 44 yeere;
sometime itt was of the cloth in graine,
itt is now but a *sigh* clout, as you may see;
It will neither hold out winde nor raine;
& Ile haue a new cloake about mee.'
Bell my Wife, l. 30. *Percy Folio MS.*, vol. ii. p. 323, ed. Hales and Furnivall.

'*Colum*, a mylke syhe, or a clansynge syfe.'—MED., in WAY.
'O.H.Germ. *siha;* O.Du. *sige* (*sijghe*); O.Icel. *sia*, a sie, *colum*.'—STRAT.

SIGHT, *sb.*, *pec.* a great number; a great quantity,—'a *sight* o' folks;'—'that cow gies a *sight* o' milk.' Com.

'. . . the greate manne broughte on hys syde a greate *syghte* of Lawyers for hys counsayle, the gentilwoman had but one man of lawe.'—LATIMER, *Sermon* ii. p. 73.

'Where is so great a strength of money, i. where is so huge a *syght* of mony.'—*Palsgrave's Acolastus*, 1540, in HAL.

Cf. **Power**.

SIKE [sei·k], (1) *v. n.* to sigh; to fetch a deep, long-drawn breath. Com. 'Sally,—
"Dunna *sike*, but send;
If 'e's alive 'e'll come,
An' if 'e's bad 'e'll mend."'

'& loked after þat ladi · for lelli he wende
þat sche here had hed in sum hurne · in þat ilk time,
to greue him in hire game · as þeiȝh he gyled were.
but whan he wist it was wast · al þat he souȝt,
he gan to *sike* & sorwe · & seide in þis wise:—'
William of Palerne, l. 691.

'on his bed side he sette him downe,
he *siked* sore & fell in swoone.'
Eger and Grine, l. 60. *Percy Folio MS.*, vol. i. p. 356, ed. Hales and Furnivall.

A.S. *sican*, to sigh.

(2) *sb.* a sigh; a sobbing breath,—''er aived sich a *sike*.' Com.

'And, with a *syk*, ryght thus she seyde hir wille.'
CHAUCER, F. 498 (Six-text ed.), Skeat.

A.S. *siccet*, a sigh, sob.

SILLS, *sb. pl.* the bottom and side pieces which form the skeleton-frame of the body of a cart or waggon—the foundation of its superstructure.—SHREWSBURY; PULVERBATCH. Qy. com.

'*Basis*, syl,' occurs in *Latin and Anglo-Saxon Glosses*, xi. cent., in Wr. vocabs., vol. ii. p. 10. See **Slotes** (1).

SILVER-LAVENDER, *sb. Santolina incana*, Lavender cotton.—PULVERBATCH.

SIMETTY [sei·miti'], *adj.* silly; half-witted.—PULVERBATCH; CLEE HILLS. ''E'll never do no good fur the Squire nor no one else—poor *simetty* thing.'

SIMNEL [sim·nul], *sb.* a species of rich plum-cake enclosed in a very hard crust, coloured with saffron, and shaped like a flattish raised pie.—SHREWSBURY. The early writers speak of *simnels* which were a fine kind of bread; thus in *Havelok the Dane* we have:—

'Wastels, *simenels* . . .'—l. 779.

Simnels seem to mean a sort of cake in the *Crieries de Paris*, v. 163, 'Chaudes tartes et *siminiaus*.'

Randle Holme says, 'A *Simnell*, is a thick copped Cake or Loaf made of white bread knodden up with Saffron and Currans.'—*Academy of Armory*, Bk. III. ch. ii. p. 293.

'*Hic artocopus*, *An*[ce] a symnelle,' is found in a *Pictorial Vocabulary*, xv. cent., with an illustration which bears a strong family likeness to the Shrewsbury *simnel* of the present day, both in form and feature—the upper rim has just the same kind of ornamental scallop round it. See Wr. vocabs., vol. i. p. 266. See '*Symnel*,' with Mr. Way's Note, in *Prompt. Parv.*, p. 456.

SIMPLE, *adj.* weakly; feeble: said of old folk. Qy. com. 'Poor owd John's gettin' mighty *simple*, 'e can 'ardly get alung,—'e's broke oncommon the las' two or three 'ears.' *Simple*, in the sense of feeble, occurs in one of the *Paston Letters*, written by Dame Elizabeth Brews; she says, 'For, cosyn,

It is but a *sympill* oke,
That [is] cut down at the first stroke.'

In a subsequent letter of the same date [A.D. 1477], by a different writer, there is another rendering of the couplet,—'I harde my lady sey,

That it was a *febill* oke,
That was kit down at the first stroke.'—vol. iii. pp. 169, 172.

Cf. *Ps.* cxiii. 6.

SINGLE-HORSE, *sb.*, *obsols.* a saddle-horse.—PULVERBATCH. This term has doubtless been retained from the time when horses were ridden either '*single*,' i. e. by one person only, on a saddle; or else 'double,' *i. e.* by two persons, one of whom was seated on a pillion at the crupper end of the saddle.

'*Rose.* And I shall be a Lady, a Captain's Lady, and ride *single*, upon a White horse with a Velvet Side-saddle.'—FARQUHAR'S *Recruiting Officer*, Act III. Scene—The Market-place [Shrewsbury].

'*Sir Peter Teazle.* And now you must have your coach—*vis-à-vis*—and three powdered footmen before your chair, . . . no recollection, I suppose, when you were content to ride *double*, behind the butler on a docked coach-horse!

Lady Teazle. No! I swear I never did that. I deny the butler and the coach-horse.'—*School for Scandal*, Act II. Sc. i. ed. 1772.

Early in the present century—about 1810—there was a high-class

Ladies' school at Ormskirk (Lancashire), where a *single-horse* and a *double-horse* were kept for the use of the pupils, with whom the *single-horse* was the 'favourite,' as its rider could out-distance her companions on the *double-horse*, and enjoy a gallop at her own sweet will. It is a true story that one of these young gentlewomen, being on the *single-horse*, made the most of her opportunities by riding a race with a butcher's boy!

SINGLET, *sb.* an under vest.—WHITCHURCH; ELLESMERE. 'Whadever did'n'ee lave off yore flannin *singlet* fur? yo'n be sure to ketch a cooth.' See *Singlet*, in HAL.

SINNA-GREEN, *sb. Sempervívum tectórum*, common Houseleek.—PULVERBATCH. ''Ow lung's yore arm bin bad?—it's despert red; get a good 'antle o' *sinna-green* an' pun it well, an' pŭt a spot o' crame to it or a bit o' lard, an' it'll cool it.'

'Howsleke, herbe, or *sengrene*.'—*Prompt. Parv.*

SINNOW [sin·u'], *sb.* a sinew.—SHREWSBURY.

'*Hic nervus*, a synow.'—*Nominale*, xv. cent., in Wr. vocabs., vol. i. p. 208.

'*Nerf.* m. a Synnow.'—COTGRAVE (*Fr. Dict.*).

'A.S. *sinu*, *seonu*; O.Fris. *sine*; O.H.Germ. *sen(e)wa*, sinew.'—STRAT. See **Sennow**.

SIRPCLOTH. See **Serpcloth**.

SIST [sis·t], (1). See **Grammar Outlines**, p. lxxxi.

> 'in the gospel thou *sist*,
> That God be law byndus y-fyre.'
>
> JOHN AUDELAY'S *Poems*, p. 6.

> 'For al dai thou *sist* with thin eien
> Hou this world wend, and ou men deien.'
>
> *MS. Digby*, in HAL.

A.S. *þu sihst*, thou seest, from *seón*, to see.

(2) *sb.* full pay-day for miners.—PULVERBATCH, *Snailbeach*; M. T. See **Sub-sist**.

SITCH [sich·], *sb.* a swamp; a boggy place.—WEM; WHITCHURCH.

'. . . a garden and lands, a messuage & backside, half a land in the Barley field near Stafford's *siche*.'—*Rent Roll of the Abbey Church*, Shrewsbury, A.D. 1637.

A few years ago there was a pool on the Sandford Estate, near to Prees, called the *Sitch*, it came nearly up to the turnpike road, but is now [1875] filled up.

Bailey—ed. 1782—has '*Siche'tum*, a small Current of Water that uses to be dry in the Summer; also a Water-furrow or Gutter. O. L.' Obviously a Latinized form of the English word.

Sitch = *syke*, the North Eng. form—a word of Scandinavian origin. Icel. *sík*, a ditch, a trench.

SIXT, sixth. Qy. com.

'The *Sixt* Peiw on the South side of the North Isle.'—GOUGH'S *History of Myddle*, p. 82.

'I haue gathered, writ, and brought into lyght the famous fryday sermons of Mayster Hugh Latimer, which he preached in Lente last past, before oure most noble King Edward the *syxt.*'—LATIMER'S *Sermons* (Thomas Some's Dedication), p. 19.

'*Trinepos*, sixte sune; *Trineptis*, sixte dohter,' occur in *Supplement to Archbp. Ælfric's Vocabulary*, x. or xi. cent., in Wr. vocabs., vol. i. p. 51. See **Grammar Outlines** (*adjectives of numeration*), p. xlvi.

SIZES, *sb. pl.* the assizes. Com. 'Theer wuz a sharp market to-day, the *sizes* bin on, an' the town's fūll o' folks—theer's nobody to be 'ong they sen, but theer's some mighty big trial gweïn on i' the nīzey-prizey cŏoürt.'

'Thei follow *Sises* and Sessions, Letes, Lawdays and Hundredes, they shold serue the kyng, but thei serue them selues.'—LATIMER'S *Sermons* (To the Reader), p. 53.

SKELLET, SKILLET [skel·it], Com. [skil·it], NEWPORT. Qy. com. *sb.* a brass pan without a lid—usually with a swivel-handle across the top—and of any size, though the term is more generally applied to a preserving-kettle.

'Let housewives make a *skillet* of my helm.'
Othello, I. iii. 273.

'*Skellet* (supposed to be from the French, *écuelle*, a porringer), A small vessel with feet for boiling.'—ASH.

Cotgrave has '*Escuellette*, a little dish.'

'O.Fr. *escuele*, *écuelle*; de [Lat.] *scutella*.'—BUR.

See *Skillet*, in WEDG. Cf. **Maslin-kettle**.

SKELLINGTON, *sb.*, *var. pr.* a skeleton.—SHREWSBURY; ELLESMERE.

SKELP [skel·p], (1) same as **Flay** (1), q. v.—PULVERBATCH.

(2) same as **Flay** (2), q. v.—WHITCHURCH.

SKEMBLING, *part.* working in a light, easy kind of way.—CLUN.

SKEN, *v. n.* to glance furtively; to peer.—WORTHEN; OSWESTRY. ''Er kep' *skennin'* around the room all the w'ile we wun talkin'.' Cf. E. *Scan*.

SKEP, *sb.* a strong, coarse basket,—same as **Kipe**, q. v.—WORTHEN, *Cherbury*.

'Sumwhat lene us bi thi *skep*;
I shal ȝou lene seide Josep.'
Cursor Mundi, MS. Coll. Trin. Cantab., f. 30, l. 4741.

Skep is a very common *East Anglian* word.

A *skep* is mentioned by Tusser amongst sundry articles of 'husbandlie furniture' for the stable, p. 35, ed. E. D. S.

'*Skeppe, Sporta, corbes.*'—*Prompt. Parv.* Cf. **Skip**.

SKER [skur'], *sb.* the ridge of a hill,—'right a-top o' the *sker*.'—WORTHEN, *Cherbury*.

'He loked abowte; thanne was he warre
Of an ermytage undir a *skerre*.'
MS. Lincoln, A. i. 17, f. 123.

See *Scar*, in HAL. 'O.Icel. *sker*, scar, cliff.'—STRAT.

SKEW [skeu·], *v. n.* to slant off; to go diagonally.—BRIDGNORTH. 'Yo' mun *skew* up w'en yo' comen to Willey.'

'*Skew* your eie towards the margent.'—*Stanihurst*, p. 17, in HAL. See **Skewt**, below.

SKEW-BALD, *sb.* a motley or parti-coloured horse, as brown (or bay) and white; but not black and white, which is *pie-bald*. Com.

'Unrip, &c. and you shall finde
Og the great commissarie, and which is worse,
Th' apparatour upon his *skew-bald* horse.'
Cleaveland's Character, &c., 1647, in WR.

See Bk. II., *Folklore*, &c., 'Superstitious Cures' (*Whooping-cough*).

SKEWT [skeu·t], *v. n.* to cross slantwise; to make a short cut by cutting off an angle. Com. 'Yo' mun gŏŏ *skewtin'* across the leasow nigh to a noud wuk tree, w'eer the cows bin, an' yo'n droppen into a lane as 'll tak' yo' to Strett'n:'—these directions were given to a wayfarer in the Lawley neighbourhood [1880].

SKEWWAYS, *adv.* obliquely; aslant.—NEWPORT; WEM. Qy. com.

SKEW-WIFF, (1) *adv.* awry; irregular; zigzag.—SHREWSBURY. Qy. com. Cf. **Cater-wiff.**

(2) [ski'ou· *or* skyou·], *sb.* the state of being awry.—WORTHEN. ''Er's got 'er bonnet on all of a *skyŏw-wiff*.'

SKILLET. See **Skellet.**

SKIM, *v. a.* to mow. Qy. com. The term *skim* is used with reference to fields which are hardly worth mowing, having no undergrowth of grass, but merely a thin surface crop of coarse blades.

SKIM-DICK, *sb.* a cheese made of skim-milk. Com. 'This is räël cheese, it hanna-d-a bit o' butter in it,' observed a farm-labourer, *apropos* of a *skim-dick.*

SKIMMETY, *adj.* scanty: said of clothes that are too spare for the person,—'whad a *skimmety* gownd!' Qy. com.

SKIMPING, same as above. Qy. com.

SKINNY, *adj., pec.* mean; miserly. Com.

SKIP, *sb.* a small waggon in which coal is brought to the surface from the 'workings.' Com. M. T. Cf. **Skep.**

SKIPPET [skip·i't], *sb.* a long-handled, spoon-shaped implement used by drainers.—CLEE HILLS. Tusser has 'skuppat' for the same kind of thing:—

'with *skuppat* and skauel, that marsh men alow.'
Husbandlie furniture, ed. E. D. S., p. 38.

SKIRT, *v. a.* to take off the outside hay from the cocks without otherwise disturbing them.—WELLINGTON. 'Mun we open the cocks, Maester?' 'No, they bin only wet o' the outside, I'll send the women to *skirt* 'em.'

SKIT, *sb.* a hoax; a practical joke.—PULVERBATCH. Qy. com. 'They played'n off a fine *skit* o' Cleeton's cowman at Stretton far—persuaden 'im as the paas'n 'ad fancied 'im fur a coachman, an' 'ired 'im!' 'Whad rar raps!'

SKITTER, *v. a.* to scatter sparsely, as of seed, or a few grains of sand, and thus differs from *scatter*, as applied to a larger quantity.—WHITCHURCH.

SKIVER [skiv·ur'], *sb.*, *obsols.* a skewer.—PULVERBATCH. 'The bŭtchers gi'en yo' plenty o' 'ŏŏd i' the *skivers*, now the mate's sellin' at tenpince an' a shillin' a pound.' 'Aye, it's a good price for timber.'

SKIVER-WOOD [ŏŏd·], *sb.*, *obsols.* wood employed for making skewers—usually Elder-wood.—*Ibid.* 'Wha'n'ee done ŏŏth that *skiver-'ŏŏd?*—yo' young dog, yo'n bin makin' w'istles stid o' *skivers*, they bin all too short—ŏŏnna raich through the fowl.'

SKULL-CAP. See **Cross-cloth**.

SLAD, (1) *sb.* the shoe or drag of a waggon wheel.—ELLESMERE. Cf. **Slade** (2), below.

(2) *sb.* a long strip of ground.—PULVERBATCH; BRIDGNORTH. Bailey—ed. 1782—gives, as an 'Old Word,' '*Slade*, a long flat Piece or Slip of Ground.'

A.S. *slǽd*, a slade, plain. Cf. **Slade** (1), below. See **Slang**.

SLADDED, *adj.* a term applied to fields when the surface soil has been washed away by very heavy rains, or when heavy rain has fallen and the land is crusted over.—CLEE HILLS. Cf. **Slerried o'er**.

SLADE [slai·d], (1) *sb.* a patch of ground in a ploughed field too wet for grain, and therefore left as greensward.—ELLESMERE, *Welshampton*. See *Slade*, in HAL. Cf. **Slad** (2), above; also **Gall** (3). See **Slade-grass**, below.

(2) *sb.* a sledge for carrying implements from one field to another. —CLEE HILLS.

'*Hec traha*, a sled.'—*Nominale*, xv. cent., in Wr. vocabs., vol. i. p. 232.

'O.N. *slæða*, to trail; *sloði*, what is *sladed* or dragged along, a brush harrow.'—WEDG.

SLADE-GRASS, *sb.* grass grown on the *slades*,—coarse, and of inferior quality; it is, when mown, usually reserved for putting on the tops of haystacks.—*Ibid.* See **Slade** (1), above.

SLAKE [slai·k *and* slee·k], *v. a.* to put out the tongue in derision. —WHITCHURCH.

SLAM [slam·], *v. a.* to close a door violently. Com. 'The girld inna saucy, but 'er shewns off 'er temper i' *slammin'* the doors an' bangin' the tubs.'

SLANG, *sb.* a long, narrow piece of land. Com. 'We bin despert short o' meadowin', theer's on'y two, an' a bit of a *slang* as yo' met'n stride across, aumust.' Cf. **Slad** (2). See **Sling** (1).

SLANNY [slan·i'], *sb.* a slattern.—PULVERBATCH; WORTHEN. 'I'd mak' that girld keep 'erself a bit tidier, — whad a *slanny* 'er looks!'

SLAT [slat·], (1) a slip of wood.—PULVERBATCH. 'Jiner, jest nail a *slat* under this box-lid, to strenthen it.' Cf. **Slob** (2).

(2) *v. a.* to plaster.—CLEE HILLS.

SLAY [slai·], *v. a.* and *v. n.*, *pec.* to dry or wither, as of grass, &c., by direct exposure to the sun.—PULVERBATCH. 'Pŭt these yarbs to *slay* i' the sun, they bin ever so much better than dried i' the 'ouse.' A.S. *sleán*, to kill. Cf. **Killow**.

SLAZY [slai·zi'], (1) poor; thin; flimsy,—in texture badly woven. —PULVERBATCH. 'I dunna like yore Dowlas-cloth, it's too *slāzy*, an' lasses none; I made our John four shirts on it, an' they wun done direc'ly—theer's nuthin' like a bit o' wham made.'

'I cannot well away with such *sleezy* stuff, with such cobweb compositions.'—Howell, in TODD.

'*Sleezy*, weak, wanting substance.'—J., in WEDG.

See *Sleezy*, in HAL. Cf. **Sayly**.

(2) *adj.* slightly constructed; badly put together.—*Ibid.* 'Them new 'ousen by the bruck bin run up despert *slāzy*.'

SLEEPERS, *sb. pl.* grains of barley which do not germinate in the process of malting.—PULVERBATCH.

SLEEPING-BEAUTY, *sb.* *Oxalis biloba*, two-lobed Wood-sorrel.—PULVERBATCH. Harriet Humphreys described this plant as having 'the most innicentest little bloom in the world.'

SLENCH [slen·sh], (1) *sb.* a hind-leg of beef from the first joint, including the upper round and part of the flank.—SHREWSBURY; WELLINGTON. Cf. **Lift-of-beef**. See **Chuck** (1).

(2) *sb.* same as **Kench** (2), q. v.—WEM. *Slenchin'* is employed like *kenchin'*, as an alternative form.

SLEP, *pret.* slept,—''E *slep* well all night.' Com.

> 'Makyng her wymmen ek to taken kep,
> And wayt on hym anyghtes whan he *slep*.'
> JOHN LYDGATE (A.D. 1420, *circa*), *The Storie of Thebes*.
> *Specim. Eng. Lit.*, III. *b.* l. 1360.

'A.S. *slápan*, pret. *slép*, now corrupted into *slept*.'

SLERRIED O'ER [slae·r'id], same as **Sladded**, q. v.—WEM. Compare 'Slorryd. . . . *Lutulentus*,' in *Prompt. Parv.*

SLIFTER [slif·tur'], *sb.* a long, narrow opening. — WHITCHURCH. 'Pool the window to, but just lave a *slifter*.'

Pegge gives '*Slifter*, a crevice or crack. Lanc.'

SLIKE [slei·k], *adj.* smooth; sleek.—PULVERBATCH. ''E gets on ŏŏth the Squire better than a 'onester mon, 'cause e's so *slike*-tongued.'

'Þo sende he after hire sone,
Þe fayrest wymman under mone;
And seyde til hire, [false] and *slike*,
Þat wicke þral, þat foule swike.'
Havelok the Dane, l. 1157.

'*Slyke*, or smothe. *Lenis*.'—*Prompt. Parv.*
'O.Icel. *slíkja*, slike (slick); *polire, levigare, blandiri*.'—STRAT.
See below.

SLIKEN [slik·n], *adj.* smooth and bright,—polished.—COLLIERY; M. T. See **Splauders**.

SLIKENSIDES, *sb.* smooth, bright sides of 'faults.' Com. M. T. Cf. **Slips**, also *Slickensides*, in HAL.

SLIM [slim·], *v. a.* to do any kind of work in a careless, superficial manner. Qy. com. 'Clane that cubbert out, Betsey, an' mind an' nod *slim* them top shilves o'er.'
Jamieson has 'To *Slim o'er*, to do anything carelessly and insufficiently.'
Compare 'O.N. *slæmr*, vilis, invalidus: *at slæma til*, to set slackly to work,' in WEDG.

SLING [sling·], (1) *sb.* a long, narrow field,—same as **Slang**, q. v.—CLEE HILLS; BRIDGNORTH. The term is sometimes employed adjectivally: 'Yo' mun gŏŏ alung the *sling* meadow, but the path inna very well bathered.'
(2) same as **Carriage**, q. v.—SHREWSBURY.

SLINK [sling·k], (1) *v. n.* to draw back, as a horse does when going to kick, or as a dog when about to bite.—CORVE DALE; WEM.
(2) *adj.* moist; slimy; slippery.—CORVE DALE. See *Slink*, in WEDG.

SLINK-VEAL, *sb.* immature veal, being the flesh of a three-day old calf.—PULVERBATCH; ELLESMERE. 'That cauve never 'eärd the Sabbath-bell—it wuz born i' the middle o' the wik an' killed fur Sunday:' said *apropos* of some poor meat supposed to be *slink-veal!*
Jamieson has '*Slink*, ill-fed veal in general.'
Pegge gives '*Slink*, a calf produced before its time. Var. Dial.'
See **Staggering-bob**.

SLIPES [slei·ps], *sb. pl.* iron plates under the 'dans' to make them drawable. Com. M. T.
'O.H.Germ. *slifan*, slipe; slide.'—STRAT. See **Dans**.

SLIPPER, *sb.*, *pec.* a skidpan for a waggon-wheel. Qy. com. Cf. **Slad** (1).

SLIPPING [slip·in], *sb.*, *obs.* a large skein of yarn, as taken off the reel.—PULVERBATCH. Qy. com. 'W'en yo' gwun up i' the cheeseroom, count 'ow many *slippin's* bin 'angin' up—I like to know whad sort of a wik's work we can shewn.'
'A *Slipping*, is as much as is wond upon the Reel at a time, which is generally about a pound of Yarn. An Hank is a *slipping* made up into a knot.'—*Academy of Armory*, Bk. III. ch. iii. p. 107.

SLIPS, *sb. pl.* smooth partings in coal and strata.—COLLIERY; M. T. 'Besides these' ['principal faults'], 'innumerable minor faults or "*slips*" and "*slikensides*," as they term them, are met with.'—*Notes on the Shropshire Coal-Field*, by T. PARTON, F.G.S., 1868.

See **Slikensides.**

SLIP-SIDE, *prep.* lying off on either hand at some little distance from a place.—PULVERBATCH. 'W'eer bin Joneses gweïn to live?' 'Toërt somew'eer *slip-side* Welli't'n, I b'lieve.'

Mr. Wright gives '*Slip-side*, the left-hand side. Leic.'

SLITHER [slidh·ur'], (1) *v. n.* to slide; to slip. Com. 'Come alung, an' we'n *slither* across the pool.' 'I darna, Mother toud me nod to gŏŏ o' the ice.'

'A heavier lurch and crash sent me *slithering* right across the saloon.'—*South Sea Bubbles*, by 'The Earl and the Doctor,' p. 235, ed. 1872.

'Du. *slidderen*, to slip, slide.'—WEDG.

(2) *sb.* a slide. Com. ''Ow bin'ee gettin' on ŏŏth the flŭd, Jim?' 'Oh! rarly, lad—Mother an' the babby bin up-stars, an' Bob an' me han got a stunnin' *slither* i' the 'ouse.'—This dialogue had reference to a flood caused by the Severn overflowing its banks, and inundating the houses in Coleham (Shrewsbury), compelling the inhabitants to take refuge in the upper rooms, when, before the waters receded, the memorably severe frost of 1878-9 set in, thus making it possible for 'Bob an' me to get a stunnin' *slither* i' the 'ouse!'

SLIVER [slei·vur'], *sb.* a long thin piece; a slice.—CLEE HILLS. 'The owd ŏŏman took a fine *sliver* off the loaf.'

> 'That he all hole, or of him some *slivere*.'
> CHAUCER, *Troilus and Cresseide*, Bk. III. l. 1015.

> 'There, on the pendant boughs her coronet weeds
> Clambering to hang, an envious *sliver* broke;
> When down her weedy trophies and herself
> Fell in the weeping brook.'
> *Hamlet*, IV. vii. 174.

Tusser has '*sliuers*,' pieces of split wood; chips.—Ed. E. D. S., p. 61. See below. Cf. **Shiver.**

SLIVING, *sb.* a branch cleft off; a splinter of wood.—*Ibid.*

The term *sliving* is more especially applied to a branch—usually of hedge-row trees—sliced off with the hatchet in 'pleaching' the hedge; but carpenters sometimes use the word thus,—'We mun tak' a *slivin'* off o' this side, an' then the lid ŏŏl fit.'

'*Slyvynge*, of a tre, or oþer lyke. *Fissula.*'—*Prompt. Parv.*

A.S. *slifan*, to cleave; to split.

SLOB [slob·], (1) *sb.* the outside cut of a tree when sawn up for planks.—SHREWSBURY; PULVERBATCH; WEM. 'Wilrit, han 'ee ever-a *slob* as yo' coulden spar'?—theer wants a bottom to the bee-bench.'

Tusser has '*slab*' with the same meaning:—

'Sawne *slab* let lie
for stable and stie.'—ed. E. D. S., p. 33.

(2) Same as **Slat** (1), q. v.—CLUN.

SLOBBER, *sb.* thin, cold rain, mixed with snow; a sloppy sleet.—SHREWSBURY; PULVERBATCH; WEM.

SLOBBERY, *adj.* cold, and wet, and sloppy,—'a *slobbery* day.'—*Ibid.*

'*Bourbon.* . . . .
Mort de ma vie! if they march along
Unfought withal, but I will sell my dukedom,
To buy a *slobbery* and a dirty farm
In that nook-shotten isle of Albion.'
K. Henry V., III. v. 13.

SLOFF [slof·], *v. n.* to eat in a slovenly, greedy manner.—PULVERBATCH. ''Ow that fellow does *sloff!*—I canna bar to see 'im o'er 'is mate, 'e's fur all the world like a noud sow ātin' grains.'

'*Sloffynge*, or on-gentyll etynge. *Voracio, devoracio, lurcacitas.*'—*Prompt. Parv.*

SLOMMACKIN', *adj.* slovenly and clumsy in appearance: said of folk,—'a great *slommackin'* wench, or chap.'—PULVERBATCH. Qy. com.

SLON [slon· *and* slaun·], *sb. Prunus spinosa*, the Sloe. Com. The fruit is usually spoken of in the double plural form,—*slons*. '*Slons* bin capital in Damson wine—yo' canna tell it from Port.' *Slon* = sloes is found in *The Treatise of Walter de Biblesworth*, xiii. cent.:—

'Le fourder que la fourdine porte.'

'*Fourder*' is glossed '*slo-thorne*,' and '*fourdine*,' '*slon*.' See Wr. vocabs., vol. i. p. 163.

A.S. *slá*, a sloe; pl. *slán*. Dan. *slaaen*; Sw. *slan*.—*Idem.*

SLOP-FROCK, *sb.* a strong linen over-garment, worn by waggoners, farm-labourers, and other like folk.—SHREWSBURY; ELLESMERE. Qy. com.

Frock is here redundant, *slop* being an old word meaning the same thing, as in the following:—

'His *overslope* nis nat worth a myte.'
CHAUCER, G. 633 (Six-text ed.), Skeat.

'*Sloppe*, garment. *Mutatorium.*'—*Prompt. Parv.*

Compare Icel. *yfirsloppr*, an upper or over garment.

Cf. **Smock-frock.**

SLOTES [sloa·ts], (1) *sb. pl.* flat bars of wood mortised into the 'sills' of a cart or waggon for the boards of the body to be nailed to. Qy. com.

'The *Slotes*, are the vnder peeces which keepe the bottom of the Cart together.'—*Academy of Armory*, Bk. III. ch. viii. p. 339.

See **Sills.**

(2) *sb. pl.* the wooden cross-bars of harrows. Qy. com.

'The *Slotes*, the cross pieces [of Harrows].'—*Academy of Armory*, Bk. III. ch. viii. p. 335.

(3) See **Sole**.

'O.Fris. *slot*; O.H.Germ. *sloz*; *vectis*.'—STRAT.

'*Vectis*, a barre, or sparre of wood.'—*Dict. Etym. Lat.* Cf. **Slat**.

SLUD [slud·], *sb.* wet mud.—SHREWSBURY. Qy. com.

SLUDGE [sluj·], same as above. Com.

SLURRY [slu·r'i'], *sb.* thin, washy mud,—more liquefied than *slud*, &c., as of half-melted snow on roads. 'I remember whad a journey I 'ad the las' time I wuz down 'ere; the snow wuz gweïn away, an' the roäds wun ancler dip i' *slurry*.'—ATCHAM; PULVERBATCH; WEM; ELLESMERE. Qy. com.

'Sloor, (*slory* . . . or cley). *Cenum, Limus*. "To slorry, or make foul, *sordido*."—GOULDM. "*Souillé*, soiled, slurried, smutched, &c.; *Souiller*, to soyle, slurrie; *Ordi*, fouled, slurried, slubbered."—COTG.' —*Prompt. Parv. and Notes*.

'O.N. *slor*, uncleanness; *slorugr*, dirty.'—WEDG.

SLUSH, same as **Slurry**. Com.

SLUT [slut·], (1) *sb.* an oven-mop made of rags.—PULVERBATCH. 'Bessey, bring the *slut* an' clane the oven out.' Dick, hearing this, dryly observed, 'Missis, yo'd'n better püt '*er* in,'—meaning that Bessey was *slut* enough for anything! See **Malkin** (1), also **Oven-sweep**.

(2) *sb.*, *obs.* a home-made candle.—PULVERBATCH. The wick of such candles was often nothing more than the cut-off hem of an under-garment; they were rudely made, and were called *sluts*, to evade the penalties which attached to making *candles* without a license, at a time when they were subject to duty.

SMAY [smai·], (1) *v. n.* to falter; to flinch.—WEM. It is often said of a horse after a journey, ''e never stumbled nor *smayed*.'

(2) *v. n.* to fail in the appetite.—PULVERBATCH; BRIDGNORTH. 'Does 'er *smay* in 'er yettin'?' was invariably asked by an old 'beast-leech' at Bridgnorth when called in professionally to a cow.

(3) *v. n.* to wear a guilty look.—PULVERBATCH. 'I know right well that bwoy sucks the eggs, fur w'en I axed 'im 'ow many theer wuz, 'e *smayed* i' the face.'

SMEG [smeg·], *sb.* a bit.—WHITCHURCH, *Tilstock*. 'We'n etten every *smeg* o' that best cheese.'

SMELLERS, *sb. pl.* cats' whiskers.—PULVERBATCH; WEM; ELLESMERE. Qy. com.

SMITE [smei·t], *sb.* a small bit; a mite.—PULVERBATCH. 'Han yo' gotten a bit o' 'bacco?' 'No, nod a *smite*.'

SMITIN, same as above.—WEM.

SMITING, *adj.*, *pec.* captivating.—PULVERBATCH. 'Polly wuz prinked fur the far, an' 'er looked right *smitin*'.'

SMOCK [smok·], *sb.*, *obs.* a woman's chemise. Com. 'My Mother-law said "Tum's wife 'ad too many fine gownds fur 'er," but I toud 'er I'd as many good *smocks* as "fine gownds," an' more than that, they wun all my own spinnin'.'

'1547. Aug. 4. Here was wedded early in the morning Thomas Munslow Smith and Alice Nycols, which wedded to him in her *smock* and bareheaded.'—*Register of Sir Thomas Boteler*, Vicar of Much Wenlock.

'"The *smok*," quod he, "that thou hast on thy bak,
Lat it be stille, and ber it forth with thee."

. . . .

Biforn the folk hir-seluen strepeth she,
And in hir *smok*, with heed and foot al bare,
Toward hir fader hous forth is she fare.'
CHAUCER, E. 890—895 (Six-text ed.), Skeat.

'*Alençon*. Doubtless he shrives this woman to her *smock*.'
1 *K. Henry VI.*, I. ii. 119.

'*Colobium*, smoc, *vel* syrc,' occurs in *Archbp. Ælfric's Vocabulary*, x. cent., and '*Interula*,' glossed '*smokke*,' in a *Metrical Vocabulary*, (perhaps) xiv. cent., in Wr. vocabs., vol. i. pp. 25, 182.

'*Interula*, a shirt, the linnen next the skin.'—*Dict. Etym. Lat.*

'O.Icel. *smokkr*; O.H.Germ. *smoccho*; smock, *interula*.'—STRAT.

See **Shift** (5).

SMOCK, SMOCK-FROCK, *sb.*, *obsols.*? an over-dress of strong linen descending below the knees, worn by farm-labourers, waggoners, &c. Com. 'Whad says our dairy-girld?—"I'd sooner 'åve a chap in a *smock-frock* than one o' them magpy-tailed bwun-polishers."'

'1798. Sept[br] 10th. Making two *smock Frocks*. 16[d].'—*Parish Accounts*, Much Wenlock.

Pegge has '*Smock-frock*, a coarse linen shirt worn over the coat by waggoners, &c., called in the South a *Gaberdine*.'

Cf. **Slop-frock**.

SMUSE. See **Muse**.

SNAG [snag·], (1) *v. a.* to trim or cut off in a rough, slovenly manner.—CLEE HILLS; BRIDGNORTH. 'W'y yo' shear a ship!—see 'ow yo'n *snagged* 'er; yo'n fat the skin off i' places an' lef' the ŏŏl on an inch lung.' Cf. **Kag** (3).

(2) *v. n.* to snap, as a little cur would. Qy. com. 'Dunna let that dog *snag* at me, keep 'im off.'

Jamieson has 'To *Snack*, to bite as a dog.' See *Snag* in WEDG.

SNAIL-HOUSEN, *sb. pl.* snail-shells.—SHREWSBURY; PULVERBATCH. Qy. com.

'*Testudo*, gehused snægl,' occurs in *Archbp. Ælfric's Vocabulary*, x. cent., in Wr. vocabs., vol. i. p. 24.

SNAKE-WEED, *sb. Mercuriális perénnis*, Dog's Mercury.—PULVERBATCH.

SNAP [snap·], *v. a.* to make hot, hasty remarks; to take a person up shortly. Com. 'Well, yo' nee'na *snap* my yed off, I on'y toud yo whad the Missis said.' '*Snap!* it's enough to make anybody *snap*, w'en they bin doin' thar best—I canna do no more.'

SNAPE [snai·p], (1) *v. a.* to check or rebuke hastily. Com. 'Dunna *snape* the poor child like that, 'e's doin' no 'arm.' ''E inna so soon *snaped* as yo' thinken, 'e's a furbidden young rascal.'

Compare Shakespeare's '*sneaping* frost,'—*Love's Labour Lost*, I. i. 100.

'*Snaipen*, O.Icel. *sneypa*? to snape, rebuke.'—STRAT. Cf. E. *Snub*.

(2) *sb.* a hasty rebuke. Com. 'I never sid sich a child as Johnny, it yo' gin 'im a bit of a *snape* 'e'll cry fur a nour.'

'My lord, I will not undergo this *sneap* without reply.'
2 *K. Henry IV.*, II. i. 133.

SNEACH [snee·ch], *v. a., obsols.* to scorch; to nip.—PULVERBATCH. The action of both extreme heat and biting cold is expressed by *sneach* and its derivatives *sneaching* and *sneachy*. 'Mind yore apparn, the fire 'll *sneach* it direc'ly.'

Compare '"As hit *snarchte* ant barst."—*Seinte Marharete*, 18, 14. O.Icel. *snerkja*? shrivel?' in STRAT.

Cf. **Snirp.**

SNEACHING, *part. adj., obsols.* scorching; nipping.—*Ibid.* (1) 'Better lave the oven-door down aw'ile, for it's *sneachin'* wut.' (2) 'The sters bin twinklin' pretty bright, theer'll be a *sneachin'* fros' to-night.'

SNEACHY, *adj., obsols.* same as above. 'The oven's despert *sneachy*;'—'a *sneachy* fros'.'—*Ibid.*

SNEAD [sned·], *sb.* the long handle of a scythe. Com.

'Scythes and *sneads*.'—*Auctioneer's Catalogue* (Stoddesden), 1870.

'These hedges are tonsile—they are to be cut and kept in order with a sythe of four foot long, and very little falcated; this is fixed on a long *sneed*, or streight handle, and does wonderfully expedite the trimming of these and the like hedges.'—EVELYN'S *Sylva* [A.D. 1664], xiii. § 2, in Nares.

See **Cogs** (1).

SNEAP. See **Snape.**

SNIDDLE, SNIDDLE-GRASS [snid·l], *sb.* a kind of coarse, broad-leaved grass, growing in marshy places.—WEM.

Mr. Wilbraham gives '*Sniddle*, or Hassocks, that kind of long grass which grows in marshy places. Lanc. The *Aira cæspitósa* of Linnæus.'

Cf. **Sniggle** (2) and **Sniggle-grass.**

SNIG [snig], (1) *v. a.* to drag timber from the place of felling to one more convenient for loading.—PULVERBATCH. Qy. com. 'I shall 'a but a poor chem to-morrow, they wanten three o' the best 'orses to *snig* timber out o' the coppy.'

(2) *sb.* a filmy substance formed by beer or vinegar in bottles or taps.—PULVERBATCH. Qy. com. 'That's fine clānin'!—w'en I went to fill the bottle, theer was a *snig* in it as big as my finger.' Cf. **Mother.**

(3) *sb.* a little slug.—CLEE HILLS.

(4) *sb.* an eel.—WELLINGTON. Qy. com. See **Sniggle** (1), below.

SNIGGER [snig·ur'], *v. a.* and *sb.* to laugh in a sneering way; a sneering laugh.—SHREWSBURY; PULVERBATCH. Qy. com.

SNIGGERING, *part. adj.* sneering.—*Ibid.* ''E's a mak'-game, *sniggerin'* fop—al'ays o' the *snigger*.'

SNIGGLE, (1) *sb.* an eel.—WELLINGTON. Qy. com.

> 'W'en wollers han lāves as large as a mouse's ear.
> Then *sniggles* they'n run, they dunna car w'eer.'
> *Local Doggerel* (Preston on the Weald-Moors).

See **Woller**.

(2) *sb.* the cæspitose root-leaves of *Erióphorum vaginatum*, Hare-tail Cotton-grass.—WHITCHURCH, *Whixall Moss*. Cf. **Sniggle-grass**, below.

SNIGGLE-BOGS, *sb. pl.* large tufts of *sniggle-grass*.—ELLESMERE. See below.

SNIGGLE-GRASS, *Aíra cæspitosa*, turfy Hair-grass.—ELLESMERE. Cf. **Sniddle-grass**, also **Snizzle-grass**.

SNIPPET, *sb.* a small bit,—'jest a *snippet*.'—PULVERBATCH.

SNIRP [snur'p·], *v. a.* to shrivel; to wither, as by great heat or extreme cold.—ATCHAM; PULVERBATCH; WORTHEN; CLUN; WEM. *Snirp* in the simple form of the verb appears to be nearly obsolete [1875], but *snirped*, its past participle, is often heard. (1) 'The oven's mighty whot, it'll *snirp* that bif if yo' put'n it in yit awilde.' (2) 'The tatoe tops bin *snirped* up ŏŏth las' night's fros', I see.'

'*Snurpe*, *v. n.* become shrivelled.—Rel. Ant., ii. 211. Sw. *snörpa*.' —COL. Cf. **Sneach**.

SNIRPED-UP, *part. adj.* cross-grained; sulky.—WEM. '*Snirped-up*, like a swinged pig's eye,' is a proverbial expression commonly applied to persons of perverse, sulky temper: it is also, but less frequently, used *apropos* to things shrivelled up.

SNIRPY, *adj.* same as above.—*Ibid.*

SNIVING [snei·vin], *part. adj.* swarming; abounding: said chiefly of insect-life, or vermin, as rats, &c., but sometimes of people.—SHREWSBURY; PULVERBATCH; WORTHEN. 'The cabbitch bin *snivin'* ŏŏth green grubs; they'n ete the laves to the very stalk.' And see example under **Sodger**.

Compare Chaucer's '*snewede*:'—

> 'Withoute bake mete was nevere his hous,
> Of flessch and fissch, and that so plentevous,
> Hit *snewede* in his hous of mete and drynke.'
> *The Prologue*, l. 345, ed. Morris.

SNIZZLE-GRASS, *sb.* turfy Hair-grass.—WELLINGTON.

'"Why it brings nowt but *snizzle-grass* an' 'ardyeds," said a farmer who was particularly careful to point out the bad qualities of a certain field, when appealing against the valuation of his farm.'—*Science Gossip*, p. 227, Oct. 1870.

See **Sniggle-grass.**

SNOFFLE [snof·l], *v. n.* to speak through the nose.—PULVERBATCH; CLUN; WEM. 'Yo' met'n as good send a pig on a narrand as a fellow that *snoffles* athatn.' Such a person is sometimes spoken of as being '*snoffle-snouted.*'

'Du. *snuffelen*, to breathe through the nose.'—WEDG.

SNOODGE [snooj·], *v. n.* to lie snug and close; to press down; to nestle: chiefly applied to the *pose* of the head,—''Er'd got 'er 'ead *snoodged* on 'is breast.'—SHREWSBURY; WORTHEN. Qy. com. See *Snudge* in WEDG.

SNOODGING, *part. adj.* sitting close: said of head-gear,—''Er'd got some little *snoodgin'* bonnet on.'—WORTHEN.

SNOW-BALLS, *sb. pl.* the flowers of *Viburnum Opulus*, common Guelder Rose. Com.

SNOW-BIRDS, *sb. pl.* Fieldfares.—CLUN. These birds are observed to come in large flocks on the approach of snow or wintry weather, whence their local name of *Snow-birds*. Cf. **Storm-cock** (1). See **Fildefare.**

SNOWL [snou·l], *v. n.* to say peevish, disagreeable things.—WORTHEN. 'The Missis is al'ays *snowlin'* an' grumpin' about.'

SOBBER [sob·ur'], *v. n.* to simmer; to boil slowly.—PULVERBATCH. 'Them tatoes ŏŏn be spiled, they'n bin *sobberin'* this 'afe 'our.' Cf. **Wallop** (1).

SOBBIN-WET, *adj.* soaking-wet. — SHREWSBURY; PULVERBATCH. 'Theer's sich a je'ow o' the grass an' tillin', my fit an' legs bin *sobbin-wet.*' [I have only heard it as *soppin-wet.*—W. W. S.] Cf. **Soggen-wet.**

SOCK [sok·], *sb.* liquid manure; the drainage of a dung-hill. Com. 'It's a downright shame that meadow inna pŭt to thar farm, fur all the *sock* o' the foud gwuz into it, an' the paas'n gets the benefit.' Cf. W. *soch*, a drain.

SOCK-HOLE, *sb.* a pit for the *sock* to drain into; a cess-pool.—NEWPORT. Qy. com.

SODDENIN-WET [sod·nin], same as **Sobbin-wet**, above.—ELLESMERE.

SODDER [sod·ur' *and* sau·dur'], *sb.* and *v. a.* solder; to solder. Com. 'I mus' tak' the coffee-pot to be *soddered*, but they maken the *sodder* so soft now, it lasses none.'

'The decoction of Veronica dronken, doth *soder* and heale all fresh and old wounds.'—LYTE'S *Herbal* [A.D. 1595], p. 31, in *Bible Word-Book.*

'Fr. *Souder*, joindre des pièces de métal ensemble. To solder or *soder.*'—CHAMB.

SODGER [soj·ur'], *sb.* a soldier. Com. 'Sosebry wuz snivin' ŏŏth *sodgers* o' Saturday—the Cavaltry bin up, an' theer wuz a ridgment o' reg'lars gwein through.'

'My humble knapsack a' my wealth,
A poor and honest *sodger*.'
ROBERT BURNS, *Poems*, p. 237, l. 6, c. 2.

SOFT-MELCHED, same as **Easy-melched**, q. v.—PULVERBATCH. See **Melch-cow**.

SOG, (1) *sb.* a blow. Qy. com. ''E gid 'im sich a *sog* i' the guts, 'e didna want another.' Cf. **Sogger**, below.

(2) *v. n.* to deal one blow.—COLLIERY. *Soggin'* is striking repeatedly.

SOGGEN [sog·i'n *and* sog·n], *sb., obsols.* a soaking.—PULVERBATCH. 'Wun yo' ketcht i' the thunder-starm o' Saturd'y?—I got a pretty *soggen*.'

'*Soggon̄*. *Aquosus*.'—*Prompt. Parv.* 'O.N. *söggr*, wet,' in WEDG.

SOGGEN-WET, *adj., obsols.* soaking-wet.—*Ibid.* Cf. **Sobbin-wet**.

SOGGER [sog·ur' *and* seg·ur'], (1) *sb.* a heavy blow.—PULVERBATCH. Qy. com. ''E gid the poor lad sich a *segger* i' the stomach tell it took 'is breath away.' Cf. **Sog** (1), above.

(2) *sb.* a thump.—*Ibid.* ''E loost the bag off 'is shŏother sich a *sogger*.'

SOLE [soa·l], PULVERBATCH. [sou·l], CLEE HILLS, *sb., obs.* a wooden collar, shaped like a bent bow, which went round the neck of a stalled beast, the ends fitted into a movable 'slote' or cross-bar at the top, and by this means the *sole* was fastened: it was employed for tethering purposes.

Tusser mentions '*soles*' amongst '*Husbandlie furniture*.' See p. 38, ed. E. D. S.

'*Soole*, beestys teyynge. *Trimembrale*. "Sole, a bowe about a beestes necke."—PALSG. "*Restis*, a sole to tie beasts."—GOULDM.'—*Prompt. Parv. and Notes*.

A.S. *solu*, a rope to moor a boat. See **Slote** (3).

SOLID, *adj.* grave; serious; sedate. Com. 'Whad's the matter, Maister?—yo' looken as *solid* as owd times.' 'No, most the pity, it's nuthin' like owd times sence these Radicals bin carryin' all afore 'em, an' pertendin' to be the farmers' friends—but gie me poor owd Băconsfild.' This was said in reference to the eventful General Election of 1880.

SOLLAR [sol·ur'], (1) *sb., obs.*? a ceiling; an upper-flooring.—PULVERBATCH. 'They'n got a bit on a 'ut o' the side o' the Wimb'ry-'ill, but theer's no *sollar* to it,' *i. e.* no ceiling,—open to the roof.

Mr. Wedgwood explains *sollar* to be 'properly, simply a flooring, then applied to floors or stages in different parts of the house. It. *solaro*, *sollato*, a floor or ceiling; *solare*, a story of any building, from *solare*, to sole, to floor, or ceil.—FLORIO (A.D. 1680).' See below.

(2) *sb., obs.*? a garret; a loft.—*Ibid.* 'Tak' them apples an' pars an' sprade 'em o' the *sollar* flur.'

'Maides, mustard seede gather, for being too ripe,

. . . .

Then dresse it and laie it in *soller* vp sweete.'

TUSSER, *Fiue Hundred Pointes of Good Husbandrie* [August].

In *Acts* i. 13; ix. 37, where the A. V. has an 'upper room or chamber,' the Wicliffite version—ed. 1388—has '*soler*.'

Grose gives '*Soller*, or *Solar*. An upper chamber or loft. From the Latin, *solarium*. S.'

'*Solarium*, up-flor,' occurs in a *Semi-Saxon Vocabulary*, xii. cent., in Wr. vocabs., vol. i. p. 93.

'*Solere*, or lofte. *Solarium*, *hectheca*, *menianum*. "Sollar a chambre, solier. Soller a lofte, *garnier*."—PALSG. "*Hecteca*, dicitur solarium dependens de parietibus cenaculi. *Menianum*, solarium, dictum a menibus, i. muris, quia muris solent addi."—ORTUS.'—*Prompt. Parv. and Notes.*

'*Solarium* . . . the *solar* in the house.'—*Dict. Etym. Lat.*

'O.Fr. *solier*; charpente, plancher, plateforme, étage, chambre haute, grenier.'—BUR.

SOLLAR HIGH, *phr.*, *obs.*? as high as the ceiling.—*Ibid.* 'Is yore pig aumust fat, John?' 'No, 'e dunna get on mighty fast, 'e's sich a piddlin' ātor,—it's time 'e wuz *sollar 'igh* [slaughtered and hung up by the heels], fur it's black-quarter at our 'ouse.' See **Sollar** (1), above.

SOND, *sb.* sand. Com. 'Theer's no *sond* to be 'ad no nigher than Exford's Green, an' it's more than it's wuth to fatch it.'

'Fer in Northumberlond the wawe hir caste,
And in the *sond* hir ship stiked so faste,
That thennes wolde it noght of al a tyde.'

CHAUCER, B. 509 (Six-text ed.), Skeat.

A.S. *sond*, sand.

SONGOW [song·oe], *v. a.* and *v. n.* to glean.—WHITCHURCH; ELLESMERE. A 'Border' word—apparently imported—which, though it obtains, is not in much use. Mr. Wilbraham gives it as a Cheshire word.

Randle Holme has 'Gleaning or Leesing or *Songoing*.'

'Dan. *sanke*, to gather, cull, glean, pick.'—WEDG.

See **Lease**, also **Swingle** (3).

SONNOCKING, *part.* loitering; idling.—CHURCH STRETTON.

SOOPLE [soop·l], (1) *adj.*, *var. pr.* supple. Com.

(2) *v. a.* to reduce inflammation by fomenting; to render pliant by external applications.—PULVERBATCH; WORTHEN. 'It's a despert bad sprain, but if yo'n get some o' owd Lewis's iles, they bin capital to *soople* the jīnt an' swage the swellin'.'

'The soveraine weede betwixt two marbles plaine
Shee pownded small, and did in peeces bruze;
And then atweene her lilly handes twaine
Into his wound the juice thereof did scruze;

And round about, as she could well it use,
The flesh therewith shee *suppled* and did steepe,
T'abate all spasme, and soke the swelling bruze.'
SPENSER, *F. Q.*, Bk. III. c. v. st. xxxiii.

'To make a thing which is hard and rough, soft; to soften, to *supple*.'—HOLLYBAND'S *Dictionarie*, 1593.

Mr. Halliwell says '*Supple* is now used only as an adjective.'

'O.Fr. *soplier, souploier;* . . . plier.'—BUR.

SOOR [soo·r'], *adj.* bad (in execution); poor (in quality); difficult; incorrigible.—SHREWSBURY; PULVERBATCH. ''E's maden a *soor* job on it.' 'They bin a *soor* lot o' ship.' 'I've got a *soor* job 'ere.' ''E's a *soor* chap, I doubt 'e'll never be no good:'—are instances of the diverse senses in which this term is used: it has a wide range of application. A story is told of the newly-appointed Rector of a certain parish, who interrogated his clerk as to what his congregation thought of his preaching. The clerk was reticent—he did not 'like to say.' The Rector was urgent. 'Well, Sir,' said the clerk, 'if I mun tell yo', they sen as yo' bin a mighty *soor* 'ond at it.'

'But cursed be he that doeth the worcke of God negligentli or gilefullie. A *soore* word for them that are neglygent in dyschargeinge theyr office, or haue done it fraudulentlye, for that is the thynge that maketh the people yll.'—LATIMER, *The Ploughers*, p. 21.

See *Sore*, in WEDG.

SORROWFUL-MONDAY, *sb.* the first Monday following the close of the harvest weeks.—PULVERBATCH. On this day the farm-labourers, resuming the usual order of work, are put upon the wonted allowance of 'drink,' of which during the harvest they have had no stint,—hence they give to it the name of *Sorrowful-Monday*.

SOSS, *v. n.* to plump down; to sit down *à l'abandon*.—WHITCHURCH. ''Er *sossed* down i' the cheer all at wunst.' The term is sometimes applied to a person who has a bad seat in the saddle,—'Theer 'e gŏŏs *sossin* on 'is 'oss.' The word *soss*—never used of hard substances—would seem to be of onomatopoetic origin.

Jamieson has '*Soss*, the flat sound caused by a heavy but soft body, when it comes hastily to the ground, or squats down.'

SOUGH [suf·], (1) *sb.* a covered drain, as from a sink; also such a one as goes through a hedge-bank from one field to another. Com.

W. *soch*, a sink, a drain. Cf. **Sock.**

(2) [soo·], *v. n.* to wail, as the wind before rain.—CLUN; WEM.

'In which ther ran a swymbel in a *swough*,
As though a storm schulde bersten every bough.'
CHAUCER, *The Knightes Tale*, l. 1121, ed. Morris.

'I saw the battle, sair and teugh,
And reeking-red ran monie a sheugh,
My heart, for fear, gae *sough* for *sough*.'
ROBERT BURNS, *Poems*, p. 230, l. 27.

Jamieson gives 'To *Souch*, *Soogh*, *Swouch*, to emit a rushing or whistling sound, with the corresponding substantive forms for a rushing, whistling sound, and also a deep sigh.'

A.S. *swógan*, to sound, to howl as the wind.

SOUGHIN' [soo·in], *sb.* the wailing sound of the wind before rain. —*Ibid.*

SOUL-CAKE [soa·l], *sb., obs.?* a dole-cake for All-Souls' Day, made of very light dough, sweetened and spiced, and of oval form.—PULVERBATCH; WEM. *Soul-cakes* were made as late as 1840 or thereabouts, and dispensed, according to old-established usage, by Mrs. (Mary) Ward of Churton, a truly venerable Dame, who, having exceeded a century of age, died in Jan. 1853.

'Aubrey, in the Remains of Gentilisme, MS. Lansd. 227, says that in his time [latter half 17th cent.] in Shropshire, &c., there was set upon the board a high heap of *soul-cakes*, lying one upon another, like the picture of the shew-bread in the old Bibles. They were about the bigness of twopenny cakes.'—BRAND's *Popular Antiquities*, vol. i. p. 393.

'*Soul-mass-Cakes* are certain Oaten Cakes, which some of the wealthier sort of persons in *Lancashire, Herefordshire*, &c. use still to give the poor on *All-Souls* day (*Novemb.* 2), who take themselves obliged to say this old verse in retribution,

God have your Saul,
Bones and All.'

BLOUNT'S *Glossographia*, p. 598.

See *N. & Q.* (5th S., x. 426).

SOULING. See Bk. II., *Folklore*, &c., 'Customs connected with Days and Seasons' (*All Souls' Day*).

SOUR-DOCK, *sb. Rumex acetosa*, common Sorrel. Com. Walter de Biblesworth says—

'Pur sauce vaut la *surele*.'

'*Sour-dokke*' is given as the gloss of '*surele*.' See Wr. vocabs., vol. i. p. 162. Cf. **Sour-sauce**, below.

SOURING, *sb.* buttermilk put into cream to prepare it for the churn when not sour enough.—PULVERBATCH. 'In winter-time a little *sourin'* put i' the crame-steän saves it [the cream] throm gweïn bitter, an' it parts sooner.'

SOUR-SAUCE, same as **Sour-dock,** above, q. v. Com.

SPAN-GUTTER, *sb.* a drain made by placing three common bricks against the face of the coal, to carry off the water to the 'sump.' The bricks are so arranged as to form a triangle—one is laid flat, the others, at each end of it, slope upwards till they meet at the apex.—COLLIERY, *Old Park*; M. T.

SPARABLES [spaar'·u'blz], *sb. pl.* shoemakers' 'sprigs'—small headless nails of brass or iron. Properly *sparrow-bills*, from their shape.—PULVERBATCH. Qy. com. 'Yo' mun get tuthree *sparables* pŭt i' the 'eels o' them boots, else yo'n be runnin' all asiden.'

'Cob clouts his shoes, and as the story tells,
His thumb-nailes par'd, afford him *sperrables*.'

Herrick, p. 266, in NARES.

Amongst 'Nails without Heads,' Randle Holme enumerates, '*Sparrow Bills*, Nails to clout Shooes withal.'—*Academy of Armory*, Bk. III. ch. vii. p. 300.

SPARE-RIB [spaa·r'ib *and* spaar'·i'p], *sb.* the rib of a bacon-pig after the flitch has been cut off. Com.

'The *Spar-Ribs*, the Ribs when they are cut from the sides of such Pork as is intended for Bacon.'—*Academy of Armory*, Bk. III. ch. iii. p. 88.

Cf. **Bald-rib.**

SPARKLE [spaa·r'kl], *sb.* a spark.—SHREWSBURY; PULVERBATCH; CLUN. 'Whad's the matter ŏŏth the child's arm?' 'W'y a *sparkle* fled out o' the fire an' burnt it.' 'Whad'n'ee pŭt to it?' 'Some sinnagreen an' crame, that's the best the thing as I knowed on.'

> 'Chylde Florent yn hys feyre wede
> Sprange owt as *sparkylle* on glede.'
> *The Emperor Octavian*, l. 962, Percy Soc., ed. 1844.

'*Sparkle*, of fyyr. *Scintilla, favilla.*'—*Prompt. Parv.*

SPARLING [spaa·r'lin], *sb.* a thin, puny little child.—PULVERBATCH. 'Inna that child a *sparlin'* fur a six yer owd?' 'Aye, it's a poor āven.' The term is sometimes used as a redundant adjective,—'it's a poor, little *sparlin'* child.' A.S. *spær*, spare + *ling*, a diminutive suffix.

SPARROW-GRASS, *sb.* asparagus. Com.

SPATTLE-SPOTTLE [spat·l], (1) SHREWSBURY; PULVERBATCH; ELLESMERE. Qy. com. [spot·l], (1) NEWPORT; LUDLOW, *Burford*, *v. a.* to splash. 'W'y 'ow yo'n dagged yore throck!' 'Oh, it inna much, it's on'y *spattled* a bit.' A.S. *spátlian*, to froth, fume.

(2) *v. a., obsols.* to slapdash with white on a black ground. The 'aister' of old-fashioned cottage fire-places is *spattled* thus:—It is first washed with a mixture of soot and buttermilk, this being dry, it is sprinkled or splashed with whitewash by means of a flat brush.—ELLESMERE. Qy. com. 'Jenny, yo' gŏŏ an' axe Betty Dulson if 'er'll lend me 'er w'itewesh brush to *spattle* the aister wuth,—we maun 'ăve it cleăn 'gen Chris'mas.' See **Aister** (1).

(3) *v. a.* to pepper,—a sportsman's phrase.—PULVERBATCH. 'Well, young fellow, w'eer han yo' bin all ŏnder?' 'I've bin all round the coppy, an' the sidelant-leasow after quice.' 'Han'ee killed any?' 'Aye, I shot three, an' *spattled* tuthree more.'

(4) *v. a.* to fritter away: said of money.—PULVERBATCH; WEM; ELLESMERE. 'Nancy Furber dunna mak' a very good ăven for a poor mon's wife, an' see the way 'er *spattles* 'er wages in bits an' dabs.' See **Spattling-money**, below.

SPATTLED, *part. past, sl.*? slightly intoxicated.—PULVERBATCH; WEM. 'Wuz the Maister drunk las' night?' 'No, 'e wunna drunk, o'y a bit *spattled*.' Cf. **Fresh** (1), also **Totty.**

SPATTLING-MONEY, *sb.* same as **Butter-money**, q. v.,—money which coming in small sums, is expended for trifling purchases.—PULVERBATCH; WEM; ELLESMERE. 'I say, Missis, yo'n too much *spattlin'-money*, I wunna a so much butter sent to markit every wik, yo' maun try an' get some more cheese from somew'eer;—that'll bring the money in, in a lump.' Compare 'spending siluer' in the following:—

'. . . so plesaunt and so seruisable
Vnto the wyf, wher as he was at table,
That she wolde suffre him no thing for to paye
For bord ne clothing, wente he neuer so gaye;
And *spending siluer* hadde he ryght ynow.'
CHAUCER, G. 1018 (Six-text ed.), Skeat.

Compare *Spattling(-money)* with 'Splarplynge or scaterynge (*spartelynge* . ., K.). *Dissipacio,*' in *Prompt. Parv.*

SPAUN [spau·n], (1) *sb.* and *v. a.*, *var. pr.* a span; to span—as by the extended hand. Qy. com. 'That young ŏŏman's mighty taper i' the middle, yo' met'n *spaun* 'er round.'

'A.S., O.H.Germ. *spannan*, span (*tendere, nectere*).'—STRAT.

(2) *sb.*, *pec.* measurement by paces, as of land,—'that plack's about three rood by my *spaun*.'—PULVERBATCH.

(3) *v. a.*, *pec.* to measure by paces.—*Ibid.* ''Ow much tatoe ground han'ee got this time?' 'Well, accordin' as I *spaun* it, about four rood—I dunna know whad they'n mak' it ŏŏth the chain.'

SPAUNER [spau·nur'], *sb.* a turn-screw; a 'wrench,' used by blacksmiths. Qy. com.

SPAWL [spau·l], *v. a.* to slice off: said of wood,—a carpenter's term.—CLUN.

SPAWLED, *part. adj.* same as **Shaked**, q. v.—SHREWSBURY.

SPEECH, *v. n.* to bulge, as of a wall,—'that wall *speeches* out above a bit.'—CLEE HILLS.

SPICE-BALLS, same as **Faggits**, q. v.—WEM; ELLESMERE.

SPICY [spei·si'], *adj.*, *pec.*, *sl.*? smartly dressed. Qy. com. 'I sid Bess at the Club, an' oncommon *spicy* 'er wuz—downright smītin.'

SPIGOT-STEAN, *sb.* a large earthen jar shaped like a barrel standing endwise, and having an orifice at the lower end to admit a spigot. Qy. com. 'Theer's two or three little casks an' a *spigot-stean* i' the catalogue, if they gwun chep I should like to 'ăve 'em, they bin so ready fur a drop o' wine or metheglin.' See **Stean.**

SPIKE-POLE, *sb.* a light pole furnished with a spike at one end, used to get down the loose portions of the roof, when the miners cannot otherwise reach it for the purpose of testing it. Com. M. T.

SPILE [spei·l], *sb.* dross; rubbish.—SHREWSBURY. Qy. com. A man complained that some 'slack' from Short Hill was full of '*spile*' that would not burn. Cf. **Spoil.**

SPINK, *sb.* the Chaffinch.—BRIDGNORTH. Probably called *Spink* from its alarm note. Grose has '*Spink*, a chaffinch. N.'

'*Hic rostellus, A*' spynke,' occurs in an *English Vocabulary*, in Wr. vocabs., vol. i. p. 189. Dr. Stratmann explains it as the '*Fringilla*.' See **Chink-chink.**

SPINNEY, *sb.* a small plantation.—LUDLOW; NEWPORT.

'. . . alas! alas!
Had her horse but been fed upon English grass,
And sheltered in Yorkshire *spinneys*.'
THOMAS HOOD, *Miss Kilmansegg*, &c., 'Her Accident.'

Mr. Halliwell says that '*spinney*, meaning a small plantation, occurs in Domesday Book.' From O.Fr. *espinnye*, 'a thorny plot, place full of briers,' Cotgrave; which is from Lat. *spinêtum*, a thicket of thorns. Cf. **Coppy**, also **Hay**.

SPINNING STREET YARN, *phr.* gossipping up and down streets or lanes instead of stopping at home to work.—SHREWSBURY; PULVERBATCH. 'It's a shame to see that great wench *spinnin' street yarn* awile the poor owd mother's lef' to do all the work.'

SPIRT [spur't], *v. n.* to 'sprit' or sprout abnormally: said of grain, &c. Com. 'They sen the corn's *spirt* sadly; but it's no ŏŏnder, the weather's bin so muckery—it'll *spirt* standin' now it's ripe.'

'1584-5. This yeare the somm' and harviest tyme was so unseasonable that husband meen could not get in their corne but mutche of it was layd flat to the grownde, and so by meanes *spirtid*, and whe' the reast that stood upp beinge ripe was rept, yet by the reason of contynuall shures was mutche *spirtid*, and in hast howsed scannt seasonid by wth unseasonablenes Rye that was beffore harvist at 15 & 1/6*d* the bushell cam to ij*s* 4*d* the bushell and all othern grayne in lycke order and rate and so lycke to coom derer.'—*Early Chronicles of Shrewsbury* (*Taylor MS.*), in *Transactions of the Shropshire Archæological and Natural History Society*.

See *Sprout*, in WEDG.

SPIRY [spei·h'r'i'], *adv.* tall and weak,—'shot up.'—PULVERBATCH; WEM. 'I dunna like bëäns set among the tatoes, they growen *spiry* an' bringen nuthin'.'

'*Spyryñ*', as corne and oþer lyke. *Spico.*'—*Prompt. Parv.*

'N. *spira*, to shoot up.'—WEDG.

SPIT, *sb.* a spadeful of soil in digging.—MUCH WENLOCK.

'Du. *spitten*, to dig.'—WEDG.

SPITTLE, *sb.* a spade.—CRAVEN ARMS; BISHOP'S CASTLE; CLUN; CLEE HILLS; CORVE DALE; LUDLOW.

SPITTLE-TREE, *sb.* the handle of a spade.—*Ibid.* See **Tree** (2).

SPLAUDERS [splau·dur'z], *sb. pl.* balls of ironstone as big as a man's hand, and as smooth as glass—'*sliken*' was the term employed by the miner in describing their appearance: they are found in the *Blue Flats*.—COLLIERY; M. T.

SPLEENY [splee·ni'], *adj.* hasty; irritable; quarrelsome.—WEM.

'. . . . . yet I know her for
A *spleeny* Lutheran; and not wholesome to
Our cause . . . . .'—*K. Henry VIII.*, III. ii. 99.

SPLOTHER [splodh·ur'], *v. n.* to 'make much ado about nothing.'—CLUN; WHITCHURCH; ELLESMERE. 'Oud yore nïze, whad bin'ee splutterin' an' *splotherin'* about?—it maks me far sick to 'ear yo.'

SPLOTHER-FOOTED, *adj.* splay-footed.—SHREWSBURY. Cf. **Wassle-footed.**

SPOIL [spwei'l *corr.* spwa'·yl], *sb.* 'débris,' as from excavations, taken down buildings, &c.—BISHOP'S CASTLE; CLUN. 'Theer'll be a sight o' *spwile* to rid away̆ w'en the church is took down; it'll do capital to fill up the 'ollow between an' the Church Bank,'—said with reference to Clun Church [1875]. Cf. **Spile.** See **W** (4) in **Grammar Outlines** (*consonants*, &c.).

SPOKE [spoa·k], *sb.* talk; conversation.—SHREWSBURY. 'I hanna 'ad no *spoke* ŏŏth 'im about it, so I canna tell whad 'e manes to do.'

SPOONTLE [spŏŏn·tl], *sb.* a spoonful. Qy. com. 'Dear 'eart alive! 'ow scăce barm is—I've bin all round the parish, an' canna get a *spŏŏntle.*' See 'Nouns compounded with -ful' in **Grammar Outlines**, p. xliii.

SPOT, (1) *sb.*, *pec.* a drop; a small quantity of liquid,—'theer's o'ny a *spot* lef';'—''ere drink this *spot.*' Com.

(2) *v. n.* to fall in large, heavy drops, as rain does, in a premonitory kind of way, sometimes. Com. 'Yo'd'n better stop w'eer yo' bin a bit, fur I doubt it's gweïn to rain.' 'Aye, it's beginnin' to *spot* now, an' theer's thunder about, an' I dunna want to be ketcht in a posh o' wet, so I ŏŏnna start—nod yet 'owever.'

SPOTTING, *part. adj.* falling in drops: said of rain,—'it's *spottin'* o' rain.' Com.

SPOTTLE. See **Spattle** (1).

SPOUT-ROAD, *sb.* same as **Cungit**, q. v.—PULVERBATCH, *Arscott*, *Longden*, &c. M. T.

SPRAD [spr'ad·], *pret.* and *part. past*, spread.—PULVERBATCH. Qy. com. 'They'n *sprad* the lime despert thin o' the 'arp-leasow—twize as much ŏŏd a done it no 'arm.'

> 'Thi body *sprad* theron was,
> Fore our syn sake.'
> JOHN AUDELAY'S *Poems*, p. 57.

> 'If oon seyde wel, another seyde the same;
> So *spradde* of hir heigh bountee the fame.'
> CHAUCER, E. 418 (Six-text ed.), Skeat.

Cf. **Sprod.**

SPRADE [spr'ai·d], *v. a.* and *v. n.* to spread. Qy. com. 'This butter 's aumust too 'ard to *sprade.*'

'A.S. *sprædan;* O.Du. *sprêden;* O.H.Germ. *spreitan*, to spread.'—STRAT. Cf. **Sprede.**

SPRADER [spr'ai·dur'], *sb.* the staff of wood which holds out the chains of team-horses, and prevents them galling their sides.—PULVERBATCH. Qy. com. Cf. **Stret-staff.**

SPRAG [spr'ag·], (1) *v. n.* to bulge, as in giving way: said of walls.—CLEE HILLS. 'That owd wall ŏŏl be down, it *sprags* out most demendous.'

'Dan. *spraga*; Swed. *spraka*, to crack.'—STRAT.

(2) *v. a.* to prop.—WEM. 'Yo' mun tak' a balk o' timber an' *sprag* up that wall.'

(3) *v. a.* to prop the coal while the men are 'holing.' Com. M. T. See **Hole.**

(4) *sb.* a short wooden prop used by the 'holers' to support the coal while they are at work. Com. M. T. 'The Mining Regulation Act' of 1873 requires that the *sprags* shall not be more than 6 ft. apart. Cf. **Gib** (1). See **Bondsmen.**

(5) *v. n.* to jerk: said of horses drawing in a team.—WEM. 'That cowt does nuthin' but *sprag* w'eer 'e is, we mun pŭt 'im i' the pin.' See **Pin.**

SPREDE [spr'ee·d], *v. a.* and *v. n.* to spread.—CLUN.

'Þe blostme ginneþ springe and *sprede*
Boþe in treo and ek on mede.'
Owl and Nightingale, l. 437.

Dan. *sprede*, to spread, See **Sprade.**

SPRENT, SPRUNT [spr'en·t], ELLESMERE. [spr'unt], PULVERBATCH; WORTHEN, *sb.* a sudden start or spring. 'I wuz joggin' quietly alung w'en the mar' gid a *sprunt* an' throwed me right o'er 'er yed.' As a verb this word appears in both forms in the early writers:—

'the greene Knight his head vp hent,
into his saddle wightilye he *sprent.*'
The Grene Knight, l. 194. *Percy Folio MS.*, vol. ii. p. 65, ed. Hales and Furnivall.

'See this sweet simpering babe,
Sweet image of thyself; see, how it *sprunts*
With joy at thy approach.'
BEN JONSON, *Devil is an Ass*, in Wedg.

SPRINGE [spr'inj·], (1) *v. n.* to bound; to spring.—SHREWSBURY; PULVERBATCH. 'The child nearly *springed* off my lap.'

'O.Fr. *Espringer*, *espringier*, . . . sauter; de l'ahal. *springan*, même signification.'—BUR.

(2) *sb.* a sudden, acute throb of pain, as of a toothache, a gathering, &c.—SHREWSBURY; PULVERBATCH. Qy. com. 'My tuth gid sich a *springe.*'

SPRINGER [spr'ing·ur'], *sb.* a rod used in thatching stacks.—ELLESMERE. Langland has 'spring' in the sense of 'rod':—

'"Who-so spareth þe *sprynge* · spilleth his children."'
Piers Pl., Text B., pass. v. l. 41.

See below.

SPRINGLE [spr'ing·l], (1) *sb.* a twig; a small branch.—PULVERBATCH. 'The robin's singin' o' the very topmust *springle* o' the plum-tree.'

'*Sprynge*, of a tre or plante. *Planta, plantula.*'—*Prompt. Parv.*

'A.Sax., O.Sax., O.H.Germ. *spring*, spring, *planta.*'—STRAT.

(2) same as **Springer**, above.—LUDLOW; ELLESMERE, *Welshampton.* Cf. **Lug** (3).

SPRING O' THE YEAR, *phr.* the season of spring. Com.

SPROD [spr'od·], *pret.* and *part. past*, spread.—CLUN; WHITCHURCH. 'We bin sprădin' the muck o' the squar' meadow, we *sprod* it o' the other isterd'y.' Cf. **Sprad.**

SPROZE, SPRUZE [spr'oa·z], WEM. [spr'ooz·], CHURCH STRETTON, *sb.* a fuss; a stir; an agitation. 'Well, I dunna mind tellin' yo' as I 'eärd they 'ad'n notice to lave the farm, but dunna yo' gŏŏ an' mak' a *sproze* about it, fur I amma sartin.' Cf. *Sprouze*, in HAL.

SPRUNT. See **Sprent.**

SPUDS [spud·z], *sb. pl.* potato-sets.—BISHOP'S CASTLE; CLUN.

SPURNS [spur'n·z], *sb. pl.* spreading roots of trees.—MUCH WENLOCK.

'. . . and their root
With long and mighty *spurns* to grapple with the land,
As nature would have said, they shall for ever stand.'
DRAYTON'S *Polyolbion* [A.D. 1613—1622], xxii. p. 1104, in Nares.

Shakespeare has *spurs* in the same sense:—

'. . . . . . the strong-based promontory
Have I made shake and by the *spurs* pluck'd up
The pine and cedar.'—*Tempest*, V. i. 47.

SQUANDERED [skwaan·dur'd], *part. past*, dispersed.—PULVERBATCH. Qy. com. 'It seems no time sence they wun all little childern runnin' about together, an' now they bin growed into men an' women, an' *squandered* up an' down the country, an' the poor owd folks bin lef' to tharselves.'

'. . and other ventures he hath *squandered* abroad.'
Merchant of Venice, I. iii. 22.

SQUARES [skwaa·r'z], *sb. pl.* hollow squares of iron averaging about six inches deep, used to hold the coal on the 'skips.' Com. M. T. See **Skip.**

SQUASH [skwash·], *v. a.* to crush. Com. 'The wench 'as *squashed* one 'afe o' the fruit I pŭt 'er to gether.'

'And thus some of them halfe dead, as being *squashed* with huge weightie stones, or shot into the breast with darts and arrowes, lay tumbling upon the ground.'—*Ammianus Marcellinus*, 1609, in WR.

SQUASHY, *adj.* soft; watery, as of fruit, &c. Com.

SQUAT [skwat·], (1) *adj.* stumpy; short, as compared with breadth,—''Ow *squat* it looks!'—CORVE DALE.

'. . . a little, wise-looking, *squat*, upright, jabbering body of a tailor.'—ROBERT BURNS, *Letters*, p. 530.

(2) *adj.* close; quiet,—'keep *squat* theer.'—LUDLOW. Cf. **Quat.**

SQUAWK [skwau·k], (1) *v. n.* to squeal, as children do,—''ow them childern dun *squawk!*' Qy. com.

(2) *v. n.* to croak; to make any discordant noise. Qy. com. 'I 'eärd a noud toäd *squawkin'*.'

SQUEDGE [skwej·], *pret.* and *part. past*, squeezed.—SHREWSBURY; PULVERBATCH. Qy. com. 'It's downright disagreeable to shake 'ands ŏŏth Will,—'e *squedge* my 'and till the jīnts cracked.' Cf. **Squoze.**

SQUEEZE-CRAB, *sb.* a person of shrunk and withered appearance,—'a reg'lar owd *squeeze-crab*.'—WORTHEN.

SQUELCH, SQUENCH [skwel·sh], PULVERBATCH. [skwen·sh], WEM, *v. a.* to allay thirst; to quench. ''ăve a dish o' warm tay, it'll *squelch* yore thirst better than anythin'.'

'Fetche pitch and flaxe, and *squench* it.'—*First Part of the Contention*, p. 59, in HAL.

SQUELT [skwel·t], *v. a.* to beat; to pommel. —LUDLOW. Mr. Wright gives '*squelt*' as a Leicestershire word, in the same sense.

SQUELTING, *sb.* a sound beating,—''e gid 'im a reg'lar good *squeltin'*.'—*Ibid.*

SQUINE [skw'ei·n], *v. n.* to squint.—OSWESTRY.

'*Lear.* I remember thine eyes well enough. Dost thou *squiny* at me?'—*K. Lear*, IV. vi. 140.

Cf. **Glyde (1).**

SQUINTER-PIP [skwin·tur' pip], *sb.* Herb Robert.—PULVERBATCH, *Arscott.* See **Dragon's-blood.**

SQUILT [skwil·t], (1) *sb.* a speck; a blemish: used with reference to the skin, and always in the negative form,—'the child's never 'ad a *squilt* on 'er.' Qy. com.

(2) *sb.* a very small quantity, as one would say, a speck,—'jest the laist *squilt* o' puddin'.'—PULVERBATCH. Qy. com.

SQUITCH [skwich·], (1) *sb.* Couch-grass.—NEWPORT. See **Scutch.**

(2) *sb.* a light, flexible stick or rod. Qy. com.

(3) *v. a.* to lash with such a rod. Qy. com.

SQUITTOCK [skwit·uk], *sb.* a small quantity. — PULVERBATCH. 'I've bin all round the parish 'untin' barm, an' I canna get a *squittock*'.

SQUOZE [skwoa·z], *pret.* and *part. past*, squeezed.—NEWPORT. Cf. **Squedge.**

SRODE. See **Shrewd.**

STAG, *sb.* a yearling turkey-cock.—SHREWSBURY; CLEE HILLS; WEM.

STAGGERING-BOB, *sb.* a very young calf, slaughtered.—PULVERBATCH. Qy. com. 'Wust'ee mane by 'aithen [heathen!] vale, Dick?' 'W'y that cauve never 'eärd the Church-bells, I'll swar—I canna bar *staggerin'-bob*.' See **Slink-veal.**

STAGGERS [stag·ur'z], *sb. pl.* strong, well-grown thorn-bushes, holly-bushes, &c.,—cropped for hedgerow purposes—taken up by the roots and replanted. sometimes to make a new fence, but more frequently to fill up gaps in an old one.—PULVERBATCH; WELLINGTON; WEM; OSWESTRY. Qy. com. 'Dun yo' think that *stagger*-fence ŏŏl grow?' 'It mun see o'er another Chris'mas-Day afore I can tell; I dunna like to see *staggers* sprout out too soon—they canna sprout an' root.'

'1793. Decr. 13—Begun to repair our fences, which is much wanted. Bought a load of *staggers* from Nuttree Bank to put in barren gapes.'—*Bailiff's Diary*, Aston, Oswestry. *Byegones*, 1877, p. 316.

STAG-WARNING, *sb.* a boys' game.—SHREWSBURY. See Bk. II., *Folklore*, &c., 'Games.'

STAIL, *sb.* a handle, as of a hay-fork, broom, &c. Com. See **Stele.**

STAIR-FOOT-HOLE [staa·r'fut oal], *sb.* the place under the stairs, which in cottages is frequently boarded in to form a kind of closet—a general receptacle for odds and ends. Com. 'Sally, look fur my buzgins, I warrant they bin i' the *star-fŭt-'ole* w'eer everything gwuz.'

STAKED [stai·kt], (1) *adj.* affected with a painful tightness at the chest, caused by indigestion.—PULVERBATCH. 'Jack's bad.' 'Whad's the matter ŏŏth 'im?' ''E's *staked*.' 'No ŏŏnder, 'e shouldna-d-a ete so much toasted cheese.'

'The brest with the *stak*. Arch. xxx. 413,' in HAL.

'In the North of France it is said of one killed or severely wounded, *il a eu son estoque*, he has had his belly-ful; from *estoquer*, to cram, satiate, "stodge." Compare Ital. *stucco*, cloyed.' See 'Glossarial Index' to *Lancelot of the Laik*, p. 127.

(2) *adj.* seriously constipated: said of brute animals only. Cf. **Steeked.**

STALL. See **Finger-stall.**

STALLED [stau·ld *and* stau·d], (1) *part. past*, fixed; set fast, as of a waggon on a heavy road,—'got *staud* o' the bonk.'—WELLINGTON; NEWPORT; WEM.

'And has all thing within thy hert *stallit*,
That may thy ȝouth oppressen or defade.'
JAMES I. OF SCOTLAND (A.D. 1423, *circa*), *The Kingis Quhair*. *Specim. Eng. Lit.*, iv. 170.

Compare Shakespeare's '*stelled*' = set, fixed.—*Lucrece*, l. 1444. *Sonnet*, xxiv. l. i.

'*Obstacula*, wid-steallas,' occurs in *Latin and Anglo-Saxon Glosses*, xi. cent., in Wr. vocabs., vol. ii. p. 89.

'A.Sax. *steall;* O.Fris., O.Du., O.H.Germ. *stal;* O.Icel. *stallr;* . . . *statio.*'—STRAT.

(2) *part. adj.* stayed from eating by being cloyed or satiated,—'the child conna finish the pŭddin'—'er's *stalled*.'—CLEE HILLS.

'Or olio that wud *staw* a sow.'
ROBERT BURNS, *Poems*, p. 72, l. 2, c. 2.

STAND, *v. a., pec.* to put; to place,—'*stand* that stean o' the setless.' Com.

STANDELF, *sb., obs.* a stone-quarry.—SHREWSBURY. The following 'Note' is taken from Owen and Blakeway's *History of Shrewsbury*:— 'The word [*standelf*] does not occur in the Glossaries, and was perhaps peculiar to Shrewsbury. In some extracts from deeds of the family of Scriven, relating to lands in the Abbey Foregate, is this passage: "In campo foriete versus Beckebury, altera versus le Whyte *stany-delf* terram spectantem capelle Be. Marie in Abbatia Salop. 30 Ed. III."'—vol. ii. p. 462. See **Delf.**

STANK [stang·k], (1) *sb.* a stake; a pile.—SHREWSBURY; PULVERBATCH; WEM. 'Yo' mun pŭt tuthree *stanks* i' the turn o' that bruck, an' wattle 'em well—it's playin' the bar ŏŏth the meadow.' '*Playin' the bar* [*bear*]' is a phrase equivalent to 'playing the deuce!'

> 'An inundation that orebears the banks
> And bounds of all religion; if some *stancks*
> Shew their emergent heads, like Seth's famed stone,
> Th' are monuments of thy devotion gone.'
>
> FLETCHER'S *Poems*, p. 167, in Nares.

'Cf. O.N. *stöng;* O.H.Germ. *stanga*, a bar, staff, pole,' in WEDG.

(2) *v. a.* to tether; to tie to a stake.—PULVERBATCH; WELLINGTON. 'Yo'd'n better *stank* that cauve i' the edgrow, else it'll mess more than it ates.'

(3) *v. a.* to mark out with stakes the limits of any ground intended for inclosure.—SHREWSBURY; PULVERBATCH; WORTHEN; WEM. 'They'n *stanked* out the scoot w'eer they bin gweïn to build the new school-'us.'

(4) *v. a.* to shore up with stakes, as of the bank of a stream.—PULVERBATCH; WELLINGTON. 'Whad a pity they dunna *stank* up that bonk, the bruck's tarrin' [tearing] that good meadow despertly.

(5) *v. a.* to dam.—PULVERBATCH; LUDLOW. '*Stank* the prill up as theer may be some waiter for the gis.'

> 'And *stanck* up the salt conducts of mine eyes,
> To watch thy shame, and weep mine obsequies.'
>
> FLETCHER'S *Poems*, p. 154, in Hal.

(6) *sb.* a dam.—PULVERBATCH; BRIDGNORTH; WELLINGTON. 'I see they'n cut sods out o' the meadow an' made a *stank* across the bruck, now we shanna 'ăve a spot o' clier waiter afore mornin'.'

'And thane Alexander and hys ostē went alle aboute that ryvere, and come tille this forsaid *stanke*, and luged thame aboute it.'—*MS. Lincoln*, A. i. 17, f. 28, in HAL.

Bailey—ed. 1782—gives 'A *Stank*, a Dam or Bank to stop Water,' as a 'North Country' word.

STARE [staeˑr'], *sb. Sturnus vulgari*, common Starling.—CHURCH STRETTON.

> 'The *stare* wyl chatre and speke of long usage,
> Though in his speche ther be no greet resoun.'
>
> LYDGATE'S *Minor Poems*, p. 150.

'"*Sturnus*, a stare," MS. Arund. 249, f. 90. "Staare a byrde, *estourneaux*," Palsgrave,' in HAL.

'A.Sax. *stær*; O.Icel. *stari*, stare; *sturnus*.'—STRAT.

Cf. **Steer** (2).

STARS [staa·r'z], *sb. pl., var. pr.* stairs. Com. 'My daughter brought the bed down 'ere, Ma'am, 'er said 'er couldna be comfortable onless 'er did,—I might fall throm the *stars*, 'er said, an' if I did it ŏŏd be a lung way fur me to fall 'edlunga.' Thus a poor woman explained how it came about that her bed was in her living-room.

START [staa·r't], *v. a., pec.* to dispatch; to send away. Com. 'I'm gweïn to Sosebry to *start* a ampot to poor Jack, 'e ŏŏnna think it's like Chris'mas if 'e dunna get summat throm wham.'

STARVE. See **Clem.**

STEAN [stee·n *and* stai·n], Com. [sti'·h'n] (*obsols.*), PULVERBATCH, *sb.* a deep earthen vessel used for various household and dairy purposes. 'I bought a right good weshin' *steän* fur a shillin'—should a 'ad to gie more i' Sosebry, on'y the mon said 'e didna want to carry it back.'

'Two cream *steens*.'—*Auctioneer's Catalogue* (Stoddesden), 1870.

'þar ys also whyt cley & reed, for to make of crokkes & *steenes* & oþer vessel.'—JOHN OF TREVISA (A.D. 1387), *Description of Britain*, *Specim. of Early Eng.*, xviii. *a.* l. 46.

'Upon an huge great Earth-pot *steane* he stood,
From whose wide mouth there flowed forth the Romane Flood.'
SPENSER, *F. Q.*, Bk. VII. c. vii. st. xlii.

See **Spigot-stean.**

STEDSTAFF [sted·staf], same as **Sprăder,** q. v.—CLEE HILLS. Cf. **Stretstaff.**

STEEKED, same as **Staked** (2), q. v.—NEWPORT.

STEEKLE [stee·kl], *v. a.* to kill; to 'settle.'—WHITCHURCH. ''E *steekled* the rot i' no time.'

STEEP [stee·p], (1) *sb.* rennet—so called from being *steeped* or soaked before it is put into the milk.—ELLESMERE.

Randle Holme gives 'Runnet or *Steep*,' amongst 'Terms used by Dairy People.'—*Academy of Armory*, Bk. III. ch. viii. p. 335.

Pegge has '*Steep*, rennet. Lanc.' See **Mawskin.**

(2) *adj.* lofty; proud.—PULVERBATCH. ''E's a mighty *steep* chap is young 'ŏŏdcock.' Layamon has 'moni *steap* mon.'—l. 1532.

'A.Sax. *steap*; O.Fris. *stâp*, steep, *altus*.'—STRAT.

STEER [stee·h'r'], (1) *sb.* an ox under three years of age.—BISHOP'S CASTLE; CLUN.

'. . . eleven heefers, foure *steares*, one bull.'—*Inventory* . . . Owlbury Manor-House, Bishop's Castle, 1625.

'Aboute his char ther wenten white alauntz,
Twenty and mo, as grete as eny *steer*.'
CHAUCER, *The Knightes Tale*, l. 1291, ed. Morris.

'*Hast.* My lord, our army is dispersed already:
Like youthful *steers* unyoked, they take their courses
East, west, north, south.'—2 *K. Henry IV.*, IV. ii. 103.

'Juvencus is a yonge oxe whan he is no lenger a calf, and he is then callyd a *steere* whan he begynneth to be helpfull unto the profit of man in eringe the erth.'—*Dialogues of Creatures Moralysed*, p. 228, in HAL.

'*Anniculus, vel trio*, steor-oxa,' and *Juvencus, vel vitula*, steor,' occur in *Archbp. Ælfric's Vocabulary*, x. cent., in Wr. vocabs., vol. i. p. 23.

'A.Sax. *steor*; O.H.Germ. *stior*; Goth. *stiur*, steer; *juvencus*.'—STRAT. Cf. **Stirk** (1).

(2) *sb.* the Starling. Com. In the *Churchwardens' Accounts* of S. Mary's, Shrewsbury, for the year 1584, is the following entry,—'For hontinge *steeres* out of the churche, and polynge downe ther nystes at the same tyme, vij^{d}.' See **Stare**.

STELCH [stel·sh], (1) *sb., obsols.* stealth.—PULVERBATCH. 'If the Maister didna gie 'im the turmits, 'e got 'em by *stelch*, fur 'e 'ad 'em, an' tumped 'em.'

(2) *sb.* the post to which cattle are tied in the stall.—PULVERBATCH; CLEE HILLS. See **Boosey-stake**.

STELE [stee·l], *sb.* a long handle, same as **Stail**, q. v.—LUDLOW, *Burford*; NEWPORT.

'And lerned men a ladel bugge · with a longe *stele*.'
Piers Pl., Text B., pass. xix. l. 274.

'And in his hand an huge Polaxe did beare,
Whose *steale* was yron-studded, but not long.'
SPENSER, *F. Q.*, Bk. V. c. xii. st. xiv.

'*Stele*, or stert of a vesselle. *Ansa*.'—*Prompt. Parv.*

'A.Sax., O.Du. *stele*, steal; *scapus, manubrium*.'—STRAT.

STEN [sten·], same as **Sprāder**, q. v.—WHITCHURCH. Cf. O.Fr. *estendre*; Lat. *extendere*, to extend.

STENT, *sb.* an allotted portion, as of work to be done in a given time,—'that's yore *stent*.'—WELLINGTON; COLLIERY.

'Erythius, that in the cart fyrste went,
Had euen nowe attaynde his iourneyes *stent*.'
THOMAS SACKVILLE (A.D. 1563), *The Mirrour for Magistrates*. *Specim. Eng. Lit.*, xxiv. 6.

STER [ste·ŭr' = stair'], *sb.* a star.—PULVERBATCH. Qy. com. 'It's lef' of raïnin' an' the *sters* bin quite bright.'

'. . . "I wil bere witnesse,
þat þo þis barne was ybore · þere blased a *sterre*,
That alle þe wyse of þis worlde · in o witte acordeden,
That such a barne was borne · in bethleem Citee."'
Piers Pl., Text B., pass. xviii. l. 231.

'We han seyn his *sterre* in the eest, and we comen to worschipe him.'—*Matt.* ii. 2. Wicliffite version—ed. A.D. 1388.

'*Sterre.* *Stella, sidus.*'—*Prompt. Parv.*

'A.S. *steorra;* O.Sax. *sterro;* O.H.Germ. *sterro;* O.Icel. *stiarna;* Goth. *stairno*, star, *stella.*'—STRAT.

See *sub voce* **H**, p. 190.

STEW [schoo· *and* steu·], *sb., pec.* a state of vexation, perplexity, or fear,—'I wuz in a fine *stew.*' Com.

STICHE [stei·ch], *v. a.* to set up; to dispose, as of sheaves, &c., in harvesting operations,—'*stiche* up them beäns i' rucks.'—ATCHAM; WEM.

'A.Sax. *stihtan;* O.Du. *stichten;* O.H.Germ. *stiftan*, to dispose.'—STRAT.

STICK [stik·], (1) *sb., pec.* a timber-tree—either standing or felled—no matter how large it may be.—CLUN.

'1770. for luging 4 *sticks* of Timber. 0 - 6 - 0.'—*Churchwardens' Accounts*, Hopton Castle (Salop).

(2) *v. a.* to kill by stabbing, as of pigs. Com.

'Thou fallest, as it were a *stiked* swyn.'
CHAUCER, C. 556 (Six-text ed.), Skeat.

'*Stykyn̄*, or sleñ. *Jugulo.*'—*Prompt. Parv.*
A.S. *stician*, to stab, pierce. See **Stucken**.

STICKINGS, *sb. pl., obsols.* pea-rods.—MUCH WENLOCK.

'1800. May 5. Paid John Wall for *Stickings*, &c. 0 - 2 - 3.'—*Parish Accounts*, Much Wenlock.

A.S. *sticca*, a stick, rod.

STILL ON, *conj.* nevertheless; notwithstanding. Qy. com. 'I toud 'em, an' toud 'em about latchin' that wicket, an' *still on* it's open every time I göö that way; but I'll püt the blacksmith's daughter [q. v.] to watch it.'

STINGE [stin·zh], *sb.* a grudge. — PULVERBATCH. 'I owed 'im a *stinge* sence 'arrŏost, an' I paid 'im afore Chris'mas.'

STINKING-COAL, *sb.* an inferior coal underlying the Penny stone. —COLLIERY; M. T.

'The *Stinking-coal* is noted for containing a great proportion of sulphuret of iron, thick seams or layers of these pyrites running in it. In consequence of this it cannot be used for smelting purposes.' —*Notes on the Shropshire Coal-Field*, by T. PARTON, F.G.S., 1868.

STINKING-ROGER, *sb. Ballota nigra*, black Horehound.—ELLESMERE.

STIRK [stur'·k], (1) *sb.* a yearling bullock.—BISHOP'S CASTLE.

'And should some Patron be so kind,
As bless you wi' a kirk,
I doubt na, Sir, but then we'll find,
Ye're still as great a *Stirk.*

. . . .

And when ye're number'd wi' the dead,
Below a grassy hillock,
Wi' justice they may mark your head—
"Here lies a famous *Bullock!*"'
ROBERT BURNS, *Poems*, p. 30, l. 35.

'*Juvencus*, styrc,' occurs in an *Anglo-Saxon Vocabulary*, xi. cent., in Wr. vocabs., vol. i. p. 78. Cf. **Steer** (1).

(2) *sb.* a two-year old heifer.—ELLESMERE.

'*Bucula, juvenca, vitula*, stirc,' is found in an *Anglo-Saxon Glossary*, x. cent., in Wr. vocabs., vol. ii. p. 126.

'*Styrk*, neet (or heefer, P.). *Juvenca*.'—*Prompt. Parv.*

Jamieson has '*Stirk, Sterk*, a bullock or heifer between one and two years old.' A.S. *styrc, stirc*, a young horned beast.

STIR-PUDDING, *sb.* a dish made by *stirring* flour into boiling milk, until it becomes a thick batter. It is eaten with treacle or sugar, and is sometimes served with a lump of butter upon it. Qy. com. A current proverbial saying—'to eat *stir-pudding* with an awl'—is applied to work attempted to be done with unsuitable tools; 'I mun gŏŏ an' fatch a spade, it's no use gweïn' ŏn ŏŏth this mattock, as good try "*to ate stir-puddin' ŏŏth an awl*."'

STITHY [stidh·i'], *sb.* a small anvil used by blacksmiths for fashioning nails upon.—SHREWSBURY; PULVERBATCH.

'As hit were dyntes of a *stithi*,
That smythes smyten in her smythi.'
Cursor Mundi, MS. Coll. Trin. Cantab. f. 138, l. 23238.

'. . . . . and the smyth
That forgeth scharpe swerdes on his *stith*.'
CHAUCER, *The Knightes Tale*, l. 1168.

Shakespeare uses *stithy* in the sense of a forge:—

'And my imaginations are as foul
As Vulcan's *stithy*.'—*Hamlet*, III. ii. 89.

Pegge has '*Stithy*, an anvil. York.'

'*Incus*, a smith's stiddie; *ab in et cudo*.'—DUNCAN'S *Appendix Etymologiæ*, A.D. 1595, E. D. S., B. xiii.

'*Stythe*, smythys instrument. *Incus*.'—*Prompt. Parv.*

'O.Icel. *steði*, stithy, *incus*.'—STRAT. See **Study**.

STIVED [stei·vd], *part. past*, stifled, as by a close oppressive atmosphere. Qy. com. *Stived* is generally used in combination with *up*. 'A good blow o' the 'ills does one some benefit after being *stived* up i the workshop so lung.'

Pegge has '*Stived*, almost suffocated. *Stived-up*, confined in a hot place. North.'

'O.Fr. *estivé*, loaden, or laden, as a ship.'—COTG.

STIVING, *part. adj.* stewing; stifling,—'sit *stivin'* i' the 'ouse.' Qy. com.

STIVY [stei·vi'], *adj.* close; hot,—''ow *stivy* this room is, open the window.' Qy. com.

STOCK [stok·], (1) *v. a.* to peck.—PULVERBATCH; CLEE HILLS. 'That savage owd 'en ŏŏl kill all these young ducks, 'er jest *stocks* 'em o' the back, an' they bin done.'

'O.Fr. *estoc, estoch*, espèce d'épée qui ne servait qu' à percer . . . de l'ahal, *stoch*, stoc, aujourdhui *stock*, ib., de *stican*, percer. De là *estocer, estochier*, frapper de l'estoc, frapper de pointe.'—BUR. See below.

(2) *v. a.* to stub up at the roots with a pointed implement,—'*stockin'* up gorst.' Com.

'The wild boar not only spoils her branches, but *stocks* up her roots.'—*Decay of Piety*.

STOCKER, *sb.* an implement used for '*stocking*' up turnips; it has two prongs and a handle four feet long.—CLEE HILLS; LUDLOW. Qy. com.

'Turnip *stocker*, &c.'—*Auctioneer's Catalogue* (Stoddesden), 1870.

STODGE [stoj·], (1) *sb.* a thick, soft mass, as of spoon-meat. Com. 'Yo' shoulden pŭt more suppin' or less bread, it's a complate *stodge*.'

(2) *v. a.* to cram; to fill to repletion,—'reg'larly *stodged*.' Com.

STODGE-FULL, *adj.* quite full; full to repletion,—''e's gotten 'is bally *stodge-full*, any-way.' Com.

STODGY, (1) *adj.* thick,—'dunna mak' the child's pap so *stodgy*.' Com.

(2) *adj.* stout; fed up.—PULVERBATCH. Qy. com. 'The Maister's gettin' quite *stodgy;* sence the lads bin growed up 'e saves 'imself a bit.'

STOKEN [stoa·kn], *adj.* stunted in growth; impoverished in condition: said of animals that have been badly fed and attended to,—'a 'ealthy young beäst, in no-ways *stoken*.'—WEM; ELLESMERE. Compare Germ. *stocken*, to stop, to stagnate. Cf. **Nuched**.

STOKES'S-BRIDGE, *sb.* a stopping-point,—'Ah! little Jack's come to *Stokes's-bridge*, I see,' *i. e.* has eaten as much as he can, and must leave what there is on the plate.—CLEE HILLS. Cf. **Staked** (1).

STOMACHFUL, (1) *adj.* high-spirited; plucky.—CLUN; WEM; ELLESMERE. ''Er's a *stomachful* little piece, 'er'll be a match fur 'im any day.'

'Disdayne he called was, and did disdayne
To be so cald, and who so did him call:
Sterne was his looke, and *full of stomache* vayne.'
SPENSER, *F. Q.*, Bk. II. c. vii. st. xli.

(2) *adj.* prone to take offence; resentful.—WORTHEN.

STOMBERED [stom·bur'd], *part. adj.* confused,—'I got *stombered* o'er it.'—COLLIERY.

STOMBERING, *part. adj.* walking in a heavy, stamping, stumbling way.—PULVERBATCH; WEM. 'Yo' gwun *stomberin'* alung like some foundered owd 'orse.' Cf. **Clontering**.

STOMBERS, *sb.*, *obsols.* a term expressive of great surprise.—PULVERBATCH. 'It gid me the *stombers* w'en 'e toud me.'

STOOK [stoo·k], *sb.* a cluster of standing sheaves, usually an even number, as six, eight, or ten.—WEM.

> 'Thus she stood amid the *stooks*,
> Praising God with sweetest looks.'
>
> THOMAS HOOD, *Ruth.*

Grose has '*Stooks.* A collection of sheaves of corn, being ten set up together, and covered by two. N.'

'Low.Du. *stuke*, stook, *strues.*'—STRAT.

Cf. **Stuck** (1), also **Mow** (1). See **Thrave.**

STOOP [stou·p *and* stoo·p], *v. a.* to tilt or incline a barrel so as to give a readier flow to its contents. Com. 'Dunna yo' *stoup* the barrel till I come an' 'elp yo', else we sha'n a the drink muddied.'

'*Stowpyn̄*. *Inclino.*'—*Prompt. Parv.*

'N. *stöypa*, to cast down; *stupa*, to fall. Sw. *stupa*, to incline, to lower, to fall. *Stupa en tunna*, to tilt a cask.'—WEDG.

STORM, *sb.*, *pec.* a hard frost.—WORTHEN, *Cherbury.* Cf. **Tempest.**

STORM-BIRDS, *sb. pl.* Seagulls, or other oceanic birds.—ELLESMERE.

STORMCOCK, (1) *sb.* the Fieldfare.—PULVERBATCH, *Hanwood.* Cf. **Snowbirds.** See **Fildefare, also Shredcock.**

(2) *sb.* the Green Woodpecker.—CLUN, *Twitchen.* See **Haihow.**

(3) *sb.* the Missel-thrush. — OSWESTRY. See **Thricecock,** also **Missel-bird.**

STOUK [stou·k], *sb.* a handle, as of any wooden or earthenware vessel.—PULVERBATCH; OSWESTRY. 'Whad, another jug crippled!—theer's one ŏŏth the nose off, an' another ŏŏth the *stouk* off—we shanna 'ăve a tidy jug lef', jest now.'

Grose has '*Stowk.* The handle of a pail. N.'

STOUL [stou·l], (1) *sb.* the stump of a copse or hedgewood tree cut down nearly to the ground, and occasionally springing forth anew. Com. 'Nobody ŏŏd think that Coppy wuz fell three 'ear agŏŏ, every *stoul* 's send up sich a lot o' sprouts, yo' canna 'ardly get through it.'

'"To go a stooling, signifies to be employed in woods, generally without the owner's leave, in cutting up such decayed *stools*, or stumps, or moots for fuel."—*MS. Devon. Gl.*,' in HAL.

'Lat. *stolo,-nis*, a shoot, sucker.'—WEDG.

(2) *v. n.* to ramify, as of young corn.—SHREWSBURY; ATCHAM; WELLINGTON; WEM; ELLESMERE. Qy. com. 'It inna begun to *stoul* yit, but gie it time an' it'll shak' 'onds': said of winter wheat looking very poor.

'I worked very hard in the copse of young ash . . . cutting out the saplings where they *stooled* too close together.'—R. D. BLACKMORE, *Lorna Doone*, A Romance of Exmoor, p. 230. ed. 1878.

Cf. **Gether.**

STRABERRY [str'ai·br'i'], *sb.*, *obsols.* a strawberry.—PULVERBATCH; BRIDGNORTH.

'The ȝyng greyn blomyt *straberry* levys amang.'
GAWIN DOUGLAS (A.D. 1513), *Prol. of the XII. Buk of Eneados. Specim. Eng. Lit.*, xiii. l. 120.

'*Hoc stragum, A*' strabery,' occurs in an *English Vocabulary*, xv. cent., in Wr. vocabs., vol. i. p. 192.

STRABERRY-WIRES, *sb. pl.*, *obsols.* strawberry-runners.—PULVERBATCH; BRIDGNORTH. 'Well, John, now 'arrŏost 's o'er, I 'ope yo'n get a bit o' time i' the garden—the *străb'ry-wires* bin all across the alley, somebody ŏŏl be breakin' thar neck some o' these days.' See **Wires.**

STRAFE [str'ai·f], (1) *sb.* a stray animal.—PULVERBATCH; CORVE DALE; CLEE HILLS; MUCH WENLOCK; WELLINGTON; OSWESTRY. 'Theer's a nice yerlin 'eifer i' the lane, as I spect's a *strafe;* pŭt 'er i' the croft, be'appen somebody ŏŏl own 'er jest now.'

'weyues and *streyues*.'—*Piers Pl.*, Prol. l. 94.

(2) *sb.* a worthless kind of fellow.—CORVE DALE; CLEE HILLS. 'Well, owd *strafe*, w'eer'st'ee bin?'—said to a man who had left his work without notice, and then returned to it.

STRAIGHT-GROWED, *adj.* well formed in figure,—'tall an' *straight-growed*.' Qy. com.

STRAKE, STROKE [str'ai·k], CRAVEN ARMS; CHURCH STRETTON. [str'oa·k], PULVERBATCH. [str'ok·], WEM; ELLESMERE, *sb.* a section of the iron band that encompasses the wheel of a cart or waggon; it is usually two feet in length, and about half the width of a large strong wheel: supposing therefore such a wheel to be three feet in circumference, it would require six *strakes* to go round about it.

'*Canthus*, the iron wherewith the cart wheel is bound, the *strake* of a cart.'—*Dict. Etym. Lat.*

'The *Stroke* is the Iron Rim about the Felloes.'—*Academy of Armory*, Bk. III. ch. iii. p. 332.

STRAMMEL. See **Scrammel.**

STRENTH [str'en·th], *sb.* a term used to denote working power in the number or capabilities of the labourers.—PULVERBATCH. Qy. com. 'I dunna know 'ow 'e manes to get 'is 'arrŏost in, w'y 'e's got no *strenth* about 'im—that owd mon aumust in 'is two-double, an' them two or three lads 'ill be now'eer.'

STRET [str'et·], *adj.* tight.—PULVERBATCH; ELLESMERE. 'Yo' mun pŭt that cheese-fillet on as *stret* as yo' can get it, else the cheese 'll bulge.'

'Streythe (streyt). *Artus*.'—*Prompt. Parv.* See **Stretten.**

STRET-STAFF [str'et· stu'f], same as **Sprăder**, q. v.—WEM.

'The *Strett Staffe* is the Staffe fixed between the Chains or Ropes to keep them from gauling the Horse sides.'—*Academy of Armory*, Bk. III. ch. viii. p. 339.

Stret-staff = *stretch-staff*, or else *strait-staff*. See **Stret**, above. Cf. **Stedstaff.**

STRETTEN [str'et·n], *v. a.* to tighten. — PULVERBATCH; WEM; ELLESMERE. 'The sackin' o' this bed wants *strett'nin'*, an' we mun *stretten* it afore it's made up.'

'*Streytyn'*, or make streyte. *Arto.*'—*Prompt. Parv.*

STRICKLE [str'ik·l], *sb., obs.* a wooden implement for striking off an even measure of corn.—PULVERBATCH.

'*Hoc osorium*, a strikylle,' occurs in a *Nominale*, xv. cent., in Wr. vocabs., vol. i. p. 233.

Mr. Wright explains it as 'A *strickle*, or piece of wood for levelling the corn in the measure.'

See **Swoggle**.

STRICKLESS [str'ik·li's], same as above.—CLEE HILLS.

'The *Strickles* is a thing that goes along with the Measure, which is a straight Board, with a Staff fixed in the side, to draw over Corn in measureing, that it exceed not the height of the Measure. Which measureing is termed Wood and Wood.'—*Academy of Armory*, Bk. III. ch. viii. p. 337. See below.

STRIKE [str'ei·k], (1) *v. a., obs.* to level the corn to the top of the measure with the '*strickless*.'—CLEE HILLS.

'"It's an ye wed the nut-brown girl,
I'll heap gold with my hand;
But an ye wed fair Annet,
I'll *strike* it with a wand."'
Lord Thomas and Fair Annet, in PERCY'S *Reliques*.

'A.Sax. *strican;* O.Du. *striken;* O.H.Germ. *strichen*, to strike, *stringere, radere, caedere.*'—STRAT.

See below; also **Strucken**.

(2) *sb.* a bushel measure; a bushel: so called, it would seem, from the usage of *striking* off the measure of corn evenly. Com.

'*The Corne. Imprimis*, twenty *strikes* of Rye, fowreteene & forty *strikes* more, two bushells of barly, twenty-six bushells of oates, Rye unthrasht, Rye upon the grownd, lj[li] ix[s] iiijd[d].'—*Inventory* . . . Owlbury Manor-House, Bishop's Castle, 1625.

'Wing, cartnaue and bushel, peck, *strike* readie hand.'—TUSSER, *Husbandlie furniture*, p. 35, ed. E. D. S.

'Some men and women, rich and nobly borne,
Gave all they had for one poore *strike* of corne.'
Taylor's Workes, 1630, i. 15, in HAL.

'A Measure, an Hoop, or a *Strick*, is 4 Pecks, or 9 Gallons. Yet some reckon but 8 gallons to the Measure, which in some places is also called a Bushel.'—*Academy of Armory*, Bk. III. ch. viii. p. 337.

See **Weights and Measures**, p. lxxxv.

(3) *v. a.* to move, as with a lever,—'w'y conna yo' *strike* it a bit?' —CLEE HILLS.

STRINE, *sb.* a water-channel. — WELLINGTON; NEWPORT. The *strines* on the Weald-moors receive all the smaller drains as tributaries.

STRIP, *v. a.* to draw the last milk from a cow.—CLUN. Cf. **Drip**, also **Stroke** (2), below.

STRIPPINGS, *sb.* the last milk drawn from the cow.—*Ibid.* Cf. **Drippings**, also **Strokings**, below.

STROKE, (1). See **Strake.**

(2) *obs.?* same as **Strip**, above. — PULVERBATCH. 'The Missis al'ays gwuz round ŏŏth the milk-bowl 'erself an' *strokes* the cows, an' if 'er gets it more than 'afe fŭll, yo'n be apt to 'ear on it.'

'Jone takes her neat rubb'd pail, and now
She trips to milk the sand-red Cow;
Where, for some sturdy foot-ball Swain,
Jone *strokes* a Sillibub or twaine.'

The Compleat Angler, ch. i. p. 35, ed. 1653.

Grose has '*Stroaking.* Milking after the calf has suckled. Exmoor.'

STROKINGS, *obs.?* same as **Strippings**, above.—*Ibid.*

'Afterings, the *Stroakings*, or last that is Milkt from a Cow.'—*Academy of Armory*, Bk. II. ch. ix. p. 173.

See **Afterings.**

STRONG [str'ung·], *adj., pec.* full; whole.—SHREWSBURY. (1) 'Joiner, this door isn't two inches thick, is it?' 'Well, Sir, it's a *strung* inch an' three-quarters.' (2) 'We'n ta'en a lodger, Ma'am, sence I sid yo' last, but I doubt we shanna mak' much out on 'im at ten shillin' a wik—'e'll sit down an' ate a *strung* 'our.'

STRUCKEN [str'uk·n], *part. past, obsols.* struck off: said of corn in the measure.—CLEE HILLS.

Milton employs the same participial form—'*strucken* mute'—in *Paradise Lost*, Book IX. l. 1064. See **Strike** (1).

STRUMPLE [str'um·pl], *sb., obs.?* the fleshy stump of a horse's tail left after 'docking.'—PULVERBATCH. Qy. com.

STUB [stub·], (1) *sb.* a stump, as of broom or gorse which has been cut down to within a few inches of the ground. Com. 'We'n gŏŏ as fare as the Brummy leasow, an' get a fyeow *stubs* awilde a bin dry.'

'ȝet þu singst worse þan þe heisugge
þat flihþ bi grunde a mong þe *stubbe*.'

Owl and Nightingale, l. 506.

'Then to the earth shee gott a thawacke;
no hurt in the world the pore man did meane;
to the ground hee cast the Ladye there;
on a *stubb* shee dang out one of her eyen.'

Marke more ffoole, l. 52. *Percy Folio MS.*, vol. iii. p. 129, ed. Hales and Furnivall.

'A.Sax. *stybb;* O.Icel. *stubbi;* stub, *stipes.*'—STRAT.

(2) *sb.* a worn-out nail drawn from a horse-shoe. Com.

STUCK (1), **STUCKLE** [stuk·, stuk·l], *sb.* a cluster of standing sheaves, usually six.—CRAVEN ARMS. See **Stook.**

STUCK (2), *pret.* stacked.—LUDLOW, *Burford.*

STUCKEN, *part. past*, stuck = stabbed = killed,—'the bŭtcher's *stŏocken* the pig.'—NEWPORT. It may be noted here *apropos* to killing pigs, that the process of 'dressing' them after they are slaughtered, varies in different parts of Salop; in the North—indeed throughout the greater part of the County—'they scauden 'em, an' 'angen 'em up by the 'eels,—back to the wall;' but in the East and South East, as about Bridgnorth and Cleobury Mortimer, 'they swingen 'em (by laying straw under them and setting it on fire), and then they 'angen 'em up by the nose,—bally to the wall.' See **Stick** (2).

STUDY, same as **Stithy**, q. v.—CLUN.

STUMP, *v. n.* to step heavily; to stamp,—''eart alive! 'ow that wench does *stump*.' Com.

STURLY [stur'li'], *adj.* stiff; standing up; staring: said of the hair or coat of an animal.—WEM. 'I spect that cow's ketcht a cooth, 'er coăt's all *sturly* like.'

SUBSIST, *sb.* part payment in advance for work.—PULVERBATCH, *Snailbeach*; M. T. See **Sist** (2).

SUCCAMORE [suk·u'moa·'h'r'], *sb.*, *var. pr.* *Acer pseudo-platanus*, the Sycamore.—SHREWSBURY; PULVERBATCH; CRAVEN ARMS. Qy. com.

SUCCOURFUL [suk·ur'ful], *adj.* yielding shelter.—PULVERBATCH; CHURCH STRETTON. A man who was advised to take up a hedge which occupied much ground, objected to do so, on the plea that it was 'mighty *succourful*' for the cattle lying out in the winter. Another man—a groom—riding through the Southern part of Shropshire, observed in reference to its undulating character, that it was 'a mighty *succourful* county.'

SUCK, *sb.*, *var. pr.* a wrought-iron ploughshare,—'a sock.' Com.

'The Sough or *Suck*, is that as Plows into the ground.'—*Academy of Armory*, Bk. III. ch. viii. p. 333.

'Drilled Prussia, compact, organic in every part from diligent plough-*sock* to shining bayonets.' — THOMAS CARLYLE, *History of Friedrich II. of Prussia*, vol. ii. p. 302, ed. 1869.

'Fr. *soc*, a ploughshare. O.Fr. *soc*, *sook*, soc: de *soccus*, ainsi nommé à cause de sa pointe recourbée comme celle d'un soulier.'—BUR.

SUCKERS, SUN-SUCKERS, *sb. pl.* the sun's rays as they sometimes appear in showery weather,—popularly believed to *suck* up the water from the earth into the sun, there to be converted into rain; and held to be a sign of coming showers.—PULVERBATCH; CHURCH STRETTON; WELLINGTON. 'We sha'n a more rain, the sun's got 'is *suckers* down.'

SUITY [soo·ti'], *adj.* even; regular.—WORTHEN; CLEE HILLS. 'The wĕăt dunna come up very *suity*, be'appen the sid wunna good.' Cf. **Shooty**.

SULLINGE [sul·inj], (1) *sb.*, *var. pr.* a syringe.—SHREWSBURY; PULVERBATCH.

(2) *v. a.* to syringe.—*Ibid.* ''Er's gweïn to the Doctor to get 'er ears *sullinged*.'

SUMMERED [sum·ur'd], (1) *part. adj.* well fed at grass.—PULVERBATCH; WEM; ELLESMERE. 'That 'eifer looks fresh, I spect 'er's bin *summered* pretty well.'

(2) *part. adj.* beer is said to be *summered*, when, from having been over-hot during the process of fermentation, it has acquired a peculiar singed taste.—PULVERBATCH; WEM. 'This drink's *summered*, Missis, I spect yo'n pŭt it together too 'ot.' *Summered* is to beer what '*mow-burnt*' is to hay.

SUMP, *sb.* a hole at the bottom of the pit-shaft, to receive the waste water of the workings. Com. M. T.

SUN-SPECKLES, *sb. pl.* freckles.—SHREWSBURY. See **Fan-peckles.**

SUN-SUCKERS. See **Suckers**.

SUP (1), *v. a.* to drink, as it were at a draught,—'mak' 'aste an' *sup* that up.'—SHREWSBURY; NEWPORT. Qy. com.

> '3 pottles of wine in a dishe
> they *supped* itt all off, as I wis,
> all there att their partinge.'
>
> *John de Reeue*, l. 627. *Percy Folio MS.*; vol. ii. p. 583, ed. Hales and Furnivall.

'*Suppynge* al vp, or al owte. *Absorbicio*.'—*Prompt. Parv.* A.S. *súpan*, to drink, to drink to excess.

(2) *sb.* a drink, enough for one draught.—*Ibid.*

(3) *v. a.* to feed animals at night.—LUDLOW, *Burford.*

> '*Lord.* Huntsman, I charge thee, tender well my hounds.
> . . . .
> . . . .
> But *sup* them well, and look unto them all:
> To-morrow I intend to hunt again.'
>
> *Taming of the Shrew*, Induction, i. 29.

See **Sup-up**, below.

SUPPING, *sb.* spoon-meat of any kind, but more especially milk and water boiled and thickened with oatmeal. Com. 'Maister, our new cowman's a rar' cratcher, whad'n'ee think 'e pŭt out o' sight this mornin'?—first 'e ete a cantle o' *suppin'*, then a 'eeler o' bread an' cheese, an' after that a apple-fŭt, rump an' stump!'

Grose gives '*Suppings*. Broth, &c. Spoon-meat. N.'

Calves' *supping* is food that they can *suck up*, made with linseed, either crushed or whole (instead of oatmeal), in milk and water or such like. A.S. *súpan*, to sup, suck up.

SUPPLE. See **Soople**.

SUPPOSE, *v. n.*, *pec.* to know with certainty. Com. 'I *suppose* the days ŏŏnna be much lunger now, we bin clos' on Midsummer, an' it's as coud as March:'—said June 20th, 1880.

SUP-UP, *v. a.* to feed and 'bed-down' animals about eight o'clock at night.—NEWPORT; WEM; ELLESMERE. Cf. **Sup** (3), above; also **Fother** (2).

SURREY [su·r'i'], *sb.*, *var. pr.* Sirrah. Com. A title of address sometimes enlarged into '*Surrey lad.*'

SWAG [swag·], (1) *v. a.* to sway, as of a heavy load of hay, &c., badly put on the waggon.—PULVERBATCH. 'See, Surrey, 'ow that löäd *swags*, it ŏŏnna oud wham, an' we sha'n lose our 'arrŏost go'se.'

'O.Icel. *sveigja*, to sway, bend.'—STRAT.

See Bk. II., *Folklore*, &c., 'Customs' (*harvest*).

(2) *v. a.* to incline heavily to one side.—*Ibid.* 'This basket's a despert 'eft to lug all the way to Dorri'ton, it farly *swags* me down.'

(3) *sb.* the inclination given to one side by a heavy weight.—*Ibid.* 'I like the owd Missis to sarve me, 'er gies a good *swag* to the scales, but as to owd Snipe, 'e canna find in 'is 'eart to gie the right weight.'

SWAGE [swai·j], (1) *v. a.* to reduce, as of a swelling or tumour, by external applications.—PULVERBATCH. 'Yedart's ancler wuz swelled oncommon bad, but I pŭt some pultis to it, an' it *swaged* it away.'

'This sely man contynued his outrage,
Til alle his goode was wasted and gone;
And they felt his expenses *swage*,
And were to hym vnkynde right anone.'

THOMAS OCCLEVE (A.D. 1420, *circa*), *De Regimine Principum*. *Specim. Eng. Lit.*, II. 601.

'*Swagynge*, or secynge. *Laxacio.*'—*Prompt. Parv.*

'O.Fr. *assouager*, adoucir, apaiser.'—BUR. Cf. **Sway** (1).

(2) *v. a.* to disperse, as of milk in the mammæ.—*Ibid.* 'Rub the elder well ŏŏth gŏoze-ile to *swage* the milk away.' Cf. **Sway** (2).

SWANKY [swaang·ki'], *sb.*, *sl.*? very weak small-beer. Qy. com.

SWAPSON [swop·sn], *sb.* a big, coarse woman. Com.

SWAR [swaar'·], *v. n.* to swear. Com. 'That's a nīnted young pippin—nod seven yer owd, an' 'e'll *swar* like a trooper.'

'And the seyd Fastolf, mevyd and passyoned gretely in his soule, seyd and *swar* . . .'—*Paston Letters*, A.D. 1468, vol. ii. p. 324.

SWARM [swaar'·m], *v. a.* and *v. n.*, *pec.* to climb a tree or pole by embracing it with the arms and legs. Com. 'Theer wuz no Sosebry Show this 'ear [1880], but they gotten up some bit of a sham fur pass-time in a fīld—pŭtten lads to *swarm* grăcy poles, run races, an' some gammocks to tice a lot o' folks to the Public.'

'"I know of a carrion crow's nest in the wood at Middleton, but it is up a tall fir tree, without any branches for a long way, and my arms are not long enough to clasp around the trunk and *swarm* up."'—G. CHRISTOPHER DAVIES, *Rambles and Adventures of Our School Field-Club*, p. 29, ed. 1875.

'He *swarmed* up into a tree,
Whyle eyther of them might other se.'

Syr Isenbras, 351, in HAL.

SWAT [swat·], (1) *sb.* sweat. Com. 'I carried three 'oops o' corn to 'Abberley mill, but it gid me a *swat*; I wuz 'bliged to bring the flour back, but I lef' the bran fur John to bring at night.' A.S. *swát*, sweat. Cf. **Swelter** (2).

(2) *pret.* sweated,—''e *swat* o'er that job.' Com.

> 'His faire steede in his prikinge
> So *swatte* that men myghte him wringe.'
> CHAUCER, B. 1966 (Six-text ed.), Skeat.

> '. . . . . . yet did he labour long,
> And *swat*, and chauf'd . . . . . .'
> SPENSER, *F. Q.*, Bk. V. c. ii. st. xlvi.

> 'Some, lucky, find a flow'ry spot,
> For which they never toil'd nor *swat*.'
> ROBERT BURNS, *Poems*, p. 35, l. 26.

A.S. *swǽtan*, from *swát*, sweat.

SWATH [swath·], *sb.* the row of grass as it falls beneath the scythe. Com.

> 'With tossing and raking and setting on cox.
> Grasse latelie in *swathes* is hay for an ox.'
> TUSSER, *Fiue Hundred Pointes of Good Husbandrie* [July].

'The *swathe* or strake of grasse, as it lyeth mowne downe with the sithe.'—*Nomenclator.*

'*Swathe*, of mowynge. *Falcidium.*'—*Prompt. Parv.*

'A.Sax. *swaðu;* O.Du. *swade*, swath, *striga.*'—STRAT.

See **Weights and Measures**, p. xciii.

SWAY [swai· *and* swee·], (1) same as **Swage** (1).—WEM; WHITCHURCH; ELLESMERE. 'Yo' maun try an' *swee* away that swellin' o' the cow's side wuth butter-milk an' gŏŏze-ile.' Cf. **Sween.**

(2) same as **Swage** (2).

SWAY-POLE [swai·], same as **Gay-pole**, q. v.—WORTHEN.

SWAYL-POLE [sweil· *corr.* swaayl· pul], *Idem.*—PULVERBATCH. 'I should think that wench is one o' the onaccountables—wha'n'ee think 'er's done?' 'I dunna know.' 'W'y pŭt gorst o' the fire, an' burnt the *swayl-pul* down, an' theer's the cauves' suppin' all o'er the brew-'us.'

SWEDLESS [swed·lis], *sb.* an infant's swaddling-band.—SHREWSBURY; PULVERBATCH; CHURCH STRETTON; ELLESMERE. 'Hanna yo' lef' off the child's *swedless* yit?' 'No, I never lave 'em off tell they tak'n thar fit, 'cause it strenthens thar back.' A.S. *sweðel*, *sweðil.*—*Idem.*

SWEEN, same as **Sway**, above.—NEWPORT.

SWEEPS, SWEEPS'-BRUSHES, *sb. Luzula campestris*, Field Wood-rush.—SHREWSBURY, *Uffington.*

SWEETING [sweet·in], *adj.* a term equivalent to willing, as applied to doing work.—WEM; ELLESMERE. 'That's as *sweetin'* lickle cowt as ever wuz pŭt in skin,' said a Welshampton man of a horse—'comin' three'—that was drawing the harrows.

SWELTER [swel·tur'], (1) *v. a.* and *v. n.* to oppress with heat, by any means; to be made excessively hot. Com. 'It's time to lave off that flannen swedless, it'll *swelter* the poor child sadly.'

'If the Suns excessive heat
Makes our bodies *swelter*,
To an Osier hedge we get
For a friendly shelter.'
The Compleat Angler, ch. xi. p. 211, ed. 1653.

Compare 'Swalteryn' for hete . . . *Exalo, sincopizo.*'—*Prompt. Parv.* A.S. *swélan*, to burn.

(2) *sb.* a state of excessive heat. Com. 'I churned three 'ours an' a 'afe this mornin', an' it pŭt me in a fine *swelter* I can tell yo'.'

'*Æstus, vel cauma*, swoloð,' is found in the *Supplement to Ælfric's Vocabulary*, x. or xi. cent., in Wr. vocabs., vol. i. p. 53. 'Hence,' says Mr. Wright, 'our modern word *swelter*.' Cf. **Bucking** (1).

SWELTRY, *adj.* very hot and close; sultry,—'we sha'n be 'ăvin' thunder I spect, it's despert *sweltry*.'

'But as we see the sunne oft times, through over *sweltrie* heate,
Changing the weather faire, great stormes and thundercraks doth threat.'—*Honours Academie*, 1610, i. 18, in HAL.

SWERD [swur'd·], (1) *sb.* a sword.—PULVERBATCH.

'In his hond is *swerd* ut-drawe.'
Havelok the Dane, l. 1802.

'Well, fetche me a *swerd* sayed he . . . Fetche me a *swerde* and deuyde the chyld betwene them.'—LATIMER, *Sermon* ii. p. 71.

'*Swerde, Gladius.*'—*Prompt. Parv.* A.S. *sweord, swurd*, a sword.

(2) *sb.* an upright bar having holes for a pin, affixed to the 'cross-tree' of a cart, by means of which the cart is set to any pitch when tilted.—CLEE HILLS.

(3) *sb.* turf; greensward,—'flay off the *swerd*.'—PULVERBATCH.
'*Swarde* of þe erþe.'—*Prompt. Parv.*
A.S. *sweard*, the surface of grass.

(4) *sb.* the rind of bacon.—PULVERBATCH. 'They bin very good to me, Ma'am,' said Betty Diggory [1856], 'they săven all the *swerds* o' bacon fur me.' 'What can you do with them, Betty?' 'Well, Ma'am, I pŭt 'em to soak, an' wesh 'em, an' 'ack 'em up, an' pŭt 'em to stew ŏŏth tuthree yarbs, awilde I gŏŏ to Church, an' a mighty nice Sunday's dinner they maken me.'

'*Swarde* or sworde of flesche. *Coriana.*'—*Prompt. Parv.*
A.S. *sweard*, the skin of bacon. See **Sword**.

SWIFTS [swif·ts], *sb.*, *obs.* a machine for holding skeins of yarn for the purpose of winding them. Qy. com. The form of the *swifts* was that of an upright gallows-shaped frame, standing about five feet from the ground, and having two reels, one at the top and the other at the bottom: these reels—for the sake of lightness—were made of spokes inserted into circular ends, they rotated upon long iron spindles, which could be withdrawn to admit of them being taken out of the frame for the yarn to be put on them. At the base of the machine was a box for holding the balls when wound. *Swifts* superseded 'yarewinds,' and in taking their place, received their name in a translated form, '*yare*,' quick, becoming *swift*. Cf. **Yarewinds.**

SWIG, *sb.* spiced ale and toast. Com. This popular Shropshire supper-dish is prepared on this wise—though perhaps with variations—a slice of 'red hot' toast is put into the *swig*-bowl, ginger and nutmeg are grated over it, sugar is added, and the bowl is filled up with cold ale. The toast—served on plates—is eaten with toasted cheese, a dish of which always accompanies the *swig*-bowl. The bowl is passed round, and each draught of ale is called a *swig*.

SWIG-BOWL, *sb.* the large bowl—like a punch-bowl—in which *swig* is served. Com.

SWILKER [swil·kur'], *v. a.* to splash about; to dash over, as of any liquid carried in an open vessel. Com. 'The wench has *swilkered* nearly all the milk out'n the pail.'

SWILL, (1) *v. a.* to wash hastily; to rinse. Com. 'Jest *swill* the men's bottles out, they wun all well scauded isterd'y.'

'Ful wel kan ich dishes *swilen*.'

Havelok the Dane, l. 919.

'Then Sir Tristeram tooke powder forth of that box,
& blent it with warme sweet milke;
& there put it vnto that horne,
& *swilled* * it about in that ilke.'

King Arthur and the King of Cornwall, l. 278. *Percy Folio MS.*, vol. i. p. 73, ed. Hales and Furnivall.

* 'i. e. rinsed it, washed it.'—*Verbum Salopiense.* Note by Bp. Percy.—*Ibid.*

'I *swyll*, I rynce or clense any maner vessell.'—Palsgrave, in Hal.
A.S. *swilian*, to wash.

(2) *v. a.* to wash by throwing an abundance of water over and about, as of a floor,—'get plenty o' waiter now, an' *swill* the causey down.'

'As fearfully as doth a galled rock
O'erhang and jutty his confounded base
Swill'd with the wild and wasteful ocean.'

K. Henry V., III. i. 14.

(3) *sb.* a thorough cleansing effected by a plentiful application of water dashed about. Com. 'Theer's so much knee-work now-a-days, w'en a scrub ŏŏth a besom an' a good *swill* ŏŏd do as well, an' be far more 'ōlesome.'

(4) *v. a.* to drink; to wash down by drinking,—''ere, ate this, an' yo' sha'n a summat to *swill* it down.' Com.

'The wretched, bloody, and usurping boar,
. . . .
Swills your warm blood like wash, and makes his trough
In your embowell'd bosoms.'—*K. Richard III.*, V. ii. 9.

(5) *sb.* sloppy pig-meat, as of scullery garbage. Com. 'Dunna gie the pig so much *swill*, let 'im a some good mate to stodge 'im up,

else we sha'n miss 'ăvin' 'im i' the 'ouse by Chris'mas.' Tusser says:—

'Remember good Gill,
Take paine with thy *swill.*'
Huswiferie, p. 171, ed. E. D. S.

'*Bróda*, wash, swile, or draffe for swine.'—*Florio*, p. 68, in HAL. Cf. **Wesh** (2).

SWILL-TUB, *sb.* a tub in which *swill* is kept. Com.

SWINGE [swinj·], *v. a.* to singe. Com. 'Mind yo' dunna *swinge* that shirt-front, the irons bin very sharp.'

'The scorching flame sore *swinged* all his face.'
SPENSER, *F. Q.*, Bk. I. c. xi. st. xxvi.

SWINGING [swinj·in], *adj.*, *obsols.* rapid; violent, in regard of motion,—'the men comen alung at a *swingin'* rate.'—PULVERBATCH. A.S. *swingan*; to swing.

SWINGLE [swing·l], (1) *sb.*, *obs.* a wooden, sword-shaped implement used to beat off the exterior coat from the fibre of hemp or flax after it had been 'tewtered.'—PULVERBATCH. Qy. com. Walter de Biblesworth—xiii. cent.—in his instructions to 'dame Muriel' upon hemp-dressing says:—

'Ne ublet pas le pesselin,
De escucher ou estonger vostre lyn.'

The interlinear glosses which are given, show the meaning to be [do not forget] 'the *swingle*,' 'to *swingle* thi flax.' See Wr. vocabs., vol. i. p. 156.

Randle Holme has, 'A *Swingle Hand*, corruptly a *Swingow Hond*: a thing like a Wooden Fauchion with a square hole or handle.'—*Academy of Armory*, Bk. III. ch. iii. p. 106.

Jamieson gives '*Swingle-wand*, the instrument with which flax is *swingled*.'

'*Swengyl*, for flax or hempe. *Excudium*.'—*Prompt. Parv.*

'A.S. *swingla* (*flagellum*), a swingle.'—STRAT.

See **Tewter**, also **Hetchel**.

(2) *v. n.* and *sb.* to swing; a swing. Com. 'Mother, may me an' Sally gŏŏ an' *swingle*?' 'W'eer?' 'I' the orchut—Ben's pŭt us a *swingle* theer.' 'Well, if yo'n mind an' nod peck out on it, yo' may gŏŏ.' A.S. *swingan*, to vibrate, swing.

(3) *sb.* a handful of gleaned corn.—CORVE DALE.

Bailey—ed. 1782—gives '*Songle*' with the same meaning, as a *Hertfordshire* word. Jamieson has '*Single*' in the like sense.

'Du. *sangh*, *sanghe*, fasciçulus spicarum.'—Kilian, in WEDG.

See **Songow**.

(4) same as **Swingle-trees**, below.—CLEE HILLS; LUDLOW.

'Bend and traces, and 2 *swingles*.'—*Auctioneer's Catalogue* (Stoddesden), 1870.

SWINGLE-TREES, *sb.* the three bars of wood, which—united and swinging together—go behind the horse and connect him with the implement he is drawing—they correspond with the 'splinter-bars' of a carriage.—SHREWSBURY; PULVERBATCH; BRIDGNORTH; NEWPORT; WHITCHURCH. Qy. com.

Pegge has '*Swingle-tree*, crooked pieces of wood, put to the traces of ploughs, &c. to keep them open. North.'

A.S. *swingan;* to swing, and *tree* = a bar of wood. Cf. **Tawtrees**.

SWINNEY [swin·i'], *adj.* dizzy. — PULVERBATCH. ''Ow bin'ee, Matty?' 'I'm right middlin', I'd sich a *swinney* feelin' i' my yed this mornin', I'd like to a fell throm the top o' the stars to the bottom.' Compare A.S. *swindan;* to languish.

SWIPPLE [swip·l], *sb.* the upper part of a flail—explained by a certain man to be 'the part as puns.'—PULVERBATCH. Qy. com.

Amongst 'The parts of a Flail or Threshal' given by Randle Holme is, 'The *Swiple*, that part as striketh out the Corn.'—*Academy of Armory*, Bk. III. ch. viii. p. 333.

Compare A.S. *swipe*, a whip; John ii. 15. See **Thrashal**.

SWISH-SWASH [swish·swash], *adv.* shaking from side to side, as of liquid in a state of agitation.—PULVERBATCH. 'Dunna gie the mar' too much waiter—'er'll gŏŏ alung *swish-swash* like buttermilk in a churn.'

SWITE [swei·t], *v. a.* to cut,—a term more especially applied to sticks.—PULVERBATCH; WEM; WHITCHURCH. In a murder case tried in Shrewsbury—March 13th, 1813—it was given in evidence against the prisoner, Rowland Preston, that he had been seen '*switing* a stick,' which stick was found on the scene of the murder, and was the convicting proof. The Judge who heard the case asked what was meant by '*switing* a stick?' and was told that it was 'cutting or shaving it.' (R—— P—— was executed on the Monday next following his trial.) *Swite* is a corruption of *thwite*, to whittle a stick, given by Palsgrave.

SWIVE [swei·v], *v. a., obsols.* to cut grain with a broad hook.—WELLINGTON. Cf. **Badge** (1). See **Swiving-hook**, below.

SWIVERS, *sb. pl., obsols.* reapers who '*swive*' the grain.—*Ibid.* The *modus operandi* of the *swivers* is to make a hit at the crop, and so keep cutting in a half circle, gathering the corn as it falls under the hook with foot and knee until they have enough to form a sheaf. They leave a much shorter stubble than the 'shearers' who reaped with a sickle. The *swivers*, who are for the most part Welshmen, go—at harvest-time—in gangs to the farm-houses to be hired for reaping. Cf. **Shearers**.

SWIVING-HOOK, *sb., obsols.* a broad reaping-hook having a smooth, keen edge, and in this respect differing from the 'shearer's' sickle, which was serrated; also it bears about the same proportion to that implement that a salmon-rod does to a light fly-rod. See **Shearers**. Cf. **Badging-hook**.

SWIZE [swei·z], *v. a.* to lift up and shake for the purpose of clearing,—a term applied to 'twins' [implements].—CLEE HILLS. 'Them twins cloggen.' 'Aye, they wanten somebody be'ind 'em to *swize* 'em up a bit.' See **Twins**.

SWOGGLE, same as **Strickle**, q. v.—BISHOP'S CASTLE.

SWORD [soa·ur'd], same as **Swerd** (4), q. v. — SHREWSBURY; NEWPORT. Qy. com.

> 'Or once a weeke perhaps, for novelty,
> Reez'd bacon *soords* shall feast his family.'
> HALL'S *Satires*, b. ii. Sat. 4, l. 15.

Mr. Nares has 'Sward. Skin . . . often corrupted to *sword* as when applied to the skin of bacon.'

SYMON [sei·mun], *sb.* a sort of red shale, same as **Calaminca**, q. v.—COLLIERY; M. T.

SYMONY GROUND, *phr.* 'faulty' ground or barren measures.—COLLIERY; M. T. A remarkable 'fault' known as the '*Great Symon* fault' traverses the coal-field.

SYNNABLE [sin·u'bl], *sb.*, *var. pr.* a syllable. — SHREWSBURY; PULVERBATCH. Qy. com. 'Yo' ŏŏnna let on to the Missis as I toud yo.' 'No danger! nod a *synnable*.'

TABOR [tab·ur'], (1) *v. n.* to tap lightly and repeatedly at intervals, as with the finger-ends; to drum.—WORTHEN. 'Theer's some one *taborin'* at the brew-'us window; yo'd'n better see who it is—be-'appen it's one o' the chaps after Sally.'

'. . . . and her maids shall lead her, ... *tabering* upon their breasts.'—Nahum ii. 7.

'*Tabowry(n). Timpaniso.*'—*Prompt. Parv.*

'O.Fr. *taborer*, tambourner.'—BUR.

(2) *v. n.*, *obsols.*? to beat time with fingers and feet in dancing country dances—somewhat after the manner of the sailor's hornpipe.—PULVERBATCH. 'Did'n'ee 'ăve a daince at the Club, Sally?' 'No, nod o' the Green, the fine folks wun saunterin' alung, clippin' one another like a bar 'uggin' a dog,—I dunna call it daincin',—so two or three on our chaps tooken the room at Clar's, an' then we coulden *tabor* away theer.'

A certain man, who had obtained local celebrity as a dancer in a 'country-footing,' was known as 'Jack the *Taborer*.'

> 'I can noither *tabre* ne trompe,' is said by a strolling minstrel.
> *Piers Pl.*, Text B., pass. xiii. l. 230.

(3) *v. a.* to beat; to thrash,—''E'll *tabor* 'is jacket fur 'im right well, if 'e ketches 'im.'—CRAVEN ARMS.

TACK [tak·], (1) *sb.* a smack; a peculiar flavour—an unpleasant taste is usually understood by the term. Com. 'The beer 'as a bit of a *tack* on it yet—I wish yo'd'n never bought that barrel, I've 'ad more trouble ŏŏth it than it's wuth; the cowper's fired it an' every-thin' to mak' it sweet.'

'He told me that three-score pound of cherries was but a kinde of washing meate, and that there was no *tacke* in them, for hee had tride it at one time.'—*Taylor's Workes*, 1630, i. 145, in HAL.

(2) *sb.* stuff of inferior quality.—SHREWSBURY; PULVERBATCH.

Qy. com. '’Ow dun yore tatoes turn out this time, John?' 'Mighty middlin', theer inna many, an' whad theer is bin poor *tack*.'

(3) *sb.* pasturage hired for temporary use; 'ley.' Qy. com. 'Yo'n got a power o' stock fur yore farm, Maister.' 'Aye, I mus' get some out on *tack*.'

Jamieson has '*Tack*, possession for a time.'

(4) *v. a.* to take animals for pasturage, on hire.—CLUN. Qy. com. 'Gran'mother, Mary Cadwallader 'as sent half-a-crown for *tackin'* the donkey, an' wants to know if you'll *tack* 'im a week or nine days longer.' See **Tak.**

TACKS, *sb. pl.* the tools or implements of trade of rat-catchers and other folk of similar *métier*.—WELLINGTON. 'My *tacks* bin at Newport, or I'd soon ketch them rots.'

W. *taclau*, implements.

TACK-WORK, *sb.* work done by contract, and paid for as per rood or acre, &c. Qy. com. 'I spect Tummas 'as a pretty good plack theer, hanna-d-'e?' 'Well, 'e's on'y nine shillin' a wik, reg'lar wages, but the Maister 'e lets 'im 'ăve a bit o' *tack-work* sometimes.'

Cf. '*Tack*, a lease,' in JAMIESON.

TADDLE [tad·l], *v. a.* and *v. n.* to pay minute attention to; to be very tender with; to feed carefully, as of a sick person or delicate young animal.—WELLINGTON; WHITCHURCH. 'After the Doctor 'ad left 'er, I *taddled* wi' 'er, an' gi'ed 'er some crame an' waiter.' Cf. **Tiddle.**

TAE [tai·], *v. a.* to take. — PULVERBATCH, *Snailbeach (Mines)*; COLLIERY; NEWPORT. 'Tell Sal to *tae* some bread an' cheese to the owd mon.'

> 'Till him he ȝeid, his knyff to tak him fra,
> Fast by the collar wallace couth him *ta*.'
>
> HENRY THE MINSTREL (A.D. 1461, *circa*), *Wallace*, Bk. I. *Specim. Eng. Lit.*, vi. l. 222.

See **A** (6) in **Grammar Outlines** (*vowels*, &c.). Cf. **Tak**, also **Tek.** See below.

TAEN, TA'EN [tai·n], *part. past*, taken,—'They'n *taen* that cowt out o' the leasow, I see.' Qy. com.

> 'So fareth loue, when he hath *tane* a sourse.'
>
> SIR THOMAS WIAT (A.D. 1540, *circa*), *Songes and Sonettes. Specim. Eng. Lit.*, xx. *h*, l. 6.

> 'Mair *taen* I'm wi' you.'
>
> ROBERT BURNS, *Poems*, p. 34, l. 12.

> 'When we have *ta'en* the grace-drink at the well,
> I'll whistle syne, and sing t'ye like mysell.'
>
> ALLAN RAMSAY, *The Gentle Shepherd*, I. i. p. 12.

Mr. Oliphant, speaking of the *Northumbrian Psalter*, A.D. 1250, *circa* (Surtees Society), says, 'In Vol. I. p. 243 we see, "when time *tane* haf I;" the first instance of *taken* being cut down to *tane*—a sure mark of the North.'—*Sources of Standard English*, p. 153.

TAG [tag·], *sb.* the twisted and pointed end of a lock of wool, as it is shorn from the fleece.—PULVERBATCH. Qy. com. 'Dunna gŏŏ so avenless about that ŏŏl, snip the end off the *tag*, an' toze it well as the grace can get among it.' The '*grace*' thus alluded to was the goose-oil which was commonly employed to soften the wool, and so fit it for the future processes of carding, &c.

'Sw. *tagg*, a point.'—WEDG. See **Toze** (1).

TAIL-ENDS, TAILINGS, *sb. pl.* the light, lean grains which fall out of the tail-end of the winnowing-machine, and are made serviceable in the poultry-yard. Com. 'Jim, bring the blind-sieve full o' *tail-ends* fur the fowls.'

Grose gives '*Tail-ends*. The refuse of wheat or other corn not saleable in the market, but kept by farmers for their own consumption. Glouc.'

See *Tail-corn* in HAL. Cf. **Oazes.**

TAILOR'S-YARD, *sb.* the three stars in the belt of Orion.—PULVERBATCH; WORTHEN; WEM; ELLESMERE.

TAILS, *sb. pl.* the plough-handles indifferently, without distinction of right or left.—CRAVEN ARMS.

Randle Holme has 'Plow *tails* or Stilts.'—*Academy of Armory*, Bk. III. ch. viii. p. 333.

See **By-tail** and **Master-tail.**

TAK [tak·], *v. a.* to take,—'Tell John to *tak* the bottle to the fild.' Com.

> 'Yet of the wyse man *tak* this sentence.'
>
> CHAUCER, B. 117 (Six-text ed.), Skeat.

> '*Pat.* But first we'll *tak* a turn up to the height,
> And see gif all our flocks be feeding right.'
>
> ALLAN RAMSAY, *The Gentle Shepherd*, I. ii. p. 12.

'Icel. *taka;* Goth. *tekan;* to take.'—STRAT.

Cf. **Tek,** also **Tae.**

TAK-AWAY, *sb.* appetite. Qy. com. 'That chap's a rar' *tak-away*, 'e ete two cantle o' suppin' fur 'is supper, an' a great lownder o' bread an' cheese.'

TAKE [tai·k *and* tak·], in combination with adverbs and prepositions, as follows. Com.

(*a*) *To take after*, to resemble in disposition. 'The child's very like 'is poor Faither in faichur, an' I 'ope 'e'll *take after* 'im, an' be as good a man, but I'm afeard 'is Mother spiles 'im.' Cf. **Favour,** also **Feature.**

(*b*) 1. *To take off*, to mimic. 'Our Jack ŏŏl *take* 'im *off* to a nicety, yo'd'n think 'twuz 'im 'isself—'e's a perty good mimic, 'e'll *take off* anybody.'

2. To depart hurriedly: usually employed in the past tense. 'The lads wun makin' a pretty riot o' Sunday night, but as soon as the Bobby shewned up yo' shoulden a sin 'ow they *tooken off*.'

(*c*) *To take on*. See **On** (3) (*f*).

(*d*) 1. *To take to*, to enter upon; to take possession of. ''E'll *tak' to* the farm at Lady Day.'

2. To adopt: said of persons or animals. (1) 'The childern bin better off than w'en they 'ad'n thar Faither; the Uncles comen forrat like men; Uncle Ben said 'e'd *take to* one, an' then the three others *tooken to* the rest—one apiece, so they bin all shooted.' (2) 'We bin likely to 'ave a lot o' cades this time—three yeows han died throm thar lambs, an' two more as 'ad'n double-couples ŏŏdna *tak' to* the secunt lamb.'

3. To become accustomed to, or attached to. 'It inna every child yo' can *take to*, but I wuz despert fond o' that little girld, an' 'er wuz mighty fond o' me.'

To be taken to, is to be surprised or astonished. (1) 'I *was taken to*, I can tell yo', w'en the Missis said so.' (2) 'I never *wuz* so *took to* in all my life w'en I 'eärd they wun gwun clane away.'

(*e*) 1. *To take up*, to answer shortly and hastily. 'Well, yo' nee'na *tak'* one *up* so sharp, jest gi'e a body time to spake.'

2. To put right; to correct. 'Yo' touden the paas'n wrang, Molly—but I didna like to *tak* yo' *up* afore 'im—it wuz Sund'y se'n-night as yo' wun at Church, nod las' Sund'y as ever wuz.'

TAKING [tai·kin *and* tak·in], *sb.* a sudden seizure of pain at the bone,—chiefly in the joints,—often ending in diseased bone or stiff joints.—PULVERBATCH; WEM. Qy. com. 'Poor Dick 'as bin lame a lungful wilde; did 'e 'urt 'is leg?' 'No, it come on itself—a *takin'* at the bwun.'

'Bless thee from whirlwinds, star-blasting, and *taking!*'—*K. Lear*, III. iv. 61.

'. . . Strike her young bones,
You *taking* airs, with lameness!'—*Ibid.* II. iv. 166.

TALE [tai·l], *v. a., obsols.* to count.—PULVERBATCH. 'I *tale* them ship to forty—'ow many bin a?' said a toll-man to a drover.

A.S. *talian*, to reckon, compute.

TALKING TO MOMMETS, *phr., obs.* self-communing in low-toned speech.—PULVERBATCH. 'Whad's the Church-bell gweïn fur?' 'A Vestry-meetin'; theer's a batch o' parish prentices to be lotted.' 'I thought theer wuz summat gweïn on; I sid owd Mister Ambler stan'in' i' the lane *talkin' to 'is mommets.*'

Mr. James Ambler was a man whose opinion was much respected, but he seldom gave it without taking counsel with himself, and was noted for '*talkin' to 'is mommets.*' He died May 1808.

The term *mommet*, thus employed, would seem to have retained some lingering sense of the O.E. *maumet*, an idol to which prayer would be addressed:—

'Do a-wei þi *Maumetes* · þei han trayed þe ofte.'
Joseph of Arimathie, l. 102.

See **Mommet** (1).

TALLANT, TALLAT [tal·unt], SHREWSBURY; PULVERBATCH; MUCH WENLOCK; WELLINGTON; WEM; OSWESTRY. Qy. com. [tal·u't],

PULVERBATCH; CRAVEN ARMS; LUDLOW, *sb.* a hay-loft. 'That bit o' clover can gŏŏ o' the *tallat*, it inna wuth măkin' a stack on.'

'You remember how you used to love hunting for eggs in the morning, and hiding up in the *tallat* with Lizzie, for me to seek you among the hay, when the sun was down.'—R. D. BLACKMORE, *Lorna Doone*, A Romance of Exmoor, p. 326, ed. 1878.

Grose gives '*Tallet* (*i. e.* top-loft), a hay-loft. Exm.'

'W. *tal*, s. m. that is over, that tops, that is fronting or upon.'—OWEN PUGHE's *Welsh Dictionary*.

TALL-BOY, *sb.* a narrow ale-glass standing high upon a stem or foot.—PULVERBATCH. Qy. com. 'Missis, the Maister wants a jug o' ale at the 'orse-block, an' two tumbler-glasses—'e said nod to sen' them *tall-boys*, kigglin'.' 'Who's ŏŏth 'im?' 'I dunna know, some gentleman; 'e says 'e ŏŏnna light.'

'She then ordered some cups, goblets, and *tall-boys* of gold, silver, and crystal to be brought, and invited us to drink.'—OZELL (first half 18th cent.), *Rabelais*, V. xlii., in Nares.

Mr. Nares says that *Tall-boy* is 'a cant term for cups or glasses, made longer or higher than common.'

TAN, *v. n.* to harp; to worry.—PULVERBATCH. 'I dunna know whad's the matter ŏŏth our Missis; 'er's bin *tan, tan, tanin'* ever sence 'er got up this mornin'.'

TANCEL [tan·si'l], *v. a.* to beat; to thrash.—SHREWSBURY; PULVERBATCH; WELLINGTON. Qy. com. 'Ŏŏn yo' lave them apples alone, an' come out o' that orchut? else I'll *tancel* yore 'ide for yo'.'

Mr. John Randall relates a story of Tom Moody, the famous 'Willey Whipper-in,' that, 'having a spite at a pike-keeper, who offended him by not opening the gate quick enough, "Tom *tancelled* his hide," and resolved the next time he went that way not to trouble him. *Driving* up to the gate, he gave a spring, and touching his horse on the flanks, went straight over, without starting a stitch or breaking a buckle [1773-96].'—*Old Sports and Sportsmen, or The Willey Country*, 1873.

Compare 'Fr. *tancer*, O.Fr. *tencer*, to rebuke, upbraid,' in PICK.

TANG [tang·], (1) *v. a.* to make a sharp, ringing noise, as with 'sounding brass,' to call the bees together when swarming.—CHURCH STRETTON. 'Mak' 'aste an' fatch the warmin'-pon an' the kay o' the 'ouse to *tang* the bees, or they'n be off, they flyen mighty 'igh.'

'Be opposite with a kinsman, surly with servants; let thy tongue *tang* arguments of state.'—*Twelfth Night*, II. v. 163.

Cf. **Ting-tang** (1).

(2) *sb.* the prong of a potato-fork.—NEWPORT; WEM; WHITCHURCH; ELLESMERE.

Randle Holme has 'The *Tangs* or Forks.'—*Academy of Armory*, Bk. III. ch. viii. p. 337.

Icel. *tangr;* the iron tongue of a knife which goes into the handle. Cf. **Tine** (1).

TANTRUMS, *sb. pl.* bursts of passionate temper. Com. Cf. **Geoltitudes**.

TAP, *v. a.* to re-sole boots or shoes. Com. 'I've made yore boots aumust as good as new; I've *tapped* an' 'eeled 'em, but I'd much ado, fur the in-sole wuz gwun.'

TARD [taa·r'd], *part. past*, torn,—'I've *tard* my throck.'—SHREWSBURY; PULVERBATCH; WEM. Qy. com.

TAR-FITCH, *sb. Ervum hirsútum*, hairy Tare.—WEM. See **Fitches.**

TASKERS, *sb. pl.* harvest-men who work by the acre, not by the day.—WELLINGTON; ELLESMERE.

'. . . . forth he goes,
Like to a harvest-man that's *task'd* to mow
Or all or lose his hire.'—*Coriolanus*, I. iii. 39.

'In 1387,—a reaper had 4*d.* a day. 1*s.* 11*d.* was paid for cutting and tying up 3 acres of wheat, *per taskam.*

'In 1388,—30 acres of oats tied up by the job (*per taskam*), 1*s.* 8*d.*' —*Notes to Piers Pl.*, p. 178, ed. Skeat, E. E. T. S.

'*Hic triturator*, A^{ce} a tasker,' occurs in a *Nominale*, xv. cent., in Wr. vocabs., vol. i. p. 218. Mr. Wright adds a note,—'*Tasker, i. e.* a thrasher. The word is now used in some dialects for a reaper; perhaps so named as working by *task* or piece.'

See **Fly-gang,** also **Tack-work.**

TASKERS'-LEASERS, *sb. pl.* the wives and children of the *taskers*, who are allowed to go into the field and glean before 'all comers' are admitted.—ELLESMERE. Perhaps some such privilege is referred to by Langland when he says—

'Ac who so *helpeth me to erie* · *or sowen here* ar I wende,
Shal haue leue, bi owre lorde · *to lese here in heruest*,
And make hem mery þere-mydde · maugre who-so bigrucccheth it.'
Piers Pl., Text B. pass. vi. ll. 67-69.

Cf. **Parlour-leasers.**

TATHER [tadh·ur'], (1) *sb.* frogs' spawn.—PULVERBATCH; WELLINGTON. Cf. **Junder** (2).

(2) *v. a.* to tie and twist and knot, as of growing corn by the wind. —PULVERBATCH. 'The winde's wassled an' *tathered* the corn till it'll be impossible to rape it, an' I canna bar mowin' w'eät—it looks so slovenly.' Cf. **Lodged.**

(3) *v. a.* and *v. n.* to entangle; to become involved—used chiefly in the preterite or participial form, as of persons or things.—*Ibid.* 'I tell yo' whad, Jim, if yo' getten blended up an' *tathered* among that lot, I've done ŏŏth yo'.'

(4) *sb.* a complicated state of things; a tangle, as of thread, &c.—PULVERBATCH; CLEE HILLS. 'Yo'n got this skein o' thrid i' sich a *tather*, it'll a to be cut.'

(5) *sb., var. pr.* a tether.—PULVERBATCH. It is said (metaphorically) of a spendthrift that ''e'll soon gŏŏ the lenth on 'is *tather*;' or of restriction imposed upon a person, that 'it'll tighten 'is *tather*.'

TATOES. See **Potatoes.**

TAW [tau·], *sb.* a large, choice marble. Com.

TAWNY OWL, *sb.* the common Brown Owl.—SHREWSBURY. See **Billy-Hooter.**

TAWTREES, TOITREES [tau·tr'iz'], PULVERBATCH, *Condover;* CRAVEN ARMS. [tot·r'i'z], WORTHEN, *Cherbury.* [toi·tr'i'z], CLUN, *sb.* same as **Swingle-trees**, q. v.

'Two sets *tawtrees.*'—*Auctioneer's Catalogue* (Longville), 1877.

TAXY-WAXY [tak·si' wak·si'], *sb.* a strong tendon in the neck of quadrupeds; cartilage, such as is seen in certain cuts of beef.—PULVERBATCH; WORTHEN. Qy. com. 'Gie the baby that piece o' *taxy waxy*, it's better than india-rubber.'

'*Paxwax*, synewe,' occurs in *Prompt. Parv.* See Mr. Way's note thereon.

TEÄRT [ti'ur'·t], (1) *adj.* sharp; biting: as of a frosty day,—'It's a mighty *teärt* day.'—CLEE HILLS. Cf. **Deurn** (2).

(2) *adj.* severe; painful.—PULVERBATCH; CLEE HILLS; MUCH WENLOCK. 'My 'and's despert bad; theer inna much to be sid, but it's that *teärt* sore I canna bar a fither to touch it.'

TED, *v. a.* to turn and spread abroad new-mown hay-grass. Com. 'I shouldna *ted* the 'ay awile the weather's so casertly, it'll keep better i' the swath.'

> 'Go sirs and away,
> to *ted* and make hay.'
>
> TUSSER, *Julies Abstract*, p. 121, ed. E. D. S.

Bailey—ed. 1782—gives '*To Ted* or *Tede* (*Grass*)' as a '*South and East Country Word.*'

'I *teede* hey, I tourne it afore it is made into cockes, je fene.'—Palsgrave in HAL. Mr. Halliwell remarks of *ted* that it is 'still in use.'

TEEM [tee·m], (1) *v. a.* and *v. n.* to pour out. Com. 'Theer's summat got i' the spout o' the tay-pot, it dunna *teem* well.'

> '& when Willie had gotten a kisse,
> I-wis shee might haue *teemed** him 3.'
>
> *Will Stewart and Iohn*, l. 144. *Percy Folio MS.*, vol. iii. p. 221, ed. Hales and Furnivall.

*'given him 3: *teem*, to pour out . . .'—Note by Mr. FURNIVALL.—*Ibid.*

(2) *v. a.* to empty.—SHREWSBURY. Qy. com. 'I axed the Maister, could 'e change me a sovereign, an' 'e *teemed* 'is pus, but 'e 'adna got it.'

> 'With swerdis swyftly thay smyte,
> Thay *teme* sadils fulle tyte.'
>
> *MS. Lincoln*, A. i. 17, f. 134, in HAL.

Jamieson has 'To *Teme*, *v. a.* to empty, *teem*, S. B.'

'*Temyñ*', or maken empty. *Vacuo, evacuo.*'—*Prompt. Parv.*

'Sw. *tömma;* Dan. *tömme;* to exhaust, empty.'—WEDG.

TEENY [tee·ni'], *adj.* very small,—tiny. Qy. com. See below.

TEENY-TINY, *adj.* an intensitive of *tiny*,—very very small.—NEWPORT. Qy. com.

'*Tiny* (a word used in *Worcester-shire* and thereabouts, as a little *tiny*) comes from the Ital. *Tini*, which is a diminutive termination.'—BLOUNT'S *Glossographia*, p. 648.

TEENY-WEENY, an intensitive of *teeny* (above). Qy. com. 'It's a pretty babby, but a *teeny-weeny* thing; yo' met'n pŭt it in a quart jug.'

'The rhyming [*sic*] form *teeny-weeny* may indicate a connection with Du. *weynigh*; G. *wenig*; little, small, few.'—WEDG.

TEERY [tee·h'r'i'], (1) *adj.* soft; smooth; mellow,—in operation.—PULVERBATCH. (1) 'If yo' pŭtten a spot o' 'ot waiter i' the churn, it'll mak' the butter work *teery*.' (2) 'The ground works nice an' *teery* after the fros'.'

Compare '*Teere*, of flowre. *Amolum*. "Pollis, vel pollen, est idem in tritico quod flos in siligine, the tere of floure."—Whitinton, Gramm., 1521.'—*Prompt. Parv. and Notes.*

(2) *adj.* tall; tapering: said of persons and plants,—'a *teery* girl,' &c.—ELLESMERE, *Welshampton*. Cf. **Spiry**.

TEG, *sb.* a sheep in its second year that has never been shorn.—CLUN; CLEE HILLS. Qy. com.

'A teg or sheepe with a little head and wooll under its belly.'—Florio, in HAL.

Ray gives 'A *Tagge*, a Sheep of the first Year, *Sussex*.'

TEG'S-WOOL, *sb.* the wool shorn off a *teg*.—*Ibid.* The wool known as *teg's-wool* is distinguished by a little curl at the end, which that of an after-shearing never has.

TELLIF [tel·if], *sb.*, *obsols.* a thick, tangled crop: said of weeds.—PULVERBATCH. 'I shall 'ăve a pretty job to 'aw them tatoes—theer's a fine *tellif* o' weeds.' Cf. **Morf**.

TEMPERSOME, *adj.* hot-tempered; passionate.—WEM; ELLESMERE.

TEMPEST, *sb.*, *pec.* a storm, more especially a thunderstorm, but without the accompaniment of high wind.—CLUN. Cf. **Storm**.

TEMPTUOUS [tem·tyus *and* tem·chus], *adj.* tempting; inviting.—PULVERBATCH. 'Thank yo', Missis, I'll tak' a bit, it looks so *tem'-tuous*—as the owd sayin' is, "the proof o' the puddin' 's i' the ătin'."'

TENSORS, *sb. pl.*, *obs.* persons who, not being burgesses, carried on business in the town as tradesmen, upon payment of certain fines.—SHREWSBURY.

'1449-50. This yeare the burgesses and *tenssars* in Shrewsbury dyd varye.'—*Early Chronicles of Shrewsbury* (*Taylor MS.*), in *Transactions of Shropshire Archæological and Natural History Society.*

The *Tensors'* fines were imposed by the Court Leet, which required that they should 'be levied before the Feast of St. Catherine [Nov. 25th].'

'In the Corporation Accounts—1519—it is ordered that "*Tensors* selling ale should pay vjd. quarterly."'—PHILLIPS'S *History of Shrewsbury*, pp. 161, 168.

See below, also see **Bibsters**.

TENSORSHIP, *sb.*, *obs.* the fine paid by *Tensors* (see above).—SHREWSBURY.

'John Bromhall, baker.—It was objected to his vote that he was no Burgess, in support of which it was proved that he pd *Tensership* several years, and that his ffather had paid toll. This *Tensership* is a ffine or acknowledgment commonly paid by persons following trade in the town that are no Burgesses. . . .'—*The Poll for the Borough of Shrewsbury*, June 29th and 30th, 1747, in *Transactions of the Shropshire Archæological and Natural History Society*.

'This Richard Muckleston . . . commenced a suite against the Towne of Shrewsbury for exacting an imposition upon him which they call *tensorship*, and did endeavour to make voyd their Charter, but they gave him his Burgesship to bee quiet.'—GOUGH'S *History of Myddle*, p. 128.

TENT, (1) *v. a.* to take charge of; to attend to, as of sheep, cattle, &c. 'Jack, the Maister wants yo' to *tent* them cows as 'e's jest turned i' the leasow.'

> 'it was a sore office, O Lord, for him
> that was a lord borne of a great degree!
> as he was *tenting* his sheepe alone,
> neither sport nor play cold hee.'
> *Lord of Learne*, l. 139. *Percy Folio MS.*, vol. i. p. 187, ed. Hales and Furnivall.

(2) *v. a.* to hinder; to watch; to 'look sharp after,'—having punishment in view.—WEM; ELLESMERE. 'I'll *tent* 'im if 'e osses to do that agen.'

> 'Ill *tent* thee, quoth Wood,
> If I can't rule my daughter, I'll rule my good.'
> *Cheshire Proverbial Saying.*

(3) *v. a.* to scare.—NEWPORT; WEM; ELLESMERE. 'Where's Will Starkey?' 'Plaze, Ma'am, 'e's *tentin'* crows off the corn.'

TERRIFY, *v. a.*, *pec.* to pain; to irritate.—SHREWSBURY; PULVERBATCH; CLEE HILLS; WEM; ELLESMERE. (1) 'This cut o' my finger *terrifies* me mightily, I canna get on ŏŏth my work.' (2) 'These gnats do so *terrify* the child—jest look at 'is for'yed, 'ow it's bitten.'

TEWTER [teu·tur' *and* choo·tur'], (1) *v. a.*, *obs.* to beat and break the hemp-stalk after it had been subjected to the action of fire as described *sub voce* **Killoddy**, q. v.—PULVERBATCH; WORTHEN. *Tewtering* was the second process of hemp-dressing. (It may be noted here that hemp and flax were treated alike.)

The verb *tewter* seems to be a variation of '*Tewtaw*, to beat, to break as flax,' given by Ash as a 'reduplication of *Tew* (from the Sax. *tawian*), to work, to beat so as to soften.'

Bailey—ed. 1782—has '*To Tew Hemp*, to beat or dress it.'

'A.S. *tawian*; O.Du. *touwen*; to taw, *subigere*.'—STRAT.

(2) *sb.*, *obs.* the implement with which the hemp-stalk was beaten, &c.—*Ibid.* The *tewter* consisted of two parts, upper and lower, respectively; the latter being a long, narrow, oaken frame, standing upon four legs, about two feet three inches in height, and furnished

with a range of four strong bars, extending its whole length. These bars were of 'cloven quarter oak'—the triangular segment of a squared block—and were fixed with the keen edge topmost. The upper part had three bars of like kind, so set as to fit the interspaces of those beneath. It was joined to the lower part at one end by a pair of 'gudgeons,' which acted as hinges in such a manner, that it could be plied up and down by means of a handle, which the operator worked with his right hand, while he held the hemp with his left, to be *tewtered* between the several parts of the implement.

Mr. Halliwell gives '*Tewter.* An instrument for breaking flax, as a brake for hemp. *Cheshire.*'

Randle Holme, however, draws no distinction between hemp and flax as regards the implements and processes required for dressing them; he mentions a '*brake*'—but not a *tewter*—amongst the former, and in the 'Terms of Art used by Hemp and Flax Dressers,' he adds, '*Braking*, is the crushing, and bruising the Stalks, between peeces of Wood with teeth like a Saw, made in them.'—*Academy of Armory*, Bk. III. ch. iii. p. 106.

See **Swingle** (1).

T-HANDLE, *sb.* a handle, as of a spade or potato-fork, having a short cross-bar at the top. Qy. com.

A *D-handle* is one that is terminated by a loop resembling the letter D reversed, thus ᗡ.

THANK YOU FOR ME, *phr.* a form of thanks for hospitality received.—PULVERBATCH; OSWESTRY. 'Now, Nelly, mak' the lady a curchey, an' say *thank you for me*, an' I'm greatly obleeged fur sich a nice tay.'

This singular expression seems to be an elliptical one, signifying, I thank you *for*—what you have given to—me,—*for* being the stress word; 'thank you *for* me.'

The Welsh have a similar idiom differenced by the emphasis, which is laid upon the final pronoun, thus:—'Supposing two persons—pedestrians—to have called at a house and asked for a draught of milk, when they have drunk it, one will say, "Diolch i chwi drosta' *I;*" or, "Diolch yn fawr iawn i' chwi drosta' *I;*" leaving his companion to convey thanks in like manner for himself.'—*Byegones*, 1878, p. 11.

Pegge gives '*Thank you for them*, an answer to an enquiry after absent friends. North. They are quite well, I thank you for them.'

THAR [dhaa·r], *pron.* their,—'It's *thar* fence, an' they mun mend it.' —SHREWSBURY; PULVERBATCH.

> 'Drink sal alle bestes of felde wide,
> Wilde asses in þar thrist sal abide.'
>
> *Metrical English Psalter*, ciii. (A.D. 1300, *ante*).
> [*Ps.* civ. 11.] *Specim. Early Eng.*, ii. l. 12.

A.S. *þæra*, of them, gen. pl. of *se*, *seo*, *þæt*.

See **Grammar Outlines** (*adjective pronouns*), p. xlviii.

THATCH-SPARROW, *sb.* common House-sparrow.—CLUN, *Twitchin.* See **Aisin-sparrow**.

THATN, THISN, *advs.* that way, this way, as of the manner of doing a thing.—CLUN, *Herefd. Border*; LUDLOW; MUCH WENLOCK; NEWPORT, *Shiffnal*.

Pegge gives '*This'n* and *That'n*, in this manner and in that manner. North.' See **Athatn, Athisn**, &c.

THAVE [thai·v], *sb.* a ewe sheep of the first year.—PULVERBATCH.

'Item, taken away uppon Draytun grounde at on time . . . CC. shepe callyd hoggys.

'Item, at a nother tyme, uppon the same ground, iiij^{xx} hoggys and xl. *theyves*.'—*Paston Letters*, A.D. 1465, vol. iii. p. 457.

Ray has 'A *Theave*; An Ewe of the first Year, *Essex*.'

Pegge gives '*Theave*, in the North, an ewe (or sheep) of three years.' He adds, 'Bailey says of one year.'

See **Hog** (1), also **Hogget**.

THETCH [thech·], *v. a.* and *sb.* to thatch; thatch.—SHREWSBURY; PULVERBATCH. Qy. com.

'And some he tauȝte to tilie · to dyche & to *thecche*.'
Piers Pl., Text B. pass. xix. l. 232.

'Blocks, rootes, pole and bough, set vpright to the *thetch*:
the neerer more handsome in winter to fetch.'
TUSSER, *Fiue Hundred Pointes of Good Husbandrie* [August].

'A.Sax. *vb.* *þeccan*; O.H.Germ. *decchen*; to thetch (thatch).'—STRAT. A.S. *sb.* *þæc*, thatch.

THETCHER, *sb.* a thatcher.—*Ibid.*

'A.Sax. *þecere*; O.H.Germ. *dechari*; a thatcher.'—STRAT.

THETCHING-PEG, *sb.* a peg used in thatching.—*Ibid.* 'Did yo' see 'ow the cow 'as 'iled the *thetch* off the pig-stў? Tak' some rushes an' tuthree *thetchin'-pegs* an' pŭt it right.'

THE-WAIN-AND-HORSES, *sb.* *Ursa Major*.—OSWESTRY. See **Charles's-Wain**, also **Jack-an'-'is-chem**, &c.

THIEF [theef·], *sb.*, *pec.* an imperfection in the wick which causes a candle to waste and to gutter. Com. 'Look at the *thief* i' the candle, 'ow it's wasting it.'

Randle Holme gives '*Thief*,' in the same sense, amongst 'Terms used by Tallow-Chandlers,' in the *Academy of Armory*, Bk. III. ch. iii. p. 102.

THILLER [thil·ur'], *sb.* a shaft-horse.—CRAVEN ARMS; CLEE HILLS; LUDLOW.

'Suit of *thiller's* gears.'—*Auctioneer's Catalogue* (Stoddesden), 1870.

'Hole bridle and saddle, whit lether and nall,
with collers and harneis, for *thiller* and all.'
TUSSER, *Husbandlie furniture*, p. 36, ed. E. D. S.

'*Thiller*, or *Thil-horse*, is that horse which is put under the *Thills* of the Cart to bear them up.'—BLOUNT'S *Glossographia*, p. 646.

Grose gives '*Thill-horse*. The shaft-horse. N.'

'*Thylle Horse*. *Veredus*.'—*Prompt. Parv.*

'A.S. *þil*, a stake . . . the pole or shafts of a carriage.'—WEDG.

THINKLE [thing·kl], *sb.* a thing-ful, as of cup, glass, &c.—PULVERBATCH; CRAVEN ARMS. '"Ăve a drop more drink, Dick.' 'No, thank yo', I'm gweïn.' 'Whad 'urry? Jest 'ăve another *thinkle.*' Cf. **Cantle**, also **Tottle**. See **Grammar Outlines** (*nouns compounded with* **ful**), p. xliii.

THIRL [thur'l·], *v. a.* and *v. n.* to pierce through; to make an opening, as out of one 'working' into another.—COLLIERY, M. T. 'Gaffer, we'n *thirled* out o' our Top-end into Smith's Level to-day.'

'and al comes of a þroly þouȝt · þat *þirles* min hert.'
William of Palerne, l. 612.

Grose gives '*Thirl.* To bore a hole, to drill. Lincolnsh.'
'*Thyrlyn̄*, or peercyn̄'. *Penetro, terebro, perforo.*'—*Prompt. Parv.*
A.S. *þyrlian;* to make a hole; to thrill, drill, pierce, bore.

THISN. See **Thatn.**

THONE, *adj.* damp; moist: said of corn, and of heavy, clammy bread.—CORVE DALE.
Ash has '*Thone* (*a local word*), damp, moist.'

THRAPE. See **Threap** below.

THRASHAL, THRASHAT [thr'ash·ul], PULVERBATCH. Qy. com. [thr'ash·ut], WEM; ELLESMERE, *sb.*, *obsols.* a flail. It consists of two parts, the *hand-staff* and the *swipple*, which are united by a band of strong leather.
Randle Holme calls this implement a '*Threshall.*'
'*Tritorium*, þerscel,' occurs in *Archbp. Ælfric's Vocabulary*, x. cent., in Wr. vocabs., vol. i. p. 16. Mr. Wright gives the explanation, 'A flail, still called in Lancashire a *threshell.*' See **Caplin,** also **Swipple.**

THRAVE [thr'ai·v], *sb.* a collective number of sheaves of corn in the straw, or of straw which has been threshed: a term always used in the singular number,—'The Maister's sen' to know if yo' can lend 'im five or six *thrave* o' straw.' Com.
'*Thrave* of Corn, was two *Shocks*, of six, or rather twelve sheaves apiece. *Stat.* 2 H. 6. *c.* 2. . . . In most Counties of *England* twenty four sheaves do now go to a *Thrave.* Twelve sheaves make a *Stook*, and two *Stooks* a *Thrave.*'—BLOUNT'S *Glossographia*, p. 647.
Grose gives '*Thrave.* A shock of corn containing 24 sheaves.'
See **Weights and Measures, &c.**, p. xciii. Cf. **Stook.**

THREAP [thr'ai·p *and* thr'eep·], *v. n.* to contradict; to dispute; to maintain an opposite opinion with obstinate pertinacity. Com. 'I knowed as that plough-bottle wunna brought in, but that imperent bwoy *thrăped* me out as it wuz.'

'"O Bell my wiffe! why dost thou fflyte?
now is now, & then was then;
wee will liue now obedyent liffe,
thou the woman, & I the man.
itts not ffor a man with a woman to *threape*
vnlesse he ffirst giue ouer the play;
wee will liue noue, as wee began."'
Bell my Wiffe, l. 61. *Percy Folio MS.*, vol. ii. p. 324, ed. Hales and Furnivall.

'Some herds, weel learn'd upo' the beuk,
Wad *threap* auld folk the thing misteuk.'
ROBERT BURNS, *Poems*, p. 80, l. 26.

'I *threpe* a mater upon one, I beare one in hande that he hath doone or said a thing amysse.'—Palsgrave, verb. f. 389, in HAL.

'A.Sax. *þreapian;* to threap, *arguere.*'—STRAT.

THREE-CORNERED, *adj., pec.* irritable; ill-conditioned: said of the temper.—WORTHEN. ''Er's in a mighty *three-cornered* 'umour to-day.' Cf. **Three-square** (2), below.

THREE-FACES-UNDER-A-HOOD, *sb. Viola tricolor,* Pansy violet, or Heart's-ease.—PULVERBATCH.
Gerarde calls it '*Three faces in a hood.*'—*Herball,* Bk. ii. p. 855.
Cf. **Two-faces-under-the-Sun.**

THREE-LEGS, same as **Nave,** q. v.—WORTHEN.

THREE-SQUARE, (1) *adj.* triangular.—LUDLOW, *Herefd. Border.*
Randle Holme says of '*Harrows*' that 'In former times Husbandmen made all these Instruments *three square.*'—*Academy of Armory,* Bk. III. ch. viii. p. 335. Cf. **Four-square.**

(2) same as **Three-cornered,** above. — PULVERBATCH. 'The Maister seems in a *three-squar'* temper this mornin'.'

THRICECOCK, *sb. Turdus viscívorus,* Missel-thrush.—NEWPORT. Cf. **Thrushcock.** See **Stormcock** (3).

THRID [thr'id·], (1) *sb.* thread. Com. 'Bring me a quarter o' mixt *thrid,* an' tell 'em to pŭt the biggest part w'ity-brown, it's the most useful.'

'There she them found all sitting round about,
The direfull distaffe standing in the mid,
And with unwearied fingers drawing out
The lines of life, from living knowledge hid.
Sad Clotho held the rocke, the whiles the *thrid*
By griesly Lachesis was spun with paine,
That cruell Atropos eftsoones undid,
With cursed knife cutting the twist in twaine.
Most wretched men, whose dayes depend on *thrids* so vaine!'
SPENSER, *F. Q.,* Bk. IV. c. ii. st. xlviii.

In explaining the 'Terms of Art used by Spinners,' Randle Holme says, 'Yarn is the single *thrid* of either Hemp or Flax.'—*Academy of Armory,* Bk. III. ch. iii. p. 107.

(2) *v. a.* to thread,—'I canna see to *thrid* the nild.'—*Ibid.*

THRIPPLES [thr'ip·lz], same as **Ripples,** q. v.—CHURCH STRETTON; CLEE HILLS; LUDLOW; NEWPORT.
'Narrow wheel cart with *thripples.*'—*Auctioneer's Catalogue* (Church Stretton), 1877.
'*Epredia,*' glossed 'the *therrepyllis,*' occurs amongst the parts of a 'wain' and cart enumerated in a *Metrical Vocabulary,* (perhaps) xiv. cent., in Wr. vocabs., vol. i. p. 181.

THROCK, *sb., var. pr.* a frock,—'Pŭt the child a clane *throck* ón afore tay.'—SHREWSBURY; PULVERBATCH. Qy. com. See **F** (2) in **Grammar Outlines** (*consonants*, &c.).

THROGGLE [thr'og·l], *v. a.* to trammel: said of any article of dress that impedes free movement.—PULVERBATCH. 'I dunna like this ŏŏllen shawl—I canna bar anythin' as *throggles* me.'

THROM, *prep., var. pr.* from.—SHREWSBURY; PULVERBATCH; CLUN; ELLESMERE. Qy. com. See **F** (2) in **Grammar Outlines** (*consonants*, &c.).

THROSH [thr'osh·], *v. a.* to thresh. Com. 'John, I want yo' to *throsh* that turmit sid, an' mind an' clane it well.'

'Light come, light go, my Faither got it a-*throshin*',' is an ironical proverbial saying (heard in the neighbourhood of Pulverbatch), applied to spendthrift waste of hardly-earned property.

'*þroshen*' is given by Dr. Stratmann as a participial form occurring in the *Ormulum* (A.D. 1200, *circa*), l. 1530.

'A.S. *þerscan*; Goth. *þriskan*; O.H.Germ. *dresken*; thresh (thrash); triturare.'—STRAT.

THROSTLE, THRUSTLE [thr'os·l, thr'us·l], *sb. Turdus músicus*, the Song-thrush. Com. Both forms obtain, but *Thrustle* is the one more usually heard.

'& eche busch ful of briddes · þat bliþeliche song,
boþe þe þrusch & þe *þrustele* · bi xxxii of boþe.'
William of Palerne, l. 820.

'Sir Thopas fil in loue-longinge
Al whan he herde the *thrustel* singe.'
CHAUCER, B. 1963 (Six-text ed.), Skeat.

'þrusche and *þrostle* and wudewale.'
Owl and Nightingale, l. 1659.

'The *throstle* with his note so true,
The wren with little quill,—'
Midsummer Night's Dream, III. i. 130.

'*Throstle*. A thrush; properly the *Missel-thrush*, but often used with latitude for any of the genus. Still current in some counties.'—NARES.

'*Thrustylle*, bryd. . . . *Merula*.'—*Prompt. Parv.*

A.S. *þrostle*;—*idem*. See **Thrushel**, also **Thrushcock**.

THROTTLE [thr'ot·l], *sb., sl.?* the throat. Com. 'That's summat wuth pŭttin' down a fellow's *throttle*.'

THROW [thr'ou·], (1) *prep., obsols.?* through,—'I sid 'im gweïn *throw* the wicket toërts the foud.'—PULVERBATCH.

'This Posie is so pickt, and choysely sorted *throw*
There is no Flower, Herbe, nor Weede, but serves some purpose now.'
GEORGE GASCOIGNE'S *Posies* (A.D. 1573), ed. Hazlitt, vol. i. p. 20.

(2) *sb.* a hole cut through a hedge as a channel to let water run off the land.—CLEE HILLS. 'Han yo' drawed them aids?' 'Iss, Maister.' 'Then gŏŏ an' cut a *throw* through the 'edge.'

Mr. Halliwell has '*Throw*, a thoroughfare; a public road. *South*.'

THROWED [thr'oa·d], *part. past*, defeated by an adverse verdict. Qy. com. 'Price an' Jones han bin 'agglin' an' wranglin' fur 'ears about that rŏŏäd; at last it wuz brought to a size trial, an' Jones wuz *throwed*.' Cf. **Cast** (4).

THRUM [thr'um·], *sb., obs.* linen-weavers' waste, used for sewing purposes.—PULVERBATCH. Qy. com. 'I'll djarn them things no lunger, fur I've used more *thrum* o'er 'em than a bin wuth, a power.'

'O Fates, come, come,
Cut thread and *thrum*.'
Midsummer Night's Dream, V. i. 291.

'*Thromm*, of a clothe. *Filamen*.'—*Prompt. Parv.*

THRUSH [thr'ush·], *v. n.* to thrust; to press, as in, or by, a throng of folk.—ATCHAM; ELLESMERE. 'They wun pushin' an' *thrushin*' sŏo, theer wuz no gettin' alung fur 'em.' Cf. **Thrutch**, below.

THRUSHCOCK, *sb.* the Missel-thrush (of both sexes).—BRIDGNORTH. Richard Barnefield—an Edgmond (Salop) man—employs the form '*Thrustle-cocke*:'—

'Or if thou wilt goe shoote at little Birds
With bow & boult (the *Thrustle-cocke* & Sparrow)
Such as our Countrey hedges can afford's;
I haue a fine bowe and an yuorie arrow;
And if thou misse, yet meate thou shalt [not] lacke.
Ile hange a bag & bottle at thy backe.'
The Affectionate Shepheard, A.D. 1594.

In Chaucer we find—

'The *thrustelcok* made eek his lay.'
Sir Thopas, B. 1959 (Six-text ed.), Skeat.

See *sub voce* **Throstle.** See also **Thricecock.**

THRUSHEL [thr'ush·u'l], same as **Throstle**, q. v.—BRIDGNORTH.
'Thrustylle, bryd (*thrusshill* or thrustyll, P.). *Merula*.'—*Prompt. Parv.*
Compare 'M.H.Germ. *droschel*;—*idem*,' in STRAT.

THRUSTY, *adj.* thirsty.—LUDLOW, *Herefd. Border.*
'. . . to quench her flaming *thrust*,' occurs in Spenser's *Faerie Queene*.
'A.Sax. *þurstig*; O.H.Germ. *durstager*, thirsty.'—STRAT.
See **R** (2) in **Grammar Outlines** (*consonants*, &c.).

THRUTCH [thr'uch·], same as **Thrush**, q. v.,—'w'eer bin'ee *thrutchin*' to?'—WEM.
'Maxfield measure, heap and *thrutch*, i. e. thrust. *Cheshire*.'—RAY's *Proverbs*, p. 59.
'A.Sax, *þryccan*; O.H.Germ. *drucchen*, thrutch; *premere, trudere*.'—STRAT.

THUMBSCALL [thum·sku'l], *sb., obs.* a piece of paper or card inserted in a book at the bottom of the page, to prevent thumb-marks.—PULVERBATCH; WORTHEN. 'Now, I've pŭt yo' a fescue an' a *thumbscall*, so mind as theer inna-d-a mark i' the book.'

THUNDER-BOWT, *sb.* *Papaver Rhœas*, common red Poppy.—SHREWSBURY; WELLINGTON. Qy. com.

THUNG, THUNK [thung·], SHREWSBURY; PULVERBATCH; ELLESMERE. Qy. com. [thung·k], WEM, *sb.*, *var. pr.* a thong—a leather boot-lace. 'I give the cobbler a penny fur two *thunks*.'

Wycliffe employs the form '*thwong*' in the same sense of a lace. 'I knelinge am not worthi for to vndo, or vnbynde, the *thwong* of his schoon.'—*Mark* i. 7 (Oxford University Press, ed. 1850).

THUNGE [thunzh·], (1) *v. n.* to thump.—WEM; ELLESMERE. Qy. com. 'Whad wun'ee doin' las' neet, *thungin'* o'er yed?—I thought the flur'd a come through.'

(2) *sb.* a thump; a heavy fall,—'I come down sich a *thunge*.' Com.

THURN, *sb.*, *var. pr.* a thorn,—'I've got a *thurn* i' my finger as terrifies me despertly.' Qy. com.

TICE, *v. a.* to allure; to tempt, or induce by temptation of some kind; to entice. Com. 'Tak' a bit o' corn i' the sarver an' *tice* the pony, it's better than runnin' 'im round an' round.'

'All these & more Ile giue thee for thy loue,
If these & more, may *tyce* thy loue away.'
RICHARD BARNEFIELD, *The Affectionate Shepheard*, A.D. 1594.

'"if I may know after this
that thou *tice* me, I-wis
thou shalt haue the law of the land."'
Sir Triamore, l. 95. *Percy Folio MS.*, vol. ii. p. 83, ed. Hales and Furnivall.

'*Tycyn̄*', or intycyn̄'. *Instigo, allicio.*'—*Prompt. Parv.*

TICKLER [tik·lur'], *sb.* a slender steel rod terminated by a hook at a right angle, used for stirring the fire slightly.—SHREWSBURY; ELLESMERE.

TICKLISH, *adj.*, *pec.* skittish; mettlesome.—PULVERBATCH. 'I dunna think the mar' 'as any vice, on'y a bit *ticklish*—ŏŏnna stan' much w'ip-cwurd.'

Bailey—ed. 1727—has '*Ticklish* [with *Horsemen*], a Horse is said to be *ticklish*, that is, too tender upon the Spur, and too sensible, that does not freely fly the Spur, but in some measure resists them, throwing himself up, when they come near and prick his Skin.'

TICKNEY, TICKNEY-WARE [tik·ni'], *sb.*, *obsols.* common, coarse earthenware.—SHREWSBURY; PULVERBATCH; WEM. 'Theer's bin three folks 'ere to-day ŏŏth *tickney*, an' w'en I wanted some dishes fur 'arrŏost nobody come nigh.' The origin of the term *tickney* may be found in the following:—

'There was a Pottery at *Ticknal* near Derby as early as the 16th century, which produced articles of a coarse hard body, of a dull brown colour, sometimes decorated with yellow slip.'—CHAFFER'S *Porcelain*, 3rd ed., p. 592.

Cf. **Crickney-ware.**

TICKNEY-MAN, TICKNEY-WOMAN [ŏŏm·u'n], *sb.*, *obsols.* an itinerant vendor of coarse, common earthenware.—*Ibid.* 'Missis, dun'ee want anythin' off the *tickney-man?*—'e's at the door.' Cf. **Crick-man**, &c.

TID (1), **TIDE** [tid·, teid·], *sb.* time; season,—an old word preserved in the compound forms, Luke's-*tid* and New-yis-*tide*. See these *ante*.

> 'Alle fra þe þai abide,
> þat þou gif þam mete in *tide*.'
> *Metrical English Psalter*, ciii. (A.D. 1300, *ante*).
> [*Ps.* civ. 27]. *Specim. Early Eng.*, ii. l. 64.

'*Vernum tempus*, lencten-tid,' occurs in an *Anglo-Saxon Vocabulary*, xi. cent., in Wr. vocabs., vol. i. p. 76.

'A.Sax., O.Sax. *tid;* O.Icel. *tid;* O.H.Germ. *zit;* tide, *tempus, hora*.' —STRAT.

TID (2), *adj.* tenderly careful of, and solicitous about.—SHREWSBURY; PULVERBATCH; WORTHEN; CLEE HILLS. 'Tum Lickus [Lucas] is despert *tid* on 'is young ŏŏman, 'e's afeard o' the winde blowin' on 'er, aumust.'

'O.Icel. *tíðe; assiduus*,' in STRAT. See below. Cf. **Choice**.

TIDDLE [tid·l], *v. a.* to nurse and nurture tenderly; same as **Taddle**, q. v.—SHREWSBURY; PULVERBATCH. 'Nancy, I'll gie yo' that little ratlin', if yo' can *tiddle* it up, it might mak' a bit of a porket.'

Bailey—ed. 1727—has '*Tiddle*, to indulge, or fondle, to make much of.' So also given by Ash.

TIDDLING, *sb.* a delicate child, or weak young animal, that needs—and receives—tender care.—SHREWSBURY; PULVERBATCH; CLUN; CLEE HILLS. 'Maister, ŏŏn'ee plaze to come an' look at my *tiddlin'* as yo' wun so good to gie me?—'e dunna look much like a ratlin' now, an' agen 'e's 'ad another bag o' male 'e'll mak' a rar' pig.'

Ash has '*Tiddling* . . a fondled child, the youngest child; a lamb brought up by hand.'

Cf. A.S. *tidder*, tender; weak; frail.

TIDY [tei·di'], *adj.* This word has a wide range of meaning beyond the ordinary one of neat; it signifies—commonly—honest, thrifty, honourable—'of good report;' pleasing, civil; pretty good, above mediocrity; considerable, as in value, size, quantity, distance, and so forth, in the idiomatic sense of good. (1) ''E's a right *tidy* mon, is John, al'ays stiddy at 'is work i' the wik, an' reg'lar at Church o' Sund'ys—it's a pity as theer inna more like 'im.' (2) ''Er's sich a *tidy* spoken ŏŏman.' (3) 'Yo'n got a *tidy* pig theer, Tummas.' (4) 'They tellen me as 'e's comen into a *tidy* property:'—'the Missis gid me a *tidy* piece o' pork:'—'we'n a *tidy* tuthree o' pars this 'ear:'—'it's a *tidy* step theer an' back; I doubt yo'n be despert tired.' Some examples of kindred usages of the term *tidy* are adduced in the following citations from early writers in the Salopian—or near akin to the Salopian—dialect:—

> 'As for a trewe *tydy* man · al tymes ylyke.'
> *Piers Pl.*, Text B. pass. xix. l. 436.

'ful spacli þe king of spayne · to spede þo nedes,
as fast ches him fifty · of ful grete lordes,
þat *tidi* men were told · & trewest of his reaume.'
William of Palerne, l. 4166.

'& talkeden bi-twene · mani *tidy* wordes.'—*Ibid.* l. 3077.

'Ne no *tidi* a-tir · in templus a-raie,
No figure of fin gold · fourme þer-inne.'
Alexander and Dindimus, l. 559.

'he ȝaf to þe kowherde · a kastel ful nobul,
þe fairest vpon fold · þat euer freke seie,
. . . .
and al þat touched þer · to a *tidi* erldome.'
William of Palerne, l. 5384.

'þe kinges sone aswiþe · let sembul miche puple,
& triȝed him to a *tidi* ost · of þe *tideȝist* burnes,
þat he miȝth in þe mene time · in any maner gadere.'
Ibid. l. 3556.

'*Tydy . . . Probus.*'—*Prompt. Parv.*

Compare 'O.Du. *tidig;* O.H.Germ. *zitiger* (*tempestivus*), tidy,' in STRAT. See **Ontidy**.

TIFT [tif·t], *sb.* a hasty quarrel. Com. 'Why did you leave your place, Sarah?' 'Well, Ma'am, the Missis an' me 'ad'n a bit of a *tift*, an' I gid 'er notice.'

TILE [tei·l], *v. a.* to bait a trap by hanging a morsel of food on a hook.—PULVERBATCH. It is said of small eaters that they 'dunna yet as much as ŏŏd *tile* a trap.'

TILL [til·], *conj., pec.* than,—'better *till* that.'—NEWPORT; ELLESMERE. Qy. com. in *N. Shr.* Cf. **Nor**.

TILLING [til·in], *sb.* the grain-crops of arable land.—SHREWSBURY; PULVERBATCH; WEM. Qy. com. 'Theer'll be no gweïn to the wakes, I can tell yo', if we dunna get the *tillin'* 'oused afore then, an' it's 'ardly likely this casertly weather.' A.S. *tylung*, crop; fruit; gain. See **Lent-tilling**.

TILTER [til·tur'], *sb. Ephemera vulgata*, the May-fly.—SHREWSBURY; CLEE HILLS. Qy. com. The *tilter* is the green and grey drake of the fly-fisherman; it derives its name from the see-saw, up-and-down flight of the fully-developed insect,—a motion more especially noticeable in the male.

TILTY [til·ti'], *adj., obsols.?* touchy.—PULVERBATCH. 'I say, Jack, none o' yore *tilty* temper this mornin'.'

TIMBERSOME [tim·bur'sum], (1) *adj., obsols.?* heavy; bulky; unwieldy.—PULVERBATCH. 'The Maister's gettin' too *timbersome* to ride them young 'orses; a stiddy owd roadster ŏŏd be best fur 'im.'

(2) *adj., obsols.* tedious; troublesome.—*Ibid.* 'I amma-d-'afe sharp to-day, the child's bin so *timbersome* all night.'

TIMERSOME [tim·ur'sum], *adj.* timid; fearful.—PULVERBATCH

MUCH WENLOCK; NEWPORT. 'Whad a *timersome*, frittened little thing yo' bin, to be afeard o' the gonder.'

Pegge has '*Timersome*, fearful. North.'

TIND [tin·d], *v. a.* and *v. n.* to ignite.—SHREWSBURY; PULVERBATCH; WORTHEN; LUDLOW. 'I canna get the fire to *tind* this mornin', the sticks bin as wet as thetch.'

When lucifer matches were first introduced (about 1834), an old man cried them about in Ludlow—with the following extempore rime—

> 'For lightin' yore candles and *tindin'* yore fire,
> These *are* the best matches! Whad *can* yo' desire?'

'No man *tendith* a lanterne, and puttith in hidlis, nether vndur a buyschel, but on a candilstike, that thei that goen in, se liȝt.'—*Luke* xi. 33. Wycliffite Version, ed. A.D. 1388.

'A.S. *tendan*, *tyndan*; Dan. *tænd*; Goth. *tandjan*, to tind, kindle, inflame.'—STRAT.

Compare Eng. *tinder*, also **Kind** (1).

TINE [tei·n], (1) *sb.* the prong of an agricultural fork.—SHREWSBURY; PULVERBATCH; CRAVEN ARMS; LUDLOW. Qy. com. in *S. Shr.* 'That fellow's broke one o' the *tines* of my sharevil diggin' up a gooseb'ry bush, stid o' gettin' a spade.' See below. Cf. **Tang** (2).

(2) *sb.* the tooth of a harrow or other similar implement. Com.

'Scuffle with 11 *tines*.'—*Auctioneer's Catalogue* (Stoddesden), 1870.

'A.Sax. *tind*; O.Icel. *tindr*; M.H.Germ. *zint*, tine, *dens*, *ramus*.'—STRAT.

(3) *v. a.* to enclose; to hedge in.—ELLESMERE, *Welshampton*. 'The mon's pŭttin' goss o' the wall to *tine* the cats out,' said Mary Price, on observing that a neighbour was enclosing his garden with furze.

'All ould tenants shall haue, severall all the yeare, a croft and a medow, or a place of medow ground, or more if he will; but the new tenant may not challenge any by costome, but [*only*] by sufferance of the ould tenants; but that they leaue to *tine* and keep so that his neighbor be harmelesse by cattel; but if the[y] be hurt, he shall be greviosely amerced, and largely make amends to his neighbor for his trespasse.—"Costomary of Tettenhall Regis." A copy made 22d July, 1604.'—*English Gilds, their Statutes and Customs*, E. E. T. S.

'*Tynyd*, or hedgydde. *Septus*.'—*Prompt. Parv.*

A.S. *tȳnan*, to hedge in, enclose.

(4) *v. a.* to mend a hedge. Qy. com. '*Tine* the glat, an' dunna mak' a crow's nist on it,' *i. e.* mend the gap substantially, by putting plenty of thorns and stakes in it.

TINED, *adj.* furnished with *tines*. Qy. com.

'Two five-*tined* turnip forks.'—*Auctioneer's Catalogue* (Longville), 1877.

'*Tynyd*, wythe a tyne,' occurs in *Prompt. Parv.*, p. 494.

See **Tine** (1) and (2), above.

TING-TANG, (1) *sb.* a peal of two bells: a term derived from the sound—the lighter bell being *ting*, the heavier, *tang*. Qy. com. 'We 'ad'n a grand weddin' at 'An'ood o' Mond'y—the *ting-tang* clattered away ŏŏth a will—they wun axed-up o' Sund'y, so they didna 'ang lung i' the bell-ropes.'

(2) *v. n.* to ring into church with two bells. Qy. com. Grose has '*Ting-tang.* The little bell of a church. N.'

Cf. **Tong** (1), also **Tang** (1).

TIPE [tei·p], *v. a.* to tip over; to throw over.—PULVERBATCH. 'I *tiped* the pail o'er ŏŏth my fūt.'

TIPLEY [tip·li'], *adj.* clean; tidy; smart,—but the term is usually employed in irony to express something 'quite other.'—PULVERBATCH. 'Han'ee sin that ŏŏman—that new comer?' 'Aye, 'er looks a *tipley* body, I should think 'er hanna weshed 'er face fur a wik o' Sund'ys.'

TISSY-BALL, *sb.* a cowslip-ball.—PULVERBATCH; WEM; ELLESMERE. Children playing with a ball of this kind, toss it up and say—

'*Tissy-ball, tissy-ball,* tell me true—
How many years have I to go through?'

Then, if they catch it as it comes down they count it for 'a year,' and so, on and on, as the ball is tossed up and caught again.

Compare 'Tytetust, or tusmose of flowrys or othyr herbys. *Olfactorium.* . . . . "A Tuttie, nosegay, posie, or tuzziemuzzie, *Fasciculus, sertum olfactorium.*"—GOULDM. See Tosty in Jennings' *W. Country Glossary*; and also "Teesty-tosty, the blossoms of cowslips collected together, tied in a globular form, and used to toss to and fro for an amusement called *teesty-tosty.* It is sometimes called simply a tosty." Donne, Hist. of the Septuagint, speaks of a "girdle of flowers and tussies of all fruits intertyed," &c.,' in *Prompt. Parv. and Notes.*

Cf. **Tossy-ball.**

TIT, *sb.* a horse. Com. 'That's a smart little *tit* o' the Maister's,—it gwuz off the ground sharpish.'

'By *tits* and such
few gaineth much.'
TUSSER, *Septembers Abstract*, ed. E. D. S., p. 31.

Grose has '*Tit.* A horse. N.'

TITHER [tidh·ur'], (1) *sb., obsols.*? the sirname Tudor.—PULVERBATCH. Mr. Halliwell gives '*Tether*, the royal name Tudor.'

(2) *v. a.* to pet, as of young things.—MUCH WENLOCK. Cf. **Tiddle.**

TITLARK, *sb. Anthus pratensis*, Meadow Pipet; and *Anthus arbóreus*, Tree Pipet, respectively. Com. Cf. Icel. *tittr*, a tit, small bird.

TITTLE-GOOSE, *sb.* a tattling, foolish woman.—PULVERBATCH. 'Han'ee 'eărd whad Nancy Bowen's bin sayin'?' 'No, I 'anna, an it dunna much matter whad sich a *tittle-goose* as 'er says.'

TITTOES, *sb. pl.* potatoes.—ELLESMERE. See **Potatoes.**

TITTOES-AN'-TOUCH, *sb.* potatoes and milk, on this wise,—a dish is lined with mashed potatoes, a well being left in the centre, which is filled with hot milk having a lump of butter in it; into this each helping of potatoes is slightly dipped.—ELLESMERE. A story is told of a farmer's wife that, as she placed before 'the men' a supper of potatoes and milk prepared in the manner here described, she said—fearing they would help themselves too lavishly to the buttered milk—'Now, chaps, yo' maunna tak' it all at wunst, yo' maun *touch* it, an' *touch* it:' whence arose the term—'*Tittoes an' touch!*'

TITTORING [tit·u'r'in], *part.* setting, or getting up, potatoes.—ELLESMERE. 'Our little Jack's gwun *tittorin'* alung wuth 'is Faither,—'e can drop tittoes as well as a mon.'

TITTY [tit·i'], *sb.* a mother's breast or milk. Com.

'*Mammille*,' glossed '*tittas*,' occurs in an *Anglo-Saxon Vocabulary*, x. or xi. cent., in Wr. vocabs., vol. i. p. 283.

'A.Sax. *titt;* O.Du. *titte;* M.H.Germ. *zitze*, tit, *uber*.'—STRAT.

TO-BOST, *v. n.* to burst asunder.—PULVERBATCH. 'Mary, yo' see an' bring that steän in to-night; if it freezes we sha'n 'ăve it *to-bost* like the tother—it wuz clane split i' two, like as if it 'ad bin cut.'

> 'þe kouherde kayred to his house · karful in hert,
> & neiȝ *to-barst* he for bale · for þe barnes sake.'
>
> *William of Palerne*, l. 374.

To-bost is especially noteworthy as an instance of preservation in the Shropshire folk-speech, of the A.S. verbal prefix *to-*, meaning *apart*, *asunder*, *in two pieces*.

To-bost = A.S. *toberstan*, to burst asunder, break, dash in pieces. See '*To-*' in the *Glossarial Index* to *William of Palerne*, p. 311.

TOËRT [toah'·r't]. See **Frommet** (1) and (2).

TOËRTLY, *adj.* thriving; promising.—PULVERBATCH. Qy. com. 'That's a *toërtly* little pig o' yores, Yedart.' 'Aye, it's a tidy ăven fur another 'ear.'

TO GO TO THE WATERS, *phr.* to go to the sea.—SHREWSBURY; MUCH WENLOCK.

'1808. August 1st. Wm Beech, Sarah Dodd & Mary Weale *to go to the salt water* £5 . 5 . 0.'—*Parish Accounts*, Much Wenlock.

Compare the French *aller aux eaux*.

TOITREES. See **Tawtrees**.

TOLLBATCH, *sb.* a miller.—WELLINGTON. See **Batch** (2).

TOLLIKY [tol·iki'], *adj.* soiled and tumbled.—PULVERBATCH; WHITCHURCH; ELLESMERE. 'These dialogues [*doyleys*] is very *tolliky*, Ma'am,' said a neat housemaid to her Mistress.

TOMMY-TAILOR, *sb.* the caterpillar of the Tiger-Moth,—*Arctia caja*. Com. Cf. **Woolly-Bear**.

TOM-NOUP [tum nou·p], *sb.* *Parus major*, the Great Titmouse. Com. It is proverbially said of a swaggering, pretentious little man that, ''E's like a *Tum-noup* on a round o' bif.' See **Nope**.

TO-MORROW-DAY, *sb.* the morrow; to-morrow.—SHREWSBURY; PULVERBATCH; ELLESMERE.

'& when it was on the *Morrow day*,
TRIAMORE was in good array
armed & well dight.'

Sir Triamore, l. 738. *Percy Folio MS.*, vol. ii. p. 105, ed. Hales and Furnivall.

TONE, *adj.* one. A form but rarely used,—'the *tone* on 'em:' 'both the *tone* an' the tother on 'em.'—NEWPORT.

'Remembrith yhow, this world hat bot o naam
Of good or ewill, efter ȝhe ar gone!
And wysly tharfor chessith yhow the *ton*
Wich most acordith to nobilitee.'

Lancelot of the Laik, l. 1822.

'The *tone* of them was Adler yonge,
The tother was Kyng Estmere.'

King Estmere, l. 5, in *Percy's Reliques*, ed. 1765.

The tone = A.S. *þæt án.* See **Grammar Outlines** (*adjectives of numeration*), p. xlvi. See also **Tother**.

TONG, (1) *sb.* the sound produced by a slow, single stroke on a church-bell; the stroke itself.—PULVERBATCH. Qy. com. 'The bell gies a *tong* or two w'en they comen out o' Church, jest to tell folks to get the dinner ready.' This was said with reference to a usage which obtained at Churton Church of sounding the bell as the congregation left, by way of conveying a timely warning to their respective households—far or near—that they were 'out,' and to have all things in readiness for their return. Cf. **Ting-tang** (1). See Bk. II., *Folklore*, &c., 'Bells.'

(2) *v. a.* and *v. n.* to cause to sound,—to sound in one tone, as of a church-bell.—*Ibid.* 'The girld never pŭt the net o' tatoes i' the biler till 'er 'eärd the bell *tong*, an' the Maister, 'e wuz fine an' crousty at the dinner bein' a bit late.'

TOP, *v. a.* to snuff a candle.—PULVERBATCH; WEM. 'Jest *top* that candle,—it's got a wick as lung as a fortnit.'

TOP AND BUT, *phr.* to chop off the tops and fibrous roots of turnips.—CLEE HILLS. See **But** (3) and (4).

TOP AND TAIL, same as above. Com. ''Er's workin' i' the filds now, *toppin' an' tailin'* turmits.'

TOP COAL, *sb.* a very valuable coal for general purposes.—COLLIERY; M. T.

'The Yard and *Top Coals* contain specimens of the *Calamite*, the *Stigmaria*, *Sigillaria*, and several genera of the *Lycopodiaceæ*.'—*Notes on the Shropshire Coal-Field*, by T. PARTON, F.G.S., 1868.

See **Coal-Field** and **Coal-Names**, pp. 90, 92.

TOP O'ER TAIL [taayl·], *adv.*, *obsols.* head over heels—completely over.—PULVERBATCH. ''E jest gid 'im a bit of a shove, an' 'e went *top o'er tail* all down the bonk.'

'& happili to þe hinde · he hit þanne formest,
& set hire a sad strok · so sore in þe necke,
þat sche *top ouer tail* · tombled ouer þe hacches.'

William of Palerne, l. 2776.

'"yee dance neither Gallyard nor hawe,
Trace nor true mesure, as I trowe,
but hopp as yee were woode."
when they began of ffoote to ffayle,
thé tumbled *top ouer tayle*,
& Master and Master they yode.'
John de Reeue, l. 534. *Percy Folio MS.*, vol. ii. p. 579, ed. Hales and Furnivall.

TOP-UP, *v. a.* to complete the top of a stack.—PULVERBATCH. Qy. com. 'Yo' mun get some rushes an' *top-up* the stack, it's too flat—we sha'n a the clover spiled.'

TORMENTIL [taur'men·til], *sb. Lamium purpúreum*, red Dead-nettle. —CRAVEN ARMS, *Stokesay*. The true *Tormentil* belongs to another genus—*Rosaceæ*—and is the plant referred to as '*Turmentylle*, herbe. *Tormentilla*,' in *Prompt. Parv.* See **Dun-nettle**.

TORRIL [tor'·il], *sb.* a weak, mean, pitiful person,—one who has a sorry appearance; a poor, ill-nourished looking animal.—PULVERBATCH; WELLINGTON. Qy. com. (1) 'Dunna yo' think as I'm gweïn to pŭt up ŏŏth a poor *torril* like 'im—I'll plaze my eye, if I plague my 'eart.' (2) 'I think yo'n feed yore cauve to djeth—it looks a poor *torril*.'

TOSSICATED [tos·i'kaitid], *adj.*, *obsols.*? harassed; worried,—'upset,' as by vexation or trouble.—PULVERBATCH. 'Poor owd Molly looks bad, 'er's bin sadly *tossicated* lately ŏŏth one thing or tother—Jack gweïn fur a sodger, an' the poor owd mon bein' 'urt, an' altogether.'

TOSSY-BALL, same as **Tissy-ball**, q. v.—SHREWSBURY.

TOT, *sb.* a small drinking-cup, holding from about quarter of a pint to half a pint. Com. 'Tak' a can o' owd beer an' a couple o' *tots*, an' gie 'em a *tot* apiece jest to finish up.' Harvest-beer is served out to the men, after dinner and supper, in small *tots*. See **Tottle**, below.

TOTHER, *adj.* other,—'one thing or *tother*;'—'this or the *tother*, w'ich yo'n a mind to.' Com.

'No man may serue tweyn lordis, for ethir he schal hate the toon, and loue the *tother*; ethir he shal susteyne the toon, and dispise the *tothir*.'—*Matt.* vi. 24, Wycliffite Version, A.D. 1388.

The *tother* = the other, that other = A.S. *þæt oþere*, where *þæt* is the neuter gender of the definite article. See **Grammar Outlines** (*adjectives of numeration*), p. xlvi. See also **Tone**.

TOTTLE, *sb.* a tot-ful.—PULVERBATCH. 'Jest gie the men a *tottle* o' owd beer apiece, after thar supper, an' tell 'em as that'll pin up the bag,' *i. e.* will be the last the occasion will afford. *To pin up the bag* is to conclude an affair—to 'finish up,' as of Harvest-supper, Christmas merry-making, or other like. Cf. **Thinkle**. See **Grammar Outlines** (*nouns compounded with* **-ful**), p. xliii.

TOTTY, *adj.* exhilarated with drink—not absolutely drunk: a man in this latter stage of intoxication, would be said to have had 'a *tot* too much.'—PULVERBATCH. ''Ow did the Maister come wham las' night—wuz 'e drunk?' 'Oh no! on'y jest a bit *totty*.'

'Then came October full of merry glee;
For yet his noule was *totty* of the must,
Which he was treading in the wine-fats see.'
SPENSER, *F. Q.*, Bk. VII. c. vii. st. xxxix.

See *Totty*, in HAL. Cf. **Fresh** (1), also **Market-peärt.**

TOUZLE [tou·zl], *v. a.* to put into disorder; to turn things over roughly; to rumple.—SHREWSBURY; PULVERBATCH; BRIDGNORTH; ELLESMERE. Qy. com. 'Dunna *touzle* that drawer o'er—it waz on'y isterd'y as I fettled it, w'en I pŭt my best gownd away.'

'May never wicked Fortune *touzle* him!
May never wicked men bamboozle him!'
ROBERT BURNS, *Poems*, p. 122, l. 31, c. 2.

Compare 'To-tused' = entirely rumpled or tumbled, in *Havelok the Dane*:—

'And bernard sone ageyn [him] nam,
Al *to-tused* and al to-torn.'—l. 1948.

Bailey—ed. 1727—has '*Tou'zled*, pulled about, tumbled, rumpled.'
'Low Du. *tuseln*, to pull or hale about; to tug.'—WEDG.
See *Tousle* in JAMIESON. Cf. **Toze**, below.

TOWTHERING [tou·dhur'in], *part. adj.* flocking, or streaming out, as sheep breaking pasture, or bees coming forth from the hive.—PULVERBATCH; WELLINGTON. 'Them ship han made a glat i' the 'edge, an' a bin *towtherin'* out o' the leasow into the lane—yo'd'n better look sharp an' fatch 'em up.' Cf. **Kaming** (1).

TOZE [toa·z], (1) *v. a.* to pull asunder, or open, the locks of wool with the fingers,—a process preparatory to carding = to *tease*, in modern English.—PULVERBATCH; CORVE DALE. See example *sub voce* **Tag.**

'What schepe that is full of wulle,
Upon his backe they *tose* and pulle.'
JOHN GOWER (A.D. 1393), *Confessio Amantis* (*Prologue*).

'Thinkest thou, for that I insinuate, or *toaze* from thee thy business, I am therefore no courtier? I am courtier cap-a-pe; and one that will either push on or pluck back thy business there: whereupon I command thee to open thy affair.'—*Winter's Tale*, IV. iv. 60.
Compare '*Touse*' in *Measure for Measure*, V. i. 313.
Bailey—ed. 1727—gives 'To *Toze*, to pull asunder, to make soft;' also, '*To'zyness*, Softness, like *tozed* Wooll.'
'Tosoñ' wulle or other lyke (tosyn or *tose* wul, S.). *Carpo.* "I toose wolle, or cotton, or suche lyke; *je force de laine*, and *je charpie de la laine*: It is a great craft to tose wolle wel."—PALSG. "Tosing, *carptura*; to tose wool or lyne, *carpo, carmino.*"—GOULDM.'—*Prompt. Parv. and Notes.*
Mr. Wedgwood says, 'To *touse* wool is to pull the flocks to pieces and lay them together again;' he refers the term to Low Du. *tuseln*; Germ. *zausen*. Cf. **Touzle**, above.

(2) *v. a.* to pluck with the claws, as cats do, when—in stretching their fore-legs—they press against any object with extended paws.—

PULVERBATCH. 'Drive that cat off—'er'll *toze* the cushion all to pieces.'

TRAMMEL [tr'am·h'l], *v. n.* to go some little distance for any purpose, as being compelled to do so, and going with reluctance.—ELLESMERE, *Welshampton.* 'I maun *trammel* all the way to Ellesmer' after that tay, I reckon, fur I conna get non' no nigher.'

TRAMMEL-NET, *sb.* a drag-net used for taking salmon and trout in the Severn.—BRIDGNORTH. This net is usually from 40 to 60 yards long, and about 5 ft. wide; one side of it is tied up at short distances with string, so as to fold over and form a kind of pouch, thus making it less easy for the fish to escape as the net drags the bottom of the river—this side is sunk with lead-weights; the opposite one is floated with corks, and has at each end a long line, by which two men—one, in a boat, the other, on the river-bank—drag the net across and down the stream. *Trammel-net* is a redundant form; *trammel* is an old word, meaning *net.* Spenser uses it—

'Her golden lockes she roundly did uptye
In breaded *tramels*, that no looser heares
Did out of order stray about her daintie eares.'
F. Q., Bk. II. c. ii. st. xv.

Bailey—ed. 1727—has '*Trammel* [*tramail, F.*] . . . . . a Sort of Net for Fowling, also for Fishing.'

See *Tramel*, in WEDG. Fr. *tramail;* It. *tramáglio*, a net; trammel.

TRANCHER [tr'an·shur'], *sb.* a wooden platter.—PULVERBATCH. 'Yo' can al'ays tell a clane sarvant by the piggins an' *tranchers.*' *Tranchers* (or trenchers) were formerly used for cold meat; they are *obsolete* for that purpose, but are still in common requisition as bread-platters.

'Fr. *tranchoir*, a platter. O.Fr. *Trencher* . . . *trancher*, trancher, tailler, couper.'—BUR.

Cf. **Trencher.** See **Piggin** (1), also **Treen.**

TRANKLEMENTS, *sb. pl.* odds and ends lying about. Com. 'Now then, young uns, clier away yore *tranklements.*'

TRAPSE [tr'ai·ps], (1) *v. n.* to walk in a slovenly way—a term generally used with regard to mud and mire, but occasionally to the dust of roads. Com.

'I hate the sight o' women going about *trapseing* from house to house in all weathers, wet or dry, and coming in with their petticoats dagged, and their shoes all over mud.'—GEORGE ELIOT, *Scenes from Clerical Life* (Amos Barton).

Ash gives '*Traipse*, To walk in a careless or sluttish manner.'

(2) *v. a.* to make dirty footmarks by heedless steps to and fro. Com. 'That careless wench comen in ŏŏth the pails jest after I'd swilled the flur, an' *trăpsed* it all o'er.'

(3) *v. n.* to walk in a heavy, sluggish way.—WEM. ''E wuz *trăpsing* alung o'er the follow as if 'e'd neither lost nur won.'

(4) *sb.* a long, dirty, tiring walk—purposeless as to results, being generally understood in the application of the term. Com. 'A fine *trăpse* I 'ad fur nuthin'!—the folks wun out w'en I got theer.'

TRASH, (1) *sb.* a slattern; a sorry, worthless kind of person.—BRIDGNORTH; WHITCHURCH; ELLESMERE. 'Er's a reg'lar *trash*—I dunna know 'ow the Missis pŭts up wuth 'er, fur I couldna.'

Compare Shakespeare's 'poor *trash* of Venice.'—*Othello*, II. i. 312.

(2) *v. n.* to walk over land in a heedless way—to trample it down so as to injure it, or the crops growing upon it.—*Ibid.* 'If the French did come 'ere, they might spile the land a bit—they met'n *trash* o'er it, but they couldna carry it away wi' 'em:' so said a farmer in the neighbourhood of Whixall. Compare Shakespeare's use of the word *trash* as a verb in *Othello*, II. i. 312. See *Trash* in NARES.

TREE (1), **TREY** [tr'ee·], Com. [tr'ai·], NEWPORT, *sb.*, *pec.* a flower-pot plant of any woody kind. 'Eh! sī that mon—'e's plontin' *treys*,' said an Edgmond child, on seeing a gardener 'bedding out' geraniums. The form *treys* appears in the *Porkington MS.*—temp. Ed. IV.—as follows:—

'Whenne the mone is in Tauro, hit is good to plante *treys* of pepyns, and whenne hit is in Cancro, in Leone, or in Libra, thanne hit is good to werche in *treys* that be new spronge . . . Also to remeve *treys* fro place to place: ʒiff it be a grete tre, or a tre that berythe the frute, chese the a fulle mone . . .'—*Early English Miscellanies in Prose and Verse*, edited by J. O. Halliwell for the Warton Club, 1855, p. 66.

'A.Sax. *treów;* O.Sax. *tris;* Goth. *triu;* O.Fris., O.Icel. *trê*, tree.'—STRAT.

TREE (2), *sb.* the handle of a spade.—PULVERBATCH. Qy. com. 'Whad's split the *tree* o' the spade?' 'The tumbril w'ĕĕl went o'er it.' '*Tre*' is found in the early writers, with the meaning of a bar or staff of wood. '*Dore-tre*,' i.e. the bar of the door, occurs in *Havelok the Dane:*—

> 'Hauelok lifte up þe *dore-tre*,
> And at a dint he slew hem þre.'—l. 1806.

Cf. **Spittle-tree.** See **Swingle-tree**, also **Tawtree.**

TREEN [tr'ee·n], *adj.* wooden,—a term applied to utensils for domestic purposes, and sometimes used elliptically to denote the things themselves.—CORVE DALE; BRIDGNORTH.

> 'Plowʒe and harwe coude he diʒt,
> *Treen* beddes was he wont to make.'
> *Cursor Mundi, MS. Coll. Trin. Cantab.*, f. 77, l. 12388.

Tusser says, '*Treene* dishes be homely;'—see 'Dinner Matters,' ed. E. D. S., p. 175.

Harrison, in his *Description of England*—A.D. 1577—speaking of things 'greatlie amended' in his day, of which one was 'Furniture of household,' says with reference to this:—'The third thing they tell of, is the exchange of vessell, as of *treene* platters into pewter, and woodden spoones into siluer or tin. For so common were all sorts of *treéne* stuffe in old time, that a man should hardlie find foure péeces of pewter (of which one was peraduenture a salt) in a good farmer's house.'

'Turnynge, or throwynge of *treyn* vessel. *Treen* is retained in E.

Anglian dialect as an adjective, wooden. See Moor's Suffolk Words, v. Treen.'—*Prompt. Parv. and Notes.*

See **Piggin** (1), also **Quaigh** (1) and **Trancher.**

TRENCHER [tr'en·shur'], *sb.* a wooden platter—same as **Trancher,** q. v. Com.

'*The little ould Buttery* some few *trenchers.*'—*Inventory* . . . Owlbury Manor-House, Bishop's Castle, 1625.

'He that waits on another man's *trencher* makes many a late dinner.'—RAY'S *Proverbs*, p. 22.

TRICKLINGS [tr'ik·linz], *sb.* sheep's dung.—PULVERBATCH. It was formerly—before the age of vaccination—a popular belief that 'ship's *tricklin's*,' duly administered, would cure the small-pox. 'Bessy, yo' mind as Granny dunna pŭt ship's *tricklin's* i' my yarb-tay, I canna tak' it if 'er does—nod if I'm marked ever so.'

TRIFLING, *adj., pec.* tedious; tiresome; troublesome: said of any employment that takes up a good deal of time, and has little to show for it.—WORTHEN, *Cherbury.* See example *sub voce* **Winberry.**

TRIG [tr'ig], (1) *v. a.* to trick out; to make spruce.—PULVERBATCH. BRIDGNORTH. 'Sally's gweïn to the Club—I warrant 'er'll *trig* out in all 'er finery.'

> 'And mak yoursells as *trig*, head, feet, and waist,
> As ye were a' to get young lads or e'en.'
>
> ALLAN RAMSAY, *The Gentle Shepherd*, II. i. p. 26.

(2) *sb.* a small gutter,—same as **Rigol** (1), q. v.—PULVERBATCH; WELLINGTON. 'Yo' nee'na cut it dip—on'y a bit of a *trig.*'

(3) *v. a.* to make shallow furrows, or *trigs*, as between seed-beds for onions, carrots, &c.,—'I *trigged* the ground afore I pŭt the seed in.'—WELLINGTON.

TRIM, *v. a., pec.* to chide; to chastise. Com. 'Yore Mother'll *trim* yo', if yo' dunna come back.'

TRIMPLE [tr'im·pl], *v. n.* to limp; to tread gingerly,—to walk as people do who suffer from corns, or tender feet, or whose shoes hurt them.—PULVERBATCH; WELLINGTON. ''Ow that chap *trimples* alung—'e met be walkin' on sparables.'

TRINDLE [tr'in·dl], (1) *sb.* the wheel of a barrow.—ELLESMERE. 'Yo' maun grace the *trindle* o' that w'ĕelbarrow, I conna bar to 'ear it squaikin'.'

> 'Wheel carriages I ha'e but few,
> Three carts, an' twa are feckly new;
> Ae auld wheelbarrow, mair for token,
> Ae leg, an' baith the trams, are broken;
> I made a poker o' the spin'le,
> An' my auld mother brunt the *trin'le.*'
>
> ROBERT BURNS, *Poems*, l. 33, p. 104.

'*Hec troilia*, a trindylle,' occurs in a *Nominale*, xv. cent., amongst other terms relating to spinning, and Mr. Wright gives the glossarial note:—'The wheel. It is still in use in the dialect of Derbyshire.'—See Wr. vocabs., vol. i. p. 217.

'A.Sax., M.H.Germ. *trendel*, trendle (*trindle*, trundle), hoop.'—STRAT. See **Trundle.**

(2) *v. a.* to wheel, as a barrow.—*Ibid.*

'M.H.Germ. *trendeln*, to trindle (trundle).'—STRAT.

(3) *v. a.* to twirl a mop rapidly—by a dexterous movement—between the hands and arms.—SHREWSBURY; PULVERBATCH. Qy. com. 'The wilrit's pŭt sich a rough stale i' the mop, it tars the skin off my arms to *trindle* it.'

(4) *sb.* a disc used by blacksmiths for measuring the circumference of wheels—a 'traveller.'—WHITCHURCH.

TROLLOP, (1) *sb.* a slattern. Com. 'I never sid sich a *trollop* as that ŏŏman—'er petticuts wun dagged 'afe a yard dip.'

(2) *sb.* an unbroken fall, a term used with reference to a person falling helplessly,—' 'E come down wi' sich a *trollop.*'—WHITCHURCH.

TROLLY, *sb.* a low, two-wheeled cart, used for the lighter kinds of field work.—PULVERBATCH; CLUN; LUDLOW; BRIDGNORTH. 'It's no use takin' the waggin fur them fyeow faggits, the *trolly* an' a couple o' 'orses ŏŏl bring 'em aisy.'

TROUSE [tr'ou·s], *sb.* hedge-cuttings,—such as are taken out in 'laying,' or 'pleaching,' a hedge, and which are serviceable in mending the gaps, &c. Com. 'Some o' that rough *trouse* ŏŏl be rar' stuff fur breastin' the 'edge to keep the ship out.'

'Provided always that they be laid with green willow bastons, and for default thereof, with vine cuttings or such *trousse*, so that they lie half a foot thick.'—Holland's *Pliny*, in WEDG.

Mr. Wedgwood says, '*Trouse* is still used in Hereford for the trimmings of hedges.' He refers the term to 'O.N. *tros*, offal, rubbish; N. *tros*, broken branches in a wood, dry, broken twigs.'

Cf. **Brouse.**

TROW [tr'oa·], (1). See **Kneading-trow.**

(2) [tr'oa·], *sb.*, *obs.* a Severn trading vessel—a barge on a very large scale—wide, flat-bottomed, and schooner-rigged, usually about 80, or from 80 to 90, tons burthen, occasionally larger still, and sometimes smaller; there were *trows* of not more than 40 tons: they used to navigate up-stream, beyond Shrewsbury, as high as Pool Quay, but no farther. *Trows* have long ceased to ply up and down Shropshire Severn, discharging and taking in cargo at the different wharfs in the course of their passage—'*nous avons changé tout çela,*' since the Age of Railways—but the name of the old vessel is still preserved [1880] as a Public-house sign, '*The Trow,*' at Jackfield (Salop).

TROWMAN, *sb.*, *obs.* the sailing-master or captain of a *trow.*

'This Indenture made the Twenty Seventh Day of August in the Twenty Sixth Year of the Reigne of our Sovereigne Lord George the second by the Grace of God of great Brittain France and Ireland King Defender of the Faith and so forth and in the Year of our Lord One Thousand Seven hundred and Fifty two Between John Rogers of the Town of Shrewsbury in the County of Salop *Trowman* and Martha his Wife of the one part and Thomas Rogers of the said

Town of Shrewsbury *Trowman* and Brother of the said John Rogers of the other part &c. &c.'

The foregoing is quoted from the preamble to a private deed which seems to relate to the transfer of some property at Frankwell (Shrewsbury): the deed itself is endorsed,—'Owner John Rogers's Settlement.'

Trowman occurs in an old Bridgnorth Burgess-list as follows:—

'Thomas Roberts of Bewdley *Trowman* 12 Sep. 1745.

'John Steward of Bewdley *Trowman* 11 May 1745.'

The persons, whose names are thus recorded, were admitted to the Freedom of Bridgnorth, on the dates specified.

'The yonger son of Charles Reve of Myddle Wood, had lived a yeare and more in Glostershire . . . . . Our officers brought him beefore Mr. Rowland Hunt, and there hee declared upon oath that his last settlement was in the Parish of ——, in Glostershire, and there an order was made to bring him. Thither hee was sent by water to Gloster; Faireley of Atcham, the *trowman*, had seven shillings to bring him thither and to maintaine him by the way.'—GOUGH's *History of Myddle*, p. 168.

See **Owner**.

TRUB [tr'ub·], *adj.* neat; tidy; trim.—PULVERBATCH. ''Is Mother wuz a mighty tidy ŏŏman—'er al'ays looked so clane an' *trub.*'

Mr. Halliwell gives '*Trub*, a slattern,' as a *Devonshire* word.

TRUCK, *sb.* dealings,—to have 'no *truck*' with a person—the term is always used with a negation—is to have nothing to do with him, to wash one's hands of him. Com.

TRUNDLE [tr'un·dl], *sb.* a brewing-vessel; a round cooler.—PULVERBATCH. 'Better part the drink, it's gettin' too warm—pŭt some i' the *trundle*.' See STRAT. *sub voce* **Trindle** (1). Cf. **Runlet**.

TUMBREL, *sb.* a heavy, broad-wheeled cart, used for carrying manure, for the most part. Com.

'Broad-wheel *tumbrel*.'—*Auctioneer's Catalogue* (Longville), 1877.

Tusser has 'Light *tumbrel* and doong crone,' in his 'husbandlie furniture:' see p. 36, ed. E. D. S.

The *Prompt. Parv.* gives '*Tomerel*, donge cart.'

TUMMY, *sb.*, *sl.*? bread and cheese—ELLESMERE; WEM. Qy. com. 'Whad'n'ee got fur yore dinner?' said a child to his school-fellow, as, lessons over, they 'opened out' their provisions. 'Only *tummy*; whad'n yo' got?' 'Mother's gid me a chitte'lin'-puff.' 'Well, yo' gie me a bit o' that, an' I'll gie yo' a bit o' my *tummy*, an' then we sha'n bŏŏth be the richer.'

TUMMY-AWK, *sb.* a dung-fork, carried at the back of the cart, and used to scrape out the manure, on the land, as it is required.—WEM; ELLESMERE. The term seems to be a ludicrous corruption of *tomahawk*. Cf. **Dunnuk**.

TUMP, (1) *sb.* a mound,—such as is raised by ants or moles.—SHREWSBURY; PULVERBATCH; WORTHEN; CORVE DALE; CLEE HILLS; LUDLOW; BRIDGNORTH; MUCH WENLOCK; WELLINGTON. 'I believe the fros' is gweïn, fur I see ŏŏnty-*tumps* throwed up i' the meadow.'

W. *twmp*, a mound. See **Anty-tump**, also **Ŏŏnty-tump**.

(2) *sb.* a store-heap of potatoes, turnips, &c. covered with straw or fern, and enclosed with earth.—*Ibid.* 'Yo'n got a rar' *tump* o' tatoes, Tummas.' 'Aye, theer's more fyarn an' mowld than tatoes, Maister.' Cf. **Bury** (2), also **Hod** (1) and **Hog** (3).

(3) *v. a.* to put potatoes, &c. into a *tump.*—*Ibid.* 'I've bin sortin' tatoes an' puttin' 'em into the trenches, fur John to *tump* w'en 'e laves off work.' See example *sub voce* **Stelch** (1). Cf. **Hod** (2), also **Hog** (3).

(4) *sb.* a clump, as of trees.—WEM; WHITCHURCH; ELLESMERE. 'We can see the *tump* o' trees at The Crimps from our 'ouse,' said a Welshampton woman.

'When he was come to the top of the long, black combe . . . . . he stopped his little nag short of the crest, and got off and looked ahead of him, from behind a *tump* of whortles.'—R. D. BLACKMORE, *Lorna Doone*, A Romance of Exmoor, p. 188, ed. 1878.

W. *twmpath*, a bush.

* **TUN-DISH,** (1) *sb.* a tin funnel for filling bottles.—SHREWSBURY; ATCHAM; PULVERBATCH; BRIDGNORTH; NEWPORT. Qy. com.

'Filling a bottle with a *tun-dish.*'—*Measure for Measure*, III. ii. 182.

(2) same as **Tunning-dish**, below.—SHREWSBURY; NEWPORT.

TUNNING-DISH, *sb.* a wooden funnel, used for filling barrels.—SHREWSBURY; ELLESMERE, *Welshampton*; WEM.

'*Hoc colum, Hoc infusorium, An^ce* tunnyng,' occurs—under the head, '*Panducsator cum suis Instrumentis*'—in a *Pictorial Vocabulary*, xv. cent., in Wr. vocabs., vol. i. p. 276.

'*Infusorium*, A tunnell, an eure.'—*Dict. Etym. Lat.*

TUNNING-GAUN, same as above.—ELLESMERE. See **Gaun** (2).

TUNPAIL, same as above.—PULVERBATCH; CRAVEN ARMS; CHURCH STRETTON; BRIDGNORTH.

'Lading-bucket and *tunpail.*'—*Auctioneer's Catalogue* (Longville), 1877.

TUP, *sb.* a ram. Com.

'O Lord, when hunger pinches sore,
Do thou stand us in need,
And send us from thy bounteous store,
A *tup* or wether head! Amen.'

ROBERT BURNS, *Poems*, p. 175, l. 18.

'*Hic vervex*, *A^me* a tuppe.'—*Nominale*, xv. cent., in Wr. vocabs., vol. i. p. 219.

'*Vervex*, A weather or sheep.'—*Dict. Etym. Lat.*

TURF, *sb.* peat, dried and cut into pieces for fuel,—each several piece is called '*a turf;*' the plural form is *turfs.*—*N. Shr.*

'Good *turffe* and peate, on mossie ground is won,
Wherewith good fires, is made for man most meete,
That burneth cleere, and yeelds a savour sweete
To those which have no nose for dayntie smell,
The finer sort, were best in court to dwell.'

CHURCHYARD'S *Poems*, p. 114, l. 4.

'For fewell, although many of the greatest woods are cutt downe, yet there is sufficient left for timber and fire-boot for most tenements. There is likewise a Turbary in Haremeare which belongs to the Lord of the Manor, and was formerly a great benefit to the neighbours; but now they have taken a trade of carriing them to Shrewsbury and selling them; soe that the Turbary is much wasted and the *Turfes* are much dearer. Soe that a yard of peates which was formerly at 8d. is now sett at 2s. Note that a yard of peates is 80 square yards, viz.:—soe many peates as can bee digged in and layd to dry upon soe much ground.'—GOUGH'S *History of Myddle*, p. 175.

'With whinnes or with furzes thy houell renew,
for *turfe* or for sedge, for to bake and to brew:
For charcole and sea cole, as also for thacke,
for tallwood and billet, as yeerlie ye lacke.'
TUSSER, *Fiue Hundred Pointes of Good Husbandrie* [June].

'*Turfe*, of flagge, swarde of þe erþe. *Cespes.* "Turfe of the fenne, *Tourbe de terre.* Turfe flagge sworde, *Tourbe.*"—PALSG. "A Turfe, *cespes, gleba.* A Turfe grafte, *turbarium.*"—CATH. ANG. The distinction above intended, seems to be retained in East Anglian dialect, according to Forby, who gives the following explanation;—"Turf, *s.* peat; fuel dug from boggy ground. The dictionaries interpret the word as meaning only the surface of the ground pared off. These we call flags, and they are cut from dry heaths as well as from bogs. The substance of the soil below these is turf. Every separate portion is a *turf*, and the plural is *turves*, which is used by Chaucer" [*C. T.*, l. 10109]. In Somerset likewise, peat cut into fuel is called *turf*, and *turves*, according to Jennings' Glossary.'—*Prompt. Parv. and Notes.*

'A.Sax. *turf;* O.Icel. *torfa;* O.H.Germ. *zurba*, turf.'—STRAT.

See **Black-Mullock**, also **Whixall-bibles**, and **Moss**.

TURMIT, *sb.* a turnip. Com.

'*Turmits*, turnips. Lanc.'—PEGGE.

TURMIT-LANTERN [lan·tun *and* lon·tun], *sb.* a lantern made by scooping out the inside of a turnip, then carving on the outside a rude representation of the human face, and placing a lighted candle within it. Com. The effect of a lantern of this kind is often hideous in the extreme. 'Jack's a dab-'ond at măkin' a *turmit-lontun;* 'e frittened the folks comin' from the daincin' the tother night out o' thar senses.'

TURN, *sb.* a dizziness to which sheep are subject,—'that ship's got the *turn*.'—WELLINGTON. Cf. **Gid.**

TURN-AGAIN-GENTLEMAN, *sb. Lilium Martagon*, Turk's cap lily.—CLUN; BRIDGNORTH.

TURNEL, *sb.* a large, oval tub used in brewing, salting, &c.—a 'cooler.'—NEWPORT; WHITCHURCH; ELLESMERE.

'Salting *turnel*.'—*Auctioneer's Catalogue* (Forton Hall, Newport), 1875. Cf. **Kneading-turnel.**

TURN THE RAIN, *phr.* to keep the rain off; to throw off the wet.—PULVERBATCH; NEWPORT. Qy. com. ''Ere, tak' this shawl, it'll *turn the rain* if theer comes on a shower, an' it ŏŏnna be much to carry, anyways.'

TUSH [tush], (1) *sb.* a boar's tusk.—PULVERBATCH; WEM. ''E wuz as foul a fellow as ever yo' sid'n, ŏŏth two lung tith jest like a bwur's *tushes*.'

'. . . thou told'st me thou wouldst hunt the boar.
O, be advised! thou know'st not what it is
With javelin's point a churlish swine to gore,
Whose *tushes* never sheathed he whetteth still,
Like to a mortal butcher bent to kill.'
SHAKESPEARE, *Venus and Adonis*, l. 617.

'*Tosche*, longe tothe, *Colomellus*, *culmus*. In Norfolk Tosh signifies, according to Forby, a tusk, a long curved tooth.'—*Prompt. Parv. and Notes.*

'A.Sax. *tusc*, *tux*; O.Fris. *tusk*, tusk (*tush*).'—STRAT.

(2) *v. a.* to drag, or shove along, as of anything too big or heavy to be lifted and carried.—PULVERBATCH. 'Can yo' carry them faggits to the 'ŏŏd-pil?' 'I dunna know, but if I canna carry 'em, be'appen I can *tush* 'em alung.'

TUSSOCK, *sb.* a clump of coarse grass. Com. *Tussocky-land* is land that has very many such clumps on it. Cf. **Sniggle-bogs.**

TUT-BALL, *sb.*, *obs.*? a game at hand-ball, chiefly played by girls.—NEWPORT, *Shiffnal.*

'*Tuts*, a term at the old game of stool-ball.'—Clarke's *Phraseologia Puerilis*, 8vo. Lond. 1655, p. 141, in HAL., ed. 1855.

See Bk. II., *Folklore*, &c., 'Games.'

TUTTY, *adj.* neat; snug,—'a *tutty* bonnet.'—WEM; ELLESMERE. Cf. **Cooty.**

TWARL [twaar'·l], *v. n.* to wrangle,—'dunna *twarl* yo' two.'—PULVERBATCH; WORTHEN.

TWARLY, *adj.* peevish; cross. Qy. com. 'W'ether it's the child's tith, or w'ether 'e's gweïn to sicken o' the maisles—'e's bin that *twarly* all day, I canna get 'im out o' 'and a bit.' Mr. Halliwell gives *Twarly* as a *Cheshire* word, with the same signification.

TWEAK [twai·k *and* twee·k], (1) *sb.* a sharp, severe attack of illness—'a pinch.'—PULVERBATCH; WEM. 'Poor ŏŏman! 'er hanna got o'er that las' bout o' sickness—it wuz a very 'eavy *tweak*.'

Bailey—ed. 1782—gives 'A Tweak [of *zwicken*, Teut. to pinch], Perplexity, Trouble, Vexation.'

'Low-German *twikken*, to pluck.'—*Bremen Wörterbuch.*

(2) *v. a.* to squeeze; to press.—PULVERBATCH; OSWESTRY. 'I canna get any more i' the ampot, Naint.' 'Yo' mun *twaik* it down, it use't to 'oud 'afe a strike, an' mus' now.' Cf. **Queak.**

TWEER-HOLE, *sb.* the ventilating passage of a blast-furnace.—COLLIERY; M. T.

'Fr. *tuyère*, a blast-pipe; O.Fr. *tuyel*, a shaft, pipe, flue.'—PICK.

TWELFT, twelfth.—SHREWSBURY; PULVERBATCH. Qy. com.

'The *twelft* day, sal sternes falle.'
Homilies in Verse (A.D. 1330, *circa*). *Specim. Early Eng.*, viii. *a.* l. 137.

'A.Sax. *twelfta*, twelfth.'—STRAT.
See **Grammar Outlines** (*adjectives of numeration*), p. xlvi.

TWINK, *sb.* the Chaffinch.—BRIDGNORTH.

'To *twink*, to twitter:—
As a swallow in the air doth sing,
With no continued song, but pausing still,
Twinks out her scattered notes in accents shrill.
Chapman, Odyss. xxi.
Twink, a chaffinch, from his twittering song.'—WEDG.

Cf. **Chink-chink, Pine-finch,** and **Spink.**

TWINS, *sb.* an agricultural implement for breaking the clods and uprooting the weeds of ploughed land, preparatory to the harrows going on. Com. *Twins* have two rows of deep, curved, broad teeth—a blacksmith said, 'the tines wun duck-fūtted.' The implement has no wheels or guides of any kind, and in this respect differs from the modern 'cultivator'; it is either single or double, and in the latter case is spoken of as '*a pair of twins*,' the several parts being coupled together: its chief work being—to use an Early English term—to *twin*, i. e. separate, the weeds from the soil, the name of *twins* has been aptly given to it.

'*Twinnen*, twin; *dividere*.'—STRAT.

Mr. Skeat says, 'From the root *two*, A.S. *twá*; compare Eng. *between*.'—*Glossarial Index* to *Man of Lawes Tale*, p. 265.

TWINTER, *v. a.* to shrivel.—PULVERBATCH; ELLESMERE. (1) 'It's likely to be a sharp fros' to-night—I'm afeard it'll *twinter* the tato-tops.' (2) 'Yo'n 'ad the oven too sharp, an' it's whad I call spilin' good mate to *twinter* it up like that.'

TWINTERED, *part. adj.* shrivelled; shrunk.—*Ibid.* 'They tellen me as the Squire's gwun sich a little *twintered* up owd mon, an' 'e wuz used to be a right brocky fellow.' See **Brocky.**

TWISTIFIED, *adj.* entangled; involved, as of affairs,—''E's left everythin' sadly *twistified*.' A coined word.—MUCH WENLOCK.

TWITTER, (1) *v. n.* to be nervous and affected in address.—PULVERBATCH. 'I canna bar to 'ear that ŏŏman talk, 'er does so mince an' *twitter*—like as if 'er couldna open 'er mouth.'

(2) *sb.* a state of nervous agitation.—PULVERBATCH. 'Theer wuz talk o' the Fenians comin' las' night, an' it pŭt everybody i' the town o' the *twitter* an' tremble.' See *Twitter* in WEDG.

TWIX, *prep.* betwixt; between.—PULVERBATCH. 'I think i' my 'eart, *twix* one thing an' another, yo'n drive me kyimet.'

'A.Sax. *twix*; O.Sax. *tuisc*, twix.'—STRAT. See **Betwix.**

TWIZE [twei·z], *adv.* twice,—'*twize* one's two.'—SHREWSBURY; PULVERBATCH; CHURCH STRETTON. Qy. com.

'"Sire, a selcouþ siȝt it is · of þis semli best;
Loo, how loueli it a-louted · lowe to vs *twiȝes*,
It bi-tokenes sum-what treuli · god turne it to gode!"'
William of Palerne, l. 3721.

Compare the M. E. *twyes*—found in Chaucer and other writers of that period—which is formed from A.S. *twy*, double, with adverbial suffix *-es*. See *Twice* in **Grammar Outlines** (*adverbs of time*).

TWO-BOWED-CHAIR [boa·d chee·h'r'], *sb.* a wooden arm-chair, of the kind often seen in old-fashioned farm-house parlours and kitchens, having a low back, which, combining with the *bows*, or arms, forms a commodious, half-circular rest for the person.—PULVERBATCH. 'The Maister wuz sittin' in 'is *two-bowed-cheer*, smokin' 'is pipe.'

TWO-DOUBLE, (1) *adj.* twofold; double. Com. This reduplicative term is applied to anything that is double, or that can be made so by folding. (1) A certain person was directed at Clunbury, to go up the village 'tell' he came to '*two-double* doors,' *i. e.* double, or folding-doors. (2) 'I never wuz out in sich coud winde—I'd a thick jacket an' cloak, an' a shawl *two-double*, an' it was like nuthin'.' See **Double-couple.**

(2) *adj.* bent, and bowed down in figure, as from the decrepitude of age, or from rheumatic affection, &c. Com. 'Poor owd Mattha [Matthew] 'uffer! 'e's aumust in 'is *two-double*—it's a pity to see 'im gwein to work.'

TWO-FACED, *adj.* double-faced; insincere. Com. 'If yo' wanten to know a 'ollow, *two-faced* fellow, yo' can see one in Tum any day.'

TWO-FACES-UNDER-THE-SUN, same as **Three-faces-under-a-hood**, q. v.—WORTHEN.

TWO-THREE [tuth·r'i'], two or three; a considerable number or quantity,—'a good *tuthree;*' 'a tidy *tuthree.*' Com. See *sub voce* **Few** in **Grammar Outlines** (*adjectives of numeration*).

TWO-TWINS. See *sub voce* **Double-couple.**

UNBEKNOWNST, *adv.* unknown—without anybody's knowledge.—WEM. 'W'en the time fur flittin' come, I just shifted my things at the edge-o'-neet, an' got out o' the 'ouse *unbeknownst.*' Cf. **Unknownst.**

UNBETHOUGHT, *part. past*, remembered; called back to mind: used with a pronoun, reflexively, for the most part. 'I should a done that wrung if I 'adna jest *unbethought* me in time.'—WHITCHURCH; ELLESMERE, *Cheshire Border.* An imported word seemingly.

'and *vnbethought** him of a while,
how he might that wilde bore beguile.'
Sir Lionell, l. 35. *Percy Folio MS.*, vol. i. p. 76, ed. Hales and Furnivall.

* 'The word still exists in Lancashire . . . . But originally the *un* was *um*, A.S. *umb*, *ymb*, about. A.S. *unbeðoht*, is unthought, inconsiderate; while *ymbþencan* is to think about.'—Note by MR. FURNIVALL.—*Ibid.*

Ash has 'Unbethink, Unbethinken (*v. t. a local word*), To bethink.'

UNGAIN, *adj.* awkward; inconvenient.—LUDLOW; BRIDGNORTH; NEWPORT.

> 'Therof the pepul wold be fayne,
> Fore to cum home aȝayne,
> That hath goon gatis *ungayne*,
> for defaute of lyȝt.'
> JOHN AUDELAY'S *Poems*, p. 14.

See **Gain** (1) and (2), also **Ongain** (1).

UNHUMAN. See **Onhuman**.

UNKED, UNKET, (1) *adj.* dreary; lonely.—CLEE HILLS. 'W'y dunna yo' stort?' 'I shall wait till the moon's up, fur the roäd's nation *unket*.'

'I had not so much as a dog with me, and the place was very *unkid* and lonesome, and the rolling clouds very desolate.'—R. D. BLACKMORE, *Lorna Doone*, A Romance of Exmoor, p. 78, ed. 1878.

(2) *adj.* awkward.—CORVE DALE. M.E. *un-*, not; and *kid*, known, with similar sense to A.S. *uncúð*, uncouth.

UNKIND, (1) *adj.* ungenial; cold; cloddy: said of soil.—PULVERBATCH; CLEE HILLS; BRIDGNORTH; WELLINGTON. 'Theer's a power o' *unkind*, clayey sile on that farm, nod fit fur anythin' but ŏŏäts.' See **Kind** (2).

(2) unthriving: said of animals.—WELLINGTON. See **Kind** (2). Cf. **Untoërtly**, below.

UNKNOWNST, same as **Unbeknownst**, q. v.—BRIDGNORTH; ELLESMERE.

UNLUCKY. See **Onlucky**.

Mr. Nares says that 'an *unlucky* boy, an *unlucky* trick [*i. e.* mischievous] would formerly have been called *unhappy*.'

'*Lafeu*. . . . . Go thy ways: let my horses be well looked to, without any tricks.

'*Clown*. If I put any tricks upon 'em, sir, they shall be jades' tricks. . . . . .

'*Lafeu*. A shrewd knave and an *unhappy*.

'*Count*. So he is. My lord that's gone made himself much sport out of him. . . .'—*All's Well that Ends Well*, IV. v. 66.

UNTIDY. See **Ontidy**.

> 'Wit[h] his *vntydy* tales · he tened ful ofte
> Conscience and his compaignye · of holicherche þe techeres.'
> *Piers Pl.*, Text B., pass. xx. l. 118.

UNTOERTLY, *adj.* unthriving; unpromising. — PULVERBATCH; BRIDGNORTH. Qy. com. 'I never thought it ŏŏd come to much, it looked *untoërtly* from the first.' See **Toërtly**.

UPHOUD, *v. a* and *v. n.* to warrant. Com. 'Yo' ŏŏdna see a prettier nor more useful tit twix 'ere an' Lunnon, I'll *up'oud* it.'

UPKEGGED, *part. adj.* upset. — WEM. 'They fund the barrel caved o'er, an' all the drink *upkegged*.'

UPRIGHT, *sb.* a chimney-sweep.—BRIDGNORTH; WELLINGTON. The marriage of one Joseph Corbett with Mary Price is recorded in the Register of Christ Church, Wellington (Salop), Oct. 17, 1859, and his 'Rank or Profession' described therein as '*Upright.*' A witness to the marriage was a certain Thomas Adams.

On March 3rd, 1880, a newspaper-hawker at Wellington—brother to a sweep—was asked if he knew any recent instance of the use of the term *upright*, as meaning a chimney-sweep? He replied, 'Yes, *not long ago*, w'en I went with my brother to put up the bands, 'e called 'imself "Thomas Adams, *upright.*"' Oddly enough, it turned out that this same Thomas Adams was the very person who had witnessed the marriage, in 1859, of Joseph Corbett, '*upright.*'

Up-wright would perhaps be a more intelligent spelling of this curious term, than that adopted in the Register, and given above, thus: *up*, a chimney, *wright*, i. e. workman. Before the Act was passed which made it illegal to do so, a sweep would actually go *up* a chimney, and, as a *wright*, or workman, follow his calling therein. Cf. *Wheel-wright*, *Ship-wright*, *Play-wright.*

UPSEDOWN [up·si'doun], *adv.* upside down. — SHREWSBURY; PULVERBATCH. 'Jack Price 'as took to runnin' a 'bus, but 'e'll mak nuthin' out—'e'll never turn the world *upsedown.*' 'No, 'e's more like to turn the w'ĕels down-side-up.'

Upsedown is found in the Wycliffite Version—A.D. 1388—'and he turnede *vpsedoun* the bordis of chaungeris, and the chayeris of men that solden culueris.'—*Matt.* xxi. 12.

Upsodown—another form of the word—is common in early writers, as, for example—

> 'Antecryst cam þanne · and al þe croppe of treuthe
> Torned it *vp so doune.* . . .'
>
> *Piers Pl.*, Text B., pass. xx. l. 53.

> 'For the lauys of this lond ben lad a wrong way,
> Both temperall and spiritual I tel ȝou treuly,
> even *up-so-doune.*'
>
> JOHN AUDELAY'S *Poems*, p. 20.

The *Promptorium Parvulorum* gives both spellings,—'*Vpsedowne* (*vp so doun*, S.). *Eversus, subversus, transversus.*'

'*Upsidedown.* For *up-so-down*, up what was down.'—WEDG.

UPSIDES, *adj.* even. COM. ''E's al'ays cuttin' at me about summat, but I'll be *upsides* ŏŏth 'im one o' these first days.'

URCHIN, *sb. Erináceus Europæus*, the Hedgehog. COM.

> 'For some like Snailes, some did like spyders shew,
> And some like ugly *Urchins* thick and short.'
>
> SPENSER, *F. Q.*, Bk. II. c. xi. st. xiii.

See *Tempest*, I. ii. 326.

'*Vrchone*, beest. *Erinacius, ericius.* "An Vrchone, *ericius, erenacius.*"—CATH. ANG. "Urchone, *herisson.* Irchen, a lytell beest full of prickes, *herison.*"—PALSG. In Italian, "*Riccio*, an vrchin or hedgehog."—FLORIO.'—*Prompt. Parv. and Notes.*

'*Ericius* . . . animal spinis coopertum quod exindè dicitur nominatim eo quòd subtegit se quando spinis suis clauditur, quibus undique protectus est contra insidius . . . . . *a hedgehog.*'—*Dict. Etym. Lat.*

'O.Fr. *Heriçon, eriçon, ireçon,* hérisson; *de ericius* . . ital. riccio, esp. erizo.'—BUR.

Cf. **Hodgen.**

UTICK, *sb. Pratíncola rubétra,* the Whinchat. — SHREWSBURY; WELLINGTON; NEWPORT. The note of this bird, '*U-tick, tick, tick,*' has given rise to its local appellation. Cf. **Haytick.**

UVVER [uv·ur'], *adj.* upper; higher in place or position,—'who lives i' the *uvver* 'ouse now?'—PULVERBATCH; WORTHEN; OSWESTRY.

'A.Sax. *ufera;* O.H.Germ. *obero,* uver (*superior*).'—STRAT.

UVVER-LIP, *sb.* the upper lip.—PULVERBATCH. 'Mother's got a despert bad coud, an' 'er *uvver-lip*'s swelled as big as two.' Compare M.E. *over-lip*—

'Hire *overlippe* wypede sche so clene,
That in hire cuppe was no ferthing sene
Of greece, whan sche dronken hadde hire draughte.'
CHAUCER, *The Prologue,* l. 133, ed. Morris.

'the *overe lippe* ant the nethere,' is given as the gloss of 'La bas levere et la levere suseyne,' in *The Treatise of Walter de Biblesworth,* xiii. cent., in Wr. vocabs., vol. i. p. 146.

UVVERMOST, *adj.* uppermost.—PULVERBATCH; LUDLOW. 'Mind 'ow yo' put'n them things i' the drawer, an' keep the Maister's collars *uvvermost.*'

'With the *overmast* lofe hit [the saltcellar] shalle be set.'—*Boke of Curtasaye,* p. 322.

See *Over* in DR. MORRIS's *Historical English Accidence,* p. 110.

A.S. *ufe-mest, yfe-mest,* highest; uppermost.

VAILS, *sb. pl., obsols.* gifts of money to servants.—SHREWSBURY; PULVERBATCH; BRIDGNORTH. 'They dunna gie very big wages, but theer's a djel o' company kep', an' the *vails* maken up—I got above a pound at the Chris'mas bout' [1840].

A Clergyman who holds a living not very remote from Shrewsbury, relates that, upon a certain occasion when he had left home to visit a friend, the Severn rose so rapidly during his absence, that he had to be driven back in his friend's carriage. The coachman, finding the usual road impassable, was obliged to make a considerable *détour,* and in doing so had to remove some hurdles to enable the carriage to pass along; arrived at their destination, the Clergyman, as a recompense to the servant-man for the trouble he had had, offered him some money, but he refused it, saying, 'No, thank you, Sir; we are not allowed to take *vails.*' This was in 1837.

'Cooke Hayward was hired with Mr. Pierpoint to bee his Cooke and caterer; his wages was £12 per annum, and his *veiles* considerable.'—GOUGH's *History of Myddle,* p. 182.

'Sept., 1766. *Vails* were abolished in Shropshire by a resolution passed at the Infirmary meeting. The grand jury at the Summer assizes had passed a similar resolution just before. It needs hardly be said that this was a fee expected by a gentleman's servants from every guest that dined at their master's table; a custom now preserved only at the official dinners given by the judges of assize upon the circuit.'—OWEN and BLAKEWAY'S *History of Shrewsbury*, vol. i. p. 583.

Vails is a contraction of *avails*, where *avail* is a substantive from the verb *avail*, meaning profit, advantage. Shakespeare has *avails* in this sense; see *All's Well that Ends Well*, III. i. 22.

VAMP, *sb.* a prop to support the shaft of a cart when the horse is taken out; also to serve as a rest for a temporary bench, or a table made of loose planks. Such a bench or table would have a *vamp* at each end. It is a rude contrivance, consisting simply of a three-forked branch of a tree, cut to the requisite length and inverted.—CORVE DALE. Cf. **Nave.**

VARJIS, *sb.*, *var. pr.* verjuice; the juice of crabs. Com. 'This fresh-drink's gwun as sour as *vargis*, an' it hanna bin brewed no time,' *i. e.* only a short time.

> 'Be sure of *vergis* (a gallond at least)
> so good for the Kitchen, so needfull for beast,
> It helpeth thy cattel, so feeble and faint,
> if timely such cattle with it thou acquaint.'
>
> TUSSER, *Fiue Hundred Pointes of Good Husbandrie* [October].

Fr. *vert*, green, and *jus*, juice. See **Crab-varjis.**

VAST, *sb.* a great quantity,—'a *vast* of timber.'—CORVE DALE.

VEERINGS, same as **Feerings**, q. v.—CLEE HILLS.

VEIL [vai·l], *sb.* the adipose membrane, or caul, of a pig's intestines. —SHREWSBURY; PULVERBATCH; WORTHEN. Qy. com. See *sub voce* **Faggits.**

VESSEL-MAID, same as **Dairy-maid**, q. v.—PULVERBATCH.

VEX, *v. n.*, *pec.* to grieve; to lament.—SHREWSBURY; CLUN; BRIDGNORTH. 'Poor Will Speake's *vexin'* sadly, 'is wife's djed o' the faiver, an' lef' 'im ŏŏth three or four little childern.'

VIRGIN-HONEY, *sb.* the honey produced from the hive of a second swarm from the parent-stock.—PULVERBATCH. Qy. com. 'Mother, whad did Mrs. Gilpin mane?—'er said as Baby wuz to 'ăve the powder in *virgin-'oney.*' 'Well, it's 'oney from the cast, an' it's quite w'ite, an' as clier as clier.' See **Cast** (7).

VIRGIN-MARY'S-COWSLIP, *sb. Pulmonaria officinális*, common Lungwort (garden plant).—CHURCH STRETTON, *Longnor.*

VIRGIN-MARY'S-HONEYSUCKLE, same as above.—CLUN; ELLESMERE. A Welshampton woman explained, that the local name given to this plant arose from a legend of the Virgin-Mother's milk having been dropped upon it—'the laves,' she said, 'han bin spotted ever sence.'

VIRGINS'-GARLANDS, *sb. pl.* chaplets of white paper-flowers, with a pair, sometimes more than one pair, of gauntlet-shaped gloves—likewise of paper—suspended from them; they were carried at young maidens' funerals, and were afterwards hung up in the Church, as mementoes of the departed. *Virgins'-garlands* still [1880] exist; as, for instance, at Minsterley, where there are several, the most recent of them being of the date, 1764. See Bk. II., *Folklore*, &c., 'Customs' (*deaths*).

VITTLE [vit·l], *sb.* provisions; victuals.—CRAVEN ARMS; CLUN. 'Yo'n brought some *vittle* fur we, Miss Nellie,' said Martha Cadwallader, to a certain young lady, as, followed by a basket-bearer, she approached the group of hay-makers, of whom Martha was one [1873].

'And, soth to sayn, *vitaille* gret plentee
They han hir yeuen . . . .'
CHAUCER, B. 443 (Six-text ed.), Skeat.

'Robin promis'd me
A' my winter *vittle;*
Fient haet he had but three
Goose feathers and a whittle.'
ROBERT BURNS, *Poems*, p. 248, l. 27.

'O.Fr. *vitaille*, de [Lat.] *victualia;* nourriture, vivres, aliments, provisions des choses nécessaires à la vie.'—BUR.

Cf. **Fittle.**

VOID, *adj.* unoccupied; vacant,—a preservation of the old sense of the term.—PULVERBATCH. 'The country's in a despert state, theer's nine or ten farms to let, an' they tellen me theer's rows an' rows o' 'ousen *void* i' the town' [1880].

'Let their habitation be *void*, and no man to dwell in their tents.'—*Ps.* lxxx. 26.

'Voyde, or vacaunt. *Vacans.*'—*Prompt. Parv.*

'O.Fr. *Vuit, vuide, void, voide;* vide . . .'—BUR.

WADDIOCK [wod·i'uk *and* wod·yuk], *sb.* a good big piece,—''Er cut me a *waddiock* o' pork-pie.' Com.

WADGE [waaj·], *sb., var. pr.* a thick slice, or lump = wedge,—'a *wadge* o' cake.'—CORVE DALE.

WADS [wod·z], *sb. pl.* the small heaps in which vetches or pease are left on the ground when cut.—CLEE HILLS; BRIDGNORTH.

WAGGONERS' WORDS TO HORSES. The Houyhnhum dialect has its varieties in common with the general dialect. But as the latter is 'improved' away by the National Schoolmaster, so the former is corrupted by the nomadic Navvy. 'Them navvies talken to thar 'orses quite different to whad we dun, an' ours bin spïlte ŏŏth 'earin' 'em as they gŏn up an' down the line,' so said an old waggoner in the neighbourhood of Shrewsbury. The following are specimens of the old *Horse-Tongue* still [1874] in use in their respective localities. Suppose a team of three horses, Leader, Pin-horse, and Shafter; the locality,—

(1) PULVERBATCH; or CRAVEN ARMS, *Stokesay*. The waggoner, standing to the left of his horses, would address them thus—Leader: '*Commoag*' [kùmmoa·g], come near; '*Gee*' [jee·], go from me; '*Jiggin*' [jig·gi'n], turn short back. The Pin-horse and Shafter alike: '*Haw-woop*' [au·woo·p]—with a rise of pitch on the latter part of the vowel—come towards; '*Heit*' [a'·yt], go from me. The whole team: '*Woo*' [wūo·], stop.

(2) SHREWSBURY, *Hanwood*. He would use these terms, to the Leader: '*Come n'arun*' [kùmnaar'·r'u'n], come near; '*Chee-haw*' [chee·au·], go from me; '*Chiggin-back*' [chig·gi'n baak], turn short back. To the Pin-horse and Shafter: '*Haw*' [au·], come towards; '*Heit*' [aeytt·], go from me. To the whole team: '*Woo*' [wūo·], stop.

(3) ELLESMERE, *Welshampton*. Here the waggoner would say to the Leader: '*Come narro*' [kùmnaar'·r'oe'], come near; '*Gee-ho*' [jee·oa], go from me; '*Gee-ho-back*' [jee·oa·'baa·k], turn short back. To the Pin-horse and Shafter: '*Haw*' [āu·], come towards; '*Heet*' [eett·], go from me. To the whole team: '*Gee-off*' [jee·oa·ff], go straight on; '*Come nether meggen woo-wo-op*' [kùm naedh·dhu'r' maeg·gi'n wù·wù·' ūp·p], come on one side, and go slowly; '*Wo-o*' [wōa],—the pronunciation of this word is equal to two long quantities with a gradual lowering of pitch—stop. *Heit* is found in Chaucer:—

> 'The carter smote, and cried as he were wood,
> *Heit* scot, *heit* brok, what spare ye for the stones.'
>
> *C. T.*, l. 7125.

See **Call-words to Animals**.

WAIDY, WEÄDY, WEEDY [wai·di', wee·h'di', wee·di'], *adj.* This term which obtains commonly throughout Salop, in one or other of the forms here given, is widely applied; it is understood to mean exceeding expectation, as regards length, quantity, durability; also, tedious, tiresome to get through, as of a piece of work, &c.—almost anything may be *waidy*, from a length of road, to a solid, 'cut and come again' piece of meat. (1) 'Yo'n find it a mighty *waidy* roăd, if yo' bin thinkin' o' walkin' from Soseb'ry to Stretton, though it dunna look so fare.' (2) 'These lung sems bin despert *waidy* sewin'—it inna like summat as yo' can get on ŏŏth.' (3) 'That's a *weädy* bit o' bif—it 'ouds out well, and theer's bin a power o' cuttin' at it.'

'A *Wheady Mile*, a Mile beyond Expectation, a tedious one. *Shrops.*' —BAILEY, ed. 1782.

See **Onweedy**.

WAIN-HUS, *sb.* a shelter-house in farm-buildings for waggons and carts when not in use.—PULVERBATCH. Qy. com. 'Tell the waggoner to pŭt the drill inside the *wain-'us*, nod to get wet.' The old word *wain*, preserved in this composite form, seems to be no longer used for the waggon itself. A.S. *wægn;* a wain or waggon, and *hús;* a house. See **Jack-and-his-Wain**, and **The-Wain-and-Horses**. See also **Hús**.

WAINY, WANTY [wai·ni', won·ti'], *adj.* irregular in shape and proportion, thus—if a piece of wood presumably three inches in diameter were required to be squared to two inches, and it would not square throughout, that would be *wainy*, or *wanty*.—CLUN. Cf. **Cater-cornelled**.

WAKES, *sb.* a country-parish festival—the Church's Saint's Dedication-Day Feast, originally, which was preceded by a Vigil = watch = *wake*. Com.

'The *Wake-day* is the day on which the Parish Church was dedicated, called So, because the Night before it they were used to watch till Morning in the Church, and feasted all the next day.'—HILMAN'S *Tusser Redivivus*, ed. 1710.

A.S. *wacan;* Swed. *vaka;* Mœso-Goth. *wakan;* to watch. See Bk. II., *Folklore*, &c., 'Wakes.'

WALEY-GALEY [wai·li' gai·li'], (1) *adj.* unsteady; tottering.—WORTHEN; PULVERBATCH. *Waley-galey* is sometimes used substantively, as one would say, 'all of a shake,'—'Come yo' childern from the stack, the lather's all of a *waley-galey*—it'll be down on some o' yo'.'

(2) *sb.* the game of see-saw, in which children, sitting or standing at each end of a plank—balanced on a prop—move alternately upwards and downwards.—*Ibid.* 'W'eer bin the lads gwun?' 'They bin playin' *waley-galey* i' the stack-yard.'

Compare '*Wawyn̄*', or waueryn, yn a myry totyr. *Oscillo.*, UG. V. Myry tottyr, chylderis game. Totyr, or myry totyr . . . *Oscillum.*—CATH. "*Oscillum*, genus ludi, cum funis suspenditur a trabe in quo pueri et puelle sedentes impelluntur huc et illuc,—a totoure."—MED. GR. "Tytter-totter, a play for childre, *balenchoeres*."—PALSG. Forby gives Titter-cum-totter, in Norfolk dialect, to ride on the ends of a balanced plank.'—*Prompt. Parv. and Notes*, pp. 518, 498.

WALLED [wau·ld], *part. adj.* boiled.—PULVERBATCH. 'Them cheese-cloths stinken o' soap enough to pïsen anybody, I toud yo' to wesh 'em i' the *walled* w'ey—now dunna let me 'ăve to tell yo' the same thing agen.'

Ray, in his '*North Country Words*,' has '*Walling*, *i. e.* Boyling, it is now in frequent Use among the Salt-boilers at *Northwych*, *Namptwych*, &c.'

'A.Sax. *weallan;* O.Sax., O.H.Germ. *wallan*, wall (*bullire*, *fervere*).'—STRAT.

See **Wallop** (1), below.

WALL-EYE, (1) *sb.* an eye, of which the iris is either streaked or parti-coloured, or else of a totally different hue to the fellow-eye, and not in harmony with the general complexion or colour.—PULVERBATCH; MUCH WENLOCK; WELLINGTON. Qy. com. Eyes of this kind are perfectly sound as regards vision; they are met with in the human subject, in horses, dogs, cats, &c., and are probably the same as the 'whally eies' of which Spenser speaks:—

'. . . a bearded Gote, whose rugged heare,
And *whally eies* (the signe of gelosy),
Was like the person selfe whom he did beare.'

F. Q., Bk. I. c. iv. st. xxiv.

Mr. Nares, who discusses the term *whally-eies* at considerable length, rejects as erroneous the gloss '*streaked eyes*' given by earlier commentators, and maintains that none other than eyes affected by the disease *glaucoma* (which imparts a clouded appearance and greenish hue to them) can be meant by it—'what are now called *wall-eyes*,' he says. This hypothesis is, however, untenable, a *wall-eye* is not primarily a diseased eye—in a horse it has the iris, either partly, or wholly white, with perfect vision—but the term is involved in confusion, it has been vaguely defined by some, wrongly by others, and loosely applied by many. The word is originally Icel. *vagleygr*, or corruptly *valdeygðr*, wall-eyed, said of a horse; lit. with a beam in the eye, from *vagl*, a beam; also a disease in the eye. It is rightly given thus, Mr. Skeat says, in VIGFUSSON'S *Icelandic Dictionary*.

(2) *sb.* a human eye which shews an undue proportion of the white, the iris being out of the centre, and inclined towards the outer corner—larger also than the fellow-eye in some cases.—PULVERBATCH; OSWESTRY. Qy. com. 'I knowed that chap as soon as ever I ketcht sight on 'is *wall-eye*.'

WALL-FLOWER, *sb. Helianthus annuus*, the Sun-flower.—CRAVEN ARMS; ELLESMERE.

'*Wall-flowers, wall-flowers*, growing up so high,

. . . .

See Bk. II., *Folklore*, &c., 'Games' (*Wall-flowers*). Cf. **Gillofer.**

WALLOP [wol·up], (1) *v. n.* to boil violently with a bubbling sound. —SHREWSBURY; ELLESMERE. 'Do them tittoes bile, Nanny?' said Mrs. Hales. 'They dunna bile, Missis, fur they *wallopen*,' was Nanny Windsor's reply.

'*Bouiller une onde*, to boyle a while or but for one bubble, or a *wallop* or two.'—Cotgrave, in WAY.

Jamieson gives '*To Wall-up, v. n.* To boil up,' also, '*To Wallop, v. n.* To move quickly, with much agitation of the body or clothes.' See **Walled**, and STRAT. *sub voce.*

(2) *v. a.* to flog.—SHREWSBURY. Qy. com.

'If I had a donkey wot wouldn't go,
Do you think I'd *wallop* him? Oh, no, no.'

Old Song.

WALL-PLIT, *sb.* the piece of timber which is placed on the top of a wall for the purpose of fastening roof-rafters to,—the 'wall-plate.' —CLUN.

WALLWORT, *sb. Sambúcus E'bulus*, dwarf Elder.—MUCH WENLOCK.

'*Hæc ebula*, A^e a walle-wurte,' occurs in a *Pictorial Vocabulary*, xv. cent., in Wr. vocabs., vol. i. p. 265.

The *Promptorium Parvulorum* gives '*Walworte*, herbe. *Ebulus*.'

WAN [wan·], *v. a.* to seize; to take firm hold of.—PULVERBATCH. 'Now then, *wan* out o' that ship, an' oud fast till I come up.' Spenser has *wan* in the sense of 'took':—

'Whylest there the varlet stood, he saw from farre
An armed knight that towardes him fast ran;
He ran on foot, as if in lucklesse warre
His forlorne steed from him the victour *wan*.'

F. Q., Bk. II. c. vi. st. xli.

Compare Lowland Scotch *To win*.

WANDLED [wan·dld], *adj.*, *obs.*? worn down with fatigue—'dead beat.'—PULVERBATCH. 'I've bin 'untin tuthree chats toërts yeätin' the oven, an' whad ööth the sticks an' the wînde, I'm aumust *wandled down.*'

WANGLING [waang·glin], *adj.* delicate; ailing; unthriving.—NEWPORT. ''Er's a poor little *wanglin'* thing, I doubt they wunna rear 'er.' *Wangling* is a weakened form of *Wankle* below.

WANKLE [wang·kl], *adj.* feeble; tottering; unsteady.—WEM.

'Forthi wil I schaw other thinges,
That er apert biseninges
Bituixe this *wankyll* werld and se,
This werldes welth to do fle.'
Homilies in Verse (A.D. 1330, *circa*). *Specim. Early Eng.*, *b.* viii. l. 97.

Ray gives '*Wankle*, Limber, flaccid, ticklish, fickle, wavering,' as a '*North Country Word.*'

'A.Sax., O.Sax. *wancol;* O.H.Germ. *wanchaler*, wankle (*instabilis*).'—STRAT.

WANT. See **Öönt.**

WANTY (1). See **Wainy.**

(2) [waan·ti' *and* won·ti'], *sb.* a short rope used in binding loads, as of hay, &c., on waggons or carts.—ATCHAM; PULVERBATCH; WELLINGTON; NEWPORT. The country-folk understand this term as meaning *one-tie*, i. e. a rope which goes *once round the load:* but the fact that the rope is used girthwise, points to the conclusion, that the word is the same, applied to a different usage, as that which Tusser employs, when he speaks of 'a panel and *wantey*,' where, the sense being that of a girth of some kind to bind a burden on a horse's back, it is rightly explained '*wamb-tie*, a belly-band,' in the *Glossary*, ed. E. D. S.

WAPPLE, WOBBLE, WOPPLE [wap·l], PULVERBATCH; ELLESMERE. [wob·l], CLEE HILLS. [wop·l], WORTHEN, a gummy secretion in the corner of the eye. 'Yo' binna-d-'afe weshed, the *wapples* bin all i' the cornels o' yore eyes.'

WAPSES [wop·siz], *sb. pl.* wasps.—NEWPORT. 'What are you about there, you fellows?' 'We'n tekkin *wapses'* neesens, Sir.'

'A.S. *wæps;* Lat. *vespa;* O.H.Germ. *wafsa*, *wefsa*, wasp (*waps*).'—STRAT.

WAR [waa·r'], *adj.* aware; conscious.—PULVERBATCH. 'Comin' down the Brummy-bonk, I 'eärd summat tussle i' the 'edge, so I went toërt it, an' wuz *war* on a great ar [hare] in a grin.' 'W'y didstna thee bring it?' 'I dar-say!—dun yo' want me to be send to the clump o' bricks [the gaol] i' Soseb'ry?'

'þan ȝede a grom of greee · in þe gardyn to pleie,
to bi-hold þe estres · & þe herberes so faire,
&, or he wiste, he was *war* · of þe white beres,
þei went a-wai a wallop · as þei wod semed.'
William of Palerne, l. 1769.

'I lokede on þe luft half · as þe ladi me tauhte;
þenne was I *war* of a wommon · wonderliche cloþed.'
Piers Pl., Text A., pass. ii. l. 8.

A.S. *wær;* O.N. *var;* having notice of, aware.

WARCH [waa·r'ch], *v. n.* to throb painfully. — PULVERBATCH; WORTHEN; NEWPORT. 'Theer'll be some change i' the weather, fur my corn *warches* despertly.'

'"Therfore be my rede," sayd syr Lucan, "it is beste that we brynge you to somme towne." "I wolde it were soo," sayd the kyng. "But I may not stonde, myn hede *werches* soo."'—SIR THOMAS MALORY (A.D. 1469), *Le Morte Darthur. Specim. Eng. Lit.*, viii. V. l. 1.

A.S. *wærc*, pain; suffering.

WARCHING, *part. adj.* throbbing.—PULVERBATCH. 'It inna so much of a pain, as a smartin', *warchin'* feel.'

WARE [waa·r'], *sb.* a weir.—PULVERBATCH. Qy. com. 'It's a good garden an' a tidy 'ouse, but I shouldna like to live so clos' to the *war'*.'

Mr. Hartshorne quotes a passage from a Treatise on Fly-Fishing—ed. Worcester, 1748, p. 14—by Richard Bowlker, a native of Ludlow or its immediate neighbourhood, where the author, speaking of trout, says, 'A little before they spawn, they make up the river towards the Spring-head, and to admiration will get through Mills, *Wares*, and Flood-gates.'—*Salopia Antiqua*, p. 610.

A.S. *wer*, a weir.

WARE-GOODS [waa·r'], *sb. pl.* goods for sale—a term applied, in contradistinction to 'live stock,' to such farm-produce as cheese or tubs of butter, when they are taken to the fair.—PULVERBATCH. 'Whad sort'n a far 'ad'n'ee las' wik?' 'Right middlin', I sid a power o' *war'-goods* pŭt by,' *i. e.* left on hand. Compare—

'Good *ware* makes quick markets.'—RAY'S *Proverbs*, p. 167.

'A.Sax. *waru;* O.Icel. *vara;* O.Du. *ware*, ware (*merx*).'—STRAT.

WAR JOWT [waa·r' jout], *phr.* beware of a jolt—an expression proper to the harvest-field; it is called out by the man at the head of the 'for'-'orse' [first horse] to the man on the load, as a warning to hold fast while the waggon crosses a 'reăn' or gutter.—PULVERBATCH. Cf. **Hold yo'**.

WARMSHIP, *sb.* warmth. Com. 'The poor owd mon wants *warmship* an' comfort worse than physic.'

WASHING-STOCK, WESHING-STOCK, *sb., obs.* a bench on which clothes were laid and beaten with a kind of bat, instead of being, as now, put into a tub and 'dollied': it was something like a butcher's block, but with two legs shorter than the others, so that it shed the water off on the side remote from the operator.—CORVE DALE; CLEE HILLS; WEM; ELLESMERE. Qy. com.

'The next morning Hopkin was found dead in Oatley Parke, haveing beene knocked on the head with the foote of a *washing stocke* which stood at Ellesmeare meare, which foot was found not far from him.'—GOUGH'S *History of Myddle*, p. 31.

It is said of a little man on a big horse that "'e looks like a frog on a *weshin'-stock*.' See **Bat** (1), also **Dolly** and **Dolly-tub**.

WASSLE [was·l], *v. a.* to beat down; to knock about.—PULVERBATCH. 'I've bin fur a burn o' ŏŏd this mornin' to yeăt the oven, an' the wīnde's farly *wassled* me down.' Compare Lowland Scotch *warsell;* to wrestle, strive; hence to knock about. See **Wazzle**.

WASSLE-BOUGH, *sb.* a bough used for beating down, as of dew from grass or grain bordering a field-path.—*Ibid.* 'I mun get a *wassle-bough*, an' *wassle* the je'ow off the grass afore the child gwuz through the craft, 'er'll be dagged above a bit else.'

WASSLE-FOOTED [fut·id], *adj.* splay-footed.—SHREWSBURY.

WASTREL [wai·str'il], (1) *sb.* a spendthrift; an idle, untrustworthy fellow,—'a ne'er-do-weel.' Com. 'Aye, poor owd John's come to the work-'us at las'—'e's al'ays been the *wastrel* o' the family ever sence I knowed 'im.'

'"It wasn't many wūrds she said,—but wūrds she said anew
To bring t'oald tinkler and her man tull what was weel ther due;
For lang i' Cārel jail they laid, an' when t'assize com on,
T'jūdge let t'oald *waistrel* lowce ageàn, but hang't his whopeful son."'
'Branthet Neuk Boggle,' in *The Folk-Speech of Cumberland*, by A. C. GIBSON, F.S.A., p. 70.

(2) *sb.* a worthless, unsound animal.—WEM. 'I doubt that cowt'll be nuthin' but a *wastrel*.'

(3) *sb.* a faulty piece of china, or such like; an imperfect brick, &c.: the term is applied to new things which are defective in some way when they leave the manufacturers' hands. Com. 'I bought it at the shop at Ironbridge, w'eer they sell *wastrels;* it's good Coalport chāney, on'y a bit asiden.' A shop of the kind here spoken of, is sometimes called a *wastrel-shop*.

(4) *adj.* imperfect; unsound,—'a *wastrel* tay-pot;'—'a *wastrel* brick.' Com.

WATCH [woch·], *sb., obs.*? minute beads, or particles of grease which appear on the surface of broth or soup.—SHREWSBURY.

WATER [wai·tur'], common pronunciation—read thus below.

WATER-SHUTTEN, WATER-SHUTTLE [shut·n], ATCHAM. [shaet·l *and* shut·l], PULVERBATCH, *adj.* made to shed water off by a due slope, &c. given to the thatch: said of stacks. ''Ow did yore stack come off, John, i' the thunder-shower?' 'Well, as luck 'ad it, we'd'n jest topped up an' made it *waiter-shettle* afore it come on.' See **Shut** (1) and (3).

WATER-SPAR, *sb. Carbonate of Baryta*, Witherite.—PULVERBATCH, *Snailbeach* (*Mines*). *Water-spar* when reduced to powder is highly poisonous, and is therefore much used for destroying rats and other vermin; so deadly are its properties, that it is said to 'pīson three times o'er,' thus: if a cat ate a rat killed by this agent, the cat would die, and if a dog ate the cat, the dog would die!

WATER-SPARROW, (1) *sb.* *Emberiza schœniclus*, the Black-headed Bunting.—SHREWSBURY. Qy. com.

(2) same as **Reed-sparrow** (1) and (2), q. v. Qy. com.

WATTLE-AND-DAB [wat·l], *sb.* and *adj.*, *obs.*? close hurdle-work plastered with clay.—PULVERBATCH. *Wattle-and-dab* cottages were constructed on this wise: standards were erected, between them twigs and branchlets were interwoven, and then moistened clay was 'dabbed' upon these 'wooden walls,' within and without, and smoothed on each side. Dwelling-places of *Wattle-and-dab* were an improvement on the clod-hut, of which latter, specimens may yet [1874] be seen on the Stiperstones and on Ponsert Hill. See *sub voce* **Outrack**.

> '". . . grace," quod Piers · "ȝe moten gyue tymbre,
> And ordeyne þat hous · ar ȝe hennes wende."
> And grace gaue hym þe crosse · with þe croune of þornes,
> That cryst vpon caluarye · for mankynde on pyned,
> And of his baptesme & blode · þat he bledde on Rode
> He made a maner morter · & mercy it hiȝte.
> And þere-with grace bigan · to make a good foundement,
> And *watteled* it and walled it · with his peynes & his passioun,
> And of al holywrit . he made a rofe after,
> And called þat hous vnite · holicherche on englisshe.'
>
> *Piers Pl.*, Text B., pass. xix. l. 323.

Wattle-and-dab, or something like it, seems to be symbolized by Langland in this description of the house built by Grace, witness the '*tymbre*,' the '*þornes*,' the '*a maner morter*,' for building materials, and the house itself '*watteled*' in course of construction.

WAUT [wau·t], *v. n.* to totter,—'look 'ow it *wauts*.'—WEM. *Waut* is the old word *walt*—to waver, to reel—with the *l* elided, just as *saut* = *salt*.

> 'þou *waltres* al in a weih · & wel y vnderstande
> whider þe balaunce bremliest · bouwes al-gate.'
>
> *William of Palerne*, l. 947.

'1589-90. This yeare and the 19*th* daye of June one John Broome the soon of Thomas Broome of Mynsterley comming to the towne w[th] a loade of poales was sooddenly murtherid by the over *waltinge* of hys wayne w[th]in a myle of the towne of Salop.'—*Early Chronicles of Shrewsbury* (*Taylor MS.*), in *Transactions of the Shropshire Archæological and Natural History Society*.

Ray gives 'To *Walt*, To totter, or lean one way, to overthrow,' as a '*North Country Word*.'

See *Waltrynge* and *Welwynge* in *Prompt. Parv.* A.S. *wealtan*, to reel; roll about. See **L** (2) in **Grammar Outlines** (*consonants*). Cf. **Wout**.

WAUTY, *adj.* unsteady; tottering.—ATCHAM.

WAUVE [wau·v], (1) *v. a.* to turn upside down for the purpose of covering: said of hollow things chiefly, such as earthenware vessels, baskets, or tubs; to cover over with the like.—PULVERBATCH; WORTHEN; CORVE DALE; CLEE HILLS. '*Wauve* a wisket o'er that 'en, if theer's never-a coop—'er'll draggle them little chickens to djeth.' See example *sub voce* **Kiver** (3).

Ray gives 'To *whoave, Chesh.*, to cover or whelm over. *We will not kill, but whoave*, Prov. *Chesh.* Spoken of a Pig or Fowl that they have overwhelmed with some Vessel in Readiness to kill.'

'Dan. *hvælve*, to arch, vault, turn bottom upwards; Sw. *hwälfwa*, to roll, turn, change, vault; O.N. *hvelfa*, *hvalfa*, to turn over, to vault.'—WEDG.

(2) *sb.* the covering of green sod—usually raised, or arched—over a grave.—CORVE DALE. 'Aye, 'e's left us, an' we'n pŭt the *wauve* o' turf o'er 'im, poor owd mon.' A.S. *hwealfa*, a vault.

WAZZLE, same as **Wassle**, q. v.—CLEE HILLS. 'The barley wuz so *wazzled* by them gulls, we couldna mow it.'

WEATHER, *sb.* storms of rain, hail, or snow,—'it looks like *weather* o' some sort.'—WELLINGTON.

'Swich housinge we han · to holde out þe *wedures*.'
Alexander and Dindimus, l. 443.

'A.Sax. *weder*; O.Sax. *wedar*; O.Icel. *veðr*; O.H.Germ. *wetar*, weather (*tempestas*).'—STRAT.

'*Tempestas* . . . a seasonable time, and faire weather, a *tempest* or *storme*.'—*Dict. Etym. Lat.*

WEATHERED, *part. adj.* damaged, but not spoilt, by too long exposure to weather—wet and bad harvesting weather: said of hay or corn. Com. ''Ow did'n yo' get yore 'ay, Mr. Jones?' 'Well, we gotten it dry at las', but it wuz a good bit *weathered*.' Tusser uses *weather* as a verb, in the sense of to *dry* in the open air:—

'Maides, mustard seede gather, for being too ripe,
and *weather* it well, er ye giue it a stripe:
Then dresse it and laie it in soller vp sweete,
least foistines make it for table vnmeete.'
Auguste husbandrie, ed. E. D. S., p. 129.

WEATHER-GALL, *sb.* the secondary rainbow.—PULVERBATCH. 'Come an' look whad a big rainbow, an' the *weather-gall's* aumust as bright as the bow.'

Mr. Halliwell says, 'I am told a second rainbow above the first is called in the Isle of Wight a *water-geal.* Carr has *weather-gall*, a secondary or broken rainbow.'

Compare Shakespeare's '*water-galls*' in *Lucrece*, l. 1588.

WED, (1) *sb.*, *obsols.* a pledge—a gage to be redeemed by some jocular fine, in the young folks' game of 'forfeits.' *To cry the weds* is to call the forfeits,—'We *cried'n the weds* an' 'ad'n rar' raps.'—PULVERBATCH; WORTHEN.

'*Wed* (Sax.), a gage or pawn; a word still retained in the Countrey sport called *Pray, my Lord, a course in your Park.*'—BLOUNT'S *Glossographia*, p. 697.

Wed is found in early writers with a nobler sense of gage:—

'. . . . . . . the which was reserued,
By Tydeus, of intencioun,
To the Kyng to make relacioun,
How his knyghtes han on her iourne spedde,
Eurich of hem his lyf left for a *wed*[*de*].'
JOHN LYDGATE (A.D. 1420, *circa*), *The Storie of Thebes.*
Specim. Eng. Lit., iii. *b.* l. 1186.

'"Nay," sayd Gray-steele, "by St. John!
this one yeere he shall not goe home,
but he shall either fight or flee,
or a *wed* in this land leaue shall hee."'
Eger and Grine, l. 952. *Percy Folio MS.*, vol. i. p. 384, ed. Hales and Furnivall.

Archbishop Trench remarks that, 'in a vast number of instances a word lives on as a verb, but has ceased to be employed as a noun; we say . . . . "to *wed*," but not "a *wed*," unless it should be urged that this survives in "*wed*-lock," a locking or binding together through the giving and receiving of a "*wed*," or pledge, namely, the ring.'—*English Past and Present*, p. 96.

'*Wedde*, or thynge leyyd yn plegge. *Vadium, pignus.*'—*Prompt. Parv.*

'A.Sax. *wedd* (*wed*); O.Icel. *veð*; Goth. *vadi*; O.H.Germ. *wetti*, gage, pledge.'—STRAT.

(2) *pret.* weeded. Com. 'I've bin mighty busy i' the garden this ōnder; I've *wed* the two īnion-beds, 'awed the forrat tatoes, an' scuffled the alleys.'

'*Wed*, fro noyowe wedys. *Runcatus.*'—*Prompt. Parv.*

WEEBLE [wee·bl], *sb.* a coleopterous insect of the family *Curculionidæ*, which comprises several species—known as *weevils*—that infest bacon, grain, &c.—PULVERBATCH. Qy. com. 'I'm afeard as the *weebles* bin got i' the shŏother o' that flitchen, I sid one o' the 'ouse-flur a bit agŏo.'

The form *wibil* occurs as the gloss of *cantarus*, in a *Vocabulary*, viii. cent., in Wr. vocabs., vol. ii. p. 103.

'A.S. *wefil*; O.Du. *wevel*; O.H.Germ. *wibil*; weevil (*curculio*).'—STRAT.

WEEDING AWAY, *phr.* gradually diminishing. — PULVERBATCH. 'I did 'ope as my coal ŏŏd a lasted till nigh Chris'mas, but I see as it's *weedin' away* sadly too fast.'

WEEDY. See **Waidy**.

WEEPING THROUGH, *phr.* dropping; oozing; leaking.—PULVERBATCH. 'I see as that barrel o' one-way-drink 's *weepin' through*, theer mus' be a new 'oop on, else we sha'n 'ăve it all about the cellar.'

WEEPY, *adj.* moist—the trickling moisture observable in badly pressed cheese.—PULVERBATCH. 'Sally, one o' the fat cheeses is *weepy*, mind to turn it on a dry place, an' notice it every day.'

WEE-WOW [wee·wou], *adj.* more on one side than on the other—ill-balanced, and shaky.—PULVERBATCH. 'I knowed well enough that loăd ŏŏd never raich wham, it wuz all *wee-wow* afore it lef' the fild.'

WEK, WEKLY [wek·], *adjs.* weak; weakly. Com. 'Well, as to bein' *wek*, poor wratch! 'e wuz al'ays *wekly* from a child, an' canna expec' to be better now.'

'1535-6. This yeare was a maltman slayne in grope lone in Shrewsburie wth the fall of a *wecke* chymney in an old howse there wch fell upon hym in tying the horse there after he had pytchyd hys loade.'—*Early Chronicles of Shrewsbury* (*Taylor MS.*), in *Transactions of the Shropshire Archæological and Natural History Society.*

WELLY [wel·i'], *adv.* nearly; well-nigh,—'*welly* clemmed,' *i. e.* nearly famished; '*welly* bos'n,' *i. e.* nearly burst, having eaten to repletion, are familiar usages of the term.—SHREWSBURY; PULVERBATCH; WELLINGTON; COLLIERY; NEWPORT; WEM; WHITCHURCH; ELLESMERE. Qy. com.

Grose has '*Welly.* Almost, nearly. N.'

A.S. *wel-neah*, well-nigh; near.

WELT, (1) *sb.* a thick, coarse, clumsy seam.—PULVERBATCH; WEM. Qy. com. 'Yo'n made this sem too broad, sich a great *welt* as this ŏŏd cripple anybody to lie on.'

(2) *sb.* the ribs of knitting at the top of a sock or stocking are called *welts*, the plural form being usually employed in this sense of the term. Com. 'It'll be a stockin' sometime—yo'n bin knittin' about a wik, an' nod out o' the *welts* yet.'

(3) *v. a.* to flog; to lash; to inflict stripes. Com. 'The schoolmaister's *welted* that poor bwoy shameful—'e ought to be complained on.'

Mr. Halliwell gives '*Welt*, to beat severely,' as a *Norfolk* word.

(4) *sb.* a raised stripe, or wale, on the skin, caused by a lash,—'Theer wuz *welts* on 'is back, as thick as my finger.' Com.

WELTING, *sb.* a sound thrashing,—''e gid the chap a right good *weltin'* as 'e ŏŏnna furget in a 'urry.' Com.

WENCH [wen·sh], *sb.* a young girl, or young woman, of peasant rank, to whom it is applied in no unworthy sense—the good old word maintaining its respectability. Com.

'Forsothe alle kast out, he takith the fadir and modir of the *wenche*, and hem that weren with him, and thei entren yn, where the *wenche* lay. And he holdinge the hond of the *wenche*, seith to hir, "Tabita, cumy," that is interpretid *or expownid*, "*Wenche*, to thee I seie, rise thou." And anon the *wenche* roos, and walkide; sothly she was of twelue ȝeer.'—*Mark* v. 40—42, Wycliffite Version, A.D. 1380.

'O ill-starr'd *wench!*
Pale as thy smock! when we shall meet at compt,
This look of thine will hurl my soul from heaven,
And fiends will snatch at it. Cold, cold, my girl!
Even like thy chastity.'—*Othello*, V. ii. 272.

'Once haruest dispatched, get *wenches* and boies,
and into the barne, afore all other toies.
Choised seede to be picked and trimlie well fide,
for seede may no longer from threshing abide.'
TUSSER, *Fiue Hundred Pointes of Good Husbandrie* [August].

'*Wenche.* *Assecla, abra, ancilla.*'—*Prompt. Parv.*

Dr. Morris says, '*Wench* is a shortened form of the O.E. *wenchel*, which in the "Ormulum" [A.D. 1200, *circa*] is applied to Isaac, and was originally a word of the common gender.'—*Historical English Accidence*, p. 84.

See *Wench* in SKEAT'S *Etymological Dictionary*.

WEP [wep·], *pret.* wept.—SHREWSBURY; PULVERBATCH. Qy. com. 'The poor Faither was despertly cut up, 'e *wep* bitterly—it's mighty 'ard to see a mon cry.'

> 'þanne of-saw he ful sone · þat semliche child,
> þat so loueliche lay & *wep* · in þat loþli caue.'
> *William of Palerne*, l. 50.

> 'But oonly for the feere thus sche cryede
> And *wep*, that it was pité for to heere.'
> CHAUCER, *The Knightes Tale*, l. 1487, ed. Morris.

Dr. Morris notes *wep* as an *obsolete* strong form.—*Historical English Accidence*, p. 157.

'A.Sax., O.Sax. *weop;* O.H.Germ. *wiof* (*pret.*), wep (*flevi*).'—STRAT.

WERRET [waer'·it], *v. a.* and *v. n.* to harass; to trouble; to torment; to worry. Com. 'What made your Mistress faint, Price?' asked the Doctor. 'Well, Sir, 'er *werrits* 'erself so.' '"*Werrits* herself!" what do you mean by that?' 'Well, Sir, *werritin'* o'er that owd S'ropshire book, 'er gies 'erself no rest o'er it; an' if I say, Ma'am, hanna yo' done plenty fur to-day? 'er only laughs, an' tells *me* nod to *werrit*—but, Sir, I dunna like these faintin'-aitches.' 'I will come up and see your Mistress,' quoth the good Doctor, and when he came, he had 'a crack' with his patient about *werriting!* [1873].

WESH, (1) *v. a.* to wash. Com.

> 'In water ich wel þe cristny her
> As Gode him-self hyt diȝte;
> For mide to *wessche* nis noþynge
> Þat man comeþ to so liȝte,
> In londe.
> . . . .'
> *William of Shoreham* (A.D. 1307—1327), *De Baptismo. Specim. Early Eng.*, vi. l. 52.

A.S. *wæscan*, *wascan*, to wash.

(2) *sb.* same as **Swill** (5), q. v. Com.

WESHING-STOCK. See **Washing-stock.**

WESH-TUB, same as **Swill-tub,** q. v. Com.

WETCHET [wech·i't *and* wech·u't], *adj.* wet in the feet; wet-shod. —PULVERBATCH; WELLINGTON. 'Jest look at yore stockin'-fit!—dun them shoes loose yo' *wetchet?*—w'y it's none sence they wun tapt.'

> 'Ac beggeres aboute Midsomer · bredlees þei soupe,
> And ȝit is wynter for hem worse · for *wete-shodde* þei gange.'
> *Piers Pl.*, Text B., pass. xiv. l. 161.

Mr. Skeat explains Langland's '*wete-shodde*'—which appears as *wet-shoed*, pass. xviii. l. 1—to be, 'with wet shoes,' 'wet-footed,' and supplements his gloss as follows,—'*Wetshod*, with water in the shoes. "Are you not *wetshod?*" have not your shoes taken in water?'—Marshall's Glossary of Yorkshire Words, 2nd ed., 1796. Compare also—

'þere men were *wetschoede*
Alle of brayn & of blode.'
Arthur, ed. Furnivall, E. E. T. S., 1864, l. 469.

In Oxfordshire it is pronounced *Watcherd* [woch·urd], and used correctly by many who have no idea of what are the component parts of the word. The opposite form, *dryshod*, is better known; see Isaiah xi. 15. The corresponding Icelandic word is *skóvátr*, lit. 'shoe-wet.'—*Notes* to *Piers Pl.*, pp. 328, 395, ed. E. E. T. S.

'*Watchet.* Wet shod, wet in the feet,' is given by Grose for *Oxfordshire.*

WHAD [wod·], *pron.* what. Com.

'By whom also thow moste mynne,
And whom he gart to do that synne,
And *whad* they were that were here ferus,
Prestes or clerkus, monkes or frerus.'
MS. Cott. Claud., A. ii. f. 146, in HAL.

See **T** (1), in **Grammar Outlines** (*consonants*).

WHAD FOR, *phr.* reason to remember, as of pain, punishment, abuse, scolding, &c.,—'that tuth gid me *whad for;*'—''e gid the chap *whad fur*, I can tell yo'.' Com.

WHAM, WHOM, WHOME [waam·, wum·], PULVERBATCH. [waam·, woam·], BRIDGNORTH. [wum·, wom·], Com., *sb.* home.

'Than preyde the ryche man Abraham
That he wide sende Lazare or sum other *wham.*'
MS. Harl., 1701, f. 44, in HAL.

'1581-2. This yeare and in the moonthe of Februarie were all the souldiars in Ireland dyschardgid, and ev'y man went *whom* to thyre countrey.'—*Early Chronicles of Shrewsbury* (*Taylor MS.*), in *Transactions of the Shropshire Archæological and Natural History Society.*

'but *whom* then came Glasgerryon,
a glad man, Lord, was hee,
"and come thou hither, Iacke, my boy,
Come hither vnto mee."'
Glasgerion, l. 21. *Percy Folio MS.*, vol. i. p. 249, ed. Hales and Furnivall.

'And yf thou wylt not so do,
Whome with the then wyll y goo.'
MS. Cantab. Ff. ii. 38, f. 210, in HAL.

'A.Sax. *hám;* O.Sax. *hêm;* O.H.Germ. *heim;* O.Icel. *heimr;* Goth. *haims*, home.'—STRAT.

WHET [wet·], *sb.* an attempt; a trial. Qy. com. 'I'm gweïn to clave that brund, it's balked me wunst or twize, but I'll 'ăve another *w'et* at it.'

'A *whet* is no let.'—RAY'S *Proverbs*, p. 168.

WHEY-SPRING, *sb.* a spot where the whey collects in imperfectly pressed cheese; it causes cracks which attract flies.—WELLINGTON. 'I doubt theer's bin a *w'ey-spring* i' this cheese, see 'ow the maggots han gotten into it.'

> 'As Mawdlin wept, so would Cisley be drest,
> for whey in hir cheeses, not halfe inough prest.
> If gentils be scrauling, call magget the py,
> if cheeses haue gentils, at Cisse by and by.'
>
> TUSSER, *A lesson for dairie maids, etc.*, p. 108, ed. E. D. S.

WHIFFLE [wif·l], (1) *v. n.* to veer; to shift; to blow inconstantly: said of the wind.—SHREWSBURY; PULVERBATCH; WORTHEN; CLEE HILLS. 'I dunna know whad to mak' o' the weather this mornin', the winde does so *w'iffle* about throm North to West—I've bin watchin' the cap o' the Wrekin, if it gwuz toërt Wenlock, we sha'n 'ăve a fine day.'

'Two days before this storm began the wind *whiffled* about to the south, and back again to the east, and blew very faintly.'—*Dampier*, in WEDG.

'Du. *weyfelen*, fluctuare, inconstantem esse, omni vento versari.'—*Kilian*,—*Ibid.*

(2) *v. n.* to move about, as if stirred by a light wind.—*Ibid.* 'I think we sha'n dry the clothes, they begin to *w'iffle* about a bit.'

WHIFFLE-MINDED, *adj.* changeable; vacillating.—PULVERBATCH; WORTHEN; WEM. 'Theer's no 'eed to be took on a fellow like 'im, 'e's so *w'iffle-minded*—'e dunna know 'is own mind two minutes together.'

WHIG [wig·], *sb.* wine-posset.—SHREWSBURY. 'Cook, yo' mus' mak' the Missis some *w'ig*, 'er's got a bad coud.' '*W'ig*,' said Cook—who was of another County—'what's that?' 'W'y, milk boiled ŏŏth winde.' 'Oh, I know; *wine-whey*, you mean.'

'*Thick Milk*, is Churned Milk gone thick. *Whigg*, is the bottom or breaking of thick Milk.'—*Academy of Armory*, Bk. III. ch. viii. p. 335.

See *Whig*, in NARES; also in HAL. W. *chwig*, whey fermented; *chwigws*, whey drink.

WHIGGED [wig·d], *adj.* broken into whey: said of a milk-pudding that has curdled in the oven.—WHITCHURCH; ELLESMERE. 'I doubt this custurt-pŭddin' 's *w'igged*, the oven's bin a bit too sharp fur it.'

Pegge gives '*Whig*, the watery part, or whey, of a baked custard. North.'

WHINNOCK [win·uk], *v. n.* to cry querulously, as a young child does.—PULVERBATCH; WELLINGTON; OSWESTRY. 'That child's done nuthin' but *w'innock* all this day; God 'elp it, it looks despert pulin'.' *Whinnock* seems to be a verbal form of *whine* + *ock* = a little cry.

'A.Sax. *hwínan;* O.Icel. *hvína*, to whine.'—STRAT.

WHIPPET-DOG, *sb.* a dog of a cross-breed, between a greyhound and a terrier.—WELLINGTON; NEWPORT.

WHIRLIGOG [wur'l·i'gog], *sb.* a turnstile.—PULVERBATCH. 'Dunna be in a 'urry, Maister, "it's one at a time 'ere," as the owd ŏŏman said, at the *w'irligog*.'

WHISK [wis·k], *sb.*, *obs.?* the game of whist. — PULVERBATCH. 'Well, theer's jest four on us, let's 'ăve a game at *w'isk* afore fotherin' time.'

'It is mentioned with other games in Taylor's Motto, 1622, sig. D. iv. It is also spelt *whisk* in the Country Gentleman's Vade-Mecum, 8vo. Lond. 1699, p. 63.'—HAL.

WHISSUN-GILLOFER [wis·n], *sb.* *Hesperis matinalis*, Single Rocket.—ELLESMERE. This plant flowers about Whitsuntide, whence the appellation. See **Gillofer**.

WHISSUN-MONDAY, WHISSUN-TUESDAY, *sbs.* the Monday and Tuesday in Whitsun-week. Com.

The forms '*Whitsun Munday*,' '*Whitsun Tuesday*,' are found in a 'Book of Common Prayer. London. Printed by *John Bill* and *Christopher Barker*, Printers to the King's Most Excellent Majesty. MDCLXII.'

WHISSUN-SUNDAY, *sb.* Whitsun-Day. Com.

'*Hec pentetoste, -tes*, whysunday,' occurs in a *Nominale*, xv. cent., in Wr. vocabs., vol. i. p. 239.

WHISSUNTIT, *sb.* Whitsuntide.—PULVERBATCH.

'Byfore, after, and *whyssone tyde*,
Eghte dayes they schullen abyde.'
MS. Cott. Claud., A. ii. f. 128, in HAL.

See **Tid** (1).

WHISSUN-WEEK, *sb.* Whitsun-week.—PULVERBATCH. Qy. com.
'Wretyn at Lederyngham, the Tewesday in *Whisson weke*.'—*Paston Letters*, temp. Hen. vi., vol. i. p. 550.

WHISTLE [wis·l], *v. n.* to sing: said of birds,—''ark at that throstle; dunnot 'e *w'istle* beautiful?'—NEWPORT.

WHITECAP, *sb.* *Ruticilla phœnicura*, the Redstart. Qy. com. *Whitecap* seems to be a gentle-folk's term. Cf. **Brand-tail**.

WHITE-CROWFOOT, *sb.* *Ranunculus aquatilis*, Water Crowfoot.—CLUN; LUDLOW. Cf. **Reits**.

WHITE FLAT IRONSTONE, *sb.* an inferior ironstone.—COLLIERY; M. T.

'*The White Flat Ironstone* contains some very interesting fossils, the characteristic plants being Lycopodiaceæ and Equisetaceæ. Associated with these are considerable quantities of Unio, scales and bones of *Megalichthys*, *Hibberti*, and *Gyracanthus Formosus*. Also, most singular fossils of undescribed Crustacea of the Trilobite family.' —*Notes on the Shropshire Coal Field*, by T. PARTON, F.G.S., 1868.

Cf. **Blue-Flats**. See **Coal-Field**.

WHITE-PUDDINGS, *sb. pl.* a kind of sweet sausages, made by filling the larger-sized 'chitterlings,' or pig's intestines—after a process of thorough cleansing—with a mixture of boiled groats, pork fat cut into small pieces, sweet herbs chopped fine, currants, sugar, and spice, and then tying them in links. They are slightly pricked to prevent them from bursting, and boiled for twenty minutes. When wanted for table they are roasted. Com. See **Chitterlings**.

WHITEY-BROWN, adj. the pale, dusky hue of unbleached calico, thread, &c., to which the term is chiefly applied. Com. 'It'll mak' yo' a rar' winter gownd, an' line it all through ŏŏth *w'itey-brown* callica.'

WHIXALL-BIBLES, *sb. pl.*, *sl.*? pieces of peat prepared for fuel on Whixall-Moss.—WHITCHURCH; ELLESMERE. See **Turf**, also **Moss.**

WHOAR-FROST [wur'· fr'os], *sb.* a hoar-frost; a white frost.—SHREWSBURY; PULVERBATCH. 'Theer wuz a bit o' *wur-fros'* i' the yarly mornin', but no danger as yo' sid'n it, yo' wunna up time enough.'

> '"ffarwell Knowsley, that litle tower
> vnderneth the holtes soe *whore**!
> euer when I thinke on that bright bower,
> white me not though my hart be sore."'
>
> *Fflodden Ffeilde*, l. 214. *Percy Folio MS.*, ed. Hales and Furnivall, vol. i. p. 237.

* 'hoar, hoary white.'—Note by BP. PERCY.—*Ibid.*

Cf. **Ketch-o'-frost.**

WHOM, WHOME. See **Wham.** See, for these and the two following words, **W** (3), in **Grammar Outlines** (*consonants*).

WHOT [wot· *and* wut·], *adj.* hot.—SHREWSBURY; PULVERBATCH. Qy. com. 'This pŭddin' 's as *w'ot* as love nine days owd.'

'1583-4. This yeare and in the sayd moonthe of December a serv'nt of Rychard Gardn' of Salop, whose name was Thomas Cott'n, was by myschance fallyn in to a furnes of *whot* boylinge lycker, and so presently boylyd to deathe.'—*Early Chronicles of Shrewsbury* (*Taylor MS.*), in *Transactions of the Shropshire Archæological and Natural History Society.*

> 'And in the midst of all
> There placed was a caudron wide and tall
> Upon a mightie fornace, burning *whott*,
> More *whott* then Actn' or flaming Mongiball,
> For day and night it brent, ne ceased not.'
>
> SPENSER, *F. Q.*, Bk. II. c. ix. st. xxix.

Grose gives '*Whott.* Hot. Exmoor.'

Mr. Halliwell observes of '*whot*,' that it is 'still in use.'

WI', *prep.* with,—'dunna thou goo alung *wi'* no sich chaps as 'im.' —BRIDGNORTH; NEWPORT; WHITCHURCH.

> 'Then hey, for a lass *wi'* a tocher, then hey, for a lass *wi'* a tocher,
> Then hey, for a lass *wi'* a tocher; the nice yellow guineas for me.'
>
> ROBERT BURNS, p. 195, ll. 15, 16.

See **With** (3).

WICKEN, WICKY, *sb. Pyrus aucupária*, Quicken-tree, or Mountain-ash.—WELLINGTON, *Wrekin.* See **Witan-tree.**

WICKET, *sb.*, *pec.* a little gate across a path, or narrow way. Com. 'Yo' canna tak' a cart that way, it's a fŭt-path an' bridle-roăd; theer's *wickets* all the way.' See example *sub voce* **Gain** (1).

> 'Bidde a-Mende [-þou] Meken him · to his Mayster ones,
> To wynne vp þe *wiket-ȝat* · þat þe wey schutte.'
>
> *Piers Pl.*, Text A., pass. vi. l. 92.

'*Wicket* . . . . . a little door (commonly) where great gates are.'—BLOUNT'S *Glossographia*, p. 700.

'*Wicket* [prob. of *guichet*, *F.*] a small door in a larger.'—BAILEY ed. 1727.

O.Fr. *wiket*, of which *guichet* is a later spelling. See BUR.

WIDDEN [wid·n], *v. a.*, *var. pr.* to widen, as in knitting a stocking. Com.

WIDDENIN'S, *sb. pl.* the spaces where a stocking is widened, in order to give shape to the leg. Com. ''Ow many bouts mun I knit atween the *wid'nin's?*' 'Three, the same as yo' pŭt'n atween the nárrowin's.'

WIDDIES, *sb. pl.* young ducklings.—PULVERBATCH; WORTHEN. See **Call-Words to Poultry** (*ducks*).

WIDGEON, *sb.* Every kind of Wild Duck except *Anas boschas*, the Mallard, is called a *Widgeon* in Salop. Com.

WIDOW, *sb.* a widower. A *widow* is called a *widow-woman*.—ELLESMERE, *Welshampton*.

Mr. Skeat says that 'the termination *-er* to *widow* is comparatively modern; cf. A.S. *wuduwa*, masc.; *wuduwe*, fem.'

WIG, *sb.* a small, oblong bun, made of very light dough, with sugar and carraway-seeds in it.—SHREWSBURY; ELLESMERE. 'Now, childern, if yo' bin good awile I'm away, I'll bring yo' a *wig* apiece throm Ellesmer' markit.'

'Wygge, brede (or bunne brede, P.). "Wygge, Eschaude."—PALSG. "*Wig* or bun, a bunn or little manchet; *Collyra*, libum."—GOULDM. In Herefordshire a small cake is called a *wig*.'—*Prompt. Parv. and Notes.*

'Echaudé, espèce de gâteau fait de pâte échaudée. Echode, *wig*, simnel.'—CHAMB.

'Du. *wegghe*, *wigghe*, a wedge, thence a mass, an oblong cake of bread or of butter.'—Kilian, in WEDG.

See Bk. II., *Folklore*, &c., 'Customs connected with Days and Seasons' (*Christmas*).

WIGGY, *adj.* said of turnips which have ceased to grow in the roots and have struck out a mass of fibres into the soil.—PULVERBATCH; ATCHAM; WEM. 'These turmits bin pretty bad to pool up, they bin that *wiggy*.'

WIK [wi·k·], *sb.* a week. Com.

'1565 It for Wm Roe the yongers table and his mans about pooling downe the window ij *wykes* ix^s iiij^d.'—*Churchwardens' Accounts of the Abbey*, Shrewsbury.

'". . . . . . par Charite, ȝif þou Conne
Eny lyf of leche Craft · lere hit me, my deore,
For summe of my seruauns · beoþ seke oþer-while,
Of alle þe *wike* heo Worcheþ not · so heor wombe akeþ."'
Piers Pl., Text A. pass. vii. l. 243.

'A.Sax. *wice*, *wuce*; O.Fris. *wike*; O.Icel. *vika*; Goth. *viko*; O.H.Germ. *wecha*, week.'—STRAT.

WIK OR NINE DAYS, *phr.* a varied form of the 'week or ten days,' so generally used to denote a period which is more than a week and less than a fortnight. Com.

WIK O' SUNDAYS, *phr.* any indefinite time,—'I hanna sid 'er fur a *wik o' Sundays.*' Com.

WIL [wi·l], *sb.*, *var. pr.* a wheel. Qy. com.

'P[d] John Chydley y[e] 21 of December 1578 for makynge of a *whyle* to a bell in saynt Gylees ij[s].'—*Churchwardens' Accounts of the Abbey*, Shrewsbury.

'A.Sax. *hweól;* O.Du. *weel, wiel;* cf. O.Icel. *hiol*, a wheel.'—STRAT.

WILD SAGE, *sb. Mentha rotundifólia*, round-leaved Mint, var. *variegata* (garden plant).—WHITCHURCH, *Tilstock.*

WILE-SICHE, *adv.* now and then; at odd times. ''E's at it every *wile-siche.*'—CLEE HILLS. Compare *wile* in the following:—

'but from þe cherl & þe child · nov chaunge we oure tale,
For i wol of þe werwolf · a *wile* nov speke.'
William of Palerne, l. 79.

'A.Sax. *hwile (tempus)*; O.Sax. *huíla;* O.H.Germ. (*h*)*wila* (*hora, momentum*); while.'—STRAT.

WILL-GILL, *sb.* an hermaphrodite.—PULVERBATCH; WELLINGTON. Qy. com.

WILLOW [wil·oe], *sb.* an active search for any missing article,—'I mun 'ave another *willow* fur it.' — ELLESMERE, *Welshampton;* OSWESTRY. This seems to be a *Welsh Border* word; the Welsh *chwilio* has emphatically the same signification. Cf. **Brevit** (2).

WIL-PIN [wi·l pin], *sb.*, *obs.* a wooden pin about seven or eight inches long with a knob at each end,—a spinner's implement used for turning the wheel of what was commonly called the *long wheel*, on which wool was spun.—PULVERBATCH. See example *sub voce* **Knobble.**

WILRIT [wi·lr'it], *sb.* a wheelwright. Qy. com.

WIMBERRY [wim·br'i'], *sb.* the fruit of *Vaccinium Myrtillus*, the Whortleberry. Com. 'Theer's a good 'it o' *wimb'ries* this time.' 'That's a rar' job fur the 'illers,' *i. e.* people who go to the hills for the purpose of gathering *wimberries.*

Mr. Thomas Wright says, 'I enjoy the peculiar feel and sound produced by trampling over the bilberry bushes as we wander through the solitude of the forest. They call them *whimberries* in Shropshire.' —*A Visit to the Scene of Comus*, in *Once a Week*, 27 Jan. 1866.

Wimberry seems to be a variation of *Winberry* = *Wine-berry.* See **Winberry.** See also **Bilberry** and **Blaeberry.**

WIMBERRY-WIRES, *sb. pl.* the stems of the shrub *Vaccinium Myrtillus*, on which the *wimberries* grow. Com. 'Theer ŏŏnna be many wimb'ries this 'ear; I wuz lookin' at the *wires* the tother day, an' they wun blowed despert scant.' See **Wires.**

WIMOTE [wei·moat], *sb. Althæa officinális*, common Marsh Mallow. —CORVE DALE.

WIM-WAM, *sb.* a turnstile.—WELLINGTON. Cf. **Whirligog.**

WINBERRY, same as **Wimberry**, *ante*, q. v.—WORTHEN, *Cherbury*. 'Me an' my boys han puck as many as six quarts o' *winb'ries* in a day, but they bin mighty trifling [tedious] to gather.' The term *winberry*, which obtains on the Western Border of Salop, has only a very limited range; it was formerly—in 1804, undoubtedly—used near Oswestry, at Cern-y-bwch, where the berries then grew plentifully, but now [1881] very few are found there, and those are called *wimberries* by the people. *Winberry* is a contraction of *wine-berry*, an old name for the fruit.

Gerarde gives in his *Herball*—1st ed., A.D. 1597—a supplementary list of old or obsolete terms; amongst them we find '*Wyneberries* is *Vaccinia*.' In the body of his work, speaking of '*Vaccinia* or Whortes,' he says that 'we in England call Whortleberries . . . . in some places *Winberries*.'—Bk. III. p. 1231.

Randle Holme says, 'Bill-Berries . . . are termed Whortle Berries or *Wind-Berries*.'—*Academy of Armory*, Bk. II. ch. v. p. 81.

Ash gives '*Wind'berry*. The whortleberry, the bilberry.'

Bailey—ed. 1782—has 'A *Wind-Berry* a Bill-berry, or Whortleberry.'

Compare the introduction of the *d* in *Winberry* with the same thing in *Winde* (1), below.

Pegge has '*Whin-berry*, a bilberry, a whortle-berry. North,'—a spelling obviously at fault, for, since 'every tree yieldeth fruit after his kind,' *Whin*, i. e. *Furze*, cannot produce *Whortleberries*. Thus—'Cwyst þu, gaderað man *win-berian* of þornum, oððe ficæppla of þyrncinum.'—*Matt.* vii. 16. A.S. Gospels, ed. THORPE.

A.S. *win-berige;* a wine-berry, a grape.

WINDE [wei·nd], (1) *sb.*, *var. pr.* wine,—'Yo'n 'ăve a glass o' *wīnde* afore yo' gŏ'n.' Com.

'1753. For Bred & *Winde* & feching it 0 - 3 - 8.'

Churchwardens' Accounts, Hopton Castle, Salop.

(2) *sb.*, *var. pr.* wind,—'Theer's a despert coud *winde* to-night.' Com.

WINDER-BITS, WINDER-RAGS [win·dur'], *sb. pl.* fragments; shreds,—'Dunna gie the child that doll, 'er'll tar it all to *winder-rags*.' Com.

WINDERS, same as above,—''E broke it all to *winders*.' Com.

WINDIN' [wei·ndin], *part. adj.* vapouring; talking foolishly—'without rime or reason,'—'Whadever bin 'ee *windin'* at now?'—WEM.

WINDROW. See **Winrow.**

WINDY [wei·ndi'], (1) *adj.* noisy; blustering; silly.—SHREWSBURY; WEM. (1) ''E's a *windy* fool.' (2) ''E's the *windiest* chap w'en 'e's 'ad a drop o' drink as ever I seed.'

(2) *adj.* A horse is said to be '*windy*' that is fresh and plays about, instead of settling to work.—WEM.

WINDY-MILL [wei·ndi'], *sb.*, *var. pr.* a wind-mill. Qy. com. A certain man observed of another that ''e wuz a crack-waggon, *windy-mill* fox!' Compare—

'To have *wind-mills* in his head.'—RAY'S *Proverbs*, p. 216.

WING, (1) *v. a.* to fling; to hurl.—WHITCHURCH; ELLESMERE. ''E ketcht out on 'im by the collar, an' *winged* 'im reet across the kitchen.'

(2) *sb., obsols.* the shoulder of a hare or rabbit when dressed for table.—PULVERBATCH; ELLESMERE. Qy. com.

'. . . him followed servants bearing on mighty dish crane already cut up, and plentifully sprinkled with salt, and meal besides; also the liver of a white goose fattened on rich figs, and *hares' wings* * torn off and served by themselves.'—HORACE, *Satires*, Bk. II. viii. 89, Globe Edition, p. 158.

* '"*hares' wings*," which the ancients thought the best part.'—Note, p. 251.

WINK-AND-PEEP, *sb. Anagallis arvénsis*, scarlet Pimpernel.—WELLINGTON. The flowers of this plant open to the morning sun, and close at noon-tide; they close also on the approach of rain; whence the pretty local name *Wink-and-Peep*.

WINLING [win·lin], *sb., var. pr.* a weanling—a term applied to a newly-weaned lamb.—PULVERBATCH. 'Whad a blaitin' theer is among the ship to-day!' 'Aye, they'n bin partin' 'em, an' the yeows bin callin' to the *winlin's*.'

WINNA, will not. See **Grammar Outlines**, p. lxxx.

'An tell them wi' a patriot-heat,
Ye *winna* bear it!'
ROBERT BURNS, *Poems*, p. 11, l. 10.

WINROW [win·r'oe], *sb.* a long row, or continuous heap, of hay, got up ready to be put into 'big cocks' for carrying. Sometimes the hay is carried direct from the *winrows*—the waggon passing between them from end to end of the field—but otherwise the 'big cocks' are made by rolling up the *winrow*. Com. 'The rain couldna ketch it at a wus time than in *winrows*; if it 'ad bin cocked, it ŏŏd a throwed it off.' *Winrow* is *windrow* with the *d* eliminated. A *windrow* is said to mean a row exposed to the action of the *wind*.

Grose gives '*Windrow*. To windrow, to rake the mown grass into rows, called windrows. Norf. and Suff.' Cf. **Quile** (= *coil*).

WINTER-PROUD, *adj.* said of wheat that, after a mild winter, shews an undue luxuriance in the early spring-tide.—PULVERBATCH; WELLINGTON; NEWPORT. 'The Barn-leasow's gettin' too *winter-proud*, the corn ŏŏd aumust cover a crow, an' that's o'er-forrat fur Febriwerry.'

WINTIE OR WRANGLE [win·ti'], *phr.* to win at any risk.—CLEE HILLS.

WINTLING [win·tlin], *sb., obs.* a young, fragile, and very small child—too small for its age.—PULVERBATCH. 'Have you seen Driver anywhere about?' 'I sid 'im at Betty Roberts's a bit agŏŏ, Sir, mindin' the *wintlin'*.' This statement seems a singular one, nevertheless it was quite true that Driver, the most sagacious and gentle of sheep-dogs, would, if called upon to do so, watch over the tiny child of a neighbouring cottager, and keep her out of harm's way, while her Mother went on some needful errand,—it was a pretty sight, the good dog lying in vigilant attitude across the threshold of the open door of the cottage, with the '*wintlin*',' thus prevented from stepping outside, nestling up to him in loving trust; and a sight which might often have been seen by the village folk in whose midst the child and the dog were, nearly half a century ago.

WIPPET, *sb.* a small creature,—'a *wippet* of a child.'—WORTHEN; WEM.

WIRES, *sb. pl.* The runners of strawberry-plants, and the stiff, angular stems of the whortleberry shrub, are respectively and alike called *wires*,—'strawberry-*wires*;'—'wimberry-*wires*.' Com.

Myrtus, glossed *wir*, appears in an *Anglo-Saxon Vocabulary*, x. or xi. cent., in Wr. vocabs., vol. i. p. 285.

WISE-MAN, WISE-WOMAN, *sb.* one—man or woman, as the case may be—who exercises the arts of divination, and deals in charms; a soothsayer.—SHREWSBURY; CORVE DALE; CLEE HILLS; LUDLOW. A.S. *wisa*, a sage, philosopher, director, wise man. Cf. **Cunning-man.** See Bk. II., *Folklore*, &c., 'Charming.'

WISEN [wei·zn], (1) *v. a.* to teach; to cause to learn wisdom,—'I should think as that ŏŏd *wisen* 'im a bit.'—SHREWSBURY; ELLESMERE.

> 'oþer-wise wold sche nouȝt · *wissen* here ladi
> bi what maner che ment · last sche were a-greued.'
> *William of Palerne*, l. 640.

'A.Sax. *wisian;* O.Sax. *wisean;* O.Icel. *visa;* O.H.Germ. *wisen;* to instruct, direct, shew.'—STRAT.

(2) *v. n.* to think upon; to reflect; to cause wisdom to bear upon, in thought,—'I'll *wisen* upon it.'—WELLINGTON.

(3) *sb.*, *var. pr.* the windpipe,—the weasand.—COLLIERY.

> 'Uppon his iron coller griped fast,
> That with the straint his *wesand* nigh he brast.'
> SPENSER, *F. Q.*, Bk. V. c. ii. st. xiv.

'*Rumen*, wasend,' occurs in an *Anglo-Saxon Vocabulary*, x. or xi. cent., in Wr. vocabs., vol. i. p. 282, where it relates to the human body.

'*Wesaunt*, of a beestys throte. *Ysofagus*.'—*Prompt. Parv.*

'A.S. *wǽsend;* O.Fris. *wasende*, the windpipe.'—WEDG.

WISK [wis·k], *sb.* a cough—the term is applied to the domestic animals of a farm, horses, cows, &c.—PULVERBATCH; OSWESTRY. 'Yo'd'n better tak a bag an' throw o'er the mar' awile 'er stan's, fur 'er's gotten a bit of a *wisk* now.' Cf. **Hoost.**

WISKET, (1) *sb.* a strong osier basket used for gardening purposes,—same as **Kipe**, q. v.—SHREWSBURY; PULVERBATCH; LUDLOW. Qy. com.

'A *Wisket*, or Straw-basket, in which Provender is given Cows or Oxen.'—*Academy of Armory*, Bk. II. ch. ix. p. 173.

Ray gives 'A *Whisket*, a Basket, a Skuttle or shallow Ped,' as a '*North Country Word*.' He also gives '*Wisket*' as an alternative spelling.

'A *whisket*, corbis, cophinus.'—COLES' *Lat. Dict.* A.D. 1677.

(2) *sb.* the wicker case in which a stone beer-bottle is carried to the field.—NEWPORT.

(3) *sb.* a wicker strainer placed over the spigot-hole within the mash-tub to prevent the grains passing through into the wort.—WHITCHURCH. Cf. **Mashing-basket.**

(4) *sb.* a satchel made of bass-matting.—NEWPORT; ELLESMERE.

WISLES [wei·zlz], *sb. pl.* potato-stalks. — PULVERBATCH; WHITCHURCH; ELLESMERE; OSWESTRY. 'The Rough-Reds bin a capital croppin' tato, an' throwen up mighty tall *wisles*.'

Randle Holme says, 'The tops of Carrats and Parsnips are by Gardiners termed *Wisalls*, and some Wisomes.'—*Academy of Armory*, Bk. II. ch. iii. p. 55.

Compare '*Wyse*, of strawbery (or pesyn, P.). *Fragus*,' in *Prompt. Parv.*

WITAN-ELM, *sb. Ulmus montána*, the Wych Elm.—CORVE DALE; LUDLOW. The employment of twigs of this tree for purposes of divination has doubtless given rise to its local name. A.S. *witan*, gen. sing. of *wita;* a wit, one who knows, a wise or cunning man: whence *witan-elm* = elm of the wise man. See **Wise-man**, also **Divining-rod** and *sub voce*.

WITAN-TREE, *sb.* the Mountain Ash.—CORVE DALE. A.S. *witan*, as for above. See Bk. II., *Folklore*, &c., 'Superstitions connected with Plants.' Cf. **Witty-tree.**

WITCHES'-STIRRUPS, *sb. pl.* matted locks in horses' manes.—CLEE HILLS.

'This is that very Mab
That plats the manes of horses in the night.'
Romeo and Juliet, I. iv. 89.

See Bk. II., *Folklore*, &c., 'Witchcraft.'

WITCHIFY, *v. a.* to bewitch; to practise witchcraft.—ELLESMERE. A coined word = M.E. *wicche*:—

'". . . . . were þei boþe here,
þei schuld *wicche* wel · ȝif þei a-wei went,
þouȝh þer were werwolfs · wiþ hem foure schore!"'
William of Palerne, l. 2539.

A.S. *wiccian*, to bewitch; to use sorcery.

WITH [with·], (1) *sb.* a tough, pliant twig, as of Honeysuckle or Willow. — PULVERBATCH. 'Yo'n find as 'oneysuckle *withs* maken the best wrathes.'

'Brydille hase he righte nane;
Seese he no better wane,
Bot a *wythe* has he tane,
And kenylles his stede.'
Sir Perceval, 421, in *Bible Word-Book*.

See **Wrathe.**

(2) *sb.* a band of twisted willow-twigs.—LUDLOW. See *Judges* xvi. 7, 8, 9.

'Wythe Bonde (*withe wythth*, S.). *Boia.* "*Boia*, torques damnatorum, quasi jugum in bove, a bos dicitur."—CATH.'—*Prompt. Parv. and Notes.*

A.S. *wiððe*, a twisted rod, a band. See **Withy**. Cf. **Wrathe.**

(3) [wi'·], BRIDGNORTH; NEWPORT; WHITCHURCH. [wudh·], BRIDGNORTH; WEM; ELLESMERE. [ŏŏdh·], SHREWSBURY; PULVERBATCH. Qy. com. in *S. Shr.*, *prep.* See **Wi'.**

WITHART [widh·ur't], *sb.* the sirname Woodward.—WHITCHURCH. A certain Clergyman asked a man who was called *Withart* what his real name was. The man could not tell, but his wife came to his aid: 'W'y,' said she, 'w'en we won married yo' know they pŭtten *Woodward* i' the beuk.' 'Aye, that's it,' said the man.

Mr. Skeat says the A.S. *widu*, wood, is found, as well as *wudu*; hence the *i* is quite correct.

WITHER [widh·ur'], *v. n.* to speak in an undertone, with an accompaniment of nods and winks. — PULVERBATCH. Qy. com. 'W'y dunna yo' spake up, an' nod *wither* an' w'isper athatn?'

WITHERINS, *sb.*, *obs.* the second floor of a malt-house where the malt was dried before going on the kiln.—PULVERBATCH; CLUN. Qy. com. See '*Wither it*,' &c., *sub voce* **Coming-floor.**

WITHER-WATHER [widh·ur' wadh·ur'], *adj.* hesitating; stopping to consider. — SHREWSBURY; PULVERBATCH; WORTHEN; WEM. Qy. com. 'Whad! yo' bin *wither-wather* yet—keepin' that poor fellow like a tŏŏăd on a pitchfork.'

WITHY [widh·i'], *sb.* the name, used generically, for all *Salices*, Willows or Osiers, which are *trees*, or which would become such, yielding *timber* after their kind. Com.

'. . . in the copse itself, where the *witheys* were gloved with silver and gold, and the primroses and the violets peeped, and the first of the wood-anemones began to star the dead ash-leaves.'—R. D. BLACKMORE, *Cradock Nowell*, A Tale of the New Forest, p. 335, ed. 1880.

'The Willow tree is called . . . in English, Sallow, *Withie*, and Willow.'—GERARDE's *Herball*, Bk. III. p. 1931.

'*Salix*,' glossed '*wiþi*,' is found in a *Semi-Saxon Vocabulary*, xii. cent., and '*wythy*' in a *Metrical Vocabulary*, xiv. cent., in Wr. vocabs., vol. i. pp. 92, 181.

'A.Sax. *wiððe*; O.Icel. *við*; O.Fris. *withthe*; O.H.Germ. *wida*; withy (withe), *salix*.'—STRAT.

Cf. **Sally.**

WITHY-BED, *sb.* a willow-plantation; an osier-holt. Qy. com. Cf. **Sally-bed.**

WITTY-BERRY, *sb.* the berry of the Mountain-Ash.—PULVERBATCH. 'The little wench thought 'erself mighty fine, ŏŏth 'er neckliss o' *witty-berries*.'

WITTY-TREE, *sb.* the Mountain-Ash.—PULVERBATCH. See **Witan-tree.**

WIZZEN-FACED, *adj.* pale-faced, with sharp, pinched features. Qy. com. ''Er's a poor *wizzen-faced* little thing, nuthin' like the rest' [others].

'A.Sax. *wisnian;* O.Icel. *visna;* O.H.Germ. *wes(e)nen;* to wizzen (*arescere*).'—STRAT.

WOBBLE, WOPPLE. See **Wapple.**

WOLLER, WULLER, *sb. Alnus glutinósa*, common Alder. Both forms obtain.—SHREWSBURY; PULVERBATCH; WORTHEN; CLUN; WELLINGTON. Cf. **Owler.**

WOODCHUCK, *sb. Gécinus víridis*, Green Woodpecker.—CLUN. See **Haihow.**

WOODEN, *adj., pec.* stupid; dull of understanding, and awkward as a consequence. Com. 'I should never a trusted a job like that to sich a *'ŏŏden* fellow as 'im.' This use of the term *wooden* seems to retain a lingering sense of the old word *wood*, mad, or of unsound or infirm mind, frequently found in the early writers. Compare—

'What schulde he studie, and make himselven *wood*,
Uppon a book in cloystre alway to powre.'
CHAUCER, *The Prologue*, l. 184, ed. Morris.

In the Wykliffite Version, Festus said to Paul, 'many lettris turnen thee to *woodnesse*.'—*Acts* xxvi. 24.

'*Woode* or madde. *Amens* . . .'—*Prompt. Parv.*

'*Amens*, mad, void of reason, or sence, *without wit or understanding*' [= stupid = *wooden*].—*Etym. Lat. Dict.*

'A.Sax. *wód;* Goth. *vóds;* O.H.Germ. *wuoter;* O.Icel. *óðr;* wood, mad.'—STRAT.

WOODFINT [wuod·fint], *sb.* the place where the cleft wood for fires is kept.—ELLESMERE.

Compare *fint* = *find* with '*Findit*, toslâf, tocleaf,' and '*Findere*, todælan,' which occur in a *Vocabulary*, xi. cent., in Wr. vocabs., vol. ii. p. 37.

Woodfill = *Woodfint.*—NEWPORT.

WOODTAPPER, *sb. Picus minor*, the Lesser Spotted Woodpecker. —BRIDGNORTH.

WOODWIND [wei·nd], *sb. Lonícera Periclýmenum*, common Honeysuckle; Woodbine.—CORVE DALE.

'*Vivorna*,' glossed '*wudu-winde*,' is found in an *Anglo-Saxon Vocabulary*, x. or xi. cent., in Wr. vocabs., vol. i. p. 286.

See '*Woodbine*' *sub voce* **Wrathe.**

WOOLERT [wul·ur't], *sb.* an owl.—CLUN. Cf. **Ŏólert.**

WOOLLY-BEAR, same as **Tommy-tailor**, q. v.—NEWPORT.

WORCH [waur'·ch], *v. a.* to cause pain; to irritate.—SHREWSBURY. (1) 'This 'ere tuth *worches* me above a bit.' (2) ''Er *worched* the poor chap despertly.' Cf. **Warch.**

WORD OF A SORT, *phr.* an admonition; a rebuke,—'I gid 'im a *word of a sort*.' Com.

WORK-BRATTLE, *adj.* industrious; diligent; inclined to work.—PULVERBATCH. 'Yo' bin al'ays desport *work-brattle* toërt night—ketchin' the day by the lag-end.'

'*Warck-brattle*, fond of work. Lanc.,' in PEGGE.

WORK I' THE BON', *phr.* to work in a band.—COLLIERY; M. T. See **Bond** (4), also **Bondsmen**.

WORRY-WHEAT, *sb. Ranunculus arvénsis*, Corn Crowfoot.—WELLINGTON, *High Ercall*. See **Devil's Curry-comb**.

WORSEN, *v. a.* to make worse,—'Yo'n *wö'sened* that a good djel, yo'd'n better a lef' it be.'—WHITCHURCH; ELLESMERE.

WORSER, *adj.* worse—a double comparative. Com.

'*York.* Damsel of France, I think I have you fast:
. . . .
. . . .
A goodly prize, fit for the devil's grace!
See, how the ugly wench doth bend her brows,
As if with Circe she would change my shape!
Pucelle. Changed to a *worser* shape thou canst not be.'
1 *King Henry VI.*, V. iii. 36.

Mr. Halliwell observes of *worser* that, it 'is still in use.'
See **Grammar Outlines**, *Adjectives* (*irregular comparisons*).

WOUT [wou·t], *v. n.* to incline on one side so as to fall; to turn over.—PULVERBATCH. 'That stack's bin cavin' this good bit, an' las' night it *wouted* o'er.' Cf. **Waut**, also **Root-wouted**.

WRACKET, *sb.* brunt; consequences. — PULVERBATCH; WEM; ELLESMERE. 'Yo' jest do whad I tell yo', an' I'll stan' the *wracket*.'

WRANG [r'ang·], *adj.* wrong.—PULVERBATCH; CHURCH STRETTON. 'Yo' bin tellin' the lady *wrang*,' said a woman at Church Stretton, coming forth from her cottage to correct a neighbour, whom she had overheard giving, what she believed to be, erroneous information upon a certain point.

'Wallace ansuerd, said; "thow art in the *wrang*."'
HENRY THE MINSTREL (A.D. 1461, *circa*), *Wallace*, Bk. I.
Specim. Eng. Lit., vi. l. 398.

'The Poets, too, a venal gang,
Wi' rhymes weel-turn'd and ready,
Wad gar you trow ye ne'er do *wrang*,
But ay unerring steady,
On sic a day.'
ROBERT BURNS, *Poems*, p. 36, l. 25.

'*Wrang*, O.Icel. *rangr*.'—STRAT.

WRATCH [r'ach·], *sb.* a term, or form of address, employed to express the feelings when pity and affection are combined = wretch. —PULVERBATCH. 'God 'elp thee *wratch!* bist'ee aumust froze? Come to the fire an' warm thee an' a tuthree broth.'

WRATHE [r'ai·dh], *sb.* the twisted band of tough twigs—'*withs*,' as they are called—which goes round a 'besom.'—PULVERBATCH. 'The Maister gid five shillin' fur a dozen birch besoms fur the barn—they wun capital good uns, an' the *wrathes* ŏŏn do agen, fur they bin made o' 'oneysuckle withs.' Compare—

> 'He bar a bordun I-bounde · wiþ a brod lyste,
> In A *weþe-bondes wyse* · *I-writhen* aboute.'
>
> *Piers Pl.*, Text A., pass. vi. l. 9—

where '*weþebonde*' means Woodbine (Honeysuckle); and compare also '*Woodbinde*, binde-weede, or *withiewinde*, because it windes about other plantes.'—Minsheu, in SKEAT'S *Notes*, p. 145, ed. E. E. T. S.

A.S. *wrað*, *wrǽð*, what is twisted, a wreath. Cf. **With** (2). See **With** (1). See also **Woodwind**.

WRECKLING. See **Reckling.**

WREKIN DOVE, *sb. Turtur auritus*, Turtle Dove.—WELLINGTON. Called *Wrekin Dove* because, while known to be a scarce bird in many parts of England, it habitually frequented the large woods about the Wrekin.

WRIT [r'it·], *pret.* wrote.—PULVERBATCH. Qy. com. 'I've sen' many a letter for 'er to Jack w'en 'e wuz a-sodgerin', but 'e never *writ* to 'er, as I know on.' *Writ*, a contraction of the participle *written*, was formerly in good use as a preterite.

> 'Maria *writ*
> The letter at Sir Toby's great importance.'
>
> *Twelfth Night*, V. i. 370.

'"I *writ* lately to Mr. Pope," Swift says, writing to Gay.'—THACKERAY'S *English Humourists.*

A.S. *wrítan*; Icel. *ríta*, to write. Cf. **Wrote**, below.

WRITING-MAISTER, *sb. Emberiza citrinella*, the Yellow Ammer. —PULVERBATCH. 'I know to a *Writin'-maister's* nist ŏŏth five young uns in it,' said a Hanwood boy. The eggs of this bird are dotted and scribbled all over, somewhat in the fashion of a child's early attempts at writing, whence the name *Writing-maister*. See **Blacksmith.**

WROSTLE [r'os·l], *v. n.*, *var. pr.* to strive; to struggle,—to wrestle. Qy. com. 'Yo' conna ate all that, Jack.' 'I'm welly bos'n, Missis, but I'll *wros'le* wuth it.' The participle, *wrostling*, is used to express an idea of size or strength,—'a great big, *wros'lin'* fellow.'

WROTE, *pret.* for *part. past*, written,—'I've *wrote* to tell 'er the raps.' Com. So Shakespeare has it:—

> '*Lucius.* Thanks, royal sir.
> My emperor hath *wrote*, I must from hence.'
>
> *Cymbeline*, III. v. 3.

Cf. **Writ**, above.

WUK, *sb.* an oak.—SHREWSBURY; PULVERBATCH; CHURCH STRETTON. Qy. com. 'The Squire 's levellin' the *wuk* this 'ear, but I ŏŏnder as 'e dunna a some o' them owd rundels down.' See **W** (3) in **Grammar Outlines** (*consonants*, &c.) for this and the following words.

WULL, will. See **Grammar Outlines,** p. lxxx.

'Poure out the wine without restraint or stay,

. . . .

Poure out to all that *wull.*'

SPENSER, *Epithalamion*, l. 252.

WULLER. See **Woller.**

WUR-FROST. See **Whoar-frost.**

WUTH [wuth·], *sb.* an oath.—SHREWSBURY; PULVERBATCH. Qy. com. 'I'll tak my *wuth* as theer inna-d-a better trottin' mar' gwuz the rŏoăd than that o' the Maister's.'

WUTMIL, *sb.* oatmeal. Qy. com.

WUTS, *sb.* oats. Qy. com.

YAL [yaa·l], *sb.* ale.—BRIDGNORTH. 'Them chaps wun aumust tossicated wi' *yal* afore a wenten i' the Jarge [George] an' Dragon, an' bygum! a gotten some spĕrits theer to top-up like; an' it made 'em right drunk, but the Missis 'ad 'em turned out then, no danger!' Cf. **Yeăl.**

YALLOW [yal·u'], *adj.* yellow. Com. 'I dunna like the waiter from the pit fur weshin', it mak's the clo'es as *yallow* as a Meadow Bout' [Marsh Marigold].

'Theise cocodrilles ben serpentes, *ȝalowe* and rayed aboven, and han four feet, and schorte thyes and grete nayles, as clees or talouns.' —SIR JOHN MANDEVILLE [A.D. 1356], *Travels*, p. 198, in Hal.

'A.Sax. *geolo;* O.H.Germ. *gelwer*, yellow.'—STRAT.

YALLOW-WORT, *sb.* a mild form of jaundice: a severer type is called the 'black jaunders.' Com. 'Poor owd Mr. Jandrell o' the Grove is very bad now; 'e's 'ad the *yallow-wort* a lung wilde, an' it's turned to the black-jaunders.' Compare—

'For the *ȝalow-souȝt*, that men callin the *jaundys*. Take hard Speynich sope and a litille stale ale in a coppe, and rubbe the sope aȝens the coppe botum tylle the ale be qwyte.'—*MS. Sloane*, 7, f. 73, in HAL.

See **Jaunders.**

YAPENNY [yaap·ni'], *sb.* a halfpenny.—BRIDGNORTH.

YAR [yaa·r'], (1) *sb.* hair,—'The child mun 'ăve 'er *yar* cut short, I doubt.' Com.

(2) *sb.* a cider hair,—a sieve used in the process of cider-making.—CLEE HILLS.

YARBALIST, *sb.* a quack whose *materia medica* is comprehended in his use of herbs; a herbalist. Com. 'Well, fur my part I hanna much opinion o' quack doctors; theer's nuthin' like the Firmary, w'eer theer's plenty o' larn'd men; an' if sich as Clement an' Burd canna cure, I shouldna a much faith in a *yarbalist.*'

YARBS, *sb. pl.* herbs. Com. 'The Maȳ-month's the best time to get *yarbs;* I sid owd Lacy busy alung the diche-bonks the tother day.' 'Aye, 'e's mighty cliver, they tellen me, an' cures a power o' folks.'

YARD-COAL, *sb.* a good coal for manufacturing purposes.—COLLIERY; M. T. See *sub voce* **Top-Coal.**

YARE, *adj.* eager; ready.—CLEE HILLS.

> 'Hwan he com hom, he wore *yare*,
> Grimes sones, forto fare
> In-to þe se, fishes to gete,
> Þat hauelok mithe wel of ete.'
>
> *Havelok the Dane*, l. 1391.

'*Pompey* . . . . . and I hope, if you have occasion to use me for your own turn, you shall find me *yare.*'—*Measure for Measure*, IV. ii. 62.

Jamieson has '*Yare.* Ready, alert, in a state of preparation.'

'A.Sax. *gearu;* O.Sax. *garu;* O.H.Germ. *gar(e)wer;* O.Icel. *görr;* yare, ready.'—STRAT.

YAREWINDS [yaa·r'winz *and* yaer'·winz], *sb., obs.* a machine for holding yarn intended to be made into skeins or wound into balls.—PULVERBATCH. The *yarewinds* consisted of a reel and stand. The reel was a stock something like the nave of a wheel, with four arms, inserted crosswise, *i. e.* at opposite diameters; these arms were perforated at regular distances from the end, to receive the tall wooden pins round which the yarn was wound. By means of the holes—about five in each arm—the pins could be adjusted to 'slippings,' or skeins, of various lengths. The stand consisted of a small block, forming an apex, as it were, to the three legs which supported it, and having in its centre a pivot upon which the reel rotated. (A tripod, to serve as a stand for the reel, would sometimes be rudely fashioned by cutting a three-forked branch to the requisite length, and inverting it.) The whole affair was about two feet and a half from the ground. When spinning was a household industry, *yarewinds* supplemented the wheel; the yarn spun and twisted on the latter being wound on the reel, as the succeeding process by which the 'slippings' were formed. Linen-yarn, when it had been made into 'slippings,' was bleached, and afterwards returned to the *yarewinds*, from which it was wound into balls for the cottage weaver. Spinning-wheels and *yarewinds* were in use about 1840, and probably at a later date still.

Walter de Biblesworth—xiii. cent.—discoursing to 'dame Muriel' upon spinning, says—

> 'A wudres ore alez;
> E vostre filoe là wudez.'

'*Wudres*' is glossed 'a *yar-wyndel*,' and the second line, 'wynde thi yarn.'—See Wr. vocabs., vol. i. p. 157.

'ȝarne wyndel, ... (or *ȝarwyndyl*). *Girgillus.* "*A gyrus, dicitur gyrgillus, instrumentum femineum, quod alio nomine dicitur volutorium, quia vertendo in gyrum inde fila devolvuntur. Filum de colo ducitur in fusum; a fuso in alabrum, vel traductorium; ab alabro in gyrgillum vel devolutorium; a gyrgillo in glomicellum.*"—CATH.'—*Prompt. Parv. and Notes*, pp. 536, 188.

'*Girgillus.* A reele to winde thread on, *winde blades.*'—*Dict. Etym. Lat.*

See **Yarnacles**, also **Yarringles**, below. Cf. **Swifts.** See **Slipping.**

YARLY [yaa·r'li'], *adj.* and *adv.* early. Com. 'They bin mighty *yarly* folks, them new-comers at Arscott, an' looken as 'ard as muntin tits' [mountain ponies].

'Nyght and day he ys in sorowe,
Late on evyn, *ȝarly* on morowe.'
MS. Cantab. Ff. ii. 38, f. 148, in HAL.

Cf. **Arly.**

YARN [yaa·r'n], (1) *v. a.* to earn. Com. 'W'en I could *yarn* money, I didna mind spendin', but now I canna get nuthin', I 'ăve to be carful.'

'When raine is a let to thy dooings abrode,
set threshers a threshing to laie on good lode:
Thresh cleane ye must bid them, though lesser they *yarn*,
and looking to thriue, haue an eie to thy barne.'
TUSSER, *Fiue Hundred Pointes of Good Husbandrie* [November].

Cf. **Arn.**

(2) *sb. Ardea cinérea*, the Heron.—WHITCHURCH, *Tilstock.* The Heron frequents the *Brown Moss* between Whitchurch and Tilstock [1874].

YARNACLES, *sb., obs.* a turning-reel for yarn to be wound upon.—NEWPORT. *Yarnacles* were, for all intents and purposes, the same as the *yarewinds* previously described, q. v.; but they were somewhat simpler in construction, the reel being merely two flat pieces of wood laid one over the other,—like a S. Andrew's Cross, in form,—with a hole in the middle to enable it to rotate on a pivot. The arms were perforated like those of the *yarewinds*, and for the same reasons; the tall pegs holding the yarn being fitted into the holes at the compass required by the skein. A pedestal, or stand of some kind, having a pivot in the centre, served for the reel to work upon. See **Yarringles**, below.

YARNEST. See *sub voce* **Earnest.**

YARRINGLES, same as **Yarnacles**, above.—WELLINGTON. Qy. com.

Randle Holme enumerates amongst 'Things belonging to Spinning,' '*Yarringle blades*, Foot or Stand, and *Yarringle Pegs*, or *Pinns.*'—*Academy of Armory*, Bk. III. ch. iii. p. 106.

Bailey—ed. 1782—gives '*Yarringles, Yarringle Blades*, an Instrument from which Hanks of yarn are wound into Clews or Balls.'

'*Hoc nirgilium*, a par garnwyndil-blades,' is enumerated amongst things pertaining to spinning, in a *Nominale*, xv. cent., in Wr. vocabs., vol. i. p. 217.

From A.S. *gearn*, yarn; and *windan*, to wind. See *Yarringles*, in HAL. See **Yarewinds.**

YASK [yaas·k], *sb.* a term used to express the sound made by a violent effort to get quit of something in the throat.—WHITCHURCH. 'Bygum! 'e wuz aumust choked, 'e gid sich a *yask*.'

'I *yeske*, I gyve a noyse out of my stomacke, *je engloute*.'—Palsgrave, in HAL.

A.S. *giscian*, to sob.

YAUL [yau·l], *v. a.* to pull, or drag roughly; to haul.—CLEE HILLS. See **H** (2) in **Grammar Outlines** (*consonants*, &c.).

YAWP [yau·p], *sb.* the nape of the neck.—CLEE HILLS. Cf. **Scuff**, &c.

YEÄL. See *sub voce* **Ale.**

YEAN [ee·n *and* yee·n], *v. n.* to bring forth lambs. Com. ''Ow bin'ee' gettin' on ŏŏth yore ship?' 'Oh! rarly; we'n got four an' twenty lombs ŏŏth ten yeows, most on 'em 'ad'n three, an' the rest double-couples, an' theer's eīghteen to *ean* yet; but we'n lost two.'

'So many days my ewes have been with young;
So many weeks ere the poor fools will *ean*.'
3 *Henry VI.*, II. v. 36.

'Eawes readie to *yeane*,
craues ground rid cleane.'
TUSSER, *Januaries abstract*, ed. E. D. S., p. 73.

Ray gives as a '*Somerset*' Proverb, 'She stamps like an Ewe upon *yeaning*.'—p. 268.

See '*Enyñ*,' with WAY'S Note, in *Prompt. Parv.*, p. 140.

'A.Sax. *eanian*; Du. *oonen*, to yean, lamb.'—STRAT.

YEAR [yee·h'r' *and* ee·h'r'], *sb. pl.* years,—'They'n bin i' that 'ouse twelve *year* nex' Miämas.' Com.

'"For sche hade brouȝt hem of bale · boþe," þei seide,
"& i-lengþed here lif · mani long *ȝere*."'
William of Palerne, l. 1040.

'Thre *yeer* and more how lasteth her vitaille?'
CHAUCER, B. 499 (Six-text ed.), Skeat.

A.S. *geár*; Icel. *ár*; Goth. *jer*, a year. The A.S. *plural* is also *geár*. See **Grammar Outlines** (*nouns of time*, &c.), p. xliii.

YEÄT [yi'·u't], *sb.* and *v. a.* heat; to heat.—PULVERBATCH. 'Theer's some sense i' querd-ŏŏd fur the oven, it ouds the *yeät*, but this poor brash keeps yo' on fillin' an' does no good.' Cf. **Yet.**

YEÄTH, YETH [yi'·uth], CHURCH STRETTON. [yeth·], SHREWSBURY; PULVERBATCH; CLUN; WEM. Qy. com., *sb.* heath. ''W'eer did the starm o'ertak' yo'?' 'Jest i' the middle o' Prees *Yeth*, an' no shelter o' ne'er-a side.' See example *sub voce* **Faggit** (1). A.S. *hǽð*, heath.

YED [yed·], *sb.* a head. Com. 'See, John, 'ow the Maister's improved yore *yed* a'ready!' This observation, addressed to 'John' by his wife, did not refer to his own '*yed*,' but to the Goat's Head on an intended sign-board—half painted, and much misrepresented, by John himself—which, the 'Maister' chancing to see, and being moved to amend, was at that moment dashing in, with true artistic skill and requisite knowledge of blazonry. See **Head.**

YEDART. See **Edward.**

YED-COLLAR. See **Head-collar.**

YED-OUT. See **Head-out.**

YED-STALL. See **Head-stall.**

YEDSTRUNG, *adj.* headstrong; stubborn. Com. ''E's a *yed-strung* young rascal, but 'e's gweïn to a Maister as ŏŏl bend 'im, or break 'im.'

YELLOP [yaal·up], *v. n.* to bark, howl, cry, as dogs do—to yelp.—WORTHEN; WEM. A.S. *gelpan*, to yelp. Cf. **Yowl.**

YELLOW HOMBER, *sb.* the Yellow Ammer.—LUDLOW; WEM. See **Homber,** also **Blacksmith.** Cf. **Golden Amber.**

YELVE [yel·v *and* yil·v], *sb.* a garden-fork.—WEM; WHITCHURCH; ELLESMERE. A *North Border* word.

'*The Parts of a Yelve.* The Barr, or Cross Bar. The Tangs, or Forks. The Socket, for the Stail to go in. The Staile. Te kaspe, is the top part on which the man holds.'—*Academy of Armory*, Bk. III. ch. viii. p. 337.

Cf. **Sharevil.**

YEOW [you· *and* yi'ou·], *sb.* a ewe. Com. See example *sub voce* **Yean.**

'Or, if he wanders up the howe,
Her living image in her *yowe*
Comes bleating to him, owre the knowe,
For bits o' bread.'
ROBERT BURNS, *Poems*, p. 33, l. 22, c. 2.

'A.Sax. *eowu*; O.H.Germ. *awi*; O.Du. *ouwe*, oie, a ewe.'—STRAT.

YEP. See **Heap.**

YEPPED [yep·t], *part. adj.* heaped. Com. 'I pŭt a *yepped* box o' coal o' the fire now jest.'

YERRIWIG [yaer'i'wig], *sb.* an earwig.—PULVERBATCH. Qy. com. 'Mother, does a *yerriwig* bite or sting?' 'Ne'er-a one, dunna yo' see as it's gotten pinsons fur a tail?—so it pinches.'

'In a Vocabulary, Harl. MS. 1002, is found, "*auriolus, Anglice a ȝerwygge.*"'—WAY, in *Prompt. Parv.*, p. 143.

See **Erriwig,** also **Arrawig.**

YERTH [yur'th·], *sb.* earth; soil. Qy. com. 'Whad bin 'ee cartin' *yerth* fur, Dick—is dirt scă'ce at yore place?' 'The Maister's 'ăvin' a mount [mound] made round the lawn, to grow primmiroses, or summat.'

'1590. Paid for carringe the *yerthe* out where the organes stood, vj[d].'—*Churchwardens' Accounts*, S. Mary's, Shrewsbury.

'Than the kynge sayde, "is my sonne deed or hurt, or on the *yerthe* felled?" "no, sir," quod the knyght, "but he is hardely matched, wherefore he hathe nede of your ayde."'—LORD BERNERS (A.D. 1523), *The Battle of Crecy*. *Specim. Eng. Lit.*, xv. *b.* l. 124.

'Nay, even the *yirth* itsel does cry,
For E'mbrugh wells are grutten dry.'
ROBERT BURNS, *Poems*, p. 137, l. 9, c. 2.

A.S. *eorðe*, earth, ground.

YES [yaes·], NEWPORT. [yaa·s], CHURCH STRETTON. [ei·s], CHURCH STRETTON, *Leebotwood.* [i'ss·], PULVERBATCH; WORTHEN; CLUN; OSWESTRY. Qy. com., *adv.* A.S. *gese; gise,* yea. See **E** (7) (8) (10) (12) in **Grammar Outlines** (*vowels,* &c.).

YET [yaet·], same as **Yeät**.—WEM; ELLESMERE.

YIT [yit· *and* it], *adv.* yet,—''E hanna bin theer *yit* as I know on.' Qy. com.

'He nevere *yit* no vileinye ne sayde
In al his lyf, unto no maner wight.'
CHAUCER, *The Prologue*, l. 70, ed. Morris.

'. . . . womman? myn our cam not *ȝit*.'—*John* ii. 4, Wycliffite Version, A.D. 1388.
A.S. *git* (*with negative*), yet.

YOCKEL [yok·h'l], *sb.* the Green Woodpecker.—ELLESMERE. See **Ecall**.

YOK [yok·], *sb.* a yoke, such as is put round the neck of a pig, to prevent it breaking through a hedge.—PULVERBATCH. 'Aye, yo' bin lucky, like Tum 'Odges, as lost five pund, an' fund a pig's *yok*.' This is proverbially said of any one who is unfortunate in sustaining losses.

'Boweth your nekke vnder that blisful *yok*
Of souueraynetee, nought of seruyse,
Which that men clepeth spousail or wedlok.'
CHAUCER, B. 113 (Six-text ed.), Skeat.

'*ȝokke. Jugum.*'—*Prompt. Parv.*
'A.Sax. *geoc, ioc;* Goth. *juk*, a yoke.'—STRAT.

YOK-FARM, *sb.* the best farm on an estate.—PULVERBATCH. 'I 'spect owd Price made a good bit o' money theer—it wuz al'ays said to be the *yok-farm* on the Lordship, an' 'e 'eld it above forty year.'
'A little farm or manor in some parts of Kent is called a *yoklet*.'—Kennett, in HAL.

YOKING [yauk·in'], *part. adj.* making a noise in the throat as if about to vomit; retching, and such like.—PULVERBATCH. 'I think the waggoner 'ad a drop too much las' night, I 'eärd 'im *yokin'* i' the back foud.'

'Ful pale he was, for-dronken, and nought red.
He *yoxeth*, and he speketh thurgh the nose.'
CHAUCER, *C. T.*, l. 4149.

See '*ȝyxyn̄*,' with WAY'S Note, in *Prompt. Parv.*, p. 539.

YORD, (1) *sb.* a small enclosure of land contiguous to a house.—PULVERBATCH. 'Run to the *yord* an' see if the gis an' gullies bin all right.'

'A *yerd* sche hadde, enclosed al aboute
With stikkes, and a drye dich withoute,
In which she hadde a cok, highte Chauntecleer,
In al the lond of crowyng nas his peer.'
CHAUCER, *The Nonne Prestes Tale*, l. 27, ed. Morris.

'ȝerd, or *ȝord. Ortus.*'—*Prompt. Parv.*
A.S. *geard*, an enclosure.

(2) *sb.* in composition—the enclosure round about a Church—the church-*yord:* the form is an old one thus.—SHREWSBURY; PULVERBATCH. Qy. com. 'I tell yo' whad I think—poor Dick's cuff soun's mighty like Churton Church-*yord*' [*i. e.* 'a Churchyard cough'].

'This yeare one Degory Waters of Salop draper dyeed the xxviij*th* day of Julii A° 1477 and was buryed in Sainct Mary's churche in Salop in Trynytie Chappel he in hys lyffe tyme buylded all the Almshowsen in St. Marys churche *yorde* and dwellyd in the Almeshowse hall there amongst them and wold also kneele amo'gst them in the same churche in a fayre longe pewe made for them and hym selfe.'—*Early Chronicles of Shrewsbury* (*Taylor MS.*), in *Transactions of the Shropshire Archæological and Natural History Society.*

YORK, *adj.* shrewd; sharp, as in driving a bargain: the term is generally understood in a sinister sense.—PULVERBATCH. 'Oh! 'e munna think to get o'er me athatn, if 'e's *york*, 'e'll fine me *york* too.'

Compare '*Yark.* Sharp, acute, quick,' which Mr. Halliwell gives as a *Devon* word.

YORN, *sb.* yarn. Com. 'I like the *yorn* scoured afore it's knit, but the owd knitters sen it grains best i' the grace,' *i. e.* works more smoothly with the grease in it, as it was spun.

'A.Sax. *gearn;* O.Icel., O.H.Germ. *garn*, yarn.'—STRAT.

YOWL [you·l], *v. n.* to howl, as dogs do. Com. 'If yo' tie'n that dog up, 'e'll *yowl* all night, an' I shanna get a wink o' sleep.'

'The kyng passed therby as the greyhound was that kept his lord and his maystre, and the greyhound aroos agayn hem, and bygan to *ȝowle* upon hem.'—*MS. Bodleian*, 546, in HAL.

'A dog winna *yowl*, an' ye hit him wi' a bane.'—*North Country Proverb.*

Grose has '*Yowl.* To cry or howl. N.'

'Low Germ. *jölen, jaulen*, yowl, howl.'—STRAT.

Cf. **Yellop.**

YOWLING, *part. adj.* crying vociferously.—SHREWSBURY; PULVERBATCH; WELLINGTON. Qy. com. 'Whad bin yo' *yowlin'* about? I'll gie yo' summat to cry fur direc'ly, as'll mak' it run aisy fur yo'.'

YOWP [you·p], *v. n.* and *sb.* to give a short bark; the bark itself.—PULVERBATCH; OSWESTRY. Qy. com. 'Nip 's a rar' dog; 'e gid a bit on a *yowp* at the ŏŏd-pil jest now, an' I knowed 'e smelt summat, or 'e ŏŏdna *yowp* athatn, so I begun to pool the ŏŏd about, an' out bouted a great big rot; 'e soon fettled that, an' went in an' fat another out—Oh! thinks I, theer's a nist 'ere, an' by-gum, theer wuz, an' thirteen young uns.'

ZAD, ZOD [zad·], WORTHEN. [zod·], Com. the letter **Z**. 'The *zods* be despert aukert!' exclaimed a young servant-girl from Bitterley (near Ludlow), taking, apparently, a retrospective view of the difficulties surmounted in learning her letters, under the tuition of her Mistress, who had set about to teach her to read and write, on finding that she could do neither (1859).

ZODICAL, *sb.* Zadkiel, used elliptically for '*Zadkiel's Almanac.*'—SHREWSBURY; ATCHAM. Qy. com. This Almanac, with its Cabalistical characters, its Hieroglyphics and Prophetic Allusions, is the Oracle of the peasantry. It would seem as if somehow they had confounded *Zadkiel*, the name of their Prophet, with *Zodiacal*, that which pertains to the signs of the seasons, in their term *Zodical*.

SUPPLEMENT TO GLOSSARY.

ALLEY, (1) *sb.* a garden-path.—PULVERBATCH. 'Yo' can play i' the gardin if yo'n mind to keep on the *alley*, 'cause yore Faither 's dug the ground.' Tusser calls a path or walk an *alley*:—

'sawe dust spred thick
makes *alley* trick.'
Septembers abstract, ed. E. D. S., p. 33.

Fr. *allée*, a passage, a walk; from *aller*, to go.

(2) *sb.* a choice kind of marble, which is highly valued by boys, and is made of white or cream-coloured marble. Com.

ANNOY, *v. a.* to damage; to spoil,—'That theer bit o' roche 'as *annoyed* my spade.'—WELLINGTON. Tusser employs *annoying* in the sense of injuring as follows:—

'Make riddance of carriage, er yeere go about,
for spoiling of plant that is newlie come out.
To carter (with oxen) this message I bring,
leaue oxen abrode for *anoieng* the spring.'
Aprils husbandrie, ed. E. D. S., p. 105—

where '*anoieng the spring*' means damaging the young shoots. See Note.—*Ibid.*

ANTELUTE [an·ti'loot], *sb., obs.*? a tea-party at a cottage, got up for the benefit of the goodwife.—ELLESMERE, *Nesscliff.* 'Now then, girls, if yo'n look sharp an' get yore work done, yo' sha'n gŏŏ to the *antelute*' [1840]. Perhaps a ludicrous corruption of *interlude*.

AULD [au·ld], *adj.* shrewd; sly; cunning.—WORTHEN. (1) 'I wuz too *auld* fur 'im—I besteds 'im.' (2) 'Our young Tum looked pretty *auld* at me w'en the paas'n said 'e supposed theer'd be a Chris'nin' fur 'im afore lung.'

BARREL, *sb., obs.* an appendage proper to the little wheel,—a reel round which the linen yarn was wound as it was spun. It was, in form, somewhat like a dumb-bell of slender proportions. The cylinder was hollow, to admit the spindle, and one of its circular ends was flat and capable of being removed: when the reel was required to be put on the spindle, this end was taken off for that purpose, and being again screwed on, the whole affair was ready for the rotatory operation of winding. The yarn was conducted to the *barrel* through the upper part of two 'wings,' as they were called,—pieces of wood, curved somewhat like the 'merry-thought' of a fowl,—permanently affixed near to the extremity of the spindle: the *barrel*, when put on at the opposite end, was pushed up to these 'wings,' which extended beyond its circumference, and thus regulated the quantity of yarn it was required to hold. See **Little Wheel** (*Supplement*). Cf. **Broach**, p. 50.

BASH, (1) *v. a.* to scare; to frighten,—'fire yore gun, an' it'll *bash* them rooks.'—WELLINGTON. Compare the M.E. *a-bascht*, which has the sense of terrified, in the following:—

'þe kyng was *a-bascht* . . . .
and his Chaumberleyn so a-ferd · þat neih he felde I-swowen.'
Joseph of Arimathie, l. 202.

'*A-baschyd*, or a-ferde. *Territus*, perterritus.'—*Prompt. Parv.*

'O.Fr. *esbahir*, to frighten; to startle: from O.Fr. *baer*, la racine dont est l'onomatopée interjective *ba*.'—BUR.

(2) *v. a.* to make ashamed; to put out of countenance.—PULVERBATCH. 'Fur shame on yo', John, talkin' so vulgar, yo'n quite *bash* these young girls.'

'His countenaunce was bold, and *bashed* not
For Guyons lookes, but scornefull eyeglaunce at him shot.'
SPENSER, *F. Q.*, Bk. II. c. iv. st. xxxvii.

BILL, *sb.* a bank-note. Qy. com. 'I hanna got no cash [coins], Maester, nuthin' but a *bill*.' Sometimes the term *Bank-bill* is used for the same thing.

BLACK-HEADED-NOB, *sb.* the Bullfinch.—ELLESMERE. See **Nope**, p. 303.

BLACK SALLY, (1) *sb. Salix caprĕa*, great Sallow, or Goat Willow.—WELLINGTON. Called *Black Sally* from the very dark tint of its green foliage.

(2) *Salix pentándra*, sweet Bay-leaved Willow.—WELLINGTON. The term *Black Sally* seems to be somewhat loosely applied to several species of Willows, growing high, and having foliage of more than ordinary depth of colour. See **Sally**, p. 360, and **Withy**, p. 487.

BLENT, *pret.* blended,—''Er *blent* it ŏop.'—NEWPORT. See example *sub voce* **Noration**, p. 304.

'Then Sir Tristeram tooke powder forth of that box,
& *blent* it with warme sweete milke.'
King Arthur and the King of Cornwall, l. 276. *Percy Folio MS.*, vol. i. p. 73, ed. Hales and Furnivall.

A.S. *blendan*, to mix, blend.

BLETCH [blech·], (1) *sb.* the black, sticky substance, into which the grease applied to the axles of cart-wheels, to machinery, &c. is converted by trituration. Com.

Compare '*Bleche* for souters, *attrament noyr*.'—Palsgrave, in WAY. 'A.S. *blæc*; O.Du. *black*; O.H.Germ. *blach*, black (*atramentum*).' —STRAT. See **Blutch**, below.

(2) *v. a.* to smear with 'bletch.' Com. 'I canna get the marks out o' yore gown, Ma'am, I've tried all as ever I can; but I doubt yo'n *bletched* it some'ow, an' *bletch* is sich a thing, yo' canna stir it.'

BLIND-NETTLE, *sb.* *Lamium galeobdolon*, Archangel; *Lamium album*, white Dead-nettle; and *Lamium purpúreum*, red Dead-nettle, are each and alike called *Blind-nettle*.—WELLINGTON.

'*Archangelica*, blinde netle,' occurs in *Archbp. Ælfric's Vocabulary*, x. cent., in Wr. vocabs., vol. i. p. 31.

Gerarde says, 'Archangell is called . . . . of some *Lamium*; in English . . *blinde Nettle*, and dead Nettle.'—*Herball*, Bk. II. p. 568, 1st ed. A.D. 1597.

The *Lamiums* known respectively as *Blind-nettle* are so called from their leaves, which while they appear to the eye like those of the stinging-nettle, are not resentful—but seemingly insensible—to the touch; so to speak *blind* or 'dead.'

See **Dea-nettle**, p. 114, also **Purple Dea-nettle**, p. 338.

BLISS, *sb.* the boundary line of an allotment of timber-felling: a term used by the wood-cutters about Cleobury Mortimer. See *sub voce* **Hag** (2), p. 192.

BLUE-ROCK, *sb.* *Columba œnas*, the Stock-Dove. A Gamekeeper's term. Com.

BLUTCH, same as **Bletch**, above—a corrupt form of the word.—CHURCH STRETTON, *Leebotwood*; WELLINGTON.

BOOTS, *sb.* *Caltha palustris*, common Marsh Marigold.—NEWPORT, *Edgmond*. This plant grows abundantly on the Wealdmoors, and some Edgmond children at the present day [1872] call the flowers *Boots*, as Richard Barnefield—an Edgmond man—did in 1594. He says, in *The Affectionate Shepheard*—

> 'Fine pretie King-cups and the yellow *Bootes*
> That growes by Riuers and by shallow Brookes.'
>
> *Complete Poems of Richard Barn[e]field*, p. 15, ed. A. B. Grosart (Roxburgh Club), 1876.

Gerarde says, *Caltha palustris* is called 'in English Marsh Marigoldes, in Cheshire and those parts it is called *Bootes*.'—*Herball*, Bk. II. p. 671, 1st ed. A.D. 1597.

'Bouts, or *Boots*, the marsh marigold, from the Fr. *bouton d'or*, in respect of the yellow flower buds.'—PRIOR'S *Popular Names of British Plants*, p. 27, ed. 1870.

Cf. **Meadow Bout** (*Supplement*). See **May-Flowers**, and *sub voce*, p. 274.

BOTTOM, *sb.*, *obs.* a ball of yarn as it was wound off the reel for the cottage weaver, or for home use.—PULVERBATCH. Qy. com. 'Come, yo' mun trindle them yarwin's [q. v.] pretty sharp, else we sha'n 'ăve owd Spake, the waiver, 'ere afore we'n got the *bottoms* ready.' In the *Midsummer Night's Dream* the weaver, who is one of the *Dramatis Personæ*, is called *Bottom*—a name borrowed, doubtless, from the *bottoms* of yarn employed in his handicraft.

BOTTOM-STALL, *sb.*, *obs.*? the foundation of a ball of yarn.—PULVERBATCH. A *bottom-stall*—which served also for a child's rattle—was often made by putting shot into a goose's wind-pipe, then drying it, and forming it into a ring, by slipping the smaller end within the other. 'I think my yorn's gettin' low, I can 'ear the *bottom-stall* rackle.'

BOUTED [bou·tid], *part. past*, sprang suddenly; bolted. Com. 'Did'n'ee 'ear o' owd Clarke's accident?' 'No, whad wuz it?' 'W'y that 'orse as 'e bought las' far *bouted* o'er the 'edge, an' throwed 'im.' 'Well, I 'eärd that 'orse wuz al'ays a *bouter*.'

> '& Gryme the spurres spared not; soe weele
> to the steeds sides he let them feele,
> his horsse *bouted* forth . . . .'
> *Eger and Grine*, l. 351. *Percy Folio MS.*, vol. i. p. 374, ed. Hales and Furnivall.

See **L** (2) in **Grammar Outlines** (*consonants*, &c.).

BOW [boa·], *sb.* mode of doing things; habits.—SHREWSBURY; PULVERBATCH. 'I'd rather take a young girl as 'ad never been out, I could sooner bring 'er up to my own *bow*.' A term borrowed from archery, probably.

BRAKE, *sb.* a plot, or parcel, of furze or fern.—WELLINGTON. 'If some o' that theer fyarn an' gorst wuz cut i' *brakes*, we met'n 'ăve some chonce to get the rabbits out.'

> 'He builded* his men in a *brake* of fearne
> a litle from that Nunery,
> sayes, "if you heare my litle horne blow,
> then looke you come to me."'
> *Robine Hood and Ffryer Tucke*, l. 11. *Percy Folio MS.*, vol. i. p. 27, ed Hales and Furnivall.

* '*for* hilded, i. e. concealed.'—Note by BP. PERCY.—*Ibid.*

'Brakebushe, or *fernebrake*. *Filicetum, filicarium*.'—*Prompt. Parv.*
'*Filicetum*. A fearnie ground.'—*Dict. Etym. Lat.*
See *Brake* (2), in HAL.

BRASE [br'ai·z], (1) *sb.* blacksmith's fuel: there are two kinds, charcoal-*brase* and coal-*brase*, of which, the former is the better and the more expensive; but both alike consist of small nuggets, quite free from dust, and producing a glowing heat.—BRIDGNORTH. *Brase* is employed in making the best quality of edge-tools, woodcutters' implements and the like. 'I'n got two or three brummocks to mak', Sir, as well as yourn, but I conna mak' 'em wi'out *brase*, an' they hanna sen' me none yit.'

'O.Du. *brase*; O.Swed. *brasa*, glowing coals.'—STRAT.
See **Brese**, below.

(2) *v. a.* to cut or slash the bark of trees,—a woodcutter's term used about Cleobury Mortimer. See *sub voce* **Hag** (2), p. 192. See *Brase*, in HAL.

BRESE [br'ee·z], *sb.* small coal sifted from the dust,—riddled slack, used by blacksmiths for general purposes.—SHREWSBURY; PULVERBATCH. Qy. com. Cf. **Brase** (1), above.

BROCK, *sb.*, *obs.* *Meles taxus*, the Badger. The term *brock* is believed to be obsolete at the present date (1881), as applied to a badger. In 1868, or thereabout, a gamekeeper on the Buildwas Park estate was heard using it; he said of certain men that, he thought 'they wun after a *brock*,' but 'they wun poachers after all.' There is a wooded mound between the Wrekin and Buildwas called the *Brockholes* Bank, from its having been the haunt of badgers in former times. *Brock*, as a part of some place-names, such as Lee *Brockhurst*, Preston *Brockhurst*, points to the same origin; and it may safely be assumed that the badger was at one time familiarly known in Salop under the appellation *brock*. Langland speaks of it by this name:—

'And go hunte hardiliche · to hares and to foxes,
To bores and to *brockes* · þat breketh adown myne hegges.'
Piers Pl., Text B., pass. vi. l. 31.

The Wycliffite Version renders *Hebrews* xi. 37: 'Thei wenten aboute in *broc* skynnes, and in skynnes of geet, nedi, angwischid, turmentid.'

Cæsar, one of Burns' '*Twa Dogs*,' says—

'. . . our gentry care as little
For delvers, ditchers, an' sic cattle,
They gang as saucy by poor folk
As I wad by a stinking *brock*.'—*Poems*, p. 3, l. 10.

'*Brok*, best, K. *Brocke*, P. *Taxus*, *castor*.'—*Prompt. Parv.*
'A.S. *broc*; Dan. *brok*, brock, badger.'—STRAT.

BROWN LINNET, *sb.* *Fringilla cannábina*, the common Linnet.—BRIDGNORTH; WELLINGTON. Qy. com. See **Gorse-bird**, &c., p. 180.

BULLIN [buol·in], *sb.*, *obs.* a receptacle for 'bottoms' of yarn.—PULVERBATCH. *Bullins*—included amongst the 'home-made' things pertaining to good housewifery—were constructed of straw, fashioned like a bee-hive; they were circular in form, and flat-bottomed. 'W'eer mun I pŭt these bottoms o' yorn, Missis?—bŏoäth *bullins* bin fŭll.' 'Yo'n fine a wisket under the stars as ŏŏl do.' See **Bottom** (*Supplement*).

BULLRUSH, *sb.* *Typha latifólia*, great Reed-mace.—WELLINGTON. Qy. com. The true Bullrush belongs to another order,—*Cyperaceæ*.

BULLS'-PATES, *sb. pl.* large root-tufts of *Aíra cæspitósa*.—WELLINGTON, *Eaton Constantine*. See **Sniggle-bogs**, p. 395.

BY, *prep.*, *pec.* about; regarding; with respect to.—WORTHEN. (1) 'Whad did they say *by* 'er?' 'Oh! they saiden as 'er wuz a nice young ŏŏman, they wun all mighty fond on 'er.' (2) 'The rots bin snivin', I dunna know whadever's to be done *by* 'em.'

'"hermitt," hee sayd, "ffor St. Charytye,
was this letter made *by** mee?"'
Sir Degree, l. 242. *Percy Folio MS.*, vol. iii. p. 27, ed. Hales and Furnivall.

* 'about, concerning.'—Note by MR. FURNIVALL.—*Ibid.* See **By**, p. 60.

CADEE, CADEE-MAN [kadee·], *sb.*, *obsols.* a man who is not regularly employed, but does odd jobs, goes on errands, carries messages, or such like.—SHREWSBURY.

Jamieson gives '*Cadie*, *s.* (1) One who gains a livelihood by running of errands, or delivering messages; a member of a Society in Edinburgh, instituted for this purpose. (2) A boy; especially as employed in running of errands, or in any inferior sort of work.'

CAG-BUTCHER, *sb.* a man who buys animals that have died a natural death; and also unsound animals, to slaughter, with the view of selling their flesh as 'butcher's-meat.'—WELLINGTON. See below.

CAG-MAG, *sb.* unwholesome, or inferior meat. — WELLINGTON; WHITCHURCH. 'I conna ate sich *cag-mag* as that, it met do fur a dog, but it inna fit fur a Christian.'

'*Cagmag*, bad food, or other coarse things. The word, in the language of Scotland, signifies an old goose. See Mr. Pennant's Tour, Appendix, p. 9.'—PEGGE.

Mr. Peacock gives '*Cag-mags*, in two several senses, (1) old geese, (2) unwholesome meat,' as a Lincolnshire word. See E. D. S., C. vi.

CARDS [ki'aar'·dz *and* kaar'·dz], *sb. pl.*, *obs.* implements of housewifery used for combing wool, and 'herdes' or 'nogs,' to prepare them for the spinning-wheel. Com. The *cards* were two flat boards, each of which was about eleven inches long by seven broad; they were covered with leather, full of teeth—bent, flexible wires set closely together. Each *card* had a handle in the centre of the long side. When the *cards* were in use the handles were at opposite points to each other. The *modus operandi* of the cards was this,—the carder laying them on her knee, with the wool or 'herdes' between them, held the lower one firmly by the handle with her left hand; then taking the handle of the upper one in her right hand, she worked the *card* towards her, repeating the process until the material undergoing it required turning or removing, when she reversed the movement, and drove it off the *cards* in thick rolls. The teeth, or wires of the *cards* for 'herdes,' or nogs, were farther apart than those in the wool-*cards*.' 'The Missis at Walleybourne wants me to card two or three pound o' 'ŏŏl fur 'er, but my 'onds bin that sore ŏŏth cardin' nogs, I'm sick o' the sight of a par o' *cards*.'

Randle Holme describes '*The Parts of a Card*' thus—

'The *Card-Board.*
The Handle.
The Leaf, is the Leather in which the Teeth or Wyer is set.
The List, is that as is nailed about to hold on the Leaf.
The Teeth, are the crooked Wyers.
The Tacks, are the small Nails which Nails the List about the Leaf to hold it on the Board.'—*Academy of Armory*, Bk. III. ch. vi. p. 285.

Ash has '*Card* . . . . The instrument with which wool is broken and made fit for spinning.'

The *Promptorium Parvulorum* gives '*Carde*, wommanys instrument. *Cardus, discerpiculum.*'

'Lat. *carduus* [a thistle]; a card, a teasel.'—STRAT.

'Ital. *Cardo*, a thistle; a carder's comb.'—MEADOWS.

CARVE [kaa·r'v], *v. n.* to thicken,—a term applied to milk in a state of preparation for the churn.—ELLESMERE, and *Cheshire Border.* 'Are you going to churn to-day?' 'No, Ma'am, the milk i' this stane inna ready, it's too thin—it hanna *carved* a bit.'

Ray gives, amongst '*North Country Words*,' 'To *carve*, or *kerve*. To grow sour, spoken of Cream. *Cheshire.* To *kerve*, or *kerme*, i. e. to curdle as sour Milk doth.'

Wilbraham has '*Carve*' in the same sense, in his *Cheshire Glossary*, ed. 1820.

CAT-TREE, *sb. Cornus sanguínea,* wild Cornel or Dogwood.—WELLINGTON. Perhaps a corruption of the old form *Gaten* or *Gater*-tree.

Gerarde says of 'the wilde Cornell tree' that it is called 'in English Houndes tree, . . Dogges berrie tree; . . . in the North countrey they call it *Gaten* tree, or *Gater* tree; the berries whereof seeme to be those which *Chaucre* calleth *Gater* berries.'—*Herball*, Bk. III. p. 1283, 1st ed. A.D. 1597.

Gerarde's reference to Chaucer is found in the *Nonne Prestes Tale*, where Pertelote says to Chauntecleer, who appears to her to need a course of alteratives—

'I schal myself to herbes techen yow,
That schul ben for youre hele,'—

and accordingly prescribes various 'simples,' amongst them, '*gaytres* beryis,' telling him to

'Pekke hem up right as thay growe, and ete hem in.'
—l. 145, ed. Morris.

CATTY-TREE, *sb. Euónymus Europæus*, common Spindle tree.—PULVERBATCH. 'Theer's a piece o' *Catty-tree* o' the fire, it stinks enough to pison a body, jest like as if a Tum-cat 'ad bin about.' The origin of the local name, *Catty-tree*, is sufficiently obvious from this! It is 'of a lothsome smell,' as old Gerarde says.

CHOP, (1) *v. a.* to set anything down hastily; to pop down.—PULVERBATCH; WELLINGTON. Qy. com. 'Jest *chop* that basket down, an' run an' fatch me a pail o' waiter to wesh the butter.' Cf. **Clap** (1), p. 81.

(2) *v. a.* to put in with a quick, sudden motion; to pop in.—*Ibid.* 'I *chopt* a ferret i' the stack, an' the rots come towtherin' out.'

Mr. Halliwell gives *Chop* in a similar sense as '*North*,' and illustrates it thus:—'"*Chopt* up in prison," put in prison, *True Tragedie of Richard III.*, p. 31.'

CHUNNER [chun·ur'], *v. n.* to mutter; to grumble,—'The owd woman went away *chunnerin'*.'—WHITCHURCH, *Cheshire Border.* Cf. **Chunder**, p. 79.

CLIER AS SACK, *phr.* extremely clear.—PULVERBATCH; WELLINGTON. Qy. com. 'It's capital fresh-drink, Missis, as *clier as Sack*, an' sharp enough to cut one's throät.'

COAL-HEARTH, *sb.* a place where charcoal has been made.—WELLINGTON.

COKE, *v. n., pec.* to make charcoal.—PULVERBATCH; WELLINGTON. 'I see they'n ruz a smoke i' the coppy, I suppose they'n begun to *coke*.'

COLD-FIRE, *sb.* fuel laid for a fire, but unlighted. Qy. com. 'Lay a *cold-fire* i' the parlour, as we can pŭt a match to in a minute, if anybody drops in.'

COME-BY-CHANCE, *sb.* an illegitimate child.—NEWPORT. 'No 'm, 't inna 'is roit nĕem, Tumkisson inna—yo' see 'e's a poor *cŏom-by-chonce* as Tumkissons tooken tŭ, an' so 'e mŏostly goos by their nĕem, bŏot 'is Mŏother's nĕem were Baarbur.' Cf. **Chance-child**, p. 70.

COW-SHAWM, *sb.* cow-dung.—WHITCHURCH. This term obtained in 1826, and *may* still exist. See **Cow-sharn**, p. 101.

CRAKER [kr'ai·kur'], *sb.* the Landrail. —WELLINGTON. Called *Craker* from its rough, grating call. Cf. **Corncrake**, p. 98, and see *sub voce*.

CRUDDLING, *part. adj.* curdling. — WORTHEN. Qy. com. A peculiar use of this word was heard, May 13th, 1881, at Marton Pool,—a man there spoke of the Pool as '*cruddlin*' in August,' thus expressively describing the 'breaking' of the water; a phenomenon, of which a scientific explanation will be given in a note at the end of this work.

Spenser says of winter that it '*cruddles* the blood.'—*Shepheard's Calender*, Februarie, l. 46.

See **Cruddled** and *sub voce*, pp. 107, 108.

DADDLE, (1) *v. n.* to trifle; to loiter; to dawdle. Qy. com. 'I'd sooner pŭt my girld to a good Missis, w'eer 'er'd larn summat better than *daddle* about ŏŏth a child.'

(2) *sb.* the hand or fist.—COLLIERY. 'Tip us yer *daddle*' is an invitation to shake hands.

DAVY WHITEHEADS [yeds], *sb.* the white cottony hairs of *Erióphorum vagínátum*, Hare-tail Cotton-grass, and of *Erióphorum angustifólium*, common Cotton-grass; both species abound on *Whixall Moss*.—WHITCHURCH. See **Sniggle** (2), p. 395.

DEAD MEN'S FINGERS, *sb. Orchis mascula*, early purple Orchis. MUCH WENLOCK, *Buildwas*, *Cressage*.

'. . . . . and long purples
That liberal shepherds give a grosser name,
But our cold maids do *dead men's fingers* call them.'
Hamlet, IV. vii. 172.

Called *Dead men's fingers*, according to Prior, 'from the pale colour and hand-like shape of the palmate tubers.'—*Popular Names of British Plants*, p. 64, ed. 1870.

See **Bloody Butchers**, p. 40.

DI [dei·], *sb.* familiar form of the name *David*.—SHREWSBURY; PULVERBATCH.

DILLY, *v. n.* to urge; to drive.—CHURCH STRETTON, *Leebotwood.* 'Yo' mun *dilly* at 'im, or 'e'll never do it.'

DIZENER [dei·znur'], *sb.* a heavy blow.—SHREWSBURY, *Montford Bridge.* Samuel Slater, describing a fight in which he had taken part, said, 'An' as 'e [his antagonist] come up, I ketcht 'im sich a *dizener*' (1855). Cf. **Dizenin'**, p. 120.

DOMENT [doo·munt], (1) *sb.* a convivial entertainment, public or private,—a term used less commonly than '*Do*,' which always means a public affair.—NEWPORT. An old woman at Edgmond said—in explanation of having a friend to tea—'It's moi bŏorthd'y to-dee, so we'n 'ăvin a bit on a *dooment*' (1874). See **Do**, p. 120.

(2) *sb.* a commotion; a fuss.—NEWPORT. 'Theer were a foine *doomeut* w'en the Missis lost 'er kays—fit to tŏorn the 'ouse insoid out, pretty noigh.'

FAIRATION, *sb.* fair dealing, as in work, play, &c.—OSWESTRY. 'Let's have *fairation*' is commonly said when trickery is suspected. A writer in *Byegones* says, with reference to the term *fairation*, 'More than thirty years ago, I remember an old man who used the word oddly, as for instance, "Let's have *fairation doos*," when those with whom he came in contact were not inclined to deal above-board.'—p. 141, 1880.

FERN-OWL, *sb. Caprimulgus Europœus*, European Goat-sucker.—BRIDGNORTH; WELLINGTON, *Wrekin.* Called *Fern-Owl*, because the bird frequently lays its eggs within the shelter of a bunch of fern-fronds: it makes no nest. See **Churn-owl**, p. 79, also **Lich-fowl**, p. 254.

FOBBED, *part. past*, tricked; imposed upon,—put off.—WELLINGTON.

'*Roderigo.* Very well! go to! I cannot go to, man; nor 'tis not very well: nay, I think it is scurvy, and begin to find myself *fobbed* in it.'—*Othello*, IV. ii. 197.

FRENCH WHEAT, *sb., obsols.*? *Polýgonum Fagopýrum*, Buck-wheat.—SHREWSBURY; ELLESMERE. Qy. com. *Buck-wheat* is now sown principally for food for Pheasants. See below.

FRENCH WHEAT-CAKES, *obs.*? cakes made of meal obtained from Buck-wheat.—SHREWSBURY; ELLESMERE. *French Wheat-Cakes* were—certainly, as made in Ellesmere—*excellent* tea-cakes, after the manner of crumpets, but less spongy; they were brown and very thin, and considerable skill was required in toasting them aright, it was said they should be turned nine times during the process, in order to attain the perfection of crispness. The art of making *French Wheat-Cakes* ceased in Ellesmere with the death of an 'expert,' one Betty Morgan—somewhere about 1846.

GIGGLING [gig·lin], *adj.* unsteady; tottering.—PULVERBATCH; WORTHEN. 'Yo'd'n better nod get up o' that *giglin'* stool, athout yo' wanten yore bwunz broke.' Cf. **Kiggling**, p. 233.

GILL [jil·], *sb.* a female ferret, or rat.—ATCHAM; WELLINGTON. Qy. com. See **Hob**, below.

GIN-RING, *sb.*, *obsols.*? the track made by the horses attached to an old-fashioned thrashing-machine, in going round and round,—usually under a covering of thatch, supported on upright poles.—WORTHEN. Qy. com. Cf. **Gin-ring**, p. 175.

GLATTING, *part.* mending gaps in hedges.—WELLINGTON. See **Glat** (1), p. 176.

GOOSE AN' GOSLINGS, GOOSE AN' GULLIES, *sb. pl.* the yellow blossoms of *Salix caprĕa.*—NEWPORT. See **Gis an' Gullies**, p. 175, and *sub voce.*

GOOSEY-GOSLINGS, same as above.—CHURCH STRETTON.

GREEN LINNET, *sb. Fringilla chloris*, the Green Finch.—BRIDGNORTH; WELLINGTON. Cf. **Linnet**, on following page.

GWERIAN, *sb.* a silly person.—OSWESTRY, *Welsh Border.* A corruption of the Welsh word '*gwirion*,' i. e. innocent. In the Authorized English Version, the well-known passage 'innocent blood' is rendered in the Welsh by '*Gwaed gwirion.*'

HEIR-WORD, *sb.* a proverbial word; a by-word.—MUCH WENLOCK; WELLINGTON. Cf. **Nay-word**, p. 298.

HOB, *sb.* a male ferret, or rat.—ATCHAM; WELLINGTON. Qy. com. See **Gill**, above.

HOMINY, *sb.*, *var. pr.* a homily.—PULVERBATCH 'Theer's no end to that fellow's story, 'e's jest like somebody readin' a *'ominy.*' See **L** (5) in **Grammar Outlines** (*consonants*, &c.).

HULLOPE [uloa·p], *interj.* a loud call, used to arouse attention, as for instance, if a horseman rode up to a house at night-fall, he would cry "*'Ullope!*'—BRIDGNORTH.

IRON GRASS, *sb. Aíra cæspitósa*, Turfy Hair-grass.—WELLINGTON, *Weald-moors.* See **Snizzle-grass**, p. 395.

JIGGLING, same as **Giggling**, q. v., preceding page.—WORTHEN.

JOHNNY O' NEELE, *sb. Chenopodium album*, white Goosefoot. Called also *John o' Neele.*—WELLINGTON, *Weald-moors.* For *Neele*, see PRIOR'S *Popular Names of British Plants*, p. 164, ed. 1870. See **Lamb-tongue**, on following page.

KEEP, *v. n.* and *v. a.*, *obsols.* to refrain from, or to restrain, tears,—"'E could 'ardly *keep.*'—NEWPORT. Shakespeare employs *keep* in the sense of *restrain*, when he makes Launce, speaking of his dog, say—

'. . . . . and I came no sooner into the dining-chamber, but he steps me to her trencher and steals her capon's leg: O, 'tis a foul thing when a cur cannot *keep* himself in all companies!'—*Two Gentlemen of Verona*, IV. iv. 11.

KETCHED [ketch·t], *part. adj.* slightly burnt and stuck to the pan in boiling: said of milk, &c.,—'The milk's a bit *ketcht* this mornin'.' —SHREWSBURY; NEWPORT. Cf. **Growed** (1), p. 188.

KNOW [noa·], *sb.* an apparition; a phantom.—'O Miss Ann, theer's the *know* of a dog, Oh! oh!'—PULVERBATCH, *Dorrington.* See Bk. II., *Folklore*, &c., 'Ghosts.'

LAKE-WEED, *sb. Polygonum amphibium*, amphibious Persicaria.—WELLINGTON.

LAMB-TONGUE, *sb. Chenopodium album*, white Goosefoot.—WELLINGTON, *Eaton Constantine.* See **Johnny-o'-Neele.**

LAND-BRIARS, *sb. pl.* the long, tangled shoots of *Rubus fruticósus*, the common Bramble, or Blackberry. The term is chiefly applied to such 'briars' as grow under trees.—WELLINGTON, *Wrekin.*

LINE [lei·n], *sb., var. pr.* a loin, as of meat.—SHREWSBURY; PULVERBATCH; NEWPORT. Qy. com. 'Plase 'm, the bŭtcher says 'e canna cut a *line* o' lamb—nuthin' less than a quarter.'

'*Kite.* . . . in short you'll be standing in your Stall an Hour and half hence, and a Gentleman will come by with a Snuff-box in his Hand, and the tip of his Handkerchief hanging out of his right Pocket; he'll ask you the Price of a *Line* of Veal, and at the same time stroak your great Dog upon the Head, and call him Chopper.

'*But.* Mercy upon us! Chopper is the Dog's name.'—FARQUHAR'S *Recruiting Officer*, Act III. Scene—A Chamber [Shrewsbury].

LINNET, *sb. Fringilla carduēlis*, the Goldfinch.—COLLIERY. Cf. **Green-linnet.**

LITTLE WHEEL, *sb., obs.* the wheel used for spinning hemp and flax.—PULVERBATCH. Qy. com. Its principal parts were,—The Stocks or Stand (usually supported by three legs). The Wheel. The Wheel-String, connecting the Wheel with the Spindle. The Spindle and Wings. The Head Standards, or two pillars, holding the Spindle between them. The Barrel. The Distaff. The Treadle. The spinner sat to this wheel, which she worked by means of the treadle.

Randle Holme says, 'There are several sorts of these kinds of *Spinning Wheeles;* some for *standing* or *going*, a second sort for *sitting*, ... is the *sitting Wheel*, generally called the *Spinning Wheel*, . . . being withal its appurtenances not above a yard high.' He describes several varieties of '*Sitting Wheels.*'—*Academy of Armory*, Bk. III. ch. vi. p. 286.

See *sub voce* **Love-spinning**, p. 263. See **Didstaff**, p. 118. See also **Barrel** (*Supplement*). Cf. **Long-wheel**, *ibid.*

LONG-RAUGHT, *adj.* a term which implies such length of arm, or commanding height, as would enable a person to reach unusually far: it is applied chiefly to men who 'can use their fists.'—WEM. 'So yo'n got well licked! an' sarve yo' reet. Whad a fule yo' mun be to gŏo wros'lin' an' fightin' wuth a good-scienced, *lung-raught* chap like Tum Jones! W'y yo' mun know as yo' wun no match fur 'im.' See **Raught**, pp. 345, 346.

LONG-WHEEL, *sb.*, *obs.* the wheel used for spinning wool. Qy. com. The principal parts of the *long-wheel*, or 'big wheel,' as it was sometimes called, were,—The Stock or Stand (usually supported by three legs). The Wheel. The Wheel-string, connecting the Wheel with the Spindle. The Spindle. The Wheel-pin. The wheel was turned by the right hand of the spinner, with the *wheel-pin*. In her left hand she held a roll of wool as it came from the *cards* [q. v.], and with finger and thumb she paid it out to the spindle, as with backward step she walked to the wheel end, thus spinning her yarn: with slow, measured pace she then went forward to the spindle, and so, with the simultaneous motion of the wheel, wound the yarn on the '*broach*' at its extremity. All the operations of the *long-wheel* were conducted by the hand of the spinner as she walked to and fro.

Randle Holme says that 'the large *Spinning-Wheele* is called a *long Wheele*, or a *going Wheele*, or a *Woollen Wheele*, because Woll is principally, nay only spun at it, and at none of the other sorts of Wheels.'—*Academy of Armory*, Bk. III. ch. vi. p. 286. See *sub voce* **Love-spinning**, p. 263. See **Wil-pin**, p. 482; also **Broach**, p. 50. Cf. **Little-wheel**, on preceding page.

MAGPIE WIDGEON, *sb. Mergus Castor*, the Goosander.—*Severn Valley* term. See **Widgeon**, p. 481.

MARCH-MONTH, MAY-MONTH, *sbs.* March and May seem to be the only month-names which obtain in the composite form here given; but March is, of the two, less generally specified thus.—PULVERBATCH; WORTHEN. 'The corn looks well now, but 'ow it'll stond the *March-month* we canna tell.' See *The* 'used before the names of months,' in **Grammar Outlines**, p. xlix.

MARIGOLD-CHEESE, *sb.*, *obs.* a cheese made of skim-milk, having the petals of Marigold-flowers strewn amongst the uncoloured curd, to which they were believed to impart a quality of mellowness. A *Marigold-cheese* was about the thickness of an ordinary cream-cheese: it was eaten as soon as it became ripe.—PULVERBATCH. See **Nuvituous**, for example, p. 305. See **Sage-cheese**, and *sub voce*, p. 359.

MATTERLESS, *adj.*, *obsols.*? unconcerned; uninterested; indifferent.—PULVERBATCH; OSWESTRY. Qy. com. 'Oh aye! if yo'n do things fur 'er, 'er'll tak' on as *matterless* as if it didna belung to 'er.'

A contributor to *Byegones*, p. 324, 1879, calls attention to this word, saying that 'it is rarely used now-a-days.' He gives the example: 'Since her's lost her son, her's gone quite *matterless*.' He adds that '*Difatter*, literally the same, is commonly used in Wales.'

MAY-MONTH. See **March-month**, above. — PULVERBATCH; WORTHEN; NEWPORT. 'I al'ays think yarbs is best gethered i' the *May-month*, they bin more juicy then than any other time.' See example *sub voce* **Yarbs**, p. 492.

MEADOW BOUT, *sb. Caltha palustris*, common Marsh Marigold.—PULVERBATCH. Fr. *bouton d'or*. See **Boots** (*Supplement*). See also **May-Flowers**, and *sub voce*, p. 274.

MILLER, *sb.* the caterpillar of the Tiger-Moth.—NEWPORT, *Market*

Drayton. Cf. **Tommy Tailor**, p. 447. See Bk. II., *Folklore*, &c., 'Superstitious Cures.'

MISTAEN, *part. past*, mistaken,—'Yo' bin *mistaen* theer, I'm sartin.'—PULVERBATCH. Qy. com.

> '*Glaud.* I trow, goodwife, if I be not *mistane*,
> He seems to be with Peggy's beauty tane.'
> ALLAN RAMSAY, *The Gentle Shepherd*, III. ii. p. 41.

See **Taen**, p. 428.

MISTOOK, *pret.* for *part. past*, mistaken,—''E'll find 'isself *mistook*, I doubt.' Com.

> '*Cassius.* Then, Brutus, I have much *mistook* your passion.'
> *Julius Cæsar*, I. ii. 48.

Shakespeare uses both forms of the participle, 'mistook' and 'mistaken.' The former is properly the form of the imperfect. In Icelandic *tók* is the imperfect, and *tekinn* the participle of *taka*. Note by WILLIAM ALDIS WRIGHT, M.A.

Milton employs '*mistook*' as a participle:—

> 'Too divine to be *mistook*.'—*Arcades*, Song 1, l. 4.

Cf. **Forsook**, pp. 158, 159.

MIT, *sb.* a shallow tub, or other like vessel used for household purposes. Qy. com. *Mit* is generally used in composition, as Butter-*mit*,—Kneading-*mit*. See for these pp. 59, 239.

MONK'S COWL, *sb. Aconitum Napéllus*, common Wolf's-bane or Monk's-hood [probably a garden plant].—LUDLOW.

So called 'from the resemblance of the upper sepal to the *cowl of a monk*.'—PRIOR'S *Popular Names of British Plants*, p. 156, ed. 1870.

Cf. **Cuckoo's Caps** [garden plant], p. 109.

MOUNTAIN FLAX, *sb. Spérgula arvénsis*, Corn Spurrey.—WELLINGTON. The so-called *Mountain Flax* is said 'to pis'n the filds an' mak' 'em all of a tether' [a tangle of weeds].

MULLIN BRIDLE, *sb.* a kind of bridle with blinkers, used for cart-horses,—'tak the *mullin bridle* an' bring up the owd mar'.'—CLEE HILLS, *Sidbury*.

NAUGHT [naut·], *adj.*, *obs.* bad; ill-flavoured; distasteful.—PULVERBATCH; WORTHEN. 'Ally 'w'eer'st'ee got this tay throm? I know right well it inna throm Bratton an' Oakley, fur it's downright *naught*.'

'It is *naught*, it is *naught*, saith the buyer: but when he is gone his way, then he boasteth.'—*Proverbs* xx. 14.

'*Touchstone*, Truly, shepherd, in respect of itself, it is a good life; but in respect that it is a shepherd's life, it is *naught*.'—*As You Like It*, III. ii. 15.

See 2 *Kings* ii. 19—22.

NAUGHTY, *obs.*? same as above: said of water,—'it's very *naughty* waiter, it inna fit to drink, else theer's plenty on it' [1834].—WORTHEN, *Brockton*. See, as for above, 2 *Kings* ii. 19—22.

NOB, (1) *sb.* same as **Blackheaded-nob**, q. v. (*Supplement*).—ELLESMERE.

(2) *sb. Leuciscus céphalus*, the Chub.—*Severn Valley* term.

NOBBLER, *sb.* a bricklayer, who is handy at odd jobs, and does not work under a regular master.—OSWESTRY.

PLONGER, PLUNGER [plonj·ur', plunj·ur'], *sb.* a long shaft used in trammel-net fishing.—BRIDGNORTH. While the net is being dragged, a man in the boat occupies himself continually with plunging the shaft into the river in order to scare the fish and send them into the net; whence the name '*plunger*' given to the shaft,—the 'watermen' call it a '*plonger*.' See **Trammel-net**, p. 451.

QUICK, QUICK-IRON, *sb.*, *obsols.* a smooth, hollow, cylindrical iron—tapering at the extremity—standing on a curved foot-stalk set in a circular base; and heated by means of a red-hot heater, fitting into the cylinder—an Italian-iron. Com. The *quick*—in general use in former days for 'getting up' most kinds of frills—was indispensable to the proper 'set' of the broad muslin borders of those comely caps worn by country-women, young and old, some fifty years ago. Such caps belong to the past, and the *quick* is passing—giving place to the gauffering-irons, which are better adapted to the modern requirements of 'little frills.' The term *Quick*, as applied to this iron, is probably due to the fact of its being *quickly* heated.

QUICKER, *v. a.*, *obsols.* to iron and 'set' frills on a *quick*.—SHREWSBURY. Qy. com. 'Now then, get on, an' *quicker* the frills o' that pillow-coat,—it'll be wanted w'en we make the bed.'

RENCH [r'en·sh], *v. a.* to rinse.—ELLESMERE. 'Now, look sharp an' pump some waiter, so as we may *rench* them clo'es out an' pŭt 'em o' the 'edge—they wunna be dry afore night else.'

'*Perluo, perpurgo*, to *rinche* faire and cleane.'—DUNCAN'S *Appendix Etymologiæ*, A.D. 1595, E. D. S., B. xiii.

Icel. *hreinsa*, to rinse, cleanse.

SCREEN, *sb.* a bench with a high back and an arm at each end, an old-fashioned piece of kitchen furniture for the fireside,—still in use. Sometimes a box with a falling lid constitutes the seat of the *screen*, forming a useful receptacle for clothes, &c. which require to be kept aired.—SHREWSBURY; NEWPORT; ELLESMERE. Qy. com. Tusser says—

'If ploughman get hatchet or whip to the *skreene*'—using *skreene* in a sense equivalent to fireside. See *Plough-Monday*, and *Note* 90, ed. E. D. S., pp. 180, 307.

Mr. Wilbraham says, '*Skreen*, *s.* A wooden settee with a very high back, sufficient to skreen those who sit on it from the external air, was with our ancestors a constant piece of furniture by all kitchen fires, and is still to be seen in the kitchens of many of our old farm-houses in Cheshire.'—*Glossary*, ed. A.D. 1820.

See **Settle**, on following page.

SETTLE, same as **Screen.**—SHREWSBURY; BRIDGNORTH; NEWPORT; ELLESMERE. This term *Settle* is becoming *unsettled*. *Screen* is found to be usurping its place, where the thing itself exists, which was aforetime known only as a *Settle*.

'*Hoc sedile, A*' lang-sedylle,' occurs in an *English Vocabulary*, xv. cent., in Wr. vocabs., vol. i. p. 197. Mr. Wright glosses '*lang-sedylle*' as 'The long wooden seat with back and arms, which is still called a *settle*.'

Cf. **Setless** (1), and see *sub voce*, p. 370.

SNIGGLE, *sb.* any kind of long, tangled, floating water-weed.—*Severn Valley* term. See **Sniggle**, p. 395.

SOUR, *adj.*, *pec.* a term applied to a log of wood, or a lump of coal, that shows tardy burning qualities.—PULVERBATCH; CLEE HILLS. 'Pŭt tuthree cobbles roun' this *sour* lump, or we sha'n 'ave a poor fire.'

STARTLEY-BUZ, *sb.* the common Cockchafer.—COLLIERY. See **Blind-buzzard** (1), p. 38; also **Huz-buz**, p. 219.

TETHER, *sb.* a tangle,—as of weeds.—WELLINGTON. See *sub voce* **Mountain Flax** (*Supplement*). Cf. **Tather** (4), p. 432.

TETHERY, *adj.* said of water-weeds, or such things as from their nature are apt to become intertwined or entangled,—'Them theer *tethery* weeds.'—WELLINGTON.

TITTIVATE [tit·i'vait], *v. a.* to smarten; to make spruce. Com. 'That bonnet's as good as new, if yo'n jest *tittivate* the trimmin' a bit.'

TOM-PUDDING, *sb.* the Little Grebe.—BRIDGNORTH, *Severn Valley.* See **Douker**, p. 123.

WIDDERSHINS, *adv.*, *obs.*? To go *widdershins* is to go the contrary way to the sun.—PULVERBATCH, *Condover*. 'A' ganging *withershins* roun and roun,' says the author of *Olrig Grange*.

Jamieson gives several forms of this word, and amongst them, '*Widdershins*,' and '*Withershins*,' with the definition,—'The contrary way, contrary to the course of the sun.' He gives the derivation, 'A.S. *wiðer*, contra, *sunne*, sol; or rather, Teut. *weder-sins*, contrario modo.'

See Bk. II., *Folklore*, &c., 'Superstitions concerning Birds.'

WINGS. See *sub voce* **Barrel** (*Supplement*).

WOOL-CARDS. See **Cards** (*Supplement*). Qy. com.

'He beareth Sable, a *Wool-Card*, Or. . . . . . the Card in its parts is Blazoned thus, the Card-Board, Or; the Leafe and List, Gules; Teeth, Argent. Some call it a Cloath-Card.

'These are termed *Wool-Cards*, from their Carding of Wool, whose Teeth then are made short, and set thick together for strength.'—*Academy of Armory*, Bk. III. ch. vi. p. 285.

YATE, YET, *sb.* a gate. This old form still lingers on, in the composition of Place-names, here and there in Salop, but otherwise does not now appear to exist, though probably it was at one time common enough in the County, as an independent word.

'I wol dô him to þe deth · and more despit ouere;
he schal heiȝe be honged · riȝt bi-fore hire *ȝate*,
þat alle þe segges of þe cite · schulle him bi-hold.'
William of Palerne, l. 3757

' "Suffre we," seide treuth · "I here & se bothe,
How a spirit speketh to helle · & bit vnspere þe *ȝatis*." '
Piers Pl., Text B., pass. xviii. l. 259.

'*ȝate. Porta, janua.*'—*Prompt. Parv.*
'A.S. *geat;* O.Sax. *gat;* O.Fris. *iet;* yat (gat), gate.'—STRAT.
See examples in **Place-Names** following.

A SHORT LIST OF PLACE-NAMES.

THE subjoined *List of Place-Names* is simply intended to afford examples of Shropshire folk-speech in the Shropshire nomenclature; but it is hoped that, though it pretends to nothing more than this, it will, as far as it goes, be found useful to some and interesting to many. Reference to the *Introduction*, p. xv, will shew that the record of '*Certain Place-names* remarkably pronounced' entered into the scheme of the *Shropshire Word-Book*.

ABBEY-FOREGATE is called **Abbey Forret** (SHREWSBURY). *Forret* is a corrupted form of *Fore-yate*, the *y* having been lost in the course of ages.

'This yeare and in the sayde moonthe of Marche 1582 the famus howse in the Abbe *foryate* in the towne of Shreusberie sytuate by a greate barne callyd the Abbotts barne was boyldid by one master Prynce Lawyar callid master Pryncs place the foondac'on began in Marche 1578 so was it iiij yeares in buyldinge to hys greate chardge, wth fame to hym and hys posterite for ev'.'—*Early Chronicles of Shrewsbury* (*Taylor MS.*), in *Transactions of the Shropshire Archæological and Natural History Society.*

Speed, describing 'Shrowesbury' (early in 17th cent.), speaks of 'Monkes *Foreyate*,'—the Abbey *Foregate* of the present day.

See **Yate**, in *Supplement.*

ALBRIGHTON is called **Aiberton** [ai·bur'tn], a chapelry 3½ miles N. SHREWSBURY. A person asking for *Albrighton*, on the spot itself, would be told that 'theer wuz no place o' that name theerabouts!' This has been proved repeatedly. The pronunciation of *Albrighton* is a very Shibboleth,—call it *Aiberton*, and its folk will at once recognize it (1876).

ALBRIGHTON is called **Auberton** [au·bur'tn], a parish 5 miles S.E. SHIFFNAL. See **L** (3) in **Grammar Outlines** (*consonants*, &c.).

BAGLEY-MOOR is called **Bagamore** [bag·u'mur']; it lies N. BASCHURCH. See **Moor**, p. 287.

BOREATTON is called **Bratton** [br'at·n]; it is about 9 miles N.W. SHREWSBURY.

BURWARTON is called **Burraton** [bu'r'at·n·], a parish 7½ miles N.E. LUDLOW. Cf. **W** (1) in **Grammar Outlines** (*consonants*, &c.).

CALVERHALL is called **Corra**, a parish S.E. WHICHURCH. See **Jack of Corra** *sub voce* **Jack** (3), p. 222.

CARADOC is called **Cwerdoc** [kwur'·duk], CHURCH STRETTON. See **W** (4) in **Grammar Outlines** (*consonants*, &c.).

CARDISTON is called **Carson** [kaa·r'sn], a parish 6 miles W. SHREWSBURY.

CLAVERLEY is called **Clarley** [klaa·r'li'], a parish 4½ miles E. BRIDGNORTH.

CLUNGUNFORD is called **Clungunnas**, a parish 7 miles E. CLUN.

'Axes and Brummocks
Say the bells of *Clungunnas*.'

Speed gives the spelling '*Clongonas*' on his map of 'Shropshyre,' dated A.D. 1610.

COLEMERE is called **Coomer**, a mere rather more than 2 miles S.E. ELLESMERE. See **L** (4) in **Grammar Outlines** (*consonants*, &c.). See *sub voce* **Moss-balls**, p. 289.

CONDOVER is called **Conder** [kun·dur'], a parish 4 miles S. SHREWSBURY. See *sub voce* **Hathorn**, p. 198; and **Rope** (1), p. 355.

'1590. Sepbr. 1. Three quarts of whit, one pottel of sak, 5 quarts, 1 pint of Claret to present sargen Owen at his sons at *Condor* vij[s] viij[d].'—*Borough Accounts*, cited in OWEN and BLAKEWAY'S *History of Shrewsbury*, vol. i. p. 394.

Speed gives the spelling *Condor* for the Village, and *Condover* for the Hundred, in his map of 'Shropshyre,' A.D. 1610.

DUDDLEWICK is called **Didlick**; a township, one mile N.W. W. STOTTESDEN. See *sub voce* **Reddins**, p. 348. See **U** (13) in **Grammar Outlines** (*vowels*, &c.). Cf. **W** (1), *ibid* (*consonants*, &c.).

DUDLESTON HEATH is called **Dilluson Yeth**; it lies N.W. ELLESMERE.

'*Dilluson Yeth*,
W'eer the divil wuz starved to djeth,'

is a saying current in the neighbourhood of Dudleston, varied sometimes by 'ketcht 'is djeth.' See **Yeth**, p. 494. See also **Starve** *sub voce* **Clem**, p. 83.

EARDINGTON is called **Yerton** [yur'·tn]; a village S. BRIDGNORTH. See citation *sub voce* **Edward**, p. 131, from FREEMAN'S *Old English History*. See also **Y** (2) in **Grammar Outlines** (*consonants*, &c.), and **ng** (6), under **G**.—*Ibid.*

ERCALL is called **Arcall** [aa·r'kul], (1) a parish—High *Ercall*—5¼ miles N.W. WELLINGTON. (2) A parish 6½ miles N.W. NEWPORT—Childs-*Ercall.* (3) A wooded hill, a spur of the Wrekin on the Wellington side, is known as the *Ercall* or *Arcall.* See *sub voce* **Hay**, p. 199.

'High *Arcall*,' and 'Childes *Arcoll*,' are given on Speed's map of 'Shropshyre,' A.D. 1610.

HAUGHMOND is called **Haymond** [ai·mun]—*Haughmond* Hill, *Haughmond* Abbey—4 miles N.E. SHREWSBURY. 'I'm gŏoin' fur a walk as fare as '*Aymon*' '*Ill*—ŏŏn'ee come alung?' See Bk. II., *Folklore*, &c., 'Legends.'

HEATH HILL is called **Yethill**; it is S. NEWPORT, near *Woodcote.* A favourite place for 'people's sports' and picnics. See **Yeth**, p. 494.

LILLESHALL is called **Linsel** [lin·si'l], a parish 3 miles S.S.W. NEWPORT. *Linsel*—itself an old contraction of the ancient form *Linleshelle*—still [1872] lingers amongst the aged people.

LYNEAL is called **Lynëa** [lin·i'u']; it lies S.E. ELLESMERE, *Flintshire Border.* *Lyneal* is thought to be a *Border* corruption of *Llynhir*; granted this, the popular form *Lynëa* would be the less 'corrupted' of the two in regard of sound.

Speed has '*Lenyall*' on his map of 'Shropshyre,' A.D. 1610.

MONTFORD is called **Monvert** *and* **Mumfort** [mon·vur't, mum·fur't], a parish 5 miles W.N.W. SHREWSBURY. See Bk. II., *Folklore*, &c., 'Ghosts.'

OAKEN-GATES is called **Wuken-yets**, *or* **yeäts** [wuk·n yaet·s *or* yi'·u'ts]; a village S.E. WELLINGTON. 'Allen o' Steppiton 'ad a 'orse stole las' night, an' they bin after it 'orse an' fŭt, but it's at *Wukenyets*, or Ketley by this, an' underground' [down the pits].

Speed, in his '*Shropshyre Described*,' speaks of '*Usiconia* now *Okenyate* neer unto the *Wrekin*,' and he marks the place as *Okenyate* in his map of 'Shropshyre,' A.D. 1610.

See **Yate** in *Supplement.* See also **W** (3) in **Grammar Outlines** (*consonants*, &c.).

OFFOXEY is called **Unket**; it is E. SHIFFNAL, *Staffordshire Border.* See **Unket** (1), p. 460.

OSBASTON is called **Trosbun** *and* **Trospun** [tr'os·bun, tr'os·pun], a township 6 miles S. OSWESTRY.

OSWESTRY is called **Ozestry** *and* **Odgestry**, a town 20 miles N.W. SHREWSBURY. *Oswestry* runs through a whole gamut of pronunciations; the two popular forms here given are, perhaps, the more familiar ones, and may be taken respectively as typical of grade-speech. *Ozestry* is a tolerably old form, since Churchyard uses it:—

'As *Ozestry*, a pretie towne full fine,
Which may be lov'd, be likte and praysed both.'
The Worthines of Wales, p. 97, l. 24.

See *Bye-gones* for various spellings of *Oswestry*, 1880, p. 71.

PONTESFORD is called **Ponsert**; it is about 7 miles S.W. SHREWSBURY. *Ponsert Hill* has a curious Legend attached to it. See Bk. II., *Folklore, &c.*, 'Legends.'

PULVERBATCH is called **Powderbatch** *and* **Powtherbatch**, *or* **Powtherbitch** [pou·dur'bach, pou·dhur'bach, pou·dhur'bi'ch], a parish 7½ miles S.S.W. SHREWSBURY. The village, *Church Pulverbatch*, is usually spoken of as *Churton*. *Castle Pulverbatch*, an adjacent hamlet, is distinctively called *Powderbatch*, *Powtherbatch*, or *Powtherbitch* by the peasant-folk thereabouts. The following lines exemplify this,—they are from the pen of a local verse-maker who flourished about the year 1770, and celebrated the neighbourhood in song—

'Cothercot up o' the 'ill,
Wilderley down i' the dale;
Churton for pretty girls,
An' *Powtherbitch* for good ale.'

Speed, in his '*Shropshyre Described*,' mentions, under the Hundreds of Shropshire, '*Pouderbach-Church*' and '*Pouderbach-Castle*;' these places appear respectively as '*Church Pōderbach*' and '*Ponderbach*' [*sic*] on his Map of 'Shropshyre,' A.D. 1610.

The Domesday spelling of *Pulverbatch* is '*Polrebec*.' See *sub voce* **Knap** (1).

QUERDOC. See **Caradoc.**

RATLINGHOPE is called **Ratchope** [r'ach·up], a parish 7 miles N.N.E. BISHOP'S CASTLE.

'1582-3. This yeare and the 17 of Marche one John Rawlyns of *Ratly choppe* in the countie of Salop beinge a begger hangid hym sellffe in an old coate or cowe house wth a lease cast ov' a beame in the same cote and there was founde in hys house bills of debt owynge hym for the soom of 50*li* or ther abouts a just reward by the dyvill uppon sutche dyssymbli'g beggers.'—*Early Chronicle of Shrewsbury* (Taylor MS.), in *Transactions of the Shropshire Archæological and Natural History Society*.

SHRAWARDINE is called **Shraden** [shr'ai·dn], a parish 6 miles W.N.W. SHREWSBURY.

SHREWSBURY is called (1) **Shrōwsbury** [shr'oa·zbr'i']; this is the classical and educated pronunciation.

'And also the seyd Fastolf hath borne grete charge and cost of alone made for the spede and helpe of the voyage whiche the Erle of *Shrowysbury* now last made into the Kynges duchie of Guyenne.'—*Paston Letters*, A.D. 1455, vol. i. p. 366.

(2) **Srōwsbury** [sr'oa·zbr'i'], the semi-refined pronunciation. See **Sh** in **Grammar Outlines** (*consonants*, &c.).

(3) **Sōsebury** [soa·zbr'i'], the pronunciation of the country-folk, commonly. 'I'll sen' yo' to *Sōseb'ry*' implies, or did imply—the saying may be obsolete now—a threat of legal proceedings, or the County Gaol, appealing to the imagination as something a little less awful than, 'I'll sen' yo' to *Bottomley Bay*' [Botany Bay].

See **Ew** (11) in **Grammar Outlines** (*vowels*, &c.), with reference to the three forms above.

(4) **Soosebury** [soo·zbr'i'] may be considered a vulgarism founded upon *Shrewsbury* = *Shroozbury*. See **Ew** (6) in **Grammar Outlines** (*vowels*, &c.); also **R** (4).—*ibid.*; (*consonants*, &c.) for the last two forms.

STOTTESDEN is called **Stotherton** [stodh·ur'tn], a parish 11 miles E.N.E. LUDLOW. *Stotherton* is the word of the peasantry. *Stottesden* is variously spelt,—*Stottesdon*, *Stoddesden*, and *Stoddesdon*,—without arbitrary rule, apparently.

WOOLSTASTON is called **Ŏosasson** [ŏos·u'su], a parish 9½ miles S.S.W. SHREWSBURY. See **W** (2), also **L** (4), in **Grammar Outlines** (*consonants*, &c.).

WORFIELD is called **Wurvil** [wur·vil], a parish 3½ miles N.E. BRIDGNORTH.

YEO EDGE is called **View Edge** [vyoo·], the ridge of an eminence S.W. STOKESAY.

Mr. Thomas Wright notices this. He says,—'The hills on the other side of the valley terminate in a point, on which there are also traces of ancient works, and which is called the *Yeo*, or (as it is pronounced) *View*, *Edge*.'—*A Pic-Nic on the Longmynd*, in *Once a Week*, 30 June, 1866.

YOCKLETON is called **Yocketon** [yok·i'tn]; a village 6 miles W. SHREWSBURY.

'14 Edward iv. Sir John Lyngien Knt., William Newport, John Leghton, Thomas Mytton, Esq[rs], and others released and confirmed to Johanna relict of Sir John Burgh, the manor of Watlesburgh, Heye, Loughton, Cardeston, *Yoketton*, Stretton, and two acres of pasture in Brodeshull for term of her life.'—PHILLIPS's *History of Shrewsbury*, p. 235.

THE BREAKING OF THE MERES.

THE following 'Note' by the well-known Author of the *Shropshire Flora, Lichen Flora,* &c. will be a valuable *addendum* to the *Shropshire Word-Book*, as affording a trustworthy, scientific explanation of the phenomenon referred to under **Break**, p. 48.

'As the Party proceeded along the margins of Ellesmere Mere, Rev. W. A. Leighton directed attention to a singular phenomenon which occurs in this lake in the month of August, and which in fact was then actually taking place. It is locally termed the "breaking-up of the water," and makes the Mere resemble the turbid state of boiling wort, when the process called "breaking" sets in. The water appears turbid, and filled with innumerable minute bodies in a certain state of motion, like boiling. These bodies when viewed under a microscope are seen to be minute globules, and each composed of a central agglomeration of spherical cellules, from each of which cylindrical filaments radiate in every direction. These filaments are broader near the central globule, and are attenuated gradually towards their apices, and are divided into short uniform cells, separated by distinct septa or joints, the cells being filled with chlorophyll of a glaucous or verdigris-green colour. The mode in which this minute plant reproduces itself has not been observed, but it is not improbable that some sort of conjugation takes place as in the conjugate confervæ, when the chlorophyll of two adjacent cells is united into a third or new cell, which forms the sporangium or winter-spore. These winter-spores are doubtless the central spherical cells above mentioned, which sink to the bottom of the lake and remain there dormant until August, when they rise to the surface, and germination takes place by throwing out the radiating filaments, which eventually again produce the sporangia, which sink as before mentioned. This little Alga is well figured in English Botany, tab. 1378, under the name of *Conferva echinulata*, from specimens sent in 1804 from a lake in Anglesea. Its proper systematic place is in Roth's genus *Rivularia*.'—*Report of the Severn Valley Naturalists' Field Club*, August 6th, 1878.

There are other Meres and Pools in Salop, besides Ellesmere Mere, that are known to '*break*.' White Mere, Crosemere, Hawkstone Mere, Marton Pool (near *Cherbury*), Berrington Pool, for instance, are subject to the marvellous troubling of their waters by some of the microscopic *algæ* during the month of August. See *Salopian Shreds and Patches*, vol. iv. p. 149. See **Cruddling** in *Supplement*.

LAST WORDS.

THE *Shropshire Word-Book* is at length finished, and very thankful I am that I have been spared to complete it with my own hand. No one can be more alive to the fact, than I myself, that it lies in the very nature of such a work to be found wanting; but I have done my best, at any rate, to keep errors out of it. The publication of the *Word-Book* in successive parts, of course led to the friendly light of criticism being shed upon its pages, while yet much remained to be done before the work appeared as a whole. I have endeavoured to turn this circumstance to good account in various ways, in the hope of making the latter portion of the work better than the former.

Through censorship it has been brought to my knowledge that misapprehensions exist in the minds of some, touching an important part of the scheme of my work, and I am anxious to do away with this, if I *can*. An objection is raised that, by assigning words to certain 'Districts,' it gives occasion for an assumption that they are not used in other parts of the County. Now I really thought I had made all safe against such a false conclusion, in the opening paragraphs of the *Introduction*, p. xv; but as I am told that I have failed to do so, I am glad to have this opportunity of asking my readers to bear in mind that, the names of the 'Districts' appended to any word must *not* be taken in a restrictive sense, as if the word did not extend beyond their limits, but rather be accepted—to use the words of Mr. Alex. J. Ellis—as 'a most important authentication.' I have placed on record as a simple fact that, in such and such 'Districts,' I have ascertained beyond all doubt that the words assigned to them *are* used, or, if obsolete, *were* used; that is all.

It by no means follows that a word heard in a certain locality is therefore confined to it. Sometimes the same word is found in localities widely apart, and not in the intervening country; sometimes the word is understood in one sense in a given locality, and in a diverse sense in another.

But all this notwithstanding, I have labelled with 'where found' upwards of **eleven thousand words**, *i.e.* **Primary words** and their **sub-meanings**, the latter being in all respects treated as **distinct words**. Having done so much, I hope to be forgiven my sins of 'omission'—which were indeed rather sins of ignorance—in cases where a word is assigned to only *some* of the 'Districts' to which it may happen to be 'Common.'

There are those who say, 'Many of the so-called *Shropshire Words* are not *peculiar* to Shropshire.' I can but reply to this, it would be a marvel if they were,—I think there are very few words indeed '*peculiar*' to any one County,—and moreover the object of my work was, as the *Title-Page* sets forth, to make 'A Glossary of the Archaic and Provincial Words, &c. *used in* Shropshire;'—this I have done, and no more to my own entire satisfaction, than to that of some, who, on the one side, say 'the *Shropshire Word-Book* is too full,' and on the other, 'there are a good many omissions!' Well, I hope we shall—mal-contents and dis-contents—find a source of satisfaction common to us all, in the reflection that, but for some such labours as these of mine, begun not a moment too soon—albeit more than eleven years ago—much that is now on record would have been past recovery, and *that* the *best* of the old-time folk-speech.

Truly the perils of Word-collectors are great, and sometimes the conclusions of Word-readers are rash. 'I wyl'—as Bp. Latimer once said in a Sermon—'furnyshe a story' to illustrate my point; it is taken from a friend's letter to me:—'You may remember that in connection with the word "*Clout*" you mention Bradley, the shoemaker's name. Richard Bradley, old John Bradley's son, tells me that some one drew his attention to the word and his name with it in your book; he said at once, "Miss Jackson must be wrong, I never heard a patch called a *clout* in my life." But strangely enough a day or two (not more) after this, a boy called at Bradley's shop with a pair of boots to be mended, and said, "Yo' mun pŭt a bit of a *clout* 'ere, an' another theer," pointing to the upper leather of the boot.'

The incident was altogether a singular one. Not only did the word *clout* bear the *onus probandi*, as recorded by me, but Richard Bradley, of whose existence I was wholly unaware, turned out to be a son of the very Bradley whom I had mentioned, and who did put *clouts* on boots and shoes—as I well knew—long, long ago. As with '*Clout*,' so with other words; they may be—often are—repudiated on no better ground than that he who denies their existence, or their special usage, has either not heard them, or not heard them so applied. I myself have often, in the course of my work, had doubts as to the authenticity of a word which I had not actually heard, but I have never discarded it without trying to find out whether I was justified in doing so. In some cases I have waited weeks and months, nay *years*, for conclusive evidence before deciding whether such a word were 'to be, or not to be,' recorded in the *Shropshire Word-Book.*

There is a point to which I particularly wish to call attention, lest hereafter it should prove a *vexata quæstio.* Two years have elapsed between the issue of the *first* Part of the *Word-Book* and this *last*, the work of compilation going on meanwhile, whence has arisen the seeming anomaly that certain dates in the book itself are subsequent to that of 1879, which appears on the *Title-Page!*

Something more there is to say, which *must* be said,—In completing the *Shropshire Word-Book* my health has utterly failed, and—my work is ended—I can do no more. But I experience this solace: Bk. II., *Folklore*, &c., so often referred to in Bk. I. (the *Word-Book*), is well provided for; she who has undertaken to edit it, Miss Burne—sometime of Edgmond, Salop—is better qualified for the task than I; she has a fuller knowledge of the subject, and has, besides, a greater gift that way. Bk. II., under her hands, promises to be a charming work; it is well-advanced, and will appear in due season—facts which give me much contentment, and heal the smart of having been obliged to relinquish that which I had hoped to do myself.

I am very grateful to all those who have so generously helped me in my self-imposed task. It has been an established joke that I was 'always *coming to words* with my friends,' but I shall do so no more. That too is ended.

For myself, I have been ill so long now that, as I lay down this work of mine, *finished*, no more fitting words occur to me, with which to close it, than—*Laus Deo.*

GEORGINA F. JACKSON.

White Friars, Chester,
June, 1881.

CORRECTIONS.

Page	xiv,	Line	4,	*for* **at** *read* **in**
,,	xxxiii,	,,	2 *from foot*,	*dele* *
,,	xxxvi,	,,	21,	*for* **th** (5) *read* **th** (3)
,,	lxxviii,	,,	*last*,	*for* **lxiii** *read* **lxvi**
,,	10,	,,	*last*,	*for* **bayȳe** *read* **baȳte**
,,	27,	,,	8,	*for* **givun** *read* **gwun**
,,	31,	,,	14 *from foot*,	*for* **wurz** *read* **wuz**
,,	52,	,,	14,	*for* **Pousbry** *read* **Ponsbry**
,,	57,	,,	10,	*for* **[bun· *or* bund]** *read* **[buon· *or* buond]**
,,	68,	,,	19 *from foot*,	*for* **Cast** (1) *read* **Cast** (3)
,,	69,	,,	11,	*for* **leaping-pole** *read* **leaping-bar**
,,	121,	,,	3,	*for* **creeping Plume-thistle** *read* **Field Madder**
,,	184,	,,	12,	*for* **duna** *read* **dunna**
,,	207,	,,	26,	*for* **Warmynchames** *read* **Warmyn-cham's**
,,	256,	,,	17 & 19 *from foot*,	*for* **-bowt** *read* **-bout**
,,	265,	,,	11, ,, ,,	*for* **Maestur** *read* **Maester**
,,	307,	,,	6, ,, ,,	*for* **glutinosus** *read* **glutinósa**
,,	338,	,,	24,	*for* **Polyporous squamosus** *read* **Polyporus, &c.**
,,	346,	,,	26,	*for* **yawl** *read* **yaul**
,,	355,	,,	10 *from foot*,	*for* **wawt** *read* **waut**
,,	442,	,,	1,	*for* **-bowt** *read* **-bout**
,,	479,	,,	7,	*for* **matinalis** *read* **matronalis**

BUNGAY: CLAY AND TAYLOR, THE CHAUCER PRESS.